PETERSON'S
COMPETITIVE COLLEGES

1996-1997

Fifteenth Edition

Peterson's
Princeton, New Jersey

Visit Peterson's Education Center on the Internet
(World Wide Web) at http://www.petersons.com

Copyright © 1996 by Peterson's.

Previous editions © 1981, 1982, 1983, 1984, 1985,
1986, 1987, 1988, 1989, 1990, 1991, 1992, 1993,
1994, 1995

Competitive Colleges is a registered trademark of
Peterson's.

ISSN 0887-0152
ISBN 1-56079-598-0

Printed in the United States of America

10   9   8   7   6   5   4   3   2   1

CONTENTS

Choosing the Right College from Among America's Best   1

Understanding the College Admission Process   3

Paying for College   7

Representative College Description   11

Comparative Descriptions of the Competitive Colleges   13

Descriptions of Competitive Arts Colleges and Conservatories   374

Majors Index   379

Competitive Colleges Indexes   430

Colleges Costing $7000 or Less   431

Colleges Reporting 50% or More Need-Based Financial Aid Recipients   431

Colleges Reporting 20% or More Non-Need-Based Financial Aid Recipients   432

Ten Largest Colleges   434

Ten Smallest Colleges   434

Colleges Accepting Fewer than Half of Their Applicants   434

Single-Sex Colleges   434

Predominantly African-American Colleges   434

Colleges with Religious Affiliation   434

Public Colleges   436

Geographical Index of Colleges   437

CHOOSING THE RIGHT COLLEGE FROM AMONG AMERICA'S BEST

Since the publication of its first edition in the spring of 1981, the purpose of Peterson's *Competitive Colleges* has been to help broaden the horizons of students like you: competitive students whose educational careers have been marked by academic or some other kind of distinction or achievement. As a competitive student, you have special needs when it comes to choosing the right college. You've excelled at what you do and you want to go on excelling. You need an educational environment that will push you, test you, help you break beyond the limits of your current potential. You require a college that "fits" exactly right, one that will help you develop your particular talents, skills, and experiences into what you uniquely can become.

Our experience at Peterson's, and that of hundreds of guidance counselors at high schools around the country, is that the search for the "right" college has perhaps never been more difficult than it is at the moment. It has always been true that, when it comes to understanding their options for college, students—especially competitive students—are often, at first, extremely limited in their thinking. It might be a worthwhile exercise for you to compile a list of the colleges mentioned whenever you and your friends discuss where you might apply. You'll probably find that everyone's list of colleges is very much alike—and strikingly narrow. With a few notable exceptions determined by the region in which you live, your specific interests, or your parents' particular alma maters, your list and those of your friends will probably include the Ivy League and a handful of other nationally known colleges and universities.

This is not surprising. Until you start to do some research, the only source of information you have about college is popular mythology, sometimes in the form of media stories but more often in the statements of enthusiastic teachers or well-intentioned relatives. Popular mythology does no real harm when it's corrected with accurate information, and it even serves the useful function of helping you begin to think. It is limiting, however; and it's often connected with a genuine misunderstanding about how the college admission process works—the same misunderstanding that is at the root of all the anxiety that competitive students frequently experience as they go about the business of applying to college.

What makes this situation especially difficult now and what concerns us at Peterson's, as well as many of our colleagues in the college admission and guidance communities, is the growing national tendency to institutionalize popular mythology in the guise of a college guide. It's one thing for your Uncle Joe to think that the only physics programs worth their salt are at MIT and Georgia Tech or for the students in your Advanced Placement class to think that their lives won't be meaningful unless they go to Harvard, Yale, or Princeton. It's quite another thing for "guides" to make such proclamations. Yet many do, with

colleges elaborately categorized and aligned in rank order and titles proclaiming that the colleges on the list are the "best this," the "most selective that," the "top 100," or the "most something else for your money."

But ask yourself: How should the quality of a college be measured? On its financial resources? Its faculty-student ratio? Its library holdings? The number of jobs students were offered by graduation? The number of articles and books published by professors? What would quality mean to you? To your best friend? To the captain of the debating team? To the star of your senior play? To the president of the science club? Quality cannot be assigned numbers and toted up for ranking. Judging a college is much harder than that. If close faculty interaction is important to you, you have to choose a college where the faculty value teaching. This may be indicated by the faculty-student ratio or the number of undergraduate courses taught by faculty. If you want to do research with some professors, you need a college where a lot is going on at the graduate level or where there is a strong commitment to undergraduate research of a high level. In this case, the number of undergraduate courses taught by professors and the faculty-student ratio probably won't be relevant.

We can leave it to the statisticians and philosophers to prove that the subjective opinion of millions of people is still subjective and that the division of a number of books by a number of students is more or less useless except in certain rigidly defined circumstances. The point is that every college or university is different, each having its own unique mission, standards, and characteristics, and you are different from all other applicants. No formula or set of statistics can adequately measure what goes on at a college. Thus, no college can be compared to any other college except in single quantifiable measures. College X may have a larger endowment than College Y. But College Y has more books and more faculty members than College X. Which is the better college? You can compare books, or endowments, or numbers of faculty members, but you can't add them up, and there's no such thing as a total of all these.

There are numbers you want to look at as you search for a college, but they have nothing to do with ranking and can't be prescribed by anyone other than you. If you love language, you might be interested in the percentage of students who scored high on the verbal section of their SATs or in the existence of programs in creative and expository writing, with graduates achieving success in related fields. If you've gotten addicted to the Internet, the number of computers on campus could be important, along with information about access to those computers in offices, libraries, and dorm rooms. Scholars might want to know what percent of the student body goes on to graduate school after receiving a bachelor's degree. If you'll need help paying for college, the amount of financial aid a college typically awards is a very important figure. The list of potentially interesting numbers is large, but you're the only one who can make up that list for you—out of your own needs and aspirations.

The editors of Peterson's *Competitive Colleges* ask you to reject the idea that artificial rankings are useful in the college admission process. We want you to think clearly and honestly about yourself and what you want from your college experience. We do make an assumption that the most influential factor in determining your experience on campus is the other students you will find there. Therefore, in selecting colleges for inclusion in this book, our focus has been on the competitiveness of the admission environment at those institutions, as evidenced by the quality of the students applying each year. The colleges selected for this book routinely attract and admit an above-average share of the nation's high-achieving students.

Good colleges typically take great care in admitting their student bodies. For them, the annual project of selecting the entering class is as Bill Fitzsimmons, Dean of Undergraduate Admission and Financial Aid at Harvard University, describes it: a process of "sculpting" the best possible class from the pool of qualified applicants. This is only in part a process of reviewing transcripts and standardized test scores. The goal of an admission committee is to bring together a community of students who can learn from one another, each one bringing particular talents, skills, and experiences that will contribute to the development of all the others.

We think you should adopt a similar approach in your attempt to find the "right" college. Construct your first—and broadest—list of possible colleges by looking at the other students on campus. Look not only for students with academic and extracurricular interests similar to yours but for students whose experiences will open up new worlds for you. Then, it's time to pay attention to the rest of the information we provide—class size, the number of computers on campus, library holdings, etc.—in terms of how this information suits your own unique needs. It's at this point only—and for you only—that it's appropriate to rank colleges. That's what this book is all about: helping you to discover the right college for you.

Best of luck in your search!

Michael Ditchkofsky
Vice President for Special Services

Peterson's would like to acknowledge the thoughtful contributions of the following reviewers: Francis D. Fergusson, President, Vassar College; David Johnson, Chancellor, University of Minnesota, Morris; Judith Rodin, President, University of Pennsylvania; and David P. Roselle, President, University of Delaware.

UNDERSTANDING THE COLLEGE ADMISSION PROCESS

by Ted Spencer, Director of Admissions at the University of Michigan

The process you are about to begin, that of choosing a college, can be very challenging, sometimes frustrating, but is most often rewarding. As Director of Admissions at a large, selective university, I would like to provide some basic information about the admission process that should help you get into the college of your choice. Although each competitive college or university has its own distinctive qualities and goals, the process of applying to them is strikingly similar. The following will give you the basic information you need to know to help you plan and apply to college.

Gathering Information

How do you get the information you need to choose a college? The fact that you are reading this article means that you have already found one of the many college information resources available today. Although colleges publish volumes of information about themselves that they are willing to mail or give out in person, another way to find out about them is through the numerous guides available, such as Peterson's *Competitive Colleges*. The major difference between the college-published brochures and the guides or handbooks is that the college information is meant to present the most appealing picture of a school and is perhaps, then, a little less objective. As a student seeking information about college, you should try to review both the information provided in the guides and handbooks and the information sent by the colleges. Your goal should be to use all of the available literature to assist you in developing your list of the top five or ten colleges in which you are interested.

Chances are, however, that if you are a top student and you have taken the PSAT (Preliminary Scholastic Assessment Test), SAT I (Scholastic Assessment Test), ACT (American College Testing) Examination, PACT (Preliminary American College Testing) Examination, or AP (Advanced Placement) Test, you will receive a great deal of material directly from many colleges and universities. Colleges purchase lists of names of students taking these exams and then screen the list for students they think will be most successful at their institutions. This results in the sending of material that is often tailored to your particular interests. Some colleges will also automatically mail course catalogs, posters, departmental brochures and pamphlets, as well as videocassettes. If you do not receive this information but would like a sample, write or call that particular college.

My advice to students is to take a look at the materials you receive and then let them help you decide (if you don't already know) about the type of college you would like to attend. Even if you already have an idea about the type of

college you plan to attend, allow the materials to help you narrow your list of top schools by comparing key facts and characteristics.

OTHER HELPFUL SOURCES

Published information about colleges, printed by the colleges, is certainly an important way to narrow your choices. But there are at least five other means of learning more about colleges and universities:

- *High School Counselors.* Although most high school counselors are overburdened, they have established positive relationships with the college representatives in your state as well as with out-of-state universities where large numbers of their students apply. As you attempt to gain more information while narrowing your choice of colleges, the high school counselor can give you a fairly accurate assessment of colleges to which you will have the best chance of gaining admission.
- *Parents.* Because most prospective students and their parents are at that stage in life in which they view the same issues in different ways, students tend to be reluctant to ask parents' opinions about college choices. However, you may find that parents are very helpful because they often are actively gathering information about the colleges that they feel are best suited for you. And not only do they gather information—you can be sure that they have thoroughly read the piles of literature that colleges have mailed to you. Ask your parents questions about what they have read and also about the colleges from which they graduated. As alumni of schools on your list, parents can be a very valuable resource.
- *College Day/Night/Fairs Visitation.* One of the best ways to help narrow your college choices is to meet with a person representing a college while they are visiting your area or high school. In fact, most admission staff spend a good portion of the fall and late spring visiting high schools and attending college fairs. In some cases, colleges will bring along students, faculty, and alumni. Before attending one of these sessions, you should prepare a list of questions you would like to ask the representatives. Most students want to know about five major areas: academic preparation, the admission process, financial aid, social life, and job preparation. Most college representatives can be extremely helpful in addressing these questions as well as the many others that you may have. It is then up to you to decide if their answers fit your criteria of the college you are seeking.
- *Alumni.* For many schools, alumni are a very important part of their admission process. In some cases, alumni conduct interviews and even serve as surrogate admis-

sion officers, particularly when admission office staff cannot travel. As recent graduates, they can talk about their own experience and can give balance to the materials you have received from the college or university.

- *Campus Visit.* Finally, try to schedule a campus visit as part of your information-gathering process. By the time you begin thinking about a campus visit, you should have narrowed down your college shopping list. Hopefully your short list of colleges will have met your personal and educational goals. Before deciding which schools to visit, you should sort the materials into piles of "definitely not interested," "definitely interested," or "could be interested." Next, in an effort to make sure that the reality lives up to the printed viewbook, you should schedule a visit and see firsthand what the college is really like. Most colleges and universities provide daily campus tours to both prospective and admitted students. The tours for prospective students are generally set up to help you answer questions about the following: class size and student-to-teacher ratio; size of the library, residence halls, and computer centers; registration and faculty advising; and retention, graduation rates, and career placement planning. Since the tours may not cover everything you came prepared to ask about, be sure to ask questions of as many staff, students, and faculty members as possible before leaving the campus.

The Admission Process

ADMISSION CRITERIA

Perhaps one of the greatest areas of frustration for students and their parents is the admission process. After you go through the process of selecting a college or narrowing your choices to a few schools, the admission process now focuses on you—your academic record and skills—and judgment will be passed on these pieces of information for admission to a particular school. One of the first things you should find out, then, about each college on your priority list is what it takes to get in, or the admission criteria:

1. Does the college or university require standardized tests—the ACT or SAT I? Do they prefer one or the other, or will they accept either?
2. Do they require SAT II Subject Tests and, if so, which ones?
3. Are Advanced Placement scores accepted and, if so, what are the minimums needed?
4. In terms of grades and class rank, what is the profile of a typical entering student?

It is also important to find out which type of admission notification system the college uses—rolling or deferred admission. On a rolling system, you find out your status within several weeks after applying; with the deferred system, notification is generally made in the spring. For the most part, public universities and colleges use rolling admission and private colleges generally use delayed notification.

THE APPLICATION

The application is the primary vehicle used to introduce yourself to the admission office. As with any introduction, you should try to make a good first impression. The first thing you should do in presenting your application is to find out what the college or university wants from you. This means you should read the application carefully to learn the following:

1. Must the application be typed, or can you print it?
2. Is there an application fee and, if so, how much is it?
3. Is there a deadline and, if so, when is it?
4. What standardized tests are required?
5. Is an essay required?
6. Is an interview required?
7. Can you send letters of recommendation?
8. How long will it take to find out the admission decision?
9. What other things can you do to improve your chances of admission?

My advice is to submit your application early. It does not guarantee admission, but it is much better than submitting it late or near the deadline. Also, don't assume that colleges using rolling admission will always have openings close to their deadlines. Regardless of when you submit it, make sure that the application is legible and that all the information requested is provided.

TRANSCRIPTS

While all of the components of the application are extremely important in the admission process, perhaps the single most important item is your transcript because it tells: (1) what courses you took; (2) which courses were college-preparatory and challenging; (3) class rank; and (4) grades and test scores.

- *Required Course Work.* Generally speaking, most colleges look at the high school transcript to see if the applicant followed a college-preparatory track while in high school. So, if you have taken four years of English, math, natural science, social sciences, and foreign language, you are on the right track. Many selective colleges require a minimum of four years of English; three years each of math, natural science, and social science; and two years of a foreign language. It is also true that some selective colleges believe students who are interested in majoring in math and science need more than the minimum requirements in those areas.
- *Challenging Courses.* As college admission staff members continue to evaluate your transcript, they also look to see how demanding your course load has been during high school. If the high school offered Advanced Placement or Honors courses, the expectation of most selective colleges is that students will have taken at least seven or more Honors classes or four or more AP courses during their four years in high school. However, if you do elect to take challenging courses, it is also important that you make good grades in those courses. Quite often, students ask, "If I take Honors and AP courses and get a 'C,' does that count more than getting a 'B' or higher in a strictly

college-prep course?" It's a difficult question to answer, because too many C's and B's can outweigh mostly A's. On the other hand, students who take the more challenging courses will be better prepared to take the more rigorous courses in college. Consequently, many colleges will give extra consideration when making their selections to the students who take the more demanding courses.

- *Transcript Trends.* Because the courses you take in high school are such a critical part of the college decision-making process, your performance in those courses indicates to colleges whether you are following an upward or downward trend. Beginning with the ninth grade, admission staff look at your transcript to see if you have started to develop good academic habits. In general, when colleges review your performance in the ninth grade, they are looking to see if you are in the college-preparatory track.

By sophomore year, students should begin choosing more demanding courses and become more involved in extracurricular activities. This will show that you are beginning to learn how to balance your academic and extracurricular commitments. Many admission officers consider the sophomore year to be the most critical and telling year for the student's future success.

The junior year is perhaps the second-most-important year in high school. The grades you earn and the courses you take will help to reinforce the trend you began in your sophomore year. At the end of your junior year, many colleges will know enough about the type of student you are to make their admission decision.

The upward and positive trend must continue, however, during your senior year. Many selective schools do not use senior grades in making their admission decisions. However, almost all do review the final transcript, so your last year needs to show a strong performance to the end. The research shows that students who finish their senior year with strong grades will start their freshman year in college with strong grades.

The Application Review Process

What's Next?
At this point, you have done all you can do. So you might as well sit back and relax, if that's possible, and wait for the letters to come in the mail. Hopefully, if you've evaluated all the college materials you were sent earlier and you prepared your application carefully and sent it to several colleges, you will be admitted to either your first, second, or third choice. It may help your peace of mind, however, to know what happens to your application after the materials have been submitted.

Once your application is received by the admission office, it is usually processed through the mailroom and then reviewed, in most cases by noncounseling staff, to determine if you have completed the application properly. If items are missing, you will receive a letter of notification identifying additional information that must be provided. Be sure to send any additional or missing information the

college requests back to them as soon as possible. Once your application is complete, it is then ready for the decision process.

Reader Review
The process by which the decision is finalized varies from school to school. Most of the private colleges and universities use a system where each application is read by at least 2 or more admission staff members. In some cases, faculty members are also used as additional readers. If all of the readers agree on the decision, a letter is sent. Under this system, if the readers do not agree, the application will be reviewed by a committee or may be forwarded to an associate dean, dean, or director of admission for the final decision. One advantage to this process is that each applicant is reviewed by several people, thereby eliminating bias.

Committee Review
At some universities, a committee reviews every application. Under that system, a committee member is assigned a number of applications to present. It is that member's responsibility to prepare background information on each applicant and then present the file to the committee for discussion and a vote. In this process, every applicant is voted on.

Counselor Review
The review process that many selective public institutions use is one in which the counselor responsible for a particular school or geographical territory makes the final decision. In this case, the counselor who makes the admission decision is also the one who identified and recruited the student, thereby lending a more personal tone to the process.

Computer-Generated Review
Many large state universities that process nearly 20,000 applications a year have developed computer-generated guidelines to admit their applicants. If applicants meet the required GPA and test scores, they are immediately notified of the decision.

Once the decisions are made using one of these methods, colleges use a variety of ways to notify students. The common methods used are early action or early decision, rolling admission, and deferred admission.

A Word of Advice

When you start the admission process, do so with the idea of exploring as many college opportunities as you can. From the very beginning, avoid focusing on just one college or, for that matter, one type of college. Look at private, public, large, small, highly selective, selective—in short, a variety of colleges and universities. Take advantage of every available resource, including students, parents, counselors, and college materials, in order to help identify the colleges that will be a great fit for you.

Finally, the most important thing you can do is to build a checklist of what you want out of the college experience and then match your list with one of the many wonderful colleges and universities just waiting for you to enroll.

Paying for College

by Don Betterton, Director of Financial Aid at Princeton University

Regardless of which college a student chooses, higher education requires a major investment of time, energy, and money. By taking advantage of a variety of available resources, most students can bring the education that is right for them within reach.

A Note of Encouragement

While there is no denying that the cost of education at a competitive college can be high, it is important to recognize that, although the rate of increase in costs in the last ten years has outpaced gains in family income, there are more options available to pay for college than ever before.

Many families find it is economically wise to spread costs out over a number of years by borrowing money for college. Although increases in federal student aid funding have fallen short of college cost increases, there remains a significant amount of government money, both federal and state, available to students. Moreover, colleges themselves have expanded their own student aid efforts considerably. In spite of rapidly increasing costs, most competitive colleges are still able to provide financial aid to all admitted students with demonstrated need.

In addition, many colleges have developed ways to assist families who are not eligible for need-based assistance. These include an increasing number of merit scholarships as well as various forms of parental loans. There also are a number of organizations that give merit awards based on a student's academic record, talent, or special characteristics. Thus, regardless of your family's income, if you are academically qualified and knowledgeable about the many different sources of aid, you should be able to attend the college of your choice.

Estimating Costs

If you have not yet settled on specific colleges and you would like to begin early financial planning, estimate a budget. Based on actual 1995–96 charges, we can estimate 1996–97 expenses at a typical competitive college as follows: tuition and fees, about $17,300; room and board, about $6,300; and an allowance for books and miscellaneous expenses, about $1,750. Thus a rough budget (excluding travel expenses) for the year is $25,350.

Identifying Resources

There are essentially four sources of funds you can use to pay for college:

1. Money from your parents
2. Need-based scholarships or grants from a college or outside organization
3. Your own contribution from savings, loans, and jobs
4. Assistance unrelated to demonstrated financial need.

All of these are considered by the financial aid office, and the aid "package" given to a student after the parental contribution has been determined usually consists of a combination of scholarships, loans, and campus work.

THE PARENTAL CONTRIBUTION

The financial aid policies of most colleges are based on the assumption that parents should contribute as much as they reasonably can to the educational expenses of their children. The amount of this contribution varies greatly, but almost every family is expected to pay something.

Because there is no limit on aid eligibility based solely on income, the best rule of thumb is *apply for financial aid if there is any reasonable doubt about your ability to meet college costs.* Since it is generally true that applying for financial aid does not affect a student's chances of being admitted, any candidate for admission should apply for aid if his or her family feels they will be unable to pay the entire cost of attendance.

Application for aid is made by completing the Free Application for Federal Student Aid (FAFSA). In addition, many competitive colleges will require you to also file a separate form called PROFILE, since they need more detailed information to award their own funds. The financial aid section of a college's admission information booklet will tell you which financial aid application is required, when it should be filed, and whether a separate aid form of the college's own design is also necessary.

Colleges use the same national system (the Federal Methodology) to determine eligibility for federal and state student aid. This process of coming up with an expected contribution from you (the student) and your parents is called "need analysis." The information on the FAFSA— parental and student income and assets, the number of family members, and the number attending college as well as other variables— is analyzed to derive the expected family contribution.

You can estimate how much your parents might be asked to contribute for college by consulting the chart on page 10. (Keep in mind that the actual parental contribution is determined on campus by a financial aid officer, using the national system as a guideline.) A more detailed analysis is furnished as part of Peterson's Financial Aid Service, a comprehensive software program that provides a personalized method of judging parental ability to pay for college expenses and gives details on college, government, and private student aid sources. It can be found in many high school guidance offices.

Competitive colleges that also require the PROFILE will have at their disposal information that they will analyze in addition to what is reported on the FAFSA. The net result of this further examination (for example, adding the value of the family home to the equation) will usually increase the expected parental contribution compared to the Federal Methodology.

Parental Borrowing

Some families who are judged to have sufficient resources to be able to finance their children's college costs find that lack of cash at any moment prevents them from paying college bills without difficulty. Other families prefer to use less current income by extending their payments over more than four years. In both instances, these families rely on borrowing to assist with college payments. Each year parental loans become a more important form of college financing.

The Federal PLUS program, part of the Federal Family Education Loan Program, is designed to help both aid and non-aid families and allows parents to pay a greater share of educational costs by borrowing at a reasonable interest rate, with the backing of the federal government. The 8–9 percent loans are available primarily from banks that offer Federal Stafford Student Loans. Many competitive colleges, state governments, and commercial lenders also have their own parental loan programs patterned along the lines of PLUS. For more information about parental loans, contact a college financial aid office or your state higher education department.

A number of competitive colleges have developed their own parental loan programs with interest rates somewhat below those of the Federal PLUS program. A college's financial aid material will explain the terms of such loans.

NEED-BASED SCHOLARSHIP OR GRANT ASSISTANCE

Need-based aid is primarily available from colleges themselves and federal and state governments. It is not necessary for a student to apply directly for a particular scholarship at a college; the financial aid office will match an eligible applicant with the appropriate fund.

The Federal Pell Grant is by far the largest single form of federal student assistance; an estimated 5 million students receive awards annually. Families with incomes of up to $25,000 (possibly higher in some cases) may be eligible for grants ranging from $250 to $2,400.

For state scholarships, students should check with the department of higher education about eligibility requirements.

Aid applicants are expected to apply directly to outside organizations for any scholarships for which they may be eligible. It is particularly important to apply for a Federal Pell Grant and a state scholarship. Application for both Pell and state scholarships is made by checking the appropriate box on the FAFSA. (Aid recipients are required to notify the college financial aid office about outside awards, as colleges take into consideration grants from all sources before assigning scholarships from their own funds.)

THE STUDENT'S OWN CONTRIBUTION

All undergraduates, not only those who apply for financial aid, can assume responsibility for meeting a portion of their college expenses by borrowing, working during the academic year and the summer, and contributing a portion of their savings. Colleges require aid recipients to provide a "self-help" contribution before awarding scholarship money because they believe students should pay a reasonable share of their own educational costs.

Student Loans

Many students will be able to borrow to help pay for college. Colleges administer three loans (all backed by the federal government): the Federal Subsidized and Unsubsidized Stafford Student Loans and the Federal Perkins Loan. Students must demonstrate financial need to be eligible for either the Subsidized Stafford Student Loan or the Perkins Loan.

Note: Rather than providing Stafford Loans, many colleges have made arrangements to participate in the Direct Loan Program. As far as the student is concerned, the loan terms are essentially the same.

Summer Employment

All students, whether or not they are receiving financial aid, should plan to work during the summer months. Students can be expected to save from $800 to $1,800 before their freshman year and $1,500 to $2,500 each summer while enrolled in college. It is worthwhile for a student to begin working while in high school to increase the chance of finding summer employment during college vacations.

Term-Time Employment

Colleges have student employment offices that find jobs for students during the school year. Aid recipients on work-study receive priority in placement, but once they have been assisted, non-aid students are helped as well. Some jobs relate closely to academic interests; others should be viewed as a source of income rather than intellectual stimulation. A standard 8- to 12-hour-per-week job does not normally interfere with academic work or extracurricular activities and results in approximately $1,500 to $2,200 in earnings during the year.

Student Savings

Student assets accumulated prior to starting college are available to help pay college bills. The need analysis system expects 35% of each year's student savings to go toward college expenses. This source can often be quite substantial, particularly when families have accumulated large sums in the student's name (or in a trust fund with the student as the beneficiary) to gain a tax advantage. Federal tax codes are now more restrictive in this area, and parents should be aware of current rules before deciding how to set aside money for college.

AID NOT REQUIRING NEED AS AN ELIGIBILITY CRITERION

There are scholarships available to students whether or not they are eligible for need-based financial aid. Awards based on merit are given by certain state scholarship programs, and National Merit Scholarship winners usually receive a $2,000 stipend regardless of family financial circumstances.

Scholarships and prizes are also awarded by community organizations and other local groups. In addition, some parents receive tuition payments for their children as employment benefits. Most colleges offer merit scholarships to a limited group of highly qualified applicants. The selection of recipients for such awards depends on unusual talent in a specific area or on overall academic excellence. To find out more about qualifying for a merit scholarship, see your high school guidance counselor or consult a scholarship guide, such as Keeslar's *Financial Aid for Higher Education* and Peterson's *Paying Less for College*. (Students should be careful about investing in computer-based scholarship searches that *promise* positive results.)

The Reserve Officers' Training Corps sponsors an extensive scholarship program that pays for tuition and books and provides $150 per month. The Army, Air Force, and Navy/Marine Corps have ROTC units at many colleges. High school guidance offices have brochures describing ROTC application procedures. For comprehensive information about financial aid programs sponsored by the military, see Peterson's *How the Military Will Help You Pay for College* (second edition).

A SIMPLE METHOD FOR ESTIMATING FAMILY CONTRIBUTION IN 1996–97

The chart that follows will enable parents to make an approximation of the yearly amount the national financial aid need analysis system will expect them to pay for college in academic year 1996–97.

To use the chart, you need to work with your income, assets, and size of your family. Read the instructions below and enter the proper amounts in the spaces provided.

1. Parents' total 1995 income before taxes

   A. Adjusted gross income (equivalent to tax return entry; use actual or estimated) _____A

   B. Nontaxable income (Social Security benefits, child support, welfare, etc.) _____B

   Total Income: A + B _____①

2. Parents' total assets

   C. Total of cash, savings, and checking accounts _____C

   D. Total value of investments (stocks, bonds, real estate other than home, etc.) _____D

   Total Assets: C + D _____②

3. Family size (include student, parents, other dependent children, and other dependents) _____③

Now find the figures on the chart that correspond to your entries in ①, ②, and ③ to determine your approximate expected parental contribution, interpolating as necessary.

4. Estimated parental contribution from chart _____④

If there will be more than one family member in college half-time or more during 1996–97, divide the figure above by the number in college.

5. Estimated parental contribution for each person in college _____⑤

6. Student's savings _____

   × .35 = _____⑥

7. Finally, add the estimated parental contribution in ⑤ and the estimated student contribution in ⑥ to arrive at the total estimated family contribution _____⑦

This number can be compared to college costs to determine an approximate level of need.

APPROXIMATE EXPECTED PARENTAL CONTRIBUTION FOR 1996–1997

ASSETS▼	FAMILY SIZE	INCOME BEFORE TAXES $ 20,000	30,000	40,000	50,000	60,000	70,000	80,000	90,000	100,000
$ 20,000										
	3	$ 400	2,000	3,800	6,700	9,900	12,500	15,500	18,500	21,500
	4	0	1,300	2,900	5,300	8,300	11,300	14,200	17,200	20,200
	5	0	700	2,200	4,200	6,800	10,100	13,100	16,100	19,100
	6	0	0	1,500	3,300	5,200	8,800	11,700	14,700	17,400
$ 30,000										
	3	$ 400	2,000	3,800	6,700	9,900	12,500	15,500	18,500	21,500
	4	0	1,300	2,900	5,300	8,300	11,300	14,200	17,200	20,200
	5	0	700	2,200	4,200	6,800	10,100	13,100	16,100	19,100
	6	0	0	1,500	3,300	5,200	8,800	11,700	14,700	17,400
$ 40,000										
	3	$ 400	2,000	3,800	6,800	10,000	12,600	15,600	18,600	21,600
	4	0	1,300	2,900	5,400	8,400	11,400	14,300	17,300	20,300
	5	0	700	2,200	4,300	6,900	10,200	13,200	16,200	19,200
	6	0	0	1,500	3,400	5,300	8,900	11,800	14,800	17,500
$ 50,000										
	3	$ 400	2,000	3,800	7,300	10,500	13,200	16,200	19,100	22,100
	4	0	1,300	2,900	5,900	9,000	11,900	14,900	18,000	20,900
	5	0	700	2,200	4,800	7,500	10,800	13,700	16,700	19,700
	6	0	0	1,500	3,700	5,800	9,400	12,400	15,400	18,100
$ 60,000										
	3	$ 400	2,000	3,800	7,900	11,100	13,700	16,700	19,700	22,700
	4	0	1,300	2,900	6,500	9,500	12,500	15,500	18,500	21,400
	5	0	700	2,200	5,200	8,000	11,300	14,300	17,300	20,300
	6	0	0	1,500	4,100	6,400	10,000	13,000	16,000	18,600
$ 70,000										
	3	$ 400	2,000	3,800	8,500	11,700	14,300	17,300	20,300	23,300
	4	0	1,300	2,900	7,000	10,100	13,000	16,000	19,000	22,000
	5	0	700	2,200	5,700	8,600	11,900	14,900	17,900	20,800
	6	0	0	1,500	4,500	6,900	10,600	13,500	16,500	19,200
$ 80,000										
	3	$ 400	2,000	3,800	9,000	12,200	14,900	17,800	21,800	23,800
	4	0	1,300	2,900	7,600	10,700	13,600	16,600	19,600	22,600
	5	0	700	2,200	6,300	9,200	12,400	15,400	18,400	21,400
	6	0	0	1,500	4,900	7,500	11,100	14,100	17,100	19,700
$ 90,000										
	3	$ 400	2,000	3,800	9,600	12,800	15,400	18,400	21,400	24,400
	4	0	1,300	2,900	8,200	11,200	14,200	17,200	20,200	23,100
	5	0	700	2,200	6,900	9,700	13,000	16,000	19,000	22,000
	6	0	0	1,500	5,400	8,100	11,700	14,700	17,700	20,300
$100,000										
	3	$ 400	2,000	3,800	10,200	13,400	16,000	19,000	22,000	25,000
	4	0	1,300	2,900	8,800	11,800	14,700	17,700	20,700	23,700
	5	0	700	2,200	7,400	10,300	13,600	16,600	19,500	22,500
	6	0	0	1,500	6,000	8,600	11,200	15,200	18,200	20,900

3 1833 02820 6073

UNIVERSITY NAME

Location • Setting • Public/Private • Institutional Control • Coed?

> Most schools have chosen to submit a brief message in order to highlight special programs or opportunities that are available or to more fully explain their particular commitment to higher education. That message appears in this box.

 ## Academics

You'll find discussions of key study and learning topics in this section of each page:

- Curriculum and courses
- Degrees awarded
- Most popular majors
- Faculty
- Class size

Computers on Campus

You'll discover information about:

- Computer resources, including purchase plans and training

- Network, e-mail, and on-line services
- Library facilities

 ## Campus Life

Here's where you'll get the story on:

- Organizations, activities, and student participation
- Fraternities and sororities
- Safety provisions
- Sports

 ## Applying

What you'll need to get in:

- Documents, high school courses, and standard tests required
- GPA minimum
- Interviews
- Deadlines
- Main contact name, address, phone, and fax

The statistical picture for each school:

GETTING IN LAST YEAR
- Number who applied
- Percent accepted
- Percent enrolled
- Percent h.s. achievers
- Average GPA
- SAT I/ACT performance*
- Number of National Merit Scholars
- Number of class presidents
- Number of valedictorians

THE STUDENT BODY
- How many students on campus and numbe who are undergrads
- Where they come from
- Percentage from in-state
- Who they are:
  —Men and women
  —Ethnic makeup
  —International students

AFTER FRESHMAN YEAR
- How many come back
- How many graduate within 4 years
- How many graduate within 5 years
- How many graduate within 6 years

AFTER GRADUATION
- Percentage pursuing further study and breakdown of 3 most popular fields
- Percentage with job offers within 6 months
- How many organizations recruit on campus
- Major academic awards won by students

WHAT YOU WILL PAY
- Tuition and fees
- Room and board
- Percent getting aid
- Average need-based and non-need aid

*SAT I scores were reported using either recentered or original (non-recentered) scores. An "(R)" printed after the SAT I performance breakdown indicates that the institution reported recentered SAT I scores while the absence of the "(R)" indicates that original scores were reported.

AGNES SCOTT COLLEGE

Decatur, Georgia • Urban setting • Private • Independent-Religious • Women

With a commitment to academic excellence, Agnes Scott is preparing effective leaders for tomorrow's global and technological world. Agnes Scott ranks 7th nationally in the percentage of graduates who earn PhDs in education and 15th in the humanities. The Atlanta Semester Program in Women, Leadership, and Social Change combines experiential learning (internships) with independent research projects and interdisciplinary academic work. Atlanta, one of the South's most dynamic and international cities, provides opportunities for fun as well as for internships, community service, and cultural events. A comparable value in terms of academic quality, personalized attention, financial strength, and a student-governed honor system cannot be found.

Academics

Agnes Scott offers a liberal arts curriculum and core academic program; more than half of graduate courses are open to undergraduates. It awards bachelor's and master's **degrees**. Challenging opportunities include advanced placement, accelerated degree programs, self-designed majors, tutorials, and Phi Beta Kappa. Special programs include internships, off-campus study, study abroad, and Naval and Air Force ROTC.

The most popular **majors** include English, psychology, and economics. A complete listing of majors at Agnes Scott appears in the Majors Index beginning on page 379.

The **faculty** at Agnes Scott has 64 full-time graduate and undergraduate teachers, 100% with terminal degrees. 94% of the faculty serve as student advisers. The student-faculty ratio is 8:1.

Computers on Campus

Students are not required to have a computer. Student rooms are linked to a campus network. 110 **computers** available in the computer center, computer labs, the learning resource center, Collaborative Learning Center, writing lab, classrooms, the library, and dormitories provide access to e-mail and on-line services. Staffed computer lab on campus (open 24 hours a day) provides training in the use of computers and software.

The 2 **libraries** have 193,924 books, 24,898 microform titles, and 774 subscriptions. They are connected to 2 national **on-line** catalogs.

Campus Life

There are 39 active **organizations** on campus, including a drama/theater group and student-run newspaper. Student **safety services** include late night transport/escort service, 24-hour emergency telephone alarm devices, and 24-hour patrols by trained security personnel.

Agnes Scott is a member of the NCAA (Division III). **Intercollegiate sports** include basketball, cross-country running, soccer, softball, tennis, volleyball.

Applying

Agnes Scott requires an essay, a high school transcript, 1 recommendation, and SAT I or ACT. It recommends 3 years of high school math and science, 2 years of high school foreign language, an interview, and 3 SAT II Subject Tests. Early, deferred, and midyear entrance are possible, with a 3/1 deadline and continuous processing to 3/15 for financial aid. **Contact:** Ms. Stephanie Balmer, Director of Admission, 141 East College Avenue, Decatur, GA 30030-3797, 404-638-6285 or toll-free 800-868-8602; fax 404-638-6414.

GETTING IN LAST YEAR
423 applied
83% were accepted
36% enrolled (125)
45% from top tenth of their h.s. class
3.42 average high school GPA
32% had SAT verbal scores over 600 (R)
35% had SAT math scores over 600 (R)
7% had SAT verbal scores over 700 (R)
6% had SAT math scores over 700 (R)

THE STUDENT BODY
Total 558, of whom 530
  are undergraduates

From 32 states and territories,
  12 other countries
57% from Georgia
100% women
14% African Americans
1% Native Americans
3% Hispanics
3% Asian Americans
3% international students

AFTER FRESHMAN YEAR
86% returned for sophomore year
51% got a degree within 4 years
56% got a degree within 5 years

AFTER GRADUATION
37% pursued further study (24% arts and
  sciences, 6% law, 4% medicine)
1 Fulbright scholar

WHAT YOU WILL PAY
Tuition and fees $14,460
Room and board $6020
68% receive need-based financial aid
Need-based college-administered scholarships and
  grants average $5225 per award
46% receive non-need financial aid
Non-need college-administered scholarships and
  grants average $6127 per award

ALBERT A. LIST COLLEGE, JEWISH THEOLOGICAL SEMINARY OF AMERICA

New York, New York • Urban setting • Private • Independent-Religious • Coed

The Albert A. List College of Jewish Studies of the Jewish Theological Seminary offers students an opportunity to earn 2 bachelor's degrees simultaneously. Students pursue one degree in a specific major of Jewish study at List College and another in the liberal arts major of their choice at Columbia University's School of General Studies or Barnard College. In small classes, students receive personal attention from faculty members, while they enjoy the warm, supportive community at List College and the exciting, diverse campus life at Columbia or Barnard.

 ## Academics

JTS offers an interdisciplinary Jewish studies curriculum and core academic program; more than half of graduate courses are open to undergraduates. It awards bachelor's, master's, and doctoral **degrees** (double bachelor's with Barnard College, Columbia University (NY)). Challenging opportunities include advanced placement, self-designed majors, tutorials, Freshman Honors College, an honors program, and a senior project. Special programs include summer session for credit, off-campus study, and study abroad.

The most popular **majors** include biblical studies, history, and philosophy. A complete listing of majors at JTS appears in the Majors Index beginning on page 379.

The **faculty** at JTS has 55 full-time graduate and undergraduate teachers, 100% with terminal degrees. 12% of the faculty serve as student advisers. The student-faculty ratio is 5:1.

 ## Computers on Campus

Students are not required to have a computer. Student rooms are linked to a campus network. 20 **computers** available in classrooms, the library, and student rooms provide access to e-mail, on-line services, and the Internet.

The **library** has 271,000 books, 9,100 microform titles, and 720 subscriptions.

 ## Campus Life

Active **organizations** on campus include drama/theater group. 90% of students participate in student government elections. Student **safety services** include late night transport/escort service, 24-hour patrols by trained security personnel, and electronically operated dormitory entrances.

This institution has no intercollegiate sports.

 ## Applying

JTS requires an essay, a high school transcript, 3 years of high school math and science, 2 recommendations, SAT I or ACT, and SAT II: Writing Test. It recommends some high school foreign language, an interview, and a minimum high school GPA of 3.0. Early, deferred, and midyear entrance are possible, with a 2/15 deadline and continuous processing to 3/1 for financial aid. **Contact:** Ms. Marci Harris Blumenthal, Director of Admissions, Room 614 Schiff, 3080 Broadway, New York, NY 10027-4649, 212-678-8832; fax 212-678-8947.

GETTING IN LAST YEAR
86 applied
74% were accepted
50% enrolled (32)
25% from top tenth of their h.s. class
3.6 average high school GPA
44% had SAT verbal scores over 600
60% had SAT math scores over 600
100% had ACT scores over 26
3% had SAT verbal scores over 700
16% had SAT math scores over 700
20% had ACT scores over 30
2 National Merit Scholars
3 valedictorians

THE STUDENT BODY
Total 476, of whom 118
  are undergraduates
From 21 states and territories,
  2 other countries
25% from New York
55% women, 45% men
0% African Americans
0% Native Americans
1% Hispanics
0% Asian Americans
3% international students

AFTER FRESHMAN YEAR
90% returned for sophomore year

AFTER GRADUATION
80% pursued further study

WHAT YOU WILL PAY
Tuition and fees $7120
Room only $3640
37% receive need-based financial aid
Need-based college-administered scholarships and
  grants average $12,000 per award
15% receive non-need financial aid
Non-need college-administered scholarships and
  grants average $6000 per award

ALBERTSON COLLEGE OF IDAHO

Caldwell, Idaho • Small-town setting • Private • Independent • Coed

Students seeking the academic rigor and intellectual diversity of a competitive liberal arts experience will feel at home at Albertson. An inviting 44-acre campus is situated at the gateway to the Pacific Northwest, surrounded by outdoor opportunities in mountains, wild rivers, deserts, and forests. The urban culture of Boise is readily accessible (20 minutes away). Students choose Albertson for its quality of teaching, easy access to faculty, and informal, residential lifestyle. Ninety-two percent of applicants to medical school have been accepted over the past 3 decades. Prelaw acceptance is similarly high. Albertson has produced 7 Rhodes Scholars—2 in the last 5 years.

Academics

Albertson offers a broad-based liberal arts curriculum and core academic program. It awards bachelor's **degrees**. Challenging opportunities include advanced placement, accelerated degree programs, self-designed majors, tutorials, an honors program, and a senior project. Special programs include internships, off-campus study, and study abroad.

The most popular **majors** include business, biology/biological sciences, and history. A complete listing of majors at Albertson appears in the Majors Index beginning on page 379.

The **faculty** at Albertson has 60 full-time teachers, 92% with terminal degrees. 96% of the faculty serve as student advisers. The student-faculty ratio is 11:1, and the average class size in core courses is 16.

Computers on Campus

Students are not required to have a computer. 120 **computers** available in the computer center, computer labs, academic buildings, classrooms, the library, and dormitories provide access to e-mail and the Internet. Staffed computer lab on campus.

The 2 **libraries** have 165,230 books, 46,353 microform titles, and 815 subscriptions.

Campus Life

There are 40 active **organizations** on campus, including a drama/theater group and student-run newspaper. 15% of eligible men and 15% of eligible women are members of 2 national **fraternities**, 1 national **sorority**, 1 local fraternity, and 2 local sororities. Student **safety services** include late night transport/escort service, 24-hour emergency telephone alarm devices, 24-hour patrols by trained security personnel, and student patrols.

Albertson is a member of the NAIA. **Intercollegiate sports** (some offering scholarships) include baseball (m), basketball (m, w), golf (m, w), skiing (downhill) (m, w), soccer (m, w), tennis (w), volleyball (w).

Applying

Albertson requires an essay, a high school transcript, 1 recommendation, and SAT I or ACT. It recommends 3 years of high school math and science, 2 years of high school foreign language, an interview, and a minimum high school GPA of 2.0. Early, deferred, and midyear entrance are possible, with rolling admissions and continuous processing to 2/15 for financial aid. **Contact:** Mr. Dennis P. Bergvall, Dean of Admissions, 2112 Cleveland Boulevard, Caldwell, ID 83605-4494, 208-459-5305 or toll-free 800-AC-IDAHO; fax 208-454-2077.

GETTING IN LAST YEAR
625 applied
84% were accepted
30% enrolled (157)
33% from top tenth of their h.s. class
3.44 average high school GPA
11% had SAT verbal scores over 600
30% had SAT math scores over 600
31% had ACT scores over 26
1% had SAT verbal scores over 700
4% had SAT math scores over 700
12% had ACT scores over 30
5 National Merit Scholars

THE STUDENT BODY
627 undergraduates
From 23 states and territories,
    12 other countries
75% from Idaho
52% women, 48% men
1% African Americans
1% Native Americans
4% Hispanics
2% Asian Americans
5% international students

AFTER FRESHMAN YEAR
82% returned for sophomore year

AFTER GRADUATION
66% had job offers within 6 months
15 organizations recruited on campus

WHAT YOU WILL PAY
Tuition and fees $14,305
Room and board $3075
84% receive need-based financial aid
Need-based college-administered scholarships and
    grants average $4532 per award
15% receive non-need financial aid
Non-need college-administered scholarships and
    grants average $4373 per award

ALBION COLLEGE

Albion, Michigan • Small-town setting • Private • Independent-Religious • Coed

Albion believes that a liberal arts education that provides practical career preparation is the ideal educational experience. To enhance that experience, opportunities for experiential learning include study in 21 countries, internships, and opportunities to undertake research with professors. Albion is a member of the Undergraduate Science Group, composed of 50 prestigious liberal arts colleges that have distinguished themselves in science education and research. Each year, an average of 25 Albion seniors attend medical school—an 87% acceptance rate in the past 5 years (52% nationally). Albion also ranks in the top 8% of 867 private undergraduate colleges in the number of alumni who are corporate executives.

Academics

Albion offers a core academic program. It awards bachelor's **degrees**. Challenging opportunities include advanced placement, self-designed majors, tutorials, an honors program, a senior project, Phi Beta Kappa, and Sigma Xi. Special programs include internships, summer session for credit, off-campus study, and study abroad.

The most popular **majors** include economics, biology/biological sciences, and English. A complete listing of majors at Albion appears in the Majors Index beginning on page 379.

The **faculty** at Albion has 107 full-time teachers, 90% with terminal degrees. 82% of the faculty serve as student advisers. The student-faculty ratio is 13:1.

Computers on Campus

Students are not required to have a computer. 120 **computers** available in the computer center, computer labs, academic buildings, classrooms, the library, and dormitories provide access to the main academic computer, off-campus computing facilities, e-mail, on-line services, and the Internet. Staffed computer lab on campus provides training in the use of computers and software.

The **library** has 287,054 books, 19,425 microform titles, and 915 subscriptions. It is connected to 7 national **on-line** catalogs.

Campus Life

There are 103 active **organizations** on campus, including a drama/theater group and student-run newspaper and radio station. 35% of students participate in student government elections. 45% of eligible men and 45% of eligible women are members of 5 national **fraternities** and 6 national **sororities**. Student **safety services** include late night transport/escort service, 24-hour emergency telephone alarm devices, 24-hour patrols by trained security personnel, student patrols, and electronically operated dormitory entrances.

Albion is a member of the NCAA (Division III). **Intercollegiate sports** include baseball (m), basketball (m, w), cross-country running (m, w), field hockey (w), football (m), golf (m, w), lacrosse (m, w), soccer (m, w), softball (w), swimming and diving (m, w), tennis (m, w), track and field (m, w), volleyball (m, w).

Applying

Albion requires a high school transcript, 1 recommendation, and SAT I or ACT. It recommends an essay, 3 years of high school math and science, some high school foreign language, and a minimum high school GPA of 3.0. Early, deferred, and midyear entrance are possible, with rolling admissions and continuous processing to 3/1 for financial aid. **Contact:** Mr. Evan Lipp, Director of Admissions, 616 East Michigan, Albion, MI 49224-1831, 517-629-0321 or toll-free 800-858-6770; fax 517-629-0509.

GETTING IN LAST YEAR
1,728 applied
91% were accepted
30% enrolled (474)
41% from top tenth of their h.s. class
3.4 average high school GPA
37% had SAT verbal scores over 600 (R)
67% had SAT math scores over 600 (R)
47% had ACT scores over 26
6% had SAT verbal scores over 700 (R)
25% had SAT math scores over 700 (R)
13% had ACT scores over 30
14 National Merit Scholars
14 class presidents
22 valedictorians

THE STUDENT BODY
1,548 undergraduates
From 30 states and territories,
  15 other countries
85% from Michigan
51% women, 49% men
3% African Americans
1% Hispanics
3% Asian Americans
1% international students

AFTER FRESHMAN YEAR
84% returned for sophomore year

58% got a degree within 4 years
63% got a degree within 5 years

AFTER GRADUATION
40% pursued further study (14% arts and
  sciences, 10% medicine, 8% law)

WHAT YOU WILL PAY
Tuition and fees $15,334
Room and board $4850
59% receive need-based financial aid
Need-based college-administered scholarships and
  grants average $8406 per award
22% receive non-need financial aid
Non-need college-administered scholarships and
  grants average $7715 per award

ALBRIGHT COLLEGE

Reading, Pennsylvania • Suburban setting • Private • Independent-Religious • Coed

Historically strong in the sciences and committed to the liberal arts, Albright College offers programs that are rigorous, flexible, and practical. A Methodist-affiliated institution that stresses the importance of values in education, Albright encourages its students to grow spiritually, socially, and culturally in an atmosphere of academic freedom. Albright's innovative Alpha Program gives students the intellectual space to investigate before choosing an area of concentration. This openness prepares them to accept the challenges of lifelong learning. An excellence in academic and preprofessional courses, well integrated with cocurricular programs, is the distinguishing hallmark of the Albright experience.

Academics

Albright offers a core academic program. It awards bachelor's **degrees**. Challenging opportunities include advanced placement, accelerated degree programs, self-designed majors, tutorials, an honors program, and a senior project. Special programs include internships, summer session for credit, and off-campus study.

The most popular **majors** include business, biology/biological sciences, and psychology. A complete listing of majors at Albright appears in the Majors Index beginning on page 379.

The **faculty** at Albright has 61 full-time teachers, 92% with terminal degrees. 100% of the faculty serve as student advisers. The student-faculty ratio is 12:1, and the average class size in core courses is 25.

Computers on Campus

Students are not required to have a computer. 225 **computers** available in the computer center, computer labs, labs in classroom buildings, classrooms, the library, the student center, and dormitories provide access to the main academic computer, off-campus computing facilities, e-mail, and the Internet. Staffed computer lab on campus provides training in the use of computers and software.

The **library** has 184,833 books, 10,081 microform titles, and 700 subscriptions. It is connected to 7 national **on-line** catalogs.

Campus Life

There are 70 active **organizations** on campus, including a drama/theater group and student-run newspaper and radio station. 90% of students participate in student government elections. 24% of eligible men and 23% of eligible women are members of 5 national **fraternities** and 3 national **sororities**. Student **safety services** include late night transport/escort service, 24-hour emergency telephone alarm devices, 24-hour patrols by trained security personnel, student patrols, and electronically operated dormitory entrances.

Albright is a member of the NCAA (Division III). **Intercollegiate sports** include badminton (w), baseball (m), basketball (m, w), cross-country running (m, w), field hockey (w), football (m), golf (m), ice hockey (m), lacrosse (m), rugby (m, w), soccer (m, w), softball (w), swimming and diving (m, w), tennis (m, w), track and field (m, w), volleyball (m, w), wrestling (m).

Applying

Albright requires an essay, a high school transcript, 2 years of high school foreign language, 2 recommendations, and SAT I or ACT. It recommends 3 years of high school math and science, an interview, and 3 SAT II Subject Tests. Early, deferred, and midyear entrance are possible, with a 2/15 deadline and continuous processing to 3/1 for financial aid. **Contact:** Mr. Gregory E. Eichhorn, Director of Admissions, Reading, PA 19612-5234, 610-921-7512 or toll-free 800-252-1856; fax 610-921-7530.

GETTING IN LAST YEAR
1,078 applied
89% were accepted
33% enrolled (312)
21% from top tenth of their h.s. class
3.07 average high school GPA
23% had SAT verbal scores over 600 (R)
20% had SAT math scores over 600 (R)
15% had ACT scores over 26
3% had SAT verbal scores over 700 (R)
3% had SAT math scores over 700 (R)
0% had ACT scores over 30
8 valedictorians

THE STUDENT BODY
1,072 undergraduates
From 23 states and territories,
 19 other countries
64% from Pennsylvania
51% women, 49% men
5% African Americans
1% Native Americans
2% Hispanics
3% Asian Americans
4% international students

AFTER FRESHMAN YEAR
80% returned for sophomore year
65% got a degree within 4 years
70% got a degree within 5 years

AFTER GRADUATION
32% pursued further study (12% arts and
 sciences, 9% law, 5% business)
39% had job offers within 6 months
40 organizations recruited on campus

WHAT YOU WILL PAY
Tuition and fees $16,575
Room and board $4820
75% receive need-based financial aid
12% receive non-need financial aid

ALFRED UNIVERSITY

Alfred, New York • Rural setting • Private • Independent • Coed

Alfred is undertaking an unprecedented building campaign to support an excellent academic program. In 1992, the University dedicated the $6.2-million Scholes Library of Ceramics, the largest library in the United States dedicated to the study of ceramics. The $5.6-million College of Business F. W. Olin Foundation building was dedicated in 1993, and the $10-million Powell Campus Center was dedicated in 1994. By early 1996, the $10-million Miller Performing Arts Center will be completed, and work will begin in the summer of 1996 on the $1.5-million McComsey Career Development Center.

Academics

Alfred offers a core academic program; fewer than half of graduate courses are open to undergraduates. It awards bachelor's, master's, and doctoral **degrees**. Challenging opportunities include advanced placement, accelerated degree programs, self-designed majors, an honors program, a senior project, and Sigma Xi. Special programs include cooperative education, internships, summer session for credit, off-campus study, study abroad, and Army ROTC.

The most popular **majors** include art/fine arts, business, and psychology. A complete listing of majors at Alfred appears in the Majors Index beginning on page 379.

The **faculty** at Alfred has 168 full-time graduate and undergraduate teachers, 90% with terminal degrees. 70% of the faculty serve as student advisers. The student-faculty ratio is 12:1.

Computers on Campus

Students are not required to have a computer. Student rooms are linked to a campus network. 400 **computers** available in the computer center, computer labs, the learn-ing resource center, academic departments, the library, and dormitories provide access to off-campus computing facilities, on-line services, and the Internet. Staffed computer lab on campus (open 24 hours a day) provides training in the use of computers and software.

The 2 **libraries** have 238,234 books, 506 microform titles, and 1,441 subscriptions.

Campus Life

There are 80 active **organizations** on campus, including a drama/theater group and student-run newspaper and radio station. 30% of eligible men and 15% of eligible women are members of 5 national **fraternities**, 2 national **sororities**, 2 local fraternities, and 3 local sororities. Student **safety services** include late night transport/escort service, 24-hour emergency telephone alarm devices, and student patrols.

Alfred is a member of the NCAA (Division III). **Intercollegiate sports** include basketball (m, w), cross-country running (m, w), equestrian sports (m, w), football (m), golf (m, w), lacrosse (m, w), skiing (downhill) (m, w), soccer (m, w), softball (w), swimming and diving (m, w), tennis (m, w), track and field (m), volleyball (w).

Applying

Alfred requires an essay, a high school transcript, 1 recommendation, SAT I or ACT, SAT II: Writing Test, and in some cases 3 years of high school math and science and an interview. It recommends 3 years of high school math and science, some high school foreign language, and an interview. Early, deferred, and midyear entrance are possible, with a 2/1 deadline and continuous processing to 4/1 for financial aid. **Contact:** Ms. Laurie Richer, Director of Admissions, Alumni Hall, Alfred, NY 14802-1205, 607-871-2115 or toll-free 800-541-9229; fax 607-871-2198.

GETTING IN LAST YEAR

1,648 applied
85% were accepted
35% enrolled (495)
20% from top tenth of their h.s. class
3.2 average high school GPA
37% had SAT verbal scores over 600 (R)
36% had SAT math scores over 600 (R)
60% had ACT scores over 26
6% had SAT verbal scores over 700 (R)
4% had SAT math scores over 700 (R)
11% had ACT scores over 30
10 National Merit Scholars

THE STUDENT BODY

Total 2,405, of whom 1,984
    are undergraduates
From 33 states and territories,
    21 other countries
69% from New York
47% women, 53% men
4% African Americans
1% Native Americans
3% Hispanics
2% Asian Americans
1% international students

AFTER FRESHMAN YEAR

83% returned for sophomore year
43% got a degree within 4 years
61% got a degree within 5 years
62% got a degree within 6 years

AFTER GRADUATION

35% pursued further study (15% engineering, 7% arts and sciences, 7% business)

WHAT YOU WILL PAY

Tuition and fees $17,948
Room and board $5716

ALLEGHENY COLLEGE

Meadville, Pennsylvania • Small-town setting • Private • Independent-Religious • Coed

One of America's oldest colleges, Allegheny stands out today for the breadth of the skills and understandings consistently developed in its students: superior professional capabilities, from writing to leadership to problem solving; skills for managing everyday life; important social abilities; talents for responsible citizenship; and values clarification. Students are actively engaged in learning through small and dynamic classes, hands-on laboratories, original research projects, and collaborations with faculty. All students complete a substantial creative or research project in the senior year, proving their abilities to complete a major assignment, work independently, analyze and synthesize, and write and speak persuasively.

Academics

Allegheny offers a multidisciplinary curriculum and core academic program. It awards bachelor's **degrees**. Challenging opportunities include advanced placement, accelerated degree programs, self-designed majors, tutorials, a senior project, and Phi Beta Kappa. Special programs include internships, off-campus study, study abroad, and Army ROTC.

The most popular **majors** include psychology, English, and political science/government. A complete listing of majors at Allegheny appears in the Majors Index beginning on page 379.

The **faculty** at Allegheny has 154 full-time teachers, 94% with terminal degrees. 100% of the faculty serve as student advisers. The student-faculty ratio is 12:1.

Computers on Campus

Students are not required to have a computer. Student rooms are linked to a campus network. 307 **computers** available in computer labs, academic buildings, and the library provide access to the main academic computer,

off-campus computing facilities, e-mail, on-line services, and the Internet. Staffed computer lab on campus (open 24 hours a day) provides training in the use of computers and software.

The 3 **libraries** have 405,712 books, 215,521 microform titles, and 1,194 subscriptions. They are connected to 5 national **on-line** catalogs.

Campus Life

There are 112 active **organizations** on campus, including a drama/theater group and student-run newspaper and radio station. 45% of students participate in student government elections. 30% of eligible men and 35% of eligible women are members of 5 national **fraternities** and 5 national **sororities**. Student **safety services** include late night transport/escort service, 24-hour emergency telephone alarm devices, 24-hour patrols by trained security personnel, student patrols, and electronically operated dormitory entrances.

Allegheny is a member of the NCAA (Division III). **Intercollegiate sports** include baseball (m), basketball (m, w), cross-country running (m, w), fencing (m, w), football (m), golf (m), ice hockey (m), lacrosse (m, w), rugby (m), skiing (downhill) (m, w), soccer (m, w), softball (w), swimming and diving (m, w), tennis (m, w), track and field (m, w), volleyball (m, w).

Applying

Allegheny requires an essay, a high school transcript, 2 recommendations, and SAT I or ACT. It recommends 3 years of high school math and science, 2 years of high school foreign language, an interview, and 2 SAT II Subject Tests. Early, deferred, and midyear entrance are possible, with a 2/15 deadline and continuous processing to 2/15 for financial aid. **Contact:** Ms. Gayle Pollock, Director of Admissions, Park Avenue, Meadville, PA 16335, 814-332-4351 or toll-free 800-521-5293; fax 814-337-0431.

GETTING IN LAST YEAR
2,811 applied
74% were accepted
27% enrolled (565)
42% from top tenth of their h.s. class
17% had SAT verbal scores over 600
45% had SAT math scores over 600
41% had ACT scores over 26
1% had SAT verbal scores over 700
9% had SAT math scores over 700
10% had ACT scores over 30
35 class presidents
20 valedictorians

THE STUDENT BODY
1,838 undergraduates
From 39 states and territories,
   16 other countries
58% from Pennsylvania
52% women, 48% men
3% African Americans
1% Native Americans
1% Hispanics
3% Asian Americans
2% international students

AFTER FRESHMAN YEAR
87% returned for sophomore year
65% got a degree within 4 years

73% got a degree within 5 years
74% got a degree within 6 years

AFTER GRADUATION
35% pursued further study (16% arts and
   sciences, 9% law, 4% business)
15 organizations recruited on campus

WHAT YOU WILL PAY
Tuition and fees $18,020
Room and board $4550
78% receive need-based financial aid
Need-based college-administered scholarships and
   grants average $8929 per award
55% receive non-need financial aid
Non-need college-administered scholarships and
   grants average $5773 per award

ALMA COLLEGE

Alma, Michigan • Small-town setting • Private • Independent-Religious • Coed

Alma's undergraduates thrive on challenging academic programs in a supportive, small-college atmosphere. The College is committed to a value-added liberal arts curriculum with opportunities for one-on-one research and publication with faculty whose first priority is teaching. Students enjoy small classes in modern facilities, including the new $7-million Heritage Center for the Performing Arts. Alma College offers excellent preparation for professional careers in business, law, medicine, the arts, and a wide range of other fields.

 ## Academics

Alma offers an interdisciplinary curriculum and core academic program. It awards bachelor's **degrees**. Challenging opportunities include advanced placement, accelerated degree programs, self-designed majors, tutorials, an honors program, a senior project, and Phi Beta Kappa. Special programs include internships, summer session for credit, off-campus study, study abroad, and Army ROTC.

The most popular **majors** include business, biology/biological sciences, and physical fitness/human movement. A complete listing of majors at Alma appears in the Majors Index beginning on page 379.

The **faculty** at Alma has 84 full-time teachers, 87% with terminal degrees. 92% of the faculty serve as student advisers. The student-faculty ratio is 14:1.

 ## Computers on Campus

Students are not required to have a computer. Student rooms are linked to a campus network. 564 **computers** available in the computer center, computer labs, the research center, faculty offices, classrooms, the library, and dormitories provide access to the main academic computer, off-campus computing facilities, e-mail, on-line services, and the Internet. Staffed computer lab on campus provides training in the use of computers and software.

The **library** has 207,600 books, 32,000 microform titles, and 1,135 subscriptions. It is connected to 4 national **on-line** catalogs.

 ## Campus Life

There are 128 active **organizations** on campus, including a drama/theater group and student-run newspaper and radio station. 60% of students participate in student government elections. 31% of eligible men and 31% of eligible women are members of 4 national **fraternities**, 3 national **sororities**, 1 local fraternity, and 1 local sorority. Student **safety services** include 24-hour emergency telephone alarm devices and 24-hour patrols by trained security personnel.

Alma is a member of the NCAA (Division III). **Intercollegiate sports** include baseball (m), basketball (m, w), cross-country running (m, w), football (m), golf (m, w), soccer (m, w), softball (w), swimming and diving (m, w), tennis (m, w), track and field (m, w), volleyball (w).

 ## Applying

Alma requires a high school transcript, 2 recommendations, SAT I or ACT, a minimum high school GPA of 2.0, and in some cases a campus interview. It recommends an essay, 3 years of high school math and science, and 2 years of high school foreign language. Early, deferred, and midyear entrance are possible, with rolling admissions and continuous processing to 2/15 for financial aid. **Contact:** Mr. John Seveland, Vice President for Enrollment and Student Affairs, 614 West Superior Street, Alma, MI 48801-1599, 517-463-7139 or toll-free 800-321-ALMA.

GETTING IN LAST YEAR
1,122 applied
94% were accepted
35% enrolled (371)
40% from top tenth of their h.s. class
3.5 average high school GPA
47% had ACT scores over 26
13% had ACT scores over 30
9 National Merit Scholars

THE STUDENT BODY
1,418 undergraduates
From 20 states and territories,
  8 other countries

95% from Michigan
56% women, 44% men
1% African Americans
1% Native Americans
1% Hispanics
2% Asian Americans
1% international students

AFTER FRESHMAN YEAR
87% returned for sophomore year
60% got a degree within 4 years
73% got a degree within 5 years
75% got a degree within 6 years

AFTER GRADUATION
27% pursued further study (11% arts and
  sciences, 5% business, 4% law)

70% had job offers within 6 months
16 organizations recruited on campus

WHAT YOU WILL PAY
Tuition and fees $13,332
Room and board $4762
76% receive need-based financial aid
Need-based college-administered scholarships and
  grants average $4530 per award
65% receive non-need financial aid
Non-need college-administered scholarships and
  grants average $6965 per award

AMERICAN UNIVERSITY

Washington, District of Columbia • Suburban setting • Private • Independent-Religious • Coed

Students who believe the world can be a better place, and want to lead their peers in making it a better place, should be at American University. That is because the University's mission, unique in higher education, is to turn ideas into service by emphasizing the liberal arts and sciences and connecting them to the issues of contemporary public affairs.

Academics

AU offers a liberal arts curriculum and core academic program. It awards associate, bachelor's, master's, doctoral, and first professional **degrees**. Challenging opportunities include advanced placement, self-designed majors, an honors program, a senior project, Phi Beta Kappa, and Sigma Xi. Special programs include cooperative education, internships, summer session for credit, off-campus study, study abroad, and Army and Air Force ROTC.

The most popular **majors** include international studies, communication, and political science/government. A complete listing of majors at AU appears in the Majors Index beginning on page 379.

The **faculty** at AU has 526 full-time graduate and undergraduate teachers, 92% with terminal degrees. The student-faculty ratio is 14:1.

Computers on Campus

Students are not required to have a computer. Student rooms are linked to a campus network. 200 **computers** available in the computer center, labs, and the student center provide access to the main academic computer, off-campus computing facilities, e-mail, on-line services, and the Internet. Staffed computer lab on campus (open 24 hours a day) provides training in the use of computers and software.

The 2 **libraries** have 618,000 books, 790,000 microform titles, and 3,500 subscriptions.

Campus Life

There are 85 active **organizations** on campus, including a drama/theater group and student-run newspaper and radio station. 20% of eligible men and 25% of eligible women are members of 7 national **fraternities** and 8 national **sororities**. Student **safety services** include late night transport/escort service, 24-hour emergency telephone alarm devices, 24-hour patrols by trained security personnel, and electronically operated dormitory entrances.

AU is a member of the NCAA (Division I). **Intercollegiate sports** (some offering scholarships) include basketball (m, w), cross-country running (m, w), field hockey (w), golf (m), lacrosse (m), soccer (m, w), swimming and diving (m, w), tennis (m, w), volleyball (w), wrestling (m).

Applying

AU requires an essay, a high school transcript, 3 years of high school math, 2 years of high school foreign language, 3 recommendations, SAT I or ACT, and a minimum high school GPA of 2.0. It recommends 4 years of high school math, 3 years of high school science, an interview, 3 SAT II Subject Tests, and a minimum high school GPA of 3.0. Early, deferred, and midyear entrance are possible, with a 2/1 deadline and continuous processing to 3/1 for financial aid. **Contact:** Ms. Marcelle D. Heerschap, Director of Admissions, 4400 Massachusetts Avenue, NW, Washington, DC 20016-8001, 202-885-6000; fax 202-885-6014.

GETTING IN LAST YEAR
5,646 applied
78% were accepted
29% enrolled (1,276)
34% from top tenth of their h.s. class
3.3 average high school GPA
26% had SAT verbal scores over 600
49% had SAT math scores over 600
56% had ACT scores over 26
3% had SAT verbal scores over 700
10% had SAT math scores over 700
17% had ACT scores over 30
29 National Merit Scholars

THE STUDENT BODY
Total 9,630, of whom 4,982
 are undergraduates
From 53 states and territories,
 110 other countries
5% from District of Columbia
60% women, 40% men
6% African Americans
0% Native Americans
5% Hispanics
4% Asian Americans
8% international students

AFTER FRESHMAN YEAR
82% returned for sophomore year
57% got a degree within 4 years
66% got a degree within 5 years

AFTER GRADUATION
125 organizations recruited on campus
4 Fulbright scholars

WHAT YOU WILL PAY
Tuition and fees $17,110
Room and board $6698

AMHERST COLLEGE

Amherst, Massachusetts • Small-town setting • Private • Independent • Coed

Amherst seeks talented students who have demonstrated their passion for learning along with a willingness to be involved in the world around them. With its dynamic, dedicated faculty, Amherst is a lively intellectual and cultural community in which students are active members; small classes and a wide variety of extracurricular offerings provide many opportunities for exploration. An open curriculum with majors ranging from neuroscience to women's and gender studies allows students substantial freedom to pursue their goals.

 ## Academics

Amherst College offers an open curriculum and no core academic program. It awards bachelor's **degrees**. Challenging opportunities include self-designed majors, an honors program, a senior project, Phi Beta Kappa, and Sigma Xi. Special programs include off-campus study and study abroad.

The most popular **majors** include English, political science/government, and economics. A complete listing of majors at Amherst College appears in the Majors Index beginning on page 379.

The **faculty** at Amherst College has 173 full-time teachers, 91% with terminal degrees. 100% of the faculty serve as student advisers. The student-faculty ratio is 10:1.

 ## Computers on Campus

Students are not required to have a computer. Student rooms are linked to a campus network. 75 **computers** available in the computer center, academic departments, the library, and dormitories provide access to e-mail. Staffed computer lab on campus provides training in the use of computers and software.

The 7 **libraries** have 807,106 books, 434,437 microform titles, and 4,731 subscriptions.

 ## Campus Life

There are 100 active **organizations** on campus, including a drama/theater group and student-run newspaper and radio station. 65% of students participate in student government elections. Student **safety services** include late night transport/escort service, 24-hour emergency telephone alarm devices, and electronically operated dormitory entrances.

Amherst College is a member of the NCAA (Division III). **Intercollegiate sports** include baseball (m), basketball (m, w), crew (m, w), cross-country running (m, w), equestrian sports (m, w), field hockey (w), football (m), golf (m, w), ice hockey (m, w), lacrosse (m, w), rugby (m, w), sailing (m, w), skiing (downhill) (m, w), soccer (m, w), softball (w), squash (m, w), swimming and diving (m, w), tennis (m, w), track and field (m, w), volleyball (m, w), water polo (m, w).

 ## Applying

Amherst College requires an essay, a high school transcript, 3 years of high school math, 3 recommendations, SAT I or ACT, and 3 SAT II Subject Tests. It recommends 4 years of high school math, 3 years of high school science, and 3 years of high school foreign language. Early, deferred, and midyear entrance are possible, with a 12/31 deadline and a 2/15 priority date for financial aid. **Contact:** Ms. Jane E. Reynolds, Dean of Admission, Route 116, South Pleasant Street, Amherst, MA 01002, 413-542-2328; fax 413-542-2040.

GETTING IN LAST YEAR
4,836 applied
19% were accepted
45% enrolled (422)
78% from top tenth of their h.s. class
67% had SAT verbal scores over 600
87% had SAT math scores over 600
24% had SAT verbal scores over 700
48% had SAT math scores over 700

THE STUDENT BODY
1,600 undergraduates
From 50 states and territories,
    25 other countries

13% from Massachusetts
44% women, 56% men
8% African Americans
1% Native Americans
9% Hispanics
12% Asian Americans
3% international students

AFTER FRESHMAN YEAR
97% returned for sophomore year
88% got a degree within 4 years
94% got a degree within 5 years
97% got a degree within 6 years

AFTER GRADUATION
34% pursued further study (21% arts and
    sciences, 8% law, 5% medicine)
2 Fulbright scholars

WHAT YOU WILL PAY
Tuition and fees $21,065
Room and board $5560
42% receive need-based financial aid
Need-based college-administered scholarships and
    grants average $14,647 per award

AUBURN UNIVERSITY

Auburn, Alabama • Small-town setting • Public • State-supported • Coed

Auburn University strives continuously to provide outstanding, economically accessible instruction to its undergraduate, graduate, and professional students, with programs in agriculture, life sciences, engineering, architecture, pharmacy, and veterinary medicine being especially well known. Auburn has been identified as 1 of 20 institutions with the most alumni serving as CEOs of Fortune 500 and Service 500 industries and is among the top 10 in providing NASA astronauts. Yet, despite the diversity of offerings and the emphasis on academic excellence, Auburn is best known for its friendliness, with a welcoming small-town environment and activities for every interest.

Academics

Auburn offers a sciences and humanities curriculum and core academic program; fewer than half of graduate courses are open to undergraduates. It awards bachelor's, master's, doctoral, and first professional **degrees**. Challenging opportunities include advanced placement, accelerated degree programs, an honors program, a senior project, and Sigma Xi. Special programs include cooperative education, internships, summer session for credit, study abroad, and Army, Naval, and Air Force ROTC.

The most popular **majors** include mechanical engineering, psychology, and finance/banking. A complete listing of majors at Auburn appears in the Majors Index beginning on page 379.

The **faculty** at Auburn has 1,131 full-time graduate and undergraduate teachers, 91% with terminal degrees. The student-faculty ratio is 16:1.

Computers on Campus

Students are not required to have a computer. Student rooms are linked to a campus network. 600 **computers**

available in computer labs, the library, and dormitories provide access to the main academic computer, e-mail, and the Internet. Staffed computer lab on campus (open 24 hours a day).

The 3 **libraries** have 2.3 million books, 2.2 million microform titles, and 19,410 subscriptions. They are connected to 13 national **on-line** catalogs.

Campus Life

There are 300 active **organizations** on campus, including a drama/theater group and student-run newspaper and radio station. 16% of eligible men and 29% of eligible women are members of 27 national **fraternities** and 18 national **sororities**. Student **safety services** include late night transport/escort service, 24-hour emergency telephone alarm devices, 24-hour patrols by trained security personnel, and electronically operated dormitory entrances.

Auburn is a member of the NCAA (Division I). **Intercollegiate sports** (some offering scholarships) include baseball (m), basketball (m, w), cross-country running (m, w), football (m), golf (m, w), gymnastics (w), soccer (w), softball (w), swimming and diving (m, w), tennis (m, w), track and field (m, w), volleyball (w).

Applying

Auburn requires a high school transcript, 3 years of high school math, SAT I or ACT, a minimum high school GPA of 2.0, and in some cases a minimum high school GPA of 3.0. It recommends 3 years of high school science and 1 year of high school foreign language. Early, deferred, and midyear entrance are possible, with a 9/1 deadline and continuous processing to 4/15 for financial aid. **Contact:** Mr. John Fletcher, Interim Director of Admissions, 202 Mary Martin Hall, Auburn University, AL 36849-0001, 334-844-4080 or toll-free 800-392-8051 (in-state).

GETTING IN LAST YEAR
9,326 applied
89% were accepted
43% enrolled (3,592)
24% from top tenth of their h.s. class
3.05 average high school GPA
13% had SAT verbal scores over 600
38% had SAT math scores over 600
29% had ACT scores over 26
1% had SAT verbal scores over 700
8% had SAT math scores over 700
8% had ACT scores over 30
37 National Merit Scholars

THE STUDENT BODY
Total 22,122, of whom 18,615
   are undergraduates

From 53 states and territories,
   51 other countries
64% from Alabama
47% women, 53% men
6% African Americans
1% Native Americans
1% Hispanics
1% Asian Americans
1% international students

AFTER FRESHMAN YEAR
33% got a degree within 4 years
61% got a degree within 5 years

AFTER GRADUATION
30% pursued further study (10% business, 6%
   arts and sciences, 4% engineering)

350 organizations recruited on campus
2 Fulbright scholars

WHAT YOU WILL PAY
Resident tuition and fees $2250
Nonresident tuition and fees $6750
Room only $1410
32% receive need-based financial aid
Need-based college-administered scholarships and
   grants average $1126 per award
26% receive non-need financial aid
Non-need college-administered scholarships and
   grants average $1433 per award

AUGUSTANA COLLEGE

Rock Island, Illinois • Suburban setting • Private • Independent-Religious • Coed

Augustana College seeks to develop in students the characteristics of liberally educated persons: clarity of thought and expression, curiosity, fair-mindedness, appreciation for the arts and cultural diversity, intellectual honesty, and a considered set of personal values and commitments. Students combine exploration of the arts, sciences, and humanities with in-depth study in their major field(s), guided by an excellent, committed faculty; they grow personally and socially through participation in wide extracurricular and cocurricular opportunities on one of the most beautiful campuses in the country. Special features include innovative interdisciplinary first-year course sequences, foreign study, and internships—both domestic and international.

Academics

Augie offers a liberal arts and sciences curriculum and core academic program. It awards bachelor's **degrees**. Challenging opportunities include advanced placement, tutorials, Freshman Honors College, an honors program, a senior project, and Phi Beta Kappa. Special programs include cooperative education, internships, summer session for credit, and study abroad.

The most popular **majors** include business, biology/biological sciences, and English. A complete listing of majors at Augie appears in the Majors Index beginning on page 379.

The **faculty** at Augie has 131 full-time teachers, 90% with terminal degrees. 92% of the faculty serve as student advisers. The student-faculty ratio is 13:1.

Computers on Campus

Students are not required to have a computer. Student rooms are linked to a campus network. 205 **computers** available in the computer center, computer labs, the learning resource center, all classroom buildings, classrooms, the library, and dormitories provide access to the main academic computer, off-campus computing facilities, e-mail, on-line services, and the Internet. Staffed computer lab on campus provides training in the use of computers and software.

The 4 **libraries** have 246,462 books, 7,806 microform titles, and 1,588 subscriptions. They are connected to 4 national **on-line** catalogs.

Campus Life

There are 109 active **organizations** on campus, including a drama/theater group and student-run newspaper and radio station. 33% of students participate in student government elections. 26% of eligible men and 30% of eligible women are members of 7 local **fraternities** and 7 local **sororities**. Student **safety services** include late night transport/escort service, 24-hour emergency telephone alarm devices, and 24-hour patrols by trained security personnel.

Augie is a member of the NCAA (Division III). **Intercollegiate sports** include baseball (m), basketball (m, w), cross-country running (m, w), football (m), golf (m), soccer (m, w), softball (w), swimming and diving (m, w), tennis (m, w), track and field (m, w), volleyball (w), wrestling (m).

Applying

Augie requires a high school transcript, SAT I or ACT, and in some cases an essay, 2 recommendations, and an interview. It recommends 3 years of high school math and science and 1 year of high school foreign language. Early, deferred, and midyear entrance are possible, with a 4/1 deadline and continuous processing to 4/1 for financial aid. **Contact:** Mr. Martin Sauer, Director of Admissions, 820 38th Street, Rock Island, IL 61201-2296, 309-794-7341 or toll-free 800-798-8100; fax 309-794-7431.

GETTING IN LAST YEAR
2,240 applied
80% were accepted
34% enrolled (605)
31% from top tenth of their h.s. class
3.4 average high school GPA
39% had ACT scores over 26
10% had ACT scores over 30
18 valedictorians

THE STUDENT BODY
2,197 undergraduates
From 32 states and territories,
   22 other countries
82% from Illinois

59% women, 41% men
3% African Americans
1% Native Americans
2% Hispanics
2% Asian Americans
3% international students

AFTER FRESHMAN YEAR
85% returned for sophomore year
68% got a degree within 4 years
73% got a degree within 5 years
75% got a degree within 6 years

AFTER GRADUATION
25% pursued further study (15% arts and
   sciences, 6% medicine, 3% law)

55% had job offers within 6 months
57 organizations recruited on campus
1 Fulbright scholar

WHAT YOU WILL PAY
Tuition and fees $14,064
Room and board $4257
68% receive need-based financial aid
Need-based college-administered scholarships and
   grants average $3930 per award
51% receive non-need financial aid
Non-need college-administered scholarships and
   grants average $3954 per award

AUGUSTANA COLLEGE

Sioux Falls, South Dakota • Urban setting • Private • Independent-Religious • Coed

The Augustana College curriculum creates a learning environment with educational bookends. First-year students take New Student Seminar, a course that facilitates a positive transition to the College community. Students complete their classes at Augustana with the Capstone course. This team-taught class stimulates seniors to recognize the relationship of their college studies to central issues of human existence. Augustana was again named a "top 10 regional liberal arts college" and a "best value" by *U.S. News & World Report*. Sioux Falls continues to be recognized as one of America's top 20 cities by *Money* magazine. The College's location affords a stimulating learning environment and opportunities for internships and employment.

Academics

Augustana offers a core academic program; fewer than half of graduate courses are open to undergraduates. It awards associate, bachelor's, and master's **degrees**. Challenging opportunities include advanced placement, accelerated degree programs, self-designed majors, tutorials, an honors program, and a senior project. Special programs include cooperative education, internships, summer session for credit, off-campus study, and study abroad.

The most popular **majors** include biology/biological sciences, education, and business. A complete listing of majors at Augustana appears in the Majors Index beginning on page 379.

The **faculty** at Augustana has 115 full-time graduate and undergraduate teachers, 85% with terminal degrees. 100% of the faculty serve as student advisers. The student-faculty ratio is 13:1.

Computers on Campus

Students are not required to have a computer. 115 **computers** available in the computer center, computer labs, academic departments, classrooms, the library, the student center, and dormitories provide access to the main academic computer, off-campus computing facilities, e-mail, on-line services, and the Internet. Staffed computer lab on campus (open 24 hours a day) provides training in the use of computers and software.

The 2 **libraries** have 221,380 books, 69,800 microform titles, and 938 subscriptions. They are connected to 2 national **on-line** catalogs.

Campus Life

There are 50 active **organizations** on campus, including a drama/theater group and student-run newspaper and radio station. 60% of students participate in student government elections. 20% of eligible men and 40% of eligible women are members of 1 local **fraternity** and 1 local **sorority**. Student **safety services** include 18-hour patrols by trained security personnel, late night transport/escort service, 24-hour emergency telephone alarm devices, and electronically operated dormitory entrances.

Augustana is a member of the NCAA (Division II). **Intercollegiate sports** (some offering scholarships) include baseball (m), basketball (m, w), cross-country running (m, w), football (m), softball (w), tennis (m, w), track and field (m, w), volleyball (w), wrestling (m).

Applying

Augustana requires a high school transcript, 1 recommendation, minimum 2.5 GPA, SAT I or ACT, and in some cases an essay. It recommends 3 years of high school math and science, some high school foreign language, and an interview. Early, deferred, and midyear entrance are possible, with rolling admissions and continuous processing to 3/1 for financial aid. **Contact:** Mr. Robert A. Preloger, Assistant to the President/Dean of Enrollment, 2001 South Summit, Sioux Falls, SD 57197, 605-336-5516 or toll-free 800-727-2844; fax 605-336-5518.

GETTING IN LAST YEAR
1,050 applied
93% were accepted
38% enrolled (372)
27% from top tenth of their h.s. class
3.44 average high school GPA
30% had ACT scores over 26
7% had ACT scores over 30
2 National Merit Scholars

THE STUDENT BODY
Total 1,778, of whom 1,592
    are undergraduates

From 39 states and territories,
    12 other countries
53% from South Dakota
65% women, 35% men
1% African Americans
1% Native Americans
1% Hispanics
1% Asian Americans
3% international students

AFTER FRESHMAN YEAR
78% returned for sophomore year
53% got a degree within 4 years

63% got a degree within 5 years
65% got a degree within 6 years

AFTER GRADUATION
20% pursued further study (5% business, 4% arts and sciences, 4% law)
85% had job offers within 6 months
60 organizations recruited on campus

WHAT YOU WILL PAY
Tuition and fees $11,780
Room and board $3372

AUSTIN COLLEGE

Sherman, Texas • Suburban setting • Private • Independent-Religious • Coed

Consistently cited among the nation's best and most affordable liberal arts colleges, Austin College is one of only a handful of nationally recognized colleges in the Southwest. It is the only institution in a 16-state area included among the "International 50," a select group of colleges with strong international studies programs. Austin has a widespread reputation for academic excellence, a strong sense of campus community, and career preparation. Its students are characterized as talented, ambitious, diverse, and service-oriented. Located in Sherman and within an hour's drive of the Dallas–Fort Worth metroplex, Austin is the oldest private college in Texas operating under its original charter.

Academics

AC offers a liberal arts curriculum and core academic program. It awards bachelor's and master's **degrees**. Challenging opportunities include advanced placement, accelerated degree programs, self-designed majors, tutorials, an honors program, and a senior project. Special programs include internships, summer session for credit, off-campus study, and study abroad.

The most popular **majors** include psychology, biology/biological sciences, and business. A complete listing of majors at AC appears in the Majors Index beginning on page 379.

The **faculty** at AC has 86 full-time graduate and undergraduate teachers, 98% with terminal degrees. 100% of the faculty serve as student advisers. The student-faculty ratio is 13:1, and the average class size in core courses is 25.

Computers on Campus

Students are not required to have a computer. Student rooms are linked to a campus network. 110 **computers** available in the computer center, computer labs, the research center, the learning resource center, psychology department, social science lab, classrooms, the library, and dormitories provide access to the main academic computer, e-mail, on-line services, and the Internet. Staffed computer lab on campus (open 24 hours a day) provides training in the use of computers and software.

The **library** has 211,000 books, 179,000 microform titles, and 862 subscriptions. It is connected to 5 national **on-line** catalogs.

Campus Life

There are 49 active **organizations** on campus, including a drama/theater group and student-run newspaper. 49% of students participate in student government elections. 26% of eligible men and 24% of eligible women are members of 10 local **fraternities** and 6 local **sororities**. Student **safety services** include late night transport/escort service, 24-hour emergency telephone alarm devices, 24-hour patrols by trained security personnel, and electronically operated dormitory entrances.

AC is a member of the NAIA. **Intercollegiate sports** include baseball (m), basketball (m, w), football (m), golf (m, w), soccer (m, w), swimming and diving (m, w), tennis (m, w), track and field (m, w), volleyball (w).

Applying

AC requires an essay, a high school transcript, 3 years of high school math and science, 2 recommendations, SAT I or ACT, and in some cases an interview. It recommends 2 years of high school foreign language and an interview. Early, deferred, and midyear entrance are possible, with a 2/1 deadline and continuous processing to 4/1 for financial aid. **Contact:** Mr. Jay Evans, Senior Associate Director of Admissions, 900 North Grand Avenue, Suite 6N, Sherman, TX 75090-4440, 903-813-3000 or toll-free 800-442-5363; fax 903-813-3198.

GETTING IN LAST YEAR
1,153 applied
79% were accepted
32% enrolled (293)
48% from top tenth of their h.s. class
51% had SAT verbal scores over 600 (R)
49% had SAT math scores over 600 (R)
41% had ACT scores over 26
10% had SAT verbal scores over 700 (R)
7% had SAT math scores over 700 (R)
10% had ACT scores over 30
4 National Merit Scholars
15 valedictorians

THE STUDENT BODY
Total 1,083, of whom 1,057
  are undergraduates

From 23 states and territories,
  14 other countries
92% from Texas
53% women, 47% men
3% African Americans
1% Native Americans
11% Hispanics
7% Asian Americans
2% international students

AFTER FRESHMAN YEAR
80% returned for sophomore year
61% got a degree within 4 years
70% got a degree within 5 years

AFTER GRADUATION
38% pursued further study (20% arts and
  sciences, 7% medicine, 6% business)
48% had job offers within 6 months
18 organizations recruited on campus

WHAT YOU WILL PAY
Tuition and fees $12,195
Room and board $4524
62% receive need-based financial aid
Need-based college-administered scholarships and
  grants average $4133 per award
27% receive non-need financial aid
Non-need college-administered scholarships and
  grants average $4476 per award

BABSON COLLEGE

Wellesley, Massachusetts • Suburban setting • Private • Independent • Coed

Babson is committed to being an international leader in management education. Through a balanced and rigorous program of management and liberal arts courses, the College educates students who are capable of initiating, managing, and implementing change. With an enrollment of over 1,700 undergraduates, Babson offers students the opportunity to participate in class discussions and other activities. Through more than 50 organizations and clubs and 30 student-run businesses, students play a role in shaping campus life. Babson's 450-acre residential campus is located 14 miles west of Boston, where students can take advantage of many social and career exploration opportunities.

Academics

Babson offers a business, management, liberal arts curriculum and core academic program; a few graduate courses are open to undergraduates. It awards bachelor's and master's **degrees**. Challenging opportunities include advanced placement, accelerated degree programs, self-designed majors, tutorials, Freshman Honors College, an honors program, and a senior project. Special programs include internships, summer session for credit, off-campus study, study abroad, and Army ROTC.

The most popular **majors** include marketing/retailing/merchandising, economics, and finance/banking. A complete listing of majors at Babson appears in the Majors Index beginning on page 379.

The **faculty** at Babson has 129 full-time graduate and undergraduate teachers, 89% with terminal degrees. 50% of the faculty serve as student advisers. The student-faculty ratio is 11:1.

Computers on Campus

Students are not required to have a computer. Student rooms are linked to a campus network. 120 **computers** available in the computer center, computer labs, classrooms, and dormitories provide access to the main academic computer, e-mail, on-line services, and the Internet. Staffed computer lab on campus (open 24 hours a day) provides training in the use of computers and software.

The **library** has 124,125 books, 346,089 microform titles, and 1,482 subscriptions. It is connected to 8 national **on-line** catalogs.

Campus Life

There are 56 active **organizations** on campus, including a drama/theater group and student-run newspaper. 12% of eligible men and 8% of eligible women are members of 4 national **fraternities** and 2 national **sororities**. Student **safety services** include late night transport/escort service, 24-hour emergency telephone alarm devices, 24-hour patrols by trained security personnel, and electronically operated dormitory entrances.

Babson is a member of the NCAA (Division III). **Intercollegiate sports** include baseball (m), basketball (m, w), cross-country running (m, w), field hockey (w), golf (m), ice hockey (m), lacrosse (m, w), rugby (m), sailing (m, w), skiing (downhill) (m, w), soccer (m, w), softball (w), squash (m, w), swimming and diving (m, w), tennis (m, w), volleyball (m, w).

Applying

Babson requires an essay, a high school transcript, 3 years of high school math, 1 recommendation, SAT I or ACT, and 2 SAT II Subject Tests. It recommends 4 years of high school math, 3 years of high school science, 2 years of high school foreign language, and an interview. Early, deferred, and midyear entrance are possible, with a 2/1 deadline and 2/15 for financial aid. **Contact:** Dr. Charles Nolan, Dean of Undergraduate Admission, Office of Undergraduate Admission, Mustard Hall, Babson Park, MA 02157-0310, 617-239-5522 or toll-free 800-488-3696; fax 617-239-4006.

GETTING IN LAST YEAR
2,349 applied
45% were accepted
37% enrolled (399)
30% from top tenth of their h.s. class
11% had SAT verbal scores over 600
52% had SAT math scores over 600
2% had SAT verbal scores over 700
15% had SAT math scores over 700
21 class presidents
3 valedictorians

THE STUDENT BODY
Total 3,378, of whom 1,725
   are undergraduates

From 43 states and territories,
   70 other countries
38% from Massachusetts
37% women, 63% men
3% African Americans
0% Native Americans
5% Hispanics
7% Asian Americans
18% international students

AFTER FRESHMAN YEAR
91% returned for sophomore year
79% got a degree within 4 years
83% got a degree within 5 years
84% got a degree within 6 years

AFTER GRADUATION
5% pursued further study (4% law, 1% business)
75% had job offers within 6 months
327 organizations recruited on campus

WHAT YOU WILL PAY
Tuition and fees $18,114
Room and board $5170
47% receive need-based financial aid
Need-based college-administered scholarships and
   grants average $9611 per award
5% receive non-need financial aid
Non-need college-administered scholarships and
   grants average $5000 per award

BALDWIN-WALLACE COLLEGE

Berea, Ohio • Suburban setting • Private • Independent-Religious • Coed

Founded in 1845, Baldwin-Wallace was among the first colleges to admit students without regard to race or gender. That spirit of inclusiveness and innovation continues today. The academic program, rooted in the liberal arts yet balanced by abundant opportunities for career exploration and application, is designed to prepare students to make a living . . . and a life worth living. It's a program committed to quality and distinguished by a personalized approach to learning that celebrates each student. "Quality education with a personal touch" is more than a slogan at B-W. It's a statement of purpose. It's who Baldwin-Wallace is.

Academics

B-W offers a liberal arts curriculum and core academic program; a few graduate courses are open to undergraduates. It awards bachelor's and master's **degrees**. Challenging opportunities include advanced placement, accelerated degree programs, self-designed majors, tutorials, an honors program, and a senior project. Special programs include internships, summer session for credit, off-campus study, study abroad, and Army and Air Force ROTC.

The most popular **majors** include business, education, and English. A complete listing of majors at B-W appears in the Majors Index beginning on page 379.

The **faculty** at B-W has 150 full-time undergraduate teachers, 76% with terminal degrees. 100% of the faculty serve as student advisers. The student-faculty ratio is 14:1.

Computers on Campus

Students are not required to have a computer. 490 **computers** available in the computer center, computer labs, all academic buildings, the library, and dormitories provide access to the main academic computer, e-mail, and the Internet. Staffed computer lab on campus provides training in the use of computers and software.

The 2 **libraries** have 230,000 books, 102,865 microform titles, and 950 subscriptions.

Campus Life

There are 40 active **organizations** on campus, including a drama/theater group and student-run newspaper and radio station. 35% of eligible men and 40% of eligible women are members of 5 national **fraternities** and 7 national **sororities**. Student **safety services** include late night transport/escort service, 24-hour emergency telephone alarm devices, 24-hour patrols by trained security personnel, student patrols, and electronically operated dormitory entrances.

B-W is a member of the NCAA (Division III). **Intercollegiate sports** include baseball (m), basketball (m, w), cross-country running (m, w), football (m), golf (m), soccer (m, w), softball (w), swimming and diving (m, w), tennis (m, w), track and field (m, w), volleyball (w), wrestling (m).

Applying

B-W requires an essay, a high school transcript, 1 recommendation, and SAT I or ACT. It recommends 3 years of high school math and science, 2 years of high school foreign language, and an interview. Deferred and midyear entrance are possible, with rolling admissions and continuous processing to 5/1 for financial aid. **Contact:** Mrs. Julie Baker, Director of Undergraduate Admission, 275 Eastland Road, Berea, OH 44017-2088, 216-826-2222.

GETTING IN LAST YEAR

1,794 applied
87% were accepted
42% enrolled (651)
23% from top tenth of their h.s. class
3.2 average high school GPA
33% had SAT verbal scores over 600 (R)
31% had SAT math scores over 600 (R)
22% had ACT scores over 26
3% had SAT verbal scores over 700 (R)
4% had SAT math scores over 700 (R)
3% had ACT scores over 30
1 National Merit Scholar
17 valedictorians

THE STUDENT BODY

Total 4,789, of whom 4,134 are undergraduates

From 32 states and territories, 21 other countries
90% from Ohio
60% women, 40% men
5% African Americans
0% Native Americans
2% Hispanics
1% Asian Americans
2% international students

AFTER FRESHMAN YEAR

80% returned for sophomore year
60% got a degree within 4 years
64% got a degree within 5 years
69% got a degree within 6 years

AFTER GRADUATION

12% pursued further study (4% business, 3% arts and sciences, 2% law)
85 organizations recruited on campus

WHAT YOU WILL PAY

Tuition and fees $12,270
Room and board $4635
74% receive need-based financial aid
Need-based college-administered scholarships and grants average $3299 per award
Non-need college-administered scholarships and grants average $3284 per award

---

BARD COLLEGE

Annandale-on-Hudson, New York • Rural setting • Private • Independent • Coed

Bard is a place to think. Its rural setting on 600 acres within the historic Hudson River Valley affords the safety and serenity conducive to serious academic study. Proximity to New York City, 90 miles to the south, provides innumerable opportunities. Typical Bard students are multitalented. The 10:1 student-faculty ratio encourages tailored programs; students develop many interests while completing specific majors. Classes are small, engaging, and rigorous. Writing and original work are emphasized across the disciplines. An Arts Division supports creative expression. About 10% of the 1,000 undergraduates are international students representing some 48 countries; students attend from all U.S. states.

 Academics

Bard offers a writing-intensive interdisciplinary curriculum and core academic program. It awards bachelor's and master's **degrees**. Challenging opportunities include advanced placement, accelerated degree programs, self-designed majors, tutorials, and a senior project. Special programs include internships, off-campus study, and study abroad.

The most popular **majors** include social science, art/fine arts, and literature. A complete listing of majors at Bard appears in the Majors Index beginning on page 379.

The **faculty** at Bard has 96 full-time undergraduate teachers, 95% with terminal degrees. 100% of the faculty serve as student advisers. The student-faculty ratio is 10:1.

 Computers on Campus

Students are not required to have a computer. 115 **computers** available in the computer center, computer labs, the research center, academic departments, and the library provide access to e-mail. Staffed computer lab on campus provides training in the use of computers and software.

The 4 **libraries** have 260,000 books, 8,700 microform titles, and 1,053 subscriptions. They are connected to 6 national **on-line** catalogs.

 Campus Life

There are 60 active **organizations** on campus, including a drama/theater group and student-run newspaper and radio station. Student **safety services** include late night transport/escort service, 24-hour emergency telephone alarm devices, 24-hour patrols by trained security personnel, student patrols, and electronically operated dormitory entrances.

Bard is a member of the NCAA (Division III) and NAIA. **Intercollegiate sports** include basketball (m, w), cross-country running (m, w), fencing (m, w), soccer (m, w), squash (m, w), tennis (m, w), volleyball (m, w).

 Applying

Bard requires an essay, a high school transcript, 3 recommendations, and in some cases a campus interview. It recommends 4 years of high school math and science, 3 years of high school foreign language, a campus interview, SAT I or ACT, SAT II Subject Tests, and a minimum high school GPA of 3.0. Early, deferred, and midyear entrance are possible, with a 1/31 deadline and a 3/15 priority date for financial aid. **Contact:** Ms. Mary Backlund, Director of Admissions, Annandale Road, Annandale-on-Hudson, NY 12504, 914-758-7472.

GETTING IN LAST YEAR

1,903 applied
53% were accepted
29% enrolled (296)
49% from top tenth of their h.s. class
3.3 average high school GPA
34 National Merit Scholars
12 class presidents
12 valedictorians

THE STUDENT BODY

Total 1,249, of whom 1,072
  are undergraduates
From 50 states and territories,
  48 other countries

26% from New York
52% women, 48% men
7% African Americans
1% Native Americans
5% Hispanics
3% Asian Americans
10% international students

AFTER FRESHMAN YEAR

90% returned for sophomore year
67% got a degree within 4 years
73% got a degree within 5 years
77% got a degree within 6 years

AFTER GRADUATION

55% pursued further study (45% arts and
  sciences, 4% law, 3% medicine)
205 organizations recruited on campus

WHAT YOU WILL PAY

Tuition and fees $21,227
Room and board $6640
68% receive need-based financial aid
Need-based college-administered scholarships and
  grants average $12,950 per award
3% receive non-need financial aid
Non-need college-administered scholarships and
  grants average $18,522 per award

BARNARD COLLEGE

New York, New York • Urban setting • Private • Independent • Women

Barnard is a small, select liberal arts college for women. Its superb faculty, about half of whom are women, are not only leading scholars but also accessible, dedicated teachers. Barnard's unique affiliation with Columbia University, which is just across the street, gives students a vast selection of courses and extracurricular activities, Division I athletic competition, and a fully coeducational social life. Adding immeasurably to a Barnard education is its location in New York City, where students have access to thousands of internships and unparalleled cultural, intellectual, and social resources.

Academics

Barnard offers a liberal arts and sciences curriculum and core academic program. It awards bachelor's **degrees**. Challenging opportunities include advanced placement, accelerated degree programs, self-designed majors, tutorials, an honors program, a senior project, Phi Beta Kappa, and Sigma Xi. Special programs include internships, off-campus study, and study abroad.

The most popular **majors** include English, psychology, and political science/government. A complete listing of majors at Barnard appears in the Majors Index beginning on page 379.

The **faculty** at Barnard has 181 full-time teachers, 93% with terminal degrees. 100% of the faculty serve as student advisers. The student-faculty ratio is 12:1.

Computers on Campus

Students are not required to have a computer. Student rooms are linked to a campus network. 120 **computers** available in the computer center, computer labs, classrooms, the library, the student center, and dormitories provide access to the main academic computer, off-campus computing facilities, e-mail, and on-line services. Staffed computer lab on campus provides training in the use of computers and software.

The **library** has 175,019 books, 14,607 microform titles, and 472 subscriptions.

Campus Life

There are 80 active **organizations** on campus, including a drama/theater group and student-run newspaper and radio station. 35% of students participate in student government elections. Student **safety services** include late night transport/escort service, 24-hour emergency telephone alarm devices, and 24-hour patrols by trained security personnel.

Barnard is a member of the NCAA (Division I). **Intercollegiate sports** include archery, basketball, crew, cross-country running, fencing, field hockey, lacrosse, soccer, swimming and diving, tennis, track and field, volleyball.

Applying

Barnard requires an essay, a high school transcript, 3 years of high school math, 3 recommendations, SAT I or ACT, and 3 SAT II Subject Tests (including SAT II: Writing Test). It recommends 3 years of high school science, 3 years of high school foreign language, and an interview. Early, deferred, and midyear entrance are possible, with a 1/15 deadline and 2/1 for financial aid. **Contact:** Ms. Doris Davis, Dean of Admissions, 3009 Broadway, New York, NY 10027, 212-854-2014; fax 212-854-6220.

GETTING IN LAST YEAR

2,973 applied
45% were accepted
40% enrolled (531)
61% from top tenth of their h.s. class
3.63 average high school GPA
51% had SAT verbal scores over 600
74% had SAT math scores over 600
85% had ACT scores over 26
5% had SAT verbal scores over 700
14% had SAT math scores over 700
16% had ACT scores over 30
3 National Merit Scholars

THE STUDENT BODY

2,276 undergraduates
From 48 states and territories,
    27 other countries
39% from New York
100% women
4% African Americans
1% Native Americans
5% Hispanics
25% Asian Americans
3% international students

AFTER FRESHMAN YEAR

95% returned for sophomore year
73% got a degree within 4 years
84% got a degree within 5 years
87% got a degree within 6 years

AFTER GRADUATION

69% had job offers within 6 months
81 organizations recruited on campus

WHAT YOU WILL PAY

Tuition and fees $19,480
Room and board $8172
60% receive need-based financial aid
Need-based college-administered scholarships and
    grants average $12,960 per award

BATES COLLEGE

Lewiston, Maine • Suburban setting • Private • Independent • Coed

Bates is the first coeducational college in New England and among the oldest such institutions in the nation. On principle, all organizations on campus are open to all students; there have never been fraternities or sororities at Bates. Another attraction is the opportunity to live in Maine, a state with unsurpassed landscape, distinctive architecture, an interesting diversity of people, and a strong sense of living history. Graduates of Bates often leave subtly changed by their 4 years in this special place.

 Academics

Bates offers a liberal arts curriculum and core academic program. It awards bachelor's **degrees**. Challenging opportunities include advanced placement, accelerated degree programs, self-designed majors, tutorials, an honors program, a senior project, and Phi Beta Kappa. Special programs include internships, off-campus study, and study abroad.

The most popular **majors** include biology/biological sciences, psychology, and English. A complete listing of majors at Bates appears in the Majors Index beginning on page 379.

The **faculty** at Bates has 146 full-time teachers, 93% with terminal degrees. 100% of the faculty serve as student advisers. The student-faculty ratio is 11:1.

 Computers on Campus

Students are not required to have a computer. Student rooms are linked to a campus network. 280 **computers** available in the computer center, computer labs, the research center, the learning resource center, classroom buildings, classrooms, and the library provide access to the main academic computer, off-campus computing facilities, e-mail, on-line services, and the Internet. Staffed computer lab on campus (open 24 hours a day) provides training in the use of computers and software.

The **library** has 605,656 books, 290,587 microform titles, and 1,919 subscriptions. It is connected to 7 national **on-line** catalogs.

 Campus Life

There are 60 active **organizations** on campus, including a drama/theater group and student-run newspaper and radio station. Student **safety services** include late night transport/escort service, 24-hour emergency telephone alarm devices, 24-hour patrols by trained security personnel, and student patrols.

Bates is a member of the NCAA (Division III). **Intercollegiate sports** include badminton (m, w), baseball (m), basketball (m, w), crew (m, w), cross-country running (m, w), equestrian sports (m, w), fencing (m, w), field hockey (w), football (m), golf (m), ice hockey (m, w), lacrosse (m, w), rugby (m, w), sailing (m, w), skiing (cross-country) (m, w), skiing (downhill) (m, w), soccer (m, w), softball (w), squash (m, w), swimming and diving (m, w), tennis (m, w), track and field (m, w), volleyball (m, w), water polo (m, w).

 Applying

Bates requires an essay, a high school transcript, and 3 recommendations. It recommends 3 years of high school math and science, some high school foreign language, and an interview. Early, deferred, and midyear entrance are possible, with a 1/15 deadline and 1/15 for financial aid. **Contact:** Mr. Wylie L. Mitchell, Dean of Admissions, 23 Campus Avenue, Lewiston, ME 04240-6028, 207-786-6000; fax 207-786-6025.

GETTING IN LAST YEAR
3,428 applied
37% were accepted
35% enrolled (437)
51% from top tenth of their h.s. class
87% had SAT verbal scores over 600 (R)
83% had SAT math scores over 600 (R)
22% had SAT verbal scores over 700 (R)
15% had SAT math scores over 700 (R)

THE STUDENT BODY
1,636 undergraduates
From 49 states and territories,
 31 other countries
13% from Maine
51% women, 49% men
2% African Americans
0% Native Americans
2% Hispanics
4% Asian Americans
3% international students

AFTER FRESHMAN YEAR
96% returned for sophomore year
87% got a degree within 6 years

WHAT YOU WILL PAY
Comprehensive fee $26,300
54% receive need-based financial aid
Need-based college-administered scholarships and
 grants average $12,069 per award
0% receive non-need financial aid

BAYLOR UNIVERSITY

Waco, Texas • Urban setting • Private • Independent-Religious • Coed

U.S. News & World Report and the *National Review College Guide* each named Baylor one of the nation's top universities. Proud of its Christian heritage, Baylor emphasizes teaching, scholarly attention to discovery, and service to others. With a low student-professor ratio, Baylor offers a more intimate, relationship-based education than is found in most major universities. Baylor administers a $69-million financial aid program and assists almost 70% of its students with loans, grants, scholarships, and campus work-study jobs. Baylor's academic quality, accessibility, and affordability make it an exceptional value in higher education today.

 ## Academics

Baylor offers an interdisciplinary curriculum and core academic program; fewer than half of graduate courses are open to undergraduates. It awards bachelor's, master's, doctoral, and first professional **degrees**. Challenging opportunities include advanced placement, accelerated degree programs, self-designed majors, an honors program, a senior project, Phi Beta Kappa, and Sigma Xi. Special programs include internships, summer session for credit, study abroad, and Air Force ROTC.

The **faculty** at Baylor has 600 full-time graduate and undergraduate teachers, 73% with terminal degrees. The student-faculty ratio is 18:1.

 ## Computers on Campus

Students are not required to have a computer. 634 **computers** available in the computer center, computer labs, the learning resource center, all major academic buildings, the library, and dormitories provide access to the main academic computer, off-campus computing facilities, e-mail, on-line services, and the Internet. Staffed computer lab on campus (open 24 hours a day) provides training in the use of computers and software.

The 9 **libraries** have 1.5 million books, 13,328 microform titles, and 9,424 subscriptions. They are connected to 5 national **on-line** catalogs.

 ## Campus Life

Active **organizations** on campus include drama/theater group and student-run newspaper and radio station. 17% of students participate in student government elections. 20% of eligible men and 30% of eligible women are members of 14 national **fraternities**, 12 national **sororities**, 3 local fraternities, and 1 local sorority. Student **safety services** include bicycle patrols, late night transport/escort service, 24-hour emergency telephone alarm devices, 24-hour patrols by trained security personnel, and electronically operated dormitory entrances.

Baylor is a member of the NCAA (Division I). **Intercollegiate sports** (some offering scholarships) include badminton (m, w), baseball (m), basketball (m, w), cross-country running (m, w), football (m), golf (m, w), lacrosse (m, w), sailing (m, w), soccer (m, w), softball (w), tennis (m, w), track and field (m, w), volleyball (m, w).

Applying

Baylor requires an essay, a high school transcript, 3 years of high school math, and SAT I or ACT. It recommends 3 years of high school science, some high school foreign language, recommendations, and a campus interview. Early, deferred, and midyear entrance are possible, with rolling admissions and continuous processing to 3/1 for financial aid. **Contact:** Ms. Teri Tippit, Director of Recruitment, PO Box 97056, Waco, TX 76798, 817-755-3435 or toll-free 800-BAYLOR U.

GETTING IN LAST YEAR
7,293 applied
84% were accepted
38% enrolled (2,339)
36% from top tenth of their h.s. class
25% had ACT scores over 26
6% had ACT scores over 30
63 National Merit Scholars

THE STUDENT BODY
Total 12,202, of whom 10,323
  are undergraduates
From 52 states and territories,
  74 other countries

78% from Texas
56% women, 44% men
5% African Americans
1% Native Americans
8% Hispanics
4% Asian Americans
2% international students

AFTER FRESHMAN YEAR
82% returned for sophomore year
43% got a degree within 4 years
67% got a degree within 5 years
70% got a degree within 6 years

AFTER GRADUATION
265 organizations recruited on campus

WHAT YOU WILL PAY
Tuition and fees $8756
Room and board $4254
Need-based college-administered scholarships and
  grants average $1190 per award
Non-need college-administered scholarships and
  grants average $2391 per award

BELLARMINE COLLEGE

Louisville, Kentucky • Suburban setting • Private • Independent-Religious • Coed

A wealth of opportunity awaits students at Bellarmine College's 120-acre campus, nestled in one of Louisville's most desirable neighborhoods. The small class size makes it easy to get to know professors and other students. Students can study in one of the 40 countries participating in the foreign exchange program. More than 50 student organizations are active on campus. Students can participate in a multitude of internship programs, which have served as a stepping stone to full-time positions. Bellarmine graduates work in leadership capacities with Fortune 500 companies both in the Louisville region and nationwide.

Academics

Bellarmine offers a liberal arts curriculum and core academic program. It awards bachelor's and master's **degrees**. Challenging opportunities include advanced placement, Freshman Honors College, an honors program, and a senior project. Special programs include internships, summer session for credit, off-campus study, study abroad, and Army and Air Force ROTC.

The most popular **majors** include business, accounting, and nursing. A complete listing of majors at Bellarmine appears in the Majors Index beginning on page 379.

The **faculty** at Bellarmine has 94 full-time graduate and undergraduate teachers, 82% with terminal degrees. 100% of the faculty serve as student advisers. The student-faculty ratio is 13:1.

Computers on Campus

Students are not required to have a computer. 80 **computers** available in the computer center, computer labs, and classrooms provide access to the Internet. Staffed computer lab on campus provides training in the use of computers and software.

The 2 **libraries** have 192,000 books, 67,177 microform titles, and 541 subscriptions. They are connected to 1 national **on-line** catalog.

Campus Life

Active **organizations** on campus include drama/theater group and student-run newspaper. 20% of eligible men are members of 1 national **fraternity** and 1 national **sorority**. Student **safety services** include 24-hour emergency telephone alarm devices and 24-hour patrols by trained security personnel.

Bellarmine is a member of the NCAA (Division II). **Intercollegiate sports** (some offering scholarships) include baseball (m), basketball (m, w), cross-country running (m, w), field hockey (w), golf (m, w), soccer (m, w), softball (w), tennis (m, w), track and field (m, w), volleyball (w).

Applying

Bellarmine requires an essay, a high school transcript, 3 years of high school math, recommendations, minimum 2.5 high school GPA, and SAT I or ACT. It recommends 3 years of high school science, 2 years of high school foreign language, and an interview. Early, deferred, and midyear entrance are possible, with an 8/1 deadline and continuous processing to 3/15 for financial aid. **Contact:** Mr. Timothy A. Sturgeon, Associate Dean of Admissions, 2001 Newburg Road, Louisville, KY 40205-0671, 502-452-8131 or toll-free 800-274-4723; fax 502-456-3331.

GETTING IN LAST YEAR

779 applied
88% were accepted
48% enrolled (329)
36% from top tenth of their h.s. class
3.35 average high school GPA
8% had SAT verbal scores over 600
22% had SAT math scores over 600
27% had ACT scores over 26
0% had SAT verbal scores over 700
3% had SAT math scores over 700
7% had ACT scores over 30
1 National Merit Scholar
14 valedictorians

THE STUDENT BODY

Total 2,359, of whom 1,908
   are undergraduates

From 28 states and territories,
   14 other countries
80% from Kentucky
59% women, 41% men
3% African Americans
0% Native Americans
1% Hispanics
1% Asian Americans
1% international students

AFTER FRESHMAN YEAR

77% returned for sophomore year
53% got a degree within 4 years
59% got a degree within 5 years
60% got a degree within 6 years

AFTER GRADUATION

20% pursued further study (5% arts and
   sciences, 5% business, 5% law)
90% had job offers within 6 months
30 organizations recruited on campus

WHAT YOU WILL PAY

Tuition and fees $9550
Room and board $3360
70% receive need-based financial aid
Need-based college-administered scholarships and
   grants average $772 per award
30% receive non-need financial aid
Non-need college-administered scholarships and
   grants average $3327 per award

BELMONT UNIVERSITY

Nashville, Tennessee • Urban setting • Private • Independent-Religious • Coed

Belmont University students receive an education that revolves around the spirit of the individual. Focusing on academic excellence and continuous improvement, the University recognizes students as central to its mission as it dedicates itself to providing students from diverse backgrounds with an academically challenging education in a Christian community. The University's vision is to be a premier teaching university that brings together the best of liberal arts and professional education in a consistently caring Christian environment. Values that fulfill this vision encourage students as well as University leadership to be honest, treat every person with respect, and listen and learn from everyone.

Academics

Belmont offers a core academic program; a few graduate courses are open to undergraduates. It awards bachelor's and master's **degrees**. Challenging opportunities include advanced placement, accelerated degree programs, tutorials, and an honors program. Special programs include cooperative education, internships, summer session for credit, study abroad, and Army ROTC.

The most popular **majors** include music business, business, and nursing. A complete listing of majors at Belmont appears in the Majors Index beginning on page 379.

The **faculty** at Belmont has 154 full-time graduate and undergraduate teachers, 67% with terminal degrees. 100% of the faculty serve as student advisers. The student-faculty ratio is 14:1.

Computers on Campus

Students are not required to have a computer. Student rooms are linked to a campus network. 200 **computers**
available in the computer center, computer labs, academic departments, and the library provide access to the main academic computer, e-mail, on-line services, and the Internet. Staffed computer lab on campus provides training in the use of computers and software.

The **library** has 133,571 books, 12,188 microform titles, and 1,100 subscriptions. It is connected to 2 national **on-line** catalogs.

Campus Life

Active **organizations** on campus include drama/theater group and student-run newspaper. 2% of eligible men and 2% of eligible women are members of 2 local **fraternities** and 2 local **sororities**. Student **safety services** include late night transport/escort service, 24-hour emergency telephone alarm devices, 24-hour patrols by trained security personnel, and electronically operated dormitory entrances.

Belmont is a member of the NAIA. **Intercollegiate sports** (some offering scholarships) include baseball (m), basketball (m, w), cross-country running (m, w), golf (m, w), soccer (m), softball (w), tennis (m, w), track and field (m, w), volleyball (w).

Applying

Belmont requires a high school transcript, recommendations, SAT I or ACT, a minimum high school GPA of 2.0, and in some cases an interview. It recommends 3 years of high school math, some high school foreign language, and SAT II Subject Tests. Early, deferred, and midyear entrance are possible, with an 8/1 deadline and continuous processing to 3/15 for financial aid. **Contact:** Dr. Kathryn Baugher, Dean of Admissions, 1900 Belmont Boulevard, Nashville, TN 37212-3757, 615-385-6785.

GETTING IN LAST YEAR
1,119 applied
74% were accepted
44% enrolled (364)
3.0 average high school GPA
35% had SAT verbal scores over 600 (R)
28% had SAT math scores over 600 (R)
25% had ACT scores over 26
6% had SAT verbal scores over 700 (R)
3% had SAT math scores over 700 (R)
6% had ACT scores over 30
3 National Merit Scholars

THE STUDENT BODY
Total 3,009, of whom 2,636 are undergraduates

From 45 states and territories, 44 other countries
66% from Tennessee
60% women, 40% men
3% African Americans
0% Native Americans
1% Hispanics
1% Asian Americans
4% international students

AFTER FRESHMAN YEAR
75% returned for sophomore year
40% got a degree within 4 years
42% got a degree within 5 years
43% got a degree within 6 years

AFTER GRADUATION
160 organizations recruited on campus

WHAT YOU WILL PAY
Tuition and fees $9550
Room and board $3840
80% receive need-based financial aid
Need-based college-administered scholarships and grants average $701 per award
Non-need college-administered scholarships and grants average $907 per award

BELOIT COLLEGE

Beloit, Wisconsin • Small-town setting • Private • Independent • Coed

The process of finding one's own direction is far too personal an adventure to be standardized. At Beloit College, there is no lengthy list of requirements, no rigid formula for choosing a major, no mold or stereotype in which one is expected to fit. Students can invent themselves at Beloit. Beloit's job—its commitment—is to provide students with resources that will allow them to develop to the fullest, starting with an extraordinary faculty in which even the most senior professors serve as advisers and mentors to first-year students and upperclassmen alike.

Academics

Beloit offers a core academic program; more than half of graduate courses are open to undergraduates. It awards bachelor's and master's **degrees**. Challenging opportunities include advanced placement, self-designed majors, tutorials, a senior project, and Phi Beta Kappa. Special programs include internships, summer session for credit, off-campus study, and study abroad.

The most popular **majors** include anthropology, biology/biological sciences, and English. A complete listing of majors at Beloit appears in the Majors Index beginning on page 379.

The **faculty** at Beloit has 83 full-time undergraduate teachers, 95% with terminal degrees. 100% of the faculty serve as student advisers. The student-faculty ratio is 11:1.

Computers on Campus

Students are not required to have a computer. 115 **computers** available in the computer center, computer labs, the library, the student center, and dormitories provide access to off-campus computing facilities, e-mail, on-line services, and the Internet. Staffed computer lab on campus provides training in the use of computers and software.

The **library** has 235,438 books, 1,295 microform titles, and 937 subscriptions. It is connected to 12 national **on-line** catalogs.

Campus Life

Active **organizations** on campus include drama/theater group and student-run newspaper and radio station. 25% of eligible men and 11% of eligible women are members of 4 national **fraternities** and 2 local **sororities**. Student **safety services** include late night transport/escort service, 24-hour emergency telephone alarm devices, and 24-hour patrols by trained security personnel.

Beloit is a member of the NCAA (Division III). **Intercollegiate sports** include baseball (m), basketball (m, w), cross-country running (m, w), fencing (m, w), football (m), golf (m), ice hockey (m), lacrosse (m, w), soccer (m, w), softball (w), swimming and diving (m, w), tennis (m, w), track and field (m, w), volleyball (w).

Applying

Beloit requires an essay, a high school transcript, SAT I or ACT, and in some cases 1 recommendation and a campus interview. It recommends 3 years of high school math and science, 2 years of high school foreign language, and an interview. Early, deferred, and midyear entrance are possible, with rolling admissions and continuous processing to 4/15 for financial aid. **Contact:** Mr. Alan G. McIvor, Vice President of Enrollment Services, 700 College Street, Beloit, WI 53511-5596, 608-363-2500 or toll-free 800-356-0751 (out-of-state).

GETTING IN LAST YEAR
1,435 applied
73% were accepted
29% enrolled (299)
28% from top tenth of their h.s. class
3.41 average high school GPA
25% had SAT verbal scores over 600
41% had SAT math scores over 600
53% had ACT scores over 26
2% had SAT verbal scores over 700
4% had SAT math scores over 700
17% had ACT scores over 30
3 National Merit Scholars

THE STUDENT BODY
Total 1,259, of whom 1,249
  are undergraduates
From 47 states and territories,
  52 other countries
23% from Wisconsin
57% women, 43% men
4% African Americans
1% Native Americans
1% Hispanics
2% Asian Americans
10% international students

AFTER FRESHMAN YEAR
94% returned for sophomore year

56% got a degree within 4 years
66% got a degree within 5 years
71% got a degree within 6 years

AFTER GRADUATION
44% pursued further study (35% arts and sciences, 3% business, 3% law)

WHAT YOU WILL PAY
Tuition and fees $17,544
Room and board $2068
69% receive need-based financial aid
15% receive non-need financial aid

BENNINGTON COLLEGE

Bennington, Vermont • Small-town setting • Private • Independent • Coed

 A Bennington education imparts more than a body of knowledge or an excellent liberal arts education. It imparts an approach to life—the belief that the way to get things done is to do them. The College was founded more than 6 decades ago on the premise that people learn best by pursuing that which most interests them and by working closely with teachers who are themselves actively engaged in their interests. Self-directedness is central; the power of the Bennington experience has everything to do with the empowerment of the student, and the result is lifelong confidence, adaptability, and independence of mind.

 ## Academics

Bennington offers an interdisciplinary curriculum and core academic program; a few graduate courses are open to undergraduates. It awards bachelor's and master's **degrees**. Challenging opportunities include self-designed majors, tutorials, and a senior project. Special programs include internships, off-campus study, and study abroad.

The most popular **majors** include literature, interdisciplinary studies, and theater arts/drama. A complete listing of majors at Bennington appears in the Majors Index beginning on page 379.

The **faculty** at Bennington has 41 full-time graduate and undergraduate teachers, 42% with terminal degrees. 100% of the faculty serve as student advisers. The student-faculty ratio is 7:1.

Computers on Campus

Students are required to have a computer. Purchase options are available. Student rooms are linked to a campus network.

40 **computers** available in the computer center, computer labs, media center, languages and cultures center, and classrooms provide access to the main academic computer, e-mail, on-line services, and the Internet. Staffed computer lab on campus provides training in the use of computers and software.

The 4 **libraries** have 118,000 books, 6,342 microform titles, and 580 subscriptions. They are connected to 1 national **on-line** catalog.

 ## Campus Life

There are 15 active **organizations** on campus, including a drama/theater group and student-run newspaper and radio station. 90% of students participate in student government elections. Student **safety services** include late night transport/escort service, 24-hour emergency telephone alarm devices, and 24-hour patrols by trained security personnel. **Intercollegiate sports** include soccer (m, w).

 ## Applying

Bennington requires an essay, a high school transcript, 2 recommendations, an interview, and SAT I or ACT. It recommends 3 years of high school math and science and 3 years of high school foreign language. Early, deferred, and midyear entrance are possible, with a 2/1 deadline and continuous processing to 3/1 for financial aid. **Contact:** Ms. Elena Ruocco Bachrach, Dean of Admissions and the Freshman Year, Bennington, VT 05201-9993, 802-442-5401 ext. 161 or toll-free 800-833-6845.

GETTING IN LAST YEAR
376 applied
64% were accepted
32% enrolled (78)
27% from top tenth of their h.s. class
3.54 average high school GPA
64% had ACT scores over 26
32% had ACT scores over 30
4 National Merit Scholars

THE STUDENT BODY
Total 387, of whom 285
 are undergraduates
From 39 states and territories

6% from Vermont
60% women, 40% men
1% African Americans
0% Native Americans
2% Hispanics
1% Asian Americans
10% international students

AFTER FRESHMAN YEAR
78% returned for sophomore year
38% got a degree within 4 years
47% got a degree within 5 years
49% got a degree within 6 years

WHAT YOU WILL PAY
Comprehensive fee $25,800
78% receive need-based financial aid
Need-based college-administered scholarships and
 grants average $14,050 per award
23% receive non-need financial aid
Non-need college-administered scholarships and
 grants average $5250 per award

BERRY COLLEGE

Mount Berry, Georgia • Small-town setting • Private • Independent • Coed

Berry College is an independent, coeducational college with fully accredited arts, sciences, and professional programs as well as specialized graduate programs in education and business administration. The College serves humanity by inspiring and educating students regardless of their economic status and emphasizes a comprehensive educational program committed to high academic standards, Christian values, and practical work experiences. The campus is an unusually beautiful environment with approximately 28,000 acres of land. Fields, forests, lakes, and mountains provide scenic beauty in a protected natural setting. The College is located in Rome, Georgia, 65 miles northwest of Atlanta and 65 miles south of Chattanooga.

 ## Academics

Berry offers an interdisciplinary curriculum and core academic program; fewer than half of graduate courses are open to undergraduates. It awards bachelor's and master's **degrees**. Challenging opportunities include advanced placement, accelerated degree programs, self-designed majors, an honors program, and a senior project. Special programs include cooperative education, internships, summer session for credit, and study abroad.

The most popular **majors** include business, education, and psychology. A complete listing of majors at Berry appears in the Majors Index beginning on page 379.

The **faculty** at Berry has 95 full-time graduate and undergraduate teachers, 86% with terminal degrees. 100% of the faculty serve as student advisers. The student-faculty ratio is 16:1.

 ## Computers on Campus

Students are not required to have a computer. 100 **computers** available in the computer center, computer labs, classroom labs, and the library provide access to e-mail, on-line services, and the Internet. Staffed computer lab on campus provides training in the use of computers and software.

The **library** has 159,629 books, 405,879 microform titles, and 1,400 subscriptions. It is connected to 4 national **on-line** catalogs.

 ## Campus Life

There are 70 active **organizations** on campus, including a drama/theater group and student-run newspaper. Student **safety services** include late night transport/escort service, 24-hour emergency telephone alarm devices, and 24-hour patrols by trained security personnel.

Berry is a member of the NAIA. **Intercollegiate sports** (some offering scholarships) include baseball (m), basketball (m, w), crew (m, w), cross-country running (m, w), equestrian sports (m, w), golf (m), rugby (m), soccer (m, w), tennis (m, w), track and field (m, w).

 ## Applying

Berry requires a high school transcript, 3 years of high school math and science, 2 years of high school foreign language, and SAT I or ACT. Early, deferred, and midyear entrance are possible, with rolling admissions and continuous processing to 4/1 for financial aid. **Contact:** Mr. George Gaddie, Dean of Admissions, Hermann Hall, Mount Berry, GA 30149-0159, 706-236-2215 or toll-free 800-237-7942.

GETTING IN LAST YEAR

2,031 applied
75% were accepted
34% enrolled (523)
36% from top tenth of their h.s. class
3.48 average high school GPA
12% had SAT verbal scores over 600
30% had SAT math scores over 600
34% had ACT scores over 26
1% had SAT verbal scores over 700
6% had SAT math scores over 700
8% had ACT scores over 30
1 National Merit Scholar

THE STUDENT BODY

Total 1,974, of whom 1,756
are undergraduates

From 36 states and territories,
29 other countries
82% from Georgia
62% women, 38% men
2% African Americans
0% Native Americans
1% Hispanics
1% Asian Americans
2% international students

AFTER FRESHMAN YEAR

67% returned for sophomore year
45% got a degree within 4 years
58% got a degree within 5 years
59% got a degree within 6 years

AFTER GRADUATION

27% pursued further study
99% had job offers within 6 months
94 organizations recruited on campus

WHAT YOU WILL PAY

Tuition and fees $9216
Room and board $4104
Need-based college-administered scholarships and
grants average $3354 per award
Non-need college-administered scholarships and
grants average $3023 per award

BETHEL COLLEGE

St. Paul, Minnesota • Suburban setting • Private • Independent-Religious • Coed

Bethel College is a Christian learning community whose goal is to foster an effective academic program and to create a supportive environment for the development of growing persons. Learning at Bethel promotes self-knowledge, appreciation of intellectual and cultural heritage, critical thinking, creative communication of ideas, and lifelong learning. Christian faith is viewed as relevant to all facets of knowledge and experience and is integrated throughout the curriculum. What makes Bethel outstanding are its excellent students, expert faculty, and dedicated staff. Bethel is committed to providing a high-quality liberal arts education to prepare tomorrow's leaders to make a difference in their community, the church, and the world.

 ## Academics

Bethel offers a core academic program; a few graduate courses are open to undergraduates. It awards associate, bachelor's, and master's **degrees**. Challenging opportunities include advanced placement, self-designed majors, Freshman Honors College, an honors program, and a senior project. Special programs include internships, summer session for credit, off-campus study, study abroad, and Army, Naval, and Air Force ROTC.

The most popular **majors** include education, nursing, and business. A complete listing of majors at Bethel appears in the Majors Index beginning on page 379.

The **faculty** at Bethel has 111 full-time undergraduate teachers, 66% with terminal degrees. The student-faculty ratio is 15:1.

 ## Computers on Campus

Students are not required to have a computer. 100 **computers** available in the computer center, computer labs, the learning resource center, dormitories, and student rooms provide access to the main academic computer and off-campus computing facilities.

The **library** has 129,000 books and 640 subscriptions.

 ## Campus Life

Active **organizations** on campus include drama/theater group and student-run newspaper and radio station. Student **safety services** include late night transport/escort service, 24-hour emergency telephone alarm devices, student patrols, and electronically operated dormitory entrances.

Bethel is a member of the NCAA (Division III). **Intercollegiate sports** include baseball (m), basketball (m, w), cross-country running (m, w), football (m), golf (m), ice hockey (m), soccer (m, w), softball (w), tennis (m, w), track and field (m, w), volleyball (w).

 ## Applying

Bethel requires an essay, a high school transcript, 2 recommendations, SAT I or ACT, PSAT, and in some cases an interview. It recommends 3 years of high school math and science and an interview. Early, deferred, and midyear entrance are possible, with rolling admissions and continuous processing to 4/15 for financial aid. **Contact:** Mr. John C. Lassen, Director of Admissions, 3900 Bethel Drive, St. Paul, MN 55112-6999, 612-638-6436 or toll-free 800-255-8706.

GETTING IN LAST YEAR
1,323 applied
76% were accepted
54% enrolled (547)
26% from top tenth of their h.s. class
38% had ACT scores over 26
7% had ACT scores over 30

THE STUDENT BODY
Total 2,348, of whom 2,195
  are undergraduates
67% from Minnesota
60% women, 40% men
1% African Americans
1% Native Americans

1% Hispanics
2% Asian Americans
1% international students

AFTER FRESHMAN YEAR
78% returned for sophomore year

WHAT YOU WILL PAY
Tuition and fees $12,260
Room and board $4460

BIRMINGHAM-SOUTHERN COLLEGE

Birmingham, Alabama • Urban setting • Private • Independent-Religious • Coed

 The College continues to be recognized as one of the nation's leading liberal arts colleges by *National Review, U.S. News & World Report,* and *Money* magazine. Special features of the curriculum are the Interim Term and the Honors Program, as well as undergraduate research, the Leadership Studies Program, service learning opportunities, and international study programs. The Interim Term (January) provides an opportunity for independent study, foreign and domestic trips, and internships with government and private organizations. The College has been recognized for its outstanding track record of graduate admission to medical, law, and graduate schools and job placement.

Academics

Birmingham-Southern offers a liberal arts curriculum and core academic program. It awards bachelor's and master's **degrees**. Challenging opportunities include advanced placement, accelerated degree programs, self-designed majors, tutorials, an honors program, a senior project, and Phi Beta Kappa. Special programs include internships, summer session for credit, off-campus study, study abroad, and Army and Air Force ROTC.

The most popular **majors** include business, biology/biological sciences, and English. A complete listing of majors at Birmingham-Southern appears in the Majors Index beginning on page 379.

The **faculty** at Birmingham-Southern has 100 full-time graduate and undergraduate teachers, 92% with terminal degrees. 100% of the faculty serve as student advisers. The student-faculty ratio is 12:1, and the average class size in core courses is 22.

Computers on Campus

Students are not required to have a computer. Student rooms are linked to a campus network. 114 **computers** available in the computer center, computer labs, the learning resource center, classroom buildings, classrooms, the library, and dormitories provide access to the main academic computer, off-campus computing facilities, e-mail, on-line services, and the Internet. Staffed computer lab on campus (open 24 hours a day) provides training in the use of computers and software.

The **library** has 200,000 books, 53,136 microform titles, and 964 subscriptions. It is connected to 1 national **on-line** catalog.

Campus Life

There are 70 active **organizations** on campus, including a drama/theater group and student-run newspaper. 60% of eligible men and 60% of eligible women are members of 6 national **fraternities** and 6 national **sororities**. Student **safety services** include late night transport/escort service, 24-hour emergency telephone alarm devices, 24-hour patrols by trained security personnel, and electronically operated dormitory entrances.

Birmingham-Southern is a member of the NAIA. **Intercollegiate sports** (some offering scholarships) include baseball (m), basketball (m), soccer (m, w), tennis (m, w).

Applying

Birmingham-Southern requires an essay, a high school transcript, 3 years of high school math and science, recommendations, SAT I or ACT, a minimum high school GPA of 2.0, and in some cases an interview. It recommends some high school foreign language. Early, deferred, and midyear entrance are possible, with a 5/1 deadline and continuous processing to 3/31 for financial aid. **Contact:** Mr. Robert Dortch, Vice President of Admissions Services, 900 Arkadelphia Road, Birmingham, AL 35254, 205-226-4686 or toll-free 800-523-5793; fax 205-226-4627.

GETTING IN LAST YEAR
756 applied
85% were accepted
38% enrolled (247)
38% from top tenth of their h.s. class
3.40 average high school GPA
51% had SAT verbal scores over 600 (R)
60% had SAT math scores over 600 (R)
63% had ACT scores over 26
14% had SAT verbal scores over 700 (R)
9% had SAT math scores over 700 (R)
26% had ACT scores over 30

THE STUDENT BODY
Total 1,562, of whom 1,446
  are undergraduates

From 30 states and territories,
  14 other countries
77% from Alabama
56% women, 44% men
13% African Americans
0% Native Americans
0% Hispanics
3% Asian Americans
1% international students

AFTER FRESHMAN YEAR
88% returned for sophomore year
69% got a degree within 4 years
70% got a degree within 5 years

AFTER GRADUATION
32% pursued further study (16% arts and
  sciences, 6% law, 6% medicine)

WHAT YOU WILL PAY
Tuition and fees $12,524
Room and board $4620
60% receive need-based financial aid
Need-based college-administered scholarships and
  grants average $1500 per award
30% receive non-need financial aid
Non-need college-administered scholarships and
  grants average $4000 per award

BOSTON COLLEGE

Chestnut Hill, Massachusetts • Suburban setting • Private • Independent-Religious • Coed

The Jesuit philosophy of education emphasizes a rigorous intellectual grounding in the liberal arts, the formation of critical leadership skills, and opportunities for reflection upon personal paths of development. The new computing and communications network provides data, voice, and cable television services to all classrooms, offices, and dorm rooms and is the latest evidence that Boston College intends to offer cutting-edge learning technologies, while always fostering respect and concern for each student.

Academics

BC offers a core academic program; more than half of graduate courses are open to undergraduates. It awards bachelor's, master's, doctoral, and first professional **degrees** (also offers continuing education program with significant enrollment not reflected in profile). Challenging opportunities include advanced placement, accelerated degree programs, self-designed majors, tutorials, Freshman Honors College, an honors program, and Phi Beta Kappa. Special programs include internships, summer session for credit, off-campus study, study abroad, and Army, Naval, and Air Force ROTC.

The most popular **majors** include English, finance/banking, and political science/government. A complete listing of majors at BC appears in the Majors Index beginning on page 379.

The **faculty** at BC has 591 full-time graduate and undergraduate teachers, 95% with terminal degrees. 100% of the faculty serve as student advisers. The student-faculty ratio is 15:1.

Computers on Campus

Students are not required to have a computer. Student rooms are linked to a campus network. 200 **computers** available in the computer center, computer labs, the learn-ing resource center, classrooms, and the library provide access to the main academic computer, off-campus computing facilities, e-mail, on-line services, and the Internet. Staffed computer lab on campus provides training in the use of computers and software.

The **library** has 1.4 million books, 2.4 million microform titles, and 15,075 subscriptions.

Campus Life

There are 140 active **organizations** on campus, including a drama/theater group and student-run newspaper and radio station. Student **safety services** include late night transport/escort service, 24-hour emergency telephone alarm devices, 24-hour patrols by trained security personnel, and electronically operated dormitory entrances.

BC is a member of the NCAA (Division I). **Intercollegiate sports** (some offering scholarships) include baseball (m), basketball (m, w), crew (m, w), cross-country running (m, w), fencing (m, w), field hockey (w), football (m), golf (m, w), ice hockey (m, w), lacrosse (m, w), rugby (m, w), sailing (m, w), skiing (downhill) (m, w), soccer (m, w), softball (w), squash (m, w), swimming and diving (m, w), tennis (m, w), track and field (m, w), volleyball (w), water polo (m), wrestling (m).

Applying

BC requires an essay, a high school transcript, 2 recommendations, SAT I or ACT, and 3 SAT II Subject Tests (including SAT II: Writing Test). It recommends 4 years of high school math, 3 years of high school science, 4 years of high school foreign language, and an interview. Early, deferred, and midyear entrance are possible, with a 1/10 deadline and a 2/1 priority date for financial aid. **Contact:** Mr. John L. Mahoney Jr., Director of Undergraduate Admission, 140 Commonwealth Avenue, Lyons Hall 120, Chestnut Hill, MA 02167-9991, 617-552-3100.

GETTING IN LAST YEAR
16,680 applied
38% were accepted
33% enrolled (2,140)
75% had SAT verbal scores over 600 (R)
84% had SAT math scores over 600 (R)
18% had SAT verbal scores over 700 (R)
20% had SAT math scores over 700 (R)
7 National Merit Scholars

THE STUDENT BODY
Total 14,695, of whom 8,896
   are undergraduates

From 51 states and territories,
   86 other countries
30% from Massachusetts
53% women, 47% men
3% African Americans
5% Hispanics
7% Asian Americans
4% international students

AFTER GRADUATION
26% pursued further study (9% arts and
   sciences, 8% law, 5% business)
1 Fulbright scholar

WHAT YOU WILL PAY
Tuition and fees $18,356
Room and board $7270
49% receive need-based financial aid
Need-based college-administered scholarships and
   grants average $8604 per award
19% receive non-need financial aid

BOSTON UNIVERSITY

Boston, Massachusetts • Urban setting • Private • Independent • Coed

The spirit of Boston University is in the possibilities:
- The excitement of living and learning in one of the world's greatest cities
- With students from 90 countries, the most culturally diverse student body in the United States
- The challenge of the honors curriculum in the College of Arts and Sciences
- An internship with Westpac Bank in Sydney, writing for a magazine in Paris, researching stories for the BBC, studying small business in Moscow, or . . . .

 ## Academics

Boston University offers a liberal arts curriculum with professional opportunities and core academic program; more than half of graduate courses are open to undergraduates. It awards bachelor's, master's, doctoral, and first professional **degrees**. Challenging opportunities include advanced placement, self-designed majors, tutorials, an honors program, a senior project, Phi Beta Kappa, and Sigma Xi. Special programs include cooperative education, internships, summer session for credit, off-campus study, study abroad, and Army, Naval, and Air Force ROTC.

The most popular **majors** include business, social science, and communication. A complete listing of majors at Boston University appears in the Majors Index beginning on page 379.

The **faculty** at Boston University has 1,816 full-time graduate and undergraduate teachers, 81% with terminal degrees. 95% of the faculty serve as student advisers. The student-faculty ratio is 13:1.

🖥 Computers on Campus

Students are not required to have a computer. Student rooms are linked to a campus network. 500 **computers** available in the computer center, computer labs, the research center, the learning resource center, academic departments, classrooms, the library, the student center, and dormitories provide access to the main academic computer, off-campus computing facilities, e-mail, on-line services, the Internet, and research and educational networks. Staffed computer lab on campus provides training in the use of computers and software.

The 24 **libraries** have 2 million books and 28,858 subscriptions.

🌲 Campus Life

There are 325 active **organizations** on campus, including a drama/theater group and student-run newspaper and radio station. 30% of students participate in student government elections. 5% of eligible men and 7% of eligible women are members of 5 national **fraternities** and 9 national **sororities**. Student **safety services** include security personnel at dormitory entrances, self-defense education, well-lit sidewalks, late night transport/escort service, 24-hour emergency telephone alarm devices, 24-hour patrols by trained security personnel, and electronically operated dormitory entrances.

Boston University is a member of the NCAA (Division I). **Intercollegiate sports** (some offering scholarships) include archery (m, w), badminton (m, w), baseball (m), basketball (m, w), crew (m, w), cross-country running (m, w), equestrian sports (m, w), fencing (m, w), field hockey (w), football (m), golf (m, w), gymnastics (m, w), ice hockey (m, w), lacrosse (m, w), rugby (m), sailing (m, w), skiing (downhill) (m, w), soccer (m, w), softball (m, w), swimming and diving (m, w), table tennis (m, w), tennis (m, w), track and field (m, w), volleyball (m, w), water polo (m, w), weight lifting (m, w), wrestling (m).

🎓 Applying

Boston University requires an essay, a high school transcript, 4 years of high school math and science, 2 recommendations, SAT I or ACT, and in some cases a campus interview, audition, portfolio, and SAT II Subject Tests (including SAT II: Writing Test). It recommends 3 years of high school foreign language and a minimum high school GPA of 3.0. Early, deferred, and midyear entrance are possible, with a 1/15 deadline and continuous processing to 2/15 for financial aid. **Contact:** Ms. Kelly Walter, Associate Director of Admissions, 121 Bay State Road, Boston, MA 02215, 617-353-2300; fax 617-353-9695.

GETTING IN LAST YEAR
23,617 applied
63% were accepted
29% enrolled (4,348)
45% from top tenth of their h.s. class
65% had SAT verbal scores over 600 (R)
64% had SAT math scores over 600 (R)
60% had ACT scores over 26
14% had SAT verbal scores over 700 (R)
12% had SAT math scores over 700 (R)
20% had ACT scores over 30
32 National Merit Scholars
77 valedictorians

THE STUDENT BODY
Total 29,025, of whom 15,097
  are undergraduates
From 54 states and territories,
  90 other countries
27% from Massachusetts
56% women, 44% men
4% African Americans
1% Native Americans
6% Hispanics
15% Asian Americans
11% international students

AFTER FRESHMAN YEAR
84% returned for sophomore year
71% got a degree within 6 years

AFTER GRADUATION
300 organizations recruited on campus
1 Fulbright scholar

WHAT YOU WILL PAY
Tuition and fees $19,700
Room and board $7100
52% receive need-based financial aid
Need-based college-administered scholarships and
  grants average $10,289 per award
11% receive non-need financial aid
Non-need college-administered scholarships and
  grants average $11,202 per award

BOWDOIN COLLEGE

Brunswick, Maine • Small-town setting • Private • Independent • Coed

Public health care in Europe, South Asian art, the effects of cognitive style on learning, gender and labor in Israeli kibbutzim, prison reform—these are some of the topics students are studying in classes and independently at Bowdoin. Bowdoin offers one of the most demanding and exciting academic programs in the country, preparing students to become leaders in their academic and professional fields and in their communities. Located just 3 miles from the ocean and 25 minutes from Portland, Maine's largest city, Bowdoin balances extremely challenging academics with an active but informal setting, creating a distinctive personality among the nation's top schools.

 Academics

Bowdoin offers a liberal arts curriculum and core academic program. It awards bachelor's **degrees**. Challenging opportunities include advanced placement, accelerated degree programs, self-designed majors, tutorials, and Phi Beta Kappa. Special programs include off-campus study and study abroad.

The most popular **majors** include political science/government, English, and economics. A complete listing of majors at Bowdoin appears in the Majors Index beginning on page 379.

The **faculty** at Bowdoin has 124 full-time teachers, 94% with terminal degrees. 100% of the faculty serve as student advisers. The student-faculty ratio is 11:1.

 Computers on Campus

Students are not required to have a computer. Student rooms are linked to a campus network. 90 **computers** available in the computer center, computer labs, the research center, academic departments, and the library provide access to the main academic computer, e-mail, and on-line services. Staffed computer lab on campus (open 24 hours a day) provides training in the use of computers and software.

The 6 **libraries** have 842,629 books and 2,110 subscriptions. They are connected to 10 national **on-line** catalogs.

 Campus Life

There are 50 active **organizations** on campus, including a drama/theater group and student-run newspaper and radio station. 40% of students participate in student government elections. 34% of eligible men and 23% of eligible women are members of 8 coed fraternities. Student **safety services** include late night transport/escort service, 24-hour emergency telephone alarm devices, 24-hour patrols by trained security personnel, student patrols, and electronically operated dormitory entrances.

Bowdoin is a member of the NCAA (Division III). **Intercollegiate sports** include baseball (m), basketball (m, w), cross-country running (m, w), field hockey (w), football (m), golf (m, w), ice hockey (m, w), lacrosse (m, w), sailing (m, w), skiing (cross-country) (m, w), skiing (downhill) (m, w), soccer (m, w), softball (w), squash (m, w), swimming and diving (m, w), tennis (m, w), track and field (m, w), volleyball (w).

 Applying

Bowdoin requires an essay, a high school transcript, and 3 recommendations. It recommends 4 years of high school math and science, 4 years of high school foreign language, and an interview. Early and deferred entrance are possible, with a 1/15 deadline and a 3/1 priority date for financial aid. **Contact:** Dr. Richard E. Steele, Dean of Admissions, College Street, Brunswick, ME 04011-2546, 207-725-3190; fax 207-725-3003.

GETTING IN LAST YEAR
4,122 applied
30% were accepted
36% enrolled (449)
72% from top tenth of their h.s. class
61% had SAT verbal scores over 600
90% had SAT math scores over 600
10% had SAT verbal scores over 700
34% had SAT math scores over 700
1 National Merit Scholar

THE STUDENT BODY
1,530 undergraduates
From 51 states and territories,
   28 other countries

14% from Maine
51% women, 49% men
2% African Americans
1% Native Americans
3% Hispanics
8% Asian Americans
2% international students

AFTER FRESHMAN YEAR
94% returned for sophomore year
85% got a degree within 4 years
91% got a degree within 5 years
92% got a degree within 6 years

AFTER GRADUATION
17% pursued further study (10% arts and
   sciences, 4% law)
76% had job offers within 6 months
64 organizations recruited on campus
5 Fulbright scholars

WHAT YOU WILL PAY
Tuition and fees $20,555
Room and board $5945
43% receive need-based financial aid

BRADLEY UNIVERSITY

Peoria, Illinois • Urban setting • Private • Independent • Coed

 Academics

Bradley offers a core academic program. It awards bachelor's and master's **degrees**. Challenging opportunities include advanced placement, accelerated degree programs, self-designed majors, tutorials, and an honors program. Special programs include cooperative education, internships, summer session for credit, study abroad, and Army ROTC.

The **faculty** at Bradley has 312 full-time graduate and undergraduate teachers, 85% with terminal degrees. 78% of the faculty serve as student advisers. The student-faculty ratio is 15:1.

 Computers on Campus

Students are not required to have a computer. Student rooms are linked to a campus network. 2,000 **computers** available in the computer center, computer labs, classrooms, the library, the student center, and dormitories provide access to e-mail and on-line services.

The **library** has 536,166 books, 30,137 microform titles, and 1,841 subscriptions.

 Campus Life

There are 220 active **organizations** on campus, including a drama/theater group and student-run newspaper and radio station. 43% of eligible men and 34% of eligible women are members of 18 national **fraternities** and 11 national **sororities**. Student **safety services** include late night transport/escort service, 24-hour emergency telephone alarm devices, 24-hour patrols by trained security personnel, and electronically operated dormitory entrances.

Bradley is a member of the NCAA (Division I). **Intercollegiate sports** (some offering scholarships) include baseball (m), basketball (m, w), cross-country running (m, w), golf (m, w), ice hockey (m), soccer (m), softball (w), swimming and diving (m, w), table tennis (m, w), tennis (m, w), volleyball (w).

 Applying

Bradley requires a high school transcript, SAT I or ACT, a minimum high school GPA of 2.0, and in some cases 3 years of high school math and science. It recommends an essay, some high school foreign language, recommendations, an interview, and a minimum high school GPA of 3.0. Early, deferred, and midyear entrance are possible, with rolling admissions and continuous processing to 3/1 for financial aid. **Contact:** Executive Director of Enrollment Management, 100 Swords Hall, Peoria, IL 61625-0002, 309-677-1000 or toll-free 800-447-6460.

GETTING IN LAST YEAR

3,710 applied
90% were accepted
30% enrolled (1,016)
31% from top tenth of their h.s. class
47% had SAT verbal scores over 600 (R)
56% had SAT math scores over 600 (R)
41% had ACT scores over 26
14% had SAT verbal scores over 700 (R)
13% had SAT math scores over 700 (R)
11% had ACT scores over 30
40 National Merit Scholars

THE STUDENT BODY

Total 5,973, of whom 5,083
    are undergraduates
From 43 states and territories,
    41 other countries
76% from Illinois
52% women, 48% men
5% African Americans
1% Native Americans
2% Hispanics
2% Asian Americans
1% international students

AFTER GRADUATION

15% pursued further study
2 Fulbright scholars

WHAT YOU WILL PAY

Tuition and fees $11,490
Room and board $4620
55% receive need-based financial aid
Need-based college-administered scholarships and
    grants average $2840 per award
32% receive non-need financial aid
Non-need college-administered scholarships and
    grants average $2700 per award

BRANDEIS UNIVERSITY

Waltham, Massachusetts • Suburban setting • Private • Independent • Coed

Brandeis features the Volen Center for Complex Systems, a nationally funded facility where faculty and students conduct interdisciplinary research studying the brain's cognitive processes; state-of-the-art sports and recreation facilities; a comprehensive program in the arts; an ideal location on a commuter rail stop 9 miles west of Boston; internships throughout the area in law, health care, government, finance, the media, public service, and the arts; opportunities for significant undergraduate research through a variety of established programs; and broad renewable financial aid, including both need- and merit-based scholarships for up to 75% of tuition for domestic and international students.

Academics

Brandeis offers an interdisciplinary curriculum and core academic program; fewer than half of graduate courses are open to undergraduates. It awards bachelor's, master's, and doctoral **degrees**. Challenging opportunities include advanced placement, self-designed majors, tutorials, a senior project, and Phi Beta Kappa. Special programs include internships, summer session for credit, off-campus study, and Army and Air Force ROTC.

The most popular **majors** include political science/government, English, and psychology. A complete listing of majors at Brandeis appears in the Majors Index beginning on page 379.

The **faculty** at Brandeis has 361 full-time graduate and undergraduate teachers, 71% with terminal degrees. 90% of the faculty serve as student advisers. The student-faculty ratio is 10:1, and the average class size in core courses is 17.

Computers on Campus

Students are not required to have a computer. Student rooms are linked to a campus network. 100 **computers** available in the computer center, computer labs, the research center, the learning resource center, science library, classrooms, the library, the student center, and dormitories provide access to off-campus computing facilities, e-mail, on-line services, and educational software. Staffed computer lab on campus provides training in the use of computers and software.

The 3 **libraries** have 981,911 books, 834,668 microform titles, and 7,064 subscriptions. They are connected to 13 national **on-line** catalogs.

Campus Life

There are 130 active **organizations** on campus, including a drama/theater group and student-run newspaper and radio station. 35% of students participate in student government elections. Student **safety services** include late night transport/escort service, 24-hour emergency telephone alarm devices, 24-hour patrols by trained security personnel, and electronically operated dormitory entrances.

Brandeis is a member of the NCAA (Division III). **Intercollegiate sports** include baseball (m), basketball (m, w), crew (m, w), cross-country running (m, w), fencing (m, w), field hockey (w), golf (m), ice hockey (m), lacrosse (m), rugby (m, w), sailing (m, w), skiing (cross-country) (m, w), soccer (m, w), softball (w), swimming and diving (m, w), tennis (m, w), track and field (m, w), volleyball (w), water polo (m, w).

Applying

Brandeis requires an essay, a high school transcript, 2 years of high school foreign language, 2 recommendations, 4 years of high school English, 1 year of high school science and history, ACT or SAT I and 3 SAT II Subject Tests. It recommends 3 years of high school math, 3 years of high school foreign language, an interview, and a minimum high school GPA of 3.0. Early, deferred, and midyear entrance are possible, with a 2/1 deadline and a 2/15 priority date for financial aid. **Contact:** Mr. Michael Kalafatas, Director of Admissions, 415 South Street, Waltham, MA 02254-9110, 617-736-3500 or toll-free 800-622-0622 (out-of-state); fax 617-736-3536.

GETTING IN LAST YEAR
4,539 applied
66% were accepted
29% enrolled (876)
57% from top tenth of their h.s. class
8 National Merit Scholars

THE STUDENT BODY
Total 4,192, of whom 2,929 are undergraduates
From 50 states and territories, 55 other countries

25% from Massachusetts
55% women, 45% men
4% African Americans
1% Native Americans
3% Hispanics
8% Asian Americans
6% international students

AFTER FRESHMAN YEAR
89% returned for sophomore year

AFTER GRADUATION
39% pursued further study (13% law, 11% arts and sciences, 9% medicine)
1 Rhodes scholar

WHAT YOU WILL PAY
Tuition and fees $20,934
Room and board $6950
59% receive need-based financial aid
12% receive non-need financial aid

BRIGHAM YOUNG UNIVERSITY

Provo, Utah • Suburban setting • Private • Independent-Religious • Coed

BYU, sponsored by The Church of Jesus Christ of Latter-day Saints, offers a range of resources and opportunities, including an extensive study-abroad program. BYU offers bachelor's degrees in 166 academic programs, master's degrees in 71, and doctorates in 33. The admission process is rigorous. The committee considers academic achievements, extracurricular strengths, and personal qualities. Students likely to benefit from BYU possess a high degree of self-discipline and enthusiasm for learning. BYU ranks in the top 10 among institutions that have National Merit Scholars. Students come from all 50 states and nearly 100 countries and bring a diversity of backgrounds and ideas.

 Academics

BYU offers an interdisciplinary curriculum and core academic program; fewer than half of graduate courses are open to undergraduates. It awards bachelor's, master's, doctoral, and first professional **degrees**. Challenging opportunities include advanced placement, accelerated degree programs, Freshman Honors College, an honors program, a senior project, and Sigma Xi. Special programs include cooperative education, internships, summer session for credit, study abroad, and Army and Air Force ROTC.

The most popular **majors** include elementary education, psychology, and English. A complete listing of majors at BYU appears in the Majors Index beginning on page 379.

The **faculty** at BYU has 1,381 full-time graduate and undergraduate teachers, 80% with terminal degrees. The student-faculty ratio is 29:1, and the average class size in core courses is 43.

 Computers on Campus

Students are not required to have a computer. 1,800 **computers** available in the computer center, computer labs, the research center, the learning resource center, classrooms, the library, the student center, and dormitories provide access to e-mail, on-line services, and the Internet. Staffed computer lab on campus.

The 2 **libraries** have 2.4 million books, 2.1 million microform titles, and 17,022 subscriptions. They are connected to 35 national **on-line** catalogs.

 Campus Life

Active **organizations** on campus include drama/theater group and student-run newspaper and radio station. 19% of students participate in student government elections. Student **safety services** include 24-hour emergency telephone alarm devices, 24-hour patrols by trained security personnel, and electronically operated dormitory entrances.

BYU is a member of the NCAA (Division I). **Intercollegiate sports** (some offering scholarships) include baseball (m), basketball (m, w), cross-country running (m, w), field hockey (w), football (m), golf (m, w), gymnastics (m, w), skiing (downhill) (m, w), soccer (m), softball (w), swimming and diving (m, w), tennis (m, w), track and field (m, w), volleyball (m, w), wrestling (m).

 Applying

BYU requires an essay, a high school transcript, 1 recommendation, an interview, minimum 3.5 high school GPA for freshmen, minimum 3.1 college GPA for transfers, and ACT. It recommends 3 years of high school math and science and 2 years of high school foreign language. Early and midyear entrance are possible, with a 2/15 deadline and continuous processing to 3/1 for financial aid. **Contact:** Mr. Erlend D. Peterson, Dean of Admissions and Records, A-183 Abraham Smoot Building, Provo, UT 84602-1001, 801-378-2539.

GETTING IN LAST YEAR
6,942 applied
70% were accepted
82% enrolled (3,990)
58% from top tenth of their h.s. class
3.72 average high school GPA
70% had ACT scores over 26
25% had ACT scores over 30
169 National Merit Scholars

THE STUDENT BODY
Total 30,465, of whom 27,625
   are undergraduates
From 53 states and territories,
   98 other countries

31% from Utah
48% women, 52% men
1% African Americans
1% Native Americans
3% Hispanics
3% Asian Americans
5% international students

AFTER FRESHMAN YEAR
57% returned for sophomore year
11% got a degree within 4 years
24% got a degree within 5 years
40% got a degree within 6 years

AFTER GRADUATION
26% pursued further study
90% had job offers within 6 months
417 organizations recruited on campus
2 Fulbright scholars

WHAT YOU WILL PAY
Tuition and fees $2450
Room and board $3740
2% receive need-based financial aid
Need-based college-administered scholarships and
   grants average $1379 per award
19% receive non-need financial aid
Non-need college-administered scholarships and
   grants average $1614 per award

BROWN UNIVERSITY

Providence, Rhode Island • Urban setting • Private • Independent • Coed

Brown is a university/college with a renowned faculty that teaches students in both the undergraduate college and the graduate school. The unique, nonrestrictive curriculum allows students freedom in selecting their courses, and they may choose their concentration from 83 areas, complete a double major, or pursue an independent concentration. The 140-acre campus is set in a residential neighborhood (National Historic District) and features state-of-the-art computing facilities and an athletics complex. A real sense of community exists on campus, as every student has an academic adviser, and there are several peer counselors in the residence halls.

Academics

Brown offers a liberal arts curriculum and no core academic program; all graduate courses are open to undergraduates. It awards bachelor's, master's, doctoral, and first professional **degrees**. Challenging opportunities include advanced placement, accelerated degree programs, self-designed majors, tutorials, a senior project, Phi Beta Kappa, and Sigma Xi. Special programs include internships, summer session for credit, off-campus study, study abroad, and Army ROTC.

The most popular **majors** include biology/biological sciences, history, and English. A complete listing of majors at Brown appears in the Majors Index beginning on page 379.

The **faculty** at Brown has 541 full-time graduate and undergraduate teachers, 98% with terminal degrees. 70% of the faculty serve as student advisers. The student-faculty ratio is 9:1.

Computers on Campus

Students are not required to have a computer. Student rooms are linked to a campus network. 400 **computers** available in the computer center, computer labs, the learn-

ing resource center, the library, the student center, and dormitories provide access to e-mail, on-line services, and the Internet. Staffed computer lab on campus provides training in the use of computers and software.

The 7 **libraries** have 2.5 million books, 1 million microform titles, and 15,090 subscriptions.

Campus Life

There are 240 active **organizations** on campus, including a drama/theater group and student-run newspaper and radio station. 43% of students participate in student government elections. 10% of eligible men and 2% of eligible women are members of 10 national **fraternities**, 2 national **sororities**, and 1 coed fraternity. Student **safety services** include late night transport/escort service, 24-hour emergency telephone alarm devices, 24-hour patrols by trained security personnel, and electronically operated dormitory entrances.

Brown is a member of the NCAA (Division I). **Intercollegiate sports** include baseball (m), basketball (m, w), crew (m, w), cross-country running (m, w), fencing (m, w), field hockey (w), football (m), golf (m, w), gymnastics (w), ice hockey (m, w), lacrosse (m, w), rugby (m, w), sailing (m, w), skiing (cross-country) (m, w), skiing (downhill) (m, w), soccer (m, w), softball (w), squash (m, w), swimming and diving (m, w), tennis (m, w), track and field (m, w), volleyball (m, w), water polo (m, w), wrestling (m).

Applying

Brown requires an essay, a high school transcript, 3 years of high school math and science, 3 years of high school foreign language, 2 recommendations, SAT I or ACT, and 3 SAT II Subject Tests. Early and deferred entrance are possible, with a 1/1 deadline and 1/1 for financial aid. **Contact:** Mr. Michael Goldberger, Director of Admission, Box 1876, Providence, RI 02912, 401-863-2378; fax 401-863-9300.

GETTING IN LAST YEAR
13,905 applied
21% were accepted
48% enrolled (1,426)
86% from top tenth of their h.s. class
89% had SAT verbal scores over 600 (R)
91% had SAT math scores over 600 (R)
78% had ACT scores over 26
49% had SAT verbal scores over 700 (R)
44% had SAT math scores over 700 (R)
49% had ACT scores over 30
75 National Merit Scholars

THE STUDENT BODY
Total 7,641, of whom 5,942
   are undergraduates

From 52 states and territories,
   68 other countries
3% from Rhode Island
53% women, 47% men
6% African Americans
1% Native Americans
5% Hispanics
15% Asian Americans
9% international students

AFTER FRESHMAN YEAR
96% returned for sophomore year
80% got a degree within 4 years
90% got a degree within 5 years
93% got a degree within 6 years

AFTER GRADUATION
30% pursued further study (10% arts and
   sciences, 10% law, 9% medicine)
300 organizations recruited on campus
1 Marshall, 14 Fulbright scholars

WHAT YOU WILL PAY
Tuition and fees $21,277
Room and board $6212
32% receive need-based financial aid
Need-based college-administered scholarships and
   grants average $11,864 per award

BRYN MAWR COLLEGE

Bryn Mawr, Pennsylvania • Suburban setting • Private • Independent • Women

Bryn Mawr, founded in 1885 to offer women the challenging education then available only to men, remains a place where women succeed beyond all stereotypical notions of "suitability." Women major in the sciences and mathematics 3 to 5 times more often than the national average (29 times the national average in physics), and Bryn Mawr ranks first in the nation in the percentage of undergraduates who earn a PhD. in the humanities and fourth in all fields. Close relationships with faculty members praised for their teaching and known for their scholarship foster an education that is active and enjoyable.

Academics

Bryn Mawr offers a liberal arts and sciences curriculum and core academic program; fewer than half of graduate courses are open to undergraduates. It awards bachelor's, master's, and doctoral **degrees**. Challenging opportunities include advanced placement, accelerated degree programs, self-designed majors, tutorials, an honors program, and Sigma Xi. Special programs include summer session for credit, off-campus study, study abroad, and Army, Naval, and Air Force ROTC.

The most popular **majors** include English, history, and political science/government. A complete listing of majors at Bryn Mawr appears in the Majors Index beginning on page 379.

The **faculty** at Bryn Mawr has 151 full-time graduate and undergraduate teachers, 99% with terminal degrees. 20% of the faculty serve as student advisers. The student-faculty ratio is 9:1.

Computers on Campus

Students are not required to have a computer. Student rooms are linked to a campus network. 150 **computers**
available in the computer center, computer labs, the library, the student center, and dormitories provide access to the main academic computer, e-mail, on-line services, and the Internet. Staffed computer lab on campus provides training in the use of computers and software.

The 5 **libraries** have 971,934 books, 122,183 microform titles, and 1,826 subscriptions. They are connected to 5 national **on-line** catalogs.

Campus Life

There are 95 active **organizations** on campus, including a drama/theater group and student-run newspaper and radio station. Student **safety services** include late night transport/escort service, 24-hour emergency telephone alarm devices, 24-hour patrols by trained security personnel, and electronically operated dormitory entrances.

Bryn Mawr is a member of the NCAA (Division III). **Intercollegiate sports** include badminton, basketball, cross-country running, fencing, field hockey, lacrosse, rugby, sailing, soccer, swimming and diving, tennis, track and field, volleyball.

Applying

Bryn Mawr requires an essay, a high school transcript, 3 years of high school math, 3 years of high school foreign language, 3 recommendations, SAT I, and 3 SAT II Subject Tests (including SAT II: Writing Test). It recommends 3 years of high school science, an interview, and ACT. Early, deferred, and midyear entrance are possible, with a 1/15 deadline and 1/15 for financial aid. **Contact:** Ms. Nancy Monnich, Director of Admissions and Financial Aid, Ely House, Bryn Mawr, PA 19010-2899, 610-526-5152 or toll-free 800-BMC-1885 (out-of-state); fax 610-526-7471.

GETTING IN LAST YEAR
1,719 applied
58% were accepted
34% enrolled (344)
62% from top tenth of their h.s. class
56% had SAT verbal scores over 600
67% had SAT math scores over 600
15% had SAT verbal scores over 700
17% had SAT math scores over 700

THE STUDENT BODY
Total 1,821, of whom 1,193
   are undergraduates
From 49 states and territories,
   44 other countries

11% from Pennsylvania
100% women
4% African Americans
1% Native Americans
3% Hispanics
17% Asian Americans
10% international students

AFTER FRESHMAN YEAR
82% got a degree within 4 years
88% got a degree within 5 years
89% got a degree within 6 years

AFTER GRADUATION
45% pursued further study (20% arts and
   sciences, 10% law, 4% medicine)
3 Fulbright scholars

WHAT YOU WILL PAY
Tuition and fees $19,810
Room and board $7085
53% receive need-based financial aid
Need-based college-administered scholarships and
   grants average $13,582 per award

BUCKNELL UNIVERSITY

Lewisburg, Pennsylvania • Small-town setting • Private • Independent • Coed

Since 1846, scholars have come together at Bucknell to ask questions and explore answers. Bucknell professors enjoy national reputations, and Bucknell students are known for their intelligence and vitality. Together, they explore a wide-ranging curriculum that includes the arts, humanities, social sciences, sciences, education, business administration, and engineering. Beginning with first-year foundation seminars, students and faculty learn to respect each other through lively classroom discussions and through collaboration in research and scholarly papers. In the supportive atmosphere of Bucknell, each person makes full use of the present and finds exciting possibilities for the future.

Academics

Bucknell offers no core academic program; fewer than half of graduate courses are open to undergraduates. It awards bachelor's and master's **degrees**. Challenging opportunities include advanced placement, accelerated degree programs, self-designed majors, an honors program, a senior project, Phi Beta Kappa, and Sigma Xi. Special programs include internships, summer session for credit, off-campus study, study abroad, and Army ROTC.

The most popular **majors** include business, economics, and biology/biological sciences. A complete listing of majors at Bucknell appears in the Majors Index beginning on page 379.

The **faculty** at Bucknell has 254 full-time graduate and undergraduate teachers, 97% with terminal degrees. 80% of the faculty serve as student advisers. The student-faculty ratio is 13:1.

Computers on Campus

Students are not required to have a computer. Student rooms are linked to a campus network. 800 **computers** available in the computer center, computer labs, classrooms, the library, and dormitories provide access to the main academic computer, e-mail, on-line services, and the Internet. Staffed computer lab on campus provides training in the use of computers and software.

The **library** has 563,080 books, 636,900 microform titles, and 4,690 subscriptions. It is connected to 2 national **on-line** catalogs.

Campus Life

There are 100 active **organizations** on campus, including a drama/theater group and student-run newspaper and radio station. 45% of eligible men and 50% of eligible women are members of 12 national **fraternities**, 8 national **sororities**, 2 local fraternities, and 2 local sororities. Student **safety services** include late night transport/escort service, 24-hour emergency telephone alarm devices, and 24-hour patrols by trained security personnel.

Bucknell is a member of the NCAA (Division I). **Intercollegiate sports** include baseball (m), basketball (m, w), crew (m, w), cross-country running (m, w), field hockey (w), football (m), golf (m), ice hockey (m), lacrosse (m, w), riflery (m, w), rugby (m, w), sailing (m, w), skiing (cross-country) (m, w), soccer (m, w), softball (w), swimming and diving (m, w), tennis (m, w), track and field (m, w), volleyball (m, w), water polo (m), wrestling (m).

Applying

Bucknell requires an essay, a high school transcript, 3 years of high school math, some high school foreign language, recommendations, and SAT I. It recommends 3 years of high school science and an interview. Early, deferred, and midyear entrance are possible, with a 1/1 deadline and a 1/1 priority date for financial aid. **Contact:** Mr. Mark D. Davies, Dean of Admissions, Freas Hall, Lewisburg, PA 17837, 717-524-1101; fax 717-524-3760.

GETTING IN LAST YEAR
6,597 applied
55% were accepted
25% enrolled (910)
50% from top tenth of their h.s. class
3.4 average high school GPA
46% had SAT verbal scores over 600 (R)
77% had SAT math scores over 600 (R)
5% had SAT verbal scores over 700 (R)
18% had SAT math scores over 700 (R)
5 National Merit Scholars
31 class presidents
28 valedictorians

THE STUDENT BODY
Total 3,558, of whom 3,342
 are undergraduates

From 42 states and territories,
 30 other countries
32% from Pennsylvania
49% women, 51% men
3% African Americans
0% Native Americans
2% Hispanics
3% Asian Americans
2% international students

AFTER FRESHMAN YEAR
84% returned for sophomore year
85% got a degree within 4 years
88% got a degree within 5 years
90% got a degree within 6 years

AFTER GRADUATION
27% pursued further study (13% arts and
 sciences, 5% law, 3% engineering)
92% had job offers within 6 months
145 organizations recruited on campus

WHAT YOU WILL PAY
Tuition and fees $20,445
Room and board $5075
60% receive need-based financial aid
Need-based college-administered scholarships and
 grants average $11,520 per award

BUENA VISTA UNIVERSITY

Storm Lake, Iowa • Small-town setting • Private • Independent-Religious • Coed

Buena Vista University's students are given the opportunity to excel through a student-professor ratio of 15:1, sophisticated technology and facilities, innovative academic programs, and career and graduate school placement services. Students can view the world through exchange programs with schools in Japan and Taiwan and January Interim programs in Europe, Australia, and other locations. They meet national and international leaders and performers on campus through the Academic & Cultural Events Series. Located in America's heartland, Buena Vista's lakeside campus offers a peaceful environment in a progressive college town.

Academics

BV offers an interdisciplinary curriculum and core academic program. It awards bachelor's and master's **degrees**. Challenging opportunities include advanced placement, self-designed majors, tutorials, an honors program, and a senior project. Special programs include internships, summer session for credit, off-campus study, and study abroad.

The most popular **majors** include business, education, and science. A complete listing of majors at BV appears in the Majors Index beginning on page 379.

The **faculty** at BV has 73 full-time undergraduate teachers, 65% with terminal degrees. 100% of the faculty serve as student advisers. The student-faculty ratio is 15:1.

Computers on Campus

Students are not required to have a computer. Student rooms are linked to a campus network. 400 **computers** available in the computer center, computer labs, the learning resource center, mass communication building, media center, classrooms, the library, the student center, and dormitories provide access to the main academic computer, e-mail, on-line services, and the Internet. Staffed computer lab on campus provides training in the use of computers and software.

The **library** has 141,652 books, 273 microform titles, and 1,130 subscriptions. It is connected to 1 national **on-line** catalog.

Campus Life

There are 40 active **organizations** on campus, including a drama/theater group and student-run newspaper and radio station. Student **safety services** include night security patrol, late night transport/escort service, 24-hour emergency telephone alarm devices, and electronically operated dormitory entrances.

BV is a member of the NCAA (Division III). **Intercollegiate sports** include baseball (m), basketball (m, w), cross-country running (m, w), football (m), golf (m, w), softball (w), swimming and diving (m, w), tennis (m, w), track and field (m, w), volleyball (w), wrestling (m).

Applying

BV requires a high school transcript, recommendations, SAT I or ACT, and in some cases an essay and an interview. It recommends 3 years of high school math and science, some high school foreign language, and a minimum high school GPA of 2.0. Early, deferred, and midyear entrance are possible, with a 6/1 deadline and continuous processing to 4/22 for financial aid. **Contact:** Mr. Mike Frantz, Director of Admissions, 610 West Fourth Street, Storm Lake, IA 50588, 712-749-2235 or toll-free 800-383-9600; fax 712-749-2037.

GETTING IN LAST YEAR
1,180 applied
92% were accepted
33% enrolled (355)
21% from top tenth of their h.s. class
3.2 average high school GPA
46% had ACT scores over 26
4% had ACT scores over 30
17 class presidents
23 valedictorians

THE STUDENT BODY
1,150 undergraduates
From 17 states and territories,
   6 other countries

78% from Iowa
51% women, 49% men
1% African Americans
1% Hispanics
1% Asian Americans
4% international students

AFTER FRESHMAN YEAR
65% returned for sophomore year
53% got a degree within 4 years
54% got a degree within 5 years
55% got a degree within 6 years

AFTER GRADUATION
16% pursued further study (7% arts and
   sciences, 4% medicine, 3% law)

95% had job offers within 6 months
70 organizations recruited on campus

WHAT YOU WILL PAY
Tuition and fees $14,078
Room and board $4017
Need-based college-administered scholarships and
   grants average $1498 per award
Non-need college-administered scholarships and
   grants average $6198 per award

BUTLER UNIVERSITY

Indianapolis, Indiana • Urban setting • Private • Independent • Coed

Nearly 4,000 students attend Butler University, an independent university composed of a college of liberal arts and sciences and 4 professional colleges. Founded in 1855, Butler offers large-university opportunities in a small-college atmosphere. Undergraduates choose from more than 60 majors while still enjoying the personal attention of a low student-faculty ratio. Butler combines a strong liberal arts foundation with practical education and career-minded professional programs. Butler also offers an active student life program featuring 80 student organizations.

Academics

Butler offers an interdisciplinary curriculum and core academic program; fewer than half of graduate courses are open to undergraduates. It awards bachelor's and master's **degrees** (also offers 6-year undergraduate doctor of pharmacy). Challenging opportunities include advanced placement, accelerated degree programs, tutorials, an honors program, a senior project, and Sigma Xi. Special programs include internships, summer session for credit, off-campus study, study abroad, and Army and Air Force ROTC.

The most popular **majors** include pharmacy/pharmaceutical sciences, biology/biological sciences, and elementary education. A complete listing of majors at Butler appears in the Majors Index beginning on page 379.

The **faculty** at Butler has 231 full-time graduate and undergraduate teachers, 83% with terminal degrees. 90% of the faculty serve as student advisers. The student-faculty ratio is 13:1, and the average class size in core courses is 18.

Computers on Campus

Students are not required to have a computer. 229 **computers** available in the computer center, labs, classrooms, the library, and dormitories provide access to the main academic computer, e-mail, and the Internet. Staffed computer lab on campus provides training in the use of computers and software.

The 2 **libraries** have 286,112 books, 235,280 microform titles, and 2,350 subscriptions. They are connected to 1 national **on-line** catalog.

Campus Life

There are 80 active **organizations** on campus, including a drama/theater group and student-run newspaper and radio station. 42% of eligible men and 38% of eligible women are members of 8 national **fraternities** and 8 national **sororities**. Student **safety services** include late night transport/escort service, 24-hour emergency telephone alarm devices, 24-hour patrols by trained security personnel, and electronically operated dormitory entrances.

Butler is a member of the NCAA (Division I). **Intercollegiate sports** (some offering scholarships) include baseball (m), basketball (m, w), crew (m, w), cross-country running (m, w), football (m), golf (m), lacrosse (m), soccer (m, w), softball (w), swimming and diving (m, w), tennis (m, w), track and field (m, w), volleyball (w).

Applying

Butler requires an essay, a high school transcript, 3 years of high school math, 2 years of high school foreign language, SAT I or ACT, and in some cases 3 years of high school science, a campus interview, and audition. It recommends SAT II Subject Tests. Early, deferred, and midyear entrance are possible, with an 8/15 deadline and continuous processing to 3/1 for financial aid. **Contact:** Ms. Carroll Davis, Director of Admission, 4600 Sunset Avenue, Indianapolis, IN 46208-3485, 317-940-8100 or toll-free 800-972-2882.

GETTING IN LAST YEAR
2,718 applied
88% were accepted
35% enrolled (849)
42% from top tenth of their h.s. class
14% had SAT verbal scores over 600
45% had SAT math scores over 600
41% had ACT scores over 26
1% had SAT verbal scores over 700
8% had SAT math scores over 700
8% had ACT scores over 30
11 National Merit Scholars
38 valedictorians

THE STUDENT BODY
Total 3,866, of whom 3,028
  are undergraduates

From 42 states and territories
66% from Indiana
60% women, 40% men
5% African Americans
0% Native Americans
1% Hispanics
2% Asian Americans
0% international students

AFTER FRESHMAN YEAR
82% returned for sophomore year
47% got a degree within 4 years
62% got a degree within 5 years
66% got a degree within 6 years

AFTER GRADUATION
20% pursued further study (15% arts and
  sciences, 2% law, 2% medicine)
70% had job offers within 6 months
300 organizations recruited on campus

WHAT YOU WILL PAY
Tuition and fees $13,990
Room and board $4730
60% receive need-based financial aid
Need-based college-administered scholarships and
  grants average $5609 per award
44% receive non-need financial aid
Non-need college-administered scholarships and
  grants average $5400 per award

CALIFORNIA INSTITUTE OF TECHNOLOGY

Pasadena, California • Suburban setting • Private • Independent • Coed

Caltech provides a research-oriented learning environment with a focus on math, science, and engineering for its 900 undergraduates and 1,000 graduate students. Because of its size, Caltech offers the advantages of a 3:1 student-faculty ratio and participation in what has been described as "a community of scientists, a scholarly intimacy that cannot be found anywhere else." In his inaugural remarks, President Everhart captured the spirit of Caltech when he said: "There need to be a few places that look ahead and dare to do the most ambitious things that human beings can accomplish. Caltech has that ambition and that daring."

 ## Academics

Caltech offers a science and math curriculum and core academic program; all graduate courses are open to undergraduates. It awards bachelor's, master's, and doctoral **degrees**. Challenging opportunities include self-designed majors, tutorials, and Sigma Xi. Special programs include internships, off-campus study, study abroad, and Army and Air Force ROTC.

The most popular **majors** include engineering and applied sciences, physics, and biology/biological sciences. A complete listing of majors at Caltech appears in the Majors Index beginning on page 379.

The **faculty** at Caltech has 295 graduate and undergraduate teachers, 100% with terminal degrees. The student-faculty ratio is 3:1.

 ## Computers on Campus

Students are not required to have a computer. Student rooms are linked to a campus network. 600 **computers**

available in the computer center, computer labs, the research center, the library, the student center, dormitories, and student rooms provide access to off-campus computing facilities, e-mail, on-line services, and the Internet. Staffed computer lab on campus (open 24 hours a day) provides training in the use of computers and software.

The 11 **libraries** have 520,733 books, 532,210 microform titles, and 4,639 subscriptions. They are connected to 4 national **on-line** catalogs.

 ## Campus Life

Active **organizations** on campus include drama/theater group and student-run newspaper. Student **safety services** include late night transport/escort service, 24-hour emergency telephone alarm devices, and 24-hour patrols by trained security personnel.

Caltech is a member of the NCAA (Division III). **Intercollegiate sports** include baseball (m), basketball (m, w), cross-country running (m, w), fencing (m, w), football (m), golf (m, w), ice hockey (m), soccer (m, w), swimming and diving (m, w), tennis (m, w), track and field (m, w), volleyball (w), water polo (m, w).

 ## Applying

Caltech requires an essay, a high school transcript, 4 years of high school math, 3 recommendations, SAT I, and 3 SAT II Subject Tests (including SAT II: Writing Test). It recommends 3 years of high school science. Early and deferred entrance are possible, with a 1/1 deadline and a 2/1 priority date for financial aid. **Contact:** Ms. Charlene Liebau, Director of Admissions, 1201 East California Boulevard, Pasadena, CA 91125-0001, 818-395-6341 or toll-free 800-568-8324; fax 818-683-3026.

GETTING IN LAST YEAR
1,900 applied
26% were accepted
44% enrolled (218)
100% from top tenth of their h.s. class
97% had SAT verbal scores over 600 (R)
100% had SAT math scores over 600 (R)
62% had SAT verbal scores over 700 (R)
99% had SAT math scores over 700 (R)
30 National Merit Scholars

THE STUDENT BODY
Total 1,973, of whom 923
 are undergraduates

From 46 states and territories,
 30 other countries
30% from California
25% women, 75% men
1% African Americans
0% Native Americans
6% Hispanics
30% Asian Americans
8% international students

AFTER FRESHMAN YEAR
97% returned for sophomore year

AFTER GRADUATION
61% pursued further study (32% arts and
 sciences, 21% engineering, 4% medicine)
1 Fulbright scholar

WHAT YOU WILL PAY
Tuition and fees $17,586
Room and board $5195
67% receive need-based financial aid
Need-based college-administered scholarships and
 grants average $13,000 per award
10% receive non-need financial aid
Non-need college-administered scholarships and
 grants average $9500 per award

CALVIN COLLEGE

Grand Rapids, Michigan • Suburban setting • Private • Independent-Religious • Coed

Calvin College is a place where knowledge and faith can grow—where students prepare to take their individual place in God's world. On Calvin's spacious campus, students, faculty, and staff form a community of supportive, committed people who savor the joyful task of serving God through intellectual curiosity, spirited interaction, and conscientious work. Nearly 4,000 students from throughout the U.S. and many other countries have found Calvin to be an ideal place for thinking, questing people who are committed to a lifetime of service in today's world.

 ## Academics

Calvin offers a Christ-centered liberal arts curriculum and core academic program; fewer than half of graduate courses are open to undergraduates. It awards bachelor's and master's **degrees**. Challenging opportunities include advanced placement, self-designed majors, tutorials, Freshman Honors College, an honors program, and a senior project. Special programs include cooperative education, internships, summer session for credit, off-campus study, and study abroad.

The most popular **majors** include education, business, and engineering (general). A complete listing of majors at Calvin appears in the Majors Index beginning on page 379.

The **faculty** at Calvin has 246 full-time graduate and undergraduate teachers, 80% with terminal degrees. 96% of the faculty serve as student advisers. The student-faculty ratio is 17:1.

 ## Computers on Campus

Students are not required to have a computer. 442 **computers** available in the computer center, computer labs, the research center, classrooms, the library, the student center, and dormitories provide access to the main academic computer, off-campus computing facilities, e-mail, on-line services, and the Internet. Staffed computer lab on campus.

The **library** has 676,130 books, 579,300 microform titles, and 2,690 subscriptions.

 ## Campus Life

There are 32 active **organizations** on campus, including a drama/theater group and student-run newspaper and radio station. Student **safety services** include crime prevention programs, crime alert bulletins, late night transport/escort service, 24-hour patrols by trained security personnel, and student patrols.

Calvin is a member of the NCAA (Division III). **Intercollegiate sports** include baseball (m), basketball (m, w), cross-country running (m, w), golf (m, w), ice hockey (m), lacrosse (m), soccer (m, w), softball (w), swimming and diving (m, w), tennis (m, w), track and field (m, w), volleyball (m, w).

 ## Applying

Calvin requires an essay, a high school transcript, 1 recommendation, SAT I or ACT, and a minimum high school GPA of 2.0. It recommends 3 years of high school math and science, 2 years of high school foreign language, and an interview. Early, deferred, and midyear entrance are possible, with rolling admissions and continuous processing to 2/15 for financial aid. **Contact:** Mr. Dale D. Kuiper, Director of Admissions, 3201 Burton Street, SE, Grand Rapids, MI 49546-4388, 616-957-6106 or toll-free 800-668-0122.

GETTING IN LAST YEAR
1,907 applied
97% were accepted
55% enrolled (1,015)
29% from top tenth of their h.s. class
3.38 average high school GPA
25% had SAT verbal scores over 600 (R)
50% had SAT math scores over 600 (R)
46% had ACT scores over 26
5% had SAT verbal scores over 700 (R)
16% had SAT math scores over 700 (R)
15% had ACT scores over 30
20 National Merit Scholars
48 valedictorians

THE STUDENT BODY
Total 3,963, of whom 3,925
  are undergraduates

From 51 states and territories,
  22 other countries
55% from Michigan
55% women, 45% men
1% African Americans
1% Native Americans
1% Hispanics
2% Asian Americans
8% international students

AFTER FRESHMAN YEAR
84% returned for sophomore year
43% got a degree within 4 years
59% got a degree within 5 years
61% got a degree within 6 years

AFTER GRADUATION
22% pursued further study (14% arts and
  sciences, 2% engineering, 2% theology)

WHAT YOU WILL PAY
Tuition and fees $10,995
Room and board $3895
66% receive need-based financial aid
Need-based college-administered scholarships and
  grants average $2500 per award
26% receive non-need financial aid
Non-need college-administered scholarships and
  grants average $1210 per award

CAPITAL UNIVERSITY

Columbus, Ohio • Suburban setting • Private • Independent-Religious • Coed

Academics

Capital offers an interdisciplinary curriculum and core academic program; a few graduate courses are open to undergraduates. It awards bachelor's, master's, and first professional **degrees**. Challenging opportunities include advanced placement and self-designed majors. Special programs include internships, summer session for credit, off-campus study, study abroad, and Army, Naval, and Air Force ROTC.

The most popular **majors** include nursing, business, and elementary education. A complete listing of majors at Capital appears in the Majors Index beginning on page 379.

The **faculty** at Capital has 124 full-time undergraduate teachers, 78% with terminal degrees. 100% of the faculty serve as student advisers. The student-faculty ratio is 16:1.

Computers on Campus

Students are not required to have a computer. Student rooms are linked to a campus network. 80 **computers** available in computer labs, academic buildings, and the library provide access to the main academic computer, off-campus computing facilities, e-mail, and the Internet. Staffed computer lab on campus provides training in the use of computers and software.

The **library** has 172,192 books, 122,390 microform titles, and 893 subscriptions.

Campus Life

There are 60 active **organizations** on campus, including a drama/theater group and student-run newspaper and radio station. 50% of students participate in student government elections. 30% of eligible men and 30% of eligible women are members of 2 national **fraternities**, 3 national **sororities**, 3 local fraternities, and 4 local sororities. Student **safety services** include late night transport/escort service, 24-hour patrols by trained security personnel, and electronically operated dormitory entrances.

Capital is a member of the NCAA (Division III). **Intercollegiate sports** include baseball (m), basketball (m, w), cross-country running (m, w), football (m), golf (m), soccer (m, w), softball (w), tennis (m, w), volleyball (w), wrestling (m).

Applying

Capital requires a high school transcript, 3 years of high school math and science, 2 years of high school foreign language, 1 recommendation, minimum 2.5 GPA for freshmen, 2.25 for transfers, SAT I or ACT, and in some cases an essay. It recommends an interview. Early, deferred, and midyear entrance are possible, with rolling admissions and continuous processing to 2/15 for financial aid. **Contact:** Ms. Beth Heiser, Director of Admission, 2199 East Main Street, Columbus, OH 43209-2394, 614-236-6101 or toll-free 800-289-6289; fax 614-236-6820.

GETTING IN LAST YEAR
2,050 applied
83% were accepted
30% enrolled (510)
25% from top tenth of their h.s. class
3.3 average high school GPA
8% had SAT verbal scores over 600
17% had SAT math scores over 600
24% had ACT scores over 26
0% had SAT verbal scores over 700
4% had SAT math scores over 700
4% had ACT scores over 30
4 National Merit Scholars
20 valedictorians

THE STUDENT BODY
Total 4,071, of whom 1,776
  are undergraduates

From 25 states and territories,
  20 other countries
90% from Ohio
64% women, 36% men
8% African Americans
0% Native Americans
0% Hispanics
2% Asian Americans
2% international students

AFTER FRESHMAN YEAR
75% returned for sophomore year
65% got a degree within 4 years

AFTER GRADUATION
15% pursued further study (8% arts and
  sciences, 4% law, 3% medicine)
87% had job offers within 6 months

WHAT YOU WILL PAY
Tuition and fees $13,700
Room and board $4000
85% receive need-based financial aid
Need-based college-administered scholarships and
  grants average $4000 per award
95% receive non-need financial aid
Non-need college-administered scholarships and
  grants average $3750 per award

CARLETON COLLEGE

Northfield, Minnesota • Small-town setting • Private • Independent • Coed

Carleton, a residential coeducational liberal arts college, is located about 35 miles south of Minneapolis–St. Paul. About 75% of Carleton students enter graduate or professional school within 5 years of graduation. Carleton ranks first of all liberal arts colleges in the number of graduates who earned PhDs in the laboratory sciences from 1986–90 and sixth in the number who earned PhDs in all fields. Two thirds of Carleton students choose to spend at least one term on an off-campus program for academic credit. A new Center for Mathematics and Computing opened in 1993, and a new biology teaching and research facility opened in 1995.

Academics

Carleton offers a liberal arts curriculum and core academic program. It awards bachelor's **degrees**. Challenging opportunities include advanced placement, accelerated degree programs, self-designed majors, a senior project, Phi Beta Kappa, and Sigma Xi. Special programs include off-campus study and study abroad.

The most popular **majors** include biology/biological sciences, English, and history. A complete listing of majors at Carleton appears in the Majors Index beginning on page 379.

The **faculty** at Carleton has 147 full-time teachers, 96% with terminal degrees. 100% of the faculty serve as student advisers. The student-faculty ratio is 11:1.

Computers on Campus

Students are not required to have a computer. 260 **computers** available in the computer center, computer labs, the research center, the learning resource center, labs, academic buildings, classrooms, and the library provide access to the main academic computer, off-campus computing facilities, e-mail, and the Internet. Staffed computer lab on campus (open 24 hours a day) provides training in the use of software.

The 2 **libraries** have 518,019 books, 265,276 microform titles, and 1,474 subscriptions.

Campus Life

There are 100 active **organizations** on campus, including a drama/theater group and student-run newspaper and radio station. 40% of students participate in student government elections. Student **safety services** include late night transport/escort service, 24-hour emergency telephone alarm devices, 24-hour patrols by trained security personnel, and student patrols.

Carleton is a member of the NCAA (Division III). **Intercollegiate sports** include baseball (m), basketball (m, w), cross-country running (m, w), fencing (m, w), field hockey (w), football (m), golf (m, w), gymnastics (w), ice hockey (m), lacrosse (m), rugby (m, w), skiing (cross-country) (m, w), skiing (downhill) (m, w), soccer (m, w), softball (w), swimming and diving (m, w), tennis (m, w), track and field (m, w), volleyball (m, w), water polo (m), wrestling (m).

Applying

Carleton requires an essay, a high school transcript, 3 years of high school math, 3 recommendations, and SAT I or ACT. It recommends 3 years of high school science, 2 years of high school foreign language, an interview, and 3 SAT II Subject Tests. Early and deferred entrance are possible, with a 2/1 deadline and a 2/15 priority date for financial aid. **Contact:** Mr. Paul Thiboutot, Dean of Admissions, 100 South College Street, Northfield, MN 55057-4001, 507-663-4190 or toll-free 800-995-2275; fax 507-663-4526.

GETTING IN LAST YEAR
2,855 applied
51% were accepted
32% enrolled (463)
73% from top tenth of their h.s. class
65% had SAT verbal scores over 600
86% had SAT math scores over 600
90% had ACT scores over 26
15% had SAT verbal scores over 700
40% had SAT math scores over 700
52% had ACT scores over 30
80 National Merit Scholars
59 valedictorians

THE STUDENT BODY
1,752 undergraduates

From 53 states and territories, 20 other countries
22% from Minnesota
50% women, 50% men
3% African Americans
1% Native Americans
4% Hispanics
9% Asian Americans
1% international students

AFTER FRESHMAN YEAR
95% returned for sophomore year
84% got a degree within 4 years
89% got a degree within 5 years
90% got a degree within 6 years

AFTER GRADUATION
20% pursued further study (11% arts and sciences, 3% law, 3% medicine)
61% had job offers within 6 months
42 organizations recruited on campus
1 Fulbright scholar

WHAT YOU WILL PAY
Tuition and fees $20,300
Room and board $4125
59% receive need-based financial aid
Need-based college-administered scholarships and grants average $10,366 per award
7% receive non-need financial aid
Non-need college-administered scholarships and grants average $848 per award

CARNEGIE MELLON UNIVERSITY

Pittsburgh, Pennsylvania • Urban setting • Private • Independent • Coed

First envisioned by steel magnate and philanthropist Andrew Carnegie, Carnegie Mellon University has steadily built upon its foundations of excellence and innovation to become one of America's leading universities. Carnegie Mellon's unique approach to education—giving students opportunities to become experts in their chosen fields while studying a broad range of course work across disciplines—will help students become leaders and problem solvers today *and* tomorrow. The University offers more than 70 majors and minors across 6 undergraduate colleges. Whether students are interested in creating the technology of tomorrow or getting their break on Broadway, a Carnegie Mellon education can take them there.

 ## Academics

CMU offers an interdisciplinary professional liberal arts and sciences curriculum and core academic program; fewer than half of graduate courses are open to undergraduates. It awards bachelor's, master's, and doctoral **degrees**. Challenging opportunities include advanced placement, accelerated degree programs, self-designed majors, an honors program, a senior project, Phi Beta Kappa, and Sigma Xi. Special programs include cooperative education, internships, summer session for credit, off-campus study, study abroad, and Army, Naval, and Air Force ROTC.

The most popular **majors** include electrical engineering, industrial administration, and architecture. A complete listing of majors at CMU appears in the Majors Index beginning on page 379.

The **faculty** at CMU has 547 full-time undergraduate teachers, 96% with terminal degrees. The student-faculty ratio is 9:1.

 ## Computers on Campus

Students are not required to have a computer. Student rooms are linked to a campus network. 397 **computers**

available in the computer center, the library, the student center, and dormitories provide access to e-mail, on-line services, and the Internet. Staffed computer lab on campus (open 24 hours a day) provides training in the use of computers and software.

The 3 **libraries** have 852,241 books, 756,985 microform titles, and 3,889 subscriptions. They are connected to 9 national **on-line** catalogs.

 ## Campus Life

Active **organizations** on campus include drama/theater group and student-run newspaper and radio station. 20% of students participate in student government elections. 25% of eligible men and 14% of eligible women are members of 14 national **fraternities** and 5 national **sororities**. Student **safety services** include late night transport/escort service and electronically operated dormitory entrances.

CMU is a member of the NCAA (Division III). **Intercollegiate sports** include baseball (m), basketball (m, w), crew (m, w), cross-country running (m, w), fencing (m, w), football (m), golf (m), ice hockey (m), lacrosse (m, w), riflery (m), rugby (m), skiing (cross-country) (m, w), soccer (m, w), swimming and diving (m, w), tennis (m, w), track and field (m, w), volleyball (m, w).

 ## Applying

CMU requires an essay, a high school transcript, 1 recommendation, SAT I or ACT, 3 SAT II Subject Tests, and in some cases 4 years of high school math and science, portfolio, audition, and SAT II: Writing Test. It recommends 2 years of high school foreign language and an interview. Early, deferred, and midyear entrance are possible, with a 2/1 deadline and continuous processing to 2/15 for financial aid. **Contact:** Mr. Michael Steidel, Director of Admissions, Warner Hall, Room 101, Pittsburgh, PA 15213-3891, 412-268-2082; fax 412-268-7838.

GETTING IN LAST YEAR
10,291 applied
54% were accepted
22% enrolled (1,237)
57% from top tenth of their h.s. class
3.43 average high school GPA
61 valedictorians

THE STUDENT BODY
Total 7,318, of whom 4,572
  are undergraduates
From 52 states and territories,
  48 other countries
26% from Pennsylvania

32% women, 68% men
4% African Americans
1% Native Americans
3% Hispanics
15% Asian Americans
12% international students

AFTER FRESHMAN YEAR
90% returned for sophomore year
57% got a degree within 4 years
68% got a degree within 5 years
70% got a degree within 6 years

AFTER GRADUATION
28% pursued further study (8% engineering, 7% arts and sciences, 6% business)

318 organizations recruited on campus
2 Fulbright scholars

WHAT YOU WILL PAY
Tuition and fees $18,760
Room and board $5850
59% receive need-based financial aid
Need-based college-administered scholarships and
  grants average $9326 per award
43% receive non-need financial aid
Non-need college-administered scholarships and
  grants average $5090 per award

CARROLL COLLEGE

Helena, Montana • Small-town setting • Private • Independent-Religious • Coed

Carroll College offers students an outstanding liberal arts education through diverse curricula, impressive facilities, and dedicated, student-oriented faculty. Carroll's superb student-faculty ratio ensures modest class sizes and a personalized education for each student. Independent studies and cooperative education programs provide opportunities to customize students' academic progress in professional surroundings. Carroll's students and faculty regularly receive national honors for their accomplishments, including Truman and Fulbright scholarships. Carroll lies midway between Glacier and Yellowstone National Parks, surrounded by world-class skiing, fishing, and wilderness areas. Together, Carroll College and Montana's capital city provide an ideal setting in which to live and learn.

 Academics

Carroll offers a core academic program. It awards associate and bachelor's **degrees**. Challenging opportunities include advanced placement, accelerated degree programs, self-designed majors, tutorials, Freshman Honors College, an honors program, and a senior project. Special programs include cooperative education, internships, summer session for credit, and study abroad.

The most popular **majors** include biology/biological sciences, nursing, and business. A complete listing of majors at Carroll appears in the Majors Index beginning on page 379.

The **faculty** at Carroll has 68 full-time teachers, 54% with terminal degrees. 100% of the faculty serve as student advisers. The student-faculty ratio is 12:1.

 Computers on Campus

Students are not required to have a computer. 90 **computers** available in the computer center, computer labs, the learning resource center, the library, and dormitories provide access to off-campus computing facilities, e-mail, on-line services, and the Internet. Staffed computer lab on campus provides training in the use of computers and software.

The **library** has 94,000 books, 25,000 microform titles, and 530 subscriptions.

 Campus Life

There are 35 active **organizations** on campus, including a drama/theater group and student-run newspaper and radio station. Student **safety services** include late night transport/escort service.

Carroll is a member of the NAIA. **Intercollegiate sports** (some offering scholarships) include basketball (m, w), football (m), swimming and diving (m, w), volleyball (w).

 Applying

Carroll requires an essay, a high school transcript, 1 recommendation, SAT I or ACT, a minimum high school GPA of 2.0, and in some cases a campus interview. It recommends 3 years of high school math and science, 2 years of high school foreign language, an interview, and a minimum high school GPA of 3.0. Early, deferred, and midyear entrance are possible, with a 7/1 deadline and continuous processing to 3/1 for financial aid. **Contact:** Ms. Candace A. Cain, Director of Admission, North Benton Avenue, Helena, MT 59625-0002, 406-447-4384 or toll-free 800-99-ADMIT.

GETTING IN LAST YEAR
673 applied
94% were accepted
47% enrolled (296)
31% from top tenth of their h.s. class
3.37 average high school GPA
25% had SAT verbal scores over 600 (R)
26% had SAT math scores over 600 (R)
29% had ACT scores over 26
3% had SAT verbal scores over 700 (R)
1% had SAT math scores over 700 (R)
6% had ACT scores over 30
21 valedictorians

THE STUDENT BODY
1,412 undergraduates

From 27 states and territories,
    14 other countries
69% from Montana
64% women, 36% men
1% African Americans
2% Native Americans
1% Hispanics
1% Asian Americans
6% international students

AFTER FRESHMAN YEAR
69% returned for sophomore year
28% got a degree within 4 years
37% got a degree within 5 years
40% got a degree within 6 years

AFTER GRADUATION
36% pursued further study (11% arts and
    sciences, 7% engineering, 6% medicine)
24 organizations recruited on campus

WHAT YOU WILL PAY
Tuition and fees $9789
Room and board $3915
59% receive need-based financial aid
Need-based college-administered scholarships and
    grants average $1383 per award
84% receive non-need financial aid
Non-need college-administered scholarships and
    grants average $3697 per award

CASE WESTERN RESERVE UNIVERSITY

Cleveland, Ohio • Urban setting • Private • Independent • Coed

Case Western Reserve admits students based on overall academic and personal qualities, not on an intended major. With superb programs in arts and sciences, engineering, and management, students can determine what major is suitable for them after they have learned about it. Only CWRU's Bachelor of Science in Nursing program requires a declared major at the time of application.

Academics

CWRU offers a quantitative, analytic, and communication skills curriculum and core academic program. It awards bachelor's, master's, doctoral, and first professional **degrees**. Challenging opportunities include advanced placement, accelerated degree programs, self-designed majors, tutorials, an honors program, a senior project, Phi Beta Kappa, and Sigma Xi. Special programs include cooperative education, internships, summer session for credit, off-campus study, and Army and Air Force ROTC.

The most popular **majors** include biology/biological sciences, mechanical engineering, and psychology. A complete listing of majors at CWRU appears in the Majors Index beginning on page 379.

The **faculty** at CWRU has 1,879 full-time graduate and undergraduate teachers, 95% with terminal degrees. 85% of the faculty serve as student advisers. The student-faculty ratio is 8:1, and the average class size in core courses is 40.

Computers on Campus

Students are not required to have a computer. Student rooms are linked to a campus network. 200 **computers** available in the computer center, computer labs, the research center, academic departments, classrooms, and the library provide access to the main academic computer, off-campus computing facilities, e-mail, on-line services, the Internet, and software library. Staffed computer lab on campus provides training in the use of computers and software.

The 7 **libraries** have 1.9 million books and 14,108 subscriptions.

Campus Life

There are 100 active **organizations** on campus, including a drama/theater group and student-run newspaper and radio station. 5% of students participate in student government elections. 33% of eligible men and 15% of eligible women are members of 17 national **fraternities**, 4 national **sororities**, and 1 local sorority. Student **safety services** include crime prevention programs, late night transport/escort service, 24-hour emergency telephone alarm devices, 24-hour patrols by trained security personnel, student patrols, and electronically operated dormitory entrances.

CWRU is a member of the NCAA (Division III). **Intercollegiate sports** include archery (m, w), badminton (m, w), baseball (m), basketball (m, w), crew (m, w), cross-country running (m, w), fencing (m, w), football (m), golf (m), ice hockey (m, w), lacrosse (m, w), racquetball (m, w), soccer (m, w), softball (m, w), squash (m, w), swimming and diving (m, w), tennis (m, w), track and field (m, w), volleyball (m, w), wrestling (m).

Applying

CWRU requires an essay, a high school transcript, 3 years of high school math, 1 recommendation, SAT I or ACT, and in some cases 3 SAT II Subject Tests. It recommends 3 years of high school science, 2 years of high school foreign language, an interview, and 3 SAT II Subject Tests. Early, deferred, and midyear entrance are possible, with a 2/1 deadline and continuous processing to 2/1 for financial aid. **Contact:** Mr. William T. Conley, Dean of Undergraduate Admissions, Tomlinson Hall, 10900 Euclid Avenue, Cleveland, OH 44106, 216-368-4450; fax 216-368-5111.

GETTING IN LAST YEAR

4,291 applied
77% were accepted
22% enrolled (732)
76% from top tenth of their h.s. class
77% had SAT verbal scores over 600 (R)
87% had SAT math scores over 600 (R)
82% had ACT scores over 26
33% had SAT verbal scores over 700 (R)
44% had SAT math scores over 700 (R)
48% had ACT scores over 30
84 National Merit Scholars
90 valedictorians

THE STUDENT BODY

Total 9,747, of whom 3,645 are undergraduates

From 49 states and territories, 40 other countries
61% from Ohio
43% women, 57% men
7% African Americans
1% Native Americans
2% Hispanics
12% Asian Americans
6% international students

AFTER FRESHMAN YEAR

91% returned for sophomore year
43% got a degree within 4 years
67% got a degree within 5 years
70% got a degree within 6 years

AFTER GRADUATION

39% pursued further study (11% arts and sciences, 11% engineering, 8% medicine)
43% had job offers within 6 months
155 organizations recruited on campus
1 Fulbright scholar

WHAT YOU WILL PAY

Tuition and fees $17,235
Room and board $4860
56% receive need-based financial aid
Need-based college-administered scholarships and grants average $6679 per award
74% receive non-need financial aid
Non-need college-administered scholarships and grants average $9058 per award

THE CATHOLIC UNIVERSITY OF AMERICA

Washington, District of Columbia • Urban setting • Private • Independent-Religious • Coed

▶The Catholic University of America, situated on 154 residential tree-lined acres in Washington, D.C., offers the beauty of a traditional collegiate campus and the excitement of the nation's capital. The national university of the Catholic Church, CUA has built its foundation from a time-honored liberal arts tradition. CUA has become a valuable resource for employers looking to fill top internships. Undergraduates work in congressional offices, executive agencies, professional organizations, research institutes, lobbying groups, and media organizations. Overseas programs include internships with the British and Irish parliaments.

Academics

CUA offers a liberal studies curriculum and core academic program; fewer than half of graduate courses are open to undergraduates. It awards bachelor's, master's, doctoral, and first professional **degrees**. Challenging opportunities include advanced placement, accelerated degree programs, self-designed majors, tutorials, Freshman Honors College, an honors program, a senior project, Phi Beta Kappa, and Sigma Xi. Special programs include internships, summer session for credit, off-campus study, study abroad, and Army, Naval, and Air Force ROTC.

The most popular **majors** include nursing, political science/government, and architecture. A complete listing of majors at CUA appears in the Majors Index beginning on page 379.

The **faculty** at CUA has 371 full-time graduate and undergraduate teachers, 95% with terminal degrees. The student-faculty ratio is 9:1.

Computers on Campus

Students are not required to have a computer. 200 **computers** available in the computer center, computer labs, the learning resource center, classrooms, the library, and dormitories provide access to the main academic computer, off-campus computing facilities, e-mail, on-line services, and the Internet. Staffed computer lab on campus provides training in the use of computers and software.

The 8 **libraries** have 1.4 million books, 1.1 million microform titles, and 9,310 subscriptions. They are connected to 4 national **on-line** catalogs.

Campus Life

There are 120 active **organizations** on campus, including a drama/theater group and student-run newspaper and radio station. 33% of students participate in student government elections. 1% of eligible men and 1% of eligible women are members of 1 national **fraternity**, 1 national **sorority**, and 1 local sorority. Student **safety services** include late night transport/escort service, 24-hour emergency telephone alarm devices, 24-hour patrols by trained security personnel, and electronically operated dormitory entrances.

CUA is a member of the NCAA (Division III). **Intercollegiate sports** include baseball (m), basketball (m, w), cross-country running (m, w), field hockey (w), football (m), soccer (m, w), softball (w), swimming and diving (m, w), tennis (m, w), track and field (m, w), volleyball (w).

Applying

CUA requires an essay, a high school transcript, 3 years of high school math, 2 years of high school foreign language, 1 recommendation, SAT I or ACT, 3 SAT II Subject Tests, and in some cases an interview. It recommends 3 years of high school science. Early, deferred, and midyear entrance are possible, with a 2/15 deadline and 1/15 for financial aid. **Contact:** Mr. David R. Gibson, Dean of Admissions and Financial Aid, Cardinal Station, Washington, DC 20064, 202-319-5305 or toll-free 800-673-2772 (out-of-state); fax 202-319-6533.

GETTING IN LAST YEAR
2,527 applied
61% were accepted
37% enrolled (570)
24% from top tenth of their h.s. class
3.1 average high school GPA
48% had SAT verbal scores over 600 (R)
45% had SAT math scores over 600 (R)
40% had ACT scores over 26
12% had SAT verbal scores over 700 (R)
4% had SAT math scores over 700 (R)
13% had ACT scores over 30

THE STUDENT BODY
Total 6,108, of whom 2,417
  are undergraduates
From 45 states and territories,
  76 other countries
3% from District of Columbia
55% women, 45% men
7% African Americans
0% Native Americans
5% Hispanics
4% Asian Americans
10% international students

AFTER FRESHMAN YEAR
85% returned for sophomore year

AFTER GRADUATION
30% pursued further study
4 Fulbright scholars

WHAT YOU WILL PAY
Tuition and fees $15,062
Room and board $6614
58% receive need-based financial aid
Need-based college-administered scholarships and
  grants average $3952 per award
48% receive non-need financial aid
Non-need college-administered scholarships and
  grants average $4821 per award

CEDARVILLE COLLEGE

Cedarville, Ohio • Rural setting • Private • Independent-Religious • Coed

Commitment to Christ and achievement characterize the education Cedarville offers. All students and faculty members testify to personal faith in Christ. A Bible minor complements every major, and relevant daily chapels encourage spiritual growth. Over 150 local and worldwide ministries provide avenues for outreach. Cedarville teams consistently finish among top universities in national academic competitions, and national, regional, and local graduate schools recruit students pursuing any of the College's 80 academic programs. The College has been recognized nationally for its pervasive and innovative campuswide computer network. Reasonable costs and financial aid make Cedarville affordable to committed Christian students aspiring to be competent professionals.

 ## Academics

Cedarville offers a biblically-integrated comprehensive liberal arts curriculum and core academic program. It awards associate and bachelor's **degrees**. Challenging opportunities include advanced placement, accelerated degree programs, an honors program, and a senior project. Special programs include internships, summer session for credit, and Army and Air Force ROTC.

The most popular **majors** include elementary education, nursing, and biology/biological sciences. A complete listing of majors at Cedarville appears in the Majors Index beginning on page 379.

The **faculty** at Cedarville has 137 full-time teachers, 64% with terminal degrees. 100% of the faculty serve as student advisers. The student-faculty ratio is 17:1.

 ## Computers on Campus

Students are not required to have a computer. Student rooms are linked to a campus network. 1,250 **computers**

available in the computer center, computer labs, academic buildings, the library, dormitories, and student rooms provide access to e-mail, the Internet, and various software packages. Staffed computer lab on campus provides training in the use of computers and software.

The **library** has 124,415 books, 1,918 microform titles, and 1,800 subscriptions. It is connected to 1,001 national **on-line** catalogs.

 ## Campus Life

There are 55 active **organizations** on campus, including a drama/theater group and student-run newspaper and radio station. Student **safety services** include late night transport/escort service, 24-hour emergency telephone alarm devices, 24-hour patrols by trained security personnel, and student patrols.

Cedarville is a member of the NAIA and NCCAA. **Intercollegiate sports** (some offering scholarships) include baseball (m), basketball (m, w), cross-country running (m, w), golf (m), soccer (m), softball (w), tennis (m, w), track and field (m, w), volleyball (w).

 ## Applying

Cedarville requires an essay, a high school transcript, 2 recommendations, SAT I or ACT, a minimum high school GPA of 3.0, and in some cases an interview. It recommends 3 years of high school math and science and 2 years of high school foreign language. Early, deferred, and midyear entrance are possible, with rolling admissions and continuous processing to 3/1 for financial aid. **Contact:** Mr. Stuart Zaharek, Associate Director of Admissions, PO Box 601, Cedarville, OH 45314-0601, 513-766-7700 or toll-free 800-CEDARVILLE.

GETTING IN LAST YEAR
1,566 applied
75% were accepted
53% enrolled (626)
32% from top tenth of their h.s. class
3.53 average high school GPA
45% had SAT verbal scores over 600 (R)
40% had SAT math scores over 600 (R)
39% had ACT scores over 26
6% had SAT verbal scores over 700 (R)
6% had SAT math scores over 700 (R)
8% had ACT scores over 30
5 National Merit Scholars
60 valedictorians

THE STUDENT BODY
2,454 undergraduates
From 48 states and territories,
   12 other countries
35% from Ohio
55% women, 45% men
1% African Americans
1% Native Americans
1% Hispanics
1% Asian Americans
1% international students

AFTER FRESHMAN YEAR
82% returned for sophomore year

43% got a degree within 4 years
54% got a degree within 5 years

AFTER GRADUATION
11% pursued further study
110 organizations recruited on campus

WHAT YOU WILL PAY
Tuition and fees $8004
Room and board $4572
52% receive need-based financial aid
Need-based college-administered scholarships and
   grants average $1013 per award
22% receive non-need financial aid
Non-need college-administered scholarships and
   grants average $1027 per award

CENTENARY COLLEGE OF LOUISIANA

Shreveport, Louisiana • Suburban setting • Private • Independent-Religious • Coed

Centenary College of Louisiana, a 65-acre campus of Georgian architecture, gardens, and shaded groves, is more than a beautiful campus. It is a community of students and faculty members who are serious about learning. The Centenary College education supports students in their quest for success in advanced study, their personal lives, and their careers. The curriculum is designed to provide broad-based and integrated general knowledge, depth in the chosen major, oral and written communication skills, and computer proficiency. The Centenary experience also includes commitment to service-based learning, career exploration through an internship, and living and learning in another culture.

 ## Academics

Centenary offers a liberal arts core curriculum. It awards bachelor's and master's **degrees**. Challenging opportunities include advanced placement, accelerated degree programs, self-designed majors, tutorials, an honors program, and a senior project. Special programs include internships, summer session for credit, off-campus study, study abroad, and Army ROTC.

The most popular **majors** include business, biology/biological sciences, and education. A complete listing of majors at Centenary appears in the Majors Index beginning on page 379.

The **faculty** at Centenary has 67 full-time graduate and undergraduate teachers, 96% with terminal degrees. 95% of the faculty serve as student advisers. The student-faculty ratio is 10:1.

 ## Computers on Campus

Students are not required to have a computer. 100 **computers** available in the computer center, computer labs, biol-ogy labs, chemistry labs, business center, the library, and dormitories provide access to e-mail, on-line services, and campus network. Staffed computer lab on campus provides training in the use of computers and software.

The 2 **libraries** have 180,000 books, 269,000 microform titles, and 1,190 subscriptions.

 ## Campus Life

There are 14 active **organizations** on campus, including a drama/theater group and student-run newspaper and radio station. 39% of students participate in student government elections. 25% of eligible men and 20% of eligible women are members of 4 national **fraternities** and 2 national **sororities**. Student **safety services** include late night transport/escort service, 24-hour emergency telephone alarm devices, 24-hour patrols by trained security personnel, and electronically operated dormitory entrances.

Centenary is a member of the NCAA (Division I). **Intercollegiate sports** (some offering scholarships) include baseball (m), basketball (m), cross-country running (m, w), golf (m), gymnastics (w), riflery (m, w), soccer (m), softball (w), tennis (m, w), volleyball (w).

 ## Applying

Centenary requires an essay, a high school transcript, recommendations, an interview, minimum 2.3 high school GPA, and SAT I or ACT. It recommends 3 years of high school math and science, some high school foreign language, and 3 SAT II Subject Tests. Early, deferred, and midyear entrance are possible, with rolling admissions and continuous processing to 3/15 for financial aid. **Contact:** Dr. Dorothy Bird Gwin, Dean of Enrollment Management, 2911 Centenary Boulevard, Shreveport, LA 71134-1188, 318-869-5131.

GETTING IN LAST YEAR

563 applied
83% were accepted
46% enrolled (215)
37% from top tenth of their h.s. class
3.4 average high school GPA
14% had SAT verbal scores over 600
33% had SAT math scores over 600
47% had ACT scores over 26
1% had SAT verbal scores over 700
8% had SAT math scores over 700
12% had ACT scores over 30

THE STUDENT BODY

Total 989, of whom 780 are undergraduates

From 23 states and territories, 9 other countries
57% from Louisiana
57% women, 43% men
6% African Americans
1% Native Americans
1% Hispanics
2% Asian Americans
2% international students

AFTER FRESHMAN YEAR

67% returned for sophomore year
39% got a degree within 4 years
51% got a degree within 5 years
53% got a degree within 6 years

AFTER GRADUATION

48% pursued further study (31% arts and sciences, 6% business, 3% law)
51% had job offers within 6 months
40 organizations recruited on campus

WHAT YOU WILL PAY

Tuition and fees $10,122
Room and board $3690
54% receive need-based financial aid
Need-based college-administered scholarships and grants average $1213 per award
37% receive non-need financial aid
Non-need college-administered scholarships and grants average $2623 per award

CENTRAL COLLEGE

Pella, Iowa • Small-town setting • Private • Independent-Religious • Coed

Whether studying ancient art in China, researching Mayan villages in Mexico, or delivering meals to homeless people in Chicago, Central College students get their education in the ultimate outdoor classroom. With 8 foreign-study programs and several off-campus learning projects to choose from, this 143-year-old liberal arts college produces students with a "WorldWise" perspective.

 ## Academics

Central offers a liberal studies curriculum emphasizing cross-cultural experience and communication skills and core academic program. It awards bachelor's **degrees**. Challenging opportunities include advanced placement, self-designed majors, tutorials, Freshman Honors College, an honors program, and a senior project. Special programs include internships, summer session for credit, off-campus study, and study abroad.

The most popular **majors** include business, elementary education, and liberal arts/general studies. A complete listing of majors at Central appears in the Majors Index beginning on page 379.

The **faculty** at Central has 84 full-time teachers, 85% with terminal degrees. 98% of the faculty serve as student advisers. The student-faculty ratio is 13:1, and the average class size in core courses is 20.

 ## Computers on Campus

Students are not required to have a computer. 115 **computers** available in the computer center, computer labs, academic buildings, the library, and dormitories provide access to the main academic computer, e-mail, and the Internet. Staffed computer lab on campus provides training in the use of computers and software.

The 3 **libraries** have 183,345 books, 53,499 microform titles, and 952 subscriptions. They are connected to 2 national **on-line** catalogs.

 ## Campus Life

There are 71 active **organizations** on campus, including a drama/theater group and student-run newspaper and radio station. 35% of students participate in student government elections. 12% of eligible men and 5% of eligible women are members of 4 local **fraternities** and 2 local **sororities**. Student **safety services** include late night transport/escort service, 24-hour emergency telephone alarm devices, student patrols, and electronically operated dormitory entrances.

Central is a member of the NCAA (Division III). **Intercollegiate sports** include baseball (m), basketball (m, w), cross-country running (m, w), football (m), golf (m, w), soccer (m, w), softball (w), tennis (m, w), track and field (m, w), volleyball (w), wrestling (m).

 ## Applying

Central requires a high school transcript, SAT I or ACT, and in some cases an essay, 3 recommendations, and an interview. It recommends 3 years of high school math and science, 2 years of high school foreign language, and an interview. Early, deferred, and midyear entrance are possible, with rolling admissions and continuous processing to 1/1 for financial aid. **Contact:** Mr. Eric Sickler, Vice President of Admission and Marketing, 812 University Street, Pella, IA 50219-1999, 515-628-5285 or toll-free 800-458-5503; fax 515-628-5316.

GETTING IN LAST YEAR
1,303 applied
87% were accepted
36% enrolled (407)
31% from top tenth of their h.s. class
3.43 average high school GPA
35% had ACT scores over 26
7% had ACT scores over 30

THE STUDENT BODY
1,453 undergraduates
From 42 states and territories,
   22 other countries
75% from Iowa

58% women, 42% men
1% African Americans
0% Native Americans
2% Hispanics
2% Asian Americans
3% international students

AFTER FRESHMAN YEAR
76% returned for sophomore year
61% got a degree within 4 years
68% got a degree within 5 years
70% got a degree within 6 years

AFTER GRADUATION
18% pursued further study (10% arts and
   sciences, 4% medicine, 2% law)

58% had job offers within 6 months
64 organizations recruited on campus

WHAT YOU WILL PAY
Tuition and fees $11,836
Room and board $3660
85% receive need-based financial aid
Need-based college-administered scholarships and
   grants average $5033 per award
15% receive non-need financial aid
Non-need college-administered scholarships and
   grants average $4499 per award

CENTRE COLLEGE

Danville, Kentucky • Small-town setting • Private • Independent • Coed

At Centre College, students are within a short drive of Lexington, Louisville, and Cincinnati, but some hardly ever feel the need to leave Danville. The College's Norton Center for the Arts takes students to another world—a world of dance with Mikhail Baryshnikov or music with the St. Louis Orchestra. Students enjoy rock 'n' roll in the new Combs Student Center, which opened with a concert by Hootie and the Blowfish. They can also interact with fascinating campus guests such as Martin Luther King III, Isaac Tigrett (a Centre alum who founded the Hard Rock Cafe and the House of Blues), actress Lynn Redgrave, singer Harry Connick Jr., or trumpet great Wynton Marsalis.

 ## Academics

Centre offers an interdisciplinary curriculum and core academic program. It awards bachelor's **degrees**. Challenging opportunities include advanced placement, self-designed majors, tutorials, a senior project, and Phi Beta Kappa. Special programs include internships, summer session for credit, off-campus study, study abroad, and Army and Air Force ROTC.

The most popular **majors** include economics, English, and history. A complete listing of majors at Centre appears in the Majors Index beginning on page 379.

The **faculty** at Centre has 83 full-time teachers, 95% with terminal degrees. 100% of the faculty serve as student advisers. The student-faculty ratio is 11:1.

 ## Computers on Campus

Students are not required to have a computer. Student rooms are linked to a campus network. 130 **computers** available in the computer center, computer labs, classroom buildings, the library, the student center, and dormitories provide access to e-mail and the Internet. Staffed computer lab on campus (open 24 hours a day) provides training in the use of computers and software.

The 2 **libraries** have 262,150 books, 53,000 microform titles, and 900 subscriptions.

 ## Campus Life

There are 66 active **organizations** on campus, including a drama/theater group and student-run newspaper. 65% of eligible men and 55% of eligible women are members of 6 national **fraternities** and 3 national **sororities**. Student **safety services** include late night transport/escort service, 24-hour emergency telephone alarm devices, 24-hour patrols by trained security personnel, and electronically operated dormitory entrances.

Centre is a member of the NCAA (Division III). **Intercollegiate sports** include baseball (m), basketball (m, w), cross-country running (m, w), field hockey (w), football (m), golf (m, w), soccer (m, w), swimming and diving (m, w), tennis (m, w), track and field (m, w), volleyball (w).

 ## Applying

Centre requires an essay, a high school transcript, 3 years of high school math, 1 recommendation, 2 years of high school social science, SAT I or ACT, and a minimum high school GPA of 2.0. It recommends 4 years of high school math and science, 2 years of high school foreign language, a campus interview, SAT II Subject Tests, and a minimum high school GPA of 3.0. Early, deferred, and midyear entrance are possible, with a 3/1 deadline and continuous processing to 3/1 for financial aid. **Contact:** Mr. Thomas B. Martin, Dean of Enrollment Management, 600 West Walnut Street, Danville, KY 40422-1394, 606-238-5350 or toll-free 800-423-6236.

GETTING IN LAST YEAR

1,156 applied
85% were accepted
31% enrolled (301)
60% from top tenth of their h.s. class
3.7 average high school GPA
30% had SAT verbal scores over 600
55% had SAT math scores over 600
75% had ACT scores over 26
4% had SAT verbal scores over 700
15% had SAT math scores over 700
26% had ACT scores over 30
9 National Merit Scholars
35 valedictorians

THE STUDENT BODY

970 undergraduates

From 41 states and territories,
  4 other countries
65% from Kentucky
50% women, 50% men
3% African Americans
0% Native Americans
1% Hispanics
1% Asian Americans
1% international students

AFTER FRESHMAN YEAR

85% returned for sophomore year
72% got a degree within 4 years
76% got a degree within 5 years

AFTER GRADUATION

40% pursued further study (21% arts and
  sciences, 10% law, 4% medicine)
60% had job offers within 6 months
20 organizations recruited on campus
1 Fulbright scholar

WHAT YOU WILL PAY

Tuition and fees $13,100
Room and board $4350
57% receive need-based financial aid
Need-based college-administered scholarships and
  grants average $3195 per award
28% receive non-need financial aid
Non-need college-administered scholarships and
  grants average $2673 per award

CHRISTENDOM COLLEGE

Front Royal, Virginia • Small-town setting • Private • Independent-Religious • Coed

A message from the school: For more than 2,000 years, Western civilization has held certain disciplines to be liberal arts. These disciplines liberate the human mind, rendering it free to think for itself and to seek and know truth. Christendom College respects this tradition. Christendom acknowledges that there is such a thing as truth and further claims to know how to lead others to discover truth. Since Christendom believes that Christ is the fullness of truth, He is the goal at Christendom College and the curriculum bears this out. Theology, as Queen of the Sciences, holds a central place among the other liberal arts studied.

Academics

Christendom offers a Western civilization curriculum and core academic program. It awards bachelor's **degrees**. Challenging opportunities include advanced placement, accelerated degree programs, and a senior project. Special programs include internships, summer session for credit, and study abroad.

The most popular **majors** include theology, history, and literature. A complete listing of majors at Christendom appears in the Majors Index beginning on page 379.

The **faculty** at Christendom has 14 full-time teachers, 71% with terminal degrees. 66% of the faculty serve as student advisers. The student-faculty ratio is 10:1.

Computers on Campus

Students are not required to have a computer. 9 **computers** available in the computer center provide access to the main academic computer. Staffed computer lab on campus provides training in the use of computers and software.

The **library** has 43,665 books, 769 microform titles, and 326 subscriptions. It is connected to 1 national **on-line** catalog.

Campus Life

There are 15 active **organizations** on campus, including a drama/theater group. Student **safety services** include late night transport/escort service and 24-hour emergency telephone alarm devices. **Intercollegiate sports** include basketball (m, w), soccer (m, w).

Applying

Christendom requires an essay, a high school transcript, 2 recommendations, and SAT I or ACT. It recommends 3 years of high school math and science, some high school foreign language, an interview, and a minimum high school GPA of 3.0. Early and midyear entrance are possible, with an 8/15 deadline and continuous processing to 4/1 for financial aid. **Contact:** Mr. Paul Heisler, Director of Admissions, 134 Christendom Drive, Front Royal, VA 22630-5103, 540-636-2900 ext. 290 or toll-free 800-877-5456; fax 540-636-1655.

GETTING IN LAST YEAR
90 applied
90% were accepted
64% enrolled (52)
3.38 average high school GPA
53% had SAT verbal scores over 600 (R)
28% had SAT math scores over 600 (R)
31% had ACT scores over 26
17% had SAT verbal scores over 700 (R)
0% had SAT math scores over 700 (R)
0% had ACT scores over 30

THE STUDENT BODY
178 undergraduates

From 40 states and territories,
  1 other country
30% from Virginia
58% women, 42% men
1% African Americans
0% Native Americans
2% Hispanics
2% Asian Americans
4% international students

AFTER FRESHMAN YEAR
86% returned for sophomore year
65% got a degree within 5 years
67% got a degree within 6 years

WHAT YOU WILL PAY
Tuition and fees $10,044
Room and board $4000
52% receive need-based financial aid
Need-based college-administered scholarships and
  grants average $1920 per award
24% receive non-need financial aid
Non-need college-administered scholarships and
  grants average $3200 per award

CHRISTIAN BROTHERS UNIVERSITY

Memphis, Tennessee • Urban setting • Private • Independent-Religious • Coed

Christian Brothers University is located in the center of the friendly Southern city of Memphis, Tennessee. Its beautiful 70-acre campus encourages a true sense of excellence and achievement that comes with the history and the tradition of the Christian Brothers. CBU offers a low student-faculty ratio and is known for the high academic caliber of its students and the caring commitment of its faculty. At Christian Brothers University, students "dream no little dreams." Outstanding acceptance rates for medical and law school students, along with a graduate placement rate of 96%, ensure that CBU's graduates are prepared for the future.

Academics

CBU offers a liberal arts curriculum and core academic program; a few graduate courses are open to undergraduates. It awards bachelor's and master's **degrees**. Challenging opportunities include advanced placement, accelerated degree programs, tutorials, an honors program, and a senior project. Special programs include cooperative education, internships, summer session for credit, off-campus study, and Army, Naval, and Air Force ROTC.

The most popular **majors** include accounting, electrical engineering, and business. A complete listing of majors at CBU appears in the Majors Index beginning on page 379.

The **faculty** at CBU has 98 full-time undergraduate teachers, 72% with terminal degrees. 90% of the faculty serve as student advisers. The student-faculty ratio is 16:1, and the average class size in core courses is 25.

Computers on Campus

Students are not required to have a computer. 250 **computers** available in the computer center, computer labs, classrooms, and the library provide access to the main academic computer, e-mail, and on-line services. Staffed computer lab on campus provides training in the use of computers and software.

The **library** has 100,000 books, 170 microform titles, and 571 subscriptions. It is connected to 3 national **on-line** catalogs.

Campus Life

There are 35 active **organizations** on campus, including a drama/theater group and student-run newspaper. 11% of students participate in student government elections. 24% of eligible men and 20% of eligible women are members of 3 national **fraternities**, 3 national **sororities**, and 1 local sorority. Student **safety services** include late night transport/escort service, 24-hour emergency telephone alarm devices, 24-hour patrols by trained security personnel, and student patrols.

CBU is a member of the NAIA. **Intercollegiate sports** (some offering scholarships) include baseball (m), basketball (m, w), cross-country running (m, w), golf (m), soccer (m, w), softball (w), tennis (m, w), volleyball (w).

Applying

CBU requires an essay, a high school transcript, SAT I or ACT, a minimum high school GPA of 2.0, and in some cases 2 recommendations. It recommends 3 years of high school math and science, some high school foreign language, an interview, and a minimum high school GPA of 3.0. Early and midyear entrance are possible, with a 7/1 deadline and continuous processing to 4/1 for financial aid. **Contact:** Mr. Michael Dausch, Dean of Admissions, 650 East Parkway South, Memphis, TN 38104-5581, 901-722-0205 ext. 210 or toll-free 800-288-7576; fax 901-722-0202.

GETTING IN LAST YEAR
826 applied
84% were accepted
47% enrolled (329)
3.0 average high school GPA
38% had ACT scores over 26
4% had ACT scores over 30

THE STUDENT BODY
Total 1,800, of whom 1,551
  are undergraduates
From 30 states and territories,
  24 other countries

71% from Tennessee
49% women, 51% men
17% African Americans
3% Asian Americans
1% international students

AFTER FRESHMAN YEAR
76% returned for sophomore year
37% got a degree within 4 years
52% got a degree within 5 years
53% got a degree within 6 years

AFTER GRADUATION
29% pursued further study

84% had job offers within 6 months
32 organizations recruited on campus

WHAT YOU WILL PAY
Tuition and fees $10,120
Room and board $3340
55% receive need-based financial aid
Need-based college-administered scholarships and
  grants average $1794 per award
35% receive non-need financial aid
Non-need college-administered scholarships and
  grants average $5300 per award

CLAREMONT MCKENNA COLLEGE

Claremont, California • Small-town setting • Private • Independent • Coed

As part of the Claremont Colleges (including Harvey Mudd, Pitzer, Pomona, and Scripps), CMC offers the "best of both worlds." All 5,000 students share facilities, cross-campus registration, and cooperative extracurricular opportunities, enabling CMC to provide the advantages of a medium-sized university with the benefits of a smaller college. With a commitment to preparing students for responsible leadership, CMC recognizes that environmental concerns are among the most important issues facing leaders today.

Academics

CMC offers a public affairs and liberal arts curriculum and core academic program. It awards bachelor's **degrees**. Challenging opportunities include advanced placement, accelerated degree programs, self-designed majors, tutorials, an honors program, a senior project, Phi Beta Kappa, and Sigma Xi. Special programs include internships, off-campus study, study abroad, and Army and Naval ROTC.

The most popular **majors** include economics, political science/government, and psychology. A complete listing of majors at CMC appears in the Majors Index beginning on page 379.

The **faculty** at CMC has 107 full-time teachers, 99% with terminal degrees. 100% of the faculty serve as student advisers. The student-faculty ratio is 9:1.

Computers on Campus

Students are not required to have a computer. Student rooms are linked to a campus network. 40 **computers** available in the computer center, computer labs, the learning resource center, research institutes, classrooms, and the library provide access to the main academic computer, off-campus computing facilities, e-mail, on-line services, and the Internet. Staffed computer lab on campus.

The 4 **libraries** have 1.9 million books, 1.2 million microform titles, and 6,800 subscriptions. They are connected to 20 national **on-line** catalogs.

Campus Life

There are 280 active **organizations** on campus, including a drama/theater group and student-run newspaper and radio station. 69% of students participate in student government elections. Student **safety services** include late night transport/escort service, 24-hour emergency telephone alarm devices, 24-hour patrols by trained security personnel, student patrols, and electronically operated dormitory entrances.

CMC is a member of the NCAA (Division III). **Intercollegiate sports** include badminton (m, w), baseball (m), basketball (m, w), cross-country running (m, w), football (m), golf (m, w), lacrosse (m, w), rugby (m, w), skiing (downhill) (m, w), soccer (m, w), softball (w), swimming and diving (m, w), tennis (m, w), track and field (m, w), volleyball (m, w), water polo (m, w).

Applying

CMC requires an essay, a high school transcript, 3 years of high school math, 2 years of high school foreign language, 2 recommendations, and SAT I or ACT. It recommends 3 years of high school science, a campus interview, and 3 SAT II Subject Tests. Early, deferred, and midyear entrance are possible, with a 1/15 deadline and a 2/1 priority date for financial aid. **Contact:** Mr. Richard C. Vos, Vice President/Dean of Admission and Financial Aid, 890 Columbia Avenue, Claremont, CA 91711-3901, 909-621-8088.

GETTING IN LAST YEAR
2,175 applied
41% were accepted
33% enrolled (288)
73% from top tenth of their h.s. class
3.83 average high school GPA
63% had SAT verbal scores over 600
91% had SAT math scores over 600
78% had ACT scores over 26
8% had SAT verbal scores over 700
44% had SAT math scores over 700
35% had ACT scores over 30
24 National Merit Scholars
12 class presidents
30 valedictorians

THE STUDENT BODY
959 undergraduates
From 43 states and territories,
   46 other countries
62% from California
44% women, 57% men
5% African Americans
1% Native Americans
10% Hispanics
21% Asian Americans
4% international students

AFTER FRESHMAN YEAR
92% returned for sophomore year
83% got a degree within 4 years
85% got a degree within 5 years

AFTER GRADUATION
46% pursued further study (13% arts and
   sciences, 11% law, 8% engineering)
38% had job offers within 6 months
96 organizations recruited on campus

WHAT YOU WILL PAY
Tuition and fees $17,980
Room and board $6260
57% receive need-based financial aid
Need-based college-administered scholarships and
   grants average $9353 per award
7% receive non-need financial aid
Non-need college-administered scholarships and
   grants average $2792 per award

CLARKSON UNIVERSITY

Potsdam, New York • Small-town setting • Private • Independent • Coed

Clarkson is a blend of vivid contrasts—high-powered academics in a cooperative and friendly community, technically oriented students who enjoy people, and a location that serves as a gateway to outstanding outdoor recreational opportunities and numerous social and cultural activities at 3 other area colleges. Clarkson's students are described as hard-working, outgoing, energized team players; the academic programs as relevant, flexible, and nationally respected; and the teachers as approachable, concerned, accomplished, and inspiring. Clarkson alumni, students, and faculty share an exceptionally strong bond and the lifetime benefits that come from a global network of personal and professional ties.

 Academics

Clarkson offers a core academic program. It awards bachelor's, master's, and doctoral **degrees**. Challenging opportunities include advanced placement, accelerated degree programs, self-designed majors, an honors program, and Sigma Xi. Special programs include cooperative education, summer session for credit, off-campus study, study abroad, and Army and Air Force ROTC.

The most popular **majors** include civil engineering, mechanical engineering, and electrical engineering. A complete listing of majors at Clarkson appears in the Majors Index beginning on page 379.

The **faculty** at Clarkson has 156 full-time graduate and undergraduate teachers, 96% with terminal degrees. The student-faculty ratio is 15:1.

 Computers on Campus

Students are required to have a computer. PCs are provided. 199 **computers** available in the computer center, computer labs, the learning resource center, classrooms, the library, the student center, and dormitories provide access to the main academic computer, off-campus computing facilities, e-mail, and on-line services.

The **library** has 224,306 books, 269,289 microform titles, and 2,716 subscriptions.

 Campus Life

Active **organizations** on campus include drama/theater group and student-run newspaper and radio station. 25% of eligible men and 30% of eligible women are members of 11 national **fraternities**, 3 national **sororities**, and 5 local fraternities. Student **safety services** include late night transport/escort service, 24-hour emergency telephone alarm devices, 24-hour patrols by trained security personnel, and electronically operated dormitory entrances.

Clarkson is a member of the NCAA (Division III). **Intercollegiate sports** (some offering scholarships) include baseball (m), basketball (m, w), cross-country running (m, w), golf (m, w), ice hockey (m), lacrosse (m, w), skiing (cross-country) (m), skiing (downhill) (m, w), soccer (m, w), swimming and diving (m, w), tennis (m, w), volleyball (w).

 Applying

Clarkson requires a high school transcript, 3 years of high school math, 1 recommendation, SAT I or ACT, and in some cases 3 years of high school science. It recommends a campus interview and SAT II Subject Tests. Early, deferred, and midyear entrance are possible, with a 3/15 deadline and a 2/15 priority date for financial aid. **Contact:** Mr. Robert Croot, Executive Director of Undergraduate Admission, Holcroft House, Potsdam, NY 13699, 315-268-6463 or toll-free 800-527-6577 (in-state), 800-527-6578 (out-of-state); fax 315-268-7647.

GETTING IN LAST YEAR

2,334 applied
31% from top tenth of their h.s. class
3.0 average high school GPA
30% had SAT verbal scores over 600
67% had SAT math scores over 600
7% had SAT verbal scores over 700
15% had SAT math scores over 700
3 National Merit Scholars
11 valedictorians

THE STUDENT BODY

Total 2,583, of whom 2,249
   are undergraduates
From 38 states and territories,
   25 other countries

69% from New York
24% women, 76% men
2% African Americans
1% Native Americans
2% Hispanics
2% Asian Americans
3% international students

AFTER FRESHMAN YEAR

83% returned for sophomore year
61% got a degree within 4 years
70% got a degree within 5 years
71% got a degree within 6 years

AFTER GRADUATION

14% pursued further study (8% arts and
   sciences, 2% law, 2% medicine)

96% had job offers within 6 months
122 organizations recruited on campus

WHAT YOU WILL PAY

Tuition and fees $17,113
Room and board $5830
83% receive need-based financial aid
Need-based college-administered scholarships and
   grants average $6771 per award
Non-need college-administered scholarships and
   grants average $4100 per award

CLARK UNIVERSITY

Worcester, Massachusetts • Urban setting • Private • Independent • Coed

Clark offers 3 exciting programs for the motivated student who seeks challenge and change: The International Studies Stream, in which students can satisfy their University requirements with classes that focus on international themes and issues; Clark's Environmental School—more than an environmental major—that combines advanced-level course work with field trips, colloquia, and research seminars exploring the interactions between humans and the environment; and the 5-year bachelor's/master's degree program, in which the fifth year is tuition-free for students maintaining a B+ grade average.

Academics

Clark offers a liberal arts and sciences curriculum and core academic program; more than half of graduate courses are open to undergraduates. It awards bachelor's, master's, doctoral, and first professional **degrees**. Challenging opportunities include advanced placement, accelerated degree programs, self-designed majors, tutorials, an honors program, a senior project, and Phi Beta Kappa. Special programs include internships, summer session for credit, off-campus study, study abroad, and Army and Air Force ROTC.

The most popular **majors** include psychology, political science/government, and business. A complete listing of majors at Clark appears in the Majors Index beginning on page 379.

The **faculty** at Clark has 168 full-time graduate and undergraduate teachers, 99% with terminal degrees. 100% of the faculty serve as student advisers. The student-faculty ratio is 11:1.

Computers on Campus

Students are not required to have a computer. Student rooms are linked to a campus network. 100 **computers** available in the computer center, computer labs, academic buildings and departments, classrooms, and the library provide access to the main academic computer, off-campus computing facilities, e-mail, and on-line services. Staffed computer lab on campus provides training in the use of software.

The 5 **libraries** have 535,000 books, 14,400 microform titles, and 1,900 subscriptions.

Campus Life

There are 74 active **organizations** on campus, including a drama/theater group and student-run newspaper and radio station. Student **safety services** include late night transport/escort service, 24-hour emergency telephone alarm devices, 24-hour patrols by trained security personnel, student patrols, and electronically operated dormitory entrances.

Clark is a member of the NCAA (Division III). **Intercollegiate sports** include baseball (m), basketball (m, w), crew (m, w), cross-country running (m, w), field hockey (w), golf (m), lacrosse (m), soccer (m, w), softball (w), swimming and diving (m, w), tennis (m, w), volleyball (w).

Applying

Clark requires an essay, a high school transcript, SAT I or ACT, and SAT II: Writing Test. It recommends 3 years of high school math and science, 2 years of high school foreign language, 2 recommendations, an interview, 2 SAT II Subject Tests, and a minimum high school GPA of 3.0. Early, deferred, and midyear entrance are possible, with a 2/1 deadline and continuous processing to 2/1 for financial aid. **Contact:** Mr. Richard W. Pierson, Dean of Admissions, Admissions House, 950 Main Street, Worcester, MA 01610-1477, 508-793-7431.

GETTING IN LAST YEAR

2,439 applied
79% were accepted
28% enrolled (532)
29% from top tenth of their h.s. class
3.03 average high school GPA
13% had SAT verbal scores over 600
31% had SAT math scores over 600
1% had SAT verbal scores over 700
5% had SAT math scores over 700

THE STUDENT BODY

Total 2,652, of whom 1,884 are undergraduates

From 38 states and territories, 70 other countries
37% from Massachusetts
57% women, 43% men
3% African Americans
3% Hispanics
5% Asian Americans
17% international students

AFTER FRESHMAN YEAR

84% returned for sophomore year
64% got a degree within 4 years
73% got a degree within 5 years
74% got a degree within 6 years

AFTER GRADUATION

28% pursued further study (14% arts and sciences, 6% business, 4% law)
77% had job offers within 6 months
83 organizations recruited on campus
3 Fulbright scholars

WHAT YOU WILL PAY

Tuition and fees $19,140
Room and board $4250
63% receive need-based financial aid
Need-based college-administered scholarships and grants average $10,066 per award
Non-need college-administered scholarships and grants average $5105 per award

---

CLEMSON UNIVERSITY

Clemson, South Carolina • Small-town setting • Public • State-supported • Coed

Recently cited by *Money* magazine as one of the nation's best honors programs among state universities, Clemson's Calhoun College is designed for academically talented, highly motivated students who are naturally inquisitive and dedicated to the life of the mind. The honors experience includes a core of interdisciplinary seminars for freshmen and sophomores and independent research projects for juniors and seniors. Housing for 300 Calhoun scholars is available in Holmes Hall, located in the heart of Clemson's beautiful campus.

 Academics

Clemson offers a core academic program; more than half of graduate courses are open to undergraduates. It awards bachelor's, master's, and doctoral **degrees**. Challenging opportunities include advanced placement, accelerated degree programs, an honors program, a senior project, and Sigma Xi. Special programs include cooperative education, internships, summer session for credit, study abroad, and Army and Air Force ROTC.

The most popular **majors** include business, finance/banking, and marketing/retailing/merchandising. A complete listing of majors at Clemson appears in the Majors Index beginning on page 379.

The **faculty** at Clemson has 1,227 full-time graduate and undergraduate teachers, 75% with terminal degrees. The student-faculty ratio is 16:1.

 Computers on Campus

Students are not required to have a computer. 1,000 **computers** available in the computer center, academic buildings, and the library provide access to the main academic computer, on-line services, and the Internet. Staffed computer lab on campus (open 24 hours a day) provides training in the use of computers and software.

The 2 **libraries** have 1.4 million books and 7,180 subscriptions.

 Campus Life

There are 260 active **organizations** on campus, including a drama/theater group and student-run newspaper and radio station. 20% of students participate in student government elections. 15% of eligible men and 26% of eligible women are members of 20 national **fraternities** and 14 national **sororities**. Student **safety services** include late night transport/escort service, 24-hour emergency telephone alarm devices, and 24-hour patrols by trained security personnel.

Clemson is a member of the NCAA (Division I). **Intercollegiate sports** (some offering scholarships) include baseball (m), basketball (m, w), bowling (m, w), crew (m, w), cross-country running (m, w), equestrian sports (m, w), fencing (m, w), field hockey (w), football (m), golf (m, w), gymnastics (m, w), lacrosse (m, w), rugby (m, w), sailing (m, w), skiing (cross-country) (m, w), skiing (downhill) (m, w), soccer (m, w), swimming and diving (m, w), table tennis (m, w), tennis (m, w), track and field (m, w), volleyball (m, w), weight lifting (m, w), wrestling (m).

 Applying

Clemson requires a high school transcript, 3 years of high school math, 2 years of high school foreign language, SAT I or ACT, and in some cases SAT II Subject Tests. It recommends an essay, 3 years of high school science, recommendations, an interview, and SAT II Subject Tests. Early, deferred, and midyear entrance are possible, with a 6/1 deadline and continuous processing to 3/1 for financial aid. **Contact:** Dr. Michael Heintze, Director of Admissions, 105 Sikes Hall, PO Box 345124, Clemson, SC 29634, 864-656-2287; fax 864-656-0622.

GETTING IN LAST YEAR
7,792 applied
80% were accepted
41% enrolled (2,575)
31% from top tenth of their h.s. class
32% had SAT verbal scores over 600 (R)
35% had SAT math scores over 600 (R)
24% had ACT scores over 26
5% had SAT verbal scores over 700 (R)
5% had SAT math scores over 700 (R)
8% had ACT scores over 30
25 National Merit Scholars

THE STUDENT BODY
Total 15,434, of whom 12,438 are undergraduates

From 48 states and territories, 37 other countries
72% from South Carolina
45% women, 55% men
9% African Americans
1% Native Americans
1% Hispanics
1% Asian Americans
1% international students

AFTER FRESHMAN YEAR
85% returned for sophomore year
38% got a degree within 4 years
66% got a degree within 5 years
72% got a degree within 6 years

AFTER GRADUATION
29% pursued further study
79% had job offers within 6 months
330 organizations recruited on campus
1 Fulbright scholar

WHAT YOU WILL PAY
Resident tuition and fees $3112
Nonresident tuition and fees $8316
Room and board $3000
45% receive need-based financial aid
Need-based college-administered scholarships and grants average $3600 per award
19% receive non-need financial aid
Non-need college-administered scholarships and grants average $4200 per award

COE COLLEGE

Cedar Rapids, Iowa • Urban setting • Private • Independent-Religious • Coed

---

At Coe College, students can walk out of their door on any day of the week and into a $5-million fitness center. Or they can walk into a beautiful library that, at a touch of a key, gives them access to libraries throughout the world. Students also have access to an electron microscope that they actually get to use. At Coe, students can experiment, perform, create, research—and, in the process, plant the seeds of a brilliant career in science, history, business, or the arts.

Academics

Coe offers a liberal arts for life curriculum and core academic program; a few graduate courses are open to undergraduates. It awards bachelor's and master's **degrees**. Challenging opportunities include advanced placement, accelerated degree programs, self-designed majors, tutorials, Freshman Honors College, an honors program, a senior project, and Phi Beta Kappa. Special programs include internships, summer session for credit, off-campus study, study abroad, and Army ROTC.

The most popular **majors** include business, psychology, and biology/biological sciences. A complete listing of majors at Coe appears in the Majors Index beginning on page 379.

The **faculty** at Coe has 89 full-time graduate and undergraduate teachers, 87% with terminal degrees. 100% of the faculty serve as student advisers. The student-faculty ratio is 12:1.

Computers on Campus

Students are not required to have a computer. Student rooms are linked to a campus network. 126 **computers** available in the computer center, computer labs, and the library provide access to the main academic computer, off-campus computing facilities, e-mail, on-line services, and the Internet. Staffed computer lab on campus provides training in the use of computers and software.

The 2 **libraries** have 184,539 books, 35,690 microform titles, and 904 subscriptions. They are connected to 1 national **on-line** catalog.

Campus Life

There are 60 active **organizations** on campus, including a drama/theater group and student-run newspaper and radio station. 50% of students participate in student government elections. 25% of eligible men and 25% of eligible women are members of 4 national **fraternities** and 3 national **sororities**. Student **safety services** include late night transport/escort service, 24-hour emergency telephone alarm devices, and 24-hour patrols by trained security personnel.

Coe is a member of the NCAA (Division III). **Intercollegiate sports** include baseball (m), basketball (m, w), cross-country running (m, w), football (m), golf (m, w), soccer (m, w), softball (w), swimming and diving (m, w), tennis (m, w), track and field (m, w), volleyball (w), wrestling (m).

Applying

Coe requires an essay, a high school transcript, 1 recommendation, and SAT I or ACT. It recommends 3 years of high school math and science, 2 years of high school foreign language, an interview, minimum 2.5 GPA, and 2 SAT II Subject Tests. Early, deferred, and midyear entrance are possible, with a 3/1 deadline and continuous processing to 3/1 for financial aid. **Contact:** Mr. Michael White, Dean of Admissions and Financial Aid, 1220 1st Avenue, NE, Cedar Rapids, IA 52402-5070, 319-399-8500 or toll-free 800-332-8404; fax 319-399-8816.

GETTING IN LAST YEAR
947 applied
86% were accepted
36% enrolled (291)
27% from top tenth of their h.s. class
3.35 average high school GPA
48% had SAT verbal scores over 600 (R)
44% had SAT math scores over 600 (R)
37% had ACT scores over 26
10% had SAT verbal scores over 700 (R)
12% had SAT math scores over 700 (R)
10% had ACT scores over 30
2 National Merit Scholars
7 valedictorians

THE STUDENT BODY
Total 1,359, of whom 1,312
   are undergraduates

From 35 states and territories,
   20 other countries
56% from Iowa
56% women, 44% men
3% African Americans
1% Native Americans
2% Hispanics
2% Asian Americans
5% international students

AFTER FRESHMAN YEAR
80% returned for sophomore year
62% got a degree within 4 years
65% got a degree within 5 years
66% got a degree within 6 years

AFTER GRADUATION
24% pursued further study (13% arts and
   sciences, 5% business, 4% law)
90% had job offers within 6 months
85 organizations recruited on campus

WHAT YOU WILL PAY
Tuition and fees $14,875
Room and board $4455
75% receive need-based financial aid
Need-based college-administered scholarships and
   grants average $5820 per award
10% receive non-need financial aid
Non-need college-administered scholarships and
   grants average $2831 per award

COLBY COLLEGE

Waterville, Maine • Small-town setting • Private • Independent • Coed

Colby, located on a 714-acre campus in central Maine, is among the oldest and most respected colleges in the nation. Colby pioneered the January Program of intensive study, has been a leader in study-abroad programs (70% of all Colby students now study in another country at some point in their college careers), and was among the first colleges to integrate computers into its academic programs. Colby's 1,700 students enjoy an 11:1 student-faculty ratio, and close interaction between the two groups is the norm rather than the exception. Colby's academic program is enhanced by a variety of extracurricular offerings.

 ## Academics

Colby offers a liberal arts curriculum and core academic program. It awards bachelor's **degrees**. Challenging opportunities include advanced placement, self-designed majors, tutorials, an honors program, a senior project, and Phi Beta Kappa. Special programs include internships, off-campus study, study abroad, and Army ROTC.

The most popular **majors** include English, biology/biological sciences, and economics. A complete listing of majors at Colby appears in the Majors Index beginning on page 379.

The **faculty** at Colby has 143 full-time teachers, 97% with terminal degrees. 100% of the faculty serve as student advisers. The student-faculty ratio is 11:1.

 ## Computers on Campus

Students are not required to have a computer. Student rooms are linked to a campus network. 135 **computers** available in the computer center, computer labs, the research center, the learning resource center, science complex, classrooms, and the library provide access to the main academic computer, off-campus computing facilities, e-mail, on-line services, and the Internet. Staffed computer lab on campus (open 24 hours a day) provides training in the use of computers and software.

The 3 **libraries** have 504,825 books, 275,620 microform titles, and 2,825 subscriptions. They are connected to 6 national **on-line** catalogs.

 ## Campus Life

There are 90 active **organizations** on campus, including a drama/theater group and student-run newspaper and radio station. 60% of students participate in student government elections.

No national or local **fraternities** or **sororities**. Student **safety services** include late night transport/escort service, 24-hour emergency telephone alarm devices, and 24-hour patrols by trained security personnel.

Colby is a member of the NCAA (Division III). **Intercollegiate sports** include baseball (m), basketball (m, w), crew (m, w), cross-country running (m, w), field hockey (w), football (m), golf (m, w), ice hockey (m, w), lacrosse (m, w), rugby (m, w), sailing (m, w), skiing (cross-country) (m, w), skiing (downhill) (m, w), soccer (m, w), softball (w), squash (m, w), swimming and diving (m, w), tennis (m, w), track and field (m, w), volleyball (m, w), water polo (m, w).

 ## Applying

Colby requires an essay, a high school transcript, 2 recommendations, and SAT I or ACT. It recommends 3 years of high school math and science, 3 years of high school foreign language, and an interview. Early, deferred, and midyear entrance are possible, with a 1/15 deadline and a 2/1 priority date for financial aid. **Contact:** Mr. Parker J. Beverage, Dean of Admissions and Financial Aid, 4800 Mayflower Hill, Waterville, ME 04901, 207-872-3168 or toll-free 800-723-3032; fax 207-872-3474.

GETTING IN LAST YEAR
4,217 applied
38% were accepted
34% enrolled (544)
65% from top tenth of their h.s. class
40% had SAT verbal scores over 600
73% had SAT math scores over 600
70% had ACT scores over 26
3% had SAT verbal scores over 700
18% had SAT math scores over 700
24% had ACT scores over 30
15 valedictorians

THE STUDENT BODY
1,785 undergraduates

From 49 states and territories,
   45 other countries
11% from Maine
55% women, 45% men
2% African Americans
1% Native Americans
2% Hispanics
4% Asian Americans
6% international students

AFTER FRESHMAN YEAR
95% returned for sophomore year
84% got a degree within 4 years
88% got a degree within 5 years
89% got a degree within 6 years

AFTER GRADUATION
14% pursued further study (8% arts and
   sciences, 3% law, 2% medicine)
80% had job offers within 6 months
51 organizations recruited on campus

WHAT YOU WILL PAY
Tuition and fees $20,990
Room and board $5650
40% receive need-based financial aid
Need-based college-administered scholarships and
   grants average $12,320 per award

COLGATE UNIVERSITY

Hamilton, New York • Rural setting • Private • Independent • Coed

When the Roper Organization asked graduates from 1980–92 "What most influenced your decision to attend Colgate," the key factor—cited on 90% of their responses—was academic reputation. Asked "how well Colgate measured up to your expectations academically," 97% of those graduates responded positively. Faculty initiative has given the college a rich mix of learning opportunities. But there is more to Colgate, including 80 student organizations, athletics and recreation at all levels, and one of the most beautiful campuses in the country.

Academics

Colgate offers an interdisciplinary curriculum and core academic program; all graduate courses are open to undergraduates. It awards bachelor's and master's **degrees**. Challenging opportunities include advanced placement, self-designed majors, tutorials, an honors program, a senior project, and Phi Beta Kappa. Special programs include off-campus study and study abroad.

The most popular **majors** include English, history, and political science/government. A complete listing of majors at Colgate appears in the Majors Index beginning on page 379.

The **faculty** at Colgate has 198 full-time undergraduate teachers, 98% with terminal degrees. 100% of the faculty serve as student advisers. The student-faculty ratio is 11:1.

Computers on Campus

Students are not required to have a computer. Student rooms are linked to a campus network. 260 **computers** available in the computer center, computer labs, the learning resource center, various academic departments, classrooms, the library, and the student center provide access to the main academic computer, e-mail, and the Internet. Staffed

computer lab on campus (open 24 hours a day) provides training in the use of computers and software.

The 2 **libraries** have 550,000 books, 67,200 microform titles, and 2,200 subscriptions. They are connected to 5 national **on-line** catalogs.

Campus Life

There are 80 active **organizations** on campus, including a drama/theater group and student-run newspaper and radio station. 37% of eligible men and 25% of eligible women are members of 8 national **fraternities**, 4 national **sororities**, and 2 local fraternities. Student **safety services** include late night transport/escort service, 24-hour emergency telephone alarm devices, 24-hour patrols by trained security personnel, student patrols, and electronically operated dormitory entrances.

Colgate is a member of the NCAA (Division I). **Intercollegiate sports** include basketball (m, w), crew (m, w), cross-country running (m, w), field hockey (w), football (m), golf (m), ice hockey (m, w), lacrosse (m, w), rugby (m, w), sailing (m, w), skiing (downhill) (m, w), soccer (m, w), softball (w), squash (m, w), swimming and diving (m, w), tennis (m, w), track and field (m, w), volleyball (m, w), water polo (m, w).

Applying

Colgate requires an essay, a high school transcript, 3 years of high school math, 3 years of high school foreign language, 3 recommendations, SAT I or ACT or 5 SAT II Subject Tests (including SAT II: Writing Test and Subject Test in math). It recommends 4 years of high school science and an interview. Early, deferred, and midyear entrance are possible, with a 1/15 deadline and a 2/1 priority date for financial aid. **Contact:** Ms. Mary F. Hill, Dean of Admission, 13 Oak Drive, Hamilton, NY 13346-1386, 315-824-7401; fax 315-824-7544.

GETTING IN LAST YEAR

6,037 applied
41% were accepted
30% enrolled (730)
59% from top tenth of their h.s. class
86% had SAT verbal scores over 600 (R)
83% had SAT math scores over 600 (R)
20% had SAT verbal scores over 700 (R)
17% had SAT math scores over 700 (R)
24 valedictorians

THE STUDENT BODY

Total 2,939, of whom 2,925
  are undergraduates

From 48 states and territories,
  44 other countries
32% from New York
52% women, 48% men
4% African Americans
1% Native Americans
3% Hispanics
5% Asian Americans
2% international students

AFTER FRESHMAN YEAR

96% returned for sophomore year

AFTER GRADUATION

70% had job offers within 6 months
82 organizations recruited on campus
1 Fulbright scholar

WHAT YOU WILL PAY

Tuition and fees $20,650
Room and board $5765
65% receive need-based financial aid
Need-based college-administered scholarships and
  grants average $13,610 per award
0% receive non-need financial aid

COLLEGE OF INSURANCE

New York, New York • Urban setting • Private • Independent • Coed

The College of Insurance is a fully accredited institution that is sponsored by more than 300 companies in the insurance and financial services industry. The College of Insurance is centrally located in the heart of the financial district, within walking distance of the World Trade Center, SoHo, Chinatown, and the South Street Seaport. The College is housed in an award-winning, self-contained building with dormitories on the top 4 floors. The College of Insurance offers qualified students the opportunity to participate in a unique cooperative work-study program.

Academics

College of Insurance offers a core academic program; a few graduate courses are open to undergraduates. It awards associate, bachelor's, and master's **degrees**. Challenging opportunities include advanced placement and a senior project. Special programs include cooperative education and summer session for credit.

The most popular **majors** include insurance and actuarial science. A complete listing of majors at College of Insurance appears in the Majors Index beginning on page 379.

The **faculty** at College of Insurance has 22 full-time undergraduate teachers, 25% with terminal degrees. The student-faculty ratio is 12:1.

Computers on Campus

Students are not required to have a computer. 16 **computers** available in computer labs.

The **library** has 96,526 books and 381 subscriptions.

Campus Life

Active **organizations** on campus include drama/theater group and student-run newspaper.

College of Insurance has 1 national **fraternity**. Student **safety services** include 24-hour emergency telephone alarm devices and 24-hour patrols by trained security personnel. **Intercollegiate sports** include bowling (m, w).

Applying

College of Insurance requires a high school transcript, 3 years of high school math, an interview, and SAT I or ACT. It recommends an essay and recommendations. Early, deferred, and midyear entrance are possible, with a 5/1 deadline and continuous processing to 6/1 for financial aid. **Contact:** Ms. Theresa C. Marro, Director of Admissions, 101 Murray Street, New York, NY 10007-2165, 212-815-9232 or toll-free 800-356-5146.

GETTING IN LAST YEAR
180 applied
54% were accepted
71% enrolled (70)
35% from top tenth of their h.s. class
0% had SAT verbal scores over 600
66% had SAT math scores over 600
0% had SAT verbal scores over 700
33% had SAT math scores over 700

THE STUDENT BODY
Total 2,210, of whom 2,045
   are undergraduates
80% from New York
52% women, 48% men
13% African Americans
10% Hispanics
8% Asian Americans
10% international students

WHAT YOU WILL PAY
Tuition and fees $12,260
Room and board $7004
Need-based college-administered scholarships and
   grants average $1521 per award
Non-need college-administered scholarships and
   grants average $5421 per award

COLLEGE OF SAINT BENEDICT
Coordinate with Saint John's University

Saint Joseph, Minnesota • Small-town setting • Private • Independent-Religious • Women

The College of Saint Benedict and Saint John's University are 2 of just 5 Catholic colleges that are recognized as selective national liberal arts institutions. Their mission is to foster learning, leadership, and wisdom for a lifetime. This is achieved through a unified curriculum stressing open inquiry, intellectual challenge, cooperative scholarship, and artistic creativity; an emphasis on the personal growth of women and men through separate residence halls, student development programming, athletics, and leadership opportunities; an experience of Benedictine values, including the formation of community built on respect for individual persons; and an entry into a heritage of leadership and service.

Academics

St. Ben's offers an interdisciplinary curriculum and core academic program. It awards bachelor's **degrees**. Challenging opportunities include advanced placement, self-designed majors, tutorials, an honors program, and a senior project. Special programs include internships, off-campus study, study abroad, and Army ROTC.

The most popular **majors** include education, nursing, and business. A complete listing of majors at St. Ben's appears in the Majors Index beginning on page 379.

The **faculty** at St. Ben's has 133 full-time teachers, 85% with terminal degrees. 100% of the faculty serve as student advisers. The student-faculty ratio is 13:1.

Computers on Campus

Students are not required to have a computer. Student rooms are linked to a campus network. 250 **computers** available in the computer center, computer labs, faculty offices, academic and administration buildings, classrooms, the library, the student center, and dormitories provide access to the main academic computer, e-mail, on-line services, and the Internet. Staffed computer lab on campus provides training in the use of computers and software.

The 3 **libraries** have 523,000 books, 103,000 microform titles, and 2,100 subscriptions. They are connected to 5 national **on-line** catalogs.

Campus Life

There are 80 active **organizations** on campus, including a drama/theater group and student-run newspaper and radio station. Student **safety services** include late night transport/escort service, 24-hour emergency telephone alarm devices, 24-hour patrols by trained security personnel, and electronically operated dormitory entrances.

St. Ben's is a member of the NCAA (Division III). **Intercollegiate sports** include basketball, crew, cross-country running, golf, lacrosse, rugby, soccer, softball, swimming and diving, tennis, track and field, volleyball.

Applying

St. Ben's requires an essay, a high school transcript, SAT I or ACT, and in some cases recommendations. It recommends 3 years of high school math and science, 2 years of high school foreign language, an interview, and a minimum high school GPA of 3.0. Early, deferred, and midyear entrance are possible, with rolling admissions and continuous processing to 8/15 for financial aid. **Contact:** Ms. Mary Milbert, Director of Admissions, 37 South College Avenue, Saint Joseph, MN 56374, 612-363-5308 or toll-free 800-544-1489; fax 612-363-6099.

GETTING IN LAST YEAR
913 applied
91% were accepted
60% enrolled (495)
38% from top tenth of their h.s. class
3.62 average high school GPA
31% had ACT scores over 26
7% had ACT scores over 30
5 National Merit Scholars

THE STUDENT BODY
1,897 undergraduates
From 29 states and territories,
    11 other countries

84% from Minnesota
100% women
1% African Americans
1% Native Americans
1% Hispanics
2% Asian Americans
2% international students

AFTER FRESHMAN YEAR
85% returned for sophomore year
57% got a degree within 4 years
64% got a degree within 5 years
66% got a degree within 6 years

AFTER GRADUATION
25% pursued further study (10% arts and
    sciences, 5% business, 5% law)

76% had job offers within 6 months
90 organizations recruited on campus

WHAT YOU WILL PAY
Tuition and fees $13,089
Room and board $4370
73% receive need-based financial aid
Need-based college-administered scholarships and
    grants average $4505 per award
13% receive non-need financial aid
Non-need college-administered scholarships and
    grants average $4150 per award

COLLEGE OF ST. SCHOLASTICA

Duluth, Minnesota • Suburban setting • Private • Independent-Religious • Coed

The College of St. Scholastica encourages visits to its beautiful 160-acre campus overlooking Lake Superior. Visitors find a community of professors and students who share a love of learning, exploring, and contributing. St. Scholastica's programs have won national honors for academic excellence and affordability. The rigorous scholarship is offset by a relaxed, small-school feel in which lifelong friendships form.

Academics

St. Scholastica offers a liberal arts core curriculum and core academic program. It awards bachelor's and master's **degrees**. Challenging opportunities include advanced placement, self-designed majors, tutorials, an honors program, and a senior project. Special programs include internships, summer session for credit, off-campus study, study abroad, and Army and Air Force ROTC.

The most popular **majors** include nursing, business, and health services administration. A complete listing of majors at St. Scholastica appears in the Majors Index beginning on page 379.

The **faculty** at St. Scholastica has 129 full-time graduate and undergraduate teachers, 67% with terminal degrees. 100% of the faculty serve as student advisers. The student-faculty ratio is 12:1, and the average class size in core courses is 19.

Computers on Campus

Students are not required to have a computer. 100 **computers** available in computer labs, classrooms, the library, and dormitories provide access to e-mail and the Internet. Staffed computer lab on campus provides training in the use of computers and software.

The 2 **libraries** have 124,565 books, 11,155 microform titles, and 750 subscriptions. They are connected to 1 national **on-line** catalog.

Campus Life

There are 40 active **organizations** on campus, including a drama/theater group and student-run newspaper. 20% of students participate in student government elections. Student **safety services** include student door monitor at night, late night transport/escort service, 24-hour emergency telephone alarm devices, and 24-hour patrols by trained security personnel.

St. Scholastica is a member of the NCAA (Division III) and NAIA. **Intercollegiate sports** include baseball (m), basketball (m, w), cross-country running (m, w), ice hockey (m), soccer (m, w), softball (w), volleyball (w).

Applying

St. Scholastica requires a high school transcript, SAT I or ACT, and in some cases an interview and a minimum high school GPA of 2.0. It recommends an essay, 3 years of high school math and science, some high school foreign language, recommendations, a campus interview, and PSAT. Early, deferred, and midyear entrance are possible, with rolling admissions and continuous processing to 3/15 for financial aid. **Contact:** Ms. Rebecca Urbanski-Junkert, Vice President for Admissions and Financial Aid, 1200 Kenwood Avenue, Duluth, MN 55811-4199, 218-723-6053 or toll-free 800-447-5444; fax 218-723-6290.

GETTING IN LAST YEAR
673 applied
89% were accepted
52% enrolled (310)
33% from top tenth of their h.s. class
4% had SAT verbal scores over 600
18% had SAT math scores over 600
49% had ACT scores over 26
0% had SAT verbal scores over 700
0% had SAT math scores over 700
19% had ACT scores over 30

THE STUDENT BODY
Total 1,895, of whom 1,551
  are undergraduates

From 21 states and territories,
  7 other countries
87% from Minnesota
72% women, 28% men
1% African Americans
2% Native Americans
1% Hispanics
1% Asian Americans
1% international students

AFTER FRESHMAN YEAR
77% returned for sophomore year
48% got a degree within 4 years
49% got a degree within 5 years

AFTER GRADUATION
19% pursued further study (16% arts and
  sciences, 1% business, 1% law)
9 organizations recruited on campus

WHAT YOU WILL PAY
Tuition and fees $12,534
Room and board $3807
85% receive need-based financial aid
Need-based college-administered scholarships and
  grants average $2222 per award
22% receive non-need financial aid
Non-need college-administered scholarships and
  grants average $1466 per award

COLLEGE OF THE HOLY CROSS

Worcester, Massachusetts • Suburban setting • Private • Independent-Religious • Coed

In a college world of shrinking resources and growing class enrollments, Holy Cross continues to fully support and refine its 150-year-old mission as a completely undergraduate Jesuit liberal arts college. An example of that commitment to open intellectual discourse is the popular First Year Program. Every one of the course offerings is taught by a faculty member, and the average class size is 15 students. The Jesuit nature of the community ensures that all its members recognize the importance of service to others and the need for social justice in daily affairs.

Academics

Holy Cross offers a liberal arts curriculum and core academic program. It awards bachelor's **degrees**. Challenging opportunities include advanced placement, accelerated degree programs, self-designed majors, tutorials, an honors program, a senior project, Phi Beta Kappa, and Sigma Xi. Special programs include internships, off-campus study, study abroad, and Army, Naval, and Air Force ROTC.

The most popular **majors** include English, economics, and history. A complete listing of majors at Holy Cross appears in the Majors Index beginning on page 379.

The **faculty** at Holy Cross has 212 full-time teachers, 94% with terminal degrees. 100% of the faculty serve as student advisers. The student-faculty ratio is 13:1.

Computers on Campus

Students are not required to have a computer. Student rooms are linked to a campus network. 130 **computers** available in the computer center, computer labs, the research center, science center, psychology labs, and the library provide access to the main academic computer, off-campus computing facilities, e-mail, and the Internet. Staffed computer lab on campus (open 24 hours a day) provides training in the use of computers and software.

The 3 **libraries** have 518,000 books, 610 microform titles, and 2,057 subscriptions. They are connected to 14 national **on-line** catalogs.

Campus Life

There are 75 active **organizations** on campus, including a drama/theater group and student-run newspaper and radio station. 42% of students participate in student government elections. Student **safety services** include late night transport/escort service, 24-hour emergency telephone alarm devices, 24-hour patrols by trained security personnel, and electronically operated dormitory entrances.

Holy Cross is a member of the NCAA (Division I). **Intercollegiate sports** include baseball (m), basketball (m, w), crew (m, w), cross-country running (m, w), fencing (m, w), field hockey (w), football (m), golf (m), ice hockey (m, w), lacrosse (m, w), rugby (m, w), sailing (m, w), soccer (m, w), softball (w), swimming and diving (m, w), tennis (m, w), track and field (m, w), volleyball (m, w), water polo (m, w).

Applying

Holy Cross requires an essay, a high school transcript, 2 recommendations, SAT I or ACT, and 3 SAT II Subject Tests (including SAT II: Writing Test). It recommends 3 years of high school math and science, some high school foreign language, and an interview. Early, deferred, and midyear entrance are possible, with a 2/1 deadline and continuous processing to 2/1 for financial aid. **Contact:** Ms. Ann Bowe McDermott, Director of Admissions, 1 College Street, Worcester, MA 01610, 508-793-2443 or toll-free 800-442-2421; fax 508-793-3888.

GETTING IN LAST YEAR
3,536 applied
50% were accepted
40% enrolled (712)
53% from top tenth of their h.s. class
32% had SAT verbal scores over 600
63% had SAT math scores over 600
14% had ACT scores over 26
3% had SAT verbal scores over 700
12% had SAT math scores over 700
0% had ACT scores over 30
6 National Merit Scholars
15 valedictorians

THE STUDENT BODY
2,738 undergraduates

From 46 states and territories,
20 other countries
40% from Massachusetts
53% women, 47% men
3% African Americans
0% Native Americans
2% Hispanics
3% Asian Americans
1% international students

AFTER FRESHMAN YEAR
94% returned for sophomore year
90% got a degree within 4 years
91% got a degree within 5 years

AFTER GRADUATION
57 organizations recruited on campus
5 Fulbright scholars

WHAT YOU WILL PAY
Tuition and fees $19,265
Room and board $6500
64% receive need-based financial aid
Need-based college-administered scholarships and grants average $9291 per award
Non-need college-administered scholarships and grants average $18,900 per award

COLLEGE OF WILLIAM AND MARY

Williamsburg, Virginia • Small-town setting • Public • State-supported • Coed

The College of William and Mary, chartered in 1693, is the second-oldest college in the United States and is known as the "alma mater of a nation." The College was first among American universities to have an interscholastic fraternity, Phi Beta Kappa, and an honor system. Committed to the principles of a liberal arts education, this "public ivy" offers undergraduate degrees in the arts and sciences. William and Mary's distinguished faculty is equally dedicated to the pursuit of research and teaching. Freshman seminars allow maximum interaction with faculty members beginning with a student's first semester.

Academics

William and Mary offers a liberal arts and sciences curriculum and core academic program; fewer than half of graduate courses are open to undergraduates. It awards bachelor's, master's, doctoral, and first professional **degrees**. Challenging opportunities include advanced placement, accelerated degree programs, self-designed majors, tutorials, Freshman Honors College, an honors program, a senior project, Phi Beta Kappa, and Sigma Xi. Special programs include summer session for credit, study abroad, and Army ROTC.

The most popular **majors** include business, biology/biological sciences, and English. A complete listing of majors at William and Mary appears in the Majors Index beginning on page 379.

The **faculty** at William and Mary has 534 full-time graduate and undergraduate teachers, 92% with terminal degrees. 30% of the faculty serve as student advisers. The student-faculty ratio is 10:1.

Computers on Campus

Students are not required to have a computer. Student rooms are linked to a campus network. 300 **computers** available in computer labs, classroom buildings, the library, and dormitories provide access to the main academic computer, off-campus computing facilities, e-mail, on-line services, and the Internet. Staffed computer lab on campus (open 24 hours a day) provides training in the use of computers and software.

The 10 **libraries** have 1.2 million books, 1.8 million microform titles, and 10,773 subscriptions. They are connected to 24 national **on-line** catalogs.

Campus Life

There are 196 active **organizations** on campus, including a drama/theater group and student-run newspaper and radio station. 35% of students participate in student government elections. 40% of eligible men and 45% of eligible women are members of 16 national **fraternities** and 13 national **sororities**. Student **safety services** include late night transport/escort service, 24-hour emergency telephone alarm devices, 24-hour patrols by trained security personnel, student patrols, and electronically operated dormitory entrances.

William and Mary is a member of the NCAA (Division I). **Intercollegiate sports** (some offering scholarships) include baseball (m), basketball (m, w), cross-country running (m, w), fencing (m, w), field hockey (w), football (m), golf (m, w), gymnastics (m, w), lacrosse (w), soccer (m, w), swimming and diving (m, w), tennis (m, w), track and field (m, w), volleyball (w).

Applying

William and Mary requires an essay, a high school transcript, SAT I or ACT, SAT II: Writing Test, and in some cases a campus interview. It recommends 4 years of high school math and science, 4 years of high school foreign language, 1 recommendation, and 3 SAT II Subject Tests. Early, deferred, and midyear entrance are possible, with a 1/15 deadline and a 2/15 priority date for financial aid. **Contact:** Ms. Virginia Carey, Dean of Admission, Richmond Road, Williamsburg, VA 23187-8795, 804-221-4223.

GETTING IN LAST YEAR
6,810 applied
49% were accepted
41% enrolled (1,372)
72% from top tenth of their h.s. class
81% had SAT verbal scores over 600 (R)
77% had SAT math scores over 600 (R)
86% had ACT scores over 26
32% had SAT verbal scores over 700 (R)
19% had SAT math scores over 700 (R)
68% had ACT scores over 30
25 National Merit Scholars
23 class presidents
75 valedictorians

THE STUDENT BODY
Total 7,709, of whom 5,480
  are undergraduates
From 50 states and territories,
  47 other countries
66% from Virginia
56% women, 44% men
7% African Americans
1% Native Americans
2% Hispanics
7% Asian Americans
2% international students

AFTER GRADUATION
34% pursued further study (13% law, 11% arts
  and sciences, 5% medicine)
47% had job offers within 6 months
150 organizations recruited on campus
1 Fulbright scholar

WHAT YOU WILL PAY
Resident tuition and fees $4738
Nonresident tuition and fees $14,428
Room and board $4372
30% receive need-based financial aid
Need-based college-administered scholarships and
  grants average $3353 per award
28% receive non-need financial aid
Non-need college-administered scholarships and
  grants average $3007 per award

THE COLLEGE OF WOOSTER

Wooster, Ohio • Small-town setting • Private • Independent-Religious • Coed

Wooster's curriculum provides students the breadth that is to be found in hundreds of course offerings and the depth that comes from 47 majors and programs of study. Small classes and an accessible faculty committed to teaching undergraduates ensure individual attention for every student. A first-year seminar links advising with teaching in a small seminar setting, while senior-year students work one-on-one with a faculty member on an Independent Study Project, a concept that was introduced into Wooster's curriculum almost 50 years ago. Wooster is one of the very few colleges that allow every student this opportunity for independent research and thought.

 ## Academics

Wooster offers an interdisciplinary curriculum and core academic program. It awards bachelor's **degrees**. Challenging opportunities include advanced placement, self-designed majors, a senior project, Phi Beta Kappa, and Sigma Xi. Special programs include internships, summer session for credit, and study abroad.

The most popular **majors** include history, biology/biological sciences, and psychology. A complete listing of majors at Wooster appears in the Majors Index beginning on page 379.

The **faculty** at Wooster has 121 full-time teachers, 95% with terminal degrees. 95% of the faculty serve as student advisers. The student-faculty ratio is 11:1.

 ## Computers on Campus

Students are not required to have a computer. Student rooms are linked to a campus network. 100 **computers** available in the computer center, computer labs, academic departments, classrooms, the library, dormitories, and student rooms provide access to the main academic computer, off-campus computing facilities, e-mail, on-line services, and the Internet. Staffed computer lab on campus (open 24 hours a day) provides training in the use of computers and software.

The 3 **libraries** have 663,805 books, 41,666 microform titles, and 1,314 subscriptions. They are connected to 3 national **on-line** catalogs.

 ## Campus Life

Active **organizations** on campus include drama/theater group and student-run newspaper and radio station. 24% of eligible men and 17% of eligible women are members of 7 local **fraternities**, 5 local **sororities**, and eating clubs, coed fraternity. Student **safety services** include residence halls connected directly to fire department, late night transport/escort service, 24-hour emergency telephone alarm devices, 24-hour patrols by trained security personnel, student patrols, and electronically operated dormitory entrances.

Wooster is a member of the NCAA (Division III). **Intercollegiate sports** include baseball (m), basketball (m, w), cross-country running (m, w), field hockey (w), football (m), golf (m), ice hockey (m), lacrosse (m, w), soccer (m, w), swimming and diving (m, w), tennis (m, w), track and field (m, w), volleyball (m, w).

 ## Applying

Wooster requires an essay, a high school transcript, 2 recommendations, and SAT I or ACT. It recommends 3 years of high school math and science, some high school foreign language, and an interview. Early and deferred entrance are possible, with a 2/15 deadline and a 2/15 priority date for financial aid. **Contact:** Dr. W. A. Hayden Schilling, Dean of Admissions, 1101 North Bever Street, Wooster, OH 44691, 216-263-2270 or toll-free 800-877-9905; fax 216-263-2594.

GETTING IN LAST YEAR
1,839 applied
89% were accepted
31% enrolled (512)
37% from top tenth of their h.s. class
55% had SAT verbal scores over 600 (R)
43% had SAT math scores over 600 (R)
58% had ACT scores over 26
11% had SAT verbal scores over 700 (R)
9% had SAT math scores over 700 (R)
18% had ACT scores over 30
9 National Merit Scholars

THE STUDENT BODY
1,683 undergraduates

From 45 states and territories,
48 other countries
48% from Ohio
52% women, 48% men
5% African Americans
0% Native Americans
1% Hispanics
1% Asian Americans
8% international students

AFTER FRESHMAN YEAR
83% returned for sophomore year
76% got a degree within 5 years
78% got a degree within 6 years

AFTER GRADUATION
22% pursued further study (12% arts and
    sciences, 5% medicine, 3% business)
61 organizations recruited on campus

WHAT YOU WILL PAY
Tuition and fees $17,600
Room and board $4640
62% receive need-based financial aid
Need-based college-administered scholarships and
    grants average $10,050 per award
Non-need college-administered scholarships and
    grants average $5800 per award

THE COLORADO COLLEGE

Colorado Springs, Colorado • Suburban setting • Private • Independent • Coed

At Colorado College, students study a liberal arts and sciences curriculum on a distinctive class schedule called the Block Plan. The year is divided into eight 3½-week segments (blocks) in which students take only one course and professors teach only one course during a segment. With no other academic obligations, students devote all their attention and time to one class. They do not have to juggle 4 different homework assignments or rush off to other classes. Courses can take place in environments most suited to learning the subject. Implemented in 1970, the Block Plan emphasizes active participation and "hands-on" learning.

 Academics

CC offers an interdisciplinary curriculum and core academic program; a few graduate courses are open to undergraduates. It awards bachelor's and master's **degrees** (master's in education only). Challenging opportunities include advanced placement, self-designed majors, tutorials, an honors program, a senior project, and Phi Beta Kappa. Special programs include internships, summer session for credit, study abroad, and Army ROTC.

The most popular **majors** include English, biology/biological sciences, and economics. A complete listing of majors at CC appears in the Majors Index beginning on page 379.

The **faculty** at CC has 155 full-time undergraduate teachers, 95% with terminal degrees. 100% of the faculty serve as student advisers. The student-faculty ratio is 12:1.

 Computers on Campus

Students are not required to have a computer. 200 **computers** available in the computer center, computer labs, academic buildings, the library, the student center, and dormitories provide access to the main academic computer, off-campus computing facilities, e-mail, on-line services, and the Internet. Staffed computer lab on campus (open 24 hours a day) provides training in the use of computers and software.

The **library** has 480,000 books, 20,000 microform titles, and 1,600 subscriptions. It is connected to 1 national **on-line** catalog.

 Campus Life

There are 60 active **organizations** on campus, including a drama/theater group and student-run newspaper and radio station. 20% of eligible men and 20% of eligible women are members of 4 national **fraternities** and 4 national **sororities**. Student **safety services** include whistle program, late night transport/escort service, 24-hour emergency telephone alarm devices, 24-hour patrols by trained security personnel, and electronically operated dormitory entrances.

CC is a member of the NCAA (Division III). **Intercollegiate sports** (some offering scholarships) include basketball (m, w), cross-country running (m, w), field hockey (m, w), football (m), ice hockey (m, w), lacrosse (m, w), rugby (m), soccer (m, w), softball (w), squash (m, w), swimming and diving (m, w), tennis (m, w), track and field (m, w), volleyball (w).

 Applying

CC requires an essay, a high school transcript, 3 recommendations, and SAT I or ACT. It recommends 3 years of high school math and science and some high school foreign language. Early and deferred entrance are possible, with a 1/15 deadline and a 2/15 priority date for financial aid. **Contact:** Mr. Terrance K. Swenson, Dean of Admission and Financial Aid, 14 East Cache La Poudre, Colorado Springs, CO 80903-3294, 719-389-6344 or toll-free 800-542-7214; fax 719-389-6816.

GETTING IN LAST YEAR
3,500 applied
51% were accepted
30% enrolled (528)
47% from top tenth of their h.s. class
96% had ACT scores over 26
71% had ACT scores over 30
11 National Merit Scholars
34 valedictorians

THE STUDENT BODY
Total 2,014, of whom 1,989
   are undergraduates

From 51 states and territories,
   23 other countries
28% from Colorado
52% women, 48% men
2% African Americans
1% Native Americans
5% Hispanics
4% Asian Americans
2% international students

AFTER FRESHMAN YEAR
92% returned for sophomore year

82% got a degree within 4 years

AFTER GRADUATION
30% pursued further study (16% arts and
   sciences, 5% law, 5% medicine)

WHAT YOU WILL PAY
Tuition and fees $18,084
Room and board $4562
50% receive need-based financial aid
Need-based college-administered scholarships and
   grants average $9000 per award
7% receive non-need financial aid

COLORADO SCHOOL OF MINES

Golden, Colorado • Small-town setting • Public • State-supported • Coed

CSM is a western school — not a typical college or university located in the West. The social atmosphere is informal and friendly, and the academic atmosphere is competitive but not cutthroat. Founded as a school of mining and geology, today CSM offers much more. From interdisciplinary, nontraditional programs in civil, electrical, and mechanical engineering to economics to environmental chemistry to chemical engineering, CSM students can choose from 14 study areas. Because CSM emphasizes hands-on experience and practical application, students prepare for their careers from their first days as freshmen.

Academics

CSM offers an engineering and applied science curriculum and no core academic program; fewer than half of graduate courses are open to undergraduates. It awards bachelor's, master's, and doctoral **degrees**. Challenging opportunities include advanced placement, accelerated degree programs, an honors program, a senior project, and Sigma Xi. Special programs include cooperative education, summer session for credit, study abroad, and Army and Air Force ROTC.

The most popular **majors** include engineering (general), chemical engineering, and computer science. A complete listing of majors at CSM appears in the Majors Index beginning on page 379.

The **faculty** at CSM has 200 full-time graduate and undergraduate teachers, 95% with terminal degrees. 90% of the faculty serve as student advisers. The student-faculty ratio is 14:1.

Computers on Campus

Students are not required to have a computer. Student rooms are linked to a campus network. 250 **computers** available in the computer center, computer labs, the research center, classroom buildings, the library, the student center, and dormitories provide access to the main academic computer, e-mail, and on-line services. Staffed computer lab on campus provides training in the use of computers and software.

The **library** has 360,000 books, 236,000 microform titles, and 2,700 subscriptions.

Campus Life

Active **organizations** on campus include drama/theater group and student-run newspaper. 10% of students participate in student government elections. 20% of eligible men and 20% of eligible women are members of 6 national **fraternities** and 2 national **sororities**. Student **safety services** include 24-hour emergency telephone alarm devices and 24-hour patrols by trained security personnel.

CSM is a member of the NCAA (Division II). **Intercollegiate sports** (some offering scholarships) include baseball (m), basketball (m, w), cross-country running (m, w), football (m), golf (m, w), lacrosse (m), rugby (m), soccer (m), softball (w), swimming and diving (m, w), tennis (m, w), track and field (m, w), volleyball (w), wrestling (m).

Applying

CSM requires a high school transcript, 4 years of high school math, 3 years of high school science, SAT I or ACT, and in some cases recommendations and an interview. It recommends some high school foreign language. Early, deferred, and midyear entrance are possible, with a 6/1 deadline and continuous processing to 3/1 for financial aid. **Contact:** Mr. Bill Young, Director of Enrollment Management, Twin Towers-1811 Elm Street, Golden, CO 80401-1887, 303-273-3227 or toll-free 800-446-9488 (out-of-state); fax 303-273-3509.

GETTING IN LAST YEAR
1,692 applied
82% were accepted
33% enrolled (452)
65% from top tenth of their h.s. class
3.75 average high school GPA
12% had SAT verbal scores over 600
80% had SAT math scores over 600
79% had ACT scores over 26
1% had SAT verbal scores over 700
10% had SAT math scores over 700
20% had ACT scores over 30

THE STUDENT BODY
Total 3,150, of whom 2,255
   are undergraduates

From 51 states and territories,
   68 other countries
69% from Colorado
24% women, 76% men
2% African Americans
1% Native Americans
6% Hispanics
5% Asian Americans
7% international students

AFTER FRESHMAN YEAR
85% returned for sophomore year
30% got a degree within 4 years
55% got a degree within 5 years
60% got a degree within 6 years

AFTER GRADUATION
15% pursued further study (8% engineering, 4%
   arts and sciences, 1% business)
85% had job offers within 6 months
95 organizations recruited on campus

WHAT YOU WILL PAY
Resident tuition and fees $4890
Nonresident tuition and fees $13,519
Room and board $4550
70% receive need-based financial aid
Need-based college-administered scholarships and
   grants average $4000 per award
15% receive non-need financial aid
Non-need college-administered scholarships and
   grants average $3500 per award

COLORADO STATE UNIVERSITY

Fort Collins, Colorado • Urban setting • Public • State-supported • Coed

Colorado State's scenic location, at the base of the Rocky Mountain foothills, provides the perfect background for intellectual and personal growth. Students describe the University as providing them with "an academically challenging and rigorous curriculum in a supportive environment," a place where they can feel at ease to be themselves and encouraged to develop their own unique talents. In addition to nearly 100 programs of study, special academic opportunities also include the popular study-abroad program, a stimulating honors program, and ROTC. Colorado State students graduate with the confidence that their education will make a difference.

Academics

Colorado State offers an interdisciplinary curriculum and core academic program. It awards bachelor's, master's, doctoral, and first professional **degrees**. Challenging opportunities include advanced placement, accelerated degree programs, self-designed majors, an honors program, a senior project, Phi Beta Kappa, and Sigma Xi. Special programs include cooperative education, internships, summer session for credit, study abroad, and Army and Air Force ROTC.

The most popular **majors** include business, liberal arts/general studies, and physical fitness/human movement. A complete listing of majors at Colorado State appears in the Majors Index beginning on page 379.

The **faculty** at Colorado State has 987 full-time graduate and undergraduate teachers, 87% with terminal degrees. 100% of the faculty serve as student advisers. The student-faculty ratio is 21:1.

Computers on Campus

Students are not required to have a computer. Student rooms are linked to a campus network. 3,500 **computers**

available in the computer center, computer labs, the research center, the learning resource center, classrooms, the library, the student center, dormitories, and student rooms provide access to the main academic computer, off-campus computing facilities, e-mail, on-line services, and the Internet. Staffed computer lab on campus provides training in the use of computers and software.

The 4 **libraries** have 1.8 million books, 1.8 million microform titles, and 20,500 subscriptions.

Campus Life

There are 300 active **organizations** on campus, including a drama/theater group and student-run newspaper and radio station. 15% of students participate in student government elections. 14% of eligible men and 14% of eligible women are members of 22 national **fraternities** and 14 national **sororities**. Student **safety services** include late night transport/escort service, 24-hour emergency telephone alarm devices, 24-hour patrols by trained security personnel, student patrols, and electronically operated dormitory entrances.

Colorado State is a member of the NCAA (Division I). **Intercollegiate sports** (some offering scholarships) include basketball (m, w), cross-country running (m, w), football (m), golf (m, w), softball (w), swimming and diving (w), tennis (m, w), track and field (m, w), volleyball (w).

Applying

Colorado State requires a high school transcript, 3 years of high school math and science, 4 years of high school English, and SAT I or ACT. It recommends an essay, 2 years of high school foreign language, recommendations, and an interview. Deferred and midyear entrance are possible, with a 7/1 deadline and continuous processing to 3/1 for financial aid. **Contact:** Ms. Mary Ontiveros, Director of Admissions, Spruce Hall, Fort Collins, CO 80523-0015, 970-491-6909; fax 970-491-7799.

GETTING IN LAST YEAR
9,435 applied
75% were accepted
37% enrolled (2,594)
26% from top tenth of their h.s. class
3.47 average high school GPA
33% had SAT verbal scores over 600 (R)
37% had SAT math scores over 600 (R)
32% had ACT scores over 26
4% had SAT verbal scores over 700 (R)
4% had SAT math scores over 700 (R)
6% had ACT scores over 30

THE STUDENT BODY
Total 21,914, of whom 18,136
   are undergraduates

From 55 states and territories,
   46 other countries
77% from Colorado
50% women, 50% men
1% African Americans
1% Native Americans
5% Hispanics
3% Asian Americans
1% international students

AFTER FRESHMAN YEAR
83% returned for sophomore year
20% got a degree within 4 years

48% got a degree within 5 years
55% got a degree within 6 years

WHAT YOU WILL PAY
Resident tuition and fees $2779
Nonresident tuition and fees $9387
Room and board $4152
52% receive need-based financial aid
Need-based college-administered scholarships and
   grants average $838 per award
22% receive non-need financial aid
Non-need college-administered scholarships and
   grants average $1004 per award

COLORADO TECHNICAL UNIVERSITY

Colorado Springs, Colorado • Suburban setting • Private • Proprietary • Coed

Colorado Technical University's mission is to provide state-of-the-practice, career-oriented education by teaching real-world, state-of-the-practice programs in selected technical, business, and health science fields. The University serves the needs of students for employment and career advancement in industry and the needs of industry for highly qualified, technically oriented professionals at the associate, bachelor's, master's, and doctoral levels.

 Academics

Colorado Tech offers an interdisciplinary curriculum and core academic program; a few graduate courses are open to undergraduates. It awards associate, bachelor's, master's, and doctoral **degrees**. Challenging opportunities include advanced placement, accelerated degree programs, tutorials, an honors program, and a senior project. Special programs include cooperative education, internships, summer session for credit, study abroad, and Army ROTC.

The most popular **majors** include computer science, electronics engineering technology, and electrical engineering. A complete listing of majors at Colorado Tech appears in the Majors Index beginning on page 379.

The **faculty** at Colorado Tech has 33 full-time graduate and undergraduate teachers, 58% with terminal degrees. 21% of the faculty serve as student advisers. The student-faculty ratio is 14:1, and the average class size in core courses is 26.

Computers on Campus

Students are not required to have a computer. 117 **computers** available in computer labs and the library provide access to on-line services. Staffed computer lab on campus provides training in the use of computers and software.

The **library** has 12,500 books, 30 microform titles, and 331 subscriptions. It is connected to 8 national **on-line** catalogs.

Campus Life

There are 6 active **organizations** on campus. Student **safety services** include 24-hour emergency telephone alarm devices.

This institution has no intercollegiate sports.

Applying

Colorado Tech requires SAT I or ACT, ACT ASSET tests in English and math, and in some cases an essay and a high school transcript. It recommends 3 years of high school math and science, an interview, and a minimum high school GPA of 3.0. Deferred and midyear entrance are possible, with rolling admissions and continuous processing to 10/1 for financial aid. **Contact:** Mr. John Richardson, Undergraduate Admissions Advisor, 4435 North Chestnut Street, Colorado Springs, CO 80907-3896, 719-598-0200; fax 719-598-3740.

GETTING IN LAST YEAR
210 applied
93% were accepted
90% enrolled (175)
42% from top tenth of their h.s. class
3.45 average high school GPA
20% had SAT verbal scores over 600 (R)
35% had SAT math scores over 600 (R)
50% had ACT scores over 26
2% had SAT verbal scores over 700 (R)
6% had SAT math scores over 700 (R)
10% had ACT scores over 30

THE STUDENT BODY
Total 1,473, of whom 1,075
　are undergraduates
97% from Colorado
19% women, 81% men
7% African Americans
1% Native Americans
6% Hispanics
3% Asian Americans
3% international students

AFTER GRADUATION
5% pursued further study (3% business, 2% engineering)

98% had job offers within 6 months
47 organizations recruited on campus

WHAT YOU WILL PAY
Tuition and fees $6468
34% receive need-based financial aid
Need-based college-administered scholarships and grants average $4000 per award
66% receive non-need financial aid
Non-need college-administered scholarships and grants average $2000 per award

COLUMBIA UNIVERSITY, COLUMBIA COLLEGE

New York, New York • Urban setting • Private • Independent • Coed

Located in the world's most international city, Columbia College, Columbia University's undergraduate liberal arts school, offers to a diverse student body a broad and solid foundation coupled with more advanced study in specific departments. More than 50 majors and interdisciplinary studies are available, and joint-degree programs take full advantage of the University's graduate and professional schools. The pace and excitement of New York color all aspects of life on campus, but students nevertheless feel a part of a small college community; the College is the Ivy League's smallest liberal arts school. Housing is guaranteed for 4 years.

 ## Academics

Columbia offers a Western civilization curriculum and core academic program; fewer than half of graduate courses are open to undergraduates. It awards bachelor's **degrees**. Challenging opportunities include advanced placement, self-designed majors, an honors program, a senior project, and Phi Beta Kappa. Special programs include summer session for credit, off-campus study, and study abroad.

The most popular **majors** include English, history, and political science/government. A complete listing of majors at Columbia appears in the Majors Index beginning on page 379.

The **faculty** at Columbia has 571 full-time teachers, 99% with terminal degrees. The student-faculty ratio is 7:1.

 ## Computers on Campus

Students are not required to have a computer. Student rooms are linked to a campus network. 400 **computers** available in the computer center, the library, and dormitories provide access to the main academic computer, e-mail, and on-line services. Staffed computer lab on campus provides training in the use of computers and software.

The 21 **libraries** have 6 million books, 4 million microform titles, and 66,000 subscriptions.

 ## Campus Life

Active **organizations** on campus include drama/theater group and student-run newspaper and radio station. 18% of eligible men and 8% of eligible women are members of 12 national **fraternities** and 7 national **sororities**. Student **safety services** include 24-hour ID check at door, late night transport/escort service, 24-hour emergency telephone alarm devices, and 24-hour patrols by trained security personnel.

Columbia is a member of the NCAA (Division I). **Intercollegiate sports** include archery (m, w), badminton (m, w), baseball (m), basketball (m, w), crew (m, w), cross-country running (m, w), equestrian sports (m, w), fencing (m, w), field hockey (w), football (m), golf (m), ice hockey (m), lacrosse (m, w), racquetball (m, w), riflery (m, w), rugby (m, w), sailing (m, w), skiing (cross-country) (m, w), soccer (m, w), softball (w), squash (m), swimming and diving (m, w), table tennis (m, w), tennis (m, w), track and field (m, w), volleyball (m, w), water polo (m), weight lifting (m), wrestling (m).

 ## Applying

Columbia requires an essay, a high school transcript, 2 recommendations, SAT I or ACT, and 3 SAT II Subject Tests (including SAT II: Writing Test). It recommends 3 years of high school math and science, 3 years of high school foreign language, and an interview. Early and deferred entrance are possible, with a 1/1 deadline and 2/1 for financial aid. **Contact:** Director of Admissions, 212 Hamilton Hall, New York, NY 10027, 212-854-2522; fax 212-854-1209.

GETTING IN LAST YEAR
8,714 applied
23% were accepted
43% enrolled (883)
84% from top tenth of their h.s. class

THE STUDENT BODY
3,573 undergraduates
From 49 states and territories, 40 other countries

19% from New York
49% women, 51% men
9% African Americans
1% Native Americans
9% Hispanics
23% Asian Americans
5% international students

AFTER FRESHMAN YEAR
96% returned for sophomore year

80% got a degree within 4 years
90% got a degree within 6 years

WHAT YOU WILL PAY
Tuition and fees $20,262
Room and board $6864
53% receive need-based financial aid
Need-based college-administered scholarships and grants average $14,338 per award

COLUMBIA UNIVERSITY, SCHOOL OF ENGINEERING AND APPLIED SCIENCE

New York, New York • Urban setting • Private • Independent • Coed

Located in the world's most international city, Columbia University's undergraduate School of Engineering and Applied Science (SEAS) offers to a diverse student body a solid and basic foundation coupled with more advanced study in specific departments; 17 engineering disciplines are offered, and joint-degree programs take full advantage of the University's other divisions, both undergraduate and graduate. The pace and excitement of New York color all aspects of life on campus, but, with only 1,000 undergraduates in SEAS, students feel part of a small-college community. Housing is guaranteed for 4 years.

 Academics

Columbia SEAS offers a core academic program. It awards bachelor's, master's, and doctoral **degrees**. Challenging opportunities include advanced placement, accelerated degree programs, tutorials, and an honors program. Special programs include internships, summer session for credit, and study abroad.

The most popular **majors** include computer science, electrical engineering, and mechanical engineering. A complete listing of majors at Columbia SEAS appears in the Majors Index beginning on page 379.

The **faculty** at Columbia SEAS has 93 full-time undergraduate teachers, 100% with terminal degrees.

 Computers on Campus

Students are not required to have a computer. Student rooms are linked to a campus network. 400 **computers** available in the computer center, computer labs, engineering departments, the library, and dormitories provide access to the main academic computer, e-mail, on-line services, and the Internet. Staffed computer lab on campus provides training in the use of computers and software.

The 21 **libraries** have 6.6 million books, 4.9 million microform titles, and 66,000 subscriptions.

 Campus Life

Active **organizations** on campus include drama/theater group and student-run newspaper and radio station. 7% of eligible men and 2% of eligible women are members of 12 national **fraternities**, 7 national **sororities**, 6 local fraternities, 2 local sororities, and 6 coed social clubs. Student **safety services** include 24-hour ID check at door, late night transport/escort service, 24-hour emergency telephone alarm devices, and 24-hour patrols by trained security personnel.

Columbia SEAS is a member of the NCAA (Division I). **Intercollegiate sports** include archery (m, w), baseball (m), basketball (m, w), crew (m, w), cross-country running (m, w), fencing (m, w), field hockey (w), football (m), golf (m), racquetball (m, w), soccer (m, w), swimming and diving (m, w), tennis (m, w), track and field (m, w), volleyball (w), water polo (m), weight lifting (m), wrestling (m).

 Applying

Columbia SEAS requires an essay, a high school transcript, 4 years of high school math, 3 years of high school science, 2 recommendations, SAT I or ACT, and 3 SAT II Subject Tests (including SAT II: Writing Test). It recommends 2 years of high school foreign language, an interview, and a minimum high school GPA of 3.0. Early and deferred entrance are possible, with a 1/1 deadline and 2/1 for financial aid. **Contact:** Director of Admissions, 212 Hamilton Hall, New York, NY 10027, 212-854-2522; fax 212-854-1209.

GETTING IN LAST YEAR
1,351 applied
50% were accepted
41% enrolled (278)
68% from top tenth of their h.s. class

THE STUDENT BODY
1,044 undergraduates
From 40 states and territories,
30 other countries

22% women, 78% men
5% African Americans
0% Native Americans
6% Hispanics
49% Asian Americans
9% international students

AFTER FRESHMAN YEAR
89% returned for sophomore year
84% got a degree within 4 years

WHAT YOU WILL PAY
Tuition and fees $20,262
Room and board $6864
Need-based college-administered scholarships and
    grants average $15,254 per award
0% receive non-need financial aid

CONCORDIA COLLEGE

Moorhead, Minnesota • Suburban setting • Private • Independent-Religious • Coed

The academic program is distinguished by its blending of liberal arts and career preparation. Both on-campus academic offerings and an extensive off-campus cooperative education program aid students in meeting career goals. The campus community is best known for its friendliness and warmth, exhibited by mutual respect between students and faculty. One of the largest colleges in the Midwest, Concordia may also be one of the "Best Buys." As a result of extraordinary donor support, the College has a reputation for outstanding faculty and strong academic programs yet has maintained a tuition rate several thousand dollars below comparable colleges.

Academics

Concordia offers a liberal arts/career preparation curriculum and core academic program. It awards bachelor's **degrees**. Challenging opportunities include advanced placement, tutorials, an honors program, and a senior project. Special programs include cooperative education, internships, summer session for credit, off-campus study, study abroad, and Army and Air Force ROTC.

The most popular **majors** include business, modern languages, and English. A complete listing of majors at Concordia appears in the Majors Index beginning on page 379.

The **faculty** at Concordia has 204 full-time teachers, 62% with terminal degrees. 100% of the faculty serve as student advisers. The student-faculty ratio is 14:1.

Computers on Campus

Students are not required to have a computer. Student rooms are linked to a campus network. 115 **computers** available in computer labs, classrooms, the library, and dormitories provide access to the main academic computer, off-campus computing facilities, e-mail, and on-line services. Staffed computer lab on campus provides training in the use of computers and software.

The 2 **libraries** have 299,500 books, 34,648 microform titles, and 1,500 subscriptions.

Campus Life

There are 30 active **organizations** on campus, including a drama/theater group and student-run newspaper and radio station. 50% of students participate in student government elections. 5% of eligible men and 5% of eligible women are members of 3 local **fraternities** and 3 local **sororities**. Student **safety services** include well-lit campus, late night transport/escort service, 24-hour emergency telephone alarm devices, 24-hour patrols by trained security personnel, and student patrols.

Concordia is a member of the NCAA (Division III). **Intercollegiate sports** include baseball (m), basketball (m, w), cross-country running (m, w), football (m), golf (m, w), ice hockey (m), soccer (m, w), softball (w), swimming and diving (w), tennis (m, w), track and field (m, w), volleyball (w), wrestling (m).

Applying

Concordia requires a high school transcript, 2 recommendations, and SAT I or ACT. It recommends 3 years of high school math and science, 2 years of high school foreign language, and an interview. Early, deferred, and midyear entrance are possible, with rolling admissions and continuous processing for financial aid. **Contact:** Mr. Lee E. Johnson, Director of Admissions, 901 8th Street South, Moorhead, MN 56562, 218-299-3004; fax 218-299-3947.

GETTING IN LAST YEAR
1,952 applied
89% were accepted
46% enrolled (803)
28% from top tenth of their h.s. class
33% had ACT scores over 26
9% had ACT scores over 30
7 National Merit Scholars
49 valedictorians

THE STUDENT BODY
2,958 undergraduates
From 37 states and territories,
 35 other countries
62% from Minnesota

59% women, 41% men
1% African Americans
1% Native Americans
1% Hispanics
2% Asian Americans
3% international students

AFTER FRESHMAN YEAR
76% returned for sophomore year
59% got a degree within 4 years
67% got a degree within 5 years
68% got a degree within 6 years

AFTER GRADUATION
20% pursued further study (8% arts and
 sciences, 4% medicine, 2% business)

70% had job offers within 6 months
60 organizations recruited on campus
2 Fulbright scholars

WHAT YOU WILL PAY
Tuition and fees $11,570
Room and board $3400
83% receive need-based financial aid
Need-based college-administered scholarships and
 grants average $5695 per award
6% receive non-need financial aid
Non-need college-administered scholarships and
 grants average $3538 per award

COOPER UNION FOR THE ADVANCEMENT OF SCIENCE AND ART

New York, New York • Urban setting • Private • Independent • Coed

> Each of Cooper Union's schools—Art, Architecture, Engineering—adheres strongly to preparation for its profession within a design-centered, problem-solving philosophy of education. A rigorous curriculum and group projects reinforce this unique atmosphere in higher education and are factors in *Money* magazine's decision to name Cooper Union "In a Class by Itself."

Academics

Cooper Union offers a world civilization and English literature curriculum and core academic program; all graduate courses are open to undergraduates. It awards bachelor's and master's **degrees**. Challenging opportunities include advanced placement, self-designed majors, tutorials, an honors program, and a senior project. Special programs include internships, summer session for credit, and off-campus study.

The most popular **majors** include art/fine arts, architecture, and electrical engineering. A complete listing of majors at Cooper Union appears in the Majors Index beginning on page 379.

The **faculty** at Cooper Union has 56 full-time graduate and undergraduate teachers, 61% with terminal degrees. 100% of the faculty serve as student advisers. The student-faculty ratio is 7:1.

Computers on Campus

Students are not required to have a computer. 160 **computers** available in the computer center, computer labs, the research center, the learning resource center, the library, and dormitories provide access to the main academic computer, off-campus computing facilities, e-mail, and on-line services. Staffed computer lab on campus provides training in the use of computers and software.

The **library** has 88,000 books, 4,700 microform titles, and 370 subscriptions.

Campus Life

There are 60 active **organizations** on campus, including a drama/theater group and student-run newspaper. 53% of students participate in student government elections. 20% of eligible men and 10% of eligible women are members of 2 national **fraternities** and 1 national **sorority**. Student **safety services** include 24-hour emergency telephone alarm devices, 24-hour patrols by trained security personnel, and electronically operated dormitory entrances. **Intercollegiate sports** include basketball (m), equestrian sports (w), soccer (m), tennis (m, w).

Applying

Cooper Union requires a high school transcript, SAT I or ACT, a minimum high school GPA of 2.0, and in some cases an essay, 4 years of high school math, 3 years of high school science, 3 recommendations, portfolio, home test, and 2 SAT II Subject Tests. It recommends a minimum high school GPA of 3.0. Early and deferred entrance are possible, with 4/15 for financial aid. **Contact:** Mr. Richard Bory, Dean of Admissions and Records, 30 Cooper Square, New York, NY 10003-7120, 212-353-4120; fax 212-353-4343.

GETTING IN LAST YEAR
2,244 applied
13% were accepted
69% enrolled (193)
80% from top tenth of their h.s. class
3.2 average high school GPA

THE STUDENT BODY
Total 1,003, of whom 923
  are undergraduates
From 37 states and territories,
  9 other countries
71% from New York

36% women, 64% men
6% African Americans
1% Native Americans
10% Hispanics
27% Asian Americans
8% international students

AFTER FRESHMAN YEAR
87% returned for sophomore year
49% got a degree within 4 years
68% got a degree within 5 years
72% got a degree within 6 years

AFTER GRADUATION
55% pursued further study (36% engineering,
  6% law, 5% arts and sciences)
59% had job offers within 6 months
29 organizations recruited on campus
1 Fulbright scholar

WHAT YOU WILL PAY
Tuition and fees $8300
Room only $5015
43% receive need-based financial aid
Need-based college-administered scholarships and
  grants average $2470 per award

CORNELL COLLEGE

Mount Vernon, Iowa • Small-town setting • Private • Independent-Religious • Coed

Since its founding in 1853, Cornell College has maintained a strong commitment to excellence in the liberal arts. Nearly 2 decades ago, the College adopted a distinctive and innovative academic calendar called One-Course-At-A-Time, which divides the traditional academic year into 9 terms, each three and a half weeks long, with a 4-day break between terms. More than 50 courses are available to students each term. Cornell's experience with single-course study now indicates that it can maximize the effect of a liberal arts education by allowing students and professors to focus their efforts exclusively on each course.

Academics

Cornell offers a core academic program. It awards bachelor's **degrees**. Challenging opportunities include advanced placement, accelerated degree programs, self-designed majors, tutorials, a senior project, and Phi Beta Kappa. Special programs include internships, off-campus study, and study abroad.

The most popular **majors** include business economics, English, and history. A complete listing of majors at Cornell appears in the Majors Index beginning on page 379.

The **faculty** at Cornell has 78 full-time teachers, 92% with terminal degrees. 100% of the faculty serve as student advisers. The student-faculty ratio is 13:1.

Computers on Campus

Students are not required to have a computer. 175 **computers** available in the computer center, computer labs, classroom buildings, the library, the student center, and dormitories provide access to e-mail and the Internet. Staffed computer lab on campus provides training in the use of computers and software.

The 2 **libraries** have 191,614 books, 214,884 microform titles, and 741 subscriptions.

Campus Life

There are 71 active **organizations** on campus, including a drama/theater group and student-run newspaper and radio station. 35% of eligible men and 35% of eligible women are members of 7 local **fraternities**, 6 local **sororities**, and 1 coed fraternity. Student **safety services** include late night transport/escort service and 24-hour emergency telephone alarm devices.

Cornell is a member of the NCAA (Division III). **Intercollegiate sports** include baseball (m), basketball (m, w), cross-country running (m, w), football (m), golf (m, w), soccer (m, w), softball (w), tennis (m, w), track and field (m, w), volleyball (m, w), wrestling (m).

Applying

Cornell requires an essay, a high school transcript, 1 recommendation, and SAT I or ACT. It recommends 3 years of high school math and science, some high school foreign language, and an interview. Early, deferred, and midyear entrance are possible, with a 3/1 deadline and continuous processing to 3/1 for financial aid. **Contact:** Mr. Larry Erenberger, Dean of Admissions and Enrollment Management, 600 First Street West, Mount Vernon, IA 52314-1098, 319-895-4477 or toll-free 800-747-1112 (out-of-state); fax 319-895-4451.

GETTING IN LAST YEAR

1,377 applied
90% were accepted
31% enrolled (387)
34% from top tenth of their h.s. class
3.43 average high school GPA
46% had ACT scores over 26
13% had ACT scores over 30

THE STUDENT BODY

1,168 undergraduates
From 44 states and territories,
  9 other countries

27% from Iowa
57% women, 43% men
3% African Americans
1% Native Americans
2% Hispanics
2% Asian Americans
1% international students

AFTER FRESHMAN YEAR

78% returned for sophomore year
67% got a degree within 4 years

AFTER GRADUATION

35% pursued further study
69% had job offers within 6 months
65 organizations recruited on campus

WHAT YOU WILL PAY

Tuition and fees $16,440
Room and board $4452
Need-based college-administered scholarships and
  grants average $13,608 per award
Non-need college-administered scholarships and
  grants average $5000 per award

CORNELL UNIVERSITY

Ithaca, New York • Small-town setting • Private • Independent • Coed

Ezra Cornell created a university that offered instruction to all who were qualified, regardless of race or gender; welcomed rich and poor; and encouraged students to choose their own programs. Cornell is still a place where a wide variety of students engage in discovery in a curriculum that is unequaled in interdisciplinary breadth.

 Academics

Cornell offers a comprehensive integration of liberal arts and professional curriculum and no core academic program; fewer than half of graduate courses are open to undergraduates. It awards bachelor's, master's, doctoral, and first professional **degrees**. Challenging opportunities include advanced placement, self-designed majors, tutorials, an honors program, a senior project, Phi Beta Kappa, and Sigma Xi. Special programs include cooperative education, internships, summer session for credit, off-campus study, study abroad, and Army, Naval, and Air Force ROTC.

The most popular **majors** include biology/biological sciences, mechanical engineering, and agricultural business. A complete listing of majors at Cornell appears in the Majors Index beginning on page 379.

The **faculty** at Cornell has 1,532 full-time graduate and undergraduate teachers, 95% with terminal degrees. The student-faculty ratio is 8:1.

Computers on Campus

Students are not required to have a computer. Student rooms are linked to a campus network. **Computers** available in the computer center, computer labs, the research center, various locations on campus, the library, the student center, dormitories, and student rooms provide access to the main academic computer, off-campus computing facilities, e-mail, on-line services, and the Internet. Staffed computer lab on campus provides training in the use of computers and software.

The 17 **libraries** have 5.8 million books, 6.7 million microform titles, and 61,705 subscriptions. They are connected to 2 national **on-line** catalogs.

Campus Life

There are 400 active **organizations** on campus, including a drama/theater group and student-run newspaper and radio station. 25% of students participate in student government elections. 32% of eligible men and 27% of eligible women are members of 43 national **fraternities**, 19 national **sororities**, and 2 local fraternities. Student **safety services** include escorts, late night transport/escort service, 24-hour emergency telephone alarm devices, 24-hour patrols by trained security personnel, and electronically operated dormitory entrances.

Cornell is a member of the NCAA (Division I). **Intercollegiate sports** include baseball (m), basketball (m, w), crew (m, w), cross-country running (m, w), equestrian sports (w), fencing (w), field hockey (w), football (m), golf (m), gymnastics (w), ice hockey (m, w), lacrosse (m, w), soccer (m, w), softball (w), squash (m), swimming and diving (m, w), tennis (m, w), track and field (m, w), volleyball (w), wrestling (m).

Applying

Cornell requires an essay, a high school transcript, 3 years of high school math, 1 recommendation, SAT I or ACT, and in some cases 3 years of high school science, 3 years of high school foreign language, a campus interview, and SAT II: Writing Test. Early, deferred, and midyear entrance are possible, with a 1/1 deadline and a 2/15 priority date for financial aid. **Contact:** Ms. Nancy Meislahn, Director of Admissions, 410 Thurston Avenue, Ithaca, NY 14850, 607-255-5241; fax 607-255-0659.

GETTING IN LAST YEAR

20,603 applied
34% were accepted
45% enrolled (3,204)
81% from top tenth of their h.s. class
84% had SAT verbal scores over 600 (R)
91% had SAT math scores over 600 (R)
32% had SAT verbal scores over 700 (R)
45% had SAT math scores over 700 (R)
60 National Merit Scholars
242 valedictorians

THE STUDENT BODY

Total 18,914, of whom 13,372
  are undergraduates

From 56 states and territories,
  80 other countries
42% from New York
47% women, 53% men
4% African Americans
1% Native Americans
6% Hispanics
17% Asian Americans
6% international students

AFTER FRESHMAN YEAR

94% returned for sophomore year
79% got a degree within 4 years
88% got a degree within 5 years
89% got a degree within 6 years

AFTER GRADUATION

32% pursued further study (13% arts and
  sciences, 8% medicine, 6% law)
500 organizations recruited on campus
1 Rhodes, 7 Fulbright scholars

WHAT YOU WILL PAY

Tuition and fees $20,066
Room and board $6762
48% receive need-based financial aid
Need-based college-administered scholarships and
  grants average $9570 per award

CREIGHTON UNIVERSITY

Omaha, Nebraska • Urban setting • Private • Independent-Religious • Coed

Emphasizing the quality of its own undergraduate preparation, Creighton University in 1996 extended a limited offer of guaranteed admission to high school seniors hoping to enroll in Creighton's professional programs in medicine, dentistry, and law. The Lied Education Center for the arts opened, adding 70,000 square feet of classroom, studio, theater, gallery, and office space to the fine arts program. Benefactors donated 3 full-tuition scholarships to the College of Business Administration, and officials announced the addition of a graduate program in information technology management. Men's and women's soccer teams continued to attract a large following, and crew was added to the list of varsity sports.

 ## Academics

Creighton offers a values-centered, globalized curriculum and core academic program. It awards associate, bachelor's, master's, doctoral, and first professional **degrees**. Challenging opportunities include advanced placement, accelerated degree programs, tutorials, an honors program, and a senior project. Special programs include internships, summer session for credit, study abroad, and Army and Air Force ROTC.

The most popular **majors** include nursing, psychology, and finance/banking. A complete listing of majors at Creighton appears in the Majors Index beginning on page 379.

The **faculty** at Creighton has 627 full-time graduate and undergraduate teachers, 88% with terminal degrees. 80% of the faculty serve as student advisers. The student-faculty ratio is 14:1.

 ## Computers on Campus

Students are not required to have a computer. Student rooms are linked to a campus network. 520 **computers** available in the computer center, computer labs, the learning resource center, classrooms, the library, and dormitories provide access to the main academic computer, e-mail, on-line services, and the Internet. Staffed computer lab on campus provides training in the use of computers and software.

The 3 **libraries** have 836,040 books, 120,752 microform titles, and 8,318 subscriptions. They are connected to 10 national **on-line** catalogs.

 ## Campus Life

There are 130 active **organizations** on campus, including a drama/theater group and student-run newspaper. 30% of students participate in student government elections. 33% of eligible men and 30% of eligible women are members of 8 national **fraternities** and 6 national **sororities**. Student **safety services** include late night transport/escort service, 24-hour emergency telephone alarm devices, 24-hour patrols by trained security personnel, student patrols, and electronically operated dormitory entrances.

Creighton is a member of the NCAA (Division I). **Intercollegiate sports** (some offering scholarships) include baseball (m), basketball (m, w), crew (m, w), cross-country running (m, w), golf (m, w), soccer (m, w), softball (w), tennis (m, w), volleyball (w).

 ## Applying

Creighton requires a high school transcript, 1 recommendation, SAT I or ACT, and a minimum high school GPA of 2.0. It recommends 3 years of high school math and science and some high school foreign language. Deferred and midyear entrance are possible, with rolling admissions and continuous processing to 4/1 for financial aid. **Contact:** Ms. Laurie R. Vinduska, Director of Admissions, 2500 California Plaza, Omaha, NE 68178-0001, 402-280-2703 or toll-free 800-282-5835 (in-state); fax 402-280-2685.

GETTING IN LAST YEAR
2,558 applied
93% were accepted
33% enrolled (786)
27% from top tenth of their h.s. class
3.49 average high school GPA
46% had ACT scores over 26
11% had ACT scores over 30

THE STUDENT BODY
Total 6,069, of whom 3,769
  are undergraduates
From 45 states and territories,
  50 other countries

46% from Nebraska
59% women, 41% men
3% African Americans
1% Native Americans
3% Hispanics
7% Asian Americans
3% international students

AFTER FRESHMAN YEAR
83% returned for sophomore year
54% got a degree within 4 years
65% got a degree within 5 years
66% got a degree within 6 years

AFTER GRADUATION
85% had job offers within 6 months
91 organizations recruited on campus
1 Fulbright scholar

WHAT YOU WILL PAY
Tuition and fees $11,562
Room and board $4548
53% receive need-based financial aid
Need-based college-administered scholarships and
  grants average $2600 per award
33% receive non-need financial aid
Non-need college-administered scholarships and
  grants average $4295 per award

DARTMOUTH COLLEGE

Hanover, New Hampshire • Rural setting • Private • Independent • Coed

Dartmouth's blending of university resources with a college's focus on undergraduate education offers small classes, outstanding research facilities, and remarkable opportunities for collaboration between faculty and students. A wide range of resources support a variety of academic, social, cultural, and extracurricular pursuits on the campus. All of this takes place within a small community that is almost entirely devoted to education.

Academics

Dartmouth offers an interdisciplinary curriculum and core academic program; more than half of graduate courses are open to undergraduates. It awards bachelor's, master's, and doctoral **degrees**. Challenging opportunities include advanced placement, accelerated degree programs, self-designed majors, tutorials, an honors program, a senior project, Phi Beta Kappa, and Sigma Xi. Special programs include summer session for credit, off-campus study, study abroad, and Army ROTC.

The most popular **majors** include political science/government, history, and engineering (general). A complete listing of majors at Dartmouth appears in the Majors Index beginning on page 379.

The **faculty** at Dartmouth has 334 full-time undergraduate teachers, 98% with terminal degrees. 75% of the faculty serve as student advisers. The student-faculty ratio is 11:1.

Computers on Campus

Students are required to have a computer. Purchase options are available. Student rooms are linked to a campus network. 6,000 **computers** available in the computer center, computer labs, the research center, the learning resource center, academic departments, classrooms, the library, the student center, dormitories, and student rooms provide access to the main academic computer, e-mail, on-line services, and the Internet. Staffed computer lab on campus (open 24 hours a day) provides training in the use of computers and software.

The 8 **libraries** have 2 million books, 1.6 million microform titles, and 19,000 subscriptions.

Campus Life

There are 290 active **organizations** on campus, including a drama/theater group and student-run newspaper and radio station. 41% of eligible men and 28% of eligible women are members of 9 national **fraternities**, 3 national **sororities**, 8 local fraternities, 5 local sororities, and 4 coed fraternities. Student **safety services** include late night transport/escort service, 24-hour emergency telephone alarm devices, 24-hour patrols by trained security personnel, and student patrols.

Dartmouth is a member of the NCAA (Division I). **Intercollegiate sports** include baseball (m), basketball (m, w), crew (m, w), cross-country running (m, w), equestrian sports (m, w), fencing (m, w), field hockey (w), football (m), golf (m, w), gymnastics (m), ice hockey (m, w), lacrosse (m, w), riflery (m, w), rugby (m, w), sailing (m, w), skiing (cross-country) (m, w), skiing (downhill) (m, w), soccer (m, w), softball (w), squash (m, w), swimming and diving (m, w), tennis (m, w), track and field (m, w), volleyball (m, w), water polo (m, w), wrestling (m).

Applying

Dartmouth requires an essay, a high school transcript, SAT I or ACT, and 3 SAT II Subject Tests. It recommends 3 years of high school math and science, some high school foreign language, and an interview. Early and deferred entrance are possible, with a 1/1 deadline and 2/1 for financial aid. **Contact:** Mr. Karl M. Furstenberg, Dean of Admissions and Financial Aid, 6016 McNutt Hall, Hanover, NH 03755, 603-646-2875; fax 603-646-1216.

GETTING IN LAST YEAR
10,004 applied
22% were accepted
49% enrolled (1,056)
90% from top tenth of their h.s. class
94% had SAT verbal scores over 600 (R)
94% had SAT math scores over 600 (R)
60% had SAT verbal scores over 700 (R)
55% had SAT math scores over 700 (R)
53 National Merit Scholars
185 valedictorians

THE STUDENT BODY
Total 5,300, of whom 4,287
    are undergraduates

From 52 states and territories,
    54 other countries
3% from New Hampshire
50% women, 50% men
7% African Americans
3% Native Americans
5% Hispanics
10% Asian Americans
7% international students

AFTER FRESHMAN YEAR
99% returned for sophomore year
93% got a degree within 4 years
95% got a degree within 5 years

AFTER GRADUATION
24% pursued further study (8% arts and
    sciences, 8% law, 6% medicine)
219 organizations recruited on campus
1 Fulbright scholar

WHAT YOU WILL PAY
Tuition and fees $20,910
Room and board $6129
Need-based college-administered scholarships and
    grants average $14,660 per award

DAVID LIPSCOMB UNIVERSITY

Nashville, Tennessee • Urban setting • Private • Independent-Religious • Coed

Since 1891, Lipscomb University has offered high-quality courses of study combined with Christian values essential to successful living. More than 100 major programs of study are offered. Lipscomb's 21st-century campuswide fiber-optic network provides PC connections in every dorm room, dorm lobby lab, and many other locations for Internet access to resources worldwide. Lipscomb University is a beautiful, quiet place with a special atmosphere that encourages learning. Nashville is one of the most exciting cities in the South. Its wide range of cultural and career opportunities enhances the academic program and each student's potential for employment following graduation.

Academics

Lipscomb University offers a core academic program; more than half of graduate courses are open to undergraduates. It awards bachelor's and master's **degrees**. Challenging opportunities include advanced placement, accelerated degree programs, self-designed majors, tutorials, an honors program, and a senior project. Special programs include internships, summer session for credit, study abroad, and Army and Air Force ROTC.

The most popular **majors** include business, (pre)medicine sequence, and education. A complete listing of majors at Lipscomb University appears in the Majors Index beginning on page 379.

The **faculty** at Lipscomb University has 101 full-time undergraduate teachers, 83% with terminal degrees. 100% of the faculty serve as student advisers. The student-faculty ratio is 16:1.

Computers on Campus

Students are not required to have a computer. Student rooms are linked to a campus network. 280 **computers**

available in the computer center, computer labs, the learning resource center, classrooms, the library, and dormitories provide access to the main academic computer, off-campus computing facilities, e-mail, on-line services, and the Internet. Staffed computer lab on campus provides training in the use of computers and software.

The 2 **libraries** have 196,391 books and 904 subscriptions.

Campus Life

There are 50 active **organizations** on campus, including a drama/theater group and student-run newspaper and radio station. 19% of eligible men and 17% of eligible women are members of 7 local **fraternities** and 8 local **sororities**. Student **safety services** include late night transport/escort service, 24-hour emergency telephone alarm devices, 24-hour patrols by trained security personnel, and electronically operated dormitory entrances.

Lipscomb University is a member of the NAIA. **Intercollegiate sports** (some offering scholarships) include baseball (m), basketball (m, w), cross-country running (m, w), golf (m), soccer (m), softball (w), tennis (m, w), volleyball (w).

Applying

Lipscomb University requires a high school transcript, 3 years of high school math and science, 2 years of high school foreign language, 2 recommendations, SAT I or ACT, and a minimum high school GPA of 2.0. It recommends an essay and an interview. Early and midyear entrance are possible, with rolling admissions and continuous processing to 2/28 for financial aid. **Contact:** Mrs. Cyndi Butler, Director of Admissions, 3901 Granny White Pike, Nashville, TN 37204-3951, 615-269-1000 ext. 1776 or toll-free 800-333-4358; fax 615-269-1804.

GETTING IN LAST YEAR
1,348 applied
89% were accepted
49% enrolled (584)
38% from top tenth of their h.s. class
3.2 average high school GPA
26% had SAT verbal scores over 600
13% had SAT math scores over 600
30% had ACT scores over 26
7% had SAT verbal scores over 700
1% had SAT math scores over 700
10% had ACT scores over 30
3 National Merit Scholars

THE STUDENT BODY
Total 2,505, of whom 2,408
    are undergraduates
From 43 states and territories,
    22 other countries
61% from Tennessee
55% women, 45% men
4% African Americans
2% Hispanics
2% Asian Americans
2% international students

AFTER FRESHMAN YEAR
70% returned for sophomore year

30% got a degree within 4 years
42% got a degree within 5 years
50% got a degree within 6 years

WHAT YOU WILL PAY
Tuition and fees $7305
Room and board $3450
Need-based college-administered scholarships and
    grants average $1041 per award
Non-need college-administered scholarships and
    grants average $1750 per award

DAVIDSON COLLEGE

Davidson, North Carolina • Small-town setting • Private • Independent-Religious • Coed

Davidson College is one of the nation's premier academic institutions, a college of the liberal arts and sciences respected for its intellectual vigor, the high quality of its faculty and students, and the achievements of its alumni. It is distinguished by its strong honor system, close interaction between professors and students, an environment that encourages both intellectual growth and community service, and a commitment to international education. Davidson places great value on student participation in extracurricular activities, intercollegiate athletics, and intramural sports. Nearby Charlotte, North Carolina, offers students the cultural, international, and internship opportunities of a major metropolitan center.

Academics

Davidson College offers a core academic program. It awards bachelor's **degrees**. Challenging opportunities include advanced placement, self-designed majors, tutorials, an honors program, a senior project, and Phi Beta Kappa. Special programs include off-campus study, study abroad, and Army and Air Force ROTC.

The most popular **majors** include history, English, and psychology. A complete listing of majors at Davidson College appears in the Majors Index beginning on page 379.

The **faculty** at Davidson College has 137 full-time teachers, 98% with terminal degrees. 100% of the faculty serve as student advisers. The student-faculty ratio is 12:1.

Computers on Campus

Students are not required to have a computer. 130 **computers** available in the computer center, computer labs, the research center, academic buildings, classrooms, and the library provide access to the main academic computer, off-campus computing facilities, e-mail, and the Internet.

Staffed computer lab on campus provides training in the use of computers and software.

The 2 **libraries** have 448,759 books, 65,183 microform titles, and 2,679 subscriptions. They are connected to 2 national **on-line** catalogs.

Campus Life

There are 100 active **organizations** on campus, including a drama/theater group and student-run newspaper and radio station. 55% of eligible men and 65% of eligible women are members of 7 national **fraternities** and 3 women's eating houses. Student **safety services** include late night transport/escort service, 24-hour emergency telephone alarm devices, 24-hour patrols by trained security personnel, and electronically operated dormitory entrances.

Davidson College is a member of the NCAA (Division I). **Intercollegiate sports** (some offering scholarships) include baseball (m), basketball (m, w), crew (m, w), cross-country running (m, w), fencing (m, w), field hockey (w), football (m), golf (m), lacrosse (m, w), rugby (m), sailing (m, w), soccer (m, w), swimming and diving (m, w), tennis (m, w), track and field (m, w), volleyball (m, w), water polo (m, w), wrestling (m).

Applying

Davidson College requires an essay, a high school transcript, 3 years of high school math, 2 years of high school foreign language, 4 recommendations, and SAT I or ACT. It recommends 3 years of high school science, a campus interview, and 3 SAT II Subject Tests (including SAT II: Writing Test). Early and deferred entrance are possible, with a 1/15 deadline and 2/15 for financial aid. **Contact:** Dr. Nancy Cable, Dean of Admission and Financial Aid, 405 North Main Street, Davidson, NC 28036-1719, 704-892-2231 or toll-free 800-768-0380; fax 704-892-2016.

GETTING IN LAST YEAR

3,061 applied
36% were accepted
38% enrolled (429)
76% from top tenth of their h.s. class
55% had SAT verbal scores over 600
87% had SAT math scores over 600
100% had ACT scores over 26
8% had SAT verbal scores over 700
33% had SAT math scores over 700
66% had ACT scores over 30
30 National Merit Scholars
57 valedictorians

THE STUDENT BODY

1,616 undergraduates

From 45 states and territories, 34 other countries
21% from North Carolina
48% women, 52% men
4% African Americans
1% Native Americans
2% Hispanics
3% Asian Americans
3% international students

AFTER FRESHMAN YEAR

98% returned for sophomore year
85% got a degree within 4 years
90% got a degree within 5 years
91% got a degree within 6 years

AFTER GRADUATION

43% pursued further study (20% arts and sciences, 11% medicine, 5% business)
1 Rhodes, 3 Fulbright scholars

WHAT YOU WILL PAY

Tuition and fees $18,626
Room and board $5364
33% receive need-based financial aid
Need-based college-administered scholarships and grants average $9623 per award
30% receive non-need financial aid
Non-need college-administered scholarships and grants average $6680 per award

DEEP SPRINGS COLLEGE

Deep Springs, California • Rural setting • Private • Independent • Men

Founded in 1917, Deep Springs College lies in an isolated desert valley of California, 1 hour from the nearest town. Its enrollment is limited to 26 students, each of whom receives a full scholarship, valued at $38,092, covering tuition, room, and board. The students, whose SAT I scores average over 1450, engage in a rigorous academic program, govern themselves (including admissions and curriculum decisions), and participate in the operation of the school-owned cattle and organic alfalfa ranch. After 2 or 3 years, they transfer to other schools, often Brown, Cornell, Harvard, or Stanford, to complete their studies.

Academics

DS offers a liberal arts and sciences curriculum and no core academic program. It awards associate **degrees**. Challenging opportunities include tutorials and an honors program. Special programs include summer session for credit and study abroad.

The **faculty** at DS has 4 full-time teachers, 100% with terminal degrees. 100% of the faculty serve as student advisers. The student-faculty ratio is 4:1.

Computers on Campus

Students are not required to have a computer. 6 **computers** available in the library.

The **library** has 25,000 books and 60 subscriptions.

Campus Life

Active **organizations** on campus include drama/theater group and student-run radio station.

This institution has no intercollegiate sports.

Applying

DS requires an essay, a high school transcript, 2 years of high school foreign language, a campus interview, SAT I, and 2 SAT II Subject Tests. Early entrance is possible, with an 11/15 deadline. **Contact:** Dr. L. Jackson Newell, President, HC 72, Box 45001, Dyer, NV 89010-9803, 619-872-2000.

GETTING IN LAST YEAR
220 applied
8% were accepted
76% enrolled (13)
100% from top tenth of their h.s. class

THE STUDENT BODY
25 undergraduates
From 17 states and territories,
 0 other countries
3% from California
100% men
0% African Americans

0% Native Americans
0% Hispanics
0% Asian Americans
0% international students

WHAT YOU WILL PAY
Comprehensive fee $0

DENISON UNIVERSITY

Granville, Ohio • Small-town setting • Private • Independent • Coed

Denison University, a 4-year, highly selective, national, residential liberal arts college for men and women, located in Granville, Ohio, is known for its curricular innovation and unique faculty/student learning partnerships. Its approximately 2,000 students come from 44 states and 31 other countries. They are intrigued by the opportunity to study such subjects as economics and mathematics in computer laboratories, to choose from 1 of the 39 academic majors and 9 preprofessional programs available, or to design their own program of study while living on the beautiful 1,200-acre hillside campus. Founded in 1831, Denison has 23,000 alumni and has recently completed a resoundingly successful $79-million capital campaign.

Academics

Denison offers a core academic program. It awards bachelor's **degrees.** Challenging opportunities include advanced placement, self-designed majors, tutorials, an honors program, a senior project, Phi Beta Kappa, and Sigma Xi. Special programs include internships, off-campus study, and study abroad.

The most popular **majors** include English, economics, and psychology. A complete listing of majors at Denison appears in the Majors Index beginning on page 379.

The **faculty** at Denison has 150 full-time teachers, 97% with terminal degrees. 98% of the faculty serve as student advisers. The student-faculty ratio is 11:1, and the average class size in core courses is 18.

Computers on Campus

Students are not required to have a computer. Student rooms are linked to a campus network. 160 **computers** available in the computer center, computer labs, the learning resource center, all academic departments, the library, and dormitories provide access to the main academic computer, e-mail, on-line services, and the Internet.

The **library** has 316,887 books, 67,199 microform titles, and 1,213 subscriptions.

Campus Life

There are 118 active **organizations** on campus, including a drama/theater group and student-run newspaper and radio station. 32% of eligible men and 42% of eligible women are members of 10 national **fraternities** and 8 national **sororities.** Student **safety services** include late night transport/escort service, 24-hour emergency telephone alarm devices, 24-hour patrols by trained security personnel, and electronically operated dormitory entrances.

Denison is a member of the NCAA (Division III). **Intercollegiate sports** include baseball (m), basketball (m, w), crew (m), cross-country running (m, w), equestrian sports (m, w), field hockey (w), football (m), golf (m), ice hockey (m), lacrosse (m, w), riflery (m, w), rugby (m, w), sailing (m, w), skiing (downhill) (m, w), soccer (m, w), softball (w), squash (m, w), swimming and diving (m, w), tennis (m, w), track and field (m, w), volleyball (w).

Applying

Denison requires an essay, a high school transcript, 2 recommendations, and SAT I or ACT. It recommends 3 years of high school math and science, 3 years of high school foreign language, an interview, and SAT II Subject Tests. Early and deferred entrance are possible, with a 2/1 deadline and a 3/1 priority date for financial aid. **Contact:** Mr. Perry Robinson, Director of Admissions, Box H, Granville, OH 43023, 614-587-6627 or toll-free 800-DENISON.

GETTING IN LAST YEAR
2,604 applied
84% were accepted
32% enrolled (701)
39% from top tenth of their h.s. class
15% had SAT verbal scores over 600
40% had SAT math scores over 600
50% had ACT scores over 26
2% had SAT verbal scores over 700
8% had SAT math scores over 700
15% had ACT scores over 30
16 National Merit Scholars
62 valedictorians

THE STUDENT BODY
1,995 undergraduates

From 44 states and territories,
   31 other countries
40% from Ohio
53% women, 47% men
4% African Americans
0% Native Americans
2% Hispanics
3% Asian Americans
3% international students

AFTER FRESHMAN YEAR
82% returned for sophomore year
75% got a degree within 4 years
77% got a degree within 5 years
78% got a degree within 6 years

AFTER GRADUATION
16% pursued further study (8% arts and
   sciences, 4% medicine, 3% law)
72% had job offers within 6 months
59 organizations recruited on campus
1 Fulbright scholar

WHAT YOU WILL PAY
Tuition and fees $18,630
Room and board $4940
44% receive need-based financial aid
Need-based college-administered scholarships and
   grants average $11,459 per award
29% receive non-need financial aid
Non-need college-administered scholarships and
   grants average $7993 per award

DEPAUL UNIVERSITY

Chicago, Illinois • Urban setting • Private • Independent-Religious • Coed

DePaul is an urban university offering over 100 undergraduate and graduate programs. A private Catholic institution founded by the Vincentian order in 1898, today DePaul reflects a wide diversity of ethnic, religious, and economic backgrounds. DePaul students study in a great city with unlimited opportunities for professional experience before graduation. Students are active participants in projects and organizations working to meet the needs of the city. DePaul continues to emphasize teaching ability as a priority for faculty selection.

 ## Academics

DePaul offers an interdisciplinary curriculum and core academic program; fewer than half of graduate courses are open to undergraduates. It awards bachelor's, master's, doctoral, and first professional **degrees**. Challenging opportunities include advanced placement, accelerated degree programs, self-designed majors, tutorials, Freshman Honors College, an honors program, and a senior project. Special programs include internships, summer session for credit, study abroad, and Army ROTC.

The most popular **majors** include accounting, finance/banking, and communication. A complete listing of majors at DePaul appears in the Majors Index beginning on page 379.

The **faculty** at DePaul has 514 full-time graduate and undergraduate teachers, 88% with terminal degrees. 89% of the faculty serve as student advisers. The student-faculty ratio is 13:1.

 ## Computers on Campus

Students are not required to have a computer. Student rooms are linked to a campus network. 850 **computers** available in the computer center, labs throughout the four campuses, classrooms, the library, the student center, and dormitories provide access to the main academic computer, e-mail, on-line services, and the Internet. Staffed computer lab on campus provides training in the use of computers and software.

The 4 **libraries** have 684,064 books, 303,132 microform titles, and 16,979 subscriptions. They are connected to 10 national **on-line** catalogs.

 ## Campus Life

There are 120 active **organizations** on campus, including a drama/theater group and student-run newspaper and radio station. 10% of students participate in student government elections. 3% of eligible men and 3% of eligible women are members of 3 national **fraternities** and 2 national **sororities**. Student **safety services** include late night transport/escort service, 24-hour emergency telephone alarm devices, 24-hour patrols by trained security personnel, and electronically operated dormitory entrances.

DePaul is a member of the NCAA (Division I). **Intercollegiate sports** (some offering scholarships) include basketball (m, w), cross-country running (m, w), golf (m, w), riflery (m, w), soccer (m, w), softball (w), tennis (m, w), track and field (m, w), volleyball (w).

 ## Applying

DePaul requires a high school transcript, 1 recommendation, SAT I or ACT, a minimum high school GPA of 2.0, and in some cases an interview, audition, and a minimum high school GPA of 3.0. It recommends 3 years of high school math and science, 2 years of high school foreign language, SAT II Subject Tests, and a minimum high school GPA of 3.0. Early, deferred, and midyear entrance are possible, with an 8/15 deadline and continuous processing to 4/1 for financial aid. **Contact:** Ms. Ellen Cohen, Director of Undergraduate Admission, 1 East Jackson Boulevard, Chicago, IL 60604-2287, 312-362-8300 or toll-free 800-4DE-PAUL (out-of-state); fax 312-362-5322.

GETTING IN LAST YEAR
5,273 applied
71% were accepted
34% enrolled (1,265)
30% from top tenth of their h.s. class
3.4 average high school GPA
14% had SAT verbal scores over 600
32% had SAT math scores over 600
32% had ACT scores over 26
1% had SAT verbal scores over 700
6% had SAT math scores over 700
7% had ACT scores over 30
39 National Merit Scholars
21 valedictorians

THE STUDENT BODY
Total 17,133, of whom 10,450
    are undergraduates
From 50 states and territories,
    74 other countries
75% from Illinois
59% women, 41% men
12% African Americans
1% Native Americans
11% Hispanics
6% Asian Americans
1% international students

AFTER FRESHMAN YEAR
86% returned for sophomore year

AFTER GRADUATION
1,000 organizations recruited on campus
1 Fulbright scholar

WHAT YOU WILL PAY
Tuition and fees $11,886
Room and board $5200
Need-based college-administered scholarships and
    grants average $3750 per award
Non-need college-administered scholarships and
    grants average $4900 per award

DEPAUW UNIVERSITY

Greencastle, Indiana • Small-town setting • Private • Independent-Religious • Coed

DePauw University provides a traditional liberal arts education complemented by one of the largest internship programs in the nation. There are extensive internship opportunities in business, science, and news media as well as in professional and not-for-profit organizations nationally and internationally. Honors programs are offered in classics, management, media, and science. DePauw offers large university facilities but small classes. Ample opportunities are available for students to personalize education and engage in collaborative research with professors. There are extensive opportunities for international study. More than half of DePauw's students volunteer for community service locally, nationally, and internationally each year.

Academics

DePauw offers a liberal arts curriculum and core academic program. It awards bachelor's **degrees**. Challenging opportunities include advanced placement, self-designed majors, tutorials, an honors program, a senior project, Phi Beta Kappa, and Sigma Xi. Special programs include internships, off-campus study, study abroad, and Army and Air Force ROTC.

The most popular **majors** include communication, creative writing, and political science/government. A complete listing of majors at DePauw appears in the Majors Index beginning on page 379.

The **faculty** at DePauw has 152 full-time teachers, 91% with terminal degrees. 92% of the faculty serve as student advisers. The student-faculty ratio is 12:1.

Computers on Campus

Students are not required to have a computer. 212 **computers** available in the computer center, computer labs, the learning resource center, the library, and dormitories provide access to the main academic computer, e-mail, on-line services, and the Internet. Staffed computer lab on campus provides training in the use of computers and software.

The 3 **libraries** have 281,685 books, 37,841 microform titles, and 1,228 subscriptions. They are connected to 4 national **on-line** catalogs.

Campus Life

There are 65 active **organizations** on campus, including a drama/theater group and student-run newspaper and radio station. 78% of eligible men and 72% of eligible women are members of 15 national **fraternities**, 9 national **sororities**, and 2 local sororities. Student **safety services** include late night transport/escort service, 24-hour emergency telephone alarm devices, and 24-hour patrols by trained security personnel.

DePauw is a member of the NCAA (Division III). **Intercollegiate sports** include baseball (m), basketball (m, w), crew (m, w), cross-country running (m, w), fencing (m, w), field hockey (w), football (m), golf (m, w), rugby (m, w), sailing (m, w), soccer (m, w), softball (w), swimming and diving (m, w), tennis (m, w), track and field (m, w), volleyball (w).

Applying

DePauw requires an essay, a high school transcript, 3 years of high school math and science, 1 recommendation, and SAT I or ACT. It recommends 2 years of high school foreign language, a campus interview, and a minimum high school GPA of 3.0. Early, deferred, and midyear entrance are possible, with a 2/15 deadline and continuous processing to 2/15 for financial aid. **Contact:** Mr. David Murray, Dean of Admissions and Associate Provost, 101 East Seminary Street, Greencastle, IN 46135-1772, 317-658-4006 or toll-free 800-447-2495; fax 317-658-4007.

GETTING IN LAST YEAR
2,234 applied
81% were accepted
32% enrolled (580)
47% from top tenth of their h.s. class
31% had SAT verbal scores over 600
64% had SAT math scores over 600
43% had ACT scores over 26
2% had SAT verbal scores over 700
20% had SAT math scores over 700
9% had ACT scores over 30
6 National Merit Scholars
36 valedictorians

THE STUDENT BODY
2,082 undergraduates

From 47 states and territories, 15 other countries
42% from Indiana
55% women, 45% men
7% African Americans
1% Native Americans
4% Hispanics
2% Asian Americans
2% international students

AFTER FRESHMAN YEAR
90% returned for sophomore year
72% got a degree within 4 years
77% got a degree within 5 years

AFTER GRADUATION
27% pursued further study (12% arts and sciences, 6% law, 4% medicine)
84% had job offers within 6 months
50 organizations recruited on campus

WHAT YOU WILL PAY
Tuition and fees $15,475
Room and board $5245
51% receive need-based financial aid
Need-based college-administered scholarships and grants average $8511 per award
30% receive non-need financial aid
Non-need college-administered scholarships and grants average $5676 per award

DICKINSON COLLEGE

Carlisle, Pennsylvania • Suburban setting • Private • Independent • Coed

A commitment to international education pervades Dickinson's liberal arts program. Its nationally recognized international study centers in Europe, Africa, and Asia and its related on-campus choices foster astute international understanding and open attractive career opportunities in the rapidly evolving global community. Dickinson has pioneered in developing innovative "hands-on" introductory physics, chemistry, and mathematics courses taught in a workshop format. It also has an established and distinguished reputation for sending students on into business, the law, and medicine; 83% of its alumni are in these fields.

Academics

Dickinson offers a liberal arts curriculum with international education thrust and core academic program. It awards bachelor's **degrees**. Challenging opportunities include advanced placement, accelerated degree programs, self-designed majors, tutorials, a senior project, and Phi Beta Kappa. Special programs include internships, summer session for credit, off-campus study, study abroad, and Army ROTC.

The most popular **majors** include political science/government, English, and history. A complete listing of majors at Dickinson appears in the Majors Index beginning on page 379.

The **faculty** at Dickinson has 183 teachers, 99% with terminal degrees. 100% of the faculty serve as student advisers. The student-faculty ratio is 10:1, and the average class size in core courses is 18.

Computers on Campus

Students are not required to have a computer. Student rooms are linked to a campus network. 295 **computers** available in the computer center, computer labs, classrooms, the library, the student center, and dormitories provide access to the main academic computer, off-campus computing facilities, e-mail, on-line services, and the Internet. Staffed computer lab on campus (open 24 hours a day) provides training in the use of computers and software.

The **library** has 421,710 books, 163,998 microform titles, and 1,735 subscriptions. It is connected to 18 national **on-line** catalogs.

Campus Life

There are 122 active **organizations** on campus, including a drama/theater group and student-run newspaper and radio station. 35% of eligible men and 35% of eligible women are members of 8 national **fraternities**, 4 national **sororities**, 1 local fraternity, and 1 local sorority. Student **safety services** include late night transport/escort service, 24-hour emergency telephone alarm devices, 24-hour patrols by trained security personnel, student patrols, and electronically operated dormitory entrances.

Dickinson is a member of the NCAA (Division III). **Intercollegiate sports** include baseball (m), basketball (m, w), cross-country running (m, w), equestrian sports (m, w), fencing (m, w), field hockey (w), football (m), golf (m), ice hockey (m), lacrosse (m, w), skiing (downhill) (m, w), soccer (m, w), softball (w), squash (m, w), swimming and diving (m, w), tennis (m, w), track and field (m, w), volleyball (m, w), wrestling (m).

Applying

Dickinson requires an essay, a high school transcript, 3 years of high school math and science, 2 years of high school foreign language, and 2 recommendations. It recommends an interview. Early, deferred, and midyear entrance are possible, with a 2/15 deadline and a 2/15 priority date for financial aid. **Contact:** Mr. R. Russell Shunk, Dean of Admissions, PO Box 1773, Carlisle, PA 17013-2896, 717-245-1231.

GETTING IN LAST YEAR
2,920 applied
84% were accepted
22% enrolled (529)
27% from top tenth of their h.s. class
55% had SAT verbal scores over 600 (R)
42% had SAT math scores over 600 (R)
6% had SAT verbal scores over 700 (R)
7% had SAT math scores over 700 (R)
17 class presidents
9 valedictorians

THE STUDENT BODY
1,840 undergraduates
From 44 states and territories,
   31 other countries

42% from Pennsylvania
57% women, 43% men
1% African Americans
0% Native Americans
2% Hispanics
3% Asian Americans
3% international students

AFTER FRESHMAN YEAR
88% returned for sophomore year
83% got a degree within 4 years
85% got a degree within 5 years
86% got a degree within 6 years

AFTER GRADUATION
12% pursued further study (7% arts and
   sciences, 2% law, 2% medicine)

97% had job offers within 6 months
33 organizations recruited on campus

WHAT YOU WILL PAY
Tuition and fees $19,750
Room and board $5270
70% receive need-based financial aid
Need-based college-administered scholarships and
   grants average $10,517 per award
Non-need college-administered scholarships and
   grants average $484 per award

DRAKE UNIVERSITY

Des Moines, Iowa • Suburban setting • Private • Independent • Coed

Drake University offers students the best of both worlds: a sound liberal arts education complemented by professional and preprofessional programs. Drake's faculty members are dedicated to teaching. From their first introductory classes through the most advanced classes in their majors, students are taught by full-time faculty members who are master teachers. Drake University is a national leader in the use of computers and educational technology. Every residence hall room is equipped with a Power Mac computer, a printer, and software. Students can retrieve library information and access national and international information networks, such as the Internet, from their residence hall rooms.

Academics

Drake offers a liberal arts curriculum with professional and pre-professional programs and no core academic program; all graduate courses are open to undergraduates. It awards bachelor's, master's, doctoral, and first professional **degrees**. Challenging opportunities include advanced placement, accelerated degree programs, self-designed majors, an honors program, a senior project, and Phi Beta Kappa. Special programs include cooperative education, internships, summer session for credit, off-campus study, study abroad, and Army and Air Force ROTC.

The most popular **majors** include pharmacy/pharmaceutical sciences, advertising, and marketing/retailing/merchandising. A complete listing of majors at Drake appears in the Majors Index beginning on page 379.

The **faculty** at Drake has 270 full-time undergraduate teachers, 92% with terminal degrees. 100% of the faculty serve as student advisers. The student-faculty ratio is 17:1.

Computers on Campus

Students are not required to have a computer. Student rooms are linked to a campus network. 1,081 **computers** available in the computer center, computer labs, academic buildings, classrooms, the library, the student center, dormitories, and student rooms provide access to the main academic computer, e-mail, on-line services, and the Internet. Staffed computer lab on campus (open 24 hours a day).

The 2 **libraries** have 729,000 books and 5,166 subscriptions. They are connected to 1 national **on-line** catalog.

Campus Life

There are 137 active **organizations** on campus, including a drama/theater group and student-run newspaper and radio station. 35% of students participate in student government elections. 34% of eligible men and 30% of eligible women are members of 11 national **fraternities** and 10 national **sororities**. Student **safety services** include 24-hour desk attendants in residences, ID checked in residence after 11 pm, late night transport/escort service, 24-hour emergency telephone alarm devices, and 24-hour patrols by trained security personnel.

Drake is a member of the NCAA (Division I). **Intercollegiate sports** (some offering scholarships) include baseball (m), basketball (m, w), crew (m, w), cross-country running (m, w), football (m), golf (m), ice hockey (m), lacrosse (m), rugby (m), soccer (m, w), softball (w), tennis (m, w), track and field (m, w), volleyball (m, w).

Applying

Drake requires a high school transcript, recommendations, SAT I or ACT, a minimum high school GPA of 2.0, and in some cases 3 years of high school math and science. It recommends an essay, 2 years of high school foreign language, and an interview. Early, deferred, and midyear entrance are possible, with rolling admissions and continuous processing to 3/1 for financial aid. **Contact:** Mr. Thomas F. Willoughby, Dean of Admission, 2507 University Avenue, Des Moines, IA 50311-4516, 515-271-3181 or toll-free 800-44 DRAKE; fax 515-271-2831.

GETTING IN LAST YEAR

2,705 applied
94% were accepted
29% enrolled (742)
35% from top tenth of their h.s. class
3.49 average high school GPA
38% had SAT verbal scores over 600 (R)
45% had SAT math scores over 600 (R)
46% had ACT scores over 26
8% had SAT verbal scores over 700 (R)
8% had SAT math scores over 700 (R)
13% had ACT scores over 30
15 National Merit Scholars
42 valedictorians

THE STUDENT BODY

Total 5,639, of whom 3,802 are undergraduates

From 40 states and territories, 50 other countries
30% from Iowa
59% women, 41% men
5% African Americans
1% Native Americans
3% Hispanics
5% Asian Americans
4% international students

AFTER FRESHMAN YEAR

80% returned for sophomore year
52% got a degree within 4 years
65% got a degree within 5 years
66% got a degree within 6 years

AFTER GRADUATION

15% pursued further study (4% arts and sciences, 4% law, 3% business)
94% had job offers within 6 months
80 organizations recruited on campus

WHAT YOU WILL PAY

Tuition and fees $14,380
Room and board $4870
67% receive need-based financial aid
Need-based college-administered scholarships and grants average $2302 per award
23% receive non-need financial aid
Non-need college-administered scholarships and grants average $4220 per award

DREW UNIVERSITY

Madison, New Jersey • Suburban setting • Private • Independent-Religious • Coed

On a forested campus 30 miles from Manhattan, Drew offers inspired teaching with an emphasis on global issues. As part of tuition, students receive personal computers, printers, and software (that they keep after graduation), and have, from their rooms, 24-hour access to electronic mail, the Internet, the campus library's automated card catalog, mainframe computer services, a telephone voice mail system, and broadband cable television. Studying in an international center for the arts, commerce, government, communications, and science, students engage in challenging internships and have an outstanding record of career and graduate/professional school placement in these fields. Off-campus and study-abroad opportunities further educate Drew students to help shape the world of the future.

Academics

Drew offers a liberal arts curriculum; more than half of graduate courses are open to undergraduates. It awards bachelor's, master's, doctoral, and first professional **degrees**. Challenging opportunities include advanced placement, self-designed majors, an honors program, a senior project, and Phi Beta Kappa. Special programs include internships, summer session for credit, off-campus study, study abroad, and Army ROTC.

The most popular **majors** include political science/government, psychology, and English. A complete listing of majors at Drew appears in the Majors Index beginning on page 379.

The **faculty** at Drew has 127 full-time graduate and undergraduate teachers, 91% with terminal degrees. 100% of the faculty serve as student advisers. The student-faculty ratio is 11:1.

Computers on Campus

Students are required to have a computer. PCs are provided. Student rooms are linked to a campus network. 2,200 **computers** available in the computer center, computer labs, the library, and dormitories provide access to the main academic computer, e-mail, on-line services, and the Internet. Staffed computer lab on campus provides training in the use of computers and software.

The **library** has 437,493 books, 294,018 microform titles, and 2,006 subscriptions. It is connected to 1 national **on-line** catalog.

Campus Life

Active **organizations** on campus include drama/theater group and student-run newspaper and radio station. Student **safety services** include late night transport/escort service, 24-hour emergency telephone alarm devices, 24-hour patrols by trained security personnel, and electronically operated dormitory entrances.

Drew is a member of the NCAA (Division III). **Intercollegiate sports** include baseball (m), basketball (m, w), cross-country running (m, w), equestrian sports (m, w), fencing (m, w), field hockey (w), lacrosse (m, w), soccer (m, w), softball (w), swimming and diving (m, w), tennis (m, w).

Applying

Drew requires an essay, a high school transcript, 2 recommendations, and SAT I or ACT. It recommends 3 years of high school math and science, 2 years of high school foreign language, an interview, and 3 SAT II Subject Tests. Early, deferred, and midyear entrance are possible, with a 2/15 deadline and 3/1 for financial aid. **Contact:** Mr. Roberto Noya, Dean of Admissions for the College of Liberal Arts, 36 Madison Avenue, Madison, NJ 07940-1493, 201-408-3739; fax 201-408-3939.

GETTING IN LAST YEAR

2,528 applied
80% were accepted
21% enrolled (433)
44% from top tenth of their h.s. class
65% had SAT verbal scores over 600 (R)
61% had SAT math scores over 600 (R)
22% had SAT verbal scores over 700 (R)
14% had SAT math scores over 700 (R)
9 National Merit Scholars

THE STUDENT BODY

Total 2,111, of whom 1,421
   are undergraduates
From 37 states and territories,
   15 other countries

57% from New Jersey
60% women, 40% men
4% African Americans
0% Native Americans
5% Hispanics
7% Asian Americans
2% international students

AFTER FRESHMAN YEAR

90% returned for sophomore year
74% got a degree within 4 years
77% got a degree within 5 years
78% got a degree within 6 years

AFTER GRADUATION

25% pursued further study (13% arts and
   sciences, 8% law, 2% medicine)

WHAT YOU WILL PAY

Tuition and fees $19,638
Room and board $5833
55% receive need-based financial aid
Need-based college-administered scholarships and
   grants average $6200 per award
48% receive non-need financial aid
Non-need college-administered scholarships and
   grants average $8100 per award

DRURY COLLEGE

Springfield, Missouri • Urban setting • Private • Independent • Coed

Preparation for the future is an advantage Drury graduates have. Students learn from full-time faculty in small-class settings with a university curriculum. Science students are co-researchers with professors, communication majors learn in the regional PBS affiliate located on campus, and architecture students are part of a national model for combining liberal arts and architecture. The Drury experience works: nearly 96% of graduates are employed or select from more than one graduate school in which to continue their education. The Drury liberal arts education helps students achieve their goals.

 ## Academics

Drury offers a global studies curriculum and core academic program; a few graduate courses are open to undergraduates. It awards bachelor's and master's **degrees**. Challenging opportunities include advanced placement, accelerated degree programs, tutorials, Freshman Honors College, an honors program, and a senior project. Special programs include internships, summer session for credit, off-campus study, study abroad, and Army ROTC.

The most popular **majors** include business, communication, and behavioral sciences. A complete listing of majors at Drury appears in the Majors Index beginning on page 379.

The **faculty** at Drury has 93 full-time undergraduate teachers, 97% with terminal degrees. 75% of the faculty serve as student advisers. The student-faculty ratio is 13:1.

 ## Computers on Campus

Students are not required to have a computer. Student rooms are linked to a campus network. 95 **computers** available in the computer center, computer labs, the research center, the learning resource center, academic departments, classrooms, the library, and the student center provide access to the main academic computer, off-campus computing facilities, e-mail, on-line services, and the Internet. Staffed computer lab on campus provides training in the use of computers and software.

The 2 **libraries** have 237,065 books, 95,935 microform titles, and 793 subscriptions.

 ## Campus Life

There are 48 active **organizations** on campus, including a drama/theater group and student-run newspaper and radio station. 25% of students participate in student government elections. 40% of eligible men and 40% of eligible women are members of 4 national **fraternities** and 4 national **sororities**. Student **safety services** include late night transport/escort service, 24-hour emergency telephone alarm devices, 24-hour patrols by trained security personnel, student patrols, and electronically operated dormitory entrances.

Drury is a member of the NCAA (Division II). **Intercollegiate sports** (some offering scholarships) include basketball (m), golf (m), soccer (m, w), swimming and diving (m, w), tennis (m, w), volleyball (w).

 ## Applying

Drury requires an essay, a high school transcript, 1 recommendation, and SAT I or ACT. It recommends 3 years of high school math and science, 1 year of high school foreign language, and a campus interview. Early and deferred entrance are possible, with rolling admissions and continuous processing to 2/15 for financial aid. **Contact:** Mr. Michael Thomas, Director of Admissions, Burnham Hall, Springfield, MO 65802-3791, 417-873-7205 or toll-free 800-922-2274 (in-state); fax 417-873-7529.

GETTING IN LAST YEAR
920 applied
93% were accepted
44% enrolled (377)
33% from top tenth of their h.s. class
3.4 average high school GPA
41% had ACT scores over 26
17% had ACT scores over 30
5 National Merit Scholars

THE STUDENT BODY
Total 1,600, of whom 1,221
    are undergraduates
From 31 states and territories,
    32 other countries

81% from Missouri
53% women, 47% men
1% African Americans
0% Native Americans
1% Hispanics
1% Asian Americans
4% international students

AFTER FRESHMAN YEAR
80% returned for sophomore year
40% got a degree within 4 years
56% got a degree within 5 years

AFTER GRADUATION
22% pursued further study (8% arts and
    sciences, 4% medicine, 3% business)
1,000 organizations recruited on campus

WHAT YOU WILL PAY
Tuition and fees $9391
Room and board $3696
Need-based college-administered scholarships and
    grants average $2500 per award
Non-need college-administered scholarships and
    grants average $3500 per award

DUKE UNIVERSITY

Durham, North Carolina • Suburban setting • Private • Independent-Religious • Coed

 Academics

Duke offers a core academic program. It awards bachelor's, master's, doctoral, and first professional **degrees**. Challenging opportunities include advanced placement, accelerated degree programs, self-designed majors, tutorials, an honors program, a senior project, Phi Beta Kappa, and Sigma Xi. Special programs include internships, summer session for credit, off-campus study, study abroad, and Army, Naval, and Air Force ROTC.

The most popular **majors** include biology/biological sciences, history, and political science/government. A complete listing of majors at Duke appears in the Majors Index beginning on page 379.

The **faculty** at Duke has 2,053 full-time graduate and undergraduate teachers, 97% with terminal degrees. The student-faculty ratio is 10:1.

 Computers on Campus

Students are not required to have a computer. Student rooms are linked to a campus network. 600 **computers** available in the computer center, computer labs, academic buildings, classrooms, the library, and dormitories provide access to the main academic computer, e-mail, on-line services, and the Internet. Staffed computer lab on campus (open 24 hours a day) provides training in the use of computers and software.

The 11 **libraries** have 4.4 million books and 33,405 subscriptions.

 Campus Life

There are 350 active **organizations** on campus, including a drama/theater group and student-run newspaper and radio station. 29% of eligible men and 42% of eligible women are members of 21 national **fraternities** and 13 national **sororities**. Student **safety services** include late night transport/escort service, 24-hour emergency telephone alarm devices, 24-hour patrols by trained security personnel, and electronically operated dormitory entrances.

Duke is a member of the NCAA (Division I). **Intercollegiate sports** (some offering scholarships) include badminton (m, w), baseball (m), basketball (m, w), crew (m, w), cross-country running (m, w), equestrian sports (m, w), fencing (m, w), field hockey (m, w), football (m, w), golf (m, w), ice hockey (m, w), lacrosse (m, w), racquetball (m, w), rugby (m, w), sailing (m, w), skiing (cross-country) (m, w), skiing (downhill) (m, w), soccer (m, w), softball (m, w), swimming and diving (m, w), tennis (m, w), track and field (m, w), volleyball (m, w), water polo (m, w), wrestling (m).

 Applying

Duke requires an essay, a high school transcript, 3 recommendations, SAT I or ACT, SAT II: Writing Test, and in some cases 3 SAT II Subject Tests. It recommends 3 years of high school math and science, 3 years of high school foreign language, an interview, audition tape for applicants with outstanding dance, dramatic, or musical talent, slides of artwork, and a minimum high school GPA of 3.0. Early, deferred, and midyear entrance are possible, with a 1/2 deadline and a 2/1 priority date for financial aid. **Contact:** Mr. Christoph Guttentag, Director of Admissions, 2138 Campus Drive, Durham, NC 27708-0586, 919-684-3214; fax 919-681-8941.

GETTING IN LAST YEAR
14,442 applied
29% were accepted
40% enrolled (1,639)
87% from top tenth of their h.s. class
90% had SAT verbal scores over 600 (R)
92% had SAT math scores over 600 (R)
92% had ACT scores over 26
43% had SAT verbal scores over 700 (R)
50% had SAT math scores over 700 (R)
70% had ACT scores over 30

THE STUDENT BODY
Total 11,512, of whom 6,264 are undergraduates

From 52 states and territories,
    44 other countries
14% from North Carolina
48% women, 52% men
8% African Americans
1% Native Americans
4% Hispanics
11% Asian Americans
2% international students

AFTER FRESHMAN YEAR
96% returned for sophomore year
91% got a degree within 4 years
94% got a degree within 5 years
95% got a degree within 6 years

AFTER GRADUATION
38% pursued further study (12% medicine, 11% arts and sciences, 11% law)
200 organizations recruited on campus
2 Rhodes, 13 Fulbright scholars

WHAT YOU WILL PAY
Tuition and fees $20,004
Room and board $6320
40% receive need-based financial aid
Need-based college-administered scholarships and grants average $13,678 per award
4% receive non-need financial aid
Non-need college-administered scholarships and grants average $13,531 per award

---

EARLHAM COLLEGE

Richmond, Indiana • Small-town setting • Private • Independent-Religious • Coed

▶ Along with exceptionally strong programs in such traditional areas as literature, psychology, and premedical study, the College leads in curricular innovation and multidisciplinary offerings. As examples, Peace and Global Studies, Human Development and Social Relations, Women's Studies, Japanese Studies, and African and African-American Studies are among the many less traditional and popular majors at Earlham. Two thirds of Earlham undergraduates live and study abroad before graduation, compared to less than 1% of all college students. They choose from 20 College programs that include opportunities in Kenya, Mexico, Jerusalem, and Japan as well as in several European countries.

 ## Academics

Earlham offers a liberal arts curriculum and core academic program. It awards bachelor's **degrees**. Challenging opportunities include advanced placement, accelerated degree programs, self-designed majors, tutorials, a senior project, and Phi Beta Kappa. Special programs include internships, off-campus study, and study abroad.

The most popular **majors** include biology/biological sciences, English, and psychology. A complete listing of majors at Earlham appears in the Majors Index beginning on page 379.

The **faculty** at Earlham has 84 full-time teachers, 90% with terminal degrees. 100% of the faculty serve as student advisers. The student-faculty ratio is 12:1.

 ## Computers on Campus

Students are not required to have a computer. 115 **computers** available in the computer center, classroom buildings, and the library provide access to the main academic computer, e-mail, on-line services, and the Internet. Staffed computer lab on campus (open 24 hours a day) provides training in the use of computers and software.

The 3 **libraries** have 352,000 books, 188,000 microform titles, and 1,260 subscriptions. They are connected to 4 national **on-line** catalogs.

 ## Campus Life

There are 60 active **organizations** on campus, including a drama/theater group and student-run newspaper and radio station. 40% of students participate in student government elections. Student **safety services** include late night transport/escort service, 24-hour emergency telephone alarm devices, and 24-hour patrols by trained security personnel.

Earlham is a member of the NCAA (Division III) and NAIA. **Intercollegiate sports** include baseball (m), basketball (m, w), cross-country running (m, w), field hockey (w), football (m), lacrosse (w), soccer (m, w), tennis (m, w), track and field (m, w), volleyball (m, w).

 ## Applying

Earlham requires an essay, a high school transcript, 3 years of high school math, 2 years of high school foreign language, 2 recommendations, and SAT I or ACT. It recommends 3 years of high school science and a campus interview. Early, deferred, and midyear entrance are possible, with a 2/15 deadline and continuous processing to 3/1 for financial aid. **Contact:** Mr. Michael Oligmueller, Dean of Admissions, 801 National Road West, Richmond, IN 47374, 317-983-1600 or toll-free 800-327-5426; fax 317-983-1560.

GETTING IN LAST YEAR
1,210 applied
80% were accepted
27% enrolled (261)
37% from top tenth of their h.s. class
62% had SAT verbal scores over 600 (R)
46% had SAT math scores over 600 (R)
48% had ACT scores over 26
20% had SAT verbal scores over 700 (R)
7% had SAT math scores over 700 (R)
10% had ACT scores over 30
5 National Merit Scholars

THE STUDENT BODY
1,017 undergraduates

From 44 states and territories,
  15 other countries
22% from Indiana
56% women, 44% men
7% African Americans
1% Native Americans
1% Hispanics
4% Asian Americans
4% international students

AFTER FRESHMAN YEAR
82% returned for sophomore year
67% got a degree within 4 years
74% got a degree within 5 years
76% got a degree within 6 years

AFTER GRADUATION
36% pursued further study (25% arts and
  sciences, 5% medicine, 4% law)
73% had job offers within 6 months
45 organizations recruited on campus

WHAT YOU WILL PAY
Tuition and fees $17,160
Room and board $4305
64% receive need-based financial aid
Need-based college-administered scholarships and
  grants average $8740 per award
Non-need college-administered scholarships and
  grants average $5040 per award

ECKERD COLLEGE

St. Petersburg, Florida • Suburban setting • Private • Independent-Religious • Coed

The Eckerd campus is a peaceful, tropical setting bordering Tampa Bay and the Gulf of Mexico. Students feel very secure in the suburban environment and have easy access to the cultural, social, and recreational opportunities of the Tampa Bay metropolitan area. Classes are small. Independent study and study-abroad experiences are encouraged. Almost all students live on campus, where a sense of community flourishes. Students enjoy a great deal of freedom in their social lives and in the design of their academic programs. Volunteer service is extensive, since the Eckerd Honor Code encourages students to be "givers" rather than "takers."

 ## Academics

Eckerd offers an interdisciplinary curriculum. It awards bachelor's **degrees**. Challenging opportunities include advanced placement, accelerated degree programs, self-designed majors, tutorials, an honors program, a senior project, and Sigma Xi. Special programs include internships, summer session for credit, off-campus study, study abroad, and Army and Air Force ROTC.

The most popular **majors** include international business, marine sciences, and business. A complete listing of majors at Eckerd appears in the Majors Index beginning on page 379.

The **faculty** at Eckerd has 92 full-time teachers, 92% with terminal degrees. 100% of the faculty serve as student advisers. The student-faculty ratio is 11:1.

 ## Computers on Campus

Students are not required to have a computer. Student rooms are linked to a campus network. 350 **computers** available in the computer center, computer labs, the learning resource center, and the library provide access to the main academic computer, off-campus computing facilities, e-mail, on-line services, and the Internet. Staffed computer lab on campus provides training in the use of computers and software.

The 2 **libraries** have 122,000 books, 14,000 microform titles, and 1,000 subscriptions. They are connected to 4 national **on-line** catalogs.

 ## Campus Life

There are 70 active **organizations** on campus, including a drama/theater group and student-run newspaper and radio station. 50% of students participate in student government elections. Student **safety services** include late night transport/escort service, 24-hour emergency telephone alarm devices, 24-hour patrols by trained security personnel, student patrols, and electronically operated dormitory entrances.

Eckerd is a member of the NCAA (Division II). **Intercollegiate sports** (some offering scholarships) include baseball (m), basketball (m, w), cross-country running (w), golf (m), sailing (m, w), soccer (m, w), softball (w), swimming and diving (m, w), tennis (m, w), volleyball (m, w).

 ## Applying

Eckerd requires an essay, a high school transcript, 3 years of high school math and science, 2 years of high school foreign language, 1 recommendation, and SAT I or ACT. It recommends an interview, SAT II Subject Tests (including SAT II: Writing Test), and a minimum high school GPA of 3.0. Early, deferred, and midyear entrance are possible, with rolling admissions and continuous processing to 3/1 for financial aid. **Contact:** Dr. Richard R. Hallin, Dean of Admissions, 4200 54th Avenue, South, St. Petersburg, FL 33711, 813-864-8331 or toll-free 800-456-9009; fax 813-866-2304.

GETTING IN LAST YEAR

1,534 applied
76% were accepted
29% enrolled (335)
34% from top tenth of their h.s. class
3.20 average high school GPA
19% had SAT verbal scores over 600
37% had SAT math scores over 600
44% had ACT scores over 26
4% had SAT verbal scores over 700
6% had SAT math scores over 700
15% had ACT scores over 30
9 National Merit Scholars
20 class presidents
25 valedictorians

THE STUDENT BODY

1,366 undergraduates

From 49 states and territories, 55 other countries
30% from Florida
52% women, 48% men
3% African Americans
1% Native Americans
4% Hispanics
2% Asian Americans
11% international students

AFTER FRESHMAN YEAR

75% returned for sophomore year
53% got a degree within 4 years
60% got a degree within 5 years
62% got a degree within 6 years

AFTER GRADUATION

45% pursued further study (16% arts and sciences, 15% business, 6% law)
45% had job offers within 6 months
175 organizations recruited on campus
1 Fulbright scholar

WHAT YOU WILL PAY

Tuition and fees $16,145
Room and board $4325
58% receive need-based financial aid
Need-based college-administered scholarships and grants average $6700 per award
24% receive non-need financial aid
Non-need college-administered scholarships and grants average $6900 per award

ELIZABETHTOWN COLLEGE

Elizabethtown, Pennsylvania • Small-town setting • Private • Independent-Religious • Coed

Elizabethtown College aims to develop sound intellectual judgment, keen moral sensitivity, and an appreciation for beauty in the world. Its educational process fosters the capacity for independent thought and commitment to personal integrity. In keeping with its tradition, the College affirms the values of peace, justice, and human dignity, as it strives to achieve a distinctive blend of the liberal arts and professional studies. This union of the world of spirit and the world of work is expressed in the College motto, "Educate for Service."

Academics

E-town offers an interdisciplinary curriculum and core academic program. It awards bachelor's **degrees**. Challenging opportunities include advanced placement, accelerated degree programs, and a senior project. Special programs include internships, summer session for credit, off-campus study, and study abroad.

The most popular **majors** include business, education, and communication. A complete listing of majors at E-town appears in the Majors Index beginning on page 379.

The **faculty** at E-town has 104 full-time teachers, 70% with terminal degrees. 97% of the faculty serve as student advisers. The student-faculty ratio is 14:1.

Computers on Campus

Students are not required to have a computer. Student rooms are linked to a campus network. 80 **computers** available in computer labs, classrooms, and the library provide access to the main academic computer, off-campus computing facilities, e-mail, and the Internet. Staffed computer lab on campus provides training in the use of computers and software.

The 2 **libraries** have 185,137 books, 117,221 microform titles, and 1,100 subscriptions. They are connected to 2 national **on-line** catalogs.

Campus Life

There are 60 active **organizations** on campus, including a drama/theater group and student-run newspaper and radio station.

No national or local **fraternities** or **sororities**. Student **safety services** include self-defense workshops, crime prevention program, late night transport/escort service, 24-hour emergency telephone alarm devices, 24-hour patrols by trained security personnel, and student patrols.

E-town is a member of the NCAA (Division III). **Intercollegiate sports** include baseball (m), basketball (m, w), cross-country running (m, w), field hockey (w), golf (m), soccer (m, w), softball (w), swimming and diving (m, w), tennis (m, w), track and field (m, w), volleyball (m, w), wrestling (m).

Applying

E-town requires an essay, a high school transcript, 2 recommendations, SAT I or ACT, a minimum high school GPA of 2.0, and in some cases a campus interview. It recommends 3 years of high school math and science, 2 years of high school foreign language, a campus interview, and a minimum high school GPA of 3.0. Early, deferred, and midyear entrance are possible, with rolling admissions and continuous processing to 4/1 for financial aid. **Contact:** Mr. Ronald D. Potier, Director of Admissions, One Alpha Drive, Elizabethtown, PA 17022-2298, 717-361-1400; fax 717-361-1365.

GETTING IN LAST YEAR
2,441 applied
74% were accepted
25% enrolled (453)
39% from top tenth of their h.s. class
11% had SAT verbal scores over 600
30% had SAT math scores over 600
45% had ACT scores over 26
1% had SAT verbal scores over 700
3% had SAT math scores over 700
0% had ACT scores over 30

THE STUDENT BODY
1,753 undergraduates
From 19 states and territories,
   22 other countries

62% from Pennsylvania
65% women, 35% men
1% African Americans
0% Native Americans
1% Hispanics
2% Asian Americans
2% international students

AFTER FRESHMAN YEAR
82% returned for sophomore year
60% got a degree within 4 years
65% got a degree within 5 years
66% got a degree within 6 years

AFTER GRADUATION
15% pursued further study

77% had job offers within 6 months
37 organizations recruited on campus

WHAT YOU WILL PAY
Tuition and fees $15,490
Room and board $4550
74% receive need-based financial aid
Need-based college-administered scholarships and
   grants average $5761 per award
40% receive non-need financial aid
Non-need college-administered scholarships and
   grants average $4527 per award

EMORY UNIVERSITY

Atlanta, Georgia • Suburban setting • Private • Independent-Religious • Coed

Selection to Emory's freshman class is very competitive. Emory seeks students who have met the high standards of an academically challenging program. An extensive review of each applicant helps the Admission Committee to understand and appreciate the many facets each student presents, including not only exemplary academic performance, but also special talents, involvements, and interests. A student's demonstrated interest in attending Emory is carefully noted and factored into all admission decisions. Emory recognizes the many variations in high school grading systems and the opportunities schools provide their students.

 ## Academics

Emory offers a broad-based liberal arts curriculum and core academic program. It awards bachelor's, master's, doctoral, and first professional **degrees**. Challenging opportunities include advanced placement, accelerated degree programs, tutorials, an honors program, a senior project, Phi Beta Kappa, and Sigma Xi. Special programs include internships, summer session for credit, off-campus study, study abroad, and Naval ROTC.

The most popular **majors** include psychology, biology/biological sciences, and political science/government. A complete listing of majors at Emory appears in the Majors Index beginning on page 379.

The **faculty** at Emory has 1,986 full-time graduate and undergraduate teachers, 98% with terminal degrees. 100% of the faculty serve as student advisers. The student-faculty ratio is 10:1.

 ## Computers on Campus

Students are not required to have a computer. Student rooms are linked to a campus network. 483 **computers** available in the computer center, computer labs, the learning resource center, law school, theological school buildings, classrooms, the library, the student center, and dormitories provide access to the main academic computer, off-campus computing facilities, e-mail, on-line services, and the Internet. Staffed computer lab on campus (open 24 hours a day) provides training in the use of computers and software.

The 7 **libraries** have 2.2 million books and 23,555 subscriptions. They are connected to 27 national **on-line** catalogs.

 ## Campus Life

There are 200 active **organizations** on campus, including a drama/theater group and student-run newspaper and radio station. 33% of eligible men and 33% of eligible women are members of 12 national **fraternities** and 10 national **sororities**. Student **safety services** include late night transport/escort service, 24-hour emergency telephone alarm devices, 24-hour patrols by trained security personnel, and student patrols.

Emory is a member of the NCAA (Division III). **Intercollegiate sports** include badminton (m, w), baseball (m), basketball (m, w), bowling (m, w), crew (m, w), cross-country running (m, w), fencing (m, w), field hockey (w), golf (m), ice hockey (m), lacrosse (m), racquetball (m, w), rugby (m), sailing (m, w), soccer (m, w), swimming and diving (m, w), tennis (m, w), track and field (m, w), volleyball (m, w), wrestling (m).

 ## Applying

Emory requires an essay, a high school transcript, 3 years of high school math and science, some high school foreign language, 1 recommendation, and SAT I or ACT. It recommends SAT II Subject Tests and a minimum high school GPA of 3.0. Early and deferred entrance are possible, with a 1/15 deadline and continuous processing to 2/15 for financial aid. **Contact:** Mr. Daniel C. Walls, Dean of Admissions, Boisfeuillet Jones Center–Office of Admissions, Atlanta, GA 30322-1100, 404-727-6036 or toll-free 800-727-6036.

GETTING IN LAST YEAR
9,508 applied
51% were accepted
26% enrolled (1,250)
80% from top tenth of their h.s. class
3.7 average high school GPA
81% had SAT verbal scores over 600 (R)
83% had SAT math scores over 600 (R)
70% had ACT scores over 26
22% had SAT verbal scores over 700 (R)
24% had SAT math scores over 700 (R)
41% had ACT scores over 30
56 National Merit Scholars

THE STUDENT BODY
Total 11,308, of whom 5,200 are undergraduates

From 49 states and territories, 44 other countries
19% from Georgia
54% women, 46% men
10% African Americans
0% Native Americans
4% Hispanics
11% Asian Americans
2% international students

AFTER FRESHMAN YEAR
92% returned for sophomore year
90% got a degree within 4 years
91% got a degree within 5 years

AFTER GRADUATION
66% pursued further study (24% arts and sciences, 22% law, 18% medicine)
1 Fulbright scholar

WHAT YOU WILL PAY
Tuition and fees $19,000
Room and board $6710
46% receive need-based financial aid
Need-based college-administered scholarships and grants average $10,930 per award
15% receive non-need financial aid
Non-need college-administered scholarships and grants average $10,077 per award

EUGENE LANG COLLEGE, NEW SCHOOL FOR SOCIAL RESEARCH

New York, New York • Urban setting • Private • Independent • Coed

Eugene Lang College offers students of diverse backgrounds the opportunity to design their own program of study within one of 5 interdisciplinary concentrations in the social sciences and the humanities. Students discuss and debate issues in small seminar courses that are never larger than 15 students. They enrich their programs with internships in a wide variety of areas, such as media and publishing, community service, and education, and they can pursue a dual degree at one of the University's 5 other divisions. The Greenwich Village location makes all the cultural treasures of the city—museums, libraries, dance, music, and theater—a distinct part of the campus.

Academics

Eugene Lang College offers an interdisciplinary, multicultural curriculum and no core academic program. It awards bachelor's **degrees**. Challenging opportunities include advanced placement, accelerated degree programs, self-designed majors, tutorials, and a senior project. Special programs include internships, summer session for credit, off-campus study, and study abroad.

The most popular **majors** include creative writing, theater arts/drama, and interdisciplinary studies. A complete listing of majors at Eugene Lang College appears in the Majors Index beginning on page 379.

The **faculty** at Eugene Lang College has 15 full-time teachers, 100% with terminal degrees. 100% of the faculty serve as student advisers. The student-faculty ratio is 9:1.

Computers on Campus

Students are not required to have a computer. 249 **computers** available in the computer center, computer labs, the learning resource center, and writing center provide access to the main academic computer, e-mail, and the Internet. Staffed computer lab on campus provides training in the use of computers and software.

The 3 **libraries** have 242,000 books, 65,000 microform titles, and 1,200 subscriptions.

Campus Life

There are 10 active **organizations** on campus, including a drama/theater group and student-run newspaper. 62% of students participate in student government elections. Student **safety services** include 24-hour desk attendants in dormitories and electronically operated dormitory entrances.

This institution has no intercollegiate sports.

Applying

Eugene Lang College requires an essay, a high school transcript, 2 recommendations, an interview, SAT I or ACT or 4 SAT II Subject Tests, a minimum high school GPA of 2.0. It recommends 3 years of high school math and science, 2 years of high school foreign language, and a minimum high school GPA of 3.0. Early, deferred, and midyear entrance are possible, with a 2/1 deadline and continuous processing to 4/1 for financial aid. **Contact:** Ms. Jennifer Fondiller, Director of Admissions, 65 West 11th Street, New York, NY 10011-8601, 212-229-5665; fax 212-229-5355.

GETTING IN LAST YEAR
306 applied
74% were accepted
36% enrolled (80)
48% from top tenth of their h.s. class
3.3 average high school GPA

THE STUDENT BODY
345 undergraduates
From 28 states and territories,
   8 other countries

42% from New York
65% women, 35% men
9% African Americans
0% Native Americans
11% Hispanics
3% Asian Americans
6% international students

AFTER FRESHMAN YEAR
70% returned for sophomore year

AFTER GRADUATION
50% pursued further study
82% had job offers within 6 months

WHAT YOU WILL PAY
Tuition and fees $16,119
Room and board $8132
68% receive need-based financial aid
Need-based college-administered scholarships and
   grants average $7749 per award

FAIRFIELD UNIVERSITY

Fairfield, Connecticut • Suburban setting • Private • Independent-Religious • Coed

Founded by the Jesuits in 1942, Fairfield is a comprehensive university and a close-knit community located in southern Connecticut. The University offers challenging programs in 3 undergraduate divisions: the College of Arts and Sciences and the Schools of Business and Nursing. Faculty and students are encouraged to participate in the larger community and in programs abroad through service and academic activities. Most of all, Fairfield serves the wider community by educating its students to be socially aware and morally responsible. The well-rounded Fairfield education is complemented by extensive extracurricular activities and Division I sports. Fairfield is a member of Phi Beta Kappa. Fairfield invites prospective students to visit its campus.

Academics

Fairfield University offers an Interdisciplinary curriculum and core academic program; fewer than half of graduate courses are open to undergraduates. It awards bachelor's and master's **degrees**. Challenging opportunities include advanced placement, tutorials, Freshman Honors College, an honors program, a senior project, and Phi Beta Kappa. Special programs include internships, summer session for credit, and study abroad.

The most popular **majors** include English, biology/biological sciences, and nursing. A complete listing of majors at Fairfield University appears in the Majors Index beginning on page 379.

The **faculty** at Fairfield University has 199 full-time graduate and undergraduate teachers, 93% with terminal degrees. 90% of the faculty serve as student advisers.

Computers on Campus

Students are not required to have a computer. Student rooms are linked to a campus network. 140 **computers** available in the computer center, computer labs, classroom buildings, and the library provide access to the main academic computer, e-mail, on-line services, and the Internet. Staffed computer lab on campus provides training in the use of computers and software.

The **library** has 322,000 books, 452,000 microform titles, and 1,850 subscriptions. It is connected to 5 national **on-line** catalogs.

Campus Life

There are 100 active **organizations** on campus, including a drama/theater group and student-run newspaper and radio station. 65% of students participate in student government elections. Student **safety services** include late night transport/escort service, 24-hour emergency telephone alarm devices, 24-hour patrols by trained security personnel, and electronically operated dormitory entrances.

Fairfield University is a member of the NCAA (Division I). **Intercollegiate sports** (some offering scholarships) include baseball (m), basketball (m, w), cross-country running (m, w), field hockey (w), football (m), golf (m), ice hockey (m), lacrosse (m), soccer (m, w), softball (w), swimming and diving (m, w), tennis (m, w), volleyball (w).

Applying

Fairfield University requires a high school transcript, 3 years of high school math and science, 2 years of high school foreign language, rank in upper 40% of high school class, minimum 2.5 GPA for transfers from two-year colleges, SAT I or ACT, a minimum high school GPA of 2.0, and in some cases 4 years of high school math and science. It recommends recommendations, an interview, and SAT II Subject Tests. Early and deferred entrance are possible, with a 3/1 deadline and 2/15 for financial aid. **Contact:** Mr. David Flynn, Dean of Admission, North Benson Road, Fairfield, CT 06430-5195, 203-254-4100; fax 203-254-4199.

GETTING IN LAST YEAR
4,841 applied
71% were accepted
23% enrolled (784)
26% from top tenth of their h.s. class
2.85 average high school GPA
12% had SAT verbal scores over 600
37% had SAT math scores over 600
1% had SAT verbal scores over 700
5% had SAT math scores over 700
4 National Merit Scholars
24 class presidents

THE STUDENT BODY
Total 4,980, of whom 2,956
  are undergraduates

From 45 states and territories,
  27 other countries
32% from Connecticut
52% women, 48% men
2% African Americans
1% Native Americans
4% Hispanics
4% Asian Americans
1% international students

AFTER FRESHMAN YEAR
89% returned for sophomore year
83% got a degree within 4 years
86% got a degree within 5 years
87% got a degree within 6 years

AFTER GRADUATION
20% pursued further study (8% arts and
  sciences, 4% law, 4% medicine)
70% had job offers within 6 months
80 organizations recruited on campus
3 Fulbright scholars

WHAT YOU WILL PAY
Tuition and fees $16,340
Room and board $6600
67% receive need-based financial aid
Need-based college-administered scholarships and
  grants average $6500 per award
Non-need college-administered scholarships and
  grants average $4300 per award

FISK UNIVERSITY

Nashville, Tennessee • Urban setting • Private • Independent-Religious • Coed

Fisk University is a private coed liberal arts institution. Since its founding in 1866, Fisk has stood as a proud symbol of achievement—the first historically black college granted a chapter of Phi Beta Kappa honor society. Students are encouraged to extend themselves and to broaden their perspectives by participating in a number of academic programs, including the exchange program and the study-abroad program. The University of Ghana has been added to the list of participating institutions. New scientific facilities are under way that will provide more opportunities for students to engage in meaningful research.

 Academics

Fisk offers a core academic program. It awards bachelor's and master's **degrees**. Challenging opportunities include advanced placement, self-designed majors, an honors program, and Phi Beta Kappa. Special programs include cooperative education, internships, off-campus study, and Army and Air Force ROTC.

The most popular **majors** include business, chemistry, and psychology. A complete listing of majors at Fisk appears in the Majors Index beginning on page 379.

The **faculty** at Fisk has 71 full-time undergraduate teachers, 75% with terminal degrees. The student-faculty ratio is 10:1.

 Computers on Campus

Students are not required to have a computer. 40 **computers** available in the computer center, computer labs, and the library provide access to the main academic computer and the Internet. Staffed computer lab on campus provides training in the use of computers and software.

The **library** has 197,000 books, 5,670 microform titles, and 330 subscriptions.

 Campus Life

Active **organizations** on campus include drama/theater group and student-run newspaper and radio station. 25% of eligible men and 35% of eligible women are members of 4 national **fraternities** and 4 national **sororities**. Student **safety services** include late night transport/escort service and 24-hour patrols by trained security personnel.

Fisk is a member of the NCAA (Division III). **Intercollegiate sports** include baseball (m), basketball (m, w), cross-country running (m, w), golf (m), tennis (m, w), track and field (m, w), volleyball (w).

 Applying

Fisk requires an essay, a high school transcript, 2 recommendations, and medical history. It recommends 3 years of high school math, some high school foreign language, SAT I or ACT, and SAT II Subject Tests. Early and midyear entrance are possible, with a 6/15 deadline and continuous processing to 4/1 for financial aid. **Contact:** Mr. Harrison F. DeShields Jr., Director of Admissions and Records, 1000 17th Avenue North, Nashville, TN 37208-3051, 615-329-8665 or toll-free 800-443-FISK.

GETTING IN LAST YEAR
1,800 applied
67% were accepted
25% enrolled (300)
15% from top tenth of their h.s. class

THE STUDENT BODY
Total 900, of whom 839
    are undergraduates
From 41 states and territories,
    11 other countries

10% from Tennessee
72% women, 28% men
98% African Americans
1% Native Americans
1% Hispanics
0% Asian Americans
11% international students

AFTER GRADUATION
58% pursued further study (15% law, 15% medicine, 10% business)

WHAT YOU WILL PAY
Tuition and fees $7055
Room and board $3948
Need-based college-administered scholarships and
    grants average $2100 per award
Non-need college-administered scholarships and
    grants average $4286 per award

FLORIDA INSTITUTE OF TECHNOLOGY

Melbourne, Florida • Small-town setting • Private • Independent • Coed

Florida Tech is excited to offer 2 new innovative programs to make its highest-quality private education more affordable. The new MERIT LOAN program allows students to borrow up to $20,000 ($5000 per year) from the University for tuition and fees. If the student then graduates with highest honors (3.8 or higher GPA), the entire loan amount is forgiven. A student who graduates with a 3.5 or higher GPA (high honors) has 50% of the loan forgiven, and a student graduating with honors (3.0 or higher GPA) has 25% of his or her loan forgiven. Florida Tech also guarantees students the opportunity to graduate in 4 years.

Academics

Florida Tech offers a core academic program; fewer than half of graduate courses are open to undergraduates. It awards bachelor's, master's, and doctoral **degrees**. Challenging opportunities include advanced placement, accelerated degree programs, tutorials, a senior project, and Sigma Xi. Special programs include cooperative education, internships, summer session for credit, off-campus study, study abroad, and Army ROTC.

The most popular **majors** include biology/biological sciences, aerospace sciences, and mechanical engineering. A complete listing of majors at Florida Tech appears in the Majors Index beginning on page 379.

The **faculty** at Florida Tech has 198 full-time graduate and undergraduate teachers, 87% with terminal degrees. 100% of the faculty serve as student advisers. The student-faculty ratio is 12:1.

Computers on Campus

Students are not required to have a computer. 400 **computers** available in the computer center, computer labs, and the library provide access to the main academic computer, off-campus computing facilities, e-mail, and on-line services. Staffed computer lab on campus provides training in the use of software.

The **library** has 264,626 books, 184,285 microform titles, and 1,700 subscriptions.

Campus Life

There are 94 active **organizations** on campus, including a drama/theater group and student-run newspaper. 10% of eligible men and 12% of eligible women are members of 7 national **fraternities** and 3 national **sororities**. Student **safety services** include late night transport/escort service, 24-hour emergency telephone alarm devices, 24-hour patrols by trained security personnel, and electronically operated dormitory entrances.

Florida Tech is a member of the NCAA (Division II). **Intercollegiate sports** (some offering scholarships) include baseball (m), basketball (m, w), crew (m, w), cross-country running (m, w), fencing (m, w), riflery (m, w), sailing (m, w), soccer (m), softball (w), tennis (m, w), volleyball (m, w).

Applying

Florida Tech requires an essay, a high school transcript, 4 years of high school math, SAT I or ACT, a minimum high school GPA of 2.0, and in some cases 3 years of high school science. It recommends some high school foreign language, recommendations, an interview, and a minimum high school GPA of 3.0. Early, deferred, and midyear entrance are possible, with rolling admissions and continuous processing to 2/1 for financial aid. **Contact:** Mr. Gregg A. Meyer, Dean of Admissions, 150 West University Boulevard, Melbourne, FL 32901-6988, 407-768-8000 ext. 8030 or toll-free 800-348-4636 (in-state), 800-888-4348 (out-of-state); fax 407-723-9468.

GETTING IN LAST YEAR

1,637 applied
83% were accepted
25% enrolled (338)
36% from top tenth of their h.s. class
3.27 average high school GPA
10% had SAT verbal scores over 600 (R)
42% had SAT math scores over 600 (R)
1% had SAT verbal scores over 700 (R)
8% had SAT math scores over 700 (R)
1 National Merit Scholar

THE STUDENT BODY

Total 4,232, of whom 1,730
  are undergraduates

From 50 states and territories,
  70 other countries
28% from Florida
32% women, 68% men
4% African Americans
1% Native Americans
6% Hispanics
2% Asian Americans
22% international students

AFTER FRESHMAN YEAR

77% returned for sophomore year
32% got a degree within 4 years
52% got a degree within 5 years
54% got a degree within 6 years

AFTER GRADUATION

20% pursued further study (8% arts and
  sciences, 8% business, 3% engineering)
80% had job offers within 6 months
50 organizations recruited on campus

WHAT YOU WILL PAY

Tuition and fees $14,346
Room and board $4264
40% receive need-based financial aid
Need-based college-administered scholarships and
  grants average $1500 per award
34% receive non-need financial aid
Non-need college-administered scholarships and
  grants average $3580 per award

FLORIDA STATE UNIVERSITY

Tallahassee, Florida • Suburban setting • Public • State-supported • Coed

Florida State University is one of the nation's most popular universities, enrolling students from all 50 states and over 100 countries. Its diverse student population participates in a Liberal Studies Program that has been nationally recognized for its effectiveness in fostering a spirit of free inquiry into humane values and for developing strong written analytical skills. Home of the National High Magnetic Field Laboratory, the Supercomputer Computations Institute, and other internationally acclaimed research centers, Florida State is one of only 88 institutions in the Research I category as classified by the Carnegie Foundation for the Advancement of Teaching. FSU invites students to explore the state of their future, Florida State University.

 Academics

Florida State offers a liberal studies curriculum and core academic program; fewer than half of graduate courses are open to undergraduates. It awards associate, bachelor's, master's, doctoral, and first professional **degrees**. Challenging opportunities include advanced placement, accelerated degree programs, an honors program, a senior project, Phi Beta Kappa, and Sigma Xi. Special programs include cooperative education, internships, summer session for credit, off-campus study, study abroad, and Army, Naval, and Air Force ROTC.

The most popular **majors** include biology/biological sciences and psychology. A complete listing of majors at Florida State appears in the Majors Index beginning on page 379.

The **faculty** at Florida State has 1,458 full-time graduate and undergraduate teachers, 87% with terminal degrees.

 Computers on Campus

Students are not required to have a computer. Student rooms are linked to a campus network. 670 **computers**

available in the computer center, computer labs, classrooms, the library, the student center, and dormitories provide access to the main academic computer, off-campus computing facilities, and e-mail. Staffed computer lab on campus provides training in the use of computers and software.

The 7 **libraries** have 2.1 million books, 4.4 million microform titles, and 18,296 subscriptions.

 Campus Life

There are 290 active **organizations** on campus, including a drama/theater group and student-run newspaper and radio station. 20% of eligible men and 20% of eligible women are members of 25 national **fraternities** and 19 national **sororities**. Student **safety services** include late night transport/escort service, 24-hour emergency telephone alarm devices, 24-hour patrols by trained security personnel, and electronically operated dormitory entrances.

Florida State is a member of the NCAA (Division I). **Intercollegiate sports** (some offering scholarships) include baseball (m), basketball (m, w), cross-country running (m, w), football (m), golf (m, w), soccer (w), softball (w), swimming and diving (m, w), tennis (m, w), track and field (m, w), volleyball (w).

 Applying

Florida State requires a high school transcript, 3 years of high school math and science, 2 years of high school foreign language, SAT I or ACT, and in some cases audition. It recommends a minimum high school GPA of 3.0. Early entrance is possible, with a 3/1 deadline and continuous processing to 3/1 for financial aid. **Contact:** Ms. Janice Finney, Associate Director of Admissions, Office of Admissions, FSU University Center, Tallahassee, FL 32306-1009, 904-644-1328.

GETTING IN LAST YEAR
13,801 applied
76% were accepted
30% enrolled (3,175)
43% from top tenth of their h.s. class
3.5 average high school GPA
37% had SAT verbal scores over 600
35% had SAT math scores over 600
32% had ACT scores over 26
6% had SAT verbal scores over 700
5% had SAT math scores over 700
8% had ACT scores over 30
91 National Merit Scholars

THE STUDENT BODY
Total 30,268, of whom 22,554
are undergraduates

From 51 states and territories,
103 other countries
89% from Florida
55% women, 45% men
10% African Americans
1% Native Americans
6% Hispanics
2% Asian Americans
1% international students

AFTER FRESHMAN YEAR
31% got a degree within 4 years
59% got a degree within 5 years
65% got a degree within 6 years

AFTER GRADUATION
867 organizations recruited on campus
3 Fulbright scholars

WHAT YOU WILL PAY
Resident tuition and fees $1798
Nonresident tuition and fees $6700
Room and board $4500
Need-based college-administered scholarships and
grants average $1273 per award
Non-need college-administered scholarships and
grants average $2879 per award

FORDHAM UNIVERSITY

New York, New York • Urban setting • Private • Independent-Religious • Coed

Fordham University has been helping students educate themselves for more than 150 years. It has encouraged young people to explore the world's knowledge, to examine its ideas, to question its truths, to engage their own minds, and to value others. The process is enhanced by a powerful setting: New York City. The Jesuit ideals of learning are served not only by the range of experience the city offers but also by the examples of excellence it provides. Combining the resources of an excellent, caring faculty and a great city, the University aims to prepare students for satisfying and productive lives.

Academics

Fordham offers a liberal arts curriculum in the Jesuit tradition and core academic program; fewer than half of graduate courses are open to undergraduates. It awards bachelor's, master's, doctoral, and first professional **degrees.** Challenging opportunities include advanced placement, accelerated degree programs, self-designed majors, tutorials, Freshman Honors College, an honors program, a senior project, Phi Beta Kappa, and Sigma Xi. Special programs include internships, summer session for credit, off-campus study, study abroad, and Army, Naval, and Air Force ROTC.

The most popular **majors** include business, communication, and English. A complete listing of majors at Fordham appears in the Majors Index beginning on page 379.

The **faculty** at Fordham has 528 full-time graduate and undergraduate teachers, 97% with terminal degrees. 30% of the faculty serve as student advisers. The student-faculty ratio is 17:1.

Computers on Campus

Students are not required to have a computer. 230 **computers** available in the computer center, computer labs, the research center, classrooms, and the library provide access to the main academic computer, e-mail, and the Internet. Staffed computer lab on campus (open 24 hours a day) provides training in the use of computers and software.

The 5 **libraries** have 1.6 million books, 1.9 million microform titles, and 9,968 subscriptions.

Campus Life

There are 130 active **organizations** on campus, including a drama/theater group and student-run newspaper and radio station. Student **safety services** include late night transport/escort service, 24-hour emergency telephone alarm devices, 24-hour patrols by trained security personnel, student patrols, and electronically operated dormitory entrances.

Fordham is a member of the NCAA (Division I). **Intercollegiate sports** (some offering scholarships) include baseball (m), basketball (m, w), crew (m, w), cross-country running (m, w), equestrian sports (m, w), football (m), golf (m), ice hockey (m), lacrosse (m, w), riflery (m, w), rugby (m), soccer (m, w), softball (w), squash (m), swimming and diving (m, w), tennis (m, w), track and field (m, w), volleyball (w), water polo (m), wrestling (m).

Applying

Fordham requires an essay, a high school transcript, 3 years of high school math, 1 recommendation, SAT I or ACT, and in some cases a campus interview. It recommends 3 years of high school science, 2 years of high school foreign language, an interview, SAT II Subject Tests, and a minimum high school GPA of 3.0. Early, deferred, and midyear entrance are possible, with a 2/1 deadline and continuous processing to 2/1 for financial aid. **Contact:** Mr. John W. Buckley, Director of Admissions, 441 E. Fordham Rd., Dealy Hall/Room 115, New York, NY 10458, 718-817-4000 or toll-free 800-FORDHAM; fax 718-367-9404.

GETTING IN LAST YEAR
4,680 applied
70% were accepted
33% enrolled (1,098)
31% from top tenth of their h.s. class
3.2 average high school GPA
15% had SAT verbal scores over 600
32% had SAT math scores over 600
2% had SAT verbal scores over 700
5% had SAT math scores over 700

THE STUDENT BODY
Total 13,909, of whom 5,795
  are undergraduates

From 42 states and territories,
  50 other countries
66% from New York
55% women, 45% men
5% African Americans
0% Native Americans
15% Hispanics
4% Asian Americans
2% international students

AFTER FRESHMAN YEAR
93% returned for sophomore year

AFTER GRADUATION
25% pursued further study (10% law, 8% arts
  and sciences, 6% business)
2 Fulbright scholars

WHAT YOU WILL PAY
Tuition and fees $15,084
Room and board $7173
90% receive need-based financial aid
Need-based college-administered scholarships and
  grants average $6800 per award
10% receive non-need financial aid
Non-need college-administered scholarships and
  grants average $6800 per award

FRANKLIN AND MARSHALL COLLEGE

Lancaster, Pennsylvania • Suburban setting • Private • Independent • Coed

Franklin & Marshall is an institution that typifies the concept of liberal learning. Whether the course is in theater or physics, classes are small, engagement is high, and discussion dominates over lecture. Beginning with the First Year Seminar, students at Franklin & Marshall are repeatedly invited to participate actively in intellectual investigation at a high level. Graduates consistently testify to the quality of an F&M education as mental preparation for life.

Academics

F & M offers a core academic program. It awards bachelor's **degrees**. Challenging opportunities include advanced placement, accelerated degree programs, self-designed majors, tutorials, a senior project, Phi Beta Kappa, and Sigma Xi. Special programs include internships, summer session for credit, off-campus study, and Army ROTC.

The most popular **majors** include political science/government, business, and English. A complete listing of majors at F & M appears in the Majors Index beginning on page 379.

The **faculty** at F & M has 152 full-time teachers, 99% with terminal degrees. 100% of the faculty serve as student advisers. The student-faculty ratio is 11:1.

Computers on Campus

Students are not required to have a computer. Student rooms are linked to a campus network. 70 **computers** available in the computer center, computer labs, academic departments, classrooms, and the library provide access to the main academic computer, off-campus computing facilities, e-mail, on-line services, and the Internet. Staffed computer lab on campus provides training in the use of computers and software.

The 2 **libraries** have 366,000 books, 258,978 microform titles, and 1,692 subscriptions. They are connected to 26 national **on-line** catalogs.

Campus Life

There are 120 active **organizations** on campus, including a drama/theater group and student-run newspaper and radio station. 70% of students participate in student government elections. 40% of eligible men and 30% of eligible women are members of 9 national **fraternities** and 3 national **sororities**. Student **safety services** include residence hall security, late night transport/escort service, 24-hour emergency telephone alarm devices, 24-hour patrols by trained security personnel, and electronically operated dormitory entrances.

F & M is a member of the NCAA (Division III). **Intercollegiate sports** include badminton (m, w), baseball (m), basketball (m, w), crew (m, w), cross-country running (m, w), fencing (m, w), field hockey (w), football (m), golf (m, w), ice hockey (m), lacrosse (m, w), rugby (m, w), soccer (m, w), softball (w), squash (m, w), swimming and diving (m, w), tennis (m, w), track and field (m, w), volleyball (m, w), wrestling (m).

Applying

F & M requires an essay, a high school transcript, 2 recommendations, and in some cases SAT I or ACT and SAT II: Writing Test. It recommends 4 years of high school math, 3 years of high school science, 3 years of high school foreign language, and an interview. Early, deferred, and midyear entrance are possible, with a 2/1 deadline and a 2/1 priority date for financial aid. **Contact:** Mr. Peter W. VanBuskirk, Dean of Admissions, PO Box 3003, Lancaster, PA 17604-3003, 717-291-3953; fax 717-291-4389.

GETTING IN LAST YEAR
3,430 applied
69% were accepted
21% enrolled (500)
53% from top tenth of their h.s. class
35% had SAT verbal scores over 600
72% had SAT math scores over 600
5% had SAT verbal scores over 700
19% had SAT math scores over 700
20 valedictorians

THE STUDENT BODY
1,866 undergraduates
From 41 states and territories,
37 other countries

35% from Pennsylvania
46% women, 54% men
3% African Americans
0% Native Americans
3% Hispanics
7% Asian Americans
7% international students

AFTER FRESHMAN YEAR
95% returned for sophomore year
78% got a degree within 5 years

AFTER GRADUATION
32% pursued further study (10% arts and sciences, 7% medicine, 6% law)

61% had job offers within 6 months
64 organizations recruited on campus
1 Fulbright scholar

WHAT YOU WILL PAY
Comprehensive fee $25,630
51% receive need-based financial aid
Need-based college-administered scholarships and grants average $11,205 per award
8% receive non-need financial aid
Non-need college-administered scholarships and grants average $4657 per award

FURMAN UNIVERSITY

Greenville, South Carolina • Suburban setting • Private • Independent • Coed

As a leading liberal arts college, Furman University is committed to helping students become responsible citizens and intellectual leaders. Furman students come from a wide range of backgrounds and share a desire to be part of an academic environment in which they are challenged to do their best intellectually and creatively. Outside the classroom, programs such as a volunteer service corps give students a chance to assist the less fortunate. The result is a caring community of scholars, where students and faculty work together to discover just how exciting the educational process can be.

Academics

Furman offers a liberal arts curriculum and core academic program. It awards bachelor's and master's **degrees**. Challenging opportunities include advanced placement, accelerated degree programs, self-designed majors, tutorials, a senior project, and Phi Beta Kappa. Special programs include cooperative education, internships, summer session for credit, study abroad, and Army ROTC.

The most popular **majors** include political science/government, physical fitness/human movement, and business. A complete listing of majors at Furman appears in the Majors Index beginning on page 379.

The **faculty** at Furman has 188 full-time undergraduate teachers, 93% with terminal degrees. 100% of the faculty serve as student advisers. The student-faculty ratio is 12:1.

Computers on Campus

Students are not required to have a computer. Student rooms are linked to a campus network. 214 **computers** available in the computer center, computer labs, academic buildings, classrooms, and the library provide access to the main academic computer, off-campus computing facilities, e-mail, on-line services, and the Internet. Staffed computer lab on campus.

The 2 **libraries** have 360,404 books, 578,037 microform titles, and 1,557 subscriptions. They are connected to 3 national **on-line** catalogs.

Campus Life

There are 128 active **organizations** on campus, including a drama/theater group and student-run newspaper and radio station. 30% of students participate in student government elections. 35% of eligible men and 35% of eligible women are members of 9 national **fraternities** and 8 national **sororities**. Student **safety services** include late night transport/escort service, 24-hour emergency telephone alarm devices, 24-hour patrols by trained security personnel, student patrols, and electronically operated dormitory entrances.

Furman is a member of the NCAA (Division I). **Intercollegiate sports** (some offering scholarships) include baseball (m), basketball (m, w), crew (m, w), cross-country running (m, w), fencing (m, w), football (m), golf (m, w), soccer (m, w), softball (w), swimming and diving (m, w), tennis (m, w), track and field (m, w), volleyball (m, w), weight lifting (m, w).

Applying

Furman requires an essay, a high school transcript, 3 years of high school math and science, some high school foreign language, essay or graded paper, and SAT I or ACT. It recommends recommendations. Early and midyear entrance are possible, with a 2/1 deadline and continuous processing to 2/15 for financial aid. **Contact:** Mr. J. Carey Thompson, Director of Admissions, 3300 Poinsett Highway, Greenville, SC 29613, 864-294-2034; fax 864-294-3127.

GETTING IN LAST YEAR
2,896 applied
80% were accepted
30% enrolled (703)
58% from top tenth of their h.s. class
3.6 average high school GPA
64% had SAT verbal scores over 600
62% had SAT math scores over 600
66% had ACT scores over 26
12% had SAT verbal scores over 700
10% had SAT math scores over 700
15% had ACT scores over 30
25 National Merit Scholars
38 valedictorians

THE STUDENT BODY
Total 2,673, of whom 2,417
are undergraduates

From 42 states and territories,
15 other countries
30% from South Carolina
54% women, 46% men
4% African Americans
0% Native Americans
1% Hispanics
2% Asian Americans
2% international students

AFTER FRESHMAN YEAR
88% returned for sophomore year
71% got a degree within 4 years
77% got a degree within 5 years

AFTER GRADUATION
33% pursued further study (25% arts and
sciences, 2% law, 2% medicine)
59% had job offers within 6 months
74 organizations recruited on campus

WHAT YOU WILL PAY
Tuition and fees $14,576
Room and board $4168
65% receive need-based financial aid
Need-based college-administered scholarships and
grants average $5223 per award
16% receive non-need financial aid
Non-need college-administered scholarships and
grants average $3775 per award

GEORGETOWN COLLEGE

Georgetown, Kentucky • Suburban setting • Private • Independent-Religious • Coed

Georgetown College distinguishes itself from many other small liberal arts colleges across the nation by offering a combination of a rigorous and respected academic program, a wealth of opportunities for leadership and involvement in extracurricular activities, and a strong commitment to Christian values and principles. While there is no shortage of schools that possess any one of these characteristics, institutions that combine any two of these qualities are less common. By placing all three side by side at unique levels and combinations, Georgetown provides a special framework that fosters intellectual, social, and spiritual growth.

 ## Academics

Georgetown offers a traditional liberal arts curriculum and core academic program; a few graduate courses are open to undergraduates. It awards bachelor's and master's **degrees**. Challenging opportunities include advanced placement, accelerated degree programs, self-designed majors, tutorials, and a senior project. Special programs include cooperative education, internships, summer session for credit, off-campus study, study abroad, and Army and Air Force ROTC.

The most popular **majors** include business, communication, and psychology. A complete listing of majors at Georgetown appears in the Majors Index beginning on page 379.

The **faculty** at Georgetown has 76 full-time undergraduate teachers, 79% with terminal degrees. 87% of the faculty serve as student advisers. The student-faculty ratio is 13:1, and the average class size in core courses is 25.

 ## Computers on Campus

Students are not required to have a computer. Student rooms are linked to a campus network. 45 **computers**

available in the computer center, classrooms, and the library provide access to the main academic computer, off-campus computing facilities, e-mail, on-line services, and the Internet. Staffed computer lab on campus provides training in the use of computers and software.

The 2 **libraries** have 131,021 books, 132,224 microform titles, and 850 subscriptions.

 ## Campus Life

There are 85 active **organizations** on campus, including a drama/theater group and student-run newspaper and radio station. 33% of eligible men and 34% of eligible women are members of 4 national **fraternities**, 3 national **sororities**, and 1 local fraternity. Student **safety services** include late night transport/escort service and 24-hour patrols by trained security personnel.

Georgetown is a member of the NAIA. **Intercollegiate sports** (some offering scholarships) include baseball (m), basketball (m, w), cross-country running (m, w), football (m), golf (m, w), soccer (m, w), softball (w), tennis (m, w), volleyball (w).

Applying

Georgetown requires an essay, a high school transcript, SAT I or ACT, and in some cases recommendations. It recommends 3 years of high school math and science and some high school foreign language. Midyear entrance is possible, with rolling admissions and continuous processing to 4/1 for financial aid. **Contact:** Mr. Michael Konopski, Director of Admissions, 400 East College Street, Georgetown, KY 40324-1696, 502-863-8009 or toll-free 800-788-9985; fax 502-868-8891.

GETTING IN LAST YEAR
793 applied
92% were accepted
42% enrolled (309)
42% from top tenth of their h.s. class
3.43 average high school GPA
36% had ACT scores over 26
8% had ACT scores over 30
1 National Merit Scholar
23 valedictorians

THE STUDENT BODY
Total 1,461, of whom 1,153
    are undergraduates
From 27 states and territories,
    9 other countries

78% from Kentucky
58% women, 42% men
2% African Americans
0% Native Americans
0% Hispanics
0% Asian Americans
1% international students

AFTER FRESHMAN YEAR
74% returned for sophomore year
32% got a degree within 4 years
44% got a degree within 5 years

AFTER GRADUATION
30 organizations recruited on campus

WHAT YOU WILL PAY
Tuition and fees $9590
Room and board $4050
63% receive need-based financial aid
Need-based college-administered scholarships and
    grants average $2692 per award
66% receive non-need financial aid
Non-need college-administered scholarships and
    grants average $2663 per award

GEORGETOWN UNIVERSITY

Washington, District of Columbia • Urban setting • Private • Independent-Religious • Coed

Georgetown's founder, John Carroll, in the spirit of revolution in 1789, saw his academy as an attempt to define the boundaries of American education. Georgetown, the oldest Catholic university in the United States, includes 5 undergraduate schools, a graduate school, and professional schools of law and medicine. It fosters a spirit of inquiry and innovation as it brings the values of the liberal arts tradition to bear on current issues. The resources of Washington, DC, provide a rich complement to the historic village of Georgetown. Students from all 50 states and more than 100 other countries find at Georgetown a unique national and international character.

 ## Academics

Georgetown offers a core academic program; fewer than half of graduate courses are open to undergraduates. It awards bachelor's, master's, doctoral, and first professional **degrees**. Challenging opportunities include advanced placement, self-designed majors, tutorials, an honors program, a senior project, Phi Beta Kappa, and Sigma Xi. Special programs include internships, summer session for credit, off-campus study, study abroad, and Army, Naval, and Air Force ROTC.

The most popular **majors** include political science/government and English. A complete listing of majors at Georgetown appears in the Majors Index beginning on page 379.

The **faculty** at Georgetown has 1,509 full-time graduate and undergraduate teachers, 90% with terminal degrees. 35% of the faculty serve as student advisers.

 ## Computers on Campus

Students are not required to have a computer. Student rooms are linked to a campus network. 300 **computers** available in the computer center, computer labs, and the library provide access to the main academic computer, e-mail, and the Internet. Staffed computer lab on campus provides training in the use of computers and software.

The 4 **libraries** have 2 million books, 2.6 million microform titles, and 26,036 subscriptions. They are connected to 5 national **on-line** catalogs.

 ## Campus Life

There are 100 active **organizations** on campus, including a drama/theater group and student-run newspaper and radio station. Student **safety services** include late night transport/escort service, 24-hour emergency telephone alarm devices, 24-hour patrols by trained security personnel, and electronically operated dormitory entrances.

Georgetown is a member of the NCAA (Division I). **Intercollegiate sports** (some offering scholarships) include baseball (m), basketball (m, w), crew (m, w), cross-country running (m, w), field hockey (w), football (m), golf (m), ice hockey (m), lacrosse (m, w), rugby (m), sailing (m, w), soccer (m, w), swimming and diving (m, w), tennis (m, w), track and field (m, w), volleyball (w).

 ## Applying

Georgetown requires an essay, a high school transcript, 2 recommendations, an interview, and SAT I or ACT. It recommends 3 years of high school math and science, some high school foreign language, and 3 SAT II Subject Tests. Early and deferred entrance are possible, with a 1/10 deadline and continuous processing to 2/1 for financial aid. **Contact:** Mr. Charles A. Deacon, Dean of Undergraduate Admissions, 57th and O Streets, NW, Washington, DC 20057, 202-687-3600; fax 202-687-5084.

GETTING IN LAST YEAR
12,831 applied
22% were accepted
49% enrolled (1,410)
73% from top tenth of their h.s. class
85% had ACT scores over 26
45% had ACT scores over 30
204 class presidents
110 valedictorians

THE STUDENT BODY
Total 12,618, of whom 6,316
   are undergraduates
From 52 states and territories,
   128 other countries

3% from District of Columbia
52% women, 48% men
7% African Americans
1% Native Americans
6% Hispanics
8% Asian Americans
10% international students

AFTER GRADUATION
25% pursued further study (12% arts and
   sciences, 8% law, 3% medicine)
1 Rhodes, 9 Fulbright scholars

WHAT YOU WILL PAY
Tuition and fees $19,402
Room and board $7466
45% receive need-based financial aid
Need-based college-administered scholarships and
   grants average $13,462 per award
10% receive non-need financial aid

THE GEORGE WASHINGTON UNIVERSITY

Washington, District of Columbia • Urban setting • Private • Independent • Coed

GW's challenging academic programs are based on a strong curriculum, specialized majors, and interconnections between scholarly theory and experiential education. Programs at GW include a Science Scholars Program in chemistry/physics, a University Honors Program, a 7-year integrated B.A./M.D. program, combined 5-year B.A./M.A. or B.A./M.S. programs, and integrated engineering/law or engineering/medicine programs, all of which have individual scholarships. Scholarships, Presidential Academic/Arts and Valedictorian, range from $2500 to $15,000.

 Academics

GW offers a core academic program; fewer than half of graduate courses are open to undergraduates. It awards associate, bachelor's, master's, doctoral, and first professional **degrees**. Challenging opportunities include advanced placement, accelerated degree programs, self-designed majors, tutorials, an honors program, a senior project, Phi Beta Kappa, and Sigma Xi. Special programs include cooperative education, internships, summer session for credit, off-campus study, study abroad, and Army, Naval, and Air Force ROTC.

The most popular **majors** include international studies, business, and biology/biological sciences. A complete listing of majors at GW appears in the Majors Index beginning on page 379.

The **faculty** at GW has 1,421 full-time graduate and undergraduate teachers, 92% with terminal degrees. The average class size in core courses is 26.

 Computers on Campus

Students are not required to have a computer. Student rooms are linked to a campus network. 550 **computers** available in the computer center, computer labs, classrooms, the library, the student center, and dormitories provide access to the main academic computer, e-mail, on-line services, and the Internet. Staffed computer lab on campus (open 24 hours a day) provides training in the use of computers and software.

The 3 **libraries** have 1.7 million books, 2 million microform titles, and 14,210 subscriptions. They are connected to 6 national **on-line** catalogs.

 Campus Life

There are 208 active **organizations** on campus, including a drama/theater group and student-run newspaper and radio station. 30% of students participate in student government elections. 19% of eligible men and 12% of eligible women are members of 12 national **fraternities** and 7 national **sororities**. Student **safety services** include student community service aides, late night transport/escort service, 24-hour emergency telephone alarm devices, 24-hour patrols by trained security personnel, and electronically operated dormitory entrances.

GW is a member of the NCAA (Division I). **Intercollegiate sports** (some offering scholarships) include baseball (m), basketball (m, w), crew (m, w), cross-country running (m, w), golf (m), gymnastics (w), soccer (m, w), swimming and diving (m, w), tennis (m, w), volleyball (w), water polo (m).

 Applying

GW requires an essay, a high school transcript, 2 recommendations, SAT I or ACT, and in some cases 3 years of high school math and 3 SAT II Subject Tests. It recommends 2 years of high school foreign language, an interview, and SAT II: Writing Test. Early, deferred, and midyear entrance are possible, with a 12/1 deadline and continuous processing to 2/1 for financial aid. **Contact:** Mr. Frederic A. Siegel, Director of Undergraduate Admissions, Office of Undergraduate Admissions, Washington, DC 20052, 202-994-6040 or toll-free 800-447-3765; fax 202-994-0325.

GETTING IN LAST YEAR
10,469 applied
55% were accepted
24% enrolled (1,395)
42% from top tenth of their h.s. class
29% had SAT verbal scores over 600
57% had SAT math scores over 600
65% had ACT scores over 26
3% had SAT verbal scores over 700
15% had SAT math scores over 700
24% had ACT scores over 30
42 National Merit Scholars
49 valedictorians

THE STUDENT BODY
Total 19,670, of whom 6,378
  are undergraduates

From 54 states and territories,
  96 other countries
10% from District of Columbia
53% women, 47% men
7% African Americans
1% Native Americans
5% Hispanics
12% Asian Americans
10% international students

AFTER FRESHMAN YEAR
91% returned for sophomore year
61% got a degree within 4 years
68% got a degree within 5 years
69% got a degree within 6 years

AFTER GRADUATION
21% pursued further study (11% arts and
  sciences, 6% law, 4% medicine)
91 organizations recruited on campus
2 Fulbright scholars

WHAT YOU WILL PAY
Tuition and fees $19,764
Room and board $6590
50% receive need-based financial aid
Need-based college-administered scholarships and
  grants average $10,558 per award
21% receive non-need financial aid
Non-need college-administered scholarships and
  grants average $7999 per award

GEORGIA INSTITUTE OF TECHNOLOGY

Atlanta, Georgia • Urban setting • Public • State-supported • Coed

Georgia Tech is ranked 3rd among engineering schools, 25th among business schools, and as the 6th-best educational value in the US by *U.S. News & World Report. Money* magazine ranks Tech as the second best buy among science/technology schools. Tech consistently ranks 1st or 2nd among public colleges in the percentage of National Merit and National Achievement Scholars and has the largest voluntary cooperative education program in America. Tech's low cost, focus on experiential education, and reputation with employers and graduate schools insures students receive the greatest return on their educational investment.

Academics

Georgia Tech offers a core academic program; fewer than half of graduate courses are open to undergraduates. It awards bachelor's, master's, and doctoral **degrees**. Challenging opportunities include advanced placement, accelerated degree programs, self-designed majors, tutorials, an honors program, a senior project, and Sigma Xi. Special programs include cooperative education, internships, summer session for credit, off-campus study, study abroad, and Army, Naval, and Air Force ROTC.

The most popular **majors** include mechanical engineering, electrical engineering, and industrial engineering. A complete listing of majors at Georgia Tech appears in the Majors Index beginning on page 379.

The **faculty** at Georgia Tech has 639 full-time graduate and undergraduate teachers, 92% with terminal degrees. The student-faculty ratio is 20:1.

Computers on Campus

Students are not required to have a computer. Student rooms are linked to a campus network. 1,400 **computers**

available in the computer center, academic buildings, the library, the student center, and dormitories provide access to the main academic computer, e-mail, and the Internet. Staffed computer lab on campus (open 24 hours a day) provides training in the use of computers and software.

The 2 **libraries** have 1.9 million books and 12,713 subscriptions. They are connected to 5 national **on-line** catalogs.

Campus Life

There are 250 active **organizations** on campus, including a drama/theater group and student-run newspaper and radio station. 30% of eligible men and 27% of eligible women are members of 31 national **fraternities** and 8 national **sororities**. Student **safety services** include late night transport/escort service, 24-hour emergency telephone alarm devices, 24-hour patrols by trained security personnel, student patrols, and electronically operated dormitory entrances.

Georgia Tech is a member of the NCAA (Division I). **Intercollegiate sports** (some offering scholarships) include baseball (m), basketball (m, w), cross-country running (m, w), football (m), golf (m), ice hockey (m), lacrosse (m), rugby (m), softball (w), swimming and diving (m), tennis (m, w), track and field (m, w), volleyball (w).

Applying

Georgia Tech requires a high school transcript, 4 years of high school math, 3 years of high school science, 2 years of high school foreign language, SAT I, and in some cases ACT. Early and midyear entrance are possible, with a 2/1 deadline and continuous processing to 3/1 for financial aid. **Contact:** Ms. Deborah Smith, Director of Admissions, 225 North Avenue, NW, Atlanta, GA 30332-0320, 404-894-4154; fax 404-853-9163.

GETTING IN LAST YEAR
7,405 applied
62% were accepted
39% enrolled (1,814)
31% had SAT verbal scores over 600
87% had SAT math scores over 600
5% had SAT verbal scores over 700
40% had SAT math scores over 700
109 National Merit Scholars

THE STUDENT BODY
Total 13,036, of whom 9,473
  are undergraduates

From 52 states and territories,
  71 other countries
27% women, 73% men
10% African Americans
1% Native Americans
4% Hispanics
11% Asian Americans
3% international students

AFTER FRESHMAN YEAR
86% returned for sophomore year
29% got a degree within 4 years

60% got a degree within 5 years

AFTER GRADUATION
20% pursued further study

WHAT YOU WILL PAY
Resident tuition and fees $2457
Nonresident tuition and fees $7638
Room and board $4896
Need-based college-administered scholarships and
  grants average $1900 per award
Non-need college-administered scholarships and
  grants average $1660 per award

GETTYSBURG COLLEGE

Gettysburg, Pennsylvania • Small-town setting • Private • Independent • Coed

 Academics

Gettysburg College offers an interdisciplinary curriculum and core academic program. It awards bachelor's **degrees**. Challenging opportunities include advanced placement, accelerated degree programs, self-designed majors, an honors program, and Phi Beta Kappa. Special programs include internships, off-campus study, and study abroad.

The most popular **majors** include business, political science/government, and psychology. A complete listing of majors at Gettysburg College appears in the Majors Index beginning on page 379.

The **faculty** at Gettysburg College has 154 full-time teachers, 95% with terminal degrees. 100% of the faculty serve as student advisers. The student-faculty ratio is 12:1.

 Computers on Campus

Students are not required to have a computer. Student rooms are linked to a campus network. 250 **computers** available in the computer center, computer labs, the learning resource center, the library, the student center, and dormitories provide access to the main academic computer, off-campus computing facilities, e-mail, on-line services, and the Internet. Staffed computer lab on campus (open 24 hours a day) provides training in the use of computers and software.

The **library** has 340,000 books, 35,000 microform titles, and 1,350 subscriptions.

 Campus Life

There are 60 active **organizations** on campus, including a drama/theater group and student-run newspaper and radio station. 55% of eligible men and 45% of eligible women are members of 11 national **fraternities** and 5 national **sororities**. Student **safety services** include late night transport/escort service, 24-hour emergency telephone alarm devices, 24-hour patrols by trained security personnel, and electronically operated dormitory entrances.

Gettysburg College is a member of the NCAA (Division III). **Intercollegiate sports** include baseball (m), basketball (m, w), cross-country running (m, w), field hockey (w), football (m), golf (m, w), lacrosse (m, w), rugby (m), soccer (m, w), softball (w), swimming and diving (m, w), tennis (m, w), track and field (m, w), volleyball (w), wrestling (m).

 Applying

Gettysburg College requires an essay, a high school transcript, 1 recommendation, SAT I or ACT, and a minimum high school GPA of 2.0. It recommends 3 years of high school math and science, some high school foreign language, a campus interview, 3 SAT II Subject Tests, and a minimum high school GPA of 3.0. Early, deferred, and midyear entrance are possible, with a 2/15 deadline and continuous processing to 2/15 for financial aid. **Contact:** Mr. Delwin K. Gustafson, Dean of Admissions, Eisenhower House, Gettysburg, PA 17325-1411, 717-337-6100 or toll-free 800-431-0803; fax 717-337-6145.

GETTING IN LAST YEAR
3,680 applied
72% were accepted
23% enrolled (605)
40% from top tenth of their h.s. class
3.5 average high school GPA
17% had SAT verbal scores over 600
40% had SAT math scores over 600
55% had ACT scores over 26
2% had SAT verbal scores over 700
6% had SAT math scores over 700
10% had ACT scores over 30

THE STUDENT BODY
2,000 undergraduates
From 40 states and territories,
    25 other countries
25% from Pennsylvania
50% women, 50% men
3% African Americans
1% Native Americans
2% Hispanics
3% Asian Americans
2% international students

AFTER FRESHMAN YEAR
92% returned for sophomore year

AFTER GRADUATION
31% pursued further study (11% arts and
    sciences, 7% law, 5% business)

WHAT YOU WILL PAY
Tuition and fees $20,834
Room and board $4522
51% receive need-based financial aid
Need-based college-administered scholarships and
    grants average $11,150 per award

GMI ENGINEERING & MANAGEMENT INSTITUTE

Flint, Michigan • Suburban setting • Private • Independent • Coed

GMI—America's Co-op College—gives students the opportunity for a head start in life. Established in 1919, GMI has a long tradition of academic excellence in engineering, science and math, and business management. Its goal is to provide students with top-notch classroom instruction and career-directed co-op work experience in business and industry. GMI's unique 5-year, fully cooperative plan of education has students alternating 12-week academic terms on campus with 12-week terms of paid work experience with a co-op employer. GMI graduates are in high demand at America's leading corporations and have the credentials for admittance into the nation's top graduate and professional schools.

Academics

GMI offers a core academic program. It awards bachelor's and master's **degrees**. Challenging opportunities include advanced placement, tutorials, an honors program, and a senior project. Special programs include cooperative education and study abroad.

The most popular **majors** include mechanical engineering, electrical engineering, and manufacturing engineering. A complete listing of majors at GMI appears in the Majors Index beginning on page 379.

The **faculty** at GMI has 150 full-time undergraduate teachers, 75% with terminal degrees. 50% of the faculty serve as student advisers. The student-faculty ratio is 12:1.

Computers on Campus

Students are not required to have a computer. Student rooms are linked to a campus network. 300 **computers** available in the computer center, labs, and classrooms provide access to the main academic computer, off-campus computing facilities, e-mail, on-line services, and the Internet. Staffed computer lab on campus (open 24 hours a day) provides training in the use of computers and software.

The 2 **libraries** have 70,000 books, 27,500 microform titles, and 750 subscriptions.

Campus Life

There are 20 active **organizations** on campus, including a drama/theater group and student-run newspaper and radio station. 54% of eligible men and 54% of eligible women are members of 13 national **fraternities** and 5 national **sororities**. Student **safety services** include late night transport/escort service, 24-hour emergency telephone alarm devices, 24-hour patrols by trained security personnel, and electronically operated dormitory entrances. **Intercollegiate sports** include ice hockey (m), soccer (m), volleyball (m).

Applying

GMI requires a high school transcript, 3 years of high school math and science, 1 recommendation, SAT I or ACT, and a minimum high school GPA of 3.0. It recommends some high school foreign language, an interview, and 2 SAT II Subject Tests. Deferred and midyear entrance are possible, with rolling admissions and continuous processing to 3/30 for financial aid. **Contact:** Mr. Phillip D. Lavender, Director of Admissions, 1700 West Third Avenue, Flint, MI 48504-4898, 810-762-7865 or toll-free 800-955-4464; fax 810-762-9837.

GETTING IN LAST YEAR
1,865 applied
75% were accepted
43% enrolled (603)
40% from top tenth of their h.s. class
3.44 average high school GPA
42% had SAT verbal scores over 600 (R)
75% had SAT math scores over 600 (R)
48% had ACT scores over 26
3% had SAT verbal scores over 700 (R)
15% had SAT math scores over 700 (R)
12% had ACT scores over 30

THE STUDENT BODY
Total 3,256, of whom 2,434
  are undergraduates

From 46 states and territories,
  12 other countries
59% from Michigan
19% women, 81% men
7% African Americans
1% Native Americans
2% Hispanics
9% Asian Americans
4% international students

AFTER FRESHMAN YEAR
87% returned for sophomore year
0% got a degree within 4 years
65% got a degree within 5 years
75% got a degree within 6 years

AFTER GRADUATION
6% pursued further study
96% had job offers within 6 months

WHAT YOU WILL PAY
Tuition and fees $13,092
Room and board $3500
76% receive need-based financial aid
Need-based college-administered scholarships and
  grants average $1818 per award
Non-need college-administered scholarships and
  grants average $2000 per award

GOSHEN COLLEGE

Goshen, Indiana • Small-town setting • Private • Independent-Religious • Coed

Goshen College is dedicated to the development of informed, articulate, sensitive, responsible Christians. As a ministry of the Mennonite Church, Goshen seeks to integrate Christian values with educational and professional life. As a community of faith and learning, Goshen strives to foster personal, intellectual, spiritual, and social growth. The College views education as a moral activity that produces servant leaders for the church and the world. Goshen has attracted national attention for its groundbreaking international education program and for providing an above-average education for a below-average price.

Academics

Goshen offers a Christian development curriculum with international emphasis and core academic program. It awards bachelor's **degrees**. Challenging opportunities include advanced placement, accelerated degree programs, self-designed majors, tutorials, and a senior project. Special programs include cooperative education, internships, summer session for credit, off-campus study, and study abroad.

The most popular **majors** include business, nursing, and elementary education. A complete listing of majors at Goshen appears in the Majors Index beginning on page 379.

The **faculty** at Goshen has 81 full-time teachers, 63% with terminal degrees. 90% of the faculty serve as student advisers. The student-faculty ratio is 11:1.

Computers on Campus

Students are not required to have a computer. 80 **computers** available in the computer center, computer labs, the library, and dormitories provide access to the main academic computer, off-campus computing facilities, e-mail, on-line services, and the Internet. Staffed computer lab on campus (open 24 hours a day) provides training in the use of computers and software.

The 2 **libraries** have 118,000 books, 100 microform titles, and 860 subscriptions. They are connected to 2 national **on-line** catalogs.

Campus Life

There are 25 active **organizations** on campus, including a drama/theater group and student-run newspaper and radio station. Student **safety services** include night security and 24-hour emergency telephone alarm devices.

Goshen is a member of the NAIA. **Intercollegiate sports** (some offering scholarships) include basketball (m, w), cross-country running (m, w), golf (m), soccer (m, w), softball (w), tennis (m, w), track and field (m, w), volleyball (w).

Applying

Goshen requires a high school transcript, 1 recommendation, and SAT I or ACT. It recommends 3 years of high school math and science, some high school foreign language, and an interview. Early, deferred, and midyear entrance are possible, with rolling admissions and continuous processing to 3/1 for financial aid. **Contact:** Ms. Martha Lehman, Director of Admissions, 1700 South Main Street, Goshen, IN 46526-4794, 219-535-7535 or toll-free 800-348-7422 (out-of-state); fax 219-535-7609.

GETTING IN LAST YEAR
552 applied
85% were accepted
51% enrolled (238)
3.32 average high school GPA
40% had SAT verbal scores over 600 (R)
28% had SAT math scores over 600 (R)
10% had SAT verbal scores over 700 (R)
6% had SAT math scores over 700 (R)
8 National Merit Scholars

THE STUDENT BODY
1,071 undergraduates
From 40 states and territories,
   34 other countries

49% from Indiana
56% women, 44% men
2% African Americans
1% Native Americans
4% Hispanics
1% Asian Americans
7% international students

AFTER FRESHMAN YEAR
85% returned for sophomore year
55% got a degree within 4 years
64% got a degree within 5 years
67% got a degree within 6 years

AFTER GRADUATION
39% pursued further study (15% arts and
   sciences, 10% medicine, 5% business)

WHAT YOU WILL PAY
Tuition and fees $9900
Room and board $3760
69% receive need-based financial aid
Need-based college-administered scholarships and
   grants average $1160 per award
76% receive non-need financial aid
Non-need college-administered scholarships and
   grants average $1308 per award

GOUCHER COLLEGE

Baltimore, Maryland • Suburban setting • Private • Independent • Coed

At Goucher, the traditional concept of the liberal arts is expanded to encompass a global perspective and an interdisciplinary way of thinking about the world. In typically small classes, Goucher professors approach education as a collaborative process between students and teachers; they take time to know the students and how they learn. As active participants in their own education, students are encouraged to tailor their course of study to their individual interests; some even create their own majors. Life at Goucher is shaped by a rigorous academic experience and a strong sense of community to which everyone contributes.

Academics

Goucher offers an interdisciplinary curriculum and core academic program; a few graduate courses are open to undergraduates. It awards bachelor's and master's **degrees**. Challenging opportunities include advanced placement, accelerated degree programs, self-designed majors, tutorials, an honors program, a senior project, and Phi Beta Kappa. Special programs include internships, off-campus study, study abroad, and Army ROTC.

The most popular **majors** include English, education, and psychology. A complete listing of majors at Goucher appears in the Majors Index beginning on page 379.

The **faculty** at Goucher has 77 full-time undergraduate teachers, 90% with terminal degrees. 100% of the faculty serve as student advisers. The student-faculty ratio is 9:1.

Computers on Campus

Students are not required to have a computer. 100 **computers** available in the computer center, academic buildings, and the library provide access to e-mail and the Internet. Staffed computer lab on campus.

The **library** has 282,500 books, 61,320 microform titles, and 1,119 subscriptions. It is connected to 1 national **on-line** catalog.

Campus Life

There are 43 active **organizations** on campus, including a drama/theater group and student-run newspaper. Student **safety services** include late night transport/escort service and electronically operated dormitory entrances.

Goucher is a member of the NCAA (Division III). **Intercollegiate sports** include basketball (m, w), cross-country running (m, w), equestrian sports (m, w), fencing (m, w), field hockey (w), lacrosse (m, w), soccer (m, w), swimming and diving (m, w), tennis (m, w), volleyball (w).

Applying

Goucher requires an essay, a high school transcript, 3 years of high school math, 2 years of high school foreign language, 3 recommendations, SAT I or ACT, SAT II: Writing Test, and a minimum high school GPA of 2.0. It recommends 3 years of high school science, an interview, 2 SAT II Subject Tests, and a minimum high school GPA of 3.0. Early, deferred, and midyear entrance are possible, with a 2/1 deadline and continuous processing to 2/15 for financial aid. **Contact:** Mr. Carlton E. Surbeck III, Director of Admissions, 1021 Dulaney Valley Road, Baltimore, MD 21204-2794, 410-337-6100 or toll-free 800-638-4278; fax 410-337-6123.

GETTING IN LAST YEAR
1,209 applied
77% were accepted
31% enrolled (284)
25% from top tenth of their h.s. class
3.27 average high school GPA
26% had SAT verbal scores over 600
40% had SAT math scores over 600
8% had SAT verbal scores over 700
13% had SAT math scores over 700
2 National Merit Scholars
3 valedictorians

THE STUDENT BODY
Total 1,276, of whom 1,065
  are undergraduates

From 40 states and territories,
  18 other countries
49% from Maryland
71% women, 29% men
8% African Americans
0% Native Americans
3% Hispanics
4% Asian Americans
4% international students

AFTER FRESHMAN YEAR
80% returned for sophomore year

AFTER GRADUATION
30% pursued further study (17% arts and
  sciences, 5% medicine, 4% business)
1 Fulbright scholar

WHAT YOU WILL PAY
Tuition and fees $16,655
Room and board $6260
48% receive need-based financial aid
Need-based college-administered scholarships and
  grants average $10,700 per award
40% receive non-need financial aid

GRINNELL COLLEGE

Grinnell, Iowa • Small-town setting • Private • Independent • Coed

Grinnell may seem like many distinguished liberal arts colleges. But, like the students it attracts, Grinnell is marked by an unusual blend of individualism, academic rigor, informality, innovation, and social justice. Free from core requirements, students design programs that fulfill their own educational needs. Intimate class settings allow faculty members to become both mentors and lifelong friends. Grinnellians feel empowered in and out of the classroom. Residential life is largely self-governing; opinions are not only heard, but treasured. Encouraged to share their distinct perspectives, students from nearly 50 states and 48 countries make Grinnell an international haven in America's heartland.

 Academics

Grinnell College offers an open curriculum and no core academic program. It awards bachelor's **degrees**. Challenging opportunities include advanced placement, accelerated degree programs, self-designed majors, tutorials, and Phi Beta Kappa. Special programs include internships, off-campus study, and study abroad.

The most popular **majors** include biology/biological sciences, English, and history. A complete listing of majors at Grinnell College appears in the Majors Index beginning on page 379.

The **faculty** at Grinnell College has 143 full-time teachers, 96% with terminal degrees. 89% of the faculty serve as student advisers. The student-faculty ratio is 10:1.

 Computers on Campus

Students are not required to have a computer. 281 **computers** available in the computer center, computer labs, science building, Carnegie Hall, classrooms, the library, and dormitories provide access to the main academic computer, off-campus computing facilities, e-mail, on-line services, and the Internet. Staffed computer lab on campus provides training in the use of computers and software.

The 3 **libraries** have 378,012 books, 8,679 microform titles, and 2,576 subscriptions. They are connected to 5 national **on-line** catalogs.

 Campus Life

There are 106 active **organizations** on campus, including a drama/theater group and student-run newspaper and radio station. 55% of students participate in student government elections. Student **safety services** include late night transport/escort service and 24-hour emergency telephone alarm devices.

Grinnell College is a member of the NCAA (Division III). **Intercollegiate sports** include baseball (m), basketball (m, w), cross-country running (m, w), football (m), golf (m, w), soccer (m, w), softball (w), swimming and diving (m, w), tennis (m, w), track and field (m, w), volleyball (w).

 Applying

Grinnell College requires an essay, a high school transcript, 3 years of high school math, 2 recommendations, and SAT I or ACT. It recommends 3 years of high school science, 3 years of high school foreign language, and an interview. Early, deferred, and midyear entrance are possible, with a 2/1 deadline and continuous processing to 2/1 for financial aid. **Contact:** Mr. Vincent Cuseo, Director of Admission, Mears Cottage, Grinnell, IA 50112-0807, 515-269-3600 or toll-free 800-247-0113 (in-state); fax 515-269-4800.

GETTING IN LAST YEAR

1,809 applied
74% were accepted
23% enrolled (307)
60% from top tenth of their h.s. class
56% had SAT verbal scores over 600
72% had SAT math scores over 600
89% had ACT scores over 26
8% had SAT verbal scores over 700
25% had SAT math scores over 700
43% had ACT scores over 30
29 National Merit Scholars
7 class presidents
35 valedictorians

THE STUDENT BODY

1,261 undergraduates

From 50 states and territories, 48 other countries
14% from Iowa
54% women, 46% men
5% African Americans
1% Native Americans
4% Hispanics
4% Asian Americans
10% international students

AFTER FRESHMAN YEAR

94% returned for sophomore year
77% got a degree within 4 years
84% got a degree within 5 years
85% got a degree within 6 years

AFTER GRADUATION

47% pursued further study (15% business, 11% arts and sciences, 11% law)
59% had job offers within 6 months
11 organizations recruited on campus
1 Fulbright scholar

WHAT YOU WILL PAY

Tuition and fees $16,628
Room and board $4782
66% receive need-based financial aid
Need-based college-administered scholarships and grants average $9754 per award
17% receive non-need financial aid
Non-need college-administered scholarships and grants average $5405 per award

GROVE CITY COLLEGE

Grove City, Pennsylvania • Small-town setting • Private • Independent-Religious • Coed

Grove City is a nationally acclaimed 4-year private Christian college of liberal arts and sciences. From its founding days, the College has endeavored to give young people the best in liberal and scientific education at the lowest possible cost and, in keeping with this historic policy, still maintains one of the lowest tuitions of an independent, high-quality college. J. Howard Pew, one of the guiding spirits in building Grove City College, stated that the College's "prime responsibility is to inculcate in the minds and hearts of youth those Christian, moral, and ethical principles without which our country cannot long endure." These principles have been part of the dynamic motivation of Grove City College.

 Academics

Grove City offers a Western civilization curriculum and core academic program. It awards bachelor's and master's **degrees**. Challenging opportunities include advanced placement, self-designed majors, and a senior project. Special programs include internships and summer session for credit.

The most popular **majors** include business and elementary education. A complete listing of majors at Grove City appears in the Majors Index beginning on page 379.

The **faculty** at Grove City has 105 full-time graduate and undergraduate teachers, 68% with terminal degrees. 65% of the faculty serve as student advisers. The student-faculty ratio is 22:1, and the average class size in core courses is 67.

 Computers on Campus

Students are required to have a computer. PCs are provided. 120 **computers** available in the computer center, engineer-ing labs, science building, and the library provide access to the main academic computer and e-mail. Staffed computer lab on campus provides training in the use of computers and software.

The **library** has 165,500 books, 270,000 microform titles, and 1,200 subscriptions.

 Campus Life

There are 123 active **organizations** on campus, including a drama/theater group and student-run newspaper and radio station. 30% of eligible men and 50% of eligible women are members of 5 local **fraternities** and 8 local **sororities**. Student **safety services** include monitored women's dormitory entrances, late night transport/escort service, 24-hour emergency telephone alarm devices, 24-hour patrols by trained security personnel, student patrols, and electronically operated dormitory entrances.

Grove City is a member of the NCAA (Division III). **Intercollegiate sports** include baseball (m), basketball (m, w), cross-country running (m, w), football (m), golf (m, w), soccer (m, w), softball (w), swimming and diving (m, w), tennis (m, w), track and field (m, w), volleyball (w).

 Applying

Grove City requires an essay, a high school transcript, 2 recommendations, and SAT I or ACT. It recommends 3 years of high school math and science, 3 years of high school foreign language, and a campus interview. Early, deferred, and midyear entrance are possible, with a 2/15 deadline and 4/15 for financial aid. **Contact:** Mr. Jeffrey C. Mincey, Director of Admissions, 100 Campus Drive, Grove City, PA 16127-2104, 412-458-2100.

GETTING IN LAST YEAR
2,570 applied
48% were accepted
51% enrolled (625)
57% from top tenth of their h.s. class
3.7 average high school GPA
25% had SAT verbal scores over 600
66% had SAT math scores over 600
64% had ACT scores over 26
2% had SAT verbal scores over 700
15% had SAT math scores over 700
18% had ACT scores over 30
3 National Merit Scholars
59 valedictorians

THE STUDENT BODY
Total 2,324, of whom 2,302
   are undergraduates

From 39 states and territories,
   19 other countries
62% from Pennsylvania
50% women, 50% men
0% African Americans
0% Native Americans
1% Hispanics
1% Asian Americans
1% international students

AFTER FRESHMAN YEAR
90% returned for sophomore year
69% got a degree within 4 years
75% got a degree within 5 years

AFTER GRADUATION
16% pursued further study (11% arts and
   sciences, 2% medicine, 1% business)
67% had job offers within 6 months
88 organizations recruited on campus

WHAT YOU WILL PAY
Tuition and fees $6174
Room and board $3474
38% receive need-based financial aid
Need-based college-administered scholarships and
   grants average $1450 per award
32% receive non-need financial aid
Non-need college-administered scholarships and
   grants average $4702 per award

GUILFORD COLLEGE

Greensboro, North Carolina • Suburban setting • Private • Independent-Religious • Coed

In each of the last 2 years the majority of graduating seniors have chosen the same 2 adjectives to describe Guilford: friendly and challenging. Although students work hard, they have solid, friendly relationships with faculty members who support the students in their course work. The College continues to believe that it is important for students to strike a balance between their studies and activities. Guilford students tend to be aware, concerned, issue-oriented, open-minded, and supportive of each other.

 ## Academics

Guilford offers an area distribution and interdisciplinary curriculum and core academic program; a few graduate courses are open to undergraduates. It awards bachelor's **degrees**. Challenging opportunities include advanced placement, accelerated degree programs, self-designed majors, tutorials, an honors program, and a senior project. Special programs include internships, summer session for credit, off-campus study, study abroad, and Army and Air Force ROTC.

The most popular **majors** include business, psychology, and criminal justice. A complete listing of majors at Guilford appears in the Majors Index beginning on page 379.

The **faculty** at Guilford has 89 full-time teachers, 87% with terminal degrees. 100% of the faculty serve as student advisers. The student-faculty ratio is 14:1.

 ## Computers on Campus

Students are not required to have a computer. Student rooms are linked to a campus network. 150 **computers** available in the computer center, computer labs, the learn-ing resource center, classroom buildings, the library, the student center, and dormitories provide access to the main academic computer, e-mail, and the Internet. Staffed computer lab on campus (open 24 hours a day) provides training in the use of computers and software.

The **library** has 223,906 books, 56 microform titles, and 1,088 subscriptions. It is connected to 15 national **on-line** catalogs.

 ## Campus Life

There are 42 active **organizations** on campus, including a drama/theater group and student-run newspaper and radio station. 62% of students participate in student government elections. Student **safety services** include late night transport/escort service, 24-hour emergency telephone alarm devices, 24-hour patrols by trained security personnel, and student patrols.

Guilford is a member of the NCAA (Division III). **Intercollegiate sports** include baseball (m), basketball (m, w), football (m), golf (m), lacrosse (m, w), rugby (m, w), soccer (m, w), tennis (m, w), volleyball (w).

 ## Applying

Guilford requires an essay, a high school transcript, 3 years of high school math, 2 years of high school foreign language, 2 recommendations, SAT I or ACT, and a minimum high school GPA of 2.0. It recommends 3 years of high school science, an interview, SAT II Subject Tests, and a minimum high school GPA of 3.0. Early, deferred, and midyear entrance are possible, with a 2/1 deadline and continuous processing to 3/1 for financial aid. **Contact:** Mr. Alton Newell, Dean of Admission, 5800 West Friendly Avenue, Greensboro, NC 27410-4173, 910-316-2124 or toll-free 800-992-7759; fax 910-316-2954.

GETTING IN LAST YEAR
1,204 applied
82% were accepted
30% enrolled (290)
29% from top tenth of their h.s. class
3.17 average high school GPA
48% had SAT verbal scores over 600 (R)
33% had SAT math scores over 600 (R)
49% had ACT scores over 26
12% had SAT verbal scores over 700 (R)
5% had SAT math scores over 700 (R)
15% had ACT scores over 30
7 valedictorians

THE STUDENT BODY
1,093 undergraduates

From 39 states and territories, 34 other countries
30% from North Carolina
51% women, 49% men
7% African Americans
1% Native Americans
2% Hispanics
1% Asian Americans
5% international students

AFTER FRESHMAN YEAR
73% returned for sophomore year
52% got a degree within 4 years
65% got a degree within 5 years
68% got a degree within 6 years

AFTER GRADUATION
22% pursued further study (12% arts and sciences, 3% medicine, 2% law)
75% had job offers within 6 months
93 organizations recruited on campus

WHAT YOU WILL PAY
Tuition and fees $14,390
Room and board $5270
61% receive need-based financial aid
Need-based college-administered scholarships and grants average $3796 per award
24% receive non-need financial aid
Non-need college-administered scholarships and grants average $4274 per award

GUSTAVUS ADOLPHUS COLLEGE

St. Peter, Minnesota • Small-town setting • Private • Independent-Religious • Coed

Gustavus Adolphus College is a national liberal arts college committed to high-quality teaching, the liberal arts and sciences, and its Lutheran heritage. Innovation in the classroom is demonstrated through the 4-1-4 calendar, 2 core curricula, the Writing Across the Curriculum program, and one of the most progressive undergraduate research programs in the country. Cost is made affordable through the Guaranteed Cost Plan, Partners in Scholarship Award for research mentoring, and the new government direct loan program. Excellent facilities include Olin Hall for physics, mathematics, and computer science; Confer Hall for humanities; and Lund Center for physical education, athletics, and health.

 Academics

Gustavus offers a liberal arts curriculum and core academic program. It awards bachelor's **degrees**. Challenging opportunities include advanced placement, accelerated degree programs, self-designed majors, tutorials, an honors program, a senior project, Phi Beta Kappa, and Sigma Xi. Special programs include cooperative education, internships, summer session for credit, off-campus study, study abroad, and Army ROTC.

The most popular **majors** include biology/biological sciences, psychology, and political science/government. A complete listing of majors at Gustavus appears in the Majors Index beginning on page 379.

The **faculty** at Gustavus has 164 full-time teachers, 83% with terminal degrees. 100% of the faculty serve as student advisers. The student-faculty ratio is 13:1.

 Computers on Campus

Students are not required to have a computer. Student rooms are linked to a campus network. 200 **computers** available in the computer center, computer labs, classrooms, and the library provide access to e-mail and the Internet. Staffed computer lab on campus provides training in the use of computers and software.

The 5 **libraries** have 233,000 books, 30,000 microform titles, and 1,200 subscriptions. They are connected to 5 national **on-line** catalogs.

 Campus Life

There are 85 active **organizations** on campus, including a drama/theater group and student-run newspaper and radio station. 60% of students participate in student government elections. 20% of eligible men and 25% of eligible women are members of 6 local **fraternities** and 6 local **sororities**. Student **safety services** include late night transport/escort service, 24-hour emergency telephone alarm devices, 24-hour patrols by trained security personnel, and electronically operated dormitory entrances.

Gustavus is a member of the NCAA (Division III). **Intercollegiate sports** include baseball (m), basketball (m, w), cross-country running (m, w), football (m), golf (m, w), gymnastics (w), ice hockey (m, w), lacrosse (m), rugby (m, w), soccer (m, w), softball (w), swimming and diving (m, w), tennis (m, w), track and field (m, w), volleyball (m, w).

 Applying

Gustavus requires an essay, a high school transcript, 2 recommendations, and SAT I or ACT. It recommends 3 years of high school math and science, some high school foreign language, and an interview. Early, deferred, and midyear entrance are possible, with a 4/1 deadline and continuous processing to 4/15 for financial aid. **Contact:** Mr. Mark Anderson, Director of Admissions, 800 College Avenue, St. Peter, MN 56082-1498, 507-933-7676 or toll-free 800-GUSTAVU(S).

GETTING IN LAST YEAR
1,801 applied
82% were accepted
42% enrolled (624)
34% from top tenth of their h.s. class
56% had SAT verbal scores over 600 (R)
50% had SAT math scores over 600 (R)
48% had ACT scores over 26
15% had SAT verbal scores over 700 (R)
10% had SAT math scores over 700 (R)
15% had ACT scores over 30
14 National Merit Scholars
55 valedictorians

THE STUDENT BODY
2,361 undergraduates

From 45 states and territories,
23 other countries
69% from Minnesota
54% women, 46% men
2% African Americans
0% Native Americans
1% Hispanics
3% Asian Americans
2% international students

AFTER FRESHMAN YEAR
88% returned for sophomore year
76% got a degree within 4 years
78% got a degree within 5 years

AFTER GRADUATION
36% pursued further study (13% arts and sciences, 7% business, 5% law)
92% had job offers within 6 months

WHAT YOU WILL PAY
Tuition and fees $14,835
Room and board $3760
73% receive need-based financial aid
Need-based college-administered scholarships and grants average $6000 per award
6% receive non-need financial aid
Non-need college-administered scholarships and grants average $3000 per award

HAMILTON COLLEGE

Clinton, New York • Rural setting • Private • Independent • Coed

Hamilton College is situated in the hills overlooking the Mohawk Valley in central New York State on a picturesque campus of more than 1,000 acres. Facilities include the new Schambach Center for the Performing Arts, fully equipped scientific laboratories, a library with almost 500,000 volumes, and a computer center with microcomputers for student use. One of America's oldest colleges, Hamilton has remained small and is committed solely to undergraduate education. The favorable student-faculty ratio assures each of Hamilton's students small classes and access to professors.

Academics

Hamilton offers a liberal arts curriculum and core academic program. It awards bachelor's **degrees**. Challenging opportunities include advanced placement, accelerated degree programs, self-designed majors, tutorials, a senior project, Phi Beta Kappa, and Sigma Xi. Special programs include internships, off-campus study, study abroad, and Army and Air Force ROTC.

The most popular **majors** include political science/government, history, and economics. A complete listing of majors at Hamilton appears in the Majors Index beginning on page 379.

The **faculty** at Hamilton has 176 full-time teachers, 98% with terminal degrees. 100% of the faculty serve as student advisers. The student-faculty ratio is 10:1.

Computers on Campus

Students are not required to have a computer. Student rooms are linked to a campus network. 200 **computers** available in the computer center, reading/writing center, the library, and the student center provide access to e-mail and on-line services. Staffed computer lab on campus provides training in the use of computers.

The 4 **libraries** have 495,048 books, 888 microform titles, and 2,801 subscriptions. They are connected to 8 national **on-line** catalogs.

Campus Life

There are 80 active **organizations** on campus, including a drama/theater group and student-run newspaper and radio station. 43% of eligible men and 6% of eligible women are members of 6 national **fraternities**, 3 local **sororities**, and 1 private society. Student **safety services** include student safety program, late night transport/escort service, and 24-hour patrols by trained security personnel.

Hamilton is a member of the NCAA (Division III). **Intercollegiate sports** include baseball (m), basketball (m, w), crew (m, w), cross-country running (m, w), fencing (m, w), field hockey (w), football (m), golf (m, w), ice hockey (m, w), lacrosse (m, w), rugby (m, w), sailing (m, w), skiing (downhill) (m, w), soccer (m, w), softball (w), squash (m, w), swimming and diving (m, w), tennis (m, w), track and field (m, w), volleyball (m, w).

Applying

Hamilton requires an essay, a high school transcript, 1 recommendation, sample of expository prose, and SAT I or ACT. It recommends 3 years of high school math and science, 3 years of high school foreign language, an interview, and 3 SAT II Subject Tests. Early and deferred entrance are possible, with a 1/15 deadline and 2/1 for financial aid. **Contact:** Mr. Richard M. Fuller, Dean of Admission and Financial Aid, 198 College Hill Road, Clinton, NY 13323-1218, 315-859-4421 or toll-free 800-843-2655; fax 315-859-4457.

GETTING IN LAST YEAR
3,650 applied
47% were accepted
29% enrolled (489)
43% from top tenth of their h.s. class
12 valedictorians

THE STUDENT BODY
1,650 undergraduates
From 43 states and territories,
44 other countries

46% from New York
46% women, 54% men
4% African Americans
0% Native Americans
3% Hispanics
4% Asian Americans
6% international students

AFTER GRADUATION
20% pursued further study (8% arts and sciences, 6% law, 5% medicine)

WHAT YOU WILL PAY
Tuition and fees $20,700
Room and board $5250
55% receive need-based financial aid
Need-based college-administered scholarships and grants average $10,630 per award

HAMLINE UNIVERSITY

St. Paul, Minnesota • Urban setting • Private • Independent-Religious • Coed

When it comes to education, Hamline students want the best. They want a school with an excellent academic reputation (membership in Phi Beta Kappa; the Hamline Plan, an award-winning curriculum) that provides interaction with professors (13:1 student-faculty ratio). They want the best of living in a metropolitan area (Minneapolis and St. Paul) and a safe, friendly environment (a residential campus). They want a liberal arts experience and a career advantage (internship opportunities). Hamline brings these qualities together and assures students that they may finish their degrees in four years, or the fifth year is tuition-free.

Academics

Hamline offers a goal-directed, interdisciplinary curriculum and core academic program; fewer than half of graduate courses are open to undergraduates. It awards bachelor's, master's, and first professional **degrees**. Challenging opportunities include advanced placement, self-designed majors, tutorials, an honors program, a senior project, and Phi Beta Kappa. Special programs include cooperative education, internships, summer session for credit, off-campus study, study abroad, and Air Force ROTC.

The most popular **majors** include psychology, English, and political science/government. A complete listing of majors at Hamline appears in the Majors Index beginning on page 379.

The **faculty** at Hamline has 131 full-time graduate and undergraduate teachers, 98% with terminal degrees. 100% of the faculty serve as student advisers. The student-faculty ratio is 13:1.

Computers on Campus

Students are not required to have a computer. 190 **computers** available in the computer center, computer labs, the research center, the learning resource center, science building, classrooms, the library, the student center, and dormitories provide access to the main academic computer, e-mail, on-line services, and the Internet. Staffed computer lab on campus provides training in the use of computers and software.

The 2 **libraries** have 312,345 books, 101,234 microform titles, and 3,453 subscriptions. They are connected to 3 national **on-line** catalogs.

Campus Life

There are 75 active **organizations** on campus, including a drama/theater group and student-run newspaper. 5% of eligible men and 5% of eligible women are members of 2 national **fraternities** and 2 local **sororities**. Student **safety services** include late night transport/escort service, 24-hour emergency telephone alarm devices, 24-hour patrols by trained security personnel, and electronically operated dormitory entrances.

Hamline is a member of the NCAA (Division III). **Intercollegiate sports** include baseball (m), basketball (m, w), cross-country running (m, w), football (m), gymnastics (w), ice hockey (m), soccer (m, w), softball (w), swimming and diving (m, w), tennis (m, w), track and field (m, w), volleyball (w).

Applying

Hamline requires an essay, a high school transcript, 2 recommendations, and SAT I or ACT. It recommends 3 years of high school math and science, 2 years of high school foreign language, and an interview. Early and deferred entrance are possible, with rolling admissions and continuous processing to 4/15 for financial aid. **Contact:** Dr. W. Scott Friedhoff, Dean of Undergraduate Admissions, 833 Snelling Avenue, St. Paul, MN 55104-1284, 612-641-2207 or toll-free 800-753-9753; fax 612-641-2458.

GETTING IN LAST YEAR
1,080 applied
83% were accepted
40% enrolled (358)
35% from top tenth of their h.s. class
3.4 average high school GPA
41% had ACT scores over 26
11% had ACT scores over 30
5 National Merit Scholars

THE STUDENT BODY
Total 2,932, of whom 1,645
   are undergraduates
From 42 states and territories,
   34 other countries

72% from Minnesota
57% women, 43% men
3% African Americans
1% Native Americans
2% Hispanics
5% Asian Americans
3% international students

AFTER FRESHMAN YEAR
82% returned for sophomore year
56% got a degree within 4 years
61% got a degree within 5 years
62% got a degree within 6 years

AFTER GRADUATION
26% pursued further study (12% arts and
   sciences, 7% law, 3% business)
84% had job offers within 6 months

WHAT YOU WILL PAY
Tuition and fees $13,808
Room and board $4342
92% receive need-based financial aid
Need-based college-administered scholarships and
   grants average $7806 per award
7% receive non-need financial aid
Non-need college-administered scholarships and
   grants average $2438 per award

HAMPDEN-SYDNEY COLLEGE

Hampden-Sydney, Virginia • Rural setting • Private • Independent-Religious • Men

The spirit of Hampden-Sydney lies in its sense of community and its preservation of tradition. Honor and civility inform the life of the College. Challenged by the curriculum, students can get help when they need it because classes are small. The greatest advantage of small-college life is that everyone can be involved. Athletics, debating, publications, fraternity life—all are part of the educational process. Many students enjoy hunting, fishing, camping, and hiking. The total experience at the College produces a man well-suited for the challenges of a job, the demands of social service, and the pleasure of personal endeavors.

Academics

Hampden-Sydney offers a liberal arts curriculum and core academic program. It awards bachelor's **degrees**. Challenging opportunities include advanced placement, accelerated degree programs, tutorials, an honors program, a senior project, Phi Beta Kappa, and Sigma Xi. Special programs include internships, summer session for credit, off-campus study, study abroad, and Army ROTC.

The most popular **majors** include economics, history, and political science/government. A complete listing of majors at Hampden-Sydney appears in the Majors Index beginning on page 379.

The **faculty** at Hampden-Sydney has 62 full-time teachers, 87% with terminal degrees. 90% of the faculty serve as student advisers. The student-faculty ratio is 13:1.

Computers on Campus

Students are not required to have a computer. Student rooms are linked to a campus network. 140 **computers** available in the computer center, computer labs, classrooms, the library, and dormitories provide access to the main academic computer, off-campus computing facilities, e-mail, on-line services, and the Internet. Staffed computer lab on campus provides training in the use of computers and software.

The **library** has 212,000 books, 39,800 microform titles, and 850 subscriptions. It is connected to 8 national **on-line** catalogs.

 Campus Life

There are 30 active **organizations** on campus, including a drama/theater group and student-run newspaper and radio station. 75% of students participate in student government elections. 37% of eligible undergraduates are members of 11 national **fraternities**. Student **safety services** include 24-hour emergency telephone alarm devices and 24-hour patrols by trained security personnel.

Hampden-Sydney is a member of the NCAA (Division III). **Intercollegiate sports** include baseball, basketball, cross-country running, fencing, football, golf, lacrosse, rugby, soccer, tennis, water polo.

 Applying

Hampden-Sydney requires an essay, a high school transcript, 3 years of high school math, 2 years of high school foreign language, 2 recommendations, and SAT I or ACT. It recommends 3 years of high school science, a campus interview, SAT II Subject Tests (including SAT II: Writing Test), and a minimum high school GPA of 2.0. Early and midyear entrance are possible, with a 3/1 deadline and continuous processing to 3/1 for financial aid. **Contact:** Ms. Anita H. Garland, Director of Admissions, PO Box 667, Hampden-Sydney, VA 23943-0667, 804-223-6120 or toll-free 800-755-0733; fax 804-223-6346.

GETTING IN LAST YEAR
817 applied
83% were accepted
42% enrolled (285)
16% from top tenth of their h.s. class
3.0 average high school GPA
16% had SAT verbal scores over 600
33% had SAT math scores over 600
28% had ACT scores over 26
2% had SAT verbal scores over 700
5% had SAT math scores over 700
9% had ACT scores over 30
2 class presidents
5 valedictorians

THE STUDENT BODY
971 undergraduates

From 31 states and territories,
   4 other countries
54% from Virginia
100% men
3% African Americans
0% Native Americans
1% Hispanics
2% Asian Americans
1% international students

AFTER FRESHMAN YEAR
78% returned for sophomore year
60% got a degree within 4 years
66% got a degree within 5 years

AFTER GRADUATION
20% pursued further study (11% arts and
   sciences, 5% law, 4% medicine)
75% had job offers within 6 months
28 organizations recruited on campus

WHAT YOU WILL PAY
Tuition and fees $14,322
Room and board $5011
50% receive need-based financial aid
Need-based college-administered scholarships and
   grants average $7000 per award
25% receive non-need financial aid
Non-need college-administered scholarships and
   grants average $4925 per award

HAMPSHIRE COLLEGE

Amherst, Massachusetts • Rural setting • Private • Independent • Coed

Hampshire College's bold, innovative approach to the liberal arts promotes self-reliance, creativity, critical thinking, and entrepreneurial spirit. Every Hampshire student has the freedom to design an individualized, interdisciplinary program of study in close collaboration with faculty mentors. Hampshire's motto, *To Know Is Not Enough,* reflects its commitment to rigorous education that goes beyond the classroom and puts learning to good use in the world. Hampshire's national reputation for excellence rests in its distinctive, contract-based academic system, where each student's progress is measured through narrative evaluations by faculty instead of credits and grades.

Academics

Hampshire offers an individually-designed curriculum and core academic program. It awards bachelor's **degrees**. Challenging opportunities include advanced placement, accelerated degree programs, self-designed majors, and a senior project. Special programs include internships, off-campus study, study abroad, and Army ROTC.

The most popular **majors** include creative writing, film studies, and art/fine arts. A complete listing of majors at Hampshire appears in the Majors Index beginning on page 379.

The **faculty** at Hampshire has 87 full-time teachers, 85% with terminal degrees. 100% of the faculty serve as student advisers. The student-faculty ratio is 12:1, and the average class size in core courses is 17.

Computers on Campus

Students are not required to have a computer. Student rooms are linked to a campus network. 125 **computers** available in the computer center, computer labs, the research center, the library, and student rooms provide access to the main academic computer, off-campus computing facilities, e-mail, on-line services, and the Internet. Staffed computer lab on campus provides training in the use of computers and software.

The **library** has 114,374 books, 223 microform titles, and 1,016 subscriptions. It is connected to 7 national **on-line** catalogs.

Campus Life

There are 80 active **organizations** on campus, including a drama/theater group and student-run newspaper. Student **safety services** include EMT On Call Program, counselor advocates, late night transport/escort service, 24-hour emergency telephone alarm devices, 24-hour patrols by trained security personnel, and student patrols. **Intercollegiate sports** include baseball (m), basketball (m, w), equestrian sports (m, w), soccer (m, w), volleyball (m, w).

Applying

Hampshire requires an essay, a high school transcript, and 2 recommendations. It recommends an interview. Early, deferred, and midyear entrance are possible, with a 2/1 deadline and continuous processing to 2/15 for financial aid. **Contact:** Ms. Audrey Smith, Director of Admissions, West Street, Amherst, MA 01002, 413-582-5471; fax 413-582-5631.

GETTING IN LAST YEAR
1,637 applied
68% were accepted
28% enrolled (314)
26% from top tenth of their h.s. class
3.14 average high school GPA
1 valedictorian

THE STUDENT BODY
1,073 undergraduates
From 46 states and territories,
   25 other countries
19% from Massachusetts

58% women, 42% men
4% African Americans
1% Native Americans
3% Hispanics
3% Asian Americans
4% international students

AFTER FRESHMAN YEAR
83% returned for sophomore year
41% got a degree within 4 years
58% got a degree within 5 years
62% got a degree within 6 years

WHAT YOU WILL PAY
Tuition and fees $22,535
Room and board $5740
61% receive need-based financial aid
Need-based college-administered scholarships and
   grants average $12,120 per award
1% receive non-need financial aid
Non-need college-administered scholarships and
   grants average $4975 per award

HARDING UNIVERSITY

Searcy, Arkansas • Small-town setting • Private • Independent-Religious • Coed

Located in the beautiful foothills of the Ozark Mountains, Harding is one of America's more highly regarded private universities. At Harding, students build lifetime friendships and, upon graduation, are highly recruited. Harding's Christian environment and challenging academic program develop students who can compete and succeed. Whether on the main campus or in the international studies program in Italy, Greece, England, or Australia, students find Harding to be a caring and serving family. From Missouri flood relief to working with orphans in Haiti or farmers in Kenya, hundreds of Harding students serve others worldwide each year.

Academics

Harding offers an interdisciplinary curriculum and core academic program; more than half of graduate courses are open to undergraduates. It awards bachelor's and master's **degrees**. Challenging opportunities include advanced placement, accelerated degree programs, self-designed majors, tutorials, Freshman Honors College, an honors program, and a senior project. Special programs include cooperative education, internships, summer session for credit, study abroad, and Army ROTC.

The most popular **majors** include business, elementary education, and communication. A complete listing of majors at Harding appears in the Majors Index beginning on page 379.

The **faculty** at Harding has 194 full-time graduate and undergraduate teachers, 72% with terminal degrees. 98% of the faculty serve as student advisers. The student-faculty ratio is 16:1.

Computers on Campus

Students are not required to have a computer. Student rooms are linked to a campus network. 275 **computers** available in the computer center, computer labs, the learning resource center, classrooms, and the library provide access to the main academic computer, off-campus computing facilities, e-mail, on-line services, and the Internet. Staffed computer lab on campus (open 24 hours a day) provides training in the use of computers and software.

The 2 **libraries** have 430,604 books, 190,217 microform titles, and 1,875 subscriptions. They are connected to 12 national **on-line** catalogs.

Campus Life

There are 52 active **organizations** on campus, including a drama/theater group and student-run newspaper and radio station. 40% of students participate in student government elections. 85% of eligible men and 80% of eligible women are members of 20 local **fraternities** and 20 local **sororities**. Student **safety services** include 24-hour emergency telephone alarm devices and 24-hour patrols by trained security personnel.

Harding is a member of the NCAA (Division II). **Intercollegiate sports** (some offering scholarships) include baseball (m), basketball (m, w), cross-country running (m, w), football (m), golf (m), tennis (m, w), track and field (m, w), volleyball (w).

Applying

Harding requires a high school transcript, 3 years of high school math and science, 2 recommendations, an interview, and SAT I or ACT. It recommends 2 years of high school foreign language. Early, deferred, and midyear entrance are possible, with a 7/1 deadline and continuous processing to 3/1 for financial aid. **Contact:** Mr. Mike Williams, Director of Admissions, Box 2255, Searcy, AR 72149-0001, 501-279-4407 or toll-free 800-477-4407; fax 501-279-4865.

GETTING IN LAST YEAR
1,694 applied
64% were accepted
81% enrolled (878)
30% from top tenth of their h.s. class
3.3 average high school GPA
44% had ACT scores over 26
14% had ACT scores over 30
17 National Merit Scholars
40 valedictorians

THE STUDENT BODY
Total 4,071, of whom 3,653
  are undergraduates
From 49 states and territories,
  36 other countries

30% from Arkansas
53% women, 47% men
3% African Americans
1% Native Americans
1% Hispanics
1% Asian Americans
4% international students

AFTER FRESHMAN YEAR
76% returned for sophomore year
39% got a degree within 4 years
54% got a degree within 5 years
60% got a degree within 6 years

AFTER GRADUATION
30% pursued further study (10% arts and
  sciences, 6% business, 6% theology)

98% had job offers within 6 months
185 organizations recruited on campus

WHAT YOU WILL PAY
Tuition and fees $6450
Room and board $3750
70% receive need-based financial aid
Need-based college-administered scholarships and
  grants average $500 per award
35% receive non-need financial aid
Non-need college-administered scholarships and
  grants average $2832 per award

HARVARD UNIVERSITY

Cambridge, Massachusetts • Urban setting • Private • Independent • Coed

Harvard and Radcliffe, the coeducational undergraduate colleges of Harvard University, offer a curriculum of 3,000 courses, the world's largest university library, a state-of-the-art Science Center, art museums, athletic facilities, and a comprehensive housing system. Excellence and diversity are the hallmarks of the experience. Students come from all 50 states and many other countries and from all educational, ethnic, and economic backgrounds. Students choose from more than 40 academic fields and pursue more than 250 different extracurricular activities. The admission process is rigorous. The committee considers academic achievement, extracurricular strengths, and personal qualities. Harvard and Radcliffe offer need-based financial aid.

Academics

Harvard offers a liberal arts curriculum and core academic program. It awards bachelor's, master's, doctoral, and first professional **degrees**. Challenging opportunities include advanced placement, accelerated degree programs, self-designed majors, tutorials, an honors program, a senior project, Phi Beta Kappa, and Sigma Xi. Special programs include summer session for credit, off-campus study, and Army, Naval, and Air Force ROTC.

The most popular **majors** include political science/government, literature, and economics. A complete listing of majors at Harvard appears in the Majors Index beginning on page 379.

The **faculty** at Harvard has 2,106 full-time graduate and undergraduate teachers, 100% with terminal degrees. The student-faculty ratio is 8:1.

Computers on Campus

Students are not required to have a computer. Student rooms are linked to a campus network. **Computers** available in the computer center, computer labs, the research center, classrooms, the library, dormitories, and student rooms provide access to the main academic computer, e-mail, on-line services, and the Internet. Staffed computer lab on campus.

The 91 **libraries** have 12.8 million books, 6.8 million microform titles, and 96,357 subscriptions.

Campus Life

There are 250 active **organizations** on campus, including a drama/theater group and student-run newspaper and radio station. 99% of eligible men and 99% of eligible women are members of "House" system. Student **safety services** include required and optional safety courses, late night transport/escort service, 24-hour emergency telephone alarm devices, 24-hour patrols by trained security personnel, and electronically operated dormitory entrances.

Harvard is a member of the NCAA (Division I). **Intercollegiate sports** include baseball (m), basketball (m, w), crew (m, w), cross-country running (m, w), fencing (m, w), field hockey (w), football (m), golf (m, w), ice hockey (m, w), lacrosse (m, w), sailing (m, w), skiing (cross-country) (m, w), skiing (downhill) (m, w), soccer (m, w), softball (w), squash (m, w), swimming and diving (m, w), tennis (m, w), track and field (m, w), volleyball (m, w), water polo (m, w), wrestling (m).

Applying

Harvard requires an essay, a high school transcript, 2 recommendations, an interview, SAT I or ACT, and 3 SAT II Subject Tests. It recommends 4 years of high school math and science, 4 years of high school foreign language, 4 years of high school English, 3 years of high school history, and ACT. Early and deferred entrance are possible, with a 1/1 deadline and a 2/1 priority date for financial aid. **Contact:** Office of Admissions and Financial Aid, Byerly Hall, 8 Garden Street, Cambridge, MA 02138, 617-495-1551.

GETTING IN LAST YEAR
17,852 applied
12% were accepted
75% enrolled (1,618)
91% from top tenth of their h.s. class
393 National Merit Scholars
474 valedictorians

THE STUDENT BODY
Total 18,480, of whom 6,643
   are undergraduates
From 53 states and territories,
   90 other countries

16% from Massachusetts
44% women, 56% men
8% African Americans
1% Native Americans
7% Hispanics
19% Asian Americans
7% international students

AFTER FRESHMAN YEAR
95% returned for sophomore year
95% got a degree within 4 years
97% got a degree within 5 years

AFTER GRADUATION
30% pursued further study
7 Rhodes, 4 Marshall, 30 Fulbright scholars

WHAT YOU WILL PAY
Tuition and fees $20,865
Room and board $6710
45% receive need-based financial aid

HARVEY MUDD COLLEGE

Claremont, California • Suburban setting • Private • Independent • Coed

Harvey Mudd College is a school of math, science, and engineering, with nearly a third of the course work in the humanities and social sciences. As one of the 6 Claremont Colleges, Harvey Mudd offers access to classes, social opportunities, and facilities at the other colleges—all within easy walking distance of one another. The student body of 650 works closely with faculty. Last year, over $2 million of undergraduate research was conducted. Students may work directly with a professor or participate in a clinic whereby a team of students solves real-world problems for high-tech companies.

 Academics

Harvey Mudd offers a science and engineering curriculum and core academic program. It awards bachelor's and master's **degrees**. Challenging opportunities include advanced placement, self-designed majors, tutorials, and a senior project. Special programs include off-campus study, study abroad, and Army and Air Force ROTC.

The most popular **majors** include engineering (general), physics, and chemistry. A complete listing of majors at Harvey Mudd appears in the Majors Index beginning on page 379.

The **faculty** at Harvey Mudd has 70 full-time undergraduate teachers, 100% with terminal degrees. 100% of the faculty serve as student advisers. The student-faculty ratio is 8:1.

 Computers on Campus

Students are not required to have a computer. Student rooms are linked to a campus network. 100 **computers** available in the computer center, computer labs, and the library provide access to the main academic computer, off-campus computing facilities, e-mail, on-line services, and the Internet. Staffed computer lab on campus (open 24 hours a day) provides training in the use of computers and software.

The 2 **libraries** have 1.9 million books, 1.3 million microform titles, and 6,029 subscriptions.

 Campus Life

Active **organizations** on campus include drama/theater group and student-run newspaper and radio station. 50% of students participate in student government elections. Student **safety services** include late night transport/escort service and 24-hour patrols by trained security personnel.

Harvey Mudd is a member of the NCAA (Division III). **Intercollegiate sports** include baseball (m), basketball (m, w), cross-country running (m, w), football (m), golf (m), soccer (m, w), softball (w), swimming and diving (m, w), tennis (m, w), track and field (m, w), volleyball (w), water polo (m).

 Applying

Harvey Mudd requires an essay, a high school transcript, 4 years of high school math, 3 years of high school science, 3 recommendations, SAT I, and 3 SAT II Subject Tests (including SAT II: Writing Test). It recommends 2 years of high school foreign language and an interview. Early and deferred entrance are possible, with a 2/1 deadline and a 2/1 priority date for financial aid. **Contact:** Ms. Patricia Coleman, Dean of Admission, 301 East 12th Street, Kingston Hall, Claremont, CA 91711-5994, 909-621-8011.

GETTING IN LAST YEAR
1,388 applied
40% were accepted
31% enrolled (177)
100% from top tenth of their h.s. class
96% had SAT verbal scores over 600 (R)
100% had SAT math scores over 600 (R)
53% had SAT verbal scores over 700 (R)
84% had SAT math scores over 700 (R)
48 National Merit Scholars

THE STUDENT BODY
Total 636, of whom 628
  are undergraduates
From 48 states and territories,
  9 other countries

48% from California
25% women, 75% men
1% African Americans
1% Native Americans
5% Hispanics
24% Asian Americans
2% international students

AFTER FRESHMAN YEAR
91% returned for sophomore year
64% got a degree within 4 years
70% got a degree within 5 years
72% got a degree within 6 years

AFTER GRADUATION
63% pursued further study (39% arts and
  sciences, 24% engineering, 1% medicine)
37 organizations recruited on campus

WHAT YOU WILL PAY
Tuition and fees $18,566
Room and board $6920
75% receive need-based financial aid
Need-based college-administered scholarships and
  grants average $10,947 per award
Non-need college-administered scholarships and
  grants average $750 per award

HAVERFORD COLLEGE

Haverford, Pennsylvania • Suburban setting • Private • Independent • Coed

Haverford College, located 10 miles west of Center City Philadelphia, is situated on a 216-acre arboretum. Founded by the Society of Friends in 1833, Haverford offers a rigorous study of the liberal arts. Students also take pride in the Honor Code, begun in 1897. The community's commitment to service is exemplified by the large percentage of students involved in volunteer activities. Haverford's commitment to academic excellence is underscored by the fact that 80% of graduates enroll in graduate school within 5 years of graduation. Prospective students are encouraged to experience the many dimensions of Haverford by visiting the campus.

 Academics

Haverford offers a liberal arts curriculum and core academic program. It awards bachelor's **degrees**. Challenging opportunities include advanced placement, accelerated degree programs, self-designed majors, tutorials, a senior project, and Phi Beta Kappa. Off-campus study is a special program.

The most popular **majors** include English, biology/biological sciences, and history. A complete listing of majors at Haverford appears in the Majors Index beginning on page 379.

The **faculty** at Haverford has 97 full-time teachers, 97% with terminal degrees. 100% of the faculty serve as student advisers. The student-faculty ratio is 10:1, and the average class size in core courses is 18.

 Computers on Campus

Students are not required to have a computer. Student rooms are linked to a campus network. 172 **computers** available in the computer center, the learning resource center, clusters throughout campus, classrooms, the library, and dormitories provide access to the main academic computer, off-campus computing facilities, e-mail, on-line services, and the Internet. Staffed computer lab on campus provides training in the use of computers and software.

The 6 **libraries** have 400,000 books, 76,000 microform titles, and 1,286 subscriptions. They are connected to 6 national **on-line** catalogs.

 Campus Life

There are 50 active **organizations** on campus, including a drama/theater group and student-run newspaper and radio station. 45% of students participate in student government elections. Student **safety services** include late night transport/escort service, 24-hour emergency telephone alarm devices, and 24-hour patrols by trained security personnel.

Haverford is a member of the NCAA (Division III). **Intercollegiate sports** include baseball (m), basketball (m, w), cross-country running (m, w), fencing (m, w), field hockey (w), lacrosse (m, w), soccer (m, w), softball (w), squash (m, w), tennis (m, w), track and field (m, w), volleyball (w), wrestling (m).

 Applying

Haverford requires an essay, a high school transcript, 3 years of high school math, 3 years of high school foreign language, 2 recommendations, SAT I, and 3 SAT II Subject Tests (including SAT II: Writing Test). It recommends 3 years of high school science and an interview. Early and deferred entrance are possible, with a 1/15 deadline and 1/31 for financial aid. **Contact:** Ms. Delsie Phillips, Director of Admissions, 370 Lancaster Avenue, Haverford, PA 19041-1392, 610-896-1350; fax 610-896-1338.

GETTING IN LAST YEAR
2,622 applied
37% were accepted
31% enrolled (306)
80% from top tenth of their h.s. class
70% had SAT verbal scores over 600
89% had SAT math scores over 600
14% had SAT verbal scores over 700
43% had SAT math scores over 700

THE STUDENT BODY
1,115 undergraduates
From 44 states and territories,
   27 other countries

14% from Pennsylvania
50% women, 50% men
4% African Americans
5% Hispanics
8% Asian Americans
2% international students

AFTER FRESHMAN YEAR
97% returned for sophomore year
83% got a degree within 4 years
89% got a degree within 5 years
90% got a degree within 6 years

AFTER GRADUATION
21% pursued further study (9% arts and
   sciences, 6% medicine, 5% law)
66% had job offers within 6 months
45 organizations recruited on campus

WHAT YOU WILL PAY
Tuition and fees $20,075
Room and board $6550
40% receive need-based financial aid
Need-based college-administered scholarships and
   grants average $13,296 per award

HENDRIX COLLEGE

Conway, Arkansas • Suburban setting • Private • Independent-Religious • Coed

A small college located at the foothills of the Ozark Mountains 30 miles from Little Rock, Hendrix is a nationally recognized liberal arts college that prepares students for the finest professional and graduate schools in the nation. The College enrolls 1,000 students who are taught by a faculty of 80 professors, all of whom have PhDs or appropriate terminal degrees in their fields. Most students complete an undergraduate research project, and many study abroad while at Hendrix. Eighty-five percent of Hendrix students live on campus, fostering an intimate community in which students and faculty members interact in all aspects of campus life.

Academics

Hendrix offers a Western civilization curriculum and core academic program. It awards bachelor's **degrees**. Challenging opportunities include advanced placement, self-designed majors, tutorials, an honors program, and a senior project. Special programs include internships, study abroad, and Army ROTC.

The most popular **majors** include biology/biological sciences, psychology, and economics. A complete listing of majors at Hendrix appears in the Majors Index beginning on page 379.

The **faculty** at Hendrix has 70 full-time teachers, 100% with terminal degrees. 100% of the faculty serve as student advisers. The student-faculty ratio is 12:1.

Computers on Campus

Students are not required to have a computer. 68 **computers** available in the computer center, terminal room, and the library provide access to the main academic computer, e-mail, on-line services, and the Internet. Staffed computer lab on campus (open 24 hours a day) provides training in the use of computers and software.

The **library** has 195,000 books, 143,608 microform titles, and 586 subscriptions.

Campus Life

There are 38 active **organizations** on campus, including a drama/theater group and student-run newspaper and radio station. Student **safety services** include late night transport/escort service, 24-hour patrols by trained security personnel, and electronically operated dormitory entrances.

Hendrix is a member of the NCAA (Division III). **Intercollegiate sports** include baseball (m), basketball (m, w), cross-country running (m, w), golf (m), rugby (m), soccer (m, w), swimming and diving (m, w), tennis (m, w), track and field (m, w), volleyball (w).

Applying

Hendrix requires an essay, a high school transcript, SAT I or ACT, and in some cases 1 recommendation and a campus interview. It recommends 3 years of high school math and science and 1 year of high school foreign language. Early, deferred, and midyear entrance are possible, with rolling admissions and continuous processing to 3/1 for financial aid. **Contact:** Mr. Rock Jones, Interim Director of Admission, 1601 Harkrider Street, Conway, AR 72032, 501-450-1362 or toll-free 800-277-9017.

GETTING IN LAST YEAR
709 applied
90% were accepted
43% enrolled (274)
44% from top tenth of their h.s. class
3.6 average high school GPA
27% had SAT verbal scores over 600
47% had SAT math scores over 600
60% had ACT scores over 26
6% had SAT verbal scores over 700
9% had SAT math scores over 700
20% had ACT scores over 30
7 National Merit Scholars
15 valedictorians

THE STUDENT BODY
959 undergraduates
From 28 states and territories,
  9 other countries
76% from Arkansas
55% women, 45% men
5% African Americans
0% Native Americans
1% Hispanics
2% Asian Americans
2% international students

AFTER FRESHMAN YEAR
76% returned for sophomore year

WHAT YOU WILL PAY
Tuition and fees $9650
Room and board $3500
Need-based college-administered scholarships and
  grants average $2692 per award
Non-need college-administered scholarships and
  grants average $2942 per award

HILLSDALE COLLEGE

Hillsdale, Michigan • Small-town setting • Private • Independent • Coed

Located in south-central Michigan, Hillsdale College provides a value-based liberal arts education grounded in the Judeo-Christian heritage and the traditions of the Western world. The refusal of government funding is what makes Hillsdale unique. The College's fierce independence is critical to the level and type of educational excellence Hillsdale is able to provide.

Academics

Hillsdale offers a great books and Western civilization curriculum and core academic program. It awards bachelor's **degrees**. Challenging opportunities include advanced placement, accelerated degree programs, tutorials, an honors program, and a senior project. Special programs include internships, summer session for credit, study abroad, and Army, Naval, and Air Force ROTC.

The most popular **majors** include business, English, and education. A complete listing of majors at Hillsdale appears in the Majors Index beginning on page 379.

The **faculty** at Hillsdale has 83 full-time teachers, 83% with terminal degrees. 99% of the faculty serve as student advisers. The student-faculty ratio is 12:1.

Computers on Campus

Students are not required to have a computer. 150 **computers** available in the computer center, computer labs, the research center, the learning resource center, classrooms, and the library provide access to the main academic computer, off-campus computing facilities, e-mail, on-line services, and the Internet. Staffed computer lab on campus provides training in the use of computers and software.

The 4 **libraries** have 175,000 books, 23,000 microform titles, and 1,800 subscriptions.

Campus Life

There are 40 active **organizations** on campus, including a drama/theater group and student-run newspaper. 45% of students participate in student government elections. 45% of eligible men and 55% of eligible women are members of 5 national **fraternities** and 4 national **sororities**. Student **safety services** include late night transport/escort service, 24-hour emergency telephone alarm devices, 24-hour patrols by trained security personnel, and electronically operated dormitory entrances.

Hillsdale is a member of the NCAA (Division II) and NAIA. **Intercollegiate sports** (some offering scholarships) include baseball (m), basketball (m, w), cross-country running (m, w), equestrian sports (w), football (m), golf (m), ice hockey (m), lacrosse (m), soccer (m), softball (w), swimming and diving (w), tennis (m, w), track and field (m, w), volleyball (w).

Applying

Hillsdale requires an essay, a high school transcript, 1 recommendation, SAT I or ACT, a minimum high school GPA of 3.0, and in some cases a campus interview. It recommends 3 years of high school math and science, 2 years of high school foreign language, and SAT II Subject Tests (including SAT II: Writing Test). Early, deferred, and midyear entrance are possible, with rolling admissions and continuous processing to 3/15 for financial aid. **Contact:** Mr. Jeffrey S. Lantis, Director of Admissions, 33 College Street, Hillsdale, MI 49242-1298, 517-437-7341 ext. 2327; fax 517-437-3923.

GETTING IN LAST YEAR
1,063 applied
76% were accepted
45% enrolled (358)
38% from top tenth of their h.s. class
3.51 average high school GPA
35% had SAT verbal scores over 600
51% had SAT math scores over 600
50% had ACT scores over 26
7% had SAT verbal scores over 700
14% had SAT math scores over 700
15% had ACT scores over 30
13 National Merit Scholars
27 valedictorians

THE STUDENT BODY
1,162 undergraduates
From 42 states and territories,
  10 other countries
55% from Michigan
51% women, 49% men
1% international students

AFTER FRESHMAN YEAR
93% returned for sophomore year
68% got a degree within 4 years
71% got a degree within 5 years
75% got a degree within 6 years

AFTER GRADUATION
23% pursued further study (7% arts and
  sciences, 5% business, 4% law)

97% had job offers within 6 months
45 organizations recruited on campus

WHAT YOU WILL PAY
Tuition and fees $11,970
Room and board $4940
65% receive need-based financial aid
Need-based college-administered scholarships and
  grants average $5000 per award
10% receive non-need financial aid
Non-need college-administered scholarships and
  grants average $6000 per award

HIRAM COLLEGE

Hiram, Ohio • Rural setting • Private • Independent-Religious • Coed

Hiram's academic calendar is unique among colleges and universities. Each 15-week semester is divided into 12-week and 3-week sessions. During the 3-week session students take only one course, which is studied inclusively. Hiram supplements classroom study through career-oriented internships and an extensive and distinctive study-abroad program that takes Hiram students all over the world. More than 40% of Hiram students participate, and all courses are taught by Hiram faculty and are a regular part of the curriculum. In August 1995, Hiram opened a new $7.2-million library.

Academics

Hiram offers a core academic program. It awards bachelor's **degrees**. Challenging opportunities include advanced placement, accelerated degree programs, self-designed majors, tutorials, a senior project, and Phi Beta Kappa. Special programs include internships, summer session for credit, and study abroad.

The most popular **majors** include biology/biological sciences, elementary education, and business. A complete listing of majors at Hiram appears in the Majors Index beginning on page 379.

The **faculty** at Hiram has 81 full-time teachers, 95% with terminal degrees. 100% of the faculty serve as student advisers. The student-faculty ratio is 12:1.

Computers on Campus

Students are not required to have a computer. Student rooms are linked to a campus network. 150 **computers** available in the computer center, computer labs, the learning resource center, academic buildings, classrooms, the library, the student center, and dormitories provide access to the main academic computer, off-campus computing facilities, e-mail, and the Internet. Staffed computer lab on campus (open 24 hours a day) provides training in the use of computers and software.

The **library** has 172,047 books, 76,265 microform titles, and 966 subscriptions.

Campus Life

There are 50 active **organizations** on campus, including a drama/theater group and student-run newspaper and radio station. Student **safety services** include late night transport/escort service, 24-hour emergency telephone alarm devices, 24-hour patrols by trained security personnel, and electronically operated dormitory entrances.

Hiram is a member of the NCAA (Division III). **Intercollegiate sports** include baseball (m), basketball (m, w), cross-country running (m, w), equestrian sports (m, w), football (m), golf (m, w), rugby (m, w), sailing (m, w), soccer (m, w), softball (w), swimming and diving (m, w), tennis (m, w), track and field (m, w), volleyball (w).

Applying

Hiram requires an essay, a high school transcript, 2 recommendations, and SAT I or ACT. It recommends 3 years of high school math and science, 2 years of high school foreign language, and a campus interview. Early and deferred entrance are possible, with a 3/15 deadline and continuous processing to 3/1 for financial aid. **Contact:** Mr. Monty L. Curtis, Vice President for Admission and College Relations, Teachout Price Hall, Hiram, OH 44234-0096, 216-569-5169 or toll-free 800-362-5280; fax 216-569-5944.

GETTING IN LAST YEAR
565 applied
88% were accepted
41% enrolled (203)
41% from top tenth of their h.s. class
3.3 average high school GPA
54% had SAT verbal scores over 600 (R)
43% had SAT math scores over 600 (R)
39% had ACT scores over 26
12% had SAT verbal scores over 700 (R)
6% had SAT math scores over 700 (R)
13% had ACT scores over 30

THE STUDENT BODY
847 undergraduates

From 20 states and territories,
8 other countries
80% from Ohio
53% women, 47% men
7% African Americans
0% Native Americans
1% Hispanics
1% Asian Americans
1% international students

AFTER FRESHMAN YEAR
83% returned for sophomore year
59% got a degree within 4 years
62% got a degree within 5 years
65% got a degree within 6 years

AFTER GRADUATION
35% pursued further study
61% had job offers within 6 months
24 organizations recruited on campus

WHAT YOU WILL PAY
Tuition and fees $15,890
Room and board $4936
95% receive need-based financial aid
Need-based college-administered scholarships and grants average $5821 per award
36% receive non-need financial aid
Non-need college-administered scholarships and grants average $4867 per award

HOBART COLLEGE

Coordinate with William Smith College

Geneva, New York • Small-town setting • Private • Independent-Religious • Men

Hobart and William Smith Colleges together offer the best features of conventionally coeducational colleges: all classes and many residences are coed and students share all campus facilities and social activities. At the same time, each College maintains its own student government, athletic program, and dean's office. Through this coordinate-college system, men and women have equal opportunities for leadership and visibility. Small classes, a dedicated faculty, and extensive opportunities for independent study and off-campus study contribute to a climate that is academically rigorous and strongly supportive. Students balance academics with involvement in over 60 clubs and athletics ranging from intramurals to intercollegiate varsity competition.

Academics

Hobart offers an interdisciplinary curriculum and core academic program. It awards bachelor's **degrees**. Challenging opportunities include advanced placement, accelerated degree programs, self-designed majors, tutorials, an honors program, a senior project, and Phi Beta Kappa. Special programs include internships, off-campus study, and study abroad.

The most popular **majors** include English, economics, and interdisciplinary studies. A complete listing of majors at Hobart appears in the Majors Index beginning on page 379.

The **faculty** at Hobart has 128 full-time teachers, 97% with terminal degrees. 95% of the faculty serve as student advisers.

Computers on Campus

Students are not required to have a computer. Student rooms are linked to a campus network. 146 **computers**

available in the computer center, computer labs, the research center, the learning resource center, honors room, classrooms, and the library provide access to the main academic computer, off-campus computing facilities, e-mail, on-line services, and the Internet. Staffed computer lab on campus provides training in the use of computers and software.

The 2 **libraries** have 320,000 books, 66,458 microform titles, and 1,871 subscriptions. They are connected to 5 national **on-line** catalogs.

Campus Life

There are 60 active **organizations** on campus, including a drama/theater group and student-run newspaper and radio station. 19% of eligible undergraduates are members of 7 national **fraternities**. Student **safety services** include late night transport/escort service, 24-hour emergency telephone alarm devices, 24-hour patrols by trained security personnel, and electronically operated dormitory entrances.

Hobart is a member of the NCAA (Division III). **Intercollegiate sports** include basketball, crew, cross-country running, football, golf, ice hockey, lacrosse, rugby, sailing, skiing (downhill), soccer, squash, tennis.

Applying

Hobart requires an essay, a high school transcript, 3 years of high school math, 2 years of high school foreign language, 2 recommendations, and SAT I or ACT. It recommends 3 years of high school science, an interview, and SAT II Subject Tests. Early and deferred entrance are possible, with a 2/1 deadline and a 2/15 priority date for financial aid. **Contact:** Ms. Mara O'Laughlin, Director of Admission, 639 South Main Street, Geneva, NY 14456-3397, 315-781-3622 or toll-free 800-852-2256; fax 315-781-3914.

GETTING IN LAST YEAR
1,375 applied
73% were accepted
23% enrolled (230)
24% from top tenth of their h.s. class
3.2 average high school GPA
36% had SAT verbal scores over 600 (R)
42% had SAT math scores over 600 (R)
39% had ACT scores over 26
6% had SAT verbal scores over 700 (R)
4% had SAT math scores over 700 (R)
10% had ACT scores over 30

THE STUDENT BODY
866 undergraduates

From 32 states and territories,
 16 other countries
46% from New York
100% men
4% African Americans
1% Native Americans
4% Hispanics
2% Asian Americans
3% international students

AFTER FRESHMAN YEAR
86% returned for sophomore year
77% got a degree within 4 years
78% got a degree within 5 years

AFTER GRADUATION
24% pursued further study (17% arts and sciences, 4% law, 2% medicine)
75% had job offers within 6 months
24 organizations recruited on campus

WHAT YOU WILL PAY
Tuition and fees $20,413
Room and board $6075
56% receive need-based financial aid
Need-based college-administered scholarships and grants average $10,721 per award
1% receive non-need financial aid
Non-need college-administered scholarships and grants average $10,000 per award

HOFSTRA UNIVERSITY

Hempstead, New York • Suburban setting • Private • Independent • Coed

Founded in 1935, Hofstra University has grown to be recognized both nationally and internationally by its resources, academic offerings, accreditations, conferences, and cultural events. Hofstra's undergraduate education places great emphasis on the role of the student in the life of the University. Hofstra also offers graduate programs in business, education, liberal arts, and law. Students have easy access to the theater and cultural life of New York City yet have a learning environment on Long Island on a 238-acre campus that is also an accredited arboretum and museum.

Academics

Hofstra offers an interdisciplinary curriculum and core academic program; fewer than half of graduate courses are open to undergraduates. It awards bachelor's, master's, doctoral, and first professional **degrees**. Challenging opportunities include advanced placement, accelerated degree programs, self-designed majors, tutorials, an honors program, a senior project, and Phi Beta Kappa. Special programs include internships, summer session for credit, study abroad, and Army ROTC.

The most popular **majors** include psychology, accounting, and marketing/retailing/merchandising. A complete listing of majors at Hofstra appears in the Majors Index beginning on page 379.

The **faculty** at Hofstra has 449 full-time graduate and undergraduate teachers, 90% with terminal degrees. 100% of the faculty serve as student advisers. The student-faculty ratio is 15:1.

Computers on Campus

Students are not required to have a computer. Student rooms are linked to a campus network. 350 **computers** available in the computer center, computer labs, the learning resource center, word processing area, classrooms, the library, the student center, and dormitories provide access to the main academic computer, off-campus computing facilities, e-mail, and the Internet. Staffed computer lab on campus provides training in the use of computers and software.

The **library** has 1.4 million books, 1.9 million microform titles, and 7,017 subscriptions. It is connected to 5 national **on-line** catalogs.

Campus Life

There are 120 active **organizations** on campus, including a drama/theater group and student-run newspaper and radio station. 10% of students participate in student government elections. 16% of eligible men and 16% of eligible women are members of 13 national **fraternities**, 10 national **sororities**, 6 local fraternities, and 3 local sororities. Student **safety services** include security booths at each residence hall, late night transport/escort service, 24-hour emergency telephone alarm devices, 24-hour patrols by trained security personnel, and student patrols.

Hofstra is a member of the NCAA (Division I). **Intercollegiate sports** (some offering scholarships) include baseball (m), basketball (m, w), cross-country running (m, w), field hockey (w), football (m), golf (m), lacrosse (m, w), soccer (m, w), softball (w), tennis (m, w), volleyball (w), wrestling (m).

Applying

Hofstra requires a high school transcript, 2 years of high school foreign language, 1 recommendation, SAT I or ACT, and in some cases an essay and a campus interview. It recommends SAT II Subject Tests. Early, deferred, and midyear entrance are possible, with rolling admissions and continuous processing to 3/1 for financial aid. **Contact:** Ms. Mary Beth Carey, Dean of Admissions, 100 Hofstra University, Hempstead, NY 11550-1090, 516-463-6700 or toll-free 800-HOFSTRA; fax 516-560-7660.

GETTING IN LAST YEAR

7,610 applied
82% were accepted
25% enrolled (1,547)
23% from top tenth of their h.s. class
3.0 average high school GPA
23% had SAT verbal scores over 600 (R)
22% had SAT math scores over 600 (R)
22% had ACT scores over 26
3% had SAT verbal scores over 700 (R)
2% had SAT math scores over 700 (R)
5% had ACT scores over 30
40 valedictorians

THE STUDENT BODY

Total 11,777, of whom 7,846
   are undergraduates

From 45 states and territories,
   67 other countries
83% from New York
53% women, 47% men
5% African Americans
1% Native Americans
5% Hispanics
5% Asian Americans
4% international students

AFTER FRESHMAN YEAR

80% returned for sophomore year
41% got a degree within 4 years

55% got a degree within 5 years
56% got a degree within 6 years

AFTER GRADUATION

158 organizations recruited on campus

WHAT YOU WILL PAY

Tuition and fees $12,360
Room and board $4390
61% receive need-based financial aid
Need-based college-administered scholarships and
   grants average $1727 per award
36% receive non-need financial aid
Non-need college-administered scholarships and
   grants average $2625 per award

HOPE COLLEGE

Holland, Michigan • Small-town setting • Private • Independent-Religious • Coed

Hope College's special niche in American higher education is influenced considerably by a blend of two important characteristics: an outright recognition as one of America's premier liberal arts colleges and, as a Christian college, an openness and freedom of inquiry that are supportive of students who wrestle with significant questions of faith and life. Hope is recognized as a leader for its collaborative research efforts conducted by students and professors. Students who desire a partnership relationship with their college professors will find the academic climate at Hope both stimulating and affirming.

 Academics

Hope offers a discipline-oriented curriculum and core academic program. It awards bachelor's **degrees**. Challenging opportunities include advanced placement, self-designed majors, tutorials, a senior project, Phi Beta Kappa, and Sigma Xi. Special programs include internships, summer session for credit, off-campus study, and study abroad.

The most popular **majors** include business, biology/biological sciences, and chemistry. A complete listing of majors at Hope appears in the Majors Index beginning on page 379.

The **faculty** at Hope has 188 full-time teachers, 89% with terminal degrees. 95% of the faculty serve as student advisers. The student-faculty ratio is 13:1, and the average class size in core courses is 35.

 Computers on Campus

Students are not required to have a computer. 260 **computers** available in the computer center, computer labs, the research center, classrooms, the library, the student center, and dormitories provide access to e-mail and the Internet.

The 2 **libraries** have 300,000 books, 178,924 microform titles, and 1,494 subscriptions. They are connected to 7 national **on-line** catalogs.

 Campus Life

There are 67 active **organizations** on campus, including a drama/theater group and student-run newspaper and radio station. 9% of eligible men and 10% of eligible women are members of 6 local **fraternities** and 6 local **sororities**. Student **safety services** include late night transport/escort service, 24-hour emergency telephone alarm devices, 24-hour patrols by trained security personnel, and electronically operated dormitory entrances.

Hope is a member of the NCAA (Division III). **Intercollegiate sports** include baseball (m), basketball (m, w), cross-country running (m, w), football (m), golf (m, w), lacrosse (m), soccer (m, w), softball (w), swimming and diving (m, w), tennis (m, w), track and field (m, w), volleyball (m, w).

 Applying

Hope requires an essay, a high school transcript, 3 years of high school math, SAT I or ACT, and in some cases 1 recommendation. It recommends 3 years of high school science, 2 years of high school foreign language, and an interview. Early, deferred, and midyear entrance are possible, with rolling admissions and continuous processing to 2/15 for financial aid. **Contact:** Office of Admissions, 69 East 10th Street, Holland, MI 49422-9000, 616-395-7850 or toll-free 800-968-7850; fax 616-395-7130.

GETTING IN LAST YEAR

1,789 applied
91% were accepted
43% enrolled (695)
37% from top tenth of their h.s. class
3.5 average high school GPA
24% had SAT verbal scores over 600
56% had SAT math scores over 600
47% had ACT scores over 26
3% had SAT verbal scores over 700
16% had SAT math scores over 700
15% had ACT scores over 30
19 National Merit Scholars
42 valedictorians

THE STUDENT BODY

2,919 undergraduates

From 42 states and territories,
   30 other countries
79% from Michigan
57% women, 43% men
1% African Americans
0% Native Americans
2% Hispanics
3% Asian Americans
2% international students

AFTER FRESHMAN YEAR

85% returned for sophomore year
53% got a degree within 4 years
68% got a degree within 5 years
69% got a degree within 6 years

AFTER GRADUATION

28% pursued further study (15% arts and
   sciences, 4% medicine, 3% law)
26% had job offers within 6 months
54 organizations recruited on campus

WHAT YOU WILL PAY

Tuition and fees $13,318
Room and board $4516
57% receive need-based financial aid
Need-based college-administered scholarships and
   grants average $3420 per award
28% receive non-need financial aid
Non-need college-administered scholarships and
   grants average $4829 per award

HOUGHTON COLLEGE

Houghton, New York • Rural setting • Private • Independent-Religious • Coed

Since 1883 Houghton College has provided an educational experience that integrates high academic quality with the Christian faith. Offering 40 majors and programs, the College has received widespread national recognition. Located on a scenic 1,300-acre campus in the countryside of western New York, the college operates an equestrian center in addition to its modern residential, academic, and recreational facilities. Houghton attracts 1,200 academically talented students annually from across the U.S. and around the world. A comprehensive financial aid program benefits more than 90% of the current student body. Numerous off-campus and study-abroad programs are available.

 ## Academics

Houghton offers an interdisciplinary curriculum and core academic program. It awards associate and bachelor's **degrees**. Challenging opportunities include advanced placement, tutorials, an honors program, and a senior project. Special programs include internships, summer session for credit, off-campus study, and Army ROTC.

The most popular **majors** include elementary education, biology/biological sciences, and psychology. A complete listing of majors at Houghton appears in the Majors Index beginning on page 379.

The **faculty** at Houghton has 90 full-time teachers, 77% with terminal degrees. 85% of the faculty serve as student advisers. The student-faculty ratio is 15:1.

 ## Computers on Campus

Students are not required to have a computer. 130 **computers** available in the computer center, computer labs, divisional offices, the library, and dormitories. Staffed computer lab on campus provides training in the use of computers and software.

The **library** has 220,000 books, 18,131 microform titles, and 822 subscriptions.

 ## Campus Life

There are 50 active **organizations** on campus, including a drama/theater group and student-run newspaper and radio station. 40% of students participate in student government elections. Student **safety services** include late night transport/escort service, 24-hour patrols by trained security personnel, and electronically operated dormitory entrances.

Houghton is a member of the NAIA. **Intercollegiate sports** (some offering scholarships) include basketball (m, w), cross-country running (m, w), field hockey (w), soccer (m, w), track and field (m, w), volleyball (w).

 ## Applying

Houghton requires an essay, a high school transcript, 1 recommendation, pastoral recommendation, and SAT I or ACT. It recommends 3 years of high school math, some high school foreign language, an interview, and a minimum high school GPA of 3.0. Early, deferred, and midyear entrance are possible, with a 3/1 deadline and continuous processing to 3/15 for financial aid. **Contact:** Mr. Timothy R. Fuller, Vice President for Alumni and Admissions, PO Box 128, Houghton, NY 14744, 716-567-9353 or toll-free 800-777-2556; fax 716-567-9522.

GETTING IN LAST YEAR
1,024 applied
79% were accepted
36% enrolled (294)
29% from top tenth of their h.s. class
3.40 average high school GPA
48% had SAT verbal scores over 600 (R)
33% had SAT math scores over 600 (R)
37% had ACT scores over 26
10% had SAT verbal scores over 700 (R)
3% had SAT math scores over 700 (R)
8% had ACT scores over 30
17 valedictorians

THE STUDENT BODY
1,271 undergraduates

From 40 states and territories,
  22 other countries
60% from New York
64% women, 36% men
2% African Americans
1% Native Americans
1% Hispanics
1% Asian Americans
5% international students

AFTER FRESHMAN YEAR
89% returned for sophomore year
62% got a degree within 4 years
65% got a degree within 5 years
66% got a degree within 6 years

AFTER GRADUATION
23% pursued further study (8% arts and
  sciences, 4% business, 4% theology)
42 organizations recruited on campus

WHAT YOU WILL PAY
Tuition and fees $10,910
Room and board $3720
82% receive need-based financial aid
Need-based college-administered scholarships and
  grants average $2647 per award
11% receive non-need financial aid
Non-need college-administered scholarships and
  grants average $2075 per award

ILLINOIS COLLEGE

Jacksonville, Illinois • Small-town setting • Private • Independent-Religious • Coed

Founded in 1829, Illinois College was the first college in Illinois to award the baccalaureate degree. The College is recognized as a best buy in education and was recently designated Bachelor of Arts 1 by the Carnegie Classification System. Illinois College offers a Phi Beta Kappa education at an annual tuition of $8600. As a premier liberal arts college, the College's goal is to prepare young women and men for a lifetime of learning and a place among the leadership of the community. The campus is a blend of historic New England charm and state-of-the-art computer-based learning facilities.

Academics

IC offers a core academic program. It awards bachelor's **degrees**. Challenging opportunities include advanced placement, accelerated degree programs, a senior project, and Phi Beta Kappa. Special programs include internships, summer session for credit, and study abroad.

The most popular **majors** include business and computer science. A complete listing of majors at IC appears in the Majors Index beginning on page 379.

The **faculty** at IC has 63 full-time teachers, 78% with terminal degrees. 87% of the faculty serve as student advisers. The student-faculty ratio is 15:1.

Computers on Campus

Students are not required to have a computer. 77 **computers** available in the computer center and computer labs provide access to the main academic computer, e-mail, and the Internet. Staffed computer lab on campus provides training in the use of computers and software.

The **library** has 135,000 books, 111 microform titles, and 620 subscriptions.

Campus Life

There are 37 active **organizations** on campus, including a drama/theater group and student-run newspaper. 40% of students participate in student government elections. 25% of eligible men and 25% of eligible women are members of 7 Greek literary societies. Student **safety services** include night security patrol, late night transport/escort service, 24-hour emergency telephone alarm devices, and electronically operated dormitory entrances.

IC is a member of the NCAA (Division III). **Intercollegiate sports** include baseball (m), basketball (m, w), cross-country running (m, w), football (m), golf (m), soccer (m, w), softball (w), tennis (m, w), track and field (m, w), volleyball (w), wrestling (m).

Applying

IC requires a high school transcript, 2 recommendations, SAT I or ACT, and in some cases an essay. It recommends 3 years of high school math and science and an interview. Early and midyear entrance are possible, with an 8/15 deadline and continuous processing to 5/1 for financial aid. **Contact:** Mr. Gale Vaughn, Director of Enrollment, 1101 West College Avenue, Jacksonville, IL 62650-2299, 217-245-3030; fax 217-245-3034.

GETTING IN LAST YEAR
823 applied
87% were accepted
31% enrolled (223)
30% from top tenth of their h.s. class
3.4 average high school GPA
12% had SAT verbal scores over 600 (R)
29% had SAT math scores over 600 (R)
33% had ACT scores over 26
0% had SAT verbal scores over 700 (R)
6% had SAT math scores over 700 (R)
6% had ACT scores over 30
2 National Merit Scholars
10 valedictorians

THE STUDENT BODY
965 undergraduates

From 15 states and territories,
 4 other countries
94% from Illinois
53% women, 47% men
1% African Americans
0% Native Americans
0% Hispanics
2% Asian Americans
1% international students

AFTER FRESHMAN YEAR
88% returned for sophomore year
44% got a degree within 4 years
50% got a degree within 5 years
51% got a degree within 6 years

AFTER GRADUATION
21% pursued further study (4% business, 4% law, 3% dentistry)

WHAT YOU WILL PAY
Tuition and fees $8600
Room and board $4000
72% receive need-based financial aid
Need-based college-administered scholarships and grants average $1199 per award
60% receive non-need financial aid
Non-need college-administered scholarships and grants average $1976 per award

ILLINOIS INSTITUTE OF TECHNOLOGY

Chicago, Illinois • Urban setting • Private • Independent • Coed

Located in the heart of Chicago, one of the world's great cities, IIT is an ideal place to study architecture, engineering, science, premed, and prelaw. Cutting-edge programs include architectural engineering and environmental engineering. IIT students get jobs! Ninety-two percent of 1995 graduates were placed in jobs or graduate school by fall. Faculty members are first-rate and accessible. Nobel Laureate Leon Lederman teaches freshman physics. Research, internship, and co-op opportunities abound. Athletics, clubs, and the recreational opportunities offered by a bowling alley and radio station are popular. On-campus housing is guaranteed. Financial aid makes IIT affordable.

Academics

IIT offers a core academic program. It awards bachelor's, master's, doctoral, and first professional **degrees**. Challenging opportunities include advanced placement, accelerated degree programs, self-designed majors, an honors program, and Sigma Xi. Special programs include cooperative education, internships, summer session for credit, study abroad, and Army, Naval, and Air Force ROTC.

The most popular **majors** include electrical engineering, mechanical engineering, and architecture. A complete listing of majors at IIT appears in the Majors Index beginning on page 379.

The **faculty** at IIT has 334 full-time undergraduate teachers, 99% with terminal degrees. The student-faculty ratio is 12:1.

Computers on Campus

Students are not required to have a computer. Student rooms are linked to a campus network. 250 **computers**

available in the computer center, computer labs, the learning resource center, academic buildings, classrooms, the library, and dormitories provide access to the main academic computer, e-mail, and the Internet. Staffed computer lab on campus provides training in the use of computers and software.

The 5 **libraries** have 400,000 books, 175,500 microform titles, and 750 subscriptions.

Campus Life

There are 75 active **organizations** on campus, including a drama/theater group and student-run newspaper and radio station. 15% of eligible men and 10% of eligible women are members of 9 national **fraternities**, 1 national **sorority**, and 1 local sorority. Student **safety services** include late night transport/escort service, 24-hour emergency telephone alarm devices, 24-hour patrols by trained security personnel, and electronically operated dormitory entrances.

IIT is a member of the NAIA. **Intercollegiate sports** (some offering scholarships) include baseball (m), basketball (m, w), cross-country running (m, w), swimming and diving (m, w), volleyball (w).

Applying

IIT requires a high school transcript, 3 years of high school math, 1 recommendation, and SAT I or ACT. It recommends an essay, 3 years of high school science, an interview, and SAT II Subject Tests. Early and deferred entrance are possible, with rolling admissions and continuous processing to 3/15 for financial aid. **Contact:** Dr. Carole L. Snow, Dean of Admission, 10 West 33rd Street, Room 101, Chicago, IL 60616, 312-567-3025 or toll-free 800-448-2329 (out-of-state); fax 312-567-6939.

GETTING IN LAST YEAR	**THE STUDENT BODY**	**AFTER GRADUATION**
1,448 applied	Total 7,157, of whom 2,546	92% had job offers within 6 months
64% were accepted	are undergraduates	96 organizations recruited on campus
25% enrolled (229)	From 49 states and territories,	
41% from top tenth of their h.s. class	72 other countries	**WHAT YOU WILL PAY**
3.51 average high school GPA	67% from Illinois	Tuition and fees $15,340
21% had SAT verbal scores over 600 (R)	24% women, 76% men	Room and board $4620
74% had SAT math scores over 600 (R)	12% African Americans	58% receive need-based financial aid
56% had ACT scores over 26	0% Native Americans	Need-based college-administered scholarships and
4% had SAT verbal scores over 700 (R)	9% Hispanics	grants average $6348 per award
34% had SAT math scores over 700 (R)	12% Asian Americans	36% receive non-need financial aid
17% had ACT scores over 30	14% international students	Non-need college-administered scholarships and
		grants average $4045 per award

ILLINOIS WESLEYAN UNIVERSITY

Bloomington, Illinois • Suburban setting • Private • Independent • Coed

Illinois Wesleyan University is a campus on the move. A $25-million Center for Natural Science Learning and Research opened in the fall of 1995, a $15.2-million athletics, recreation, and wellness complex opened the previous fall, and a $1 million-plus computer networking project was launched in the summer of 1995. IWU offers liberal arts and professional programs in a College of Liberal Arts, College of Fine Arts, and a 4-year School of Nursing. IWU students are encouraged to pursue multiple interests simultaneously, and they often double major in diverse fields, from music and biology to physics and business administration.

 ## Academics

IWU offers a liberal arts curriculum and core academic program. It awards bachelor's **degrees**. Challenging opportunities include advanced placement, accelerated degree programs, self-designed majors, an honors program, and Sigma Xi. Special programs include internships, summer session for credit, off-campus study, study abroad, and Army ROTC.

The most popular **majors** include business, biology/biological sciences, and English. A complete listing of majors at IWU appears in the Majors Index beginning on page 379.

The **faculty** at IWU has 138 full-time teachers, 92% with terminal degrees. 90% of the faculty serve as student advisers. The student-faculty ratio is 13:1.

 ## Computers on Campus

Students are not required to have a computer. Student rooms are linked to a campus network. 352 **computers** available in the computer center, computer labs, special labs, classrooms, the library, and dormitories provide access to off-campus computing facilities, e-mail, on-line services, and the Internet. Staffed computer lab on campus provides training in the use of computers and software.

The **library** has 218,737 books, 109,032 microform titles, and 1,045 subscriptions.

 ## Campus Life

There are 60 active **organizations** on campus, including a drama/theater group and student-run newspaper and radio station. 25% of eligible men and 25% of eligible women are members of 6 national **fraternities** and 5 national **sororities**. Student **safety services** include student/administration security committee, late night transport/escort service, 24-hour emergency telephone alarm devices, and 24-hour patrols by trained security personnel.

IWU is a member of the NCAA (Division III). **Intercollegiate sports** include baseball (m), basketball (m, w), cross-country running (m, w), football (m), golf (m), sailing (m, w), soccer (m, w), softball (w), swimming and diving (m, w), tennis (m, w), track and field (m, w), volleyball (w).

 ## Applying

IWU requires an essay, a high school transcript, SAT I or ACT, and a minimum high school GPA of 2.0. It recommends 3 years of high school math and science, 3 years of high school foreign language, 3 recommendations, a campus interview, and a minimum high school GPA of 3.0. Early, deferred, and midyear entrance are possible, with rolling admissions and a 3/1 priority date for financial aid.
Contact: Mr. James R. Ruoti, Dean of Admissions, 1312 North Park Street, Bloomington, IL 61702-2900, 309-556-3031 or toll-free 800-332-2498; fax 309-556-3411.

GETTING IN LAST YEAR
2,674 applied
64% were accepted
30% enrolled (513)
47% from top tenth of their h.s. class
64% had SAT verbal scores over 600 (R)
64% had SAT math scores over 600 (R)
70% had ACT scores over 26
15% had SAT verbal scores over 700 (R)
17% had SAT math scores over 700 (R)
23% had ACT scores over 30
12 National Merit Scholars

THE STUDENT BODY
1,875 undergraduates

From 33 states and territories,
    24 other countries
84% from Illinois
51% women, 49% men
2% African Americans
1% Native Americans
1% Hispanics
4% Asian Americans
3% international students

AFTER FRESHMAN YEAR
95% returned for sophomore year
72% got a degree within 4 years
77% got a degree within 5 years
78% got a degree within 6 years

AFTER GRADUATION
29% pursued further study (14% arts and
    sciences, 5% law, 4% medicine)
80% had job offers within 6 months
41 organizations recruited on campus

WHAT YOU WILL PAY
Tuition and fees $16,410
Room and board $4424
65% receive need-based financial aid
Need-based college-administered scholarships and
    grants average $7777 per award
20% receive non-need financial aid
Non-need college-administered scholarships and
    grants average $4473 per award

IOWA STATE UNIVERSITY OF SCIENCE AND TECHNOLOGY

Ames, Iowa • Suburban setting • Public • State-supported • Coed

Iowa State University offers all the advantages of a major university along with the friendliness and warmth of a residential campus. Iowa State's students are exceptional academically, diverse racially and culturally, and active socially. Along with a strong academic experience, students also have opportunities to further develop their leadership skills and interpersonal relationships through any one of 500 student organizations, 60 intramural sports, 19 residence halls, 36 fraternities, 20 sororities, and a multitude of arts and recreational activities.

 ## Academics

Iowa State offers no core academic program; fewer than half of graduate courses are open to undergraduates. It awards bachelor's, master's, doctoral, and first professional **degrees**. Challenging opportunities include advanced placement, accelerated degree programs, self-designed majors, tutorials, Freshman Honors College, an honors program, a senior project, Phi Beta Kappa, and Sigma Xi. Special programs include cooperative education, internships, summer session for credit, off-campus study, study abroad, and Army, Naval, and Air Force ROTC.

The most popular **majors** include finance/banking, mechanical engineering, and elementary education. A complete listing of majors at Iowa State appears in the Majors Index beginning on page 379.

The **faculty** at Iowa State has 1,560 full-time graduate and undergraduate teachers, 87% with terminal degrees. 33% of the faculty serve as student advisers. The student-faculty ratio is 14:1.

 ## Computers on Campus

Students are not required to have a computer. Student rooms are linked to a campus network. 1,600 **computers** available in the computer center, computer labs, the learning resource center, classrooms, the library, the student center, and dormitories provide access to the main academic computer, off-campus computing facilities, e-mail, on-line services, and the Internet. Staffed computer lab on campus (open 24 hours a day) provides training in the use of computers and software.

The 2 **libraries** have 2.1 million books, 2.7 million microform titles, and 21,201 subscriptions. They are connected to 34 national **on-line** catalogs.

 ## Campus Life

There are 500 active **organizations** on campus, including a drama/theater group and student-run newspaper and radio station. 8% of students participate in student government elections. 15% of eligible men and 15% of eligible women are members of 35 national **fraternities**, 20 national **sororities**, and 1 local fraternity. Student **safety services** include vehicle assistance, crime prevention programs, late night transport/escort service, 24-hour emergency telephone alarm devices, 24-hour patrols by trained security personnel, and student patrols.

Iowa State is a member of the NCAA (Division I). **Intercollegiate sports** (some offering scholarships) include baseball (m), basketball (m, w), cross-country running (m, w), football (m), golf (m, w), gymnastics (w), soccer (w), softball (w), swimming and diving (m, w), tennis (w), track and field (m, w), volleyball (w), wrestling (m).

 ## Applying

Iowa State requires a high school transcript, 3 years of high school math and science, rank in upper half of high school class or achievement of a satisfactory combination of high school rank and ACT/SAT I scores, and in some cases 2 years of high school foreign language. It recommends 2 years of high school foreign language. Early, deferred, and midyear entrance are possible, with rolling admissions and continuous processing to 3/1 for financial aid. **Contact:** Mr. Phil Caffrey, Associate Director for Freshman Admissions, 314 Alumni Hall, Ames, IA 50011, 515-294-5836 or toll-free 800-262-3810; fax 515-294-2592.

GETTING IN LAST YEAR
9,088 applied
91% were accepted
41% enrolled (3,412)
27% from top tenth of their h.s. class
3.39 average high school GPA
35% had ACT scores over 26
10% had ACT scores over 30
54 National Merit Scholars
170 valedictorians

THE STUDENT BODY
Total 24,431, of whom 20,208 are undergraduates
From 52 states and territories, 84 other countries
77% from Iowa

43% women, 57% men
3% African Americans
0% Native Americans
2% Hispanics
2% Asian Americans
6% international students

AFTER FRESHMAN YEAR
82% returned for sophomore year
20% got a degree within 4 years
54% got a degree within 5 years
62% got a degree within 6 years

AFTER GRADUATION
17% pursued further study (8% arts and sciences, 3% engineering, 2% veterinary medicine)

76% had job offers within 6 months
1,000 organizations recruited on campus
1 Fulbright scholar

WHAT YOU WILL PAY
Resident tuition and fees $2574
Nonresident tuition and fees $8192
Room and board $3382
61% receive need-based financial aid
Need-based college-administered scholarships and grants average $850 per award
18% receive non-need financial aid
Non-need college-administered scholarships and grants average $1587 per award

JAMES MADISON UNIVERSITY

Harrisonburg, Virginia • Small-town setting • Public • State-supported • Coed

James Madison University has been described as the "Ultimate University." It is a close-knit community that possesses a unique atmosphere for living and learning. The special kind of spirit on campus emphasizes excellence in all aspects of a student's life. Students are challenged both inside and outside the classroom by talented and caring faculty and staff and by other JMU students who are friendly, diverse, and actively involved in their own educations. A beautiful campus, supportive environment, and strong commitment to students' preparation for the 21st century combine to make JMU a distinctive institution.

 Academics

JMU offers a major concentration/liberal studies curriculum and core academic program; fewer than half of graduate courses are open to undergraduates. It awards bachelor's, master's, and doctoral **degrees**. Challenging opportunities include advanced placement, accelerated degree programs, Freshman Honors College, an honors program, and a senior project. Special programs include internships, summer session for credit, study abroad, and Army ROTC.

The most popular **majors** include psychology, English, and political science/government. A complete listing of majors at JMU appears in the Majors Index beginning on page 379.

The **faculty** at JMU has 528 full-time graduate and undergraduate teachers, 83% with terminal degrees. 75% of the faculty serve as student advisers. The student-faculty ratio is 18:1, and the average class size in core courses is 25.

 Computers on Campus

Students are not required to have a computer. Student rooms are linked to a campus network. 500 **computers** available in the computer center, computer labs, academic buildings, classrooms, the library, and dormitories provide access to e-mail and the Internet. Staffed computer lab on campus (open 24 hours a day) provides training in the use of computers and software.

The 2 **libraries** have 353,786 books, 1.3 million microform titles, and 2,956 subscriptions.

 Campus Life

There are 230 active **organizations** on campus, including a drama/theater group and student-run newspaper and radio station. 15% of students participate in student government elections. 20% of eligible men and 18% of eligible women are members of 18 national **fraternities** and 12 national **sororities**. Student **safety services** include late night transport/escort service, 24-hour emergency telephone alarm devices, 24-hour patrols by trained security personnel, student patrols, and electronically operated dormitory entrances.

JMU is a member of the NCAA (Division I). **Intercollegiate sports** (some offering scholarships) include archery (m, w), baseball (m), basketball (m, w), cross-country running (m, w), fencing (w), field hockey (w), football (m), golf (m, w), gymnastics (m, w), lacrosse (w), soccer (m, w), swimming and diving (m, w), tennis (m, w), track and field (m, w), volleyball (w), wrestling (m).

 Applying

JMU requires an essay, a high school transcript, English proficiency for foreign students, SAT I or ACT, a minimum high school GPA of 2.0, and in some cases some high school foreign language. It recommends 3 years of high school math and science. Early and midyear entrance are possible, with a 1/15 deadline and a 2/15 priority date for financial aid. **Contact:** Mrs. Roxie Shabazz, Director of Admissions, Office of Admissions, Harrisonburg, VA 22807, 540-568-6147.

GETTING IN LAST YEAR
12,314 applied
57% were accepted
36% enrolled (2,539)
32% from top tenth of their h.s. class
40% had SAT verbal scores over 600 (R)
43% had SAT math scores over 600 (R)
4% had SAT verbal scores over 700 (R)
3% had SAT math scores over 700 (R)
25 National Merit Scholars

THE STUDENT BODY
Total 11,927, of whom 10,503
  are undergraduates
From 43 states and territories,
  46 other countries

71% from Virginia
54% women, 46% men
6% African Americans
1% Native Americans
2% Hispanics
4% Asian Americans
1% international students

AFTER FRESHMAN YEAR
92% returned for sophomore year
58% got a degree within 4 years
79% got a degree within 5 years
82% got a degree within 6 years

AFTER GRADUATION
19% pursued further study

73% had job offers within 6 months
201 organizations recruited on campus

WHAT YOU WILL PAY
Resident tuition and fees $4014
Nonresident tuition and fees $8294
Room and board $4680
35% receive need-based financial aid
Need-based college-administered scholarships and
  grants average $3000 per award
24% receive non-need financial aid
Non-need college-administered scholarships and
  grants average $12,538 per award

JOHN CARROLL UNIVERSITY

University Heights, Ohio • Suburban setting • Private • Independent-Religious • Coed

John Carroll University, founded in 1886, is one of 28 Catholic colleges and universities operated in the United States by the Society of Jesus. In the Jesuit tradition of leadership, faith, and service, John Carroll provides its students with a rigorous education rooted in the liberal arts and focused on questions of moral and ethical values. John Carroll offers more than 85 student organizations, community volunteer service opportunities, and academic honor societies to foster leadership activities outside the classroom.

 ## Academics

Carroll offers a Jesuit core curriculum and core academic program; fewer than half of graduate courses are open to undergraduates. It awards bachelor's and master's **degrees**. Challenging opportunities include advanced placement, accelerated degree programs, self-designed majors, tutorials, an honors program, and a senior project. Special programs include cooperative education, internships, summer session for credit, off-campus study, study abroad, and Army ROTC.

The most popular **majors** include communication, English, and biology/biological sciences. A complete listing of majors at Carroll appears in the Majors Index beginning on page 379.

The **faculty** at Carroll has 208 full-time undergraduate teachers, 87% with terminal degrees. 100% of the faculty serve as student advisers. The student-faculty ratio is 15:1.

 ## Computers on Campus

Students are not required to have a computer. Student rooms are linked to a campus network. 200 **computers** available in the computer center, computer labs, the learning resource center, classrooms, the library, the student center, and dormitories provide access to the main academic computer, off-campus computing facilities, e-mail, on-line services, and the Internet. Staffed computer lab on campus provides training in the use of computers and software.

The **library** has 564,640 books, 176,034 microform titles, and 1,831 subscriptions. It is connected to 6 national **on-line** catalogs.

 ## Campus Life

There are 87 active **organizations** on campus, including a drama/theater group and student-run newspaper and radio station. 55% of students participate in student government elections. 32% of eligible men and 35% of eligible women are members of 8 local **fraternities** and 6 local **sororities**. Student **safety services** include late night transport/escort service, 24-hour emergency telephone alarm devices, and 24-hour patrols by trained security personnel.

Carroll is a member of the NCAA (Division III). **Intercollegiate sports** include baseball (m), basketball (m, w), cross-country running (m, w), football (m), golf (m), ice hockey (m), lacrosse (m, w), rugby (m, w), sailing (m, w), skiing (cross-country) (m, w), skiing (downhill) (m, w), soccer (m, w), softball (w), swimming and diving (m, w), tennis (m, w), track and field (m, w), volleyball (m, w), wrestling (m).

Applying

Carroll requires a high school transcript, 3 years of high school math, 2 years of high school foreign language, 1 recommendation, and SAT I or ACT. It recommends an essay, 3 years of high school science, a campus interview, and SAT II Subject Tests. Early, deferred, and midyear entrance are possible, with rolling admissions and continuous processing to 3/1 for financial aid. **Contact:** Ms. Laryn Runco, Director of Admission, 20700 North Park Boulevard, University Heights, OH 44118-4581, 216-397-4294; fax 216-397-4256.

GETTING IN LAST YEAR

2,415 applied
90% were accepted
39% enrolled (847)
3.23 average high school GPA
51% had SAT verbal scores over 600 (R)
44% had SAT math scores over 600 (R)
26% had ACT scores over 26
6% had SAT verbal scores over 700 (R)
8% had SAT math scores over 700 (R)
5% had ACT scores over 30
6 National Merit Scholars
21 valedictorians

THE STUDENT BODY

Total 4,397, of whom 3,545
  are undergraduates

From 31 states and territories,
  13 other countries
66% from Ohio
51% women, 49% men
4% African Americans
0% Native Americans
1% Hispanics
3% Asian Americans
1% international students

AFTER FRESHMAN YEAR

87% returned for sophomore year
62% got a degree within 4 years
73% got a degree within 5 years
74% got a degree within 6 years

AFTER GRADUATION

25% pursued further study (20% arts and
  sciences, 4% law, 2% medicine)

WHAT YOU WILL PAY

Tuition and fees $13,122
Room and board $5550
68% receive need-based financial aid
Need-based college-administered scholarships and
  grants average $3642 per award
76% receive non-need financial aid
Non-need college-administered scholarships and
  grants average $2650 per award

JOHNS HOPKINS UNIVERSITY

Baltimore, Maryland • Urban setting • Private • Independent • Coed

The School of Arts and Sciences and the Whiting School of Engineering are the heart of a small but unusually diverse coeducational university. Johns Hopkins was founded in 1876 as the first true American university modeled after the European research university. With a favorable student-faculty ratio, most classes are small and give students an excellent opportunity for advanced studies and creative investigation.

 Academics

Johns Hopkins offers an interdisciplinary curriculum; all graduate courses are open to undergraduates. It awards bachelor's, master's, and doctoral **degrees**. Challenging opportunities include advanced placement, accelerated degree programs, self-designed majors, tutorials, a senior project, Phi Beta Kappa, and Sigma Xi. Special programs include cooperative education, internships, summer session for credit, off-campus study, study abroad, and Army and Air Force ROTC.

The most popular **majors** include biology/biological sciences, biomedical engineering, and international studies. A complete listing of majors at Johns Hopkins appears in the Majors Index beginning on page 379.

The **faculty** at Johns Hopkins has 361 full-time graduate and undergraduate teachers, 99% with terminal degrees. 70% of the faculty serve as student advisers. The student-faculty ratio is 10:1.

 Computers on Campus

Students are not required to have a computer. Student rooms are linked to a campus network. 230 **computers** available in the computer center, academic buildings, the library, and dormitories provide access to the main academic computer, off-campus computing facilities, e-mail, on-line services, and the Internet. Staffed computer lab on campus provides training in the use of computers and software.

The 7 **libraries** have 2.3 million books, 2 million microform titles, and 20,000 subscriptions.

 Campus Life

There are 150 active **organizations** on campus, including a drama/theater group and student-run newspaper and radio station. 55% of students participate in student government elections. 30% of eligible men and 25% of eligible women are members of 13 national **fraternities** and 5 national **sororities**. Student **safety services** include late night transport/escort service, 24-hour emergency telephone alarm devices, 24-hour patrols by trained security personnel, student patrols, and electronically operated dormitory entrances.

Johns Hopkins is a member of the NCAA (Division III). **Intercollegiate sports** (some offering scholarships) include baseball (m), basketball (m, w), crew (m, w), cross-country running (m, w), fencing (m, w), field hockey (w), football (m), golf (m), ice hockey (m), lacrosse (m, w), riflery (m, w), rugby (m), soccer (m, w), squash (w), swimming and diving (m, w), tennis (m, w), track and field (m, w), volleyball (w), water polo (m, w), wrestling (m).

 Applying

Johns Hopkins requires an essay, a high school transcript, 1 recommendation, SAT I, 3 SAT II Subject Tests (including SAT II: Writing Test), and in some cases ACT. It recommends 3 years of high school math and science, 3 years of high school foreign language, and an interview. Early, deferred, and midyear entrance are possible, with a 1/1 deadline and a 2/1 priority date for financial aid. **Contact:** Mr. Paul White, Director of Undergraduate Admissions, 3400 North Charles Street, Baltimore, MD 21218-2699, 410-516-8171.

GETTING IN LAST YEAR

7,877 applied
42% were accepted
26% enrolled (876)
76% from top tenth of their h.s. class
3.8 average high school GPA
59% had SAT verbal scores over 600 (R)
90% had SAT math scores over 600 (R)
91% had ACT scores over 26
11% had SAT verbal scores over 700 (R)
53% had SAT math scores over 700 (R)
48% had ACT scores over 30
38 National Merit Scholars
64 valedictorians

THE STUDENT BODY

Total 4,847, of whom 3,444
   are undergraduates

From 52 states and territories,
   36 other countries
14% from Maryland
39% women, 61% men
5% African Americans
1% Native Americans
3% Hispanics
23% Asian Americans
5% international students

AFTER FRESHMAN YEAR

94% returned for sophomore year
80% got a degree within 4 years
85% got a degree within 5 years
86% got a degree within 6 years

AFTER GRADUATION

67% pursued further study (26% medicine, 14% arts and sciences, 11% engineering)
40% had job offers within 6 months
115 organizations recruited on campus
11 Fulbright scholars

WHAT YOU WILL PAY

Tuition and fees $19,700
Room and board $7050
50% receive need-based financial aid
Need-based college-administered scholarships and grants average $11,350 per award
6% receive non-need financial aid
Non-need college-administered scholarships and grants average $12,000 per award

JUNIATA COLLEGE

Huntingdon, Pennsylvania • Small-town setting • Private • Independent • Coed

Students who can be described as intelligent, independent, creative, determined, friendly, active, or unique; students who rise to academic challenges; those who are intrigued by environments rich with lakes, mountains, fresh air, and natural beauty; those who are hungry to discover who they are and what they are capable of—these students owe it to themselves to consider Juniata College. At Juniata, students will have the opportunity to explore their interests and prepare for a useful life and a successful career. Juniata's traditions include excellence in academics, small classes, a close-knit community, a familylike atmosphere, and many surprises, including Mountain Day.

Academics

Juniata offers an interdisciplinary curriculum and core academic program; a few graduate courses are open to undergraduates. It awards bachelor's **degrees**. Challenging opportunities include advanced placement, accelerated degree programs, self-designed majors, tutorials, Freshman Honors College, an honors program, and a senior project. Special programs include internships, summer session for credit, off-campus study, and study abroad.

The most popular **majors** include business, education, and natural sciences. A complete listing of majors at Juniata appears in the Majors Index beginning on page 379.

The **faculty** at Juniata has 75 full-time teachers, 92% with terminal degrees. 100% of the faculty serve as student advisers. The student-faculty ratio is 13:1.

Computers on Campus

Students are not required to have a computer. Student rooms are linked to a campus network. 250 **computers** available in the computer center, computer labs, academic buildings, classrooms, the library, dormitories, and student rooms provide access to the main academic computer, e-mail, and the Internet. Staffed computer lab on campus provides training in the use of computers and software.

The **library** has 129,809 books, 9,435 microform titles, and 895 subscriptions.

Campus Life

There are 75 active **organizations** on campus, including a drama/theater group and student-run newspaper and radio station. Student **safety services** include late night transport/escort service, 24-hour emergency telephone alarm devices, and 24-hour patrols by trained security personnel.

Juniata is a member of the NCAA (Division III). **Intercollegiate sports** include baseball (m), basketball (m, w), cross-country running (w), field hockey (w), football (m), lacrosse (m), rugby (m), skiing (downhill) (m), soccer (m, w), softball (w), swimming and diving (w), tennis (w), track and field (m, w), volleyball (m, w).

Applying

Juniata requires an essay, a high school transcript, 2 years of high school foreign language, 1 recommendation, SAT I or ACT, and in some cases an interview. It recommends 3 years of high school math and science and SAT II Subject Tests. Early, deferred, and midyear entrance are possible, with rolling admissions and continuous processing to 3/1 for financial aid. **Contact:** Mr. David Hawsey III, Dean of Enrollment, 1700 Moore Street, Huntingdon, PA 16652-2119, 814-641-3420 ext. 420 or toll-free 800-526-1970; fax 814-641-3100.

GETTING IN LAST YEAR
1,017 applied
85% were accepted
33% enrolled (284)
3.1 average high school GPA
42% had SAT verbal scores over 600
37% had SAT math scores over 600
29% had ACT scores over 26
9% had SAT verbal scores over 700
3% had SAT math scores over 700
3% had ACT scores over 30
3 National Merit Scholars

THE STUDENT BODY
1,065 undergraduates

From 28 states and territories,
   13 other countries
79% from Pennsylvania
56% women, 44% men
1% African Americans
0% Native Americans
1% Hispanics
1% Asian Americans
4% international students

AFTER FRESHMAN YEAR
85% returned for sophomore year
70% got a degree within 4 years

AFTER GRADUATION
35% pursued further study (20% arts and
   sciences, 6% medicine, 5% law)
90% had job offers within 6 months

WHAT YOU WILL PAY
Tuition and fees $16,480
Room and board $4700
80% receive need-based financial aid
Need-based college-administered scholarships and
   grants average $7910 per award

KALAMAZOO COLLEGE

Kalamazoo, Michigan • Suburban setting • Private • Independent • Coed

---

A Kalamazoo College education prepares students to better understand, live successfully within, and provide enlightened leadership to a richly diverse and increasingly complex world. The College is nationally recognized for its "Kalamazoo Plan," which includes on-campus immersion in the liberal arts and sciences, a meaningful career internship, a senior individualized project, and study abroad. Over 85% of Kalamazoo students choose to study abroad at one of the College's centers in Africa, Asia, Europe, and Latin America. Kalamazoo students graduate with excellent academic qualifications and impressive hands-on experiences that prepare them for success in graduate programs and careers.

Academics

K-College offers a liberal arts and sciences curriculum and core academic program. It awards bachelor's **degrees**. Challenging opportunities include advanced placement, tutorials, a senior project, Phi Beta Kappa, and Sigma Xi. Special programs include cooperative education, internships, off-campus study, study abroad, and Army ROTC.

The most popular **majors** include economics, biology/biological sciences, and English. A complete listing of majors at K-College appears in the Majors Index beginning on page 379.

The **faculty** at K-College has 89 full-time teachers, 90% with terminal degrees. 95% of the faculty serve as student advisers. The student-faculty ratio is 11:1.

Computers on Campus

Students are not required to have a computer. Student rooms are linked to a campus network. 80 **computers**
available in the computer center, computer labs, and classrooms provide access to e-mail, on-line services, and the Internet. Staffed computer lab on campus (open 24 hours a day).

The **library** has 317,459 books, 18,748 microform titles, and 1,300 subscriptions. It is connected to 5 national **on-line** catalogs.

Campus Life

There are 36 active **organizations** on campus, including a drama/theater group and student-run newspaper and radio station. 59% of students participate in student government elections. Student **safety services** include late night transport/escort service, 24-hour emergency telephone alarm devices, 24-hour patrols by trained security personnel, and electronically operated dormitory entrances.

K-College is a member of the NCAA (Division III). **Intercollegiate sports** include baseball (m), basketball (m, w), cross-country running (m, w), football (m), golf (m, w), soccer (m, w), softball (w), swimming and diving (m, w), tennis (m, w), volleyball (w).

Applying

K-College requires an essay, a high school transcript, 2 recommendations, and SAT I or ACT. It recommends 3 years of high school math and science, some high school foreign language, an interview, and a minimum high school GPA of 3.0. Early, deferred, and midyear entrance are possible, with a 2/15 deadline and continuous processing to 2/15 for financial aid. **Contact:** Ms. Teresa M. Lahti, Dean of Admission, Mandelle Hall, Kalamazoo, MI 49006-3295, 616-337-7166 or toll-free 800-253-3602; fax 616-337-7390.

GETTING IN LAST YEAR

1,358 applied
92% were accepted
28% enrolled (350)
55% from top tenth of their h.s. class
3.6 average high school GPA
37% had SAT verbal scores over 600
66% had SAT math scores over 600
72% had ACT scores over 26
4% had SAT verbal scores over 700
11% had SAT math scores over 700
32% had ACT scores over 30
11 National Merit Scholars
27 valedictorians

THE STUDENT BODY

1,272 undergraduates
From 38 states and territories,
    30 other countries
69% from Michigan
58% women, 42% men
3% African Americans
1% Native Americans
1% Hispanics
5% Asian Americans
4% international students

AFTER FRESHMAN YEAR

83% returned for sophomore year
63% got a degree within 4 years

72% got a degree within 5 years
74% got a degree within 6 years

AFTER GRADUATION

15 organizations recruited on campus

WHAT YOU WILL PAY

Tuition and fees $17,284
Room and board $5421
51% receive need-based financial aid
Need-based college-administered scholarships and
    grants average $3720 per award
45% receive non-need financial aid
Non-need college-administered scholarships and
    grants average $3975 per award

KENTUCKY WESLEYAN COLLEGE

Owensboro, Kentucky • Suburban setting • Private • Independent-Religious • Coed

 Academics

Kentucky Wesleyan offers a broad-based cultural curriculum and core academic program. It awards associate and bachelor's **degrees**. Challenging opportunities include advanced placement, self-designed majors, tutorials, and a senior project. Special programs include internships, summer session for credit, off-campus study, and study abroad.

The most popular **majors** include nursing, business, and criminal justice. A complete listing of majors at Kentucky Wesleyan appears in the Majors Index beginning on page 379.

The **faculty** at Kentucky Wesleyan has 48 full-time teachers, 70% with terminal degrees. 100% of the faculty serve as student advisers. The student-faculty ratio is 10:1.

 Computers on Campus

Students are not required to have a computer. Student rooms are linked to a campus network. 50 **computers** available in the computer center, computer labs, faculty offices, classrooms, the library, dormitories, and student rooms provide access to the main academic computer, e-mail, and the Internet. Staffed computer lab on campus.

The **library** has 94,934 books, 54,903 microform titles, and 459 subscriptions. It is connected to 1 national **on-line** catalog.

 Campus Life

There are 40 active **organizations** on campus, including a drama/theater group and student-run newspaper and radio station. 14% of eligible men and 33% of eligible women are members of 3 national **fraternities** and 2 national **sororities**. Student **safety services** include 12-hour patrols by trained security personnel and late night transport/escort service.

Kentucky Wesleyan is a member of the NCAA (Division II). **Intercollegiate sports** (some offering scholarships) include baseball (m), basketball (m, w), football (m), golf (m), soccer (m, w), softball (w), tennis (m, w), volleyball (w).

 Applying

Kentucky Wesleyan requires an essay, a high school transcript, 3 years of high school math and science, SAT I or ACT, and in some cases recommendations and an interview. It recommends 2 years of high school foreign language and recommendations. Early, deferred, and midyear entrance are possible, with rolling admissions and continuous processing to 3/1 for financial aid. **Contact:** Ms. Gloria Smith Kunik, Director of Enrollment Services, 3000 Frederica Street, Owensboro, KY 42302-1039, 502-926-3111 ext. 143 or toll-free 800-999-0592; fax 502-926-3196.

GETTING IN LAST YEAR
487 applied
79% were accepted
39% enrolled (151)
32% from top tenth of their h.s. class
3.18 average high school GPA
42% had SAT verbal scores over 600 (R)
33% had SAT math scores over 600 (R)
25% had ACT scores over 26
8% had SAT verbal scores over 700 (R)
8% had SAT math scores over 700 (R)
5% had ACT scores over 30
3 National Merit Scholars
3 valedictorians

THE STUDENT BODY
635 undergraduates

From 21 states and territories,
 4 other countries
78% from Kentucky
55% women, 45% men
4% African Americans
0% Native Americans
0% Hispanics
1% Asian Americans
1% international students

AFTER FRESHMAN YEAR
60% returned for sophomore year
44% got a degree within 4 years
46% got a degree within 5 years
48% got a degree within 6 years

AFTER GRADUATION
30% pursued further study (15% arts and
 sciences, 4% business, 4% medicine)
97% had job offers within 6 months
8 organizations recruited on campus

WHAT YOU WILL PAY
Tuition and fees $9100
Room and board $4300
77% receive need-based financial aid
Need-based college-administered scholarships and
 grants average $2326 per award
60% receive non-need financial aid
Non-need college-administered scholarships and
 grants average $2424 per award

KENYON COLLEGE

Gambier, Ohio • Rural setting • Private • Independent • Coed

> Ranked in the top 30 undergraduate colleges for academic reputation and in the top 25 for quality of teaching, Kenyon is also one of only a handful of colleges included on 3 "Top 50" lists: whose graduates earn PhDs in the sciences or humanities, whose graduates are major corporate executives, and whose students study abroad. Students cite quality of teaching, accessibility of faculty, and a strong sense of community as reasons they chose Kenyon. Half of the classes have 15 or fewer students. Kenyon's 800-acre campus set in the quintessential college town has been described as one of the most beautiful in the country.

 Academics

Kenyon offers a liberal arts and sciences curriculum and core academic program. It awards bachelor's **degrees**. Challenging opportunities include advanced placement, self-designed majors, tutorials, an honors program, a senior project, and Phi Beta Kappa. Special programs include internships, off-campus study, and study abroad.

The most popular **majors** include English, history, and psychology. A complete listing of majors at Kenyon appears in the Majors Index beginning on page 379.

The **faculty** at Kenyon has 133 full-time teachers, 93% with terminal degrees. 100% of the faculty serve as student advisers. The student-faculty ratio is 10:1.

 Computers on Campus

Students are not required to have a computer. Student rooms are linked to a campus network. 219 **computers** available in computer labs, the research center, classrooms, the library, dormitories, and student rooms provide access to the main academic computer, off-campus computing facilities, e-mail, on-line services, the Internet, and commercial databases. Staffed computer lab on campus provides training in the use of computers and software.

The **library** has 423,306 books, 343,675 microform titles, and 1,211 subscriptions. It is connected to 4 national **on-line** catalogs.

 Campus Life

There are 107 active **organizations** on campus, including a drama/theater group and student-run newspaper and radio station. 37% of students participate in student government elections. 25% of eligible men and 2% of eligible women are members of 7 national **fraternities**, 1 local fraternity, 2 local **sororities**, and 2 Community service clubs, social clubs. Student **safety services** include late night transport/escort service, 24-hour emergency telephone alarm devices, 24-hour patrols by trained security personnel, and student patrols.

Kenyon is a member of the NCAA (Division III). **Intercollegiate sports** include baseball (m), basketball (m, w), cross-country running (m, w), field hockey (w), football (m), golf (m, w), lacrosse (m, w), soccer (m, w), swimming and diving (m, w), tennis (m, w), track and field (m, w), volleyball (w).

 Applying

Kenyon requires an essay, a high school transcript, 3 years of high school math, 3 years of high school foreign language, 1 recommendation, SAT I or ACT, and a minimum high school GPA of 2.0. It recommends 4 years of high school math, 3 years of high school science, 4 years of high school foreign language, an interview, and a minimum high school GPA of 3.0. Early, deferred, and midyear entrance are possible, with a 2/15 deadline and 2/15 for financial aid. **Contact:** Mr. John W. Anderson, Dean of Admissions, Ransom Hall, Gambier, OH 43022-9623, 614-427-5776 or toll-free 800-848-2468; fax 614-427-2634.

GETTING IN LAST YEAR

2,303 applied
71% were accepted
27% enrolled (441)
40% from top tenth of their h.s. class
3.53 average high school GPA
72% had SAT verbal scores over 600 (R)
60% had SAT math scores over 600 (R)
82% had ACT scores over 26
24% had SAT verbal scores over 700 (R)
13% had SAT math scores over 700 (R)
30% had ACT scores over 30
30 National Merit Scholars
20 class presidents
15 valedictorians

THE STUDENT BODY

1,516 undergraduates
From 47 states and territories,
  22 other countries
25% from Ohio
52% women, 48% men
4% African Americans
1% Native Americans
3% Hispanics
4% Asian Americans
2% international students

AFTER FRESHMAN YEAR

89% returned for sophomore year
81% got a degree within 4 years

84% got a degree within 5 years
85% got a degree within 6 years

AFTER GRADUATION

53 organizations recruited on campus

WHAT YOU WILL PAY

Tuition and fees $21,830
Room and board $3940
40% receive need-based financial aid
Need-based college-administered scholarships and
  grants average $11,138 per award
10% receive non-need financial aid
Non-need college-administered scholarships and
  grants average $7346 per award

KNOX COLLEGE

Galesburg, Illinois • Small-town setting • Private • Independent • Coed

For more than 150 years, Knox College has offered students the chance to work closely with distinguished teachers. Knox provides a superior liberal arts program with special strengths in the sciences and creative arts. A college of exceptional diversity, Knox enjoys an open, easygoing campus culture that allows students to take charge of their own lives and to flourish; students can go anywhere with a Knox degree. Knox is eleventh among liberal arts colleges in the percentage of graduates who earn math/science PhDs and thirtieth in the percentage of graduates who become business executives.

 ## Academics

Knox offers an interdisciplinary curriculum and core academic program. It awards bachelor's **degrees**. Challenging opportunities include advanced placement, self-designed majors, tutorials, a senior project, Phi Beta Kappa, and Sigma Xi. Special programs include internships, off-campus study, and study abroad.

The most popular **majors** include political science/government, sociology, and biology/biological sciences. A complete listing of majors at Knox appears in the Majors Index beginning on page 379.

The **faculty** at Knox has 94 full-time teachers, 86% with terminal degrees. 75% of the faculty serve as student advisers. The student-faculty ratio is 12:1.

 ## Computers on Campus

Students are not required to have a computer. Student rooms are linked to a campus network. 130 **computers** available in the computer center, computer labs, the learning resource center, all academic buildings, classrooms, the library, and the student center provide access to the main academic computer, e-mail, on-line services, and the Internet. Staffed computer lab on campus (open 24 hours a day) provides training in the use of computers and software.

The 3 **libraries** have 273,170 books, 95,155 microform titles, and 732 subscriptions. They are connected to 5 national **on-line** catalogs.

 ## Campus Life

There are 68 active **organizations** on campus, including a drama/theater group and student-run newspaper and radio station. 35% of eligible men and 15% of eligible women are members of 5 national **fraternities** and 2 national **sororities**. Student **safety services** include late night transport/escort service and 24-hour emergency telephone alarm devices.

Knox is a member of the NCAA (Division III). **Intercollegiate sports** include baseball (m), basketball (m, w), cross-country running (m, w), football (m), golf (m, w), soccer (m, w), softball (w), swimming and diving (m, w), tennis (m, w), track and field (m, w), volleyball (w), wrestling (m).

 ## Applying

Knox requires an essay, a high school transcript, 3 years of high school math and science, 2 recommendations, and SAT I or ACT. It recommends 2 years of high school foreign language and an interview. Early, deferred, and midyear entrance are possible, with a 2/15 deadline and continuous processing to 3/1 for financial aid. **Contact:** Mr. Paul Steenis, Director of Admissions, Admissions Office, Box K-148, Galesburg, IL 61401, 309-341-7100 or toll-free 800-678-KNOX; fax 309-341-7070.

GETTING IN LAST YEAR

1,070 applied
81% were accepted
36% enrolled (308)
48% from top tenth of their h.s. class
55% had SAT verbal scores over 600
51% had SAT math scores over 600
54% had ACT scores over 26
14% had SAT verbal scores over 700
13% had SAT math scores over 700
16% had ACT scores over 30
11 National Merit Scholars
19 valedictorians

THE STUDENT BODY

1,127 undergraduates

From 42 states and territories,
33 other countries
57% from Illinois
54% women, 46% men
5% African Americans
1% Native Americans
3% Hispanics
5% Asian Americans
7% international students

AFTER FRESHMAN YEAR

86% returned for sophomore year
67% got a degree within 4 years
72% got a degree within 5 years
73% got a degree within 6 years

AFTER GRADUATION

32% pursued further study (20% arts and sciences, 6% medicine, 4% business)
68% had job offers within 6 months
46 organizations recruited on campus

WHAT YOU WILL PAY

Tuition and fees $17,778
Room and board $4662
80% receive need-based financial aid
Need-based college-administered scholarships and grants average $9020 per award
10% receive non-need financial aid
Non-need college-administered scholarships and grants average $5950 per award

LAFAYETTE COLLEGE

Easton, Pennsylvania • Suburban setting • Private • Independent-Religious • Coed

Lafayette College has achieved a unique niche in American higher education: liberal arts and engineering programs in a small-college setting. Lafayette offers small classes, interdisciplinary first-year seminars, and student-faculty collaborative research on a residential campus located in eastern Pennsylvania close to New York and Philadelphia.

Academics

Lafayette offers an interdisciplinary curriculum and core academic program. It awards bachelor's **degrees**. Challenging opportunities include advanced placement, accelerated degree programs, self-designed majors, tutorials, an honors program, Phi Beta Kappa, and Sigma Xi. Special programs include internships, summer session for credit, off-campus study, study abroad, and Army ROTC.

The most popular **majors** include biology/biological sciences, business economics, and psychology. A complete listing of majors at Lafayette appears in the Majors Index beginning on page 379.

The **faculty** at Lafayette has 180 full-time teachers, 100% with terminal degrees. 63% of the faculty serve as student advisers. The student-faculty ratio is 11:1.

Computers on Campus

Students are not required to have a computer. Student rooms are linked to a campus network. 250 **computers** available in the computer center, classroom buildings, the library, and dormitories provide access to the main academic computer, off-campus computing facilities, e-mail, on-line services, and the Internet. Staffed computer lab on campus (open 24 hours a day) provides training in the use of computers and software.

The 2 **libraries** have 436,107 books and 1,705 subscriptions. They are connected to 5 national **on-line** catalogs.

Campus Life

There are 95 active **organizations** on campus, including a drama/theater group and student-run newspaper and radio station. 25% of students participate in student government elections. 50% of eligible men and 70% of eligible women are members of 11 national **fraternities**, 6 national **sororities**, and 2 social dorms. Student **safety services** include late night transport/escort service, 24-hour emergency telephone alarm devices, 24-hour patrols by trained security personnel, student patrols, and electronically operated dormitory entrances.

Lafayette is a member of the NCAA (Division I). **Intercollegiate sports** include baseball (m), basketball (m, w), crew (m, w), cross-country running (m, w), equestrian sports (m, w), fencing (m, w), field hockey (w), football (m), golf (m), lacrosse (m, w), rugby (m, w), skiing (downhill) (m, w), soccer (m, w), softball (w), squash (m), swimming and diving (m, w), tennis (m, w), track and field (m, w), volleyball (w), weight lifting (m, w), wrestling (m).

Applying

Lafayette requires an essay, a high school transcript, 3 years of high school math, 2 years of high school foreign language, and 1 recommendation. It recommends 3 years of high school science and an interview. Early and deferred entrance are possible, with a 1/15 deadline and continuous processing to 2/15 for financial aid. **Contact:** Dr. Gary Ripple, Director of Admissions, 118 Markle Hall, Easton, PA 18042-1798, 610-250-5100; fax 610-250-5355.

GETTING IN LAST YEAR
4,010 applied
60% were accepted
24% enrolled (588)
37% from top tenth of their h.s. class
1 National Merit Scholar

THE STUDENT BODY
2,219 undergraduates
From 39 states and territories,
    50 other countries
31% from Pennsylvania

44% women, 56% men
4% African Americans
1% Native Americans
2% Hispanics
4% Asian Americans
4% international students

AFTER FRESHMAN YEAR
94% returned for sophomore year
82% got a degree within 4 years
83% got a degree within 5 years
86% got a degree within 6 years

AFTER GRADUATION
25% pursued further study (12% arts and
    sciences, 6% law, 3% engineering)

WHAT YOU WILL PAY
Tuition and fees $19,621
Room and board $6000
51% receive need-based financial aid
Need-based college-administered scholarships and
    grants average $11,845 per award

LAKE FOREST COLLEGE

Lake Forest, Illinois • Suburban setting • Private • Independent • Coed

Lake Forest College is situated in the remarkably beautiful community of Lake Forest, Illinois' safest city, with a population of more than 5,000. Chicago is located just 30 miles south of the campus, where students enhance their liberal arts education through the world-renowned resources of this great city. Over 80% of LFC students strengthen their education through domestic and international internships, practicums, and the College's extensive study-abroad program. On campus, the distinguished faculty offer students high-quality teaching and the unique opportunity to conduct independent research. Students enjoy the tree-lined campus near the shore of Lake Michigan.

Academics

Lake Forest offers a liberal arts curriculum and core academic program. It awards bachelor's and master's **degrees**. Challenging opportunities include advanced placement, accelerated degree programs, self-designed majors, tutorials, Freshman Honors College, a senior project, Phi Beta Kappa, and Sigma Xi. Special programs include internships, summer session for credit, off-campus study, and study abroad.

The most popular **majors** include psychology, English, and business economics. A complete listing of majors at Lake Forest appears in the Majors Index beginning on page 379.

The **faculty** at Lake Forest has 72 full-time undergraduate teachers, 95% with terminal degrees. 100% of the faculty serve as student advisers. The student-faculty ratio is 11:1, and the average class size in core courses is 19.

Computers on Campus

Students are not required to have a computer. Student rooms are linked to a campus network. 196 **computers** available in the computer center, computer labs, the research center, the learning resource center, labs, classrooms, the library, the student center, and dormitories provide access to the main academic computer, e-mail, and on-line services. Staffed computer lab on campus (open 24 hours a day) provides training in the use of computers and software.

The 2 **libraries** have 275,569 books, 101,709 microform titles, and 1,170 subscriptions.

Campus Life

There are 46 active **organizations** on campus, including a drama/theater group and student-run newspaper and radio station. 60% of students participate in student government elections. 21% of eligible men and 19% of eligible women are members of 1 national **fraternity**, 3 local fraternities, and 3 local **sororities**. Student **safety services** include late night transport/escort service, 24-hour emergency telephone alarm devices, 24-hour patrols by trained security personnel, and student patrols.

Lake Forest is a member of the NCAA (Division III). **Intercollegiate sports** include baseball (m), basketball (m, w), cross-country running (m, w), fencing (m, w), football (m), ice hockey (m), lacrosse (m, w), sailing (m, w), soccer (m, w), softball (w), swimming and diving (m, w), tennis (m, w), volleyball (m, w), water polo (m).

Applying

Lake Forest requires an essay, a high school transcript, 2 recommendations, and SAT I or ACT. It recommends 3 years of high school math, 2 years of high school foreign language, and an interview. Early, deferred, and midyear entrance are possible, with a 3/1 deadline and continuous processing to 3/1 for financial aid. **Contact:** Mr. William G. Motzer Jr., Director of Admissions, 555 North Sheridan Road, Lake Forest, IL 60045-2399, 847-735-5000; fax 847-735-6291.

GETTING IN LAST YEAR
1,055 applied
72% were accepted
35% enrolled (266)
32% from top tenth of their h.s. class
3.3 average high school GPA
33% had SAT verbal scores over 600 (R)
28% had SAT math scores over 600 (R)
39% had ACT scores over 26
8% had SAT verbal scores over 700 (R)
4% had SAT math scores over 700 (R)
7% had ACT scores over 30
1 National Merit Scholar
15 class presidents
4 valedictorians

THE STUDENT BODY
Total 1,039, of whom 1,028
  are undergraduates

From 48 states and territories,
  34 other countries
41% from Illinois
55% women, 45% men
6% African Americans
1% Native Americans
5% Hispanics
4% Asian Americans
8% international students

AFTER FRESHMAN YEAR
74% returned for sophomore year
56% got a degree within 4 years
63% got a degree within 5 years

AFTER GRADUATION
21% pursued further study (8% arts and
  sciences, 5% law, 3% medicine)
65% had job offers within 6 months
56 organizations recruited on campus

WHAT YOU WILL PAY
Tuition and fees $19,000
Room and board $4400
71% receive need-based financial aid
Need-based college-administered scholarships and
  grants average $10,992 per award
2% receive non-need financial aid
Non-need college-administered scholarships and
  grants average $8879 per award

LA SALLE UNIVERSITY

Philadelphia, Pennsylvania • Urban setting • Private • Independent-Religious • Coed

La Salle University offers one of the country's most respected honors programs. Established in 1963 to meet the needs of La Salle's most gifted students, the program has become a national model and has been praised by the National Collegiate Honors Council for its "extraordinary record in terms of garnering Fulbright, Danforth and Marshall Fellowships." La Salle has been ranked among the nation's leading colleges by *U.S. News & World Report, Money* magazine, *Barron's,* and the *New York Times.*

Academics

La Salle offers a core academic program. It awards associate, bachelor's, and master's **degrees**. Challenging opportunities include advanced placement, accelerated degree programs, self-designed majors, tutorials, Freshman Honors College, an honors program, and a senior project. Special programs include cooperative education, internships, summer session for credit, off-campus study, study abroad, and Army, Naval, and Air Force ROTC.

The most popular **majors** include accounting, (pre)medicine sequence, and communication. A complete listing of majors at La Salle appears in the Majors Index beginning on page 379.

The **faculty** at La Salle has 228 full-time undergraduate teachers, 88% with terminal degrees. 80% of the faculty serve as student advisers. The student-faculty ratio is 14:1.

Computers on Campus

Students are not required to have a computer. 350 **computers** available in the computer center, computer labs, the research center, the learning resource center, classrooms, the library, and the student center provide access to the main academic computer, e-mail, on-line services, and the Internet. Staffed computer lab on campus provides training in the use of computers and software.

The **library** has 347,000 books, 36,470 microform titles, and 1,650 subscriptions. It is connected to 3 national **on-line** catalogs.

Campus Life

There are 115 active **organizations** on campus, including a drama/theater group and student-run newspaper and radio station. 15% of eligible men and 13% of eligible women are members of 8 national **fraternities**, 8 national **sororities**, 1 local fraternity, and 1 local sorority. Student **safety services** include late night transport/escort service, 24-hour emergency telephone alarm devices, 24-hour patrols by trained security personnel, student patrols, and electronically operated dormitory entrances.

La Salle is a member of the NCAA (Division I) and NAIA. **Intercollegiate sports** (some offering scholarships) include baseball (m), basketball (m, w), crew (m, w), cross-country running (m, w), field hockey (w), golf (m, w), soccer (m, w), softball (w), swimming and diving (m, w), tennis (m, w), track and field (m, w), volleyball (w), wrestling (m).

Applying

La Salle requires an essay, a high school transcript, 3 years of high school math, 2 years of high school foreign language, 1 recommendation, and SAT I or ACT. It recommends a campus interview and SAT II Subject Tests. Early, deferred, and midyear entrance are possible, with a 4/1 deadline and continuous processing to 2/15 for financial aid. **Contact:** Mr. Christopher P. Lydon, Director of Admission and Financial Aid, Administration Building, Philadelphia, PA 19141-1199, 215-951-1500 or toll-free 800-382-1910; fax 215-951-1488.

GETTING IN LAST YEAR
2,742 applied
79% were accepted
34% enrolled (742)
21% from top tenth of their h.s. class
36% had SAT verbal scores over 600 (R)
28% had SAT math scores over 600 (R)
4% had SAT verbal scores over 700 (R)
3% had SAT math scores over 700 (R)
3 National Merit Scholars
12 class presidents
9 valedictorians

THE STUDENT BODY
Total 5,449, of whom 4,073
  are undergraduates

From 24 states and territories,
  12 other countries
68% from Pennsylvania
54% women, 46% men
10% African Americans
0% Native Americans
3% Hispanics
3% Asian Americans
2% international students

AFTER FRESHMAN YEAR
86% returned for sophomore year
69% got a degree within 4 years
73% got a degree within 5 years

AFTER GRADUATION
11% pursued further study
1 Fulbright scholar

WHAT YOU WILL PAY
Tuition and fees $13,160
Room and board $5970
79% receive need-based financial aid
Need-based college-administered scholarships and
  grants average $5459 per award
6% receive non-need financial aid
Non-need college-administered scholarships and
  grants average $4000 per award

LAWRENCE UNIVERSITY

Appleton, Wisconsin • Small-town setting • Private • Independent • Coed

Lawrence University is committed to the development of intellect and talent, the acquisition of knowledge and understanding, and the cultivation of judgment and values. Its graduates earn Fulbrights, Watsons, Rhodes, and other prestigious fellowships for continuing their education beyond the undergraduate level. Every year, Lawrence students have the highest academic profile of any institution of higher learning in Wisconsin. Research opportunities with faculty members, an outstanding laser physics laboratory, an excellent conservatory of music offering a 5-year double-degree program, and especially strong interdisciplinary areas of study are among the most attractive programs available at Lawrence.

Academics

Lawrence offers a core academic program. It awards bachelor's **degrees**. Challenging opportunities include advanced placement, self-designed majors, tutorials, an honors program, a senior project, and Phi Beta Kappa. Special programs include internships, off-campus study, and study abroad.

The most popular **majors** include biology/biological sciences, English, and psychology. A complete listing of majors at Lawrence appears in the Majors Index beginning on page 379.

The **faculty** at Lawrence has 109 full-time teachers, 97% with terminal degrees. 100% of the faculty serve as student advisers. The student-faculty ratio is 10:1.

Computers on Campus

Students are not required to have a computer. Student rooms are linked to a campus network. 140 **computers** available in the computer center, computer labs, the learning resource center, academic buildings, the library, and dormitories provide access to the main academic computer, off-campus computing facilities, e-mail, on-line services, and the Internet. Staffed computer lab on campus provides training in the use of computers and software.

The **library** has 336,957 books, 102,910 microform titles, and 1,357 subscriptions. It is connected to 3 national **on-line** catalogs.

Campus Life

There are 120 active **organizations** on campus, including a drama/theater group and student-run newspaper. 37% of eligible men and 18% of eligible women are members of 5 national **fraternities** and 3 national **sororities**. Student **safety services** include evening patrols by trained security personnel, late night transport/escort service, 24-hour emergency telephone alarm devices, student patrols, and electronically operated dormitory entrances.

Lawrence is a member of the NCAA (Division III). **Intercollegiate sports** include baseball (m), basketball (m, w), crew (m, w), cross-country running (m, w), fencing (m, w), football (m), golf (m), ice hockey (m), lacrosse (m, w), rugby (w), soccer (m, w), softball (w), swimming and diving (m, w), tennis (m, w), track and field (m, w), volleyball (w), wrestling (m).

Applying

Lawrence requires an essay, a high school transcript, 2 recommendations, audition for music majors, and SAT I or ACT. It recommends 3 years of high school math and science, 2 years of high school foreign language, an interview, and a minimum high school GPA of 3.0. Early, deferred, and midyear entrance are possible, with a 2/1 deadline and continuous processing to 3/15 for financial aid. **Contact:** Mr. Steven T. Syverson, Dean of Admissions and Financial Aid, 706 East College Avenue, Appleton, WI 54912-0599, 414-832-6500 or toll-free 800-227-0982; fax 414-832-6782.

GETTING IN LAST YEAR
1,546 applied
69% were accepted
31% enrolled (327)
46% from top tenth of their h.s. class
3.55 average high school GPA
62% had SAT verbal scores over 600 (R)
60% had SAT math scores over 600 (R)
66% had ACT scores over 26
27% had SAT verbal scores over 700 (R)
16% had SAT math scores over 700 (R)
30% had ACT scores over 30
7 National Merit Scholars
18 valedictorians

THE STUDENT BODY
1,216 undergraduates
From 43 states and territories,
  39 other countries
45% from Wisconsin
52% women, 48% men
2% African Americans
1% Native Americans
2% Hispanics
4% Asian Americans
7% international students

AFTER FRESHMAN YEAR
82% returned for sophomore year
59% got a degree within 4 years

70% got a degree within 5 years
71% got a degree within 6 years

AFTER GRADUATION
27% pursued further study (24% arts and
  sciences, 1% business, 1% law)
72% had job offers within 6 months
33 organizations recruited on campus

WHAT YOU WILL PAY
Tuition and fees $18,057
Room and board $4038
Need-based college-administered scholarships and
  grants average $10,238 per award
Non-need college-administered scholarships and
  grants average $6354 per award

LEHIGH UNIVERSITY

Bethlehem, Pennsylvania • Suburban setting • Private • Independent • Coed

Lehigh University is a comprehensive national university located on a spectacular 1600-acre campus in Bethlehem, Pennsylvania. The University comprises 3 undergraduate colleges—Arts and Sciences, Business and Economics, and Engineering and Applied Sciences; a graduate school; and a graduate-level College of Education. Since its founding in 1865, Lehigh's philosophy has been to prepare young people for a rewarding and successful life. The hallmarks of a Lehigh education are close student-faculty interaction and experiential learning both inside and outside the classroom.

Academics

Lehigh offers an interdisciplinary curriculum and no core academic program; fewer than half of graduate courses are open to undergraduates. It awards bachelor's, master's, and doctoral **degrees**. Challenging opportunities include advanced placement, accelerated degree programs, self-designed majors, tutorials, an honors program, a senior project, Phi Beta Kappa, and Sigma Xi. Special programs include cooperative education, internships, summer session for credit, off-campus study, study abroad, and Army ROTC.

The most popular **majors** include mechanical engineering, civil engineering, and accounting. A complete listing of majors at Lehigh appears in the Majors Index beginning on page 379.

The **faculty** at Lehigh has 410 full-time graduate and undergraduate teachers, 98% with terminal degrees. The student-faculty ratio is 11:1.

Computers on Campus

Students are not required to have a computer. Student rooms are linked to a campus network. 500 **computers** available in the computer center, computer labs, the research center, the learning resource center, academic buildings, classrooms, the library, the student center, and dormitories provide access to the main academic computer, off-campus computing facilities, e-mail, on-line services, and the Internet. Staffed computer lab on campus (open 24 hours a day) provides training in the use of computers and software.

The 3 **libraries** have 1.1 million books, 1.7 million microform titles, and 10,510 subscriptions. They are connected to 9 national **on-line** catalogs.

Campus Life

There are 130 active **organizations** on campus, including a drama/theater group and student-run newspaper and radio station. 48% of eligible men and 48% of eligible women are members of 28 national **fraternities** and 8 national **sororities**. Student **safety services** include late night transport/escort service, 24-hour emergency telephone alarm devices, 24-hour patrols by trained security personnel, student patrols, and electronically operated dormitory entrances.

Lehigh is a member of the NCAA (Division I). **Intercollegiate sports** (some offering scholarships) include baseball (m), basketball (m, w), crew (m, w), cross-country running (m, w), equestrian sports (m, w), field hockey (w), football (m, w), golf (m), gymnastics (w), ice hockey (m), lacrosse (m, w), riflery (m, w), rugby (m), sailing (m, w), skiing (downhill) (m, w), soccer (m, w), softball (w), squash (m), swimming and diving (m, w), tennis (m, w), track and field (m, w), volleyball (m, w), water polo (m), wrestling (m).

Applying

Lehigh requires a high school transcript, 2 years of high school foreign language, 1 recommendation, graded writing sample, SAT I or ACT, and in some cases 4 years of high school math and 3 years of high school science. It recommends a campus interview. Early, deferred, and midyear entrance are possible, with a 2/15 deadline and a 2/15 priority date for financial aid. **Contact:** Mrs. Patricia G. Boig, Director of Admissions, 27 Memorial Drive West, Bethlehem, PA 18015-3094, 610-758-3100; fax 610-758-4361.

GETTING IN LAST YEAR
6,483 applied
60% were accepted
27% enrolled (1,046)
40% from top tenth of their h.s. class
42% had SAT verbal scores over 600 (R)
66% had SAT math scores over 600 (R)
32% had ACT scores over 26
6% had SAT verbal scores over 700 (R)
11% had SAT math scores over 700 (R)
11% had ACT scores over 30
10 National Merit Scholars

THE STUDENT BODY
Total 6,255, of whom 4,357
  are undergraduates

From 45 states and territories,
  44 other countries
33% from Pennsylvania
37% women, 63% men
3% African Americans
1% Native Americans
2% Hispanics
5% Asian Americans
4% international students

AFTER FRESHMAN YEAR
91% returned for sophomore year
84% got a degree within 5 years

AFTER GRADUATION
23% pursued further study (7% arts and
  sciences, 6% law, 5% engineering)

WHAT YOU WILL PAY
Tuition and fees $20,500
Room and board $6020
52% receive need-based financial aid
Need-based college-administered scholarships and
  grants average $10,855 per award
Non-need college-administered scholarships and
  grants average $6850 per award

LE MOYNE COLLEGE

Syracuse, New York • Suburban setting • Private • Independent-Religious • Coed

Le Moyne provides a rigorous and personalized academic experience. To strengthen problem-solving, critical thinking, and communication skills and to better understand the world in which we live, all students integrate a humanities core sequence into the exploration of their chosen discipline. A spirit of academic excellence is nurtured on the suburban Syracuse campus, where classes average 21 students and are taught exclusively by professors. It is important to provide this fine education at a reasonable cost. In fact, it is this combination of high quality and reasonable net cost that has allowed Le Moyne to distinguish itself as "One of America's Best Colleges."

Academics

Le Moyne offers a Western culture curriculum and core academic program. It awards bachelor's and master's **degrees**. Challenging opportunities include advanced placement, accelerated degree programs, an honors program, and a senior project. Special programs include internships, summer session for credit, off-campus study, and Army and Air Force ROTC.

The most popular **majors** include accounting, business, and psychology. A complete listing of majors at Le Moyne appears in the Majors Index beginning on page 379.

The **faculty** at Le Moyne has 121 full-time graduate and undergraduate teachers, 92% with terminal degrees. 62% of the faculty serve as student advisers. The student-faculty ratio is 13:1, and the average class size in core courses is 19.

Computers on Campus

Students are not required to have a computer. Student rooms are linked to a campus network. 150 **computers** available in the computer center, computer labs, the learning resource center, science center, the library, and dormitories provide access to the main academic computer, e-mail, on-line services, and the Internet. Staffed computer lab on campus provides training in the use of computers and software.

The **library** has 215,395 books, 298 microform titles, and 1,730 subscriptions. It is connected to 5 national **on-line** catalogs.

Campus Life

There are 70 active **organizations** on campus, including a drama/theater group and student-run newspaper and radio station. 40% of students participate in student government elections. Student **safety services** include late night transport/escort service, 24-hour patrols by trained security personnel, and electronically operated dormitory entrances.

Le Moyne is a member of the NCAA (Division II). **Intercollegiate sports** (some offering scholarships) include baseball (m), basketball (m, w), cross-country running (m, w), golf (m), lacrosse (m, w), soccer (m, w), softball (w), swimming and diving (m, w), tennis (m, w), volleyball (w).

Applying

Le Moyne requires a high school transcript, 3 years of high school math and science, 3 years of high school foreign language, 1 recommendation, SAT I or ACT, and in some cases an essay. It recommends an essay and an interview. Early, deferred, and midyear entrance are possible, with a 3/15 deadline and a 2/15 priority date for financial aid. **Contact:** Mr. Dennis R. DePerro, Dean of Enrollment Management, Syracuse, NY 13214, 315-445-4707 or toll-free 800-333-4733.

GETTING IN LAST YEAR
1,719 applied
78% were accepted
30% enrolled (403)
20% from top tenth of their h.s. class
3.2 average high school GPA
25% had SAT verbal scores over 600 (R)
23% had SAT math scores over 600 (R)
26% had ACT scores over 26
2% had SAT verbal scores over 700 (R)
2% had SAT math scores over 700 (R)
8% had ACT scores over 30

THE STUDENT BODY
Total 2,425, of whom 1,809
  are undergraduates

From 25 states and territories,
  8 other countries
94% from New York
59% women, 41% men
4% African Americans
1% Native Americans
3% Hispanics
2% Asian Americans
1% international students

AFTER FRESHMAN YEAR
87% returned for sophomore year
72% got a degree within 4 years
76% got a degree within 5 years
78% got a degree within 6 years

AFTER GRADUATION
26% pursued further study (17% arts and
  sciences, 4% business, 4% medicine)
61 organizations recruited on campus

WHAT YOU WILL PAY
Tuition and fees $12,060
Room and board $5040
70% receive need-based financial aid
Need-based college-administered scholarships and
  grants average $6300 per award
30% receive non-need financial aid
Non-need college-administered scholarships and
  grants average $2850 per award

LETOURNEAU UNIVERSITY

Longview, Texas • Suburban setting • Private • Independent-Religious • Coed

---

Set apart by a special "spirit of ingenuity," LeTourneau University continues to expand on the excellence and inventive zeal of its heritage. Always striving to excel, LeTourneau was the first evangelical Christian college to receive professional accreditation by the Accreditation Board for Engineering and Technology (ABET). The University provides solid programs in more than 40 majors, with special emphasis on aviation, business, engineering, and technology. Set in the beautiful pine woods and lakes of East Texas, the spacious contemporary campus is home to innovative students from virtually every state and 25 nations. At LeTourneau, "Faith brings us together, ingenuity sets us apart."

 Academics

LeTourneau offers a core academic program; a few graduate courses are open to undergraduates. It awards associate, bachelor's, and master's **degrees**. Challenging opportunities include advanced placement and a senior project. Special programs include cooperative education, internships, summer session for credit, and off-campus study.

The most popular **majors** include aviation technology, electrical engineering, and mechanical engineering. A complete listing of majors at LeTourneau appears in the Majors Index beginning on page 379.

The **faculty** at LeTourneau has 55 full-time graduate and undergraduate teachers, 71% with terminal degrees. 95% of the faculty serve as student advisers. The student-faculty ratio is 15:1, and the average class size in core courses is 24.

 Computers on Campus

Students are not required to have a computer. 300 **computers** available in the computer center, computer labs, and the library provide access to on-line services and the Internet. Staffed computer lab on campus.

The **library** has 12,202 books, 520 microform titles, and 1,636 subscriptions. It is connected to 2 national **on-line** catalogs.

 Campus Life

There are 27 active **organizations** on campus, including a drama/theater group and student-run newspaper. 47% of students participate in student government elections. 3% of eligible men are members of societies. Student **safety services** include late night transport/escort service, 24-hour emergency telephone alarm devices, 24-hour patrols by trained security personnel, and electronically operated dormitory entrances.

LeTourneau is a member of the NAIA. **Intercollegiate sports** (some offering scholarships) include baseball (m), basketball (m, w), cross-country running (m, w), soccer (m), track and field (m, w), volleyball (w).

 Applying

LeTourneau requires an essay, a high school transcript, 2 recommendations, SAT I or ACT, a minimum high school GPA of 2.0, and in some cases 3 years of high school math and a campus interview. It recommends 3 years of high school science. Early, deferred, and midyear entrance are possible, with an 8/15 deadline and continuous processing to 2/15 for financial aid. **Contact:** Mr. Howard Wilson, Director of Admissions, 2100 South Mobberly, Longview, TX 75607-7001, 903-233-3400 ext. 240 or toll-free 800-759-8811; fax 903-233-3411.

GETTING IN LAST YEAR
23% from top tenth of their h.s. class
3.31 average high school GPA
32% had ACT scores over 26
6% had ACT scores over 30
2 National Merit Scholars
5 valedictorians

THE STUDENT BODY
Total 2,256, of whom 2,089 are undergraduates
From 47 states and territories, 27 other countries

71% from Texas
37% women, 63% men
4% African Americans
1% Native Americans
4% Hispanics
1% Asian Americans
3% international students

AFTER FRESHMAN YEAR
66% returned for sophomore year
27% got a degree within 4 years
49% got a degree within 5 years
55% got a degree within 6 years

AFTER GRADUATION
5% pursued further study (2% engineering, 1% business, 1% law)

WHAT YOU WILL PAY
Tuition and fees $11,030
Room and board $4630
77% receive need-based financial aid
Need-based college-administered scholarships and grants average $1937 per award
14% receive non-need financial aid
Non-need college-administered scholarships and grants average $2046 per award

LEWIS & CLARK COLLEGE

Portland, Oregon • Suburban setting • Private • Independent • Coed

Lewis & Clark College is a national college with a global reach. Its students are motivated, reflective, intellectually curious, adventurous, and politically, environmentally, and culturally aware . . . and busy! As fast as change occurs in today's world, Lewis & Clark believes students need a college experience that will make them versatile professionals and creative and ethical leaders, no matter what the endeavor. The College's liberal arts and sciences curriculum builds strong skills of analysis and communication, emphasizes international and cross-cultural learning, and fosters an informed respect for the environment. The classes are small, often conducted in seminar style, and taught by faculty members whose first priority is teaching.

Academics

L & C offers a liberal arts and sciences curriculum with international focus and core academic program; a few graduate courses are open to undergraduates. It awards bachelor's, master's, and first professional **degrees**. Challenging opportunities include advanced placement, accelerated degree programs, self-designed majors, tutorials, an honors program, and a senior project. Special programs include internships, summer session for credit, off-campus study, study abroad, and Army, Naval, and Air Force ROTC.

The most popular **majors** include English, psychology, and international studies. A complete listing of majors at L & C appears in the Majors Index beginning on page 379.

The **faculty** at L & C has 179 full-time graduate and undergraduate teachers, 93% with terminal degrees. 99% of the faculty serve as student advisers. The student-faculty ratio is 13:1, and the average class size in core courses is 20.

Computers on Campus

Students are not required to have a computer. Student rooms are linked to a campus network. 149 **computers** available in the computer center, computer labs, computer rooms, the library, and dormitories provide access to the main academic computer, off-campus computing facilities, e-mail, and the Internet. Staffed computer lab on campus provides training in the use of computers and software.

The 2 **libraries** have 284,350 books, 274,335 microform titles, and 1,885 subscriptions. They are connected to 13 national **on-line** catalogs.

Campus Life

There are 60 active **organizations** on campus, including a drama/theater group and student-run newspaper and radio station. 21% of students participate in student government elections. Student **safety services** include late night transport/escort service, 24-hour emergency telephone alarm devices, 24-hour patrols by trained security personnel, student patrols, and electronically operated dormitory entrances.

L & C is a member of the NAIA. **Intercollegiate sports** include baseball (m), basketball (m, w), crew (m, w), cross-country running (m, w), football (m), golf (m, w), lacrosse (m, w), rugby (m, w), sailing (m, w), skiing (cross-country) (m, w), skiing (downhill) (m, w), soccer (m, w), softball (w), swimming and diving (m, w), tennis (m, w), track and field (m, w), volleyball (m, w).

Applying

L & C requires an essay, a high school transcript, 2 recommendations, SAT I or ACT or academic portfolio, a minimum high school GPA of 2.0, and in some cases individualized portfolio. It recommends 3 years of high school math and science, 2 years of high school foreign language, and an interview. Early, deferred, and midyear entrance are possible, with a 2/1 deadline and continuous processing to 2/15 for financial aid. **Contact:** Mr. Michael Sexton, Dean of Admissions and Student Financial Services, 0615 Southwest Palatine Hill Road, Portland, OR 97219-7879, 503-768-7040 or toll-free 800-444-4111 (out-of-state); fax 503-768-7055.

GETTING IN LAST YEAR

3,011 applied
77% were accepted
20% enrolled (458)
36% from top tenth of their h.s. class
3.2 average high school GPA
27% had SAT verbal scores over 600 (R)
44% had SAT math scores over 600 (R)
55% had ACT scores over 26
5% had SAT verbal scores over 700 (R)
13% had SAT math scores over 700 (R)
21% had ACT scores over 30
12 National Merit Scholars
25 valedictorians

THE STUDENT BODY

Total 3,255, of whom 1,833
    are undergraduates

From 47 states and territories,
    37 other countries
32% from Oregon
57% women, 43% men
2% African Americans
1% Native Americans
3% Hispanics
10% Asian Americans
9% international students

AFTER FRESHMAN YEAR

77% returned for sophomore year
68% got a degree within 5 years

AFTER GRADUATION

29% pursued further study (13% arts and
    sciences, 10% law, 2% medicine)
57% had job offers within 6 months
31 organizations recruited on campus

WHAT YOU WILL PAY

Tuition and fees $16,820
Room and board $5070
52% receive need-based financial aid
Need-based college-administered scholarships and
    grants average $9328 per award
15% receive non-need financial aid
Non-need college-administered scholarships and
    grants average $5145 per award

LINFIELD COLLEGE

McMinnville, Oregon • Small-town setting • Private • Independent-Religious • Coed

> Distinctive features of Linfield College include the opportunity for student research in the Science Division and Linfield Research Institute, the annual Oregon Nobel Laureate Symposium, award-winning theater and music programs, popular study-abroad programs, a new physical education/recreation complex, and nationally competitive athletic programs.

 Academics

Linfield offers a core academic program; a few graduate courses are open to undergraduates. It awards bachelor's **degrees**. Challenging opportunities include advanced placement, accelerated degree programs, an honors program, and a senior project. Special programs include internships, summer session for credit, off-campus study, study abroad, and Air Force ROTC.

The most popular **majors** include business, elementary education, and psychology. A complete listing of majors at Linfield appears in the Majors Index beginning on page 379.

The **faculty** at Linfield has, 92% with terminal degrees. 100% of the faculty serve as student advisers. The student-faculty ratio is 13:1.

 Computers on Campus

Students are not required to have a computer. Student rooms are linked to a campus network. 150 **computers** available in the computer center, computer labs, the learning resource center, classrooms, the library, and dormitories provide access to the main academic computer, e-mail, on-line services, and the Internet. Staffed computer lab on campus provides training in the use of computers and software.

The 2 **libraries** have 132,265 books, 116,363 microform titles, and 1,130 subscriptions.

 Campus Life

There are 60 active **organizations** on campus, including a drama/theater group and student-run newspaper and radio station. 46% of students participate in student government elections. 25% of eligible men and 25% of eligible women are members of 3 national **fraternities**, 2 national **sororities**, 1 local fraternity, and 1 local sorority. Student **safety services** include late night transport/escort service, 24-hour emergency telephone alarm devices, 24-hour patrols by trained security personnel, and student patrols.

Linfield is a member of the NAIA. **Intercollegiate sports** include baseball (m), basketball (m, w), cross-country running (m, w), football (m), golf (m, w), lacrosse (m), soccer (m, w), softball (w), swimming and diving (m, w), tennis (m, w), track and field (m, w), volleyball (w).

 Applying

Linfield requires an essay, a high school transcript, 2 recommendations, and SAT I or ACT. It recommends 3 years of high school math and science, some high school foreign language, and an interview. Early, deferred, and midyear entrance are possible, with a 2/15 deadline and continuous processing to 2/1 for financial aid. **Contact:** Mr. John W. Reed, Dean of Enrollment Services, 900 South Baker Street, McMinnville, OR 97128-6894, 503-434-2213 or toll-free 800-640-2287; fax 503-434-2472.

GETTING IN LAST YEAR
1,933 applied
79% were accepted
29% enrolled (445)
38% from top tenth of their h.s. class
3.62 average high school GPA
13% had SAT verbal scores over 600
33% had SAT math scores over 600
46% had ACT scores over 26
0% had SAT verbal scores over 700
8% had SAT math scores over 700
13% had ACT scores over 30
4 National Merit Scholars
29 valedictorians

THE STUDENT BODY
Total 1,588, of whom 1,541
    are undergraduates

From 28 states and territories,
    34 other countries
59% from Oregon
56% women, 44% men
1% African Americans
1% Native Americans
1% Hispanics
4% Asian Americans
5% international students

AFTER FRESHMAN YEAR
80% returned for sophomore year
58% got a degree within 4 years

62% got a degree within 5 years
64% got a degree within 6 years

AFTER GRADUATION
15% pursued further study (8% arts and
    sciences, 2% business, 2% medicine)
83% had job offers within 6 months

WHAT YOU WILL PAY
Tuition and fees $14,397
Room and board $4380
68% receive need-based financial aid
Need-based college-administered scholarships and
    grants average $3258 per award
Non-need college-administered scholarships and
    grants average $4147 per award

LOUISIANA STATE UNIVERSITY AND AGRICULTURAL AND MECHANICAL COLLEGE

Baton Rouge, Louisiana • Urban setting • Public • State-supported • Coed

Louisiana State University, the state's only Research University I under the Carnegie Foundation designation, is one of Louisiana's most selective and comprehensive institutions. Some students enjoy the traditional college experience, while others enhance their college programs by participating in Academic Program Abroad, National Student Exchange, and the Honors College. LSU's campus is listed among the 20 best campuses in America in Thomas A. Gaines's *The Campus as a Work of Art*.

Academics

LSU offers a core academic program; fewer than half of graduate courses are open to undergraduates. It awards bachelor's, master's, doctoral, and first professional **degrees**. Challenging opportunities include advanced placement, self-designed majors, Freshman Honors College, an honors program, a senior project, Phi Beta Kappa, and Sigma Xi. Special programs include cooperative education, internships, summer session for credit, off-campus study, study abroad, and Army, Naval, and Air Force ROTC.

The most popular **majors** include psychology, liberal arts/general studies, and elementary education. A complete listing of majors at LSU appears in the Majors Index beginning on page 379.

The **faculty** at LSU has 1,204 full-time graduate and undergraduate teachers, 78% with terminal degrees. The student-faculty ratio is 18:1, and the average class size in core courses is 28.

Computers on Campus

Students are not required to have a computer. Student rooms are linked to a campus network. 5,000 **computers** available in the computer center, computer labs, business, engineering colleges, the library, and dormitories provide access to the main academic computer, off-campus computing facilities, e-mail, on-line services, and the Internet. Staffed computer lab on campus provides training in the use of computers and software.

The 8 **libraries** have 2.9 million books and 14,537 subscriptions. They are connected to 10 national **on-line** catalogs.

Campus Life

There are 186 active **organizations** on campus, including a drama/theater group and student-run newspaper and radio station. 13% of students participate in student government elections. 14% of eligible men and 15% of eligible women are members of 20 national **fraternities** and 15 national **sororities**. Student **safety services** include self-defense education, crime prevention programs, late night transport/escort service, 24-hour emergency telephone alarm devices, 24-hour patrols by trained security personnel, and electronically operated dormitory entrances.

LSU is a member of the NCAA (Division I). **Intercollegiate sports** (some offering scholarships) include baseball (m), basketball (m, w), cross-country running (m, w), football (m), golf (m, w), gymnastics (w), soccer (w), swimming and diving (m, w), tennis (m, w), track and field (m, w), volleyball (w).

Applying

LSU requires a high school transcript, 3 years of high school math and science, 2 years of high school foreign language, minimum high school GPA of 2.0 overall with GPA of 2.3 in high school requirements, SAT I or ACT, and in some cases 1 recommendation. Early and midyear entrance are possible, with a 6/1 deadline and continuous processing to 3/1 for financial aid. **Contact:** Ms. Lisa Harris, Director of Admissions, Thomas Boyd Hall, Baton Rouge, LA 70803-3103, 504-388-1175.

GETTING IN LAST YEAR
6,886 applied
80% were accepted
62% enrolled (3,428)
27% from top tenth of their h.s. class
3.11 average high school GPA
30% had ACT scores over 26
7% had ACT scores over 30
33 National Merit Scholars
93 valedictorians

THE STUDENT BODY
Total 25,897, of whom 20,374
   are undergraduates
From 52 states and territories,
   101 other countries

86% from Louisiana
51% women, 49% men
9% African Americans
0% Native Americans
2% Hispanics
4% Asian Americans
3% international students

AFTER FRESHMAN YEAR
78% returned for sophomore year
15% got a degree within 4 years
37% got a degree within 5 years
46% got a degree within 6 years

AFTER GRADUATION
22% pursued further study

880 organizations recruited on campus
2 Fulbright scholars

WHAT YOU WILL PAY
Resident tuition and fees $2663
Nonresident tuition and fees $5963
Room and board $3610
31% receive need-based financial aid
Need-based college-administered scholarships and
   grants average $900 per award
37% receive non-need financial aid
Non-need college-administered scholarships and
   grants average $2971 per award

LOYOLA COLLEGE

Baltimore, Maryland • Suburban setting • Private • Independent-Religious • Coed

 Traditional academic standards are central to Jesuit education. Loyola's curriculum is rigorous, and the faculty's expectations for students are high. The aim is to challenge students and to try to develop their skills and abilities. Hard work is required for a good education, and Loyola is interested in admitting students who have been ambitious in their course selection in high school and who have shown that they can do well in academic work.

Academics

Loyola offers a core academic program; fewer than half of graduate courses are open to undergraduates. It awards bachelor's, master's, and doctoral **degrees**. Challenging opportunities include advanced placement, an honors program, a senior project, and Phi Beta Kappa. Special programs include internships, summer session for credit, off-campus study, study abroad, and Army and Air Force ROTC.

The **faculty** at Loyola has 221 full-time undergraduate teachers, 88% with terminal degrees. 90% of the faculty serve as student advisers. The student-faculty ratio is 14:1.

Computers on Campus

Students are not required to have a computer. Student rooms are linked to a campus network. 168 **computers** available in the computer center, academic buildings, dormitories, and student rooms provide access to the main academic computer, e-mail, and the Internet. Staffed computer lab on campus (open 24 hours a day) provides training in the use of computers and software.

The **library** has 322,105 books, 38 microform titles, and 2,084 subscriptions. It is connected to 2 national **on-line** catalogs.

Campus Life

Active **organizations** on campus include drama/theater group and student-run newspaper and radio station. Student **safety services** include late night transport/escort service, 24-hour emergency telephone alarm devices, 24-hour patrols by trained security personnel, student patrols, and electronically operated dormitory entrances.

Loyola is a member of the NCAA (Division I). **Intercollegiate sports** (some offering scholarships) include baseball (m), basketball (m, w), crew (m, w), cross-country running (m, w), field hockey (w), golf (m), ice hockey (m), lacrosse (m, w), rugby (m, w), sailing (m, w), soccer (m, w), swimming and diving (m, w), tennis (m, w), track and field (m, w), volleyball (m, w).

Applying

Loyola requires an essay, a high school transcript, 3 years of high school math and science, 2 years of high school foreign language, SAT I, and in some cases 1 recommendation. It recommends an interview. Early and deferred entrance are possible, with a 2/1 deadline and continuous processing to 2/1 for financial aid. **Contact:** Mr. William Bossemeyer, Director of Admissions, 4501 North Charles Street, Baltimore, MD 21210-2699, 410-617-2000 ext. 2252 or toll-free 800-221-9107 Ext. 2252 (in-state); fax 410-617-2176.

GETTING IN LAST YEAR
5,536 applied
63% were accepted
23% enrolled (801)
30% from top tenth of their h.s. class
3.3 average high school GPA
19% had SAT verbal scores over 600
43% had SAT math scores over 600
2% had SAT verbal scores over 700
9% had SAT math scores over 700

THE STUDENT BODY
Total 6,364, of whom 3,236
    are undergraduates
From 36 states and territories,
    11 other countries
47% from Maryland

55% women, 45% men
4% African Americans
0% Native Americans
2% Hispanics
3% Asian Americans
2% international students

AFTER FRESHMAN YEAR
91% returned for sophomore year
69% got a degree within 4 years
75% got a degree within 5 years
76% got a degree within 6 years

AFTER GRADUATION
22% pursued further study (9% arts and
    sciences, 3% law, 2% business)

WHAT YOU WILL PAY
Tuition and fees $14,510
Room and board $6360
41% receive need-based financial aid
Need-based college-administered scholarships and
    grants average $5230 per award
Non-need college-administered scholarships and
    grants average $6670 per award

LOYOLA UNIVERSITY CHICAGO

Chicago, Illinois • Urban setting • Private • Independent-Religious • Coed

---

Chicago offers an ideal environment to enrich students' academic experience, with its world-class museums and performing arts; professional sports; culturally rich diversity; and international headquarters for media, commerce, medicine, and banking. Loyola's partnership with the city of Chicago adds an extra dimension—vast resources for internships, fieldwork, and independent exploration—rare in universities of Loyola's affiliation (Jesuit, Catholic), size (medium), and ranking (national research university). Extraordinary resources include a distinguished and dedicated faculty (97% with the PhD) teaching classes averaging 25 students while mentoring new students' living and learning experience through the Loyola Freshman Year Experience.

 ## Academics

Loyola offers a core academic program. It awards bachelor's, master's, doctoral, and first professional **degrees** (also offers adult part-time program with significant enrollment not reflected in profile). Challenging opportunities include advanced placement, accelerated degree programs, an honors program, Phi Beta Kappa, and Sigma Xi. Special programs include internships, summer session for credit, off-campus study, study abroad, and Army, Naval, and Air Force ROTC.

The most popular **majors** include psychology, communication, and biology/biological sciences. A complete listing of majors at Loyola appears in the Majors Index beginning on page 379.

The **faculty** at Loyola has 536 full-time graduate and undergraduate teachers, 97% with terminal degrees. The student-faculty ratio is 13:1.

 ## Computers on Campus

Students are not required to have a computer. Student rooms are linked to a campus network. 318 **computers** available in the computer center, computer labs, academic buildings, the library, and dormitories provide access to the main academic computer, e-mail, on-line services, and the Internet. Staffed computer lab on campus provides training in the use of computers and software.

The 4 **libraries** have 1.3 million books, 1.2 million microform titles, and 11,545 subscriptions.

 ## Campus Life

There are 136 active **organizations** on campus, including a drama/theater group and student-run newspaper and radio station. 8% of eligible men and 7% of eligible women are members of 6 national **fraternities** and 9 national **sororities**. Student **safety services** include late night transport/escort service, 24-hour emergency telephone alarm devices, 24-hour patrols by trained security personnel, and electronically operated dormitory entrances.

Loyola is a member of the NCAA (Division I). **Intercollegiate sports** (some offering scholarships) include basketball (m, w), cross-country running (m, w), golf (m, w), soccer (m, w), softball (w), track and field (m, w), volleyball (m, w).

 ## Applying

Loyola requires a high school transcript and SAT I or ACT. It recommends an essay, 3 years of high school math and science, some high school foreign language, and an interview. Early and midyear entrance are possible, with a 4/1 deadline and continuous processing to 3/1 for financial aid. **Contact:** Mr. Robert Blust, Director of Admissions, 820 North Michigan Avenue, Chicago, IL 60611-2196, 312-915-6500 or toll-free 800-262-2373.

GETTING IN LAST YEAR
3,812 applied
86% were accepted
36% enrolled (1,186)
33% from top tenth of their h.s. class
17% had SAT verbal scores over 600
39% had SAT math scores over 600
39% had ACT scores over 26
2% had SAT verbal scores over 700
7% had SAT math scores over 700
11% had ACT scores over 30
21 valedictorians

THE STUDENT BODY
Total 14,001, of whom 7,978
 are undergraduates
From 50 states and territories,
 67 other countries
86% from Illinois
61% women, 39% men
5% African Americans
1% Native Americans
7% Hispanics
14% Asian Americans
1% international students

AFTER FRESHMAN YEAR
18% returned for sophomore year
35% got a degree within 4 years
59% got a degree within 5 years
62% got a degree within 6 years

WHAT YOU WILL PAY
Tuition and fees $14,700
Room and board $5910
75% receive need-based financial aid
Need-based college-administered scholarships and
 grants average $4935 per award
Non-need college-administered scholarships and
 grants average $6766 per award

LUTHER COLLEGE

Decorah, Iowa • Small-town setting • Private • Independent-Religious • Coed

A Phi Beta Kappa institution, Luther is one of the top colleges in the Midwest. Luther's 800-acre campus is noteworthy for its size, modern buildings, and natural beauty. The College offers more than 60 majors and preprofessional and certificate programs leading to the Bachelor of Arts degree. Of Luther's 154 full-time faculty members, 82% hold an earned doctorate or terminal degree. The 2,400-member student body comes from 34 states and 50 countries. Cocurricular activities include intercollegiate sports for men and women and 10 music ensembles. The College's strong academic program includes internship, professional semester, and extensive study-abroad opportunities.

Academics

Luther offers a core academic program. It awards bachelor's **degrees**. Challenging opportunities include advanced placement, self-designed majors, tutorials, an honors program, a senior project, and Phi Beta Kappa. Special programs include internships, summer session for credit, off-campus study, and study abroad.

The most popular **majors** include biology/biological sciences, business, and elementary education. A complete listing of majors at Luther appears in the Majors Index beginning on page 379.

The **faculty** at Luther has 154 full-time teachers, 82% with terminal degrees. 100% of the faculty serve as student advisers. The student-faculty ratio is 13:1.

Computers on Campus

Students are not required to have a computer. Student rooms are linked to a campus network. 350 **computers** available in the computer center, computer labs, all classroom buildings, classrooms, the library, and dormitories provide access to the main academic computer, off-campus computing facilities, e-mail, on-line services, and the Internet. Staffed computer lab on campus provides training in the use of computers and software.

The **library** has 309,484 books, 21,505 microform titles, and 1,139 subscriptions. It is connected to 8 national **on-line** catalogs.

Campus Life

There are 90 active **organizations** on campus, including a drama/theater group and student-run newspaper and radio station. 15% of eligible men and 18% of eligible women are members of 1 national **fraternity**, 4 local fraternities, and 4 local **sororities**. Student **safety services** include door monitors, 24-hour emergency telephone alarm devices, 24-hour patrols by trained security personnel, and electronically operated dormitory entrances.

Luther is a member of the NCAA (Division III). **Intercollegiate sports** include baseball (m), basketball (m, w), cross-country running (m, w), football (m), golf (m, w), soccer (m, w), softball (w), swimming and diving (m, w), tennis (m, w), track and field (m, w), volleyball (w), wrestling (m).

Applying

Luther requires an essay, a high school transcript, 2 years of high school foreign language, 1 recommendation, 3 years of high school social science, and SAT I or ACT. It recommends 3 years of high school math and science and an interview. Early, deferred, and midyear entrance are possible, with a 6/1 deadline and continuous processing to 3/1 for financial aid. **Contact:** Dr. David Sallee, Dean for Enrollment Management, 700 College Drive, Decorah, IA 52101-1045, 319-387-1287 or toll-free 800-458-8437; fax 319-387-2159.

GETTING IN LAST YEAR
1,786 applied
91% were accepted
36% enrolled (591)
36% from top tenth of their h.s. class
3.61 average high school GPA
24% had SAT verbal scores over 600
52% had SAT math scores over 600
46% had ACT scores over 26
2% had SAT verbal scores over 700
18% had SAT math scores over 700
13% had ACT scores over 30
8 National Merit Scholars
42 valedictorians

THE STUDENT BODY
2,386 undergraduates

From 34 states and territories,
  50 other countries
36% from Iowa
61% women, 39% men
1% African Americans
1% Hispanics
2% Asian Americans
6% international students

AFTER FRESHMAN YEAR
88% returned for sophomore year
67% got a degree within 4 years
76% got a degree within 5 years

AFTER GRADUATION
24% pursued further study (13% arts and
  sciences, 3% law, 3% medicine)

67% had job offers within 6 months
49 organizations recruited on campus

WHAT YOU WILL PAY
Tuition and fees $14,100
Room and board $3600
72% receive need-based financial aid
Need-based college-administered scholarships and
  grants average $3000 per award
11% receive non-need financial aid
Non-need college-administered scholarships and
  grants average $2600 per award

LYON COLLEGE

Batesville, Arkansas • Small-town setting • Private • Independent-Religious • Coed

Lyon's powerful sense of community, commitment to honor, and dedication to the education of the total person make it a place where students grow in remarkable ways. A college of fewer than 1,000 students located in the beautiful foothills of the Ozark Mountains, Lyon offers access to talented teacher-scholars as part of a stimulating academic community organized around a residential house system. A strong endowment supports a challenging academic program and exceptional opportunities in such areas as study abroad and student research. Lyon students are noted for their enthusiasm, involvement, and high acceptance rates into graduate and professional schools.

 Academics

Lyon offers a liberal education curriculum and core academic program. It awards bachelor's **degrees**. Challenging opportunities include advanced placement, self-designed majors, tutorials, and a senior project. Special programs include internships, summer session for credit, and study abroad.

The most popular **majors** include biology/biological sciences, elementary education, and chemistry. A complete listing of majors at Lyon appears in the Majors Index beginning on page 379.

The **faculty** at Lyon has 42 full-time teachers, 93% with terminal degrees. 100% of the faculty serve as student advisers. The student-faculty ratio is 11:1, and the average class size in core courses is 20.

 Computers on Campus

Students are not required to have a computer. 64 **computers** available in the computer center, computer labs, the research center, the learning resource center, classrooms, and the library provide access to off-campus computing facilities, e-mail, on-line services, and the Internet. Staffed computer lab on campus provides training in the use of computers and software.

The **library** has 120,000 books, 34,000 microform titles, and 900 subscriptions. It is connected to 5 national **on-line** catalogs.

 Campus Life

There are 30 active **organizations** on campus, including a drama/theater group and student-run newspaper. 85% of students participate in student government elections. 25% of eligible men and 23% of eligible women are members of 2 national **fraternities**, 2 national **sororities**, 1 local fraternity, and 1 local sorority. Student **safety services** include late night transport/escort service, 24-hour emergency telephone alarm devices, and 24-hour patrols by trained security personnel.

Lyon is a member of the NCAA (Division II) and NAIA. **Intercollegiate sports** (some offering scholarships) include baseball (m), basketball (m, w), cross-country running (m, w), golf (m), soccer (m, w), tennis (m, w), volleyball (w).

 Applying

Lyon requires an essay, a high school transcript, 3 years of high school math and science, 2 years of high school foreign language, 4 years of English, 3 years of social science, and SAT I or ACT. It recommends 1 recommendation and an interview. Early, deferred, and midyear entrance are possible, with rolling admissions and continuous processing to 4/1 for financial aid. **Contact:** Ms. Kristine Penix, Associate Director of Admissions, 2300 Highland Drive, Batesville, AR 72503-2317, 501-698-4250 or toll-free 800-423-2542 (out-of-state); fax 501-698-4622.

GETTING IN LAST YEAR

777 applied
46% were accepted
47% enrolled (168)
51% from top tenth of their h.s. class
3.47 average high school GPA
19% had SAT verbal scores over 600
50% had SAT math scores over 600
49% had ACT scores over 26
0% had SAT verbal scores over 700
9% had SAT math scores over 700
12% had ACT scores over 30

THE STUDENT BODY

586 undergraduates

From 23 states and territories,
5 other countries
79% from Arkansas
57% women, 43% men
4% African Americans
1% Native Americans
1% Hispanics
2% Asian Americans
1% international students

AFTER FRESHMAN YEAR

65% returned for sophomore year
35% got a degree within 4 years
42% got a degree within 5 years
44% got a degree within 6 years

AFTER GRADUATION

20% pursued further study (6% medicine, 5% arts and sciences, 2% business)
75% had job offers within 6 months
16 organizations recruited on campus

WHAT YOU WILL PAY

Tuition and fees $9110
Room and board $4076
67% receive need-based financial aid
Need-based college-administered scholarships and grants average $3613 per award
17% receive non-need financial aid
Non-need college-administered scholarships and grants average $6488 per award

MACALESTER COLLEGE

St. Paul, Minnesota • Urban setting • Private • Independent-Religious • Coed

---

The intellectual partnering of distinguished faculty and talented students is at the core of Macalester's academic program. A $500-million endowment enables Macalester to support this interaction with top facilities and an 11:1 student-faculty ratio that will drop to 10:1 in the next few years. A residential, campus-centered college, Macalester is located in a historic and serene neighborhood several miles from the city centers of Minneapolis and St. Paul. Macalester students come from virtually every state and over 80 other countries; over half ranked in the top 10% of their high school class.

 Academics

Mac offers a core academic program. It awards bachelor's **degrees**. Challenging opportunities include advanced placement, self-designed majors, tutorials, an honors program, a senior project, and Phi Beta Kappa. Special programs include internships, off-campus study, study abroad, and Naval and Air Force ROTC.

The most popular **majors** include history, English, and psychology. A complete listing of majors at Mac appears in the Majors Index beginning on page 379.

The **faculty** at Mac has 139 full-time teachers, 92% with terminal degrees. 100% of the faculty serve as student advisers. The student-faculty ratio is 11:1.

 Computers on Campus

Students are not required to have a computer. Student rooms are linked to a campus network. 350 **computers** available in the computer center, computer labs, academic departments, the library, and dormitories provide access to the main academic computer, e-mail, on-line services, and the Internet. Staffed computer lab on campus provides training in the use of computers and software.

The **library** has 360,724 books, 61,425 microform titles, and 1,496 subscriptions. It is connected to 7 national **on-line** catalogs.

 Campus Life

There are 70 active **organizations** on campus, including a drama/theater group and student-run newspaper and radio station. 32% of students participate in student government elections. Student **safety services** include late night transport/escort service, 24-hour emergency telephone alarm devices, 24-hour patrols by trained security personnel, and electronically operated dormitory entrances.

Mac is a member of the NCAA (Division III). **Intercollegiate sports** include baseball (m), basketball (m, w), crew (m, w), cross-country running (m, w), fencing (m, w), football (m), golf (m, w), ice hockey (m, w), rugby (m, w), skiing (cross-country) (m, w), soccer (m, w), softball (w), swimming and diving (m, w), tennis (m, w), track and field (m, w), volleyball (m, w), water polo (m, w), weight lifting (m, w).

 Applying

Mac requires an essay, a high school transcript, 3 recommendations, and SAT I or ACT. It recommends 3 years of high school math and science, 3 years of high school foreign language, a campus interview, and SAT II Subject Tests. Early and deferred entrance are possible, with a 1/15 deadline and a 2/8 priority date for financial aid. **Contact:** Mr. William M. Shain, Dean of Admissions, 1600 Grand Avenue, St. Paul, MN 55105-1899, 612-696-6357 or toll-free 800-231-7974; fax 612-696-6724.

GETTING IN LAST YEAR
2,880 applied
54% were accepted
28% enrolled (437)
54% from top tenth of their h.s. class
63% had SAT verbal scores over 600
77% had SAT math scores over 600
87% had ACT scores over 26
10% had SAT verbal scores over 700
28% had SAT math scores over 700
42% had ACT scores over 30
48 National Merit Scholars

THE STUDENT BODY
1,768 undergraduates

From 49 states and territories,
   81 other countries
23% from Minnesota
55% women, 45% men
4% African Americans
1% Native Americans
4% Hispanics
5% Asian Americans
10% international students

AFTER FRESHMAN YEAR
88% returned for sophomore year
65% got a degree within 4 years
78% got a degree within 5 years
79% got a degree within 6 years

AFTER GRADUATION
29% pursued further study (19% arts and
   sciences, 3% law, 3% medicine)
97 organizations recruited on campus
1 Rhodes, 1 Fulbright scholar

WHAT YOU WILL PAY
Tuition and fees $16,686
Room and board $4975
70% receive need-based financial aid
Need-based college-administered scholarships and
   grants average $9594 per award
5% receive non-need financial aid
Non-need college-administered scholarships and
   grants average $2805 per award

MARIETTA COLLEGE

Marietta, Ohio • Small-town setting • Private • Independent • Coed

Marietta College, a 4-year, private liberal arts college, has a long-standing history of academic excellence. Proud to have the 16th-oldest chapter of Phi Beta Kappa, Marietta is also consistently ranked among the top 10 by *U.S. News & World Report's Best Liberal Arts Colleges in the Midwest.* Approximately 1,200 students, representing 35 states and 7 other countries, can choose from over 30 majors. There is a low student-faculty ratio and a premier leadership program. Marietta students involve themselves in many clubs and organizations, including athletics, student government, radio and television stations, and the student newspaper.

 Academics

Marietta offers an interdisciplinary curriculum and core academic program; a few graduate courses are open to undergraduates. It awards associate, bachelor's, and master's **degrees**. Challenging opportunities include advanced placement, accelerated degree programs, self-designed majors, tutorials, Freshman Honors College, an honors program, a senior project, and Phi Beta Kappa. Special programs include internships, summer session for credit, off-campus study, and Army ROTC.

The most popular **majors** include business, communication, and education. A complete listing of majors at Marietta appears in the Majors Index beginning on page 379.

The **faculty** at Marietta has 73 full-time undergraduate teachers, 50% with terminal degrees. 80% of the faculty serve as student advisers. The student-faculty ratio is 13:1.

 Computers on Campus

Students are not required to have a computer. 200 **computers** available in the computer center, computer labs, departmental labs, the library, and the student center provide access to e-mail, on-line services, and the Internet. Staffed computer lab on campus provides training in the use of computers and software.

The **library** has 241,394 books, 10,826 microform titles, and 873 subscriptions.

 Campus Life

There are 65 active **organizations** on campus, including a drama/theater group and student-run newspaper and radio station. 21% of eligible men and 37% of eligible women are members of 4 national **fraternities** and 4 national **sororities**. Student **safety services** include late night transport/escort service, 24-hour emergency telephone alarm devices, 24-hour patrols by trained security personnel, student patrols, and electronically operated dormitory entrances.

Marietta is a member of the NCAA (Division III). **Intercollegiate sports** include baseball (m), basketball (m, w), crew (m, w), football (m), golf (m), lacrosse (m), soccer (m, w), softball (w), tennis (m, w), volleyball (w).

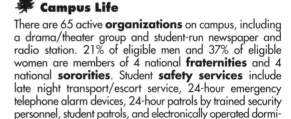 **Applying**

Marietta requires an essay, a high school transcript, 3 years of high school math and science, 1 recommendation, SAT I or ACT, and a minimum high school GPA of 2.0. It recommends some high school foreign language, an interview, SAT II Subject Tests, and a minimum high school GPA of 3.0. Deferred and midyear entrance are possible, with rolling admissions and continuous processing to 3/1 for financial aid. **Contact:** Ms. Marke Vickers, Dean of Admission, 215 Fifth Street, Marietta, OH 45750-4000, 614-376-4602 or toll-free 800-331-7896; fax 614-376-8888.

GETTING IN LAST YEAR
1,497 applied
79% were accepted
25% enrolled (296)
12% from top tenth of their h.s. class
3.12 average high school GPA
9% had SAT verbal scores over 600 (R)
22% had SAT math scores over 600 (R)
28% had ACT scores over 26
0% had SAT verbal scores over 700 (R)
5% had SAT math scores over 700 (R)
13% had ACT scores over 30

THE STUDENT BODY
Total 1,167, of whom 1,108
  are undergraduates
From 35 states and territories,
  7 other countries
50% from Ohio
48% women, 52% men
1% African Americans
1% Native Americans
1% Hispanics
1% Asian Americans
2% international students

AFTER GRADUATION
14% pursued further study (9% arts and
  sciences, 3% law, 1% business)
19 organizations recruited on campus

WHAT YOU WILL PAY
Tuition and fees $14,850
Room and board $4030
83% receive need-based financial aid
Need-based college-administered scholarships and
  grants average $9440 per award
20% receive non-need financial aid

MARLBORO COLLEGE

Marlboro, Vermont • Rural setting • Private • Independent • Coed

With 270 students, Marlboro chooses to remain one of the smallest liberal arts colleges in the world as part of its commitment to keeping its 8:1 student-faculty ratio. Its intimate size is ideal for pursuing a personal approach to education and for building meaningful friendships. Such small size stimulates one-on-one relationships between students and faculty. At the heart of a Marlboro education is the Oxford-style tutorial system for upperclass students. Tutorials make it virtually impossible for any Marlboro student to fade into the background. The result is a community in which ideas are exchanged both in and out of the classroom.

 Academics

Marlboro offers a self-designed, interdisciplinary curriculum and no core academic program. It awards bachelor's and master's **degrees**. Challenging opportunities include advanced placement, accelerated degree programs, self-designed majors, tutorials, an honors program, and a senior project. Special programs include internships, summer session for credit, and off-campus study.

The **faculty** at Marlboro has 32 full-time undergraduate teachers, 57% with terminal degrees. 100% of the faculty serve as student advisers. The student-faculty ratio is 8:1.

 Computers on Campus

Students are not required to have a computer. 22 **computers** available in the computer center and the learning resource center provide access to off-campus computing facilities, e-mail, and the Internet. Staffed computer lab on campus (open 24 hours a day) provides training in the use of computers and software.

The **library** has 63,000 books, 70 microform titles, and 192 subscriptions. It is connected to 2 national **on-line** catalogs.

 Campus Life

There are 12 active **organizations** on campus, including a drama/theater group and student-run newspaper. 70% of students participate in student government elections. Student **safety services** include late night transport/escort service and 24-hour emergency telephone alarm devices. **Intercollegiate sports** include skiing (cross-country) (m, w), skiing (downhill) (m, w), soccer (m, w), volleyball (m, w).

 Applying

Marlboro requires an essay, a high school transcript, 1 recommendation, a campus interview, sample of expository prose, and SAT I or ACT. It recommends 3 years of high school math and science, some high school foreign language, SAT II Subject Tests, and a minimum high school GPA of 3.0. Early, deferred, and midyear entrance are possible, with rolling admissions and continuous processing to 3/1 for financial aid. **Contact:** Mr. Wayne R. Wood, Director of Admissions, South Road, Marlboro, VT 05344, 802-257-4333 ext. 237 or toll-free 800-343-0049 (out-of-state).

GETTING IN LAST YEAR
217 applied
88% were accepted
38% enrolled (72)
56% had SAT verbal scores over 600 (R)
26% had SAT math scores over 600 (R)
14% had SAT verbal scores over 700 (R)
4% had SAT math scores over 700 (R)

THE STUDENT BODY
270 undergraduates
From 35 states and territories,
8 other countries

12% from Vermont
58% women, 42% men
1% African Americans
0% Native Americans
1% Hispanics
1% Asian Americans
6% international students

AFTER FRESHMAN YEAR
59% returned for sophomore year

AFTER GRADUATION
33% pursued further study (30% arts and
sciences, 1% business, 1% law)
67% had job offers within 6 months

WHAT YOU WILL PAY
Tuition and fees $19,882
Room and board $6445
75% receive need-based financial aid
Need-based college-administered scholarships and
grants average $9000 per award
Non-need college-administered scholarships and
grants average $5000 per award

MARQUETTE UNIVERSITY

Milwaukee, Wisconsin • Urban setting • Private • Independent-Religious • Coed

---

Since 1881, Marquette University has challenged students to work toward reaching their potential in every facet of their lives. A Jesuit university, Marquette places emphasis on the liberal arts, Christian ideals, and humanistic concern for others. Nearly 95% of the faculty members hold the PhD or equivalent terminal degrees, and all are expected to teach and to do research. Marquette's diverse, residential student body hails from all 50 states and almost 80 other countries. Marquette's campus is adjacent to downtown Milwaukee and 1 mile west of Lake Michigan.

 ## Academics

Marquette offers a core academic program; fewer than half of graduate courses are open to undergraduates. It awards associate, bachelor's, master's, doctoral, and first professional **degrees**. Challenging opportunities include advanced placement, accelerated degree programs, self-designed majors, tutorials, Freshman Honors College, an honors program, a senior project, Phi Beta Kappa, and Sigma Xi. Special programs include cooperative education, internships, summer session for credit, off-campus study, study abroad, and Army, Naval, and Air Force ROTC.

The most popular **majors** include mechanical engineering, accounting, and electrical engineering. A complete listing of majors at Marquette appears in the Majors Index beginning on page 379.

The **faculty** at Marquette has 581 full-time graduate and undergraduate teachers, 95% with terminal degrees. The student-faculty ratio is 15:1.

 ## Computers on Campus

Students are not required to have a computer. Student rooms are linked to a campus network. 800 **computers** available in the computer center, computer labs, classrooms, the library, and dormitories provide access to the main academic computer, off-campus computing facilities, e-mail, on-line services, and the Internet. Staffed computer lab on campus (open 24 hours a day) provides training in the use of computers and software.

The 3 **libraries** have 1 million books, 382,861 microform titles, and 9,220 subscriptions. They are connected to 6 national **on-line** catalogs.

 ## Campus Life

There are 164 active **organizations** on campus, including a drama/theater group and student-run newspaper and radio station. 10% of eligible men and 10% of eligible women are members of 7 national **fraternities** and 7 national **sororities**. Student **safety services** include late night transport/escort service, 24-hour emergency telephone alarm devices, 24-hour patrols by trained security personnel, and student patrols.

Marquette is a member of the NCAA (Division I). **Intercollegiate sports** (some offering scholarships) include baseball (m), basketball (m, w), crew (m, w), cross-country running (m, w), football (m), golf (m), ice hockey (m), lacrosse (m), riflery (m, w), rugby (m), sailing (m, w), skiing (downhill) (m, w), soccer (m, w), softball (w), swimming and diving (m, w), tennis (m, w), track and field (m, w), volleyball (m, w), wrestling (m).

 ## Applying

Marquette requires an essay, a high school transcript, SAT I or ACT, a minimum high school GPA of 2.0, and in some cases 3 years of high school math and science. It recommends 2 years of high school foreign language, recommendations, an interview, and a minimum high school GPA of 3.0. Deferred and midyear entrance are possible, with rolling admissions and continuous processing to 3/1 for financial aid. **Contact:** Mr. Raymond A. Brown, Dean of Admissions, 615 North 11th Street, Milwaukee, WI 53201-1881, 414-288-7302 or toll-free 800-222-6544.

GETTING IN LAST YEAR
5,487 applied
29% from top tenth of their h.s. class
3.00 average high school GPA
12% had SAT verbal scores over 600
38% had SAT math scores over 600
44% had ACT scores over 26
1% had SAT verbal scores over 700
9% had SAT math scores over 700
10% had ACT scores over 30
17 National Merit Scholars
68 valedictorians

THE STUDENT BODY
Total 10,774, of whom 6,914
are undergraduates

From 55 states and territories,
77 other countries
47% from Wisconsin
52% women, 48% men
5% African Americans
1% Native Americans
4% Hispanics
5% Asian Americans
5% international students

AFTER FRESHMAN YEAR
88% returned for sophomore year
54% got a degree within 4 years
75% got a degree within 5 years
77% got a degree within 6 years

AFTER GRADUATION
25% pursued further study (8% medicine, 5% law, 4% arts and sciences)
70% had job offers within 6 months
106 organizations recruited on campus
1 Fulbright scholar

WHAT YOU WILL PAY
Tuition and fees $13,230
Room and board $5100
Need-based college-administered scholarships and grants average $7400 per award
Non-need college-administered scholarships and grants average $4800 per award

---

MARYLAND INSTITUTE, COLLEGE OF ART

Baltimore, Maryland • Urban setting • Private • Independent • Coed

The Maryland Institute, College of Art, founded in 1826, is the nation's oldest fully accredited, degree-granting art college. Its curriculum integrates concentrated studio experience in the visual arts with the study of liberal arts ideas and theory. Students are encouraged to take risks, break new ground, and make connections between words, images, and ideas. The high caliber of the Institute's academic program and outstanding faculty is reflected in a recent national survey that ranked the Institute among the nation's top 3 visual arts colleges. The Institute's Baltimore campus, student housing designed especially for artists, academic and student life facilities, and on-site career services reflect its academic philosophy.

Academics

Maryland Institute, College of Art offers a studio and liberal arts curriculum and core academic program. It awards bachelor's and master's **degrees**. Challenging opportunities include advanced placement, self-designed majors, an honors program, and a senior project. Special programs include internships, summer session for credit, off-campus study, study abroad, and Army ROTC.

The most popular **majors** include art/fine arts, illustration, and painting/drawing. A complete listing of majors at Maryland Institute, College of Art appears in the Majors Index beginning on page 379.

The **faculty** at Maryland Institute, College of Art has 65 full-time graduate and undergraduate teachers, 87% with terminal degrees. 40% of the faculty serve as student advisers. The student-faculty ratio is 6:1.

Computers on Campus

Students are required to have a computer. Purchase options are available. 121 **computers** available in the computer center, computer labs, the learning resource center, and classrooms provide access to e-mail and the Internet. Staffed computer lab on campus (open 24 hours a day) provides training in the use of computers and software.

The **library** has 51,000 books and 235 subscriptions.

Campus Life

Active **organizations** on campus include student-run newspaper. Student **safety services** include late night transport/escort service, 24-hour patrols by trained security personnel, and student patrols.

This institution has no intercollegiate sports.

Applying

Maryland Institute, College of Art requires an essay, a high school transcript, and art portfolio. It recommends 2 recommendations, an interview, and SAT I or ACT. Early, deferred, and midyear entrance are possible, with rolling admissions and continuous processing to 3/1 for financial aid. **Contact:** Ms. Theresa M. Lynch-Bedoya, Dean of Admissions, 1300 Mount Royal Avenue, Baltimore, MD 21217-4192, 410-225-2294.

GETTING IN LAST YEAR
811 applied
66% were accepted
38% enrolled (204)
13% from top tenth of their h.s. class
14% had SAT verbal scores over 600 (R)
18% had SAT math scores over 600 (R)
1% had SAT verbal scores over 700 (R)
1% had SAT math scores over 700 (R)

THE STUDENT BODY
Total 924, of whom 817
    are undergraduates
From 41 states and territories,
    44 other countries

29% from Maryland
53% women, 47% men
5% African Americans
1% Native Americans
5% Hispanics
7% Asian Americans
7% international students

AFTER FRESHMAN YEAR
77% returned for sophomore year
41% got a degree within 4 years
48% got a degree within 5 years
51% got a degree within 6 years

AFTER GRADUATION
22% pursued further study (22% arts and
    sciences)

WHAT YOU WILL PAY
Tuition and fees $15,100
Room and board $5440
70% receive need-based financial aid
Need-based college-administered scholarships and
    grants average $2582 per award
11% receive non-need financial aid
Non-need college-administered scholarships and
    grants average $1507 per award

MARYVILLE UNIVERSITY OF SAINT LOUIS

St. Louis, Missouri • Suburban setting • Private • Independent • Coed

---

 Maryville University of Saint Louis is committed to integrating the liberal arts with professional education by providing innovative and interactive programs with the business, education, health care, cultural, and arts communities it serves. Academic programs are grounded in the humanizing values and ideals that move and guide society—all in the spirit of the liberal arts. In addition, these programs provide opportunities for students to perfect their skills in settings beyond the classroom, gain self-confidence, and profit from the energy of experience.

Academics

Maryville offers an integrated professional liberal education curriculum and core academic program; fewer than half of graduate courses are open to undergraduates. It awards bachelor's and master's **degrees**. Challenging opportunities include advanced placement, accelerated degree programs, tutorials, Freshman Honors College, an honors program, and a senior project. Special programs include cooperative education, internships, summer session for credit, off-campus study, study abroad, and Army ROTC.

The most popular **majors** include business, nursing, and accounting. A complete listing of majors at Maryville appears in the Majors Index beginning on page 379.

The **faculty** at Maryville has 85 full-time graduate and undergraduate teachers, 71% with terminal degrees. 100% of the faculty serve as student advisers. The student-faculty ratio is 14:1.

Computers on Campus

Students are not required to have a computer. 191 **computers** available in the computer center, computer labs, career management, nursing, and housing offices, the library, and dormitories provide access to the main academic computer, off-campus computing facilities, e-mail, and the Internet. Staffed computer lab on campus.

The **library** has 144,072 books, 517 microform titles, and 774 subscriptions.

Campus Life

There are 30 active **organizations** on campus, including a drama/theater group and student-run newspaper. 10% of students participate in student government elections. Student **safety services** include video/audio security system in residence halls, emergency phones throughout the campus, late night transport/escort service, 24-hour emergency telephone alarm devices, 24-hour patrols by trained security personnel, and electronically operated dormitory entrances.

Maryville is a member of the NCAA (Division III). **Intercollegiate sports** include baseball (m), basketball (m, w), cross-country running (m, w), golf (m, w), soccer (m, w), softball (w), tennis (m, w), volleyball (w).

Applying

Maryville requires a high school transcript, 3 years of high school math and science, SAT I or ACT, a minimum high school GPA of 2.0, and in some cases an essay, recommendations, a campus interview, and audition, portfolio. Early, deferred, and midyear entrance are possible, with rolling admissions and continuous processing to 2/1 for financial aid. **Contact:** Dr. Martha Wade, Dean of Admissions and Enrollment Management, Gander Hall, St. Louis, MO 63141-7299, 314-529-9350 or toll-free 800-627-9855; fax 314-542-9085.

GETTING IN LAST YEAR
696 applied
74% were accepted
38% enrolled (198)
23% from top tenth of their h.s. class
3.29 average high school GPA
8% had SAT verbal scores over 600
33% had SAT math scores over 600
27% had ACT scores over 26
0% had SAT verbal scores over 700
4% had SAT math scores over 700
4% had ACT scores over 30
6 valedictorians

THE STUDENT BODY
Total 3,378, of whom 2,835
    are undergraduates
From 18 states and territories,
    33 other countries
86% from Missouri
71% women, 29% men
4% African Americans
1% Native Americans
1% Hispanics
1% Asian Americans
6% international students

AFTER FRESHMAN YEAR
69% returned for sophomore year

AFTER GRADUATION
53 organizations recruited on campus

WHAT YOU WILL PAY
Tuition and fees $9800
Room and board $4750
38% receive need-based financial aid
Need-based college-administered scholarships and
    grants average $3105 per award
30% receive non-need financial aid
Non-need college-administered scholarships and
    grants average $2820 per award

MARY WASHINGTON COLLEGE

Fredericksburg, Virginia • Small-town setting • Public • State-supported • Coed

Academic excellence, personal attention to students, outstanding value: together these terms best describe Mary Washington College. As Virginia's public college of the liberal arts and sciences, Mary Washington is distinctive. Its students come from throughout the country and the world to study on the beautiful, neoclassical campus, which is located in historic Fredericksburg, just 50 miles south of Washington, D.C. The College recently installed one of the nation's most advanced fiber-optic campus networks. Residence halls feature in-room phone and voice-mail service, full computer access, and video services. The College features a strong undergraduate research program and offers outstanding internship opportunities due to its convenient location.

Academics

Mary Washington offers a writing-intensive liberal arts curriculum and core academic program; a few graduate courses are open to undergraduates. It awards bachelor's and master's **degrees**. Challenging opportunities include advanced placement, accelerated degree programs, self-designed majors, tutorials, a senior project, and Phi Beta Kappa. Special programs include cooperative education, internships, summer session for credit, and study abroad.

The most popular **majors** include business, psychology, and English. A complete listing of majors at Mary Washington appears in the Majors Index beginning on page 379.

The **faculty** at Mary Washington has 170 full-time undergraduate teachers, 88% with terminal degrees. 90% of the faculty serve as student advisers. The student-faculty ratio is 17:1.

Computers on Campus

Students are not required to have a computer. Student rooms are linked to a campus network. 147 **computers** available in the computer center, computer labs, and the library provide access to e-mail and the Internet. Staffed computer lab on campus (open 24 hours a day) provides training in the use of computers and software.

The **library** has 338,000 books, 360,000 microform titles, and 1,700 subscriptions. It is connected to 20 national **on-line** catalogs.

Campus Life

There are 85 active **organizations** on campus, including a drama/theater group and student-run newspaper and radio station. Student **safety services** include late night transport/escort service, 24-hour emergency telephone alarm devices, 24-hour patrols by trained security personnel, student patrols, and electronically operated dormitory entrances.

Mary Washington is a member of the NCAA (Division III). **Intercollegiate sports** include baseball (m), basketball (m, w), crew (m, w), cross-country running (m, w), equestrian sports (m, w), field hockey (w), lacrosse (m, w), rugby (m, w), soccer (m, w), softball (w), swimming and diving (m, w), tennis (m, w), track and field (m, w), volleyball (m, w).

Applying

Mary Washington requires an essay, a high school transcript, 3 years of high school math and science, 3 years of high school foreign language, and SAT I. It recommends 3 SAT II Subject Tests. Early, deferred, and midyear entrance are possible, with a 2/1 deadline and 3/1 for financial aid. **Contact:** Dr. Martin A. Wilder Jr., Vice President for Admissions and Financial Aid, 1301 College Avenue, Fredericksburg, VA 22401-5358, 540-654-2000 or toll-free 800-468-5614.

GETTING IN LAST YEAR
4,035 applied
57% were accepted
33% enrolled (766)
37% from top tenth of their h.s. class
3.47 average high school GPA
24% had SAT verbal scores over 600
39% had SAT math scores over 600
2% had SAT verbal scores over 700
5% had SAT math scores over 700
2 National Merit Scholars
20 valedictorians

THE STUDENT BODY
Total 3,529, of whom 3,464
  are undergraduates

From 40 states and territories,
  16 other countries
70% from Virginia
65% women, 35% men
6% African Americans
0% Native Americans
2% Hispanics
3% Asian Americans
1% international students

AFTER FRESHMAN YEAR
90% returned for sophomore year
65% got a degree within 4 years
73% got a degree within 5 years
75% got a degree within 6 years

AFTER GRADUATION
20% pursued further study
67% had job offers within 6 months
64 organizations recruited on campus

WHAT YOU WILL PAY
Resident tuition and fees $3300
Nonresident tuition and fees $8190
Room and board $5024
42% receive need-based financial aid
Need-based college-administered scholarships and
  grants average $1500 per award
25% receive non-need financial aid
Non-need college-administered scholarships and
  grants average $1820 per award

MASSACHUSETTS INSTITUTE OF TECHNOLOGY

Cambridge, Massachusetts • Urban setting • Private • Independent • Coed

Academics

MIT offers a science and technology-based general curriculum and core academic program; all graduate courses are open to undergraduates. It awards bachelor's, master's, and doctoral **degrees**. Challenging opportunities include advanced placement, accelerated degree programs, self-designed majors, tutorials, a senior project, Phi Beta Kappa, and Sigma Xi. Special programs include cooperative education, internships, summer session for credit, off-campus study, and Army, Naval, and Air Force ROTC.

The most popular **majors** include mechanical engineering, electrical engineering, and computer science. A complete listing of majors at MIT appears in the Majors Index beginning on page 379.

The **faculty** at MIT has 938 full-time graduate and undergraduate teachers, 99% with terminal degrees. 60% of the faculty serve as student advisers. The student-faculty ratio is 5:1.

Computers on Campus

Students are not required to have a computer. Student rooms are linked to a campus network. 700 **computers** available in the computer center, computer labs, the research center, the learning resource center, academic buildings, classrooms, the library, the student center, dormitories, and student rooms provide access to the main academic computer, off-campus computing facilities, e-mail, on-line services, and the Internet. Staffed computer lab on campus (open 24 hours a day) provides training in the use of computers and software.

The 23 **libraries** have 2.4 million books, 2.1 million microform titles, and 21,453 subscriptions. They are connected to 32 national **on-line** catalogs.

Campus Life

There are 280 active **organizations** on campus, including a drama/theater group and student-run newspaper and radio station. 35% of students participate in student government elections. 50% of eligible men and 26% of eligible women are members of 28 national **fraternities**, 5 national **sororities**, 2 local fraternities, and social clubs. Student **safety services** include late night transport/escort service, 24-hour emergency telephone alarm devices, 24-hour patrols by trained security personnel, student patrols, and electronically operated dormitory entrances.

MIT is a member of the NCAA (Division III). **Intercollegiate sports** include baseball (m), basketball (m, w), crew (m, w), cross-country running (m, w), fencing (m, w), field hockey (w), football (m), golf (m), gymnastics (m, w), ice hockey (m, w), lacrosse (m, w), riflery (m, w), rugby (m, w), sailing (m, w), skiing (cross-country) (m, w), skiing (downhill) (m, w), soccer (m, w), softball (w), squash (m), swimming and diving (m, w), tennis (m, w), track and field (m, w), volleyball (m, w), water polo (m), wrestling (m).

Applying

MIT requires an essay, a high school transcript, 2 recommendations, an interview, SAT I or ACT, and 3 SAT II Subject Tests. It recommends 4 years of high school math and science and 2 years of high school foreign language. Early and deferred entrance are possible, with a 1/1 deadline and a 1/19 priority date for financial aid. **Contact:** Mr. Michael C. Behnke, Director of Admissions, 77 Massachusetts Avenue, Room 3-107, Cambridge, MA 02139-4307, 617-253-4791; fax 617-258-8304.

GETTING IN LAST YEAR

7,958 applied
27% were accepted
53% enrolled (1,116)
97% from top tenth of their h.s. class
93% had SAT verbal scores over 600 (R)
100% had SAT math scores over 600 (R)
94% had ACT scores over 26
56% had SAT verbal scores over 700 (R)
83% had SAT math scores over 700 (R)
73% had ACT scores over 30
129 National Merit Scholars
264 valedictorians

THE STUDENT BODY

Total 9,960, of whom 4,495
  are undergraduates

From 53 states and territories,
  100 other countries
8% from Massachusetts
38% women, 62% men
6% African Americans
1% Native Americans
9% Hispanics
29% Asian Americans
8% international students

AFTER FRESHMAN YEAR

96% returned for sophomore year
77% got a degree within 4 years
86% got a degree within 5 years
89% got a degree within 6 years

AFTER GRADUATION

50% pursued further study (20% engineering,
  13% arts and sciences, 12% medicine)
41% had job offers within 6 months
440 organizations recruited on campus
1 Rhodes, 3 Marshall, 2 Fulbright scholars

WHAT YOU WILL PAY

Tuition and fees $21,612
Room and board $6150
59% receive need-based financial aid
Need-based college-administered scholarships and
  grants average $12,820 per award

MESSIAH COLLEGE

Grantham, Pennsylvania • Small-town setting • Private • Independent-Religious • Coed

Messiah College is a 4-year Christian college of the liberal and applied arts and sciences. The main campus is located in Grantham, Pa., 10 miles southwest of Harrisburg, the state capital. A small urban campus is located in Philadelphia adjacent to Temple University. Messiah College seeks to integrate faith and learning, to provide strong academic emphasis in traditional liberal arts and professional programs of study. Presently, approximately 2,400 students are pursuing undergraduate degrees in more than 50 academic programs, including business, science, math, nursing, education, engineering, and other liberal arts curricula. The College is accredited by the Middle States Association of Colleges and Schools. Merit and need-based scholarships and grants are available for eligible students.

Academics

Messiah College offers a core academic program. It awards bachelor's **degrees**. Challenging opportunities include advanced placement, accelerated degree programs, self-designed majors, an honors program, and a senior project. Special programs include internships, summer session for credit, off-campus study, and study abroad.

The most popular **majors** include elementary education, nursing, and biology/biological sciences. A complete listing of majors at Messiah College appears in the Majors Index beginning on page 379.

The **faculty** at Messiah College has 128 full-time teachers, 60% with terminal degrees. 100% of the faculty serve as student advisers. The student-faculty ratio is 15:1.

Computers on Campus

Students are not required to have a computer. Student rooms are linked to a campus network. 300 **computers** available in the computer center, computer labs, the research center, the learning resource center, classrooms, the library, and dormitories provide access to the main academic computer, off-campus computing facilities, e-mail, on-line services, and the Internet. Staffed computer lab on campus provides training in the use of computers and software.

The **library** has 200,000 books, 5,000 microform titles, and 1,500 subscriptions. It is connected to 2 national **on-line** catalogs.

Campus Life

There are 58 active **organizations** on campus, including a drama/theater group and student-run newspaper and radio station. No national or local **fraternities** or **sororities**. Student **safety services** include late night transport/escort service, 24-hour emergency telephone alarm devices, and 24-hour patrols by trained security personnel.

Messiah College is a member of the NCAA (Division III). **Intercollegiate sports** include baseball (m), basketball (m, w), cross-country running (m, w), field hockey (w), golf (m), lacrosse (m, w), soccer (m, w), softball (w), tennis (m, w), track and field (m, w), volleyball (w), wrestling (m).

Applying

Messiah College requires an essay, a high school transcript, 2 recommendations, SAT I or ACT, and in some cases some high school foreign language. It recommends 3 years of high school math and science and a campus interview. Early, deferred, and midyear entrance are possible, with rolling admissions and a 4/1 priority date for financial aid. **Contact:** Mr. William G. Strausbaugh, Vice President of Enrollment Management, Old Main Building, Grantham, PA 17027, 717-691-6000 or toll-free 800-382-1349 (in-state), 800-233-4220 (out-of-state); fax 717-691-6025.

GETTING IN LAST YEAR
1,876 applied
86% were accepted
42% enrolled (673)
32% from top tenth of their h.s. class
16% had SAT verbal scores over 600
32% had SAT math scores over 600
38% had ACT scores over 26
2% had SAT verbal scores over 700
5% had SAT math scores over 700
7% had ACT scores over 30
5 National Merit Scholars
31 valedictorians

THE STUDENT BODY
2,428 undergraduates

From 38 states and territories,
  13 other countries
50% from Pennsylvania
60% women, 40% men
2% African Americans
1% Native Americans
2% Hispanics
2% Asian Americans
1% international students

AFTER FRESHMAN YEAR
83% returned for sophomore year
61% got a degree within 4 years
65% got a degree within 5 years
67% got a degree within 6 years

AFTER GRADUATION
30% pursued further study (8% arts and
  sciences, 8% business, 4% medicine)
95% had job offers within 6 months
100 organizations recruited on campus

WHAT YOU WILL PAY
Tuition and fees $10,954
Room and board $5040
43% receive need-based financial aid
Need-based college-administered scholarships and
  grants average $3606 per award
12% receive non-need financial aid
Non-need college-administered scholarships and
  grants average $1634 per award

MIAMI UNIVERSITY

Oxford, Ohio • Small-town setting • Public • State-related • Coed

---

Students receive an outstanding education at Miami, which ranks 8th nationally for its unusually strong commitment to undergraduate teaching, according to *U.S. News & World Report*. Miami students study abroad, conduct research with faculty, and run more than 300 clubs. This 7th-oldest public university encompasses a campus of Georgian brick buildings in the college town of Oxford, north of Cincinnati. With a 90% freshman retention rate, Miami offers 1st-year academic advising in residence halls; state-of-the-art facilities, including a new recreation center; and an education founded in the liberal arts.

Academics

Miami University offers a liberal arts curriculum and core academic program; more than half of graduate courses are open to undergraduates. It awards bachelor's, master's, and doctoral **degrees**. Challenging opportunities include advanced placement, accelerated degree programs, self-designed majors, tutorials, an honors program, a senior project, Phi Beta Kappa, and Sigma Xi. Special programs include cooperative education, internships, summer session for credit, off-campus study, study abroad, and Army, Naval, and Air Force ROTC.

The most popular **majors** include elementary education, accounting, and marketing/retailing/merchandising. A complete listing of majors at Miami University appears in the Majors Index beginning on page 379.

The **faculty** at Miami University has 767 full-time graduate and undergraduate teachers, 89% with terminal degrees. The student-faculty ratio is 17:1.

Computers on Campus

Students are not required to have a computer. Student rooms are linked to a campus network. 700 **computers** available in the computer center, computer labs, the learning resource center, academic buildings, classrooms, the

library, and dormitories provide access to the main academic computer, off-campus computing facilities, e-mail, on-line services, and the Internet. Staffed computer lab on campus provides training in the use of computers and software.

The 4 **libraries** have 2 million books, 1.2 million microform titles, and 6,014 subscriptions. They are connected to 5 national **on-line** catalogs.

Campus Life

There are 325 active **organizations** on campus, including a drama/theater group and student-run newspaper and radio station. 20% of students participate in student government elections. 31% of eligible men and 34% of eligible women are members of 28 national **fraternities** and 22 national **sororities**. Student **safety services** include late night transport/escort service, 24-hour emergency telephone alarm devices, 24-hour patrols by trained security personnel, and student patrols.

Miami University is a member of the NCAA (Division I). **Intercollegiate sports** (some offering scholarships) include archery (m, w), baseball (m), basketball (m, w), cross-country running (m, w), equestrian sports (m, w), fencing (m, w), field hockey (w), football (m), golf (m), gymnastics (m, w), ice hockey (m), lacrosse (m), racquetball (m, w), rugby (m), sailing (m, w), soccer (m, w), softball (w), swimming and diving (m, w), tennis (m, w), track and field (m, w), volleyball (m, w), wrestling (m).

Applying

Miami University requires a high school transcript, 3 years of high school math and science, 2 years of high school foreign language, and SAT I or ACT. It recommends an essay and 1 recommendation. Early and midyear entrance are possible, with a 1/31 deadline and continuous processing to 2/15 for financial aid. **Contact:** Dr. James S. McCoy, Assistant Vice President for Enrollment Services, Glos Admissions Center, Oxford, OH 45056, 513-529-2531.

GETTING IN LAST YEAR

10,723 applied
74% were accepted
41% enrolled (3,244)
41% from top tenth of their h.s. class
52% had SAT verbal scores over 600 (R)
62% had SAT math scores over 600 (R)
48% had ACT scores over 26
8% had SAT verbal scores over 700 (R)
9% had SAT math scores over 700 (R)
10% had ACT scores over 30
74 class presidents

THE STUDENT BODY

Total 15,601, of whom 14,119
  are undergraduates

From 50 states and territories,
  35 other countries
72% from Ohio
54% women, 46% men
3% African Americans
1% Native Americans
1% Hispanics
2% Asian Americans
1% international students

AFTER FRESHMAN YEAR

92% returned for sophomore year
73% got a degree within 4 years
81% got a degree within 5 years
82% got a degree within 6 years

AFTER GRADUATION

36% pursued further study (17% arts and
  sciences, 12% law, 5% medicine)
336 organizations recruited on campus

WHAT YOU WILL PAY

Resident tuition and fees $4884
Nonresident tuition and fees $10,314
Room and board $4210
28% receive need-based financial aid
Need-based college-administered scholarships and
  grants average $1686 per award
38% receive non-need financial aid
Non-need college-administered scholarships and
  grants average $3314 per award

MICHIGAN STATE UNIVERSITY

East Lansing, Michigan • Small-town setting • Public • State-supported • Coed

---

Dedicated to undergraduate education, Michigan State University, the nation's premier land-grant institution, offers 11 degree-granting colleges that support 150 academic programs of study, 360 student groups, 90 overseas study programs, a campus of unparalleled beauty, and Big Ten athletics—few institutions have it all. The Honors College offers enriched curricula in all majors, and 2 residential programs, Lyman Briggs School and James Madison College, integrate academic pursuits and living environment. Undergraduate research opportunities exist in majors ranging from advertising and biochemistry to criminal justice and engineering. Joint freshman admission programs are administered by the Colleges of Human Medicine and Veterinary Medicine.

Academics

Michigan State offers a core academic program; fewer than half of graduate courses are open to undergraduates. It awards bachelor's, master's, doctoral, and first professional **degrees**. Challenging opportunities include advanced placement, self-designed majors, tutorials, Freshman Honors College, an honors program, a senior project, Phi Beta Kappa, and Sigma Xi. Special programs include cooperative education, internships, summer session for credit, study abroad, and Army and Air Force ROTC.

The most popular **majors** include accounting, advertising, and criminal justice. A complete listing of majors at Michigan State appears in the Majors Index beginning on page 379.

The **faculty** at Michigan State has 2,468 full-time undergraduate teachers, 95% with terminal degrees.

Computers on Campus

Students are not required to have a computer. 2,500 **computers** available in the computer center, computer labs, the library, the student center, and dormitories provide access to the main academic computer, e-mail, and the Internet. Staffed computer lab on campus.

The 16 **libraries** have 3.9 million books and 28,000 subscriptions.

Campus Life

There are 350 active **organizations** on campus, including a drama/theater group and student-run newspaper and radio station. 8% of eligible men and 8% of eligible women are members of 35 national **fraternities** and 19 national **sororities**. Student **safety services** include self-defense workshops, late night transport/escort service, 24-hour emergency telephone alarm devices, and 24-hour patrols by trained security personnel.

Michigan State is a member of the NCAA (Division I). **Intercollegiate sports** (some offering scholarships) include baseball (m), basketball (m, w), cross-country running (m, w), equestrian sports (m, w), fencing (m), field hockey (w), football (m), golf (m, w), gymnastics (m, w), ice hockey (m), lacrosse (m), soccer (m), swimming and diving (m, w), tennis (m, w), track and field (m, w), volleyball (w), wrestling (m).

Applying

Michigan State requires a high school transcript and SAT I or ACT. It recommends 3 years of high school math, 2 years of high school foreign language, and 2 years of high school science, 4 years of high school English, 3 years of high school social science. Deferred and midyear entrance are possible, with a 7/30 deadline and continuous processing for financial aid. **Contact:** Dr. William H. Turner, Director of Admissions, 250 Administration Building, East Lansing, MI 48824-1020, 517-355-8332.

GETTING IN LAST YEAR
19,663 applied
82% were accepted
40% enrolled (6,420)
20% from top tenth of their h.s. class
3.31 average high school GPA
11% had SAT verbal scores over 600
32% had SAT math scores over 600
25% had ACT scores over 26
1% had SAT verbal scores over 700
8% had SAT math scores over 700
5% had ACT scores over 30
47 National Merit Scholars

THE STUDENT BODY
Total 40,647, of whom 31,329
  are undergraduates

From 54 states and territories,
  70 other countries
91% from Michigan
52% women, 48% men
8% African Americans
1% Native Americans
2% Hispanics
4% Asian Americans
3% international students

AFTER FRESHMAN YEAR
85% returned for sophomore year
35% got a degree within 4 years
64% got a degree within 5 years
69% got a degree within 6 years

AFTER GRADUATION
617 organizations recruited on campus
1 Rhodes, 1 Fulbright scholar

WHAT YOU WILL PAY
Resident tuition and fees $4522
Nonresident tuition and fees $11,377
Room and board $3828
44% receive need-based financial aid
Need-based college-administered scholarships and
  grants average $1235 per award
Non-need college-administered scholarships and
  grants average $2206 per award

MICHIGAN TECHNOLOGICAL UNIVERSITY

Houghton, Michigan • Small-town setting • Public • State-supported • Coed

Michigan Tech is recognized as one of the nation's leading universities for undergraduate and graduate education in science and engineering. MTU's state-of-the-art campus is located near Lake Superior in Michigan's beautiful Upper Peninsula. *Money Guide* ranks Michigan Tech among the top 10 scientific and technical universities in the nation, and *U.S. News & World Report* includes Michigan Tech with the top 50 best values among national universities. MTU is one of Michigan's 4 nationally recognized research universities.

 ## Academics

Michigan Tech offers an interdisciplinary curriculum and core academic program; fewer than half of graduate courses are open to undergraduates. It awards associate, bachelor's, master's, and doctoral **degrees**. Challenging opportunities include advanced placement, self-designed majors, tutorials, a senior project, and Sigma Xi. Special programs include cooperative education, internships, summer session for credit, off-campus study, study abroad, and Army and Air Force ROTC.

The most popular **majors** include mechanical engineering, electrical engineering, and civil engineering. A complete listing of majors at Michigan Tech appears in the Majors Index beginning on page 379.

The **faculty** at Michigan Tech has 347 full-time graduate and undergraduate teachers, 84% with terminal degrees. 17% of the faculty serve as student advisers. The student-faculty ratio is 17:1.

 ## Computers on Campus

Students are not required to have a computer. Student rooms are linked to a campus network. 885 **computers** available in the computer center, computer labs, the research center, the learning resource center, classrooms, and dormitories provide access to e-mail, on-line services, and the Internet. Staffed computer lab on campus provides training in the use of computers and software.

The **library** has 795,312 books, 440,508 microform titles, and 5,048 subscriptions. It is connected to 1 national **on-line** catalog.

 ## Campus Life

There are 200 active **organizations** on campus, including a drama/theater group and student-run newspaper and radio station. 16% of students participate in student government elections. 13% of eligible men and 16% of eligible women are members of 12 national **fraternities**, 4 national **sororities**, 4 local fraternities, 4 local sororities, and social clubs. Student **safety services** include late night transport/escort service, 24-hour emergency telephone alarm devices, and 24-hour patrols by trained security personnel.

Michigan Tech is a member of the NCAA (Division II). **Intercollegiate sports** (some offering scholarships) include basketball (m, w), cross-country running (m, w), football (m), ice hockey (m), skiing (cross-country) (m, w), swimming and diving (m, w), tennis (m, w), track and field (m, w), volleyball (w).

 ## Applying

Michigan Tech requires a high school transcript, and in some cases 3 years of high school math. It recommends 3 years of high school science, some high school foreign language, an interview, SAT I or ACT, and SAT II Subject Tests. Deferred and midyear entrance are possible, with rolling admissions and 3/1 for financial aid. **Contact:** Ms. Nancy Rehling, Director of Undergraduate Admissions, 1400 Townsend Drive, Houghton, MI 49931-1295, 906-487-2335; fax 906-487-3343.

GETTING IN LAST YEAR
2,577 applied
94% were accepted
44% enrolled (1,074)
37% from top tenth of their h.s. class
3.48 average high school GPA
43% had SAT verbal scores over 600 (R)
68% had SAT math scores over 600 (R)
52% had ACT scores over 26
12% had SAT verbal scores over 700 (R)
19% had SAT math scores over 700 (R)
13% had ACT scores over 30
15 National Merit Scholars
56 valedictorians

THE STUDENT BODY
Total 6,390, of whom 5,699
   are undergraduates

From 41 states and territories,
   44 other countries
78% from Michigan
26% women, 74% men
2% African Americans
1% Native Americans
1% Hispanics
1% Asian Americans
4% international students

AFTER FRESHMAN YEAR
83% returned for sophomore year
21% got a degree within 4 years
52% got a degree within 5 years
62% got a degree within 6 years

AFTER GRADUATION
24% pursued further study

90% had job offers within 6 months
158 organizations recruited on campus

WHAT YOU WILL PAY
Resident tuition and fees $3843
Nonresident tuition and fees $8733
Room and board $4137
40% receive need-based financial aid
Need-based college-administered scholarships and
   grants average $850 per award
31% receive non-need financial aid
Non-need college-administered scholarships and
   grants average $3037 per award

MIDDLEBURY COLLEGE

Middlebury, Vermont • Small-town setting • Private • Independent • Coed

Literary study, global understanding based on language and cultural competence, environmental studies grounded in science, application of learning to the real world—these form the core of the academic excellence at Middlebury. The campus is beautiful, with its own ski area and golf course, as well as a contemporary arts center, sophisticated computer networks, multimedia workstations for language study, state-of-the-art scientific equipment, and large libraries with on-line connections all over the world. To have gone to Middlebury is to have a lifetime of opportunities, made possible by the very best liberal arts education.

Academics

Middlebury offers a core academic program. It awards bachelor's, master's, and doctoral **degrees**. Challenging opportunities include advanced placement, self-designed majors, an honors program, and Phi Beta Kappa. Special programs include internships, off-campus study, and study abroad.

The most popular **majors** include English, psychology, and history. A complete listing of majors at Middlebury appears in the Majors Index beginning on page 379.

The **faculty** at Middlebury has 251 undergraduate teachers, 95% with terminal degrees. 100% of the faculty serve as student advisers. The student-faculty ratio is 11:1.

Computers on Campus

Students are not required to have a computer. Student rooms are linked to a campus network. 200 **computers** available in the computer center, computer labs, classrooms, the library, and dormitories provide access to e-mail and the Internet. Staffed computer lab on campus (open 24 hours a day) provides training in the use of computers and software.

The 4 **libraries** have 751,161 books, 265,439 microform titles, and 1,894 subscriptions.

Campus Life

There are 90 active **organizations** on campus, including a drama/theater group and student-run newspaper and radio station.

Middlebury has 6 social houses, commons system. Student **safety services** include late night transport/escort service.

Middlebury is a member of the NCAA (Division III). **Intercollegiate sports** include baseball (m), basketball (m, w), cross-country running (m, w), field hockey (w), football (m), golf (m, w), ice hockey (m, w), lacrosse (m, w), skiing (cross-country) (m, w), skiing (downhill) (m, w), soccer (m, w), squash (w), swimming and diving (m, w), tennis (m, w), track and field (m, w).

Applying

Middlebury requires a high school transcript, 3 recommendations, ACT or 3 SAT II Subject Tests (including SAT II Writing Test and 1 quantitative SAT II Test) or 3 Advanced Placement Tests (including AP English and 1 quantitative AP Test) or 3 I.B. Subsidiary Tests (including I.B. Languages and 1 quantitative I.B. Test). It recommends 4 years of high school math, 3 years of high school science, 4 years of high school foreign language, an interview, and 4 years of high school English, 3 years of high school history. Early and deferred entrance are possible, with a 1/1 deadline and a 1/15 priority date for financial aid. **Contact:** Mr. John Hanson, Director of Admissions, Emma Willard House, Middlebury, VT 05753-6002, 802-388-3711 ext. 5153.

GETTING IN LAST YEAR
3,818 applied
35% were accepted
45% enrolled (585)
65% from top tenth of their h.s. class

THE STUDENT BODY
2,041 undergraduates
From 50 states and territories,
73 other countries

5% from Vermont
50% women, 50% men
2% African Americans
1% Native Americans
3% Hispanics
6% Asian Americans
9% international students

AFTER FRESHMAN YEAR
94% returned for sophomore year

AFTER GRADUATION
33% pursued further study
36 organizations recruited on campus

WHAT YOU WILL PAY
Comprehensive fee $27,020
Need-based college-administered scholarships and grants average $15,120 per award

MILLIKIN UNIVERSITY

Decatur, Illinois • Suburban setting • Private • Independent-Religious • Coed

Millikin remains true to its founding mission of combining the liberal arts with professional education. Nearly every major offers opportunities for internships and other hands-on experience. Career planning services are readily available, and the placement rate of graduates is consistently above 95%. International study is available at more than 20 sites. With its combination of liberal arts and career preparation and a size that is small enough to be personal and large enough to offer diversity, Millikin offers the best of both worlds. The University is most often described as friendly and academically challenging.

Academics

Millikin offers an interdisciplinary curriculum and core academic program; a few graduate courses are open to undergraduates. It awards bachelor's **degrees**. Challenging opportunities include advanced placement, self-designed majors, tutorials, an honors program, and a senior project. Special programs include internships, summer session for credit, off-campus study, and study abroad.

The most popular **majors** include nursing, elementary education, and business. A complete listing of majors at Millikin appears in the Majors Index beginning on page 379.

The **faculty** at Millikin has 128 full-time teachers, 91% with terminal degrees. 100% of the faculty serve as student advisers. The student-faculty ratio is 14:1.

Computers on Campus

Students are not required to have a computer. Student rooms are linked to a campus network. 132 **computers** available in the computer center, computer labs, the learn-ing resource center, specialized labs, and the library provide access to e-mail, on-line services, and the Internet. Staffed computer lab on campus.

The **library** has 150,212 books, 19,204 microform titles, and 959 subscriptions. It is connected to 12 national **on-line** catalogs.

Campus Life

There are 78 active **organizations** on campus, including a drama/theater group and student-run newspaper and radio station. 35% of students participate in student government elections. 32% of eligible men and 19% of eligible women are members of 7 national **fraternities** and 4 national **sororities**. Student **safety services** include late night transport/escort service, 24-hour emergency telephone alarm devices, 24-hour patrols by trained security personnel, and electronically operated dormitory entrances.

Millikin is a member of the NCAA (Division III). **Intercollegiate sports** include baseball (m), basketball (m, w), cross-country running (m, w), football (m), golf (m), soccer (m, w), softball (w), swimming and diving (m, w), tennis (m, w), track and field (m, w), volleyball (w), wrestling (m).

Applying

Millikin requires a high school transcript, 3 recommendations, SAT I or ACT, and a minimum high school GPA of 2.0. It recommends 3 years of high school math and science, 2 years of high school foreign language, and an interview. Deferred and midyear entrance are possible, with rolling admissions and continuous processing to 8/1 for financial aid. **Contact:** Mr. Lin Stoner, Dean of Admission, 1184 West Main Street, Decatur, IL 62522, 217-424-6210 or toll-free 800-373-7733; fax 217-424-3993.

GETTING IN LAST YEAR
1,322 applied
91% were accepted
41% enrolled (496)
24% from top tenth of their h.s. class
3.1 average high school GPA
28% had SAT verbal scores over 600 (R)
34% had SAT math scores over 600 (R)
27% had ACT scores over 26
6% had SAT verbal scores over 700 (R)
0% had SAT math scores over 700 (R)
5% had ACT scores over 30
26 valedictorians

THE STUDENT BODY
1,883 undergraduates

From 27 states and territories,
  12 other countries
87% from Illinois
58% women, 42% men
5% African Americans
1% Hispanics
1% Asian Americans
1% international students

AFTER FRESHMAN YEAR
80% returned for sophomore year
60% got a degree within 4 years
64% got a degree within 5 years

AFTER GRADUATION
18% pursued further study (11% arts and
  sciences, 5% medicine, 1% business)
80% had job offers within 6 months
92 organizations recruited on campus

WHAT YOU WILL PAY
Tuition and fees $12,687
Room and board $4596
88% receive need-based financial aid
Need-based college-administered scholarships and
  grants average $6940 per award
4% receive non-need financial aid
Non-need college-administered scholarships and
  grants average $3664 per award

MILLSAPS COLLEGE

Jackson, Mississippi • Urban setting • Private • Independent-Religious • Coed

 ## Academics

Millsaps College offers an interdisciplinary curriculum and core academic program. It awards bachelor's and master's **degrees**. Challenging opportunities include advanced placement, tutorials, an honors program, a senior project, and Phi Beta Kappa. Special programs include internships, summer session for credit, off-campus study, study abroad, and Army ROTC.

The most popular **majors** include English, business, and biology/biological sciences. A complete listing of majors at Millsaps College appears in the Majors Index beginning on page 379.

The **faculty** at Millsaps College has 85 full-time graduate and undergraduate teachers, 91% with terminal degrees. 80% of the faculty serve as student advisers. The student-faculty ratio is 14:1.

 ## Computers on Campus

Students are not required to have a computer. Student rooms are linked to a campus network. 125 **computers** available in the computer center, computer labs, student labs, the library, the student center, dormitories, and student rooms provide access to the main academic computer, off-campus computing facilities, e-mail, on-line services, and the Internet. Staffed computer lab on campus (open 24 hours a day) provides training in the use of computers and software.

The **library** has 283,993 books, 72,393 microform titles, and 786 subscriptions. It is connected to 3 national **on-line** catalogs.

 ## Campus Life

There are 60 active **organizations** on campus, including a drama/theater group and student-run newspaper. 60% of students participate in student government elections. 62% of eligible men and 60% of eligible women are members of 6 national **fraternities** and 5 national **sororities**. Student **safety services** include late night transport/escort service, 24-hour emergency telephone alarm devices, 24-hour patrols by trained security personnel, student patrols, and electronically operated dormitory entrances.

Millsaps College is a member of the NCAA (Division III). **Intercollegiate sports** include baseball (m), basketball (m, w), cross-country running (m, w), football (m), golf (m), soccer (m, w), tennis (m, w), volleyball (w).

 ## Applying

Millsaps College requires an essay, a high school transcript, and SAT I or ACT. It recommends 3 years of high school math and science, some high school foreign language, recommendations, an interview, 4 years of high school English, and SAT II Subject Tests. Early, deferred, and midyear entrance are possible, with a 4/1 deadline and continuous processing to 3/1 for financial aid. **Contact:** Ms. Florence W. Hines, Director of Admissions, 1701 North State Street, Jackson, MS 39210-0001, 601-974-1050 or toll-free 800-352-1050; fax 601-974-1059.

GETTING IN LAST YEAR
988 applied
86% were accepted
31% enrolled (260)
39% from top tenth of their h.s. class
3.25 average high school GPA
60% had SAT verbal scores over 600 (R)
55% had SAT math scores over 600 (R)
52% had ACT scores over 26
18% had SAT verbal scores over 700 (R)
5% had SAT math scores over 700 (R)
17% had ACT scores over 30
20 National Merit Scholars
35 class presidents
32 valedictorians

THE STUDENT BODY
Total 1,430, of whom 1,294 are undergraduates
From 24 states and territories, 4 other countries
60% from Mississippi
51% women, 49% men
5% African Americans
0% Native Americans
1% Hispanics
3% Asian Americans
1% international students

AFTER FRESHMAN YEAR
84% returned for sophomore year

AFTER GRADUATION
48% pursued further study (24% arts and sciences, 8% business, 8% law)
38% had job offers within 6 months
54 organizations recruited on campus
1 Fulbright scholar

WHAT YOU WILL PAY
Tuition and fees $12,700
Room and board $4770
57% receive need-based financial aid
Need-based college-administered scholarships and grants average $4720 per award
22% receive non-need financial aid
Non-need college-administered scholarships and grants average $5100 per award

MILLS COLLEGE

Oakland, California • Urban setting • Private • Independent • Women

Mills can change a woman's life. Recent highly publicized research has demonstrated why women in coed colleges aren't equal; the students who went on strike in 1990 to keep Mills a women's college already knew. Mills knows how to teach women. Even in their first year, students can discover the excitement of original hands-on research (most students don't experience this until graduate school). All Mills' resources are committed to women. Since half the professors at Mills are women, students have successful role models in every field. And internship opportunities provide wide career experience. When women graduate from Mills, they know they can succeed. And that confidence makes all the difference.

 Academics

Mills offers a multicultural and interdisciplinary curriculum and core academic program; more than half of graduate courses are open to undergraduates. It awards bachelor's and master's **degrees**. Challenging opportunities include advanced placement, accelerated degree programs, self-designed majors, tutorials, a senior project, and Phi Beta Kappa. Special programs include cooperative education, internships, and off-campus study.

The most popular **majors** include English, political, legal, and economic analysis, and communication. A complete listing of majors at Mills appears in the Majors Index beginning on page 379.

The **faculty** at Mills has 73 full-time graduate and undergraduate teachers, 99% with terminal degrees. 95% of the faculty serve as student advisers. The student-faculty ratio is 12:1.

 Computers on Campus

Students are not required to have a computer. 122 **computers** available in the computer center, student lounge, academic buildings, the library, the student center, and dormitories provide access to the main academic computer, off-campus computing facilities, e-mail, on-line services, and the Internet. Staffed computer lab on campus provides training in the use of computers and software.

The 2 **libraries** have 219,244 books, 8,142 microform titles, and 738 subscriptions. They are connected to 5 national **on-line** catalogs.

 Campus Life

There are 40 active **organizations** on campus, including a drama/theater group and student-run newspaper. Student **safety services** include late night transport/escort service, 24-hour emergency telephone alarm devices, and 24-hour patrols by trained security personnel.

Mills is a member of the NCAA (Division III). **Intercollegiate sports** include basketball, crew, cross-country running, tennis, volleyball.

 Applying

Mills requires a high school transcript, 3 recommendations, essay or graded paper, and SAT I or ACT. It recommends 3 years of high school math and science, 2 years of high school foreign language, an interview, and 3 SAT II Subject Tests. Deferred and midyear entrance are possible, with rolling admissions and a 2/15 priority date for financial aid. **Contact:** Ms. Genevieve Ann Flaherty, Dean of Admission and Financial Aid, 5000 MacArthur Boulevard, Oakland, CA 94613-1000, 510-430-2135 or toll-free 800-87-MILLS.

GETTING IN LAST YEAR
568 applied
82% were accepted
29% enrolled (133)
28% from top tenth of their h.s. class
3.4 average high school GPA
51% had SAT verbal scores over 600 (R)
28% had SAT math scores over 600 (R)
38% had ACT scores over 26
11% had SAT verbal scores over 700 (R)
3% had SAT math scores over 700 (R)
0% had ACT scores over 30

THE STUDENT BODY
Total 1,169, of whom 871
  are undergraduates
From 36 states and territories,
  14 other countries
82% from California
100% women
7% African Americans
1% Native Americans
6% Hispanics
11% Asian Americans
3% international students

AFTER FRESHMAN YEAR
73% returned for sophomore year
56% got a degree within 4 years
65% got a degree within 5 years

WHAT YOU WILL PAY
Tuition and fees $14,640
Room and board $6180
78% receive need-based financial aid
Need-based college-administered scholarships and
  grants average $6608 per award
8% receive non-need financial aid
Non-need college-administered scholarships and
  grants average $72,295 per award

MILWAUKEE SCHOOL OF ENGINEERING

Milwaukee, Wisconsin • Urban setting • Private • Independent • Coed

Oscar Werwath, a practicing engineer and a graduate of European technical schools, organized MSOE in 1903. He was the first to plan an American educational institution based on an applications-oriented curriculum. Leaders of business and industry cooperated in the college's development, and a close relationship was established that continues today. MSOE offers 13 bachelor's degrees, 2 associate degrees, 3 master's degrees, and 10 certificate programs. MSOE is located near the center of downtown Milwaukee, just a few blocks from the theater district and Lake Michigan and with easy access to Milwaukee's business and industrial centers and major cultural and artistic facilities.

 ## Academics

MSOE offers a core academic program; a few graduate courses are open to undergraduates. It awards associate, bachelor's, and master's **degrees**. Challenging opportunities include advanced placement, an honors program, and a senior project. Special programs include internships, summer session for credit, study abroad, and Army and Air Force ROTC.

The most popular **majors** include electrical engineering, mechanical engineering, and architectural engineering. A complete listing of majors at MSOE appears in the Majors Index beginning on page 379.

The **faculty** at MSOE has 103 full-time graduate and undergraduate teachers, 35% with terminal degrees. The student-faculty ratio is 13:1.

 ## Computers on Campus

Students are not required to have a computer. Student rooms are linked to a campus network. 200 **computers** available in the computer center, computer labs, the learning resource center, labs, classrooms, the library, and the student center provide access to the main academic computer, off-campus computing facilities, e-mail, on-line services, and the Internet. Staffed computer lab on campus provides training in the use of computers and software.

The **library** has 60,000 books, 30 microform titles, and 529 subscriptions. It is connected to 3 national **on-line** catalogs.

 ## Campus Life

There are 57 active **organizations** on campus, including a drama/theater group and student-run newspaper and radio station. 10% of eligible men and 15% of eligible women are members of 1 national **fraternity**, 1 national **sorority**, 4 local fraternities, and 1 local sorority. Student **safety services** include late night transport/escort service and 24-hour patrols by trained security personnel.

MSOE is a member of the NCAA (Division III). **Intercollegiate sports** include baseball (m), basketball (m, w), cross-country running (m, w), golf (m), ice hockey (m), soccer (m), softball (w), tennis (m, w), volleyball (w), wrestling (m).

 ## Applying

MSOE requires an essay, a high school transcript, SAT I or ACT, and in some cases 3 years of high school science. It recommends 3 years of high school math, 1 recommendation, and an interview. Deferred and midyear entrance are possible, with rolling admissions and continuous processing to 3/15 for financial aid. **Contact:** Mr. T. Owen Smith, Dean of Admissions, Student Life and Campus Center, Milwaukee, WI 53202-3109, 414-277-7202 or toll-free 800-332-6763; fax 414-277-7475.

GETTING IN LAST YEAR
1,159 applied
90% were accepted
49% enrolled (513)
33% from top tenth of their h.s. class
3.2 average high school GPA
42% had ACT scores over 26
11% had ACT scores over 30

THE STUDENT BODY
Total 3,007, of whom 2,577
  are undergraduates
From 25 states and territories,
  27 other countries

61% from Wisconsin
16% women, 84% men
3% African Americans
1% Native Americans
2% Hispanics
4% Asian Americans
5% international students

AFTER FRESHMAN YEAR
30% got a degree within 4 years
50% got a degree within 5 years
52% got a degree within 6 years

AFTER GRADUATION
8% pursued further study (5% engineering)

WHAT YOU WILL PAY
Tuition and fees $13,305
Room and board $3615
Need-based college-administered scholarships and
  grants average $1700 per award
Non-need college-administered scholarships and
  grants average $3372 per award

MONMOUTH COLLEGE

Monmouth, Illinois • Small-town setting • Private • Independent-Religious • Coed

A school rich in traditions, Monmouth College was founded in 1853 by determined Presbyterian pioneers. Situated on 35 rolling acres in the heart of a quiet community, its campus features an appealing blend of stately old buildings and state-of-the-art facilities. Monmouth's commitment to providing a broad-based liberal arts education is reflected in a faculty totally dedicated to undergraduate teaching. A freshman seminar gives all students a firm foothold for pursuing their education, and a senior capstone course helps them solidify what they have learned. With an enrollment of just 1,000, the College offers ample opportunities for individual leadership in curricular and extracurricular activities.

Academics

Monmouth offers a core academic program. It awards bachelor's **degrees**. Challenging opportunities include advanced placement, self-designed majors, tutorials, an honors program, and a senior project. Special programs include internships, summer session for credit, off-campus study, and Army ROTC.

The most popular **majors** include business, education, and biology/biological sciences. A complete listing of majors at Monmouth appears in the Majors Index beginning on page 379.

The **faculty** at Monmouth has 53 full-time teachers, 90% with terminal degrees. 100% of the faculty serve as student advisers. The student-faculty ratio is 14:1, and the average class size in core courses is 20.

Computers on Campus

Students are not required to have a computer. 105 **computers** available in the computer center, computer labs, classrooms, and the library provide access to the main academic computer, off-campus computing facilities, e-mail, on-line services, and the Internet. Staffed computer lab on campus provides training in the use of computers and software.

The **library** has 250,000 books, 70,000 microform titles, and 1,300 subscriptions.

Campus Life

Active **organizations** on campus include drama/theater group and student-run newspaper and radio station. 62% of students participate in student government elections. 27% of eligible men and 35% of eligible women are members of 3 national **fraternities** and 3 national **sororities**. Student **safety services** include night security and late night transport/escort service.

Monmouth is a member of the NCAA (Division III). **Intercollegiate sports** include baseball (m), basketball (m, w), cross-country running (m, w), football (m), soccer (m, w), softball (w), track and field (m, w), volleyball (w), wrestling (m).

Applying

Monmouth requires a high school transcript, 3 years of high school math, SAT I or ACT, and in some cases an essay. It recommends 3 years of high school science, 2 years of high school foreign language, 2 recommendations, and an interview. Early, deferred, and midyear entrance are possible, with a 5/1 deadline and continuous processing to 4/30 for financial aid. **Contact:** Mr. Richard Valentine, Vice President for Enrollment, 700 East Broadway, Monmouth, IL 61462-1998, 309-457-2131 or toll-free 800-747-2687; fax 309-457-2141.

GETTING IN LAST YEAR
1,078 applied
80% were accepted
36% enrolled (310)
22% from top tenth of their h.s. class
3.15 average high school GPA
22% had ACT scores over 26
2% had ACT scores over 30
17 class presidents
15 valedictorians

THE STUDENT BODY
923 undergraduates
From 22 states and territories,
   18 other countries

85% from Illinois
60% women, 40% men
1% African Americans
0% Native Americans
2% Hispanics
1% Asian Americans
6% international students

AFTER FRESHMAN YEAR
85% returned for sophomore year
57% got a degree within 4 years
62% got a degree within 5 years
63% got a degree within 6 years

AFTER GRADUATION
34% pursued further study (18% business, 8% arts and sciences, 4% law)
88% had job offers within 6 months
12 organizations recruited on campus

WHAT YOU WILL PAY
Tuition and fees $14,175
Room and board $4275
65% receive need-based financial aid
Need-based college-administered scholarships and grants average $6125 per award
38% receive non-need financial aid
Non-need college-administered scholarships and grants average $3866 per award

---

Morehouse College

Atlanta, Georgia • Urban setting • Private • Independent • Men

 Academics

Morehouse College offers a core academic program. It awards bachelor's **degrees**. Challenging opportunities include advanced placement, tutorials, an honors program, a senior project, and Phi Beta Kappa. Special programs include cooperative education, internships, summer session for credit, off-campus study, study abroad, and Army, Naval, and Air Force ROTC.

The most popular **majors** include biology/biological sciences, engineering (general), and political science/government. A complete listing of majors at Morehouse College appears in the Majors Index beginning on page 379.

The **faculty** at Morehouse College has 150 full-time teachers, 72% with terminal degrees. 100% of the faculty serve as student advisers. The student-faculty ratio is 17:1.

 Computers on Campus

Students are not required to have a computer. 325 **computers** available in the computer center, science building, writing skills lab, the library, and dormitories.

The **library** has 560,000 books, 110,000 microform titles, and 1,000 subscriptions.

 Campus Life

Active **organizations** on campus include drama/theater group and student-run newspaper. 3% of eligible undergraduates are members of 5 national **fraternities**. Student **safety services** include late night transport/escort service.

Morehouse College is a member of the NCAA (Division II). **Intercollegiate sports** (some offering scholarships) include basketball, cross-country running, football, swimming and diving, tennis, track and field.

 Applying

Morehouse College requires an essay, a high school transcript, 3 years of high school math, minimum 2.8 high school GPA, SAT I or ACT, and in some cases recommendations and an interview. It recommends 3 years of high school science, some high school foreign language, and a minimum high school GPA of 3.0. Early, deferred, and midyear entrance are possible, with a 2/15 deadline and 4/1 for financial aid. **Contact:** Mr. André Pattillo, Director of Admissions, 830 Westview Drive, Atlanta, GA 30314, 404-215-2632 or toll-free 800-851-1254; fax 404-659-6536.

GETTING IN LAST YEAR
3,263 applied
57% were accepted
38% enrolled (704)
28% from top tenth of their h.s. class
3.0 average high school GPA
32% had ACT scores over 26
5% had ACT scores over 30
27 valedictorians

THE STUDENT BODY
2,992 undergraduates
From 41 states and territories,
   18 other countries
18% from Georgia
100% men
98% African Americans
2% international students

WHAT YOU WILL PAY
Tuition and fees $10,430
Room and board $5770
Need-based college-administered scholarships and
   grants average $4500 per award
Non-need college-administered scholarships and
   grants average $1800 per award

MOUNT HOLYOKE COLLEGE

South Hadley, Massachusetts • Small-town setting • Private • Independent • Women

Located in a small town in the Connecticut River Valley of Massachusetts, Mount Holyoke College is a liberal arts college for women, the oldest of its kind in the United States. Believing that the ability to make sound decisions is one of the chief benefits of a liberal education, the College gives its students primary responsibility for planning and achieving their educational goals. To this end, it offers a high degree of independence and a wide range of opportunities, including all that come with membership in the Five College Consortium with Amherst, Hampshire, and Smith colleges and the University of Massachusetts.

 ## Academics

Mount Holyoke offers a core academic program; a few graduate courses are open to undergraduates. It awards bachelor's and master's **degrees**. Challenging opportunities include advanced placement, accelerated degree programs, self-designed majors, tutorials, an honors program, Phi Beta Kappa, and Sigma Xi. Special programs include internships, off-campus study, study abroad, and Army and Air Force ROTC.

The most popular **majors** include English, political science/government, and biology/biological sciences. A complete listing of majors at Mount Holyoke appears in the Majors Index beginning on page 379.

The **faculty** at Mount Holyoke has 181 full-time graduate and undergraduate teachers, 96% with terminal degrees. The student-faculty ratio is 9:1.

 ## Computers on Campus

Students are not required to have a computer. 245 **computers** available in the computer center, classroom buildings, the library, and dormitories. Staffed computer lab on campus provides training in the use of computers and software.

The 2 **libraries** have 623,336 books, 15,120 microform titles, and 1,811 subscriptions.

 ## Campus Life

There are 100 active **organizations** on campus, including a drama/theater group and student-run newspaper and radio station. Student **safety services** include late night transport/escort service, 24-hour emergency telephone alarm devices, 24-hour patrols by trained security personnel, and student patrols.

Mount Holyoke is a member of the NCAA (Division III). **Intercollegiate sports** include basketball, crew, cross-country running, equestrian sports, field hockey, golf, lacrosse, soccer, squash, swimming and diving, tennis, track and field, volleyball.

 ## Applying

Mount Holyoke requires an essay, a high school transcript, 3 years of high school math, 2 recommendations, an interview, SAT I and 3 SAT II Subject Tests (including SAT II: Writing Test) or ACT. It recommends 3 years of high school science and 4 years of high school foreign language. Early and deferred entrance are possible, with a 1/15 deadline and 2/1 for financial aid. **Contact:** Ms. Anita Smith, Director of Admissions, College Street, South Hadley, MA 01075-1414, 413-538-2023; fax 413-538-2409.

GETTING IN LAST YEAR
2,033 applied
65% were accepted
38% enrolled (500)
58% from top tenth of their h.s. class
31% had SAT verbal scores over 600
48% had SAT math scores over 600
5% had SAT verbal scores over 700
11% had SAT math scores over 700

THE STUDENT BODY
Total 1,957, of whom 1,946
    are undergraduates
From 49 states and territories,
    52 other countries

20% from Massachusetts
100% women
4% African Americans
1% Native Americans
4% Hispanics
8% Asian Americans
13% international students

AFTER FRESHMAN YEAR
94% returned for sophomore year
79% got a degree within 4 years
81% got a degree within 5 years

AFTER GRADUATION
33% pursued further study (22% arts and
    sciences, 5% law, 3% medicine)
2 Fulbright scholars

WHAT YOU WILL PAY
Tuition and fees $20,290
Room and board $5950
Need-based college-administered scholarships and
    grants average $14,600 per award

MOUNT UNION COLLEGE

Alliance, Ohio • Suburban setting • Private • Independent-Religious • Coed

Mount Union College has established a reputation for producing successful graduates in a wide array of occupations. The College affirms the importance of reason, open inquiry, living faith, and individual worth. Mount Union's mission is to prepare students for meaningful work, fulfilling lives, and responsible citizenship. Mount Union strives to provide the best education possible for each of its students so that its graduates have developed communication skills, critical thinking, a sensitivity to social responsibility, and a concern for human needs.

 ## Academics

Mount Union offers a core academic program. It awards bachelor's **degrees**. Challenging opportunities include advanced placement, accelerated degree programs, self-designed majors, tutorials, an honors program, and a senior project. Special programs include cooperative education, internships, summer session for credit, off-campus study, study abroad, and Army and Air Force ROTC.

The most popular **majors** include business, education, and accounting. A complete listing of majors at Mount Union appears in the Majors Index beginning on page 379.

The **faculty** at Mount Union has 85 full-time teachers, 78% with terminal degrees. 100% of the faculty serve as student advisers. The student-faculty ratio is 16:1, and the average class size in core courses is 18.

 ## Computers on Campus

Students are not required to have a computer. Student rooms are linked to a campus network. 130 **computers** available in computer labs, personal computer lab, and the library provide access to e-mail and the Internet. Staffed computer lab on campus provides training in the use of computers and software.

The 3 **libraries** have 215,397 books, 29,523 microform titles, and 868 subscriptions. They are connected to 3 national **on-line** catalogs.

 ## Campus Life

There are 75 active **organizations** on campus, including a drama/theater group and student-run newspaper and radio station. 35% of eligible men and 35% of eligible women are members of 5 national **fraternities**, 4 national **sororities**, and 1 local sorority. Student **safety services** include 24-hour locked dormitory entrances with outside phone, 24-hour patrols by trained security personnel, and electronically operated dormitory entrances.

Mount Union is a member of the NCAA (Division III). **Intercollegiate sports** include baseball (m), basketball (m, w), cross-country running (m, w), football (m), golf (m), soccer (m, w), softball (w), swimming and diving (m, w), tennis (m, w), track and field (m, w), volleyball (w), wrestling (m).

 ## Applying

Mount Union requires an essay, a high school transcript, 1 recommendation, SAT I or ACT, and a minimum high school GPA of 2.0. It recommends 3 years of high school math and science, 2 years of high school foreign language, and a campus interview. Early, deferred, and midyear entrance are possible, with rolling admissions and continuous processing to 5/1 for financial aid. **Contact:** Mr. Greg King, Director of Admissions and Enrollment Management, 1972 Clark Avenue, Alliance, OH 44601-3993, 216-823-2590 or toll-free 800-334-6682 (in-state), 800-992-6682 (out-of-state); fax 216-821-0425.

GETTING IN LAST YEAR
1,518 applied
82% were accepted
43% enrolled (533)
25% from top tenth of their h.s. class
25% had ACT scores over 26
5% had ACT scores over 30

THE STUDENT BODY
1,583 undergraduates
From 22 states and territories,
    22 other countries

80% from Ohio
49% women, 51% men
5% African Americans
1% Native Americans
1% Hispanics
1% Asian Americans
5% international students

AFTER FRESHMAN YEAR
87% returned for sophomore year
63% got a degree within 4 years
65% got a degree within 5 years

AFTER GRADUATION
27% pursued further study (12% arts and
    sciences, 5% law, 4% business)
94% had job offers within 6 months
25 organizations recruited on campus

WHAT YOU WILL PAY
Tuition and fees $13,480
Room and board $3650
Need-based college-administered scholarships and
    grants average $5982 per award

MUHLENBERG COLLEGE

Allentown, Pennsylvania • Suburban setting • Private • Independent-Religious • Coed

> Muhlenberg offers merit scholarships ranging in value from $1000 to $7000, renewable annually based on a 3.0 GPA. Last year, 50 students enrolled with a merit award. Merit recipients typically scored 1250 or better on the combined SAT and ranked in the top 10% of their high school classes. Two Honors Programs—Muhlenberg Scholar and Dana Associates—also carry an annual stipend.

 ## Academics

Muhlenberg offers an interdisciplinary curriculum and core academic program. It awards bachelor's **degrees**. Challenging opportunities include advanced placement, accelerated degree programs, self-designed majors, tutorials, an honors program, a senior project, and Phi Beta Kappa. Special programs include internships, summer session for credit, off-campus study, study abroad, and Army ROTC.

The most popular **majors** include biology/biological sciences, psychology, and English. A complete listing of majors at Muhlenberg appears in the Majors Index beginning on page 379.

The **faculty** at Muhlenberg has 126 full-time teachers, 86% with terminal degrees. 90% of the faculty serve as student advisers. The student-faculty ratio is 13:1.

 ## Computers on Campus

Students are not required to have a computer. Student rooms are linked to a campus network. 150 **computers** available in the computer center, computer labs, the library, and dormitories provide access to the main academic computer, e-mail, and the Internet. Staffed computer lab on campus provides training in the use of computers and software.

The **library** has 200,000 books, 437 microform titles, and 900 subscriptions. It is connected to 2 national **on-line** catalogs.

 ## Campus Life

There are 80 active **organizations** on campus, including a drama/theater group and student-run newspaper and radio station. 45% of eligible men and 40% of eligible women are members of 4 national **fraternities** and 4 national **sororities**. Student **safety services** include late night transport/escort service, 24-hour emergency telephone alarm devices, 24-hour patrols by trained security personnel, and electronically operated dormitory entrances.

Muhlenberg is a member of the NCAA (Division III). **Intercollegiate sports** include baseball (m), basketball (m, w), cross-country running (m, w), field hockey (w), football (m), golf (m), lacrosse (w), soccer (m, w), softball (w), tennis (m, w), track and field (m, w), volleyball (w), wrestling (m).

 ## Applying

Muhlenberg requires an essay, a high school transcript, 3 years of high school math, 2 years of high school foreign language, 2 recommendations, and SAT I or ACT. It recommends 3 years of high school science and a campus interview. Early, deferred, and midyear entrance are possible, with a 2/15 deadline and a 2/15 priority date for financial aid. **Contact:** Mr. Christopher Hooker-Haring, Dean of Admissions, 2400 Chew Street, Allentown, PA 18104-5586, 610-821-3200; fax 610-821-3234.

GETTING IN LAST YEAR
2,586 applied
74% were accepted
25% enrolled (487)
26% from top tenth of their h.s. class
3.3 average high school GPA
46% had SAT verbal scores over 600 (R)
40% had SAT math scores over 600 (R)
24% had ACT scores over 26
7% had SAT verbal scores over 700 (R)
7% had SAT math scores over 700 (R)
1% had ACT scores over 30
18 class presidents
7 valedictorians

THE STUDENT BODY
1,874 undergraduates

From 35 states and territories,
12 other countries
34% from Pennsylvania
53% women, 47% men
2% African Americans
0% Native Americans
2% Hispanics
4% Asian Americans
1% international students

AFTER FRESHMAN YEAR
92% returned for sophomore year
83% got a degree within 4 years
84% got a degree within 5 years

AFTER GRADUATION
30% pursued further study (15% arts and sciences, 6% law, 4% medicine)
63% had job offers within 6 months

WHAT YOU WILL PAY
Tuition and fees $17,550
Room and board $4720
53% receive need-based financial aid
Need-based college-administered scholarships and grants average $8430 per award
10% receive non-need financial aid
Non-need college-administered scholarships and grants average $5000 per award

NEBRASKA WESLEYAN UNIVERSITY

Lincoln, Nebraska • Suburban setting • Private • Independent-Religious • Coed

A Nebraska Wesleyan education is driven by the differences among and within all students. Strong relationships with the faculty enable students to develop and refine interests, talents, and critical thinking and communication skills necessary to be competitive. Superior research facilities provide experience for students as early as their first year. The benefits of integrated advising, orientation, and career services are evident in Nebraska Wesleyan's high retention, graduation, and graduate/professional school placement rates. Development of leadership skills is well within reach of all students through more than 80 honoraries, clubs, and organizations, and through service learning and local, national, and international volunteer opportunities.

Academics

NWU offers a core academic program; a few graduate courses are open to undergraduates. It awards bachelor's **degrees**. Challenging opportunities include advanced placement and a senior project. Special programs include internships, summer session for credit, off-campus study, study abroad, and Army and Air Force ROTC.

The most popular **majors** include business, biology/biological sciences, and psychology. A complete listing of majors at NWU appears in the Majors Index beginning on page 379.

The **faculty** at NWU has 91 full-time teachers, 81% with terminal degrees. 89% of the faculty serve as student advisers. The student-faculty ratio is 13:1.

Computers on Campus

Students are not required to have a computer. 70 **computers** available in the computer center, computer labs, the learning resource center, classrooms, the library, and dormitories provide access to e-mail. Staffed computer lab on campus provides training in the use of computers and software.

The **library** has 165,058 books, 19 microform titles, and 768 subscriptions. It is connected to 4 national **on-line** catalogs.

Campus Life

There are 80 active **organizations** on campus, including a drama/theater group and student-run newspaper. 42% of eligible men and 34% of eligible women are members of 3 national **fraternities**, 2 national **sororities**, 1 local fraternity, and 1 local sorority. Student **safety services** include late night transport/escort service, 24-hour patrols by trained security personnel, and electronically operated dormitory entrances.

NWU is a member of the NCAA (Division III) and NAIA. **Intercollegiate sports** include baseball (m), basketball (m, w), cross-country running (m, w), football (m), golf (m, w), soccer (m, w), softball (w), tennis (m, w), track and field (m, w), volleyball (w).

Applying

NWU requires a high school transcript, ACT, a minimum high school GPA of 2.0, and in some cases an essay and resumé of activities. It recommends some high school foreign language, recommendations, an interview, and SAT I. Early, deferred, and midyear entrance are possible, with a 3/15 deadline and continuous processing to 7/15 for financial aid. **Contact:** Mr. Ken Sieg, Director of Admissions, 5000 Saint Paul Avenue, Lincoln, NE 68504-2796, 402-465-2218 or toll-free 800-541-3818 (in-state); fax 402-465-2179.

GETTING IN LAST YEAR

1,044 applied
84% were accepted
41% enrolled (362)
19% from top tenth of their h.s. class
29% had ACT scores over 26
7% had ACT scores over 30
3 National Merit Scholars
12 valedictorians

THE STUDENT BODY

1,584 undergraduates
From 23 states and territories,
   12 other countries

93% from Nebraska
60% women, 40% men
3% African Americans
0% Native Americans
2% Hispanics
1% Asian Americans
1% international students

AFTER FRESHMAN YEAR

80% returned for sophomore year
50% got a degree within 4 years
65% got a degree within 5 years
67% got a degree within 6 years

AFTER GRADUATION

21 organizations recruited on campus
1 Fulbright scholar

WHAT YOU WILL PAY

Tuition and fees $10,316
Room and board $3420
62% receive need-based financial aid
Need-based college-administered scholarships and
   grants average $2695 per award
68% receive non-need financial aid
Non-need college-administered scholarships and
   grants average $1480 per award

NEW COLLEGE OF THE UNIVERSITY OF SOUTH FLORIDA

Sarasota, Florida • Suburban setting • Public • State-supported • Coed

Descriptions such as highly rigorous, intellectually sophisticated, and innovative apply to New College and to the manner in which individuals are selected to become a part of the student body. A significant level of intellectual sophistication is required to successfully negotiate the admissions process; there are 5 writing samples required, including a graded paper. Innovativeness is also a central tenet in the selection process. Students are considered and notified on a rolling basis (an approach that is rare for highly selective colleges), and applicants are never put on a waiting list.

Academics

New College of USF offers an interdisciplinary curriculum and no core academic program. It awards bachelor's **degrees**. Challenging opportunities include accelerated degree programs, self-designed majors, tutorials, an honors program, and a senior project. Special programs include internships, off-campus study, study abroad, and Army and Air Force ROTC.

The most popular **majors** include biology/biological sciences, literature, and psychology. A complete listing of majors at New College of USF appears in the Majors Index beginning on page 379.

The **faculty** at New College of USF has 53 full-time teachers, 95% with terminal degrees. 100% of the faculty serve as student advisers. The student-faculty ratio is 11:1, and the average class size in core courses is 19.

Computers on Campus

Students are not required to have a computer. Student rooms are linked to a campus network. 40 **computers** available in the computer center, natural sciences building, the library, and the student center provide access to the main academic computer, e-mail, and the Internet. Staffed computer lab on campus provides training in the use of computers and software.

The **library** has 247,000 books, 400,000 microform titles, and 829 subscriptions. It is connected to 4 national **on-line** catalogs.

Campus Life

There are 20 active **organizations** on campus, including a drama/theater group and student-run newspaper. Student **safety services** include late night transport/escort service, 24-hour emergency telephone alarm devices, and 24-hour patrols by trained security personnel.

This institution has no intercollegiate sports.

Applying

New College of USF requires an essay, a high school transcript, 3 years of high school math and science, 2 years of high school foreign language, 2 recommendations, graded writing sample, SAT I or ACT, and in some cases a campus interview. It recommends an interview and a minimum high school GPA of 3.0. Early and deferred entrance are possible, with rolling admissions and continuous processing to 2/1 for financial aid. **Contact:** Ms. Kathleen Rillion, Acting Director of Admissions, 5700 North Tamiami Trail, Sarasota, FL 34243-2197, 941-359-4269.

GETTING IN LAST YEAR
524 applied
59% were accepted
46% enrolled (143)
61% from top tenth of their h.s. class
3.87 average high school GPA
69% had SAT verbal scores over 600
83% had SAT math scores over 600
92% had ACT scores over 26
16% had SAT verbal scores over 700
30% had SAT math scores over 700
50% had ACT scores over 30
21 National Merit Scholars

THE STUDENT BODY
586 undergraduates

From 40 states and territories,
7 other countries
58% from Florida
46% women, 54% men
2% African Americans
0% Native Americans
5% Hispanics
8% Asian Americans
2% international students

AFTER FRESHMAN YEAR
80% returned for sophomore year
36% got a degree within 4 years
54% got a degree within 5 years
59% got a degree within 6 years

AFTER GRADUATION
42% pursued further study (31% arts and
    sciences, 6% law, 2% medicine)
55% had job offers within 6 months
1 Fulbright scholar

WHAT YOU WILL PAY
Resident tuition and fees $2066
Nonresident tuition and fees $7949
Room and board $3847
57% receive need-based financial aid
Need-based college-administered scholarships and
    grants average $2852 per award
57% receive non-need financial aid
Non-need college-administered scholarships and
    grants average $2336 per award

NEW JERSEY INSTITUTE OF TECHNOLOGY

Newark, New Jersey • Urban setting • Public • State-supported • Coed

The Albert Dorman Honors College is one of the nation's leading technologically oriented honors programs. Admission is highly selective; successful applicants generally rank in the top 10% of their high schools, with SAT I scores above 1250. Honors College scholars receive at least a one-half tuition scholarship award. Exceptionally well-prepared students may be eligible for additional scholarships and partial room grants. All degree programs are available through the Albert Dorman Honors College.

 ## Academics

NJIT offers a technology and applied science curriculum and core academic program. It awards bachelor's, master's, and doctoral **degrees**. Challenging opportunities include advanced placement, tutorials, Freshman Honors College, an honors program, a senior project, and Sigma Xi. Special programs include cooperative education, internships, summer session for credit, off-campus study, study abroad, and Air Force ROTC.

The most popular **majors** include engineering technology, electrical engineering, and mechanical engineering. A complete listing of majors at NJIT appears in the Majors Index beginning on page 379.

The **faculty** at NJIT has 348 full-time graduate and undergraduate teachers, 98% with terminal degrees. 100% of the faculty serve as student advisers. The student-faculty ratio is 14:1, and the average class size in core courses is 25.

 ## Computers on Campus

Students are required to have a computer. PCs are provided. Student rooms are linked to a campus network. 1,200 **computers** available in the computer center, computer labs, the research center, the learning resource center, classrooms, the library, the student center, dormitories, and student rooms provide access to the main academic computer, off-campus computing facilities, e-mail, on-line services, and the Internet. Staffed computer lab on campus provides training in the use of computers and software.

The 2 **libraries** have 157,000 books, 3,730 microform titles, and 1,129 subscriptions. They are connected to 2 national **on-line** catalogs.

 ## Campus Life

There are 50 active **organizations** on campus, including a drama/theater group and student-run newspaper and radio station. 15% of eligible men and 8% of eligible women are members of 10 national **fraternities**, 5 national **sororities**, 4 local fraternities, and 4 local sororities. Student **safety services** include bicycle patrols, sexual assault response team, late night transport/escort service, 24-hour emergency telephone alarm devices, 24-hour patrols by trained security personnel, and electronically operated dormitory entrances.

NJIT is a member of the NCAA (Division III). **Intercollegiate sports** include baseball (m), basketball (m, w), cross-country running (m, w), fencing (m, w), golf (m, w), soccer (m), softball (w), tennis (m, w), volleyball (m, w).

 ## Applying

NJIT requires a high school transcript, 4 years of high school math, SAT I or ACT, 1 SAT II Subject Test, and in some cases an essay and an interview. It recommends 3 years of high school science and 1 recommendation. Early and midyear entrance are possible, with a 4/1 deadline and continuous processing to 3/15 for financial aid. **Contact:** Ms. Kathy Kelly, Director of Admissions, University Heights, Newark, NJ 07102-1982, 201-596-3300 or toll-free 800-222-NJIT (in-state); fax 201-802-1854.

GETTING IN LAST YEAR
1,916 applied
67% were accepted
44% enrolled (564)
27% from top tenth of their h.s. class
12% had SAT verbal scores over 600
55% had SAT math scores over 600
2% had SAT verbal scores over 700
16% had SAT math scores over 700
3 valedictorians

THE STUDENT BODY
Total 7,885, of whom 5,042
   are undergraduates
From 19 states and territories,
   66 other countries

90% from New Jersey
18% women, 82% men
13% African Americans
2% Native Americans
13% Hispanics
18% Asian Americans
4% international students

AFTER FRESHMAN YEAR
85% returned for sophomore year
35% got a degree within 4 years
60% got a degree within 5 years
70% got a degree within 6 years

AFTER GRADUATION
20% pursued further study (12% engineering,
   3% arts and sciences, 2% business)
70% had job offers within 6 months
100 organizations recruited on campus

WHAT YOU WILL PAY
Resident tuition and fees $5220
Nonresident tuition and fees $9564
Room and board $4956
60% receive need-based financial aid
Need-based college-administered scholarships and
   grants average $682 per award
35% receive non-need financial aid
Non-need college-administered scholarships and
   grants average $1609 per award

NEW MEXICO INSTITUTE OF MINING AND TECHNOLOGY

Socorro, New Mexico • Small-town setting • Public • State-supported • Coed

New Mexico Tech is able to offer an exceptional education in science and engineering due in large part to its faculty. One recent graduate said, "Many of Tech's faculty are amazingly friendly, congenial, and humorous—characteristics cultivated by the informal Tech atmosphere. Here, students *know* professors. Most professors give their home phone numbers to students; they encourage questions. Tech's faculty and staff overall do an outstanding job of providing a good education." Faculty members bring research into their classrooms and employ students in their research labs; more than 50% of undergraduates work in research positions.

Academics

New Mexico Tech offers a science and engineering curriculum and core academic program; more than half of graduate courses are open to undergraduates. It awards associate, bachelor's, master's, and doctoral **degrees**. Challenging opportunities include advanced placement, self-designed majors, tutorials, a senior project, and Sigma Xi. Special programs include cooperative education, internships, summer session for credit, off-campus study, and study abroad.

The most popular **majors** include environmental engineering, electrical engineering, and physics. A complete listing of majors at New Mexico Tech appears in the Majors Index beginning on page 379.

The **faculty** at New Mexico Tech has 103 full-time graduate and undergraduate teachers, 96% with terminal degrees. 85% of the faculty serve as student advisers. The student-faculty ratio is 11:1, and the average class size in core courses is 23.

Computers on Campus

Students are not required to have a computer. Student rooms are linked to a campus network. 150 **computers** available in the computer center, computer labs, the research center, technical communications lab, most academic departments, classrooms, and the library provide access to off-campus computing facilities, e-mail, on-line services, and the Internet. Staffed computer lab on campus provides training in the use of computers and software.

The 2 **libraries** have 242,500 books, 180,000 microform titles, and 900 subscriptions. They are connected to 1 national **on-line** catalog.

Campus Life

There are 60 active **organizations** on campus, including a drama/theater group and student-run newspaper and radio station. 6% of students participate in student government elections. Student **safety services** include late night transport/escort service, 24-hour emergency telephone alarm devices, and 24-hour patrols by trained security personnel.

This institution has no intercollegiate sports.

Applying

New Mexico Tech requires a high school transcript, 3 years of high school math and science, some high school foreign language, SAT I or ACT, a minimum high school GPA of 2.0, and in some cases 2 recommendations. It recommends an interview and SAT II Subject Tests. Early, deferred, and midyear entrance are possible, with an 8/1 deadline and continuous processing to 3/1 for financial aid. **Contact:** Ms. Louise E. Chamberlin, Director of Admissions, Brown Hall, Socorro, NM 87801, 505-835-5424 or toll-free 800-428-TECH; fax 505-835-5989.

GETTING IN LAST YEAR
753 applied
74% were accepted
35% enrolled (195)
35% from top tenth of their h.s. class
3.3 average high school GPA
55% had ACT scores over 26
20% had ACT scores over 30
5 National Merit Scholars
7 valedictorians

THE STUDENT BODY
Total 1,494, of whom 1,251 are undergraduates

From 47 states and territories, 33 other countries
73% from New Mexico
36% women, 64% men
1% African Americans
3% Native Americans
19% Hispanics
3% Asian Americans
3% international students

AFTER FRESHMAN YEAR
65% returned for sophomore year
31% got a degree within 5 years
35% got a degree within 6 years

AFTER GRADUATION
32% pursued further study (20% arts and sciences, 10% engineering, 1% law)
28 organizations recruited on campus

WHAT YOU WILL PAY
Resident tuition and fees $1928
Nonresident tuition and fees $6206
Room and board $3426
50% receive need-based financial aid
Need-based college-administered scholarships and grants average $575 per award
47% receive non-need financial aid
Non-need college-administered scholarships and grants average $1681 per award

NEW YORK UNIVERSITY

New York, New York • Urban setting • Private • Independent • Coed

NYU is one of the most distinguished private universities in the United States—a world-renowned research university devoted to scholarship, teaching, and learning. The preeminence of its faculty, the extraordinary range and quality of its resources, and its interaction with New York City offer undergraduates the opportunity to learn and grow in an intellectual environment. University facilities include one of the largest open-stack research libraries in the nation; institutes famous for research in applied mathematics, physics, and fine arts; foreign language and cultural centers offering lectures, films, and concerts; art galleries and exhibition spaces; and advanced computer and recreational facilities.

 ## Academics

NYU offers a core academic program; fewer than half of graduate courses are open to undergraduates. It awards associate, bachelor's, master's, doctoral, and first professional **degrees**. Challenging opportunities include advanced placement, self-designed majors, tutorials, Freshman Honors College, an honors program, a senior project, Phi Beta Kappa, and Sigma Xi. Special programs include internships, summer session for credit, off-campus study, study abroad, and Air Force ROTC.

The most popular **majors** include business, theater arts/drama, and social science. A complete listing of majors at NYU appears in the Majors Index beginning on page 379.

The **faculty** at NYU has 1,305 full-time graduate and undergraduate teachers, 99% with terminal degrees. The student-faculty ratio is 13:1.

 ## Computers on Campus

Students are not required to have a computer. Student rooms are linked to a campus network. 859 **computers**

available in the computer center, computer labs, classrooms, the library, the student center, and dormitories provide access to the main academic computer, e-mail, on-line services, and the Internet. Staffed computer lab on campus (open 24 hours a day) provides training in the use of computers and software.

The 8 **libraries** have 3.6 million books, 3 million microform titles, and 29,244 subscriptions.

 ## Campus Life

There are 230 active **organizations** on campus, including a drama/theater group and student-run newspaper and radio station. 7% of eligible men and 6% of eligible women are members of 11 national **fraternities**, 3 national **sororities**, and 7 local sororities. Student **safety services** include 24-hour security in residence halls, late night transport/escort service, 24-hour emergency telephone alarm devices, 24-hour patrols by trained security personnel, student patrols, and electronically operated dormitory entrances.

NYU is a member of the NCAA (Division III). **Intercollegiate sports** include basketball (m, w), cross-country running (m, w), fencing (m, w), golf (m), soccer (m, w), swimming and diving (m, w), tennis (m, w), track and field (m, w), volleyball (m, w), wrestling (m).

 ## Applying

NYU requires an essay, a high school transcript, 3 years of high school math and science, 2 years of high school foreign language, 2 recommendations, SAT I or ACT, a minimum high school GPA of 3.0, and in some cases a campus interview and SAT II Subject Tests. It recommends SAT II Subject Tests. Early, deferred, and midyear entrance are possible, with a 1/15 deadline and a 2/15 priority date for financial aid. **Contact:** Director of Admissions, 22 Washington Square North, New York, NY 10012-1019, 212-998-4500; fax 212-995-4902.

GETTING IN LAST YEAR
16,491 applied
46% were accepted
38% enrolled (2,901)
49% from top tenth of their h.s. class
3.5 average high school GPA
75% had SAT verbal scores over 600 (R)
73% had SAT math scores over 600 (R)
22% had SAT verbal scores over 700 (R)
18% had SAT math scores over 700 (R)
72 National Merit Scholars

THE STUDENT BODY
Total 35,825, of whom 16,396
  are undergraduates

From 52 states and territories,
  120 other countries
60% from New York
59% women, 41% men
10% African Americans
0% Native Americans
8% Hispanics
19% Asian Americans
6% international students

AFTER FRESHMAN YEAR
88% returned for sophomore year

AFTER GRADUATION
73% pursued further study (38% arts and
  sciences, 14% medicine, 13% law)
70% had job offers within 6 months
400 organizations recruited on campus
5 Fulbright scholars

WHAT YOU WILL PAY
Tuition and fees $19,748
Room and board $7550
66% receive need-based financial aid
Need-based college-administered scholarships and
  grants average $6619 per award
Non-need college-administered scholarships and
  grants average $4200 per award

NORTH CAROLINA STATE UNIVERSITY

Raleigh, North Carolina • Suburban setting • Public • State-supported • Coed

Students select NCSU for its strong programs, outstanding academic reputation, location in the renowned Research Triangle Park area of North Carolina, low cost, and friendly atmosphere. Students from all 50 states and 97 other countries like the excitement of a large campus and the incredible opportunities it offers, such as cooperative education, study abroad, and extensive scholars programming. Each year hundreds of graduates are accepted into medical and law schools and other areas of professional study.

Academics

NC State offers an interdisciplinary curriculum and core academic program; fewer than half of graduate courses are open to undergraduates. It awards associate, bachelor's, master's, and doctoral **degrees**. Challenging opportunities include advanced placement, self-designed majors, tutorials, an honors program, a senior project, Phi Beta Kappa, and Sigma Xi. Special programs include cooperative education, internships, summer session for credit, off-campus study, study abroad, and Army, Naval, and Air Force ROTC.

The most popular **majors** include business, electrical engineering, and mechanical engineering. A complete listing of majors at NC State appears in the Majors Index beginning on page 379.

The **faculty** at NC State has 2,382 full-time graduate and undergraduate teachers, 92% with terminal degrees. 100% of the faculty serve as student advisers.

Computers on Campus

Students are not required to have a computer. Student rooms are linked to a campus network. 4,100 **computers** available in the computer center, computer labs, the research center, the learning resource center, classrooms, the library, the student center, and dormitories provide access to the main academic computer, off-campus computing facilities, e-mail, on-line services, and the Internet. Staffed computer lab on campus (open 24 hours a day) provides training in the use of computers and software.

The 5 **libraries** have 2.2 million books, 3.7 million microform titles, and 18,086 subscriptions. They are connected to 8 national **on-line** catalogs.

Campus Life

There are 300 active **organizations** on campus, including a drama/theater group and student-run newspaper and radio station. 30% of students participate in student government elections. 20% of eligible men and 22% of eligible women are members of 25 national **fraternities** and 10 national **sororities**. Student **safety services** include late night transport/escort service, 24-hour emergency telephone alarm devices, 24-hour patrols by trained security personnel, student patrols, and electronically operated dormitory entrances.

NC State is a member of the NCAA (Division I). **Intercollegiate sports** (some offering scholarships) include baseball (m), basketball (m, w), cross-country running (m, w), fencing (m, w), football (m), golf (m, w), gymnastics (m, w), ice hockey (m), lacrosse (m), racquetball (m, w), riflery (m, w), rugby (m, w), sailing (m, w), skiing (downhill) (m, w), soccer (m, w), swimming and diving (m, w), tennis (m, w), track and field (m, w), volleyball (m, w), water polo (m, w), weight lifting (m, w), wrestling (m).

Applying

NC State requires a high school transcript, 3 years of high school math and science, 2 years of high school foreign language, 4 years of high school English, 2 years of high school social studies, SAT I or ACT, SAT II Subject Test in math, and in some cases recommendations and an interview. It recommends an essay and a minimum high school GPA of 3.0. Early and midyear entrance are possible, with a 2/1 deadline and continuous processing to 3/1 for financial aid. **Contact:** Dr. George R. Dixon, Director of Admissions, Box 7103, 112 Peele Hall, Raleigh, NC 27695, 919-515-2434; fax 919-515-5039.

GETTING IN LAST YEAR

11,233 applied
63% were accepted
50% enrolled (3,528)
57% from top tenth of their h.s. class
3.67 average high school GPA
36% had SAT verbal scores over 600 (R)
38% had SAT math scores over 600 (R)
69% had ACT scores over 26
1% had SAT verbal scores over 700 (R)
2% had SAT math scores over 700 (R)
14% had ACT scores over 30
34 National Merit Scholars
98 class presidents
375 valedictorians

THE STUDENT BODY

Total 27,537, of whom 18,821
  are undergraduates

From 52 states and territories,
  97 other countries
82% from North Carolina
42% women, 58% men
12% African Americans
1% Native Americans
2% Hispanics
3% Asian Americans
4% international students

AFTER FRESHMAN YEAR

91% returned for sophomore year
34% got a degree within 4 years
67% got a degree within 5 years
80% got a degree within 6 years

AFTER GRADUATION

29% pursued further study (12% business, 8% engineering, 4% medicine)

70% had job offers within 6 months
475 organizations recruited on campus
2 Fulbright scholars

WHAT YOU WILL PAY

Resident tuition and fees $1686
Nonresident tuition and fees $9848
Room and board $3856
44% receive need-based financial aid
Need-based college-administered scholarships and
  grants average $890 per award
Non-need college-administered scholarships and
  grants average $1737 per award

NORTH CENTRAL COLLEGE

Naperville, Illinois • Suburban setting • Private • Independent-Religious • Coed

Located 29 miles west of Chicago and in the Illinois Research and Development Corridor, North Central College provides unlimited internship and career opportunities. NCC is a comprehensive college that offers more than 50 areas of concentration in preprofessional, liberal arts, and science disciplines. A student-faculty ratio of 14:1 facilitates personalized study, while the Leadership, Ethics, and Values Program provides a unique educational philosophy. Cocurricular opportunities include community service, mock trial, Model UN, performing arts, Students in Free Enterprise, student government, forensics, the radio station, campus ministry, and Division III varsity athletics. More than 90% of freshmen receive some type of financial assistance.

Academics

North Central offers a leadership curriculum and core academic program; more than half of graduate courses are open to undergraduates. It awards bachelor's and master's **degrees**. Challenging opportunities include advanced placement, accelerated degree programs, self-designed majors, tutorials, an honors program, and a senior project. Special programs include cooperative education, internships, summer session for credit, off-campus study, study abroad, and Army, Naval, and Air Force ROTC.

The most popular **majors** include business, broadcasting, and computer science. A complete listing of majors at North Central appears in the Majors Index beginning on page 379.

The **faculty** at North Central has 100 full-time graduate and undergraduate teachers, 87% with terminal degrees. 100% of the faculty serve as student advisers. The student-faculty ratio is 14:1.

Computers on Campus

Students are not required to have a computer. Student rooms are linked to a campus network. 110 **computers** available in the computer center, computer labs, the library, and dormitories provide access to the main academic computer, e-mail, and the Internet. Staffed computer lab on campus provides training in the use of computers and software.

The **library** has 116,503 books and 664 subscriptions. It is connected to 1 national **on-line** catalog.

Campus Life

Active **organizations** on campus include drama/theater group and student-run newspaper and radio station. Student **safety services** include late night transport/escort service.

North Central is a member of the NCAA (Division III). **Intercollegiate sports** include baseball (m), basketball (m, w), cross-country running (m, w), football (m), golf (m, w), soccer (m), softball (w), swimming and diving (m, w), tennis (m, w), track and field (m, w), volleyball (w), wrestling (m).

Applying

North Central requires a high school transcript, SAT I or ACT, a minimum high school GPA of 2.0, and in some cases an interview. It recommends an essay, 3 years of high school math and science, some high school foreign language, and recommendations. Early, deferred, and midyear entrance are possible, with rolling admissions and continuous processing to 7/1 for financial aid. **Contact:** Mr. Fred A. Schebor, Dean of Admission, 30 North Brainard Street, Naperville, IL 60566-7063, 708-420-3414.

GETTING IN LAST YEAR
1,103 applied
81% were accepted
37% enrolled (330)
24% from top tenth of their h.s. class
19% had SAT verbal scores over 600
50% had SAT math scores over 600
39% had ACT scores over 26
2% had SAT verbal scores over 700
10% had SAT math scores over 700
9% had ACT scores over 30

THE STUDENT BODY
Total 2,489, of whom 1,682
  are undergraduates

From 23 states and territories,
  8 other countries,
87% from Illinois
54% women, 46% men
4% African Americans
3% Hispanics
3% Asian Americans
1% international students

AFTER FRESHMAN YEAR
76% returned for sophomore year
50% got a degree within 4 years
55% got a degree within 5 years

AFTER GRADUATION
12% pursued further study
87% had job offers within 6 months
25 organizations recruited on campus
1 Fulbright scholar

WHAT YOU WILL PAY
Tuition and fees $12,633
Room and board $4692
Need-based college-administered scholarships and
  grants average $3722 per award
Non-need college-administered scholarships and
  grants average $4407 per award

NORTHWESTERN COLLEGE

Orange City, Iowa • Rural setting • Private • Independent-Religious • Coed

Academics

Northwestern offers a Western civilization and interdisciplinary curriculum and core academic program. It awards associate and bachelor's **degrees**. Challenging opportunities include advanced placement, accelerated degree programs, self-designed majors, an honors program, and a senior project. Special programs include cooperative education, internships, summer session for credit, off-campus study, and study abroad.

The most popular **majors** include business, elementary education, and biology/biological sciences. A complete listing of majors at Northwestern appears in the Majors Index beginning on page 379.

The **faculty** at Northwestern has 61 full-time teachers, 70% with terminal degrees. 98% of the faculty serve as student advisers. The student-faculty ratio is 16:1.

Computers on Campus

Students are not required to have a computer. Student rooms are linked to a campus network. 180 **computers** available in the computer center, the learning resource center, Demco Business Center, Kresge Education Center, classrooms, the library, and dormitories provide access to the main academic computer, e-mail, on-line services, and the Internet. Staffed computer lab on campus provides training in the use of computers and software.

The 2 **libraries** have 108,000 books, 3,500 microform titles, and 500 subscriptions.

Campus Life

There are 30 active **organizations** on campus, including a drama/theater group and student-run newspaper and radio station. 65% of students participate in student government elections. Student **safety services** include 24-hour emergency telephone alarm devices and electronically operated dormitory entrances.

Northwestern is a member of the NAIA. **Intercollegiate sports** (some offering scholarships) include baseball (m), basketball (m, w), cross-country running (m, w), football (m), golf (m, w), soccer (m, w), softball (w), tennis (m, w), track and field (m, w), volleyball (w), wrestling (m).

Applying

Northwestern requires a high school transcript, 1 recommendation, and SAT I or ACT. It recommends 3 years of high school math and science and an interview. Deferred and midyear entrance are possible, with rolling admissions and continuous processing to 4/1 for financial aid.
Contact: Mr. Ronald K. DeJong, Director of Admissions, 101 College Lane, Orange City, IA 51041-1996, 712-737-7000 or toll-free 800-747-4757 (in-state); fax 712-737-7164.

GETTING IN LAST YEAR
1,113 applied
92% were accepted
39% enrolled (405)
28% from top tenth of their h.s. class
3.2 average high school GPA
28% had ACT scores over 26
4% had ACT scores over 30

THE STUDENT BODY
1,198 undergraduates
From 23 states and territories,
   13 other countries

65% from Iowa
57% women, 43% men
1% African Americans
1% Native Americans
1% Hispanics
1% Asian Americans
4% international students

AFTER FRESHMAN YEAR
89% returned for sophomore year
37% got a degree within 4 years
46% got a degree within 5 years
49% got a degree within 6 years

AFTER GRADUATION
13% pursued further study (7% theology, 3% medicine, 2% business)
93% had job offers within 6 months

WHAT YOU WILL PAY
Tuition and fees $10,400
Room and board $3175
82% receive need-based financial aid
Need-based college-administered scholarships and grants average $2120 per award
20% receive non-need financial aid
Non-need college-administered scholarships and grants average $2250 per award

NORTHWESTERN UNIVERSITY

Evanston, Illinois • Suburban setting • Private • Independent • Coed

Northwestern, on the shore of Lake Michigan just north of Chicago, combines the accessibility of 6 small colleges with the resources and opportunities of a major university. The College of Arts and Sciences, the Schools of Education and Social Policy, of Music, and of Speech; the Medill School of Journalism; and the McCormick School of Engineering and Applied Science offer a sound foundation in the liberal arts as an integral part of a student's education. Northwestern's 7,500 undergraduates come from 49 states and a variety of backgrounds. Fifty-one percent are women, and approximately 29 percent are minority group members.

 Academics

Northwestern offers a core academic program; fewer than half of graduate courses are open to undergraduates. It awards bachelor's, master's, doctoral, and first professional **degrees**. Challenging opportunities include advanced placement, accelerated degree programs, self-designed majors, tutorials, an honors program, a senior project, Phi Beta Kappa, and Sigma Xi. Special programs include cooperative education, internships, summer session for credit, off-campus study, study abroad, and Army, Naval, and Air Force ROTC.

The most popular **majors** include economics, political science/government, and journalism. A complete listing of majors at Northwestern appears in the Majors Index beginning on page 379.

The **faculty** at Northwestern has 1,831 full-time undergraduate teachers, 100% with terminal degrees. 100% of the faculty serve as student advisers.

 Computers on Campus

Students are not required to have a computer. Student rooms are linked to a campus network. 530 **computers**

available in the computer center, academic buildings, the library, the student center, and dormitories provide access to the main academic computer, e-mail, on-line services, and the Internet. Staffed computer lab on campus provides training in the use of computers and software.

The 11 **libraries** have 3.7 million books, 2.9 million microform titles, and 38,626 subscriptions. They are connected to 15 national **on-line** catalogs.

 Campus Life

There are 250 active **organizations** on campus, including a drama/theater group and student-run newspaper and radio station. 35% of students participate in student government elections. 40% of eligible men and 39% of eligible women are members of 21 national **fraternities** and 11 national **sororities**. Student **safety services** include late night transport/escort service, 24-hour emergency telephone alarm devices, 24-hour patrols by trained security personnel, and electronically operated dormitory entrances.

Northwestern is a member of the NCAA (Division I). **Intercollegiate sports** (some offering scholarships) include baseball (m), basketball (m, w), fencing (w), field hockey (w), football (m), golf (m, w), soccer (m, w), softball (w), swimming and diving (m, w), tennis (m, w), volleyball (w), wrestling (m).

 Applying

Northwestern requires an essay, a high school transcript, 1 recommendation, SAT I or ACT, and in some cases an audition for music majors and SAT II Subject Tests. It recommends 3 years of high school math and science, 2 years of high school foreign language, and an interview. Early, deferred, and midyear entrance are possible, with a 1/1 deadline and continuous processing to 2/15 for financial aid. **Contact:** Ms. Carol Lunkenheimer, Director of Admissions, 1801 Hinman Avenue, Evanston, IL 60208, 847-491-7271.

GETTING IN LAST YEAR
12,918 applied
40% were accepted
38% enrolled (1,950)
81% from top tenth of their h.s. class
86% had SAT verbal scores over 600 (R)
89% had SAT math scores over 600 (R)
90% had ACT scores over 26
32% had SAT verbal scores over 700 (R)
39% had SAT math scores over 700 (R)
52% had ACT scores over 30
118 National Merit Scholars

THE STUDENT BODY
Total 12,196, of whom 7,570
  are undergraduates
From 49 states and territories,
  42 other countries
25% from Illinois
51% women, 49% men
6% African Americans
1% Native Americans
3% Hispanics
19% Asian Americans
3% international students

AFTER FRESHMAN YEAR
96% returned for sophomore year

AFTER GRADUATION
39% pursued further study
3 Fulbright scholars

WHAT YOU WILL PAY
Tuition and fees $17,184
Room and board $5781
56% receive need-based financial aid
Need-based college-administered scholarships and
  grants average $9150 per award

OBERLIN COLLEGE

Oberlin, Ohio • Small-town setting • Private • Independent • Coed

As long as there has been an Oberlin, Oberlinians have been changing the world. Oberlin was the first coeducational school in the United States and a historic leader in educating African American students. Among primarily undergraduate institutions, Oberlin ranks first for the number of students who go on to earn PhD degrees. Its alumni, who include 3 Nobel laureates, are leaders in law, scientific and scholarly research, medicine, the arts, theology, communication, business, and government. Oberlin also offers a 5-year double-degree program, combining studies at the Conservatory of Music and the College of Arts and Sciences.

 Academics

Oberlin offers a liberal arts curriculum and no core academic program; a few graduate courses are open to undergraduates. It awards bachelor's **degrees.** Challenging opportunities include advanced placement, self-designed majors, tutorials, an honors program, a senior project, Phi Beta Kappa, and Sigma Xi. Special programs include internships, off-campus study, and study abroad.

The most popular **majors** include English, biology/biological sciences, and history. A complete listing of majors at Oberlin appears in the Majors Index beginning on page 379.

The **faculty** at Oberlin has 175 full-time teachers, 95% with terminal degrees. 100% of the faculty serve as student advisers. The student-faculty ratio is 12:1.

 Computers on Campus

Students are not required to have a computer. Student rooms are linked to a campus network. 240 **computers** available in the computer center, classrooms, the library, the student center, and dormitories provide access to the main academic computer, off-campus computing facilities, e-mail, on-line services, and the Internet. Staffed computer lab on campus provides training in the use of computers and software.

The 4 **libraries** have 1.1 million books, 327,428 microform titles, and 2,759 subscriptions.

 Campus Life

There are 100 active **organizations** on campus, including a drama/theater group and student-run newspaper and radio station. Student **safety services** include crime prevention programs, late night transport/escort service, 24-hour emergency telephone alarm devices, 24-hour patrols by trained security personnel, and electronically operated dormitory entrances.

Oberlin is a member of the NCAA (Division III). **Intercollegiate sports** include baseball (m), basketball (m, w), cross-country running (m, w), equestrian sports (m, w), fencing (m, w), field hockey (w), football (m), ice hockey (m), lacrosse (m, w), racquetball (m, w), rugby (m, w), soccer (m, w), softball (w), squash (m, w), swimming and diving (m, w), tennis (m, w), track and field (m, w), volleyball (m, w), water polo (m).

 Applying

Oberlin requires an essay, a high school transcript, 2 recommendations, and SAT I or ACT. It recommends 4 years of high school math, 3 years of high school science, 3 years of high school foreign language, an interview, and 3 SAT II Subject Tests. Early, deferred, and midyear entrance are possible, with a 1/15 deadline and continuous processing to 2/15 for financial aid. **Contact:** Ms. Debra Chermonte, Director of College Admissions, 101 North Professor Street, Oberlin, OH 44074-1090, 216-775-8411 or toll-free 800-622-OBIE.

GETTING IN LAST YEAR

3,728 applied
72% were accepted
25% enrolled (668)
50% from top tenth of their h.s. class
3.46 average high school GPA
83% had SAT verbal scores over 600 (R)
76% had SAT math scores over 600 (R)
78% had ACT scores over 26
36% had SAT verbal scores over 700 (R)
17% had SAT math scores over 700 (R)
33% had ACT scores over 30
30 National Merit Scholars
24 valedictorians

THE STUDENT BODY

2,823 undergraduates
From 51 states and territories,
  45 other countries
9% from Ohio
58% women, 42% men
8% African Americans
1% Native Americans
4% Hispanics
10% Asian Americans
5% international students

AFTER FRESHMAN YEAR

89% returned for sophomore year
81% got a degree within 6 years

AFTER GRADUATION

34% pursued further study
1 Fulbright scholar

WHAT YOU WILL PAY

Tuition and fees $20,746
Room and board $5970
55% receive need-based financial aid
Need-based college-administered scholarships and
  grants average $12,618 per award
5% receive non-need financial aid
Non-need college-administered scholarships and
  grants average $4446 per award

OCCIDENTAL COLLEGE

Los Angeles, California • Urban setting • Private • Independent • Coed

Occidental College offers abundant opportunities for students to live and learn within a community of scholars dedicated to providing leadership for an increasingly complex and global society. Since its founding in 1887, Occidental College has been committed to education in the best tradition of liberal arts. The College encourages a broad understanding of many fields of knowledge, erasing boundaries of subjects as one comes to realize the relationships among them and providing a foundation for lifelong learning. Students and faculty alike are willing to consider new ideas with an open mind and an enthusiasm for the ideals of multiculturalism that is the hallmark of the "Oxy" experience.

Academics

Occidental offers an interdisciplinary curriculum and core academic program; a few graduate courses are open to undergraduates. It awards bachelor's and master's **degrees**. Challenging opportunities include advanced placement, self-designed majors, tutorials, an honors program, a senior project, and Phi Beta Kappa. Special programs include internships, summer session for credit, off-campus study, study abroad, and Army, Naval, and Air Force ROTC.

The most popular **majors** include psychology, English, and biology/biological sciences. A complete listing of majors at Occidental appears in the Majors Index beginning on page 379.

The **faculty** at Occidental has 141 full-time undergraduate teachers, 96% with terminal degrees. 94% of the faculty serve as student advisers. The student-faculty ratio is 11:1.

Computers on Campus

Students are not required to have a computer. Student rooms are linked to a campus network. 100 **computers** available in the computer center, computer labs, the research center, the learning resource center, classrooms, the library, and dormitories provide access to e-mail and the Internet. Staffed computer lab on campus.

The 3 **libraries** have 458,680 books, 394,026 microform titles, and 1,317 subscriptions. They are connected to 8 national **on-line** catalogs.

Campus Life

There are 80 active **organizations** on campus, including a drama/theater group and student-run newspaper and radio station. 15% of eligible men and 15% of eligible women are members of 3 national **fraternities** and 3 local **sororities**. Student **safety services** include community policing services, late night transport/escort service, 24-hour emergency telephone alarm devices, 24-hour patrols by trained security personnel, student patrols, and electronically operated dormitory entrances.

Occidental is a member of the NCAA (Division III) and NAIA. **Intercollegiate sports** include badminton (m, w), baseball (m), basketball (m, w), cross-country running (m, w), equestrian sports (m, w), fencing (m, w), field hockey (w), football (m), golf (m, w), lacrosse (m, w), rugby (m), skiing (downhill) (m, w), soccer (m, w), softball (w), swimming and diving (m, w), tennis (m, w), track and field (m, w), volleyball (m, w), water polo (m, w).

Applying

Occidental requires an essay, a high school transcript, 2 years of high school foreign language, 3 recommendations, and SAT I or ACT. It recommends 3 years of high school math and science, an interview, and SAT II Subject Tests. Early and deferred entrance are possible, with a 1/15 deadline and 2/1 for financial aid. **Contact:** Mr. Thomas A. Matos, Dean of Admissions, 1600 Campus Road, Los Angeles, CA 90041-3392, 213-259-2700 or toll-free 800-825-5262; fax 213-259-2958.

GETTING IN LAST YEAR
2,086 applied
66% were accepted
29% enrolled (407)
56% from top tenth of their h.s. class
21% had SAT verbal scores over 600
51% had SAT math scores over 600
3% had SAT verbal scores over 700
13% had SAT math scores over 700
6 National Merit Scholars
19 valedictorians

THE STUDENT BODY
Total 1,617, of whom 1,580 are undergraduates

From 42 states and territories, 23 other countries
64% from California
57% women, 43% men
6% African Americans
1% Native Americans
20% Hispanics
18% Asian Americans
5% international students

AFTER FRESHMAN YEAR
92% returned for sophomore year
67% got a degree within 4 years
70% got a degree within 5 years
71% got a degree within 6 years

AFTER GRADUATION
50% pursued further study (25% arts and sciences, 9% medicine, 6% law)
35% had job offers within 6 months
62 organizations recruited on campus

WHAT YOU WILL PAY
Tuition and fees $17,992
Room and board $5660
62% receive need-based financial aid
Need-based college-administered scholarships and grants average $12,788 per award
13% receive non-need financial aid
Non-need college-administered scholarships and grants average $5876 per award

OGLETHORPE UNIVERSITY

Atlanta, Georgia • Suburban setting • Private • Independent • Coed

It's not just the rigorous academic program, the small class discussions, and the motivating professors that make Oglethorpe different. It's the location—near the center of one of the country's most exciting, dynamic, international cities—Atlanta. A revamped honors program and a dynamic Urban Leadership Program are gaining much recognition from city leaders as Oglethorpe helps connect students to the rich resources of Atlanta. Internships are available in virtually every major and are very popular among the student body.

 Academics

Oglethorpe offers a primary sources curriculum and core academic program; more than half of graduate courses are open to undergraduates. It awards bachelor's and master's **degrees**. Challenging opportunities include advanced placement, accelerated degree programs, self-designed majors, tutorials, an honors program, and a senior project. Special programs include cooperative education, internships, summer session for credit, off-campus study, study abroad, and Army and Air Force ROTC.

The most popular **majors** include business, psychology, and accounting. A complete listing of majors at Oglethorpe appears in the Majors Index beginning on page 379.

The **faculty** at Oglethorpe has 48 full-time graduate and undergraduate teachers, 95% with terminal degrees. 100% of the faculty serve as student advisers. The student-faculty ratio is 10:1, and the average class size in core courses is 22.

 Computers on Campus

Students are not required to have a computer. 57 **computers** available in the computer center, computer labs, and the library provide access to the Internet. Staffed computer lab on campus.

The **library** has 113,529 books, 2 microform titles, and 732 subscriptions. It is connected to 1 national **on-line** catalog.

 Campus Life

There are 40 active **organizations** on campus, including a drama/theater group and student-run newspaper and radio station. 38% of eligible men and 25% of eligible women are members of 4 national **fraternities** and 2 national **sororities**. Student **safety services** include late night transport/escort service, 24-hour emergency telephone alarm devices, 24-hour patrols by trained security personnel, student patrols, and electronically operated dormitory entrances.

Oglethorpe is a member of the NCAA (Division III). **Intercollegiate sports** include baseball (m), basketball (m, w), cross-country running (m, w), golf (m), soccer (m, w), tennis (m, w), track and field (m, w), volleyball (w).

 Applying

Oglethorpe requires an essay, a high school transcript, 3 years of high school math, 1 recommendation, SAT I or ACT, and in some cases an interview. It recommends 3 years of high school science, some high school foreign language, an interview, and minimum 2.5 GPA. Early, deferred, and midyear entrance are possible, with an 8/1 deadline and continuous processing to 3/1 for financial aid. **Contact:** Mr. Dennis T. Matthews, Associate Dean for Enrollment Management, 4484 Peachtree Road, NE, Atlanta, GA 30319-2797, 404-364-8307 or toll-free 800-428-4484; fax 404-364-8500.

GETTING IN LAST YEAR
671 applied
81% were accepted
35% enrolled (193)
43% from top tenth of their h.s. class
3.62 average high school GPA
58% had SAT verbal scores over 600 (R)
42% had SAT math scores over 600 (R)
60% had ACT scores over 26
15% had SAT verbal scores over 700 (R)
6% had SAT math scores over 700 (R)
14% had ACT scores over 30
5 National Merit Scholars
5 class presidents
7 valedictorians

THE STUDENT BODY
Total 1,313, of whom 1,260
  are undergraduates
From 31 states and territories,
  30 other countries
49% from Georgia
56% women, 44% men
4% African Americans
1% Native Americans
3% Hispanics
5% Asian Americans
7% international students

AFTER FRESHMAN YEAR
80% returned for sophomore year
45% got a degree within 4 years

51% got a degree within 5 years
53% got a degree within 6 years

AFTER GRADUATION
35% pursued further study (15% business, 12% arts and sciences, 5% medicine)

WHAT YOU WILL PAY
Tuition and fees $14,030
Room and board $4650
66% receive need-based financial aid
Need-based college-administered scholarships and grants average $3034 per award
89% receive non-need financial aid
Non-need college-administered scholarships and grants average $6412 per award

OHIO NORTHERN UNIVERSITY

Ada, Ohio • Small-town setting • Private • Independent-Religious • Coed

National recognition, small classes, excellent facilities, strong faculty members who teach all classes, and a rich and diverse curriculum are just some of the features that set Ohio Northern apart from other colleges in the Midwest. But what truly makes ONU unique is its students. They reflect the value of service to others, which is the product of the individual attention they receive from the faculty, staff, and administration of ONU.

 Academics

Ohio Northern offers no core academic program; a few graduate courses are open to undergraduates. It awards bachelor's and first professional **degrees**. Challenging opportunities include advanced placement, tutorials, a senior project, and Sigma Xi. Special programs include cooperative education, internships, summer session for credit, study abroad, and Army and Air Force ROTC.

The most popular **majors** include pharmacy/pharmaceutical sciences, mechanical engineering, and elementary education. A complete listing of majors at Ohio Northern appears in the Majors Index beginning on page 379.

The **faculty** at Ohio Northern has 178 full-time graduate and undergraduate teachers, 79% with terminal degrees. 95% of the faculty serve as student advisers. The student-faculty ratio is 13:1.

Computers on Campus

Students are not required to have a computer. Student rooms are linked to a campus network. 324 **computers** available in the computer center, computer labs, academic buildings, the library, and dormitories provide access to the main academic computer, off-campus computing facilities, e-mail, on-line services, and the Internet. Staffed computer lab on campus.

The 2 **libraries** have 416,673 books, 88,725 microform titles, and 4,248 subscriptions. They are connected to 2 national **on-line** catalogs.

Campus Life

There are 25 active **organizations** on campus, including a drama/theater group and student-run newspaper and radio station. 30% of eligible men and 30% of eligible women are members of 8 national **fraternities** and 5 national **sororities**. Student **safety services** include late night transport/escort service, 24-hour emergency telephone alarm devices, 24-hour patrols by trained security personnel, and electronically operated dormitory entrances.

Ohio Northern is a member of the NCAA (Division III). **Intercollegiate sports** include baseball (m), basketball (m, w), cross-country running (m, w), football (m), golf (m), soccer (m, w), softball (w), swimming and diving (m, w), tennis (m, w), track and field (m, w), volleyball (w), wrestling (m).

Applying

Ohio Northern requires a high school transcript, 3 years of high school math, and SAT I or ACT. It recommends an essay, 3 years of high school science, 2 years of high school foreign language, recommendations, and a campus interview. Early, deferred, and midyear entrance are possible, with an 8/15 deadline and continuous processing to 5/1 for financial aid. **Contact:** Ms. Karen Condeni, Dean of Admissions and Financial Aid, Lehr Memorial Building, Ada, OH 45810, 419-772-2260; fax 419-772-2313.

GETTING IN LAST YEAR
2,253 applied
48% were accepted
68% enrolled (737)
41% from top tenth of their h.s. class
3.4 average high school GPA
34% had ACT scores over 26
7% had ACT scores over 30
56 valedictorians

THE STUDENT BODY
Total 2,997, of whom 2,642
  are undergraduates
From 36 states and territories,
  23 other countries

86% from Ohio
49% women, 51% men
3% African Americans
1% Hispanics
1% Asian Americans
3% international students

AFTER FRESHMAN YEAR
81% returned for sophomore year
33% got a degree within 4 years
60% got a degree within 5 years
65% got a degree within 6 years

AFTER GRADUATION
16% pursued further study (6% arts and
  sciences, 3% law, 2% engineering)
192 organizations recruited on campus

WHAT YOU WILL PAY
Tuition and fees $17,970
Room and board $4500
78% receive need-based financial aid
Need-based college-administered scholarships and
  grants average $6860 per award
22% receive non-need financial aid
Non-need college-administered scholarships and
  grants average $5520 per award

THE OHIO STATE UNIVERSITY

Columbus, Ohio • Urban setting • Public • State-supported • Coed

More students choose Ohio State than any other single-campus university in the country. Ohio State offers nearly 200 major areas of study, more than 11,000 courses, and over 500 student organizations. As the state's leading center for teaching, research, and public service, it has the faculty, facilities, academic programs, and support services that few universities can match. Ohio State continues to attract a competitive student body, and its tuition costs and fees are also competitive.

Academics

Ohio State offers a core academic program; more than half of graduate courses are open to undergraduates. It awards associate, bachelor's, master's, doctoral, and first professional **degrees**. Challenging opportunities include advanced placement, accelerated degree programs, self-designed majors, tutorials, an honors program, a senior project, Phi Beta Kappa, and Sigma Xi. Special programs include cooperative education, internships, summer session for credit, off-campus study, study abroad, and Army, Naval, and Air Force ROTC.

The most popular **majors** include elementary education, psychology, and journalism. A complete listing of majors at Ohio State appears in the Majors Index beginning on page 379.

The **faculty** at Ohio State has 2,827 full-time graduate and undergraduate teachers. The student-faculty ratio is 13:1.

Computers on Campus

Students are not required to have a computer. 1,110 **computers** available in the computer center, computer labs, the research center, the learning resource center, labs, the library, the student center, and dormitories provide access to e-mail. Staffed computer lab on campus.

The 51 **libraries** have 4.9 million books, 4 million microform titles, and 33,368 subscriptions. They are connected to 5 national **on-line** catalogs.

Campus Life

There are 550 active **organizations** on campus, including a drama/theater group and student-run newspaper and radio station. 11% of eligible men and 12% of eligible women are members of 39 national **fraternities** and 24 national **sororities**. Student **safety services** include late night transport/escort service, 24-hour emergency telephone alarm devices, 24-hour patrols by trained security personnel, and student patrols.

Ohio State is a member of the NCAA (Division I). **Intercollegiate sports** (some offering scholarships) include baseball (m), basketball (m, w), cross-country running (m, w), fencing (m, w), field hockey (w), football (m), golf (m, w), gymnastics (m, w), ice hockey (m), lacrosse (m), riflery (m, w), soccer (m, w), softball (w), swimming and diving (m, w), tennis (m, w), track and field (m, w), volleyball (m, w), wrestling (m).

Applying

Ohio State requires a high school transcript, 3 years of high school math, 2 years of high school foreign language, 2 years each of natural science and social science, 1 year of visual/performing arts, 4 years of English, and SAT I or ACT. It recommends 3 years of high school science and recommendations. Early and midyear entrance are possible, with a 2/15 deadline and continuous processing to 2/15 for financial aid. **Contact:** Ms. Lori Faur, Admissions Information and Application Requests, 3rd Floor, Lincoln Tower, Columbus, OH 43210, 614-292-3980; fax 614-292-4818.

GETTING IN LAST YEAR
15,887 applied
90% were accepted
41% enrolled (5,794)
21% from top tenth of their h.s. class
30% had SAT verbal scores over 600 (R)
35% had SAT math scores over 600 (R)
26% had ACT scores over 26
6% had SAT verbal scores over 700 (R)
7% had SAT math scores over 700 (R)
7% had ACT scores over 30
96 National Merit Scholars
150 valedictorians

THE STUDENT BODY
Total 48,676, of whom 35,475
 are undergraduates
From 54 states and territories,
 78 other countries
91% from Ohio
47% women, 53% men
7% African Americans
1% Native Americans
2% Hispanics
5% Asian Americans
4% international students

AFTER FRESHMAN YEAR
77% returned for sophomore year
21% got a degree within 4 years
51% got a degree within 5 years
59% got a degree within 6 years

WHAT YOU WILL PAY
Resident tuition and fees $3273
Nonresident tuition and fees $9813
Room and board $4668
Need-based college-administered scholarships and
 grants average $4422 per award

OHIO UNIVERSITY

Athens, Ohio • Small-town setting • Public • State-supported • Coed

Chartered in 1804, Ohio University symbolizes America's early commitment to higher education. Its historic campus provides a setting matched by only a handful of other universities in the country. Students choose Ohio University mainly because of its academic strength, but the beautiful setting and college-town atmosphere are also factors in their decision. Ohio University is the central focus of Athens, Ohio, located approximately 75 miles southeast of Columbus. The University encourages prospective students to come for a visit and experience its beauty and academic excellence.

Academics

OU offers a core academic program; a few graduate courses are open to undergraduates. It awards associate, bachelor's, master's, doctoral, and first professional **degrees**. Challenging opportunities include advanced placement, accelerated degree programs, self-designed majors, tutorials, an honors program, a senior project, Phi Beta Kappa, and Sigma Xi. Special programs include cooperative education, internships, summer session for credit, study abroad, and Army and Air Force ROTC.

The most popular **majors** include education, communication, and psychology. A complete listing of majors at OU appears in the Majors Index beginning on page 379.

The **faculty** at OU has 887 full-time graduate and undergraduate teachers, 93% with terminal degrees. 100% of the faculty serve as student advisers. The student-faculty ratio is 18:1, and the average class size in core courses is 26.

Computers on Campus

Students are not required to have a computer. Student rooms are linked to a campus network. 903 **computers** available in the computer center, computer labs, classroom buildings, the library, the student center, and dormitories provide access to the main academic computer, off-campus computing facilities, e-mail, on-line services, and the Internet. Staffed computer lab on campus (open 24 hours a day) provides training in the use of computers and software.

The **library** has 1.7 million books, 2.3 million microform titles, and 11,600 subscriptions. It is connected to 6 national **on-line** catalogs.

Campus Life

There are 338 active **organizations** on campus, including a drama/theater group and student-run newspaper and radio station. 11% of eligible men and 16% of eligible women are members of 19 national **fraternities** and 12 national **sororities**. Student **safety services** include security lighting, late night transport/escort service, 24-hour emergency telephone alarm devices, 24-hour patrols by trained security personnel, and electronically operated dormitory entrances.

OU is a member of the NCAA (Division I). **Intercollegiate sports** (some offering scholarships) include baseball (m), basketball (m, w), cross-country running (m, w), equestrian sports (m, w), field hockey (w), football (m), golf (m), ice hockey (m), lacrosse (m, w), rugby (m, w), soccer (m, w), softball (w), swimming and diving (m, w), track and field (m, w), volleyball (m, w), water polo (m), weight lifting (m), wrestling (m).

Applying

OU requires a high school transcript and SAT I or ACT. It recommends an essay, 3 years of high school math and science, 2 years of high school foreign language, 2 recommendations, and an interview. Early, deferred, and midyear entrance are possible, with a 2/1 deadline and continuous processing to 3/15 for financial aid. **Contact:** Mr. N. Kip Howard, Director of Admissions, 120 Chubb Hall, Athens, OH 45701-2979, 614-593-4100; fax 614-593-0560.

GETTING IN LAST YEAR
11,746 applied
72% were accepted
40% enrolled (3,415)
19% from top tenth of their h.s. class
3.2 average high school GPA
29% had SAT verbal scores over 600 (R)
29% had SAT math scores over 600 (R)
26% had ACT scores over 26
4% had SAT verbal scores over 700 (R)
3% had SAT math scores over 700 (R)
4% had ACT scores over 30
10 National Merit Scholars
62 valedictorians

THE STUDENT BODY
Total 19,143, of whom 16,271 are undergraduates

From 52 states and territories, 100 other countries
89% from Ohio
54% women, 46% men
4% African Americans
1% Native Americans
1% Hispanics
1% Asian Americans
2% international students

AFTER FRESHMAN YEAR
84% returned for sophomore year
55% got a degree within 4 years
69% got a degree within 5 years
70% got a degree within 6 years

AFTER GRADUATION
79% had job offers within 6 months

450 organizations recruited on campus
1 Fulbright scholar

WHAT YOU WILL PAY
Resident tuition and fees $3666
Nonresident tuition and fees $7905
Room and board $4260
43% receive need-based financial aid
Need-based college-administered scholarships and grants average $1738 per award
30% receive non-need financial aid
Non-need college-administered scholarships and grants average $4166 per award

OHIO WESLEYAN UNIVERSITY

Delaware, Ohio • Small-town setting • Private • Independent-Religious • Coed

---

Ohio Wesleyan is one of the nation's most balanced selective liberal arts colleges. Students praise the faculty for their dedication to teaching and active encouragement in the classroom. Students balance their academic experience with strong participation in community service, athletics, and student government. Each year the University offers a speaker series and seminar classes that focus on a major public issue of concern (National Colloquium). Loren Pope, author of *Beyond the Ivy League*, says "Ohio Wesleyan has a much more diverse, cosmopolitan, and friendly student body than a lot of the selective east and west coast schools."

Academics

Ohio Wesleyan offers an interdisciplinary curriculum and core academic program. It awards bachelor's **degrees**. Challenging opportunities include advanced placement, self-designed majors, tutorials, Freshman Honors College, an honors program, a senior project, Phi Beta Kappa, and Sigma Xi. Special programs include internships, summer session for credit, off-campus study, and study abroad.

The most popular **majors** include psychology, biology/biological sciences, and economics. A complete listing of majors at Ohio Wesleyan appears in the Majors Index beginning on page 379.

The **faculty** at Ohio Wesleyan has 125 full-time teachers, 94% with terminal degrees. 95% of the faculty serve as student advisers. The student-faculty ratio is 13:1, and the average class size in core courses is 16.

Computers on Campus

Students are not required to have a computer. Student rooms are linked to a campus network. 170 **computers** available in the computer center, computer labs, academic departments, the library, and dormitories provide access to the main academic computer, e-mail, on-line services, and the Internet. Staffed computer lab on campus provides training in the use of computers and software.

The 4 **libraries** have 485,501 books, 51,460 microform titles, and 1,079 subscriptions. They are connected to 7 national **on-line** catalogs.

Campus Life

There are 100 active **organizations** on campus, including a drama/theater group and student-run newspaper and radio station. 50% of students participate in student government elections. 50% of eligible men and 30% of eligible women are members of 11 national **fraternities** and 7 national **sororities**. Student **safety services** include late night transport/escort service, 24-hour emergency telephone alarm devices, 24-hour patrols by trained security personnel, and electronically operated dormitory entrances.

Ohio Wesleyan is a member of the NCAA (Division III). **Intercollegiate sports** include baseball (m), basketball (m, w), cross-country running (m, w), equestrian sports (m, w), field hockey (w), football (m), golf (m), ice hockey (m), lacrosse (m, w), rugby (m, w), sailing (m, w), soccer (m, w), swimming and diving (m, w), tennis (m, w), track and field (m, w), volleyball (w).

Applying

Ohio Wesleyan requires an essay, a high school transcript, 3 years of high school math, 2 recommendations, and SAT I or ACT. It recommends 3 years of high school science, 3 years of high school foreign language, and an interview. Early, deferred, and midyear entrance are possible, with a 3/1 deadline and continuous processing to 3/1 for financial aid. **Contact:** Mr. Douglas C. Thompson, Dean of Admission, Slocum Hall, Delaware, OH 43015, 614-368-3020 or toll-free 800-922-8953; fax 614-368-3314.

GETTING IN LAST YEAR
2,234 applied
84% were accepted
26% enrolled (480)
28% from top tenth of their h.s. class
3.4 average high school GPA
21% had SAT verbal scores over 600
46% had SAT math scores over 600
41% had ACT scores over 26
1% had SAT verbal scores over 700
15% had SAT math scores over 700
18% had ACT scores over 30
20 valedictorians

THE STUDENT BODY
1,712 undergraduates

From 43 states and territories, 41 other countries,
50% from Ohio
51% women, 49% men
4% African Americans
1% Native Americans
1% Hispanics
2% Asian Americans
8% international students

AFTER FRESHMAN YEAR
80% returned for sophomore year
72% got a degree within 4 years
73% got a degree within 5 years
74% got a degree within 6 years

AFTER GRADUATION
30% pursued further study (7% medicine, 6% law, 5% arts and sciences)
28 organizations recruited on campus
1 Fulbright scholar

WHAT YOU WILL PAY
Tuition and fees $17,569
Room and board $5876
59% receive need-based financial aid
Need-based college-administered scholarships and grants average $10,172 per award
21% receive non-need financial aid
Non-need college-administered scholarships and grants average $8866 per award

---

OKLAHOMA STATE UNIVERSITY

Stillwater, Oklahoma • Small-town setting • Public • State-supported • Coed

For more than a century, Oklahoma State University has fueled the dreams of students from 50 states and more than 100 nations. It's a place where one's imagination can become one's future. A nationally-acclaimed Honors Program means collaboration, not competition, with special honors sections, personal advising, priority enrollment, and special housing. Selected freshmen become Research Scholars and work with faculty mentors on critical national projects in lasers, biotechnology, environmental sciences, manufacturing, material sciences, and public policy. Engineering, accounting, mathematics, agricultural sciences and natural resources, music and performing arts, biological sciences, creative writing, and hotel and restaurant management are nationally recognized programs.

 Academics

OSU offers an interdisciplinary curriculum and core academic program; more than half of graduate courses are open to undergraduates. It awards bachelor's, master's, doctoral, and first professional **degrees**. Challenging opportunities include advanced placement, accelerated degree programs, self-designed majors, tutorials, an honors program, a senior project, and Sigma Xi. Special programs include cooperative education, internships, summer session for credit, off-campus study, study abroad, and Army and Air Force ROTC.

The most popular **majors** include education, management information systems, and marketing/retailing/merchandising. A complete listing of majors at OSU appears in the Majors Index beginning on page 379.

The **faculty** at OSU has 832 full-time graduate and undergraduate teachers, 90% with terminal degrees. The student-faculty ratio is 21:1, and the average class size in core courses is 45.

 Computers on Campus

Students are not required to have a computer. Student rooms are linked to a campus network. 1,000 **computers**

available in the computer center, computer labs, the research center, the learning resource center, labs, classrooms, the library, the student center, and dormitories provide access to the main academic computer, off-campus computing facilities, e-mail, on-line services, and the Internet. Staffed computer lab on campus provides training in the use of computers and software.

The **library** has 1.7 million books, 3.1 million microform titles, and 17,311 subscriptions. It is connected to 16 national **on-line** catalogs.

 Campus Life

There are 329 active **organizations** on campus, including a student-run newspaper and radio station. 10% of students participate in student government elections. 17% of eligible men and 16% of eligible women are members of 25 national **fraternities** and 13 national **sororities**. Student **safety services** include 24-hour emergency telephone alarm devices, 24-hour patrols by trained security personnel, and student patrols.

OSU is a member of the NCAA (Division I). **Intercollegiate sports** (some offering scholarships) include baseball (m), basketball (m, w), cross-country running (m, w), football (m), golf (m, w), soccer (w), softball (w), tennis (m, w), track and field (m, w), wrestling (m).

 Applying

OSU requires a high school transcript, 3 years of high school math, 4 years of high school English, 2 years each of high school history and science, SAT I or ACT, and a minimum high school GPA of 3.0. It recommends 2 years of high school foreign language. Early and midyear entrance are possible, with rolling admissions and continuous processing to 3/1 for financial aid. **Contact:** High School and College Relations, 104 Whitehurst Hall, Stillwater, OK 74078, 405-744-5358 or toll-free 800-233-5019 (in-state), 800-852-1255 (out-of-state); fax 405-744-5285.

GETTING IN LAST YEAR
4,355 applied
96% were accepted
59% enrolled (2,470)
30% from top tenth of their h.s. class
3.43 average high school GPA
33% had ACT scores over 26
10% had ACT scores over 30
23 National Merit Scholars
280 valedictorians

THE STUDENT BODY
Total 19,125, of whom 14,564
  are undergraduates

From 50 states and territories,
  100 other countries
83% from Oklahoma
46% women, 54% men
3% African Americans
7% Native Americans
2% Hispanics
2% Asian Americans
7% international students

AFTER FRESHMAN YEAR
76% returned for sophomore year
16% got a degree within 4 years

41% got a degree within 5 years
49% got a degree within 6 years

WHAT YOU WILL PAY
Resident tuition and fees $1698
Nonresident tuition and fees $4470
Room and board $3816
43% receive need-based financial aid
Need-based college-administered scholarships and
  grants average $1020 per award
19% receive non-need financial aid
Non-need college-administered scholarships and
  grants average $1450 per award

Pacific Lutheran University

Tacoma, Washington • Suburban setting • Private • Independent-Religious • Coed

When Russia's international airline, Aeroflot, wanted to learn Western accounting systems, it sent 80 of its executives to Pacific Lutheran; when Israel needed a world authority on the Holocaust, a PLU history professor was chosen; when Chinese officials needed to know how to deal with social changes brought about by free enterprise, a PLU anthropology professor was consulted; and when Russia's universities wanted an economics text on market economics, they chose a text by a PLU economics professor. These and many other top-flight scholars teach undergraduates at PLU because teaching is their first love.

 Academics

PLU offers a liberal arts and professional curriculum and core academic program. It awards bachelor's and master's **degrees**. Challenging opportunities include advanced placement, accelerated degree programs, self-designed majors, tutorials, Freshman Honors College, an honors program, and a senior project. Special programs include cooperative education, internships, summer session for credit, study abroad, and Army ROTC.

The most popular **majors** include business, education, and biology/biological sciences. A complete listing of majors at PLU appears in the Majors Index beginning on page 379.

The **faculty** at PLU has 233 full-time graduate and undergraduate teachers, 80% with terminal degrees. 95% of the faculty serve as student advisers. The student-faculty ratio is 15:1.

 Computers on Campus

Students are not required to have a computer. Student rooms are linked to a campus network. 200 **computers** available in the computer center, computer labs, science building, classrooms, the library, and dormitories provide access to the main academic computer, off-campus computing facilities, e-mail, on-line services, and the Internet. Staffed computer lab on campus provides training in the use of computers and software.

The **library** has 422,166 books, 75,605 microform titles, and 1,992 subscriptions. It is connected to 3 national **on-line** catalogs.

 Campus Life

There are 45 active **organizations** on campus, including a drama/theater group and student-run newspaper and radio station. 20% of students participate in student government elections. Student **safety services** include late night transport/escort service, 24-hour emergency telephone alarm devices, 24-hour patrols by trained security personnel, and student patrols.

PLU is a member of the NAIA. **Intercollegiate sports** include baseball (m), basketball (m, w), crew (m, w), cross-country running (m, w), football (m), golf (m, w), lacrosse (m, w), skiing (cross-country) (m, w), skiing (downhill) (m, w), soccer (m, w), softball (w), swimming and diving (m, w), tennis (m, w), track and field (m, w), volleyball (m, w), wrestling (m).

 Applying

PLU requires an essay, a high school transcript, 2 years of high school foreign language, 2 recommendations, minimum 2.5 GPA, SAT I or ACT, and in some cases an interview. It recommends 3 years of high school math and science. Early, deferred, and midyear entrance are possible, with rolling admissions and continuous processing to 3/1 for financial aid. **Contact:** Dr. Laura Polcyn, Dean of Admissions, Administration Building, Room 109, Tacoma, WA 98447, 206-535-7151 or toll-free 800-274-6758.

GETTING IN LAST YEAR
1,682 applied
97% were accepted
41% enrolled (668)
30% from top tenth of their h.s. class
3.5 average high school GPA
11% had SAT verbal scores over 600 (R)
31% had SAT math scores over 600 (R)
1% had SAT verbal scores over 700 (R)
7% had SAT math scores over 700 (R)
3 National Merit Scholars
33 valedictorians

THE STUDENT BODY
Total 3,579, of whom 3,166 are undergraduates

From 37 states and territories, 28 other countries
76% from Washington
61% women, 39% men
3% African Americans
1% Native Americans
2% Hispanics
5% Asian Americans
4% international students

AFTER FRESHMAN YEAR
78% returned for sophomore year
36% got a degree within 4 years
58% got a degree within 5 years
60% got a degree within 6 years

AFTER GRADUATION
9% pursued further study (3% law, 3% medicine, 2% arts and sciences)
50 organizations recruited on campus
2 Fulbright scholars

WHAT YOU WILL PAY
Tuition and fees $13,856
Room and board $4644
74% receive need-based financial aid
Need-based college-administered scholarships and grants average $4593 per award
16% receive non-need financial aid
Non-need college-administered scholarships and grants average $3366 per award

PENNSYLVANIA STATE UNIVERSITY
UNIVERSITY PARK CAMPUS

State College, Pennsylvania • Small-town setting • Public • State-related • Coed

Recognized nationally as one of the finest public universities, Penn State offers its students a broad curriculum filled with opportunity and challenge. Foremost amongst those challenges is the University Scholars Program, a University-wide honors program. University Scholars enroll in small honors classes and seminars, work closely with honors advisers, and conduct independent study and research projects. Computer accounts, registration priority, and extended library privileges support honors study. Students are encouraged to take advantage of the University's extensive study-abroad, externship, and internship programs.

Academics

Penn State offers a core academic program. It awards associate, bachelor's, master's, and doctoral **degrees**. Challenging opportunities include advanced placement, self-designed majors, Freshman Honors College, an honors program, a senior project, Phi Beta Kappa, and Sigma Xi. Special programs include cooperative education, internships, summer session for credit, study abroad, and Army, Naval, and Air Force ROTC.

The most popular **majors** include engineering (general), science, and business. A complete listing of majors at Penn State appears in the Majors Index beginning on page 379.

The **faculty** at Penn State has 1,856 full-time graduate and undergraduate teachers, 90% with terminal degrees. The student-faculty ratio is 19:1.

Computers on Campus

Students are not required to have a computer. Student rooms are linked to a campus network. 2,954 **computers** available in the computer center, computer labs, the learning resource center, classrooms, the library, and dormitories provide access to the main academic computer, off-campus computing facilities, e-mail, on-line services, and the Internet.

Staffed computer lab on campus (open 24 hours a day) provides training in the use of computers and software.

The 8 **libraries** have 2.6 million books and 24,901 subscriptions.

Campus Life

There are 400 active **organizations** on campus, including a drama/theater group and student-run newspaper and radio station. 20% of students participate in student government elections. 15% of eligible men and 15% of eligible women are members of 55 national **fraternities** and 25 national **sororities**. Student **safety services** include late night transport/escort service, 24-hour emergency telephone alarm devices, 24-hour patrols by trained security personnel, student patrols, and electronically operated dormitory entrances.

Penn State is a member of the NCAA (Division I). **Intercollegiate sports** (some offering scholarships) include baseball (m), basketball (m, w), cross-country running (m, w), equestrian sports (m, w), fencing (m, w), field hockey (w), football (m), golf (m, w), gymnastics (m, w), ice hockey (m), lacrosse (m, w), rugby (m, w), skiing (downhill) (m, w), soccer (m, w), softball (w), swimming and diving (m, w), table tennis (m), tennis (m, w), track and field (m, w), volleyball (m, w), water polo (m, w), weight lifting (m, w), wrestling (m).

Applying

Penn State requires a high school transcript, 3 years of high school math and science, SAT I or ACT, and in some cases some high school foreign language. Midyear entrance is possible, with rolling admissions and continuous processing to 2/15 for financial aid. **Contact:** Dr. John J. Romano, Vice Provost for Enrollment Management and Administration, 201 Shields Building, University Park, PA 16802-1503, 814-865-5471.

GETTING IN LAST YEAR
22,361 applied
51% were accepted
38% enrolled (4,310)
45% from top tenth of their h.s. class
3.68 average high school GPA
16% had SAT verbal scores over 600
54% had SAT math scores over 600
2% had SAT verbal scores over 700
14% had SAT math scores over 700

THE STUDENT BODY
Total 39,646, of whom 32,790 are undergraduates

From 52 states and territories
81% from Pennsylvania
44% women, 56% men
3% African Americans
1% Native Americans
2% Hispanics
5% Asian Americans
1% international students

AFTER FRESHMAN YEAR
93% returned for sophomore year
49% got a degree within 4 years

78% got a degree within 5 years
80% got a degree within 6 years

AFTER GRADUATION
936 organizations recruited on campus
1 Marshall, 15 Fulbright scholars

WHAT YOU WILL PAY
Resident tuition and fees $5258
Nonresident tuition and fees $11,310
Room and board $4040

PEPPERDINE UNIVERSITY

Malibu, California • Small-town setting • Private • Independent-Religious • Coed

 Academics

Pepperdine offers an interdisciplinary curriculum and core academic program. It awards bachelor's, master's, doctoral, and first professional **degrees**. The university is organized into four colleges: Seaver, the School of Law, the School of Business and Management, and the Graduate School of Education and Psychology. Seaver College is the undergraduate, residential, liberal arts school of the University and is committed to providing education of outstanding academic quality with particular attention to Christian values. Challenging opportunities include advanced placement, accelerated degree programs, self-designed majors, tutorials, an honors program, and a senior project. Special programs include internships, summer session for credit, study abroad, and Army, Naval, and Air Force ROTC.

The most popular **majors** include business, communication, and international studies. A complete listing of majors at Pepperdine appears in the Majors Index beginning on page 379.

The **faculty** at Pepperdine has 170 full-time undergraduate teachers, 98% with terminal degrees. 100% of the faculty serve as student advisers. The student-faculty ratio is 13:1.

 Computers on Campus

Students are not required to have a computer. Student rooms are linked to a campus network. 292 **computers** available in the computer center, electronic classrooms, the library, the student center, and dormitories.

The 2 **libraries** have 789,868 books, 86,938 microform titles, and 2,489 subscriptions. They are connected to 20 national **on-line** catalogs.

 Campus Life

There are 50 active **organizations** on campus, including a drama/theater group and student-run newspaper and radio station. 18% of eligible men and 20% of eligible women are members of 4 local **fraternities** and 6 local **sororities**. Student **safety services** include late night transport/escort service and student patrols.

Pepperdine is a member of the NCAA (Division I). **Intercollegiate sports** (some offering scholarships) include baseball (m), basketball (m, w), cross-country running (m, w), golf (m, w), ice hockey (m), lacrosse (m), rugby (m), soccer (m, w), swimming and diving (w), tennis (m, w), volleyball (m, w), water polo (m).

 Applying

Pepperdine requires an essay, a high school transcript, 3 years of high school math, 2 recommendations, and SAT I or ACT. It recommends 3 years of high school science, 2 years of high school foreign language, an interview, and SAT II Subject Tests. Early and midyear entrance are possible, with a 2/1 deadline and continuous processing to 2/15 for financial aid. **Contact:** Mr. Paul Long, Dean of Admission, 24255 Pacific Coast Highway, Malibu, CA 90263-0001, 310-456-4392; fax 310-456-4861.

GETTING IN LAST YEAR
3,179 applied
75% were accepted
24% enrolled (584)
85% from top tenth of their h.s. class
3.41 average high school GPA
13% had SAT verbal scores over 600 (R)
39% had SAT math scores over 600 (R)
1% had SAT verbal scores over 700 (R)
7% had SAT math scores over 700 (R)
3 National Merit Scholars

THE STUDENT BODY
Total 7,833, of whom 2,716
   are undergraduates

From 51 states and territories,
   54 other countries
61% from California
57% women, 43% men
3% African Americans
1% Native Americans
8% Hispanics
7% Asian Americans
9% international students

AFTER FRESHMAN YEAR
85% returned for sophomore year

AFTER GRADUATION
52% pursued further study (21% business, 18% arts and sciences, 8% law)
40% had job offers within 6 months
112 organizations recruited on campus

WHAT YOU WILL PAY
Tuition and fees $19,260
Room and board $6880
53% receive need-based financial aid
Need-based college-administered scholarships and grants average $7799 per award
46% receive non-need financial aid
Non-need college-administered scholarships and grants average $3900 per award

---

PITZER COLLEGE

Claremont, California • Suburban setting • Private • Independent • Coed

A liberal arts college of more than 800 students, Pitzer offers close, personal attention within the university environment of The Claremont Colleges (which include Pomona, Scripps, Claremont McKenna, and Harvey Mudd colleges). Students may enroll at classes offered by any of the campuses and enjoy such shared resources as a major library, the $16.5-million Keck Science Center, theaters, recreational and competitive sports, and social activities. Pitzer's interdisciplinary and multicultural curriculum emphasizes self-direction and independent thought and provides a large number of community-service internship opportunities. Pitzer's award-winning study-abroad program provides intensive language and culture immersion in countries from Australia to Zimbabwe.

 ## Academics

Pitzer offers an interdisciplinary curriculum and core academic program. It awards bachelor's **degrees**. Challenging opportunities include advanced placement, self-designed majors, tutorials, an honors program, a senior project, and Sigma Xi. Special programs include cooperative education, internships, off-campus study, and study abroad.

The most popular **majors** include psychology, sociology, and anthropology. A complete listing of majors at Pitzer appears in the Majors Index beginning on page 379.

The **faculty** at Pitzer has 65 full-time teachers, 99% with terminal degrees. 100% of the faculty serve as student advisers. The student-faculty ratio is 12:1.

 ## Computers on Campus

Students are not required to have a computer. 45 **computers** available in the computer center, computer labs, the research center, language lab, and the library provide access to the main academic computer, e-mail, on-line services, and the Internet. Staffed computer lab on campus provides training in the use of computers and software.

The 2 **libraries** have 1.9 million books, 1.2 million microform titles, and 6,800 subscriptions. They are connected to 20 national **on-line** catalogs.

 ## Campus Life

There are 19 active **organizations** on campus, including a drama/theater group and student-run newspaper and radio station. 50% of students participate in student government elections. Student **safety services** include late night transport/escort service, 24-hour emergency telephone alarm devices, 24-hour patrols by trained security personnel, and electronically operated dormitory entrances.

Pitzer is a member of the NCAA (Division III). **Intercollegiate sports** include badminton (m, w), baseball (m), basketball (m, w), cross-country running (m, w), fencing (m, w), football (m), golf (m), soccer (m, w), softball (w), swimming and diving (m, w), tennis (m, w), track and field (m, w), volleyball (w), water polo (m), wrestling (m).

 ## Applying

Pitzer requires an essay, a high school transcript, 2 recommendations, and SAT I or ACT. It recommends 3 years of high school math and science, 2 years of high school foreign language, an interview, and 3 SAT II Subject Tests (including SAT II: Writing Test). Early, deferred, and midyear entrance are possible, with a 2/1 deadline and 2/1 for financial aid. **Contact:** Dr. Willam D. Tingley, Vice President for Admission and Financial Aid, 1050 North Mills Avenue, Claremont, CA 91711-6110, 909-621-8129 or toll-free 800-748-9371; fax 909-621-8770.

GETTING IN LAST YEAR
1,219 applied
80% were accepted
21% enrolled (199)
3.24 average high school GPA
52% had ACT scores over 26
13% had ACT scores over 30

THE STUDENT BODY
837 undergraduates
From 42 states and territories,
   26 other countries

42% from California
52% women, 48% men
7% African Americans
1% Native Americans
16% Hispanics
17% Asian Americans
10% international students

AFTER FRESHMAN YEAR
78% returned for sophomore year
67% got a degree within 4 years
70% got a degree within 5 years

AFTER GRADUATION
38% pursued further study (17% arts and
   sciences, 7% law, 6% business)
75% had job offers within 6 months
25 organizations recruited on campus
1 Rhodes, 2 Fulbright scholars

WHAT YOU WILL PAY
Tuition and fees $20,270
Room and board $6208
38% receive need-based financial aid
Need-based college-administered scholarships and
   grants average $11,300 per award

POLYTECHNIC UNIVERSITY, BROOKLYN CAMPUS

Brooklyn, New York • Urban setting • Private • Independent • Coed

Academics

Polytechnic offers a core academic program; fewer than half of graduate courses are open to undergraduates. It awards bachelor's, master's, and doctoral **degrees**. Challenging opportunities include advanced placement, accelerated degree programs, tutorials, an honors program, a senior project, and Sigma Xi. Special programs include cooperative education, summer session for credit, and Army and Air Force ROTC.

The most popular **majors** include electrical engineering and mechanical engineering. A complete listing of majors at Polytechnic appears in the Majors Index beginning on page 379.

The **faculty** at Polytechnic has 151 full-time graduate and undergraduate teachers, 95% with terminal degrees. 10% of the faculty serve as student advisers. The student-faculty ratio is 15:1, and the average class size in core courses is 25.

Computers on Campus

Students are not required to have a computer. Student rooms are linked to a campus network. 350 **computers** available in the computer center, computer labs, the research center, classrooms, and the library provide access to the main academic computer, e-mail, on-line services, and the Internet. Staffed computer lab on campus provides training in the use of computers and software.

The **library** has 197,300 books, 199 microform titles, and 1,621 subscriptions.

Campus Life

There are 47 active **organizations** on campus, including a student-run newspaper. 30% of students participate in student government elections. 6% of eligible men are members of 3 national **fraternities**. Student **safety services** include 24-hour patrols by trained security personnel.

Polytechnic is a member of the NCAA (Division III). **Intercollegiate sports** include baseball (m), basketball (m), cross-country running (m, w), lacrosse (m), soccer (m), tennis (m, w), volleyball (w), wrestling (m).

Applying

Polytechnic requires an essay, a high school transcript, 3 years of high school math and science, recommendations, and SAT I or ACT. It recommends some high school foreign language, an interview, and SAT II Subject Tests (including SAT II: Writing Test). Deferred and midyear entrance are possible, with rolling admissions and continuous processing to 3/1 for financial aid. **Contact:** Mr. Peter Grant Jordan, Dean of Admissions, Six Metrotech Center, Brooklyn, NY 11201-2990, 718-260-3100 or toll-free 800-POLYTECH; fax 718-260-3136.

GETTING IN LAST YEAR

658 applied
67% were accepted
57% enrolled (253)
65% from top tenth of their h.s. class
3.5 average high school GPA
7% had SAT verbal scores over 600
62% had SAT math scores over 600
0% had SAT verbal scores over 700
13% had SAT math scores over 700
7 valedictorians

THE STUDENT BODY

Total 2,258, of whom 1,164 are undergraduates

From 19 states and territories, 19 other countries
92% from New York
16% women, 84% men
12% African Americans
1% Native Americans
11% Hispanics
33% Asian Americans
4% international students

AFTER FRESHMAN YEAR

78% returned for sophomore year

AFTER GRADUATION

16% pursued further study (11% engineering, 4% business, 1% arts and sciences)
96% had job offers within 6 months
60 organizations recruited on campus
1 Fulbright scholar

WHAT YOU WILL PAY

Tuition and fees $17,585
Room and board $3610
Need-based college-administered scholarships and grants average $4064 per award
Non-need college-administered scholarships and grants average $7693 per award

POLYTECHNIC UNIVERSITY, FARMINGDALE CAMPUS

Farmingdale, New York • Suburban setting • Private • Independent • Coed

 Academics

Polytechnic offers an interdisciplinary core curriculum and core academic program; fewer than half of graduate courses are open to undergraduates. It awards bachelor's, master's, and doctoral **degrees**. Challenging opportunities include advanced placement, accelerated degree programs, tutorials, an honors program, and a senior project. Special programs include cooperative education, summer session for credit, off-campus study, and Army and Air Force ROTC.

The most popular **majors** include electrical engineering, mechanical engineering, and aerospace engineering. A complete listing of majors at Polytechnic appears in the Majors Index beginning on page 379.

The **faculty** at Polytechnic has 151 full-time graduate and undergraduate teachers, 95% with terminal degrees. 10% of the faculty serve as student advisers. The student-faculty ratio is 15:1, and the average class size in core courses is 25.

 Computers on Campus

Students are not required to have a computer. Student rooms are linked to a campus network. 86 **computers** available in the computer center, computer labs, the research center, and the library provide access to the main academic computer, e-mail, on-line services, and the Internet. Staffed computer lab on campus provides training in the use of computers and software.

The **library** has 35,000 books and 110 subscriptions. It is connected to 1 national **on-line** catalog.

 Campus Life

There are 24 active **organizations** on campus, including a drama/theater group and student-run newspaper. 70% of students participate in student government elections. 15% of eligible men and 15% of eligible women are members of 1 national **fraternity**, 1 local fraternity, 1 local **sorority**, and 1 coed fraternity. Student **safety services** include patrols by trained security personnel and electronically operated dormitory entrances.

Polytechnic is a member of the NCAA (Division III). **Intercollegiate sports** include baseball (m), basketball (m), cross-country running (m, w), lacrosse (m), soccer (m), tennis (m, w), volleyball (w).

 Applying

Polytechnic requires an essay, a high school transcript, 3 years of high school math and science, recommendations, and SAT I or ACT. It recommends some high school foreign language, an interview, and SAT II Subject Tests (including SAT II: Writing Test). Early, deferred, and midyear entrance are possible, with rolling admissions and continuous processing to 3/1 for financial aid. **Contact:** Mr. Steve Kerge, Associate Dean of Admissions, Long Island Center, Main Building, Farmingdale, NY 11735-3995, 516-755-4200 or toll-free 800-POLYTECH; fax 516-755-4404.

GETTING IN LAST YEAR
246 applied
85% were accepted
44% enrolled (92)
65% from top tenth of their h.s. class
3.5 average high school GPA
11% had SAT verbal scores over 600
63% had SAT math scores over 600
0% had SAT verbal scores over 700
15% had SAT math scores over 700
2 valedictorians

THE STUDENT BODY
Total 637, of whom 361
  are undergraduates

From 11 states and territories,
  10 other countries
85% from New York
12% women, 88% men
5% African Americans
0% Native Americans
16% Hispanics
18% Asian Americans
2% international students

AFTER FRESHMAN YEAR
78% returned for sophomore year

AFTER GRADUATION
16% pursued further study (11% engineering,
  4% business, 1% arts and sciences)
98% had job offers within 6 months
60 organizations recruited on campus

WHAT YOU WILL PAY
Tuition and fees $17,350
Room and board $4400
Need-based college-administered scholarships and
  grants average $3371 per award
Non-need college-administered scholarships and
  grants average $8696 per award

POMONA COLLEGE

Claremont, California • Suburban setting • Private • Independent • Coed

Pomona College is located in Claremont, California, 35 miles east of Los Angeles, and is the founding member of the Claremont Colleges. Recognized as one of the nation's premier liberal arts colleges, Pomona offers a comprehensive undergraduate curriculum and enrolls students from around the nation and across class and ethnicity. With financial resources among the strongest of any national liberal arts college, Pomona offers a broad range of resources and opportunities, including an extensive study-abroad program. The community enjoys academic, cultural, and extracurricular activities usually found only at large universities, with all of the benefits and advantages of a small college.

Academics

Pomona offers a perception, analysis, and communication skills curriculum and core academic program. It awards bachelor's **degrees**. Challenging opportunities include advanced placement, self-designed majors, a senior project, Phi Beta Kappa, and Sigma Xi. Special programs include internships, off-campus study, and study abroad.

The most popular **majors** include biology/biological sciences, political science/government, and psychology. A complete listing of majors at Pomona appears in the Majors Index beginning on page 379.

The **faculty** at Pomona has 154 full-time teachers, 100% with terminal degrees. 100% of the faculty serve as student advisers. The student-faculty ratio is 9:1.

Computers on Campus

Students are not required to have a computer. Student rooms are linked to a campus network. 180 **computers** available in the computer center, computer labs, classroom buildings, classrooms, the library, the student center, and dormitories provide access to the main academic computer,

off-campus computing facilities, e-mail, and the Internet. Staffed computer lab on campus provides training in the use of computers and software.

The 4 **libraries** have 1.9 million books, 1.2 million microform titles, and 6,800 subscriptions. They are connected to 20 national **on-line** catalogs.

Campus Life

There are 280 active **organizations** on campus, including a drama/theater group and student-run newspaper and radio station. 88% of students participate in student government elections. 4% of eligible men and 2% of eligible women are members of 3 local **fraternities** and 4 local coed fraternities. Student **safety services** include late night transport/escort service, 24-hour emergency telephone alarm devices, 24-hour patrols by trained security personnel, and electronically operated dormitory entrances.

Pomona is a member of the NCAA (Division III). **Intercollegiate sports** include baseball (m), basketball (m, w), cross-country running (m, w), football (m), golf (m), soccer (m, w), softball (w), swimming and diving (m, w), tennis (m, w), track and field (m, w), volleyball (w), water polo (m, w).

Applying

Pomona requires an essay, a high school transcript, 3 years of high school math, 2 recommendations, SAT I or ACT, and a minimum high school GPA of 2.0. It recommends 3 years of high school science, 3 years of high school foreign language, an interview, portfolio or tapes for art and performing arts programs, and 3 SAT II Subject Tests (including SAT II: Writing Test). Early and deferred entrance are possible, with a 1/1 deadline and 2/11 for financial aid. **Contact:** Mr. Bruce Poch, Dean of Admissions, 333 North College Way, Claremont, CA 91711, 909-621-8134; fax 909-621-8403.

GETTING IN LAST YEAR
3,586 applied
34% were accepted
32% enrolled (392)
84% from top tenth of their h.s. class
93% had SAT verbal scores over 600 (R)
93% had SAT math scores over 600 (R)
92% had ACT scores over 26
53% had SAT verbal scores over 700 (R)
51% had SAT math scores over 700 (R)
58% had ACT scores over 30
45 National Merit Scholars
18 class presidents
48 valedictorians

THE STUDENT BODY
1,402 undergraduates
From 46 states and territories,
   23 other countries
44% from California
48% women, 52% men
5% African Americans
1% Native Americans
12% Hispanics
21% Asian Americans
4% international students

AFTER FRESHMAN YEAR
98% returned for sophomore year

AFTER GRADUATION
35% pursued further study (20% arts and
   sciences, 6% law, 6% medicine)
111 organizations recruited on campus
2 Fulbright scholars

WHAT YOU WILL PAY
Tuition and fees $18,880
Room and board $7500
54% receive need-based financial aid
Need-based college-administered scholarships and
   grants average $12,290 per award

PRESBYTERIAN COLLEGE

Clinton, South Carolina • Small-town setting • Private • Independent-Religious • Coed

Presbyterian College—with 43 national and international scholarship recipients in recent years—provides an environment that nurtures the best and brightest. Students respect and live by a strong Honor Code, and well over half volunteer for community service. Students also may study under PC's Service Learning Program, participate in a comprehensive Honors Program, or study abroad in locations around the world. To prepare for graduate school and the job market, students may intern or conduct research alongside professors. A scholarship program for outstanding students is supported by one of the largest endowments per student in the region.

Academics

Presbyterian College offers a career-oriented, liberal arts curriculum and core academic program; a few graduate courses are open to undergraduates. It awards bachelor's **degrees**. Challenging opportunities include advanced placement, accelerated degree programs, tutorials, Freshman Honors College, an honors program, and a senior project. Special programs include internships, summer session for credit, off-campus study, study abroad, and Army ROTC.

The most popular **majors** include business, education, and biology/biological sciences. A complete listing of majors at Presbyterian College appears in the Majors Index beginning on page 379.

The **faculty** at Presbyterian College has 76 full-time teachers, 90% with terminal degrees. 99% of the faculty serve as student advisers. The student-faculty ratio is 15:1, and the average class size in core courses is 21.

Computers on Campus

Students are not required to have a computer. Student rooms are linked to a campus network. 130 **computers**

available in the computer center, computer labs, academic buildings, classrooms, and the library provide access to the main academic computer, e-mail, on-line services, and the Internet. Staffed computer lab on campus provides training in the use of computers and software.

The **library** has 145,000 books, 100 microform titles, and 810 subscriptions. It is connected to 3 national **on-line** catalogs.

Campus Life

There are 90 active **organizations** on campus, including a drama/theater group and student-run newspaper and radio station. 75% of students participate in student government elections. 44% of eligible men and 42% of eligible women are members of 6 national **fraternities**, 3 national **sororities**, and Minority Social Club. Student **safety services** include late night transport/escort service, 24-hour emergency telephone alarm devices, 24-hour patrols by trained security personnel, and electronically operated dormitory entrances.

Presbyterian College is a member of the NCAA (Division II). **Intercollegiate sports** (some offering scholarships) include baseball (m), basketball (m, w), football (m), golf (m, w), riflery (m, w), soccer (m, w), tennis (m, w), track and field (m), volleyball (w).

Applying

Presbyterian College requires an essay, a high school transcript, 2 years of high school foreign language, 1 recommendation, SAT I or ACT, and a minimum high school GPA of 2.0. It recommends 3 years of high school math and science and an interview. Early, deferred, and midyear entrance are possible, with a 4/1 deadline and continuous processing to 3/1 for financial aid. **Contact:** Mr. Eddie G. Rogers, Associate Director of Admissions, South Broad Street, Clinton, SC 29325, 803-833-8228 or toll-free 800-476-7272; fax 803-833-8481.

GETTING IN LAST YEAR
1,198 applied
82% were accepted
36% enrolled (354)
35% from top tenth of their h.s. class
3.3 average high school GPA
34% had SAT verbal scores over 600 (R)
63% had SAT math scores over 600 (R)
38% had ACT scores over 26
4% had SAT verbal scores over 700 (R)
15% had SAT math scores over 700 (R)
3% had ACT scores over 30
1 National Merit Scholar
23 class presidents
4 valedictorians

THE STUDENT BODY
1,186 undergraduates
From 23 states and territories,
  7 other countries
47% from South Carolina
49% women, 51% men
4% African Americans
1% Native Americans
1% Hispanics
1% Asian Americans
1% international students

AFTER FRESHMAN YEAR
90% returned for sophomore year
74% got a degree within 4 years
75% got a degree within 5 years

AFTER GRADUATION
25% pursued further study
70% had job offers within 6 months
35 organizations recruited on campus

WHAT YOU WILL PAY
Tuition and fees $13,454
Room and board $3834
39% receive need-based financial aid
Need-based college-administered scholarships and
  grants average $4721 per award
78% receive non-need financial aid
Non-need college-administered scholarships and
  grants average $3350 per award

PRINCETON UNIVERSITY

Princeton, New Jersey • Suburban setting • Private • Independent • Coed

Academics

Princeton offers a core academic program. It awards bachelor's, master's, and doctoral **degrees**. Challenging opportunities include advanced placement, accelerated degree programs, self-designed majors, an honors program, a senior project, Phi Beta Kappa, and Sigma Xi. Special programs include internships, off-campus study, and Army and Air Force ROTC.

The most popular **majors** include history, political science/government, and English. A complete listing of majors at Princeton appears in the Majors Index beginning on page 379.

The **faculty** at Princeton has 731 full-time undergraduate teachers, 84% with terminal degrees. 21% of the faculty serve as student advisers. The student-faculty ratio is 5:1.

Computers on Campus

Students are not required to have a computer. Student rooms are linked to a campus network. 400 **computers** available in the computer center, computer labs, the research center, academic departments, classrooms, the library, and dormitories provide access to the main academic computer, off-campus computing facilities, e-mail, on-line services, and the Internet.

The 23 **libraries** have 5 million books, 3 million microform titles, and 30,000 subscriptions.

Campus Life

There are 200 active **organizations** on campus, including a drama/theater group and student-run newspaper and radio station. 70% of eligible men and 70% of eligible women are members of 11 eating clubs. Student **safety services** include late night transport/escort service, 24-hour emergency telephone alarm devices, 24-hour patrols by trained security personnel, student patrols, and electronically operated dormitory entrances.

Princeton is a member of the NCAA (Division I) and NAIA. **Intercollegiate sports** include baseball (m), basketball (m, w), crew (m, w), cross-country running (m, w), fencing (m, w), field hockey (w), football (m), golf (m, w), ice hockey (m, w), lacrosse (m, w), soccer (m, w), softball (w), squash (m, w), swimming and diving (m, w), tennis (m, w), track and field (m, w), volleyball (m, w), water polo (m, w), wrestling (m).

Applying

Princeton requires an essay, a high school transcript, recommendations, SAT I, and in some cases SAT II Subject Tests. It recommends 4 years of high school math, 3 years of high school science, 4 years of high school foreign language, an interview, and 3 SAT II Subject Tests. Early and deferred entrance are possible, with a 1/2 deadline and continuous processing to 2/1 for financial aid. **Contact:** Mr. Fred A. Hargadon, Dean of Admission, West College, Princeton, NJ 08544-1019, 609-258-3060.

GETTING IN LAST YEAR
14,363 applied
14% were accepted
57% enrolled (1,189)
90% from top tenth of their h.s. class

THE STUDENT BODY
Total 6,419, of whom 4,609
   are undergraduates
From 52 states and territories,
   69 other countries
13% from New Jersey

46% women, 54% men
7% African Americans
1% Native Americans
6% Hispanics
11% Asian Americans
5% international students

AFTER FRESHMAN YEAR
96% returned for sophomore year
87% got a degree within 4 years
94% got a degree within 5 years
95% got a degree within 6 years

AFTER GRADUATION
30% pursued further study (11% arts and
   sciences, 9% medicine, 5% law)
280 organizations recruited on campus
1 Rhodes, 3 Marshall, 16 Fulbright scholars

WHAT YOU WILL PAY
Tuition and fees $22,000
Room and board $6325
44% receive need-based financial aid
Need-based college-administered scholarships and
   grants average $13,800 per award

PROVIDENCE COLLEGE

Providence, Rhode Island • Suburban setting • Private • Independent-Religious • Coed

Intellectual zeal, high standards, shared values, a sense of community, and a willingness to help others—these are the qualities that shape the character of Providence College. PC is the only US college under the stewardship of the Dominican Friars, whose intellectual heritage dates back to the 13th century. PC's special attractions include the Liberal Arts Honors Program and an acclaimed 2-year Development of Western Civilization Program, opportunities to pursue research and independent study with faculty scholars, strong prelaw and premedical advisory programs, and the Feinstein Institute for Public Service offering the first known major and minor in public and community service studies.

 ## Academics

PC offers a liberal arts curriculum and core academic program; all graduate courses are open to undergraduates. It awards associate, bachelor's, master's, and doctoral **degrees**. Challenging opportunities include advanced placement, self-designed majors, tutorials, an honors program, and a senior project. Special programs include internships, summer session for credit, study abroad, and Army ROTC.

The most popular **majors** include business, education, and English. A complete listing of majors at PC appears in the Majors Index beginning on page 379.

The **faculty** at PC has 280 full-time graduate and undergraduate teachers, 82% with terminal degrees. 98% of the faculty serve as student advisers. The student-faculty ratio is 13:1, and the average class size in core courses is 25.

 ## Computers on Campus

Students are not required to have a computer. Student rooms are linked to a campus network. 144 **computers**

available in the computer center, computer labs, the learning resource center, classrooms, and the library provide access to e-mail, on-line services, and the Internet. Staffed computer lab on campus provides training in the use of computers and software.

The **library** has 331,000 books, 27,500 microform titles, and 1,850 subscriptions. It is connected to 3 national **on-line** catalogs.

 ## Campus Life

There are 85 active **organizations** on campus, including a drama/theater group and student-run newspaper and radio station. Student **safety services** include late night transport/escort service, 24-hour emergency telephone alarm devices, 24-hour patrols by trained security personnel, student patrols, and electronically operated dormitory entrances.

PC is a member of the NCAA (Division I). **Intercollegiate sports** (some offering scholarships) include baseball (m), basketball (m, w), cross-country running (m, w), field hockey (w), golf (m), ice hockey (m, w), lacrosse (m), racquetball (m, w), rugby (m, w), soccer (m, w), softball (w), swimming and diving (m, w), tennis (m, w), track and field (m, w), volleyball (w).

 ## Applying

PC requires an essay, a high school transcript, SAT I or ACT, and in some cases 3 years of high school science. It recommends 3 years of high school math, 3 years of high school foreign language, recommendations, a campus interview, 3 SAT II Subject Tests, and a minimum high school GPA of 3.0. Early, deferred, and midyear entrance are possible, with a 1/15 deadline and a 2/1 priority date for financial aid. **Contact:** Mr. William DiBrienza, Dean of Admissions and Financial Aid, Eaton Street and River Avenue, Providence, RI 02918, 401-865-2535 or toll-free 800-721-6444; fax 401-865-2826.

GETTING IN LAST YEAR
3,836 applied
75% were accepted
33% enrolled (962)
27% from top tenth of their h.s. class
10% had SAT verbal scores over 600
33% had SAT math scores over 600
1% had SAT verbal scores over 700
5% had SAT math scores over 700
36 National Merit Scholars
27 class presidents
17 valedictorians

THE STUDENT BODY
Total 5,493, of whom 3,500 are undergraduates

From 40 states and territories, 12 other countries
16% from Rhode Island
60% women, 40% men
4% African Americans
0% Native Americans
2% Hispanics
2% Asian Americans
1% international students

AFTER FRESHMAN YEAR
96% returned for sophomore year
89% got a degree within 4 years
91% got a degree within 5 years

AFTER GRADUATION
32% pursued further study (12% arts and sciences, 7% business, 7% law)

WHAT YOU WILL PAY
Tuition and fees $15,500
Room and board $6475
55% receive need-based financial aid
Need-based college-administered scholarships and grants average $7000 per award
9% receive non-need financial aid
Non-need college-administered scholarships and grants average $10,227 per award

PURDUE UNIVERSITY

West Lafayette, Indiana • Suburban setting • Public • State-supported • Coed

Located in the heart of the Midwest, Purdue University is a land-grant institution founded in 1869. Beginning with academic areas in agriculture and mechanics arts, Purdue now offers more than 200 programs that range from pharmacy and restaurant/hotel management to engineering and linguistics. Purdue students come from all 50 states and more than 70 countries. They bring to campus a diversity of backgrounds and ideas that complement their academic preparation. With its international reputation for academic excellence, highly regarded faculty, and competitive student body, Purdue offers more than just a college degree: it offers an educational experience for now and for the future.

 Academics

Purdue offers no core academic program; fewer than half of graduate courses are open to undergraduates. It awards associate, bachelor's, master's, and doctoral **degrees**. Challenging opportunities include advanced placement, accelerated degree programs, self-designed majors, an honors program, a senior project, Phi Beta Kappa, and Sigma Xi. Special programs include cooperative education, internships, summer session for credit, study abroad, and Army, Naval, and Air Force ROTC.

The most popular **majors** include mechanical engineering, communication, and electrical engineering. A complete listing of majors at Purdue appears in the Majors Index beginning on page 379.

The **faculty** at Purdue has 2,019 full-time graduate and undergraduate teachers, 86% with terminal degrees. The student-faculty ratio is 17:1.

 Computers on Campus

Students are not required to have a computer. Student rooms are linked to a campus network. 2,000 **computers** available in the computer center, computer labs, individual schools, the student center, and dormitories provide access to the main academic computer, e-mail, on-line services, and the Internet. Staffed computer lab on campus.

The 16 **libraries** have 2.1 million books, 2.2 million microform titles, and 14,257 subscriptions.

 Campus Life

There are 560 active **organizations** on campus, including a drama/theater group and student-run newspaper and radio station. 6% of students participate in student government elections. 21% of eligible men and 18% of eligible women are members of 39 national **fraternities**, 16 national **sororities**, 6 local fraternities, and 7 local sororities. Student **safety services** include late night transport/escort service, 24-hour emergency telephone alarm devices, and student patrols.

Purdue is a member of the NCAA (Division I). **Intercollegiate sports** (some offering scholarships) include archery (m, w), baseball (m), basketball (m, w), crew (m, w), cross-country running (m, w), equestrian sports (m, w), fencing (m, w), football (m), golf (m, w), gymnastics (m, w), ice hockey (m), lacrosse (m, w), racquetball (m, w), riflery (m, w), rugby (m, w), sailing (m, w), soccer (m, w), softball (w), squash (m, w), swimming and diving (m, w), table tennis (m, w), tennis (m, w), track and field (m, w), volleyball (m, w), water polo (m, w), wrestling (m).

 Applying

Purdue requires a high school transcript, SAT I or ACT, and in some cases 3 years of high school math and science. It recommends 3 years of high school math and science and some high school foreign language. Early and midyear entrance are possible, with rolling admissions and continuous processing to 3/1 for financial aid. **Contact:** Office of Admissions, Schleman Hall, West Lafayette, IN 47907-1080, 317-494-1776.

GETTING IN LAST YEAR
16,714 applied
90% were accepted
41% enrolled (5,967)
27% from top tenth of their h.s. class
19% had SAT verbal scores over 600 (R)
33% had SAT math scores over 600 (R)
38% had ACT scores over 26
2% had SAT verbal scores over 700 (R)
6% had SAT math scores over 700 (R)
9% had ACT scores over 30
33 National Merit Scholars
145 valedictorians

THE STUDENT BODY
Total 34,685, of whom 27,982
   are undergraduates

From 55 states and territories,
   73 other countries
74% from Indiana
43% women, 57% men
4% African Americans
0% Native Americans
2% Hispanics
4% Asian Americans
3% international students

AFTER FRESHMAN YEAR
31% got a degree within 4 years

AFTER GRADUATION
56% had job offers within 6 months

658 organizations recruited on campus
2 Fulbright scholars

WHAT YOU WILL PAY
Resident tuition and fees $3056
Nonresident tuition and fees $10,128
Room and board $4300
53% receive need-based financial aid
Need-based college-administered scholarships and
   grants average $956 per award
Non-need college-administered scholarships and
   grants average $2474 per award

QUINCY UNIVERSITY

Quincy, Illinois • Small-town setting • Private • Independent-Religious • Coed

More students than ever are applying to Quincy University—and with good reason. Quincy University is the place to be. Personal attention is paramount throughout the student's education. Freshmen participate in the "First-Year Experience," a program designed to assist first-year students in their transition from high school to university life. This seminar format allows students to develop critical reading and writing skills, as well as to hone their oral communication and analytical thinking skills. Graduates realize the benefits of a Quincy University education, with over 93% being employed or continuing in graduate school within 90 days of graduation.

 ## Academics

Quincy University offers a liberal arts/career preparation curriculum and core academic program; all graduate courses are open to undergraduates. It awards associate, bachelor's, and master's **degrees**. Challenging opportunities include advanced placement, accelerated degree programs, self-designed majors, tutorials, Freshman Honors College, an honors program, and a senior project. Special programs include internships and summer session for credit.

The most popular **majors** include business, elementary education, and accounting. A complete listing of majors at Quincy University appears in the Majors Index beginning on page 379.

The **faculty** at Quincy University has 66 full-time graduate and undergraduate teachers, 75% with terminal degrees. 100% of the faculty serve as student advisers. The student-faculty ratio is 12:1.

 ## Computers on Campus

Students are not required to have a computer. Student rooms are linked to a campus network. 196 **computers** available in the computer center, computer labs, honors houses, classrooms, the library, and dormitories provide access to the main academic computer, off-campus computing facilities, e-mail, on-line services, and the Internet. Staffed computer lab on campus provides training in the use of computers and software.

The **library** has 232,101 books, 139,670 microform titles, and 620 subscriptions. It is connected to 7 national **on-line** catalogs.

 ## Campus Life

There are 41 active **organizations** on campus, including a drama/theater group and student-run newspaper and radio station. 75% of students participate in student government elections. 5% of eligible men are members of 1 national **fraternity**. Student **safety services** include 24-hour weekend patrols, 20-hour patrols Monday through Thursday, late night transport/escort service, 24-hour emergency telephone alarm devices, student patrols, and electronically operated dormitory entrances.

Quincy University is a member of the NCAA (Division II). **Intercollegiate sports** (some offering scholarships) include baseball (m), basketball (m, w), cross-country running (m, w), football (m), soccer (m, w), softball (w), tennis (m, w), volleyball (m, w).

 ## Applying

Quincy University requires a high school transcript, 1 recommendation, and SAT I or ACT. It recommends 3 years of high school math and science, some high school foreign language, an interview, and a minimum high school GPA of 2.0. Early, deferred, and midyear entrance are possible, with rolling admissions and continuous processing to 4/1 for financial aid. **Contact:** Mr. Frank Bevec, Director of Admissions, 1800 College Avenue, Quincy, IL 62301-2699, 217-222-8020 ext. 5215 or toll-free 800-688-4295; fax 217-228-5479.

GETTING IN LAST YEAR
1,098 applied
72% were accepted
33% enrolled (261)
23% from top tenth of their h.s. class
3.1 average high school GPA
32% had ACT scores over 26
8% had ACT scores over 30
1 National Merit Scholar

THE STUDENT BODY
Total 1,105, of whom 1,024
   are undergraduates
From 30 states and territories,
   15 other countries

67% from Illinois
50% women, 50% men
6% African Americans
1% Hispanics
1% Asian Americans
2% international students

AFTER FRESHMAN YEAR
80% returned for sophomore year
48% got a degree within 4 years
52% got a degree within 5 years
55% got a degree within 6 years

AFTER GRADUATION
20% pursued further study (11% arts and
   sciences, 4% business, 3% law)
98% had job offers within 6 months
18 organizations recruited on campus

WHAT YOU WILL PAY
Tuition and fees $10,910
Room and board $4380
80% receive need-based financial aid
Need-based college-administered scholarships and
   grants average $3954 per award
68% receive non-need financial aid
Non-need college-administered scholarships and
   grants average $4261 per award

RANDOLPH-MACON WOMAN'S COLLEGE

Lynchburg, Virginia • Suburban setting • Private • Independent-Religious • Women

A singular education, self-awareness, and involvement—these are priorities at Randolph-Macon Woman's College. Students seize opportunities to study abroad, participate in internships, conduct original research with faculty members, become active in campus organizations, and volunteer in the community. They discover new interests. The supportive and engaging atmosphere fosters academic excellence and leadership potential, with 70% of all classes having 15 or fewer students. Contemporary facilities and advanced technology afford women a competitive edge for career prospects. The College provides a setting for learning and living that prepares women for meaningful personal and professional lives.

 ## Academics

R-MWC offers a liberal arts and sciences curriculum and core academic program. It awards bachelor's **degrees**. Challenging opportunities include advanced placement, accelerated degree programs, self-designed majors, tutorials, an honors program, a senior project, and Phi Beta Kappa. Special programs include internships, summer session for credit, off-campus study, and study abroad.

The most popular **majors** include English, political science/government, and psychology. A complete listing of majors at R-MWC appears in the Majors Index beginning on page 379.

The **faculty** at R-MWC has 68 full-time teachers, 95% with terminal degrees. 100% of the faculty serve as student advisers. The student-faculty ratio is 9:1.

 ## Computers on Campus

Students are not required to have a computer. Student rooms are linked to a campus network. 70 **computers**

available in the computer center, computer labs, the research center, the learning resource center, multimedia rooms, classrooms, and the library provide access to the main academic computer, off-campus computing facilities, e-mail, on-line services, and the Internet. Staffed computer lab on campus (open 24 hours a day).

The **library** has 165,800 books, 368 microform titles, and 855 subscriptions. It is connected to 3 national **on-line** catalogs.

 ## Campus Life

There are 30 active **organizations** on campus, including a drama/theater group and student-run radio station. Student **safety services** include late night transport/escort service, 24-hour emergency telephone alarm devices, and 24-hour patrols by trained security personnel.

R-MWC is a member of the NCAA (Division III). **Intercollegiate sports** include basketball, equestrian sports, field hockey, lacrosse, soccer, softball, swimming and diving, tennis, volleyball.

 ## Applying

R-MWC requires an essay, a high school transcript, 2 recommendations, and SAT I or ACT. It recommends 3 years of high school math and science, 3 years of high school foreign language, an interview, and 2 SAT II Subject Tests. Early, deferred, and midyear entrance are possible, with a 3/1 deadline and continuous processing to 3/1 for financial aid. **Contact:** Ms. Jean H. Stewart, Director of Admissions, 2500 Rivermont Avenue, Lynchburg, VA 24503-1526, 804-947-8100 or toll-free 800-745-7692 (in-state).

GETTING IN LAST YEAR
624 applied
90% were accepted
34% enrolled (189)
34% from top tenth of their h.s. class
22% had SAT verbal scores over 600
30% had SAT math scores over 600
39% had ACT scores over 26
4% had SAT verbal scores over 700
7% had SAT math scores over 700
8% had ACT scores over 30
3 valedictorians

THE STUDENT BODY
724 undergraduates

From 47 states and territories, 21 other countries
37% from Virginia
100% women
5% African Americans
0% Native Americans
2% Hispanics
2% Asian Americans
7% international students

AFTER FRESHMAN YEAR
84% returned for sophomore year
59% got a degree within 4 years
60% got a degree within 5 years
61% got a degree within 6 years

AFTER GRADUATION
20% pursued further study (14% arts and sciences, 3% law, 2% medicine)

WHAT YOU WILL PAY
Tuition and fees $15,090
Room and board $6330
Need-based college-administered scholarships and grants average $3190 per award
Non-need college-administered scholarships and grants average $1941 per award

REED COLLEGE

Portland, Oregon • Suburban setting • Private • Independent • Coed

Reed's traditional, integrated curriculum provides a context for rigorous study, with a focus on individual responsibility and tolerance for different viewpoints. Students possess a high degree of self-discipline, intellectual curiosity, independence, and genuine enthusiasm for learning. One national survey of professors ranked Reed first in faculty commitment to teaching. Results show Reed ranks first among national undergraduate institutions in percentage of graduates earning PhDs. Reed has produced 30 Rhodes scholars since 1915, a number met by only one other liberal arts college. Graduates remember Reed as "a 4-year-long debate" where the activity of learning was paramount.

 Academics

Reed offers a core academic program; a few graduate courses are open to undergraduates. It awards bachelor's and master's **degrees**. Challenging opportunities include advanced placement, accelerated degree programs, self-designed majors, tutorials, a senior project, and Phi Beta Kappa. Special programs include off-campus study, study abroad, and Army ROTC.

The most popular **majors** include biology/biological sciences, English, and history. A complete listing of majors at Reed appears in the Majors Index beginning on page 379.

The **faculty** at Reed has 100 full-time graduate and undergraduate teachers, 85% with terminal degrees. 90% of the faculty serve as student advisers. The student-faculty ratio is 10:1.

 Computers on Campus

Students are not required to have a computer. Student rooms are linked to a campus network. 140 **computers**

available in the computer center, computer labs, various academic departments, and the library provide access to the main academic computer, off-campus computing facilities, e-mail, on-line services, and the Internet. Staffed computer lab on campus (open 24 hours a day) provides training in the use of computers and software.

The 2 **libraries** have 394,111 books, 54,674 microform titles, and 1,752 subscriptions. They are connected to 73 national **on-line** catalogs.

 Campus Life

Active **organizations** on campus include drama/theater group and student-run newspaper and radio station. Student **safety services** include 24-hour emergency dispatch, late night transport/escort service, 24-hour emergency telephone alarm devices, 24-hour patrols by trained security personnel, student patrols, and electronically operated dormitory entrances. **Intercollegiate sports** include basketball (m), crew (m, w), fencing (m, w), rugby (m, w), sailing (m, w), skiing (cross-country) (m, w), skiing (downhill) (m, w), soccer (m, w).

 Applying

Reed requires an essay, a high school transcript, 2 recommendations, SAT I or ACT, and in some cases 3 SAT II Subject Tests. It recommends 3 years of high school math and science, some high school foreign language, an interview, 3 SAT II Subject Tests, and a minimum high school GPA of 3.0. Early, deferred, and midyear entrance are possible, with a 2/1 deadline and 3/1 for financial aid. **Contact:** Mr. Robert Mansueto, Dean of Admission, 3203 Southeast Woodstock Boulevard, Portland, OR 97202-8199, 503-777-7511 or toll-free 800-547-4750 (out-of-state).

GETTING IN LAST YEAR

1,825 applied
84% were accepted
23% enrolled (354)
50% from top tenth of their h.s. class
3.7 average high school GPA
89% had SAT verbal scores over 600 (R)
84% had SAT math scores over 600 (R)
85% had ACT scores over 26
50% had SAT verbal scores over 700 (R)
26% had SAT math scores over 700 (R)
43% had ACT scores over 30
14 National Merit Scholars
24 valedictorians

THE STUDENT BODY

Total 1,290, of whom 1,276
  are undergraduates

From 47 states and territories,
  23 other countries
14% from Oregon
52% women, 48% men
1% African Americans
1% Native Americans
4% Hispanics
9% Asian Americans
7% international students

AFTER FRESHMAN YEAR

87% returned for sophomore year
41% got a degree within 4 years

61% got a degree within 5 years
66% got a degree within 6 years

AFTER GRADUATION

57% pursued further study (36% arts and
  sciences, 7% law, 5% business)
24 organizations recruited on campus
2 Fulbright scholars

WHAT YOU WILL PAY

Tuition and fees $20,760
Room and board $5750
45% receive need-based financial aid
Need-based college-administered scholarships and
  grants average $18,050 per award

RENSSELAER POLYTECHNIC INSTITUTE

Troy, New York • Suburban setting • Private • Independent • Coed

Rensselaer undergraduates have numerous opportunities to conduct research through the University-funded Undergraduate Research Program and to gain valuable job experience by participation in the Cooperative Education Program. Among successful Rensselaer graduates are Washington Roebling, chief engineer of the Brooklyn Bridge; Nancy Fitzroy, the first woman president of the American Society of Mechanical Engineers; and William Mow, founder of Bugle Boy Industries.

 ## Academics

Rensselaer offers an interactive curriculum and core academic program; more than half of graduate courses are open to undergraduates. It awards bachelor's, master's, and doctoral **degrees**. Challenging opportunities include advanced placement, accelerated degree programs, self-designed majors, tutorials, an honors program, a senior project, and Sigma Xi. Special programs include cooperative education, internships, summer session for credit, off-campus study, study abroad, and Army, Naval, and Air Force ROTC.

The most popular **majors** include mechanical engineering, electrical engineering, and computer science. A complete listing of majors at Rensselaer appears in the Majors Index beginning on page 379.

The **faculty** at Rensselaer has 341 full-time undergraduate teachers, 99% with terminal degrees. The student-faculty ratio is 12:1.

 ## Computers on Campus

Students are not required to have a computer. Student rooms are linked to a campus network. 618 **computers** available in the computer center, computer labs, academic buildings, classrooms, the library, and dormitories provide access to the main academic computer, off-campus computing facilities, e-mail, on-line services, and the Internet. Staffed

computer lab on campus (open 24 hours a day) provides training in the use of computers and software.

The 2 **libraries** have 441,000 books, 602,267 microform titles, and 3,662 subscriptions. They are connected to 21 national **on-line** catalogs.

 ## Campus Life

There are 114 active **organizations** on campus, including a drama/theater group and student-run newspaper and radio station. 40% of eligible men and 40% of eligible women are members of 29 national **fraternities**, 5 national **sororities**, 1 local fraternity, 1 local sorority, and 1 coed fraternity. Student **safety services** include campus foot patrols at night, late night transport/escort service, 24-hour emergency telephone alarm devices, 24-hour patrols by trained security personnel, and electronically operated dormitory entrances.

Rensselaer is a member of the NCAA (Division III). **Intercollegiate sports** (some offering scholarships) include baseball (m), basketball (m, w), crew (m, w), cross-country running (m, w), equestrian sports (m, w), fencing (m, w), field hockey (w), football (m), golf (m), ice hockey (m, w), lacrosse (m, w), racquetball (m, w), rugby (m), skiing (cross-country) (m, w), skiing (downhill) (m, w), soccer (m, w), softball (w), swimming and diving (m, w), tennis (m, w), track and field (m, w), volleyball (m, w), wrestling (m).

 ## Applying

Rensselaer requires an essay, a high school transcript, 4 years of high school math, 3 years of high school science, 1 recommendation, SAT I or ACT, and in some cases 3 SAT II Subject Tests. It recommends some high school foreign language, a campus interview, and 3 SAT II Subject Tests. Early, deferred, and midyear entrance are possible, with a 1/1 deadline and a 2/15 priority date for financial aid. **Contact:** Ms. Teresa Duffy, Dean of Admissions, Sage and Eaton Streets, Troy, NY 12180-3590, 518-276-6216 or toll-free 800-448-6562; fax 518-276-4072.

GETTING IN LAST YEAR
4,543 applied
85% were accepted
25% enrolled (963)
56% from top tenth of their h.s. class
25% had SAT verbal scores over 600
82% had SAT math scores over 600
1% had SAT verbal scores over 700
31% had SAT math scores over 700
26 National Merit Scholars
62 valedictorians

THE STUDENT BODY
Total 6,400, of whom 4,360
   are undergraduates
From 53 states and territories,
   53 other countries

41% from New York
24% women, 76% men
4% African Americans
1% Native Americans
5% Hispanics
14% Asian Americans
6% international students

AFTER FRESHMAN YEAR
90% returned for sophomore year
44% got a degree within 4 years
65% got a degree within 5 years
68% got a degree within 6 years

AFTER GRADUATION
18% pursued further study
79% had job offers within 6 months
266 organizations recruited on campus

WHAT YOU WILL PAY
Tuition and fees $18,555
Room and board $6155
Need-based college-administered scholarships and
   grants average $8074 per award
Non-need college-administered scholarships and
   grants average $6689 per award

RHODE ISLAND SCHOOL OF DESIGN

Providence, Rhode Island • Urban setting • Private • Independent • Coed

 Rhode Island School of Design has been successfully educating aspiring artists and designers for fulfilling lives and careers in the visual arts for more than 117 years. Widely recognized today by professional artists and designers, educators, and comparative college guides as one of the leading colleges for the visual arts, RISD offers an unsurpassed environment to challenge students' ideas and perfect their talents. The combination of a faculty of 300 artists, the student body of 1,980 drawn from around the country and 50 nations around the world, and the campus of 40 buildings housing extensive studios and numerous specialized art-making facilities creates an environment that will encourage and support students' goals.

Academics

RISD offers a core academic program; a few graduate courses are open to undergraduates. It awards bachelor's and master's **degrees**. Challenging opportunities include advanced placement, tutorials, and a senior project. Special programs include internships, off-campus study, and study abroad.

The most popular **majors** include illustration, architecture, and graphic arts. A complete listing of majors at RISD appears in the Majors Index beginning on page 379.

The **faculty** at RISD has 122 full-time graduate and undergraduate teachers, 71% with terminal degrees. The student-faculty ratio is 12:1.

 ## Computers on Campus

Students are not required to have a computer. 240 **computers** available in the computer center, academic departments, the library, and dormitories provide access to e-mail and the Internet. Staffed computer lab on campus provides training in the use of computers and software.

The **library** has 80,000 books and 393 subscriptions.

 ## Campus Life

There are 60 active **organizations** on campus, including a drama/theater group and student-run newspaper. Student **safety services** include late night transport/escort service, 24-hour emergency telephone alarm devices, 24-hour patrols by trained security personnel, and electronically operated dormitory entrances.

This institution has no intercollegiate sports.

 ## Applying

RISD requires an essay, a high school transcript, portfolio, drawing assignments, SAT I or ACT, and in some cases 3 years of high school math. It recommends 3 recommendations. Early and deferred entrance are possible, with a 1/21 deadline and a 2/15 priority date for financial aid. **Contact:** Mr. Edward Newhall, Director of Admissions, 62 Prospect Street, Providence, RI 02903-2784, 401-454-6300 or toll-free 800-364-RISD (in-state); fax 401-454-6309.

GETTING IN LAST YEAR
1,496 applied
58% were accepted
44% enrolled (377)
20% from top tenth of their h.s. class
3.0 average high school GPA
18% had SAT verbal scores over 600
36% had SAT math scores over 600
1% had SAT verbal scores over 700
8% had SAT math scores over 700

THE STUDENT BODY
Total 1,987, of whom 1,815
  are undergraduates

From 50 states and territories,
  52 other countries
8% from Rhode Island
56% women, 44% men
2% African Americans
1% Native Americans
2% Hispanics
7% Asian Americans
19% international students

AFTER FRESHMAN YEAR
94% returned for sophomore year
85% got a degree within 5 years

AFTER GRADUATION
5% pursued further study (5% arts and sciences)

WHAT YOU WILL PAY
Tuition and fees $17,780
Room and board $6618
61% receive need-based financial aid
Need-based college-administered scholarships and
  grants average $5958 per award
Non-need college-administered scholarships and
  grants average $2500 per award

RHODES COLLEGE

Memphis, Tennessee • Suburban setting • Private • Independent-Religious • Coed

Rhodes offers something that is not found around most highly selective national liberal arts colleges—a big city. Memphis is a hub of commerce and culture with local theaters, touring Broadway shows, a symphony, concerts, professional sports, restaurants, and shops. There are also many opportunities for internships—60% of Rhodes' students gain internship experience during their 4 years. Rhodes is distinctive for its commitment to community service and for broad involvement by students in their own self-governance. Central to Rhodes is a completely student-run honor system.

Academics

Rhodes offers a traditional liberal arts curriculum with international emphasis and core academic program; fewer than half of graduate courses are open to undergraduates. It awards bachelor's and master's **degrees** (master's in accounting only). Challenging opportunities include advanced placement, accelerated degree programs, self-designed majors, tutorials, an honors program, a senior project, and Phi Beta Kappa. Special programs include cooperative education, internships, summer session for credit, off-campus study, study abroad, and Army and Air Force ROTC.

The most popular **majors** include English, biology/biological sciences, and international studies. A complete listing of majors at Rhodes appears in the Majors Index beginning on page 379.

The **faculty** at Rhodes has 115 full-time graduate and undergraduate teachers, 99% with terminal degrees. 100% of the faculty serve as student advisers. The student-faculty ratio is 12:1, and the average class size in core courses is 18.

Computers on Campus

Students are not required to have a computer. Student rooms are linked to a campus network. 125 **computers** available in the computer center, computer labs, departmental offices, classrooms, and the library provide access to the main academic computer, off-campus computing facilities, e-mail, on-line services, and the Internet. Staffed computer lab on campus provides training in the use of computers and software.

The 4 **libraries** have 238,000 books, 6,300 microform titles, and 1,195 subscriptions. They are connected to 2 national **on-line** catalogs.

Campus Life

There are 88 active **organizations** on campus, including a drama/theater group and student-run newspaper. 51% of eligible men and 53% of eligible women are members of 6 national **fraternities** and 7 national **sororities**. Student **safety services** include 24-hour monitored security cameras in parking areas, fenced campus with monitored access at night, late night transport/escort service, 24-hour emergency telephone alarm devices, 24-hour patrols by trained security personnel, and student patrols.

Rhodes is a member of the NCAA (Division III). **Intercollegiate sports** include baseball (m), basketball (m, w), cross-country running (m, w), equestrian sports (m, w), football (m), golf (m, w), lacrosse (m), rugby (m), soccer (m, w), swimming and diving (m, w), tennis (m, w), track and field (m, w), volleyball (w).

Applying

Rhodes requires an essay, a high school transcript, 3 years of high school math, 2 years of high school foreign language, 2 recommendations, 2 years of high school science, and SAT I or ACT. It recommends an interview. Early, deferred, and midyear entrance are possible, with a 2/1 deadline and continuous processing to 3/1 for financial aid. **Contact:** Mr. David J. Wottle, Dean of Admissions and Financial Aid, 2000 North Parkway, Memphis, TN 38112-1690, 901-726-3700 or toll-free 800-844-5969 (out-of-state); fax 901-726-3719.

GETTING IN LAST YEAR
2,345 applied
70% were accepted
24% enrolled (391)
56% from top tenth of their h.s. class
3.6 average high school GPA
43% had SAT verbal scores over 600 (R)
71% had SAT math scores over 600 (R)
78% had ACT scores over 26
6% had SAT verbal scores over 700 (R)
17% had SAT math scores over 700 (R)
31% had ACT scores over 30
16 National Merit Scholars
19 class presidents
34 valedictorians

THE STUDENT BODY
Total 1,441, of whom 1,435
    are undergraduates

From 42 states and territories,
    18 other countries
33% from Tennessee
56% women, 44% men
3% African Americans
0% Native Americans
1% Hispanics
4% Asian Americans
3% international students

AFTER FRESHMAN YEAR
90% returned for sophomore year
72% got a degree within 4 years
76% got a degree within 5 years
77% got a degree within 6 years

AFTER GRADUATION
40% pursued further study (19% arts and
    sciences, 8% law, 7% medicine)

80% had job offers within 6 months
29 organizations recruited on campus
1 Fulbright scholar

WHAT YOU WILL PAY
Tuition and fees $15,920
Room and board $4912
45% receive need-based financial aid
Need-based college-administered scholarships and
    grants average $8239 per award
32% receive non-need financial aid
Non-need college-administered scholarships and
    grants average $7381 per award

RICE UNIVERSITY

Houston, Texas • Urban setting • Private • Independent • Coed

Adjacent to the largest medical center in the country and the Houston museum district, Rice University offers students access to a wide range of educational and cultural opportunities. Much of Rice's distinctiveness stems from combining the characteristics of a relatively small liberal arts college with those of a true research university. In addition, the university maintains one of the few remaining honor systems in the country as well as a residential college system. Recognized as one of the best educational bargains in the country, Rice offers need-based assistance as well as athletic, academic, and minority scholarships.

Academics

Rice University offers an interdisciplinary curriculum and core academic program; more than half of graduate courses are open to undergraduates. It awards bachelor's, master's, doctoral, and first professional **degrees**. Challenging opportunities include advanced placement, accelerated degree programs, self-designed majors, an honors program, a senior project, Phi Beta Kappa, and Sigma Xi. Special programs include internships, summer session for credit, off-campus study, study abroad, and Army and Naval ROTC.

The most popular **majors** include political science/government, English, and history. A complete listing of majors at Rice University appears in the Majors Index beginning on page 379.

The **faculty** at Rice University has 428 full-time graduate and undergraduate teachers, 100% with terminal degrees. The student-faculty ratio is 9:1.

Computers on Campus

Students are not required to have a computer. Student rooms are linked to a campus network. 185 **computers**

available in the computer center, computer labs, academic department buildings, the library, and dormitories provide access to e-mail, on-line services, and the Internet. Staffed computer lab on campus (open 24 hours a day) provides training in the use of computers and software.

The **library** has 1.8 million books, 1.8 million microform titles, and 13,100 subscriptions.

Campus Life

There are 80 active **organizations** on campus, including a drama/theater group and student-run newspaper and radio station. Student **safety services** include late night transport/escort service, 24-hour emergency telephone alarm devices, 24-hour patrols by trained security personnel, and electronically operated dormitory entrances.

Rice University is a member of the NCAA (Division I). **Intercollegiate sports** (some offering scholarships) include baseball (m), basketball (m, w), crew (m, w), cross-country running (m, w), football (m), golf (m), lacrosse (m), riflery (m, w), rugby (m), sailing (m, w), soccer (m, w), swimming and diving (m, w), tennis (m, w), track and field (m, w), volleyball (w).

Applying

Rice University requires an essay, a high school transcript, 3 years of high school math, 2 years of high school foreign language, 2 recommendations, SAT I or ACT, 3 SAT II Subject Tests (including SAT II: Writing Test), and in some cases 3 years of high school science. It recommends an interview. Early and deferred entrance are possible, with a 1/2 deadline and continuous processing for financial aid.
Contact: Ms. Julie M. Browning, Director of Admissions, MS 17, Houston, TX 77005, 713-527-4036 or toll-free 800-527-OWLS (out-of-state).

GETTING IN LAST YEAR
6,843 applied
26% were accepted
38% enrolled (696)
75% from top tenth of their h.s. class
244 National Merit Scholars

THE STUDENT BODY
Total 4,051, of whom 2,645
    are undergraduates
From 50 states and territories,
    30 other countries
47% from Texas
45% women, 55% men
7% African Americans

1% Native Americans
10% Hispanics
15% Asian Americans
2% international students

AFTER FRESHMAN YEAR
95% returned for sophomore year
68% got a degree within 4 years
86% got a degree within 5 years
88% got a degree within 6 years

AFTER GRADUATION
60% pursued further study (23% law, 15% arts
    and sciences, 9% business)
1 Marshall, 4 Fulbright scholars

WHAT YOU WILL PAY
Tuition and fees $12,222
Room and board $5900
35% receive need-based financial aid
Need-based college-administered scholarships and
    grants average $4191 per award
43% receive non-need financial aid
Non-need college-administered scholarships and
    grants average $4016 per award

RIPON COLLEGE

Ripon, Wisconsin • Small-town setting • Private • Independent • Coed

---

> Ripon College has an unrivaled commitment to the liberal arts and a dedicated teaching faculty to ensure its fulfillment. The traditional, residential nature of Ripon creates a distinctive academic and social community. This atmosphere offers the best educational value, and scholarship and financial aid programs represent the commitment to making Ripon affordable.

Academics

Ripon offers a core academic program. It awards bachelor's **degrees**. Challenging opportunities include advanced placement, accelerated degree programs, self-designed majors, tutorials, a senior project, and Phi Beta Kappa. Special programs include internships, off-campus study, study abroad, and Army ROTC.

The most popular **majors** include history, English, and biology/biological sciences. A complete listing of majors at Ripon appears in the Majors Index beginning on page 379.

The **faculty** at Ripon has 70 full-time teachers, 90% with terminal degrees. 100% of the faculty serve as student advisers. The student-faculty ratio is 10:1.

Computers on Campus

Students are not required to have a computer. Student rooms are linked to a campus network. 140 **computers** available in the computer center, computer labs, classrooms, the library, and dormitories provide access to e-mail, on-line services, and the Internet. Staffed computer lab on campus provides training in the use of computers and software.

The **library** has 161,396 books, 18,672 microform titles, and 715 subscriptions. It is connected to 2 national **on-line** catalogs.

Campus Life

There are 80 active **organizations** on campus, including a drama/theater group and student-run newspaper and radio station. 55% of eligible men and 28% of eligible women are members of 3 national **fraternities**, 2 national **sororities**, 2 local fraternities, and 1 local sorority. Student **safety services** include late night transport/escort service, 24-hour emergency telephone alarm devices, 24-hour patrols by trained security personnel, student patrols, and electronically operated dormitory entrances.

Ripon is a member of the NCAA (Division III). **Intercollegiate sports** include baseball (m), basketball (m, w), cross-country running (m, w), fencing (m, w), football (m), golf (m), ice hockey (m, w), lacrosse (m, w), riflery (m, w), rugby (m), soccer (m, w), softball (w), swimming and diving (m, w), tennis (m, w), track and field (m, w), volleyball (m, w).

Applying

Ripon requires an essay, a high school transcript, 1 recommendation, SAT I or ACT, and a minimum high school GPA of 2.0. It recommends 3 years of high school math and science, some high school foreign language, and an interview. Early, deferred, and midyear entrance are possible, with a 3/15 deadline and continuous processing to 3/1 for financial aid. **Contact:** Mr. Paul J. Weeks, Vice President and Dean of Admission, 300 Seward Street, Ripon, WI 54971, 414-748-8102 or toll-free 800-947-4766.

GETTING IN LAST YEAR

592 applied
83% were accepted
39% enrolled (189)
30% from top tenth of their h.s. class
3.29 average high school GPA
24% had SAT verbal scores over 600 (R)
52% had SAT math scores over 600 (R)
37% had ACT scores over 26
3% had SAT verbal scores over 700 (R)
11% had SAT math scores over 700 (R)
9% had ACT scores over 30

THE STUDENT BODY

769 undergraduates

From 39 states and territories,
15 other countries
61% from Wisconsin
50% women, 50% men
1% African Americans
1% Native Americans
2% Hispanics
2% Asian Americans
4% international students

AFTER FRESHMAN YEAR

89% returned for sophomore year

AFTER GRADUATION

30% pursued further study (23% arts and sciences, 5% medicine, 2% law)
95% had job offers within 6 months
61 organizations recruited on campus

WHAT YOU WILL PAY

Tuition and fees $17,000
Room and board $4400
75% receive need-based financial aid
Need-based college-administered scholarships and grants average $9031 per award
10% receive non-need financial aid
Non-need college-administered scholarships and grants average $4887 per award

ROCHESTER INSTITUTE OF TECHNOLOGY

Rochester, New York • Suburban setting • Private • Independent • Coed

Respected internationally as a leader in career-oriented education, RIT has been an innovative pacesetter since 1829. RIT offers outstanding teaching, a strong foundation in the liberal arts and sciences, modern classroom facilities, and work experience gained through the university's cooperative education program. Innovative programs include microelectronic engineering, imaging science, film/video, biotechnology, international business, and the programs of RIT's National Technical Institute for the Deaf (NTID). RIT draws students from every state and more than 70 other countries.

 Academics

RIT offers a humanities and social sciences curriculum and core academic program; fewer than half of graduate courses are open to undergraduates. It awards associate, bachelor's, master's, and doctoral **degrees**. Challenging opportunities include advanced placement, self-designed majors, tutorials, and a senior project. Special programs include cooperative education, internships, summer session for credit, off-campus study, study abroad, and Army, Naval, and Air Force ROTC.

The most popular **majors** include engineering technology, engineering (general), and business. A complete listing of majors at RIT appears in the Majors Index beginning on page 379.

The **faculty** at RIT has 695 full-time graduate and undergraduate teachers, 75% with terminal degrees. 90% of the faculty serve as student advisers. The student-faculty ratio is 12:1.

 Computers on Campus

Students are not required to have a computer. Student rooms are linked to a campus network. 800 **computers** available in the computer center, computer labs, classrooms, the library, and dormitories provide access to the main academic computer, off-campus computing facilities, e-mail, on-line services, the Internet, and course registration and student account information. Staffed computer lab on campus provides training in the use of computers and software.

The **library** has 346,771 books, 232,701 microform titles, and 4,796 subscriptions. It is connected to 2 national **on-line** catalogs.

 Campus Life

There are 75 active **organizations** on campus, including a drama/theater group and student-run newspaper and radio station. 10% of eligible men and 10% of eligible women are members of 15 national **fraternities**, 9 national **sororities**, 1 local fraternity, and 1 local sorority. Student **safety services** include late night transport/escort service, 24-hour emergency telephone alarm devices, 24-hour patrols by trained security personnel, and student patrols.

RIT is a member of the NCAA (Division III). **Intercollegiate sports** include baseball (m), basketball (m, w), crew (m, w), cross-country running (m, w), fencing (m, w), ice hockey (m, w), lacrosse (m, w), rugby (m, w), soccer (m, w), softball (w), swimming and diving (m, w), tennis (m, w), track and field (m, w), volleyball (m, w), water polo (m, w), wrestling (m).

 Applying

RIT requires an essay, a high school transcript, SAT I or ACT, and in some cases 3 years of high school math and science, a portfolio for art majors, and a minimum high school GPA of 3.0. It recommends recommendations and an interview. Early, deferred, and midyear entrance are possible, with a 7/1 deadline and continuous processing to 3/15 for financial aid. **Contact:** Mr. Daniel Shelley, Director of Admissions, 60 Lomb Memorial Drive, Rochester, NY 14623-5604, 716-475-6631; fax 716-475-7424.

GETTING IN LAST YEAR
5,635 applied
76% were accepted
38% enrolled (1,647)
27% from top tenth of their h.s. class
3.7 average high school GPA
13% had SAT verbal scores over 600
48% had SAT math scores over 600
46% had ACT scores over 26
1% had SAT verbal scores over 700
12% had SAT math scores over 700
11% had ACT scores over 30
15 National Merit Scholars
35 valedictorians

THE STUDENT BODY
Total 12,600, of whom 10,552
  are undergraduates

From 50 states and territories,
  70 other countries
60% from New York
34% women, 66% men
5% African Americans
1% Native Americans
3% Hispanics
5% Asian Americans
5% international students

AFTER FRESHMAN YEAR
86% returned for sophomore year
62% got a degree within 6 years

AFTER GRADUATION
10% pursued further study
90% had job offers within 6 months
400 organizations recruited on campus

WHAT YOU WILL PAY
Tuition and fees $14,937
Room and board $5898
70% receive need-based financial aid
Need-based college-administered scholarships and
  grants average $5700 per award
20% receive non-need financial aid
Non-need college-administered scholarships and
  grants average $3600 per award

ROCKHURST COLLEGE

Kansas City, Missouri • Urban setting • Private • Independent-Religious • Coed

Rockhurst College prides itself on teaching students not just what to think, but how to think. The Rockhurst method of critical questioning is based on the 450-year-old Jesuit tradition. Rockhurst's 35-acre campus in Kansas City's cultural district hosts a learning community characterized by close student-faculty interaction; highly ranked academic excellence in the liberal arts, management, and allied health; and an award-winning service learning program. Rockhurst prepares students for success after graduation: "Famous Rocks," as its distinguished alumni are known, serve in leadership roles throughout the nation in many fields. Rockhurst challenges prospective students to "climb the Rock" by visiting campus.

 Academics

Rockhurst offers an interdisciplinary curriculum and core academic program; fewer than half of graduate courses are open to undergraduates. It awards bachelor's and master's **degrees**. Challenging opportunities include advanced placement, accelerated degree programs, tutorials, Freshman Honors College, an honors program, and a senior project. Special programs include cooperative education, internships, summer session for credit, off-campus study, study abroad, and Army ROTC.

The most popular **majors** include nursing, psychology, and biology/biological sciences. A complete listing of majors at Rockhurst appears in the Majors Index beginning on page 379.

The **faculty** at Rockhurst has 137 full-time graduate and undergraduate teachers, 79% with terminal degrees. 88% of the faculty serve as student advisers. The student-faculty ratio is 11:1.

 Computers on Campus

Students are not required to have a computer. 300 **computers** available in the computer center, computer labs, classrooms, the library, and dormitories provide access to the main academic computer, e-mail, on-line services, and the Internet. Staffed computer lab on campus provides training in the use of computers and software.

The **library** has 105,285 books, 20,361 microform titles, and 695 subscriptions. It is connected to 2 national **on-line** catalogs.

 Campus Life

There are 35 active **organizations** on campus, including a drama/theater group and student-run newspaper and radio station. 50% of students participate in student government elections. 27% of eligible men and 12% of eligible women are members of 4 national **fraternities** and 2 national **sororities**. Student **safety services** include closed circuit TV, 24-hour emergency telephone alarm devices, 24-hour patrols by trained security personnel, student patrols, and electronically operated dormitory entrances.

Rockhurst is a member of the NAIA. **Intercollegiate sports** (some offering scholarships) include baseball (m), basketball (m, w), cross-country running (m, w), golf (m, w), soccer (m, w), tennis (m, w), volleyball (w).

 Applying

Rockhurst requires a high school transcript, 1 recommendation, SAT I or ACT, and a minimum high school GPA of 2.0. It recommends 3 years of high school math and science, 2 years of high school foreign language, an interview, 4 years of high school English, 3 years of high school social sciences, and some high school fine arts. Early, deferred, and midyear entrance are possible, with rolling admissions and continuous processing to 4/1 for financial aid. **Contact:** Mr. Jack Reichmeier, Director of Admissions, 1100 Rockhurst Road, Kansas City, MO 64110-2561, 816-501-4100 or toll-free 800-842-6776; fax 816-501-4588.

GETTING IN LAST YEAR
970 applied
90% were accepted
33% enrolled (289)
27% from top tenth of their h.s. class
29% had ACT scores over 26
5% had ACT scores over 30
11 valedictorians

THE STUDENT BODY
Total 2,886, of whom 2,140 are undergraduates
From 29 states and territories, 17 other countries

72% from Missouri
58% women, 42% men
7% African Americans
1% Native Americans
5% Hispanics
2% Asian Americans
1% international students

AFTER FRESHMAN YEAR
83% returned for sophomore year
49% got a degree within 4 years
57% got a degree within 5 years
58% got a degree within 6 years

AFTER GRADUATION
22% pursued further study (15% arts and sciences, 3% business, 3% law)

72% had job offers within 6 months
71 organizations recruited on campus

WHAT YOU WILL PAY
Tuition and fees $11,240
Room and board $4490
38% receive need-based financial aid
Need-based college-administered scholarships and grants average $1198 per award
56% receive non-need financial aid
Non-need college-administered scholarships and grants average $1496 per award

ROLLINS COLLEGE

Winter Park, Florida • Suburban setting • Private • Independent • Coed

In order to ensure a smooth transition from secondary school to college, Rollins offers the Rollins Conference, a first-semester program for freshmen. Students may choose from more than 25 different Conference courses, and sections are limited to 17 students each. The faculty member for the section is the students' first-year academic adviser. Two upperclass peer mentors are assigned to each section, providing academic and social support during the first year. In addition, the freshmen coordinator works closely with all freshmen and supervises peer mentors.

 ## Academics

Rollins offers a liberal arts curriculum and core academic program; a few graduate courses are open to undergraduates. It awards bachelor's and master's **degrees**. Challenging opportunities include advanced placement, accelerated degree programs, self-designed majors, tutorials, an honors program, a senior project, and Sigma Xi. Special programs include internships, off-campus study, and study abroad.

The most popular **majors** include psychology, economics, and English. A complete listing of majors at Rollins appears in the Majors Index beginning on page 379.

The **faculty** at Rollins has 146 full-time graduate and undergraduate teachers, 92% with terminal degrees. 91% of the faculty serve as student advisers. The student-faculty ratio is 12:1.

 ## Computers on Campus

Students are not required to have a computer. 150 **computers** available in the computer center, computer labs, writing center, classrooms, the library, and dormitories provide access to the main academic computer, off-campus computing facilities, e-mail, and on-line services. Staffed computer lab on campus provides training in the use of computers and software.

The **library** has 264,658 books, 37,758 microform titles, and 1,546 subscriptions. It is connected to 3 national **on-line** catalogs.

 ## Campus Life

There are 54 active **organizations** on campus, including a drama/theater group and student-run newspaper and radio station. 50% of students participate in student government elections. 35% of eligible men and 35% of eligible women are members of 5 national **fraternities**, 5 national **sororities**, 1 local fraternity, and 1 local sorority. Student **safety services** include late night transport/escort service, 24-hour emergency telephone alarm devices, 24-hour patrols by trained security personnel, and electronically operated dormitory entrances.

Rollins is a member of the NCAA (Division II). **Intercollegiate sports** (some offering scholarships) include baseball (m), basketball (m, w), crew (m, w), cross-country running (m, w), golf (m, w), sailing (m, w), soccer (m, w), softball (w), tennis (m, w), volleyball (w).

 ## Applying

Rollins requires an essay, a high school transcript, 3 years of high school math, 1 recommendation, and SAT I or ACT. It recommends 3 years of high school science, 2 years of high school foreign language, an interview, and 3 SAT II Subject Tests. Early, deferred, and midyear entrance are possible, with a 2/15 deadline and continuous processing to 3/1 for financial aid. **Contact:** Mr. David Erdmann, Dean of Admissions and Student Financial Planning, 1000 Holt Avenue, Winter Park, FL 32789-4499, 407-646-2161; fax 407-646-2600.

GETTING IN LAST YEAR
1,800 applied
70% were accepted
33% enrolled (412)
38% from top tenth of their h.s. class
16% had SAT verbal scores over 600
35% had SAT math scores over 600
34% had ACT scores over 26
1% had SAT verbal scores over 700
6% had SAT math scores over 700
5% had ACT scores over 30

THE STUDENT BODY
Total 3,281, of whom 1,422
 are undergraduates

From 42 states and territories,
 24 other countries
45% from Florida
55% women, 45% men
4% African Americans
1% Native Americans
6% Hispanics
3% Asian Americans
3% international students

AFTER FRESHMAN YEAR
88% returned for sophomore year
71% got a degree within 4 years
73% got a degree within 5 years
74% got a degree within 6 years

AFTER GRADUATION
20% pursued further study (8% arts and
 sciences, 3% business, 3% law)
70% had job offers within 6 months
39 organizations recruited on campus

WHAT YOU WILL PAY
Tuition and fees $17,995
Room and board $5555
40% receive need-based financial aid
Need-based college-administered scholarships and
 grants average $9247 per award
20% receive non-need financial aid
Non-need college-administered scholarships and
 grants average $5700 per award

ROSE-HULMAN INSTITUTE OF TECHNOLOGY

Terre Haute, Indiana • Rural setting • Private • Independent • Coed

Academics

Rose-Hulman offers an engineering and science curriculum and core academic program; fewer than half of graduate courses are open to undergraduates. It awards bachelor's and master's **degrees**. Challenging opportunities include advanced placement, an honors program, and a senior project. Special programs include internships, off-campus study, study abroad, and Army and Air Force ROTC.

The **faculty** at Rose-Hulman has 115 full-time undergraduate teachers, 95% with terminal degrees. 100% of the faculty serve as student advisers. The student-faculty ratio is 13:1.

Computers on Campus

Students are required to have a computer. Purchase options are available. Student rooms are linked to a campus network. 300 **computers** available in the computer center, computer labs, the learning resource center, academic buildings, classrooms, the library, and the student center provide access to the main academic computer, off-campus computing facilities, e-mail, on-line services, and the Internet. Staffed computer lab on campus (open 24 hours a day) provides training in the use of computers and software.

The **library** has 68,000 books and 392 subscriptions. It is connected to 2 national **on-line** catalogs.

Campus Life

There are 70 active **organizations** on campus, including a drama/theater group and student-run newspaper and radio station. 40% of students participate in student government elections. 40% of eligible men are members of 8 national **fraternities**. Student **safety services** include late night transport/escort service, 24-hour emergency telephone alarm devices, 24-hour patrols by trained security personnel, and electronically operated dormitory entrances.

Rose-Hulman is a member of the NCAA (Division III). **Intercollegiate sports** include baseball (m), basketball (m, w), cross-country running (m, w), football (m), golf (m), riflery (m, w), soccer (m), tennis (m), track and field (m, w), volleyball (w), wrestling (m).

Applying

Rose-Hulman requires a high school transcript, 4 years of high school math, 1 recommendation, and SAT I or ACT. It recommends 3 years of high school science. Rolling admissions and a 3/1 priority date for financial aid. **Contact:** Mr. Charles G. Howard, Dean of Admissions, 5500 Wabash Avenue, Terre Haute, IN 47803-3920, 812-877-8213 or toll-free 800-552-0725 (in-state), 800-248-7448 (out-of-state); fax 812-877-8941.

GETTING IN LAST YEAR
3,507 applied
58% were accepted
23% enrolled (462)
65% from top tenth of their h.s. class
37% had SAT verbal scores over 600
93% had SAT math scores over 600
100% had ACT scores over 26
11% had SAT verbal scores over 700
50% had SAT math scores over 700
80% had ACT scores over 30
23 National Merit Scholars

THE STUDENT BODY
Total 1,520, of whom 1,450
 are undergraduates

From 41 states and territories,
 6 other countries
55% from Indiana
6% women, 94% men
2% African Americans
1% Native Americans
1% Hispanics
2% Asian Americans
4% international students

AFTER FRESHMAN YEAR
90% returned for sophomore year
73% got a degree within 4 years
75% got a degree within 5 years

AFTER GRADUATION
20% pursued further study (12% engineering,
 4% arts and sciences, 2% business)
99% had job offers within 6 months
285 organizations recruited on campus

WHAT YOU WILL PAY
Tuition and fees $15,735
Room and board $4700
Need-based college-administered scholarships and
 grants average $2000 per award
Non-need college-administered scholarships and
 grants average $2000 per award

RUTGERS, THE STATE UNIVERSITY OF NEW JERSEY, COLLEGE OF ENGINEERING

Piscataway, New Jersey • Small-town setting • Public • State-supported • Coed

The College of Engineering maintains 2 principal objectives: the sound technical and cultural education of its students and the advancement of knowledge through research. Its programs emphasize a thorough understanding of fundamental engineering principles, methods of analysis, and reasoning. The College offers 4-year degree programs in 8 major areas: applied sciences in engineering and bioresource, ceramic, chemical, civil, electrical, industrial, and mechanical engineering. In addition, students can specialize in areas such as aerospace, agricultural, biochemical, biomedical, computer, environmental, food, and packaging engineering.

Academics

Rutgers, The State University of New Jersey, College of Engineering offers a core academic program. It awards bachelor's **degrees** (master of science, master of philosophy, and doctor of philosophy are offered through the Graduate School, New Brunswick). Challenging opportunities include advanced placement, self-designed majors, tutorials, an honors program, and a senior project. Special programs include internships, summer session for credit, off-campus study, study abroad, and Army and Air Force ROTC.

The most popular **majors** include mechanical engineering, electrical engineering, and civil engineering. A complete listing of majors at Rutgers, The State University of New Jersey, College of Engineering appears in the Majors Index beginning on page 379.

The **faculty** at Rutgers, The State University of New Jersey, College of Engineering has 127 full-time teachers, 98% with terminal degrees. The student-faculty ratio is 11:1, and the average class size in core courses is 47.

Computers on Campus

Students are not required to have a computer. Student rooms are linked to a campus network. 690 **computers** available in the computer center, computer labs, the research center, the learning resource center, various locations on campus, classrooms, the library, the student center, dormitories, and student rooms provide access to the main academic computer, off-campus computing facilities, e-mail, on-line services, and the Internet. Staffed computer lab on campus (open 24 hours a day) provides training in the use of computers and software.

The 15 **libraries** have 4.4 million books, 2.8 million microform titles, and 18,274 subscriptions. They are connected to 26 national **on-line** catalogs.

Campus Life

There are 400 active **organizations** on campus, including a drama/theater group and student-run newspaper and radio station. 25% of students participate in student government elections. 11% of eligible men and 7% of eligible women are members of 31 national **fraternities**, 11 national **sororities**, and 4 local sororities. Student **safety services** include late night transport/escort service, 24-hour emergency telephone alarm devices, 24-hour patrols by trained security personnel, student patrols, and electronically operated dormitory entrances.

Rutgers, The State University of New Jersey, College of Engineering is a member of the NCAA (Division I). **Intercollegiate sports** (some offering scholarships) include baseball (m), basketball (m, w), crew (m, w), cross-country running (m, w), fencing (m, w), field hockey (w), football (m), golf (m, w), gymnastics (w), lacrosse (m, w), soccer (m, w), softball (w), swimming and diving (m, w), tennis (m, w), track and field (m, w), volleyball (w), wrestling (m).

Applying

Rutgers, The State University of New Jersey, College of Engineering requires a high school transcript, 4 years of high school math, 1 course each in chemistry and physics, SAT I or ACT, and in some cases 3 SAT II Subject Tests. Early and deferred entrance are possible, with a 1/15 deadline and continuous processing to 3/1 for financial aid. **Contact:** Dr. Elizabeth Mitchell, Asst. Vice President for University Undergraduate Admissions, PO Box 2101, New Brunswick, NJ 08903-2101, 908-445-3770; fax 908-445-0237.

GETTING IN LAST YEAR

3,005 applied
76% were accepted
24% enrolled (542)
32% from top tenth of their h.s. class
36% had SAT verbal scores over 600 (R)
78% had SAT math scores over 600 (R)
4% had SAT verbal scores over 700 (R)
25% had SAT math scores over 700 (R)
1 National Merit Scholar
14 valedictorians

THE STUDENT BODY

2,278 undergraduates
From 24 states and territories,
   37 other countries
86% from New Jersey
18% women, 82% men
6% African Americans
1% Native Americans
6% Hispanics
23% Asian Americans
5% international students

AFTER GRADUATION

500 organizations recruited on campus

WHAT YOU WILL PAY

Resident tuition and fees $5214
Nonresident tuition and fees $9562
Room and board $4936
54% receive need-based financial aid
Need-based college-administered scholarships and
   grants average $1450 per award
38% receive non-need financial aid
Non-need college-administered scholarships and
   grants average $3074 per award

RUTGERS, THE STATE UNIVERSITY OF NEW JERSEY, COLLEGE OF PHARMACY

Piscataway, New Jersey • Small-town setting • Public • State-supported • Coed

> The College of Pharmacy is one of the most selective and competitive programs in the nation. The 5-year BS curriculum prepares students for practicing the profession of pharmacy in community pharmacies and hospitals as well as in the pharmaceutical industry. Students develop high levels of comprehension and professional problem-solving skills.

 ## Academics

Rutgers, The State University of New Jersey, College of Pharmacy offers a core academic program. It awards bachelor's and doctoral **degrees**. In addition to the master of science and doctor of philosophy degrees offered through the Graduate School, New Brunswick, a two year doctor of pharmacy degree (Pharm. D) is offered through the College of Pharmacy. Challenging opportunities include advanced placement, tutorials, an honors program, and a senior project. Special programs include internships, summer session for credit, off-campus study, study abroad, and Army and Air Force ROTC.

The **faculty** at Rutgers, The State University of New Jersey, College of Pharmacy has 54 full-time graduate and undergraduate teachers, 98% with terminal degrees. The student-faculty ratio is 14:1, and the average class size in core courses is 47.

 ## Computers on Campus

Students are not required to have a computer. Student rooms are linked to a campus network. 690 **computers** available in the computer center, computer labs, the research center, the learning resource center, various locations on campus, classrooms, the library, the student center, dormitories, and student rooms provide access to the main academic computer, off-campus computing facilities, e-mail, on-line services, and the Internet. Staffed computer lab on campus (open 24 hours a day) provides training in the use of computers and software.

The 15 **libraries** have 4.4 million books, 2.8 million microform titles, and 18,274 subscriptions. They are connected to 26 national **on-line** catalogs.

 ## Campus Life

There are 400 active **organizations** on campus, including a drama/theater group and student-run newspaper and radio station. 11% of eligible men and 7% of eligible women are members of 31 national **fraternities**, 11 national **sororities**, and 4 local sororities. Student **safety services** include late night transport/escort service, 24-hour emergency telephone alarm devices, 24-hour patrols by trained security personnel, student patrols, and electronically operated dormitory entrances.

Rutgers, The State University of New Jersey, College of Pharmacy is a member of the NCAA (Division I). **Intercollegiate sports** (some offering scholarships) include baseball (m), basketball (m, w), crew (m, w), cross-country running (m, w), fencing (m, w), field hockey (w), football (m), golf (m, w), gymnastics (w), lacrosse (m, w), soccer (m, w), softball (w), swimming and diving (m, w), tennis (m, w), track and field (m, w), volleyball (w), wrestling (m).

 ## Applying

Rutgers, The State University of New Jersey, College of Pharmacy requires a high school transcript, 3 years of high school math, 2 years of high school foreign language, 1 course each in biology and chemistry, SAT I or ACT, and in some cases 3 SAT II Subject Tests. Early and deferred entrance are possible, with a 1/15 deadline and continuous processing to 3/1 for financial aid. **Contact:** Dr. Elizabeth Mitchell, Asst. Vice President for University Undergraduate Admissions, PO Box 2101, Piscataway, NJ 08855-0789, 908-445-3770; fax 908-445-0237.

GETTING IN LAST YEAR

1,567 applied
37% were accepted
34% enrolled (198)
74% from top tenth of their h.s. class
59% had SAT verbal scores over 600 (R)
82% had SAT math scores over 600 (R)
9% had SAT verbal scores over 700 (R)
32% had SAT math scores over 700 (R)
2 National Merit Scholars
9 valedictorians

THE STUDENT BODY

Total 983, of whom 914
  are undergraduates

From 19 states and territories,
  11 other countries
86% from New Jersey
62% women, 38% men
6% African Americans
1% Native Americans
8% Hispanics
40% Asian Americans
2% international students

AFTER GRADUATION

500 organizations recruited on campus

WHAT YOU WILL PAY

Resident tuition and fees $5214
Nonresident tuition and fees $9562
Room and board $4936
69% receive need-based financial aid
Need-based college-administered scholarships and
  grants average $1540 per award
44% receive non-need financial aid
Non-need college-administered scholarships and
  grants average $2900 per award

RUTGERS, THE STATE UNIVERSITY OF NEW JERSEY, COOK COLLEGE

New Brunswick, New Jersey • Small-town setting • Public • State-supported • Coed

Cook College offers an extensive range of academic programs in the life, environmental, marine and coastal, and agricultural sciences. Students choose from 26 majors with nearly 60 more specialized options. While all programs are based on a strong foundation in the physical and biological sciences, the social and human dimensions of scientific practice form a special emphasis within the curriculum. Advanced technology centers offer exceptional facilities for independent research, allowing undergraduates the opportunity to turn scientific theory into practice. Cook College students graduate with the skill and confidence to pursue careers or advanced-degree programs.

Academics

Rutgers, The State University of New Jersey, Cook College offers a core academic program. It awards bachelor's **degrees**. Challenging opportunities include advanced placement, self-designed majors, tutorials, an honors program, and a senior project. Special programs include cooperative education, internships, summer session for credit, off-campus study, study abroad, and Army and Air Force ROTC.

The most popular **majors** include environmental sciences, biology/biological sciences, and business economics. A complete listing of majors at Rutgers, The State University of New Jersey, Cook College appears in the Majors Index beginning on page 379.

The **faculty** at Rutgers, The State University of New Jersey, Cook College has 95 full-time teachers, 98% with terminal degrees. The student-faculty ratio is 17:1, and the average class size in core courses is 47.

Computers on Campus

Students are not required to have a computer. Student rooms are linked to a campus network. 690 **computers** available in the computer center, computer labs, the research center, the learning resource center, various locations on campus, classrooms, the library, the student center, dormitories, and student rooms provide access to the main academic computer, off-campus computing facilities, e-mail, on-line services, and the Internet. Staffed computer lab on campus (open 24 hours a day) provides training in the use of computers and software.

The 15 **libraries** have 4.4 million books, 2.8 million microform titles, and 18,274 subscriptions. They are connected to 26 national **on-line** catalogs.

Campus Life

There are 400 active **organizations** on campus, including a drama/theater group and student-run newspaper and radio station. 15% of students participate in student government elections. 11% of eligible men and 7% of eligible women are members of 31 national **fraternities**, 11 national **sororities**, and 4 local sororities. Student **safety services** include late night transport/escort service, 24-hour emergency telephone alarm devices, 24-hour patrols by trained security personnel, student patrols, and electronically operated dormitory entrances.

Rutgers, The State University of New Jersey, Cook College is a member of the NCAA (Division I). **Intercollegiate sports** (some offering scholarships) include baseball (m), basketball (m, w), crew (m, w), cross-country running (m, w), fencing (m, w), field hockey (w), football (m), golf (m, w), gymnastics (w), lacrosse (m, w), soccer (m, w), softball (w), swimming and diving (m, w), tennis (m, w), track and field (m, w), volleyball (w), wrestling (m).

Applying

Rutgers, The State University of New Jersey, Cook College requires a high school transcript, 3 years of high school math, 2 years of high school science, SAT I or ACT, and in some cases 3 SAT II Subject Tests. It recommends 4 years of high school math. Early and deferred entrance are possible, with a 1/15 deadline and continuous processing to 3/1 for financial aid. **Contact:** Dr. Elizabeth Mitchell, Asst. Vice President for University Undergraduate Admissions, PO Box 2101, New Brunswick, NJ 08903-0231, 908-445-3770; fax 908-445-0237.

GETTING IN LAST YEAR
6,919 applied
64% were accepted
14% enrolled (629)
25% from top tenth of their h.s. class
36% had SAT verbal scores over 600 (R)
46% had SAT math scores over 600 (R)
4% had SAT verbal scores over 700 (R)
8% had SAT math scores over 700 (R)
7 valedictorians

THE STUDENT BODY
3,147 undergraduates

From 26 states and territories,
19 other countries
91% from New Jersey
50% women, 50% men
5% African Americans
1% Native Americans
6% Hispanics
11% Asian Americans
1% international students

AFTER GRADUATION
500 organizations recruited on campus

WHAT YOU WILL PAY
Resident tuition and fees $5231
Nonresident tuition and fees $9579
Room and board $4936
53% receive need-based financial aid
Need-based college-administered scholarships and grants average $1370 per award
31% receive non-need financial aid
Non-need college-administered scholarships and grants average $3120 per award

RUTGERS, THE STATE UNIVERSITY OF NEW JERSEY, DOUGLASS COLLEGE

New Brunswick, New Jersey • Small-town setting • Public • State-supported • Women

Douglass is the largest women's college in the United States. It is dedicated to the development, advancement, and achievement of women in contemporary society and has the range of academic programs, research facilities, and social activities possible only in large coeducational universities. Douglass offers majors in the arts and sciences as well as several professional programs. Features include language and cultural residences, an alumnae career externship program, a math-science residence hall, and an honors program. The College is a national center for research, public service, and community outreach programs focusing on women and is the site of the University's model women's studies program.

Academics

Rutgers, The State University of New Jersey, Douglass College offers a core academic program. It awards bachelor's **degrees**. Challenging opportunities include advanced placement, self-designed majors, tutorials, an honors program, a senior project, and Phi Beta Kappa. Special programs include internships, summer session for credit, off-campus study, study abroad, and Army and Air Force ROTC.

The most popular **majors** include psychology, English, and biology/biological sciences. A complete listing of majors at Rutgers, The State University of New Jersey, Douglass College appears in the Majors Index beginning on page 379.

The **faculty** at Rutgers, The State University of New Jersey, Douglass College has 763 full-time teachers, 98% with terminal degrees. The student-faculty ratio is 18:1, and the average class size in core courses is 47.

Computers on Campus

Students are not required to have a computer. Student rooms are linked to a campus network. 690 **computers** available in the computer center, computer labs, the research center, the learning resource center, classrooms, the library, the student center, dormitories, and student rooms provide access to the main academic computer, off-campus computing facilities, e-mail, on-line services, and the Internet. Staffed computer lab on campus (open 24 hours a day) provides training in the use of computers and software.

The 15 **libraries** have 4.4 million books, 2.8 million microform titles, and 18,274 subscriptions. They are connected to 26 national **on-line** catalogs.

Campus Life

There are 400 active **organizations** on campus, including a drama/theater group and student-run newspaper and radio station. 7% of eligible undergraduates are members of 11 national **sororities** and 4 local sororities. Student **safety services** include late night transport/escort service, 24-hour emergency telephone alarm devices, 24-hour patrols by trained security personnel, student patrols, and electronically operated dormitory entrances.

Rutgers, The State University of New Jersey, Douglass College is a member of the NCAA (Division I). **Intercollegiate sports** (some offering scholarships) include basketball, crew, cross-country running, fencing, field hockey, golf, gymnastics, lacrosse, soccer, softball, swimming and diving, tennis, track and field, volleyball.

Applying

Rutgers, The State University of New Jersey, Douglass College requires a high school transcript, 3 years of high school math, 2 years of high school foreign language, 2 years of high school science, SAT I or ACT, and in some cases 3 SAT II Subject Tests. It recommends 4 years of high school math. Early and deferred entrance are possible, with a 1/15 deadline and continuous processing to 3/1 for financial aid. **Contact:** Dr. Elizabeth Mitchell, Asst. Vice President for University Undergraduate Admissions, PO Box 2101, New Brunswick, NJ 08903-0270, 908-445-3770; fax 908-445-0237.

GETTING IN LAST YEAR

5,319 applied
73% were accepted
16% enrolled (603)
20% from top tenth of their h.s. class
32% had SAT verbal scores over 600 (R)
29% had SAT math scores over 600 (R)
6% had SAT verbal scores over 700 (R)
5% had SAT math scores over 700 (R)
4 National Merit Scholars
6 valedictorians

THE STUDENT BODY

2,973 undergraduates
From 26 states and territories,
  21 other countries
94% from New Jersey
100% women
11% African Americans
1% Native Americans
7% Hispanics
14% Asian Americans
1% international students

AFTER GRADUATION

500 organizations recruited on campus

WHAT YOU WILL PAY

Resident tuition and fees $4798
Nonresident tuition and fees $8719
Room and board $4936
52% receive need-based financial aid
Need-based college-administered scholarships and
  grants average $1359 per award
36% receive non-need financial aid
Non-need college-administered scholarships and
  grants average $2048 per award

RUTGERS, THE STATE UNIVERSITY OF NEW JERSEY, RUTGERS COLLEGE

New Brunswick, New Jersey • Small-town setting • Public • State-supported • Coed

Rutgers College is the eighth-oldest institution of higher learning in America, predating many of the Ivy League schools. Rutgers has always been dedicated to "the education of youth in the learned languages, liberal and useful arts and sciences." Times have changed, but the College's philosophy remains the same: to provide a broad liberal arts experience. Rutgers College students select a major and a minor from a full range of liberal arts and preprofessional subjects. General education requirements provide a mastery of writing and quantitative skills and an understanding of the natural and social sciences, humanities, and non-Western cultures.

 Academics

Rutgers, The State University of New Jersey, Rutgers College offers a core academic program. It awards bachelor's **degrees**. Challenging opportunities include advanced placement, self-designed majors, tutorials, an honors program, a senior project, Phi Beta Kappa, and Sigma Xi. Special programs include internships, summer session for credit, off-campus study, study abroad, and Army and Air Force ROTC.

The most popular **majors** include psychology, biology/biological sciences, and English. A complete listing of majors at Rutgers, The State University of New Jersey, Rutgers College appears in the Majors Index beginning on page 379.

The **faculty** at Rutgers, The State University of New Jersey, Rutgers College has 763 full-time teachers, 98% with terminal degrees. The student-faculty ratio is 18:1, and the average class size in core courses is 47.

 Computers on Campus

Students are not required to have a computer. Student rooms are linked to a campus network. 690 **computers** available in the computer center, computer labs, the research center, the learning resource center, various locations on campus, classrooms, the library, the student center, dormitories, and student rooms provide access to the main academic computer, off-campus computing facilities, e-mail, on-line services, and the Internet. Staffed computer lab on campus (open 24 hours a day) provides training in the use of computers and software.

The 15 **libraries** have 4.4 million books, 2.8 million microform titles, and 18,274 subscriptions. They are connected to 26 national **on-line** catalogs.

 **Campus Life**

There are 400 active **organizations** on campus, including a drama/theater group and student-run newspaper and radio station. 11% of students participate in student government elections. 11% of eligible men and 7% of eligible women are members of 31 national **fraternities**, 11 national **sororities**, and 4 local sororities. Student **safety services** include late night transport/escort service, 24-hour emergency telephone alarm devices, 24-hour patrols by trained security personnel, student patrols, and electronically operated dormitory entrances.

Rutgers, The State University of New Jersey, Rutgers College is a member of the NCAA (Division I). **Intercollegiate sports** (some offering scholarships) include baseball (m), basketball (m, w), crew (m, w), cross-country running (m, w), fencing (m, w), field hockey (w), football (m), golf (m, w), gymnastics (w), lacrosse (m, w), soccer (m, w), softball (w), swimming and diving (m, w), tennis (m, w), track and field (m, w), volleyball (w), wrestling (m).

 Applying

Rutgers, The State University of New Jersey, Rutgers College requires a high school transcript, 3 years of high school math, 2 years of high school foreign language, 2 years of high school science, SAT I or ACT, and in some cases 3 SAT II Subject Tests. It recommends 4 years of high school math. Early and deferred entrance are possible, with a 1/15 deadline and continuous processing to 3/1 for financial aid. **Contact:** Dr. Elizabeth Mitchell, Asst. Vice President for University Undergraduate Admissions, PO Box 2101, New Brunswick, NJ 08903-2101, 908-445-3770; fax 908-445-0237.

GETTING IN LAST YEAR
15,978 applied
53% were accepted
24% enrolled (2,056)
39% from top tenth of their h.s. class
54% had SAT verbal scores over 600 (R)
62% had SAT math scores over 600 (R)
11% had SAT verbal scores over 700 (R)
17% had SAT math scores over 700 (R)
14 National Merit Scholars
22 valedictorians

THE STUDENT BODY
9,573 undergraduates

From 43 states and territories,
   51 other countries
88% from New Jersey
50% women, 50% men
7% African Americans
1% Native Americans
11% Hispanics
18% Asian Americans
2% international students

AFTER GRADUATION
500 organizations recruited on campus
3 Fulbright scholars

WHAT YOU WILL PAY
Resident tuition and fees $4836
Nonresident tuition and fees $8757
Room and board $4936
56% receive need-based financial aid
Need-based college-administered scholarships and
   grants average $1505 per award
34% receive non-need financial aid
Non-need college-administered scholarships and
   grants average $4059 per award

ST. JOHN'S COLLEGE

Annapolis, Maryland • Small-town setting • Private • Independent • Coed

Great Books Program: St. John's offers an integrated liberal arts and sciences curriculum structured around seminar discussions of major works of Western civilization. These discussions are supported by tutorials in mathematics, music, language, and the physical sciences. Only original sources are read, and all classes are small discussion groups.

 Academics

St. John's offers a great books curriculum and core academic program; a few graduate courses are open to undergraduates. It awards bachelor's and master's **degrees**. Challenging opportunities include tutorials and a senior project. Special programs include off-campus study and study abroad.

The **faculty** at St. John's has 57 full-time graduate and undergraduate teachers, 58% with terminal degrees. 100% of the faculty serve as student advisers. The student-faculty ratio is 8:1.

 Computers on Campus

Students are not required to have a computer. 12 **computers** available in the computer center and the library provide access to e-mail and the Internet. Staffed computer lab on campus provides training in the use of computers and software.

The 2 **libraries** have 98,596 books, 75 microform titles, and 126 subscriptions. They are connected to 1 national **on-line** catalog.

 Campus Life

There are 35 active **organizations** on campus, including a drama/theater group and student-run newspaper. 50% of students participate in student government elections. Student **safety services** include late night transport/escort service, 24-hour emergency telephone alarm devices, 24-hour patrols by trained security personnel, and electronically operated dormitory entrances.

This institution has no intercollegiate sports.

 Applying

St. John's requires an essay, a high school transcript, 3 years of high school math, and 2 recommendations. It recommends 3 years of high school science, 2 years of high school foreign language, an interview, and SAT I or ACT. Early, deferred, and midyear entrance are possible, with rolling admissions and continuous processing to 2/15 for financial aid. **Contact:** Mr. John Christensen, Director of Admissions, PO Box 2800, Annapolis, MD 21404, 410-263-2371 ext. 222 or toll-free 800-727-9238.

GETTING IN LAST YEAR
338 applied
86% were accepted
38% enrolled (112)
32% from top tenth of their h.s. class
1 National Merit Scholar

THE STUDENT BODY
Total 513, of whom 419
  are undergraduates
From 45 states and territories,
  9 other countries
14% from Maryland

48% women, 52% men
2% African Americans
1% Native Americans
4% Hispanics
3% Asian Americans
5% international students

AFTER FRESHMAN YEAR
81% returned for sophomore year
53% got a degree within 4 years
61% got a degree within 5 years
64% got a degree within 6 years

AFTER GRADUATION
58% pursued further study (42% arts and
  sciences, 7% law, 6% medicine)
10 organizations recruited on campus

WHAT YOU WILL PAY
Tuition and fees $18,830
Room and board $5890
55% receive need-based financial aid
Need-based college-administered scholarships and
  grants average $10,780 per award

ST. JOHN'S COLLEGE

Santa Fe, New Mexico • Small-town setting • Private • Independent • Coed

St. Johns's appeals to students who value good books, love to read, and are passionate about discourse and debate. There are no lectures and virtually no tests or electives. Instead, there are discussion-based classes of 20 students where professors are as likely as students to be asked to defend their points of view. Great Books provide the direction, context, and stimulus for conversation. The entire student body adheres to the same all-required arts and sciences curriculum. Seventy-five percent of the College's alumni obtain graduate and professional degrees in law, medicine, humanities, natural sciences, business, journalism, fine and performing arts, or architecture.

Academics

St. John's offers a great books, interdisciplinary, arts and sciences curriculum and core academic program; a few graduate courses are open to undergraduates. It awards bachelor's and master's **degrees**. Challenging opportunities include tutorials and a senior project. Special programs include off-campus study and study abroad.

The **faculty** at St. John's has 45 full-time undergraduate teachers, 60% with terminal degrees. 100% of the faculty serve as student advisers. The student-faculty ratio is 8:1.

Computers on Campus

Students are not required to have a computer. 9 **computers** available in science, lab buildings and the library provide access to e-mail, on-line services, and the Internet. Staffed computer lab on campus provides training in the use of computers and software.

The **library** has 60,000 books and 160 subscriptions. It is connected to 1 national **on-line** catalog.

Campus Life

Active **organizations** on campus include drama/theater group and student-run newspaper. No national or local **fraternities** or **sororities**. Student **safety services** include late night transport/escort service, 24-hour emergency telephone alarm devices, 24-hour patrols by trained security personnel, student patrols, and electronically operated dormitory entrances.

This institution has no intercollegiate sports.

Applying

St. John's requires an essay, a high school transcript, 3 recommendations, and in some cases an interview. It recommends 3 years of high school math and science, 2 years of high school foreign language, an interview, and SAT I or ACT. Early, deferred, and midyear entrance are possible, with rolling admissions and continuous processing to 2/15 for financial aid. **Contact:** Mr. Larry Clendenin, Director of Admissions, 1160 Camino Cruz Blanca, Santa Fe, NM 87501-4599, 505-984-6060 or toll-free 800-331-5232.

GETTING IN LAST YEAR
286 applied
82% were accepted
50% enrolled (116)
33% from top tenth of their h.s. class
84% had SAT verbal scores over 600 (R)
58% had SAT math scores over 600 (R)
67% had ACT scores over 26
37% had SAT verbal scores over 700 (R)
15% had SAT math scores over 700 (R)
23% had ACT scores over 30
5 National Merit Scholars
11 valedictorians

THE STUDENT BODY
Total 426, of whom 379
  are undergraduates

From 51 states and territories,
  7 other countries
11% from New Mexico
45% women, 55% men
1% African Americans
1% Native Americans
7% Hispanics
3% Asian Americans
2% international students

AFTER FRESHMAN YEAR
80% returned for sophomore year
68% got a degree within 6 years

AFTER GRADUATION
58% pursued further study (42% arts and
  sciences, 7% law, 6% medicine)
17 organizations recruited on campus

WHAT YOU WILL PAY
Tuition and fees $18,720
Room and board $6055
65% receive need-based financial aid
Need-based college-administered scholarships and
  grants average $11,325 per award
0% receive non-need financial aid

SAINT JOHN'S UNIVERSITY

Coordinate with College of Saint Benedict

Collegeville, Minnesota • Rural setting • Private • Independent-Religious • Men

 ## Academics

St. John's offers an interdisciplinary curriculum and core academic program; fewer than half of graduate courses are open to undergraduates. It awards bachelor's and master's **degrees**. Challenging opportunities include advanced placement, self-designed majors, tutorials, an honors program, and a senior project. Special programs include internships, off-campus study, study abroad, and Army ROTC.

The most popular **majors** include business, biology/biological sciences, and psychology. A complete listing of majors at St. John's appears in the Majors Index beginning on page 379.

The **faculty** at St. John's has 130 full-time graduate and undergraduate teachers, 85% with terminal degrees. 100% of the faculty serve as student advisers. The student-faculty ratio is 13:1, and the average class size in core courses is 21.

 ## Computers on Campus

Students are not required to have a computer. Student rooms are linked to a campus network. 250 **computers** available in the computer center, computer labs, academic buildings, classrooms, the library, the student center, and dormitories provide access to the main academic computer, e-mail, on-line services, and the Internet. Staffed computer lab on campus provides training in the use of computers and software.

The 3 **libraries** have 523,000 books, 103,000 microform titles, and 2,100 subscriptions. They are connected to 5 national **on-line** catalogs.

 ## Campus Life

There are 80 active **organizations** on campus, including a drama/theater group and student-run newspaper and radio station. Student **safety services** include late night transport/escort service, 24-hour emergency telephone alarm devices, and 24-hour patrols by trained security personnel.

St. John's is a member of the NCAA (Division III). **Intercollegiate sports** include baseball, basketball, crew, cross-country running, football, golf, ice hockey, lacrosse, rugby, soccer, swimming and diving, tennis, track and field, wrestling.

 ## Applying

St. John's requires an essay, a high school transcript, SAT I or ACT, and in some cases recommendations. It recommends 3 years of high school math and science, 2 years of high school foreign language, an interview, and a minimum high school GPA of 3.0. Early, deferred, and midyear entrance are possible, with rolling admissions and continuous processing to 3/1 for financial aid. **Contact:** Ms. Mary Milbert, Director of Admissions, The Great Hall, Collegeville, MN 56321, 612-363-2196 or toll-free 800-24 JOHNS; fax 612-363-2115.

GETTING IN LAST YEAR
894 applied
87% were accepted
55% enrolled (430)
18% from top tenth of their h.s. class
3.4 average high school GPA
31% had ACT scores over 26
8% had ACT scores over 30
2 National Merit Scholars

THE STUDENT BODY
Total 1,820, of whom 1,692
   are undergraduates
From 29 states and territories,
   25 other countries

80% from Minnesota
100% men
1% African Americans
1% Native Americans
1% Hispanics
2% Asian Americans
3% international students

AFTER FRESHMAN YEAR
85% returned for sophomore year
61% got a degree within 4 years
72% got a degree within 5 years

AFTER GRADUATION
25% pursued further study (10% arts and
   sciences, 5% business, 5% law)
70% had job offers within 6 months
90 organizations recruited on campus

WHAT YOU WILL PAY
Tuition and fees $13,089
Room and board $4224
70% receive need-based financial aid
Need-based college-administered scholarships and
   grants average $4528 per award
8% receive non-need financial aid
Non-need college-administered scholarships and
   grants average $3494 per award

SAINT JOSEPH'S UNIVERSITY

Philadelphia, Pennsylvania • Suburban setting • Private • Independent-Religious • Coed

Saint Joseph's, Philadelphia's Jesuit university, recently added 5 accelerated–degree programs in cooperation with Thomas Jefferson University's College of Allied Health. Students in diagnostic imaging, laboratory sciences, nursing, occupational therapy, and physical therapy have the opportunity to earn degrees from both institutions, giving them a distinct competitive advantage when entering the job market. In the field of physical therapy, students participate in a 6-year program leading to a bachelor's degree in biology and a bachelor's and master's degree in physical therapy. Other allied health sciences are 5-year programs leading to a bachelor's degree in biology and a bachelor's degree in the desired field.

Academics

SJU offers a core academic program; fewer than half of graduate courses are open to undergraduates. It awards associate, bachelor's, and master's **degrees**. Challenging opportunities include advanced placement, accelerated degree programs, self-designed majors, tutorials, an honors program, a senior project, and Sigma Xi. Special programs include cooperative education, internships, summer session for credit, off-campus study, study abroad, and Army, Naval, and Air Force ROTC.

The most popular **majors** include accounting, food marketing, and psychology. A complete listing of majors at SJU appears in the Majors Index beginning on page 379.

The **faculty** at SJU has 168 full-time graduate and undergraduate teachers, 94% with terminal degrees. 100% of the faculty serve as student advisers. The student-faculty ratio is 16:1, and the average class size in core courses is 22.

Computers on Campus

Students are not required to have a computer. Student rooms are linked to a campus network. 215 **computers**

available in the computer center, academic buildings, classrooms, the library, and dormitories provide access to e-mail and the Internet. Staffed computer lab on campus.

The 2 **libraries** have 324,000 books, 727,000 microform titles, and 2,000 subscriptions. They are connected to 3 national **on-line** catalogs.

Campus Life

There are 73 active **organizations** on campus, including a drama/theater group and student-run newspaper and radio station. 19% of eligible men and 13% of eligible women are members of 4 national **fraternities** and 3 national **sororities**. Student **safety services** include 24-hour shuttle/escort service, bicycle patrols, late night transport/escort service, 24-hour emergency telephone alarm devices, 24-hour patrols by trained security personnel, and electronically operated dormitory entrances.

SJU is a member of the NCAA (Division I). **Intercollegiate sports** (some offering scholarships) include baseball (m), basketball (m, w), crew (m, w), cross-country running (m, w), field hockey (w), golf (m), lacrosse (m, w), soccer (m), softball (w), tennis (m, w), track and field (m, w).

Applying

SJU requires an essay, a high school transcript, 3 years of high school math, 2 years of high school foreign language, 1 recommendation, and SAT I or ACT. It recommends 3 years of high school science, a campus interview, and a minimum high school GPA of 2.0. Early, deferred, and midyear entrance are possible, with rolling admissions and a 3/1 priority date for financial aid. **Contact:** Mr. David Conway, Dean of Enrollment Management, 5600 City Avenue, Philadelphia, PA 19131-1376, 610-660-1300.

GETTING IN LAST YEAR
2,791 applied
73% were accepted
39% enrolled (804)
39% from top tenth of their h.s. class

THE STUDENT BODY
Total 6,938, of whom 3,989
   are undergraduates
From 28 states and territories,
   67 other countries

53% from Pennsylvania
53% women, 47% men
8% African Americans
0% Native Americans
2% Hispanics
2% Asian Americans
4% international students

AFTER FRESHMAN YEAR
85% returned for sophomore year
69% got a degree within 4 years

75% got a degree within 5 years
76% got a degree within 6 years

AFTER GRADUATION
35% pursued further study (13% arts and
   sciences, 12% business, 5% law)
96 organizations recruited on campus
1 Fulbright scholar

WHAT YOU WILL PAY
Tuition and fees $13,750
Room and board $6500

ST. LAWRENCE UNIVERSITY

Canton, New York • Small-town setting • Private • Independent • Coed

St. Lawrence prepares students for life after college in all its dimensions. A tight-knit community prepares students for involvement in other communities after graduation. Eleven international study possibilities offer students the opportunity to succeed in an ever-smaller world. Distinguished environmental studies and outdoor education programs take advantage of the University's location and prepare the student to assume stewardship responsibilities for, as well as enjoyable use of, the earth. A program in the first year emphasizing writing, speaking, faculty attention, and how to handle independence helps students make the most of their college experiences.

Academics

St. Lawrence offers an interdisciplinary international curriculum and core academic program; fewer than half of graduate courses are open to undergraduates. It awards bachelor's and master's **degrees**. Challenging opportunities include advanced placement, self-designed majors, tutorials, an honors program, a senior project, and Phi Beta Kappa. Special programs include internships, summer session for credit, off-campus study, study abroad, and Air Force ROTC.

The most popular **majors** include economics, English, and political science/government. A complete listing of majors at St. Lawrence appears in the Majors Index beginning on page 379.

The **faculty** at St. Lawrence has 154 full-time undergraduate teachers, 93% with terminal degrees. 99% of the faculty serve as student advisers. The student-faculty ratio is 12:1.

Computers on Campus

Students are not required to have a computer. Student rooms are linked to a campus network. 600 **computers** available in the computer center, computer labs, classrooms, the library, and dormitories provide access to the main academic computer, off-campus computing facilities, e-mail, on-line services, and the Internet. Staffed computer lab on campus (open 24 hours a day) provides training in the use of computers and software.

The 3 **libraries** have 440,000 books, 462,000 microform titles, and 2,400 subscriptions.

Campus Life

There are 75 active **organizations** on campus, including a drama/theater group and student-run newspaper and radio station. 50% of students participate in student government elections. 23% of eligible men and 30% of eligible women are members of 7 national **fraternities**, 4 national **sororities**, and 1 local sorority. Student **safety services** include late night transport/escort service, 24-hour emergency telephone alarm devices, 24-hour patrols by trained security personnel, and student patrols.

St. Lawrence is a member of the NCAA (Division III). **Intercollegiate sports** include baseball (m), basketball (m, w), crew (m), cross-country running (m, w), equestrian sports (m, w), field hockey (w), football (m), ice hockey (m, w), lacrosse (m, w), rugby (m), skiing (cross-country) (m, w), skiing (downhill) (m, w), soccer (m, w), swimming and diving (m, w), tennis (m, w), track and field (m, w), volleyball (w).

Applying

St. Lawrence requires an essay, a high school transcript, 3 years of high school math and science, 3 years of high school foreign language, 2 recommendations, SAT I or ACT, and 1 SAT II Subject Test. It recommends an interview and 2 SAT II Subject Tests. Early, deferred, and midyear entrance are possible, with a 2/15 deadline and 2/15 for financial aid. **Contact:** Mr. Joel Wincowski, Dean of Admissions and Financial Aid, Payson Hall, Admissions, Canton, NY 13617-1455, 315-379-5261; fax 315-379-5502.

GETTING IN LAST YEAR
2,833 applied
60% were accepted
33% enrolled (572)
28% from top tenth of their h.s. class
41% had SAT verbal scores over 600 (R)
41% had SAT math scores over 600 (R)
8% had SAT verbal scores over 700 (R)
3% had SAT math scores over 700 (R)
16 valedictorians

THE STUDENT BODY
Total 2,106, of whom 1,976
   are undergraduates
From 42 states and territories,
   21 other countries

49% from New York
50% women, 50% men
2% African Americans
1% Native Americans
2% Hispanics
2% Asian Americans
4% international students

AFTER FRESHMAN YEAR
85% returned for sophomore year
75% got a degree within 4 years
80% got a degree within 5 years
82% got a degree within 6 years

AFTER GRADUATION
20% pursued further study (10% arts and
   sciences, 4% law, 3% medicine)
74% had job offers within 6 months

WHAT YOU WILL PAY
Tuition and fees $19,765
Room and board $5885
70% receive need-based financial aid
Need-based college-administered scholarships and
   grants average $11,898 per award
1% receive non-need financial aid
Non-need college-administered scholarships and
   grants average $10,000 per award

St. Louis College of Pharmacy

St. Louis, Missouri • Urban setting • Private • Independent • Coed

The St. Louis College of Pharmacy is located in the heart of St. Louis' central west-end medical community and is the oldest college of its type west of the Mississippi River. The College is a national leader in pharmacy education, offering an integration of pharmaceutical knowledge and skills with a sound preparation in the basic sciences and liberal arts. The College strives to improve the well-being of society by preparing students to lead useful and satisfying lives, to contribute and lead in their communities, and to advance the profession of pharmacy.

Academics

St. Louis College of Pharmacy offers a core academic program; more than half of graduate courses are open to undergraduates. It awards bachelor's and master's **degrees**. Challenging opportunities include advanced placement, tutorials, and a senior project. Special programs include internships, summer session for credit, study abroad, and Army and Air Force ROTC.

The **faculty** at St. Louis College of Pharmacy has 55 full-time graduate and undergraduate teachers, 75% with terminal degrees. 64% of the faculty serve as student advisers. The student-faculty ratio is 12:1.

Computers on Campus

Students are not required to have a computer. Student rooms are linked to a campus network. 60 **computers** available in computer labs, the library, and the student center provide access to the main academic computer, e-mail, on-line services, and the Internet. Staffed computer lab on campus provides training in the use of computers and software.

The 4 **libraries** have 31,342 books and 490 subscriptions. They are connected to 2 national **on-line** catalogs.

Campus Life

There are 15 active **organizations** on campus, including a drama/theater group and student-run newspaper. 70% of eligible men and 65% of eligible women are members of 4 national **fraternities** and 1 national **sorority**. Student **safety services** include late night transport/escort service, 24-hour emergency telephone alarm devices, 24-hour patrols by trained security personnel, and electronically operated dormitory entrances.

St. Louis College of Pharmacy is a member of the NAIA. **Intercollegiate sports** include basketball (m), volleyball (w).

Applying

St. Louis College of Pharmacy requires an essay, a high school transcript, 3 years of high school math, ACT, a minimum high school GPA of 2.0, and in some cases SAT I. It recommends 3 years of high school science, some high school foreign language, an interview, and a minimum high school GPA of 3.0. Midyear entrance is possible, with rolling admissions and continuous processing to 6/30 for financial aid. **Contact:** Ms. Lisa Boeschen, Director of Admissions, 4588 Parkview Place, St. Louis, MO 63110-1088, 314-367-8700 ext. 1072 or toll-free 800-278-5267 (in-state); fax 314-367-2784.

GETTING IN LAST YEAR
298 applied
81% were accepted
66% enrolled (158)
48% from top tenth of their h.s. class
3.6 average high school GPA
45% had ACT scores over 26
8% had ACT scores over 30
14 valedictorians

THE STUDENT BODY
Total 851, of whom 795
   are undergraduates

From 15 states and territories,
   1 other country
48% from Missouri
61% women, 39% men
3% African Americans
0% Native Americans
1% Hispanics
9% Asian Americans
1% international students

AFTER FRESHMAN YEAR
92% returned for sophomore year

AFTER GRADUATION
6% pursued further study (2% arts and sciences, 2% business, 1% law)

WHAT YOU WILL PAY
Tuition and fees $10,470
Room and board $4600
Need-based college-administered scholarships and
   grants average $800 per award
Non-need college-administered scholarships and
   grants average $1300 per award

SAINT LOUIS UNIVERSITY

St. Louis, Missouri • Urban setting • Private • Independent-Religious • Coed

For almost 180 years, Saint Louis University has had a reputation for excellence in education. In its history, Saint Louis has accomplished a list of firsts that makes it a true center of higher learning: first university west of the Mississippi; first Catholic college in the United States to have faculty in schools of philosophy, theology, medicine, law, and business; first federally certified air college (Parks College of Engineering and Aviation); and first freestanding European campus (Madrid, Spain) operated by an American university. Saint Louis' academic reputation is the foundation of its success today.

 ## Academics

SLU offers a traditional liberal arts curriculum and core academic program; fewer than half of graduate courses are open to undergraduates. It awards associate, bachelor's, master's, doctoral, and first professional **degrees**. Challenging opportunities include advanced placement, accelerated degree programs, self-designed majors, tutorials, an honors program, a senior project, Phi Beta Kappa, and Sigma Xi. Special programs include internships, summer session for credit, off-campus study, study abroad, and Army and Air Force ROTC.

The most popular **majors** include business, political science/government, and communication. A complete listing of majors at SLU appears in the Majors Index beginning on page 379.

The **faculty** at SLU has 1,193 full-time graduate and undergraduate teachers, 95% with terminal degrees. 100% of the faculty serve as student advisers. The average class size in core courses is 28.

 ## Computers on Campus

Students are not required to have a computer. Student rooms are linked to a campus network. 500 **computers** available in the computer center, computer labs, the learning resource center, academic buildings, the library, and dormitories provide access to the main academic computer, off-campus computing facilities, e-mail, and the Internet. Staffed computer lab on campus provides training in the use of computers and software.

The 4 **libraries** have 1.4 million books, 114,384 microform titles, and 13,834 subscriptions. They are connected to 4 national **on-line** catalogs.

 ## Campus Life

There are 60 active **organizations** on campus, including a drama/theater group and student-run newspaper and radio station. 24% of students participate in student government elections. 16% of eligible men and 10% of eligible women are members of 9 national **fraternities** and 5 national **sororities**. Student **safety services** include late night transport/escort service, 24-hour emergency telephone alarm devices, 24-hour patrols by trained security personnel, student patrols, and electronically operated dormitory entrances.

SLU is a member of the NCAA (Division I). **Intercollegiate sports** (some offering scholarships) include baseball (m), basketball (m, w), cross-country running (m, w), field hockey (w), golf (m), ice hockey (m), riflery (m, w), rugby (m), soccer (m), softball (w), swimming and diving (m, w), tennis (m, w), volleyball (w).

 ## Applying

SLU requires a high school transcript, minimum 2.5 GPA, ACT, and in some cases an essay. It recommends 3 years of high school math and science, some high school foreign language, recommendations, an interview, and SAT I. Deferred and midyear entrance are possible, with rolling admissions and continuous processing to 4/1 for financial aid. **Contact:** Mr. Scott Belobrajdic, Director of Undergraduate Admissions, 221 North Grand Boulevard, St. Louis, MO 63103-2097, 314-977-2500 or toll-free 800-758-3678 (out-of-state); fax 314-977-3874.

GETTING IN LAST YEAR
3,694 applied
86% were accepted
33% enrolled (1,049)
32% from top tenth of their h.s. class
48% had ACT scores over 26
15% had ACT scores over 30
11 National Merit Scholars

THE STUDENT BODY
Total 10,719, of whom 6,123
  are undergraduates
From 49 states and territories
53% from Missouri
53% women, 47% men

9% African Americans
1% Native Americans
2% Hispanics
4% Asian Americans
5% international students

AFTER FRESHMAN YEAR
84% returned for sophomore year
46% got a degree within 4 years
60% got a degree within 5 years
64% got a degree within 6 years

AFTER GRADUATION
16% pursued further study (16% arts and
  sciences)

78% had job offers within 6 months
93 organizations recruited on campus
1 Fulbright scholar

WHAT YOU WILL PAY
Tuition and fees $12,880
Room and board $4900
59% receive need-based financial aid
Need-based college-administered scholarships and
  grants average $3957 per award
19% receive non-need financial aid
Non-need college-administered scholarships and
  grants average $5799 per award

SAINT MARY'S COLLEGE

Notre Dame, Indiana • Suburban setting • Private • Independent-Religious • Women

Academics

Saint Mary's offers a core academic program. It awards bachelor's **degrees**. Challenging opportunities include advanced placement, self-designed majors, and a senior project. Special programs include internships, off-campus study, study abroad, and Army, Naval, and Air Force ROTC.

The most popular **majors** include business, elementary education, and communication. A complete listing of majors at Saint Mary's appears in the Majors Index beginning on page 379.

The **faculty** at Saint Mary's has 114 full-time teachers, 95% with terminal degrees. 100% of the faculty serve as student advisers. The student-faculty ratio is 11:1.

Computers on Campus

Students are not required to have a computer. Student rooms are linked to a campus network. 110 **computers** available in the computer center, computer labs, the learning resource center, classroom buildings, the library, and dormitories provide access to the main academic computer, off-campus computing facilities, e-mail, and the Internet. Staffed computer lab on campus (open 24 hours a day) provides training in the use of computers and software.

The **library** has 195,424 books, 6,164 microform titles, and 1,077 subscriptions. It is connected to 1 national **on-line** catalog.

Campus Life

There are 116 active **organizations** on campus, including a drama/theater group and student-run newspaper. Student **safety services** include late night transport/escort service, 24-hour emergency telephone alarm devices, 24-hour patrols by trained security personnel, and electronically operated dormitory entrances.

Saint Mary's is a member of the NCAA (Division III). **Intercollegiate sports** include basketball, crew, gymnastics, sailing, skiing (downhill), soccer, softball, swimming and diving, tennis, track and field, volleyball.

Applying

Saint Mary's requires an essay, a high school transcript, 3 years of high school math, 2 years of high school foreign language, 1 recommendation, SAT I or ACT, and 3 SAT II Subject Tests (including SAT II: Writing Test). It recommends 3 years of high school science and an interview. Early, deferred, and midyear entrance are possible, with a 3/1 deadline and continuous processing to 3/1 for financial aid. **Contact:** Ms. Mary Pat Nolan, Director of Admission, 116 LeMans Hall, Notre Dame, IN 46556, 219-284-4587 or toll-free 800-551-7621.

GETTING IN LAST YEAR
819 applied
85% were accepted
55% enrolled (386)
31% from top tenth of their h.s. class
3.56 average high school GPA
41% had SAT verbal scores over 600
30% had SAT math scores over 600
32% had ACT scores over 26
3% had SAT verbal scores over 700
1% had SAT math scores over 700
5% had ACT scores over 30
12 National Merit Scholars
5 class presidents
7 valedictorians

THE STUDENT BODY
1,579 undergraduates
From 47 states and territories,
   20 other countries
20% from Indiana
100% women
2% African Americans
1% Native Americans
3% Hispanics
2% Asian Americans
2% international students

AFTER FRESHMAN YEAR
85% returned for sophomore year
73% got a degree within 4 years

78% got a degree within 5 years
80% got a degree within 6 years

AFTER GRADUATION
90% had job offers within 6 months
92 organizations recruited on campus

WHAT YOU WILL PAY
Tuition and fees $14,910
Room and board $4970
67% receive need-based financial aid
Need-based college-administered scholarships and
   grants average $7000 per award
12% receive non-need financial aid
Non-need college-administered scholarships and
   grants average $5000 per award

SAINT MARY'S COLLEGE OF CALIFORNIA

Moraga, California • Suburban setting • Private • Independent-Religious • Coed

It has been said that Saint Mary's College is "a classic example of a school committed to teaching students *how* to think rather than *what* to think." It is home to some of the "happiest students in the nation," has a safe and beautiful campus, and is a "good buy." Saint Mary's intimate academic community of 2,200 undergraduates is located 20 miles east of San Francisco. Operated and owned by the Christian Brothers, the College is committed to providing students with a comprehensive liberal arts education that includes reading and discussing the Great Books.

Academics

Saint Mary's offers a core academic program. It awards bachelor's and master's **degrees**. Challenging opportunities include advanced placement, self-designed majors, tutorials, an honors program, and a senior project. Special programs include internships, off-campus study, and Army, Naval, and Air Force ROTC.

The most popular **majors** include business, biology/biological sciences, and communication. A complete listing of majors at Saint Mary's appears in the Majors Index beginning on page 379.

The **faculty** at Saint Mary's has 164 full-time undergraduate teachers, 91% with terminal degrees. 100% of the faculty serve as student advisers. The student-faculty ratio is 14:1, and the average class size in core courses is 19.

Computers on Campus

Students are not required to have a computer. Student rooms are linked to a campus network. 116 **computers** available in the computer center, computer labs, classrooms,

and the library provide access to the main academic computer, off-campus computing facilities, e-mail, on-line services, and the Internet. Staffed computer lab on campus provides training in the use of computers and software.

The **library** has 185,460 books, 198,177 microform titles, and 1,110 subscriptions.

Campus Life

There are 32 active **organizations** on campus, including a drama/theater group and student-run newspaper and radio station. Student **safety services** include late night transport/escort service, 24-hour emergency telephone alarm devices, and 24-hour patrols by trained security personnel.

Saint Mary's is a member of the NCAA (Division I). **Intercollegiate sports** (some offering scholarships) include baseball (m), basketball (m, w), crew (m, w), cross-country running (m, w), football (m), golf (m), ice hockey (m), lacrosse (m, w), rugby (m), soccer (m, w), softball (w), tennis (m, w), volleyball (w).

Applying

Saint Mary's requires an essay, a high school transcript, 1 recommendation, SAT I or ACT, a minimum high school GPA of 2.0, and in some cases 3 years of high school science, an interview, and a minimum high school GPA of 3.0. It recommends 3 years of high school math, some high school foreign language, and a minimum high school GPA of 3.0. Early, deferred, and midyear entrance are possible, with a 3/1 deadline and continuous processing to 3/2 for financial aid. **Contact:** Mr. Michael Tressel, Director of Admissions, PO Box 4800, Moraga, CA 94575, 510-631-4224; fax 510-376-7193.

GETTING IN LAST YEAR
2,457 applied
86% were accepted
23% enrolled (487)
39% from top tenth of their h.s. class
3.37 average high school GPA
32% had SAT verbal scores over 600 (R)
32% had SAT math scores over 600 (R)
15% had ACT scores over 26
3% had SAT verbal scores over 700 (R)
2% had SAT math scores over 700 (R)
2% had ACT scores over 30
1 National Merit Scholar

THE STUDENT BODY
Total 4,318, of whom 2,142
   are undergraduates

From 36 states and territories,
   21 other countries
76% from California
54% women, 46% men
4% African Americans
1% Native Americans
14% Hispanics
10% Asian Americans
4% international students

AFTER FRESHMAN YEAR
85% returned for sophomore year
61% got a degree within 4 years
65% got a degree within 5 years
66% got a degree within 6 years

AFTER GRADUATION
35% pursued further study (10% business, 10% law, 6% medicine)
44% had job offers within 6 months
100 organizations recruited on campus

WHAT YOU WILL PAY
Tuition and fees $14,250
Room and board $6608
55% receive need-based financial aid
Need-based college-administered scholarships and grants average $5776 per award
3% receive non-need financial aid
Non-need college-administered scholarships and grants average $5223 per award

ST. MARY'S COLLEGE OF MARYLAND

St. Mary's City, Maryland • Rural setting • Public • State-supported • Coed

St. Mary's College of Maryland, with its distinctive identity as a public honors college, is emerging as one of the finest liberal arts and sciences colleges in the country. A lively academic atmosphere combines with the serene yet stunning natural beauty of a riverfront campus to create a challenging and memorable college experience for more than 1,400 students. Construction in recent years includes 40 town house student residences, a new library, and a new state-of-the-art science building. Newly opened are 40 additional town house residences, and both the student center and the gymnasium are scheduled for expansion soon.

 Academics

St. Mary's offers a liberal arts and sciences curriculum and core academic program. It awards bachelor's **degrees**. Challenging opportunities include advanced placement, self-designed majors, tutorials, Freshman Honors College, and a senior project. Special programs include internships, summer session for credit, off-campus study, and study abroad.

The most popular **majors** include psychology, biology/biological sciences, and economics. A complete listing of majors at St. Mary's appears in the Majors Index beginning on page 379.

The **faculty** at St. Mary's has 105 full-time teachers, 97% with terminal degrees. 85% of the faculty serve as student advisers. The student-faculty ratio is 13:1, and the average class size in core courses is 25.

 Computers on Campus

Students are not required to have a computer. 155 **computers** available in the computer center, computer labs, the research center, classrooms, and the library provide access to the main academic computer, off-campus computing facilities, e-mail, on-line services, and the Internet. Staffed computer lab on campus provides training in the use of computers and software.

The **library** has 152,392 books, 32,841 microform titles, and 1,601 subscriptions. It is connected to 3 national **on-line** catalogs.

 Campus Life

There are 45 active **organizations** on campus, including a drama/theater group and student-run newspaper and radio station. 33% of students participate in student government elections. Student **safety services** include late night transport/escort service, 24-hour emergency telephone alarm devices, 24-hour patrols by trained security personnel, student patrols, and electronically operated dormitory entrances.

St. Mary's is a member of the NCAA (Division III). **Intercollegiate sports** include baseball (m), basketball (m, w), crew (m, w), fencing (m, w), field hockey (w), golf (m, w), lacrosse (m, w), rugby (m), sailing (m, w), soccer (m, w), swimming and diving (m, w), tennis (m, w), volleyball (m, w), wrestling (m).

 Applying

St. Mary's requires an essay, a high school transcript, 3 years of high school math and science, 2 years of high school foreign language, and SAT I or ACT. It recommends 4 years of high school foreign language, 3 recommendations, and a campus interview. Early and midyear entrance are possible, with a 1/15 deadline and a 3/1 priority date for financial aid. **Contact:** Mr. Richard Edgar, Director of Admissions, Admissions Office, St. Mary's City, MD 20686, 301-862-0292 or toll-free 800-492-7181; fax 301-862-0906.

GETTING IN LAST YEAR
1,588 applied
54% were accepted
41% enrolled (352)
46% from top tenth of their h.s. class
3.5 average high school GPA
83% had SAT verbal scores over 600 (R)
78% had SAT math scores over 600 (R)
27% had SAT verbal scores over 700 (R)
14% had SAT math scores over 700 (R)
10 National Merit Scholars
43 valedictorians

THE STUDENT BODY
1,443 undergraduates
From 37 states and territories,
   24 other countries

84% from Maryland
57% women, 43% men
10% African Americans
0% Native Americans
2% Hispanics
4% Asian Americans
1% international students

AFTER FRESHMAN YEAR
84% returned for sophomore year
57% got a degree within 4 years
71% got a degree within 5 years
73% got a degree within 6 years

AFTER GRADUATION
37% pursued further study (27% arts and sciences, 5% law, 2% business)

72% had job offers within 6 months
8 organizations recruited on campus
1 Fulbright scholar

WHAT YOU WILL PAY
Resident tuition and fees $6005
Nonresident tuition and fees $9555
Room and board $5220
16% receive need-based financial aid
Need-based college-administered scholarships and
   grants average $2600 per award
50% receive non-need financial aid
Non-need college-administered scholarships and
   grants average $3326 per award

ST. NORBERT COLLEGE

De Pere, Wisconsin • Suburban setting • Private • Independent-Religious • Coed

Recognized nationally for its academic program, St. Norbert College provides students with the resources necessary to compete with the nation's best. With a faculty determined to provide the best possible instruction and advising, the College is committed to helping students achieve their goals. The College community, steeped in the values of the Norbertine tradition, encourages students to discover ways in which they can enrich their lives, society, and the world. Students considering St. Norbert are welcome to visit the campus, sit in on classes, and meet with faculty members.

 Academics

St. Norbert offers a liberal arts and sciences curriculum and core academic program; a few graduate courses are open to undergraduates. It awards bachelor's and master's **degrees**. Challenging opportunities include advanced placement, accelerated degree programs, self-designed majors, tutorials, an honors program, and a senior project. Special programs include cooperative education, internships, summer session for credit, off-campus study, study abroad, and Army ROTC.

The most popular **majors** include business, elementary education, and communication. A complete listing of majors at St. Norbert appears in the Majors Index beginning on page 379.

The **faculty** at St. Norbert has 114 full-time undergraduate teachers, 86% with terminal degrees. 100% of the faculty serve as student advisers. The student-faculty ratio is 15:1, and the average class size in core courses is 30.

 Computers on Campus

Students are not required to have a computer. Student rooms are linked to a campus network. 95 **computers** available in the computer center and the library provide access to the main academic computer, e-mail, on-line services, and the Internet. Staffed computer lab on campus provides training in the use of computers and software.

The **library** has 173,446 books, 25,379 microform titles, and 812 subscriptions.

 Campus Life

There are 75 active **organizations** on campus, including a drama/theater group and student-run newspaper and radio station. 30% of students participate in student government elections. 41% of eligible men and 57% of eligible women are members of 3 national **fraternities**, 1 national **sorority**, 2 local fraternities, 3 local sororities, and 12 social clubs. Student **safety services** include late night transport/escort service, 24-hour emergency telephone alarm devices, and 24-hour patrols by trained security personnel.

St. Norbert is a member of the NCAA (Division III). **Intercollegiate sports** include baseball (m), basketball (m, w), cross-country running (m, w), football (m), golf (m, w), ice hockey (m), soccer (m, w), softball (w), tennis (m, w), track and field (m, w), volleyball (w).

 Applying

St. Norbert requires an essay, a high school transcript, 3 years of high school math, 1 recommendation, and SAT I or ACT. It recommends 3 years of high school science, 2 years of high school foreign language, and an interview. Early, deferred, and midyear entrance are possible, with rolling admissions and continuous processing to 3/1 for financial aid. **Contact:** Mr. Craig Wesley, Dean of Admission, 100 Grant Street, Office of Admission, De Pere, WI 54115-2099, 414-337-3005 or toll-free 800-236-4878.

GETTING IN LAST YEAR
1,404 applied
92% were accepted
40% enrolled (520)
26% from top tenth of their h.s. class
3.25 average high school GPA
27% had ACT scores over 26
4% had ACT scores over 30

THE STUDENT BODY
Total 2,135, of whom 2,097
  are undergraduates
From 29 states and territories,
  21 other countries

70% from Wisconsin
56% women, 44% men
1% African Americans
1% Native Americans
1% Hispanics
1% Asian Americans
3% international students

AFTER FRESHMAN YEAR
84% returned for sophomore year
71% got a degree within 4 years

AFTER GRADUATION
20% pursued further study (12% arts and
  sciences, 4% law, 2% business)

71% had job offers within 6 months
44 organizations recruited on campus

WHAT YOU WILL PAY
Tuition and fees $13,040
Room and board $4655
64% receive need-based financial aid
Need-based college-administered scholarships and
  grants average $5097 per award
25% receive non-need financial aid
Non-need college-administered scholarships and
  grants average $3710 per award

St. Olaf College

Northfield, Minnesota • Small-town setting • Private • Independent-Religious • Coed

St. Olaf College strives to instill in its students the moral sensitivity and critical thinking necessary for knowledgeable and responsible citizenship of the world. An undergraduate residential institution of the Evangelical Lutheran Church in America, St. Olaf provides an education committed to the liberal arts, rooted in the Christian gospel, and incorporating a global perspective. Its nationally ranked science and mathematics departments, widely acclaimed international studies program, superb choral tradition, and competitive membership in the Minnesota Intercollegiate Athletic Conference are special features. St. Olaf has been widely recognized as one of America's leading colleges and as a "best buy" among the nation's liberal arts institutions.

 Academics

St. Olaf offers an interdisciplinary curriculum and core academic program. It awards bachelor's **degrees**. Challenging opportunities include advanced placement, accelerated degree programs, self-designed majors, tutorials, a senior project, and Phi Beta Kappa. Special programs include internships, summer session for credit, off-campus study, and study abroad.

The most popular **majors** include biology/biological sciences, economics, and English. A complete listing of majors at St. Olaf appears in the Majors Index beginning on page 379.

The **faculty** at St. Olaf has 255 full-time teachers, 79% with terminal degrees. 100% of the faculty serve as student advisers. The student-faculty ratio is 11:1.

 Computers on Campus

Students are not required to have a computer. 450 **computers** available in the computer center, computer labs, all academic buildings, the library, and dormitories provide access to the main academic computer, e-mail, on-line services, and the Internet. Staffed computer lab on campus (open 24 hours a day) provides training in the use of computers and software.

The 4 **libraries** have 444,287 books, 55,425 microform titles, and 1,757 subscriptions. They are connected to 1 national **on-line** catalog.

 Campus Life

There are 80 active **organizations** on campus, including a drama/theater group and student-run newspaper and radio station. 25% of students participate in student government elections. Student **safety services** include late night transport/escort service, 24-hour emergency telephone alarm devices, 24-hour patrols by trained security personnel, and electronically operated dormitory entrances.

St. Olaf is a member of the NCAA (Division III). **Intercollegiate sports** include baseball (m), basketball (m, w), cross-country running (m, w), football (m), golf (m, w), ice hockey (m), skiing (cross-country) (m, w), skiing (downhill) (m, w), soccer (m, w), softball (w), swimming and diving (m, w), tennis (m, w), track and field (m, w), volleyball (w), wrestling (m).

 Applying

St. Olaf requires an essay, a high school transcript, 2 recommendations, SAT I or ACT, PSAT, and a minimum high school GPA of 3.0. It recommends 3 years of high school math and science, 2 years of high school foreign language, and an interview. Early, deferred, and midyear entrance are possible, with rolling admissions and continuous processing to 3/1 for financial aid. **Contact:** Ms. Barbara Lundberg, Director of Admissions, 1520 St. Olaf Avenue, Northfield, MN 55057-1098, 507-646-3025 or toll-free 800-800-3025 (in-state); fax 507-646-3549.

GETTING IN LAST YEAR
2,333 applied
74% were accepted
43% enrolled (748)
38% from top tenth of their h.s. class
3.5 average high school GPA
30% had SAT verbal scores over 600
56% had SAT math scores over 600
56% had ACT scores over 26
6% had SAT verbal scores over 700
17% had SAT math scores over 700
18% had ACT scores over 30
32 National Merit Scholars

THE STUDENT BODY
2,936 undergraduates

From 49 states and territories,
    34 other countries
55% from Minnesota
58% women, 42% men
1% African Americans
1% Native Americans
1% Hispanics
4% Asian Americans
2% international students

AFTER FRESHMAN YEAR
83% returned for sophomore year
73% got a degree within 4 years
79% got a degree within 5 years

AFTER GRADUATION
31% pursued further study
66% had job offers within 6 months
36 organizations recruited on campus
3 Fulbright scholars

WHAT YOU WILL PAY
Tuition and fees $15,080
Room and board $3850
64% receive need-based financial aid
Need-based college-administered scholarships and
    grants average $5608 per award
5% receive non-need financial aid
Non-need college-administered scholarships and
    grants average $3362 per award

SAMFORD UNIVERSITY

Birmingham, Alabama • Suburban setting • Private • Independent-Religious • Coed

Samford University is the largest private accredited university in Alabama, yet with 4,600 students, it is an ideal size. More than half the undergraduates reside on campus. Students from 40 states and 32 other countries enjoy a beautiful setting characterized by Georgian-Colonial architecture. The institution takes seriously its Christian heritage and is consistently listed in rankings of Southeastern institutions. Faculty members have earned degrees from more than 160 colleges and universities, with nearly 80% holding the terminal degree in their field. Excellent opportunity to "stretch" academically, socially, physically, and spiritually is provided, along with special opportunities in computer competency, in international experiences, and in externships.

 Academics

Samford offers a liberal arts curriculum and core academic program. It awards associate, bachelor's, master's, and first professional **degrees**. Challenging opportunities include advanced placement, accelerated degree programs, self-designed majors, and a senior project. Special programs include cooperative education, internships, summer session for credit, off-campus study, study abroad, and Army and Air Force ROTC.

The most popular **majors** include liberal arts/general studies and business. A complete listing of majors at Samford appears in the Majors Index beginning on page 379.

The **faculty** at Samford has 257 full-time graduate and undergraduate teachers, 79% with terminal degrees. 60% of the faculty serve as student advisers. The student-faculty ratio is 14:1.

 Computers on Campus

Students are not required to have a computer. 268 **computers** available in the computer center, computer labs, vari-ous schools, and the library provide access to e-mail. Staffed computer lab on campus provides training in the use of computers and software.

The 5 **libraries** have 756,738 books, 248,453 microform titles, and 2,101 subscriptions. They are connected to 2 national **on-line** catalogs.

 Campus Life

There are 110 active **organizations** on campus, including a drama/theater group and student-run newspaper and radio station. 30% of students participate in student government elections. 30% of eligible men and 41% of eligible women are members of 5 national **fraternities** and 8 national **sororities**. Student **safety services** include 24-hour patrols by trained security personnel and electronically operated dormitory entrances.

Samford is a member of the NCAA (Division I). **Intercollegiate sports** (some offering scholarships) include baseball (m), basketball (m), cross-country running (m, w), football (m), golf (m, w), softball (w), tennis (m, w), track and field (m, w), volleyball (w).

 Applying

Samford requires an essay, a high school transcript, 2 recommendations, SAT I or ACT, and a minimum high school GPA of 3.0. It recommends 3 years of high school math and science, some high school foreign language, and a campus interview. Early, deferred, and midyear entrance are possible, with rolling admissions and continuous processing to 3/1 for financial aid. **Contact:** Dr. Don Belcher, Dean of Admissions and Financial Aid, Samford Hall, Birmingham, AL 35229-0002, 205-870-2901 or toll-free 800-888-7218; fax 205-870-2171.

GETTING IN LAST YEAR
1,713 applied
85% were accepted
44% enrolled (647)
36% from top tenth of their h.s. class
3.49 average high school GPA
40% had SAT verbal scores over 600 (R)
35% had SAT math scores over 600 (R)
37% had ACT scores over 26
8% had SAT verbal scores over 700 (R)
5% had SAT math scores over 700 (R)
12% had ACT scores over 30
19 National Merit Scholars
24 valedictorians

THE STUDENT BODY
Total 4,630, of whom 3,102
  are undergraduates
From 40 states and territories
48% from Alabama
62% women, 38% men
5% African Americans
0% Native Americans
1% Hispanics
1% Asian Americans
1% international students

AFTER FRESHMAN YEAR
82% returned for sophomore year
43% got a degree within 4 years

57% got a degree within 5 years
60% got a degree within 6 years

AFTER GRADUATION
23 organizations recruited on campus

WHAT YOU WILL PAY
Tuition and fees $8648
Room and board $3844
35% receive need-based financial aid
Need-based college-administered scholarships and
  grants average $1291 per award
53% receive non-need financial aid
Non-need college-administered scholarships and
  grants average $4192 per award

SANTA CLARA UNIVERSITY

Santa Clara, California • Suburban setting • Private • Independent-Religious • Coed

Students who are interested in a strong academic program, a commitment to social justice, California weather and diversity, and a learning environment where professors know their students should consider Santa Clara University. In addition to the undergraduate divisions of arts and sciences, business, and engineering, special programs are offered in environmental studies, international business, studies abroad, and courses that incorporate community service. Santa Clara is looking for students who have taken solid, college-prep courses in high school and who are prepared to excel in a rigorous collegiate program. The University particularly welcomes students who share a concern for and commitment to solving societal problems.

Academics

Santa Clara offers an education of the whole person curriculum and core academic program; a few graduate courses are open to undergraduates. It awards bachelor's, master's, doctoral, and first professional **degrees**. Challenging opportunities include advanced placement, self-designed majors, tutorials, Freshman Honors College, an honors program, a senior project, Phi Beta Kappa, and Sigma Xi. Special programs include cooperative education, internships, summer session for credit, and Army, Naval, and Air Force ROTC.

The most popular **majors** include finance/banking, political science/government, and English. A complete listing of majors at Santa Clara appears in the Majors Index beginning on page 379.

The **faculty** at Santa Clara has 341 full-time graduate and undergraduate teachers, 88% with terminal degrees. 100% of the faculty serve as student advisers. The student-faculty ratio is 10:1, and the average class size in core courses is 31.

 Computers on Campus

Students are not required to have a computer. Student rooms are linked to a campus network. 350 **computers** available in the computer center, computer labs, classrooms, the library, and the student center provide access to the main academic computer, e-mail, and the Internet. Staffed computer lab on campus provides training in the use of computers and software.

The **library** has 608,273 books, 36,991 microform titles, and 4,831 subscriptions.

Campus Life

There are 100 active **organizations** on campus, including a drama/theater group and student-run newspaper and radio station. 15% of eligible men and 16% of eligible women are members of 4 national **fraternities** and 3 national **sororities**. Student **safety services** include late night transport/escort service and 24-hour emergency telephone alarm devices.

Santa Clara is a member of the NCAA (Division I). **Intercollegiate sports** (some offering scholarships) include baseball (m), basketball (m, w), crew (m, w), cross-country running (m, w), golf (m, w), lacrosse (m, w), rugby (m, w), soccer (m, w), softball (w), tennis (m, w), volleyball (m, w), water polo (m).

 Applying

Santa Clara requires an essay, a high school transcript, 3 years of high school math, 3 years of high school foreign language, 1 recommendation, SAT I or ACT, and in some cases 3 years of high school science. It recommends an interview. 2/1 deadline and continuous processing to 2/1 for financial aid. **Contact:** Ms. Charlene Aguilar, Director of Undergraduate Admissions, 500 El Camino Real, Santa Clara, CA 95053-0001, 408-554-4700; fax 408-554-5255.

GETTING IN LAST YEAR
4,270 applied
76% were accepted
32% enrolled (1,043)
37% from top tenth of their h.s. class
3.45 average high school GPA
13% had SAT verbal scores over 600 (R)
51% had SAT math scores over 600 (R)
1% had SAT verbal scores over 700 (R)
12% had SAT math scores over 700 (R)
8 National Merit Scholars
49 valedictorians

THE STUDENT BODY
Total 7,654, of whom 4,100
   are undergraduates

From 43 states and territories,
   79 other countries
67% from California
52% women, 48% men
3% African Americans
1% Native Americans
14% Hispanics
21% Asian Americans
4% international students

AFTER FRESHMAN YEAR
92% returned for sophomore year
75% got a degree within 4 years
82% got a degree within 5 years

AFTER GRADUATION
21% pursued further study
250 organizations recruited on campus

WHAT YOU WILL PAY
Tuition and fees $14,772
Room and board $6522
64% receive need-based financial aid
Need-based college-administered scholarships and
   grants average $6600 per award
4% receive non-need financial aid
Non-need college-administered scholarships and
   grants average $11,160 per award

SARAH LAWRENCE COLLEGE

Bronxville, New York • Suburban setting • Private • Independent • Coed

Sarah Lawrence, a private, coeducational liberal arts college founded in 1926, is a lively community of students, scholars, and artists just 30 minutes from midtown Manhattan. In its unique seminar/conference system, each course consists of 2 parts: the seminar, enrolling about 15 students, and the conference, a private biweekly meeting with the seminar professor. In conference, student and teacher create a project that extends the seminar material and connects it to the student's interests. To prepare for this rigorous work, all first-year students enroll in a First-Year Studies Seminar. This seminar teacher will be the student's don, or adviser, throughout his or her Sarah Lawrence years.

 ## Academics

Sarah Lawrence offers an interdisciplinary curriculum and core academic program. It awards bachelor's and master's **degrees**. Challenging opportunities include advanced placement, self-designed majors, and tutorials. Special programs include internships, off-campus study, and study abroad.

The most popular **majors** include literature, creative writing, and theater arts/drama. A complete listing of majors at Sarah Lawrence appears in the Majors Index beginning on page 379.

The **faculty** at Sarah Lawrence has 165 full-time undergraduate teachers, 92% with terminal degrees. 100% of the faculty serve as student advisers. The student-faculty ratio is 6:1.

 ## Computers on Campus

Students are not required to have a computer. 46 **computers** available in the computer center provide access to e-mail. Staffed computer lab on campus provides training in the use of computers and software.

The 3 **libraries** have 217,907 books, 16,737 microform titles, and 1,111 subscriptions. They are connected to 7 national **on-line** catalogs.

Campus Life

There are 30 active **organizations** on campus, including a drama/theater group and student-run newspaper. 40% of students participate in student government elections. No national or local **fraternities** or **sororities**. Student **safety services** include late night transport/escort service, 24-hour emergency telephone alarm devices, 24-hour patrols by trained security personnel, student patrols, and electronically operated dormitory entrances. **Intercollegiate sports** include crew (m, w), equestrian sports (m, w), tennis (m, w), volleyball (w).

 ## Applying

Sarah Lawrence requires an essay, a high school transcript, 3 recommendations, SAT I or ACT or any 3 SAT II Subject Tests. It recommends 3 years of high school math and science, some high school foreign language, an interview, and a minimum high school GPA of 3.0. Early, deferred, and midyear entrance are possible, with a 2/1 deadline and 2/1 for financial aid. **Contact:** Mr. Robert M. Kinnally, Dean of Admissions, One Mead Way, Bronxville, NY 10708, 914-395-2510 or toll-free 800-888-2858; fax 914-395-2668.

GETTING IN LAST YEAR
1,284 applied
59% were accepted
31% enrolled (233)
51% from top tenth of their h.s. class
3.3 average high school GPA
74% had SAT verbal scores over 600 (R)
37% had SAT math scores over 600 (R)
55% had ACT scores over 26
22% had SAT verbal scores over 700 (R)
3% had SAT math scores over 700 (R)
18% had ACT scores over 30

THE STUDENT BODY
Total 1,279, of whom 1,035
    are undergraduates

From 48 states and territories,
    24 other countries
24% from New York
76% women, 24% men
6% African Americans
1% Native Americans
6% Hispanics
5% Asian Americans
4% international students

AFTER FRESHMAN YEAR
90% returned for sophomore year
70% got a degree within 4 years
75% got a degree within 5 years
80% got a degree within 6 years

AFTER GRADUATION
35% pursued further study
1 Fulbright scholar

WHAT YOU WILL PAY
Tuition and fees $20,708
Room and board $6838
61% receive need-based financial aid
Need-based college-administered scholarships and
    grants average $13,390 per award
0% receive non-need financial aid

SCRIPPS COLLEGE

Claremont, California • Suburban setting • Private • Independent • Women

From its founding in 1926 as one of the few institutions in the West dedicated to educating women for professional careers as well as personal intellectual growth, Scripps College has championed the qualities of mind and spirit described by its founder, newspaper entrepreneur and philanthropist Ellen Browning Scripps. Scripps remains a women's college because it believes that having women at the core of its concerns provides the very best environment for intellectually ambitious women to learn from a distinguished teaching faculty and from each other. Scripps emphasizes a challenging liberal arts curriculum based on interdisciplinary humanistic studies.

 Academics

Scripps offers an interdisciplinary curriculum and core academic program. It awards bachelor's **degrees**. Challenging opportunities include advanced placement, self-designed majors, tutorials, a senior project, and Phi Beta Kappa. Special programs include internships, off-campus study, study abroad, and Army and Air Force ROTC.

The most popular **majors** include psychology and biology/biological sciences. A complete listing of majors at Scripps appears in the Majors Index beginning on page 379.

The **faculty** at Scripps has 61 full-time teachers, 100% with terminal degrees. 100% of the faculty serve as student advisers. The student-faculty ratio is 9:1.

 Computers on Campus

Students are not required to have a computer. Student rooms are linked to a campus network. 65 **computers** available in the computer center, computer labs, the learn-

ing resource center, classrooms, and dormitories provide access to the main academic computer, off-campus computing facilities, e-mail, and the Internet. Staffed computer lab on campus provides training in the use of computers and software.

The 2 **libraries** have 1.9 million books and 1.2 million microform titles. They are connected to 20 national **on-line** catalogs.

 Campus Life

There are 200 active **organizations** on campus, including a drama/theater group and student-run newspaper and radio station. 40% of students participate in student government elections. Student **safety services** include late night transport/escort service, 24-hour emergency telephone alarm devices, 24-hour patrols by trained security personnel, and electronically operated dormitory entrances.

Scripps is a member of the NCAA (Division III). **Intercollegiate sports** include basketball, cross-country running, golf, soccer, softball, swimming and diving, tennis, track and field, volleyball.

 Applying

Scripps requires an essay, a high school transcript, 3 recommendations, graded writing sample, and SAT I or ACT. It recommends 4 years of high school math, 3 years of high school science, 3 years of high school foreign language, an interview, 3 SAT II Subject Tests, and a minimum high school GPA of 3.0. Early, deferred, and midyear entrance are possible, with a 2/1 deadline and a 2/1 priority date for financial aid. **Contact:** Ms. Patricia F. Goldsmith, Dean of Admission and Financial Aid, 1030 Columbia Avenue, Claremont, CA 91711-3948, 909-621-8149 or toll-free 800-770-1333; fax 909-621-8323.

GETTING IN LAST YEAR
914 applied
80% were accepted
29% enrolled (215)
50% from top tenth of their h.s. class
3.44 average high school GPA
62% had SAT verbal scores over 600 (R)
49% had SAT math scores over 600 (R)
44% had ACT scores over 26
14% had SAT verbal scores over 700 (R)
5% had SAT math scores over 700 (R)
13% had ACT scores over 30
4 National Merit Scholars
15 valedictorians

THE STUDENT BODY
684 undergraduates

From 37 states and territories,
    15 other countries
56% from California
100% women
4% African Americans
1% Native Americans
7% Hispanics
20% Asian Americans
4% international students

AFTER FRESHMAN YEAR
88% returned for sophomore year
69% got a degree within 4 years
70% got a degree within 5 years

AFTER GRADUATION
22% pursued further study (18% arts and
    sciences, 2% law, 1% business)
150 organizations recruited on campus

WHAT YOU WILL PAY
Tuition and fees $18,180
Room and board $7500
45% receive need-based financial aid
Need-based college-administered scholarships and
    grants average $11,537 per award
10% receive non-need financial aid
Non-need college-administered scholarships and
    grants average $7844 per award

SHEPHERD COLLEGE

Shepherdstown, West Virginia • Small-town setting • Public • State-supported • Coed

Since Shepherd College is located only one hour's drive from the Baltimore and Washington Beltways, it offers numerous internships and co-op programs with government agencies, scientific research centers, and corporations in the area. It is also the home of the Center for the Study of the Civil War and the professional Equity Contemporary American Theater Festival. The Honors Program offers a stimulating curriculum for its students.

 Academics

Shepherd offers a core academic program. It awards associate and bachelor's **degrees**. Challenging opportunities include advanced placement, accelerated degree programs, an honors program, and a senior project. Special programs include cooperative education, internships, summer session for credit, and Army and Air Force ROTC.

The most popular **majors** include business, education, and nursing. A complete listing of majors at Shepherd appears in the Majors Index beginning on page 379.

The **faculty** at Shepherd has 120 full-time teachers, 78% with terminal degrees. 100% of the faculty serve as student advisers. The student-faculty ratio is 14:1.

 Computers on Campus

Students are not required to have a computer. Student rooms are linked to a campus network. 202 **computers** available in the computer center, computer labs, the learning resource center, and the library provide access to the main academic computer, e-mail, on-line services, and the Internet. Staffed computer lab on campus provides training in the use of computers and software.

The **library** has 156,706 books, 149,469 microform titles, and 952 subscriptions. It is connected to 4 national **on-line** catalogs.

 Campus Life

There are 70 active **organizations** on campus, including a drama/theater group and student-run newspaper and radio station. 40% of students participate in student government elections. 25% of eligible men and 25% of eligible women are members of 5 national **fraternities** and 3 national **sororities**. Student **safety services** include late night transport/escort service, 24-hour emergency telephone alarm devices, 24-hour patrols by trained security personnel, and electronically operated dormitory entrances.

Shepherd is a member of the NCAA (Division II). **Intercollegiate sports** (some offering scholarships) include baseball (m), basketball (m, w), cross-country running (m, w), football (m), golf (m, w), soccer (m), softball (w), tennis (m, w), volleyball (w).

 Applying

Shepherd requires an essay, a high school transcript, 3 years of high school math and science, 3 recommendations, and SAT I or ACT. It recommends 2 years of high school foreign language and a campus interview. Early, deferred, and midyear entrance are possible, with a 2/1 deadline and continuous processing to 3/1 for financial aid. **Contact:** Mr. Karl L. Wolf, Director of Admissions, McMurran Hall, Shepherdstown, WV 25443, 304-876-5212 or toll-free 800-344-5231; fax 304-876-3101.

GETTING IN LAST YEAR
1,800 applied
60% were accepted
61% enrolled (660)
3.06 average high school GPA
20% had ACT scores over 26
2% had ACT scores over 30
6 National Merit Scholars
25 class presidents
35 valedictorians

THE STUDENT BODY
3,602 undergraduates

From 35 states and territories,
  12 other countries
72% from West Virginia
60% women, 40% men
6% African Americans
1% Native Americans
2% Hispanics
1% Asian Americans
1% international students

AFTER FRESHMAN YEAR
77% returned for sophomore year

AFTER GRADUATION
93% had job offers within 6 months
142 organizations recruited on campus

WHAT YOU WILL PAY
Resident tuition and fees $2064
Nonresident tuition and fees $4694
Room and board $3970
39% receive need-based financial aid
39% receive non-need financial aid
Non-need college-administered scholarships and
  grants average $535 per award

SIENA COLLEGE

Loudonville, New York • Suburban setting • Private • Independent-Religious • Coed

Siena's top-flight faculty members call forth the best Siena students have to give, and the students do the same for the faculty members. Siena people are competitive but not at each other's expense. A caring network of faculty, friars, students, and staff ensures a complete education for each individual student. The curriculum includes 23 majors in 3 divisions—arts, science, and business. In addition, there are more than 15 preprofessional and special academic programs. Siena's 152-acre campus is located in Loudonville, a suburb of Albany, New York, the state capital.

 Academics

Siena offers a core academic program; a few graduate courses are open to undergraduates. It awards bachelor's and master's **degrees**. Challenging opportunities include advanced placement, tutorials, an honors program, and a senior project. Special programs include internships, summer session for credit, off-campus study, and Army and Air Force ROTC.

The most popular **majors** include accounting, marketing/retailing/merchandising, and biology/biological sciences. A complete listing of majors at Siena appears in the Majors Index beginning on page 379.

The **faculty** at Siena has 162 full-time undergraduate teachers, 81% with terminal degrees. 100% of the faculty serve as student advisers. The student-faculty ratio is 16:1.

 Computers on Campus

Students are not required to have a computer. 500 **computers** available in the computer center, computer labs, academic buildings, and classrooms provide access to the main academic computer, e-mail, and the Internet. Staffed computer lab on campus (open 24 hours a day) provides training in the use of computers and software.

The **library** has 257,617 books, 30,341 microform titles, and 1,658 subscriptions.

 Campus Life

There are 77 active **organizations** on campus, including a drama/theater group and student-run newspaper and radio station. Student **safety services** include call boxes in parking lots and on roadways, late night transport/escort service, 24-hour emergency telephone alarm devices, 24-hour patrols by trained security personnel, and electronically operated dormitory entrances.

Siena is a member of the NCAA (Division I). **Intercollegiate sports** (some offering scholarships) include baseball (m), basketball (m, w), cross-country running (m, w), equestrian sports (m, w), fencing (m, w), field hockey (w), football (m), golf (m), ice hockey (m), lacrosse (m, w), rugby (m), skiing (downhill) (m, w), soccer (m, w), softball (m), tennis (m, w), track and field (m, w), volleyball (w).

 Applying

Siena requires an essay, a high school transcript, 3 years of high school math and science, 1 recommendation, SAT I or ACT, and in some cases a campus interview. It recommends 2 years of high school foreign language and SAT II Subject Tests. Early, deferred, and midyear entrance are possible, with a 3/1 deadline and continuous processing to 2/1 for financial aid. **Contact:** Mr. Edward Jones, Dean of Admissions, 515 Loudon Road, Loudonville, NY 12211-1462, 518-783-2423 or toll-free 800-45-SIENA.

GETTING IN LAST YEAR
2,447 applied
81% were accepted
30% enrolled (593)
17% from top tenth of their h.s. class
22% had SAT verbal scores over 600 (R)
29% had SAT math scores over 600 (R)
28% had ACT scores over 26
2% had SAT verbal scores over 700 (R)
2% had SAT math scores over 700 (R)
1% had ACT scores over 30

THE STUDENT BODY
Total 3,288, of whom 3,270
  are undergraduates

From 27 states and territories,
  6 other countries
82% from New York
55% women, 45% men
2% African Americans
1% Native Americans
2% Hispanics
3% Asian Americans
1% international students

AFTER FRESHMAN YEAR
83% returned for sophomore year
74% got a degree within 4 years
79% got a degree within 5 years
80% got a degree within 6 years

AFTER GRADUATION
25% pursued further study
144 organizations recruited on campus

WHAT YOU WILL PAY
Tuition and fees $11,650
Room and board $5270
73% receive need-based financial aid
Need-based college-administered scholarships and
  grants average $4425 per award
12% receive non-need financial aid

Simon's Rock College of Bard

Great Barrington, Massachusetts • Small-town setting • Private • Independent • Coed

In fall 1993, Simon's Rock installed its own Internet node. Students now have free access to the system and individual accounts to use as they wish. The influence of this system on society in general and the College in particular is likely to be profound. William Gibson's *Neuromancer* has already made its way into the curriculum. The admissions office is keenly interested in applicants with network experience. Interested students should send electronic mail to brian@plato.simons-rock.edu for more information.

 Academics

Simon's Rock offers an interdisciplinary curriculum and core academic program. It awards associate and bachelor's **degrees**. Challenging opportunities include tutorials, an honors program, and a senior project. Special programs include internships, off-campus study, and study abroad.

The **faculty** at Simon's Rock has 36 full-time teachers, 100% with terminal degrees. 100% of the faculty serve as student advisers. The student-faculty ratio is 9:1.

 Computers on Campus

Students are not required to have a computer. 20 **computers** available in the computer center, computer labs, the library, and dormitories provide access to off-campus computing facilities, e-mail, and on-line services. Staffed computer lab on campus provides training in the use of computers and software.

The **library** has 65,000 books, 140 microform titles, and 325 subscriptions. It is connected to 3 national **on-line** catalogs.

 Campus Life

Active **organizations** on campus include drama/theater group and student-run newspaper. Student **safety services** include late night transport/escort service, 24-hour emergency telephone alarm devices, and electronically operated dormitory entrances.

Simon's Rock is a member of the NSCAA. **Intercollegiate sports** include basketball (m, w), soccer (m, w), tennis (m, w).

 Applying

Simon's Rock requires an essay, a high school transcript, 2 recommendations, a campus interview, parent application, SAT I or ACT, and PSAT. Early, deferred, and midyear entrance are possible, with a 6/15 deadline and continuous processing to 6/15 for financial aid. **Contact:** Mr. Brian R. Hopewell, Director of Admissions, 84 Alford Road, Great Barrington, MA 01230-9702, 413-528-0771 ext. 313 or toll-free 800-235-7186; fax 413-528-7334.

GETTING IN LAST YEAR
381 applied
60% were accepted
54% enrolled (124)

THE STUDENT BODY
304 undergraduates
From 34 states and territories,
  5 other countries
12% from Massachusetts
62% women, 38% men

4% African Americans
1% Native Americans
2% Hispanics
8% Asian Americans
3% international students

AFTER GRADUATION
33% pursued further study (33% arts and
  sciences)
56% had job offers within 6 months

WHAT YOU WILL PAY
Tuition and fees $19,770
Room and board $5860
85% receive need-based financial aid
Need-based college-administered scholarships and
  grants average $9000 per award
19% receive non-need financial aid
Non-need college-administered scholarships and
  grants average $23,019 per award

SIMPSON COLLEGE

Indianola, Iowa • Small-town setting • Private • Independent-Religious • Coed

Simpson College combines the best of a liberal arts education with outstanding career preparation and extracurricular programs. Activities range from an award-winning music program to nationally recognized NCAA Division III teams. Located 12 miles from Des Moines, Simpson offers the friendliness of a small town and the advantages of a metropolitan area. Outstanding facilities have been enhanced with recent multimillion-dollar expansions and renovations, including the state-of-the-art Carver Science Center, named after Simpson's most distinguished alumnus, George Washington Carver. The beautiful 63-acre tree-lined campus provides a setting that nurtures creativity, energy, and productivity.

Academics

Simpson offers a liberal arts curriculum and core academic program. It awards bachelor's **degrees**. Challenging opportunities include advanced placement, accelerated degree programs, self-designed majors, tutorials, Freshman Honors College, an honors program, and a senior project. Special programs include cooperative education, internships, summer session for credit, off-campus study, and study abroad.

The most popular **majors** include business, accounting, and biology/biological sciences. A complete listing of majors at Simpson appears in the Majors Index beginning on page 379.

The **faculty** at Simpson has 73 full-time teachers, 78% with terminal degrees. 93% of the faculty serve as student advisers. The student-faculty ratio is 13:1.

Computers on Campus

Students are not required to have a computer. 200 **computers** available in the computer center, computer labs, fraternities, the library, and dormitories provide access to the main academic computer, off-campus computing facilities, e-mail, and the Internet. Staffed computer lab on campus provides training in the use of computers and software.

The **library** has 155,761 books, 61 microform titles, and 586 subscriptions. It is connected to 4 national **on-line** catalogs.

Campus Life

There are 81 active **organizations** on campus, including a drama/theater group and student-run newspaper and radio station. 40% of students participate in student government elections. 32% of eligible men and 30% of eligible women are members of 3 national **fraternities**, 4 national **sororities**, and 1 local fraternity. Student **safety services** include late night transport/escort service, 24-hour emergency telephone alarm devices, 24-hour patrols by trained security personnel, student patrols, and electronically operated dormitory entrances.

Simpson is a member of the NCAA (Division III). **Intercollegiate sports** include baseball (m), basketball (m, w), cross-country running (m, w), football (m), golf (m, w), rugby (m), soccer (m, w), softball (w), swimming and diving (m, w), tennis (m, w), track and field (m, w), volleyball (w), wrestling (m).

Applying

Simpson requires a high school transcript, 1 recommendation, and SAT I or ACT. It recommends 3 years of high school math and science, 3 years of high school foreign language, an interview, and rank in top half of graduating class. Early, deferred, and midyear entrance are possible, with rolling admissions and continuous processing to 4/20 for financial aid. **Contact:** Mr. John Kellogg, Vice President of Enrollment and Planning, 701 North C Street, Indianola, IA 50125-1297, 515-961-1624 or toll-free 800-362-2454; fax 515-961-1498.

GETTING IN LAST YEAR
1,069 applied
89% were accepted
38% enrolled (358)
22% from top tenth of their h.s. class
32% had ACT scores over 26
6% had ACT scores over 30

THE STUDENT BODY
1,685 undergraduates
From 25 states and territories,
  7 other countries

93% from Iowa
51% women, 49% men
1% African Americans
0% Native Americans
1% Hispanics
1% Asian Americans
1% international students

AFTER FRESHMAN YEAR
81% returned for sophomore year
49% got a degree within 4 years
58% got a degree within 5 years

AFTER GRADUATION
78 organizations recruited on campus

WHAT YOU WILL PAY
Tuition and fees $12,170
Room and board $3980
87% receive need-based financial aid
Need-based college-administered scholarships and
  grants average $3667 per award
13% receive non-need financial aid
Non-need college-administered scholarships and
  grants average $3970 per award

SKIDMORE COLLEGE

Saratoga Springs, New York • Small-town setting • Private • Independent • Coed

Skidmore College, located on a beautiful 850-acre campus, is a liberal arts college with a history of innovation and imagination. An interdisciplinary liberal studies curriculum challenges students to explore broadly. A rich cocurricular program provides further opportunities for personal growth and leadership. Among the largest majors are business, studio art, English, psychology, government, and biology/chemistry. A total of 2,129 students from 47 states and 24 countries live and learn in Skidmore's lively intellectual climate and beautiful campus surroundings.

Academics

Skidmore College offers an interdisciplinary curriculum and core academic program; a few graduate courses are open to undergraduates. It awards bachelor's and master's **degrees**. Challenging opportunities include advanced placement, accelerated degree programs, self-designed majors, tutorials, a senior project, and Phi Beta Kappa. Special programs include internships, summer session for credit, off-campus study, study abroad, and Army and Air Force ROTC.

The most popular **majors** include business, English, and psychology. A complete listing of majors at Skidmore College appears in the Majors Index beginning on page 379.

The **faculty** at Skidmore College has 201 full-time graduate and undergraduate teachers, 93% with terminal degrees. 100% of the faculty serve as student advisers. The student-faculty ratio is 11:1.

Computers on Campus

Students are not required to have a computer. Student rooms are linked to a campus network. 200 **computers** available in the computer center, computer labs, classroom buildings, the library, the student center, and dormitories provide access to the main academic computer, e-mail, on-line services, and the Internet. Staffed computer lab on campus (open 24 hours a day) provides training in the use of computers and software.

The **library** has 410,000 books, 267,000 microform titles, and 1,700 subscriptions. It is connected to 8 national **on-line** catalogs.

Campus Life

There are 80 active **organizations** on campus, including a drama/theater group and student-run newspaper and radio station. Student **safety services** include late night transport/escort service, 24-hour emergency telephone alarm devices, 24-hour patrols by trained security personnel, and electronically operated dormitory entrances.

Skidmore College is a member of the NCAA (Division III). **Intercollegiate sports** include baseball (m), basketball (m, w), crew (m, w), equestrian sports (m, w), field hockey (w), golf (m), ice hockey (m, w), lacrosse (m, w), skiing (downhill) (m, w), soccer (m, w), softball (w), swimming and diving (m, w), tennis (m, w), volleyball (w).

Applying

Skidmore College requires an essay, a high school transcript, 3 years of high school math and science, 3 years of high school foreign language, 2 recommendations, and SAT I or ACT. It recommends an interview and 3 SAT II Subject Tests. Early, deferred, and midyear entrance are possible, with a 2/1 deadline and 2/1 for financial aid. **Contact:** Ms. Mary Lou Bates, Director of Admissions, North Broadway, Saratoga Springs, NY 12866-1632, 518-584-5000 ext. 2213 or toll-free 800-867-6007; fax 518-581-7462.

GETTING IN LAST YEAR
4,673 applied
65% were accepted
20% enrolled (610)
20% from top tenth of their h.s. class
59% had ACT scores over 26
3% had ACT scores over 30

THE STUDENT BODY
Total 2,183, of whom 2,129
   are undergraduates
From 47 states and territories,
   24 other countries
32% from New York
60% women, 40% men

2% African Americans
1% Native Americans
5% Hispanics
4% Asian Americans
1% international students

AFTER FRESHMAN YEAR
88% returned for sophomore year
70% got a degree within 4 years
78% got a degree within 5 years

AFTER GRADUATION
24% pursued further study (18% arts and
   sciences, 3% law, 1% business)

92% had job offers within 6 months
103 organizations recruited on campus
1 Fulbright scholar

WHAT YOU WILL PAY
Tuition and fees $19,950
Room and board $5890
31% receive need-based financial aid
Need-based college-administered scholarships and
   grants average $12,480 per award
19% receive non-need financial aid
Non-need college-administered scholarships and
   grants average $6000 per award

SMITH COLLEGE

Northampton, Massachusetts • Urban setting • Private • Independent • Women

Students choose Smith because it is one of the most outstanding and highly selective liberal arts colleges in the United States. From its founding in 1871, the College has been committed to helping women develop fully their intellects and talents by providing them with the highest quality undergraduate education. Smith has taken a progressive, expansive, and student-oriented view of its role as a liberal arts college. Each student has the freedom and responsibility to design a course of studies to fit her individual needs and interests, since there are no core course requirements outside of a student's major.

Academics

Smith offers an open curriculum and no core academic program. It awards bachelor's, master's, and doctoral **degrees**. Challenging opportunities include advanced placement, accelerated degree programs, self-designed majors, tutorials, an honors program, a senior project, Phi Beta Kappa, and Sigma Xi. Special programs include internships, off-campus study, study abroad, and Army and Air Force ROTC.

The most popular **majors** include art/fine arts, political science/government, and psychology. A complete listing of majors at Smith appears in the Majors Index beginning on page 379.

The **faculty** at Smith has 269 full-time graduate and undergraduate teachers, 97% with terminal degrees. 100% of the faculty serve as student advisers. The student-faculty ratio is 10:1.

Computers on Campus

Students are not required to have a computer. Student rooms are linked to a campus network. 230 **computers**

available in the computer center, resource centers, special needs computer room, and the library provide access to the main academic computer, e-mail, on-line services, and the Internet. Staffed computer lab on campus provides training in the use of computers and software.

The 4 **libraries** have 1.15 million books and 2,579 subscriptions. They are connected to 5 national **on-line** catalogs.

Campus Life

There are 93 active **organizations** on campus, including a drama/theater group and student-run newspaper and radio station. 30% of students participate in student government elections. Student **safety services** include self-defense workshops, emergency telephones, late night transport/escort service, 24-hour emergency telephone alarm devices, and 24-hour patrols by trained security personnel.

Smith is a member of the NCAA (Division III). **Intercollegiate sports** include basketball, crew, cross-country running, equestrian sports, field hockey, lacrosse, skiing (downhill), soccer, softball, squash, swimming and diving, tennis, track and field, volleyball.

Applying

Smith requires an essay, a high school transcript, 2 recommendations, and SAT I or ACT. It recommends 3 years of high school math and science, 3 years of high school foreign language, an interview, and 3 SAT II Subject Tests. Early and deferred entrance are possible, with a 1/15 deadline and 2/1 for financial aid. **Contact:** Ms. Nanci Tessier, Director of Admissions, 7 College Lane, Northampton, MA 01063, 413-585-2500; fax 413-585-2527.

GETTING IN LAST YEAR
3,334 applied
49% were accepted
39% enrolled (631)
57% from top tenth of their h.s. class
87% had SAT verbal scores over 600 (R)
70% had SAT math scores over 600 (R)
91% had ACT scores over 26
30% had SAT verbal scores over 700 (R)
9% had SAT math scores over 700 (R)
27% had ACT scores over 30
25 valedictorians

THE STUDENT BODY
Total 3,184, of whom 2,668
   are undergraduates

From 52 states and territories,
   68 other countries
18% from Massachusetts
100% women
4% African Americans
1% Native Americans
4% Hispanics
11% Asian Americans
8% international students

AFTER FRESHMAN YEAR
88% returned for sophomore year
81% got a degree within 4 years
83% got a degree within 5 years
84% got a degree within 6 years

AFTER GRADUATION
17% pursued further study (12% arts and
   sciences, 3% law, 2% medicine)
4 Fulbright scholars

WHAT YOU WILL PAY
Tuition and fees $19,814
Room and board $6670
55% receive need-based financial aid
Need-based college-administered scholarships and
   grants average $13,122 per award

SOUTH DAKOTA SCHOOL OF MINES AND TECHNOLOGY

Rapid City, South Dakota • Suburban setting • Public • State-supported • Coed

South Dakota School of Mines and Technology is one of only a select few moderately sized, affordably priced universities that emphasize Bachelor of Science, Master of Science, and doctorate-level programs exclusively in the areas of engineering and science. This specialization enhances the School's national and international reputation for academic excellence, makes its graduates highly sought by industry, allows the School to furnish classrooms and laboratories with the latest in high-tech state-of-the-art scientific equipment, and provides a greater degree of fellowship among students, making it easy for students to study and work together in a group effort.

Academics

SDSM & T offers a general curriculum and core academic program; fewer than half of graduate courses are open to undergraduates. It awards bachelor's, master's, and doctoral **degrees**. Challenging opportunities include advanced placement, self-designed majors, a senior project, and Sigma Xi. Special programs include cooperative education, summer session for credit, study abroad, and Army ROTC.

The most popular **majors** include mechanical engineering, computer science, and electrical engineering. A complete listing of majors at SDSM & T appears in the Majors Index beginning on page 379.

The **faculty** at SDSM & T has 102 full-time graduate and undergraduate teachers, 78% with terminal degrees. 69% of the faculty serve as student advisers. The student-faculty ratio is 16:1.

Computers on Campus

Students are not required to have a computer. Student rooms are linked to a campus network. 130 **computers**

available in the computer center, computer labs, classrooms, the library, the student center, and dormitories provide access to the main academic computer, off-campus computing facilities, e-mail, and on-line services. Staffed computer lab on campus provides training in the use of computers and software.

The 2 **libraries** have 155,886 books, 194,614 microform titles, and 959 subscriptions.

Campus Life

Active **organizations** on campus include drama/theater group and student-run newspaper and radio station. 19% of eligible men and 21% of eligible women are members of 4 national **fraternities** and 2 national **sororities**. Student **safety services** include late night transport/escort service, 24-hour emergency telephone alarm devices, and 24-hour patrols by trained security personnel.

SDSM & T is a member of the NAIA. **Intercollegiate sports** (some offering scholarships) include basketball (m, w), cross-country running (m, w), football (m), tennis (m), track and field (m, w), volleyball (w).

Applying

SDSM & T requires a high school transcript, 3 years of high school math and science, SAT I or ACT, and a minimum high school GPA of 2.0. It recommends some high school foreign language. Rolling admissions and continuous processing to 4/15 for financial aid. **Contact:** Mr. Chuck Colombe, Director of Admissions, 501 East Saint Joseph Street, Rapid City, SD 57701-3995, 605-394-2400 or toll-free 800-544-8162; fax 605-394-6721 ext. 2400.

GETTING IN LAST YEAR
704 applied
69% were accepted
77% enrolled (375)
27% from top tenth of their h.s. class
26% had SAT verbal scores over 600
64% had SAT math scores over 600
37% had ACT scores over 26
0% had SAT verbal scores over 700
5% had SAT math scores over 700
7% had ACT scores over 30
2 National Merit Scholars
18 valedictorians

THE STUDENT BODY
Total 2,356, of whom 2,099
    are undergraduates
From 38 states and territories,
    17 other countries
68% from South Dakota
33% women, 67% men
1% African Americans
3% Native Americans
1% Hispanics
1% Asian Americans
10% international students

AFTER FRESHMAN YEAR
45% got a degree within 5 years

AFTER GRADUATION
13% pursued further study (7% engineering, 2% business, 2% medicine)

WHAT YOU WILL PAY
Resident tuition and fees $3241
Nonresident tuition and fees $6250
Room and board $3240
Need-based college-administered scholarships and grants average $1134 per award
Non-need college-administered scholarships and grants average $405 per award

---

SOUTHERN METHODIST UNIVERSITY

Dallas, Texas • Suburban setting • Private • Independent-Religious • Coed

SMU offers an education as individual as each of its students, with as many as 70 majors in the humanities, sciences, business, engineering, and the arts. Small classes taught by full-time faculty members provide personal attention and mentoring opportunities. SMU offers more than 10 study-abroad programs and a summer campus near Taos, New Mexico. SMU's diverse student body represents all 50 states, many countries, and numerous faiths; 20% are members of minority groups. Seventy-two percent of undergraduates receive financial assistance. SMU's park-like campus is just 5 miles north of downtown Dallas, a dynamic center of commerce and culture.

 ## Academics

SMU offers a liberal arts and professional curriculum and core academic program; fewer than half of graduate courses are open to undergraduates. It awards bachelor's, master's, doctoral, and first professional **degrees**. Challenging opportunities include advanced placement, self-designed majors, tutorials, an honors program, Phi Beta Kappa, and Sigma Xi. Special programs include cooperative education, internships, summer session for credit, study abroad, and Army and Air Force ROTC.

The most popular **majors** include finance/banking, psychology, and advertising. A complete listing of majors at SMU appears in the Majors Index beginning on page 379.

The **faculty** at SMU has 485 full-time graduate and undergraduate teachers, 88% with terminal degrees. The student-faculty ratio is 12:1.

 ## Computers on Campus

Students are not required to have a computer. 299 **computers** available in the computer center, computer labs, the research center, the learning resource center, various locations on campus, classrooms, the library, the student center, and dormitories provide access to the main academic computer, off-campus computing facilities, e-mail, and the Internet. Staffed computer lab on campus provides training in the use of computers and software.

The 8 **libraries** have 3 million books, 679,904 microform titles, and 6,220 subscriptions. They are connected to 3 national **on-line** catalogs.

 ## Campus Life

There are 135 active **organizations** on campus, including a drama/theater group and student-run newspaper and radio station. 24% of students participate in student government elections. 32% of eligible men and 47% of eligible women are members of 15 national **fraternities** and 11 national **sororities**. Student **safety services** include late night transport/escort service, 24-hour emergency telephone alarm devices, 24-hour patrols by trained security personnel, and electronically operated dormitory entrances.

SMU is a member of the NCAA (Division I). **Intercollegiate sports** (some offering scholarships) include basketball (m, w), cross-country running (m, w), football (m), golf (m, w), soccer (m, w), swimming and diving (m, w), tennis (m, w), track and field (m, w), volleyball (w).

 ## Applying

SMU requires an essay, a high school transcript, 3 years of high school math and science, 2 years of high school foreign language, 1 recommendation, SAT I or ACT, and in some cases SAT II Subject Tests. Early, deferred, and midyear entrance are possible, with a 4/1 deadline and continuous processing to 1/15 for financial aid. **Contact:** Mr. Ron W. Moss, Director of Admission and Enrollment Management, 6425 Boaz Street, Dallas, TX 75275, 214-768-2058 or toll-free 800-323-0672.

GETTING IN LAST YEAR
3,869 applied
90% were accepted
35% enrolled (1,229)
32% from top tenth of their h.s. class
3.2 average high school GPA
39% had SAT verbal scores over 600 (R)
43% had SAT math scores over 600 (R)
39% had ACT scores over 26
7% had SAT verbal scores over 700 (R)
7% had SAT math scores over 700 (R)
10% had ACT scores over 30

THE STUDENT BODY
Total 9,172, of whom 5,297
   are undergraduates

From 50 states and territories,
   66 other countries
60% from Texas
53% women, 47% men
6% African Americans
1% Native Americans
9% Hispanics
6% Asian Americans
2% international students

AFTER FRESHMAN YEAR
84% returned for sophomore year
58% got a degree within 4 years
69% got a degree within 5 years
71% got a degree within 6 years

AFTER GRADUATION
5% had job offers within 6 months
170 organizations recruited on campus

WHAT YOU WILL PAY
Tuition and fees $15,228
Room and board $5206
38% receive need-based financial aid
Need-based college-administered scholarships and
   grants average $3525 per award
32% receive non-need financial aid
Non-need college-administered scholarships and
   grants average $3416 per award

SOUTHWESTERN UNIVERSITY

Georgetown, Texas • Suburban setting • Private • Independent-Religious • Coed

Southwestern is a national liberal arts college recognized for a high-quality academic program and priced well below most comparable schools. In the past 2 years, Southwestern accepted a chapter of Phi Beta Kappa, had a teacher named U.S. Professor of the Year, received a $6.5-million, state-of-the-art academic building from the F. W. Olin Foundation, and was selected to join the Southern Collegiate Athletic Association in Division III of the NCAA. Located north of Austin, SU offers a values-centered mission, a broad-based curriculum, and extensive study-abroad opportunities to its 1,250 students.

 Academics

SU offers a liberal arts and sciences curriculum and core academic program. It awards bachelor's **degrees**. Challenging opportunities include advanced placement, accelerated degree programs, self-designed majors, tutorials, an honors program, a senior project, and Phi Beta Kappa. Special programs include internships, summer session for credit, and study abroad.

The most popular **majors** include psychology, biology/biological sciences, and business. A complete listing of majors at SU appears in the Majors Index beginning on page 379.

The **faculty** at SU has 86 full-time teachers, 93% with terminal degrees. 100% of the faculty serve as student advisers. The student-faculty ratio is 12:1.

 Computers on Campus

Students are not required to have a computer. 150 **computers** available in the computer center, computer labs, academic departments, the library, and dormitories provide access to the main academic computer, off-campus computing facilities, e-mail, on-line services, and the Internet. Staffed computer lab on campus provides training in the use of computers and software.

The **library** has 259,872 books, 33,872 microform titles, and 1,404 subscriptions. It is connected to 3 national **on-line** catalogs.

 Campus Life

There are 86 active **organizations** on campus, including a drama/theater group and student-run newspaper. 40% of students participate in student government elections. 36% of eligible men and 38% of eligible women are members of 4 national **fraternities** and 4 national **sororities**. Student **safety services** include late night transport/escort service, 24-hour emergency telephone alarm devices, 24-hour patrols by trained security personnel, student patrols, and electronically operated dormitory entrances.

SU is a member of the NCAA (Division III). **Intercollegiate sports** include baseball (m), basketball (m, w), cross-country running (m, w), golf (m, w), soccer (m, w), tennis (m, w), volleyball (w).

 Applying

SU requires an essay, a high school transcript, 1 recommendation, SAT I or ACT, and in some cases an interview. It recommends 4 years of high school math, 3 years of high school science, 2 years of high school foreign language, and an interview. Early, deferred, and midyear entrance are possible, with a 2/15 deadline and continuous processing to 3/1 for financial aid. **Contact:** Mr. John W. Lind, Vice President for Enrollment Management, University at Maple, Georgetown, TX 78626, 512-863-1200 or toll-free 800-252-3166; fax 512-863-9601.

GETTING IN LAST YEAR
1,229 applied
76% were accepted
35% enrolled (328)
46% from top tenth of their h.s. class
3.4 average high school GPA
57% had SAT verbal scores over 600 (R)
55% had SAT math scores over 600 (R)
56% had ACT scores over 26
17% had SAT verbal scores over 700 (R)
11% had SAT math scores over 700 (R)
12% had ACT scores over 30
11 National Merit Scholars
33 class presidents
17 valedictorians

THE STUDENT BODY
1,261 undergraduates

From 35 states and territories,
  14 other countries
87% from Texas
56% women, 44% men
3% African Americans
1% Native Americans
11% Hispanics
5% Asian Americans
2% international students

AFTER FRESHMAN YEAR
85% returned for sophomore year
56% got a degree within 4 years
67% got a degree within 5 years
68% got a degree within 6 years

AFTER GRADUATION
31% pursued further study (14% arts and
  sciences, 6% medicine, 4% business)
94% had job offers within 6 months
26 organizations recruited on campus
1 Fulbright scholar

WHAT YOU WILL PAY
Tuition and fees $12,700
Room and board $4870
61% receive need-based financial aid
Need-based college-administered scholarships and
  grants average $7170 per award
10% receive non-need financial aid
Non-need college-administered scholarships and
  grants average $3774 per award

SPELMAN COLLEGE

Atlanta, Georgia • Urban setting • Private • Independent • Women

Located in Atlanta, Georgia, Spelman College is a historically black, privately endowed, 4-year, liberal arts college for women. Founded in 1881 as the Atlanta Baptist Female Seminary, Spelman today is one of America's top liberal arts colleges, providing academic excellence for women. Spelman's commitment to excellence is demonstrated by its dedicated and accessible faculty and low student-faculty ratio of 14:1, as well as by the outstanding success of students and alumnae.

Academics

Spelman offers a core academic program. It awards bachelor's **degrees**. Challenging opportunities include advanced placement, accelerated degree programs, self-designed majors, an honors program, and a senior project. Special programs include internships, off-campus study, study abroad, and Army, Naval, and Air Force ROTC.

The most popular **majors** include psychology, economics, and English. A complete listing of majors at Spelman appears in the Majors Index beginning on page 379.

The **faculty** at Spelman has 134 full-time teachers, 78% with terminal degrees. 85% of the faculty serve as student advisers.

Computers on Campus

Students are not required to have a computer. 105 **computers** available in the computer center, academic buildings, classrooms, and the library provide access to off-campus computing facilities, e-mail, and the Internet. Staffed computer lab on campus provides training in the use of computers and software.

The **library** has 404,991 books, 69,750 microform titles, and 2,693 subscriptions.

Campus Life

Active **organizations** on campus include drama/theater group and student-run newspaper. 61% of students participate in student government elections. 15% of eligible undergraduates are members of 4 national **sororities**. Student **safety services** include late night transport/escort service, 24-hour emergency telephone alarm devices, 24-hour patrols by trained security personnel, and electronically operated dormitory entrances. **Intercollegiate sports** include basketball, tennis, track and field, volleyball.

Applying

Spelman requires an essay, a high school transcript, 2 recommendations, SAT I or ACT, and in some cases an interview. It recommends 3 years of high school math and science and 2 years of high school foreign language. Early and midyear entrance are possible, with a 2/1 deadline and continuous processing to 4/1 for financial aid. **Contact:** Ms. Victoria Valle, Director of Admissions and Orientation Services, 350 Spelman Lane, SW, Atlanta, GA 30314-4399, 404-681-3643 ext. 2188 or toll-free 800-982-2411 (out-of-state); fax 404-223-1449.

GETTING IN LAST YEAR
2,933 applied
47% were accepted
35% enrolled (481)
47% from top tenth of their h.s. class
27% had ACT scores over 26
3% had ACT scores over 30
10 National Merit Scholars
52 class presidents

THE STUDENT BODY
1,961 undergraduates

From 45 states and territories,
   21 other countries
21% from Georgia
100% women
98% African Americans
0% Native Americans
0% Hispanics
0% Asian Americans
2% international students

AFTER FRESHMAN YEAR
90% returned for sophomore year

AFTER GRADUATION
38% pursued further study

WHAT YOU WILL PAY
Tuition and fees $8875
Room and board $5890
Need-based college-administered scholarships and
   grants average $992 per award
Non-need college-administered scholarships and
   grants average $2211 per award

STANFORD UNIVERSITY

Stanford, California • Suburban setting • Private • Independent • Coed

---

Renowned for the quality of its faculty (12 Nobel laureates, 4 Pulitzer Prize winners, 14 MacArthur Prizes, 20 National Medal of Science winners), Stanford University is equally proud of its graduates, which include 75 Rhodes Scholars and 50 Marshall Scholars. Stanford students are both challenged and warmly supported by their faculty mentors, and share in an invigorating and open intellectual environment. Undergraduates are encouraged to undertake original research. The University fosters personal and intellectual growth in a residential setting, and admits students it believes will contribute to the sum of human knowledge and enrich human experience through the creative arts.

Academics

Stanford offers a core academic program. It awards bachelor's, master's, doctoral, and first professional **degrees**. Challenging opportunities include advanced placement, accelerated degree programs, self-designed majors, tutorials, an honors program, a senior project, Phi Beta Kappa, and Sigma Xi. Special programs include internships, summer session for credit, off-campus study, study abroad, and Army, Naval, and Air Force ROTC.

The most popular **majors** include biology/biological sciences and economics. A complete listing of majors at Stanford appears in the Majors Index beginning on page 379.

The **faculty** at Stanford has 1,433 full-time graduate and undergraduate teachers, 99% with terminal degrees.

Computers on Campus

Students are not required to have a computer. 7,100 **computers** available in the computer center, computer labs, computer clusters, classrooms, the library, the student center, and dormitories provide access to e-mail and the Internet.

The 18 **libraries** have 6.5 million books, 4.5 million microform titles, and 43,800 subscriptions.

Campus Life

There are 494 active **organizations** on campus, including a drama/theater group and student-run newspaper and radio station. 10% of eligible men and 10% of eligible women are members of 21 national **fraternities**, 10 national **sororities**, and 6 eating clubs. Student **safety services** include late night transport/escort service, 24-hour emergency telephone alarm devices, 24-hour patrols by trained security personnel, and electronically operated dormitory entrances.

Stanford is a member of the NCAA (Division I) and NAIA. **Intercollegiate sports** (some offering scholarships) include baseball (m), basketball (m, w), crew (m, w), cross-country running (m, w), equestrian sports (m, w), fencing (m, w), field hockey (m, w), football (m), golf (m, w), gymnastics (m, w), lacrosse (w), racquetball (m, w), rugby (m, w), sailing (m, w), skiing (cross-country) (m, w), skiing (downhill) (m, w), soccer (m, w), softball (w), squash (m, w), swimming and diving (m, w), tennis (m, w), track and field (m, w), volleyball (m, w), water polo (m, w), wrestling (m).

Applying

Stanford requires an essay, a high school transcript, 3 recommendations, and SAT I or ACT. It recommends 3 years of high school math and science, some high school foreign language, and SAT II Subject Tests. Early and deferred entrance are possible, with a 12/15 deadline and continuous processing to 4/15 for financial aid. **Contact:** Mr. John Bunnell, Associate Dean of Admissions, Old Union Building, Room 232, Stanford, CA 94305-9991, 415-723-2091; fax 415-725-2846.

GETTING IN LAST YEAR
15,390 applied
19% were accepted
55% enrolled (1,601)
87% from top tenth of their h.s. class
75% had SAT verbal scores over 600
93% had SAT math scores over 600
29% had SAT verbal scores over 700
64% had SAT math scores over 700

THE STUDENT BODY
Total 14,044, of whom 6,577
   are undergraduates

From 52 states and territories,
   59 other countries
46% from California
50% women, 50% men
8% African Americans
1% Native Americans
12% Hispanics
24% Asian Americans
5% international students

AFTER FRESHMAN YEAR
97% returned for sophomore year

AFTER GRADUATION
450 organizations recruited on campus
3 Rhodes, 1 Marshall, 16 Fulbright scholars

WHAT YOU WILL PAY
Tuition and fees $19,797
Room and board $7054
Need-based college-administered scholarships and
   grants average $13,376 per award
Non-need college-administered scholarships and
   grants average $19,695 per award

STATE UNIVERSITY OF NEW YORK AT BINGHAMTON

Binghamton, New York • Suburban setting • Public • State-supported • Coed

Mid-sized Binghamton University, in upstate New York's scenic southern tier, is known for the excellent teaching and solid research of its outstanding, accessible faculty. At Binghamton, challenging academic programs combine with virtually unlimited opportunities for student participation in all areas of campus life. More than 150 campus organizations offer activities for every interest. In a community that values excellence and independence, Binghamton students excel.

Academics

Binghamton University offers a core academic program; fewer than half of graduate courses are open to undergraduates. It awards bachelor's, master's, and doctoral **degrees**. Challenging opportunities include advanced placement, accelerated degree programs, self-designed majors, tutorials, an honors program, a senior project, and Phi Beta Kappa. Special programs include internships, summer session for credit, off-campus study, study abroad, and Air Force ROTC.

The most popular **majors** include English, psychology, and biology/biological sciences. A complete listing of majors at Binghamton University appears in the Majors Index beginning on page 379.

The **faculty** at Binghamton University has 448 full-time graduate and undergraduate teachers, 95% with terminal degrees. 100% of the faculty serve as student advisers. The student-faculty ratio is 21:1.

Computers on Campus

Students are not required to have a computer. Student rooms are linked to a campus network. 1,000 **computers** available in the computer center, computer labs, the learning resource center, the library, and dormitories provide access to the main academic computer, e-mail, on-line services, and the Internet. Staffed computer lab on campus provides training in the use of computers and software.

The 3 **libraries** have 1.5 million books, 1.4 million microform titles, and 9,264 subscriptions.

Campus Life

There are 150 active **organizations** on campus, including a drama/theater group and student-run newspaper and radio station. 15% of eligible men and 15% of eligible women are members of 17 national **fraternities**, 11 national **sororities**, 4 local fraternities, and 3 local sororities. Student **safety services** include safety awareness programs, late night transport/escort service, 24-hour emergency telephone alarm devices, 24-hour patrols by trained security personnel, and electronically operated dormitory entrances.

Binghamton University is a member of the NCAA (Division III). **Intercollegiate sports** include baseball (m), basketball (m, w), bowling (m), crew (m, w), cross-country running (m, w), equestrian sports (m, w), fencing (m, w), golf (m), lacrosse (m, w), racquetball (m, w), rugby (m, w), skiing (downhill) (m, w), soccer (m, w), softball (w), swimming and diving (m, w), tennis (m, w), track and field (m, w), volleyball (m, w), wrestling (m).

Applying

Binghamton University requires an essay, a high school transcript, SAT I or ACT, and in some cases 3 years of high school math and science, some high school foreign language, and 1 recommendation. It recommends 3 years of high school math and science, some high school foreign language, and portfolio, audition. Early, deferred, and midyear entrance are possible, with a 2/15 deadline and continuous processing to 3/1 for financial aid. **Contact:** Mr. Geoffrey D. Gould, Director of Admissions, PO Box 6001, Binghamton, NY 13902-6001, 607-777-2171.

GETTING IN LAST YEAR
16,348 applied
40% were accepted
28% enrolled (1,790)
59% from top tenth of their h.s. class
19% had SAT verbal scores over 600
64% had SAT math scores over 600
56% had ACT scores over 26
2% had SAT verbal scores over 700
15% had SAT math scores over 700
14% had ACT scores over 30

THE STUDENT BODY
Total 11,952, of whom 9,273 are undergraduates

From 33 states and territories, 48 other countries
93% from New York
54% women, 46% men
5% African Americans
1% Native Americans
5% Hispanics
13% Asian Americans
2% international students

AFTER FRESHMAN YEAR
93% returned for sophomore year
67% got a degree within 4 years
80% got a degree within 5 years

AFTER GRADUATION
35% pursued further study
175 organizations recruited on campus
3 Fulbright scholars

WHAT YOU WILL PAY
Resident tuition and fees $3910
Nonresident tuition and fees $8810
Room and board $4654
Need-based college-administered scholarships and grants average $700 per award
Non-need college-administered scholarships and grants average $2300 per award

STATE UNIVERSITY OF NEW YORK AT BUFFALO

Buffalo, New York • Suburban setting • Public • State-supported • Coed

Students are invited to learn more about the University at Buffalo, New York's premier public research university—an academic community in which undergraduates can explore an exceptional range of possible futures with faculty and graduate students working on the leading edge in their fields. UB offers the most comprehensive selection of undergraduate and graduate programs in the State University of New York system. Students are encouraged to explore the possibilities, in a community of student and faculty scholars, among 30 programs in the arts and sciences and extensive offerings in the health sciences, management, engineering, architecture, nursing, medicine, and biomedical sciences and pharmacy.

 Academics

UB offers an interdisciplinary curriculum and core academic program. It awards bachelor's, master's, doctoral, and first professional **degrees**. Challenging opportunities include advanced placement, self-designed majors, tutorials, Freshman Honors College, an honors program, a senior project, Phi Beta Kappa, and Sigma Xi. Special programs include internships, summer session for credit, off-campus study, study abroad, and Army ROTC.

The most popular **majors** include business, social science, and psychology. A complete listing of majors at UB appears in the Majors Index beginning on page 379.

The **faculty** at UB has 1,286 full-time graduate and undergraduate teachers, 97% with terminal degrees. The student-faculty ratio is 14:1, and the average class size in core courses is 24.

 Computers on Campus

Students are not required to have a computer. Student rooms are linked to a campus network. 750 **computers** available in the computer center, computer labs, academic buildings, classrooms, the library, and dormitories provide access to the main academic computer, e-mail, on-line services, and the Internet. Staffed computer lab on campus provides training in the use of computers and software.

The 8 **libraries** have 2.9 million books, 4.6 million microform titles, and 21,818 subscriptions.

 Campus Life

There are 150 active **organizations** on campus, including a drama/theater group and student-run newspaper and radio station. 1% of eligible men and 1% of eligible women are members of 11 national **fraternities**, 7 national **sororities**, 4 local fraternities, and 6 local sororities. Student **safety services** include self-defense programs, awareness programs, late night transport/escort service, 24-hour emergency telephone alarm devices, and 24-hour patrols by trained security personnel.

UB is a member of the NCAA (Division I). **Intercollegiate sports** (some offering scholarships) include basketball (m, w), cross-country running (m, w), football (m), soccer (m, w), swimming and diving (m, w), tennis (m, w), track and field (m, w), volleyball (w), wrestling (m).

 Applying

UB requires a high school transcript, SAT I or ACT, and in some cases recommendations and portfolio, audition. It recommends 3 years of high school math and science and 3 years of high school foreign language. Early entrance and early decision are possible, with rolling admissions and continuous processing to 3/1 for financial aid. **Contact:** Mr. Kevin M. Durkin, Director of Admissions, Capen Hall, Room 17, North Campus, Buffalo, NY 14260-1660, 716-645-6900; fax 716-645-6411.

GETTING IN LAST YEAR
15,461 applied
69% were accepted
25% enrolled (2,685)
22% from top tenth of their h.s. class
3.2 average high school GPA
33% had SAT verbal scores over 600 (R)
49% had SAT math scores over 600 (R)
6% had SAT verbal scores over 700 (R)
7% had SAT math scores over 700 (R)

THE STUDENT BODY
Total 24,493, of whom 16,150
  are undergraduates
From 34 states and territories,
  61 other countries

96% from New York
45% women, 55% men
7% African Americans
1% Native Americans
4% Hispanics
11% Asian Americans
2% international students

AFTER FRESHMAN YEAR
86% returned for sophomore year
30% got a degree within 4 years
55% got a degree within 5 years
59% got a degree within 6 years

AFTER GRADUATION
35% pursued further study

442 organizations recruited on campus
3 Fulbright scholars

WHAT YOU WILL PAY
Resident tuition and fees $4060
Nonresident tuition and fees $8960
Room and board $5276
60% receive need-based financial aid
Need-based college-administered scholarships and
  grants average $648 per award
5% receive non-need financial aid
Non-need college-administered scholarships and
  grants average $3073 per award

STATE UNIVERSITY OF NEW YORK COLLEGE AT GENESEO

Geneseo, New York • Small-town setting • Public • State-supported • Coed

The *New York Times* cited Geneseo as "one of the nation's most selective, highly regarded colleges." This reputation is derived not only from the extraordinarily able students who enroll but also from the College's total dedication to a single mission: teaching undergraduates. Geneseo offers a personal atmosphere in which students, faculty, and staff are concerned about each other. Students have the opportunity to study with others who have demonstrated a seriousness of purpose and a high level of academic achievement. The Geneseo experience is created by a collegiate environment, small size, excellent curricular offerings, and idyllic location.

Academics

Geneseo College offers an interdisciplinary curriculum and core academic program. It awards bachelor's and master's **degrees**. Challenging opportunities include advanced placement, tutorials, an honors program, and a senior project. Special programs include internships, summer session for credit, off-campus study, and Army and Air Force ROTC.

The most popular **majors** include psychology, business, and education. A complete listing of majors at Geneseo College appears in the Majors Index beginning on page 379.

The **faculty** at Geneseo College has 239 full-time graduate and undergraduate teachers, 85% with terminal degrees. 95% of the faculty serve as student advisers. The student-faculty ratio is 20:1.

Computers on Campus

Students are not required to have a computer. 550 **computers** available in the computer center, computer labs, academic departments, the library, the student center, and dormitories provide access to the main academic computer, e-mail, on-line services, and the Internet. Staffed computer lab on campus provides training in the use of computers and software.

The 2 **libraries** have 521,558 books and 3,156 subscriptions.

Campus Life

There are 155 active **organizations** on campus, including a drama/theater group and student-run newspaper and radio station. 10% of students participate in student government elections. 19% of eligible men and 15% of eligible women are members of 4 national **fraternities**, 3 national **sororities**, 5 local fraternities, and 8 local sororities. Student **safety services** include late night transport/escort service, 24-hour emergency telephone alarm devices, 24-hour patrols by trained security personnel, and student patrols.

Geneseo College is a member of the NCAA (Division III). **Intercollegiate sports** include basketball (m, w), crew (m, w), cross-country running (m, w), equestrian sports (w), ice hockey (m), lacrosse (m, w), racquetball (m, w), rugby (m, w), soccer (m, w), softball (w), squash (m, w), swimming and diving (m, w), tennis (w), track and field (m, w), volleyball (m, w).

Applying

Geneseo College requires an essay, a high school transcript, and SAT I or ACT. It recommends 4 years of high school math and science, 3 years of high school foreign language, recommendations, and a campus interview. Early, deferred, and midyear entrance are possible, with a 2/15 deadline and continuous processing to 2/15 for financial aid. **Contact:** Ms. Jill Conlon, Director of Admissions, Erwin Building, Geneseo, NY 14454-1401, 716-245-5571.

GETTING IN LAST YEAR
8,934 applied
54% were accepted
25% enrolled (1,210)
46% from top tenth of their h.s. class
22% had SAT verbal scores over 600
59% had SAT math scores over 600
59% had ACT scores over 26
2% had SAT verbal scores over 700
9% had SAT math scores over 700
10% had ACT scores over 30

THE STUDENT BODY
Total 5,719, of whom 5,334 are undergraduates

From 22 states and territories,
9 other countries
98% from New York
64% women, 36% men
2% African Americans
1% Native Americans
4% Hispanics
6% Asian Americans
1% international students

AFTER FRESHMAN YEAR
89% returned for sophomore year
69% got a degree within 4 years
78% got a degree within 5 years

AFTER GRADUATION
35% pursued further study
44% had job offers within 6 months
31 organizations recruited on campus

WHAT YOU WILL PAY
Resident tuition and fees $3859
Nonresident tuition and fees $8759
Room and board $4500
49% receive need-based financial aid
Need-based college-administered scholarships and grants average $2800 per award
7% receive non-need financial aid
Non-need college-administered scholarships and grants average $630 per award

STATE UNIVERSITY OF NEW YORK COLLEGE OF ENVIRONMENTAL SCIENCE AND FORESTRY

Syracuse, New York • Urban setting • Public • State-supported • Coed

ESF is the only college in the country with academic programs focused exclusively on the natural environment. Located on a 12-acre site adjacent to Syracuse University, ESF's core academic programs in the basic sciences, environmental sciences, engineering, and landscape architecture are supplemented by the vast array of course offerings at SU. Students at this small, distinguished professional college with an international reputation will discover a world of opportunity in both ESF's and SU's academic, athletic, and social life.

Academics

ESF offers an engineering, natural science, and design curriculum and core academic program; fewer than half of graduate courses are open to undergraduates. It awards bachelor's, master's, and doctoral **degrees**. Challenging opportunities include advanced placement, an honors program, and a senior project. Special programs include internships, off-campus study, and Army and Air Force ROTC.

The most popular **majors** include environmental biology, environmental engineering, and environmental sciences. A complete listing of majors at ESF appears in the Majors Index beginning on page 379.

The **faculty** at ESF has 106 full-time undergraduate teachers, 90% with terminal degrees. 85% of the faculty serve as student advisers.

Computers on Campus

Students are not required to have a computer. 100 **computers** available in the computer center, academic buildings, and the library. Staffed computer lab on campus provides training in the use of computers and software.

The 2 **libraries** have 114,398 books, 91,000 microform titles, and 1,767 subscriptions.

Campus Life

There are 300 active **organizations** on campus, including a drama/theater group and student-run newspaper and radio station. 25% of eligible men and 25% of eligible women are members of 25 national **fraternities**, 13 national **sororities**, and 1 local fraternity. Student **safety services** include 24-hour emergency telephone alarm devices and 24-hour patrols by trained security personnel.

This institution has no intercollegiate sports.

Applying

ESF requires an essay, a high school transcript, 4 years of high school math and science, and SAT I or ACT. It recommends recommendations and an interview. Early and deferred entrance are possible, with rolling admissions and continuous processing to 3/1 for financial aid. **Contact:** Ms. Susan Sanford, Associate Director of Admissions, 1 Forestry Drive, Syracuse, NY 13210-2779, 315-470-6600 or toll-free 800-777-7ESF; fax 315-470-6933.

GETTING IN LAST YEAR
820 applied
16% were accepted
61% enrolled (79)
39% from top tenth of their h.s. class
3.5 average high school GPA
59% had SAT verbal scores over 600 (R)
60% had SAT math scores over 600 (R)
10% had SAT verbal scores over 700 (R)
13% had SAT math scores over 700 (R)

THE STUDENT BODY
Total 1,772, of whom 1,069
   are undergraduates

From 11 states and territories,
   3 other countries
90% from New York
33% women, 67% men
3% African Americans
1% Native Americans
2% Hispanics
2% Asian Americans
1% international students

AFTER FRESHMAN YEAR
91% returned for sophomore year
92% got a degree within 4 years

AFTER GRADUATION
79% had job offers within 6 months
25 organizations recruited on campus

WHAT YOU WILL PAY
Resident tuition and fees $3413
Nonresident tuition and fees $8313
Room and board $6910
82% receive need-based financial aid
Need-based college-administered scholarships and
   grants average $300 per award
16% receive non-need financial aid
Non-need college-administered scholarships and
   grants average $3400 per award

STATE UNIVERSITY OF NEW YORK MARITIME COLLEGE

Throgs Neck, New York • Suburban setting • Public • State-supported • Coed

Maritime graduates may pursue on-shore careers in industry, government service, or the professions; careers at sea as civilian officers in the Merchant Marine; or careers in the Navy, Marine Corps, Coast Guard, Air Force, or NOAA. The College offers BS or BE degrees in engineering, business administration/marine transportation, naval architecture, marine environmental science, and a humanities concentration. The annual 2-month Summer Sea Term aboard the training ship *Empire State* provides hands-on training to cadets who, under supervision, assume responsibility for the ship's operation in preparation for the U.S. Merchant Marine Officer's license. Graduates have a 95% job placement rate within 2 months of graduation in maritime and related industries.

 Academics

Maritime College offers a core academic program; fewer than half of graduate courses are open to undergraduates. It awards associate, bachelor's, and master's **degrees**. Challenging opportunities include advanced placement, tutorials, and a senior project. Special programs include internships, summer session for credit, study abroad, and Naval and Air Force ROTC.

The most popular **majors** include business, marine engineering, and electrical engineering. A complete listing of majors at Maritime College appears in the Majors Index beginning on page 379.

The **faculty** at Maritime College has 60 full-time undergraduate teachers. 81% of the faculty serve as student advisers.

 Computers on Campus

Students are not required to have a computer. 85 **computers** available in the computer center, student lounge, and the library provide access to the main academic computer.

The **library** has 76,854 books and 354 subscriptions. It is connected to 2 national **on-line** catalogs.

 Campus Life

Active **organizations** on campus include student-run newspaper. 4% of eligible men are members of 1 local **fraternity**. Student **safety services** include late night transport/escort service, 24-hour emergency telephone alarm devices, 24-hour patrols by trained security personnel, and student patrols.

Maritime College is a member of the NCAA (Division III). **Intercollegiate sports** include basketball (m, w), crew (m, w), cross-country running (m, w), ice hockey (m), lacrosse (m), riflery (m, w), rugby (m), sailing (m, w), soccer (m), swimming and diving (m, w), tennis (m, w), volleyball (w), wrestling (m).

Applying

Maritime College requires a high school transcript, 3 years of high school math and science, 1 recommendation, medical history, SAT I or ACT, and a minimum high school GPA of 2.0. It recommends an essay, some high school foreign language, an interview, and SAT II Subject Tests. Early, deferred, and midyear entrance are possible, with rolling admissions and continuous processing to 5/1 for financial aid. **Contact:** Mr. Peter Cooney, Director of Admissions and Financial Aid, 6 Pennyfield Avenue, Throgs Neck, NY 10465, 718-409-7220 or toll-free 800-654-1874 (in-state), 800-642-1874 (out-of-state); fax 718-409-7392.

GETTING IN LAST YEAR
797 applied
58% were accepted
46% enrolled (210)
8% from top tenth of their h.s. class
2.5 average high school GPA
7% had SAT verbal scores over 600
22% had SAT math scores over 600
0% had SAT verbal scores over 700
6% had SAT math scores over 700

THE STUDENT BODY
Total 825, of whom 653
are undergraduates

From 22 states and territories
78% from New York
10% women, 90% men
5% African Americans
1% Native Americans
6% Hispanics
5% Asian Americans
9% international students

AFTER GRADUATION
3% pursued further study (2% engineering, 1% business)

WHAT YOU WILL PAY
Resident tuition and fees $4080
Nonresident tuition and fees $8980
Room and board $5000
Need-based college-administered scholarships and grants average $2383 per award
Non-need college-administered scholarships and grants average $2301 per award

STETSON UNIVERSITY

DeLand, Florida • Small-town setting • Private • Independent • Coed

Stetson expects students to make a difference, personally and professionally. The University believes students learn best how to do this by doing. Therefore, students may be found managing an investment portfolio of more than $1 million, operating a campus outlet for an international firm, or conducting biology research with pygmy rattlesnakes in a nearby wildlife preserve. Beyond the classroom, students practice social responsibility by building Habitat for Humanity houses and working with at-risk youngsters in Youth Motivators. With a strong emphasis on student-professor interaction and liberal learning, Stetson offers a total environment that supports students' development as mature, responsible adults.

 ## Academics

Stetson offers a comprehensive curriculum and core academic program; fewer than half of graduate courses are open to undergraduates. It awards bachelor's, master's, and first professional **degrees**. Challenging opportunities include advanced placement, accelerated degree programs, self-designed majors, an honors program, a senior project, and Phi Beta Kappa. Special programs include internships, summer session for credit, off-campus study, study abroad, and Army ROTC.

The most popular **majors** include business, education, and psychology. A complete listing of majors at Stetson appears in the Majors Index beginning on page 379.

The **faculty** at Stetson has 155 full-time undergraduate teachers, 90% with terminal degrees. 100% of the faculty serve as student advisers. The student-faculty ratio is 11:1.

 ## Computers on Campus

Students are not required to have a computer. 120 **computers** available in the computer center, computer labs, the research center, science hall, classrooms, and the library. Staffed computer lab on campus.

The 3 **libraries** have 313,261 books, 6,532 microform titles, and 1,300 subscriptions. They are connected to 1 national **on-line** catalog.

 ## Campus Life

There are 80 active **organizations** on campus, including a drama/theater group and student-run newspaper and radio station. 35% of eligible men and 35% of eligible women are members of 6 national **fraternities** and 6 national **sororities**. Student **safety services** include late night transport/escort service, 24-hour emergency telephone alarm devices, and 24-hour patrols by trained security personnel.

Stetson is a member of the NCAA (Division I). **Intercollegiate sports** (some offering scholarships) include baseball (m), basketball (m, w), crew (m, w), cross-country running (m, w), golf (m, w), soccer (m, w), softball (w), tennis (m, w), volleyball (w).

 ## Applying

Stetson requires an essay, a high school transcript, 3 years of high school math and science, some high school foreign language, recommendations, and SAT I or ACT. It recommends an interview and SAT II Subject Tests. Early and midyear entrance are possible, with a 3/15 deadline and continuous processing to 3/15 for financial aid. **Contact:** Mr. James R. Beasley, Dean of Admissions, Griffith Hall, DeLand, FL 32720-3781, 904-822-7100 or toll-free 800-688-0101; fax 904-822-8832.

GETTING IN LAST YEAR
1,722 applied
85% were accepted
32% enrolled (474)
30% from top tenth of their h.s. class
3.45 average high school GPA
12% had SAT verbal scores over 600
31% had SAT math scores over 600
28% had ACT scores over 26
2% had SAT verbal scores over 700
4% had SAT math scores over 700
5% had ACT scores over 30

THE STUDENT BODY
Total 2,897, of whom 1,950
    are undergraduates

From 38 states and territories,
    42 other countries
78% from Florida
57% women, 43% men
3% African Americans
0% Native Americans
5% Hispanics
2% Asian Americans
6% international students

AFTER FRESHMAN YEAR
80% returned for sophomore year
53% got a degree within 4 years

64% got a degree within 5 years
66% got a degree within 6 years

WHAT YOU WILL PAY
Tuition and fees $13,700
Room and board $4800
59% receive need-based financial aid
Need-based college-administered scholarships and
    grants average $3080 per award
30% receive non-need financial aid
Non-need college-administered scholarships and
    grants average $4196 per award

STEVENS INSTITUTE OF TECHNOLOGY

Hoboken, New Jersey • Urban setting • Private • Independent • Coed

Stevens continues to enjoy an outstanding reputation among leaders in research and technology. The mission of Stevens is to sustain a community of individuals who are dedicated to the achievement of excellence and who share a vision related to engineering, management, and applied and pure science. Because of the distinctive approach of the Institute, success is a by-product of the Stevens education. Each undergraduate program—science, engineering, humanities, and computer science—calls for study in a variety of fields within and outside the discipline. This comprehensive approach prepares Stevens graduates with a thorough understanding of science and technology and their implications for society.

 ## Academics

Stevens offers a core academic program; more than half of graduate courses are open to undergraduates. It awards bachelor's, master's, and doctoral **degrees**. Challenging opportunities include advanced placement, accelerated degree programs, tutorials, Freshman Honors College, an honors program, a senior project, and Sigma Xi. Special programs include cooperative education, internships, summer session for credit, off-campus study, study abroad, and Army and Air Force ROTC.

The most popular **majors** include electrical engineering, mechanical engineering, and civil engineering. A complete listing of majors at Stevens appears in the Majors Index beginning on page 379.

The **faculty** at Stevens has 115 full-time graduate and undergraduate teachers, 92% with terminal degrees. 90% of the faculty serve as student advisers. The student-faculty ratio is 11:1.

 ## Computers on Campus

Students are required to have a computer. PCs are provided. Student rooms are linked to a campus network. 1,550 computers available in the computer center, computer labs, the research center, the learning resource center, the library, the student center, dormitories, and student rooms provide access to e-mail, on-line services, and the Internet. Staffed computer lab on campus provides training in the use of computers and software.

The **library** has 106,288 books, 850 microform titles, and 2,640 subscriptions.

 ## Campus Life

There are 50 active **organizations** on campus, including a drama/theater group and student-run newspaper and radio station. Stevens has 10 national **fraternities** and 3 national **sororities**. Student **safety services** include late night transport/escort service, 24-hour emergency telephone alarm devices, 24-hour patrols by trained security personnel, and electronically operated dormitory entrances.

Stevens is a member of the NCAA (Division III). **Intercollegiate sports** include archery (m, w), baseball (m, w), basketball (m), bowling (m), cross-country running (m), fencing (m, w), golf (m), lacrosse (m), rugby (m), sailing (m, w), skiing (cross-country) (m, w), skiing (downhill) (m, w), soccer (m, w), squash (m), tennis (m, w), volleyball (m, w), wrestling (m).

 ## Applying

Stevens requires a high school transcript, 4 years of high school math, 3 years of high school science, an interview, and SAT I. It recommends an essay, some high school foreign language, recommendations, and SAT II Subject Tests. Early and deferred entrance are possible, with a 3/1 deadline and continuous processing to 3/1 for financial aid. **Contact:** Mrs. Maureen P. Weatherall, Dean of Undergraduate Admissions and Financial Aid, Stevens Center, Hoboken, NJ 07030, 201-216-5194 or toll-free 800-458-5323; fax 201-216-8348.

GETTING IN LAST YEAR
1,935 applied
63% were accepted
33% enrolled (405)
51% from top tenth of their h.s. class
50% had SAT verbal scores over 600 (R)
64% had SAT math scores over 600 (R)
20% had SAT verbal scores over 700 (R)
7% had SAT math scores over 700 (R)

THE STUDENT BODY
Total 2,639, of whom 1,313
  are undergraduates

From 40 states and territories,
  20 other countries
55% from New Jersey
25% women, 75% men
7% African Americans
11% Hispanics
15% Asian Americans
10% international students

AFTER FRESHMAN YEAR
80% returned for sophomore year

AFTER GRADUATION
15% pursued further study (6% arts and
  sciences, 6% engineering, 1% dentistry)
170 organizations recruited on campus

WHAT YOU WILL PAY
Tuition and fees $17,770
Room and board $5740
80% receive need-based financial aid
Need-based college-administered scholarships and
  grants average $5400 per award
Non-need college-administered scholarships and
  grants average $6000 per award

SWARTHMORE COLLEGE

Swarthmore, Pennsylvania • Suburban setting • Private • Independent • Coed

Swarthmore is a selective college of liberal arts and engineering, located 11 miles southwest of Philadelphia. Founded as a coeducational institution in 1864, it is nonsectarian but reflects many traditions and values of its Quaker founders. Swarthmore's Honors Program provides an option to study in small seminars during the junior and senior years. The campus occupies over 330 acres of woodland and is officially designated an arboretum. A small school by deliberate policy, its enrollment is about 1,350, with a student-faculty ratio of about 9:1. It attracts students from 50 states and approximately 40 overseas countries.

Academics

Swarthmore offers a liberal arts curriculum and core academic program. It awards bachelor's **degrees**. Challenging opportunities include advanced placement, self-designed majors, tutorials, an honors program, a senior project, Phi Beta Kappa, and Sigma Xi. Special programs include internships, off-campus study, study abroad, and Army, Naval, and Air Force ROTC.

The most popular **majors** include literature, biology/biological sciences, and political science/government. A complete listing of majors at Swarthmore appears in the Majors Index beginning on page 379.

The **faculty** at Swarthmore has 157 full-time teachers, 93% with terminal degrees. 89% of the faculty serve as student advisers. The student-faculty ratio is 9:1, and the average class size in core courses is 18.

Computers on Campus

Students are not required to have a computer. Student rooms are linked to a campus network. 100 **computers** available in the computer center, computer labs, the learn-

ing resource center, labs, and the library provide access to the main academic computer, off-campus computing facilities, e-mail, on-line services, and the Internet. Staffed computer lab on campus provides training in the use of computers and software.

The 5 **libraries** have 1 million books, 190,000 microform titles, and 5,335 subscriptions. They are connected to 25 national **on-line** catalogs.

Campus Life

There are 150 active **organizations** on campus, including a drama/theater group and student-run newspaper and radio station. 40% of students participate in student government elections. 5% of eligible men are members of 1 national **fraternity** and 1 local fraternity. Student **safety services** include late night transport/escort service, 24-hour patrols by trained security personnel, and electronically operated dormitory entrances.

Swarthmore is a member of the NCAA (Division III). **Intercollegiate sports** include badminton (w), baseball (m), basketball (m, w), cross-country running (m, w), field hockey (w), football (m), golf (m), ice hockey (m), lacrosse (m, w), rugby (m, w), soccer (m, w), softball (w), squash (m), swimming and diving (m, w), tennis (m, w), track and field (m, w), volleyball (w), wrestling (m).

Applying

Swarthmore requires an essay, a high school transcript, 2 recommendations, SAT I or ACT, and 3 SAT II Subject Tests (including SAT II: Writing Test). It recommends 3 years of high school math and science, some high school foreign language, and an interview. Early and deferred entrance are possible, with a 1/1 deadline and a 2/1 priority date for financial aid. **Contact:** Office of Admissions, 500 College Avenue, Swarthmore, PA 19081-1397, 610-328-8300; fax 610-328-8673.

GETTING IN LAST YEAR
3,512 applied
34% were accepted
30% enrolled (354)
87% from top tenth of their h.s. class
78% had SAT verbal scores over 600 (R)
93% had SAT math scores over 600 (R)
28% had SAT verbal scores over 700 (R)
54% had SAT math scores over 700 (R)
32 National Merit Scholars
50 valedictorians

THE STUDENT BODY
1,353 undergraduates
From 53 states and territories,
    42 other countries

12% from Pennsylvania
52% women, 48% men
6% African Americans
0% Native Americans
5% Hispanics
11% Asian Americans
5% international students

AFTER FRESHMAN YEAR
89% returned for sophomore year
86% got a degree within 4 years
96% got a degree within 5 years
97% got a degree within 6 years

AFTER GRADUATION
24% pursued further study (15% arts and
    sciences, 6% medicine, 3% law)

76 organizations recruited on campus
3 Fulbright scholars

WHAT YOU WILL PAY
Tuition and fees $20,186
Room and board $6880
48% receive need-based financial aid
Need-based college-administered scholarships and
    grants average $13,722 per award
2% receive non-need financial aid
Non-need college-administered scholarships and
    grants average $19,992 per award

SWEET BRIAR COLLEGE

Sweet Briar, Virginia • Rural setting • Private • Independent • Women

Sweet Briar women take charge and revel in their accomplishments. This attitude helps graduates compete confidently in graduate school and in the corporate world as scientists and writers, lawyers and judges, and dancers and art historians. Sweet Briar attracts women who enjoy being involved not only in a first-rate academic program but also in meaningful activities outside the classroom. A hands-on, one-on-one approach to the sciences, a 4-year honors program, and superior study-abroad programs encourage bright students to excel. Sweet Briar students are taken seriously, and professors take an interest in their intellectual development and personal growth.

 ## Academics

Sweet Briar offers a core academic program. It awards bachelor's **degrees**. Challenging opportunities include advanced placement, accelerated degree programs, self-designed majors, tutorials, an honors program, a senior project, and Phi Beta Kappa. Special programs include internships, off-campus study, study abroad, and Army ROTC.

The most popular **majors** include psychology, political science/government, and English. A complete listing of majors at Sweet Briar appears in the Majors Index beginning on page 379.

The **faculty** at Sweet Briar has 74 full-time teachers, 94% with terminal degrees. 71% of the faculty serve as student advisers. The student-faculty ratio is 8:1.

 ## Computers on Campus

Students are not required to have a computer. Student rooms are linked to a campus network. 300 **computers** available in the computer center, computer labs, the learn-ing resource center, academic support center, classrooms, the library, and dormitories provide access to the main academic computer, off-campus computing facilities, e-mail, and on-line services. Staffed computer lab on campus (open 24 hours a day) provides training in the use of computers and software.

The 4 **libraries** have 230,000 books, 350,000 microform titles, and 1,047 subscriptions. They are connected to 4 national **on-line** catalogs.

 ## Campus Life

There are 43 active **organizations** on campus, including a drama/theater group and student-run newspaper and radio station. Student **safety services** include front gate security, late night transport/escort service, 24-hour patrols by trained security personnel, and electronically operated dormitory entrances.

Sweet Briar is a member of the NCAA (Division III). **Intercollegiate sports** include basketball, equestrian sports, fencing, field hockey, golf, lacrosse, soccer, softball, swimming and diving, tennis, volleyball.

 ## Applying

Sweet Briar requires an essay, a high school transcript, 3 years of high school math, 2 years of high school foreign language, 2 recommendations, 4 years of high school English, 3 years of high school social studies, 2 years of high school science, and SAT I or ACT. It recommends an interview and 3 SAT II Subject Tests. Early and deferred entrance are possible, with a 2/15 deadline and continuous processing to 3/1 for financial aid. **Contact:** Ms. Nancy E. Church, Executive Director of Admissions and Financial Aid, PO Box B, Sweet Briar, VA 24595, 804-381-6142 or toll-free 800-381-6142; fax 804-381-6152.

GETTING IN LAST YEAR
497 applied
85% were accepted
41% enrolled (174)
30% from top tenth of their h.s. class
3.2 average high school GPA
5 class presidents
3 valedictorians

THE STUDENT BODY
731 undergraduates
From 41 states and territories,
    17 other countries

29% from Virginia
100% women
6% African Americans
0% Native Americans
2% Hispanics
3% Asian Americans
4% international students

AFTER FRESHMAN YEAR
79% returned for sophomore year
62% got a degree within 4 years
63% got a degree within 5 years

AFTER GRADUATION
23% pursued further study (15% arts and
    sciences, 3% law, 2% business)

WHAT YOU WILL PAY
Tuition and fees $15,115
Room and board $6385
60% receive need-based financial aid
Need-based college-administered scholarships and
    grants average $10,404 per award
16% receive non-need financial aid
Non-need college-administered scholarships and
    grants average $5690 per award

SYRACUSE UNIVERSITY

Syracuse, New York • Urban setting • Private • Independent • Coed

---

Syracuse University strives to provide an enriching, high-quality educational experience. Faculty members encourage interaction through small classes and integrate research into teaching. A continued commitment to the liberal arts complements professional teaching in all schools and colleges. Students' individual needs are met through the University's enhanced system of orientation and advising, expanded use of introductory courses, and increased selection of minors. Syracuse students augment their course work with internships, travel-abroad opportunities, and a wide variety of extracurricular activities.

Academics

SU offers a professional and liberal arts curriculum and core academic program. It awards bachelor's, master's, doctoral, and first professional **degrees**. Challenging opportunities include advanced placement, accelerated degree programs, self-designed majors, tutorials, an honors program, a senior project, Phi Beta Kappa, and Sigma Xi. Special programs include cooperative education, internships, summer session for credit, off-campus study, study abroad, and Army and Air Force ROTC.

The most popular **majors** include psychology, broadcasting, and architecture. A complete listing of majors at SU appears in the Majors Index beginning on page 379.

The **faculty** at SU has 817 full-time graduate and undergraduate teachers, 87% with terminal degrees. 100% of the faculty serve as student advisers. The student-faculty ratio is 11:1.

Computers on Campus

Students are not required to have a computer. Student rooms are linked to a campus network. 1,000 **computers** available in the computer center, computer labs, academic buildings, classrooms, the library, the student center, and dormitories provide access to off-campus computing facilities, e-mail, and the Internet. Staffed computer lab on campus (open 24 hours a day) provides training in the use of computers and software.

The 7 **libraries** have 2.8 million books, 3.3 million microform titles, and 16,300 subscriptions. They are connected to 5 national **on-line** catalogs.

Campus Life

There are 250 active **organizations** on campus, including a drama/theater group and student-run newspaper and radio station. 16% of eligible men and 25% of eligible women are members of 22 national **fraternities**, 18 national **sororities**, 1 local fraternity, and 1 local sorority. Student **safety services** include crime prevention programs, late night transport/escort service, 24-hour emergency telephone alarm devices, 24-hour patrols by trained security personnel, and electronically operated dormitory entrances.

SU is a member of the NCAA (Division I). **Intercollegiate sports** (some offering scholarships) include baseball (m, w), basketball (m, w), crew (m, w), cross-country running (m, w), equestrian sports (m, w), fencing (m, w), field hockey (w), football (m), gymnastics (m, w), ice hockey (m), lacrosse (m, w), racquetball (m, w), rugby (m), sailing (m, w), skiing (downhill) (m, w), soccer (m, w), softball (w), swimming and diving (m, w), tennis (w), track and field (m, w), volleyball (m, w), wrestling (m).

Applying

SU requires an essay, a high school transcript, 3 years of high school math and science, 2 years of high school foreign language, 1 recommendation, SAT I or ACT, a minimum high school GPA of 2.0, and in some cases an audition for drama and music majors, portfolio for art and architecture majors, 4 years of English, 3 years of social studies and a minimum high school GPA of 3.0. It recommends an interview. Early, deferred, and midyear entrance are possible, with a 2/1 deadline and 2/15 for financial aid. **Contact:** Office of Admissions, 201 Tolley Administration Building, Syracuse, NY 13244-0003, 315-443-3611.

GETTING IN LAST YEAR
10,150 applied
66% were accepted
36% enrolled (2,409)
33% from top tenth of their h.s. class
18% had SAT verbal scores over 600
39% had SAT math scores over 600
2% had SAT verbal scores over 700
9% had SAT math scores over 700
22 valedictorians

THE STUDENT BODY
Total 14,636, of whom 10,097 are undergraduates

From 53 states and territories, 98 other countries
42% from New York
51% women, 49% men
9% African Americans
1% Native Americans
6% Hispanics
5% Asian Americans
4% international students

AFTER FRESHMAN YEAR
88% returned for sophomore year
69% got a degree within 5 years

AFTER GRADUATION
20% pursued further study (7% business, 5% law, 3% engineering)

160 organizations recruited on campus
3 Fulbright scholars

WHAT YOU WILL PAY
Tuition and fees $16,280
Room and board $7150
63% receive need-based financial aid
Need-based college-administered scholarships and grants average $7200 per award
11% receive non-need financial aid
Non-need college-administered scholarships and grants average $4500 per award

---

TAYLOR UNIVERSITY

Upland, Indiana • Rural setting • Private • Independent • Coed

Taylor University seeks Christian scholars who wish to experience thoughtful and rigorous academic studies thoroughly integrated with biblical Christianity. It seeks students who will respond to a supportive campus community that expects responsible decision making in the context of Christian freedom. It seeks students who will endeavor to translate their 4-year experience into lifelong learning and ministering the redemptive love of Jesus Christ to a world in need. Taylor's president, Dr. Jay Kesler, and the outstanding Christian faculty invite students to consider the call to become a part of Taylor's exceptional student body and begin their own Taylor tradition.

Academics

Taylor offers a Christian liberal arts curriculum and core academic program. It awards associate and bachelor's **degrees**. Challenging opportunities include advanced placement, accelerated degree programs, self-designed majors, tutorials, an honors program, and a senior project. Special programs include internships, summer session for credit, off-campus study, and study abroad.

The most popular **majors** include business, elementary education, and psychology. A complete listing of majors at Taylor appears in the Majors Index beginning on page 379.

The **faculty** at Taylor has 101 full-time teachers, 63% with terminal degrees. 100% of the faculty serve as student advisers. The student-faculty ratio is 18:1.

Computers on Campus

Students are not required to have a computer. Student rooms are linked to a campus network. 186 **computers** available in computer labs, the learning resource center, the library, and dormitories provide access to the main academic computer, e-mail, on-line services, and the Internet. Staffed computer lab on campus provides training in the use of computers and software.

The **library** has 175,000 books, 100 microform titles, and 690 subscriptions. It is connected to 10 national **on-line** catalogs.

Campus Life

There are 30 active **organizations** on campus, including a drama/theater group and student-run newspaper and radio station. Student **safety services** include late night transport/escort service, 24-hour patrols by trained security personnel, and student patrols.

Taylor is a member of the NAIA. **Intercollegiate sports** (some offering scholarships) include baseball (m), basketball (m, w), cross-country running (m, w), equestrian sports (m, w), football (m), golf (m), soccer (m, w), softball (w), tennis (m, w), track and field (m, w), volleyball (m, w).

Applying

Taylor requires an essay, a high school transcript, 3 years of high school math and science, 2 recommendations, and SAT I or ACT. It recommends 2 years of high school foreign language, an interview, and a minimum high school GPA of 3.0. Deferred and midyear entrance are possible, with rolling admissions and continuous processing to 3/1 for financial aid. **Contact:** Mr. Stephen R. Mortland, Director of Admissions, 500 West Reade Avenue, Upland, IN 46989-1001, 317-998-5134 or toll-free 800-882-3456.

GETTING IN LAST YEAR
1,707 applied
61% were accepted
41% enrolled (420)
42% from top tenth of their h.s. class
3.6 average high school GPA
22% had SAT verbal scores over 600
47% had SAT math scores over 600
53% had ACT scores over 26
4% had SAT verbal scores over 700
11% had SAT math scores over 700
7% had ACT scores over 30
30 valedictorians

THE STUDENT BODY
1,829 undergraduates

From 45 states and territories,
  20 other countries
29% from Indiana
52% women, 48% men
2% African Americans
1% Native Americans
1% Hispanics
2% Asian Americans
3% international students

AFTER FRESHMAN YEAR
89% returned for sophomore year
49% got a degree within 4 years
68% got a degree within 5 years
71% got a degree within 6 years

AFTER GRADUATION
13% pursued further study (6% arts and
  sciences, 3% theology, 2% medicine)
114 organizations recruited on campus

WHAT YOU WILL PAY
Tuition and fees $11,914
Room and board $4150
56% receive need-based financial aid
Need-based college-administered scholarships and
  grants average $2600 per award
23% receive non-need financial aid
Non-need college-administered scholarships and
  grants average $1700 per award

TEXAS A&M UNIVERSITY

College Station, Texas • Suburban setting • Public • State-supported • Coed

---

▶ An internationally acclaimed research university, Texas A&M is widely recognized for the strength of its undergraduate curricular and extracurricular programs. Expanding frontiers of knowledge, from the humanities and social sciences to business studies, science, and engineering, Texas A&M's distinguished faculty includes Pulitzer and Nobel prize recipients. An outstanding student body is attracted from 50 states and 100 countries to pursue degrees in over 150 fields of study. The University's 5,000-acre main campus is home to the cyclotron, supercomputer, visualization lab, art galleries, recreation centers, and fitness facilities. More than 700 recognized student organizations provide unparalleled opportunities for leadership development.

 ## Academics

Texas A&M offers an interdisciplinary curriculum and core academic program; fewer than half of graduate courses are open to undergraduates. It awards bachelor's, master's, doctoral, and first professional **degrees**. Challenging opportunities include advanced placement, accelerated degree programs, tutorials, an honors program, and Sigma Xi. Special programs include cooperative education, internships, summer session for credit, off-campus study, study abroad, and Army, Naval, and Air Force ROTC.

The most popular **majors** include psychology, accounting, and management information systems. A complete listing of majors at Texas A&M appears in the Majors Index beginning on page 379.

The **faculty** at Texas A&M has 1,844 full-time graduate and undergraduate teachers, 77% with terminal degrees. The student-faculty ratio is 27:1.

 ## Computers on Campus

Students are not required to have a computer. Student rooms are linked to a campus network. 1,700 **computers**

available in the computer center, computer labs, the research center, the learning resource center, various locations on campus, classrooms, the library, the student center, and dormitories provide access to the main academic computer, off-campus computing facilities, e-mail, and on-line services. Staffed computer lab on campus (open 24 hours a day) provides training in the use of computers and software.

The 4 **libraries** have 2.2 million books, 4.4 million microform titles, and 16,000 subscriptions. They are connected to 16 national **on-line** catalogs.

 ## Campus Life

There are 700 active **organizations** on campus, including a drama/theater group and student-run newspaper and radio station. 25% of students participate in student government elections. 8% of eligible men and 11% of eligible women are members of 29 national **fraternities**, 15 national **sororities**, 5 local fraternities, and 4 local sororities. Student **safety services** include late night transport/escort service, 24-hour emergency telephone alarm devices, 24-hour patrols by trained security personnel, and electronically operated dormitory entrances.

Texas A&M is a member of the NCAA (Division I). **Intercollegiate sports** (some offering scholarships) include baseball (m), basketball (m, w), cross-country running (m, w), football (m), golf (m, w), riflery (m, w), soccer (w), softball (w), swimming and diving (m, w), tennis (m, w), track and field (m, w), volleyball (w).

 ## Applying

Texas A&M requires a high school transcript, SAT I or ACT, and in some cases recommendations. It recommends 2 years of high school foreign language and 2 SAT II Subject Tests. Early, deferred, and midyear entrance are possible, with a 3/1 deadline and continuous processing to 4/1 for financial aid. **Contact:** Mr. Gary R. Engelgau, Executive Director of Admissions and Records, 217 John J. Koldus Building, College Station, TX 77843-1265, 409-845-3741.

GETTING IN LAST YEAR
15,888 applied
69% were accepted
56% enrolled (6,072)
49% from top tenth of their h.s. class
43% had SAT verbal scores over 600 (R)
53% had SAT math scores over 600 (R)
43% had ACT scores over 26
9% had SAT verbal scores over 700 (R)
13% had SAT math scores over 700 (R)
13% had ACT scores over 30
194 National Merit Scholars

THE STUDENT BODY
Total 41,790, of whom 34,371
 are undergraduates

From 55 states and territories
86% from Texas
44% women, 56% men
3% African Americans
0% Native Americans
10% Hispanics
4% Asian Americans
6% international students

AFTER FRESHMAN YEAR
87% returned for sophomore year
24% got a degree within 4 years
59% got a degree within 5 years
67% got a degree within 6 years

AFTER GRADUATION
47% had job offers within 6 months
804 organizations recruited on campus
2 Fulbright scholars

WHAT YOU WILL PAY
Resident tuition and fees $2288
Nonresident tuition and fees $8048
Room and board $2200
Need-based college-administered scholarships and
 grants average $1300 per award
Non-need college-administered scholarships and
 grants average $1685 per award

THOMAS AQUINAS COLLEGE

Santa Paula, California • Rural setting • Private • Independent-Religious • Coed

 The College's curriculum is based on the Great Books, the original works of the principal philosophers, theologians, scientists, mathematicians, poets, and writers of Western civilization. This unique program attracts students of exceptional ability and diverse backgrounds to a community of learning. Conventional lectures are replaced by small seminars, tutorials, and laboratories in which faculty lead rigorous and lively conversations about classic works in the arts and sciences. The unified, required curriculum integrates the essential intellectual disciplines of a classical liberal education. The College's academic program and community life are guided by the philosophic and religious traditions of the Catholic Church.

Academics

TAC offers a great books curriculum and core academic program. It awards bachelor's **degrees**. A senior project is a challenging opportunity. Study abroad is a special program.

The **faculty** at TAC has 23 full-time teachers, 73% with terminal degrees. 48% of the faculty serve as student advisers. The student-faculty ratio is 10:1, and the average class size in core courses is 15.

 ## Computers on Campus

Students are not required to have a computer. 8 **computers** available in the library, the student center, and dormitories.

The **library** has 40,000 books and 45 subscriptions.

 ## Campus Life

There is 1 active **organization** on campus. Student **safety services** include 24-hour emergency telephone alarm devices and student patrols.

This institution has no intercollegiate sports.

 ## Applying

TAC requires an essay, a high school transcript, 2 years of high school foreign language, 3 recommendations, SAT I or ACT, and in some cases an interview. It recommends 3 years of high school math and science. Early and deferred entrance are possible, with rolling admissions and continuous processing to 9/1 for financial aid. **Contact:** Mr. Thomas J. Susanka Jr., Director of Admissions, 10000 North Ojai Road, Santa Paula, CA 93060-9980, 805-525-4417 ext. 359 or toll-free 800-634-9797; fax 805-525-0620.

GETTING IN LAST YEAR
122 applied
79% were accepted
75% enrolled (72)
36% from top tenth of their h.s. class
3.48 average high school GPA
82% had SAT verbal scores over 600 (R)
44% had SAT math scores over 600 (R)
57% had ACT scores over 26
29% had SAT verbal scores over 700 (R)
7% had SAT math scores over 700 (R)
21% had ACT scores over 30

THE STUDENT BODY
232 undergraduates

From 37 states and territories,
    10 other countries
34% from California
43% women, 57% men
1% African Americans
0% Native Americans
6% Hispanics
0% Asian Americans
15% international students

AFTER FRESHMAN YEAR
82% returned for sophomore year
60% got a degree within 4 years
63% got a degree within 5 years
65% got a degree within 6 years

AFTER GRADUATION
22% pursued further study (16% arts and
    sciences, 3% law, 3% medicine)
64% had job offers within 6 months
1 organization recruited on campus

WHAT YOU WILL PAY
Tuition and fees $13,900
Room and board $5300
90% receive need-based financial aid
Need-based college-administered scholarships and
    grants average $9295 per award

TRANSYLVANIA UNIVERSITY

Lexington, Kentucky • Urban setting • Private • Independent-Religious • Coed

Today, in its 216th year, Transylvania is a distinguished liberal arts college enrolling nearly 1,000 students. A strong commitment to undergraduate teaching and small classes are among Transylvania's distinctive assets. Students repeatedly cite their personal relationships with faculty members as being among the most valuable aspects of their Transylvania experience. Transylvania's location in Lexington, at the heart of Kentucky's beautiful Bluegrass region, provides students with an exceptional range of cultural and recreational activities. Now in its third century, Transylvania is consistently ranked among the nation's top liberal arts colleges.

Academics

Transylvania offers an interdisciplinary liberal arts curriculum and core academic program. It awards bachelor's **degrees**. Challenging opportunities include advanced placement, accelerated degree programs, self-designed majors, and tutorials. Special programs include internships, summer session for credit, off-campus study, study abroad, and Army and Air Force ROTC.

The most popular **majors** include business, biology/biological sciences, and psychology. A complete listing of majors at Transylvania appears in the Majors Index beginning on page 379.

The **faculty** at Transylvania has 62 full-time teachers, 92% with terminal degrees. 100% of the faculty serve as student advisers. The student-faculty ratio is 14:1, and the average class size in core courses is 18.

Computers on Campus

Students are not required to have a computer. Student rooms are linked to a campus network. 115 **computers** available in the computer center, computer labs, the research center, the learning resource center, academic buildings, classrooms, the library, the student center, and dormitories provide access to the main academic computer, off-campus computing facilities, e-mail, on-line services, and the Internet. Staffed computer lab on campus provides training in the use of computers and software.

The **library** has 115,000 books, 64 microform titles, and 580 subscriptions. It is connected to 2 national **on-line** catalogs.

Campus Life

There are 43 active **organizations** on campus, including a drama/theater group and student-run newspaper and radio station. 26% of students participate in student government elections. 60% of eligible men and 62% of eligible women are members of 4 national **fraternities** and 4 national **sororities**. Student **safety services** include late night transport/escort service, 24-hour emergency telephone alarm devices, and 24-hour patrols by trained security personnel.

Transylvania is a member of the NAIA. **Intercollegiate sports** (some offering scholarships) include baseball (m), basketball (m, w), cross-country running (m, w), field hockey (w), golf (m), soccer (m, w), softball (w), swimming and diving (m, w), tennis (m, w).

Applying

Transylvania requires an essay, a high school transcript, 3 years of high school math, 2 recommendations, minimum 2.25 GPA, SAT I or ACT, and in some cases an interview. It recommends 3 years of high school science, some high school foreign language, and an interview. Early, deferred, and midyear entrance are possible, with a 3/1 deadline and continuous processing to 3/15 for financial aid. **Contact:** Mr. John O. Gaines, Acting Director of Admissions, 300 North Broadway, Lexington, KY 40508-1797, 606-233-8242 or toll-free 800-872-6798; fax 606-233-8797.

GETTING IN LAST YEAR
855 applied
93% were accepted
34% enrolled (273)
56% from top tenth of their h.s. class
3.41 average high school GPA
19% had SAT verbal scores over 600
43% had SAT math scores over 600
55% had ACT scores over 26
1% had SAT verbal scores over 700
12% had SAT math scores over 700
16% had ACT scores over 30
2 National Merit Scholars
42 valedictorians

THE STUDENT BODY
926 undergraduates

From 26 states and territories,
 11 other countries
80% from Kentucky
53% women, 47% men
2% African Americans
0% Native Americans
1% Hispanics
3% Asian Americans
1% international students

AFTER FRESHMAN YEAR
77% returned for sophomore year
56% got a degree within 4 years
63% got a degree within 5 years

AFTER GRADUATION
35% pursued further study (16% arts and
 sciences, 7% medicine, 6% law)
55% had job offers within 6 months
20 organizations recruited on campus

WHAT YOU WILL PAY
Tuition and fees $12,020
Room and board $4630
45% receive need-based financial aid
Need-based college-administered scholarships and
 grants average $5826 per award
42% receive non-need financial aid
Non-need college-administered scholarships and
 grants average $7600 per award

TRENTON STATE COLLEGE

Trenton, New Jersey • Suburban setting • Public • State-supported • Coed

Trenton State College is a highly selective institution that has received consistent national recognition for its commitment to quality. The College enrolls bright and creative students who contribute actively to campus life and to their own intellectual growth. They join a community of learners dedicated to the ideals of public service, excellence, diversity, and community. In a learning partnership with faculty, TSC students enhance their skills, expand their knowledge, and formulate the values and attitudes necessary to assume the responsibilities of an increasingly complex society. TSC graduates take their places as productive citizens and as future leaders in their professions.

Academics

TSC offers an interdisciplinary curriculum and core academic program; fewer than half of graduate courses are open to undergraduates. It awards bachelor's and master's **degrees**. Challenging opportunities include advanced placement, tutorials, an honors program, and a senior project. Special programs include internships, summer session for credit, off-campus study, study abroad, and Army and Air Force ROTC.

The most popular **majors** include elementary education, criminal justice, and English. A complete listing of majors at TSC appears in the Majors Index beginning on page 379.

The **faculty** at TSC has 316 full-time undergraduate teachers, 82% with terminal degrees. 98% of the faculty serve as student advisers. The average class size in core courses is 25.

Computers on Campus

Students are not required to have a computer. Student rooms are linked to a campus network. 500 **computers** available in the computer center, computer labs, academic buildings, classrooms, the library, the student center, and dormitories provide access to the main academic computer, off-campus computing facilities, e-mail, on-line services, and the Internet. Staffed computer lab on campus provides training in the use of computers and software.

The **library** has 500,000 books, 200,000 microform titles, and 1,563 subscriptions. It is connected to 7 national **on-line** catalogs.

Campus Life

There are 140 active **organizations** on campus, including a drama/theater group and student-run newspaper and radio station. 16% of students participate in student government elections. 19% of eligible men and 19% of eligible women are members of 11 national **fraternities**, 13 national **sororities**, 3 local fraternities, and 3 local sororities. Student **safety services** include late night transport/escort service, 24-hour emergency telephone alarm devices, 24-hour patrols by trained security personnel, student patrols, and electronically operated dormitory entrances.

TSC is a member of the NCAA (Division III). **Intercollegiate sports** include baseball (m), basketball (m, w), cross-country running (m, w), field hockey (w), football (m), golf (m), lacrosse (w), soccer (m, w), softball (w), swimming and diving (m, w), tennis (m, w), track and field (m, w), wrestling (m).

Applying

TSC requires an essay, a high school transcript, 3 years of high school math and science, SAT I, SAT II: Writing Test, and in some cases an interview. It recommends 2 years of high school foreign language and recommendations. Early and deferred entrance are possible, with a 3/1 deadline and continuous processing to 4/15 for financial aid. **Contact:** Mr. Frank Cooper, Acting Director of Admissions, Green Hall, Trenton, NJ 08650-4700, 609-771-2131 or toll-free 800-345-0967 (in-state), 800-345-7354 (out-of-state).

GETTING IN LAST YEAR
5,946 applied
45% were accepted
41% enrolled (1,088)
55% from top tenth of their h.s. class
53% had SAT verbal scores over 600 (R)
56% had SAT math scores over 600 (R)
9% had SAT verbal scores over 700 (R)
8% had SAT math scores over 700 (R)
19 valedictorians

THE STUDENT BODY
Total 6,666, of whom 5,747
  are undergraduates

From 23 states and territories,
  20 other countries
92% from New Jersey
60% women, 40% men
7% African Americans
1% Native Americans
6% Hispanics
5% Asian Americans
1% international students

AFTER FRESHMAN YEAR
91% returned for sophomore year
42% got a degree within 4 years
68% got a degree within 5 years
73% got a degree within 6 years

AFTER GRADUATION
250 organizations recruited on campus
1 Marshall scholar

WHAT YOU WILL PAY
Resident tuition and fees $4168
Nonresident tuition and fees $6585
Room and board $5600
42% receive need-based financial aid
Need-based college-administered scholarships and
  grants average $600 per award
36% receive non-need financial aid
Non-need college-administered scholarships and
  grants average $1850 per award

TRINITY COLLEGE

Hartford, Connecticut • Urban setting • Private • Independent • Coed

Trinity offers its students the distinctive combination of a beautiful hilltop campus in a thriving capital city. Students find hundreds of internship and volunteer opportunities and cultural or entertainment activities in Hartford. More than 50% pursue internships in business, politics, law, medicine, education, and the arts. Community Outreach, the organization that coordinates some 20 volunteer projects, involves more than 400 students in community service work annually. Long considered one of America's premier liberal arts colleges, Trinity is one of only a few such distinguished institutions that can provide its students with the rich opportunities available only in a major metropolitan area.

Academics

Trinity College offers a core academic program; more than half of graduate courses are open to undergraduates. It awards bachelor's and master's **degrees**. Challenging opportunities include advanced placement, accelerated degree programs, self-designed majors, tutorials, a senior project, and Phi Beta Kappa. Special programs include internships, summer session for credit, off-campus study, study abroad, and Army ROTC.

The most popular **majors** include history, English, and psychology. A complete listing of majors at Trinity College appears in the Majors Index beginning on page 379.

The **faculty** at Trinity College has 163 full-time undergraduate teachers, 98% with terminal degrees. 100% of the faculty serve as student advisers. The student-faculty ratio is 10:1.

Computers on Campus

Students are not required to have a computer. Student rooms are linked to a campus network. 150 **computers** available in the computer center, academic departments, and the library provide access to the main academic computer, off-campus computing facilities, e-mail, on-line services, and the Internet. Staffed computer lab on campus (open 24 hours a day) provides training in the use of computers and software.

The 3 **libraries** have 893,858 books, 302,116 microform titles, and 2,273 subscriptions. They are connected to 2 national **on-line** catalogs.

Campus Life

There are 80 active **organizations** on campus, including a drama/theater group and student-run newspaper and radio station. 30% of students participate in student government elections. 30% of eligible men and 10% of eligible women are members of 6 coed fraternities. Student **safety services** include late night transport/escort service, 24-hour emergency telephone alarm devices, 24-hour patrols by trained security personnel, and electronically operated dormitory entrances.

Trinity College is a member of the NCAA (Division III). **Intercollegiate sports** include baseball (m), basketball (m, w), crew (m, w), cross-country running (m, w), equestrian sports (m, w), fencing (m, w), field hockey (w), football (m), golf (m), ice hockey (m, w), lacrosse (m, w), rugby (m, w), sailing (m, w), skiing (downhill) (m, w), soccer (m, w), softball (w), squash (m, w), swimming and diving (m, w), tennis (m, w), track and field (m, w), volleyball (m, w), water polo (m, w), wrestling (m).

Applying

Trinity College requires an essay, a high school transcript, 3 years of high school math, 2 years of high school foreign language, 3 recommendations, SAT I or ACT, and SAT II: Writing Test. It recommends 3 years of high school science and an interview. Early and deferred entrance are possible, with a 1/15 deadline and 2/1 for financial aid. **Contact:** Dr. David M. Borus, Dean of Admissions and Financial Aid, 300 Summit Street, Hartford, CT 06106-3100, 203-297-2180; fax 203-297-2287.

GETTING IN LAST YEAR
3,054 applied
57% were accepted
29% enrolled (509)
43% from top tenth of their h.s. class
71% had SAT verbal scores over 600 (R)
67% had SAT math scores over 600 (R)
52% had ACT scores over 26
14% had SAT verbal scores over 700 (R)
8% had SAT math scores over 700 (R)
16% had ACT scores over 30

THE STUDENT BODY
Total 2,142, of whom 1,944
    are undergraduates
From 47 states and territories,
    23 other countries
28% from Connecticut
50% women, 50% men
6% African Americans
0% Native Americans
4% Hispanics
5% Asian Americans
2% international students

AFTER FRESHMAN YEAR
94% returned for sophomore year
84% got a degree within 4 years
90% got a degree within 5 years

WHAT YOU WILL PAY
Tuition and fees $20,230
Room and board $6130
45% receive need-based financial aid
Need-based college-administered scholarships and
    grants average $13,000 per award

TRINITY UNIVERSITY

San Antonio, Texas • Urban setting • Private • Independent-Religious • Coed

Trinity University is a highly selective liberal arts and sciences institution that also offers several professional programs that are nationally cited as models in their fields. Trinity offers its students a unique undergraduate experience. Class sizes are small, research labs and other facilities equal to those of moderate-sized Ph.D.-granting institutions are devoted exclusively to undergraduates, and contact with professors is frequent and personal (Trinity employs no graduate assistants and extraordinarily few part-time faculty members.) The 117-acre campus is known for its beauty and for its unique skyline view of downtown San Antonio, one of America's most interesting multicultural cities.

Academics

Trinity offers a six understandings curriculum and core academic program; a few graduate courses are open to undergraduates. It awards bachelor's and master's **degrees**. Challenging opportunities include advanced placement, accelerated degree programs, tutorials, and Phi Beta Kappa. Special programs include internships, summer session for credit, study abroad, and Air Force ROTC.

The **faculty** at Trinity has 220 full-time graduate and undergraduate teachers, 96% with terminal degrees. 97% of the faculty serve as student advisers. The student-faculty ratio is 11:1, and the average class size in core courses is 20.

Computers on Campus

Students are not required to have a computer. Student rooms are linked to a campus network. 400 **computers** available in the computer center and the student center provide access to the main academic computer, e-mail, and the Internet. Staffed computer lab on campus (open 24 hours a day) provides training in the use of computers and software.

The **library** has 784,530 books, 281,784 microform titles, and 2,378 subscriptions.

Campus Life

Active **organizations** on campus include drama/theater group and student-run newspaper and radio station. 30% of eligible men and 33% of eligible women are members of 6 local **fraternities** and 5 local **sororities**. Student **safety services** include late night transport/escort service, 24-hour emergency telephone alarm devices, 24-hour patrols by trained security personnel, and student patrols.

Trinity is a member of the NCAA (Division III). **Intercollegiate sports** include baseball (m), basketball (m, w), cross-country running (m, w), football (m), golf (m), soccer (m, w), softball (w), swimming and diving (m, w), tennis (m, w), track and field (m, w), volleyball (m, w).

Applying

Trinity requires an essay, a high school transcript, 3 years of high school math and science, 2 years of high school foreign language, recommendations, and SAT I or ACT. It recommends an interview. Early, deferred, and midyear entrance are possible, with a 2/1 deadline and a 2/1 priority date for financial aid. **Contact:** Dr. George Boyd, Director of Admissions, 715 Stadium Drive, San Antonio, TX 78212-7200, 210-736-7207 or toll-free 800-TRINITY.

GETTING IN LAST YEAR
2,442 applied
79% were accepted
32% enrolled (615)
63% from top tenth of their h.s. class
3.8 average high school GPA
73% had ACT scores over 26
17% had ACT scores over 30
39 National Merit Scholars

THE STUDENT BODY
Total 2,482, of whom 2,227
    are undergraduates
From 48 states and territories,
    18 other countries

64% from Texas
51% women, 49% men
2% African Americans
1% Native Americans
8% Hispanics
9% Asian Americans
3% international students

AFTER FRESHMAN YEAR
85% returned for sophomore year
64% got a degree within 4 years
76% got a degree within 5 years
78% got a degree within 6 years

AFTER GRADUATION
56% pursued further study (33% arts and
    sciences, 10% law, 3% engineering)

10% had job offers within 6 months
85 organizations recruited on campus
1 Rhodes, 4 Fulbright scholars

WHAT YOU WILL PAY
Tuition and fees $13,044
Room and board $5545
43% receive need-based financial aid
Need-based college-administered scholarships and
    grants average $12,784 per award
25% receive non-need financial aid
Non-need college-administered scholarships and
    grants average $3263 per award

TRUMAN STATE UNIVERSITY

Kirksville, Missouri • Small-town setting • Public • State-supported • Coed

"By any name, Northeast/Truman might be the right place for your educational buck to stop," says *Money Guide* (1996 edition) about the school ranked as the 3rd "Best Buy" nationally. Truman has embraced the challenge of becoming an uncommon public university, where undergraduates are encouraged to succeed and are given the support to flourish. With a foundation in the liberal arts and sciences and dynamic classrooms advocating the acquisition of knowledge, a Truman education helps students learn to love learning. Extensive cocurricular opportunities in undergraduate research, student government, and performing arts build upon that foundation, preparing Truman students for life.

Academics

Truman offers a liberal arts and sciences curriculum and core academic program; fewer than half of graduate courses are open to undergraduates. It awards bachelor's and master's **degrees**. Challenging opportunities include advanced placement, accelerated degree programs, an honors program, and a senior project. Special programs include internships, summer session for credit, off-campus study, study abroad, and Army ROTC.

The most popular **majors** include business, biology/biological sciences, and psychology. A complete listing of majors at Truman appears in the Majors Index beginning on page 379.

The **faculty** at Truman has 341 full-time graduate and undergraduate teachers, 79% with terminal degrees. 81% of the faculty serve as student advisers. The student-faculty ratio is 16:1.

Computers on Campus

Students are not required to have a computer. Student rooms are linked to a campus network. 950 **computers** available in computer labs, academic buildings, the library, and dormitories provide access to the main academic computer, e-mail, on-line services, and the Internet. Staffed computer lab on campus provides training in the use of computers and software.

The 2 **libraries** have 355,190 books, 294,305 microform titles, and 1,969 subscriptions. They are connected to 25 national **on-line** catalogs.

Campus Life

There are 153 active **organizations** on campus, including a drama/theater group and student-run newspaper and radio station. 15% of students participate in student government elections. 28% of eligible men and 21% of eligible women are members of 17 national **fraternities**, 10 national **sororities**, and 1 local sorority. Student **safety services** include patrols by commissioned officers, late night transport/escort service, 24-hour emergency telephone alarm devices, 24-hour patrols by trained security personnel, and student patrols.

Truman is a member of the NCAA (Division II). **Intercollegiate sports** (some offering scholarships) include baseball (m), basketball (m, w), cross-country running (m, w), equestrian sports (m, w), football (m), golf (m, w), rugby (m, w), soccer (m, w), softball (w), swimming and diving (m, w), tennis (m, w), track and field (m, w), volleyball (w), wrestling (m).

Applying

Truman requires an essay, a high school transcript, 3 years of high school math and science, 2 years of high school foreign language, SAT I or ACT, and in some cases recommendations. It recommends a minimum high school GPA of 3.0. Early, deferred, and midyear entrance are possible, with a 3/1 deadline and continuous processing to 4/30 for financial aid. **Contact:** Ms. Kathy Rieck, Dean of Admission and Records, 205 McClain Hall, Kirksville, MO 63501-4221, 816-785-4114 or toll-free 800-892-7792 (in-state); fax 816-785-4181.

GETTING IN LAST YEAR
6,587 applied
74% were accepted
31% enrolled (1,504)
34% from top tenth of their h.s. class
3.57 average high school GPA
52% had ACT scores over 26
18% had ACT scores over 30
17 National Merit Scholars
115 class presidents
65 valedictorians

THE STUDENT BODY
Total 6,287, of whom 6,043
   are undergraduates
From 42 states and territories,
   50 other countries

70% from Missouri
57% women, 43% men
3% African Americans
1% Native Americans
2% Hispanics
2% Asian Americans
2% international students

AFTER FRESHMAN YEAR
84% returned for sophomore year
56% got a degree within 4 years
58% got a degree within 5 years
59% got a degree within 6 years

AFTER GRADUATION
40% pursued further study (26% arts and
   sciences, 5% business, 3% law)

55% had job offers within 6 months
220 organizations recruited on campus
1 Fulbright scholar

WHAT YOU WILL PAY
Resident tuition and fees $2890
Nonresident tuition and fees $5170
Room and board $3624
45% receive need-based financial aid
Need-based college-administered scholarships and
   grants average $272 per award
59% receive non-need financial aid
Non-need college-administered scholarships and
   grants average $1881 per award

TUFTS UNIVERSITY

Medford, Massachusetts • Suburban setting • Private • Independent • Coed

Tufts is located on a residential campus and enrolls students from 50 states and more than 60 countries. Undergraduate colleges in liberal arts and engineering and 7 graduate schools are available. Over 40 departmental majors and 16 interdisciplinary programs in liberal arts and professional degree programs in chemical, civil and environmental, electrical, mechanical, and interdisciplinary engineering programs prepare students for leadership. Typically, 40% of Tufts students pursue study abroad. Students enjoy the advantages of Boston, an active campus, and the accessibility of faculty members for whom research and scholarship are balanced by a commitment to teaching.

Academics

Tufts offers a core academic program; fewer than half of graduate courses are open to undergraduates. It awards bachelor's, master's, doctoral, and first professional **degrees**. Challenging opportunities include advanced placement, self-designed majors, tutorials, an honors program, a senior project, Phi Beta Kappa, and Sigma Xi. Special programs include internships, summer session for credit, off-campus study, study abroad, and Army, Naval, and Air Force ROTC.

The most popular **majors** include English and biology/biological sciences. A complete listing of majors at Tufts appears in the Majors Index beginning on page 379.

The **faculty** at Tufts has 565 full-time graduate and undergraduate teachers, 99% with terminal degrees. 99% of the faculty serve as student advisers. The student-faculty ratio is 13:1.

Computers on Campus

Students are not required to have a computer. Student rooms are linked to a campus network. 254 **computers** available in the computer center, computer labs, CAD lab, the library, the student center, and dormitories provide access to the main academic computer, off-campus computing facilities, e-mail, on-line services, and the Internet. Staffed computer lab on campus provides training in the use of computers and software.

The 8 **libraries** have 836,000 books, 1 million microform titles, and 4,956 subscriptions. They are connected to 1 national **on-line** catalog.

Campus Life

There are 130 active **organizations** on campus, including a drama/theater group and student-run newspaper and radio station. 15% of eligible men and 4% of eligible women are members of 11 national **fraternities** and 4 national **sororities**. Student **safety services** include security lighting, call boxes to campus police, late night transport/escort service, 24-hour emergency telephone alarm devices, 24-hour patrols by trained security personnel, and electronically operated dormitory entrances.

Tufts is a member of the NCAA (Division III). **Intercollegiate sports** include baseball (m), basketball (m, w), crew (m, w), cross-country running (m, w), field hockey (w), football (m), golf (m), ice hockey (m), lacrosse (m, w), sailing (m, w), soccer (m, w), softball (w), squash (m, w), swimming and diving (m, w), tennis (m, w), track and field (m, w), volleyball (w).

Applying

Tufts requires an essay, a high school transcript, 1 recommendation, SAT I or ACT, and 3 SAT II Subject Tests (including SAT II: Writing Test). It recommends 3 years of high school math and science, 3 years of high school foreign language, and an interview. Early and deferred entrance are possible, with a 1/1 deadline and 2/1 for financial aid. **Contact:** Mr. David D. Cuttino, Dean of Undergraduate Admissions, Bendetson Hall, Medford, MA 02155, 617-627-3170; fax 617-627-3860.

GETTING IN LAST YEAR
8,510 applied
43% were accepted
32% enrolled (1,158)
62% from top tenth of their h.s. class
76% had SAT verbal scores over 600 (R)
85% had SAT math scores over 600 (R)
79% had ACT scores over 26
22% had SAT verbal scores over 700 (R)
25% had SAT math scores over 700 (R)
28% had ACT scores over 30
22 National Merit Scholars

THE STUDENT BODY
Total 8,097, of whom 4,531
  are undergraduates

From 52 states and territories,
  64 other countries
27% from Massachusetts
52% women, 48% men
4% African Americans
5% Hispanics
14% Asian Americans
8% international students

AFTER FRESHMAN YEAR
98% returned for sophomore year
90% got a degree within 4 years

AFTER GRADUATION
33% pursued further study (11% law, 10%
  business, 9% medicine)

155 organizations recruited on campus
1 Marshall, 10 Fulbright scholars

WHAT YOU WILL PAY
Tuition and fees $21,086
Room and board $6250
40% receive need-based financial aid
Need-based college-administered scholarships and
  grants average $12,226 per award
Non-need college-administered scholarships and
  grants average $750 per award

TULANE UNIVERSITY

New Orleans, Louisiana • Urban setting • Private • Independent • Coed

With 5,000 full-time undergraduate students in 5 divisions, Tulane University offers the personal attention and teaching excellence traditionally associated with liberal arts colleges together with the facilities and interdisciplinary resources found only at major research universities—with both complemented by the exciting, historic setting of New Orleans. Senior faculty members regularly teach introductory and lower-level courses, and 74% of the classes have 25 or fewer students. The close student-teacher relationship pays off. Tulane graduates are among the country's most likely to be selected for several prestigious fellowships that support graduate study abroad.

 Academics

Tulane offers a core academic program; fewer than half of graduate courses are open to undergraduates. It awards associate, bachelor's, master's, doctoral, and first professional **degrees**. Challenging opportunities include advanced placement, accelerated degree programs, self-designed majors, tutorials, Freshman Honors College, an honors program, a senior project, Phi Beta Kappa, and Sigma Xi. Special programs include internships, summer session for credit, off-campus study, study abroad, and Army, Naval, and Air Force ROTC.

The most popular **majors** include biology/biological sciences, English, and psychology. A complete listing of majors at Tulane appears in the Majors Index beginning on page 379.

The **faculty** at Tulane has 452 full-time graduate and undergraduate teachers, 98% with terminal degrees. The student-faculty ratio is 10:1.

 Computers on Campus

Students are not required to have a computer. Student rooms are linked to a campus network. 500 **computers** available in the computer center, computer labs, the learning resource center, academic buildings, classrooms, the library, the student center, and dormitories provide access to the main academic computer, off-campus computing facilities, e-mail, on-line services, and the Internet. Staffed computer lab on campus provides training in the use of computers and software.

The **library** has 2.1 million books, 2.4 million microform titles, and 16,500 subscriptions.

 Campus Life

There are 200 active **organizations** on campus, including a drama/theater group and student-run newspaper and radio station. 32% of eligible men and 35% of eligible women are members of 16 national **fraternities** and 8 national **sororities**. Student **safety services** include late night transport/escort service, 24-hour emergency telephone alarm devices, 24-hour patrols by trained security personnel, student patrols, and electronically operated dormitory entrances.

Tulane is a member of the NCAA (Division I). **Intercollegiate sports** (some offering scholarships) include baseball (m), basketball (m, w), crew (m, w), cross-country running (m, w), equestrian sports (m, w), fencing (m, w), field hockey (m, w), football (m), golf (m, w), gymnastics (m, w), ice hockey (m, w), lacrosse (m, w), riflery (m, w), rugby (m), sailing (m, w), soccer (m, w), softball (w), swimming and diving (m, w), tennis (m, w), track and field (m, w), volleyball (m, w), water polo (m, w).

 Applying

Tulane requires an essay, a high school transcript, 1 recommendation, and SAT I or ACT. It recommends 3 years of high school math and science, 3 years of high school foreign language, and SAT II Subject Tests. Early, deferred, and midyear entrance are possible, with a 1/15 deadline and continuous processing to 1/15 for financial aid. **Contact:** Mr. Richard Whiteside, Dean of Admission and Enrollment Management, 210 Gibson Hall, New Orleans, LA 70118-5669, 504-865-5731 or toll-free 800-873-9283; fax 504-862-8715.

GETTING IN LAST YEAR
8,707 applied
72% were accepted
20% enrolled (1,239)
56% from top tenth of their h.s. class
40% had SAT verbal scores over 600
70% had SAT math scores over 600
9% had SAT verbal scores over 700
22% had SAT math scores over 700

THE STUDENT BODY
Total 11,158, of whom 6,327
    are undergraduates
From 52 states and territories,
    100 other countries

20% from Louisiana
50% women, 50% men
10% African Americans
1% Native Americans
5% Hispanics
5% Asian Americans
4% international students

AFTER FRESHMAN YEAR
85% returned for sophomore year
70% got a degree within 4 years
73% got a degree within 5 years

AFTER GRADUATION
57% pursued further study (22% arts and
    sciences, 16% law, 9% medicine)

504 organizations recruited on campus
1 Marshall, 5 Fulbright scholars

WHAT YOU WILL PAY
Tuition and fees $20,386
Room and board $6130
33% receive need-based financial aid
Need-based college-administered scholarships and
    grants average $14,514 per award
21% receive non-need financial aid

UNION COLLEGE

Schenectady, New York • Suburban setting • Private • Independent • Coed

Union College, one of the oldest colleges in America, is located in the small city of Schenectady, about 3 hours north of New York City. Its distinctive curriculum combines the traditional liberal arts with engineering study. Three basic tenets undergird a Union education: commitments to lifelong learning, the liberal arts, and a close working relationship between students and faculty. People from many different backgrounds come to Union, attracted by these values and the opportunities they imply: small classes, excellent access to superb facilities, a caring and committed faculty, and an academic program of depth and diversity.

Academics

Union College offers a core academic program; more than half of graduate courses are open to undergraduates. It awards bachelor's, master's, and doctoral **degrees**. Challenging opportunities include advanced placement, accelerated degree programs, self-designed majors, tutorials, a senior project, Phi Beta Kappa, and Sigma Xi. Special programs include summer session for credit, off-campus study, study abroad, and Army, Naval, and Air Force ROTC.

The most popular **majors** include psychology, political science/government, and economics. A complete listing of majors at Union College appears in the Majors Index beginning on page 379.

The **faculty** at Union College has 174 full-time undergraduate teachers, 96% with terminal degrees. 100% of the faculty serve as student advisers. The student-faculty ratio is 11:1.

Computers on Campus

Students are not required to have a computer. Student rooms are linked to a campus network. 200 **computers** available in the computer center, computer labs, academic buildings, classrooms, the library, and the student center provide access to the main academic computer, off-campus computing facilities, e-mail, on-line services, and the Internet. Staffed computer lab on campus (open 24 hours a day) provides training in the use of computers and software.

The **library** has 502,115 books, 36,322 microform titles, and 1,970 subscriptions. It is connected to 4 national **on-line** catalogs.

Campus Life

There are 90 active **organizations** on campus, including a drama/theater group and student-run newspaper and radio station. 40% of students participate in student government elections. 37% of eligible men and 30% of eligible women are members of 14 national **fraternities**, 4 national **sororities**, and 1 coed fraternity. Student **safety services** include late night transport/escort service, 24-hour emergency telephone alarm devices, 24-hour patrols by trained security personnel, student patrols, and electronically operated dormitory entrances.

Union College is a member of the NCAA (Division III). **Intercollegiate sports** include baseball (m), basketball (m, w), crew (m, w), cross-country running (m, w), fencing (m), field hockey (w), football (m), ice hockey (m), lacrosse (m, w), rugby (m, w), skiing (cross-country) (m, w), skiing (downhill) (m, w), soccer (m, w), softball (w), swimming and diving (m, w), tennis (m, w), track and field (m, w), volleyball (w).

Applying

Union College requires an essay, a high school transcript, 2 recommendations, 3 SAT II Subject Tests (including SAT II: Writing Test) or ACT, and in some cases 3 years of high school math and science. It recommends 2 years of high school foreign language and an interview. Early and deferred entrance are possible, with a 2/1 deadline and a 2/1 priority date for financial aid. **Contact:** Mr. Daniel Lundquist, Vice President for Admissions and Financial Aid, Becker Hall, Schenectady, NY 12308-2311, 518-388-6112; fax 518-388-6986.

GETTING IN LAST YEAR
3,550 applied
52% were accepted
28% enrolled (515)
47% from top tenth of their h.s. class

THE STUDENT BODY
Total 2,330, of whom 2,063
   are undergraduates
From 38 states and territories,
   13 other countries
51% from New York

47% women, 53% men
3% African Americans
0% Native Americans
3% Hispanics
6% Asian Americans
2% international students

AFTER FRESHMAN YEAR
92% returned for sophomore year
78% got a degree within 4 years
85% got a degree within 5 years

AFTER GRADUATION
35% pursued further study (14% arts and
   sciences, 10% medicine, 8% law)
65 organizations recruited on campus

WHAT YOU WILL PAY
Tuition and fees $19,972
Room and board $6234
57% receive need-based financial aid
Need-based college-administered scholarships and
   grants average $11,800 per award

UNION UNIVERSITY

Jackson, Tennessee • Small-town setting • Private • Independent-Religious • Coed

Union University, located between Memphis and Nashville in the growing community of Jackson, Tennessee, offers a full liberal arts curriculum in more than 40 fields of study. A student-faculty ratio of 14:1 guarantees individual attention to student needs, and most majors offer senior seminars to promote research and exchange of ideas. As a Christian university, Union inspires its graduates to pursue goals that stretch higher than the corporate ladder reaches. Union's goal is to bring out the very best in each student, both inside and out of the classroom.

 ## Academics

Union offers a liberal arts curriculum and core academic program. It awards bachelor's and master's **degrees**. Challenging opportunities include advanced placement, accelerated degree programs, an honors program, and a senior project. Special programs include internships, summer session for credit, and off-campus study.

The most popular **majors** include nursing, education, and business. A complete listing of majors at Union appears in the Majors Index beginning on page 379.

The **faculty** at Union has 104 full-time graduate and undergraduate teachers, 55% with terminal degrees. The student-faculty ratio is 14:1, and the average class size in core courses is 24.

 ## Computers on Campus

Students are not required to have a computer. 140 **computers** available in the computer center, computer labs, classrooms, the library, and dormitories provide access to the main academic computer, e-mail, and the Internet. Staffed computer lab on campus (open 24 hours a day) provides training in the use of computers and software.

The **library** has 197,242 books, 850 microform titles, and 1,125 subscriptions. It is connected to 5 national **on-line** catalogs.

 ## Campus Life

There are 45 active **organizations** on campus, including a drama/theater group and student-run newspaper and radio station. 9% of eligible men and 12% of eligible women are members of 3 national **fraternities** and 3 national **sororities**. Student **safety services** include 24-hour patrols by trained security personnel.

Union is a member of the NAIA. **Intercollegiate sports** (some offering scholarships) include baseball (m), basketball (m, w), golf (m), softball (w), tennis (m, w).

 ## Applying

Union requires a high school transcript, 3 years of high school math and science, SAT I or ACT, a minimum high school GPA of 2.0, and in some cases an essay, some high school foreign language, recommendations, and an interview. Early and midyear entrance are possible, with a 2/1 deadline and continuous processing to 2/1 for financial aid. **Contact:** Mr. Carroll Griffin, Director of Admissions, Highway 45 Bypass North, Jackson, TN 38305, 901-661-5000 or toll-free 800-33 UNION; fax 901-661-5177.

GETTING IN LAST YEAR
865 applied
88% were accepted
50% enrolled (379)
36% had ACT scores over 26
9% had ACT scores over 30
39 valedictorians

THE STUDENT BODY
Total 1,973, of whom 1,845
  are undergraduates
From 32 states and territories,
  8 other countries

74% from Tennessee
62% women, 38% men
4% African Americans
0% Native Americans
0% Hispanics
0% Asian Americans
1% international students

AFTER FRESHMAN YEAR
43% got a degree within 4 years
53% got a degree within 5 years
57% got a degree within 6 years

AFTER GRADUATION
40% pursued further study

WHAT YOU WILL PAY
Tuition and fees $7030
Room and board $2700
Non-need college-administered scholarships and
  grants average $1200 per award

UNITED STATES AIR FORCE ACADEMY

Colorado Springs, Colorado • Suburban setting • Public • Federally supported • Coed

The Air Force Academy challenge requires a well-rounded academic, physical, and leadership background. Cadets must accept discipline, be competitive, and have a desire to serve others with a sense of duty and morality. Applicants should prepare early to meet the admissions requirements, competition, and demands they will face at the Academy.

Academics

USAFA offers a broad-based curriculum and core academic program; a few graduate courses are open to undergraduates. It awards bachelor's **degrees**. Challenging opportunities include advanced placement, self-designed majors, tutorials, and a senior project. Special programs include internships, summer session for credit, off-campus study, and study abroad.

The most popular **majors** include behavioral sciences, civil engineering, and business. A complete listing of majors at USAFA appears in the Majors Index beginning on page 379.

The **faculty** at USAFA has 547 full-time teachers, 48% with terminal degrees. 90% of the faculty serve as student advisers. The student-faculty ratio is 8:1, and the average class size in core courses is 19.

Computers on Campus

Students are required to have a computer. PCs are provided. Student rooms are linked to a campus network. 4,800 **computers** available in the computer center, computer labs, the library, dormitories, and student rooms provide access to off-campus computing facilities, e-mail, and the Internet. Staffed computer lab on campus provides training in the use of computers and software.

The 4 **libraries** have 690,000 books, 572,000 microform titles, and 2,268 subscriptions. They are connected to 12 national **on-line** catalogs.

Campus Life

There are 70 active **organizations** on campus, including a drama/theater group and student-run newspaper and radio station. Student **safety services** include self defense education, well-lit campus, late night transport/escort service, 24-hour emergency telephone alarm devices, and 24-hour patrols by trained security personnel.

USAFA is a member of the NCAA (Division I-Men; Division II-Women). **Intercollegiate sports** include baseball (m), basketball (m, w), bowling (m, w), cross-country running (m, w), equestrian sports (m, w), fencing (m, w), football (m), golf (m), gymnastics (m, w), ice hockey (m), lacrosse (m, w), racquetball (m, w), riflery (m, w), rugby (m, w), skiing (cross-country) (m, w), skiing (downhill) (m, w), soccer (m, w), softball (w), squash (m), swimming and diving (m, w), tennis (m, w), track and field (m, w), volleyball (m, w), water polo (m), weight lifting (m), wrestling (m).

Applying

USAFA requires an essay, a high school transcript, an interview, authorized nomination, and SAT I or ACT. It recommends 4 years of high school math and science, 2 years of high school foreign language, and SAT II Subject Tests. Early entrance is possible, with a 1/31 deadline. **Contact:** Mr. Rolland Stoneman, Director of Selections, USAF Academy, CO 80840-5025, 719-472-2520 or toll-free 800-443-9266.

GETTING IN LAST YEAR
8,538 applied
22% were accepted
73% enrolled (1,340)
66% from top tenth of their h.s. class
3.8 average high school GPA
77% had SAT verbal scores over 600 (R)
86% had SAT math scores over 600 (R)
15% had SAT verbal scores over 700 (R)
21% had SAT math scores over 700 (R)
224 National Merit Scholars
172 class presidents
132 valedictorians

THE STUDENT BODY
4,117 undergraduates
From 50 states and territories,
    24 other countries
4% from Colorado
15% women, 85% men
6% African Americans
1% Native Americans
7% Hispanics
4% Asian Americans
1% international students

AFTER FRESHMAN YEAR
90% returned for sophomore year
77% got a degree within 4 years

AFTER GRADUATION
6% pursued further study (2% medicine, 1% arts and sciences)
100% had job offers within 6 months

WHAT YOU WILL PAY
Comprehensive fee $0

UNITED STATES COAST GUARD ACADEMY

New London, Connecticut • Suburban setting • Public • Federally supported • Coed

---

The United States Coast Guard Academy, located halfway between New York City and Boston on Connecticut's shoreline, is committed to the development of professional career Coast Guard officers. Not only as an academic institution, but also as a multimissioned training facility for today's officer, the Academy provides solid academic studies, hands-on leadership experiences, and military training necessary to be successful in the world's premier maritime service. Whether it is rescuing a stranded mariner or enforcing maritime laws, the U.S. Coast Guard can be found in all corners of the world, supporting and shaping national policy every day.

 ## Academics

USCGA offers an engineering curriculum and core academic program. It awards bachelor's **degrees**. Challenging opportunities include tutorials, an honors program, and a senior project. Special programs include summer session for credit, off-campus study, and study abroad.

The most popular **majors** include marine engineering, business, and marine sciences. A complete listing of majors at USCGA appears in the Majors Index beginning on page 379.

The **faculty** at USCGA has 111 full-time teachers, 30% with terminal degrees. 77% of the faculty serve as student advisers. The student-faculty ratio is 10:1.

 ## Computers on Campus

Students are required to have a computer. PCs are provided. Student rooms are linked to a campus network. 120 **computers** available in the computer center, computer labs, engineering, science, math, computer science departments, the library, dormitories, and student rooms provide access to the main academic computer, off-campus computing facilities, e-mail, and the Internet. Staffed computer lab on campus provides training in the use of computers and software.

The **library** has 150,000 books, 61,000 microform titles, and 1,690 subscriptions. It is connected to 2 national **on-line** catalogs.

 ## Campus Life

Active **organizations** on campus include drama/theater group and student-run newspaper. Student **safety services** include 24-hour emergency telephone alarm devices and 24-hour patrols by trained security personnel.

USCGA is a member of the NCAA (Division III). **Intercollegiate sports** include baseball (m), basketball (m, w), bowling (m, w), crew (m, w), cross-country running (m, w), football (m), ice hockey (m), lacrosse (m), riflery (m, w), rugby (m), sailing (m, w), soccer (m, w), softball (w), swimming and diving (m), tennis (m), track and field (m, w), volleyball (m, w), wrestling (m).

 ## Applying

USCGA requires an essay, a high school transcript, 3 years of high school math, 3 recommendations, SAT I or ACT, and in some cases an interview. It recommends 3 years of high school science. 12/15 deadline. **Contact:** Capt. R. W. Thorne, Director of Admissions, 15 Mohegan Avenue, New London, CT 06320-4195, 203-444-8500; fax 203-444-8289.

GETTING IN LAST YEAR

2,009 applied
22% were accepted
56% enrolled (243)
73% from top tenth of their h.s. class
31% had SAT verbal scores over 600
76% had SAT math scores over 600
61% had ACT scores over 26
2% had SAT verbal scores over 700
19% had SAT math scores over 700
10% had ACT scores over 30

9 class presidents
12 valedictorians

THE STUDENT BODY

862 undergraduates
From 50 states and territories,
    13 other countries
7% from Connecticut
34% women, 66% men
7% African Americans
2% Native Americans
7% Hispanics
9% Asian Americans
1% international students

AFTER FRESHMAN YEAR

81% returned for sophomore year
70% got a degree within 4 years
71% got a degree within 5 years

WHAT YOU WILL PAY

Comprehensive fee $0

UNITED STATES MERCHANT MARINE ACADEMY

Kings Point, New York • Suburban setting • Public • Federally supported • Coed

The United States Merchant Marine Academy is a 4-year federal service academy dedicated to educating and training young men and women as officers in America's merchant marine and U.S. Naval Reserve and as future leaders of the maritime and transportation industries. The Academy, in Kings Point, Long Island, offers accredited programs in marine transportation and engineering leading to a BS degree, a U.S. merchant marine officer's license, and a Naval Reserve commission. Students spend two 6-month periods at sea aboard U.S. cargo ships as part of their training. There are about 950 men and women at the Academy.

Academics

United States Merchant Marine Academy offers a maritime and intermodal transportation curriculum and core academic program. It awards bachelor's **degrees**. An honors program is a challenging opportunity. Special programs include cooperative education, internships, and study abroad.

The **faculty** at United States Merchant Marine Academy has 74 full-time teachers, 85% with terminal degrees. The student-faculty ratio is 11:1.

Computers on Campus

Students are required to have a computer. Student rooms are linked to a campus network. 1,200 **computers** available in the computer center, independent study labs, classrooms, the library, and dormitories provide access to e-mail, on-line services, and the Internet. Staffed computer lab on campus provides training in the use of computers and software.

The **library** has 232,576 books, 161,576 microform titles, and 985 subscriptions. It is connected to 5 national **on-line** catalogs.

Campus Life

There are 45 active **organizations** on campus, including a drama/theater group and student-run newspaper. 100% of eligible men and 100% of eligible women are members of Ethnic Culture Club. Student **safety services** include 24-hour patrols by trained security personnel.

United States Merchant Marine Academy is a member of the NCAA (Division III). **Intercollegiate sports** include baseball (m), basketball (m), crew (m, w), cross-country running (m, w), football (m), golf (m, w), ice hockey (m), lacrosse (m), riflery (m, w), rugby (m), sailing (m, w), soccer (m), softball (w), swimming and diving (m, w), tennis (m, w), track and field (m, w), volleyball (m, w), water polo (m), wrestling (m).

Applying

United States Merchant Marine Academy requires an essay, a high school transcript, 3 years of high school math, 1 recommendation, SAT I or ACT, and in some cases SAT II Subject Tests. It recommends 3 years of high school science, 2 years of high school foreign language, and a campus interview. 3/1 deadline and continuous processing to 3/15 for financial aid. **Contact:** Capt. James M. Skinner, USMS, Director of Admissions, Wiley Hall, Kings Point, NY 11024, 516-773-5391 or toll-free 800-732-6267 (out-of-state); fax 516-773-5390.

GETTING IN LAST YEAR
758 applied
43% were accepted
82% enrolled (266)
34% from top tenth of their h.s. class
74% had SAT verbal scores over 600 (R)
75% had SAT math scores over 600 (R)
24% had SAT verbal scores over 700 (R)
15% had SAT math scores over 700 (R)

THE STUDENT BODY
950 undergraduates
From 53 states and territories,
  6 other countries
14% from New York
10% women, 90% men
1% African Americans
1% Native Americans
4% Hispanics
4% Asian Americans
4% international students

AFTER FRESHMAN YEAR
90% returned for sophomore year

AFTER GRADUATION
2% pursued further study (1% business, 1% engineering)

WHAT YOU WILL PAY
Comprehensive fee $0

UNITED STATES MILITARY ACADEMY

West Point, New York • Small-town setting • Public • Federally supported • Coed

---

West Point is a challenging test and a personal triumph, rewarding young men and women with a wealth of academic, military leadership, and life experiences. It provides each a foundation for career success as an Army officer, developing leadership skills that are essential in motivating and guiding young soldiers to become the best they can be. West Point is tough and it should be. But it is worth it. One cadet says it best: "The person I have become is so much better than the person who first came here."

Academics

West Point offers a leaders of character for the national defense curriculum and core academic program. It awards bachelor's **degrees**. Challenging opportunities include advanced placement, tutorials, and an honors program. Special programs include summer session for credit, off-campus study, and study abroad.

The most popular **majors** include mechanical engineering, civil engineering, and history. A complete listing of majors at West Point appears in the Majors Index beginning on page 379.

The **faculty** at West Point has 529 full-time teachers, 34% with terminal degrees. 80% of the faculty serve as student advisers. The student-faculty ratio is 8:1, and the average class size in core courses is 15.

Computers on Campus

Students are required to have a computer. PCs are provided. Student rooms are linked to a campus network. 5,500 **computers** available in the computer center, computer labs, the research center, the learning resource center, classrooms, the library, dormitories, and student rooms provide access to the main academic computer, e-mail, on-line services, and the Internet. Staffed computer lab on campus (open 24 hours a day) provides training in the use of computers and software.

The 2 **libraries** have 429,580 books, 1,223 microform titles, and 2,000 subscriptions. They are connected to 2 national **on-line** catalogs.

Campus Life

There are 114 active **organizations** on campus, including a drama/theater group and student-run radio station. Student **safety services** include 24-hour emergency telephone alarm devices and 24-hour patrols by trained security personnel.

West Point is a member of the NCAA (Division I). **Intercollegiate sports** include baseball (m), basketball (m, w), bowling (m, w), crew (m, w), cross-country running (m, w), equestrian sports (m, w), fencing (m, w), football (m), golf (m), gymnastics (m), ice hockey (m), lacrosse (m, w), racquetball (m, w), riflery (m, w), rugby (m), sailing (m, w), skiing (cross-country) (m, w), skiing (downhill) (m, w), soccer (m, w), softball (w), squash (m, w), swimming and diving (m, w), tennis (m, w), track and field (m, w), volleyball (m, w), water polo (m), weight lifting (m, w), wrestling (m).

Applying

West Point requires an essay, a high school transcript, 4 recommendations, authorized nomination, medical and physical aptitude exams, proof of age (between 17 and 21 at matriculation), proof of U.S. citizenship (except students nominated by agreement between U.S. and another country), unmarried, not pregnant, no legal obligation to support a child, and SAT I or ACT. It recommends 4 years of high school math, 3 years of high school science, 2 years of high school foreign language, and an interview. Early action is possible, with a 3/21 deadline. **Contact:** Col. Michael C. Jones, Director of Admissions, 606 Thayer Road, West Point, NY 10996, 914-938-4041; fax 914-938-3021.

GETTING IN LAST YEAR
12,429 applied
13% were accepted
73% enrolled (1,187)
60% from top tenth of their h.s. class
30% had SAT verbal scores over 600
84% had SAT math scores over 600
78% had ACT scores over 26
3% had SAT verbal scores over 700
24% had SAT math scores over 700
34% had ACT scores over 30
223 National Merit Scholars

202 class presidents
82 valedictorians

THE STUDENT BODY
4,091 undergraduates
From 52 states and territories,
   20 other countries
8% from New York
12% women, 88% men
7% African Americans
1% Native Americans
4% Hispanics

5% Asian Americans
1% international students

AFTER FRESHMAN YEAR
92% returned for sophomore year
75% got a degree within 4 years
80% got a degree within 5 years

AFTER GRADUATION
2% pursued further study (2% medicine)
1 Rhodes, 1 Marshall scholar

WHAT YOU WILL PAY
Comprehensive fee $0

UNITED STATES NAVAL ACADEMY

Annapolis, Maryland • Small-town setting • Public • Federally supported • Coed

---

 Academics

Naval Academy offers a leadership-intensive curriculum and core academic program. It awards bachelor's **degrees**. Challenging opportunities include advanced placement, tutorials, an honors program, and Sigma Xi. Special programs include summer session for credit and study abroad.

The most popular **majors** include political science/government, aerospace engineering, and oceanography. A complete listing of majors at Naval Academy appears in the Majors Index beginning on page 379.

The **faculty** at Naval Academy has 650 full-time teachers.

 Computers on Campus

Students are required to have a computer. PCs are provided. Student rooms are linked to a campus network. 6,100 **computers** available in the computer center, the library, and dormitories provide access to the main academic computer, off-campus computing facilities, e-mail, and on-line services. Staffed computer lab on campus provides training in the use of computers and software.

The **library** has 750,000 books and 2,100 subscriptions.

 Campus Life

Active **organizations** on campus include drama/theater group and student-run radio station. Student **safety services** include front gate security, 24-hour emergency telephone alarm devices, 24-hour patrols by trained security personnel, and student patrols.

Naval Academy is a member of the NCAA (Division I). **Intercollegiate sports** include baseball (m), basketball (m, w), crew (m, w), cross-country running (m, w), football (m), golf (m), gymnastics (m), ice hockey (m), lacrosse (m, w), riflery (m, w), rugby (m, w), sailing (m, w), skiing (downhill) (m, w), soccer (m, w), softball (w), squash (m), swimming and diving (m, w), tennis (m), track and field (m, w), volleyball (m, w), water polo (m), wrestling (m).

 Applying

Naval Academy requires an essay, a high school transcript, 2 recommendations, authorized nomination, SAT I or ACT, and a minimum high school GPA of 2.0. It recommends 4 years of high school math and science, 2 years of high school foreign language, and an interview. 3/20 deadline. **Contact:** Capt. John W. Renard, Retd., Dean of Admissions, 117 Decatur Road, Annapolis, MD 21402-5000, 410-293-4336 or toll-free 800-638-9156; fax 410-293-4348.

GETTING IN LAST YEAR
10,422 applied
14% were accepted
79% enrolled (1,165)
61% from top tenth of their h.s. class
38% had SAT verbal scores over 600
84% had SAT math scores over 600
4% had SAT verbal scores over 700
31% had SAT math scores over 700

THE STUDENT BODY
4,080 undergraduates
From 54 states and territories, 20 other countries
2% from Maryland
14% women, 86% men
7% African Americans
1% Native Americans
6% Hispanics
4% Asian Americans
1% international students

AFTER FRESHMAN YEAR
86% returned for sophomore year
100% got a degree within 4 years

AFTER GRADUATION
1% pursued further study (1% medicine)
100% had job offers within 6 months
2 Marshall scholars

WHAT YOU WILL PAY
Comprehensive fee $0

UNIVERSITY AT ALBANY, STATE UNIVERSITY OF NEW YORK

Albany, New York • Suburban setting • Public • State-supported • Coed

Founded in 1848, the University at Albany is the flagship campus of the State University of New York. Located in the capital of New York State, the University is respected for its diversified curriculum, its commitment to undergraduate scholarship, and the ability of its faculty and staff to personalize the educational process. The University offers more than 75 majors in humanities, fine arts, social and behavioral sciences, science, mathematics, the School of Business, the Rockefeller College of Public Affairs, and the School of Social Welfare. The University is the home of the New York State Writers Institute.

Academics

University at Albany offers a general education curriculum and core academic program; fewer than half of graduate courses are open to undergraduates. It awards bachelor's, master's, and doctoral **degrees**. Challenging opportunities include advanced placement, self-designed majors, tutorials, Freshman Honors College, an honors program, a senior project, Phi Beta Kappa, and Sigma Xi. Special programs include internships, summer session for credit, off-campus study, study abroad, and Army, Naval, and Air Force ROTC.

The most popular **majors** include English, psychology, and business. A complete listing of majors at University at Albany appears in the Majors Index beginning on page 379.

The **faculty** at University at Albany has 694 full-time graduate and undergraduate teachers, 96% with terminal degrees. The student-faculty ratio is 16:1.

Computers on Campus

Students are not required to have a computer. Student rooms are linked to a campus network. 500 **computers** available in the computer center, computer labs, the research center, the learning resource center, special user rooms, classrooms, the library, and dormitories provide access to the main academic computer, off-campus computing facilities, e-mail, on-line services, and the Internet. Staffed computer lab on campus (open 24 hours a day) provides training in the use of computers and software.

The **library** has 1.8 million books, 2.7 million microform titles, and 5,500 subscriptions.

Campus Life

There are 160 active **organizations** on campus, including a drama/theater group and student-run newspaper and radio station. 20% of eligible men and 15% of eligible women are members of 15 national **fraternities**, 5 national **sororities**, 5 local fraternities, and 6 local sororities. Student **safety services** include late night transport/escort service, 24-hour emergency telephone alarm devices, 24-hour patrols by trained security personnel, and electronically operated dormitory entrances.

University at Albany is a member of the NCAA (Division II). **Intercollegiate sports** include baseball (m), basketball (m, w), crew (m, w), cross-country running (m, w), football (m), lacrosse (m, w), rugby (m, w), soccer (m, w), tennis (w), track and field (m, w), volleyball (w).

Applying

University at Albany requires a high school transcript, SAT I or ACT, and in some cases 3 years of high school math and science portfolio, and an audition. It recommends an essay, 3 years of high school math and science, and some high school foreign language. Early, deferred, and midyear entrance are possible, with rolling admissions and continuous processing to 3/15 for financial aid. **Contact:** Dr. Michelleen Treadwell, Director of Admissions, 1400 Washington Avenue, Albany, NY 12222-0001, 518-442-5435.

GETTING IN LAST YEAR
14,967 applied
62% were accepted
20% enrolled (1,900)
14% from top tenth of their h.s. class
11% had SAT verbal scores over 600
44% had SAT math scores over 600
1% had SAT verbal scores over 700
7% had SAT math scores over 700

THE STUDENT BODY
Total 14,412, of whom 10,197
 are undergraduates

From 23 states and territories,
 29 other countries
97% from New York
48% women, 52% men
9% African Americans
1% Native Americans
7% Hispanics
9% Asian Americans
1% international students

AFTER FRESHMAN YEAR
90% returned for sophomore year
60% got a degree within 4 years

69% got a degree within 5 years
71% got a degree within 6 years

AFTER GRADUATION
45% pursued further study

WHAT YOU WILL PAY
Resident tuition and fees $3956
Nonresident tuition and fees $8856
Room and board $4836
Need-based college-administered scholarships and
 grants average $1550 per award
Non-need college-administered scholarships and
 grants average $2000 per award

THE UNIVERSITY OF ALABAMA IN HUNTSVILLE

Huntsville, Alabama • Urban setting • Public • State-supported • Coed

Huntsville, one of America's fastest growing small cities, a nationally known center for research and development, and a highly desirable place to live, creates unique opportunities for students and graduates to help support themselves through interesting part-time employment. Some take traditional jobs on campus or in the community, others work on innovative and creative research grants and contracts, while others take advantage of the University's excellent co-op program with local business, industry, and government. Students are encouraged to consider the special advantages that UAH and Huntsville have to offer.

Academics

UAH offers an interdisciplinary curriculum and core academic program; fewer than half of graduate courses are open to undergraduates. It awards bachelor's, master's, and doctoral **degrees**. Challenging opportunities include advanced placement, an honors program, a senior project, and Sigma Xi. Special programs include cooperative education, internships, summer session for credit, off-campus study, and Army and Air Force ROTC.

The most popular **majors** include nursing, electrical engineering, and mechanical engineering. A complete listing of majors at UAH appears in the Majors Index beginning on page 379.

The **faculty** at UAH has 283 full-time graduate and undergraduate teachers, 88% with terminal degrees. The student-faculty ratio is 10:1.

Computers on Campus

Students are not required to have a computer. Student rooms are linked to a campus network. 250 **computers** available in the computer center, computer labs, the library, and the student center provide access to the main academic computer, off-campus computing facilities, e-mail, and on-line services. Staffed computer lab on campus provides training in the use of computers and software.

The **library** has 426,344 books, 413,909 microform titles, and 3,105 subscriptions. It is connected to 5 national **on-line** catalogs.

Campus Life

There are 50 active **organizations** on campus, including a drama/theater group and student-run newspaper. 10% of eligible men and 12% of eligible women are members of 5 national **fraternities**, 5 national **sororities**, and social clubs. Student **safety services** include late night transport/ escort service, 24-hour emergency telephone alarm devices, 24-hour patrols by trained security personnel, and electronically operated dormitory entrances.

UAH is a member of the NCAA (Division II). **Intercollegiate sports** (some offering scholarships) include basketball (m, w), cross-country running (m, w), ice hockey (m), soccer (m), softball (w), tennis (m, w), volleyball (w).

Applying

UAH requires a high school transcript, SAT I or ACT, and in some cases a campus interview. It recommends 3 years of high school math and science and some high school foreign language. Early, deferred, and midyear entrance are possible, with an 8/15 deadline and continuous processing to 4/1 for financial aid. **Contact:** Ms. Sabrina Williams, Assistant Registrar/Admissions, University Center 119, Huntsville, AL 35899, 205-895-6070 or toll-free 800-UAH-CALL (in-state); fax 205-895-6754.

GETTING IN LAST YEAR
1,495 applied
74% were accepted
51% enrolled (561)
32% from top tenth of their h.s. class
3.28 average high school GPA
28% had SAT verbal scores over 600 (R)
34% had SAT math scores over 600 (R)
25% had ACT scores over 26
6% had SAT verbal scores over 700 (R)
6% had SAT math scores over 700 (R)
6% had ACT scores over 30
9 National Merit Scholars

THE STUDENT BODY
Total 7,264, of whom 5,533 are undergraduates

From 50 states and territories,
20 other countries
83% from Alabama
49% women, 51% men
11% African Americans
1% Native Americans
2% Hispanics
3% Asian Americans
4% international students

AFTER FRESHMAN YEAR
71% returned for sophomore year
23% got a degree within 5 years
39% got a degree within 6 years

AFTER GRADUATION
201 organizations recruited on campus
3 Fulbright scholars

WHAT YOU WILL PAY
Resident tuition and fees $2620
Nonresident tuition and fees $5240
Room and board $3370
27% receive need-based financial aid
Need-based college-administered scholarships and grants average $1000 per award
11% receive non-need financial aid
Non-need college-administered scholarships and grants average $1800 per award

UNIVERSITY OF ARIZONA

Tucson, Arizona • Urban setting • Public • State-supported • Coed

Surrounded by mountains and the dramatic beauty of the Sonoran desert, the University of Arizona offers a top-drawer education in a resort-like setting. Some of the nation's highest-ranked departments make their homes here. Tucson's clear skies provide an ideal setting for one of the country's best astronomy programs. Anthropology, nursing, management information systems, and creative writing are also nationally ranked. The University balances a strong research component with an emphasis on teaching—faculty rolls include Nobel- and Pulitzer-prize holders.

Academics

UA offers a core academic program; fewer than half of graduate courses are open to undergraduates. It awards bachelor's, master's, doctoral, and first professional **degrees**. Challenging opportunities include advanced placement, self-designed majors, tutorials, Freshman Honors College, an honors program, a senior project, Phi Beta Kappa, and Sigma Xi. Special programs include cooperative education, internships, summer session for credit, study abroad, and Army, Naval, and Air Force ROTC.

The most popular **majors** include psychology, political science/government, and accounting. A complete listing of majors at UA appears in the Majors Index beginning on page 379.

The **faculty** at UA has 1,469 full-time undergraduate teachers, 97% with terminal degrees. The student-faculty ratio is 19:1.

Computers on Campus

Students are not required to have a computer. Student rooms are linked to a campus network. **Computers** avail-able in the computer center, computer labs, the research center, the learning resource center, classrooms, the library, dormitories, and student rooms provide access to the Internet. Staffed computer lab on campus provides training in the use of computers and software.

The 6 **libraries** have 4 million books, 4.7 million microform titles, and 26,150 subscriptions.

Campus Life

Active **organizations** on campus include drama/theater group and student-run newspaper and radio station. 15% of eligible men and 15% of eligible women are members of 21 national **fraternities**, 14 national **sororities**, 1 local fraternity, and 2 local sororities. Student **safety services** include late night transport/escort service and 24-hour patrols by trained security personnel.

UA is a member of the NCAA (Division I). **Intercollegiate sports** (some offering scholarships) include baseball (m), basketball (m, w), cross-country running (m, w), football (m), golf (m, w), gymnastics (w), ice hockey (m), lacrosse (m), rugby (m), soccer (m, w), softball (w), swimming and diving (m, w), tennis (m, w), track and field (m, w), volleyball (m, w).

Applying

UA requires a high school transcript, 3 years of high school math, SAT I or ACT, and in some cases 3 years of high school science, recommendations, an interview, and a minimum high school GPA of 3.0. It recommends 3 years of high school science and some high school foreign language. Early, deferred, and midyear entrance are possible, with a 3/1 deadline and continuous processing to 3/1 for financial aid. **Contact:** Ms. Lori Goldman, Interim Director of Admissions, Nugent Building, Tucson, AZ 85721, 520-621-3237; fax 520-621-9799.

GETTING IN LAST YEAR
16,308 applied
84% were accepted
33% enrolled (4,557)
30% from top tenth of their h.s. class
3.27 average high school GPA
31% had SAT verbal scores over 600 (R)
34% had SAT math scores over 600 (R)
28% had ACT scores over 26
5% had SAT verbal scores over 700 (R)
4% had SAT math scores over 700 (R)
8% had ACT scores over 30
64 National Merit Scholars

THE STUDENT BODY
Total 34,777, of whom 26,153
  are undergraduates

From 52 states and territories,
  79 other countries
72% from Arizona
51% women, 49% men
3% African Americans
2% Native Americans
14% Hispanics
5% Asian Americans
3% international students

AFTER FRESHMAN YEAR
77% returned for sophomore year
19% got a degree within 4 years

43% got a degree within 5 years
50% got a degree within 6 years

WHAT YOU WILL PAY
Resident tuition and fees $1950
Nonresident tuition and fees $7978
Room and board $4190
50% receive need-based financial aid
Need-based college-administered scholarships and
  grants average $1515 per award
16% receive non-need financial aid
Non-need college-administered scholarships and
  grants average $2476 per award

UNIVERSITY OF CALIFORNIA, BERKELEY

Berkeley, California • Urban setting • Public • State-supported • Coed

Berkeley is widely recognized as one of the best universities in the world. Its rich culture and ethnic diversity help to produce the wide range of opinion and perspective essential to a great university. *U.S. News & World Report* recently ranked Cal the best public university in the nation. A seminar program ensures that freshmen can take small classes taught by distinguished scholars. Undergraduates also undertake research, publishing the results in *Cal Science*. More students who earn bachelor's degrees at Berkeley complete PhDs than graduates of any other university in the country.

Academics

Cal offers a core academic program. It awards bachelor's, master's, doctoral, and first professional **degrees**. Challenging opportunities include advanced placement, accelerated degree programs, self-designed majors, tutorials, an honors program, Phi Beta Kappa, and Sigma Xi. Special programs include cooperative education, internships, summer session for credit, off-campus study, study abroad, and Army, Naval, and Air Force ROTC.

The most popular **majors** include English, molecular biology, and political science/government. A complete listing of majors at Cal appears in the Majors Index beginning on page 379.

The **faculty** at Cal has 1,787 graduate and undergraduate teachers, 95% with terminal degrees. The student-faculty ratio is 16:1.

Computers on Campus

Students are not required to have a computer. Student rooms are linked to a campus network. **Computers** available in the computer center, computer labs, the learning resource center, academic departments, classrooms, the library, the student center, dormitories, and student rooms provide access to the main academic computer, e-mail, on-line services, and the Internet. Staffed computer lab on campus provides training in the use of computers and software.

The **library** has 8 million books and 89,750 subscriptions.

Campus Life

There are 350 active **organizations** on campus, including a drama/theater group and student-run newspaper and radio station. 14% of eligible men and 13% of eligible women are members of 41 national **fraternities** and 15 national **sororities**. Student **safety services** include Office of Emergency Preparedness, late night transport/escort service, 24-hour emergency telephone alarm devices, 24-hour patrols by trained security personnel, and electronically operated dormitory entrances.

Cal is a member of the NCAA (Division I). **Intercollegiate sports** (some offering scholarships) include baseball (m), basketball (m, w), crew (m, w), cross-country running (m, w), field hockey (w), football (m), golf (m, w), gymnastics (m, w), rugby (m), skiing (downhill) (m, w), soccer (m, w), softball (w), squash (m, w), swimming and diving (m, w), tennis (m, w), track and field (m, w), volleyball (m, w), water polo (m).

Applying

Cal requires an essay, a high school transcript, 3 years of high school math, 2 years of high school foreign language, minimum 3.3 high school GPA, minimum 2.4 college GPA for transfer students, SAT I or ACT, and 3 SAT II Subject Tests (including SAT II: Writing Test). It recommends 4 years of high school math, 3 years of high school science, and 3 years of high school foreign language. Early entrance is possible, with an 11/30 deadline and continuous processing to 3/2 for financial aid. **Contact:** Office of Undergraduate Admission, 110 Sproul Hall, # 5800, Berkeley, CA 94720, 510-642-3175; fax 510-642-7333.

GETTING IN LAST YEAR
22,811 applied
39% were accepted
39% enrolled (3,405)
96% from top tenth of their h.s. class
3.84 average high school GPA
40% had SAT verbal scores over 600
78% had SAT math scores over 600
8% had SAT verbal scores over 700
44% had SAT math scores over 700

THE STUDENT BODY
Total 29,630, of whom 21,176
  are undergraduates

From 53 states and territories,
  100 other countries
88% from California
48% women, 52% men
6% African Americans
1% Native Americans
14% Hispanics
39% Asian Americans
4% international students

AFTER FRESHMAN YEAR
94% returned for sophomore year
73% got a degree within 5 years
80% got a degree within 6 years

WHAT YOU WILL PAY
Resident tuition and fees $4354
Nonresident tuition and fees $12,053
Room and board $6466
51% receive need-based financial aid

UNIVERSITY OF CALIFORNIA, DAVIS

Davis, California • Suburban setting • Public • State-supported • Coed

 ## Academics

UC Davis offers an interdisciplinary education curriculum based on specialization in the major and core academic program; fewer than half of graduate courses are open to undergraduates. It awards bachelor's, master's, doctoral, and first professional **degrees**. Challenging opportunities include advanced placement, self-designed majors, tutorials, Freshman Honors College, an honors program, a senior project, Phi Beta Kappa, and Sigma Xi. Special programs include internships, summer session for credit, study abroad, and Army and Air Force ROTC.

The most popular **majors** include psychology and biology/biological sciences. A complete listing of majors at UC Davis appears in the Majors Index beginning on page 379.

The **faculty** at UC Davis has 1,293 full-time graduate and undergraduate teachers, 99% with terminal degrees. The student-faculty ratio is 19:1.

 ## Computers on Campus

Students are not required to have a computer. 600 **computers** available in the computer center, computer labs, various locations on campus, classrooms, the library, and dormitories provide access to the main academic computer, off-campus computing facilities, e-mail, on-line services, the Internet, and specialized software packages. Staffed computer lab on campus.

The 6 **libraries** have 2.8 million books, 3.5 million microform titles, and 47,133 subscriptions. They are connected to 5 national **on-line** catalogs.

 ## Campus Life

There are 316 active **organizations** on campus, including a drama/theater group and student-run newspaper and radio station. 10% of students participate in student government elections. 10% of eligible men and 9% of eligible women are members of 21 national **fraternities**, 14 national **sororities**, and 3 state fraternities and 4 state sororities. Student **safety services** include rape prevention programs, late night transport/escort service, 24-hour emergency telephone alarm devices, 24-hour patrols by trained security personnel, student patrols, and electronically operated dormitory entrances.

UC Davis is a member of the NCAA (Division II). **Intercollegiate sports** include baseball (m), basketball (m, w), cross-country running (m, w), football (m), golf (m), gymnastics (w), soccer (m, w), softball (w), swimming and diving (m, w), tennis (m, w), track and field (m, w), volleyball (w), water polo (m), wrestling (m).

 ## Applying

UC Davis requires an essay, a high school transcript, 3 years of high school math, 2 years of high school foreign language, SAT I or ACT, and 3 SAT II Subject Tests (including SAT II: Writing Test). It recommends 4 years of high school math, 3 years of high school science, and 3 years of high school foreign language. Deferred and midyear entrance are possible, with an 11/30 deadline and continuous processing to 3/2 for financial aid. **Contact:** Dr. Gary Tudor, Director of Undergraduate Admissions, Davis, CA 95616, 916-752-2971.

GETTING IN LAST YEAR
17,722 applied
71% were accepted
26% enrolled (3,287)
3.70 average high school GPA
39% had SAT verbal scores over 600
50% had SAT math scores over 600
31% had ACT scores over 26
6% had SAT verbal scores over 700
7% had SAT math scores over 700
7% had ACT scores over 30
25 National Merit Scholars

THE STUDENT BODY
Total 23,092, of whom 18,001
   are undergraduates
From 46 states and territories,
   100 other countries
96% from California
52% women, 48% men
4% African Americans
1% Native Americans
11% Hispanics
31% Asian Americans
2% international students

AFTER FRESHMAN YEAR
90% returned for sophomore year
42% got a degree within 4 years
69% got a degree within 5 years
71% got a degree within 6 years

WHAT YOU WILL PAY
Resident tuition and fees $4174
Nonresident tuition and fees $11,873
Room and board $5520
46% receive need-based financial aid
Need-based college-administered scholarships and
   grants average $2069 per award
16% receive non-need financial aid
Non-need college-administered scholarships and
   grants average $2887 per award

UNIVERSITY OF CALIFORNIA, LOS ANGELES

Los Angeles, California • Urban setting • Public • State-supported • Coed

 Academics

UCLA offers a core academic program. It awards bachelor's, master's, doctoral, and first professional **degrees**. Challenging opportunities include advanced placement, self-designed majors, an honors program, Phi Beta Kappa, and Sigma Xi. Special programs include internships, summer session for credit, off-campus study, study abroad, and Army, Naval, and Air Force ROTC.

The most popular **majors** include biology/biological sciences, psychology, and economics. A complete listing of majors at UCLA appears in the Majors Index beginning on page 379.

The **faculty** at UCLA has 3,275 graduate and undergraduate teachers. The student-faculty ratio is 17:1.

 Computers on Campus

Students are not required to have a computer. **Computers** available in the computer center, the library, the student center, and dormitories. Staffed computer lab on campus.

The 15 **libraries** have 6.6 million books, 5.8 million microform titles, and 96,121 subscriptions.

 Campus Life

Active **organizations** on campus include drama/theater group and student-run newspaper and radio station. 12% of eligible men and 10% of eligible women are members of 29 national **fraternities**, 16 national **sororities**, 4 local fraternities, and 2 local sororities. Student **safety services** include late night transport/escort service, 24-hour emergency telephone alarm devices, and student patrols.

UCLA is a member of the NCAA (Division I). **Intercollegiate sports** (some offering scholarships) include baseball (m), basketball (m, w), cross-country running (m, w), football (m), golf (m, w), gymnastics (w), soccer (m, w), softball (w), swimming and diving (w), tennis (m, w), track and field (m, w), volleyball (m, w), water polo (m, w).

 Applying

UCLA requires an essay, a high school transcript, 3 years of high school math and science, 2 years of high school foreign language, SAT I or ACT, and 3 SAT II Subject Tests. Early entrance is possible, with an 11/30 deadline and continuous processing to 3/2 for financial aid. **Contact:** Dr. Rae Lee Siporin, Director of Undergraduate Admissions, 405 Hilgard Avenue, Los Angeles, CA 90095, 310-825-3101.

GETTING IN LAST YEAR

25,464 applied
42% were accepted
33% enrolled (3,576)
3.92 average high school GPA
20% had SAT verbal scores over 600 (R)
63% had SAT math scores over 600 (R)
1% had SAT verbal scores over 700 (R)
21% had SAT math scores over 700 (R)
73 National Merit Scholars

THE STUDENT BODY

Total 34,713, of whom 23,769
 are undergraduates
From 50 states and territories,
 100 other countries
95% from California
51% women, 49% men
6% African Americans
1% Native Americans
18% Hispanics
35% Asian Americans
3% international students

AFTER FRESHMAN YEAR

94% returned for sophomore year
71% got a degree within 5 years
77% got a degree within 6 years

WHAT YOU WILL PAY

Resident tuition and fees $3894
Nonresident tuition and fees $11,593
Room and board $5755
Need-based college-administered scholarships and
 grants average $1787 per award
Non-need college-administered scholarships and
 grants average $1500 per award

UNIVERSITY OF CALIFORNIA, RIVERSIDE

Riverside, California • Suburban setting • Public • State-supported • Coed

University of California, Riverside, is one of the 8 general campuses of the University of California, the finest public university in the world. It is a major research institution of 8,900 students with a strong commitment to undergraduate education. Ninety-eight percent of the faculty hold doctorates, classes are small, and freshmen complete their bachelor's degrees in an average of 4.1 years. Extensive undergraduate research and academic internship opportunities exist and placement rates to law, medical, business, and Ph.D. programs are excellent. Ample on-campus housing and financial aid are available and support services and campus life activities are extensive.

Academics

UCR offers an interdisciplinary curriculum and core academic program; more than half of graduate courses are open to undergraduates. It awards bachelor's, master's, and doctoral **degrees**. Challenging opportunities include advanced placement, accelerated degree programs, self-designed majors, tutorials, Freshman Honors College, an honors program, a senior project, Phi Beta Kappa, and Sigma Xi. Special programs include cooperative education, internships, summer session for credit, study abroad, and Army and Air Force ROTC.

The most popular **majors** include business, biology/biological sciences, and psychology. A complete listing of majors at UCR appears in the Majors Index beginning on page 379.

The **faculty** at UCR has 537 full-time graduate and undergraduate teachers, 98% with terminal degrees. 50% of the faculty serve as student advisers. The student-faculty ratio is 16:1.

Computers on Campus

Students are not required to have a computer. 190 **computers** available in the computer center, computer labs, vari-

ous locations on campus, the library, the student center, and dormitories provide access to the main academic computer, off-campus computing facilities, e-mail, on-line services, and the Internet. Staffed computer lab on campus provides training in the use of computers and software.

The 5 **libraries** have 1.7 million books, 1.4 million microform titles, and 13,296 subscriptions. They are connected to 6 national **on-line** catalogs.

Campus Life

There are 180 active **organizations** on campus, including a drama/theater group and student-run newspaper and radio station. 12% of eligible men and 13% of eligible women are members of 11 national **fraternities**, 9 national **sororities**, 3 local fraternities, 3 local sororities, and 2 coed fraternities. Student **safety services** include late night transport/escort service, 24-hour emergency telephone alarm devices, 24-hour patrols by trained security personnel, student patrols, and electronically operated dormitory entrances.

UCR is a member of the NCAA (Division II). **Intercollegiate sports** (some offering scholarships) include baseball (m), basketball (m, w), cross-country running (m, w), softball (w), tennis (m, w), track and field (m, w), volleyball (w).

Applying

UCR requires an essay, a high school transcript, 3 years of high school math, 2 years of high school foreign language, SAT I or ACT, 3 SAT II Subject Tests (including SAT II: Writing Test), and a minimum high school GPA of 2.0. It recommends 3 years of high school science. Early and midyear entrance are possible, with an 11/30 deadline and continuous processing to 3/2 for financial aid. **Contact:** Ms. Laurie Nelson, Associate Admissions Officer, 900 University Avenue, Riverside, CA 92521-0102, 909-787-3411.

GETTING IN LAST YEAR
9,885 applied
78% were accepted
21% enrolled (1,596)
70% from top tenth of their h.s. class
3.63 average high school GPA
10% had SAT verbal scores over 600
33% had SAT math scores over 600
20% had ACT scores over 26
2% had SAT verbal scores over 700
9% had SAT math scores over 700
4% had ACT scores over 30

THE STUDENT BODY
Total 8,906, of whom 7,433
    are undergraduates
From 21 states and territories,
    11 other countries
97% from California
53% women, 47% men
5% African Americans
1% Native Americans
19% Hispanics
39% Asian Americans
1% international students

AFTER FRESHMAN YEAR
86% returned for sophomore year
47% got a degree within 4 years
64% got a degree within 5 years
67% got a degree within 6 years

AFTER GRADUATION
38% pursued further study
54% had job offers within 6 months
92 organizations recruited on campus
1 Fulbright scholar

WHAT YOU WILL PAY
Resident tuition and fees $4093
Nonresident tuition and fees $11,792
Room and board $5430
57% receive need-based financial aid

UNIVERSITY OF CALIFORNIA, SAN DIEGO

La Jolla, California • Suburban setting • Public • State-supported • Coed

The 5 colleges that comprise UCSD—Revelle, John Muir, Thurgood Marshall, Earl Warren, and Eleanor Roosevelt—are modeled on the Cambridge and Oxford systems found in Great Britain. This idea provides for a small college setting within the context of a large university. Each college has its own educational philosophy and traditions, its own set of general education (GE) requirements, and its own academic and student affairs staffs. When applying to UCSD, students select a college that best matches their personal interests and career goals to the way they prefer to learn. It is important to note that students may pursue any UCSD major through any of the 5 colleges.

 ## Academics

UCSD offers a core academic program. It awards bachelor's, master's, and doctoral **degrees**. Challenging opportunities include advanced placement, accelerated degree programs, self-designed majors, Freshman Honors College, an honors program, a senior project, and Phi Beta Kappa. Special programs include internships, summer session for credit, off-campus study, and study abroad.

The most popular **majors** include biology/biological sciences, psychology, and political science/government. A complete listing of majors at UCSD appears in the Majors Index beginning on page 379.

The **faculty** at UCSD has 1,139 full-time graduate and undergraduate teachers, 95% with terminal degrees. The student-faculty ratio is 19:1.

 ## Computers on Campus

Students are not required to have a computer. Student rooms are linked to a campus network. 700 **computers**

available in the computer center, each academic college, the library, and the student center provide access to the main academic computer, off-campus computing facilities, e-mail, on-line services, and the Internet. Staffed computer lab on campus (open 24 hours a day) provides training in the use of computers and software.

The 7 **libraries** have 2.2 million books, 2 million microform titles, and 24,414 subscriptions.

 ## Campus Life

Active **organizations** on campus include drama/theater group and student-run newspaper and radio station. 10% of eligible men and 10% of eligible women are members of 14 national **fraternities** and 8 national **sororities**. Student **safety services** include crime prevention programs and late night transport/escort service.

UCSD is a member of the NCAA (Division III). **Intercollegiate sports** include baseball (m), basketball (m, w), crew (m, w), cross-country running (m, w), fencing (m, w), golf (m, w), soccer (m, w), softball (w), swimming and diving (m, w), tennis (m, w), track and field (m, w), volleyball (m, w), water polo (m, w).

 ## Applying

UCSD requires an essay, a high school transcript, 3 years of high school math, 2 years of high school foreign language, SAT I or ACT, and 3 SAT II Subject Tests (including SAT II: Writing Test). It recommends 3 years of high school science. Early entrance is possible, with an 11/30 deadline and continuous processing to 5/1 for financial aid. **Contact:** Mr. Tim Johnston, Acting Director of Student Outreach and Recruitment, 9500 Gilman Drive, La Jolla, CA 92093-5003, 619-534-4831.

GETTING IN LAST YEAR
25,769 applied
45% were accepted
26% enrolled (2,998)
95% from top tenth of their h.s. class
3.8 average high school GPA
17% had SAT verbal scores over 600
62% had SAT math scores over 600
2% had SAT verbal scores over 700
16% had SAT math scores over 700

THE STUDENT BODY
Total 18,324, of whom 14,846
   are undergraduates

96% from California
49% women, 51% men
3% African Americans
1% Native Americans
12% Hispanics
34% Asian Americans
1% international students

AFTER FRESHMAN YEAR
71% returned for sophomore year
62% got a degree within 4 years
92% got a degree within 5 years

AFTER GRADUATION
35% pursued further study
7 Fulbright scholars

WHAT YOU WILL PAY
Resident tuition and fees $4198
Nonresident tuition and fees $11,897
Room and board $6627
42% receive need-based financial aid
Need-based college-administered scholarships and
   grants average $4224 per award
Non-need college-administered scholarships and
   grants average $895 per award

UNIVERSITY OF CALIFORNIA, SANTA BARBARA

Santa Barbara, California • Suburban setting • Public • State-supported • Coed

The University of California, Santa Barbara, is one of the few residential public university campuses in the state, which gives its students the opportunity to learn from renowned scholars in a setting that fosters personal interaction. Just 50 years old, UC Santa Barbara has become one of the top 50 research campuses in the country, having gained prominence in fields ranging from physics and engineering to religious studies and music. When a new professional School of Environmental Science and Management admitted its first students in fall 1994, the University began to play a pivotal role in training the environmental problem-solvers of the future.

 Academics

UCSB offers a core academic program. It awards bachelor's, master's, and doctoral **degrees**. Challenging opportunities include advanced placement, accelerated degree programs, self-designed majors, Freshman Honors College, an honors program, a senior project, Phi Beta Kappa, and Sigma Xi. Special programs include cooperative education, internships, summer session for credit, study abroad, and Army ROTC.

The most popular **majors** include business economics, political science/government, and sociology. A complete listing of majors at UCSB appears in the Majors Index beginning on page 379.

The **faculty** at UCSB has 684 full-time graduate and undergraduate teachers, 100% with terminal degrees. The student-faculty ratio is 19:1.

 Computers on Campus

Students are not required to have a computer. 2,000 **computers** available in the computer center, computer labs, departmental labs, the library, the student center, and dormitories provide access to e-mail, on-line services, and the Internet. Staffed computer lab on campus provides training in the use of computers and software.

The **library** has 2.2 million books and 24,325 subscriptions.

 Campus Life

There are 250 active **organizations** on campus, including a drama/theater group and student-run newspaper and radio station. 15% of eligible men and 16% of eligible women are members of 18 national **fraternities**, 14 national **sororities**, 3 local fraternities, and 4 local sororities. Student **safety services** include late night transport/escort service and 24-hour emergency telephone alarm devices.

UCSB is a member of the NCAA (Division I). **Intercollegiate sports** (some offering scholarships) include baseball (m), basketball (m, w), bowling (m, w), crew (m, w), cross-country running (m, w), fencing (m, w), golf (m, w), gymnastics (m, w), lacrosse (m, w), rugby (m), sailing (m, w), skiing (downhill) (m, w), soccer (m, w), softball (w), swimming and diving (m, w), tennis (m, w), track and field (m, w), volleyball (m, w), water polo (m, w).

 Applying

UCSB requires an essay, a high school transcript, 3 years of high school math, 2 years of high school foreign language, 4 years of high school English, 1 year of high school U.S. history, SAT I or ACT, 3 SAT II Subject Tests (including SAT II: Writing Test), and in some cases an interview. It recommends 3 years of high school science. Early and midyear entrance are possible, with an 11/30 deadline and continuous processing to 3/2 for financial aid. **Contact:** Mr. William Villa, Director of Admissions/Relations with Schools, 1234 Cheadle Hall, Santa Barbara, CA 93106, 805-893-2485.

GETTING IN LAST YEAR
18,291 applied
81% were accepted
23% enrolled (3,361)
3.5 average high school GPA
29% had SAT verbal scores over 600 (R)
39% had SAT math scores over 600 (R)
23% had ACT scores over 26
4% had SAT verbal scores over 700 (R)
5% had SAT math scores over 700 (R)
6% had ACT scores over 30

THE STUDENT BODY
Total 18,224, of whom 15,934
are undergraduates

From 49 states and territories,
50 other countries
95% from California
53% women, 47% men
3% African Americans
1% Native Americans
12% Hispanics
17% Asian Americans
1% international students

AFTER FRESHMAN YEAR
84% returned for sophomore year
39% got a degree within 4 years
65% got a degree within 5 years
70% got a degree within 6 years

AFTER GRADUATION
22% pursued further study
56% had job offers within 6 months
5 Fulbright scholars

WHAT YOU WILL PAY
Resident tuition and fees $4098
Nonresident tuition and fees $11,797
Room and board $5990
Need-based college-administered scholarships and
grants average $2974 per award
Non-need college-administered scholarships and
grants average $3528 per award

UNIVERSITY OF CALIFORNIA, SANTA CRUZ

Santa Cruz, California • Small-town setting • Public • State-supported • Coed

Since 1965, the University of California, Santa Cruz, has grown, one college at a time, to almost 10,000 students. Ninety percent are undergraduates pursuing majors in humanities, natural sciences, social sciences, and arts. Graduate students earn education credentials, graduate certificates, and degrees in 22 fields. Thirteen of the faculty are members of the National Academy of Sciences and 19 belong to the American Academy of Arts and Sciences. UCSC students win National Science Foundation Fellowships, Fullbrights, and other awards in numbers far exceeding expectations for a campus of this size. New facilities include the Science Library, a visual arts painting studio, the Earth and Marine Sciences and Social Sciences buildings, and a music center.

Academics

UCSC offers a core academic program. It awards bachelor's, master's, and doctoral **degrees**. Challenging opportunities include advanced placement, self-designed majors, a senior project, Phi Beta Kappa, and Sigma Xi. Special programs include internships, summer session for credit, off-campus study, and study abroad.

The most popular **majors** include biology/biological sciences, psychology, and literature. A complete listing of majors at UCSC appears in the Majors Index beginning on page 379.

The **faculty** at UCSC has 400 full-time graduate and undergraduate teachers, 98% with terminal degrees. The student-faculty ratio is 19:1.

Computers on Campus

Students are not required to have a computer. 200 **computers** available in the computer center, each academic col-

lege, and the student center provide access to the main academic computer, off-campus computing facilities, e-mail, and on-line services. Staffed computer lab on campus (open 24 hours a day) provides training in the use of computers and software.

The 10 **libraries** have 1 million books, 548,215 microform titles, and 10,004 subscriptions.

Campus Life

Active **organizations** on campus include drama/theater group and student-run newspaper and radio station. 25% of students participate in student government elections. Student **safety services** include evening main gate security, late night transport/escort service, 24-hour emergency telephone alarm devices, and 24-hour patrols by trained security personnel.

UCSC is a member of the NCAA (Division III). **Intercollegiate sports** include basketball (m, w), fencing (m, w), lacrosse (m, w), rugby (m), sailing (m, w), soccer (m), swimming and diving (m, w), tennis (m, w), volleyball (m, w), water polo (m, w).

Applying

UCSC requires an essay, a high school transcript, 3 years of high school math, 2 years of high school foreign language, SAT I or ACT, and 3 SAT II Subject Tests (including SAT II: Writing Test). It recommends 3 years of high school science. 11/30 deadline and continuous processing to 3/2 for financial aid. **Contact:** Mr. J. Michael Thompson, Associate Vice Chancellor of Enrollment Management, Admissions Office, Cook House, Santa Cruz, CA 95064, 408-459-4008; fax 408-459-4452.

GETTING IN LAST YEAR
11,439 applied
83% were accepted
19% enrolled (1,823)
94% from top tenth of their h.s. class
39% had SAT verbal scores over 600 (R)
33% had SAT math scores over 600 (R)
27% had ACT scores over 26
7% had SAT verbal scores over 700 (R)
4% had SAT math scores over 700 (R)
2% had ACT scores over 30

THE STUDENT BODY
Total 9,923, of whom 8,876
   are undergraduates

From 48 states and territories,
   36 other countries
96% from California
60% women, 40% men
3% African Americans
1% Native Americans
16% Hispanics
14% Asian Americans
2% international students

AFTER FRESHMAN YEAR
80% returned for sophomore year
40% got a degree within 4 years
59% got a degree within 5 years
65% got a degree within 6 years

AFTER GRADUATION
50% pursued further study
8 Fulbright scholars

WHAT YOU WILL PAY
Resident tuition and fees $4136
Nonresident tuition and fees $11,835
Room and board $6222
Need-based college-administered scholarships and
   grants average $7200 per award
Non-need college-administered scholarships and
   grants average $2817 per award

UNIVERSITY OF CHICAGO

Chicago, Illinois • Urban setting • Private • Independent • Coed

---

The College of the University of Chicago is the liberal arts college at the heart of one of the world's great research centers, where 65 Nobel prize winners have studied, researched, or taught. The College offers the Common Core, the country's oldest and most extensive general education curriculum.

Academics

Chicago offers a liberal education curriculum and core academic program; more than half of graduate courses are open to undergraduates. It awards bachelor's, master's, doctoral, and first professional **degrees**. Challenging opportunities include advanced placement, accelerated degree programs, self-designed majors, tutorials, a senior project, Phi Beta Kappa, and Sigma Xi. Special programs include internships, summer session for credit, off-campus study, study abroad, and Army and Air Force ROTC.

The most popular **majors** include economics, biology/biological sciences, and English. A complete listing of majors at Chicago appears in the Majors Index beginning on page 379.

The **faculty** at Chicago has 1,282 full-time graduate and undergraduate teachers, 100% with terminal degrees. The student-faculty ratio is 6:1.

Computers on Campus

Students are not required to have a computer. Student rooms are linked to a campus network. 1,000 **computers** available in the computer center, computer labs, the research center, the learning resource center, classroom buildings, classrooms, the library, dormitories, and student rooms provide access to the main academic computer, off-campus computing facilities, e-mail, on-line services, and the Internet. Staffed computer lab on campus provides training in the use of software.

The 9 **libraries** have 5.7 million books, 2 million microform titles, and 47,000 subscriptions. They are connected to 7 national **on-line** catalogs.

Campus Life

There are 150 active **organizations** on campus, including a drama/theater group and student-run newspaper and radio station. 14% of eligible men and 5% of eligible women are members of 9 national **fraternities** and 2 national **sororities**. Student **safety services** include late night transport/escort service, 24-hour emergency telephone alarm devices, 24-hour patrols by trained security personnel, and electronically operated dormitory entrances.

Chicago is a member of the NCAA (Division III). **Intercollegiate sports** include baseball (m), basketball (m, w), cross-country running (m, w), fencing (m), football (m), soccer (m, w), softball (w), swimming and diving (m, w), tennis (m, w), track and field (m, w), volleyball (w), wrestling (m).

Applying

Chicago requires an essay, a high school transcript, 3 recommendations, and SAT I or ACT. It recommends 4 years of high school math and science, 3 years of high school foreign language, and an interview. Early and deferred entrance are possible, with a 1/15 deadline and a 2/1 priority date for financial aid. **Contact:** Mr. Theodore O'Neill, Dean of Admissions, 1116 East 59th Street, Chicago, IL 60637-1513, 312-702-8650; fax 312-702-4199.

GETTING IN LAST YEAR
5,843 applied
54% were accepted
31% enrolled (986)
75% from top tenth of their h.s. class
64% had SAT verbal scores over 600
89% had SAT math scores over 600
85% had ACT scores over 26
21% had SAT verbal scores over 700
44% had SAT math scores over 700
50% had ACT scores over 30
146 National Merit Scholars

THE STUDENT BODY
Total 11,875, of whom 3,453
  are undergraduates

From 52 states and territories,
  43 other countries
26% from Illinois
44% women, 56% men
4% African Americans
0% Native Americans
4% Hispanics
26% Asian Americans
4% international students

AFTER FRESHMAN YEAR
93% returned for sophomore year
80% got a degree within 4 years
84% got a degree within 5 years
86% got a degree within 6 years

AFTER GRADUATION
35% pursued further study (17% arts and
  sciences, 8% law, 7% medicine)
1 Rhodes, 1 Marshall, 14 Fulbright scholars

WHAT YOU WILL PAY
Tuition and fees $20,193
Room and board $6668
Need-based college-administered scholarships and
  grants average $10,416 per award
Non-need college-administered scholarships and
  grants average $9671 per award

UNIVERSITY OF COLORADO AT BOULDER

Boulder, Colorado • Urban setting • Public • State-supported • Coed

The University of Colorado at Boulder, a major research and teaching university, is located in one of the most spectacular environments in the country at the foot of the Rocky Mountains. Ranking 10th among all public universities in federally funded research, the University offers tremendous academic diversity, with faculty committed to bringing their research into the classroom. Students may participate in honors programs, an undergraduate research program, and several residential programs.

Academics

CU-Boulder offers a research and teaching-oriented curriculum and no core academic program; fewer than half of graduate courses are open to undergraduates. It awards bachelor's, master's, doctoral, and first professional **degrees**. Challenging opportunities include advanced placement, accelerated degree programs, self-designed majors, tutorials, Freshman Honors College, an honors program, a senior project, Phi Beta Kappa, and Sigma Xi. Special programs include cooperative education, internships, summer session for credit, off-campus study, study abroad, and Army, Naval, and Air Force ROTC.

The most popular **majors** include psychology, English, and environmental biology. A complete listing of majors at CU-Boulder appears in the Majors Index beginning on page 379.

The **faculty** at CU-Boulder has 1,093 full-time graduate and undergraduate teachers, 99% with terminal degrees. The student-faculty ratio is 22:1.

Computers on Campus

Students are not required to have a computer. Student rooms are linked to a campus network. 1,500 **computers** available in the computer center, computer labs, the research center, the learning resource center, classroom buildings, classrooms, the library, the student center, and dormitories provide access to the main academic computer, off-campus computing facilities, e-mail, on-line services, the Internet, and standard and academic software. Staffed computer lab on campus (open 24 hours a day) provides training in the use of computers and software.

The 7 **libraries** have 2.6 million books and 29,406 subscriptions.

Campus Life

There are 351 active **organizations** on campus, including a drama/theater group and student-run newspaper and radio station. 10% of students participate in student government elections. 15% of eligible men and 13% of eligible women are members of 17 national **fraternities**, 9 national **sororities**, and 1 local sorority. Student **safety services** include university police department, late night transport/escort service, 24-hour emergency telephone alarm devices, 24-hour patrols by trained security personnel, and student patrols.

CU-Boulder is a member of the NCAA (Division I). **Intercollegiate sports** (some offering scholarships) include baseball (m), basketball (m, w), crew (m, w), cross-country running (m, w), fencing (m, w), field hockey (w), football (m), golf (m, w), ice hockey (m), lacrosse (m, w), racquetball (m, w), riflery (m, w), rugby (m, w), skiing (cross-country) (m, w), skiing (downhill) (m, w), soccer (m, w), softball (w), swimming and diving (m, w), tennis (m, w), track and field (m, w), volleyball (w), water polo (m, w), weight lifting (m, w), wrestling (m).

Applying

CU-Boulder requires a high school transcript, 3 years of high school math and science, 2 years of high school foreign language, SAT I or ACT, a minimum high school GPA of 2.0, and in some cases 4 years of high school math and 3 years of high school foreign language. It recommends an essay, recommendations, and a minimum high school GPA of 3.0. Early, deferred, and midyear entrance are possible, with a 2/15 deadline and continuous processing to 4/1 for financial aid. **Contact:** Admissions Counselor, Campus Box 30, Boulder, CO 80309-0030, 303-492-6301; fax 303-492-7115.

GETTING IN LAST YEAR
15,066 applied
80% were accepted
35% enrolled (4,182)
23% from top tenth of their h.s. class
43% had SAT verbal scores over 600 (R)
51% had SAT math scores over 600 (R)
42% had ACT scores over 26
6% had SAT verbal scores over 700 (R)
6% had SAT math scores over 700 (R)
9% had ACT scores over 30

THE STUDENT BODY
Total 24,440, of whom 19,640
  are undergraduates

From 52 states and territories,
  91 other countries
67% from Colorado
47% women, 53% men
2% African Americans
1% Native Americans
6% Hispanics
6% Asian Americans
2% international students

AFTER FRESHMAN YEAR
79% returned for sophomore year
46% got a degree within 4 years
63% got a degree within 5 years

AFTER GRADUATION
28% pursued further study
350 organizations recruited on campus
4 Fulbright scholars

WHAT YOU WILL PAY
Resident tuition and fees $2769
Nonresident tuition and fees $13,837
Room and board $4123
10% receive need-based financial aid
Need-based college-administered scholarships and
  grants average $1845 per award
35% receive non-need financial aid
Non-need college-administered scholarships and
  grants average $1180 per award

UNIVERSITY OF CONNECTICUT

Storrs, Connecticut • Rural setting • Public • State-supported • Coed

UConn provides an academic and social environment that develops the skills students need in order to be successful. Its programs enhance students' independence, sense of responsibility, initiative, and the desire to take an active role in their undergraduate experience and a leading role in all aspects of their education. The process of making choices, asking questions, and solving problems prepares students for the competition, shifting terrain, and expectations of graduate school or the demands of a global, competitive economy. UConn's academic and social offerings reflect the growing links between cultures and countries and emphasize the sophisticated skills needed by citizens in the global marketplace.

 Academics

UCONN offers a liberal education curriculum through professional training and core academic program; fewer than half of graduate courses are open to undergraduates. It awards associate, bachelor's, master's, doctoral, and first professional **degrees**. Challenging opportunities include advanced placement, accelerated degree programs, self-designed majors, an honors program, Phi Beta Kappa, and Sigma Xi. Special programs include cooperative education, internships, summer session for credit, off-campus study, study abroad, and Army and Air Force ROTC.

The most popular **majors** include biology/biological sciences, education, and psychology. A complete listing of majors at UCONN appears in the Majors Index beginning on page 379.

The **faculty** at UCONN has 1,068 full-time graduate and undergraduate teachers, 93% with terminal degrees. The student-faculty ratio is 17:1.

 Computers on Campus

Students are not required to have a computer. Student rooms are linked to a campus network. 1,800 **computers** available in the computer center, departmental labs, the library, the student center, and dormitories provide access to the main academic computer, e-mail, and on-line services. Staffed computer lab on campus provides training in the use of computers and software.

The 4 **libraries** have 2 million books, 2.9 million microform titles, and 8,476 subscriptions. They are connected to 12 national **on-line** catalogs.

 Campus Life

There are 250 active **organizations** on campus, including a drama/theater group and student-run newspaper and radio station. 13% of eligible men and 7% of eligible women are members of 17 national **fraternities** and 9 national **sororities**. Student **safety services** include late night transport/escort service and 24-hour emergency telephone alarm devices.

UCONN is a member of the NCAA (Division I). **Intercollegiate sports** (some offering scholarships) include baseball (m), basketball (m, w), cross-country running (m, w), field hockey (w), golf (m), ice hockey (m), soccer (m, w), softball (w), swimming and diving (m, w), tennis (m, w), track and field (m, w), volleyball (w).

 Applying

UCONN requires an essay, a high school transcript, 3 years of high school math, 2 years of high school foreign language, SAT I or ACT, and in some cases 3 years of high school science. It recommends recommendations. Early, deferred, and midyear entrance are possible, with a 4/1 deadline and continuous processing to 3/1 for financial aid. **Contact:** Dr. Ann L. Huckenbeck, Director of Admissions, 2131 Hillside Road, U-88, Storrs, CT 06269, 860-486-3137; fax 860-486-1909.

GETTING IN LAST YEAR
9,886 applied
70% were accepted
29% enrolled (2,021)
23% from top tenth of their h.s. class
34% had SAT verbal scores over 600
32% had SAT math scores over 600
5% had SAT verbal scores over 700
5% had SAT math scores over 700
13 National Merit Scholars
20 valedictorians

THE STUDENT BODY
Total 15,735, of whom 11,333
   are undergraduates

88% from Connecticut
50% women, 50% men
4% African Americans
1% Native Americans
3% Hispanics
6% Asian Americans
1% international students

AFTER FRESHMAN YEAR
86% returned for sophomore year
40% got a degree within 4 years
65% got a degree within 5 years
70% got a degree within 6 years

AFTER GRADUATION
15% pursued further study

65% had job offers within 6 months
206 organizations recruited on campus
3 Fulbright scholars

WHAT YOU WILL PAY
Resident tuition and fees $4974
Nonresident tuition and fees $13,244
Room and board $5302
39% receive need-based financial aid
Need-based college-administered scholarships and
   grants average $8522 per award
9% receive non-need financial aid
Non-need college-administered scholarships and
   grants average $7012 per award

UNIVERSITY OF DALLAS

Irving, Texas • Suburban setting • Private • Independent-Religious • Coed

The University of Dallas, the Catholic university for independent thinkers, is where debate and discourse are a way of life. The professors guide students in an environment of intellectual inquiry that engages the imagination. UD's distinctive and comprehensive core curriculum emphasizes the use of original texts. Reading great books, sharing a common body of knowledge with other students, and discussing ideas are important parts of a student's education. UD's classical education comes to life on its Rome campus, where nearly 85% of sophomores spend a semester exploring the cities, works of art, and historic landmarks that they have studied in their core courses.

Academics

UD offers an ancient and modern Western civilization curriculum and core academic program; fewer than half of graduate courses are open to undergraduates. It awards bachelor's, master's, and doctoral **degrees**. Challenging opportunities include advanced placement, accelerated degree programs, self-designed majors, tutorials, a senior project, and Phi Beta Kappa. Special programs include internships, summer session for credit, off-campus study, study abroad, and Army and Air Force ROTC.

The most popular **majors** include biology/biological sciences, English, and political science/government. A complete listing of majors at UD appears in the Majors Index beginning on page 379.

The **faculty** at UD has 95 full-time graduate and undergraduate teachers, 95% with terminal degrees. 75% of the faculty serve as student advisers. The student-faculty ratio is 13:1, and the average class size in core courses is 20.

Computers on Campus

Students are not required to have a computer. Student rooms are linked to a campus network. 70 **computers** available in science buildings and the library provide access to the main academic computer, e-mail, and the Internet. Staffed computer lab on campus provides training in the use of computers and software.

The **library** has 295,018 books, 75,565 microform titles, and 1,074 subscriptions. It is connected to 1 national **on-line** catalog.

Campus Life

There are 43 active **organizations** on campus, including a drama/theater group and student-run newspaper. Student **safety services** include late night transport/escort service, 24-hour emergency telephone alarm devices, 24-hour patrols by trained security personnel, and electronically operated dormitory entrances.

UD is a member of the NAIA. **Intercollegiate sports** include basketball (m, w), golf (m, w), soccer (m, w), tennis (m, w), volleyball (w).

Applying

UD requires an essay, a high school transcript, 1 recommendation, SAT I or ACT, and in some cases a campus interview. It recommends 3 years of high school math and science, 2 years of high school foreign language, and an interview. Early, deferred, and midyear entrance are possible, with a 3/1 deadline and continuous processing to 3/1 for financial aid. **Contact:** Mr. Fred Zuker, Dean of Admissions and Financial Aid, 1845 East Northgate Drive, Irving, TX 75062-4799, 214-721-5266; fax 214-721-5017.

GETTING IN LAST YEAR
722 applied
91% were accepted
38% enrolled (248)
34% from top tenth of their h.s. class
34% had SAT verbal scores over 600
48% had SAT math scores over 600
59% had ACT scores over 26
7% had SAT verbal scores over 700
11% had SAT math scores over 700
16% had ACT scores over 30
6 National Merit Scholars

THE STUDENT BODY
Total 2,746, of whom 1,103 are undergraduates

From 46 states and territories, 15 other countries
61% from Texas
54% women, 46% men
2% African Americans
1% Native Americans
13% Hispanics
10% Asian Americans
2% international students

AFTER FRESHMAN YEAR
88% returned for sophomore year
47% got a degree within 4 years
54% got a degree within 5 years
56% got a degree within 6 years

AFTER GRADUATION
58% pursued further study (32% arts and sciences, 16% medicine, 6% business)
95% had job offers within 6 months
50 organizations recruited on campus
2 Fulbright scholars

WHAT YOU WILL PAY
Tuition and fees $11,430
Room and board $4830
70% receive need-based financial aid
Need-based college-administered scholarships and grants average $5536 per award
80% receive non-need financial aid
Non-need college-administered scholarships and grants average $2739 per award

UNIVERSITY OF DELAWARE

Newark, Delaware • Small-town setting • Public • State-related • Coed

Delaware has had a longstanding commitment to undergraduate teaching and research. Delaware's graduation rate, one of the highest among the 50 major public universities, is further evidence of this commitment. Some of the nation's brightest students enroll in the University Honors Program. The enrollment of approximately 15,000 undergraduates is ideal for high-achieving students seeking the diversity and richness of opportunity of a large university and the qualities and spirit of a small, personal campus. A major advantage of the campus location is its proximity to Washington, Philadelphia, and New York.

Academics

Delaware offers an interdisciplinary curriculum and core academic program; all graduate courses are open to undergraduates. It awards associate, bachelor's, master's, and doctoral **degrees**. Challenging opportunities include advanced placement, accelerated degree programs, self-designed majors, tutorials, an honors program, a senior project, Phi Beta Kappa, and Sigma Xi. Special programs include cooperative education, internships, summer session for credit, off-campus study, study abroad, and Army and Air Force ROTC.

The most popular **majors** include English, psychology, and elementary education. A complete listing of majors at Delaware appears in the Majors Index beginning on page 379.

The **faculty** at Delaware has 969 full-time graduate and undergraduate teachers, 88% with terminal degrees. The student-faculty ratio is 15:1.

Computers on Campus

Students are not required to have a computer. Student rooms are linked to a campus network. 700 **computers** available in the computer center, computer labs, 28 sites throughout campus, the library, the student center, dormitories, and student rooms provide access to the main academic computer, e-mail, on-line services, and the Internet. Staffed computer lab on campus provides training in the use of computers and software.

The 4 **libraries** have 2.1 million books, 2.6 million microform titles, and 19,000 subscriptions.

Campus Life

There are 150 active **organizations** on campus, including a drama/theater group and student-run newspaper and radio station. 18% of eligible men and 18% of eligible women are members of 25 national **fraternities** and 15 national **sororities**. Student **safety services** include late night transport/escort service, 24-hour emergency telephone alarm devices, 24-hour patrols by trained security personnel, student patrols, and electronically operated dormitory entrances.

Delaware is a member of the NCAA (Division I). **Intercollegiate sports** (some offering scholarships) include baseball (m), basketball (m, w), crew (m, w), cross-country running (m, w), field hockey (w), football (m), golf (m), ice hockey (m), lacrosse (m, w), rugby (m, w), soccer (m, w), softball (w), swimming and diving (m, w), tennis (m, w), track and field (m, w), volleyball (w).

Applying

Delaware requires a high school transcript, 2 years of high school foreign language, SAT I, and in some cases an essay and 1 recommendation. It recommends SAT II Subject Tests. Early, deferred, and midyear entrance are possible, with a 3/1 deadline and continuous processing to 3/15 for financial aid. **Contact:** Dr. Bruce Walker, Associate Provost for Admissions and Student Financial Aid, 116 Hullihen Hall, South College Avenue, Newark, DE 19716, 302-831-8123; fax 302-831-6905.

GETTING IN LAST YEAR
13,860 applied
73% were accepted
32% enrolled (3,179)
23% from top tenth of their h.s. class
3.2 average high school GPA
45 National Merit Scholars
42 valedictorians

THE STUDENT BODY
Total 17,892, of whom 14,668
   are undergraduates
From 46 states and territories,
   85 other countries
42% from Delaware

57% women, 43% men
5% African Americans
1% Native Americans
2% Hispanics
3% Asian Americans
1% international students

AFTER FRESHMAN YEAR
85% returned for sophomore year
48% got a degree within 4 years
69% got a degree within 5 years
71% got a degree within 6 years

AFTER GRADUATION
20% pursued further study (9% arts and
   sciences, 4% law, 3% business)

75% had job offers within 6 months
1 Fulbright scholar

WHAT YOU WILL PAY
Resident tuition and fees $4286
Nonresident tuition and fees $11,156
Room and board $4420
62% receive need-based financial aid
Need-based college-administered scholarships and
   grants average $4300 per award
18% receive non-need financial aid
Non-need college-administered scholarships and
   grants average $5000 per award

UNIVERSITY OF DENVER

Denver, Colorado • Suburban setting • Private • Independent • Coed

 Academics

DU offers an interdisciplinary curriculum and core academic program; more than half of graduate courses are open to undergraduates. It awards bachelor's, master's, doctoral, and first professional **degrees**. Challenging opportunities include advanced placement, accelerated degree programs, self-designed majors, tutorials, Freshman Honors College, an honors program, a senior project, Phi Beta Kappa, and Sigma Xi. Special programs include cooperative education, internships, summer session for credit, study abroad, and Army and Air Force ROTC.

The most popular **majors** include international business, biology/biological sciences, and communication. A complete listing of majors at DU appears in the Majors Index beginning on page 379.

The **faculty** at DU has 390 full-time graduate and undergraduate teachers, 90% with terminal degrees. 75% of the faculty serve as student advisers. The student-faculty ratio is 13:1.

 Computers on Campus

Students are not required to have a computer. Student rooms are linked to a campus network. 534 **computers** available in the computer center, computer labs, the research center, the learning resource center, classrooms, the library, the student center, and dormitories provide access to the main academic computer, off-campus computing facilities, e-mail, on-line services, the Internet, and campus-wide information system. Staffed computer lab on campus provides training in the use of computers and software.

The **library** has 1.1 million books, 912,115 microform titles, and 5,330 subscriptions. It is connected to 3 national **on-line** catalogs.

 Campus Life

There are 60 active **organizations** on campus, including a drama/theater group and student-run newspaper and radio station. 28% of students participate in student government elections. 62% of eligible men and 36% of eligible women are members of 9 national **fraternities** and 5 national **sororities**. Student **safety services** include 24-hour locked dormitory entrances, late night transport/escort service, 24-hour emergency telephone alarm devices, 24-hour patrols by trained security personnel, and electronically operated dormitory entrances.

DU is a member of the NCAA (Division II). **Intercollegiate sports** (some offering scholarships) include baseball (m), basketball (m, w), football (m), golf (m), gymnastics (w), ice hockey (m), lacrosse (m, w), rugby (m), skiing (cross-country) (m, w), skiing (downhill) (m, w), soccer (m, w), swimming and diving (m, w), tennis (m, w), volleyball (m, w).

Applying

DU requires an essay, a high school transcript, 3 years of high school math and science, 2 years of high school foreign language, 2 recommendations, and SAT I or ACT. It recommends an interview and a minimum high school GPA of 2.0. Early, deferred, and midyear entrance are possible, with rolling admissions and continuous processing to 2/19 for financial aid. **Contact:** Ms. Susan Hunt, Director of Admission Counseling, 2199 South University Boulevard, Denver, CO 80208, 303-871-2036 or toll-free 800-525-9495 (out-of-state); fax 303-871-3301.

GETTING IN LAST YEAR
2,783 applied
81% were accepted
29% enrolled (659)
33% from top tenth of their h.s. class
3.46 average high school GPA
37% had SAT verbal scores over 600 (R)
30% had SAT math scores over 600 (R)
39% had ACT scores over 26
5% had SAT verbal scores over 700 (R)
5% had SAT math scores over 700 (R)
6% had ACT scores over 30

THE STUDENT BODY
Total 8,515, of whom 2,825
   are undergraduates

From 52 states and territories,
   92 other countries
42% from Colorado
51% women, 49% men
2% African Americans
1% Native Americans
5% Hispanics
5% Asian Americans
12% international students

AFTER FRESHMAN YEAR
81% returned for sophomore year
58% got a degree within 4 years
68% got a degree within 5 years
70% got a degree within 6 years

AFTER GRADUATION
19% pursued further study
100% had job offers within 6 months
188 organizations recruited on campus

WHAT YOU WILL PAY
Tuition and fees $16,284
Room and board $5115
55% receive need-based financial aid
Need-based college-administered scholarships and
   grants average $4166 per award
21% receive non-need financial aid
Non-need college-administered scholarships and
   grants average $3269 per award

UNIVERSITY OF DETROIT MERCY

Detroit, Michigan • Urban setting • Private • Independent-Religious • Coed

University of Detroit Mercy is Michigan's largest, most comprehensive Catholic university, offering a value-oriented, person-centered education. Small class size and a faculty-student ratio of 1:14 ensure that students will receive individual support and one-on-one interaction with professors. Undergraduate, graduate, and professional degrees are available in over 60 academic fields. A nationally recognized Cooperative Education Program enables students to acquire on-the-job experience with prominent national and international employers. Located in a dynamic urban area, UDM offers unlimited opportunities for enrichment and enjoyment.

Academics

U of D Mercy offers a core academic program; fewer than half of graduate courses are open to undergraduates. It awards associate, bachelor's, master's, doctoral, and first professional **degrees**. Challenging opportunities include advanced placement, accelerated degree programs, self-designed majors, tutorials, an honors program, and a senior project. Special programs include cooperative education, internships, summer session for credit, off-campus study, study abroad, and Army ROTC.

The most popular **majors** include nursing, engineering (general), and architecture. A complete listing of majors at U of D Mercy appears in the Majors Index beginning on page 379.

The **faculty** at U of D Mercy has 283 full-time graduate and undergraduate teachers, 81% with terminal degrees. The student-faculty ratio is 14:1.

Computers on Campus

Students are not required to have a computer. 200 **computers** available in the computer center, computer labs, classrooms, the library, and the student center provide access to the main academic computer, e-mail, and the Internet.

The 5 **libraries** have 645,039 books, 88,650 microform titles, and 5,505 subscriptions. They are connected to 3 national **on-line** catalogs.

Campus Life

Active **organizations** on campus include drama/theater group and student-run newspaper and radio station. 22% of eligible men and 13% of eligible women are members of 7 national **fraternities**, 7 local fraternities, and 3 local **sororities**. Student **safety services** include late night transport/escort service.

U of D Mercy is a member of the NCAA (Division I). **Intercollegiate sports** (some offering scholarships) include baseball (m), basketball (m, w), cross-country running (m, w), fencing (m, w), golf (m, w), riflery (m, w), soccer (m, w), softball (w), track and field (m, w).

Applying

U of D Mercy requires a high school transcript, SAT I or ACT, and in some cases 3 years of high school math and science, some high school foreign language, 1 recommendation, and an interview. It recommends recommendations. Early and deferred entrance are possible, with an 8/15 deadline and continuous processing to 4/1 for financial aid. **Contact:** Dr. Robert Johnson, Dean of Enrollment Management, PO Box 19900, Detroit, MI 48219-0900, 313-993-1245.

GETTING IN LAST YEAR
1,429 applied
85% were accepted
40% enrolled (483)
24% from top tenth of their h.s. class
3.13 average high school GPA
23% had ACT scores over 26
5% had ACT scores over 30

THE STUDENT BODY
Total 7,524, of whom 4,503
    are undergraduates

From 29 states and territories,
    26 other countries
93% from Michigan
66% women, 34% men
40% African Americans
0% Native Americans
3% Hispanics
2% Asian Americans
2% international students

AFTER FRESHMAN YEAR
79% returned for sophomore year

25% got a degree within 4 years
41% got a degree within 5 years
51% got a degree within 6 years

AFTER GRADUATION
20% pursued further study (6% business, 4% engineering, 3% arts and sciences)

WHAT YOU WILL PAY
Tuition and fees $11,675
Room and board $3253

UNIVERSITY OF EVANSVILLE

Evansville, Indiana • Suburban setting • Private • Independent-Religious • Coed

Discover the difference! The University of Evansville seeks students whose expectations know no boundaries. The private, liberal arts and sciences University is an appropriate size for learning, with over 80 major areas of study. More than 3,000 undergraduates from 48 states and more than 50 countries are usually in classes of 25 or fewer, giving them the opportunity to enjoy stimulating debate and discussion. Outside the classroom, Evansville's students enjoy Division I athletics as well as more than 120 social and academic organizations. Students also have the opportunity to strengthen their understanding of a different culture at Evansville's campus at Harlaxton College in Grantham, England.

Academics

UE offers a world cultures curriculum and core academic program. It awards associate, bachelor's, and master's **degrees**. Challenging opportunities include advanced placement, tutorials, Freshman Honors College, an honors program, and a senior project. Special programs include cooperative education, internships, summer session for credit, and study abroad.

The most popular **majors** include accounting, electrical engineering, and elementary education. A complete listing of majors at UE appears in the Majors Index beginning on page 379.

The **faculty** at UE has 176 full-time graduate and undergraduate teachers, 83% with terminal degrees. 60% of the faculty serve as student advisers. The student-faculty ratio is 13:1.

Computers on Campus

Students are not required to have a computer. Student rooms are linked to a campus network. 300 **computers** available in computer labs, classrooms, and the library provide access to e-mail, on-line services, and the Internet. Staffed computer lab on campus provides training in the use of computers and software.

The **library** has 244,500 books, 338,273 microform titles, and 1,258 subscriptions.

Campus Life

There are 130 active **organizations** on campus, including a drama/theater group and student-run newspaper and radio station. 30% of eligible men and 20% of eligible women are members of 5 national **fraternities** and 4 national **sororities**. Student **safety services** include late night transport/escort service, 24-hour emergency telephone alarm devices, and 24-hour patrols by trained security personnel.

UE is a member of the NCAA (Division I). **Intercollegiate sports** (some offering scholarships) include baseball (m), basketball (m, w), cross-country running (m, w), football (m), golf (m), soccer (m, w), softball (w), swimming and diving (m, w), tennis (m, w), volleyball (w).

Applying

UE requires an essay, a high school transcript, 1 recommendation, SAT I or ACT, and in some cases 3 years of high school math and science and a campus interview. It recommends 3 years of high school math and science, 2 years of high school foreign language, and a campus interview. Early, deferred, and midyear entrance are possible, with a 2/15 deadline and continuous processing to 3/1 for financial aid. **Contact:** Mr. Clint Kaiser, Associate Director of Admission, 1800 Lincoln Avenue, Evansville, IN 47722-0002, 812-479-2468 or toll-free 800-992-5877 (in-state), 800-423-8633 (out-of-state); fax 812-479-2320.

GETTING IN LAST YEAR
2,874 applied
86% were accepted
32% enrolled (785)
35% from top tenth of their h.s. class
40% had SAT verbal scores over 600 (R)
38% had SAT math scores over 600 (R)
50% had ACT scores over 26
7% had SAT verbal scores over 700 (R)
7% had SAT math scores over 700 (R)
12% had ACT scores over 30
4 National Merit Scholars
39 valedictorians

THE STUDENT BODY
Total 3,185, of whom 3,091
   are undergraduates
From 48 states and territories,
   52 other countries
55% from Indiana
53% women, 47% men
3% African Americans
0% Native Americans
1% Hispanics
1% Asian Americans
5% international students

AFTER GRADUATION
12% pursued further study (4% arts and
   sciences, 2% business, 2% medicine)
1 Fulbright scholar

WHAT YOU WILL PAY
Tuition and fees $12,630
Room and board $3950
Need-based college-administered scholarships and
   grants average $4644 per award
Non-need college-administered scholarships and
   grants average $4733 per award

UNIVERSITY OF FLORIDA

Gainesville, Florida • Suburban setting • Public • State-supported • Coed

---

Belonging to a tradition of great universities, UF participates in a conversation among scholars and students that prepares generations of educated people to address the problems of society. UF is a public land-grant research university, with 39,000 students from all 50 states and over 100 countries. As one of the most comprehensive institutions in the United States, it encompasses virtually all academic and professional disciplines. It is the oldest and largest university in Florida and a member of the prestigious American Association of Universities. UF's faculty and staff are dedicated to the common pursuit of the University's mission of teaching, research, and service.

 ## Academics

UF offers a diverse, interdisciplinary curriculum and core academic program; more than half of graduate courses are open to undergraduates. It awards bachelor's, master's, doctoral, and first professional **degrees**. Challenging opportunities include advanced placement, accelerated degree programs, self-designed majors, tutorials, an honors program, a senior project, Phi Beta Kappa, and Sigma Xi. Special programs include cooperative education, internships, summer session for credit, off-campus study, study abroad, and Army, Naval, and Air Force ROTC.

The most popular **majors** include psychology, finance/banking, and English. A complete listing of majors at UF appears in the Majors Index beginning on page 379.

The **faculty** at UF has 2,225 full-time graduate and undergraduate teachers, 97% with terminal degrees. 86% of the faculty serve as student advisers. The student-faculty ratio is 17:1.

 ## Computers on Campus

Students are not required to have a computer. Student rooms are linked to a campus network. 612 **computers** available in the computer center, computer labs, the research center, the learning resource center, labs, classrooms, the library, the student center, dormitories, and student rooms provide access to the main academic computer, e-mail, and the Internet. Staffed computer lab on campus (open 24 hours a day) provides training in the use of computers and software.

The 16 **libraries** have 3.1 million books and 24,191 subscriptions. They are connected to 20 national **on-line** catalogs.

 ## Campus Life

There are 450 active **organizations** on campus, including a drama/theater group and student-run newspaper and radio station. 15% of eligible men and 15% of eligible women are members of 28 national **fraternities** and 18 national **sororities**. Student **safety services** include crime and rape prevention programs, late night transport/escort service, 24-hour emergency telephone alarm devices, 24-hour patrols by trained security personnel, student patrols, and electronically operated dormitory entrances.

UF is a member of the NCAA (Division I). **Intercollegiate sports** (some offering scholarships) include baseball (m), basketball (m, w), cross-country running (m, w), football (m), golf (m, w), gymnastics (w), softball (w), swimming and diving (m, w), tennis (m, w), track and field (m, w), volleyball (w).

 ## Applying

UF requires a high school transcript, 3 years of high school math and science, 2 years of high school foreign language, SAT I or ACT, and 3 SAT II Subject Tests (including SAT II: Writing Test). Early and midyear entrance are possible, with a 2/1 deadline and continuous processing to 4/15 for financial aid. **Contact:** Admissions Office, PO Box 11400, Gainesville, FL 32611-4000, 904-392-1365.

GETTING IN LAST YEAR
12,724 applied
67% were accepted
44% enrolled (3,699)
50% from top tenth of their h.s. class
61% had ACT scores over 26
16% had ACT scores over 30
127 National Merit Scholars

THE STUDENT BODY
Total 39,439, of whom 29,637
   are undergraduates
From 52 states and territories,
   114 other countries

92% from Florida
53% women, 47% men
6% African Americans
9% Hispanics
6% Asian Americans

AFTER FRESHMAN YEAR
90% returned for sophomore year
32% got a degree within 4 years
58% got a degree within 5 years

AFTER GRADUATION
27% pursued further study
450 organizations recruited on campus
6 Fulbright scholars

WHAT YOU WILL PAY
Resident tuition and fees $1705
Nonresident tuition and fees $7403
Room and board $4310
36% receive need-based financial aid
Need-based college-administered scholarships and
   grants average $1450 per award
37% receive non-need financial aid
Non-need college-administered scholarships and
   grants average $1450 per award

UNIVERSITY OF GEORGIA

Athens, Georgia • Suburban setting • Public • State-supported • Coed

Because of the school's growing national preeminence, merit scholarships that now include full-tuition HOPE Scholarships for Georgia residents, and limited space for new freshmen, the University of Georgia is more competitive in admission and classroom performance than ever. The average freshman SAT I score is now almost 100 points higher than 10 years ago, and 1 out of 5 freshmen have scores in the top 90th percentile nationally. The Honors Program, one of the oldest and largest in the country, provides a strengthened liberal arts foundation for undergraduates through many honors course alternatives as well as faculty-guided individual research and progress into graduate-level work.

Academics

UGA offers a core academic program; fewer than half of graduate courses are open to undergraduates. It awards associate, bachelor's, master's, doctoral, and first professional **degrees**. Challenging opportunities include advanced placement, accelerated degree programs, self-designed majors, an honors program, a senior project, Phi Beta Kappa, and Sigma Xi. Special programs include cooperative education, internships, summer session for credit, off-campus study, study abroad, and Army and Air Force ROTC.

The most popular **majors** include English, accounting, and political science/government. A complete listing of majors at UGA appears in the Majors Index beginning on page 379.

The **faculty** at UGA has 1,985 full-time graduate and undergraduate teachers, 94% with terminal degrees.

Computers on Campus

Students are not required to have a computer. Student rooms are linked to a campus network. 800 **computers**

available in the computer center, computer labs, the research center, various campus facilities, the library, the student center, and dormitories provide access to the main academic computer, off-campus computing facilities, e-mail, on-line services, and the Internet. Staffed computer lab on campus (open 24 hours a day) provides training in the use of computers and software.

The 3 **libraries** have 3.3 million books, 5.3 million microform titles, and 48,190 subscriptions. They are connected to 125 national **on-line** catalogs.

Campus Life

There are 405 active **organizations** on campus, including a drama/theater group and student-run newspaper and radio station. 19% of eligible men and 23% of eligible women are members of 26 national **fraternities** and 22 national **sororities**. Student **safety services** include late night transport/escort service, 24-hour emergency telephone alarm devices, 24-hour patrols by trained security personnel, and electronically operated dormitory entrances.

UGA is a member of the NCAA (Division I). **Intercollegiate sports** (some offering scholarships) include baseball (m), basketball (m, w), cross-country running (m, w), football (m), golf (m, w), gymnastics (w), soccer (m, w), swimming and diving (m, w), tennis (m, w), track and field (m, w), volleyball (m, w).

Applying

UGA requires a high school transcript, 3 years of high school math and science, 2 years of high school foreign language, and SAT I or ACT. Early and deferred entrance are possible, with a 2/1 deadline and continuous processing to 3/1 for financial aid. **Contact:** Dr. John Albright, Associate Director of Admissions, Terrell Hall, Athens, GA 30602 .

GETTING IN LAST YEAR
13,401 applied
59% were accepted
47% enrolled (3,695)
53% from top tenth of their h.s. class
3.43 average high school GPA
19% had SAT verbal scores over 600
43% had SAT math scores over 600
2% had SAT verbal scores over 700
8% had SAT math scores over 700
1 National Merit Scholar

THE STUDENT BODY
Total 30,149, of whom 23,572
  are undergraduates

From 52 states and territories,
  99 other countries
84% from Georgia
53% women, 47% men
7% African Americans
1% Native Americans
1% Hispanics
2% Asian Americans
2% international students

AFTER FRESHMAN YEAR
85% returned for sophomore year
36% got a degree within 4 years
62% got a degree within 5 years
66% got a degree within 6 years

AFTER GRADUATION
504 organizations recruited on campus
1 Rhodes, 2 Fulbright scholars

WHAT YOU WILL PAY
Resident tuition and fees $2508
Nonresident tuition and fees $6795
Room and board $3820
Need-based college-administered scholarships and
  grants average $900 per award
Non-need college-administered scholarships and
  grants average $1400 per award

THE UNIVERSITY OF IOWA

Iowa City, Iowa • Small-town setting • Public • State-supported • Coed

Iowa offers strong undergraduate programs in diverse areas, such as the health sciences, traditional liberal arts, and preprofessional programs. Undergraduates are exposed to outstanding opportunities and facilities, from the world-renowned Writer's Workshop to the top-ranked College of Medicine and University of Iowa Hospitals and Clinics, the largest university-owned teaching hospital in the United States. Popular undergraduate areas of study include business administration, engineering, communications, English, psychology, and premedical studies.

 Academics

Iowa offers a liberal arts curriculum and core academic program; fewer than half of graduate courses are open to undergraduates. It awards bachelor's, master's, doctoral, and first professional **degrees**. Challenging opportunities include advanced placement, accelerated degree programs, self-designed majors, tutorials, an honors program, a senior project, Phi Beta Kappa, and Sigma Xi. Special programs include cooperative education, internships, summer session for credit, off-campus study, study abroad, and Army and Air Force ROTC.

The most popular **majors** include business, psychology, and English. A complete listing of majors at Iowa appears in the Majors Index beginning on page 379.

The **faculty** at Iowa has 1,747 full-time graduate and undergraduate teachers, 99% with terminal degrees. The student-faculty ratio is 15:1.

 Computers on Campus

Students are not required to have a computer. 1,200 **computers** available in the computer center, computer labs, the research center, classroom buildings, classrooms, the library, the student center, and dormitories provide access to the main academic computer, e-mail, and the Internet. Staffed computer lab on campus (open 24 hours a day) provides training in the use of computers and software.

The **library** has 3.5 million books and 40,009 subscriptions. It is connected to 16 national **on-line** catalogs.

 Campus Life

There are 337 active **organizations** on campus, including a drama/theater group and student-run newspaper and radio station. 14% of eligible men and 15% of eligible women are members of 25 national **fraternities** and 19 national **sororities**. Student **safety services** include late night transport/escort service, 24-hour emergency telephone alarm devices, and 24-hour patrols by trained security personnel.

Iowa is a member of the NCAA (Division I). **Intercollegiate sports** (some offering scholarships) include badminton (m, w), baseball (m), basketball (m, w), bowling (m, w), crew (m, w), cross-country running (m, w), field hockey (w), football (m), golf (m, w), gymnastics (m, w), ice hockey (m, w), lacrosse (m, w), rugby (m, w), sailing (m, w), soccer (m), softball (w), swimming and diving (m, w), table tennis (m, w), tennis (m, w), track and field (m, w), volleyball (m, w), wrestling (m).

 Applying

Iowa requires a high school transcript, 3 years of high school math and science, 2 years of high school foreign language, and SAT I or ACT. It recommends a campus interview. Early, deferred, and midyear entrance are possible, with a 5/15 deadline and continuous processing to 1/1 for financial aid. **Contact:** Mr. Michael Barron, Director of Admissions, Calvin Hall, Iowa City, IA 52242, 319-335-3847 or toll-free 800-553-4692; fax 319-335-1535.

GETTING IN LAST YEAR
9,940 applied
86% were accepted
42% enrolled (3,578)
21% from top tenth of their h.s. class
3.4 average high school GPA
37% had ACT scores over 26
9% had ACT scores over 30
24 National Merit Scholars
126 valedictorians

THE STUDENT BODY
Total 27,597, of whom 18,740 are undergraduates
From 52 states and territories, 78 other countries
69% from Iowa
53% women, 47% men
2% African Americans
1% Native Americans
2% Hispanics
4% Asian Americans
2% international students

WHAT YOU WILL PAY
Resident tuition and fees $2558
Nonresident tuition and fees $8808
Room and board $3550
75% receive need-based financial aid
Need-based college-administered scholarships and grants average $1590 per award
Non-need college-administered scholarships and grants average $1704 per award

UNIVERSITY OF KANSAS

Lawrence, Kansas • Suburban setting • Public • State-supported • Coed

Academics

KU offers a core academic program; fewer than half of graduate courses are open to undergraduates. It awards bachelor's, master's, doctoral, and first professional **degrees** (The University of Kansas is a single institution with academic programs and facilities at two primary locations: Lawrence and Kansas City. Undergraduate, graduate, and professional education are the principal missions of the Lawrence campus, with medicine and related health professional education the focus of the Kansas City campus). Challenging opportunities include advanced placement, self-designed majors, tutorials, an honors program, a senior project, Phi Beta Kappa, and Sigma Xi. Special programs include cooperative education, internships, summer session for credit, study abroad, and Army, Naval, and Air Force ROTC.

The most popular **majors** include journalism, business, and psychology. A complete listing of majors at KU appears in the Majors Index beginning on page 379.

The **faculty** at KU has 1,673 full-time graduate and undergraduate teachers, 96% with terminal degrees. The student-faculty ratio is 14:1.

Computers on Campus

Students are not required to have a computer. Student rooms are linked to a campus network. 550 **computers** available in the computer center, computer labs, classrooms, the library, and dormitories provide access to the main academic computer, off-campus computing facilities, e-mail, on-line services, and the Internet. Staffed computer lab on campus (open 24 hours a day) provides training in the use of computers and software.

The 12 **libraries** have 3.4 million books, 2.9 million microform titles, and 32,504 subscriptions. They are connected to 18 national **on-line** catalogs.

Campus Life

There are 300 active **organizations** on campus, including a drama/theater group and student-run newspaper and radio station. 12% of students participate in student government elections. 21% of eligible men and 23% of eligible women are members of 27 national **fraternities** and 18 national **sororities**. Student **safety services** include late night transport/escort service, 24-hour emergency telephone alarm devices, 24-hour patrols by trained security personnel, and electronically operated dormitory entrances.

KU is a member of the NCAA (Division I). **Intercollegiate sports** (some offering scholarships) include baseball (m), basketball (m, w), crew (m, w), cross-country running (m, w), fencing (m, w), football (m), golf (m, w), ice hockey (m), lacrosse (m), racquetball (m, w), rugby (m, w), soccer (m, w), softball (w), swimming and diving (m, w), tennis (m, w), track and field (m, w), volleyball (w).

Applying

KU requires a high school transcript, SAT I or ACT, and in some cases a minimum high school GPA of 3.0. It recommends 3 years of high school math and science and 2 years of high school foreign language. Early and midyear entrance are possible, with a 4/1 deadline, 2/1 deadline for nonresidents and continuous processing to 3/1 for financial aid. **Contact:** Ms. Deborah Boulware, Director of Admissions, 126 Strong Hall, Lawrence, KS 66045-1910, 913-864-3911.

GETTING IN LAST YEAR
8,234 applied
68% were accepted
64% enrolled (3,555)
31% had ACT scores over 26
8% had ACT scores over 30
58 National Merit Scholars

THE STUDENT BODY
Total 27,639, of whom 18,657 are undergraduates
From 54 states and territories, 109 other countries

70% from Kansas
51% women, 49% men
3% African Americans
1% Native Americans
2% Hispanics
3% Asian Americans
5% international students

AFTER FRESHMAN YEAR
75% returned for sophomore year
25% got a degree within 4 years

51% got a degree within 5 years
58% got a degree within 6 years

WHAT YOU WILL PAY
Resident tuition and fees $2182
Nonresident tuition and fees $7900
Room and board $3544
Need-based college-administered scholarships and grants average $1012 per award
Non-need college-administered scholarships and grants average $2521 per award

---

UNIVERSITY OF MARYLAND COLLEGE PARK

College Park, Maryland • Suburban setting • Public • State-supported • Coed

Maryland is one of the nation's leading public research institutions and the flagship of the University of Maryland System. That means Maryland takes the lead when it comes to educating some of the country's most promising students. Innovative living-learning programs, undergraduate research opportunities, outstanding faculty and students, and the widest range of choices—for courses, housing, recreation, and activities—combine with a superb location in the Washington-Baltimore area to make Maryland the university to choose for a first-rate education.

 Academics

University of Maryland College Park offers a core academic program; fewer than half of graduate courses are open to undergraduates. It awards bachelor's, master's, and doctoral **degrees**. Challenging opportunities include advanced placement, accelerated degree programs, self-designed majors, tutorials, Freshman Honors College, an honors program, a senior project, Phi Beta Kappa, and Sigma Xi. Special programs include cooperative education, internships, summer session for credit, off-campus study, study abroad, and Naval and Air Force ROTC.

The most popular **majors** include political science/ government, computer science, and electrical engineering. A complete listing of majors at University of Maryland College Park appears in the Majors Index beginning on page 379.

The **faculty** at University of Maryland College Park has 1,196 full-time graduate and undergraduate teachers, 97% with terminal degrees. The student-faculty ratio is 13:1.

 Computers on Campus

Students are not required to have a computer. Student rooms are linked to a campus network. 1,700 **computers** available in the computer center, computer labs, academic buildings, the library, and dormitories provide access to the main academic computer, off-campus computing facilities, e-mail, on-line services, and the Internet. Staffed computer lab on campus (open 24 hours a day) provides training in the use of computers and software.

The 7 **libraries** have 2.5 million books and 25,926 subscriptions.

 Campus Life

There are 274 active **organizations** on campus, including a drama/theater group and student-run newspaper and radio station. 12% of eligible men and 15% of eligible women are members of 26 national **fraternities** and 20 national **sororities**. Student **safety services** include campus police, late night transport/escort service, 24-hour emergency telephone alarm devices, student patrols, and electronically operated dormitory entrances.

University of Maryland College Park is a member of the NCAA (Division I). **Intercollegiate sports** (some offering scholarships) include baseball (m), basketball (m, w), cross-country running (m, w), field hockey (w), football (m), golf (m), gymnastics (w), lacrosse (m, w), soccer (m, w), softball (w), swimming and diving (m, w), tennis (m, w), track and field (m, w), volleyball (w), wrestling (m).

 Applying

University of Maryland College Park requires a high school transcript, 3 years of high school math, 2 years of high school foreign language, SAT I or ACT, and in some cases an essay, recommendations, and a campus interview. It recommends 3 years of high school science. Early and midyear entrance are possible, with a 4/30 deadline and continuous processing to 2/15 for financial aid. **Contact:** Dr. Linda Clement, Director of Admissions, 130 Mitchell Building, College Park, MD 20742, 301-314-8385 or toll-free 800-422-5867.

GETTING IN LAST YEAR
14,956 applied
68% were accepted
36% enrolled (3,632)
30% from top tenth of their h.s. class
3.23 average high school GPA
47% had SAT verbal scores over 600 (R)
58% had SAT math scores over 600 (R)
8% had SAT verbal scores over 700 (R)
10% had SAT math scores over 700 (R)
27 National Merit Scholars

THE STUDENT BODY
Total 30,646, of whom 22,922
   are undergraduates

From 50 states and territories,
   113 other countries
75% from Maryland
47% women, 53% men
13% African Americans
1% Native Americans
4% Hispanics
14% Asian Americans
3% international students

AFTER FRESHMAN YEAR
85% returned for sophomore year
31% got a degree within 4 years
59% got a degree within 5 years
66% got a degree within 6 years

AFTER GRADUATION
31% pursued further study (12% arts and
   sciences, 12% dentistry, 4% business)
448 organizations recruited on campus
4 Fulbright scholars

WHAT YOU WILL PAY
Resident tuition and fees $4169
Nonresident tuition and fees $10,228
Room and board $5251
Need-based college-administered scholarships and
   grants average $1190 per award
Non-need college-administered scholarships and
   grants average $3318 per award

UNIVERSITY OF MASSACHUSETTS AMHERST

Amherst, Massachusetts • Small-town setting • Public • State-supported • Coed

The operative word for students at UMass Amherst is "choice." More than 90 academic majors, the largest library at a public school in the Northeast, and 2,000 courses per semester provide for almost limitless academic exploration. The Honors Program gives students the opportunity to work more closely with faculty. Through the Five College Consortium, students can choose classes at Amherst, Hampshire, Mount Holyoke, and Smith Colleges at no extra charge. And the campus enjoys a friendly New England college-town setting.

 ## Academics

UMass Amherst offers an interdisciplinary curriculum and core academic program; all graduate courses are open to undergraduates. It awards associate, bachelor's, master's, and doctoral **degrees**. Challenging opportunities include advanced placement, self-designed majors, tutorials, an honors program, a senior project, Phi Beta Kappa, and Sigma Xi. Special programs include cooperative education, internships, summer session for credit, off-campus study, study abroad, and Army and Air Force ROTC.

The most popular **majors** include psychology, communication, and hotel and restaurant management. A complete listing of majors at UMass Amherst appears in the Majors Index beginning on page 379.

The **faculty** at UMass Amherst has 1,146 full-time graduate and undergraduate teachers, 96% with terminal degrees. The student-faculty ratio is 18:1, and the average class size in core courses is 70.

 ## Computers on Campus

Students are not required to have a computer. Student rooms are linked to a campus network. 1,000 **computers** available in the computer center, computer labs, the research center, the learning resource center, academic buildings, classrooms, the library, and dormitories provide access to the main academic computer, off-campus computing facilities, e-mail, on-line services, and the Internet. Staffed computer lab on campus provides training in the use of computers and software.

The 3 **libraries** have 2.7 million books, 2.1 million microform titles, and 15,641 subscriptions. They are connected to 8 national **on-line** catalogs.

 ## Campus Life

There are 246 active **organizations** on campus, including a drama/theater group and student-run newspaper and radio station. 20% of students participate in student government elections. 8% of eligible men and 6% of eligible women are members of 21 national **fraternities**, 12 national **sororities**, 1 local fraternity, and 1 local sorority. Student **safety services** include locked dormitories at night and during weekends, late night transport/escort service, 24-hour emergency telephone alarm devices, 24-hour patrols by trained security personnel, and electronically operated dormitory entrances.

UMass Amherst is a member of the NCAA (Division I). **Intercollegiate sports** (some offering scholarships) include baseball (m), basketball (m, w), crew (w), cross-country running (m, w), field hockey (w), football (m), gymnastics (m, w), ice hockey (m), lacrosse (m, w), skiing (cross-country) (m, w), skiing (downhill) (m, w), soccer (m, w), softball (w), swimming and diving (m, w), tennis (m, w), track and field (m, w), volleyball (m, w), water polo (m, w).

 ## Applying

UMass Amherst requires an essay, a high school transcript, 3 years of high school math, 2 years of high school foreign language, SAT I or ACT, and in some cases 3 years of high school science. It recommends recommendations and SAT II Subject Tests. Early, deferred, and midyear entrance are possible, with a 2/1 deadline and continuous processing to 3/1 for financial aid. **Contact:** Ms. Arlene Cash, Director of Undergraduate Admissions, Box 30120, Amherst, MA 01003-0120, 413-545-0222.

GETTING IN LAST YEAR
17,562 applied
78% were accepted
28% enrolled (3,861)
12% from top tenth of their h.s. class
2.8 average high school GPA
29% had SAT verbal scores over 600 (R)
31% had SAT math scores over 600 (R)
4% had SAT verbal scores over 700 (R)
4% had SAT math scores over 700 (R)

THE STUDENT BODY
Total 22,916, of whom 17,904
  are undergraduates

From 51 states and territories,
  71 other countries
73% from Massachusetts
48% women, 52% men
4% African Americans
1% Native Americans
4% Hispanics
6% Asian Americans
3% international students

AFTER FRESHMAN YEAR
76% returned for sophomore year

AFTER GRADUATION
26% pursued further study (4% arts and
  sciences, 3% business, 3% law)
2 Fulbright scholars

WHAT YOU WILL PAY
Resident tuition and fees $5514
Nonresident tuition and fees $11,860
Room and board $4188
54% receive need-based financial aid
Need-based college-administered scholarships and
  grants average $6580 per award
Non-need college-administered scholarships and
  grants average $5372 per award

UNIVERSITY OF MIAMI

Coral Gables, Florida • Suburban setting • Private • Independent • Coed

The University of Miami is moderate in size for a major research university (8,000 undergraduates) but comprehensive with 130 majors. UM features the intimacy of a small school by virtue of its residential college system, where students live with a faculty master and associate masters. Three fourths of all undergraduate classes have 25 or fewer students. Study-abroad programs are available in 22 countries and 51 universities. The location of the University in suburban Coral Gables is just a Metrorail ride away from booming Metropolitan Miami—a city of the 21st century—and offers students a magnificent array of cultural and career opportunities.

 Academics

UM offers a general education curriculum and core academic program. It awards bachelor's, master's, doctoral, and first professional **degrees**. Challenging opportunities include advanced placement, accelerated degree programs, self-designed majors, tutorials, an honors program, a senior project, Phi Beta Kappa, and Sigma Xi. Special programs include internships, summer session for credit, study abroad, and Army and Air Force ROTC.

The most popular **majors** include psychology, biology/biological sciences, and nursing. A complete listing of majors at UM appears in the Majors Index beginning on page 379.

The **faculty** at UM has 1,884 full-time graduate and undergraduate teachers, 95% with terminal degrees. The student-faculty ratio is 8:1.

 Computers on Campus

Students are not required to have a computer. 2,000 **computers** available in the computer center, computer labs, the research center, the learning resource center, academic departments, classrooms, the library, the student center, and dormitories provide access to the main academic computer, off-campus computing facilities, e-mail, on-line services, and the Internet. Staffed computer lab on campus (open 24 hours a day).

The 3 **libraries** have 2 million books, 3 million microform titles, and 19,550 subscriptions. They are connected to 4 national **on-line** catalogs.

 Campus Life

There are 200 active **organizations** on campus, including a drama/theater group and student-run newspaper and radio station. 10% of students participate in student government elections. 13% of eligible men and 11% of eligible women are members of 15 national **fraternities** and 9 national **sororities**. Student **safety services** include crime prevention and safety workshops, residential college crime watch, late night transport/escort service, 24-hour emergency telephone alarm devices, 24-hour patrols by trained security personnel, student patrols, and electronically operated dormitory entrances.

UM is a member of the NCAA (Division I). **Intercollegiate sports** (some offering scholarships) include baseball (m), basketball (m, w), crew (m, w), cross-country running (m, w), football (m), golf (w), swimming and diving (m, w), tennis (m, w), track and field (m, w).

 Applying

UM requires an essay, a high school transcript, 1 recommendation, SAT I or ACT, and in some cases SAT II Subject Tests. It recommends 3 years of high school math and science, some high school foreign language, and an interview. Early, deferred, and midyear entrance are possible, with a 3/1 deadline and continuous processing to 2/15 for financial aid. **Contact:** Mr. Edward M. Gillis, Associate Dean of Enrollments, PO Box 248025, Coral Gables, FL 33124, 305-284-4323.

GETTING IN LAST YEAR
10,564 applied
58% were accepted
28% enrolled (1,701)
44% from top tenth of their h.s. class
15% had SAT verbal scores over 600
39% had SAT math scores over 600
39% had ACT scores over 26
2% had SAT verbal scores over 700
10% had SAT math scores over 700
11% had ACT scores over 30
10 National Merit Scholars
28 valedictorians

THE STUDENT BODY
Total 13,541, of whom 8,289
  are undergraduates
From 51 states and territories,
  108 other countries
56% from Florida
50% women, 50% men
11% African Americans
1% Native Americans
30% Hispanics
7% Asian Americans
10% international students

AFTER FRESHMAN YEAR
79% returned for sophomore year
60% got a degree within 5 years
63% got a degree within 6 years

AFTER GRADUATION
205 organizations recruited on campus
2 Fulbright scholars

WHAT YOU WILL PAY
Tuition and fees $18,583
Room and board $7101

UNIVERSITY OF MICHIGAN

Ann Arbor, Michigan • Suburban setting • Public • State-supported • Coed

The University of Michigan, Ann Arbor, is one of the nation's top-ranked public universities that is consistently rated among the top 25 academic institutions in the country. Nearly every one of the University's 17 academic schools and colleges is rated among the top in its field. Students and faculty members come from over 104 different countries and all 50 states. The academic and personal growth achieved by students is unique and diverse, and Michigan graduates are prepared to face the challenges the 21st century will have to offer. A friendly and beautiful campus, extensive resources, dedicated faculty, and exceptional students—this is the Wolverine Spirit, the Michigan tradition.

Academics

Michigan offers no core academic program; more than half of graduate courses are open to undergraduates. It awards bachelor's, master's, doctoral, and first professional **degrees**. Challenging opportunities include advanced placement, accelerated degree programs, self-designed majors, tutorials, an honors program, a senior project, Phi Beta Kappa, and Sigma Xi. Special programs include cooperative education, internships, summer session for credit, off-campus study, study abroad, and Army, Naval, and Air Force ROTC.

The most popular **majors** include psychology, biology/biological sciences, and mechanical engineering. A complete listing of majors at Michigan appears in the Majors Index beginning on page 379.

The **faculty** at Michigan has 2,813 full-time graduate and undergraduate teachers, 95% with terminal degrees. The student-faculty ratio is 12:1.

Computers on Campus

Students are not required to have a computer. Student rooms are linked to a campus network. 3,500 **computers** available in the computer center, computer labs, the learning resource center, academic buildings, the library, the student center, dormitories, and student rooms provide access to the main academic computer, off-campus computing facilities, e-mail, on-line services, and the Internet. Staffed computer lab on campus (open 24 hours a day) provides training in the use of computers and software.

The 18 **libraries** have 6.8 million books, 5.3 million microform titles, and 70,118 subscriptions. They are connected to 12 national **on-line** catalogs.

Campus Life

There are 500 active **organizations** on campus, including a drama/theater group and student-run newspaper and radio station. 20% of eligible men and 20% of eligible women are members of 36 national **fraternities**, 22 national **sororities**, 2 local fraternities, and 1 local sorority. Student **safety services** include bicycle patrols, late night transport/escort service, 24-hour emergency telephone alarm devices, 24-hour patrols by trained security personnel, and electronically operated dormitory entrances.

Michigan is a member of the NCAA (Division I). **Intercollegiate sports** (some offering scholarships) include baseball (m), basketball (m, w), crew (w), cross-country running (m, w), field hockey (w), football (m), golf (m, w), gymnastics (m, w), ice hockey (m), soccer (m, w), softball (m), swimming and diving (m, w), tennis (m, w), track and field (m, w), volleyball (w), wrestling (m).

Applying

Michigan requires an essay, a high school transcript, SAT I or ACT, and in some cases 3 years of high school math, recommendations, and an interview. It recommends 3 years of high school science and some high school foreign language. Early, deferred, and midyear entrance are possible, with a 2/1 deadline and continuous processing to 2/1 for financial aid. **Contact:** Mr. Ted Spencer, Director of Undergraduate Admissions, 515 East Jefferson, Ann Arbor, MI 48109-1316, 313-764-7433; fax 313-936-0740.

GETTING IN LAST YEAR
18,993 applied
69% were accepted
39% enrolled (5,149)
64% from top tenth of their h.s. class
3.6 average high school GPA
29% had SAT verbal scores over 600
76% had SAT math scores over 600
70% had ACT scores over 26
4% had SAT verbal scores over 700
30% had SAT math scores over 700
27% had ACT scores over 30
50 National Merit Scholars

THE STUDENT BODY
Total 36,687, of whom 23,575
   are undergraduates

From 54 states and territories,
   72 other countries
66% from Michigan
49% women, 51% men
9% African Americans
1% Native Americans
5% Hispanics
11% Asian Americans
3% international students

AFTER FRESHMAN YEAR
94% returned for sophomore year
61% got a degree within 4 years
82% got a degree within 5 years
85% got a degree within 6 years

AFTER GRADUATION
900 organizations recruited on campus
1 Marshall, 13 Fulbright scholars

WHAT YOU WILL PAY
Resident tuition and fees $5546
Nonresident tuition and fees $17,070
Room and board $4897
38% receive need-based financial aid
Need-based college-administered scholarships and
   grants average $3300 per award
8% receive non-need financial aid
Non-need college-administered scholarships and
   grants average $2500 per award

UNIVERSITY OF MICHIGAN–DEARBORN

Dearborn, Michigan • Suburban setting • Public • State-supported • Coed

Since its founding 35 years ago, the University of Michigan–Dearborn has been distinguished by its commitment to provide outstanding educational opportunities to nearly 8,000 of the most academically qualified students in southeastern Michigan. While many UM-Dearborn students work full- or part-time, many others elect to participate in internships and co-op placements that provide an opportunity for them to combine practical on-the-job experience with the University of Michigan tradition of scholarship and excellence. It is understandable why new UM-Dearborn students have identified academic reputation and excellent jobs after graduation as the 2 primary reasons for enrolling at UM-Dearborn.

Academics

UM-D offers a core academic program. It awards bachelor's and master's **degrees**. Challenging opportunities include accelerated degree programs, self-designed majors, and an honors program. Special programs include cooperative education, internships, summer session for credit, off-campus study, study abroad, and Army, Naval, and Air Force ROTC.

The most popular **majors** include mechanical engineering, electrical engineering, and psychology. A complete listing of majors at UM-D appears in the Majors Index beginning on page 379.

The **faculty** at UM-D has 219 full-time undergraduate teachers, 84% with terminal degrees. The student-faculty ratio is 21:1.

Computers on Campus

Students are not required to have a computer. 350 **computers** available in the computer center, computer labs, and engineering and writing labs. Staffed computer lab on campus provides training in the use of computers and software.

The **library** has 299,792 books, 432,298 microform titles, and 1,169 subscriptions.

Campus Life

Active **organizations** on campus include drama/theater group and student-run newspaper and radio station. 6% of eligible men and 5% of eligible women are members of 8 national **fraternities** and 4 national **sororities**. Student **safety services** include late night transport/escort service, 24-hour emergency telephone alarm devices, and 24-hour patrols by trained security personnel.

UM-D is a member of the NAIA. **Intercollegiate sports** (some offering scholarships) include basketball (m, w), volleyball (w).

Applying

UM-D requires a high school transcript, SAT I or ACT, and in some cases recommendations and an interview. It recommends 3 years of high school math and science and some high school foreign language. Early entrance is possible, with rolling admissions and continuous processing to 4/1 for financial aid. **Contact:** Ms. Carol S. Mack, Director of Admissions, 4901 Evergreen Road, Dearborn, MI 48128-1491, 313-593-5100.

GETTING IN LAST YEAR

1,903 applied
73% were accepted
52% enrolled (721)
3.24 average high school GPA
25% had ACT scores over 26
4% had ACT scores over 30

THE STUDENT BODY

Total 7,534, of whom 6,135
   are undergraduates
From 7 states and territories
99% from Michigan
54% women, 46% men
7% African Americans
1% Native Americans
2% Hispanics
4% Asian Americans

WHAT YOU WILL PAY

Resident tuition and fees $3872
Nonresident tuition and fees $10,610
Need-based college-administered scholarships and
   grants average $715 per award
Non-need college-administered scholarships and
   grants average $1092 per award

UNIVERSITY OF MINNESOTA, MORRIS

Morris, Minnesota • Small-town setting • Public • State-supported • Coed

"A unique opportunity" best describes the University of Minnesota, Morris. It is one of only a few public liberal arts colleges in the country, making it a rare find for serious students. The emphasis is on undergraduate learning where classes are small and faculty members actually interact with their students. Equally rare for a public institution is its selectivity, where nearly half of the students come from the top 10% of their graduating class. The rigorous academic program is also balanced with a close-knit community where active participation is key to a successful college experience. UMM is also exceptional because it is affordable. Costs are reasonable and help from scholarships and financial aid programs are also available, allowing the very best students access to a quality liberal arts education. UMM brings together quality and affordability for a rare value among so many choices in undergraduate education.

Academics

UMM offers a liberal arts curriculum and core academic program. It awards bachelor's **degrees**. Challenging opportunities include advanced placement, accelerated degree programs, self-designed majors, tutorials, Freshman Honors College, an honors program, and a senior project. Special programs include internships, summer session for credit, off-campus study, and study abroad.

The most popular **majors** include education, biology/biological sciences, and English. A complete listing of majors at UMM appears in the Majors Index beginning on page 379.

The **faculty** at UMM has 128 full-time teachers, 83% with terminal degrees. 100% of the faculty serve as student advisers. The student-faculty ratio is 15:1.

Computers on Campus

Students are not required to have a computer. Student rooms are linked to a campus network. 140 **computers** available in the computer center, computer labs, the research center, the learning resource center, science building, the library, the student center, dormitories, and student rooms provide access to the main academic computer, off-campus computing facilities, e-mail, on-line services, and the Internet.

The **library** has 166,000 books, 19,307 microform titles, and 900 subscriptions.

Campus Life

There are 80 active **organizations** on campus, including a drama/theater group and student-run newspaper and radio station. 40% of students participate in student government elections. 1% of eligible men and 2% of eligible women are members of 1 national **fraternity** and 2 local **sororities**. Student **safety services** include late night transport/escort service, 24-hour patrols by trained security personnel, and electronically operated dormitory entrances. **Intercollegiate sports** include baseball (m), basketball (m, w), football (m), golf (m, w), softball (w), tennis (m, w), track and field (m, w), volleyball (w), wrestling (m).

Applying

UMM requires a high school transcript, 3 years of high school math and science, 2 years of high school foreign language, SAT I or ACT, and in some cases an essay. It recommends an essay and recommendations. Early, deferred, and midyear entrance are possible, with a 3/15 deadline and continuous processing to 4/1 for financial aid. **Contact:** Dr. Rodney M. Oto, Director of Admissions and Financial Aid, Behmler Hall, Morris, MN 56267, 612-589-6035 or toll-free 800-992-8863; fax 612-589-1673.

GETTING IN LAST YEAR
1,280 applied
85% were accepted
49% enrolled (535)
46% from top tenth of their h.s. class
35% had SAT verbal scores over 600
51% had SAT math scores over 600
46% had ACT scores over 26
3% had SAT verbal scores over 700
23% had SAT math scores over 700
11% had ACT scores over 30
7 National Merit Scholars
52 valedictorians

THE STUDENT BODY
1,952 undergraduates

From 22 states and territories,
11 other countries
79% from Minnesota
55% women, 45% men
4% African Americans
3% Native Americans
1% Hispanics
3% Asian Americans
1% international students

AFTER FRESHMAN YEAR
87% returned for sophomore year
39% got a degree within 4 years
60% got a degree within 5 years

AFTER GRADUATION
28% pursued further study (16% arts and sciences, 4% business, 4% law)
76% had job offers within 6 months
35 organizations recruited on campus

WHAT YOU WILL PAY
Resident tuition and fees $4188
Nonresident tuition and fees $11,535
Room and board $3474
Need-based college-administered scholarships and grants average $1033 per award
Non-need college-administered scholarships and grants average $1632 per award

---

UNIVERSITY OF MINNESOTA, TWIN CITIES CAMPUS

Minneapolis, Minnesota • Urban setting • Public • State-supported • Coed

On this beautiful Big Ten campus in the heart of the Twin Cities of Minneapolis and St. Paul, the hallmarks are quality and opportunity. The quality of a U of M–Twin Cities education is a matter of record. And so are the opportunities—about 150 undergraduate and 180 graduate and professional degree programs, many nationally ranked; an Undergraduate Research Opportunities Program that is a national model; one of the largest study-abroad programs in the country; the fifteenth-largest university library system in the country; extraordinary opportunities for internships, employment, and personal enrichment in the culturally rich and thriving Twin Cities area; and more than 500 student organizations.

 ## Academics

U of M–Twin Cities Campus offers a diversified core curriculum and core academic program; more than half of graduate courses are open to undergraduates. It awards bachelor's, master's, doctoral, and first professional **degrees**. Challenging opportunities include advanced placement, accelerated degree programs, self-designed majors, tutorials, Freshman Honors College, an honors program, a senior project, Phi Beta Kappa, and Sigma Xi. Special programs include cooperative education, internships, summer session for credit, off-campus study, study abroad, and Army, Naval, and Air Force ROTC.

The most popular **majors** include mechanical engineering, electrical engineering, and psychology. A complete listing of majors at U of M–Twin Cities Campus appears in the Majors Index beginning on page 379.

The **faculty** at U of M–Twin Cities Campus has 2,663 full-time graduate and undergraduate teachers, 91% with terminal degrees. The student-faculty ratio is 15:1.

 ## Computers on Campus

Students are not required to have a computer. Student rooms are linked to a campus network. 20,000 **comput-**ers available in the computer center, computer labs, the learning resource center, the library, the student center, and dormitories provide access to the main academic computer, e-mail, on-line services, and the Internet.

The 18 **libraries** have 5 million books and 52,018 subscriptions. They are connected to 4 national **on-line** catalogs.

 ## Campus Life

Active **organizations** on campus include drama/theater group and student-run newspaper and radio station. 3% of eligible men and 3% of eligible women are members of 27 national **fraternities**, 15 national **sororities**, and 2 local sororities. Student **safety services** include victim assistance programs, safety/security orientation, security lighting, vehicle assistance, late night transport/escort service, 24-hour emergency telephone alarm devices, 24-hour patrols by trained security personnel, student patrols, and electronically operated dormitory entrances.

U of M–Twin Cities Campus is a member of the NCAA (Division I). **Intercollegiate sports** (some offering scholarships) include baseball (m), basketball (m, w), cross-country running (m, w), football (m), golf (m, w), gymnastics (m, w), ice hockey (m, w), swimming and diving (m, w), tennis (m, w), track and field (m, w), volleyball (w), wrestling (m).

  ## Applying

U of M–Twin Cities Campus requires a high school transcript, 3 years of high school math and science, 2 years of high school foreign language, SAT I or ACT, and in some cases SAT I and a minimum high school GPA of 3.0. It recommends a minimum high school GPA of 2.0. Early, deferred, and midyear entrance are possible, with rolling admissions and continuous processing to 4/30 for financial aid. **Contact:** Dr. Wayne Sigler, Director of Admissions, 240 Williamson, Minneapolis, MN 55455-0213, 612-625-2006 or toll-free 800-752-1000; fax 612-626-1693.

GETTING IN LAST YEAR	THE STUDENT BODY	AFTER FRESHMAN YEAR
13,271 applied	Total 36,995, of whom 23,715	81% returned for sophomore year
62% were accepted	are undergraduates	14% got a degree within 4 years
53% enrolled (4,356)	From 55 states and territories,	38% got a degree within 5 years
26% from top tenth of their h.s. class	85 other countries	49% got a degree within 6 years
20% had SAT verbal scores over 600 (R)	74% from Minnesota	
53% had SAT math scores over 600 (R)	49% women, 51% men	**WHAT YOU WILL PAY**
36% had ACT scores over 26	4% African Americans	Resident tuition and fees $3857
2% had SAT verbal scores over 700 (R)	1% Native Americans	Nonresident tuition and fees $10,344
17% had SAT math scores over 700 (R)	2% Hispanics	Room and board $4085
9% had ACT scores over 30	8% Asian Americans	
136 valedictorians	2% international students	

UNIVERSITY OF MISSOURI–COLUMBIA

Columbia, Missouri • Small-town setting • Public • State-supported • Coed

Academics

MU offers a core academic program. It awards bachelor's, master's, doctoral, and first professional **degrees**. Challenging opportunities include advanced placement, accelerated degree programs, self-designed majors, tutorials, Freshman Honors College, an honors program, a senior project, Phi Beta Kappa, and Sigma Xi. Special programs include cooperative education, internships, summer session for credit, off-campus study, study abroad, and Army, Naval, and Air Force ROTC.

The most popular **majors** include business, education, and psychology. A complete listing of majors at MU appears in the Majors Index beginning on page 379.

The **faculty** at MU has 1,538 full-time graduate and undergraduate teachers, 87% with terminal degrees. The student-faculty ratio is 19:1.

Computers on Campus

Students are not required to have a computer. Student rooms are linked to a campus network. 800 **computers** available in the computer center, computer labs, classrooms, the library, the student center, and dormitories provide access to e-mail and on-line services. Staffed computer lab on campus (open 24 hours a day) provides training in the use of computers and software.

The 11 **libraries** have 2.6 million books, 5.1 million microform titles, and 22,973 subscriptions. They are connected to 200 national **on-line** catalogs.

Campus Life

There are 376 active **organizations** on campus, including a drama/theater group and student-run newspaper and radio station. 11% of students participate in student government elections. 24% of eligible men and 24% of eligible women are members of 32 national **fraternities** and 18 national **sororities**. Student **safety services** include late night transport/escort service, 24-hour emergency telephone alarm devices, and electronically operated dormitory entrances.

MU is a member of the NCAA (Division I). **Intercollegiate sports** (some offering scholarships) include baseball (m), basketball (m, w), cross-country running (m, w), football (m), golf (m, w), gymnastics (w), softball (w), swimming and diving (m, w), tennis (m, w), track and field (m, w), volleyball (w), wrestling (m).

Applying

MU requires a high school transcript, 3 years of high school math, and ACT. It recommends 3 years of high school science and 2 years of high school foreign language. Early, deferred, and midyear entrance are possible, with a 5/1 deadline and a 3/1 priority date for financial aid. **Contact:** Ms. Georgeanne Porter, Director of Undergraduate Admissions, 130 Jesse Hall, Columbia, MO 65211, 314-882-7786 or toll-free 800-225-6075 (in-state); fax 314-882-7887.

GETTING IN LAST YEAR
8,441 applied
90% were accepted
51% enrolled (3,845)
32% from top tenth of their h.s. class
45% had ACT scores over 26
17% had ACT scores over 30
61 National Merit Scholars

THE STUDENT BODY
Total 22,313, of whom 16,784
  are undergraduates

From 50 states and territories,
  117 other countries
88% from Missouri
52% women, 48% men
6% African Americans
1% Native Americans
1% Hispanics
2% Asian Americans
3% international students

AFTER FRESHMAN YEAR
82% returned for sophomore year

WHAT YOU WILL PAY
Resident tuition and fees $3771
Nonresident tuition and fees $10,395
Room and board $3599
41% receive need-based financial aid
Need-based college-administered scholarships and
  grants average $980 per award
Non-need college-administered scholarships and
  grants average $2010 per award

UNIVERSITY OF MISSOURI–KANSAS CITY

Kansas City, Missouri • Urban setting • Public • State-supported • Coed

 Academics

UMKC offers a core academic program; fewer than half of graduate courses are open to undergraduates. It awards bachelor's, master's, doctoral, and first professional **degrees**. Challenging opportunities include advanced placement, accelerated degree programs, self-designed majors, an honors program, and a senior project. Special programs include cooperative education, internships, summer session for credit, off-campus study, study abroad, and Army ROTC.

The most popular **majors** include biology/biological sciences, liberal arts/general studies, and business. A complete listing of majors at UMKC appears in the Majors Index beginning on page 379.

The **faculty** at UMKC has 527 full-time graduate and undergraduate teachers, 94% with terminal degrees. The student-faculty ratio is 10:1.

 Computers on Campus

Students are not required to have a computer. Student rooms are linked to a campus network. 400 **computers** available in the computer center, computer labs, the research center, the learning resource center, classrooms, the library, the student center, and dormitories provide access to the main academic computer, off-campus computing facilities, e-mail, and on-line services. Staffed computer lab on campus provides training in the use of computers and software.

The 4 **libraries** have 962,529 books, 531,092 microform titles, and 8,793 subscriptions. They are connected to 8 national **on-line** catalogs.

 Campus Life

There are 75 active **organizations** on campus, including a drama/theater group and student-run newspaper. 5% of eligible men and 4% of eligible women are members of 4 national **fraternities**, 3 national **sororities**, and 1 local sorority. Student **safety services** include late night transport/escort service, 24-hour emergency telephone alarm devices, and 24-hour patrols by trained security personnel.

UMKC is a member of the NCAA (Division I). **Intercollegiate sports** (some offering scholarships) include basketball (m, w), cross-country running (m, w), golf (m, w), riflery (m, w), soccer (m), softball (w), tennis (m, w), track and field (m, w), volleyball (w).

 Applying

UMKC requires a high school transcript, 3 years of high school math, 4 years of high school English, 2 years each of science and social science, 1 year of fine arts, and ACT. Early, deferred, and midyear entrance are possible, with rolling admissions and continuous processing to 3/15 for financial aid. **Contact:** Mr. Melvin C. Tyler, Director of Admissions, 5100 Rockhill Road, Kansas City, MO 64110-2499, 816-235-1111; fax 816-235-1717.

GETTING IN LAST YEAR
2,155 applied
61% were accepted
47% enrolled (609)
30% from top tenth of their h.s. class
42% had ACT scores over 26
15% had ACT scores over 30

THE STUDENT BODY
Total 10,209, of whom 5,447
   are undergraduates
From 38 states and territories,
   70 other countries

76% from Missouri
55% women, 45% men
9% African Americans
1% Native Americans
3% Hispanics
5% Asian Americans
6% international students

AFTER FRESHMAN YEAR
72% returned for sophomore year
11% got a degree within 4 years
24% got a degree within 5 years
41% got a degree within 6 years

AFTER GRADUATION
85% had job offers within 6 months
384 organizations recruited on campus

WHAT YOU WILL PAY
Resident tuition and fees $3799
Nonresident tuition and fees $10,423
Room and board $3750
Need-based college-administered scholarships and
   grants average $713 per award
Non-need college-administered scholarships and
   grants average $2702 per award

UNIVERSITY OF MISSOURI–ROLLA

Rolla, Missouri • Small-town setting • Public • State-supported • Coed

The University of Missouri–Rolla has an outstanding engineering, science, and liberal arts curriculum that produces graduates able to meet the complex challenges of a changing world. Rolla faculty members are renowned scholars and researchers as well as teachers who care about their students. Leaders learn from leaders. The UMR Promise program guarantees that all graduates who follow a balanced prescribed program will have a career opportunity within 6 months of graduation or the University will offer the student a one-year tuition grant for additional study at UM–Rolla.

 Academics

UMR offers a core academic program; more than half of graduate courses are open to undergraduates. It awards bachelor's, master's, and doctoral **degrees**. Challenging opportunities include advanced placement, tutorials, an honors program, a senior project, and Sigma Xi. Special programs include cooperative education, summer session for credit, off-campus study, study abroad, and Army and Air Force ROTC.

The most popular **majors** include mechanical engineering, civil engineering, and electrical engineering. A complete listing of majors at UMR appears in the Majors Index beginning on page 379.

The **faculty** at UMR has 333 full-time graduate and undergraduate teachers, 94% with terminal degrees. The student-faculty ratio is 14:1.

 Computers on Campus

Students are not required to have a computer. Student rooms are linked to a campus network. 625 **computers** available in the computer center, computer labs, the learning resource center, classrooms, the library, and dormitories provide access to the main academic computer, off-campus computing facilities, e-mail, and on-line services. Staffed computer lab on campus (open 24 hours a day) provides training in the use of computers and software.

The **library** has 455,302 books, 509,889 microform titles, and 1,405 subscriptions. It is connected to 3 national **on-line** catalogs.

 Campus Life

There are 138 active **organizations** on campus, including a drama/theater group and student-run newspaper and radio station. 28% of eligible men and 20% of eligible women are members of 21 national **fraternities** and 5 national **sororities**. Student **safety services** include Pro Active Crime Prevention Programs, late night transport/escort service, 24-hour emergency telephone alarm devices, 24-hour patrols by trained security personnel, student patrols, and electronically operated dormitory entrances.

UMR is a member of the NCAA (Division II). **Intercollegiate sports** (some offering scholarships) include baseball (m), basketball (m, w), cross-country running (m, w), football (m), golf (m), soccer (m, w), softball (w), swimming and diving (m), tennis (m), track and field (m, w).

Applying

UMR requires a high school transcript, 3 years of high school math, and SAT I or ACT. It recommends 3 years of high school science and some high school foreign language. Early, deferred, and midyear entrance are possible, with a 7/1 deadline and continuous processing to 3/1 for financial aid. **Contact:** Mr. Dave Allen, Director of Admissions and Financial Aid, 102 Parker Hall, Rolla, MO 65401-0249, 573-341-4164.

GETTING IN LAST YEAR
2,242 applied
97% were accepted
38% enrolled (828)
50% from top tenth of their h.s. class
30% had SAT verbal scores over 600
75% had SAT math scores over 600
70% had ACT scores over 26
3% had SAT verbal scores over 700
32% had SAT math scores over 700
38% had ACT scores over 30
27 National Merit Scholars

THE STUDENT BODY
Total 5,426, of whom 4,386
 are undergraduates
From 50 states and territories,
 52 other countries
75% from Missouri
24% women, 76% men
3% African Americans
1% Native Americans
1% Hispanics
3% Asian Americans
3% international students

AFTER FRESHMAN YEAR
78% returned for sophomore year
9% got a degree within 4 years
40% got a degree within 5 years
53% got a degree within 6 years

WHAT YOU WILL PAY
Resident tuition and fees $4483
Nonresident tuition and fees $11,704
Room and board $3422
39% receive need-based financial aid
51% receive non-need financial aid
Non-need college-administered scholarships and
 grants average $2957 per award

UNIVERSITY OF NEW HAMPSHIRE

Durham, New Hampshire • Small-town setting • Public • State-supported • Coed

UNH offers an excellent education at a reasonable cost to students with a broad range of interests. Over 100 majors, 2,000 courses, and 100 student clubs and organizations are offered. Programs that provide valuable experience include the honors program, undergraduate research, internships, study abroad, and national exchange. UNH's location also caters to a wide range of interests. The campus itself is in a small-town setting surrounded by woods and farms; within 20 minutes is the Atlantic coastline, and just over an hour away are the White Mountains, Boston, Massachusetts, and Portland, Maine.

 Academics

UNH offers an interdisciplinary curriculum and core academic program; fewer than half of graduate courses are open to undergraduates. It awards associate, bachelor's, master's, and doctoral **degrees**. Challenging opportunities include advanced placement, accelerated degree programs, self-designed majors, tutorials, an honors program, a senior project, Phi Beta Kappa, and Sigma Xi. Special programs include internships, summer session for credit, off-campus study, study abroad, and Army and Air Force ROTC.

The most popular **majors** include business, English, and biology/biological sciences. A complete listing of majors at UNH appears in the Majors Index beginning on page 379.

The **faculty** at UNH has 629 full-time graduate and undergraduate teachers, 90% with terminal degrees. 100% of the faculty serve as student advisers. The student-faculty ratio is 18:1.

 Computers on Campus

Students are not required to have a computer. Student rooms are linked to a campus network. 200 **computers** available in the computer center, computer labs, classrooms, and the student center provide access to the main academic computer, off-campus computing facilities, e-mail, on-line services, and the Internet. Staffed computer lab on campus.

The 5 **libraries** have 1 million books, 714,199 microform titles, and 6,500 subscriptions.

 Campus Life

There are 100 active **organizations** on campus, including a drama/theater group and student-run newspaper and radio station. 35% of students participate in student government elections. 10% of eligible men and 10% of eligible women are members of 10 national **fraternities**, 6 national **sororities**, and 1 local fraternity. Student **safety services** include late night transport/escort service, 24-hour emergency telephone alarm devices, 24-hour patrols by trained security personnel, student patrols, and electronically operated dormitory entrances.

UNH is a member of the NCAA (Division I). **Intercollegiate sports** (some offering scholarships) include badminton (m, w), baseball (m), basketball (m, w), crew (m), cross-country running (m, w), equestrian sports (m, w), fencing (m, w), field hockey (w), football (m), golf (m, w), gymnastics (w), ice hockey (m, w), lacrosse (m, w), rugby (m, w), sailing (w), skiing (cross-country) (m, w), skiing (downhill) (m, w), soccer (m, w), softball (w), squash (m, w), swimming and diving (m, w), tennis (m, w), track and field (m, w), volleyball (m, w).

 Applying

UNH requires an essay, a high school transcript, 4 years of high school math, 1 recommendation, and SAT I or ACT. It recommends 4 years of high school science, 3 years of high school foreign language, a campus interview, and SAT II Subject Tests. Early, deferred, and midyear entrance are possible, with a 2/1 deadline and continuous processing to 3/1 for financial aid. **Contact:** Mr. David Kraus, Director of Admissions, Grant House, 4 Garrison Avenue, Durham, NH 03824, 603-862-1360.

GETTING IN LAST YEAR
10,026 applied
77% were accepted
32% enrolled (2,440)
24% from top tenth of their h.s. class
3.0 average high school GPA
30% had SAT verbal scores over 600 (R)
32% had SAT math scores over 600 (R)
3% had SAT verbal scores over 700 (R)
4% had SAT math scores over 700 (R)

THE STUDENT BODY
Total 12,414, of whom 10,620
    are undergraduates
From 44 states and territories,
    30 other countries

60% from New Hampshire
57% women, 43% men
1% African Americans
1% Native Americans
1% Hispanics
2% Asian Americans
1% international students

AFTER FRESHMAN YEAR
85% returned for sophomore year
50% got a degree within 4 years
68% got a degree within 5 years
75% got a degree within 6 years

AFTER GRADUATION
175 organizations recruited on campus
2 Fulbright scholars

WHAT YOU WILL PAY
Resident tuition and fees $5054
Nonresident tuition and fees $13,724
Room and board $4150
59% receive need-based financial aid
Need-based college-administered scholarships and
    grants average $2702 per award
31% receive non-need financial aid
Non-need college-administered scholarships and
    grants average $5245 per award

UNIVERSITY OF NORTH CAROLINA AT ASHEVILLE

Asheville, North Carolina • Suburban setting • Public • State-supported • Coed

 Academics

UNCA offers a liberal arts curriculum. It awards bachelor's and master's **degrees**. Challenging opportunities include advanced placement, accelerated degree programs, self-designed majors, an honors program, a senior project, and Sigma Xi. Special programs include internships, summer session for credit, off-campus study, and study abroad.

The most popular **majors** include business, psychology, and biology/biological sciences. A complete listing of majors at UNCA appears in the Majors Index beginning on page 379.

The **faculty** at UNCA has 153 full-time graduate and undergraduate teachers, 82% with terminal degrees. 100% of the faculty serve as student advisers. The student-faculty ratio is 12:1.

 Computers on Campus

Students are not required to have a computer. Student rooms are linked to a campus network. 400 **computers** available in the computer center, computer labs, classroom buildings, the library, and dormitories provide access to the main academic computer, off-campus computing facilities, e-mail, and on-line services. Staffed computer lab on campus provides training in the use of computers and software.

The 2 **libraries** have 321,649 books, 59,302 microform titles, and 2,004 subscriptions. They are connected to 4 national **on-line** catalogs.

 Campus Life

There are 70 active **organizations** on campus, including a drama/theater group and student-run newspaper. 8% of eligible men and 6% of eligible women are members of 3 national **fraternities**, 2 national **sororities**, 1 local fraternity, and 1 local sorority. Student **safety services** include late night transport/escort service, 24-hour patrols by trained security personnel, and electronically operated dormitory entrances.

UNCA is a member of the NCAA (Division I). **Intercollegiate sports** (some offering scholarships) include baseball (m), basketball (m, w), cross-country running (m, w), golf (m), soccer (m, w), softball (w), tennis (m, w), track and field (m, w), volleyball (w).

 Applying

UNCA requires a high school transcript, 3 years of high school math and science, 4 years of high school English, 2 years of high school social studies, SAT I or ACT, and in some cases recommendations and an interview. It recommends an essay, 2 years of high school foreign language, SAT II Subject Tests, and a minimum high school GPA of 3.0. Early, deferred, and midyear entrance are possible, with a 4/15 deadline and continuous processing to 3/1 for financial aid. **Contact:** Mr. John White, Director of Admissions, University Heights, Asheville, NC 28804-3299, 704-251-6481.

GETTING IN LAST YEAR

2,117 applied
59% were accepted
32% enrolled (397)
27% from top tenth of their h.s. class
3.54 average high school GPA
37% had SAT verbal scores over 600 (R)
34% had SAT math scores over 600 (R)
29% had ACT scores over 26
5% had SAT verbal scores over 700 (R)
3% had SAT math scores over 700 (R)
0% had ACT scores over 30
6 National Merit Scholars
5 valedictorians

THE STUDENT BODY

Total 3,222, of whom 3,176
    are undergraduates

From 39 states and territories,
    42 other countries
89% from North Carolina
56% women, 44% men
4% African Americans
0% Native Americans
1% Hispanics
1% Asian Americans
1% international students

AFTER FRESHMAN YEAR

79% returned for sophomore year
17% got a degree within 4 years
35% got a degree within 5 years
41% got a degree within 6 years

AFTER GRADUATION

47% pursued further study (18% business, 2% law, 2% medicine)
1 Fulbright scholar

WHAT YOU WILL PAY

Resident tuition and fees $1708
Nonresident tuition and fees $7748
Room and board $2678
27% receive need-based financial aid
Need-based college-administered scholarships and grants average $900 per award
24% receive non-need financial aid
Non-need college-administered scholarships and grants average $1933 per award

UNIVERSITY OF NORTH CAROLINA AT CHAPEL HILL

Chapel Hill, North Carolina • Suburban setting • Public • State-supported • Coed

The University of North Carolina at Chapel Hill was the first state university to open its doors and the nation's only public university to award degrees in the 18th century. The University was chartered in 1789, and the cornerstone for the first state university building, Old East, was laid in 1793. Now part of the 16-campus UNC System, Carolina has earned a worldwide reputation for vital teaching, cutting-edge research, and distinguished public service. Among the nation's most comprehensive institutions, units include schools of business, education, journalism and mass communication, law, information and library science, and social work, along with dentistry, medicine, nursing, pharmacy, and public health.

Academics

UNC Chapel Hill offers a liberal arts curriculum and core academic program. It awards bachelor's, master's, doctoral, and first professional **degrees**. Challenging opportunities include advanced placement, accelerated degree programs, self-designed majors, an honors program, Phi Beta Kappa, and Sigma Xi. Special programs include internships, summer session for credit, off-campus study, study abroad, and Army, Naval, and Air Force ROTC.

The most popular **majors** include biology/biological sciences, business, and psychology. A complete listing of majors at UNC Chapel Hill appears in the Majors Index beginning on page 379.

The **faculty** at UNC Chapel Hill has 2,328 full-time graduate and undergraduate teachers, 94% with terminal degrees.

Computers on Campus

Students are not required to have a computer. 460 **computers** available in the computer center, computer labs, the learning resource center, classrooms, the library, the student center, and dormitories provide access to the main academic computer, off-campus computing facilities, e-mail, on-line services, and the Internet. Staffed computer lab on campus provides training in the use of computers and software.

The 16 **libraries** have 4.3 million books, 3.9 million microform titles, and 43,840 subscriptions.

Campus Life

There are 350 active **organizations** on campus, including a drama/theater group and student-run newspaper and radio station. 17% of eligible men and 17% of eligible women are members of 28 national **fraternities**, 15 national **sororities**, and 1 local sorority. Student **safety services** include late night transport/escort service, 24-hour emergency telephone alarm devices, 24-hour patrols by trained security personnel, student patrols, and electronically operated dormitory entrances.

UNC Chapel Hill is a member of the NCAA (Division I). **Intercollegiate sports** include baseball (m), basketball (m, w), cross-country running (m, w), fencing (m, w), field hockey (w), football (m), golf (m, w), gymnastics (w), lacrosse (m, w), soccer (m, w), softball (w), swimming and diving (m, w), tennis (m, w), track and field (m, w), volleyball (w), wrestling (m).

Applying

UNC Chapel Hill requires a high school transcript, 3 years of high school math and science, 2 years of high school foreign language, 4 years of high school English, 2 years of high school social studies, and SAT I or ACT. Early action is possible, with a 1/15 deadline and continuous processing to 3/1 for financial aid. **Contact:** Dr. James Walters, Associate Provost/Director of Undergraduate Admissions, CB #2200, Jackson Hall, Chapel Hill, NC 27599, 919-966-3621.

GETTING IN LAST YEAR
16,063 applied
35% were accepted
58% enrolled (3,239)
73% from top tenth of their h.s. class
3.8 average high school GPA
59% had SAT verbal scores over 600 (R)
59% had SAT math scores over 600 (R)
54% had ACT scores over 26
16% had SAT verbal scores over 700 (R)
13% had SAT math scores over 700 (R)
22% had ACT scores over 30
254 National Merit Scholars
220 class presidents
226 valedictorians

THE STUDENT BODY
Total 24,439, of whom 15,702
  are undergraduates
From 53 states and territories,
  55 other countries
82% from North Carolina
60% women, 40% men
10% African Americans
1% Native Americans
1% Hispanics
5% Asian Americans
1% international students

AFTER FRESHMAN YEAR
63% got a degree within 4 years
82% got a degree within 5 years

AFTER GRADUATION
33% pursued further study
69% had job offers within 6 months
200 organizations recruited on campus
2 Marshall, 4 Fulbright scholars

WHAT YOU WILL PAY
Resident tuition and fees $1685
Nonresident tuition and fees $9801
Room and board $4350
Need-based college-administered scholarships and
  grants average $1120 per award
Non-need college-administered scholarships and
  grants average $1620 per award

UNIVERSITY OF NOTRE DAME

Notre Dame, Indiana • Suburban setting • Private • Independent-Religious • Coed

▶ Notre Dame is a Catholic university that attracts students from all states and many other countries. The unique Freshman Year of Studies program, dynamic faculty, supportive residence hall system, and new state-of-the-art classroom building are special features. Many students pursue second majors or concentrations. Notre Dame provides exceptional academic opportunities in a friendly environment on a beautiful campus. Community service, music, drama, and recreational sports are major aspects of student life. Most varsity sports attain national rankings or win conference championships each year.

 Academics

Notre Dame offers a liberal arts core curriculum and core academic program; fewer than half of graduate courses are open to undergraduates. It awards bachelor's, master's, doctoral, and first professional **degrees**. Challenging opportunities include advanced placement, accelerated degree programs, tutorials, Freshman Honors College, an honors program, a senior project, Phi Beta Kappa, and Sigma Xi. Special programs include summer session for credit, off-campus study, study abroad, and Army, Naval, and Air Force ROTC.

The most popular **majors** include accounting and political science/government. A complete listing of majors at Notre Dame appears in the Majors Index beginning on page 379.

The **faculty** at Notre Dame has 648 full-time graduate and undergraduate teachers, 96% with terminal degrees. 50% of the faculty serve as student advisers. The student-faculty ratio is 12:1.

Computers on Campus

Students are not required to have a computer. Student rooms are linked to a campus network. 490 **computers** available in the computer center, computer labs, various academic departments, classrooms, the library, and the student center provide access to the main academic computer, e-mail, on-line services, and the Internet. Staffed computer lab on campus (open 24 hours a day) provides training in the use of computers and software.

The 9 **libraries** have 2.1 million books, 2.5 million microform titles, and 22,640 subscriptions. They are connected to 3 national **on-line** catalogs.

Campus Life

There are 200 active **organizations** on campus, including a drama/theater group and student-run newspaper and radio station. No national or local **fraternities** or **sororities**. Student **safety services** include late night transport/escort service, 24-hour emergency telephone alarm devices, 24-hour patrols by trained security personnel, and electronically operated dormitory entrances.

Notre Dame is a member of the NCAA (Division I). **Intercollegiate sports** (some offering scholarships) include baseball (m), basketball (m, w), crew (m, w), cross-country running (m, w), equestrian sports (m, w), fencing (m, w), football (m), golf (m, w), gymnastics (m, w), ice hockey (m), lacrosse (m, w), rugby (m), sailing (m, w), skiing (downhill) (m, w), soccer (m, w), softball (w), swimming and diving (m, w), tennis (m, w), track and field (m, w), volleyball (m, w), water polo (m).

Applying

Notre Dame requires an essay, a high school transcript, 3 years of high school science, 2 years of high school foreign language, 1 recommendation, SAT I or ACT, and in some cases 4 years of high school math. It recommends 4 years of high school math and SAT II Subject Tests. Early and deferred entrance are possible, with a 1/5 deadline and continuous processing to 2/15 for financial aid. **Contact:** Mr. Kevin M. Rooney, Director of Admissions, 113 Main Building, Notre Dame, IN 46556, 219-631-7505.

GETTING IN LAST YEAR
9,999 applied
39% were accepted
49% enrolled (1,906)
82% from top tenth of their h.s. class
43% had SAT verbal scores over 600
84% had SAT math scores over 600
82% had ACT scores over 26
5% had SAT verbal scores over 700
37% had SAT math scores over 700
45% had ACT scores over 30
45 National Merit Scholars
248 class presidents
260 valedictorians

THE STUDENT BODY
Total 10,000, of whom 7,600
   are undergraduates

From 52 states and territories,
   35 other countries
9% from Indiana
43% women, 57% men
3% African Americans
1% Native Americans
6% Hispanics
4% Asian Americans
2% international students

AFTER FRESHMAN YEAR
97% returned for sophomore year
93% got a degree within 4 years
94% got a degree within 5 years

AFTER GRADUATION
33% pursued further study (11% arts and
   sciences, 9% law, 8% medicine)
60% had job offers within 6 months
251 organizations recruited on campus
11 Fulbright scholars

WHAT YOU WILL PAY
Tuition and fees $17,971
Room and board $4500
60% receive need-based financial aid
Need-based college-administered scholarships and
   grants average $7100 per award
Non-need college-administered scholarships and
   grants average $13,000 per award

UNIVERSITY OF OKLAHOMA

Norman, Oklahoma • Suburban setting • Public • State-supported • Coed

The University of Oklahoma is dedicated to academic excellence enhanced by Sooner pride and tradition. OU has attracted its share of outstanding students. The University of Oklahoma now has the highest percentage of National Merit Scholars of any comprehensive public university in America. OU provides outstanding opportunities that include study abroad, a technologically advanced campus, and an emphasis on student leadership. Most OU professors are involved in the discovery and creation of new knowledge. They are leaders in their fields and have plenty to offer in the classroom. OU provides a major college experience in a private college atmosphere.

 ## Academics

OU offers a core academic program; more than half of graduate courses are open to undergraduates. It awards bachelor's, master's, doctoral, and first professional **degrees**. Challenging opportunities include advanced placement, accelerated degree programs, self-designed majors, tutorials, an honors program, a senior project, Phi Beta Kappa, and Sigma Xi. Special programs include cooperative education, internships, summer session for credit, off-campus study, study abroad, and Army, Naval, and Air Force ROTC.

The most popular **majors** include psychology, accounting, and management information systems. A complete listing of majors at OU appears in the Majors Index beginning on page 379.

The **faculty** at OU has 841 full-time graduate and undergraduate teachers, 85% with terminal degrees.

 ## Computers on Campus

Students are not required to have a computer. Student rooms are linked to a campus network. 600 **computers** available in the computer center, computer labs, the research center, academic units, classrooms, the library, the student center, dormitories, and student rooms provide access to the main academic computer, off-campus computing facilities, e-mail, on-line services, and the Internet. Staffed computer lab on campus (open 24 hours a day) provides training in the use of computers and software.

The 8 **libraries** have 2.5 million books, 3.4 million microform titles, and 16,600 subscriptions. They are connected to 4 national **on-line** catalogs.

 ## Campus Life

There are 213 active **organizations** on campus, including a drama/theater group and student-run newspaper. 20% of students participate in student government elections. 18% of eligible men and 18% of eligible women are members of 22 national **fraternities** and 15 national **sororities**. Student **safety services** include crime prevention programs, late night transport/escort service, 24-hour emergency telephone alarm devices, 24-hour patrols by trained security personnel, and student patrols.

OU is a member of the NCAA (Division I). **Intercollegiate sports** (some offering scholarships) include baseball (m), basketball (m, w), cross-country running (m, w), football (m), golf (m, w), gymnastics (m, w), softball (w), tennis (m, w), track and field (m, w), volleyball (w), wrestling (m).

 ## Applying

OU requires a high school transcript, 3 years of high school math, 2 years of history (including one year of American history), 2 years of high school lab science, 4 units of high school English, SAT I or ACT, a minimum high school GPA of 3.0, and in some cases an essay. It recommends some high school foreign language. Early and midyear entrance are possible, with a 7/15 deadline and continuous processing to 3/1 for financial aid. **Contact:** Ms. Leslie Baumert, Director of Prospective Student Services, 407 West Boyd, Norman, OK 73019, 405-325-2151 or toll-free 800-234-6868; fax 405-325-7478.

GETTING IN LAST YEAR
5,503 applied
88% were accepted
56% enrolled (2,699)
31% from top tenth of their h.s. class
36% had ACT scores over 26
14% had ACT scores over 30
179 National Merit Scholars

THE STUDENT BODY
Total 19,964, of whom 15,527
  are undergraduates
From 50 states and territories,
  83 other countries

78% from Oklahoma
45% women, 55% men
7% African Americans
7% Native Americans
3% Hispanics
5% Asian Americans
7% international students

AFTER FRESHMAN YEAR
79% returned for sophomore year
17% got a degree within 4 years
38% got a degree within 5 years
45% got a degree within 6 years

AFTER GRADUATION
212 organizations recruited on campus
1 Fulbright scholar

WHAT YOU WILL PAY
Resident tuition and fees $1962
Nonresident tuition and fees $5427
Room and board $3808
61% receive need-based financial aid
Need-based college-administered scholarships and
  grants average $1205 per award
39% receive non-need financial aid
Non-need college-administered scholarships and
  grants average $2759 per award

UNIVERSITY OF PENNSYLVANIA

Philadelphia, Pennsylvania • Urban setting • Private • Independent • Coed

---

The University of Pennsylvania was founded over 250 years ago by Benjamin Franklin. Based upon his ideas, Penn was the first college to instruct students in the sciences, economics, modern languages, public law, and applied mathematics. It opened the nation's first medical school in 1765 and, in 1779, became the nation's first university. Today, Penn has 4 undergraduate schools and 12 graduate and professional schools.

 ## Academics

Penn offers a core academic program; fewer than half of graduate courses are open to undergraduates. It awards associate, bachelor's, master's, doctoral, and first professional **degrees**. Challenging opportunities include advanced placement, accelerated degree programs, self-designed majors, tutorials, an honors program, a senior project, Phi Beta Kappa, and Sigma Xi. Special programs include internships, summer session for credit, off-campus study, study abroad, and Army, Naval, and Air Force ROTC.

The most popular **majors** include finance/banking, history, and psychology. A complete listing of majors at Penn appears in the Majors Index beginning on page 379.

The **faculty** at Penn has 2,174 full-time graduate and undergraduate teachers, 99% with terminal degrees. The student-faculty ratio is 5:1.

 ## Computers on Campus

Students are not required to have a computer. Student rooms are linked to a campus network. 555 **computers** available in the computer center, computer labs, the research center, classroom buildings, classrooms, the library, the student center, and dormitories provide access to the main academic computer, off-campus computing facilities, and e-mail. Staffed computer lab on campus (open 24 hours a day).

The 14 **libraries** have 4.2 million books and 33,384 subscriptions. They are connected to 11 national **on-line** catalogs.

 ## Campus Life

There are 306 active **organizations** on campus, including a drama/theater group and student-run newspaper and radio station. 30% of eligible men and 30% of eligible women are members of 29 national **fraternities** and 14 national **sororities**. Student **safety services** include late night transport/escort service, 24-hour emergency telephone alarm devices, 24-hour patrols by trained security personnel, and student patrols.

Penn is a member of the NCAA (Division I). **Intercollegiate sports** include baseball (m), basketball (m, w), crew (m, w), cross-country running (m, w), fencing (m, w), field hockey (w), football (m), golf (m), gymnastics (w), lacrosse (m, w), soccer (m, w), softball (w), squash (m, w), swimming and diving (m, w), tennis (m, w), track and field (m, w), volleyball (w), wrestling (m).

 ## Applying

Penn requires an essay, a high school transcript, 2 recommendations, SAT I or ACT, and 3 SAT II Subject Tests (including SAT II: Writing Test). It recommends 3 years of high school math and science, 3 years of high school foreign language, and an interview. Early and deferred entrance are possible, with a 1/1 deadline and a 2/15 priority date for financial aid. **Contact:** Mr. Willis J. Stetson Jr., Dean of Admissions, 1 College Hall, Levy Park, Philadelphia, PA 19104, 215-898-7507.

GETTING IN LAST YEAR
15,074 applied
33% were accepted
48% enrolled (2,384)
86% from top tenth of their h.s. class
85% had SAT verbal scores over 600 (R)
92% had SAT math scores over 600 (R)
34% had SAT verbal scores over 700 (R)
44% had SAT math scores over 700 (R)
71 class presidents
159 valedictorians

THE STUDENT BODY
Total 22,148, of whom 11,504
   are undergraduates

21% from Pennsylvania
48% women, 52% men
7% African Americans
1% Native Americans
5% Hispanics
21% Asian Americans
8% international students

AFTER FRESHMAN YEAR
94% returned for sophomore year
79% got a degree within 4 years
86% got a degree within 5 years
87% got a degree within 6 years

AFTER GRADUATION
26% pursued further study (8% law, 8% medicine, 4% arts and sciences)
67% had job offers within 6 months
475 organizations recruited on campus
8 Fulbright scholars

WHAT YOU WILL PAY
Tuition and fees $19,898
Room and board $7500
41% receive need-based financial aid
Need-based college-administered scholarships and grants average $12,500 per award

UNIVERSITY OF PITTSBURGH

Pittsburgh, Pennsylvania • Urban setting • Public • State-related • Coed

The University of Pittsburgh offers students a tremendous array of academic, cocurricular, and extracurricular opportunities, which students can combine to creatively define their own levels of challenge and innovation. University of Pittsburgh students pursue self-designed, double, or triple majors; internships; teaching and research assistantships; dual degrees; and study-abroad opportunities. Through the University Honors College, academically motivated students also participate in small, in-depth honors courses and pursue the prestigious Bachelor of Philosophy degree. Many win national and international scholarships. The University awards 4-year merit scholarships, including some covering full tuition, room, and board, to freshmen.

Academics

Pitt offers a core academic program. It awards bachelor's, master's, doctoral, and first professional **degrees**. Challenging opportunities include advanced placement, self-designed majors, an honors program, a senior project, Phi Beta Kappa, and Sigma Xi. Special programs include cooperative education, internships, summer session for credit, off-campus study, study abroad, and Army, Naval, and Air Force ROTC.

The most popular **majors** include psychology, communication, and nursing. A complete listing of majors at Pitt appears in the Majors Index beginning on page 379.

The **faculty** at Pitt has 2,849 full-time graduate and undergraduate teachers, 90% with terminal degrees. The student-faculty ratio is 15:1.

Computers on Campus

Students are not required to have a computer. 600 **computers** available in the computer center, computer labs, the library, and dormitories provide access to the main academic computer, e-mail, on-line services, and the Internet. Staffed computer lab on campus provides training in the use of computers and software.

The 27 **libraries** have 3.3 million books, 3.3 million microform titles, and 23,290 subscriptions.

Campus Life

There are 352 active **organizations** on campus, including a drama/theater group and student-run newspaper and radio station. 14% of eligible men and 11% of eligible women are members of 21 national **fraternities** and 15 national **sororities**. Student **safety services** include on-call van transportation, late night transport/escort service, 24-hour emergency telephone alarm devices, 24-hour patrols by trained security personnel, and electronically operated dormitory entrances.

Pitt is a member of the NCAA (Division I). **Intercollegiate sports** (some offering scholarships) include baseball (m), basketball (m, w), cross-country running (m, w), football (m), gymnastics (w), soccer (m), softball (w), swimming and diving (m, w), tennis (w), track and field (m, w), volleyball (w), wrestling (m).

Applying

Pitt requires a high school transcript and SAT I or ACT. It recommends an essay, 3 years of high school math and science, 3 years of high school foreign language, recommendations, and an interview. Early, deferred, and midyear entrance are possible, with rolling admissions and continuous processing to 3/1 for financial aid. **Contact:** Dr. Betsy A. Porter, Director of Admissions and Financial Aid, Bruce Hall, Second Floor, Pittsburgh, PA 15261, 412-624-7488; fax 412-648-8815.

GETTING IN LAST YEAR
7,825 applied
66% were accepted
39% enrolled (2,022)
27% from top tenth of their h.s. class

THE STUDENT BODY
Total 26,083, of whom 16,447 are undergraduates

From 50 states and territories, 52 other countries
88% from Pennsylvania
52% women, 48% men
9% African Americans
1% Native Americans
1% Hispanics
3% Asian Americans
1% international students

AFTER GRADUATION
301 organizations recruited on campus
8 Fulbright scholars

WHAT YOU WILL PAY
Resident tuition and fees $5638
Nonresident tuition and fees $11,724
Room and board $4834
Need-based college-administered scholarships and grants average $606 per award

UNIVERSITY OF PITTSBURGH AT JOHNSTOWN

Johnstown, Pennsylvania • Suburban setting • Public • State-related • Coed

At the University of Pittsburgh at Johnstown, learning isn't limited to the boundaries of the campus. There is a variety of opportunities to learn more about the world around us. The Semester-at-Sea allows students to pursue course work while they travel the world on an ocean liner. Students can spend a term in the nation's capital through the Washington Semester. An International Studies Certificate provides an international perspective for any major or degree. And the President's Scholars Program identifies students who show extra intellectual potential, provides special advising and registration provisions, and rewards accomplishments with scholarship assistance.

 Academics

Pitt-Johnstown offers a comprehensive curriculum and core academic program. It awards associate and bachelor's **degrees**. Challenging opportunities include advanced placement, accelerated degree programs, self-designed majors, and a senior project. Special programs include internships, summer session for credit, off-campus study, and study abroad.

The most popular **majors** include business economics, elementary education, and biology/biological sciences. A complete listing of majors at Pitt-Johnstown appears in the Majors Index beginning on page 379.

The **faculty** at Pitt-Johnstown has 149 full-time teachers, 68% with terminal degrees. 89% of the faculty serve as student advisers. The student-faculty ratio is 20:1.

 Computers on Campus

Students are not required to have a computer. 171 **computers** available in the computer center, computer labs, and the library provide access to e-mail. Staffed computer lab on campus provides training in the use of computers and software.

The **library** has 133,265 books, 17,863 microform titles, and 662 subscriptions. It is connected to 35 national **on-line** catalogs.

 Campus Life

There are 81 active **organizations** on campus, including a drama/theater group and student-run newspaper and radio station. 10% of eligible men and 10% of eligible women are members of 5 national **fraternities**, 5 national **sororities**, 1 local fraternity, and 1 local sorority. Student **safety services** include late night transport/escort service and 24-hour patrols by trained security personnel.

Pitt-Johnstown is a member of the NCAA (Division II). **Intercollegiate sports** (some offering scholarships) include baseball (m), basketball (m, w), cross-country running (w), soccer (m), track and field (w), volleyball (w), wrestling (m).

 Applying

Pitt-Johnstown requires an essay, a high school transcript, 2 years of high school foreign language, 2 years of high school science, SAT I or ACT, a minimum high school GPA of 2.0, and in some cases a campus interview. It recommends 3 years of high school math. Early, deferred, and midyear entrance are possible, with rolling admissions and continuous processing to 4/1 for financial aid. **Contact:** Mr. James F. Gyure, Director of Admissions, 133 Biddle Hall, Johnstown, PA 15904-2990, 814-269-7050 or toll-free 800-765-4875; fax 814-269-7044.

GETTING IN LAST YEAR
1,806 applied
80% were accepted
48% enrolled (701)
24% from top tenth of their h.s. class
3.0 average high school GPA
5% had SAT verbal scores over 600
17% had SAT math scores over 600
3% had ACT scores over 26
0% had SAT verbal scores over 700
1% had SAT math scores over 700
0% had ACT scores over 30
7 valedictorians

THE STUDENT BODY
3,149 undergraduates

From 11 states and territories,
 1 other country
98% from Pennsylvania
52% women, 48% men
2% African Americans
1% Native Americans
1% Hispanics
1% Asian Americans
1% international students

AFTER FRESHMAN YEAR
82% returned for sophomore year
59% got a degree within 4 years

61% got a degree within 5 years
62% got a degree within 6 years

WHAT YOU WILL PAY
Resident tuition and fees $5656
Nonresident tuition and fees $11,742
Room and board $4480
82% receive need-based financial aid
Need-based college-administered scholarships and
 grants average $830 per award
31% receive non-need financial aid
Non-need college-administered scholarships and
 grants average $1966 per award

UNIVERSITY OF PUGET SOUND

Tacoma, Washington • Suburban setting • Private • Independent • Coed

Fundamental to the Puget Sound education is the commitment to the liberal arts and sciences. The University offers a challenging liberal arts and sciences education with 61 academic major options and 4 highly regarded professional schools. Students receive a broad-based, balanced education. Puget Sound is proud of the national recognition it has received for its programs, including Prelude and Passages (orientation program), the Honors Program in the Classics, the Business Leadership Program, and the Pacific Rim Study Program. Puget Sound students engage an academic program with high levels of challenge and support on a campus enhanced by the natural beauty of the Pacific Northwest.

 ## Academics

Puget Sound offers a liberal arts curriculum and core academic program; a few graduate courses are open to undergraduates. It awards bachelor's and master's **degrees**. Challenging opportunities include advanced placement, tutorials, an honors program, a senior project, and Phi Beta Kappa. Special programs include cooperative education, internships, summer session for credit, study abroad, and Army ROTC.

The most popular **majors** include business, English, and political science/government. A complete listing of majors at Puget Sound appears in the Majors Index beginning on page 379.

The **faculty** at Puget Sound has 206 full-time undergraduate teachers, 80% with terminal degrees. 100% of the faculty serve as student advisers. The student-faculty ratio is 13:1, and the average class size in core courses is 24.

 ## Computers on Campus

Students are not required to have a computer. 136 **computers** available in the computer center, computer labs, the learning resource center, the library, and dormitories provide access to the main academic computer, off-campus computing facilities, e-mail, on-line services, and the Internet. Staffed computer lab on campus (open 24 hours a day) provides training in the use of computers and software.

The **library** has 380,465 books and 1,970 subscriptions. It is connected to 60 national **on-line** catalogs.

 ## Campus Life

There are 38 active **organizations** on campus, including a drama/theater group and student-run newspaper and radio station. 30% of students participate in student government elections. 30% of eligible men and 30% of eligible women are members of 6 national **fraternities** and 6 national **sororities**. Student **safety services** include 24-hour locked residences, late night transport/escort service, 24-hour emergency telephone alarm devices, 24-hour patrols by trained security personnel, student patrols, and electronically operated dormitory entrances.

Puget Sound is a member of the NAIA. **Intercollegiate sports** include baseball (m), basketball (m, w), crew (m, w), cross-country running (m, w), football (m), golf (m, w), lacrosse (m, w), sailing (m, w), skiing (downhill) (m, w), soccer (m, w), softball (w), swimming and diving (m, w), tennis (m, w), track and field (m, w), volleyball (w).

 ## Applying

Puget Sound requires an essay, a high school transcript, 2 recommendations, and SAT I or ACT. It recommends 4 years of high school math and science, 2 years of high school foreign language, an interview, and a minimum high school GPA of 3.0. Early, deferred, and midyear entrance are possible, with a 2/1 deadline and continuous processing to 2/1 for financial aid. **Contact:** Dr. George H. Mills, Vice President for Enrollment, 1500 North Warner Street, Tacoma, WA 98416-0005, 206-756-3211; fax 206-756-3500.

GETTING IN LAST YEAR
4,112 applied
78% were accepted
21% enrolled (657)
44% from top tenth of their h.s. class
3.55 average high school GPA
55% had SAT verbal scores over 600 (R)
57% had SAT math scores over 600 (R)
52% had ACT scores over 26
11% had SAT verbal scores over 700 (R)
9% had SAT math scores over 700 (R)
18% had ACT scores over 30
21 National Merit Scholars

THE STUDENT BODY
Total 3,073, of whom 2,756
    are undergraduates

From 46 states and territories,
    12 other countries
42% from Washington
59% women, 41% men
2% African Americans
1% Native Americans
3% Hispanics
10% Asian Americans
1% international students

AFTER FRESHMAN YEAR
84% returned for sophomore year
55% got a degree within 4 years
71% got a degree within 5 years
73% got a degree within 6 years

AFTER GRADUATION
23% pursued further study
1 Fulbright scholar

WHAT YOU WILL PAY
Tuition and fees $17,450
Room and board $4720
65% receive need-based financial aid
Need-based college-administered scholarships and
    grants average $4560 per award
40% receive non-need financial aid
Non-need college-administered scholarships and
    grants average $5105 per award

UNIVERSITY OF REDLANDS

Redlands, California • Small-town setting • Private • Independent • Coed

At the University of Redlands, students explore connections, blurring the barriers often artificially imposed between academic disciplines, between the classroom and the real world, and between their own views and the way others see things. Academics are combined with a community-based residential life and a range of opportunities to gain first-hand experience through internships, international study, and original faculty-directed research. Students take ownership of their education with the active support of professors who are truly committed to student participation in the learning process; they coax, challenge, captivate, support, nourish, and actively engage in an exchange of stimulating and provocative ideas.

 Academics

Redlands offers a liberal arts curriculum and core academic program; fewer than half of graduate courses are open to undergraduates. It awards bachelor's and master's **degrees**. Challenging opportunities include advanced placement, self-designed majors, tutorials, Freshman Honors College, an honors program, a senior project, and Phi Beta Kappa. Special programs include internships, off-campus study, study abroad, and Army and Air Force ROTC.

The most popular **majors** include liberal arts/general studies, social science, and business. A complete listing of majors at Redlands appears in the Majors Index beginning on page 379.

The **faculty** at Redlands has 106 full-time undergraduate teachers, 88% with terminal degrees. The student-faculty ratio is 13:1.

Computers on Campus

Students are not required to have a computer. 150 **computers** available in the computer center, computer labs, various academic departments, and classrooms provide access to the main academic computer, e-mail, and on-line services. Staffed computer lab on campus provides training in the use of computers and software.

The **library** has 225,000 books, 45,000 microform titles, and 1,623 subscriptions.

 Campus Life

There are 60 active **organizations** on campus, including a drama/theater group and student-run newspaper and radio station. 60% of students participate in student government elections. 14% of eligible men and 16% of eligible women are members of 6 local **fraternities** and 4 local **sororities**. Student **safety services** include safety whistles, late night transport/escort service, 24-hour emergency telephone alarm devices, 24-hour patrols by trained security personnel, student patrols, and electronically operated dormitory entrances.

Redlands is a member of the NCAA (Division III). **Intercollegiate sports** include baseball (m), basketball (m, w), cross-country running (m, w), football (m), golf (m, w), soccer (m, w), softball (w), swimming and diving (m, w), tennis (m, w), track and field (m, w), volleyball (w), water polo (m, w).

 Applying

Redlands requires an essay, a high school transcript, 2 recommendations, SAT I or ACT, and in some cases 3 years of high school science. It recommends 3 years of high school math, some high school foreign language, an interview, and a minimum high school GPA of 3.0. Early, deferred, and midyear entrance are possible, with a 3/1 deadline and continuous processing to 2/15 for financial aid. **Contact:** Mr. Paul Driscoll, Dean of Admissions, 1200 East Colton Avenue, Redlands, CA 92373-0999, 909-335-4074 or toll-free 800-455-5064; fax 909-335-4089.

GETTING IN LAST YEAR
1,619 applied
80% were accepted
22% enrolled (286)
3.47 average high school GPA
5 National Merit Scholars
8 class presidents

THE STUDENT BODY
Total 3,723, of whom 2,757
   are undergraduates

From 45 states and territories,
   35 other countries
60% from California
51% women, 49% men
2% African Americans
1% Native Americans
11% Hispanics
9% Asian Americans
7% international students

AFTER GRADUATION
30% pursued further study

WHAT YOU WILL PAY
Tuition and fees $17,335
Room and board $6515
60% receive need-based financial aid
15% receive non-need financial aid

UNIVERSITY OF RICHMOND

Richmond, Virginia • Suburban setting • Private • Independent-Religious • Coed

---

▶ Students who attend Richmond find a rigorous intellectual experience that prepares them for the best graduate schools and the most challenging occupations in our society. Richmond's campus—350 acres of stately pines, rolling hills, and a magnificent lake—is located 6 miles from the capital of Virginia. Many of Richmond's top students are rewarded with merit-based scholarships, which range from one-half tuition to a full scholarship covering all expenses for 4 years. Student scholars benefit from an average class size of 19, ample opportunities in undergraduate research, and no graduate assistants.

 ## Academics

University of Richmond offers a liberal arts curriculum and core academic program; fewer than half of graduate courses are open to undergraduates. It awards associate, bachelor's, master's, and first professional **degrees**. Challenging opportunities include advanced placement, accelerated degree programs, self-designed majors, tutorials, an honors program, a senior project, Phi Beta Kappa, and Sigma Xi. Special programs include internships, summer session for credit, off-campus study, study abroad, and Army ROTC.

The most popular **majors** include business, biology/biological sciences, and political science/government. A complete listing of majors at University of Richmond appears in the Majors Index beginning on page 379.

The **faculty** at University of Richmond has 271 full-time graduate and undergraduate teachers, 95% with terminal degrees. The student-faculty ratio is 11:1, and the average class size in core courses is 19.

 ## Computers on Campus

Students are not required to have a computer. Student rooms are linked to a campus network. 500 **computers** available in the computer center, computer labs, the learning resource center, classrooms, and the library provide access to the main academic computer, off-campus computing facilities, e-mail, on-line services, and the Internet. Staffed computer lab on campus provides training in the use of computers and software.

The 5 **libraries** have 647,791 books, 276,000 microform titles, and 7,327 subscriptions. They are connected to 9 national **on-line** catalogs.

 ## Campus Life

There are 174 active **organizations** on campus, including a drama/theater group and student-run newspaper and radio station. 50% of students participate in student government elections. 51% of eligible men and 61% of eligible women are members of 11 national **fraternities** and 9 national **sororities**. Student **safety services** include late night transport/escort service, 24-hour emergency telephone alarm devices, 24-hour patrols by trained security personnel, and electronically operated dormitory entrances.

University of Richmond is a member of the NCAA (Division I). **Intercollegiate sports** (some offering scholarships) include baseball (m), basketball (m, w), crew (m, w), cross-country running (m, w), equestrian sports (w), fencing (m, w), field hockey (w), football (m), golf (m), lacrosse (m, w), rugby (m), soccer (m, w), swimming and diving (m, w), tennis (m, w), track and field (m, w), volleyball (m, w), water polo (m, w).

 ## Applying

University of Richmond requires an essay, a high school transcript, 3 years of high school math, 1 recommendation, SAT I or ACT, 3 SAT II Subject Tests (including SAT II: Writing Test), and a minimum high school GPA of 2.0. It recommends 3 years of high school science and 2 years of high school foreign language. Early and deferred entrance are possible, with a 2/1 deadline and 2/25 for financial aid. **Contact:** Ms. Pamela Spence, Dean of Admissions, Sarah Brunet Hall, Richmond Way, Richmond, VA 23173, 804-289-8640; fax 804-287-6003.

GETTING IN LAST YEAR
5,204 applied
53% were accepted
29% enrolled (797)
53% from top tenth of their h.s. class
75% had SAT verbal scores over 600 (R)
78% had SAT math scores over 600 (R)
66% had ACT scores over 26
17% had SAT verbal scores over 700 (R)
14% had SAT math scores over 700 (R)
18% had ACT scores over 30
24 National Merit Scholars
29 valedictorians

THE STUDENT BODY
Total 4,320, of whom 3,501
    are undergraduates

From 44 states and territories,
    40 other countries
19% from Virginia
50% women, 50% men
4% African Americans
0% Native Americans
2% Hispanics
3% Asian Americans
4% international students

AFTER FRESHMAN YEAR
92% returned for sophomore year
79% got a degree within 4 years
83% got a degree within 5 years
84% got a degree within 6 years

AFTER GRADUATION
26% pursued further study (14% arts and
    sciences, 7% law, 4% medicine)
58% had job offers within 6 months
331 organizations recruited on campus
1 Fulbright scholar

WHAT YOU WILL PAY
Tuition and fees $15,500
Room and board $3435
27% receive need-based financial aid
Need-based college-administered scholarships and
    grants average $6890 per award
33% receive non-need financial aid
Non-need college-administered scholarships and
    grants average $8330 per award

UNIVERSITY OF ROCHESTER

Rochester, New York • Suburban setting • Private • Independent • Coed

Founded in 1850, the University of Rochester is one of the leading private universities in the country. Programs are available in 7 divisions, including Arts and Sciences, Engineering, Nursing, Education, Business, Medicine, and the Eastman School of Music. Special undergraduate opportunities include Quest, Take Five, management certificate, Rochester Early Medical Scholars, 3-2 programs, and study abroad.

Academics

U of R offers a core academic program; more than half of graduate courses are open to undergraduates. It awards bachelor's, master's, and doctoral **degrees**. Challenging opportunities include advanced placement, self-designed majors, an honors program, Phi Beta Kappa, and Sigma Xi. Special programs include internships, summer session for credit, off-campus study, study abroad, and Army, Naval, and Air Force ROTC.

The most popular **majors** include psychology, political science/government, and economics. A complete listing of majors at U of R appears in the Majors Index beginning on page 379.

The **faculty** at U of R has 1,231 full-time graduate and undergraduate teachers, 99% with terminal degrees. The student-faculty ratio is 12:1.

Computers on Campus

Students are not required to have a computer. 265 **computers** available in the computer center, academic buildings, various locations on campus, the library, and dormitories provide access to the main academic computer and on-line services. Staffed computer lab on campus (open 24 hours a day) provides training in the use of computers and software.

The **library** has 2.8 million books and 10,284 subscriptions. It is connected to 10 national **on-line** catalogs.

Campus Life

Active **organizations** on campus include drama/theater group and student-run newspaper and radio station. 24% of students participate in student government elections. 25% of eligible men and 20% of eligible women are members of 16 national **fraternities** and 9 national **sororities**. Student **safety services** include late night transport/escort service, 24-hour emergency telephone alarm devices, 24-hour patrols by trained security personnel, and electronically operated dormitory entrances.

U of R is a member of the NCAA (Division III). **Intercollegiate sports** include baseball (m), basketball (m, w), crew (m, w), cross-country running (m, w), equestrian sports (m, w), field hockey (w), football (m), golf (m, w), ice hockey (m), lacrosse (m, w), rugby (m), skiing (cross-country) (m, w), skiing (downhill) (m, w), soccer (m, w), softball (w), squash (m, w), swimming and diving (m, w), tennis (m, w), track and field (m, w), volleyball (m, w).

Applying

U of R requires an essay, a high school transcript, 1 recommendation, SAT I or ACT, and in some cases audition, portfolio. It recommends 3 years of high school math and science, 2 years of high school foreign language, an interview, and SAT II Subject Tests. Early, deferred, and midyear entrance are possible, with a 1/31 deadline and continuous processing to 1/1 for financial aid. **Contact:** Mr. Wayne A. Locust, Director of Admissions, Meliora Hall, Intercampus Drive, Rochester, NY 14627-0001, 716-275-3221; fax 716-461-4595.

GETTING IN LAST YEAR
9,195 applied
61% were accepted
22% enrolled (1,227)
56% from top tenth of their h.s. class
30% had SAT verbal scores over 600
64% had SAT math scores over 600
68% had ACT scores over 26
3% had SAT verbal scores over 700
21% had SAT math scores over 700
26% had ACT scores over 30
10 National Merit Scholars

THE STUDENT BODY
Total 8,120, of whom 5,182
  are undergraduates

From 52 states and territories,
  75 other countries
50% from New York
49% women, 51% men
7% African Americans
1% Native Americans
4% Hispanics
10% Asian Americans
10% international students

AFTER FRESHMAN YEAR
93% returned for sophomore year
65% got a degree within 4 years

73% got a degree within 5 years
77% got a degree within 6 years

WHAT YOU WILL PAY
Tuition and fees $19,175
Room and board $6730
67% receive need-based financial aid
Need-based college-administered scholarships and
  grants average $10,500 per award
10% receive non-need financial aid
Non-need college-administered scholarships and
  grants average $5500 per award

UNIVERSITY OF SCRANTON

Scranton, Pennsylvania • Urban setting • Private • Independent-Religious • Coed

The Jesuit tradition at the University of Scranton focuses on care for the whole person (cura personalis). In an educational context, this means preparation not only for a career but also for life. Over the last 5 years, an average of 95% of graduates have been working or attending graduate school full-time within 6 months of graduation. This year 49 graduates entered medical school, 40 entered law school, and 2 were named Fulbright Scholars. Scranton is truly where potential becomes achievement in the Jesuit tradition.

 Academics

Scranton offers a flexible liberal arts curriculum and core academic program; fewer than half of graduate courses are open to undergraduates. It awards associate, bachelor's, and master's **degrees**. Challenging opportunities include advanced placement, accelerated degree programs, self-designed majors, tutorials, Freshman Honors College, an honors program, a senior project, and Sigma Xi. Special programs include internships, summer session for credit, off-campus study, and Army and Air Force ROTC.

The most popular **majors** include biology/biological sciences, accounting, and communication. A complete listing of majors at Scranton appears in the Majors Index beginning on page 379.

The **faculty** at Scranton has 253 full-time graduate and undergraduate teachers, 84% with terminal degrees. 60% of the faculty serve as student advisers. The student-faculty ratio is 14:1.

 Computers on Campus

Students are not required to have a computer. Student rooms are linked to a campus network. 321 **computers** available in the computer center, computer labs, the research center, the learning resource center, various academic departments, classrooms, the library, the student center, dormitories, and student rooms provide access to the main academic computer, off-campus computing facilities, e-mail, on-line services, and the Internet. Staffed computer lab on campus provides training in the use of computers and software.

The **library** has 340,630 books, 307,500 microform titles, and 2,052 subscriptions. It is connected to 7 national **on-line** catalogs.

 Campus Life

There are 80 active **organizations** on campus, including a drama/theater group and student-run newspaper and radio station. Student **safety services** include late night transport/escort service, 24-hour emergency telephone alarm devices, 24-hour patrols by trained security personnel, student patrols, and electronically operated dormitory entrances.

Scranton is a member of the NCAA (Division III). **Intercollegiate sports** include baseball (m), basketball (m, w), bowling (m, w), crew (m, w), cross-country running (m, w), equestrian sports (m, w), field hockey (w), golf (m), ice hockey (m), lacrosse (m, w), rugby (m, w), skiing (downhill) (m, w), soccer (m, w), softball (w), swimming and diving (m, w), tennis (m, w), track and field (m, w), volleyball (m, w), wrestling (m).

 Applying

Scranton requires a high school transcript, 3 years of high school math, 2 years of high school foreign language, 2 recommendations, SAT I or ACT, and in some cases 3 years of high school science. It recommends a campus interview. Early, deferred, and midyear entrance are possible, with a 3/1 deadline and continuous processing to 2/15 for financial aid. **Contact:** Rev. Bernard R. McIlhenny, SJ, Dean of Admissions, Room 406, Saint Thomas Hall, Scranton, PA 18510-4622, 717-941-7540; fax 717-941-6369.

GETTING IN LAST YEAR
4,783 applied
64% were accepted
30% enrolled (927)
26% from top tenth of their h.s. class
3.0 average high school GPA
29% had SAT verbal scores over 600 (R)
33% had SAT math scores over 600 (R)
4% had SAT verbal scores over 700 (R)
3% had SAT math scores over 700 (R)
7 National Merit Scholars
23 class presidents
15 valedictorians

THE STUDENT BODY
Total 4,931, of whom 4,163
   are undergraduates

From 27 states and territories,
   18 other countries
47% from Pennsylvania
55% women, 45% men
1% African Americans
0% Native Americans
2% Hispanics
2% Asian Americans
1% international students

AFTER FRESHMAN YEAR
88% returned for sophomore year
73% got a degree within 4 years
83% got a degree within 5 years

AFTER GRADUATION
20% pursued further study (7% arts and
   sciences, 5% law, 4% medicine)
66% had job offers within 6 months
75 organizations recruited on campus
4 Fulbright scholars

WHAT YOU WILL PAY
Tuition and fees $14,740
Room and board $6074
80% receive need-based financial aid
Need-based college-administered scholarships and
   grants average $3865 per award
20% receive non-need financial aid
Non-need college-administered scholarships and
   grants average $4212 per award

UNIVERSITY OF SOUTHERN CALIFORNIA

Los Angeles, California • Urban setting • Private • Independent • Coed

As one of the country's leading private research universities, USC provides outstanding teachers, excellent facilities, and an incredible array of academic offerings, including honors programs and undergraduate research opportunities. With a student-faculty ratio of 14:1 and small classes, students work with world-acclaimed professors in every discipline as participants, not spectators. USC offers over 170 undergraduate majors in the College of Letters, Arts and Sciences and 15 professional schools. Over 450 possible combinations are available for double majors, dual majors, and major-minor programs.

Academics

USC offers an interdisciplinary curriculum and core academic program; fewer than half of graduate courses are open to undergraduates. It awards bachelor's, master's, doctoral, and first professional **degrees**. Challenging opportunities include advanced placement, accelerated degree programs, self-designed majors, tutorials, Freshman Honors College, an honors program, a senior project, Phi Beta Kappa, and Sigma Xi. Special programs include cooperative education, internships, summer session for credit, off-campus study, study abroad, and Army, Naval, and Air Force ROTC.

The most popular **majors** include business, communication, and political science/government. A complete listing of majors at USC appears in the Majors Index beginning on page 379.

The **faculty** at USC has 1,629 full-time graduate and undergraduate teachers, 94% with terminal degrees. The student-faculty ratio is 14:1.

Computers on Campus

Students are not required to have a computer. 5,000 **computers** available in the computer center, computer labs, classrooms, the library, and the student center provide access to the main academic computer, off-campus computing facilities, e-mail, on-line services, and the Internet. Staffed computer lab on campus (open 24 hours a day) provides training in the use of computers and software.

The 18 **libraries** have 1 million books, 3.9 million microform titles, and 21,000 subscriptions.

Campus Life

There are 450 active **organizations** on campus, including a drama/theater group and student-run newspaper and radio station. 18% of eligible men and 20% of eligible women are members of 26 national **fraternities** and 12 national **sororities**. Student **safety services** include late night transport/escort service, 24-hour emergency telephone alarm devices, 24-hour patrols by trained security personnel, student patrols, and electronically operated dormitory entrances.

USC is a member of the NCAA (Division I). **Intercollegiate sports** (some offering scholarships) include baseball (m), basketball (m, w), crew (w), cross-country running (w), football (m), golf (m, w), sailing (m, w), soccer (w), swimming and diving (m, w), tennis (m, w), track and field (m, w), volleyball (m, w), water polo (m).

Applying

USC requires an essay, a high school transcript, SAT I or ACT, and in some cases recommendations. It recommends 3 years of high school math and science, 2 years of high school foreign language, recommendations, an interview, and SAT II Subject Tests. Early, deferred, and midyear entrance are possible, with a 2/1 deadline and continuous processing to 2/1 for financial aid. **Contact:** Mr. Duncan Murdoch, Director of Admissions, 700 Childs Way, Los Angeles, CA 90089-0911, 213-740-1111; fax 213-740-6364.

GETTING IN LAST YEAR
12,642 applied
70% were accepted
30% enrolled (2,608)
44% from top tenth of their h.s. class
3.57 average high school GPA
21% had SAT verbal scores over 600
55% had SAT math scores over 600
46% had ACT scores over 26
4% had SAT verbal scores over 700
17% had SAT math scores over 700
18% had ACT scores over 30
100 National Merit Scholars

THE STUDENT BODY
Total 27,589, of whom 14,543
  are undergraduates
From 52 states and territories,
  109 other countries
69% from California
47% women, 53% men
7% African Americans
1% Native Americans
15% Hispanics
23% Asian Americans
10% international students

WHAT YOU WILL PAY
Tuition and fees $18,598
Room and board $6438
61% receive need-based financial aid
Need-based college-administered scholarships and
  grants average $13,988 per award
10% receive non-need financial aid
Non-need college-administered scholarships and
  grants average $6898 per award

UNIVERSITY OF TENNESSEE, KNOXVILLE

Knoxville, Tennessee • Urban setting • Public • State-supported • Coed

The University of Tennessee, Knoxville, is committed to the development of individuals and society through the cultivation of the human mind and spirit. The University wants its students to think critically, acquire wisdom and insight, and be committed to the pursuit of truth in all endeavors. Opportunity abounds with over 100 academic majors and 300 clubs and organizations. In honors classes, outstanding faculty teach small groups of talented students, including more than 120 National Merit Scholars. The educational experience is enhanced by one of the nation's most technologically advanced libraries, a dynamic theater facility, and modern robotics and image laboratories.

Academics

UT Knoxville offers a comprehensive curriculum and no core academic program; fewer than half of graduate courses are open to undergraduates. It awards bachelor's, master's, doctoral, and first professional **degrees**. Challenging opportunities include advanced placement, accelerated degree programs, self-designed majors, tutorials, an honors program, a senior project, Phi Beta Kappa, and Sigma Xi. Special programs include cooperative education, internships, summer session for credit, off-campus study, study abroad, and Army and Air Force ROTC.

The most popular **majors** include psychology, accounting, and business. A complete listing of majors at UT Knoxville appears in the Majors Index beginning on page 379.

The **faculty** at UT Knoxville has 1,522 full-time graduate and undergraduate teachers, 82% with terminal degrees. 85% of the faculty serve as student advisers. The student-faculty ratio is 17:1.

Computers on Campus

Students are not required to have a computer. 1,500 **computers** available in the computer center, classrooms, the library, the student center, and dormitories.

The 7 **libraries** have 2.1 million books, 1.9 million microform titles, and 14,676 subscriptions. They are connected to 4 national **on-line** catalogs.

Campus Life

There are 300 active **organizations** on campus, including a drama/theater group and student-run newspaper and radio station. 16% of eligible men and 16% of eligible women are members of 26 national **fraternities** and 19 national **sororities**. Student **safety services** include late night transport/escort service, 24-hour emergency telephone alarm devices, and 24-hour patrols by trained security personnel.

UT Knoxville is a member of the NCAA (Division I). **Intercollegiate sports** (some offering scholarships) include baseball (m), basketball (m, w), crew (w), cross-country running (m, w), football (m), golf (m, w), soccer (w), softball (w), swimming and diving (m, w), tennis (m, w), track and field (m, w), volleyball (w).

Applying

UT Knoxville requires a high school transcript, 3 years of high school math, 2 years of high school foreign language, SAT I or ACT, a minimum high school GPA of 2.0, and in some cases an essay, recommendations, and an interview. Early, deferred, and midyear entrance are possible, with a 7/1 deadline and continuous processing to 2/15 for financial aid. **Contact:** Dr. Gordon Stanley, Director of Admissions, 320 Student Services Building, Knoxville, TN 37996, 423-974-2184 or toll-free 800-221-8657 (instate).

GETTING IN LAST YEAR
8,305 applied
72% were accepted
59% enrolled (3,506)
27% from top tenth of their h.s. class
3.17 average high school GPA
33% had SAT verbal scores over 600 (R)
32% had SAT math scores over 600 (R)
26% had ACT scores over 26
6% had SAT verbal scores over 700 (R)
6% had SAT math scores over 700 (R)
6% had ACT scores over 30
30 National Merit Scholars

THE STUDENT BODY
Total 25,704, of whom 18,735
    are undergraduates
From 49 states and territories,
    69 other countries
85% from Tennessee
49% women, 51% men
5% African Americans
1% Native Americans
1% Hispanics
4% Asian Americans
2% international students

AFTER FRESHMAN YEAR
75% returned for sophomore year
25% got a degree within 4 years
48% got a degree within 5 years
55% got a degree within 6 years

WHAT YOU WILL PAY
Resident tuition and fees $2164
Nonresident tuition and fees $6294
Room and board $3418
Need-based college-administered scholarships and
    grants average $1200 per award
Non-need college-administered scholarships and
    grants average $1200 per award

UNIVERSITY OF TEXAS AT AUSTIN

Austin, Texas • Urban setting • Public • State-supported • Coed

In the 112 years of its existence, UT has grown from a small, 40-acre, one-building campus into an internationally recognized institution. With its current enrollment of just under 48,000 students, the University offers more than 250 graduate and undergraduate degree programs in virtually all major academic disciplines. Approximately 50 honors programs are available to undergraduates in the humanities, the sciences, communication, and business. The University of Texas at Austin extends well beyond the boundaries of the main campus, incorporating research centers around Austin and across the state that keep the University at the forefront of study.

 Academics

UT Austin offers a core academic program. It awards bachelor's, master's, doctoral, and first professional **degrees**. Challenging opportunities include advanced placement, accelerated degree programs, self-designed majors, an honors program, Phi Beta Kappa, and Sigma Xi. Special programs include cooperative education, internships, summer session for credit, study abroad, and Army, Naval, and Air Force ROTC.

The **faculty** at UT Austin has 2,194 full-time graduate and undergraduate teachers, 91% with terminal degrees. The student-faculty ratio is 19:1.

 Computers on Campus

Students are not required to have a computer. Student rooms are linked to a campus network. 500 **computers** available in the computer center, computer labs, classrooms, the library, the student center, and dormitories provide access

to the main academic computer, off-campus computing facilities, e-mail, and on-line services. Staffed computer lab on campus (open 24 hours a day) provides training in the use of computers and software.

The 19 **libraries** have 6.8 million books, 4.9 million microform titles, and 51,338 subscriptions.

 Campus Life

There are 697 active **organizations** on campus, including a drama/theater group and student-run newspaper and radio station. 11% of eligible men and 13% of eligible women are members of 34 national **fraternities** and 20 national **sororities**. Student **safety services** include late night transport/escort service, 24-hour emergency telephone alarm devices, 24-hour patrols by trained security personnel, student patrols, and electronically operated dormitory entrances.

UT Austin is a member of the NCAA (Division I). **Intercollegiate sports** (some offering scholarships) include baseball (m), basketball (m, w), cross-country running (m, w), football (m), golf (m, w), soccer (w), softball (w), swimming and diving (m, w), tennis (m, w), track and field (m, w), volleyball (w).

 Applying

UT Austin requires a high school transcript, 3 years of high school math, 2 years of high school foreign language, SAT I or ACT, and in some cases an essay and SAT II: Writing Test. It recommends 3 years of high school science. Midyear entrance is possible, with a 2/1 deadline and continuous processing to 4/1 for financial aid. **Contact:** Ms. Shirley F. Binder, Director of Admissions, Red River and Martin Luther King Blvd., Austin, TX 78712, 512-475-7399.

GETTING IN LAST YEAR

15,542 applied
62% were accepted
66% enrolled (6,352)
46% from top tenth of their h.s. class
54% had SAT verbal scores over 600 (R)
64% had SAT math scores over 600 (R)
48% had ACT scores over 26
11% had SAT verbal scores over 700 (R)
15% had SAT math scores over 700 (R)
8% had ACT scores over 30
217 National Merit Scholars

THE STUDENT BODY

Total 47,905, of whom 35,088
   are undergraduates
From 52 states and territories,
   115 other countries
91% from Texas
48% women, 52% men
4% African Americans
1% Native Americans
15% Hispanics
12% Asian Americans
3% international students

AFTER FRESHMAN YEAR

59% returned for sophomore year
31% got a degree within 4 years
57% got a degree within 5 years
65% got a degree within 6 years

WHAT YOU WILL PAY

Resident tuition and fees $2208
Nonresident tuition and fees $7968
Room and board $4550
90% receive need-based financial aid
Need-based college-administered scholarships and
   grants average $2200 per award
15% receive non-need financial aid
Non-need college-administered scholarships and
   grants average $1800 per award

UNIVERSITY OF THE SOUTH

Sewanee, Tennessee • Small-town setting • Private • Independent-Religious • Coed

The University of the South (Sewanee) is consistently ranked among the top tier of national liberal arts institutions. Sewanee is committed to an academic curriculum that focuses on the liberal arts. The campus is located on 10,000 acres atop Tennessee's Cumberland Plateau between Chattanooga and Nashville. Sewanee has an impressive record of academic achievement: 22 Rhodes scholars, 19 NCAA Postgraduate Scholarship recipients, and 89% of undergraduates who apply to medical and dental schools are accepted.

 ## Academics

Sewanee offers a liberal arts curriculum and core academic program; fewer than half of graduate courses are open to undergraduates. It awards bachelor's, master's, doctoral, and first professional **degrees**. Challenging opportunities include advanced placement, accelerated degree programs, self-designed majors, tutorials, an honors program, a senior project, Phi Beta Kappa, and Sigma Xi. Special programs include internships, summer session for credit, and study abroad.

The most popular **majors** include English, natural resource management, and art/fine arts. A complete listing of majors at Sewanee appears in the Majors Index beginning on page 379.

The **faculty** at Sewanee has 115 full-time graduate and undergraduate teachers, 94% with terminal degrees. 100% of the faculty serve as student advisers. The student-faculty ratio is 11:1.

 ## Computers on Campus

Students are not required to have a computer. Student rooms are linked to a campus network. 92 **computers** available in the computer center, computer labs, various academic locations, classrooms, and the library provide access to the main academic computer, off-campus computing facilities, e-mail, and on-line services. Staffed computer lab on campus (open 24 hours a day) provides training in the use of computers and software.

The **library** has 453,121 books, 246,754 microform titles, and 2,665 subscriptions. It is connected to 7 national **on-line** catalogs.

 ## Campus Life

There are 110 active **organizations** on campus, including a drama/theater group and student-run newspaper and radio station. 62% of eligible men and 65% of eligible women are members of 11 national **fraternities** and 7 local **sororities**. Student **safety services** include security lighting, late night transport/escort service, 24-hour emergency telephone alarm devices, and 24-hour patrols by trained security personnel.

Sewanee is a member of the NCAA (Division III). **Intercollegiate sports** include baseball (m), basketball (m, w), crew (m, w), cross-country running (m, w), equestrian sports (m, w), fencing (m, w), field hockey (w), football (m), golf (m, w), lacrosse (m, w), rugby (m, w), skiing (cross-country) (m, w), skiing (downhill) (m, w), soccer (m, w), swimming and diving (m, w), tennis (m, w), track and field (m, w), volleyball (w).

 ## Applying

Sewanee requires an essay, a high school transcript, 3 years of high school math, 2 years of high school foreign language, 2 recommendations, and SAT I or ACT. It recommends 3 years of high school science, a campus interview, and SAT II Subject Tests. Early, deferred, and midyear entrance are possible, with a 2/1 deadline and continuous processing to 3/1 for financial aid. **Contact:** Mr. Robert M. Hedrick, Director of Admission, 735 University Avenue, Sewanee, TN 37383-1000, 615-598-1238 or toll-free 800-522-2234; fax 615-598-1667.

GETTING IN LAST YEAR
1,864 applied
64% were accepted
31% enrolled (370)
53% from top tenth of their h.s. class
3.36 average high school GPA
63% had SAT verbal scores over 600 (R)
91% had SAT math scores over 600 (R)
91% had ACT scores over 26
16% had SAT verbal scores over 700 (R)
24% had SAT math scores over 700 (R)
24% had ACT scores over 30
5 National Merit Scholars

THE STUDENT BODY
Total 1,322, of whom 1,242
  are undergraduates

From 45 states and territories,
  17 other countries
18% from Tennessee
50% women, 50% men
2% African Americans
1% Native Americans
1% Hispanics
1% Asian Americans
2% international students

AFTER FRESHMAN YEAR
91% returned for sophomore year
87% got a degree within 4 years
88% got a degree within 5 years

AFTER GRADUATION
35% pursued further study (14% arts and
  sciences, 6% law, 5% business)
28 organizations recruited on campus

WHAT YOU WILL PAY
Tuition and fees $16,315
Room and board $4280
42% receive need-based financial aid
Need-based college-administered scholarships and
  grants average $10,529 per award
14% receive non-need financial aid
Non-need college-administered scholarships and
  grants average $5901 per award

UNIVERSITY OF TULSA

Tulsa, Oklahoma • Urban setting • Private • Independent-Religious • Coed

Academics

TU offers a liberal arts curriculum and core academic program; fewer than half of graduate courses are open to undergraduates. It awards bachelor's, master's, doctoral, and first professional **degrees**. Challenging opportunities include advanced placement, self-designed majors, an honors program, a senior project, Phi Beta Kappa, and Sigma Xi. Special programs include internships, summer session for credit, and study abroad.

The most popular **majors** include accounting, psychology, and communication. A complete listing of majors at TU appears in the Majors Index beginning on page 379.

The **faculty** at TU has 317 full-time graduate and undergraduate teachers, 96% with terminal degrees. 100% of the faculty serve as student advisers. The student-faculty ratio is 11:1.

Computers on Campus

Students are not required to have a computer. Student rooms are linked to a campus network. 500 **computers** available in the computer center, computer labs, classrooms, the library, and dormitories provide access to the main academic computer, off-campus computing facilities, e-mail, on-line services, and the Internet. Staffed computer lab on campus (open 24 hours a day) provides training in the use of computers and software.

The 3 **libraries** have 1.3 million books, 2.4 million microform titles, and 3,485 subscriptions. They are connected to 5 national **on-line** catalogs.

Campus Life

There are 140 active **organizations** on campus, including a drama/theater group and student-run newspaper. 21% of eligible men and 19% of eligible women are members of 7 national **fraternities** and 7 national **sororities**. Student **safety services** include late night transport/escort service, 24-hour emergency telephone alarm devices, 24-hour patrols by trained security personnel, and electronically operated dormitory entrances.

TU is a member of the NCAA (Division I). **Intercollegiate sports** (some offering scholarships) include basketball (m, w), crew (w), cross-country running (m, w), football (m), golf (m, w), soccer (m, w), softball (w), tennis (m, w), track and field (m, w), volleyball (w).

Applying

TU requires a high school transcript, 1 recommendation, SAT I or ACT, and a minimum high school GPA of 2.0. It recommends an essay, 3 years of high school math and science, 2 years of high school foreign language, an interview, and a minimum high school GPA of 3.0. Early, deferred, and midyear entrance are possible, with rolling admissions and continuous processing to 2/15 for financial aid. **Contact:** Mr. John C. Corso, Assoc. Vice President for Administration/Dean of Admission, Tulsa, OK 74104-3189, 918-631-2307 or toll-free 800-331-3050; fax 918-631-3172.

GETTING IN LAST YEAR
1,808 applied
82% were accepted
37% enrolled (545)
36% from top tenth of their h.s. class
3.55 average high school GPA
22% had SAT verbal scores over 600
44% had SAT math scores over 600
41% had ACT scores over 26
3% had SAT verbal scores over 700
12% had SAT math scores over 700
10% had ACT scores over 30
14 National Merit Scholars

THE STUDENT BODY
Total 4,386, of whom 3,025
   are undergraduates

From 40 states and territories,
   57 other countries
66% from Oklahoma
52% women, 48% men
7% African Americans
6% Native Americans
3% Hispanics
2% Asian Americans
10% international students

AFTER FRESHMAN YEAR
75% returned for sophomore year

AFTER GRADUATION
30% pursued further study (11% business, 10%
   arts and sciences, 5% engineering)

1 Fulbright scholar

WHAT YOU WILL PAY
Tuition and fees $12,300
Room and board $4360
75% receive need-based financial aid
Need-based college-administered scholarships and
   grants average $6450 per award
45% receive non-need financial aid
Non-need college-administered scholarships and
   grants average $2000 per award

UNIVERSITY OF UTAH

Salt Lake City, Utah • Urban setting • Public • State-supported • Coed

 Academics

U of U offers a liberal arts and professional curriculum and core academic program. It awards bachelor's, master's, doctoral, and first professional **degrees**. Challenging opportunities include advanced placement, accelerated degree programs, self-designed majors, tutorials, an honors program, Phi Beta Kappa, and Sigma Xi. Special programs include cooperative education, internships, summer session for credit, off-campus study, study abroad, and Army, Naval, and Air Force ROTC.

The most popular **majors** include sociology, political science/government, and accounting. A complete listing of majors at U of U appears in the Majors Index beginning on page 379.

The **faculty** at U of U has 1,475 full-time graduate and undergraduate teachers, 97% with terminal degrees. 20% of the faculty serve as student advisers. The student-faculty ratio is 23:1.

 Computers on Campus

Students are not required to have a computer. Student rooms are linked to a campus network. 3,000 **computers** available in the computer center, computer labs, the research center, the learning resource center, several academic departments, the library, the student center, and dormitories provide access to the main academic computer, off-campus computing facilities, e-mail, on-line services, and the Internet. Staffed computer lab on campus provides training in the use of computers and software.

The 3 **libraries** have 2.3 million books, 3.1 million microform titles, and 21,807 subscriptions.

 Campus Life

There are 250 active **organizations** on campus, including a drama/theater group and student-run newspaper and radio station. 12% of students participate in student government elections. 3% of eligible men and 3% of eligible women are members of 8 national **fraternities**, 6 national **sororities**, 1 local fraternity, and 1 local sorority. Student **safety services** include late night transport/escort service, 24-hour emergency telephone alarm devices, 24-hour patrols by trained security personnel, student patrols, and electronically operated dormitory entrances.

U of U is a member of the NCAA (Division I). **Intercollegiate sports** (some offering scholarships) include baseball (m), basketball (m, w), bowling (m, w), cross-country running (m, w), football (m), golf (m), gymnastics (w), ice hockey (m), racquetball (m, w), rugby (m), skiing (cross-country) (m, w), skiing (downhill) (m, w), soccer (m, w), softball (w), swimming and diving (m, w), table tennis (m, w), tennis (m, w), track and field (m, w), volleyball (w).

 Applying

U of U requires a high school transcript, 2 years of high school foreign language, SAT I or ACT, and a minimum high school GPA of 2.0. It recommends 3 years of high school math and science and a minimum high school GPA of 3.0. Early, deferred, and midyear entrance are possible, with a 7/1 deadline and continuous processing to 3/1 for financial aid. **Contact:** Mrs. Pat Goldsmith, Director of High School Services, 250 South Student Services Building, Salt Lake City, UT 84112, 801-581-8761 or toll-free 800-444-8638; fax 801-585-3034.

GETTING IN LAST YEAR

6,093 applied
89% were accepted
50% enrolled (2,728)
27% from top tenth of their h.s. class
3.44 average high school GPA
19% had SAT verbal scores over 600
40% had SAT math scores over 600
37% had ACT scores over 26
4% had SAT verbal scores over 700
11% had SAT math scores over 700
13% had ACT scores over 30
43 National Merit Scholars
30 class presidents
40 valedictorians

THE STUDENT BODY

Total 25,423, of whom 20,369
 are undergraduates
From 55 states and territories,
 110 other countries
91% from Utah
45% women, 55% men
1% African Americans
1% Native Americans
3% Hispanics
3% Asian Americans
3% international students

AFTER FRESHMAN YEAR

59% returned for sophomore year

AFTER GRADUATION

24% pursued further study
60% had job offers within 6 months
269 organizations recruited on campus
2 Fulbright scholars

WHAT YOU WILL PAY

Resident tuition and fees $2508
Nonresident tuition and fees $7707
Room and board $6318
37% receive need-based financial aid
Need-based college-administered scholarships and
 grants average $868 per award
9% receive non-need financial aid
Non-need college-administered scholarships and
 grants average $1563 per award

UNIVERSITY OF VERMONT

Burlington, Vermont • Small-town setting • Public • State-supported • Coed

---

▶The University of Vermont is distinctive among state universities for its unusual balance of students—at least half are from outside Vermont. UVM's mission focuses on teaching undergraduates, including offering students a unique opportunity to work with faculty on research projects. All undergraduates receive a liberal education through the College of Arts and Sciences.

Academics

UVM offers a liberal arts and professional curriculum and no core academic program; more than half of graduate courses are open to undergraduates. It awards associate, bachelor's, master's, doctoral, and first professional **degrees**. Challenging opportunities include advanced placement, self-designed majors, an honors program, Phi Beta Kappa, and Sigma Xi. Special programs include cooperative education, internships, summer session for credit, study abroad, and Army and Air Force ROTC.

The most popular **majors** include business, political science/government, and psychology. A complete listing of majors at UVM appears in the Majors Index beginning on page 379.

The **faculty** at UVM has 874 full-time graduate and undergraduate teachers, 86% with terminal degrees. 60% of the faculty serve as student advisers. The student-faculty ratio is 13:1.

Computers on Campus

Students are not required to have a computer. 500 **computers** available in the computer center, computer labs, engineering and business administration buildings, the library, the student center, and dormitories provide access to the main academic computer, off-campus computing facilities, e-mail, on-line services, and the Internet. Staffed computer lab on campus.

The 4 **libraries** have 2.2 million books, 275,000 microform titles, and 18,625 subscriptions. They are connected to 2 national **on-line** catalogs.

Campus Life

There are 100 active **organizations** on campus, including a drama/theater group and student-run newspaper and radio station. 7% of eligible men and 7% of eligible women are members of 13 national **fraternities**, 6 national **sororities**, and 2 local fraternities. Student **safety services** include late night transport/escort service, 24-hour emergency telephone alarm devices, and 24-hour patrols by trained security personnel.

UVM is a member of the NCAA (Division I). **Intercollegiate sports** (some offering scholarships) include baseball (m), basketball (m, w), crew (m, w), cross-country running (m, w), fencing (m, w), field hockey (w), golf (m), gymnastics (m, w), ice hockey (m, w), lacrosse (m, w), rugby (m, w), skiing (cross-country) (m, w), skiing (downhill) (m, w), soccer (m, w), softball (w), swimming and diving (m, w), tennis (m, w), track and field (m, w), volleyball (m, w), wrestling (m).

Applying

UVM requires an essay, a high school transcript, 3 years of high school math, 2 years of high school foreign language, and SAT I or ACT. It recommends 2 recommendations and an interview. Early, deferred, and midyear entrance are possible, with a 2/1 deadline and continuous processing to 3/1 for financial aid. **Contact:** Ms. Barbara A. O'Reilly, Director of Admissions, Clement House, 194 South Prospect Street, Burlington, VT 05401-3596, 802-656-3370; fax 802-656-8611.

GETTING IN LAST YEAR
7,979 applied
81% were accepted
29% enrolled (1,889)
15% from top tenth of their h.s. class
33% had SAT verbal scores over 600 (R)
33% had SAT math scores over 600 (R)
3% had SAT verbal scores over 700 (R)
2% had SAT math scores over 700 (R)

THE STUDENT BODY
Total 9,111, of whom 7,539
  are undergraduates
From 49 states and territories,
  31 other countries

42% from Vermont
54% women, 46% men
1% African Americans
1% Native Americans
1% Hispanics
2% Asian Americans
1% international students

AFTER FRESHMAN YEAR
82% returned for sophomore year
54% got a degree within 4 years
70% got a degree within 5 years
75% got a degree within 6 years

AFTER GRADUATION
18% pursued further study
78% had job offers within 6 months
102 organizations recruited on campus

WHAT YOU WILL PAY
Resident tuition and fees $6909
Nonresident tuition and fees $16,605
Room and board $4632
Need-based college-administered scholarships and
  grants average $3000 per award
Non-need college-administered scholarships and
  grants average $7715 per award

UNIVERSITY OF VIRGINIA

Charlottesville, Virginia • Suburban setting • Public • State-supported • Coed

Established in 1825, the University of Virginia today continues to be influenced by the spirit of its founder, Thomas Jefferson. His powerful convictions—the idea that the University exists to train young people for public affairs and that the liberal arts constitute the foundation for any education—continue to inspire the students and faculty and to guide the development of its programs. Mr. Jefferson's vision of the University as a community where scholars and students work closely together remains paramount. Deemed a "public ivy" and consistently rated as one of the best institutions in the country, the University has achieved national stature for teaching, research, and public service.

 ## Academics

UVA offers no core academic program; more than half of graduate courses are open to undergraduates. It awards bachelor's, master's, doctoral, and first professional **degrees**. Challenging opportunities include advanced placement, accelerated degree programs, self-designed majors, tutorials, an honors program, a senior project, Phi Beta Kappa, and Sigma Xi. Special programs include internships, summer session for credit, study abroad, and Army, Naval, and Air Force ROTC.

The most popular **majors** include business, English, and psychology. A complete listing of majors at UVA appears in the Majors Index beginning on page 379.

The **faculty** at UVA has 1,768 full-time graduate and undergraduate teachers, 90% with terminal degrees. 100% of the faculty serve as student advisers. The student-faculty ratio is 14:1.

 ## Computers on Campus

Students are not required to have a computer. Student rooms are linked to a campus network. 950 **computers** available in the computer center, computer labs, the library, and dormitories provide access to the main academic computer, off-campus computing facilities, e-mail, on-line services, and the Internet. Staffed computer lab on campus (open 24 hours a day) provides training in the use of computers and software.

The 16 **libraries** have 4.2 million books, 140,000 microform titles, and 37,132 subscriptions.

 ## Campus Life

There are 300 active **organizations** on campus, including a drama/theater group and student-run newspaper and radio station. 28% of eligible men and 30% of eligible women are members of 38 national **fraternities**, 22 national **sororities**, and 1 local fraternity. Student **safety services** include late night transport/escort service, 24-hour emergency telephone alarm devices, 24-hour patrols by trained security personnel, and electronically operated dormitory entrances.

UVA is a member of the NCAA (Division I). **Intercollegiate sports** (some offering scholarships) include baseball (m), basketball (m, w), crew (w), cross-country running (m, w), field hockey (w), football (m), golf (m), lacrosse (m, w), soccer (m, w), softball (w), swimming and diving (m, w), tennis (m, w), track and field (m, w), volleyball (w), wrestling (m).

 ## Applying

UVA requires an essay, a high school transcript, 4 years of high school math, 2 years of high school foreign language, 1 recommendation, SAT I, and 3 SAT II Subject Tests (including SAT II: Writing Test). It recommends 3 years of high school science. Early entrance and early decision are possible, with a 1/2 deadline and continuous processing to 3/1 for financial aid. **Contact:** Mr. John A. Blackburn, Dean of Admission, PO Box 9017, Charlottesville, VA 22903, 804-982-3200; fax 804-924-3587.

GETTING IN LAST YEAR
15,578 applied
37% were accepted
50% enrolled (2,876)
79% from top tenth of their h.s. class
79% had SAT verbal scores over 600 (R)
81% had SAT math scores over 600 (R)
25% had SAT verbal scores over 700 (R)
28% had SAT math scores over 700 (R)
177 valedictorians

THE STUDENT BODY
Total 18,055, of whom 11,949
   are undergraduates

From 53 states and territories,
   86 other countries
66% from Virginia
53% women, 47% men
11% African Americans
0% Native Americans
2% Hispanics
10% Asian Americans
2% international students

AFTER FRESHMAN YEAR
97% returned for sophomore year
82% got a degree within 4 years
91% got a degree within 5 years
93% got a degree within 6 years

AFTER GRADUATION
450 organizations recruited on campus
1 Fulbright scholar

WHAT YOU WILL PAY
Resident tuition and fees $4614
Nonresident tuition and fees $13,922
Room and board $3862
32% receive need-based financial aid
Need-based college-administered scholarships and
   grants average $6150 per award
6% receive non-need financial aid
Non-need college-administered scholarships and
   grants average $10,200 per award

UNIVERSITY OF WASHINGTON

Seattle, Washington • Urban setting • Public • State-supported • Coed

Academics

UW offers a core academic program; fewer than half of graduate courses are open to undergraduates. It awards bachelor's, master's, doctoral, and first professional **degrees**. Challenging opportunities include advanced placement, accelerated degree programs, self-designed majors, an honors program, a senior project, Phi Beta Kappa, and Sigma Xi. Special programs include cooperative education, internships, summer session for credit, and Army, Naval, and Air Force ROTC.

The **faculty** at UW has 2,994 full-time graduate and undergraduate teachers, 99% with terminal degrees. The student-faculty ratio is 9:1, and the average class size in core courses is 31.

Computers on Campus

Students are not required to have a computer. 285 **computers** available in the computer center, computer labs, the research center, the learning resource center, academic departments, classrooms, the library, the student center, dormitories, and student rooms provide access to the main academic computer and e-mail. Staffed computer lab on campus (open 24 hours a day) provides training in the use of computers and software.

The 22 **libraries** have 5.3 million books, 6 million microform titles, and 56,500 subscriptions.

Campus Life

There are 300 active **organizations** on campus, including a drama/theater group and student-run newspaper and radio station. 18% of eligible men and 14% of eligible women are members of 29 national **fraternities** and 16 national **sororities**. Student **safety services** include late night transport/escort service, 24-hour emergency telephone alarm devices, 24-hour patrols by trained security personnel, and electronically operated dormitory entrances.

UW is a member of the NCAA (Division I). **Intercollegiate sports** (some offering scholarships) include baseball (m), basketball (m, w), crew (m, w), cross-country running (m, w), football (m), golf (m, w), gymnastics (w), soccer (m, w), softball (w), swimming and diving (m, w), tennis (m, w), track and field (m, w), volleyball (w), wrestling (m).

Applying

UW requires a high school transcript, 3 years of high school math, 2 years of high school foreign language, and SAT I or ACT. Early and midyear entrance are possible, with a 2/1 deadline and a 2/28 priority date for financial aid. **Contact:** Ms. Stephanie Preston, Assistant Director of Admissions, 1410 Northeast Campus Parkway, Seattle, WA 98195, 206-543-9686; fax 206-685-3655.

GETTING IN LAST YEAR

12,527 applied
65% were accepted
46% enrolled (3,701)
40% from top tenth of their h.s. class
0% had SAT verbal scores over 600
75% had SAT math scores over 600
0% had SAT verbal scores over 700
0% had SAT math scores over 700
22 National Merit Scholars

THE STUDENT BODY

Total 33,996, of whom 24,838
  are undergraduates

From 52 states and territories,
  56 other countries
90% from Washington
50% women, 50% men
3% African Americans
1% Native Americans
4% Hispanics
20% Asian Americans
2% international students

AFTER FRESHMAN YEAR

30% got a degree within 4 years
62% got a degree within 5 years

AFTER GRADUATION

450 organizations recruited on campus
8 Fulbright scholars

WHAT YOU WILL PAY

Resident tuition and fees $3019
Nonresident tuition and fees $8523
Room and board $4329
Need-based college-administered scholarships and
  grants average $4379 per award

UNIVERSITY OF WISCONSIN–MADISON

Madison, Wisconsin • Urban setting • Public • State-supported • Coed

At Wisconsin, "the largest small school in the country," world-class undergraduate learning opportunities are provided by a faculty that has been placed in the top ten nationally by every scholarly college and university ranking done this century. Close contact to this faculty is ensured because over 85% of all classes include fewer than 30 students. Rich honors programs provide students with the opportunity to engage in original research with faculty mentors dedicated to making the resources of one of the world's great teaching and research universities available to all undergraduate scholars.

Academics

Wisconsin offers no core academic program; more than half of graduate courses are open to undergraduates. It awards bachelor's, master's, doctoral, and first professional **degrees**. Challenging opportunities include advanced placement, accelerated degree programs, self-designed majors, tutorials, Freshman Honors College, an honors program, a senior project, Phi Beta Kappa, and Sigma Xi. Special programs include cooperative education, internships, summer session for credit, study abroad, and Army, Naval, and Air Force ROTC.

The most popular **majors** include political science/government, history, and mechanical engineering. A complete listing of majors at Wisconsin appears in the Majors Index beginning on page 379.

The **faculty** at Wisconsin has 2,395 full-time undergraduate teachers, 96% with terminal degrees. 40% of the faculty serve as student advisers. The student-faculty ratio is 12:1.

Computers on Campus

Students are not required to have a computer. Student rooms are linked to a campus network. 2,800 **computers** available in the computer center, computer labs, the research center, the learning resource center, the library, the student center, and dormitories provide access to the main academic computer, e-mail, on-line services, and the Internet. Staffed computer lab on campus provides training in the use of computers and software.

The 40 **libraries** have 5.3 million books, 2 million microform titles, and 55,300 subscriptions.

Campus Life

There are 900 active **organizations** on campus, including a drama/theater group and student-run newspaper and radio station. 10% of students participate in student government elections. 15% of eligible men and 15% of eligible women are members of 27 national **fraternities**, 10 national **sororities**, and 10 eating clubs, social clubs. Student **safety services** include late night transport/escort service, 24-hour emergency telephone alarm devices, 24-hour patrols by trained security personnel, and electronically operated dormitory entrances.

Wisconsin is a member of the NCAA (Division I). **Intercollegiate sports** (some offering scholarships) include basketball (m, w), crew (m, w), cross-country running (m, w), football (m), golf (m, w), ice hockey (m, w), lacrosse (w), rugby (m), sailing (m), soccer (m, w), softball (w), swimming and diving (m, w), tennis (m, w), track and field (m, w), volleyball (m, w), wrestling (m).

Applying

Wisconsin requires a high school transcript, 3 years of high school math, 2 years of high school foreign language, SAT I or ACT, and in some cases recommendations. It recommends an essay and 3 years of high school science. Early, deferred, and midyear entrance are possible, with a 2/1 deadline and continuous processing to 3/1 for financial aid. **Contact:** Office of Admissions, 140 Peterson Office Building, 750 University Avenue, Madison, WI 53706-1490, 608-262-3961; fax 608-262-1429.

GETTING IN LAST YEAR
16,403 applied
71% were accepted
44% enrolled (5,164)
43% from top tenth of their h.s. class
3.51 average high school GPA
60% had SAT verbal scores over 600 (R)
70% had SAT math scores over 600 (R)
64% had ACT scores over 26
16% had SAT verbal scores over 700 (R)
19% had SAT math scores over 700 (R)
23% had ACT scores over 30

THE STUDENT BODY
Total 37,890, of whom 26,361
  are undergraduates

From 53 states and territories,
  76 other countries
64% from Wisconsin
51% women, 49% men
4% African Americans
1% Native Americans
4% Hispanics
5% Asian Americans
6% international students

AFTER FRESHMAN YEAR
97% returned for sophomore year
35% got a degree within 4 years

72% got a degree within 5 years
86% got a degree within 6 years

WHAT YOU WILL PAY
Resident tuition and fees $2870
Nonresident tuition and fees $9580
Room and board $4520
41% receive need-based financial aid
Need-based college-administered scholarships and
  grants average $840 per award
30% receive non-need financial aid
Non-need college-administered scholarships and
  grants average $1619 per award

URSINUS COLLEGE

Collegeville, Pennsylvania • Suburban setting • Private • Independent-Religious • Coed

Ursinus is a small, residential, highly competitive college located in Collegeville, Pennsylvania, 30 miles from Philadelphia, offering the safety and beauty of a small town and access to a vibrant metropolitan community. The main objective of Ursinus's traditional liberal arts curriculum is to prepare students for the professions. Most graduates go on to earn advanced-level degrees through professional or graduate course work, particularly in the areas of medicine, law, and social sciences. Ursinus is committed to a policy of both need-based and merit-based financial aid and awards Ursinus College Scholarships to students who have demonstrated academic and extracurricular leadership.

Academics

Ursinus offers an interdisciplinary curriculum and core academic program. It awards bachelor's **degrees**. Challenging opportunities include advanced placement, accelerated degree programs, self-designed majors, tutorials, an honors program, a senior project, Phi Beta Kappa, and Sigma Xi. Special programs include internships, summer session for credit, off-campus study, and study abroad.

The **faculty** at Ursinus has 95 full-time teachers, 81% with terminal degrees. 100% of the faculty serve as student advisers. The student-faculty ratio is 12:1, and the average class size in core courses is 20.

Computers on Campus

Students are not required to have a computer. Student rooms are linked to a campus network. 200 **computers** available in the computer center, computer labs, the research center, academic buildings, classrooms, the library, and dormitories provide access to the main academic computer, off-campus computing facilities, e-mail, on-line services, and the Internet. Staffed computer lab on campus provides training in the use of computers and software.

The **library** has 185,000 books, 155,000 microform titles, and 900 subscriptions.

Campus Life

There are 75 active **organizations** on campus, including a drama/theater group and student-run newspaper and radio station. 55% of eligible men and 50% of eligible women are members of 1 national **fraternity**, 8 local fraternities, and 5 local **sororities**. Student **safety services** include late night transport/escort service and 24-hour patrols by trained security personnel.

Ursinus is a member of the NCAA (Division III). **Intercollegiate sports** include baseball (m), basketball (m, w), cross-country running (m, w), field hockey (w), football (m), golf (m, w), gymnastics (w), lacrosse (m, w), soccer (m), softball (w), swimming and diving (m, w), tennis (m, w), track and field (m, w), volleyball (w), wrestling (m).

Applying

Ursinus requires an essay, a high school transcript, 3 years of high school math, 2 years of high school foreign language, 3 recommendations, SAT I or ACT, and in some cases 3 years of high school science. It recommends a campus interview and 3 SAT II Subject Tests. Early, deferred, and midyear entrance are possible, with a 2/15 deadline and continuous processing to 2/15 for financial aid. **Contact:** Mr. Richard G. Di Feliciantonio, Director of Admissions and Enrollment, Main Street, Collegeville, PA 19426-1000, 610-409-3200 ext. 2224; fax 610-489-0627.

GETTING IN LAST YEAR
1,486 applied
81% were accepted
26% enrolled (317)
42% from top tenth of their h.s. class
47% had SAT verbal scores over 600 (R)
46% had SAT math scores over 600 (R)
7% had SAT verbal scores over 700 (R)
5% had SAT math scores over 700 (R)

THE STUDENT BODY
1,245 undergraduates
From 20 states and territories,
15 other countries

67% from Pennsylvania
52% women, 48% men
4% African Americans
0% Native Americans
2% Hispanics
4% Asian Americans
3% international students

AFTER FRESHMAN YEAR
92% returned for sophomore year
72% got a degree within 4 years
74% got a degree within 5 years

AFTER GRADUATION
30% pursued further study (15% arts and sciences, 10% medicine, 3% law)

62% had job offers within 6 months
50 organizations recruited on campus

WHAT YOU WILL PAY
Tuition and fees $15,690
Room and board $5330
80% receive need-based financial aid
Need-based college-administered scholarships and grants average $7800 per award
12% receive non-need financial aid
Non-need college-administered scholarships and grants average $5800 per award

UTICA COLLEGE OF SYRACUSE UNIVERSITY

Utica, New York • Suburban setting • Private • Independent • Coed

At Utica College students find the small classes, excellent advising, and personal attention of a small liberal arts college, but they enjoy the broad curriculum and diverse student body of a large university. And, upon graduation, Utica College students receive the internationally recognized Syracuse University degree. Utica College students choose among 5 academic divisions and 35 majors in both the liberal arts/science and professional career programs. Prospective students who visit the campus for an interview and tour notice the friendly, warm atmosphere. Personal attention to each student is the hallmark of Utica College.

 ## Academics

Utica College offers a core academic program. It awards bachelor's **degrees**. Challenging opportunities include advanced placement, accelerated degree programs, tutorials, Freshman Honors College, an honors program, and a senior project. Special programs include cooperative education, internships, summer session for credit, off-campus study, study abroad, and Army and Air Force ROTC.

The most popular **majors** include business, criminal justice, and occupational therapy. A complete listing of majors at Utica College appears in the Majors Index beginning on page 379.

The **faculty** at Utica College has 105 full-time teachers, 92% with terminal degrees. 100% of the faculty serve as student advisers. The student-faculty ratio is 13:1.

 ## Computers on Campus

Students are not required to have a computer. 131 **computers** available in the computer center, classroom buildings, the library, and dormitories. Staffed computer lab on campus provides training in the use of computers and software.

The **library** has 169,995 books, 355 microform titles, and 1,087 subscriptions.

 ## Campus Life

There are 60 active **organizations** on campus, including a drama/theater group and student-run newspaper and radio station. 27% of students participate in student government elections. 3% of eligible men and 3% of eligible women are members of 5 national **fraternities**, 4 national **sororities**, 1 local fraternity, and 2 local sororities. Student **safety services** include late night transport/escort service, 24-hour emergency telephone alarm devices, 24-hour patrols by trained security personnel, and electronically operated dormitory entrances.

Utica College is a member of the NCAA (Division III). **Intercollegiate sports** include baseball (m), basketball (m, w), cross-country running (m, w), golf (m, w), lacrosse (m), soccer (m, w), softball (w), swimming and diving (m, w), tennis (m, w), volleyball (w).

 ## Applying

Utica College requires a high school transcript, a minimum high school GPA of 2.0, and in some cases an essay, SAT I or ACT, and a minimum high school GPA of 3.0. It recommends an essay, 3 years of high school math and science, some high school foreign language, recommendations, and an interview. Early, deferred, and midyear entrance are possible, with rolling admissions and continuous processing to 2/15 for financial aid. **Contact:** Ms. Leslie North, Director of Admissions, 1600 Burrstone Road, Hubbard Hall, Utica, NY 13502-4892, 315-792-3006 or toll-free 800-782-8884; fax 315-792-3292.

GETTING IN LAST YEAR
1,139 applied
82% were accepted
28% enrolled (263)
15% from top tenth of their h.s. class
2 valedictorians

THE STUDENT BODY
1,762 undergraduates
From 25 states and territories,
    9 other countries
86% from New York
64% women, 36% men
7% African Americans

0% Native Americans
2% Hispanics
1% Asian Americans
1% international students

AFTER FRESHMAN YEAR
71% returned for sophomore year
32% got a degree within 4 years
46% got a degree within 5 years
49% got a degree within 6 years

AFTER GRADUATION
9% pursued further study (7% arts and sciences,
    1% law, 1% medicine)

79% had job offers within 6 months
110 organizations recruited on campus

WHAT YOU WILL PAY
Tuition and fees $13,406
Room and board $5122
74% receive need-based financial aid
Need-based college-administered scholarships and
    grants average $4336 per award
4% receive non-need financial aid
Non-need college-administered scholarships and
    grants average $5637 per award

VALPARAISO UNIVERSITY

Valparaiso, Indiana • Small-town setting • Private • Independent-Religious • Coed

Valparaiso, a Lutheran university, is the school of choice for those who seek excellence in education. *U.S. News & World Report* rates Valparaiso the number one regional university in the Midwest, and a "Best Buy." More than 65% of entering freshmen placed in the upper quarter of their high school class and nearly half ranked in the top tenth. VU ranks in the upper 10% of the nation's schools for enrollment of National Merit Scholars. Nearby Chicago provides opportunities for academic study, the arts, and entertainment.

Academics

Valpo offers a liberal arts curriculum and core academic program; fewer than half of graduate courses are open to undergraduates. It awards associate, bachelor's, master's, and first professional **degrees**. Challenging opportunities include advanced placement, accelerated degree programs, self-designed majors, Freshman Honors College, an honors program, and a senior project. Special programs include cooperative education, internships, summer session for credit, off-campus study, and study abroad.

The most popular **majors** include nursing, business, and elementary education. A complete listing of majors at Valpo appears in the Majors Index beginning on page 379.

The **faculty** at Valpo has 227 full-time graduate and undergraduate teachers, 81% with terminal degrees. The student-faculty ratio is 12:1.

Computers on Campus

Students are not required to have a computer. Student rooms are linked to a campus network. 350 **computers** available in the computer center, computer labs, classrooms, the library, dormitories, and student rooms provide access to the main academic computer, off-campus computing facilities, e-mail, on-line services, and the Internet. Staffed computer lab on campus provides training in the use of computers and software.

The 2 **libraries** have 530,000 books, 333,000 microform titles, and 3,753 subscriptions. They are connected to 8 national **on-line** catalogs.

Campus Life

There are 150 active **organizations** on campus, including a drama/theater group and student-run newspaper and radio station. 32% of eligible men and 23% of eligible women are members of 10 national **fraternities** and 8 local **sororities**. Student **safety services** include late night transport/escort service, 24-hour emergency telephone alarm devices, 24-hour patrols by trained security personnel, and electronically operated dormitory entrances.

Valpo is a member of the NCAA (Division I). **Intercollegiate sports** (some offering scholarships) include baseball (m), basketball (m, w), cross-country running (m, w), football (m), soccer (m, w), softball (w), swimming and diving (m, w), tennis (m, w), volleyball (w).

Applying

Valpo requires a high school transcript, SAT I or ACT, and in some cases 3 years of high school math and science and a campus interview. It recommends an essay, 3 years of high school math and science, 2 years of high school foreign language, and recommendations. Early, deferred, and midyear entrance are possible, with rolling admissions and continuous processing to 3/1 for financial aid. **Contact:** Ms. Karen Foust, Director of Admissions, Kretzmann Hall, Valparaiso, IN 46383-6493, 219-464-5011 or toll-free 800-348-2611 (out-of-state); fax 219-464-5381.

GETTING IN LAST YEAR
2,408 applied
86% were accepted
34% enrolled (708)
37% from top tenth of their h.s. class
15% had SAT verbal scores over 600
43% had SAT math scores over 600
40% had ACT scores over 26
1% had SAT verbal scores over 700
10% had SAT math scores over 700
14% had ACT scores over 30
11 National Merit Scholars
30 valedictorians

THE STUDENT BODY
Total 3,524, of whom 2,755 are undergraduates

From 43 states and territories, 39 other countries
39% from Indiana
56% women, 44% men
4% African Americans
1% Native Americans
2% Hispanics
2% Asian Americans
4% international students

AFTER FRESHMAN YEAR
87% returned for sophomore year
55% got a degree within 4 years
70% got a degree within 5 years
73% got a degree within 6 years

AFTER GRADUATION
25% pursued further study
90% had job offers within 6 months
60 organizations recruited on campus

WHAT YOU WILL PAY
Tuition and fees $12,860
Room and board $3450
70% receive need-based financial aid
Need-based college-administered scholarships and grants average $2935 per award
38% receive non-need financial aid
Non-need college-administered scholarships and grants average $3400 per award

VANDERBILT UNIVERSITY

Nashville, Tennessee • Urban setting • Private • Independent • Coed

Vanderbilt University enrolls America's most talented students, who are challenged daily to expand their intellectual horizons and free their imaginations. Dialogue, service, the Honor Code, the search for knowledge and personal fulfillment—a Vanderbilt education enhances the life of every student. Vanderbilt alumni carry with them not only knowledge gained in classes, but a lifelong connection to a special community of learners. Vanderbilt is committed to enrolling talented, motivated students from diverse backgrounds. The University offers a full range of financial aid and financing options for those who need assistance.

Academics

Vanderbilt offers an interdisciplinary curriculum and core academic program. It awards bachelor's, master's, doctoral, and first professional **degrees**. Challenging opportunities include advanced placement, accelerated degree programs, self-designed majors, tutorials, an honors program, a senior project, Phi Beta Kappa, and Sigma Xi. Special programs include internships, summer session for credit, off-campus study, study abroad, and Army, Naval, and Air Force ROTC.

The most popular **majors** include English, human development, and psychology. A complete listing of majors at Vanderbilt appears in the Majors Index beginning on page 379.

The **faculty** at Vanderbilt has 1,668 full-time graduate and undergraduate teachers, 97% with terminal degrees. The student-faculty ratio is 8:1, and the average class size in core courses is 24.

Computers on Campus

Students are not required to have a computer. 400 **computers** available in the computer center, computer labs, the learning resource center, labs, classrooms, the library, and dormitories provide access to the main academic computer, off-campus computing facilities, e-mail, on-line services, and productivity and educational software. Staffed computer lab on campus provides training in the use of computers and software.

The 8 **libraries** have 2.3 million books and 17,450 subscriptions. They are connected to 6 national **on-line** catalogs.

Campus Life

Active **organizations** on campus include drama/theater group and student-run newspaper and radio station. 38% of eligible men and 50% of eligible women are members of 17 national **fraternities** and 12 national **sororities**. Student **safety services** include late night transport/escort service, 24-hour emergency telephone alarm devices, 24-hour patrols by trained security personnel, student patrols, and electronically operated dormitory entrances.

Vanderbilt is a member of the NCAA (Division I). **Intercollegiate sports** (some offering scholarships) include baseball (m), basketball (m, w), crew (m, w), cross-country running (m, w), equestrian sports (m, w), fencing (m, w), football (m), golf (m, w), ice hockey (m), lacrosse (m, w), riflery (m, w), rugby (m, w), sailing (m, w), skiing (downhill) (m, w), soccer (m, w), squash (m, w), table tennis (m), tennis (m, w), volleyball (m), water polo (m), weight lifting (m).

Applying

Vanderbilt requires an essay, a high school transcript, 3 years of high school math, 2 recommendations, SAT I or ACT, 3 SAT II Subject Tests (including SAT II: Writing Test), and in some cases 3 years of high school science and some high school foreign language. Early and deferred entrance are possible, with a 1/15 deadline and continuous processing to 2/15 for financial aid. **Contact:** Dr. Neill Sanders, Dean of Undergraduate Admissions, 2305 West End Avenue, Nashville, TN 37203-1700, 615-322-2561.

GETTING IN LAST YEAR
8,878 applied
58% were accepted
30% enrolled (1,539)
78% from top tenth of their h.s. class
77% had SAT verbal scores over 600
85% had SAT math scores over 600
78% had ACT scores over 26
20% had SAT verbal scores over 700
24% had SAT math scores over 700
34% had ACT scores over 30
89 National Merit Scholars
9 class presidents

THE STUDENT BODY
Total 10,074, of whom 5,792
   are undergraduates

From 54 states and territories,
   31 other countries
13% from Tennessee
46% women, 54% men
4% African Americans
0% Native Americans
3% Hispanics
7% Asian Americans
2% international students

AFTER FRESHMAN YEAR
92% returned for sophomore year
75% got a degree within 4 years
82% got a degree within 5 years
83% got a degree within 6 years

AFTER GRADUATION
29% pursued further study (10% arts and
   sciences, 7% law, 7% medicine)
63% had job offers within 6 months
243 organizations recruited on campus
1 Fulbright scholar

WHAT YOU WILL PAY
Tuition and fees $19,422
Room and board $6656
35% receive need-based financial aid
Need-based college-administered scholarships and
   grants average $7710 per award
21% receive non-need financial aid
Non-need college-administered scholarships and
   grants average $7064 per award

Vassar College

Poughkeepsie, New York • Suburban setting • Private • Independent • Coed

Since its founding in 1861, Vassar has held a place in the forefront of liberal arts education. Today, it seeks students who value learning and who want to take charge of their own education. Vassar offers a rigorous program that is both diverse and coherent; students learn with the support of a dedicated and distinguished faculty, most of whom live on the school's 1,000-acre Hudson Valley campus. The nearby cities of Poughkeepsie and New York offer opportunities for education and entertainment; Vassar also offers a vital extracurricular program, including varsity sports and widespread participation in drama, dance, music, and writing.

 Academics

Vassar offers a liberal arts curriculum and no core academic program. It awards bachelor's and master's **degrees**. Challenging opportunities include advanced placement, accelerated degree programs, self-designed majors, a senior project, Phi Beta Kappa, and Sigma Xi. Special programs include internships, off-campus study, and study abroad.

The most popular **majors** include English, political science/government, and psychology. A complete listing of majors at Vassar appears in the Majors Index beginning on page 379.

The **faculty** at Vassar has 202 full-time undergraduate teachers, 95% with terminal degrees. 100% of the faculty serve as student advisers. The student-faculty ratio is 11:1, and the average class size in core courses is 15.

 Computers on Campus

Students are not required to have a computer. Student rooms are linked to a campus network. 300 **computers** available in the computer center, computer labs, academic buildings, the library, and dormitories provide access to e-mail, on-line services, and the Internet. Staffed computer lab on campus (open 24 hours a day) provides training in the use of computers and software.

The **library** has 762,000 books, 350,000 microform titles, and 3,900 subscriptions.

 Campus Life

There are 70 active **organizations** on campus, including a drama/theater group and student-run newspaper and radio station. 40% of students participate in student government elections. Student **safety services** include late night transport/escort service, 24-hour emergency telephone alarm devices, 24-hour patrols by trained security personnel, student patrols, and electronically operated dormitory entrances.

Vassar is a member of the NCAA (Division III). **Intercollegiate sports** include baseball (m), basketball (m, w), crew (m, w), cross-country running (m, w), fencing (m, w), field hockey (w), golf (m, w), lacrosse (m, w), rugby (m, w), sailing (m, w), soccer (m, w), squash (m, w), swimming and diving (m, w), tennis (m, w), volleyball (m, w).

 Applying

Vassar requires an essay, a high school transcript, 2 recommendations, SAT I or ACT, and 3 SAT II Subject Tests. It recommends 3 years of high school math and science, 3 years of high school foreign language, and an interview. Early and deferred entrance are possible, with a 1/1 deadline and 1/1 for financial aid. **Contact:** Mr. Richard Moll, Interim Director of Admissions, Raymond Avenue, Poughkeepsie, NY 12601, 914-437-7300; fax 914-437-7063.

GETTING IN LAST YEAR
3,943 applied
48% were accepted
34% enrolled (653)
58% from top tenth of their h.s. class
56% had SAT verbal scores over 600 (R)
68% had SAT math scores over 600 (R)
91% had ACT scores over 26
9% had SAT verbal scores over 700 (R)
15% had SAT math scores over 700 (R)
32% had ACT scores over 30
24 National Merit Scholars
24 class presidents
28 valedictorians

THE STUDENT BODY
Total 2,346, of whom 2,344 are undergraduates

From 51 states and territories, 30 other countries
32% from New York
62% women, 38% men
6% African Americans
1% Native Americans
5% Hispanics
9% Asian Americans
3% international students

AFTER FRESHMAN YEAR
92% returned for sophomore year
78% got a degree within 4 years

86% got a degree within 5 years
87% got a degree within 6 years

AFTER GRADUATION
20% pursued further study (13% arts and sciences, 5% law, 2% medicine)
66% had job offers within 6 months
1 Fulbright scholar

WHAT YOU WILL PAY
Tuition and fees $20,330
Room and board $6150
60% receive need-based financial aid
Need-based college-administered scholarships and grants average $12,525 per award

VILLANOVA UNIVERSITY

Villanova, Pennsylvania • Suburban setting • Private • Independent-Religious • Coed

Villanova seeks to enroll academically talented and diverse individuals through a comprehensive scholarship program. In 1995–96, Villanova offered more than 200 full and partial merit-based scholarships totaling $2 million. Full-tuition Presidential Scholarships are awarded to selected students who have a minimum score of 1350 on the SAT I, rank in the top 5% of their high school class, and submit their application for admission by December 15.

Academics

Villanova offers an interdisciplinary curriculum and core academic program; fewer than half of graduate courses are open to undergraduates. It awards associate, bachelor's, master's, doctoral, and first professional **degrees**. Challenging opportunities include advanced placement, accelerated degree programs, tutorials, an honors program, a senior project, Phi Beta Kappa, and Sigma Xi. Special programs include internships, summer session for credit, off-campus study, study abroad, and Army, Naval, and Air Force ROTC.

The most popular **majors** include political science/government, communication, and business. A complete listing of majors at Villanova appears in the Majors Index beginning on page 379.

The **faculty** at Villanova has 463 full-time undergraduate teachers, 90% with terminal degrees.

Computers on Campus

Students are not required to have a computer. Student rooms are linked to a campus network. 400 **computers** available in the computer center, computer labs, the research center, the learning resource center, departmental labs, and classrooms provide access to the main academic computer, off-campus computing facilities, e-mail, on-line services, and the Internet. Staffed computer lab on campus provides training in the use of computers and software.

The 2 **libraries** have 650,000 books, 72,574 microform titles, and 2,865 subscriptions. They are connected to 5 national **on-line** catalogs.

Campus Life

Active **organizations** on campus include drama/theater group and student-run newspaper and radio station. 25% of students participate in student government elections. 29% of eligible men and 48% of eligible women are members of 13 national **fraternities**, 8 national **sororities**, and 1 local fraternity. Student **safety services** include late night transport/escort service, 24-hour emergency telephone alarm devices, 24-hour patrols by trained security personnel, and electronically operated dormitory entrances.

Villanova is a member of the NCAA (Division I). **Intercollegiate sports** (some offering scholarships) include baseball (m), basketball (m, w), crew (m, w), cross-country running (m, w), field hockey (w), football (m), golf (m), lacrosse (m, w), rugby (m), sailing (m, w), soccer (m, w), softball (w), swimming and diving (w), tennis (m, w), track and field (m, w), volleyball (m, w), water polo (m), weight lifting (m, w).

Applying

Villanova requires an essay, a high school transcript, 3 years of high school math and science, some high school foreign language, SAT I or ACT, and in some cases 4 years of high school math, 2 years of high school foreign language, and 2 SAT II Subject Tests. It recommends recommendations. Early and deferred entrance are possible, with a 1/15 deadline and continuous processing to 2/15 for financial aid. **Contact:** Mr. Stephen Merritt, Director of Undergraduate Admissions, Austin Hall, Villanova, PA 19085-1699, 610-519-4000 or toll-free 800-338-7927; fax 610-519-6450.

GETTING IN LAST YEAR
7,976 applied
74% were accepted
28% enrolled (1,669)
51% had SAT verbal scores over 600 (R)
56% had SAT math scores over 600 (R)
7% had SAT verbal scores over 700 (R)
10% had SAT math scores over 700 (R)
6 National Merit Scholars
22 valedictorians

THE STUDENT BODY
Total 10,514, of whom 6,729
  are undergraduates
From 49 states and territories,
  21 other countries

31% from Pennsylvania
49% women, 51% men
2% African Americans
1% Native Americans
2% Hispanics
3% Asian Americans
9% international students

AFTER FRESHMAN YEAR
93% returned for sophomore year
75% got a degree within 4 years
83% got a degree within 5 years
84% got a degree within 6 years

AFTER GRADUATION
22% pursued further study (10% arts and
  sciences, 6% law, 3% medicine)
59% had job offers within 6 months
236 organizations recruited on campus
1 Fulbright scholar

WHAT YOU WILL PAY
Tuition and fees $16,560
Room and board $7180
49% receive need-based financial aid
Need-based college-administered scholarships and
  grants average $5105 per award
14% receive non-need financial aid
Non-need college-administered scholarships and
  grants average $12,382 per award

VIRGINIA POLYTECHNIC INSTITUTE AND STATE UNIVERSITY

Blacksburg, Virginia • Small-town setting • Public • State-supported • Coed

Excellence in academics and athletics go hand-in-hand at Virginia Tech, Virginia's largest and most diverse university. Student successes most recently have included a Rhodes Scholarship award and, in NCAA Division I athletics, the NIT basketball and Big East football championships, including a Sugar Bowl victory for the Hokies in 1995.

Academics

Virginia Tech offers a liberal arts and sciences curriculum and core academic program. It awards associate, bachelor's, master's, and doctoral **degrees**. Challenging opportunities include advanced placement, accelerated degree programs, tutorials, an honors program, a senior project, Phi Beta Kappa, and Sigma Xi. Special programs include cooperative education, internships, summer session for credit, off-campus study, study abroad, and Army, Naval, and Air Force ROTC.

The most popular **majors** include psychology, mechanical engineering, and marketing/retailing/merchandising. A complete listing of majors at Virginia Tech appears in the Majors Index beginning on page 379.

The **faculty** at Virginia Tech has 1,424 full-time graduate and undergraduate teachers, 87% with terminal degrees. The student-faculty ratio is 17:1.

Computers on Campus

Student rooms are linked to a campus network. 2,000 **computers** available in computer labs, academic buildings, classrooms, the library, and dormitories provide access to e-mail, on-line services, and the Internet. Staffed computer lab on campus provides training in the use of computers and software.

The 4 **libraries** have 1.9 million books, 5.9 million microform titles, and 17,743 subscriptions. They are connected to 9 national **on-line** catalogs.

Campus Life

There are 437 active **organizations** on campus, including a drama/theater group and student-run newspaper and radio station. 13% of eligible men and 22% of eligible women are members of 33 national **fraternities**, 16 national **sororities**, and 1 local fraternity. Student **safety services** include late night transport/escort service, 24-hour emergency telephone alarm devices, 24-hour patrols by trained security personnel, and student patrols.

Virginia Tech is a member of the NCAA (Division I). **Intercollegiate sports** (some offering scholarships) include baseball (m), basketball (m, w), bowling (m, w), crew (m, w), cross-country running (m, w), equestrian sports (m, w), fencing (m, w), field hockey (m, w), football (m), golf (m), gymnastics (m, w), lacrosse (m, w), rugby (m, w), soccer (m, w), swimming and diving (m, w), tennis (m, w), track and field (m, w), volleyball (m, w), weight lifting (m, w), wrestling (m).

Applying

Virginia Tech requires a high school transcript, 3 years of high school math, SAT I or ACT, 2 SAT II Subject Tests (including SAT II: Writing Test), and in some cases 4 years of high school math and 3 years of high school science. It recommends 3 years of high school science, 2 years of high school foreign language, and a minimum high school GPA of 3.0. Early, deferred, and midyear entrance are possible, with a 2/1 deadline and continuous processing to 2/15 for financial aid. **Contact:** Office of Undergraduate Admissions, 104 Burruss Hall, Blacksburg, VA 24061-0202, 540-231-6267; fax 540-231-3242.

GETTING IN LAST YEAR
14,779 applied
79% were accepted
40% enrolled (4,708)
30% from top tenth of their h.s. class
12% had SAT verbal scores over 600
43% had SAT math scores over 600
2% had SAT verbal scores over 700
10% had SAT math scores over 700
39 National Merit Scholars

THE STUDENT BODY
Total 23,674, of whom 19,496
  are undergraduates
From 50 states and territories,
  100 other countries
79% from Virginia
41% women, 59% men
5% African Americans
0% Native Americans
2% Hispanics
7% Asian Americans
1% international students

AFTER GRADUATION
378 organizations recruited on campus
1 Rhodes, 1 Fulbright scholar

WHAT YOU WILL PAY
Resident tuition and fees $4087
Nonresident tuition and fees $10,739
Room and board $3120
45% receive need-based financial aid
Need-based college-administered scholarships and
  grants average $1788 per award
16% receive non-need financial aid

WABASH COLLEGE

Crawfordsville, Indiana • Small-town setting • Private • Independent • Men

As a college for men, Wabash helps students achieve their full potential—intellectually, athletically, emotionally, and artistically. Wabash prepares students for leadership in an ever-changing world. The College helps them learn to think clearly and openly and to explore a variety of interests. Independence and responsibility are emphasized and defined by the Gentlemen's Rule, which calls on students to conduct themselves as gentlemen at all times. With the guidance of professors who are accessible, a support staff that cares, and a nationwide network of alumni willing to offer assistance and encouragement, Wabash men frequently surpass even their own expectations.

 Academics

Wabash offers an interdisciplinary curriculum and core academic program. It awards bachelor's **degrees**. Challenging opportunities include advanced placement, accelerated degree programs, self-designed majors, tutorials, and Phi Beta Kappa. Off-campus study is a special program.

The most popular **majors** include psychology, biology/biological sciences, and English. A complete listing of majors at Wabash appears in the Majors Index beginning on page 379.

The **faculty** at Wabash has 71 full-time teachers, 94% with terminal degrees. 100% of the faculty serve as student advisers. The student-faculty ratio is 10:1.

 Computers on Campus

Students are not required to have a computer. Student rooms are linked to a campus network. 103 **computers** available in the computer center, computer labs, the learning resource center, classrooms, and the library provide access to the main academic computer, off-campus computing facilities, e-mail, and the Internet. Staffed computer lab on campus (open 24 hours a day) provides training in the use of computers and software.

The **library** has 251,886 books, 8,631 microform titles, and 877 subscriptions. It is connected to 6 national **on-line** catalogs.

 Campus Life

There are 30 active **organizations** on campus, including a drama/theater group and student-run newspaper. 65% of students participate in student government elections. 75% of eligible undergraduates are members of 10 national **fraternities**. Student **safety services** include 24-hour emergency telephone alarm devices.

Wabash is a member of the NCAA (Division III). **Intercollegiate sports** include baseball, basketball, crew, cross-country running, football, golf, ice hockey, rugby, sailing, soccer, swimming and diving, tennis, track and field, water polo, wrestling.

 Applying

Wabash requires an essay, a high school transcript, 3 years of high school math, 1 recommendation, and SAT I or ACT. It recommends 3 years of high school science, 2 years of high school foreign language, an interview, and minimum 2.7 high school GPA. Early, deferred, and midyear entrance are possible, with a 3/1 deadline and continuous processing to 3/1 for financial aid. **Contact:** Mr. Gregory Birk, Director of Admissions, 502 West Wabash Avenue, Crawfordsville, IN 47933-0352, 317-361-6225 or toll-free 800-345-5385.

GETTING IN LAST YEAR
779 applied
78% were accepted
37% enrolled (227)
37% from top tenth of their h.s. class
3.51 average high school GPA
44% had SAT verbal scores over 600 (R)
57% had SAT math scores over 600 (R)
51% had ACT scores over 26
8% had SAT verbal scores over 700 (R)
10% had SAT math scores over 700 (R)
15% had ACT scores over 30
3 National Merit Scholars
15 valedictorians

THE STUDENT BODY
790 undergraduates

From 34 states and territories,
17 other countries
74% from Indiana
100% men
4% African Americans
1% Native Americans
3% Hispanics
4% Asian Americans
4% international students

AFTER FRESHMAN YEAR
84% returned for sophomore year
75% got a degree within 4 years
76% got a degree within 5 years

AFTER GRADUATION
45% pursued further study (12% arts and sciences, 12% law, 10% medicine)
39% had job offers within 6 months
19 organizations recruited on campus

WHAT YOU WILL PAY
Tuition and fees $13,950
Room and board $4405
67% receive need-based financial aid
Need-based college-administered scholarships and grants average $7808 per award
28% receive non-need financial aid
Non-need college-administered scholarships and grants average $7184 per award

---

WAKE FOREST UNIVERSITY

Winston-Salem, North Carolina • Suburban setting • Private • Independent • Coed

Academics

Wake Forest offers a classical liberal arts curriculum and core academic program. It awards bachelor's, master's, doctoral, and first professional **degrees**. Challenging opportunities include advanced placement, accelerated degree programs, self-designed majors, an honors program, a senior project, Phi Beta Kappa, and Sigma Xi. Special programs include internships, summer session for credit, off-campus study, study abroad, and Army ROTC.

The most popular **majors** include business, biology/biological sciences, and psychology. A complete listing of majors at Wake Forest appears in the Majors Index beginning on page 379.

The **faculty** at Wake Forest has 976 full-time graduate and undergraduate teachers, 90% with terminal degrees. 80% of the faculty serve as student advisers. The student-faculty ratio is 13:1.

Computers on Campus

Students are not required to have a computer. Student rooms are linked to a campus network. 248 **computers** available in the computer center, computer labs, classrooms, the library, the student center, and dormitories provide access to the main academic computer, off-campus computing facilities, e-mail, on-line services, and the Internet. Staffed computer lab on campus provides training in the use of computers and software.

The 3 **libraries** have 1.3 million books, 362,470 microform titles, and 17,535 subscriptions. They are connected to 6 national **on-line** catalogs.

Campus Life

There are 100 active **organizations** on campus, including a drama/theater group and student-run newspaper and radio station. 42% of eligible men and 51% of eligible women are members of 15 national **fraternities** and 10 national **sororities**. Student **safety services** include late night transport/escort service.

Wake Forest is a member of the NCAA (Division I). **Intercollegiate sports** (some offering scholarships) include baseball (m), basketball (m, w), cross-country running (m, w), equestrian sports (m, w), field hockey (w), football (m), golf (m, w), ice hockey (m), lacrosse (m, w), soccer (m, w), tennis (m, w), track and field (m, w).

Applying

Wake Forest requires an essay, a high school transcript, 3 years of high school math, 2 years of high school foreign language, 1 recommendation, and SAT I. It recommends 3 years of high school science and 3 SAT II Subject Tests. Early and deferred entrance are possible, with a 1/15 deadline and continuous processing to 3/1 for financial aid. **Contact:** Mr. William G. Starling, Director of Admissions, PO Box 7305, Winston-Salem, NC 27109, 910-759-5201.

GETTING IN LAST YEAR
6,342 applied
43% were accepted
36% enrolled (965)
71% from top tenth of their h.s. class
42% had SAT verbal scores over 600
76% had SAT math scores over 600
5% had SAT verbal scores over 700
26% had SAT math scores over 700
24 National Merit Scholars
65 class presidents
67 valedictorians

THE STUDENT BODY
Total 5,913, of whom 3,740
  are undergraduates

From 50 states and territories,
  29 other countries
31% from North Carolina
50% women, 50% men
7% African Americans
1% Hispanics
2% Asian Americans
2% international students

AFTER FRESHMAN YEAR
93% returned for sophomore year
75% got a degree within 4 years
86% got a degree within 5 years
87% got a degree within 6 years

AFTER GRADUATION
32% pursued further study (16% arts and
  sciences, 6% law, 6% medicine)
1 Fulbright scholar

WHAT YOU WILL PAY
Tuition and fees $14,750
Room and board $4585
31% receive need-based financial aid
Need-based college-administered scholarships and
  grants average $6545 per award
34% receive non-need financial aid
Non-need college-administered scholarships and
  grants average $8869 per award

WARTBURG COLLEGE

Waverly, Iowa • Small-town setting • Private • Independent-Religious • Coed

Wartburg College affirms the role of faith and values in preparing students for lives of leadership and service. It challenges students to accept responsibility and assume leadership in addressing issues facing their communities and the world. The Institute for Leadership Education provides academic course work, mentoring relationships, and practical experience to help students develop leadership skills. The College's Global and Multicultural Program offers cultural immersions for one month, a term, or an entire year in settings throughout the world. Campus life is enriched by the presence and participation of international students from more than 20 countries.

 ## Academics

Wartburg offers an interdisciplinary curriculum and core academic program. It awards bachelor's **degrees**. Challenging opportunities include advanced placement, accelerated degree programs, self-designed majors, tutorials, and a senior project. Special programs include internships, summer session for credit, off-campus study, and study abroad.

The most popular **majors** include education, business, and biology/biological sciences. A complete listing of majors at Wartburg appears in the Majors Index beginning on page 379.

The **faculty** at Wartburg has 92 full-time teachers, 91% with terminal degrees. 100% of the faculty serve as student advisers. The student-faculty ratio is 14:1, and the average class size in core courses is 19.

 ## Computers on Campus

Students are not required to have a computer. Student rooms are linked to a campus network. 120 **computers** available in the computer center, computer labs, classroom technology center, classrooms, and the library provide access to the main academic computer, off-campus computing facilities, and e-mail. Staffed computer lab on campus (open 24 hours a day) provides training in the use of computers and software.

The **library** has 122,016 books, 5,822 microform titles, and 744 subscriptions. It is connected to 1 national **on-line** catalog.

 ## Campus Life

There are 75 active **organizations** on campus, including a drama/theater group and student-run newspaper and radio station. 50% of students participate in student government elections. Student **safety services** include late night transport/escort service, 24-hour patrols by trained security personnel, and electronically operated dormitory entrances.

Wartburg is a member of the NCAA (Division III). **Intercollegiate sports** include baseball (m), basketball (m, w), cross-country running (m, w), football (m), golf (m, w), soccer (m, w), softball (w), tennis (m, w), track and field (m, w), volleyball (w), wrestling (m).

 ## Applying

Wartburg requires a high school transcript, recommendations, SAT I or ACT, and in some cases an interview. It recommends 3 years of high school math and science, 2 years of high school foreign language, and an interview. Deferred and midyear entrance are possible, with rolling admissions and continuous processing to 3/1 for financial aid. **Contact:** Mr. Doug Bowman, Director of Admissions, 222 Ninth Street, NW, Waverly, IA 50677-1033, 319-352-8264 or toll-free 800-772-2085; fax 319-352-8579.

GETTING IN LAST YEAR
1,158 applied
85% were accepted
36% enrolled (359)
35% from top tenth of their h.s. class
2.85 average high school GPA
46% had SAT verbal scores over 600 (R)
36% had SAT math scores over 600 (R)
42% had ACT scores over 26
14% had SAT verbal scores over 700 (R)
7% had SAT math scores over 700 (R)
9% had ACT scores over 30
1 National Merit Scholar

THE STUDENT BODY
1,433 undergraduates

From 27 states and territories,
  20 other countries
73% from Iowa
58% women, 42% men
6% African Americans
0% Native Americans
1% Hispanics
1% Asian Americans
3% international students

AFTER FRESHMAN YEAR
88% returned for sophomore year
54% got a degree within 4 years
62% got a degree within 5 years
63% got a degree within 6 years

AFTER GRADUATION
20% pursued further study
96% had job offers within 6 months
30 organizations recruited on campus

WHAT YOU WILL PAY
Tuition and fees $12,370
Room and board $3730
77% receive need-based financial aid
Need-based college-administered scholarships and
  grants average $4446 per award
24% receive non-need financial aid
Non-need college-administered scholarships and
  grants average $4634 per award

WASHINGTON AND JEFFERSON COLLEGE

Washington, Pennsylvania • Small-town setting • Private • Independent • Coed

Washington and Jefferson College, located 30 miles south of Pittsburgh, is the eleventh-oldest college in the United States. Since 1781, the College has actively pursued a course of academic excellence through attention to individual needs. This personalized approach to education distinguishes Washington and Jefferson from other colleges. Nationally recognized programs in prelaw and prehealth, averaging over 90% placement, and a strong and varied liberal arts curriculum offer endless opportunities for the bright, creative, and motivated student. An involved faculty, superior academic programs, and an inquisitive student body combine to continue the rich tradition of achievement.

Academics

W & J offers an interdisciplinary curriculum and core academic program. It awards bachelor's **degrees**. Challenging opportunities include advanced placement, accelerated degree programs, self-designed majors, tutorials, an honors program, and Phi Beta Kappa. Special programs include internships, summer session for credit, off-campus study, study abroad, and Army ROTC.

The **faculty** at W & J has 89 full-time teachers, 92% with terminal degrees. The student-faculty ratio is 11:1.

Computers on Campus

Students are not required to have a computer. 200 **computers** available in the computer center, computer labs, classrooms, the library, and the student center provide access to the main academic computer, e-mail, and the Internet. Staffed computer lab on campus provides training in the use of computers and software.

The **library** has 195,000 books, 5,400 microform titles, and 715 subscriptions. It is connected to 1 national **on-line** catalog.

Campus Life

There are 87 active **organizations** on campus, including a drama/theater group and student-run newspaper and radio station. 53% of eligible men and 67% of eligible women are members of 10 national **fraternities** and 4 national **sororities**. Student **safety services** include late night transport/escort service, 24-hour emergency telephone alarm devices, 24-hour patrols by trained security personnel, and electronically operated dormitory entrances.

W & J is a member of the NCAA (Division III). **Intercollegiate sports** include baseball (m), basketball (m, w), cross-country running (m, w), football (m), golf (m), lacrosse (m), soccer (m, w), softball (w), swimming and diving (m, w), tennis (m, w), track and field (m, w), volleyball (w), wrestling (m).

Applying

W & J requires a high school transcript, 3 years of high school math and science, 2 years of high school foreign language, SAT I or ACT, and 3 SAT II Subject Tests (including SAT II: Writing Test). It recommends an essay, recommendations, and an interview. Early, deferred, and midyear entrance are possible, with a 3/1 deadline and continuous processing to 3/15 for financial aid. **Contact:** Mr. Thomas P. O'Connor, Director of Admissions, 60 South Lincoln Street, Washington, PA 15301-4801, 412-223-6025; fax 412-223-5271.

GETTING IN LAST YEAR
1,140 applied
91% were accepted
27% enrolled (281)
31% from top tenth of their h.s. class
8% had SAT verbal scores over 600
33% had SAT math scores over 600
0% had SAT verbal scores over 700
3% had SAT math scores over 700

THE STUDENT BODY
1,128 undergraduates

From 30 states and territories,
    3 other countries
70% from Pennsylvania
44% women, 56% men
5% African Americans
1% Native Americans
1% Hispanics
2% Asian Americans
1% international students

AFTER FRESHMAN YEAR
92% returned for sophomore year

AFTER GRADUATION
45% pursued further study (18% medicine, 17% law, 5% business)
55% had job offers within 6 months

WHAT YOU WILL PAY
Tuition and fees $16,840
Room and board $4205
Need-based college-administered scholarships and grants average $8509 per award
Non-need college-administered scholarships and grants average $4012 per award

WASHINGTON AND LEE UNIVERSITY

Lexington, Virginia • Small-town setting • Private • Independent • Coed

Washington and Lee continues in its traditional mold of academic excellence and unparalleled value per educational dollar, striving always to provide a top-quality education at the lowest possible cost to students and families. To that end, the University has recently completed a $150-million capital campaign, raising endowment resources to $400 million. The goals of the campaign include a strengthened endowment for educational programs and faculty support, increased revenues for both need-based and non-need-based financial assistance to students, and expansion and improvement of campus facilities. Washington and Lee truly adheres to its Latin motto, *Non In Cautus Futuri*—Not Unmindful of the Future.

Academics

W & L offers a liberal arts curriculum and core academic program; a few graduate courses are open to undergraduates. It awards bachelor's and first professional **degrees**. Challenging opportunities include advanced placement, accelerated degree programs, self-designed majors, tutorials, an honors program, a senior project, and Phi Beta Kappa. Special programs include internships, off-campus study, and study abroad.

The most popular **majors** include history, economics, and business. A complete listing of majors at W & L appears in the Majors Index beginning on page 379.

The **faculty** at W & L has 166 full-time graduate and undergraduate teachers, 96% with terminal degrees. 92% of the faculty serve as student advisers. The student-faculty ratio is 11:1.

Computers on Campus

Students are not required to have a computer. Student rooms are linked to a campus network. 195 **computers** available in the computer center, computer labs, academic buildings, upperclass residence hall, classrooms, the library, and dormitories provide access to the main academic computer, e-mail, on-line services, and the Internet. Staffed computer lab on campus (open 24 hours a day) provides training in the use of computers and software.

The 2 **libraries** have 445,552 books, 120,000 microform titles, and 1,600 subscriptions. They are connected to 5 national **on-line** catalogs.

Campus Life

Active **organizations** on campus include drama/theater group and student-run newspaper and radio station. 80% of eligible men and 65% of eligible women are members of 15 national **fraternities** and 4 national **sororities**. Student **safety services** include late night transport/escort service, 24-hour emergency telephone alarm devices, 24-hour patrols by trained security personnel, and electronically operated dormitory entrances.

W & L is a member of the NCAA (Division III). **Intercollegiate sports** include baseball (m), basketball (m, w), cross-country running (m, w), fencing (m, w), field hockey (w), football (m), golf (m), ice hockey (m, w), lacrosse (m, w), rugby (m), soccer (m, w), softball (w), swimming and diving (m, w), tennis (m, w), track and field (m, w), volleyball (m, w), water polo (m), wrestling (m).

Applying

W & L requires an essay, a high school transcript, 3 years of high school math, 2 years of high school foreign language, 3 recommendations, ACT or SAT I and 3 unrelated SAT II Subject Tests (including SAT II: Writing Test). It recommends 3 years of high school science and an interview. Early and deferred entrance are possible, with a 1/15 deadline and a 2/1 priority date for financial aid. **Contact:** Mr. William M. Hartog, Dean of Admissions and Financial Aid, Gilliam Admissions House, Lexington, VA 24450, 540-463-8710.

GETTING IN LAST YEAR

3,346 applied
32% were accepted
41% enrolled (435)
76% from top tenth of their h.s. class
65% had SAT verbal scores over 600
88% had SAT math scores over 600
98% had ACT scores over 26
10% had SAT verbal scores over 700
33% had SAT math scores over 700
37% had ACT scores over 30
25 National Merit Scholars
35 class presidents
37 valedictorians

THE STUDENT BODY

Total 1,995, of whom 1,618
  are undergraduates

From 49 states and territories,
  20 other countries
12% from Virginia
40% women, 60% men
3% African Americans
0% Native Americans
1% Hispanics
1% Asian Americans
2% international students

AFTER FRESHMAN YEAR

92% returned for sophomore year
87% got a degree within 4 years
90% got a degree within 5 years
91% got a degree within 6 years

AFTER GRADUATION

24% pursued further study (9% arts and
  sciences, 7% law, 5% medicine)
69% had job offers within 6 months
46 organizations recruited on campus
2 Fulbright scholars

WHAT YOU WILL PAY

Tuition and fees $14,655
Room and board $5310
35% receive need-based financial aid
Need-based college-administered scholarships and
  grants average $8085 per award
15% receive non-need financial aid
Non-need college-administered scholarships and
  grants average $6895 per award

WASHINGTON COLLEGE

Chestertown, Maryland • Small-town setting • Private • Independent • Coed

Washington College has initiated a new $40,000 scholarship program expressly for National Honor Society members. Washington College NHS Scholarships are $10,000 annual awards renewable through the completion of 8 semesters (full-time enrollment and cumulative GPA of 3.0–4.0 required). To be eligible for WC/NHS Scholarship consideration a student must apply for freshman admission no later than February 1 of the senior year, be admitted to Washington College, maintain NHS membership through graduation, and remit a $300 enrollment deposit no later than May 1 of the senior year. For more information, students can contact the Admission Office or visit the WC Web Site at http://www.washcoll.edu.

Academics

WC offers a core academic program. It awards bachelor's and master's **degrees**. Challenging opportunities include advanced placement, self-designed majors, tutorials, and a senior project. Special programs include internships, off-campus study, and study abroad.

The most popular **majors** include English, psychology, and business. A complete listing of majors at WC appears in the Majors Index beginning on page 379.

The **faculty** at WC has 65 full-time undergraduate teachers, 95% with terminal degrees. 89% of the faculty serve as student advisers. The student-faculty ratio is 12:1.

Computers on Campus

Students are not required to have a computer. Student rooms are linked to a campus network. 80 **computers** available in the computer center, computer labs, study center, the library, and dormitories provide access to the main academic computer, off-campus computing facilities, e-mail, on-line services, and the Internet. Staffed computer lab on campus provides training in the use of computers and software.

The **library** has 210,746 books, 181,334 microform titles, and 814 subscriptions. It is connected to 3 national **on-line** catalogs.

Campus Life

There are 50 active **organizations** on campus, including a drama/theater group and student-run newspaper. 25% of eligible men and 25% of eligible women are members of 3 national **fraternities** and 3 national **sororities**. Student **safety services** include late night transport/escort service, 24-hour emergency telephone alarm devices, and 24-hour patrols by trained security personnel.

WC is a member of the NCAA (Division III). **Intercollegiate sports** include baseball (m), basketball (m, w), crew (m, w), field hockey (w), ice hockey (m, w), lacrosse (m, w), rugby (m), sailing (m, w), soccer (m, w), softball (w), swimming and diving (m, w), tennis (m, w), volleyball (w).

Applying

WC requires an essay, a high school transcript, 3 years of high school math, 2 years of high school foreign language, 2 recommendations, and SAT I. It recommends 3 years of high school science and an interview. Early, deferred, and midyear entrance are possible, with a 2/15 deadline and continuous processing to 2/15 for financial aid. **Contact:** Mr. Kevin Coveney, Vice President for Admissions, 300 Washington Avenue, Chestertown, MD 21620-1197, 410-778-7700 or toll-free 800-422-1782; fax 410-778-7287.

GETTING IN LAST YEAR

1,037 applied
89% were accepted
26% enrolled (242)
35% from top tenth of their h.s. class
3.1 average high school GPA
15% had SAT verbal scores over 600
20% had SAT math scores over 600
2% had SAT verbal scores over 700
3% had SAT math scores over 700

THE STUDENT BODY

Total 992, of whom 928
  are undergraduates

From 30 states and territories,
  30 other countries
47% from Maryland
56% women, 44% men
6% African Americans
0% Native Americans
2% Hispanics
2% Asian Americans
8% international students

AFTER FRESHMAN YEAR

88% returned for sophomore year
65% got a degree within 4 years
69% got a degree within 5 years

AFTER GRADUATION

30% pursued further study (20% arts and
  sciences, 4% law, 2% business)
1 Fulbright scholar

WHAT YOU WILL PAY

Tuition and fees $16,440
Room and board $5558
60% receive need-based financial aid
Need-based college-administered scholarships and
  grants average $7010 per award
20% receive non-need financial aid
Non-need college-administered scholarships and
  grants average $9146 per award

WASHINGTON UNIVERSITY

St. Louis, Missouri • Suburban setting • Private • Independent • Coed

Learning across disciplines is a way of life at Washington University. Students enrolled in one of the undergraduate schools—Architecture, Art, Arts and Sciences, Business, and Engineering and Applied Science—are able to enroll in courses offered by any of the others. Students are challenged both in the classroom and in labs and studios where they work side by side with their professors on research and other special projects.

Academics

Washington offers an interdisciplinary curriculum and core academic program; all graduate courses are open to undergraduates. It awards bachelor's, master's, doctoral, and first professional **degrees**. Challenging opportunities include advanced placement, accelerated degree programs, self-designed majors, tutorials, Phi Beta Kappa, and Sigma Xi. Special programs include cooperative education, internships, summer session for credit, off-campus study, study abroad, and Army and Air Force ROTC.

The most popular **majors** include engineering (general), psychology, and business. A complete listing of majors at Washington appears in the Majors Index beginning on page 379.

The **faculty** at Washington has 1,998 full-time graduate and undergraduate teachers, 98% with terminal degrees. 90% of the faculty serve as student advisers. The student-faculty ratio is 6:1, and the average class size in core courses is 17.

Computers on Campus

Students are not required to have a computer. Student rooms are linked to a campus network. 1,000 **computers** available in the computer center, computer labs, the research center, every school, classrooms, the library, and dormitories provide access to the main academic computer, off-campus computing facilities, e-mail, on-line services, and the Internet. Staffed computer lab on campus provides training in the use of computers and software.

The 14 **libraries** have 3.1 million books, 2.7 million microform titles, and 18,968 subscriptions. They are connected to 7 national **on-line** catalogs.

Campus Life

There are 200 active **organizations** on campus, including a drama/theater group and student-run newspaper and radio station. 24% of students participate in student government elections. 30% of eligible men and 30% of eligible women are members of 11 national **fraternities** and 6 national **sororities**. Student **safety services** include late night transport/escort service, 24-hour emergency telephone alarm devices, 24-hour patrols by trained security personnel, and electronically operated dormitory entrances.

Washington is a member of the NCAA (Division III). **Intercollegiate sports** include baseball (m), basketball (m, w), crew (m, w), cross-country running (m, w), football (m), ice hockey (m), lacrosse (m), soccer (m, w), swimming and diving (m, w), tennis (m, w), track and field (m, w), volleyball (m, w).

Applying

Washington requires an essay, a high school transcript, 1 recommendation, and SAT I or ACT. It recommends 3 years of high school math and science, 2 years of high school foreign language, an interview, and a minimum high school GPA of 3.0. Early, deferred, and midyear entrance are possible, with a 1/15 deadline and 2/15 for financial aid.
Contact: Ms. Nanette Clift, Director of Recruitment, Campus Box 1089, 1 Brookings Drive, St. Louis, MO 63130-4899, 314-935-6000 or toll-free 800-638-0700; fax 314-935-4290.

GETTING IN LAST YEAR
9,380 applied
56% were accepted
23% enrolled (1,185)
67% from top tenth of their h.s. class
34% had SAT verbal scores over 600
82% had SAT math scores over 600
82% had ACT scores over 26
4% had SAT verbal scores over 700
28% had SAT math scores over 700
39% had ACT scores over 30
58 National Merit Scholars
33 class presidents
83 valedictorians

THE STUDENT BODY
Total 11,482, of whom 4,993
  are undergraduates

From 52 states and territories,
  83 other countries
16% from Missouri
47% women, 53% men
5% African Americans
1% Native Americans
2% Hispanics
14% Asian Americans
6% international students

AFTER FRESHMAN YEAR
93% returned for sophomore year
75% got a degree within 4 years

83% got a degree within 5 years
84% got a degree within 6 years

AFTER GRADUATION
47% pursued further study
250 organizations recruited on campus
5 Fulbright scholars

WHAT YOU WILL PAY
Tuition and fees $19,291
Room and board $6032
45% receive need-based financial aid
Need-based college-administered scholarships and
  grants average $10,500 per award
6% receive non-need financial aid
Non-need college-administered scholarships and
  grants average $10,600 per award

WEBB INSTITUTE

Glen Cove, New York • Suburban setting • Private • Independent • Primarily men

Academics

Webb Institute offers a core academic program. It awards bachelor's **degrees**. A senior project is a challenging opportunity. Special programs include cooperative education, internships, and study abroad.

The **faculty** at Webb Institute has 9 full-time teachers, 44% with terminal degrees. 78% of the faculty serve as student advisers. The student-faculty ratio is 6:1.

Computers on Campus

Students are not required to have a computer. 28 **computers** available in the computer center, classrooms, and dormitories provide access to e-mail. Staffed computer lab on campus (open 24 hours a day) provides training in the use of computers and software.

The **library** has 49,839 books, 311 microform titles, and 255 subscriptions. It is connected to 1 national **on-line** catalog.

Campus Life

84% of students participate in student government elections. **Intercollegiate sports** include basketball (m, w), sailing (m, w), soccer (m, w), tennis (m, w).

Applying

Webb Institute requires a high school transcript, 2 recommendations, an interview, SAT I, and 3 SAT II Subject Tests (including SAT II: Writing Test). Early decision is possible, with a 2/15 deadline and continuous processing to 7/1 for financial aid. **Contact:** Mr. William G. Murray, Director of Admissions, Crescent Beach Road, Glen Cove, NY 11542-1398, 516-671-2213.

GETTING IN LAST YEAR
87 applied
37% were accepted
72% enrolled (23)
92% from top tenth of their h.s. class
3.4 average high school GPA
96% had SAT verbal scores over 600 (R)
100% had SAT math scores over 600 (R)
38% had SAT verbal scores over 700 (R)
54% had SAT math scores over 700 (R)

THE STUDENT BODY
79 undergraduates
From 19 states and territories,
  0 other countries

23% from New York
15% women, 85% men
0% African Americans
0% Native Americans
0% Hispanics
3% Asian Americans
0% international students

AFTER FRESHMAN YEAR
88% returned for sophomore year
64% got a degree within 4 years
72% got a degree within 5 years
76% got a degree within 6 years

AFTER GRADUATION
14% pursued further study (14% engineering)

WHAT YOU WILL PAY
Tuition and fees $0
Room and board $5500
22% receive need-based financial aid
Need-based college-administered scholarships and
  grants average $400 per award
8% receive non-need financial aid
Non-need college-administered scholarships and
  grants average $1200 per award

WELLESLEY COLLEGE

Wellesley, Massachusetts • Suburban setting • Private • Independent • Women

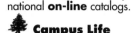 Academics

Wellesley offers a core academic program. It awards bachelor's **degrees** (double bachelor's with Massachusetts Institute of Technology). Challenging opportunities include advanced placement, accelerated degree programs, self-designed majors, an honors program, Phi Beta Kappa, and Sigma Xi. Special programs include internships, off-campus study, study abroad, and Army, Naval, and Air Force ROTC.

The most popular **majors** include political science/government, economics, and English. A complete listing of majors at Wellesley appears in the Majors Index beginning on page 379.

The **faculty** at Wellesley has 241 full-time teachers, 97% with terminal degrees. The student-faculty ratio is 10:1.

Computers on Campus

Students are not required to have a computer. Student rooms are linked to a campus network. 200 **computers** available in the computer center, computer labs, the research center, the learning resource center, science center, social science building, classrooms, the library, and dormitories. Staffed computer lab on campus (open 24 hours a day) provides training in the use of computers and software.

The 4 **libraries** have 704,404 books, 75,098 microform titles, and 2,399 subscriptions. They are connected to 5 national **on-line** catalogs.

Campus Life

There are 140 active **organizations** on campus, including a drama/theater group and student-run newspaper and radio station. Student **safety services** include late night transport/escort service, 24-hour emergency telephone alarm devices, 24-hour patrols by trained security personnel, and electronically operated dormitory entrances.

Wellesley is a member of the NCAA (Division III). **Intercollegiate sports** include basketball, crew, cross-country running, fencing, field hockey, lacrosse, rugby, sailing, skiing (downhill), soccer, softball, squash, swimming and diving, tennis, track and field, volleyball.

Applying

Wellesley requires an essay, a high school transcript, 3 recommendations, SAT I or ACT, and 3 SAT II Subject Tests (including SAT II: Writing Test). It recommends 3 years of high school math and science, some high school foreign language, and an interview. Early and deferred entrance are possible, with a 1/15 deadline and 1/15 for financial aid. **Contact:** Ms. Janet Lavin, Dean of Admission, 240 Green Hall, Wellesley, MA 02181, 617-283-2270; fax 617-283-3678.

GETTING IN LAST YEAR
3,411 applied
39% were accepted
44% enrolled (585)
83% from top tenth of their h.s. class
91% had SAT verbal scores over 600 (R)
82% had SAT math scores over 600 (R)
43% had SAT verbal scores over 700 (R)
25% had SAT math scores over 700 (R)

THE STUDENT BODY
2,299 undergraduates
From 53 states and territories,
    62 other countries

22% from Massachusetts
100% women
6% African Americans
1% Native Americans
5% Hispanics
25% Asian Americans
6% international students

AFTER FRESHMAN YEAR
94% returned for sophomore year
86% got a degree within 4 years
87% got a degree within 5 years
88% got a degree within 6 years

AFTER GRADUATION
33% pursued further study (16% arts and
    sciences, 7% medicine, 4% law)
1 Marshall, 3 Fulbright scholars

WHAT YOU WILL PAY
Tuition and fees $19,610
Room and board $6200
55% receive need-based financial aid
Need-based college-administered scholarships and
    grants average $11,429 per award

WELLS COLLEGE

Aurora, New York • Rural setting • Private • Independent • Women

Wells College believes the 21st century will be a time of unprecedented opportunity for women. Those women who are prepared for leadership roles will have a distinct advantage. Wells students are being prepared to become the 21st-century leaders in a variety of fields: business, government, the arts, science, medicine, and education. The classroom experience and the cocurricular experience are both documented by transcripts that students will present to prospective employers and graduate schools. The Women's Leadership Institute and a focus on leadership issues in the classroom and in student life give Wells women the 21st-century advantage.

 Academics

Wells offers a liberal arts curriculum and core academic program. It awards bachelor's **degrees**. Challenging opportunities include advanced placement, accelerated degree programs, self-designed majors, tutorials, a senior project, and Phi Beta Kappa. Special programs include internships, off-campus study, study abroad, and Army and Air Force ROTC.

The most popular **majors** include psychology, English, and biology/biological sciences. A complete listing of majors at Wells appears in the Majors Index beginning on page 379.

The **faculty** at Wells has 48 full-time teachers, 96% with terminal degrees. 100% of the faculty serve as student advisers. The student-faculty ratio is 8:1.

 Computers on Campus

Students are not required to have a computer. 60 **computers** available in the computer center, computer labs, Zabriskie Hall of Science, Morgan Hall, Macmillan Hall, and the library provide access to e-mail and on-line services. Staffed computer lab on campus (open 24 hours a day).

The 5 **libraries** have 242,451 books, 10,434 microform titles, and 472 subscriptions.

 Campus Life

There are 35 active **organizations** on campus, including a drama/theater group and student-run newspaper. 95% of students participate in student government elections. Student **safety services** include late night transport/escort service, 24-hour emergency telephone alarm devices, and 24-hour patrols by trained security personnel.

Wells is a member of the NCAA (Division III). **Intercollegiate sports** include field hockey, lacrosse, soccer, swimming and diving, tennis.

 Applying

Wells requires an essay, a high school transcript, 2 recommendations, and SAT I or ACT. It recommends 3 years of high school math and science, 3 years of high school foreign language, an interview, and SAT II Subject Tests. Early and deferred entrance are possible, with a 3/1 deadline and continuous processing to 4/1 for financial aid. **Contact:** Ms. Susan Raith Sloan, Director of Admissions, Route 90, Aurora, NY 13026, 315-364-3264 or toll-free 800-952-9355; fax 315-364-3362.

GETTING IN LAST YEAR

307 applied
89% were accepted
37% enrolled (100)
38% from top tenth of their h.s. class
3.0 average high school GPA
33% had SAT verbal scores over 600 (R)
33% had SAT math scores over 600 (R)
26% had ACT scores over 26
8% had SAT verbal scores over 700 (R)
9% had SAT math scores over 700 (R)
6% had ACT scores over 30

THE STUDENT BODY

425 undergraduates
From 32 states and territories,
   4 other countries
64% from New York
100% women
5% African Americans
1% Native Americans
4% Hispanics
7% Asian Americans
2% international students

AFTER FRESHMAN YEAR

85% returned for sophomore year
95% got a degree within 4 years
100% got a degree within 5 years

WHAT YOU WILL PAY

Tuition and fees $17,440
Room and board $5900
80% receive need-based financial aid
Need-based college-administered scholarships and
   grants average $9600 per award
4% receive non-need financial aid

WESLEYAN COLLEGE

Macon, Georgia • Suburban setting • Private • Independent-Religious • Women

Academics

Wesleyan offers a goal-oriented, liberal arts curriculum and core academic program. It awards bachelor's **degrees**. Challenging opportunities include advanced placement, self-designed majors, tutorials, an honors program, and a senior project. Special programs include internships, summer session for credit, and study abroad.

The most popular **majors** include business, English, and psychology. A complete listing of majors at Wesleyan appears in the Majors Index beginning on page 379.

The **faculty** at Wesleyan has 44 full-time teachers, 91% with terminal degrees. 100% of the faculty serve as student advisers. The student-faculty ratio is 10:1.

Computers on Campus

Students are required to have a computer. PCs are provided. Student rooms are linked to a campus network. 450 **computers** available in the computer center, computer labs, classrooms, dormitories, and student rooms provide access to e-mail and the Internet. Staffed computer lab on campus provides training in the use of computers and software.

The **library** has 138,211 books, 23,487 microform titles, and 586 subscriptions.

Campus Life

There are 48 active **organizations** on campus, including a drama/theater group and student-run newspaper. 40% of students participate in student government elections. Student **safety services** include late night transport/escort service, 24-hour emergency telephone alarm devices, 24-hour patrols by trained security personnel, and electronically operated dormitory entrances.

Wesleyan is a member of the NCAA (Division III). **Intercollegiate sports** include basketball, equestrian sports, soccer, softball, tennis, volleyball.

Applying

Wesleyan requires an essay, a high school transcript, 3 years of high school math and science, 2 recommendations, and SAT I or ACT. It recommends some high school foreign language, an interview, and a minimum high school GPA of 2.0. Early, deferred, and midyear entrance are possible, with rolling admissions and continuous processing to 3/1 for financial aid. **Contact:** Lynne Henderson, Director of Admissions, 4760 Forsyth Road, Macon, GA 31297-4299, 912-757-5206 or toll-free 800-447-6610; fax 912-757-4030.

GETTING IN LAST YEAR
319 applied
91% were accepted
47% enrolled (136)
32% from top tenth of their h.s. class
3.4 average high school GPA
28% had SAT verbal scores over 600
20% had SAT math scores over 600
30% had ACT scores over 26
5% had SAT verbal scores over 700
1% had SAT math scores over 700
3% had ACT scores over 30

THE STUDENT BODY
445 undergraduates

From 21 states and territories, 5 other countries
64% from Georgia
100% women
17% African Americans
0% Native Americans
3% Hispanics
4% Asian Americans
2% international students

AFTER FRESHMAN YEAR
71% returned for sophomore year
44% got a degree within 4 years

AFTER GRADUATION
29 organizations recruited on campus

WHAT YOU WILL PAY
Tuition and fees $12,700
Room and board $4800
73% receive need-based financial aid
Need-based college-administered scholarships and grants average $6127 per award
22% receive non-need financial aid
Non-need college-administered scholarships and grants average $6147 per award

WESLEYAN UNIVERSITY

Middletown, Connecticut • Small-town setting • Private • Independent • Coed

For more than 160 years, Wesleyan University has championed the values of a liberal education in the arts and sciences. It seeks to train minds and open hearts and asks students to contribute to the good of society and to the world. About 30% of the undergraduates are members of minority groups, while 12% are the first in their families to attend college. Wesleyan is committed to meeting the full demonstrated financial need of all students.

 Academics

Wesleyan offers an interdisciplinary liberal arts and sciences curriculum and no core academic program; all graduate courses are open to undergraduates. It awards bachelor's, master's, and doctoral **degrees**. Challenging opportunities include advanced placement, accelerated degree programs, self-designed majors, tutorials, a senior project, Phi Beta Kappa, and Sigma Xi. Special programs include cooperative education, internships, off-campus study, study abroad, and Army, Naval, and Air Force ROTC.

The most popular **majors** include English, political science/government, and history. A complete listing of majors at Wesleyan appears in the Majors Index beginning on page 379.

The **faculty** at Wesleyan has 278 full-time graduate and undergraduate teachers, 95% with terminal degrees. 100% of the faculty serve as student advisers. The student-faculty ratio is 11:1.

 Computers on Campus

Students are not required to have a computer. Student rooms are linked to a campus network. 250 **computers** available in the computer center, computer labs, the research center, and the library provide access to the main academic computer, off-campus computing facilities, e-mail, and the Internet. Staffed computer lab on campus (open 24 hours a day) provides training in the use of computers and software.

The 4 **libraries** have 1.2 million books, 228,000 microform titles, and 3,166 subscriptions.

 Campus Life

There are 200 active **organizations** on campus, including a drama/theater group and student-run newspaper and radio station. 8% of eligible men and 2% of eligible women are members of 6 national **fraternities**, 3 national **sororities**, 2 local fraternities, and 6 eating clubs. Student **safety services** include late night transport/escort service, 24-hour emergency telephone alarm devices, 24-hour patrols by trained security personnel, student patrols, and electronically operated dormitory entrances.

Wesleyan is a member of the NCAA (Division III). **Intercollegiate sports** include baseball (m), basketball (m, w), crew (m, w), cross-country running (m, w), equestrian sports (m, w), field hockey (w), football (m), golf (m), ice hockey (m, w), lacrosse (m, w), rugby (m, w), sailing (m, w), skiing (cross-country) (m, w), skiing (downhill) (m, w), soccer (m, w), squash (m, w), swimming and diving (m, w), tennis (m, w), track and field (m, w), volleyball (m, w), water polo (m, w), wrestling (m).

Applying

Wesleyan requires an essay, a high school transcript, 3 recommendations, SAT I, and 3 SAT II Subject Tests (including SAT II: Writing Test). It recommends 4 years of high school math and science, 4 years of high school foreign language, an interview, and ACT. Early and deferred entrance are possible, with a 1/15 deadline and 2/1 for financial aid. **Contact:** Ms. Barbara-Jan Wilson, Dean of Admissions and Financial Aid, High Street, Middletown, CT 06459-0260, 860-685-3000; fax 860-685-3001.

GETTING IN LAST YEAR
5,500 applied
36% were accepted
36% enrolled (711)
65% from top tenth of their h.s. class
87% had SAT verbal scores over 600 (R)
83% had SAT math scores over 600 (R)
44% had SAT verbal scores over 700 (R)
29% had SAT math scores over 700 (R)
68 National Merit Scholars
27 class presidents
28 valedictorians

THE STUDENT BODY
Total 3,244, of whom 2,716
   are undergraduates
From 51 states and territories,
   38 other countries
9% from Connecticut
52% women, 48% men
8% African Americans
0% Native Americans
7% Hispanics
11% Asian Americans
3% international students

AFTER GRADUATION
12% pursued further study (6% arts and
   sciences, 3% medicine, 2% law)
186 organizations recruited on campus
1 Marshall, 2 Fulbright scholars

WHAT YOU WILL PAY
Tuition and fees $20,820
Room and board $5810
41% receive need-based financial aid
Need-based college-administered scholarships and
   grants average $15,733 per award

Westminster Choir College of Rider University

Princeton, New Jersey • Small-town setting • Private • Independent • Coed

Carnegie Hall, The Academy of Music, Avery Fisher Hall, the Kennedy Center—these are the major stages and concert halls where Westminster students sing. They also perform with major orchestras including the New York Philharmonic, the Philadelphia Orchestra, and the New Jersey Symphony Orchestra. These are only a few of the many musical opportunities available at Westminster Choir College of Rider University. Whether a student's musical dream is to be a performer, a music educator, a church musician, or a composer, Westminster's distinctive programs help young singers, organists, composers, and pianists live their dreams.

Academics

Westminster offers a music curriculum and no core academic program; a few graduate courses are open to undergraduates. It awards bachelor's and master's **degrees**. Challenging opportunities include advanced placement, an honors program, and a senior project. Special programs include internships, summer session for credit, and off-campus study.

The most popular **majors** include music education, sacred music, and voice. A complete listing of majors at Westminster appears in the Majors Index beginning on page 379.

The **faculty** at Westminster has 37 full-time graduate and undergraduate teachers, 91% with terminal degrees. 75% of the faculty serve as student advisers. The student-faculty ratio is 7:1.

Computers on Campus

Students are not required to have a computer. Student rooms are linked to a campus network. 60 **computers** available in the computer center, computer labs, the research center, the learning resource center, music computing lab, classrooms, the library, and the student center provide access to the main academic computer, e-mail, on-line services, and the Internet. Staffed computer lab on campus provides training in the use of computers and software.

The **library** has 55,000 books, 414 microform titles, and 160 subscriptions.

Campus Life

Active **organizations** on campus include drama/theater group and student-run newspaper and radio station. Student **safety services** include security guards 4 p.m.- 7 a.m., late night transport/escort service, and 24-hour emergency telephone alarm devices.

This institution has no intercollegiate sports.

Applying

Westminster requires an essay, a high school transcript, 3 recommendations, audition, music test, and SAT I or ACT. It recommends 3 years of high school math and science, 2 years of high school foreign language, an interview, and a minimum high school GPA of 2.0. Early, deferred, and midyear entrance are possible, with rolling admissions and continuous processing to 3/1 for financial aid. **Contact:** Ms. Janet F. Daugherty, Assistant Director of Admissions, 101 Walnut Lane, Princeton, NJ 08540-3899, 609-921-7144 ext. 209 or toll-free 800-96-CHOIR; fax 609-921-8829.

GETTING IN LAST YEAR
274 applied
22% were accepted
93% enrolled (56)
3.0 average high school GPA
30% had ACT scores over 26
15% had ACT scores over 30
1 class president

THE STUDENT BODY
Total 407, of whom 272
 are undergraduates
From 38 states and territories,
 11 other countries
32% from New Jersey
57% women, 43% men
7% African Americans
0% Native Americans
4% Hispanics

6% Asian Americans
14% international students

AFTER FRESHMAN YEAR
86% returned for sophomore year

WHAT YOU WILL PAY
Tuition and fees $14,135
Room and board $6100
75% receive need-based financial aid
65% receive non-need financial aid

WHEATON COLLEGE

Wheaton, Illinois • Suburban setting • Private • Independent-Religious • Coed

> Convinced that "all truth is God's truth," Wheaton College actively pursues the integration of biblical Christianity and rigorous study in the liberal arts with the goal of serving Christ in the world. Wheaton's national reputation rests upon a dedicated faculty known for its outstanding teaching and scholarship and a student body committed to academic achievement, leadership, and Christian service. Wheaton typically ranks in the top 1 percent of all colleges and universities in the percentage of its freshman class who are National Merit Scholars.

 ## Academics

Wheaton offers a liberal arts curriculum and core academic program; more than half of graduate courses are open to undergraduates. It awards bachelor's, master's, and doctoral **degrees**. Challenging opportunities include advanced placement, self-designed majors, and a senior project. Special programs include internships, summer session for credit, off-campus study, study abroad, and Army ROTC.

The most popular **majors** include literature, psychology, and music. A complete listing of majors at Wheaton appears in the Majors Index beginning on page 379.

The **faculty** at Wheaton has 165 full-time graduate and undergraduate teachers, 88% with terminal degrees. 95% of the faculty serve as student advisers. The student-faculty ratio is 15:1.

 ## Computers on Campus

Students are not required to have a computer. 96 **computers** available in computer labs provide access to the main academic computer, off-campus computing facilities, e-mail, and the Internet. Staffed computer lab on campus provides training in the use of computers and software.

The 2 **libraries** have 313,576 books, 196,136 microform titles, and 1,576 subscriptions. They are connected to 2 national **on-line** catalogs.

 ## Campus Life

There are 56 active **organizations** on campus, including a drama/theater group and student-run newspaper and radio station. 50% of students participate in student government elections. Student **safety services** include late night transport/escort service and 24-hour patrols by trained security personnel.

Wheaton is a member of the NCAA (Division III). **Intercollegiate sports** include baseball (m), basketball (m, w), crew (m, w), cross-country running (m, w), equestrian sports (m, w), field hockey (w), football (m), golf (m), ice hockey (m), lacrosse (m, w), soccer (m, w), softball (w), swimming and diving (m, w), tennis (m, w), track and field (m, w), volleyball (m, w), wrestling (m).

 ## Applying

Wheaton requires an essay, a high school transcript, 2 recommendations, an interview, and SAT I or ACT. It recommends 3 years of high school math and science, 2 years of high school foreign language, and SAT II Subject Tests. Early and deferred entrance are possible, with a 2/1 deadline and continuous processing to 3/15 for financial aid. **Contact:** Mr. Dan Crabtree, Director of Admissions, 501 East College Avenue, Wheaton, IL 60187-5571, 708-752-5011 or toll-free 800-222-2419 (out-of-state).

GETTING IN LAST YEAR
1,823 applied
53% were accepted
56% enrolled (549)
59% from top tenth of their h.s. class
3.64 average high school GPA
47% had SAT verbal scores over 600
75% had SAT math scores over 600
82% had ACT scores over 26
7% had SAT verbal scores over 700
28% had SAT math scores over 700
34% had ACT scores over 30
43 National Merit Scholars

THE STUDENT BODY
Total 2,695, of whom 2,317
   are undergraduates

From 50 states and territories,
   8 other countries
22% from Illinois
52% women, 48% men
2% African Americans
1% Native Americans
3% Hispanics
6% Asian Americans
1% international students

AFTER FRESHMAN YEAR
91% returned for sophomore year
70% got a degree within 4 years

81% got a degree within 5 years
82% got a degree within 6 years

AFTER GRADUATION
140 organizations recruited on campus

WHAT YOU WILL PAY
Tuition and fees $12,300
Room and board $4370
54% receive need-based financial aid
Need-based college-administered scholarships and
   grants average $5796 per award
15% receive non-need financial aid
Non-need college-administered scholarships and
   grants average $933 per award

WHITMAN COLLEGE

Walla Walla, Washington • Small-town setting • Private • Independent • Coed

Whitman combines the educational values of the best liberal arts colleges of the East with the outdoor vigor of the Pacific Northwest. An active student-faculty research program, required senior projects, and comprehensive examinations challenge students in all areas of the arts and sciences. Over 75% of graduates pursue advanced degrees in areas such as law, business, medicine, and education; 35% participate in study-abroad programs around the world. Over 80% of students receive merit and/or need-based assistance, ranging from $2000 to $19,500 per year, which is supported by generous alumni and a sizable endowment of $170 million.

Academics

Whitman College offers an antiquity or modernity curriculum and core academic program. It awards bachelor's **degrees**. Challenging opportunities include advanced placement, accelerated degree programs, self-designed majors, tutorials, an honors program, a senior project, Phi Beta Kappa, and Sigma Xi. Special programs include internships, off-campus study, and study abroad.

The most popular **majors** include English, political science/government, and economics. A complete listing of majors at Whitman College appears in the Majors Index beginning on page 379.

The **faculty** at Whitman College has 100 full-time teachers, 91% with terminal degrees. 90% of the faculty serve as student advisers. The student-faculty ratio is 11:1.

Computers on Campus

Students are not required to have a computer. Student rooms are linked to a campus network. 100 **computers** available in computer labs, the learning resource center,

academic buildings, and the library provide access to the main academic computer, e-mail, and the Internet. Staffed computer lab on campus provides training in the use of computers and software.

The 2 **libraries** have 315,116 books, 13,000 microform titles, and 2,000 subscriptions. They are connected to 3 national **on-line** catalogs.

Campus Life

There are 35 active **organizations** on campus, including a drama/theater group and student-run newspaper and radio station. 50% of students participate in student government elections. 31% of eligible men and 38% of eligible women are members of 4 national **fraternities**, 4 national **sororities**, and 1 local sorority. Student **safety services** include security telephones, late night transport/escort service, 24-hour emergency telephone alarm devices, 24-hour patrols by trained security personnel, student patrols, and electronically operated dormitory entrances.

Whitman College is a member of the NAIA. **Intercollegiate sports** include baseball (m), basketball (m, w), cross-country running (m, w), golf (m, w), skiing (cross-country) (m, w), skiing (downhill) (m, w), soccer (m, w), swimming and diving (m, w), tennis (m, w), track and field (m, w), volleyball (w).

Applying

Whitman College requires an essay, a high school transcript, 1 recommendation, and SAT I or ACT. It recommends 3 years of high school math and science, 2 years of high school foreign language, an interview, and SAT II Subject Tests. Early, deferred, and midyear entrance are possible, with a 2/15 deadline and 2/15 for financial aid. **Contact:** Mr. John Bogley, Director of Admission, Walla Walla, WA 99362-2083, 509-527-5176; fax 509-527-4967.

GETTING IN LAST YEAR
2,125 applied
49% were accepted
38% enrolled (393)
57% from top tenth of their h.s. class
3.83 average high school GPA
77% had SAT verbal scores over 600 (R)
76% had SAT math scores over 600 (R)
71% had ACT scores over 26
25% had SAT verbal scores over 700 (R)
17% had SAT math scores over 700 (R)
30% had ACT scores over 30
16 National Merit Scholars
48 valedictorians

THE STUDENT BODY
1,325 undergraduates
From 26 states and territories,
  9 other countries
40% from Washington
51% women, 49% men
1% African Americans
1% Native Americans
1% Hispanics
7% Asian Americans
2% international students

AFTER FRESHMAN YEAR
86% returned for sophomore year

AFTER GRADUATION
20% pursued further study (9% arts and
  sciences, 6% law, 3% medicine)
25 organizations recruited on campus
1 Fulbright scholar

WHAT YOU WILL PAY
Tuition and fees $17,785
Room and board $5160
60% receive need-based financial aid
Need-based college-administered scholarships and
  grants average $7948 per award
27% receive non-need financial aid
Non-need college-administered scholarships and
  grants average $4143 per award

WHITTIER COLLEGE

Whittier, California • Suburban setting • Private • Independent • Coed

The National Endowment for the Humanities has recognized Whittier College's curriculum as a model for liberal arts colleges, and Whittier has produced Rhodes Scholars. Though the College deserves the recognition, students shouldn't choose Whittier for its status. They should appreciate, instead, its substance: a powerful curriculum, organized around the way people actually learn; a system of resident Faculty Masters, at whose homes students exchange insights on the world's events and cultures; team-taught and "paired" courses; natural arenas for heated discussion and mind-opening challenges; and professors who claim their success only when students declare their own.

Academics

Whittier offers an individualized liberal arts curriculum and core academic program. It awards bachelor's, master's, and first professional **degrees**. Challenging opportunities include advanced placement, accelerated degree programs, self-designed majors, tutorials, an honors program, and a senior project. Special programs include internships, summer session for credit, study abroad, and Army and Air Force ROTC.

The most popular **majors** include business, English, and biology/biological sciences. A complete listing of majors at Whittier appears in the Majors Index beginning on page 379.

The **faculty** at Whittier has 117 full-time graduate and undergraduate teachers, 90% with terminal degrees. 100% of the faculty serve as student advisers. The student-faculty ratio is 14:1.

Computers on Campus

Students are not required to have a computer. Student rooms are linked to a campus network. 81 **computers**

available in the computer center, computer labs, writing center, academic departments, the library, dormitories, and student rooms provide access to e-mail and the Internet. Staffed computer lab on campus provides training in the use of computers and software.

The 2 **libraries** have 340,080 books, 174,156 microform titles, and 1,357 subscriptions. They are connected to 1 national **on-line** catalog.

Campus Life

There are 39 active **organizations** on campus, including a drama/theater group and student-run newspaper and radio station. 33% of students participate in student government elections. 17% of eligible men and 24% of eligible women are members of 4 local **fraternities** and 5 local **sororities**. Student **safety services** include late night transport/escort service, 24-hour patrols by trained security personnel, and electronically operated dormitory entrances.

Whittier is a member of the NCAA (Division III). **Intercollegiate sports** include baseball (m), basketball (m, w), cross-country running (m, w), football (m), golf (m), lacrosse (m), soccer (m, w), softball (w), swimming and diving (m, w), tennis (m, w), track and field (m, w), volleyball (w), water polo (m, w).

Applying

Whittier requires an essay, a high school transcript, 2 recommendations, and SAT I or ACT. It recommends 3 years of high school math and science, 2 years of high school foreign language, an interview, and SAT II Subject Tests. Early, deferred, and midyear entrance are possible, with rolling admissions and continuous processing to 2/15 for financial aid. **Contact:** Mr. Doug Locker, Director of Admission, 13406 East Philadelphia Street, Whittier, CA 90608-0634, 310-907-4238.

GETTING IN LAST YEAR
1,896 applied
66% were accepted
27% enrolled (336)
24% from top tenth of their h.s. class
3.0 average high school GPA
24% had SAT verbal scores over 600 (R)
17% had SAT math scores over 600 (R)
16% had ACT scores over 26
3% had SAT verbal scores over 700 (R)
3% had SAT math scores over 700 (R)
1% had ACT scores over 30
3 valedictorians

THE STUDENT BODY
Total 2,167, of whom 1,316
  are undergraduates

From 30 states and territories,
  16 other countries
75% from California
55% women, 45% men
5% African Americans
1% Native Americans
29% Hispanics
10% Asian Americans
3% international students

AFTER FRESHMAN YEAR
72% returned for sophomore year
48% got a degree within 4 years
58% got a degree within 5 years

AFTER GRADUATION
28% pursued further study (5% arts and
  sciences, 2% law, 2% medicine)
48% had job offers within 6 months
14 organizations recruited on campus
1 Rhodes scholar

WHAT YOU WILL PAY
Tuition and fees $17,187
Room and board $5813
69% receive need-based financial aid
Need-based college-administered scholarships and
  grants average $4531 per award
12% receive non-need financial aid
Non-need college-administered scholarships and
  grants average $7615 per award

WILLAMETTE UNIVERSITY

Salem, Oregon • Urban setting • Private • Independent-Religious • Coed

Academics

Willamette offers a traditional liberal arts and interdisciplinary curriculum and core academic program. It awards bachelor's, master's, and first professional **degrees**. Challenging opportunities include advanced placement, accelerated degree programs, self-designed majors, tutorials, and a senior project. Special programs include internships, off-campus study, study abroad, and Air Force ROTC.

The most popular **majors** include economics, psychology, and biology/biological sciences. A complete listing of majors at Willamette appears in the Majors Index beginning on page 379.

The **faculty** at Willamette has 164 full-time graduate and undergraduate teachers, 90% with terminal degrees. 100% of the faculty serve as student advisers. The average class size in core courses is 15.

🖥 Computers on Campus

Students are not required to have a computer. Student rooms are linked to a campus network. 200 **computers** available in the computer center, computer labs, science center, classrooms, the library, the student center, and dormitories provide access to the main academic computer, off-campus computing facilities, e-mail, on-line services, and the Internet. Staffed computer lab on campus (open 24 hours a day) provides training in the use of computers and software.

The 3 **libraries** have 247,892 books, 7,646 microform titles, and 1,448 subscriptions. They are connected to 3 national **on-line** catalogs.

Campus Life

There are 96 active **organizations** on campus, including a drama/theater group and student-run newspaper. 75% of students participate in student government elections. 30% of eligible men and 23% of eligible women are members of 6 national **fraternities** and 3 national **sororities**. Student **safety services** include late night transport/escort service, 24-hour emergency telephone alarm devices, 24-hour patrols by trained security personnel, student patrols, and electronically operated dormitory entrances.

Willamette is a member of the NCAA (Division III) and NAIA. **Intercollegiate sports** include baseball (m), basketball (m, w), crew (m, w), cross-country running (m, w), football (m), golf (m, w), lacrosse (m), rugby (m, w), soccer (m, w), softball (w), swimming and diving (m, w), tennis (m, w), track and field (m, w), volleyball (w).

Applying

Willamette requires an essay, a high school transcript, 3 years of high school math and science, 3 years of high school foreign language, 1 recommendation, SAT I or ACT, a minimum high school GPA of 3.0, and in some cases an interview. It recommends an interview. Early, deferred, and midyear entrance are possible, with a 2/1 deadline and continuous processing to 2/1 for financial aid. **Contact:** Mr. James M. Sumner, Dean of Admissions, 900 State Street, Salem, OR 97301-3931, 503-370-6303; fax 503-375-5363.

GETTING IN LAST YEAR

2,097 applied
70% were accepted
30% enrolled (436)
51% from top tenth of their h.s. class
3.75 average high school GPA
58% had SAT verbal scores over 600 (R)
57% had SAT math scores over 600 (R)
55% had ACT scores over 26
10% had SAT verbal scores over 700 (R)
9% had SAT math scores over 700 (R)
14% had ACT scores over 30
11 National Merit Scholars
16 class presidents
38 valedictorians

THE STUDENT BODY

Total 2,525, of whom 1,713
  are undergraduates

From 34 states and territories,
  17 other countries
50% from Oregon
56% women, 44% men
1% African Americans
1% Native Americans
4% Hispanics
6% Asian Americans
2% international students

AFTER FRESHMAN YEAR

87% returned for sophomore year
65% got a degree within 4 years
75% got a degree within 5 years
76% got a degree within 6 years

AFTER GRADUATION

24% pursued further study (10% arts and
  sciences, 3% law, 3% medicine)
53% had job offers within 6 months
1 Fulbright scholar

WHAT YOU WILL PAY

Tuition and fees $18,390
Room and board $5070
67% receive need-based financial aid
Need-based college-administered scholarships and
  grants average $7560 per award
10% receive non-need financial aid
Non-need college-administered scholarships and
  grants average $5237 per award

WILLIAM JEWELL COLLEGE

Liberty, Missouri • Small-town setting • Private • Independent-Religious • Coed

William Jewell College has long been recognized as the "Campus of Achievement." Through curricular and cocurricular activities and the College's metropolitan locale, students can participate in the life of the College and community rather than sit on the sidelines. An excellent teaching faculty administers such innovative curricular programs as the Oxbridge Tutorial Honors Alternative, an American adaptation of the educational methods of the great English universities, Oxford and Cambridge. Graduates are self-confident and prepared for the rigors of postgraduate challenges. William Jewell graduates are leaders in a variety of fields.

Academics

William Jewell offers a core academic program. It awards bachelor's **degrees**. Challenging opportunities include advanced placement, accelerated degree programs, self-designed majors, tutorials, Freshman Honors College, an honors program, and a senior project. Special programs include cooperative education, internships, summer session for credit, off-campus study, and study abroad.

The most popular **majors** include business, nursing, and psychology. A complete listing of majors at William Jewell appears in the Majors Index beginning on page 379.

The **faculty** at William Jewell has 90 full-time teachers, 72% with terminal degrees. 94% of the faculty serve as student advisers. The student-faculty ratio is 13:1.

Computers on Campus

Students are not required to have a computer. Student rooms are linked to a campus network. 90 **computers** available in the computer center, computer labs, the learning resource center, academic departments, classrooms, the library, the student center, and dormitories provide access to e-mail, on-line services, and the Internet. Staffed computer lab on campus provides training in the use of computers and software.

The 2 **libraries** have 225,278 books, 162,446 microform titles, and 893 subscriptions. They are connected to 5 national **on-line** catalogs.

Campus Life

There are 20 active **organizations** on campus, including a drama/theater group and student-run newspaper and radio station. 50% of students participate in student government elections. 45% of eligible men and 55% of eligible women are members of 4 national **fraternities** and 4 national **sororities**. Student **safety services** include late night transport/escort service, 24-hour emergency telephone alarm devices, 24-hour patrols by trained security personnel, and electronically operated dormitory entrances.

William Jewell is a member of the NAIA. **Intercollegiate sports** (some offering scholarships) include baseball (m), basketball (m, w), cross-country running (m, w), football (m), golf (m), soccer (m), softball (w), tennis (m, w), track and field (m, w), volleyball (w).

Applying

William Jewell requires an essay, a high school transcript, 2 recommendations, SAT I or ACT, a minimum high school GPA of 2.0, and in some cases a minimum high school GPA of 3.0. It recommends 4 years of high school math and science, 2 years of high school foreign language, and an interview. Early, deferred, and midyear entrance are possible, with a 3/15 deadline and continuous processing to 3/1 for financial aid. **Contact:** Mr. Vic Davolt, Interim Director of Admission, 500 College Hill, Liberty, MO 64068-1843, 816-781-7700 ext. 5137 or toll-free 800-753-7009; fax 816-781-3164.

GETTING IN LAST YEAR
708 applied
84% were accepted
47% enrolled (279)
36% from top tenth of their h.s. class
3.54 average high school GPA
52% had SAT verbal scores over 600 (R)
48% had SAT math scores over 600 (R)
38% had ACT scores over 26
13% had SAT verbal scores over 700 (R)
4% had SAT math scores over 700 (R)
13% had ACT scores over 30
3 National Merit Scholars

THE STUDENT BODY
1,250 undergraduates

From 30 states and territories,
  13 other countries
75% from Missouri
60% women, 40% men
2% African Americans
1% Native Americans
1% Hispanics
1% Asian Americans
2% international students

AFTER FRESHMAN YEAR
86% returned for sophomore year
58% got a degree within 5 years

AFTER GRADUATION
29% pursued further study (17% arts and
  sciences, 5% business, 2% law)
73% had job offers within 6 months
100 organizations recruited on campus

WHAT YOU WILL PAY
Tuition and fees $10,580
Room and board $2970
66% receive need-based financial aid
Need-based college-administered scholarships and
  grants average $1513 per award
31% receive non-need financial aid
Non-need college-administered scholarships and
  grants average $4152 per award

WILLIAMS COLLEGE

Williamstown, Massachusetts • Small-town setting • Private • Independent • Coed

---

Williams is a community of learning where students and faculty are active and responsible partners. The College emphasizes the continuities between curriculum and extracurricular life, formal education and the lifelong quest for understanding, and commitment to excellence in teaching and support for artistic endeavor and scholarly research. Williams admits students without regard to financial need and provides financial assistance to meet 100% of demonstrated need. The College is dedicated to being a multicultural community in order to enrich the exchange of ideas, to anticipate the diverse world in which its graduates function, and to enhance the educational environment for all its members.

 Academics

Williams offers a liberal arts curriculum and core academic program; fewer than half of graduate courses are open to undergraduates. It awards bachelor's and master's **degrees**. Challenging opportunities include advanced placement, accelerated degree programs, self-designed majors, tutorials, an honors program, a senior project, Phi Beta Kappa, and Sigma Xi. Special programs include internships, off-campus study, and study abroad.

The most popular **majors** include history, English, and political science/government. A complete listing of majors at Williams appears in the Majors Index beginning on page 379.

The **faculty** at Williams has 226 full-time undergraduate teachers, 95% with terminal degrees. The student-faculty ratio is 11:1.

 Computers on Campus

Students are not required to have a computer. Student rooms are linked to a campus network. 150 **computers** available in the computer center, computer labs, the research center, the learning resource center, academic buildings, and the library provide access to the main academic computer, off-campus computing facilities, e-mail, on-line services, and the Internet. Staffed computer lab on campus provides training in the use of computers and software.

The 8 **libraries** have 748,711 books, 448,711 microform titles, and 2,678 subscriptions. They are connected to 7 national **on-line** catalogs.

 Campus Life

There are 115 active **organizations** on campus, including a drama/theater group and student-run newspaper and radio station. Student **safety services** include late night transport/escort service, 24-hour emergency telephone alarm devices, 24-hour patrols by trained security personnel, student patrols, and electronically operated dormitory entrances.

Williams is a member of the NCAA (Division III). **Intercollegiate sports** include baseball (m), basketball (m, w), crew (m, w), cross-country running (m, w), equestrian sports (m, w), field hockey (w), football (m), golf (m, w), ice hockey (m, w), lacrosse (m, w), rugby (m, w), sailing (m, w), skiing (cross-country) (m, w), skiing (downhill) (m, w), soccer (m, w), softball (w), squash (m, w), swimming and diving (m, w), tennis (m, w), track and field (m, w), volleyball (m, w), water polo (m, w), wrestling (m).

 Applying

Williams requires an essay, a high school transcript, 4 years of high school math, 4 years of high school foreign language, 2 recommendations, SAT I or ACT, and 3 SAT II Subject Tests. It recommends 3 years of high school science and an interview. Early, deferred, and midyear entrance are possible, with a 1/1 deadline and 2/1 for financial aid. **Contact:** Mr. Philip F. Smith, Dean of Admission, 988 Main Street, Williamstown, MA 01267, 413-597-2211.

GETTING IN LAST YEAR
4,996 applied
26% were accepted
40% enrolled (525)
82% from top tenth of their h.s. class
73% had SAT verbal scores over 600
89% had SAT math scores over 600
92% had ACT scores over 26
29% had SAT verbal scores over 700
59% had SAT math scores over 700
60% had ACT scores over 30
39 National Merit Scholars

THE STUDENT BODY
Total 2,104, of whom 2,053
  are undergraduates

From 54 states and territories,
  40 other countries
11% from Massachusetts
49% women, 51% men
6% African Americans
1% Native Americans
7% Hispanics
11% Asian Americans
3% international students

AFTER FRESHMAN YEAR
96% returned for sophomore year
93% got a degree within 4 years
96% got a degree within 5 years

AFTER GRADUATION
18% pursued further study (11% arts and
  sciences, 4% medicine, 3% law)
63% had job offers within 6 months
114 organizations recruited on campus

WHAT YOU WILL PAY
Tuition and fees $20,790
Room and board $5990
47% receive need-based financial aid
Need-based college-administered scholarships and
  grants average $13,110 per award

WILLIAM SMITH COLLEGE

Coordinate with Hobart College

Geneva, New York • Small-town setting • Private • Independent • Women

Hobart and William Smith Colleges together offer the best features of conventionally coeducational colleges: all classes and many residences are coed and students share all campus facilities and social activities. At the same time, each College maintains its own student government, athletic program, and dean's office. Through this coordinate-college system, men and women have equal opportunities for leadership and visibility. Small classes, a dedicated faculty, and extensive opportunities for independent study and off-campus study contribute to a climate that is academically rigorous and strongly supportive. Students balance academics with involvement in over 60 clubs and athletics ranging from intramurals to intercollegiate varsity competition.

Academics

William Smith offers an interdisciplinary curriculum and core academic program. It awards bachelor's **degrees**. Challenging opportunities include advanced placement, accelerated degree programs, self-designed majors, tutorials, an honors program, a senior project, and Phi Beta Kappa. Special programs include internships, off-campus study, and study abroad.

The most popular **majors** include English, psychology, and interdisciplinary studies. A complete listing of majors at William Smith appears in the Majors Index beginning on page 379.

The **faculty** at William Smith has 128 full-time teachers, 97% with terminal degrees. 95% of the faculty serve as student advisers. The student-faculty ratio is 13:1.

Computers on Campus

Students are not required to have a computer. Student rooms are linked to a campus network. 146 **computers**

available in the computer center, computer labs, the research center, the learning resource center, honors room, classrooms, and the library provide access to the main academic computer, off-campus computing facilities, e-mail, on-line services, and the Internet. Staffed computer lab on campus provides training in the use of computers and software.

The 2 **libraries** have 320,000 books, 66,438 microform titles, and 1,871 subscriptions.

Campus Life

There are 60 active **organizations** on campus, including a drama/theater group and student-run newspaper and radio station. Student **safety services** include late night transport/escort service, 24-hour emergency telephone alarm devices, 24-hour patrols by trained security personnel, and electronically operated dormitory entrances.

William Smith is a member of the NCAA (Division III). **Intercollegiate sports** include basketball, crew, cross-country running, field hockey, ice hockey, lacrosse, sailing, skiing (downhill), soccer, swimming and diving, tennis.

Applying

William Smith requires an essay, a high school transcript, 3 years of high school math, 2 years of high school foreign language, 2 recommendations, and SAT I or ACT. It recommends 3 years of high school science, an interview, and SAT II Subject Tests. Early and deferred entrance are possible, with a 2/1 deadline and a 2/15 priority date for financial aid. **Contact:** Ms. Mara O'Laughlin, Director of Admissions, 629 South Main Street, Geneva, NY 14456, 315-781-3472 or toll-free 800-245-0100; fax 315-781-3471.

GETTING IN LAST YEAR
1,411 applied
79% were accepted
23% enrolled (254)
30% from top tenth of their h.s. class
3.36 average high school GPA
48% had SAT verbal scores over 600 (R)
32% had SAT math scores over 600 (R)
32% had ACT scores over 26
8% had SAT verbal scores over 700 (R)
3% had SAT math scores over 700 (R)
10% had ACT scores over 30

THE STUDENT BODY
898 undergraduates

From 37 states and territories,
  11 other countries
52% from New York
100% women
5% African Americans
1% Native Americans
5% Hispanics
2% Asian Americans
3% international students

AFTER FRESHMAN YEAR
86% returned for sophomore year
80% got a degree within 4 years
82% got a degree within 5 years

AFTER GRADUATION
25% pursued further study (17% arts and
  sciences, 4% law, 2% medicine)
75% had job offers within 6 months
24 organizations recruited on campus

WHAT YOU WILL PAY
Tuition and fees $20,413
Room and board $6075
62% receive need-based financial aid
Need-based college-administered scholarships and
  grants average $11,775 per award
1% receive non-need financial aid
Non-need college-administered scholarships and
  grants average $10,000 per award

WOFFORD COLLEGE

Spartanburg, South Carolina • Urban setting • Private • Independent-Religious • Coed

Founded in 1854 and related to the United Methodist church, Wofford was South Carolina's first independent college to receive a chapter of Phi Beta Kappa. It continues to be recognized for effectively using technology to teach the liberal arts and for preparing students for postgraduate studies in medicine, law, and other fields. Each week, Wofford's 1,100 students volunteer to provide more than 1,500 service hours at nearby human service agencies. Social life revolves around more than 50 organizations and a Southern Conference NCAA Division I athletics program. The campus is also the summer training camp home of the NFL's Carolina Panthers.

 Academics

Wofford offers a core academic program. It awards bachelor's **degrees**. Challenging opportunities include advanced placement, accelerated degree programs, self-designed majors, tutorials, and Phi Beta Kappa. Special programs include internships, summer session for credit, off-campus study, study abroad, and Army ROTC.

The most popular **majors** include biology/biological sciences, English, and psychology. A complete listing of majors at Wofford appears in the Majors Index beginning on page 379.

The **faculty** at Wofford has 66 full-time teachers, 91% with terminal degrees. 92% of the faculty serve as student advisers. The student-faculty ratio is 15:1.

 Computers on Campus

Students are not required to have a computer. 118 **computers** available in the computer center, all academic build-ings, classrooms, and the library provide access to the main academic computer, e-mail, on-line services, and the Internet. Staffed computer lab on campus provides training in the use of computers and software.

The **library** has 176,090 books, 48,099 microform titles, and 642 subscriptions.

 Campus Life

Active **organizations** on campus include drama/theater group and student-run newspaper. 75% of students participate in student government elections. 50% of eligible men and 58% of eligible women are members of 8 national **fraternities** and 3 national **sororities**. Student **safety services** include late night transport/escort service, 24-hour emergency telephone alarm devices, 24-hour patrols by trained security personnel, and electronically operated dormitory entrances.

Wofford is a member of the NCAA. **Intercollegiate sports** (some offering scholarships) include baseball (m), basketball (m, w), cross-country running (m, w), fencing (m, w), football (m), golf (m, w), riflery (m, w), soccer (m, w), tennis (m, w), track and field (w), volleyball (w).

 Applying

Wofford requires an essay, a high school transcript, and SAT I or ACT. It recommends 3 years of high school math and science, some high school foreign language, recommendations, an interview, and SAT II Subject Tests. Early, deferred, and midyear entrance are possible, with a 2/1 deadline and continuous processing to 3/15 for financial aid. **Contact:** Mr. Brand R. Stille Jr., Director of Admissions, 429 North Church Street, Spartanburg, SC 29303-3663, 864-597-4130; fax 864-597-4149.

GETTING IN LAST YEAR
1,134 applied
87% were accepted
29% enrolled (286)
42% from top tenth of their h.s. class
24% had SAT verbal scores over 600
46% had SAT math scores over 600
1% had SAT verbal scores over 700
9% had SAT math scores over 700
3 National Merit Scholars
5 class presidents
14 valedictorians

THE STUDENT BODY
1,113 undergraduates

From 29 states and territories,
    4 other countries
67% from South Carolina
45% women, 55% men
6% African Americans
0% Native Americans
1% Hispanics
2% Asian Americans
1% international students

AFTER FRESHMAN YEAR
90% returned for sophomore year

AFTER GRADUATION
37% pursued further study (17% arts and
    sciences, 8% medicine, 6% law)
54% had job offers within 6 months

WHAT YOU WILL PAY
Tuition and fees $13,795
Room and board $4185
49% receive need-based financial aid
Need-based college-administered scholarships and
    grants average $7341 per award
27% receive non-need financial aid
Non-need college-administered scholarships and
    grants average $6304 per award

WORCESTER POLYTECHNIC INSTITUTE

Worcester, Massachusetts • Suburban setting • Private • Independent • Coed

▶ WPI's facilities and faculty are outstanding, the extracurricular and athletic programs are excellent, and the campus setting is attractive. However, it is the academic program—the way in which each student, individually, is able to reach his or her goals—that provides the margin of difference. The WPI Plan involves in-depth project-research work not only in a student's major field but also in the humanities and the linkage between technology and social issues. Approximately one third of the students do one of these projects overseas or in Washington, DC, and more than 200 outside agencies and corporations sponsor projects.

 ## Academics

WPI offers a hands-on, project-oriented curriculum and no core academic program. It awards bachelor's, master's, and doctoral **degrees**. Challenging opportunities include advanced placement, accelerated degree programs, self-designed majors, a senior project, and Sigma Xi. Special programs include cooperative education, summer session for credit, off-campus study, study abroad, and Army, Naval, and Air Force ROTC.

The most popular **majors** include mechanical engineering, electrical engineering, and civil engineering. A complete listing of majors at WPI appears in the Majors Index beginning on page 379.

The **faculty** at WPI has 203 full-time undergraduate teachers, 95% with terminal degrees. The student-faculty ratio is 12:1.

 ## Computers on Campus

Students are not required to have a computer. Student rooms are linked to a campus network. 850 **computers** available in the computer center, computer labs, and the library provide access to the main academic computer, off-campus computing facilities, e-mail, on-line services, and the Internet. Staffed computer lab on campus (open 24 hours a day) provides training in the use of computers and software.

The **library** has 300,000 books, 785,000 microform titles, and 1,400 subscriptions.

 ## Campus Life

There are 65 active **organizations** on campus, including a drama/theater group and student-run newspaper and radio station. 35% of eligible men and 40% of eligible women are members of 12 national **fraternities** and 2 national **sororities**. Student **safety services** include late night transport/escort service, 24-hour emergency telephone alarm devices, 24-hour patrols by trained security personnel, and student patrols.

WPI is a member of the NCAA (Division III). **Intercollegiate sports** include baseball (m), basketball (m, w), bowling (m, w), crew (m, w), cross-country running (m, w), fencing (m, w), field hockey (w), football (m), golf (m), ice hockey (m), lacrosse (m, w), rugby (m, w), sailing (m, w), skiing (downhill) (m, w), soccer (m, w), softball (w), swimming and diving (m, w), tennis (m, w), track and field (m, w), volleyball (m, w), water polo (m, w), wrestling (m).

 ## Applying

WPI requires a high school transcript, 4 years of high school math, 2 recommendations, SAT I or ACT, and 3 SAT II Subject Tests (including SAT II: Writing Test). It recommends an essay, 3 years of high school science, and an interview. Early and deferred entrance are possible, with a 2/15 deadline and 3/1 for financial aid. **Contact:** Mr. Robert G. Voss, Executive Director of Admissions and Financial Aid, 100 Institute Road, Worcester, MA 01609-2247, 508-831-5286; fax 508-831-5875.

GETTING IN LAST YEAR

2,480 applied
85% were accepted
28% enrolled (589)
47% from top tenth of their h.s. class
25% had SAT verbal scores over 600 (R)
80% had SAT math scores over 600 (R)
95% had ACT scores over 26
3% had SAT verbal scores over 700 (R)
34% had SAT math scores over 700 (R)
50% had ACT scores over 30
13 National Merit Scholars

THE STUDENT BODY

Total 3,593, of whom 2,588
  are undergraduates

From 49 states and territories,
  57 other countries
47% from Massachusetts
21% women, 79% men
1% African Americans
1% Native Americans
2% Hispanics
6% Asian Americans
6% international students

AFTER FRESHMAN YEAR

94% returned for sophomore year

AFTER GRADUATION

22% pursued further study (11% engineering,
  5% arts and sciences, 3% business)

75% had job offers within 6 months
160 organizations recruited on campus

WHAT YOU WILL PAY

Tuition and fees $17,336
Room and board $5652
75% receive need-based financial aid
Need-based college-administered scholarships and
  grants average $7800 per award
Non-need college-administered scholarships and
  grants average $5320 per award

XAVIER UNIVERSITY

Cincinnati, Ohio • Suburban setting • Private • Independent-Religious • Coed

Academics

Xavier offers a liberal arts curriculum and core academic program. It awards associate, bachelor's, and master's **degrees**. Challenging opportunities include advanced placement, accelerated degree programs, an honors program, and a senior project. Special programs include internships, summer session for credit, off-campus study, study abroad, and Army and Air Force ROTC.

The most popular **majors** include business, education, and communication. A complete listing of majors at Xavier appears in the Majors Index beginning on page 379.

The **faculty** at Xavier has 231 full-time graduate and undergraduate teachers, 70% with terminal degrees. The student-faculty ratio is 15:1.

Computers on Campus

Students are not required to have a computer. Student rooms are linked to a campus network. 425 **computers** available in the computer center, classroom building labs, the library, and dormitories provide access to the main academic computer, e-mail, and the Internet. Staffed computer lab on campus provides training in the use of computers and software.

The 3 **libraries** have 350,000 books, 459,327 microform titles, and 1,557 subscriptions.

Campus Life

There are 75 active **organizations** on campus, including a drama/theater group and student-run newspaper. Student **safety services** include late night transport/escort service, 24-hour emergency telephone alarm devices, 24-hour patrols by trained security personnel, and electronically operated dormitory entrances.

Xavier is a member of the NCAA (Division I). **Intercollegiate sports** (some offering scholarships) include baseball (m), basketball (m, w), crew (m, w), cross-country running (m, w), fencing (m, w), golf (m, w), riflery (m, w), rugby (m, w), sailing (m, w), soccer (m, w), swimming and diving (m, w), tennis (m, w), volleyball (m, w), wrestling (m).

Applying

Xavier requires a high school transcript, SAT I or ACT, and a minimum high school GPA of 2.0. It recommends an essay, 3 years of high school math and science, 2 years of high school foreign language, recommendations, a campus interview, and a minimum high school GPA of 3.0. Early, deferred, and midyear entrance are possible, with rolling admissions and continuous processing to 2/15 for financial aid. **Contact:** Director of Admissions, 3800 Victory Parkway, Cincinnati, OH 45207-5311, 513-745-3301 or toll-free 800-344-4698; fax 513-745-4319.

GETTING IN LAST YEAR
2,456 applied
91% were accepted
31% enrolled (701)
29% from top tenth of their h.s. class
3.25 average high school GPA
35% had SAT verbal scores over 600 (R)
33% had SAT math scores over 600 (R)
37% had ACT scores over 26
6% had SAT verbal scores over 700 (R)
4% had SAT math scores over 700 (R)
8% had ACT scores over 30
15 valedictorians

THE STUDENT BODY
Total 6,127, of whom 3,756
  are undergraduates

From 45 states and territories,
  40 other countries
69% from Ohio
59% women, 41% men
7% African Americans
0% Native Americans
2% Hispanics
2% Asian Americans
3% international students

AFTER FRESHMAN YEAR
86% returned for sophomore year
53% got a degree within 4 years

67% got a degree within 5 years
68% got a degree within 6 years

AFTER GRADUATION
21% pursued further study (12% arts and
  sciences, 5% medicine, 3% law)

WHAT YOU WILL PAY
Tuition and fees $12,270
Room and board $5190
Need-based college-administered scholarships and
  grants average $2227 per award
Non-need college-administered scholarships and
  grants average $4315 per award

YALE UNIVERSITY

New Haven, Connecticut • Urban setting • Private • Independent • Coed

Students and faculty at Yale are excited by the thought-provoking discussions they find in classes, dining halls, and dormitory rooms. Yale is committed to undergraduate teaching, and every professor at Yale College teaches undergraduate classes. Yale's most distinctive feature is its residential college system, in which each student belongs to an intimate community that is a microcosm of the larger Yale community. In the colleges, academic life merges with other interests, and the result is an environment in which students come to know and respect one another as colleagues and friends. Yale College is a center for arts and athletics, music and drama, religion, politics, and community service.

Academics

Yale offers a liberal arts curriculum and core academic program. It awards bachelor's, master's, doctoral, and first professional **degrees**. Challenging opportunities include advanced placement, accelerated degree programs, self-designed majors, tutorials, an honors program, a senior project, Phi Beta Kappa, and Sigma Xi. Special programs include summer session for credit, study abroad, and Army and Air Force ROTC.

The most popular **majors** include history, English, and biology/biological sciences. A complete listing of majors at Yale appears in the Majors Index beginning on page 379.

The **faculty** at Yale has 2,802 graduate and undergraduate teachers, 96% with terminal degrees. 100% of the faculty serve as student advisers. The student-faculty ratio is 6:1.

Computers on Campus

Students are not required to have a computer. Student rooms are linked to a campus network. 250 **computers**

available in the computer center, computer labs, classrooms, the library, and dormitories provide access to e-mail and on-line services. Staffed computer lab on campus provides training in the use of computers and software.

The 21 **libraries** have 10.2 million books and 54,601 subscriptions.

Campus Life

There are 300 active **organizations** on campus, including a drama/theater group and student-run newspaper and radio station. Student **safety services** include late night transport/escort service, 24-hour emergency telephone alarm devices, 24-hour patrols by trained security personnel, and electronically operated dormitory entrances.

Yale is a member of the NCAA (Division I). **Intercollegiate sports** include baseball (m), basketball (m, w), crew (m, w), cross-country running (m, w), fencing (m, w), field hockey (w), football (m), golf (m, w), gymnastics (w), ice hockey (m, w), lacrosse (m, w), soccer (m, w), softball (w), squash (m, w), swimming and diving (m, w), tennis (m, w), track and field (m, w), volleyball (w).

Applying

Yale requires an essay, a high school transcript, 3 recommendations, SAT I or ACT, and 3 SAT II Subject Tests. It recommends 3 years of high school math and science, some high school foreign language, and an interview. Early and deferred entrance are possible, with a 12/31 deadline and 2/1 for financial aid. **Contact:** Admissions Counselor, PO Box 208234, New Haven, CT 06520, 203-432-1900; fax 203-432-7329.

GETTING IN LAST YEAR
12,620 applied
20% were accepted
54% enrolled (1,369)
95% from top tenth of their h.s. class
96% had SAT verbal scores over 600 (R)
96% had SAT math scores over 600 (R)
69% had SAT verbal scores over 700 (R)
69% had SAT math scores over 700 (R)

THE STUDENT BODY
Total 10,986, of whom 5,326
  are undergraduates
From 55 states and territories,
  51 other countries

10% from Connecticut
49% women, 51% men
9% African Americans
1% Native Americans
7% Hispanics
17% Asian Americans
5% international students

AFTER FRESHMAN YEAR
98% returned for sophomore year
87% got a degree within 4 years
93% got a degree within 5 years

AFTER GRADUATION
35% pursued further study (11% arts and
  sciences, 11% medicine, 8% law)
62% had job offers within 6 months
1 Marshall, 26 Fulbright scholars

WHAT YOU WILL PAY
Tuition and fees $21,000
Room and board $6630
42% receive need-based financial aid
Need-based college-administered scholarships and
  grants average $15,710 per award

YESHIVA UNIVERSITY

New York, New York • Urban setting • Private • Independent • Men

Academics

YU offers a liberal arts and business joined with Jewish studies programs curriculum and core academic program; fewer than half of graduate courses are open to undergraduates. It awards bachelor's, master's, doctoral, and first professional **degrees** (Yeshiva College and Stern College for Women are coordinate undergraduate colleges of arts and sciences for men and women, respectively. Sy Syms School of Business offers programs at both campuses). Challenging opportunities include advanced placement, self-designed majors, tutorials, an honors program, and a senior project. Special programs include internships, summer session for credit, off-campus study, and study abroad.

The most popular **majors** include psychology, biology/biological sciences, and accounting. A complete listing of majors at YU appears in the Majors Index beginning on page 379.

The **faculty** at YU has 736 full-time graduate and undergraduate teachers, 94% with terminal degrees. 6% of the faculty serve as student advisers. The student-faculty ratio is 9:1.

Computers on Campus

Students are not required to have a computer. 142 **computers** available in the computer center, computer labs, labs, and the library provide access to the main academic computer, e-mail, on-line services, and the Internet. Staffed computer lab on campus provides training in the use of computers and software.

The 7 **libraries** have 995,312 books, 79,432 microform titles, and 9,760 subscriptions.

 ## Campus Life

Active **organizations** on campus include drama/theater group and student-run newspaper and radio station. 60% of students participate in student government elections. Student **safety services** include late night transport/escort service, 24-hour emergency telephone alarm devices, and 24-hour patrols by trained security personnel.

YU is a member of the NCAA (Division III). **Intercollegiate sports** include basketball (m, w), cross-country running (m), fencing (m), golf (m), tennis (m, w), volleyball (m), wrestling (m).

 ## Applying

YU requires a high school transcript, 2 years of high school foreign language, 2 recommendations, an interview, and SAT I or ACT. It recommends an essay and SAT II Subject Tests. Early, deferred, and midyear entrance are possible, with a 2/15 deadline and continuous processing to 4/15 for financial aid. **Contact:** Mr. Michael Kranzler, Director of Admissions, 500 West 185th Street, New York, NY 10033-3201, 212-960-5400 ext. 277; fax 212-960-0043.

GETTING IN LAST YEAR
1,354 applied
84% were accepted
69% enrolled (788)
3.4 average high school GPA
34% had SAT verbal scores over 600
70% had SAT math scores over 600
6% had SAT verbal scores over 700
22% had SAT math scores over 700

THE STUDENT BODY
Total 5,433, of whom 2,325 are undergraduates

From 31 states and territories, 30 other countries
57% from New York
43% women, 57% men
5% international students

AFTER FRESHMAN YEAR
83% returned for sophomore year

AFTER GRADUATION
97% had job offers within 6 months
50 organizations recruited on campus

WHAT YOU WILL PAY
Tuition and fees $13,430
Room and board $6300
75% receive need-based financial aid
Need-based college-administered scholarships and grants average $3343 per award
25% receive non-need financial aid
Non-need college-administered scholarships and grants average $4100 per award

DESCRIPTIONS OF COMPETITIVE ARTS COLLEGES AND CONSERVATORIES

The listings below show the autonomous colleges specializing in art and/or music that have highly selective application/acceptance ratios.

Art Center College of Design
Pasadena, California 91103

Founded 1930; suburban setting; independent; coed; awards B, M.

Enrollment 1,334 total; 1,251 undergraduates (200 freshmen).
Faculty 427 total; 59 full-time; student-faculty ratio is 5:1.
Expenses (1996–97) Tuition: $15,440.
Majors Advertising, art/fine arts, commercial art, environmental design, film studies, graphic arts, illustration, industrial design, painting/drawing, photography.
Applying Required: high school transcript, essay, portfolio. Recommended: Minimum 3.0 high school GPA, some foreign language, interview. SAT I or ACT required for some.
Application deadlines Rolling, 3/1 priority date for financial aid.
Contact Ms. Kit Brown, Vice President of Student Services, 818-396-2373.

California Institute of the Arts
Valencia, California 91355

Founded 1961; suburban setting; independent; coed; awards B, M.

Enrollment 1079 total; 712 undergraduates (96 freshmen).
Faculty 212 total; student-faculty ratio is 8:1.
Expenses (1995–96) Comprehensive fee of $22,160 includes tuition ($16,400), mandatory fees ($60), and room and board ($5700).
Majors Art/fine arts, commercial art, computer graphics, dance, film studies, graphic arts, illustration, jazz, music, photography, piano/organ, sculpture, stringed instruments, studio art, theater arts/drama, voice.
Applying Required: essay, high school transcript, portfolio or audition. Interview, recommendations, test scores required for some.
Application deadlines 2/1, 3/1 priority date for financial aid.
Contact Mr. Kenneth Young, Director of Admissions, 805-255-1050 Ext. 7863.

Cleveland Institute of Music
Cleveland, Ohio 44106

Founded 1920; urban setting; independent; coed; awards B, M, D.

Enrollment 341 total; 266 undergraduates (59 freshmen).
Faculty 94 total; 26 full-time; student-faculty ratio is 10:1.
Expenses (1995–96) Comprehensive fee of $20,766 includes tuition ($14,756), mandatory fees ($1155), and room and board ($4855).
Majors Audio engineering, music, music education, piano/organ, stringed instruments, voice, wind and percussion instruments.
Applying Required: essay, high school transcript, 2 recommendations, audition, SAT I or ACT. Recommended: 3 years of high school math and science, some high school foreign language, interview.
Application deadlines 12/15, 3/1 priority date for financial aid.
Contact Mr. William Fay, Director of Admission, 216-795-3107.
From the College Ranked as one of the foremost schools of music in the United States, CIM's curriculum is based upon solid, traditional musical values while incorporating liberal arts instruction and new technologies that equip students to meet the challenges of the 21st century. Graduates are admitted routinely to leading graduate schools, are winners of major competitions, and occupy important performance and teaching positions throughout the world.

Corcoran School of Art
Washington, District of Columbia 20006

Founded 1890; urban setting; independent; coed; awards B.

Enrollment 325 total; all undergraduates (84 freshmen).
Faculty 113 total; 58 full-time; student-faculty ratio is 10:1.
Expenses (1995–96) Tuition: $11,550. Room only: $4360.
Majors Applied art, art/fine arts, ceramic art and design, commercial art, graphic arts, painting/drawing, photography, printmaking, sculpture, studio art.
Applying Required: high school transcript, portfolio, minimum 2.0 high school GPA. Recommended: SAT I or ACT, letters of recommendation, campus interview.
Application deadlines Rolling, 3/15 priority date for financial aid.
Contact Mr. Mark Sistek, Director of Admissions, 202-628-9484 Ext. 700.

Curtis Institute of Music
Philadelphia, Pennsylvania 19103

> Founded 1924; urban setting; independent; coed; awards B, M.

Enrollment 156 total; 140 undergraduates (36 freshmen).
Faculty 84 total; 2 full-time.
Expenses (1995–96) Tuition: $0. Mandatory fees: $600.
Majors Music, piano/organ, stringed instruments, voice, wind and percussion instruments.
Applying Required: high school transcript, recommendations, audition, SAT I. Recommended: 3 years of high school math and science, some high school foreign language. TSWE required for some.
Application deadlines 1/15, 6/1 for financial aid.
Contact Ms. Judi L. Gattone, Admissions and Financial Aid Officer, 215-893-5262.

Fashion Institute of Technology
New York, New York 10001

> Founded 1944; urban setting; state and locally supported; coed; awards A, B, M.

Enrollment 8,489 total; 8,430 undergraduates (1,732 freshmen).
Faculty 919 total; 159 full-time; student-faculty ratio is 14:1.
Expenses (1995–96) State resident tuition: $2300. Nonresident tuition: $5450. Mandatory fees: $210. Room and board: $5174.
Majors Advertising, applied art, art/fine arts, commercial art, communications, fashion design and technology, fashion merchandising, illustration, industrial administration, interior design, jewelry and metalsmithing, management engineering, marketing/retailing/merchandising, photography, textile arts, textiles and clothing.
Applying Required: essay, high school transcript, portfolio for art and design majors; SAT I required for some.
Application deadlines Rolling, 3/15 priority date for financial aid.
Contact Mr. Jim Pidgeon, Director of Admissions, 212-760-7675.
The Fashion Institute of Technology is a specialized college of SUNY and is located near the corporate and business centers of major companies in fashion and apparel design and manufacture, textiles, advertising, photography, jewelry, and interior design and decoration. Students come from all parts of the United States and 60 other countries to study art, design, business, or technology. The college offers a 2-year AAS degree or a 4-year BS or BFA. All programs are structured to provide a practical approach in the major, a core curriculum in liberal arts, and an opportunity to learn through co-op and internships.

Juilliard School
New York, New York 10023

> Founded 1905; urban setting; independent; coed; awards B, M, D.

Enrollment 832 total; 484 undergraduates (107 freshmen).
Faculty 234 total; 184 full-time; student-faculty ratio is 4:1.
Expenses (1995–96) Comprehensive fee of $19,900 includes tuition ($13,000), mandatory fees ($600), and room and board ($6300).
Majors Dance, music, opera, piano/organ, stringed instruments, theater arts/drama, voice, wind and percussion instruments.
Applying Required: high school transcript, audition. Essay required for some.
Application deadlines 1/8, 2/15 priority date for financial aid.
Contact Mrs. Mary K. Gray, Director of Admissions, 212-799-5000 Ext. 223.

Manhattan School of Music
New York, New York 10027

> Founded 1917; urban setting; independent; coed; awards B, M, D.

Enrollment 886 total; 439 undergraduates (94 freshmen).
Faculty 309 total; student-faculty ratio is 10:1.
Expenses (1995–96) Tuition: $14,200. Mandatory fees: $680. Room only: $4160.
Majors Jazz, music, piano/organ, stringed instruments, voice, wind and percussion instruments.
Applying Required: high school transcript, essay, minimum 2.0 GPA, audition. Recommended: SAT I or ACT, 3 years of high school math and science, some high school foreign language, recommendations, interview, minimum 3.0 GPA.
Application deadlines 4/1, 4/15 priority date for financial aid.
Contact Ms. Carolyn Disnew, Director of Admission, 212-749-2802 Ext. 2.
From the College By selecting MSM, students choose to work with faculty members who are performers with international reputations who choose to be with exceptional students from around the world in an environment of intensity, genuine friendliness, and cooperation. With extensive performance opportunities in New York—the heart of music in America—and the chance to freelance and develop professional contacts, students undergo remarkable changes: they begin to function as professional musicians while still in school. This powerful convergence gives MSM students the best chance to go as far as their talent, intelligence, and courage can take them.

Mannes College of Music
New York, New York 10024

> Founded 1916; urban setting; independent; coed; awards B, M.

Enrollment 5,781 university (New School for Social Research) total; 265 unit total; 127 undergraduates (21 freshmen).
Faculty 216 total; 15 full-time; student-faculty ratio is 5:1.
Expenses (1995–96) Tuition ($13,700), mandatory fees ($225), and room only ($5500).
Majors Jazz, music, opera, piano/organ, stringed instruments, voice, wind and percussion instruments.
Applying Required: high school transcript, 1 recommendation, audition. Recommended: 3 years of high school math and science, campus interview.
Application deadlines 7/15, 7/15 priority date for financial aid.
Contact Ms. Marilyn Groves, Director of Admissions and Registration, 212-580-0210 Ext. 46.
From the College Founded in 1916 by David and Clara Damrosch Mannes, who were then world renowned as a violin-piano duo, the Mannes College of Music is recognized—nationally and internationally—as among the finest professional music conservatories. As such, its primary focus is on the training of outstanding young musicians who are preparing for professional careers in performance, unlike college and university music departments, which more often prepare students for careers in fields other than performance. Mannes is also distinguished by a relatively small enrollment that permits the close and supportive environment of a craft shop.

Massachusetts College of Art
Boston, Massachusetts 02115

> Founded 1873; urban setting; state-supported; coed; awards B, M.

Enrollment 1,479 total; 1,367 undergraduates (230 freshmen).
Faculty 184 total; 63 full-time; student-faculty ratio is 12:1.
Expenses (1995–96) State resident tuition: $1463. Nonresident tuition: $6422. Mandatory fees: $2644. Room and board: $5412.
Majors Applied art, architecture, art education, art/fine arts, art history, ceramic art and design, commercial art, computer graphics, fashion design and technology, film and video, graphic arts, illustration, industrial design, jewelry and metalsmithing, painting/drawing, photography, printmaking, sculpture, studio art, textile arts.
Applying Required: essay, high school transcript, 3 years of high school math and science, 2 years of high school foreign language, portfolio, SAT I. Recommended: recommendations, campus interview.
Application deadlines 12/1 for early decision, 3/1, 5/1 priority date for financial aid.

Contact Ms. Kay Ransdell, Director of Admissions, 617-232-1555 Ext. 235.
From the College Unique among institutions of higher education, Massachusetts College of Art is a state-assisted, free-standing college of art, design, and art education. Rigorous, innovative, and multicultural, the curriculum is supplemented by a schedule of exhibitions and visiting artists, cross-registration options, and programs of study abroad. Newly renovated, state-of-the-art facilities meet advanced health and safety standards and offer students extraordinary art-making opportunities. The student body represents a variety of experiences and backgrounds and includes citizens of 60 countries and many states. The College is located in the heart of Boston's cultural area, adjacent to major museums and other colleges.

New England Conservatory of Music
Boston, Massachusetts 02115

> Founded 1867; urban setting; independent; coed; awards B, M, D.

Enrollment 752 total; 358 undergraduates (61 freshmen).
Faculty 191 total; 55 full-time.
Expenses (1995–96) Comprehensive fee of $23,850 includes tuition ($16,200) and room and board ($7650).
Majors Jazz, music, music education, music history, opera, piano/organ, stringed instruments, voice, wind and percussion instruments.
Applying Required: essay, high school transcript, 1 recommendation, audition, SAT I or ACT.
Application deadlines 1/15, 3/1 priority date for financial aid.
Contact Ms. Allison T. Ball, Dean of Enrollment Services, 617-262-1120 Ext. 430.

New York School of Interior Design
New York, New York 10021

> Founded 1916; urban setting; independent; coed; awards A, B.

Enrollment 409 total, all undergraduates (98 freshmen).
Faculty 98 total; 3 full-time; student-faculty ratio is 12:1.
Expenses (1995–96) Tuition: $11,520. Mandatory fees: $50.
Major Interior design.
Applying Required: essay, high school transcript, 2 recommendations, portfolio (for BFA applicants), SAT I or ACT. Recommended: interview. Interview required for some.
Application deadlines Rolling, 7/1 priority date for financial aid.
Contact Ms. Jessica Aguayo, Admissions Associate, 212-472-1500 ext. 23 or toll-free 800-336-9743.
From the College Manhattan, with its world-famous museums, showrooms, and architectural landmarks, is home to the New York School of Interior Design (NYSID). NYSID was the first and only single-major college in the United States dedicated solely to the study of interior design, a

tradition that continues today. Because of its reputation in the design industry, many NYSID graduates have gone on to find work in the best design and architectural firms in New York City and around the world. The Bachelor of Fine Arts degree is a FIDER-accredited program.

North Carolina School of the Arts
Winston-Salem, North Carolina 27117-2189

Founded 1963; urban setting; state-supported; coed; awards B, M.

Enrollment 658 total; 605 undergraduates (136 freshmen).
Faculty 109 total; 73 full-time; student-faculty ratio is 7:1.
Expenses (1995–96) State resident tuition: $1308. Nonresident tuition: $9159. Mandatory fees: $756. Room and board: $3706.
Majors Dance, film and video production, film studies, music, theater arts/drama.
Applying Required: high school transcript, 3 years of high school math and science, 2 recommendations, audition, SAT I or ACT. Recommended: 2 years of high school foreign language. Essay, interview required for some.
Application deadlines Rolling, 3/1 priority date for financial aid.
Contact Ms. Carol J. Palm, Director of Admissions, 919-770-3291 or toll-free 800-282-2787.
From the College The School of the Arts was the first state-supported residential arts school of its kind in the nation, established in 1963. This accredited school became part of the 16-campus University of North Carolina in 1972. Five individual schools—Dance, Design and Production, Drama, Filmmaking, and Music—make up the School of the Arts. Because the School's mission is to train students for professional careers in the performing arts, performance is an integral part of training. The School's diverse enrollment offers the student the opportunity to live and work in a close and supportive environment with artists in other fields, from different backgrounds, and from different areas of the world.

Parsons School of Design, New School for Social Research
New York, New York 10011

Founded 1896; urban setting; independent; coed; awards A, B, M.

Enrollment 5,781 university total; 1,933 unit total; 1,810 undergraduates (387 freshmen).
Faculty 413 total; 17 full-time; student-faculty ratio is 14:1.
Expenses (1995–96) Comprehensive fee of $22,600 includes tuition ($16,070), mandatory fees ($280), and room and board ($7450).
Majors Architecture, art education, art/fine arts, ceramic art and design, commercial art, environmental design, fashion design and technology, fashion merchandising, graphic arts, illustration, industrial design, interior design, jewelry and metalsmithing, painting/drawing, photography, sculpture, textile arts.
Applying Required: high school transcript, campus interview, portfolio, at-home examination, SAT I or ACT. Recommended: recommendations. Essay, recommendations required for some.
Application deadlines Rolling, 4/1 priority date for financial aid.
Contact Ms. Nadine M. Bourgeois, Director of Admissions, 212-229-8910 or toll-free 800-252-0852.
From the College For nearly 100 years, Parsons graduates have soared to positions of leadership in art, design, and marketing. Heads of their own companies and top executives in major firms, their accomplishments have won them prestige, industry awards, and brand-name status. Ideas taught at Parsons educate students in what makes one design solution good, another better, and a third best. Parsons also looks to the future. A new Fashion Design Computing Center, Foundation Year Computing Lab, and AUTOCAD Interior Design and Environmental Design Lab complement Parsons' existing Computer Design Center and make Parsons one of the most technologically advanced design schools in America.

Rutgers, The State University of New Jersey, Mason Gross School of the Arts
New Brunswick, New Jersey 08903

Founded 1976; small-town setting; state-supported; coed; awards B, M, D.

Enrollment 48,135 university total; 682 unit total; 452 undergraduates (106 freshmen).
Faculty 79 full-time; student-faculty ratio is 11:1.
Expenses (1995–96) State resident tuition: $3786. Nonresident tuition: $7707. Mandatory fees: range from $1012 to $1076, according to college affiliation. Room and board: $4936.
Majors Art/fine arts, ceramic art and design, dance, film studies, graphic arts, jazz, music, music education, painting/drawing, photography, printmaking, sculpture, theater arts/drama.
Applying Required: high school transcript, 3 years of high school math, audition or portfolio or interview, SAT I or ACT. Recommended: 4 years of high school math, 2 years of high school foreign language. 3 SAT II Subject Tests required for some.
Application deadlines 1/15, 3/1 priority date for financial aid.
Contact Dr. Elizabeth Mitchell, Assistant Vice President for University Undergraduate Admissions, 908-445-3770.
From the College Mason Gross School of the Arts is designed for students who aspire to professional careers in the creative and performing arts. MGSA's well-equipped arts facilities include a new comprehensive visual arts center in downtown New Brunswick, 5 theaters, a scene shop, prop-building and costume design shops, a sculpture studio, numerous art galleries, an 800-seat concert hall, an electronic studio based on the Synclavier II, recital halls,

and 4 large dance studios. The School is committed to maintaining high standards in the arts through the quality of its programs, faculty, and facilities and is dedicated to encouraging creativity, originality, and professionalism in its students.

San Francisco Conservatory of Music
San Francisco, California 94122

Founded 1917; urban setting; independent; coed; awards B, M.

Enrollment 255 total; 148 undergraduates (28 freshmen).

Faculty 65 total; 24 full-time; student-faculty ratio is 7:1.
Expenses (1995–96) Tuition: $14,500. Mandatory fees: $250.
Majors Music, opera, piano/organ, stringed instruments, voice, wind and percussion instruments.
Applying Required: high school transcript, 2 recommendations, audition, SAT I or ACT. Recommended: some high school foreign language.
Application deadlines 3/1, 3/1 priority date for financial aid.
Contact Ms. Joan Gordon, Admissions Officer, 415-759-3431.

MAJORS INDEX

Agnes Scott College
Anthropology, art/fine arts, art history, biblical studies, biology/biological sciences, chemistry, classics, creative writing, economics, English, French, German, Greek, history, international relations, Latin, literature, mathematics, music, philosophy, physics, political science/government, psychobiology, psychology, religious studies, sociology, Spanish, theater arts/drama.

Albert A. List College, Jewish Theological Seminary of America
Biblical studies, history, Judaic studies, literature, museum studies, music, philosophy, religious studies.

Albertson College of Idaho
Accounting, anthropology, art/fine arts, biology/biological sciences, business administration/commerce/management, chemistry, computer science, creative writing, economics, elementary education, English, French, German, history, (pre)law sequence, mathematics, (pre)medicine sequence, music, philosophy, physical education, physical fitness/exercise science, physics, political science/government, psychology, religious studies, science education, secondary education, sociology, Spanish, sports administration, theater arts/drama.

Albion College
American studies, anthropology, art/fine arts, biology/biological sciences, business administration/commerce/management, chemistry, communication, economics, elementary education, English, environmental sciences, environmental studies, French, geology, German, history, human services, international studies, (pre)law sequence, mathematics, (pre)medicine sequence, modern languages, music, philosophy, physical education, physics, political science/government, psychology, public affairs and policy studies, religious studies, secondary education, sociology, Spanish, theater arts/drama, (pre)veterinary medicine sequence, women's studies.

Albright College
Accounting, American studies, biochemistry, biology/biological sciences, business administration/commerce/management, chemistry, child care/child and family studies, cognitive science, computer science, criminal justice, (pre)dentistry sequence, economics, elementary education, English, environmental sciences, fashion design and technology, fashion merchandising, finance/banking, forestry, French, history, human ecology, interdisciplinary studies, international business, (pre)law sequence, marketing/retailing/merchandising, mathematics, medical technology, (pre)medicine sequence, natural resource management, philosophy, political science/government, psychobiology, psychology, religious studies, secondary education, Spanish, textiles and clothing, theater arts/drama, (pre)veterinary medicine sequence.

Alfred University
Accounting, applied art, art education, art/fine arts, art therapy, bilingual/bicultural education, biology/biological sciences, biomedical technologies, business administration/commerce/management, business economics, business education, ceramic art and design, ceramic engineering, ceramic sciences, chemistry, clinical psychology, commercial art, communication, computer information systems, computer science, criminal justice, (pre)dentistry sequence, earth science, ecology, economics, education, electrical engineering, elementary education, English, environmental sciences, experimental psychology, finance/banking, forestry, French, geology, German,

gerontology, graphic arts, health services administration, history, interdisciplinary studies, international business, (pre)law sequence, liberal arts/general studies, literature, marketing/retailing/merchandising, mathematics, mechanical engineering, medical laboratory technology, (pre)medicine sequence, modern languages, painting/drawing, philosophy, photography, physics, political science/government, printmaking, psychology, public administration, science, science education, sculpture, secondary education, sociology, Spanish, studio art, theater arts/drama, (pre)veterinary medicine sequence.

Allegheny College
Anthropology, art/fine arts, art history, biochemistry, biology/biological sciences, chemistry, classics, communication, computer science, (pre)dentistry sequence, economics, education, elementary education, English, environmental sciences, environmental studies, French, geology, German, Greek, history, international studies, Latin, (pre)law sequence, marine sciences, mathematics, (pre)medicine sequence, modern languages, music, philosophy, physics, political science/government, psychology, religious studies, Russian, secondary education, sociology, Spanish, speech/rhetoric/public address/debate, studio art, theater arts/drama, (pre)veterinary medicine sequence, women's studies.

Alma College
Accounting, art education, art/fine arts, athletic training, biochemistry, biology/biological sciences, business administration/commerce/management, chemistry, communication, computer information systems, computer science, dance, (pre)dentistry sequence, early childhood education, ecology, economics, education, elementary education, English, finance/banking, French, German, gerontology, health science, history, humanities, international business, journalism, (pre)law sequence, liberal arts/general studies, literature, marketing/retailing/merchandising, mathematics, medical illustration, (pre)medicine sequence, modern languages, music, music education, occupational therapy, painting/drawing, philosophy, physical fitness/exercise science, physics, political science/government, psychology, public health, recreation and leisure services, religious studies, retail management, science, secondary education, social science, sociology, Spanish, sports medicine, stringed instruments, teaching English as a second language, theater arts/drama, (pre)veterinary medicine sequence, voice, wind and percussion instruments, women's studies.

American University
Accounting, American studies, anthropology, applied art, applied mathematics, art/fine arts, art history, audio engineering, biology/biological sciences, broadcasting, business administration/commerce/management, chemistry, communication, computer information systems, computer science, criminal justice, criminology, early childhood education, ecology, economics, education, elementary education, English, environmental studies, European studies, film and video production, film studies, finance/banking, French, German, Germanic languages and literature, graphic arts, history, interdisciplinary studies, international business, international economics, international relations, international studies, Japanese, journalism, Judaic studies, labor and industrial relations, Latin American studies, (pre)law sequence, legal studies, liberal arts/general studies, literature, management information systems, marketing/retailing/merchandising, mathematics, (pre)medicine sequence, modern languages, music, Near and Middle Eastern studies, peace studies, philosophy, physics, political science/government, psychology,

public administration, public affairs and policy studies, public relations, radio and television studies, real estate, religious studies, Russian, Russian and Slavic studies, science, social science, sociology, Spanish, special education, statistics, studio art, theater arts/drama, urban studies, women's studies.

Amherst College

American studies, anthropology, art/fine arts, Asian/Oriental studies, astronomy, biology/biological sciences, black/African-American studies, chemistry, classics, computer science, dance, economics, English, European studies, French, geology, German, Greek, history, interdisciplinary studies, Latin, legal studies, mathematics, music, neurosciences, philosophy, physics, political science/government, psychology, religious studies, Romance languages, Russian, sociology, Spanish, theater arts/drama, women's studies.

Art Center College of Design

Advertising, art/fine arts, commercial art, environmental design, film studies, graphic arts, illustration, industrial design, painting/drawing, photography.

Auburn University

Accounting, adult and continuing education, aerospace engineering, agricultural business, agricultural economics, agricultural education, agricultural engineering, agricultural sciences, agronomy/soil and crop sciences, animal sciences, anthropology, applied art, applied mathematics, architecture, art/fine arts, aviation administration, biochemistry, biology/biological sciences, biomedical sciences, botany/plant sciences, broadcasting, business administration/commerce/management, business economics, business education, chemical engineering, chemistry, child care/child and family studies, child psychology/child development, civil engineering, commercial art, communication, computer engineering, computer science, construction management, corrections, criminal justice, dairy sciences, (pre)dentistry sequence, dietetics, early childhood education, earth science, East European and Soviet studies, economics, education, electrical engineering, elementary education, engineering (general), English, entomology, environmental design, environmental sciences, fashion merchandising, finance/banking, fish and game management, food sciences, forest engineering, forestry, forest technology, French, geography, geological engineering, geology, German, graphic arts, health education, health services administration, history, home economics, home economics education, horticulture, hotel and restaurant management, human resources, industrial arts, industrial design, industrial engineering, interior design, international business, journalism, laboratory technologies, landscape architecture/design, Latin American studies, law enforcement/police sciences, (pre)law sequence, management information systems, marine biology, marketing/retailing/merchandising, materials engineering, mathematics, mechanical engineering, medical laboratory technology, medical technology, (pre)medicine sequence, microbiology, middle school education, molecular biology, music, music education, nursing, nutrition, ornamental horticulture, pest control technology, pharmacy/pharmaceutical sciences, philosophy, physical education, physical fitness/exercise science, physics, piano/organ, political science/government, poultry sciences, psychology, public administration, public relations, radio and television studies, recreation and leisure services, rehabilitation therapy, religious studies, science education, secondary education, social work, sociology, Spanish, special education, speech pathology and audiology, speech/rhetoric/public address/debate, speech therapy, studio art, textile arts, textile engineering, textiles and clothing, theater arts/drama, transportation technologies, (pre)veterinary medicine sequence, vocational education, wildlife management, wood sciences, zoology.

Augustana College (IL)

Accounting, anthropology, art education, art/fine arts, art history, Asian/Oriental studies, astrophysics, athletic training, biology/biological sciences, black/African-American studies, business administration/commerce/management, chemistry, Chinese, classics, communication, computer science, creative writing, (pre)dentistry sequence, earth science, economics, education, elementary education, engineering physics, English, environmental studies, European studies, finance/banking, French, geography, geology, German, Greek, history, Japanese, jazz, journalism, Latin, Latin American studies, (pre)law sequence, liberal arts/general studies, literature, marketing/retailing/merchandising, mathematics, medical technology, (pre)medicine sequence, music, music education, occupational therapy, philosophy, physical education, physics, piano/organ, political science/government, psychology, public administration, religious studies, sacred music, Scandinavian languages/studies, secondary education, sociology, Spanish, speech pathology and audiology, speech/rhetoric/public address/debate, speech therapy, stringed instruments, studio art, theater arts/drama, (pre)veterinary medicine sequence, voice, wind and percussion instruments, women's studies.

Augustana College (SD)

Accounting, art education, biochemistry, biology/biological sciences, business administration/commerce/management, chemistry, communication, computer science, (pre)dentistry sequence, early childhood education, ecology, economics, education, elementary education, engineering physics, English, French, German, health services administration, history, international studies, journalism, (pre)law sequence, liberal arts/general studies, management information systems, mathematics, medical technology, (pre)medicine sequence, music, music education, nursing, philosophy, physical education, physical fitness/exercise science, physics, political science/government, psychology, religious studies, Romance languages, secondary education, social work, sociology, special education, speech pathology and audiology, theater arts/drama, (pre)veterinary medicine sequence.

Austin College

American studies, art/fine arts, biology/biological sciences, business administration/commerce/management, chemistry, classics, communication, (pre)dentistry sequence, economics, English, French, German, history, interdisciplinary studies, international studies, Latin, Latin American studies, (pre)law sequence, mathematics, (pre)medicine sequence, music, philosophy, physical education, physics, political science/government, psychology, religious studies, sociology, Spanish, speech/rhetoric/public address/debate.

Babson College

Accounting, American studies, business administration/commerce/management, communication, economics, finance/banking, international business, management information systems, marketing/retailing/merchandising, operations research.

Baldwin-Wallace College

Accounting, art education, art/fine arts, art history, arts administration, athletic training, biology/biological sciences, broadcasting, business administration/commerce/management, business education, chemistry, communication, computer information systems, computer science, criminal justice, dance, (pre)dentistry sequence, economics, education, elementary education, engineering sciences, English, environmental sciences, finance/banking, French, geology, German, health education, history, home economics, home economics education, human services, interdisciplinary studies, international studies, Japanese, (pre)law sequence, marketing/retailing/merchandising, mathematics, medical technology, (pre)medicine sequence, middle school education, music, music business, music education, music history, music therapy, philosophy, physical education, physics, piano/organ, political science/government, psychology, religious studies, science education, secondary education, sociology, Spanish, special education, speech pathology and audiology, sports administration, stringed instruments, studio art, theater arts/drama, (pre)veterinary medicine sequence, voice, wind and percussion instruments.

Bard College
Adult and continuing education, American studies, anthropology, archaeology, art/fine arts, art history, Asian/Oriental studies, biology/biological sciences, chemistry, Chinese, city/community/regional planning, classics, comparative literature, creative writing, dance, (pre)dentistry sequence, East European and Soviet studies, ecology, economics, English, environmental sciences, environmental studies, ethnic studies, European studies, film and video production, film studies, French, German, Germanic languages and literature, Greek, history, history of science, humanities, interdisciplinary studies, international economics, international studies, Italian, jazz, Latin, (pre)law sequence, literature, mathematics, (pre)medicine sequence, medieval studies, modern languages, music, music history, natural sciences, painting/drawing, philosophy, photography, physical sciences, physics, political science/government, psychology, religious studies, Romance languages, Russian, Russian and Slavic studies, science, sculpture, social science, sociology, Spanish, studio art, theater arts/drama, (pre)veterinary medicine sequence, voice.

Barnard College
African studies, American studies, anthropology, applied mathematics, architecture, art history, Asian/Oriental studies, astronomy, biochemistry, biology/biological sciences, black/African-American studies, chemistry, classics, comparative literature, computer science, dance, East Asian studies, East European and Soviet studies, economics, education, English, environmental sciences, European studies, French, German, Germanic languages and literature, history, interdisciplinary studies, Italian, Latin, Latin American studies, mathematics, (pre)medicine sequence, medieval studies, music, Near and Middle Eastern studies, philosophy, physics, political science/government, psychobiology, psychology, religious studies, Russian, Russian and Slavic studies, Slavic languages, sociology, South Asian studies, Spanish, statistics, theater arts/drama, urban studies, women's studies.

Bates College
African studies, American studies, anthropology, art/fine arts, biochemistry, biology/biological sciences, chemistry, classics, East Asian studies, economics, English, environmental studies, French, geology, German, history, interdisciplinary studies, mathematics, medieval studies, music, philosophy, physics, political science/government, psychology, religious studies, Russian, sociology, Spanish, speech/rhetoric/public address/debate, theater arts/drama, women's studies.

Baylor University
Accounting, African studies, American studies, anthropology, applied art, archaeology, architecture, art education, art/fine arts, art history, Asian/Oriental studies, aviation technology, biblical languages, biology/biological sciences, broadcasting, business administration/commerce/management, business economics, business education, chemistry, child care/child and family studies, child psychology/child development, classics, commercial art, communication, computer engineering, computer information systems, computer programming, computer science, (pre)dentistry sequence, dietetics, early childhood education, earth science, ecology, economics, education, electrical

engineering, elementary education, engineering (general), English, environmental sciences, environmental studies, family and consumer studies, fashion design and technology, fashion merchandising, finance/banking, forestry, French, geology, geophysics, German, Greek, health education, health science, history, home economics, home economics education, human resources, insurance, interdisciplinary studies, interior design, international business, international studies, journalism, Latin, Latin American studies, (pre)law sequence, management information systems, marketing/retailing/merchandising, mathematics, mechanical engineering, medical technology, (pre)medicine sequence, museum studies, music, music education, music history, neurosciences, nursing, operations research, optometry, philosophy, physical education, physical fitness/exercise science, physical sciences, physics, piano/organ, political science/government, psychology, public administration, reading education, real estate, recreation and leisure services, religious studies, Russian, Russian and Slavic studies, sacred music, science, science education, secondary education, social work, sociology, Spanish, special education, speech pathology and audiology, speech/rhetoric/public address/debate, speech therapy, stringed instruments, studio art, technical writing, telecommunications, theater arts/drama, urban studies, voice, wind and percussion instruments.

Bellarmine College
Accounting, actuarial science, art education, art/fine arts, arts administration, biology/biological sciences, business administration/commerce/management, chemistry, communication, computer engineering, computer information systems, computer science, (pre)dentistry sequence, economics, education, elementary education, English, history, jazz, (pre)law sequence, mathematics, (pre)medicine sequence, middle school education, music, music education, nursing, philosophy, political science/government, psychology, science education, secondary education, sociology, special education, studio art, theology, (pre)veterinary medicine sequence.

Belmont University
Accounting, advertising, applied mathematics, art education, art/fine arts, behavioral sciences, biblical languages, biblical studies, bilingual/bicultural education, biochemistry, biology/biological sciences, broadcasting, business administration/commerce/management, business economics, business education, chemistry, child psychology/child development, communication, computer information systems, computer management, computer programming, computer science, early childhood education, economics, education, elementary education, engineering sciences, English, finance/banking, Greek, guidance and counseling, health education, health services administration, history, hospitality services, hotel and restaurant management, international business, journalism, (pre)law sequence, marketing/retailing/merchandising, mathematics, medical technology, (pre)medicine sequence, ministries, music, music business, music education, music history, nursing, pastoral studies, pharmacology, philosophy, physical education, physics, piano/organ, political science/government, psychology, radio and television studies, reading education, recreation and leisure services, retail management, sacred music, science, secretarial studies/office management, social work, sociology, Spanish, special education, speech/rhetoric/public address/debate, studio art, theater arts/drama, (pre)veterinary medicine sequence, voice, Western civilization and culture.

Beloit College
Anthropology, art education, art/fine arts, art history, Asian/Oriental studies, biochemistry, biology/biological sciences, business administration/commerce/management, cell biology, chemistry, classics, communication, comparative literature, computer science, creative writing, (pre)dentistry sequence, economics, education,

elementary education, English, environmental biology, environmental sciences, European studies, French, geology, German, history, interdisciplinary studies, international relations, journalism, Latin American studies, (pre)law sequence, literature, mathematics, (pre)medicine sequence, modern languages, molecular biology, museum studies, music, music education, philosophy, physics, political science/government, psychology, religious studies, Romance languages, Russian, Russian and Slavic studies, science education, secondary education, sociology, Spanish, studio art, theater arts/drama, women's studies.

Bennington College
Anthropology, architecture, art/fine arts, art history, biochemistry, biology/biological sciences, ceramic art and design, chemistry, child psychology/child development, Chinese, comparative literature, computer science, computer technologies, creative writing, dance, early childhood education, ecology, economics, education, English, environmental biology, environmental sciences, environmental studies, European studies, film studies, French, German, Germanic languages and literature, Greek, history, history of philosophy, humanities, interdisciplinary studies, international relations, international studies, Japanese, jazz, Latin, (pre)law sequence, liberal arts/general studies, literature, mathematics, (pre)medicine sequence, modern languages, music, music history, natural sciences, opera, painting/drawing, philosophy, photography, physics, piano/organ, political science/government, printmaking, psychology, science, science education, sculpture, social science, sociology, Spanish, stringed instruments, studio art, theater arts/drama, (pre)veterinary medicine sequence, voice, women's studies.

Berry College
Accounting, animal sciences, applied art, art education, art/fine arts, athletic training, behavioral sciences, biochemistry, biology/biological sciences, business administration/commerce/management, business economics, chemistry, communication, computer science, consumer services, (pre)dentistry sequence, early childhood education, economics, education, elementary education, English, family and consumer studies, family services, fashion merchandising, finance/banking, food services management, French, German, health education, history, home economics, home economics education, horticulture, hotel and restaurant management, information science, interdisciplinary studies, international studies, (pre)law sequence, marketing/retailing/merchandising, mathematics, (pre)medicine sequence, middle school education, music, music business, music education, philosophy, physical education, physical fitness/exercise science, physics, piano/organ, political science/government, psychology, religious studies, science education, secondary education, social science, sociology, Spanish, sports administration, studio art, theater arts/drama, (pre)veterinary medicine sequence, voice.

Bethel College (MN)
Accounting, adult and continuing education, art education, art/fine arts, art history, athletic training, biblical studies, biology/biological sciences, business administration/commerce/management, chemistry, child care/child and family studies, communication, computer science, creative writing, (pre)dentistry sequence, early childhood education, economics, education, elementary education, English, finance/banking, health education, history, international relations, international studies, (pre)law sequence, literature, management information systems, mathematics, (pre)medicine sequence, ministries, molecular biology, music, music education, nursing, philosophy, physical education, physics, political science/government, psychology, sacred music, science education, secondary education, social work, Spanish, speech/rhetoric/public address/debate, studio art, theater arts/drama, theology, (pre)veterinary medicine sequence.

Birmingham-Southern College
Accounting, art education, art/fine arts, art history, biology/biological sciences, business administration/commerce/management, chemistry, computer science, dance, (pre)dentistry sequence, early childhood education, economics, education, elementary education, English, French, German, graphic arts, history, human resources, interdisciplinary studies, (pre)law sequence, mathematics, (pre)medicine sequence, music, music education, music history, nursing, philosophy, physics, piano/organ, political science/government, psychology, religious studies, sculpture, secondary education, sociology, Spanish, studio art, theater arts/drama, voice.

Boston College
Accounting, American studies, art history, biochemistry, biology/biological sciences, business administration/commerce/management, chemistry, classics, communication, computer information systems, computer science, (pre)dentistry sequence, early childhood education, economics, education, elementary education, English, environmental sciences, finance/banking, French, geology, geophysics, German, Germanic languages and literature, Greek, Hispanic studies, history, human development, human resources, interdisciplinary studies, Italian, Latin, (pre)law sequence, linguistics, management information systems, marketing/retailing/merchandising, mathematics, (pre)medicine sequence, music, nursing, operations research, philosophy, physics, political science/government, psychology, Romance languages, Russian, Russian and Slavic studies, science, secondary education, Slavic languages, sociology, Spanish, special education, studio art, theater arts/drama, theology.

Boston University
Accounting, advertising, aerospace engineering, African studies, American studies, anthropology, archaeology, art education, art/fine arts, art history, astronomy, astrophysics, athletic training, bilingual/bicultural education, biochemistry, biology/biological sciences, biomedical engineering, biomedical technologies, biotechnology, broadcasting, business administration/commerce/management, chemistry, classics, communication, comparative literature, computer engineering, computer information systems, computer science, (pre)dentistry sequence, early childhood education, earth science, East Asian studies, East European and Soviet studies, economics, education, electrical engineering, elementary education, engineering (general), engineering management, English, environmental sciences, environmental studies, film studies, finance/banking, food services management, French, geography, geology, German, Germanic languages and literature, graphic arts, Greek, health education, health science, Hispanic studies, history, hospitality services, hotel and restaurant management, interdisciplinary studies, international relations, international studies, Italian, journalism, Latin, Latin American studies, (pre)law sequence, liberal arts/general studies, linguistics, literature, management information systems, manufacturing engineering, marine biology, marine sciences, marketing/retailing/merchandising, mathematics, mechanical engineering, medical assistant technologies, medical technology, (pre)medicine sequence, mental health/rehabilitation counseling, modern languages, molecular biology, music, music education, music history, occupational therapy, opera, operations research, painting/drawing, paralegal studies, philosophy, photography, physical education, physical fitness/exercise science, physical therapy, physics, physiology, piano/organ, planetary and space sciences, political science/government, psychology, public relations, recreation and leisure services, rehabilitation therapy, religious studies, Russian, Russian and Slavic studies, sacred music, science education, sculpture, secondary education, social science, social work, sociology, Spanish, special education, speech pathology and audiology, speech therapy, sports medicine, statistics, stringed

instruments, studio art, systems engineering, teaching English as a second language, theater arts/drama, urban studies, voice, wind and percussion instruments.

Bowdoin College

African studies, anthropology, archaeology, art/fine arts, art history, Asian/Oriental studies, biochemistry, biology/biological sciences, black/African-American studies, chemistry, classics, computer science, dance, economics, English, environmental studies, film studies, French, geology, German, history, Latin American studies, mathematics, (pre)medicine sequence, music, neurosciences, philosophy, physics, political science/government, psychobiology, psychology, religious studies, Romance languages, Russian, sociology, Spanish, studio art, theater arts/drama.

Bradley University

Accounting, advertising, applied art, art education, art/fine arts, art history, biochemistry, biology/biological sciences, biotechnology, broadcasting, business administration/commerce/management, business economics, ceramic art and design, chemistry, civil engineering, communication, computer engineering, computer information systems, computer programming, computer science, construction engineering, construction management, criminal justice, (pre)dentistry sequence, dietetics, early childhood education, ecology, economics, education, electrical engineering, electrical engineering technology, elementary education, engineering physics, English, environmental biology, environmental sciences, fashion merchandising, film studies, finance/banking, French, geology, German, graphic arts, history, home economics, industrial engineering, interior design, international business, international studies, jewelry and metalsmithing, journalism, law enforcement/police sciences, (pre)law sequence, liberal arts/general studies, management information systems, manufacturing engineering, manufacturing technology, marketing/retailing/merchandising, mathematics, mechanical engineering, mechanical engineering technology, medical technology, (pre)medicine sequence, music, music education, nursing, nutrition, painting/drawing, philosophy, photography, physical therapy, physics, piano/organ, political science/government, psychology, radio and television studies, religious studies, sculpture, secondary education, social work, sociology, Spanish, special education, stringed instruments, studio art, theater arts/drama, (pre)veterinary medicine sequence, voice, wind and percussion instruments.

Brandeis University

African studies, American studies, anthropology, archaeology, art/fine arts, art history, biochemistry, biology/biological sciences, biophysics, black/African-American studies, chemistry, classics, cognitive science, comparative literature, computer science, creative writing, economics, engineering physics, English, European studies, French, German, Germanic languages and literature, Greek, history, history of philosophy, international economics, Italian, Judaic studies, Latin, Latin American studies, linguistics, literature, mathematics, music, music history, Near and Middle Eastern studies, neurosciences, philosophy, physics, political science/government, psychology, Russian, Russian and Slavic studies, science, sociology, Spanish, studio art, theater arts/drama.

Brigham Young University

Accounting, actuarial science, advertising, aerospace sciences, agricultural business, agricultural economics, agricultural sciences, agronomy/soil and crop sciences, American studies, animal sciences, anthropology, applied art, art education, art/fine arts, art history, Asian/Oriental studies, astronomy, athletic training, biblical languages, bilingual/bicultural education, biochemistry, biology/biological sciences, biophysics, biotechnology, botany/plant sciences,

broadcasting, business administration/commerce/management, business economics, business education, Canadian studies, cartography, ceramic art and design, chemical engineering, chemistry, child care/child and family studies, child psychology/child development, Chinese, civil engineering, classics, communication, community services, comparative literature, computer engineering, computer information systems, computer science, conservation, construction management, dance, (pre)dentistry sequence, dietetics, drafting and design, early childhood education, earth science, East Asian studies, ecology, economics, education, electrical and electronics technologies, electrical engineering, electrical engineering technology, electronics engineering technology, elementary education, engineering (general), engineering and applied sciences, engineering technology, English, entomology, European studies, family and consumer studies, family services, farm and ranch management, fashion design and technology, fashion merchandising, film studies, finance/banking, food sciences, food services management, French, geography, geological engineering, geology, German, Germanic languages and literature, graphic arts, Greek, health education, health science, history, home economics, home economics education, horticulture, human development, humanities, illustration, industrial administration, industrial arts, industrial design, information science, interior design, international business, international relations, Italian, Japanese, journalism, Latin, Latin American studies, (pre)law sequence, linguistics, literature, management information systems, manufacturing engineering, manufacturing technology, marketing/retailing/merchandising, mathematics, mechanical engineering, (pre)medicine sequence, Mexican-American/Chicano studies, microbiology, middle school education, military science, molecular biology, music, music education, Near and Middle Eastern studies, nursing, nutrition, ornamental horticulture, painting/drawing, parks management, philosophy, photography, physical education, physical fitness/exercise science, physical sciences, physical therapy, physics, piano/organ, political science/government, Portuguese, printing technologies, printmaking, psychology, public affairs and policy studies, public relations, radio and television studies, range management, recreational facilities management, recreation and leisure services, recreation therapy, retail management, Russian, science education, sculpture, secondary education, social science, social work, sociology, Southeast Asian studies, Spanish, special education, speech pathology and audiology, sports administration, statistics, studio art, textiles and clothing, theater arts/drama, tourism and travel, (pre)veterinary medicine sequence, vocational education, voice, wildlife biology, wildlife management, zoology.

Brown University

American studies, anthropology, applied mathematics, art/fine arts, art history, Asian/Oriental studies, behavioral sciences, biochemistry, biology/biological sciences, biomedical engineering, biomedical sciences, biophysics, black/African-American studies, chemical engineering, chemistry, Chinese, civil engineering, classics, cognitive science, comparative literature, computer engineering, computer science, creative writing, dance, East Asian studies, ecology, economics, education, electrical engineering, engineering (general), engineering sciences, English, environmental sciences, environmental studies, film and video production, film studies, French, geochemistry, geology, geophysics, German, Germanic languages and literature, Greek, Hispanic studies, history, international relations, international studies, Italian, Judaic studies, Latin, Latin American studies, linguistics, literature, marine biology, materials engineering, mathematics, mechanical engineering, medieval studies, modern languages, molecular biology, music, Near and Middle Eastern studies, neurosciences, philosophy, physics, political science/government, Portuguese, psychology, religious studies, Russian, Russian and Slavic studies, Slavic languages, sociology, South Asian studies, Spanish, studio art, theater arts/drama, urban studies, women's studies.

Bryn Mawr College

African studies, American studies, anthropology, archaeology, art/fine arts, art history, Asian/Oriental studies, astronomy, behavioral sciences, biochemistry, biology/biological sciences, black/African-American studies, chemistry, classics, comparative literature, computer science, East Asian studies, economics, English, French, geology, German, Greek, Hispanic studies, history, international economics, Italian, Latin, Latin American studies, mathematics, music, neurosciences, philosophy, physics, political science/government, psychology, religious studies, Romance languages, Russian, Russian and Slavic studies, sociology, Spanish, urban studies, women's studies.

Bucknell University

Accounting, animal sciences, anthropology, art/fine arts, art history, biochemistry, biology/biological sciences, business administration/commerce/management, cell biology, chemical engineering, chemistry, child psychology/child development, civil engineering, classics, computer engineering, computer science, (pre)dentistry sequence, early childhood education, economics, education, electrical engineering, elementary education, engineering management, English, environmental sciences, experimental psychology, French, geography, geology, German, history, international studies, Japanese, Latin American studies, mathematics, mechanical engineering, (pre)medicine sequence, modern languages, music, music education, music history, philosophy, physics, piano/organ, political science/government, psychology, religious studies, Russian, secondary education, sociology, Spanish, statistics, studio art, theater arts/drama, (pre)veterinary medicine sequence, voice, women's studies.

Buena Vista University

Accounting, art/fine arts, arts administration, athletic training, biology/biological sciences, business administration/commerce/management, business economics, business education, chemistry, communication, computer information systems, computer science, criminal justice, (pre)dentistry sequence, economics, education, elementary education, English, finance/banking, history, international business, (pre)law sequence, liberal arts/general studies, management information systems, marketing/retailing/merchandising, mathematics, (pre)medicine sequence, modern languages, music, music education, natural sciences, philosophy, physical education, physics, political science/government, psychology, public relations, radio and television studies, science, science education, secondary education, social science, social work, Spanish, special education, speech/rhetoric/public address/debate, theater arts/drama, (pre)veterinary medicine sequence.

Butler University

Accounting, actuarial science, arts administration, biology/biological sciences, broadcasting, business administration/commerce/management, business economics, chemistry, communication, computer science, dance, (pre)dentistry sequence, early childhood education, economics, elementary education, English, finance/banking, French, German, Greek, history, international business, international studies, journalism, Latin, (pre)law sequence, marketing/retailing/merchandising, mathematics, (pre)medicine sequence, modern languages, music, music business, music education, music history, pharmacy/pharmaceutical sciences, philosophy, physician's assistant studies, physics, piano/organ, political science/government, psychology, radio and television studies, religious studies, Romance languages, secondary education, sociology, Spanish, special education, speech pathology and audiology, speech/rhetoric/public

address/debate, stringed instruments, telecommunications, theater arts/drama, (pre)veterinary medicine sequence, voice, wind and percussion instruments.

California Institute of Technology

Aerospace engineering, applied mathematics, astronomy, astrophysics, biochemistry, biology/biological sciences, cell biology, chemical engineering, chemistry, civil engineering, computer engineering, computer science, economics, electrical engineering, engineering and applied sciences, engineering physics, environmental engineering, geochemistry, geology, geophysics, history, literature, materials sciences, mathematics, mechanical engineering, molecular biology, neurosciences, nuclear physics, physical sciences, physics, planetary and space sciences, social science.

California Institute of the Arts

Art/fine arts, commercial art, computer graphics, dance, film studies, graphic arts, illustration, jazz, music, photography, piano/organ, sculpture, stringed instruments, studio art, theater arts/drama, voice.

Calvin College

Accounting, art education, art/fine arts, art history, athletic training, biblical studies, bilingual/bicultural education, biochemistry, biology/biological sciences, business administration/commerce/management, business economics, chemistry, civil engineering, classics, communication, computer science, criminal justice, (pre)dentistry sequence, economics, education, electrical engineering, elementary education, engineering (general), English, environmental sciences, European studies, film studies, French, geography, geology, German, Germanic languages and literature, Greek, history, humanities, interdisciplinary studies, Japanese, journalism, Latin, (pre)law sequence, liberal arts/general studies, linguistics, literature, mathematics, mechanical engineering, medical technology, (pre)medicine sequence, music, music education, music history, natural sciences, nursing, occupational therapy, philosophy, physical education, physical fitness/exercise science, physical sciences, physics, political science/government, psychology, recreation and leisure services, religious education, religious studies, sacred music, science, science education, secondary education, social science, social work, sociology, Spanish, special education, speech pathology and audiology, speech/rhetoric/public address/debate, sports medicine, studio art, telecommunications, theater arts/drama, theology, (pre)veterinary medicine sequence, voice.

Capital University

Accounting, art education, art/fine arts, art therapy, biology/biological sciences, business administration/commerce/management, chemistry, communication, computer science, criminology, (pre)dentistry sequence, economics, education, elementary education, English, finance/banking, French, health education, history, interdisciplinary studies, international studies, jazz, (pre)law sequence, liberal arts/general studies, literature, marketing/retailing/merchandising, mathematics, (pre)medicine sequence, modern languages, music, music business, music education, nursing, philosophy, physical education, piano/organ, political science/government, psychology, public administration, public relations, radio and television studies, religious studies, science education, secondary education, social work, sociology, Spanish, speech/rhetoric/public address/debate, sports medicine, stringed instruments, studio art, (pre)veterinary medicine sequence, voice, wind and percussion instruments.

Carleton College

Anthropology, art history, Asian/Oriental studies, biology/biological sciences, chemistry, classics, computer science, ecology, economics, English, French, geology, German, Greek, history, Latin, Latin American studies, (pre)law sequence, mathematics, (pre)medicine sequence, music, philosophy, physics, political science/government, psychology, religious studies, Romance languages, Russian, Russian and Slavic studies, sociology, Spanish, studio art, women's studies.

Carnegie Mellon University

Accounting, applied art, applied mathematics, architecture, art/fine arts, behavioral sciences, biochemistry, bioengineering, biology/biological sciences, biomedical engineering, biomedical sciences, biophysics, business administration/commerce/management, business economics, cell biology, ceramic art and design, chemical engineering, chemistry, child psychology/child development, city/community/regional planning, civil engineering, clinical psychology, commercial art, communication, comparative literature, computer engineering, computer information systems, computer management, computer programming, computer science, creative writing, (pre)dentistry sequence, economics, electrical engineering, electronics engineering, engineering (general), engineering and applied sciences, engineering design, engineering management, engineering mechanics, engineering sciences, English, environmental engineering, environmental sciences, European studies, experimental psychology, finance/banking, French, genetics, German, Germanic languages and literature, graphic arts, Hispanic studies, history, humanities, illustration, industrial administration, industrial design, information science, jewelry and metalsmithing, journalism, labor and industrial relations, (pre)law sequence, liberal arts/general studies, linguistics, literature, management information systems, manufacturing engineering, marketing/retailing/merchandising, materials engineering, materials sciences, mathematics, mechanical engineering, (pre)medicine sequence, metallurgical engineering, metallurgy, microbiology, modern languages, molecular biology, music, music education, opera, operations research, painting/drawing, philosophy, physics, piano/organ, political science/government, polymer science, printing technologies, psychology, public administration, public affairs and policy studies, publishing, robotics, sculpture, social science, sociology, Spanish, speech/rhetoric/public address/debate, statistics, stringed instruments, studio art, systems engineering, systems science, technical writing, technology and public affairs, textile arts, theater arts/drama, toxicology, urban studies, (pre)veterinary medicine sequence, voice, Western civilization and culture, wind and percussion instruments.

Carroll College (MT)

Accounting, biology/biological sciences, business administration/commerce/management, business economics, chemistry, communication, computer engineering, (pre)dentistry sequence, education, elementary education, engineering (general), English, finance/banking, French, history, international relations, Latin, (pre)law sequence, liberal arts/general studies, mathematics, medical records services, medical technology, (pre)medicine sequence, nursing, philosophy, physical education, political science/government, psychology, public administration, public relations, religious education, religious studies, science education, secondary education, social science, social work, sociology, Spanish, speech/rhetoric/public address/debate, sports administration, teaching English as a second language, technical writing, theater arts/drama, theology, (pre)veterinary medicine sequence.

Case Western Reserve University

Accounting, aerospace engineering, American studies, anthropology, applied mathematics, art education, art history, Asian/Oriental studies, astronomy, audio engineering, biochemistry, biology/biological sciences, biomedical engineering, business administration/commerce/management, chemical engineering, chemistry, civil engineering, classics, communication, comparative literature, computer engineering, computer science, (pre)dentistry sequence, dietetics, earth science, economics, electrical engineering, engineering (general), English,

environmental sciences, European studies, finance/banking, fluid and thermal sciences, French, geology, German, gerontology, Greek, history, history of science, international studies, Latin, (pre)law sequence, literature, management information systems, materials engineering, materials sciences, mathematics, mechanical engineering, medical technology, (pre)medicine sequence, music, music education, natural sciences, nursing, nutrition, operations research, philosophy, physics, political science/government, polymer science, psychology, religious studies, sociology, Spanish, speech pathology and audiology, statistics, systems engineering, theater arts/drama, (pre)veterinary medicine sequence.

The Catholic University of America

Accounting, American studies, anthropology, architectural engineering, architecture, art education, art/fine arts, art history, biochemistry, biology/biological sciences, biomedical engineering, business administration/commerce/management, chemistry, civil engineering, classics, communication, computer engineering, computer science, construction engineering, early childhood education, economics, education, electrical engineering, elementary education, engineering (general), English, finance/banking, French, German, Greek, history, human resources, interdisciplinary studies, international economics, international studies, Italian, Latin, mathematics, mechanical engineering, medical technology, (pre)medicine sequence, medieval studies, modern languages, music, music education, music history, nursing, peace studies, philosophy, physics, piano/organ, political science/government, psychology, religious studies, Romance languages, secondary education, social work, sociology, Spanish, studio art, theater arts/drama, (pre)veterinary medicine sequence, voice, wind and percussion instruments.

Cedarville College

Accounting, American studies, athletic training, behavioral sciences, biblical studies, biology/biological sciences, broadcasting, business administration/commerce/management, business economics, business education, chemistry, communication, computer information systems, criminal justice, (pre)dentistry sequence, early childhood education, economics, education, electrical engineering, elementary education, English, environmental biology, finance/banking, health education, history, international business, international economics, international studies, (pre)law sequence, marketing/retailing/merchandising, mathematics, mechanical engineering, medical technology, (pre)medicine sequence, music, music education, nursing, pastoral studies, philosophy, physical education, political science/government, psychology, public administration, radio and television studies, sacred music, science, science education, secondary education, secretarial studies/office management, social science, social work, sociology, Spanish, special education, speech/rhetoric/public address/debate, technical writing, theater arts/drama, theology, (pre)veterinary medicine sequence, voice.

Centenary College of Louisiana

Accounting, art education, art/fine arts, arts administration, biblical studies, biochemistry, biology/biological sciences, biophysics, business administration/commerce/management, business economics, chemistry, communication, dance, (pre)dentistry sequence, early childhood education, earth science, economics, education, elementary education, engineering and applied sciences, English, environmental sciences, environmental studies, film studies, French, geology, German, health education, health science, history, interdisciplinary studies, (pre)law sequence, liberal arts/general studies, literature, mathematics, (pre)medicine sequence, middle school education, military science, music, music education, occupational therapy, painting/drawing, philosophy, physical education, physical sciences, physical therapy, physics, piano/organ, political science/government, psychology, religious education, religious studies, sacred music, science education, secondary education, social science, sociology, Spanish, speech pathology and audiology, speech/rhetoric/public address/debate, stringed instruments, studio art, theater arts/drama, (pre)veterinary medicine sequence, voice, wind and percussion instruments.

Central College (IA)
Accounting, art education, art/fine arts, Asian/Oriental studies, biology/biological sciences, business administration/commerce/management, chemistry, communication, computer information systems, computer science, economics, education, elementary education, English, environmental studies, European studies, French, German, history, international business, international studies, Latin American studies, liberal arts/general studies, linguistics, mathematics, music, music education, philosophy, physical education, physics, political science/government, psychology, recreation and leisure services, religious studies, secondary education, sociology, Spanish, theater arts/drama, urban studies.

Centre College
Anthropology, art/fine arts, art history, biochemistry, biology/biological sciences, chemistry, classics, computer science, (pre)dentistry sequence, economics, elementary education, English, French, German, history, international relations, (pre)law sequence, mathematics, (pre)medicine sequence, molecular biology, music, philosophy, physics, political science/government, psychobiology, psychology, religious studies, secondary education, sociology, Spanish, theater arts/drama.

Christendom College
Classics, French, history, literature, philosophy, political science/government, theology.

Christian Brothers University
Accounting, biology/biological sciences, business administration/commerce/management, chemical engineering, chemistry, civil engineering, communication, computer information systems, computer science, (pre)dentistry sequence, economics, education, electrical engineering, elementary education, engineering physics, English, finance/banking, history, (pre)law sequence, marketing/retailing/merchandising, mathematics, mechanical engineering, (pre)medicine sequence, natural science, physics, psychology.

Claremont McKenna College
Accounting, American studies, art/fine arts, Asian/Oriental studies, biochemistry, biology/biological sciences, black/African-American studies, chemistry, Chinese, classics, computer science, (pre)dentistry sequence, economics, engineering management, English, environmental sciences, environmental studies, European studies, film studies, French, German, Greek, history, international business, international economics, international relations, international studies, Italian, Japanese, Latin, Latin American studies, (pre)law sequence, legal studies, literature, management engineering, mathematics, (pre)medicine sequence, Mexican-American/Chicano studies, modern languages, music, philosophy, physics, political science/government, psychobiology, psychology, religious studies, Russian, Spanish, theater arts/drama, women's studies.

Clarkson University
Accounting, aerospace engineering, applied mathematics, biochemical technology, biochemistry, biology/biological sciences, business administration/commerce/management, business economics, cell biology, chemical engineering, chemistry, civil engineering, computer engineering, computer information systems, computer management, computer science, economics, electrical engineering, engineering (general), engineering management, engineering sciences, environmental engineering, environmental health sciences, finance/

banking, history, humanities, industrial engineering, interdisciplinary studies, (pre)law sequence, liberal arts/general studies, management engineering, management information systems, manufacturing engineering, marketing/retailing/merchandising, materials engineering, mathematics, mechanical engineering, (pre)medicine sequence, microbiology, occupational safety and health, operations research, physics, political science/government, psychology, social science, sociology, surveying engineering, technical writing, toxicology, transportation engineering, water resources.

Clark University
Art/fine arts, art history, Asian/Oriental studies, biochemistry, biology/biological sciences, business administration/commerce/management, chemistry, classics, communication, comparative literature, computer science, (pre)dentistry sequence, earth science, ecology, economics, education, elementary education, engineering (general), English, environmental sciences, environmental studies, ethnic studies, film studies, French, geography, German, Germanic languages and literature, graphic arts, history, interdisciplinary studies, international relations, international studies, Judaic studies, (pre)law sequence, literature, mathematics, (pre)medicine sequence, middle school education, modern languages, molecular biology, music, natural resource management, neurosciences, peace studies, philosophy, physics, political science/government, psychology, Romance languages, secondary education, sociology, Spanish, studio art, theater arts/drama, (pre)veterinary medicine sequence.

Clemson University
Accounting, agricultural business, agricultural economics, agricultural education, agricultural engineering, agricultural sciences, agronomy/soil and crop sciences, animal sciences, applied mathematics, architecture, art/fine arts, biochemistry, biology/biological sciences, botany/plant sciences, business administration/commerce/management, ceramic engineering, chemical engineering, chemistry, city/community/regional planning, civil engineering, communication, computer engineering, computer information systems, computer science, construction management, dairy sciences, early childhood education, earth science, economics, education, electrical engineering, elementary education, engineering (general), English, entomology, finance/banking, food sciences, forestry, French, geology, German, graphic arts, health science, history, horticulture, industrial arts, industrial engineering, international business, landscape architecture/design, (pre)law sequence, liberal arts/general studies, marketing/retailing/merchandising, mathematics, mechanical engineering, medical technology, (pre)medicine sequence, microbiology, modern languages, nursing, occupational safety and health, ornamental horticulture, parks management, philosophy, physics, political science/government, poultry sciences, psychology, reading education, recreation and leisure services, science education, secondary education, sociology, Spanish, special education, textiles and clothing, tourism and travel, (pre)veterinary medicine sequence, vocational education, wildlife biology, wildlife management, wood sciences.

Cleveland Institute of Music
Audio engineering, music, music education, piano/organ, stringed instruments, voice, wind and percussion instruments.

Coe College
Accounting, American studies, art education, art/fine arts, Asian/Oriental studies, athletic training, biochemistry, biology/biological sciences, black/African-American studies, business administration/commerce/management, chemistry, classics, computer science, (pre)dentistry sequence, economics, education, elementary education, English, environmental studies, French, German, history, interdisciplinary studies, (pre)law sequence, liberal arts/general

studies, literature, mathematics, medical technology, (pre)medicine sequence, music, music education, nursing, philosophy, physical education, physical sciences, physics, political science/government, psychology, public relations, religious studies, science, science education, secondary education, sociology, Spanish, studio art, theater arts/drama, (pre)veterinary medicine sequence.

Colby College

American studies, anthropology, art/fine arts, art history, biochemistry, biology/biological sciences, black/African-American studies, business administration/commerce/management, cell biology, chemistry, classics, computer science, earth science, East Asian studies, economics, English, environmental studies, French, geology, German, history, international studies, Latin American studies, mathematics, molecular biology, music, philosophy, physics, political science/government, psychology, religious studies, Russian and Slavic studies, sociology, Spanish, theater arts/drama, women's studies.

Colgate University

African studies, anthropology, art/fine arts, art history, Asian/Oriental studies, astronomy, astrophysics, biochemistry, biology/biological sciences, black/African-American studies, chemistry, Chinese, classics, computer science, East Asian studies, economics, education, English, French, geography, geology, German, Greek, history, humanities, international relations, Japanese, Latin, Latin American studies, mathematics, molecular biology, music, Native American studies, natural sciences, neurosciences, peace studies, philosophy, physical sciences, physics, political science/government, psychology, religious studies, Romance languages, Russian, Russian and Slavic studies, social science, sociology, Spanish, theater arts/drama, women's studies.

College of Insurance

Actuarial science, business administration/commerce/management, insurance.

College of Saint Benedict

Accounting, art education, art/fine arts, art history, biology/biological sciences, business administration/commerce/management, chemistry, classics, communication, computer science, (pre)dentistry sequence, dietetics, economics, education, elementary education, English, forestry, French, German, Greek, history, humanities, Latin, (pre)law sequence, liberal arts/general studies, mathematics, medical technology, (pre)medicine sequence, medieval studies, ministries, music, music education, natural sciences, nursing, nutrition, occupational therapy, peace studies, pharmacy/pharmaceutical sciences, philosophy, physical therapy, physics, political science/government, psychology, religious education, religious studies, sacred music, secondary education, social science, social work, sociology, Spanish, studio art, theater arts/drama, theology, (pre)veterinary medicine sequence.

College of St. Scholastica

Accounting, behavioral sciences, bilingual/bicultural education, biology/biological sciences, business administration/commerce/management, chemistry, communication, computer information systems, (pre)dentistry sequence, dietetics, early childhood education, education, elementary education, English, family and consumer studies, fashion merchandising, food services management, health science, health services administration, history, home economics, home economics education, humanities, interdisciplinary studies, international business, (pre)law sequence, liberal arts/general studies, mathematics, medical records services, medical technology, (pre)medicine sequence, ministries, music, music education, natural sciences, nursing, occupational therapy, pastoral studies, physical fitness/exercise science, physical therapy, piano/organ, psychology, religious

education, religious studies, science education, secondary education, social work, sociology, sports administration, (pre)veterinary medicine sequence.

College of the Holy Cross

Accounting, anthropology, art/fine arts, art history, Asian/Oriental studies, biology/biological sciences, black/African-American studies, chemistry, classics, computer science, (pre)dentistry sequence, economics, English, environmental studies, European studies, French, German, gerontology, history, international studies, Italian, Latin American studies, (pre)law sequence, mathematics, (pre)medicine sequence, modern languages, music, Near and Middle Eastern studies, peace studies, philosophy, physics, political science/government, psychobiology, psychology, religious studies, Russian, sociology, Spanish, studio art, theater arts/drama, (pre)veterinary medicine sequence, women's studies.

College of William and Mary

American studies, anthropology, art/fine arts, art history, biology/biological sciences, business administration/commerce/management, chemistry, classics, comparative literature, computer science, East Asian studies, economics, English, environmental sciences, European studies, French, geology, German, Greek, history, interdisciplinary studies, international studies, Latin, Latin American studies, linguistics, mathematics, modern languages, music, philosophy, physical education, physics, political science/government, psychology, public affairs and policy studies, religious studies, Russian and Slavic studies, sociology, Spanish, speech/rhetoric/public address/debate, theater arts/drama, urban studies.

The College of Wooster

African studies, archaeology, art/fine arts, art history, Asian/Oriental studies, biochemistry, biology/biological sciences, black/African-American studies, business economics, chemistry, classics, communication, comparative literature, computer science, (pre)dentistry sequence, economics, English, European studies, French, geology, German, Greek, history, international relations, Latin, Latin American studies, (pre)law sequence, mathematics, (pre)medicine sequence, music, music education, music history, music therapy, philosophy, physics, political science/government, psychology, religious studies, Russian, sociology, South Asian studies, Spanish, speech pathology and audiology, speech/rhetoric/public address/debate, studio art, theater arts/drama, urban studies, (pre)veterinary medicine sequence, voice.

The Colorado College

Anthropology, art/fine arts, art history, biochemistry, biology/biological sciences, chemistry, classics, comparative literature, creative writing, dance, (pre)dentistry sequence, economics, English, environmental sciences, environmental studies, French, geology, German, history, interdisciplinary studies, international economics, international studies, (pre)law sequence, liberal arts/general studies, mathematics, (pre)medicine sequence, music, peace studies, philosophy, physics, political science/government, psychology, religious studies, Romance languages, Russian, sociology, Spanish, theater arts/drama, (pre)veterinary medicine sequence, women's studies.

Colorado School of Mines

Chemical engineering, chemistry, civil engineering, computer science, economics, electrical engineering, engineering (general), engineering and applied sciences, engineering physics, engineering sciences, geological engineering, geophysical engineering, materials sciences, mathematics, mechanical engineering, metallurgical engineering, mining and mineral engineering, petroleum/natural gas engineering, physics.

Colorado State University

Accounting, actuarial science, agricultural business, agricultural economics, agricultural education, agricultural engineering, agricultural sciences, agronomy/soil and crop sciences, American studies, animal sciences, anthropology, applied mathematics, art education, art/fine arts, art history, biochemistry, biology/biological sciences, botany/plant sciences, business administration/commerce/management, ceramic art and design, chemical engineering, chemistry, child care/child and family studies, civil engineering, computer information systems, computer science, construction management, creative writing, dance, (pre)dentistry sequence, dietetics, economics, electrical engineering, engineering physics, engineering sciences, English, entomology, environmental engineering, environmental health sciences, equestrian studies, family and consumer studies, farm and ranch management, fashion merchandising, finance/banking, fish and game management, food sciences, forestry, French, geology, German, graphic arts, history, home economics, home economics education, horticulture, hotel and restaurant management, human development, humanities, industrial arts, interior design, jewelry and metalsmithing, journalism, landscape architecture/design, (pre)law sequence, liberal arts/general studies, marketing/retailing/merchandising, mathematics, mechanical engineering, (pre)medicine sequence, microbiology, music, music education, music therapy, natural resource management, nutrition, occupational therapy, ornamental horticulture, painting/drawing, parks management, philosophy, photography, physical education, physical fitness/exercise science, physical sciences, physics, political science/government, printmaking, psychology, public relations, range management, real estate, recreational facilities management, sculpture, social science, social work, sociology, Spanish, speech/rhetoric/public address/debate, statistics, studio art, technical writing, textiles and clothing, theater arts/drama, (pre)veterinary medicine sequence, water resources, wildlife biology, zoology.

Colorado Technical University

Business administration/commerce/management, computer engineering, computer science, electrical engineering, electronics engineering technology, management information systems, telecommunications.

Columbia University, Columbia College (NY)

African studies, anthropology, archaeology, architecture, art/fine arts, art history, astronomy, astrophysics, biochemistry, biology/biological sciences, biophysics, black/African-American studies, chemistry, classics, comparative literature, computer science, dance, East Asian studies, East European and Soviet studies, economics, English, environmental sciences, film studies, French, geochemistry, geology, geophysics, German, Germanic languages and literature, Greek, Hispanic studies, history, interdisciplinary studies, Italian, Latin, Latin American studies, mathematics, medieval studies, music, Near and Middle Eastern studies, philosophy, physics, political science/government, psychology, religious studies, Russian, Russian and Slavic studies, sociology, Spanish, statistics, theater arts/drama, urban studies, Western civilization and culture, women's studies.

Columbia University, School of Engineering and Applied Science

Applied mathematics, bioengineering, chemical engineering, civil engineering, computer engineering, computer science, electrical engineering, engineering mechanics, environmental engineering, industrial engineering, materials sciences, mechanical engineering, metallurgical engineering, metallurgy, mining and mineral engineering, operations research, physics.

Concordia College (Moorhead, MN)

Accounting, advertising, art education, art/fine arts, art history, biology/biological sciences, broadcasting, business administration/commerce/management, business economics, business education, chemistry, child care/child and family studies, classics, communication, computer science, creative writing, criminal justice, (pre)dentistry sequence, dietetics, economics, education, elementary education, English, environmental studies, family and consumer studies, French, German, health education, health services administration, history, home economics, home economics education, humanities, international business, international relations, journalism, Latin, (pre)law sequence, mathematics, medical technology, (pre)medicine sequence, music, music education, nursing, nutrition, philosophy, physical education, physics, piano/organ, political science/government, psychology, radio and television studies, recreation and leisure services, religious studies, Russian and Slavic studies, Scandinavian languages/studies, science education, secondary education, secretarial studies/office management, social work, sociology, Spanish, speech/rhetoric/public address/debate, studio art, textiles and clothing, theater arts/drama, (pre)veterinary medicine sequence, voice, wind and percussion instruments.

Cooper Union for the Advancement of Science and Art

Architecture, art/fine arts, chemical engineering, civil engineering, electrical engineering, engineering (general), graphic arts, mechanical engineering.

The Corcoran School of Art

Applied art, art/fine arts, ceramic art and design, commercial art, graphic arts, painting/drawing, photography, printmaking, sculpture, studio art.

Cornell College

Anthropology, architecture, art education, art/fine arts, art history, behavioral sciences, biochemistry, biology/biological sciences, business administration/commerce/management, business economics, business education, chemistry, classics, computer science, (pre)dentistry sequence, ecology, economics, education, elementary education, English, environmental sciences, environmental studies, ethnic studies, French, geology, German, history, interdisciplinary studies, international business, international relations, international studies, Latin American studies, (pre)law sequence, liberal arts/general studies, mathematics, medical technology, (pre)medicine sequence, medieval studies, modern languages, molecular biology, music, music education, philosophy, physical education, physics, political science/government, psychology, religious studies, Russian, Russian and Slavic studies, secondary education, sociology, Spanish, speech/rhetoric/public address/debate, studio art, theater arts/drama, (pre)veterinary medicine sequence, women's studies.

Cornell University

African studies, agricultural business, agricultural economics, agricultural education, agricultural engineering, agricultural sciences, agricultural technologies, agronomy/soil and crop sciences, American studies, anatomy, animal sciences, anthropology, applied art, archaeology, architectural technologies, architecture, art/fine arts, art history, Asian/Oriental studies, astronomy, atmospheric sciences, behavioral sciences, biochemistry, bioengineering, biology/biological sciences, biometrics, black/African-American studies, botany/plant sciences, business administration/commerce/management, cell biology, chemical engineering, chemistry, child care/child and family studies, child psychology/child development, Chinese, city/community/regional planning, civil engineering, classics, communication, community services, comparative literature, computer information systems, computer science, consumer services, creative writing, dairy sciences, dance, dietetics, East Asian studies, East European and Soviet studies, ecology, economics, education, electrical engineering, engineering (general), engineering physics, engineering sciences, English, entomology, environmental design, environmental engineering, environmental sciences, European studies, family and consumer studies, family services, farm and ranch management, food sciences, food services management, French, genetics, geological engineering, geology, German, Germanic languages and literature, Greek, Hebrew, Hispanic studies, history, history of science, home economics education, horticulture, hotel and restaurant management, human development, human ecology, human services, industrial engineering, interdisciplinary studies, international studies, Italian, Japanese, Judaic studies, labor and industrial relations, labor studies, landscape architecture/design, Latin, Latin American studies, (pre)law sequence, liberal arts/general studies, linguistics, marine sciences, materials engineering, materials sciences, mathematics, mechanical engineering, (pre)medicine sequence, medieval studies, meteorology, microbiology, modern languages, molecular biology, music, Native American studies, natural resource management, Near and Middle Eastern studies, neurosciences, nutrition, operations research, ornamental horticulture, painting/drawing, pest control technology, philosophy, photography, physics, physiology, political science/government, poultry sciences, psychology, public affairs and policy studies, religious studies, Romance languages, Russian, Russian and Slavic studies, sculpture, Slavic languages, social work, sociobiology, sociology, Southeast Asian studies, Spanish, statistics, textile arts, textiles and clothing, theater arts/drama, urban studies, (pre)veterinary medicine sequence, women's studies, zoology.

Creighton University

Accounting, American studies, art education, art/fine arts, atmospheric sciences, biology/biological sciences, business economics, chemistry, classics, communication, computer science, economics, education, elementary education, English, environmental sciences, finance/banking, French, German, Greek, history, international business, international studies, journalism, Latin, management information systems, marketing/retailing/merchandising, mathematics, ministries, modern languages, music, nursing, occupational therapy, pharmacy/pharmaceutical sciences, philosophy, physical fitness/exercise science, physical therapy, physics, political science/government, psychology, social work, sociology, Spanish, special education, speech/rhetoric/public address/debate, statistics, theater arts/drama, theology.

The Curtis Institute of Music

Music, piano/organ, stringed instruments, voice, wind and percussion instruments.

Dartmouth College

Anthropology, applied art, archaeology, art/fine arts, art history, Asian/Oriental studies, biochemistry, biology/biological sciences, black/African-American studies, chemistry, classics, cognitive science, comparative literature, computer science, earth science, economics, education, engineering (general), engineering sciences, English, environmental sciences, film studies, French, geography, German, Hispanic studies, history, Italian, linguistics, mathematics, (pre)medicine sequence, music, Native American studies, philosophy, physics, political science/government, psychology, religious studies, Romance languages, Russian, sociology, Spanish, studio art, theater arts/drama, women's studies.

David Lipscomb University

Accounting, American studies, art/fine arts, athletic training, biblical languages, biblical studies, biochemistry, biology/biological sciences, business administration/commerce/management, business economics,

chemistry, commercial art, communication, computer information systems, computer science, (pre)dentistry sequence, dietetics, education, elementary education, engineering sciences, English, family and consumer studies, fashion merchandising, finance/banking, food services management, French, German, health education, history, home economics, (pre)law sequence, liberal arts/general studies, marketing/retailing/merchandising, mathematics, (pre)medicine sequence, middle school education, ministries, music, music education, nursing, philosophy, physical education, physical fitness/exercise science, physics, piano/organ, political science/government, psychology, public administration, public relations, secondary education, social work, Spanish, speech/rhetoric/public address/debate, stringed instruments, studio art, theology, urban studies, (pre)veterinary medicine sequence, voice, wind and percussion instruments.

Davidson College

Anthropology, art/fine arts, art history, biology/biological sciences, chemistry, classics, economics, English, French, German, history, mathematics, music, philosophy, physics, political science/government, psychology, religious studies, sociology, Spanish, studio art, theater arts/drama.

Deep Springs College

Liberal arts/general studies.

Denison University

Anthropology, art/fine arts, art history, biochemistry, biology/biological sciences, black/African-American studies, chemistry, classics, communication, computer science, creative writing, dance, East Asian studies, economics, English, environmental sciences, environmental studies, film studies, French, geology, German, history, international studies, Latin American studies, mathematics, music, music education, philosophy, physical education, physics, political science/government, psychology, religious studies, sociology, Spanish, speech/rhetoric/public address/debate, studio art, theater arts/drama, women's studies.

DePaul University

Accounting, actuarial science, adult and continuing education, advertising, African studies, American studies, anthropology, applied art, applied mathematics, art history, arts administration, audio engineering, biochemistry, biology/biological sciences, black/African-American studies, business administration/commerce/management, business economics, chemistry, city/community/regional planning, commercial art, communication, comparative literature, computer graphics, computer information systems, computer programming, computer science, computer technologies, creative writing, criminal justice, (pre)dentistry sequence, early childhood education, ecology, economics, education, electrical and electronics technologies, elementary education, English, environmental sciences, finance/banking, French, geography, German, graphic arts, guidance and counseling, history, human development, human resources, information science, interdisciplinary studies, international business, international relations, international studies, Italian, Japanese, jazz, Judaic studies, Latin American studies, (pre)law sequence, legal studies, linguistics, literature, management information systems, marketing/retailing/merchandising, mathematics, medical laboratory technology, (pre)medicine sequence, military science, modern languages, music, music business, music education, nursing, operations research, painting/drawing, philosophy, physical education, physics, piano/organ, political science/government, psychology, religious education, religious studies, sculpture, secondary education, social science, sociology, Spanish, statistics, stringed instruments, studio art, theater arts/drama, tourism and travel, urban studies, (pre)veterinary medicine sequence, voice, wind and percussion instruments, women's studies.

DePauw University
Anthropology, art history, Asian/Oriental studies, biology/biological sciences, chemistry, classics, communication, computer science, creative writing, earth science, East Asian studies, economics, elementary education, English, French, geology, German, Greek, history, interdisciplinary studies, Latin, literature, mathematics, medical technology, music, music business, music education, philosophy, physical education, physics, political science/government, psychology, religious studies, Romance languages, Russian and Slavic studies, sociology, Spanish, studio art, women's studies.

Dickinson College
American studies, anthropology, art/fine arts, biology/biological sciences, chemistry, computer science, East Asian studies, economics, English, environmental sciences, environmental studies, French, geology, German, Greek, history, international studies, Italian, Judaic studies, Latin, mathematics, music, philosophy, physics, political science/government, psychology, public affairs and policy studies, religious studies, Russian, Russian and Slavic studies, sociology, Spanish, theater arts/drama.

Drake University
Accounting, actuarial science, advertising, applied art, art education, art/fine arts, art history, Asian/Oriental studies, astronomy, biology/biological sciences, broadcasting, business administration/commerce/management, business education, chemistry, clinical psychology, commercial art, communication, computer information systems, computer science, (pre)dentistry sequence, earth science, economics, education, educational administration, elementary education, English, environmental sciences, experimental psychology, finance/banking, French, geography, German, gerontology, graphic arts, history, insurance, interior design, international business, international relations, journalism, Latin American studies, (pre)law sequence, literature, marine sciences, marketing/retailing/merchandising, mathematics, medical technology, (pre)medicine sequence, military science, music, music business, music education, nursing, painting/drawing, pharmacy/pharmaceutical sciences, philosophy, physical sciences, physics, piano/organ, political science/government, printmaking, psychology, public relations, radio and television studies, religious studies, sacred music, science, science education, sculpture, secondary education, social science, sociology, Spanish, speech/rhetoric/public address/debate, stringed instruments, studio art, theater arts/drama, (pre)veterinary medicine sequence, voice, wind and percussion instruments, women's studies.

Drew University
American studies, anthropology, applied mathematics, art/fine arts, art history, behavioral sciences, biochemistry, biology/biological sciences, chemistry, classics, computer science, economics, English, French, German, history, interdisciplinary studies, Italian, liberal arts/general studies, mathematics, music, philosophy, physics, political science/government, psychobiology, psychology, religious studies, Russian, Russian and Slavic studies, sociology, Spanish, studio art, theater arts/drama.

Drury College
Accounting, architecture, art education, art/fine arts, art history, behavioral sciences, biology/biological sciences, business administration/commerce/management, chemistry, communication, criminology, (pre)dentistry sequence, economics, education, elementary education, English, French, German, history, (pre)law sequence, mathematics, medical technology, (pre)medicine sequence, music, music education, nursing, philosophy, physical education, physical

fitness/exercise science, physics, political science/government, psychology, religious studies, secondary education, sociology, Spanish, special education, studio art, theater arts/drama, (pre)veterinary medicine sequence.

Duke University
Anatomy, anthropology, art/fine arts, art history, Asian/Oriental studies, biology/biological sciences, biomedical engineering, black/African-American studies, chemistry, civil engineering, classics, computer science, East European and Soviet studies, economics, electrical engineering, English, environmental sciences, European studies, French, geology, Germanic languages and literature, Greek, history, international studies, Italian, Latin, Latin American studies, literature, materials sciences, mathematics, mechanical engineering, medieval studies, music, philosophy, physics, political science/government, psychology, public affairs and policy studies, religious studies, Russian, Russian and Slavic studies, Slavic languages, sociology, Spanish, theater arts/drama, women's studies.

Earlham College
African studies, anthropology, art/fine arts, astronomy, biology/biological sciences, black/African-American studies, chemistry, classics, computer science, East Asian studies, economics, education, elementary education, English, environmental studies, French, geology, German, history, human development, international studies, Japanese, Judaic studies, (pre)law sequence, legal studies, literature, mathematics, (pre)medicine sequence, museum studies, music, peace studies, philosophy, physics, political science/government, psychology, religious studies, secondary education, sociology, Spanish, theater arts/drama, (pre)veterinary medicine sequence, women's studies.

Eckerd College
American studies, anthropology, art/fine arts, biology/biological sciences, business administration/commerce/management, chemistry, comparative literature, computer science, creative writing, (pre)dentistry sequence, economics, English, environmental studies, French, German, history, human development, humanities, interdisciplinary studies, international business, international relations, international studies, (pre)law sequence, literature, marine sciences, mathematics, medical technology, (pre)medicine sequence, modern languages, music, philosophy, physics, political science/government, psychology, religious studies, Russian, sociology, Spanish, theater arts/drama, (pre)veterinary medicine sequence, women's studies.

Elizabethtown College
Accounting, actuarial science, anthropology, applied mathematics, art/fine arts, biochemistry, biology/biological sciences, biotechnology, broadcasting, business administration/commerce/management, business economics, chemistry, child psychology/child development, communication, computer engineering, computer information systems, computer science, (pre)dentistry sequence, early childhood education, economics, education, elementary education, engineering (general), engineering physics, English, environmental sciences, finance/banking, French, German, history, industrial engineering, international business, international studies, (pre)law sequence, literature, marketing/retailing/merchandising, mathematics, medical technology, (pre)medicine sequence, modern languages, music, music education, music therapy, occupational therapy, peace studies, philosophy, physical therapy, physics, political science/government, psychology, public administration, public relations, radio and television studies, religious studies, science, science education, secondary education, social science, social work, sociology, Spanish, statistics, theater arts/drama, toxicology, (pre)veterinary medicine sequence.

Emory University

Accounting, African studies, anthropology, art history, Asian/Oriental studies, biology/biological sciences, biomedical sciences, black/African-American studies, business administration/commerce/management, business economics, chemistry, classics, comparative literature, computer science, creative writing, East European and Soviet studies, economics, education, elementary education, English, film studies, finance/banking, French, Germanic languages and literature, Greek, history, human ecology, international studies, Italian, Judaic studies, Latin, Latin American studies, liberal arts/general studies, literature, marketing/retailing/merchandising, mathematics, medieval studies, music, nursing, philosophy, physics, political science/government, psychology, religious studies, Russian, secondary education, sociology, Spanish, theater arts/drama, women's studies.

Eugene Lang College, New School for Social Research

Anthropology, creative writing, economics, education, English, history, humanities, interdisciplinary studies, international studies, liberal arts/general studies, literature, music history, philosophy, political science/government, psychology, religious studies, science, social science, sociology, theater arts/drama, urban studies, women's studies.

Fairfield University

Accounting, American studies, art/fine arts, biology/biological sciences, business administration/commerce/management, chemistry, clinical psychology, communication, computer information systems, computer science, economics, English, finance/banking, French, German, history, international studies, management information systems, marketing/retailing/merchandising, mathematics, modern languages, music history, neurosciences, nursing, philosophy, physics, political science/government, psychology, religious studies, secondary education, sociology, Spanish.

Fashion Institute of Technology

Advertising, applied art, commercial art, fashion design and technology, fashion merchandising, illustration, industrial administration, industrial design, interior design, management engineering, manufacturing technology, marketing/retailing/merchandising, textile arts, textiles and clothing.

Fisk University

Accounting, art/fine arts, biology/biological sciences, business administration/commerce/management, chemistry, economics, English, finance/banking, French, health services administration, history, mathematics, music, music education, philosophy, physics, political science/government, psychology, public administration, religious studies, sociology, Spanish, speech/rhetoric/public address/debate, theater arts/drama.

Florida Institute of Technology

Accounting, aerospace engineering, aerospace sciences, applied mathematics, astronomy, astrophysics, aviation administration, behavioral sciences, biochemistry, biology/biological sciences, business administration/commerce/management, cell biology, chemical engineering, chemistry, civil engineering, clinical psychology, communication, computer engineering, computer management, computer programming, computer science, data processing, (pre)dentistry sequence, economics, education, electrical engineering, environmental biology, environmental engineering, environmental sciences, finance/banking, flight training, hospitality services, hotel and restaurant management, humanities, interdisciplinary studies, (pre)law sequence, liberal arts/general studies, marine biology, marine engineering, marketing/retailing/merchandising, mathematics, mechanical engineering, (pre)medicine sequence, microbiology, molecular biology, naval architecture, ocean engineering,

oceanography, physics, planetary and space sciences, psychology, science education, secondary education, technical writing, (pre)veterinary medicine sequence.

Florida State University

Accounting, actuarial science, advertising, American studies, anthropology, applied mathematics, archaeology, art education, art/fine arts, art history, art therapy, Asian/Oriental studies, bilingual/bicultural education, biochemistry, biology/biological sciences, botany/plant sciences, broadcasting, business administration/commerce/management, cell biology, chemical engineering, chemistry, child psychology/child development, civil engineering, classics, clinical psychology, communication, comparative literature, computer engineering, computer science, corrections, creative writing, criminal justice, criminology, dance, (pre)dentistry sequence, dietetics, early childhood education, East Asian studies, East European and Soviet studies, ecology, economics, education, electrical engineering, electronics engineering, elementary education, English, environmental engineering, environmental sciences, environmental studies, evolutionary biology, experimental psychology, family and consumer studies, family services, fashion design and technology, fashion merchandising, film and video production, film studies, finance/banking, food sciences, food services management, French, geography, geology, German, graphic arts, Greek, health education, history, home economics, home economics education, hotel and restaurant management, humanities, human resources, industrial engineering, information science, insurance, interior design, international business, international relations, Italian, Latin, Latin American studies, law enforcement/police sciences, (pre)law sequence, linguistics, literature, management information systems, marine biology, marketing/retailing/merchandising, mathematics, mechanical engineering, (pre)medicine sequence, meteorology, molecular biology, music, music education, music history, music therapy, neurosciences, nursing, nutrition, painting/drawing, parks management, philosophy, photography, physical education, physics, physiology, piano/organ, political science/government, printmaking, psychology, public relations, radio and television studies, reading education, real estate, recreation and leisure services, rehabilitation therapy, religious studies, Russian, Russian and Slavic studies, science education, sculpture, secondary education, Slavic languages, social science, social work, sociology, Spanish, special education, speech pathology and audiology, speech/rhetoric/public address/debate, sports administration, statistics, stringed instruments, studio art, systems engineering, textile arts, textiles and clothing, theater arts/drama, urban studies, (pre)veterinary medicine sequence, voice, wind and percussion instruments, zoology.

Fordham University

Accounting, African studies, American studies, anthropology, art/fine arts, art history, bilingual/bicultural education, biology/biological sciences, black/African-American studies, broadcasting, business administration/commerce/management, business economics, chemistry, classics, communication, comparative literature, computer information systems, computer management, computer science, creative writing, criminal justice, (pre)dentistry sequence, East European and Soviet studies, economics, education, elementary education, English, film studies, finance/banking, French, German, Germanic languages and literature, graphic arts, Greek, Hispanic studies, history, information science, interdisciplinary studies, international business, international relations, international studies, Italian, journalism, Latin, Latin American studies, (pre)law sequence, liberal arts/general studies, literature, management information systems, marketing/retailing/merchandising, mathematics, medical technology, (pre)medicine sequence, medieval studies, modern languages, music history, natural sciences, Near and Middle Eastern studies, peace studies, philosophy, photography, physical sciences, physics, political science/government, psychology, public administration, radio and television studies, religious studies, Romance languages, Russian, Russian and Slavic studies, science, science education, secondary education, social science, sociology, Spanish, studio art, theater arts/drama, theology, urban studies, (pre)veterinary medicine sequence, women's studies.

Franklin and Marshall College

Accounting, American studies, anthropology, art/fine arts, art history, biology/biological sciences, business administration/commerce/management, chemistry, classics, economics, English, French, geology, German, Greek, history, interdisciplinary studies, Latin, mathematics, music, neurosciences, philosophy, physics, political science/government, psychobiology, psychology, religious studies, sociology, Spanish, theater arts/drama.

Furman University

Accounting, art/fine arts, Asian/Oriental studies, biology/biological sciences, business administration/commerce/management, chemistry, computer science, economics, education, English, environmental sciences, French, German, Greek, history, Latin, mathematics, music, music education, music history, philosophy, physical fitness/exercise science, physics, political science/government, psychology, religious studies, sacred music, sociology, Spanish, theater arts/drama, urban studies.

Georgetown College

Accounting, American studies, art/fine arts, biology/biological sciences, business administration/commerce/management, chemistry, communication, computer information systems, computer science, (pre)dentistry sequence, early childhood education, ecology, education, elementary education, English, environmental sciences, European studies, finance/banking, French, German, history, international business, (pre)law sequence, management information systems, marketing/retailing/merchandising, mathematics, medical technology, (pre)medicine sequence, music, music education, nursing, philosophy, physical education, physics, piano/organ, political science/government, psychology, recreation and leisure services, religious studies, secondary education, sociology, Spanish, speech/rhetoric/public address/debate, theater arts/drama, voice.

Georgetown University

Accounting, American studies, Arabic, art/fine arts, biology/biological sciences, business administration/commerce/management, chemistry, Chinese, classics, computer science, (pre)dentistry sequence, economics, English, finance/banking, French, German, history, interdisciplinary studies, international business, international economics, international relations, Italian, Japanese, liberal arts/general studies, linguistics, marketing/retailing/merchandising, mathematics, (pre)medicine sequence, nursing, philosophy, physics, political science/government, Portuguese, psychology, religious studies, Russian, sociology, Spanish.

The George Washington University

Accounting, American studies, anthropology, applied mathematics, archaeology, art/fine arts, art history, Asian/Oriental studies, biology/biological sciences, business administration/commerce/management, business economics, chemistry, Chinese, civil engineering, classics, communication, computer engineering, computer science, criminal justice, dance, (pre)dentistry sequence, East Asian studies, economics, electrical engineering, emergency medical technology, engineering (general), engineering and applied sciences, English, environmental engineering, environmental sciences, European studies, finance/banking, French, geography, geology, Germanic languages and literature, history, humanities, human resources, human services, information science, interdisciplinary studies, international business,

international studies, journalism, Judaic studies, laboratory technologies, Latin American studies, (pre)law sequence, liberal arts/general studies, marketing/retailing/merchandising, mathematics, mechanical engineering, medical technology, (pre)medicine sequence, music, Near and Middle Eastern studies, philosophy, physical fitness/exercise science, physician's assistant studies, physics, political science/government, psychology, public affairs and policy studies, radio and television studies, radiological sciences, religious studies, Russian, Russian and Slavic studies, sociology, Spanish, speech pathology and audiology, speech/rhetoric/public address/debate, statistics, studio art, systems engineering, theater arts/drama.

Georgia Institute of Technology

Aerospace engineering, applied mathematics, architecture, atmospheric sciences, biology/biological sciences, business administration/commerce/management, ceramic engineering, chemical engineering, chemistry, civil engineering, computer engineering, computer science, construction management, construction technologies, earth science, economics, electrical engineering, engineering mechanics, engineering sciences, history of science, industrial design, industrial engineering, international studies, literature, materials engineering, mathematics, mechanical engineering, nuclear engineering, physics, psychology, technology and public affairs, textile engineering, textiles and clothing.

Gettysburg College

Accounting, anthropology, art/fine arts, art history, biochemistry, biology/biological sciences, business administration/commerce/management, chemistry, classics, computer science, (pre)dentistry sequence, economics, education, elementary education, English, environmental studies, French, German, Greek, history, international business, international economics, international relations, international studies, Latin, Latin American studies, (pre)law sequence, liberal arts/general studies, literature, marine biology, mathematics, (pre)medicine sequence, modern languages, music, music education, philosophy, physical education, physics, political science/government, psychology, religious studies, Romance languages, science, science education, secondary education, social science, sociology, South Asian studies, Spanish, studio art, theater arts/drama, (pre)veterinary medicine sequence, Western civilization and culture, women's studies.

GMI Engineering & Management Institute

Accounting, applied mathematics, business administration/commerce/management, computer engineering, computer information systems, computer science, electrical engineering, engineering physics, environmental sciences, industrial administration, industrial engineering, management information systems, manufacturing engineering, marketing/retailing/merchandising, mechanical engineering, statistics, systems engineering.

Goshen College

Accounting, art education, art/fine arts, art therapy, biblical studies, bilingual/bicultural education, biology/biological sciences, broadcasting, business administration/commerce/management, business education, chemistry, child care/child and family studies, communication, computer information systems, computer science, (pre)dentistry sequence, dietetics, early childhood education, economics, education, elementary education, English, family services, German, Hispanic studies, history, journalism, (pre)law sequence, liberal arts/general studies, mathematics, (pre)medicine sequence, music, music education, natural sciences, nursing, nutrition, physical education, physical sciences, physics, political science/government, psychology, religious studies, science education, secondary education, social work, sociology, Spanish, teaching English as a second language, theater arts/drama, (pre)veterinary medicine sequence.

Goucher College

American studies, anthropology, applied art, applied mathematics, art education, art/fine arts, art history, arts administration, behavioral sciences, biochemistry, biology/biological sciences, biomedical sciences, black/African-American studies, business administration/commerce/management, business economics, cell biology, chemistry, cognitive science, communication, computer programming, computer science, creative writing, dance, dance therapy, (pre)dentistry sequence, early childhood education, economics, education, elementary education, English, environmental biology, European studies, evolutionary biology, experimental psychology, French, German, historic preservation, history, interdisciplinary studies, international relations, international studies, Latin American studies, (pre)law sequence, liberal arts/general studies, marine biology, mathematics, (pre)medicine sequence, microbiology, modern languages, molecular biology, music, music history, peace studies, philosophy, physics, political science/government, psychology, public affairs and policy studies, radio and television studies, religious studies, Romance languages, Russian, Russian and Slavic studies, science, science education, secondary education, social science, social work, sociology, Spanish, special education, studio art, theater arts/drama, urban studies, (pre)veterinary medicine sequence, voice, wind and percussion instruments, women's studies.

Grinnell College

American studies, anthropology, art/fine arts, biology/biological sciences, black/African-American studies, chemistry, Chinese, classics, computer science, (pre)dentistry sequence, economics, English, environmental studies, European studies, French, German, history, interdisciplinary studies, Latin American studies, (pre)law sequence, linguistics, mathematics, (pre)medicine sequence, music, philosophy, physical sciences, physics, political science/government, psychology, religious studies, Russian, Russian and Slavic studies, science, sociology, Spanish, technology and public affairs, theater arts/drama, (pre)veterinary medicine sequence, women's studies.

Grove City College

Accounting, biochemistry, biology/biological sciences, business administration/commerce/management, business economics, chemistry, communication, computer management, (pre)dentistry sequence, early childhood education, economics, electrical engineering, elementary education, English, finance/banking, French, history, industrial administration, international studies, (pre)law sequence, literature, marketing/retailing/merchandising, mathematics, mechanical engineering, (pre)medicine sequence, ministries, modern languages, molecular biology, music business, music education, philosophy, physics, political science/government, psychology, religious studies, science education, secondary education, Spanish, (pre)veterinary medicine sequence.

Guilford College

Accounting, anthropology, art/fine arts, biology/biological sciences, black/African-American studies, business administration/commerce/management, chemistry, communication, criminal justice, (pre)dentistry sequence, early childhood education, economics, education, elementary education, English, environmental studies, French, geology, German, history, humanities, international studies, (pre)law sequence, liberal arts/general studies, mathematics, (pre)medicine sequence, medieval studies, music, peace studies, philosophy, physical education, physician's assistant studies, physics, political science/government, psychology, religious studies, secondary education, sociology, Spanish, sports administration, sports medicine, theater arts/drama, (pre)veterinary medicine sequence, women's studies.

Gustavus Adolphus College

Accounting, American studies, anthropology, art education, art/fine arts, arts administration, athletic training, biochemistry, biology/biological sciences, business administration/commerce/management, business economics, chemistry, classics, communication, computer science, criminal justice, dance, (pre)dentistry sequence, economics, education, elementary education, English, French, geography, geology, German, health education, history, interdisciplinary studies, international business, Latin American studies, (pre)law sequence, mathematics, (pre)medicine sequence, music, music education, nursing, occupational therapy, philosophy, physical education, physical therapy, physics, political science/government, psychology, religious studies, Russian, Russian and Slavic studies, sacred music, Scandinavian languages/studies, secondary education, social science, sociology, Spanish, speech/rhetoric/public address/debate, theater arts/drama, (pre)veterinary medicine sequence.

Hamilton College

African studies, American studies, anthropology, art/fine arts, art history, Asian/Oriental studies, biochemistry, biology/biological sciences, chemistry, classics, comparative literature, computer science, creative writing, dance, East Asian studies, economics, English, French, geology, German, Greek, history, international studies, Latin, linguistics, literature, mathematics, modern languages, molecular biology, music, Near and Middle Eastern studies, philosophy, physics, political science/government, psychobiology, psychology, public affairs and policy studies, religious studies, Russian and Slavic studies, sociology, Spanish, studio art, theater arts/drama, Western civilization and culture, women's studies.

Hamline University

Anthropology, art/fine arts, art history, Asian/Oriental studies, athletic training, biology/biological sciences, business administration/commerce/management, chemistry, communication, criminal justice, (pre)dentistry sequence, East Asian studies, East European and Soviet studies, economics, education, elementary education, English, environmental sciences, environmental studies, European studies, French, German, health education, history, international business, international economics, international studies, Judaic studies, Latin American studies, (pre)law sequence, legal studies, mathematics, medical technology, (pre)medicine sequence, music, music education, occupational therapy, paralegal studies, philosophy, physical education, physical fitness/exercise science, physical therapy, physics, political science/government, psychology, public administration, religious studies, Russian and Slavic studies, science education, secondary education, social science, sociology, Spanish, studio art, theater arts/drama, urban studies, (pre)veterinary medicine sequence, women's studies.

Hampden-Sydney College

Art/fine arts, biochemistry, biology/biological sciences, biophysics, business economics, chemistry, classics, computer science, economics, English, French, German, Greek, history, humanities, Latin, mathematics, philosophy, physics, political science/government, psychology, public affairs and policy studies, religious studies, Spanish.

Hampshire College

African studies, agricultural sciences, American studies, anatomy, animal sciences, anthropology, applied mathematics, archaeology, architecture, art/fine arts, art history, Asian/Oriental studies, astronomy, astrophysics, bacteriology, behavioral sciences, biochemistry, biology/biological sciences, biophysics, black/African-American studies, botany/plant sciences, Canadian studies, cell biology, chemistry, child care/child and family studies, child psychology/child development, city/community/regional planning, cognitive science, communication, community services, comparative literature, computer graphics, computer programming, computer science, conservation, creative writing, dance, early childhood education, earth science, East Asian studies, East European and Soviet studies, ecology, economics, education, elementary education, English, environmental biology, environmental design, environmental health sciences, environmental sciences, environmental studies, ethnic studies, European studies, evolutionary biology, family and consumer studies, film and video production, film studies, genetics, geochemistry, geography, geology, geophysics, graphic arts, health science, Hispanic studies, history, history of philosophy, history of science, human development, humanities, information science, interdisciplinary studies, international business, international economics, international relations, international studies, Islamic studies, jazz, journalism, Judaic studies, labor and industrial relations, labor studies, Latin American studies, legal studies, liberal arts/general studies, linguistics, literature, marine biology, marine sciences, mathematics, (pre)medicine sequence, medieval studies, Mexican-American/Chicano studies, microbiology, molecular biology, music, music history, Native American studies, natural sciences, Near and Middle Eastern studies, neurosciences, nutrition, oceanography, painting/drawing, peace studies, philosophy, photography, physical fitness/exercise science, physical sciences, physics, physiology, political science/government, psychobiology, psychology, public affairs and policy studies, public health, radio and television studies, religious studies, Russian and Slavic studies, science, sculpture, secondary education, social science, sociobiology, sociology, solar technologies, South Asian studies, Southeast Asian studies, statistics, studio art, telecommunications, theater arts/drama, urban studies, (pre)veterinary medicine sequence, women's studies.

Harding University

Accounting, advertising, American studies, art education, art/fine arts, art history, biblical languages, biblical studies, biochemistry, biology/biological sciences, business administration/commerce/management, business education, chemistry, communication, computer information systems, computer programming, computer science, data processing, (pre)dentistry sequence, dietetics, early childhood education, economics, education, elementary education, English, fashion merchandising, finance/banking, food marketing, food services management, French, history, home economics, home economics education, interior design, international studies, journalism, (pre)law sequence, marketing/retailing/merchandising, mathematics, (pre)medicine sequence, modern languages, music, music education, nursing, painting/drawing, physical education, physics, piano/organ, political science/government, psychology, public administration, public relations, radio and television studies, religious education, religious studies, science, science education, secondary education, social science, social work, sociology, Spanish, special education, speech pathology and audiology, speech/rhetoric/public address/debate, sports administration, stringed instruments, systems science, theater arts/drama, theology, (pre)veterinary medicine sequence, voice.

Harvard University

African languages, African studies, American studies, anthropology, applied mathematics, Arabic, archaeology, art/fine arts, art history, Asian/Oriental studies, astronomy, astrophysics, biblical languages, biochemistry, bioengineering, biology/biological sciences, biomedical engineering, biophysics, black/African-American studies, cell biology, chemistry, Chinese, classics, comparative literature, computer science, earth science, East Asian studies, East European and Soviet studies, ecology, economics, engineering (general), engineering and applied sciences, engineering physics, engineering sciences, English, environmental design, environmental engineering, environmental sciences, environmental studies, ethnic studies, European studies, folklore, French, geology, geophysics, German, Germanic languages

and literature, Greek, Hebrew, Hispanic studies, history, history of philosophy, history of science, humanities, information science, interdisciplinary studies, Italian, Japanese, Judaic studies, Latin, linguistics, literature, materials engineering, mathematics, mechanical engineering, medieval studies, modern languages, molecular biology, music, music history, Near and Middle Eastern studies, neurosciences, philosophy, physical sciences, physics, planetary and space sciences, political science/government, Portuguese, psychology, religious studies, Romance languages, Russian, Russian and Slavic studies, Scandinavian languages/studies, science, Slavic languages, social science, sociology, South Asian studies, Southeast Asian studies, Spanish, statistics, systems engineering, urban studies, Western civilization and culture, women's studies.

Harvey Mudd College

Biology/biological sciences, chemistry, computer science, engineering (general), mathematics, physics.

Haverford College

African studies, anthropology, archaeology, art/fine arts, art history, astronomy, biochemistry, biology/biological sciences, biophysics, chemistry, classics, comparative literature, computer science, East Asian studies, economics, education, English, French, geology, German, Greek, history, international studies, Italian, Latin, Latin American studies, (pre)law sequence, mathematics, (pre)medicine sequence, music, neurosciences, peace studies, philosophy, physics, political science/government, psychology, religious studies, Romance languages, Russian, sociology, Spanish, urban studies, (pre)veterinary medicine sequence, women's studies.

Hendrix College

Accounting, American studies, art/fine arts, biology/biological sciences, business economics, chemistry, communication, (pre)dentistry sequence, economics, education, elementary education, English, French, German, history, humanities, international business, international studies, (pre)law sequence, mathematics, (pre)medicine sequence, music, philosophy, physical education, physics, political science/government, psychology, religious studies, sociology, Spanish, theater arts/drama, (pre)veterinary medicine sequence.

Hillsdale College

Accounting, American studies, art/fine arts, biology/biological sciences, business administration/commerce/management, chemistry, classics, comparative literature, computer science, (pre)dentistry sequence, early childhood education, economics, education, elementary education, English, European studies, finance/banking, French, German, history, interdisciplinary studies, international studies, marketing/retailing/merchandising, mathematics, (pre)medicine sequence, music, philosophy, physical education, physics, political science/government, psychology, religious studies, secondary education, sociology, Spanish, speech/rhetoric/public address/debate, theater arts/drama, (pre)veterinary medicine sequence.

Hiram College

Art/fine arts, art history, biology/biological sciences, business administration/commerce/management, chemistry, classics, communication, computer science, (pre)dentistry sequence, economics, elementary education, English, French, German, history, international business, international economics, (pre)law sequence, mathematics, (pre)medicine sequence, music, philosophy, physics, political science/government, psychobiology, psychology, religious studies, secondary education, social science, sociology, Spanish, studio art, theater arts/drama, (pre)veterinary medicine sequence.

Hobart College

American studies, anthropology, architecture, art/fine arts, art history, Asian/Oriental studies, biochemistry, biology/biological sciences, black/African-American studies, chemistry, Chinese, classics, comparative literature, computer science, dance, (pre)dentistry sequence, economics, English, environmental studies, French, geology, German, Greek, history, interdisciplinary studies, Japanese, Judaic studies, Latin, (pre)law sequence, mathematics, (pre)medicine sequence, medieval studies, modern languages, music, philosophy, physics, political science/government, psychology, religious studies, Russian, Russian and Slavic studies, sociology, Spanish, studio art, theater arts/drama, urban studies, (pre)veterinary medicine sequence, women's studies.

Hofstra University

Accounting, African studies, American studies, anthropology, art education, art/fine arts, art history, Asian/Oriental studies, athletic training, biochemistry, biology/biological sciences, black/African-American studies, broadcasting, business administration/commerce/management, business education, chemistry, classics, communication, computer information systems, computer science, dance, economics, education, electrical engineering, elementary education, engineering (general), engineering sciences, English, environmental sciences, film and video production, film studies, finance/banking, French, geography, geology, German, Hebrew, history, humanities, industrial engineering, interdisciplinary studies, international business, Italian, journalism, Judaic studies, liberal arts/general studies, marketing/retailing/merchandising, mathematics, mechanical engineering, modern languages, music, music business, music education, music history, natural sciences, philosophy, physical education, physical fitness/exercise science, physics, political science/government, psychology, radio and television studies, Russian, science, science education, secondary education, social science, sociology, Spanish, speech pathology and audiology, speech/rhetoric/public address/debate, theater arts/drama.

Hope College

Accounting, art education, art/fine arts, art history, biochemistry, biology/biological sciences, business administration/commerce/management, chemistry, classics, communication, computer science, dance, dance therapy, (pre)dentistry sequence, economics, education, elementary education, engineering physics, English, environmental sciences, French, geochemistry, geology, geophysics, German, history, humanities, interdisciplinary studies, international studies, Latin, mathematics, medical technology, (pre)medicine sequence, music, music education, nursing, philosophy, physical education, physical fitness/exercise science, physics, political science/government, psychology, religious education, religious studies, science education, secondary education, social work, sociology, Spanish, special education, sports medicine, studio art, theater arts/drama, (pre)veterinary medicine sequence.

Houghton College

Accounting, art education, art/fine arts, biblical studies, biology/biological sciences, business administration/commerce/management, chemistry, communication, creative writing, (pre)dentistry sequence, early childhood education, education, elementary education, English, French, history, humanities, international studies, (pre)law sequence, literature, mathematics, medical laboratory technology, medical technology, (pre)medicine sequence, ministries, music, music education, natural sciences, pastoral studies, philosophy, physical education, physical sciences, physics, piano/organ, political science/government, psychology, recreation and leisure services, religious education, religious studies, sacred music, science, science education, secondary

education, social science, sociology, Spanish, stringed instruments, (pre)veterinary medicine sequence, voice, wind and percussion instruments.

Illinois College

Accounting, art/fine arts, biology/biological sciences, business administration/commerce/management, business economics, chemistry, communication, computer information systems, computer science, cytotechnology, (pre)dentistry sequence, economics, education, elementary education, English, finance/banking, French, German, history, interdisciplinary studies, international studies, (pre)law sequence, liberal arts/general studies, management information systems, mathematics, medical technology, (pre)medicine sequence, music, occupational therapy, philosophy, physical education, physics, political science/government, psychology, religious studies, secondary education, sociology, Spanish, speech/rhetoric/public address/debate, theater arts/drama, (pre)veterinary medicine sequence.

Illinois Institute of Technology

Aerospace engineering, applied mathematics, architectural engineering, architecture, biology/biological sciences, chemical engineering, chemistry, civil engineering, computer engineering, computer science, electrical engineering, environmental engineering, (pre)law sequence, manufacturing technology, materials engineering, mechanical engineering, (pre)medicine sequence, metallurgical engineering, physics, political science/government, psychology.

Illinois Wesleyan University

Accounting, applied art, art/fine arts, art history, arts administration, biology/biological sciences, business administration/commerce/management, chemistry, computer science, (pre)dentistry sequence, economics, education, elementary education, English, European studies, French, German, graphic arts, history, insurance, interdisciplinary studies, international business, international studies, Latin American studies, (pre)law sequence, liberal arts/general studies, mathematics, medical technology, (pre)medicine sequence, music, music business, music education, nursing, painting/drawing, philosophy, physics, piano/organ, political science/government, psychology, religious studies, sacred music, science education, secondary education, sociology, Spanish, stringed instruments, studio art, theater arts/drama, (pre)veterinary medicine sequence, voice, wind and percussion instruments.

Iowa State University of Science and Technology

Accounting, advertising, aerospace engineering, agricultural business, agricultural education, agricultural engineering, agricultural sciences, agricultural technologies, agronomy/soil and crop sciences, animal sciences, anthropology, applied art, architecture, art/fine arts, biochemistry, biology/biological sciences, biophysics, botany/plant sciences, broadcasting, business administration/commerce/management, ceramic engineering, chemical engineering, chemistry, child care/child and family studies, child psychology/child development, city/community/regional planning, civil engineering, communication, community services, computer engineering, computer science, construction engineering, consumer services, dairy sciences, (pre)dentistry sequence, dietetics, early childhood education, earth science, ecology, economics, education, electrical engineering, elementary education, engineering (general), engineering sciences, English, entomology, environmental studies, family and consumer studies, family services, farm and ranch management, fashion design and technology, fashion merchandising, finance/banking, fish and game management, food sciences, food services management, food services technology, forestry, French, genetics, geology, German, graphic arts, health education, history, home economics, home economics education, horticulture, hotel and restaurant management, industrial engineering, interdisciplinary studies, interior design, international studies, journalism, landscape architecture/design, (pre)law sequence, liberal arts/general studies, linguistics, management information systems, marketing/retailing/merchandising, mathematics, mechanical engineering, medical illustration, (pre)medicine sequence, metallurgical engineering, meteorology, microbiology, music, music education, naval sciences, nutrition, ornamental horticulture, philosophy, physical education, physics, political science/government, psychology, public administration, religious studies, Russian, secondary education, social work, sociology, Spanish, speech/rhetoric/public address/debate, statistics, textiles and clothing, theater arts/drama, transportation technologies, (pre)veterinary medicine sequence, vocational education, wildlife biology, zoology.

James Madison University

Accounting, anthropology, art/fine arts, art history, biology/biological sciences, business administration/commerce/management, business economics, chemistry, communication, computer information systems, computer science, (pre)dentistry sequence, dietetics, early childhood education, economics, elementary education, English, finance/banking, French, geography, geology, German, health science, history, hospitality services, international business, international studies, (pre)law sequence, liberal arts/general studies, library science, marketing/retailing/merchandising, mathematics, medical technology, (pre)medicine sequence, modern languages, music, nursing, philosophy, physical education, political science/government, psychology, public administration, religious studies, Russian, secretarial studies/office management, social science, social work, sociology, Spanish, special education, speech pathology and audiology, theater arts/drama, (pre)veterinary medicine sequence.

John Carroll University

Accounting, art history, Asian/Oriental studies, biology/biological sciences, business administration/commerce/management, chemistry, classics, communication, computer science, (pre)dentistry sequence, early childhood education, East Asian studies, economics, education, electrical engineering, elementary education, engineering physics, English, environmental studies, finance/banking, French, German, gerontology, Greek, history, humanities, interdisciplinary studies, international economics, international studies, Judaic studies, Latin, (pre)law sequence, literature, marketing/retailing/merchandising, mathematics, (pre)medicine sequence, neurosciences, philosophy, physical education, physics, political science/government, psychology, public administration, religious education, religious studies, science, secondary education, sociology, Spanish, special education, (pre)veterinary medicine sequence.

Johns Hopkins University

Anthropology, Arabic, art history, astronomy, astrophysics, behavioral sciences, bioengineering, biology/biological sciences, biomedical engineering, biophysics, chemical engineering, chemistry, civil engineering, classics, cognitive science, computer engineering, computer science, creative writing, earth science, East Asian studies, economics, electrical engineering, engineering (general), engineering mechanics, English, environmental engineering, environmental sciences, French, geography, German, Hispanic studies, history, history of science, humanities, international studies, Italian, Latin American studies, liberal arts/general studies, materials engineering, materials sciences, mathematics, mechanical engineering, music, natural sciences, Near and Middle Eastern studies, philosophy, physics, planetary and space sciences, political science/government, psychobiology, psychology, Russian, social science, sociology, Spanish.

Juilliard School

Dance, music, opera, piano/organ, stringed instruments, theater arts/drama, voice, wind and percussion instruments.

Juniata College

Accounting, American studies, anthropology, applied mathematics, art/fine arts, art history, arts administration, behavioral sciences, biochemistry, biology/biological sciences, botany/plant sciences, business administration/commerce/management, business economics, chemistry, communication, computer science, criminal justice, criminology, cytotechnology, (pre)dentistry sequence, drug and alcohol/substance abuse counseling, early childhood education, earth science, East European and Soviet studies, ecology, economics, education, elementary education, engineering (general), engineering sciences, English, environmental biology, environmental sciences, environmental studies, European studies, experimental psychology, finance/banking, French, genetics, geology, German, health science, history, humanities, human resources, human services, interdisciplinary studies, international business, international relations, international studies, journalism, labor and industrial relations, (pre)law sequence, liberal arts/general studies, literature, management information systems, marine biology, marine sciences, marketing/retailing/merchandising, mathematics, medical technology, (pre)medicine sequence, microbiology, molecular biology, music, natural sciences, peace studies, philosophy, physics, political science/government, psychology, public administration, public relations, radiological technology, religious studies, Russian, science, science education, secondary education, social science, social work, sociology, Spanish, speech/rhetoric/public address/debate, studio art, (pre)veterinary medicine sequence, voice, Western civilization and culture, wildlife biology.

Kalamazoo College

African studies, anthropology, art/fine arts, art history, biology/biological sciences, black/African-American studies, business administration/commerce/management, business economics, chemistry, Chinese, classics, computer science, (pre)dentistry sequence, economics, English, environmental sciences, European studies, French, German, Greek, health science, history, human development, human resources, human services, international business, international economics, international studies, Italian, Japanese, Latin, (pre)law sequence, literature, mathematics, (pre)medicine sequence, modern languages, music, philosophy, physics, political science/government, psychology, public affairs and policy studies, religious studies, Romance languages, Russian, secondary education, sociology, Spanish, studio art, theater arts/drama, (pre)veterinary medicine sequence, women's studies.

Kentucky Wesleyan College

Accounting, art education, art/fine arts, biology/biological sciences, business administration/commerce/management, chemistry, communication, computer science, criminal justice, (pre)dentistry sequence, elementary education, English, environmental studies, history, human resources, (pre)law sequence, mathematics, medical technology, (pre)medicine sequence, middle school education, modern languages, music, music education, nursing, philosophy, physical education, physics, political science/government, psychology, radio and television studies, religious studies, secondary education, social science, sociology, speech/rhetoric/public address/debate, telecommunications, theater arts/drama, (pre)veterinary medicine sequence.

Kenyon College

American studies, anthropology, art/fine arts, art history, Asian/Oriental studies, biochemistry, biology/biological sciences, black/

African-American studies, chemistry, classics, computer science, creative writing, dance, (pre)dentistry sequence, economics, English, environmental studies, French, German, Greek, history, humanities, interdisciplinary studies, international studies, Latin, (pre)law sequence, literature, mathematics, (pre)medicine sequence, modern languages, molecular biology, music, natural sciences, philosophy, physics, political science/government, psychology, religious studies, Romance languages, sociology, Spanish, studio art, theater arts/drama, (pre)veterinary medicine sequence, women's studies.

Knox College

American studies, anthropology, art/fine arts, art history, biochemistry, biology/biological sciences, black/African-American studies, chemistry, classics, computer science, creative writing, economics, education, elementary education, English, environmental studies, French, German, history, interdisciplinary studies, international relations, (pre)law sequence, literature, mathematics, (pre)medicine sequence, modern languages, music, philosophy, physics, political science/government, psychology, religious studies, Russian, Russian and Slavic studies, secondary education, sociology, Spanish, studio art, theater arts/drama, (pre)veterinary medicine sequence, women's studies.

Lafayette College

American studies, anthropology, art/fine arts, art history, biochemistry, biology/biological sciences, business economics, chemical engineering, chemistry, civil engineering, computer science, economics, electrical engineering, engineering (general), English, environmental engineering, French, geology, German, history, international studies, mathematics, mechanical engineering, music, music history, philosophy, physics, political science/government, psychology, religious studies, Russian and Slavic studies, sociology, Spanish, studio art.

Lake Forest College

African studies, American studies, anthropology, art history, Asian/Oriental studies, biology/biological sciences, business economics, chemistry, city/community/regional planning, comparative literature, computer science, (pre)dentistry sequence, economics, education, elementary education, English, environmental sciences, European studies, finance/banking, French, German, history, international relations, international studies, Latin American studies, (pre)law sequence, mathematics, (pre)medicine sequence, music, Near and Middle Eastern studies, philosophy, physics, political science/government, psychology, public administration, secondary education, sociology, Spanish, studio art, urban studies, (pre)veterinary medicine sequence, women's studies.

La Salle University

Accounting, applied mathematics, art education, art/fine arts, art history, biochemistry, biology/biological sciences, broadcasting, business administration/commerce/management, business economics, business education, chemistry, classics, communication, computer information systems, computer programming, computer science, creative writing, criminal justice, (pre)dentistry sequence, early childhood education, earth science, economics, education, elementary education, English, environmental sciences, film studies, finance/banking, French, geology, German, Germanic languages and literature, Greek, health services administration, history, human resources, information science, international business, international economics, international studies, Italian, journalism, labor and industrial relations, labor studies, Latin, (pre)law sequence, liberal arts/general studies, literature, management information systems, marketing/retailing/merchandising, mathematics, (pre)medicine sequence, modern languages, music, music history, nursing, philosophy, physics, political science/government, psychology, public

administration, radio and television studies, religious education, religious studies, retail management, Russian, Russian and Slavic studies, science education, secondary education, social science, social work, sociology, Spanish, special education, speech/rhetoric/public address/debate, theology, (pre)veterinary medicine sequence, women's studies.

Lawrence University

Anthropology, art history, biology/biological sciences, chemistry, classics, cognitive science, computer science, (pre)dentistry sequence, East Asian studies, ecology, economics, English, environmental sciences, French, geology, German, history, international economics, international studies, (pre)law sequence, linguistics, mathematics, (pre)medicine sequence, music, music education, neurosciences, philosophy, physics, piano/organ, political science/government, psychology, religious studies, Russian, Russian and Slavic studies, secondary education, Slavic languages, Spanish, stringed instruments, studio art, theater arts/drama, (pre)veterinary medicine sequence, voice, wind and percussion instruments, women's studies.

Lehigh University

Accounting, American studies, anthropology, applied mathematics, architecture, art/fine arts, behavioral sciences, biochemistry, biology/biological sciences, business administration/commerce/management, business economics, chemical engineering, chemistry, civil engineering, classics, cognitive science, computer engineering, computer science, (pre)dentistry sequence, East Asian studies, economics, electrical engineering, engineering and applied sciences, engineering mechanics, engineering physics, English, environmental sciences, finance/banking, French, geology, geophysics, German, history, industrial engineering, international business, international relations, journalism, (pre)law sequence, marketing/retailing/merchandising, materials engineering, mathematics, mechanical engineering, (pre)medicine sequence, metallurgy, modern languages, molecular biology, music, natural sciences, neurosciences, philosophy, physics, political science/government, psychology, religious studies, Russian and Slavic studies, social science, sociology, Spanish, statistics, technical writing, theater arts/drama, urban studies, (pre)veterinary medicine sequence.

Le Moyne College

Accounting, actuarial science, biology/biological sciences, business administration/commerce/management, business education, chemistry, communication, computer science, criminal justice, (pre)dentistry sequence, economics, education, elementary education, English, finance/banking, French, history, human resources, international business, international studies, labor and industrial relations, (pre)law sequence, marketing/retailing/merchandising, mathematics, (pre)medicine sequence, modern languages, operations research, philosophy, physics, political science/government, psychology, religious studies, science, science education, secondary education, sociology, Spanish, special education, statistics, teaching English as a second language, urban studies, (pre)veterinary medicine sequence.

LeTourneau University

Accounting, aircraft and missile maintenance, aviation technology, biblical studies, biology/biological sciences, business administration/commerce/management, chemistry, computer engineering, computer science, computer technologies, (pre)dentistry sequence, electrical engineering, electrical engineering technology, engineering (general), engineering technology, English, flight training, history, industrial administration, (pre)law sequence, marketing/retailing/merchandising, mathematics, mechanical engineering, mechanical engineering technology, (pre)medicine sequence, ministries, natural sciences, physical education, physics, psychology, public administration, religious studies, secondary education, sports administration, (pre)veterinary medicine sequence, welding engineering, welding technology.

Lewis & Clark College

Anthropology, art/fine arts, biochemistry, biology/biological sciences, business administration/commerce/management, chemistry, communication, computer science, (pre)dentistry sequence, East Asian studies, economics, English, French, German, Hispanic studies, history, international studies, (pre)law sequence, mathematics, (pre)medicine sequence, modern languages, music, philosophy, physics, political science/government, psychology, religious studies, sociology, Spanish, theater arts/drama, (pre)veterinary medicine sequence.

Linfield College

Accounting, anthropology, art education, art/fine arts, arts administration, biology/biological sciences, botany/plant sciences, business administration/commerce/management, chemistry, child psychology/child development, communication, computer science, creative writing, (pre)dentistry sequence, early childhood education, earth science, ecology, economics, education, elementary education, English, finance/banking, French, German, health education, history, humanities, information science, international business, Japanese, journalism, (pre)law sequence, liberal arts/general studies, mathematics, medical technology, (pre)medicine sequence, modern languages, music, music education, natural sciences, nursing, philosophy, physical education, physics, political science/government, psychology, public relations, radio and television studies, religious studies, science, science education, secondary education, sociology, Spanish, studio art, systems science, theater arts/drama, (pre)veterinary medicine sequence.

Louisiana State University and Agricultural and Mechanical College

Accounting, advertising, agricultural business, agricultural economics, agricultural education, agricultural engineering, agronomy/soil and crop sciences, animal sciences, anthropology, architecture, art/fine arts, art history, Asian/Oriental studies, astronomy, biochemistry, black/African-American studies, botany/plant sciences, broadcasting, business administration/commerce/management, business economics, business education, ceramic art and design, chemical engineering, chemistry, child care/child and family studies, civil engineering, classics, communication, computer engineering, computer science, construction management, construction technologies, consumer services, corrections, criminology, culinary arts, dairy sciences, (pre)dentistry sequence, dietetics, earth science, economics, electrical engineering, elementary education, English, entomology, environmental engineering, environmental sciences, family and consumer studies, family services, fashion merchandising, finance/banking, fish and game management, food sciences, forestry, French, geography, geology, German, graphic arts, Greek, health science, history, home economics education, horticulture, human services, industrial arts, industrial engineering, interior design, international economics, Italian, jewelry and metalsmithing, journalism, Judaic studies, landscape architecture/design, Latin, (pre)law sequence, liberal arts/general studies, linguistics, literature, management information systems, marketing/retailing/merchandising, mathematics, mechanical engineering, (pre)medicine sequence, microbiology, music, music education, nutrition, occupational safety and health, painting/drawing, petroleum/natural gas engineering, philosophy, photography, physical education, physical fitness/exercise science, physics, piano/organ, political science/government, poultry sciences, printmaking, psychology, public relations, religious studies, Russian, Russian and Slavic studies, sculpture, secondary education, sociology, Spanish, speech pathology and audiology, speech/rhetoric/public address/

debate, statistics, stringed instruments, studio art, surveying technology, textiles and clothing, theater arts/drama, (pre)veterinary medicine sequence, vocational education, voice, wildlife management, wind and percussion instruments, women's studies, zoology.

Loyola College

Accounting, advertising, art/fine arts, art history, biology/biological sciences, business administration/commerce/management, business economics, chemistry, classics, communication, computer engineering, computer science, creative writing, (pre)dentistry sequence, economics, education, electrical engineering, elementary education, engineering (general), engineering sciences, English, finance/banking, French, German, history, interdisciplinary studies, international business, journalism, Latin, (pre)law sequence, management information systems, marketing/retailing/merchandising, mathematics, (pre)medicine sequence, military science, ministries, modern languages, music, pastoral studies, philosophy, photography, physics, political science/government, psychology, public relations, secondary education, sociology, Spanish, speech pathology and audiology, studio art, theater arts/drama, theology, (pre)veterinary medicine sequence.

Loyola University Chicago

Accounting, anthropology, art/fine arts, biology/biological sciences, business administration/commerce/management, business economics, chemistry, classics, communication, computer information systems, computer science, criminal justice, (pre)dentistry sequence, economics, elementary education, English, finance/banking, food sciences, French, German, Greek, history, Italian, Latin, (pre)law sequence, management information systems, marketing/retailing/merchandising, mathematics, (pre)medicine sequence, music, nursing, nutrition, philosophy, physics, political science/government, psychology, social work, sociology, Spanish, special education, speech/rhetoric/public address/debate, statistics, theater arts/drama, theology, (pre)veterinary medicine sequence.

Luther College

Accounting, African studies, anthropology, art education, art/fine arts, arts administration, biology/biological sciences, black/African-American studies, business administration/commerce/management, chemistry, classics, communication, computer science, cytotechnology, dance, (pre)dentistry sequence, early childhood education, economics, education, elementary education, English, environmental biology, French, German, Greek, health education, Hebrew, history, interdisciplinary studies, international business, international studies, Latin, Latin American studies, (pre)law sequence, management information systems, marine biology, mathematics, medical technology, (pre)medicine sequence, modern languages, museum studies, music, music business, music education, nursing, philosophy, physical education, physics, political science/government, psychobiology, psychology, religious studies, Scandinavian languages/studies, secondary education, social work, sociology, Spanish, special education, speech pathology and audiology, speech/rhetoric/public address/debate, sports administration, sports medicine, statistics, theater arts/drama, (pre)veterinary medicine sequence.

Lyon College

Accounting, art/fine arts, biology/biological sciences, chemistry, economics, elementary education, English, history, human resources, journalism, mathematics, music, philosophy, political science/government, psychology, religious studies, secondary education, Spanish, theater arts/drama.

Macalester College

Anthropology, art history, biology/biological sciences, chemistry, classics, communication, computer science, East Asian studies, economics, English, environmental studies, French, geography, geology, German, Greek, history, humanities, international studies, Latin, Latin American studies, linguistics, mathematics, music, philosophy, physics, political science/government, psychology, religious studies, Russian, Russian and Slavic studies, social science, sociology, Spanish, studio art, theater arts/drama, urban studies, women's studies.

Manhattan School of Music
Jazz, music, piano/organ, stringed instruments, voice, wind and percussion instruments.

Mannes College of Music, New School for Social Research
Jazz, music, opera, piano/organ, stringed instruments, voice, wind and percussion instruments.

Marietta College
Accounting, adult and continuing education, advertising, art/fine arts, athletic training, biochemistry, biology/biological sciences, business administration/commerce/management, chemistry, communication, computer information systems, computer science, (pre)dentistry sequence, economics, education, elementary education, engineering (general), English, environmental sciences, French, geology, history, human resources, industrial engineering, international business, journalism, (pre)law sequence, liberal arts/general studies, marketing/retailing/merchandising, mathematics, (pre)medicine sequence, modern languages, music, petroleum/natural gas engineering, philosophy, physics, political science/government, psychology, public relations, radio and television studies, secondary education, Spanish, speech/rhetoric/public address/debate, sports medicine, studio art, theater arts/drama, (pre)veterinary medicine sequence.

Marlboro College
African studies, American studies, anthropology, applied mathematics, art/fine arts, art history, Asian/Oriental studies, astronomy, astrophysics, behavioral sciences, biblical studies, biochemistry, biology/biological sciences, botany/plant sciences, cell biology, ceramic art and design, chemistry, child psychology/child development, classics, comparative literature, computer science, conservation, creative writing, dance, (pre)dentistry sequence, earth science, East Asian studies, East European and Soviet studies, ecology, economics, energy management technologies, English, environmental biology, environmental design, environmental education, environmental sciences, ethnic studies, European studies, experimental psychology, film studies, folklore, forestry, French, German, Greek, history, history of philosophy, human ecology, humanities, interdisciplinary studies, international economics, international studies, Italian, jazz, Latin, Latin American studies, (pre)law sequence, linguistics, literature, marine biology, mathematics, (pre)medicine sequence, medieval studies, microbiology, modern languages, molecular biology, music, music history, natural sciences, painting/drawing, peace studies, philosophy, photography, physical sciences, physics, piano/organ, planetary and space sciences, political science/government, Portuguese, psychology, religious studies, Romance languages, Russian, Russian and Slavic studies, sacred music, Scandinavian languages/studies, sculpture, social science, social work, sociology, solar technologies, Spanish, stringed instruments, studio art, theater arts/drama, (pre)veterinary medicine sequence, voice, wind and percussion instruments, women's studies, wood sciences.

Marquette University
Accounting, advertising, anthropology, biochemistry, biology/biological sciences, biomedical engineering, broadcasting, business administration/commerce/management, business economics, chemistry, civil engineering, classics, communication, computer engineering, computer information systems, computer science,

construction engineering, criminal justice, criminology, dental services, (pre)dentistry sequence, economics, education, electrical engineering, electronics engineering, elementary education, engineering (general), English, environmental engineering, finance/banking, French, German, history, human development, humanities, human resources, industrial engineering, interdisciplinary studies, international business, international relations, journalism, (pre)law sequence, management information systems, manufacturing engineering, marketing/retailing/merchandising, materials engineering, mathematics, mechanical engineering, medical laboratory technology, (pre)medicine sequence, middle school education, molecular biology, natural sciences, nursing, philosophy, physics, political science/government, psychology, public relations, secondary education, social science, social work, sociology, Spanish, speech pathology and audiology, speech/rhetoric/public address/debate, statistics, systems engineering, theater arts/drama, theology, transportation engineering, urban studies, water resources.

Maryland Institute, College of Art
Applied art, art education, art/fine arts, ceramic art and design, commercial art, graphic arts, illustration, interior design, painting/drawing, photography, printmaking, sculpture, studio art, textile arts.

Maryville University of Saint Louis
Accounting, actuarial science, art education, art/fine arts, biology/biological sciences, business administration/commerce/management, chemistry, communication, computer information systems, (pre)dentistry sequence, early childhood education, education, elementary education, English, health services administration, history, humanities, interior design, (pre)law sequence, liberal arts/general studies, management information systems, marketing/retailing/merchandising, mathematics, medical technology, (pre)medicine sequence, middle school education, music, music therapy, nursing, occupational therapy, philosophy, physical therapy, political science/government, psychology, religious studies, science, science education, secondary education, sociology, studio art.

Mary Washington College
American studies, art/fine arts, art history, biology/biological sciences, business administration/commerce/management, chemistry, classics, computer science, (pre)dentistry sequence, economics, elementary education, English, environmental sciences, French, geography, geology, German, historic preservation, history, interdisciplinary studies, international studies, Latin, (pre)law sequence, liberal arts/general studies, mathematics, (pre)medicine sequence, modern languages, music, music education, philosophy, physics, political science/government, psychology, religious studies, secondary education, sociology, Spanish, studio art, theater arts/drama, (pre)veterinary medicine sequence.

Massachusetts College of Art
Applied art, architecture, art education, art/fine arts, art history, ceramic art and design, commercial art, computer graphics, fashion design and technology, film and video production, graphic arts, illustration, industrial design, jewelry and metalsmithing, painting/drawing, photography, printmaking, sculpture, studio art, textile arts.

Massachusetts Institute of Technology
Aerospace engineering, aerospace sciences, American studies, anthropology, applied mathematics, archaeology, architectural engineering, architecture, art history, astronomy, astrophysics, atmospheric sciences, bacteriology, biochemistry, bioengineering, biology/biological sciences, biomedical engineering, biophysics, business administration/commerce/management, business economics, cell biology, ceramic engineering, chemical engineering, chemistry, city/community/regional planning, civil engineering, cognitive science, communication, computer engineering, computer information systems,

computer programming, computer science, construction engineering, construction management, creative writing, (pre)dentistry sequence, earth science, economics, electrical engineering, electronics engineering, engineering (general), engineering and applied sciences, engineering design, engineering management, engineering physics, environmental design, environmental engineering, environmental health sciences, environmental sciences, fluid and thermal sciences, French, genetics, geochemistry, geological engineering, geology, geophysical engineering, geophysics, German, health science, history, history of science, humanities, information science, interdisciplinary studies, international studies, Latin American studies, (pre)law sequence, liberal arts/general studies, linguistics, literature, management engineering, management information systems, manufacturing engineering, manufacturing technology, marine biology, marine engineering, materials engineering, materials sciences, mathematics, mechanical engineering, (pre)medicine sequence, medieval studies, metallurgical engineering, metallurgical technology, metallurgy, meteorology, microbiology, mining and mineral engineering, molecular biology, music, naval architecture, naval sciences, neurosciences, nuclear engineering, nuclear physics, ocean engineering, pharmacy/pharmaceutical sciences, philosophy, photography, physical sciences, physics, physiology, planetary and space sciences, plastics engineering, political science/government, polymer science, psychology, robotics, Russian, Russian and Slavic studies, science, Spanish, statistics, systems science, technology and public affairs, theater arts/drama, transportation engineering, urban studies, (pre)veterinary medicine sequence, women's studies.

Messiah College

Accounting, art education, art/fine arts, art history, behavioral sciences, biblical studies, biochemistry, biology/biological sciences, business administration/commerce/management, chemistry, civil engineering, civil engineering technology, clinical psychology, communication, computer information systems, computer science, (pre)dentistry sequence, dietetics, early childhood education, economics, education, electrical engineering, elementary education, engineering (general), English, environmental sciences, experimental psychology, family services, French, geography, German, history, humanities, human resources, international business, journalism, (pre)law sequence, liberal arts/general studies, marketing/retailing/merchandising, mathematics, mechanical engineering, medical technology, (pre)medicine sequence, ministries, modern languages, music, music education, natural sciences, nursing, pastoral studies, philosophy, physical education, physics, political science/government, psychology, radio and television studies, recreation and leisure services, recreation therapy, religious education, religious studies, science education, secondary education, social science, social work, sociology, Spanish, speech/rhetoric/public address/debate, sports medicine, stringed instruments, theater arts/drama, theology, (pre)veterinary medicine sequence, voice.

Miami University

Accounting, American studies, anthropology, architecture, art education, art/fine arts, art history, athletic training, biology/biological sciences, black/African-American studies, botany/plant sciences, broadcasting, business administration/commerce/management, business economics, chemistry, child care/child and family studies, classics, communication, computer science, creative writing, (pre)dentistry sequence, dietetics, early childhood education, earth science, economics, education, elementary education, engineering management, engineering physics, English, environmental design, family and consumer studies, finance/banking, French, geography, geology, German, Greek, health education, history, home economics, home economics education, human resources, interdisciplinary studies, interior design, international relations, international studies, journalism,

Latin, (pre)law sequence, linguistics, management information systems, manufacturing engineering, marketing/retailing/merchandising, mathematics, medical technology, (pre)medicine sequence, microbiology, middle school education, music, music education, nursing, operations research, paper and pulp sciences, philosophy, physical education, physical fitness/exercise science, physics, political science/government, psychology, public administration, public relations, purchasing/inventory management, religious studies, Russian, science education, secondary education, social work, sociology, Spanish, special education, speech pathology and audiology, speech/rhetoric/public address/debate, speech therapy, sports administration, sports medicine, statistics, studio art, systems science, theater arts/drama, urban studies, (pre)veterinary medicine sequence, zoology.

Michigan State University

Accounting, advertising, agricultural education, agricultural sciences, agronomy/soil and crop sciences, American studies, animal sciences, anthropology, art education, art/fine arts, art history, Asian/Oriental studies, astrophysics, biochemistry, biology/biological sciences, biotechnology, botany/plant sciences, business administration/commerce/management, chemical engineering, chemistry, child psychology/child development, city/community/regional planning, civil engineering, communication, community services, computer engineering, computer science, construction management, criminal justice, (pre)dentistry sequence, dietetics, early childhood education, earth science, East Asian studies, economics, education, electrical engineering, elementary education, engineering mechanics, engineering technology, English, entomology, environmental studies, family and consumer studies, family services, fashion design and technology, fashion merchandising, finance/banking, fish and game management, food sciences, food services management, forestry, French, geography, geology, German, history, home economics, home economics education, horticulture, hotel and restaurant management, humanities, human resources, interdisciplinary studies, interior design, international relations, journalism, laboratory technologies, landscape architecture/design, Latin, (pre)law sequence, linguistics, marketing/retailing/merchandising, materials engineering, materials sciences, mathematics, mechanical engineering, medical technology, (pre)medicine sequence, microbiology, music, music education, music therapy, natural resource management, nursing, nutrition, parks management, philosophy, physical education, physical fitness/exercise science, physical sciences, physics, physiology, political science/government, psychology, public administration, public affairs and policy studies, purchasing/inventory management, religious studies, Russian, science education, secondary education, social science, social work, sociology, Spanish, special education, speech pathology and audiology, statistics, stringed instruments, studio art, telecommunications, theater arts/drama, (pre)veterinary medicine sequence, veterinary technology, voice, wildlife management, women's studies, zoology.

Michigan Technological University

Accounting, applied mathematics, biochemistry, bioengineering, biology/biological sciences, biomedical engineering, biotechnology, business administration/commerce/management, business economics, chemical engineering, chemistry, civil engineering, computer engineering, computer information systems, computer programming, computer science, construction engineering, (pre)dentistry sequence, earth science, ecology, economics, electrical engineering, electrical engineering technology, engineering (general), engineering management, engineering mechanics, engineering physics, engineering technology, English, environmental engineering, finance/banking, forestry, geological engineering, geology, geophysics, history, liberal arts/general studies, management information systems, manufacturing engineering, marketing/retailing/merchandising, materials engineering, mathematics, mechanical engineering, mechanical engineering technology, medical technology, (pre)medicine sequence, metallurgical engineering, microbiology, mining and mineral engineering, physical sciences, physics, science education, secondary education, social science, statistics, surveying technology, technical writing, (pre)veterinary medicine sequence, wood sciences.

Middlebury College
American studies, anthropology, art/fine arts, art history, biochemistry, biology/biological sciences, chemistry, Chinese, classics, computer science, dance, (pre)dentistry sequence, East Asian studies, East European and Soviet studies, economics, education, elementary education, English, environmental studies, film studies, French, geography, geology, German, history, humanities, international economics, international studies, Italian, Japanese, (pre)law sequence, liberal arts/general studies, literature, mathematics, (pre)medicine sequence, modern languages, molecular biology, music, natural sciences, painting/drawing, philosophy, physical sciences, physics, political science/government, psychology, religious studies, Romance languages, Russian, Russian and Slavic studies, science, secondary education, social science, sociology, Southeast Asian studies, Spanish, studio art, theater arts/drama, (pre)veterinary medicine sequence, women's studies.

Millikin University
Accounting, American studies, art education, art/fine arts, arts administration, art therapy, athletic training, behavioral sciences, biology/biological sciences, business administration/commerce/management, business economics, chemistry, commercial art, communication, computer graphics, computer management, computer science, creative writing, (pre)dentistry sequence, economics, education, elementary education, English, experimental psychology, finance/banking, French, German, history, human resources, human services, interdisciplinary studies, international business, international studies, (pre)law sequence, liberal arts/general studies, literature, management information systems, marketing/retailing/merchandising, mathematics, (pre)medicine sequence, modern languages, music, music business, music education, nursing, philosophy, physical education, physics, political science/government, psychology, religious studies, sacred music, science, science education, secondary education, social science, social work, sociology, Spanish, studio art, theater arts/drama, (pre)veterinary medicine sequence, voice.

Millsaps College
Accounting, art/fine arts, biology/biological sciences, business administration/commerce/management, chemistry, classics, computer science, economics, education, elementary education, English, French, geology, Greek, history, Latin, mathematics, music, music education, philosophy, physics, piano/organ, political science/government, psychology, religious studies, sacred music, sociology, Spanish, theater arts/drama, voice.

Mills College
American studies, anthropology, art/fine arts, art history, biochemistry, biology/biological sciences, business economics, chemistry, child psychology/child development, communication, comparative literature, computer science, creative writing, dance, early childhood education, economics, education, elementary education, English, environmental sciences, ethnic studies, French, Germanic languages and literature, Hispanic studies, history, interdisciplinary studies, international studies, liberal arts/general studies, mathematics, (pre)medicine sequence, music, philosophy, political, legal, and economic analysis, psychology, social science, sociology, statistics, studio art, theater arts/drama, women's studies.

Milwaukee School of Engineering
Architectural engineering, biomedical engineering, business administration/commerce/management, computer engineering, electrical engineering, electrical engineering technology, industrial engineering, manufacturing technology, mechanical engineering, mechanical engineering technology, nursing, technical writing.

Monmouth College
Accounting, art/fine arts, biology/biological sciences, business administration/commerce/management, chemistry, classics, communication, computer science, economics, education, elementary education, English, environmental sciences, French, Greek, history, humanities, Latin, liberal arts/general studies, mathematics, military science, modern languages, music, natural sciences, philosophy, physical education, physics, political science/government, psychology, religious studies, secondary education, sociology, Spanish, special education, speech/rhetoric/public address/debate, theater arts/drama.

Morehouse College
Accounting, actuarial science, architecture, art/fine arts, biology/biological sciences, business administration/commerce/management, chemistry, computer science, (pre)dentistry sequence, economics, education, engineering (general), English, finance/banking, French, German, history, insurance, interdisciplinary studies, international studies, (pre)law sequence, marketing/retailing/merchandising, mathematics, (pre)medicine sequence, music, philosophy, physical education, physics, political science/government, psychology, real estate, religious studies, sociology, Spanish, theater arts/drama, urban studies.

Mount Holyoke College
American studies, anthropology, art history, Asian/Oriental studies, astronomy, biochemistry, biology/biological sciences, black/African-American studies, chemistry, classics, computer science, dance, economics, education, English, environmental studies, European studies, French, geography, geology, German, Greek, history, international studies, Italian, Judaic studies, Latin, Latin American studies, mathematics, medieval studies, music, philosophy, physics, political science/government, psychobiology, psychology, religious studies, Romance languages, Russian, Russian and Slavic studies, sociology, Spanish, statistics, studio art, theater arts/drama, women's studies.

Mount Union College
Accounting, American studies, art education, art/fine arts, Asian/Oriental studies, astronomy, biology/biological sciences, business administration/commerce/management, chemistry, communication, computer information systems, computer science, cytotechnology, (pre)dentistry sequence, economics, education, elementary education, English, French, geology, health education, history, information science, interdisciplinary studies, international business, international economics, Japanese, (pre)law sequence, liberal arts/general studies, mathematics, medical technology, (pre)medicine sequence, music, music education, philosophy, physical education, physics, political science/government, psychology, religious studies, secondary education, sociology, Spanish, special education, sports administration, sports medicine, theater arts/drama.

Muhlenberg College
Accounting, American studies, art/fine arts, art history, biochemistry, biology/biological sciences, business administration/commerce/management, chemistry, classics, communication, computer information systems, computer science, dance, (pre)dentistry sequence, economics, elementary education, English, environmental studies, French, German, Greek, history, human resources, information science, international

economics, international studies, Latin, (pre)law sequence, mathematics, (pre)medicine sequence, music, natural sciences, philosophy, physical sciences, physics, political science/government, psychology, religious studies, Russian and Slavic studies, secondary education, social science, social work, sociology, Spanish, studio art, theater arts/drama, (pre)veterinary medicine sequence.

Nebraska Wesleyan University

Art/fine arts, biochemistry, biology/biological sciences, business administration/commerce/management, chemistry, communication, computer information systems, computer science, economics, elementary education, English, French, German, history, interdisciplinary studies, international business, international studies, mathematics, middle school education, music, music education, nursing, paralegal studies, philosophy, physical education, physical fitness/exercise science, physics, political science/government, psychobiology, psychology, religious studies, science education, social work, sociology, Spanish, special education, sports administration, theater arts/drama.

New College of the University of South Florida

Anthropology, art/fine arts, art history, behavioral sciences, biology/biological sciences, cell biology, ceramic art and design, chemistry, child psychology/child development, classics, comparative literature, ecology, economics, environmental biology, environmental studies, European studies, evolutionary biology, experimental psychology, French, genetics, German, Germanic languages and literature, Greek, history, history of philosophy, interdisciplinary studies, Latin, (pre)law sequence, liberal arts/general studies, literature, marine biology, marine sciences, mathematics, (pre)medicine sequence, medieval studies, modern languages, molecular biology, music, music history, natural sciences, painting/drawing, philosophy, physics, political science/government, psychology, public affairs and policy studies, religious studies, Russian, sculpture, social science, sociology, Spanish, studio art, urban studies.

New England Conservatory of Music

Jazz, music, music education, music history, opera, piano/organ, stringed instruments, voice, wind and percussion instruments.

New Jersey Institute of Technology

Actuarial science, applied mathematics, architecture, business administration/commerce/management, chemical engineering, chemistry, civil engineering, civil engineering technology, computer engineering, computer science, (pre)dentistry sequence, electrical engineering, electrical engineering technology, engineering (general), engineering and applied sciences, engineering sciences, engineering technology, industrial engineering, information science, (pre)law sequence, manufacturing engineering, manufacturing technology, materials engineering, materials sciences, mathematics, mechanical engineering, mechanical engineering technology, (pre)medicine sequence, physics, statistics, surveying technology, systems engineering, technology and public affairs.

New Mexico Institute of Mining and Technology

Applied mathematics, astrophysics, atmospheric sciences, behavioral sciences, biology/biological sciences, business administration/commerce/management, chemical engineering, chemistry, computer programming, computer science, (pre)dentistry sequence, electrical engineering, electronics engineering, engineering (general), engineering mechanics, engineering sciences, environmental biology, environmental engineering, environmental sciences, experimental psychology, geochemistry, geology, geophysics, interdisciplinary studies, liberal arts/general studies, materials engineering,

mathematics, medical technology, (pre)medicine sequence, metallurgical engineering, mining and mineral engineering, petroleum/natural gas engineering, physics, psychology, science, science education, technical writing, (pre)veterinary medicine sequence.

New York School of Interior Design

Interior design.

New York University

Accounting, actuarial science, adult and continuing education, African studies, anthropology, applied mathematics, Arabic, archaeology, art education, art/fine arts, art history, Asian/Oriental studies, astronomy, audio engineering, behavioral sciences, biochemistry, biology/biological sciences, black/African-American studies, broadcasting, business administration/commerce/management, business economics, chemical engineering, chemistry, child psychology/child development, Chinese, city/community/regional planning, civil engineering, classics, communication, comparative literature, computer information systems, computer science, creative writing, dance, (pre)dentistry sequence, dietetics, early childhood education, earth science, East Asian studies, economics, education, electrical engineering, elementary education, engineering (general), engineering physics, English, environmental engineering, environmental sciences, European studies, film and video production, film studies, finance/banking, food sciences, food services management, French, German, Germanic languages and literature, graphic arts, Greek, Hebrew, Hispanic studies, history, hotel and restaurant management, humanities, information science, interdisciplinary studies, international business, international relations, Islamic studies, Italian, Japanese, jazz, journalism, Judaic studies, Latin, Latin American studies, (pre)law sequence, liberal arts/general studies, linguistics, literature, marketing/retailing/merchandising, materials engineering, mathematics, mechanical engineering, (pre)medicine sequence, medieval studies, middle school education, modern languages, music, music business, music education, music history, natural sciences, Near and Middle Eastern studies, neurosciences, nursing, nutrition, opera, operations research, painting/drawing, peace studies, philosophy, photography, physical therapy, physics, piano/organ, political science/government, Portuguese, psychology, radio and television studies, religious studies, retail management, Romance languages, Russian, Russian and Slavic studies, science education, sculpture, secondary education, Slavic languages, social science, social work, sociology, Spanish, special education, speech pathology and audiology, statistics, studio art, theater arts/drama, tourism and travel, urban studies, (pre)veterinary medicine sequence, voice, wind and percussion instruments, women's studies.

North Carolina School of the Arts

Dance, film and video production, film studies, music, theater arts/drama.

North Carolina State University

Accounting, aerospace engineering, African studies, agricultural business, agricultural economics, agricultural education, agricultural engineering, agricultural sciences, agronomy/soil and crop sciences, animal sciences, anthropology, applied mathematics, architecture, biochemistry, biology/biological sciences, botany/plant sciences, business administration/commerce/management, chemical engineering, chemistry, civil engineering, communication, comparative literature, computer engineering, computer science, conservation, construction engineering, construction management, criminal justice, (pre)dentistry sequence, economics, education, electrical engineering, English, entomology, environmental design, environmental engineering, environmental sciences, film studies, fish and game management, food sciences, forestry, French, geology, geophysics, German, history, horticulture, humanities, human resources, industrial design, industrial engineering, interdisciplinary studies, Japanese, journalism, landscape architecture/design, liberal arts/general studies, linguistics, marketing/retailing/merchandising, materials engineering, mathematics, mechanical engineering, medical technology, (pre)medicine sequence, meteorology, microbiology, natural resource management, nuclear engineering, nutrition, ornamental horticulture, paper and pulp sciences, parks management, philosophy, physical education, physics, political science/government, poultry sciences, psychology, public affairs and policy studies, recreational facilities management, Russian and Slavic studies, science education, secondary education, social science, social work, sociology, Spanish, speech therapy, statistics, technical writing, textile engineering, textiles and clothing, tourism and travel, (pre)veterinary medicine sequence, vocational education, wildlife biology, women's studies, wood sciences, zoology.

North Central College

Accounting, actuarial science, anthropology, art education, art/fine arts, athletic training, biochemistry, biology/biological sciences, broadcasting, business administration/commerce/management, business education, chemistry, classics, communication, computer information systems, computer science, (pre)dentistry sequence, early childhood education, economics, education, elementary education, English, finance/banking, French, German, graphic arts, Greek, health education, history, humanities, international business, international relations, Japanese, Latin, (pre)law sequence, liberal arts/general studies, literature, management information systems, marketing/retailing/merchandising, mathematics, (pre)medicine sequence, modern languages, music, natural sciences, philosophy, physical education, physical fitness/exercise science, physics, piano/organ, political science/government, psychology, public relations, reading education, religious studies, science education, secondary education, social science, sociology, Spanish, speech/rhetoric/public address/debate, sports medicine, theater arts/drama, (pre)veterinary medicine sequence, voice.

Northwestern College (IA)

Accounting, art/fine arts, athletic training, biology/biological sciences, business administration/commerce/management, business education, chemistry, communication, computer science, economics, education, elementary education, English, environmental sciences, French, history, humanities, mathematics, medical technology, music, music education, philosophy, physical education, political science/government, psychology, recreation and leisure services, religious studies, secondary education, social work, sociology, Spanish, theater arts/drama, theology.

Northwestern University

American studies, anthropology, applied mathematics, art/fine arts, art history, Asian/Oriental studies, astronomy, astrophysics, behavioral sciences, biochemistry, bioengineering, biology/biological sciences, biomedical engineering, black/African-American studies, broadcasting, cell biology, chemical engineering, chemistry, child psychology/child development, city/community/regional planning, civil engineering, classics, cognitive science, communication, comparative literature, computer engineering, computer science, dance, (pre)dentistry sequence, economics, education, electrical engineering, engineering (general), engineering and applied sciences, engineering sciences, English, environmental engineering, environmental sciences, ethnic studies, film studies, French, geology, German, Germanic languages and literature, Hispanic studies, history, human development, humanities, industrial engineering, interdisciplinary studies, Italian, journalism, Latin American studies, linguistics, literature, materials engineering, materials sciences, mathematics, mechanical engineering, (pre)medicine sequence, microbiology, molecular biology,

music, music education, music history, neurosciences, opera, philosophy, physics, piano/organ, political science/government, Portuguese, psychology, radio and television studies, religious studies, secondary education, Slavic languages, sociology, Spanish, speech pathology and audiology, speech/rhetoric/public address/debate, speech therapy, statistics, stringed instruments, studio art, theater arts/drama, urban studies, voice, wind and percussion instruments.

Oberlin College

Anthropology, archaeology, art/fine arts, art history, biochemistry, biology/biological sciences, black/African-American studies, chemistry, classics, comparative literature, computer science, creative writing, dance, East Asian studies, ecology, economics, English, environmental studies, French, geology, German, Greek, history, jazz, Judaic studies, Latin, Latin American studies, legal studies, mathematics, music, music education, music history, Near and Middle Eastern studies, neurosciences, philosophy, physics, piano/organ, political science/government, psychobiology, psychology, religious studies, Romance languages, Russian, Russian and Slavic studies, sociology, Spanish, stringed instruments, studio art, theater arts/drama, voice, wind and percussion instruments, women's studies.

Occidental College

American studies, anthropology, art/fine arts, art history, Asian/Oriental studies, behavioral sciences, biochemistry, biology/biological sciences, chemistry, Chinese, classics, cognitive science, comparative literature, (pre)dentistry sequence, East Asian studies, East European and Soviet studies, economics, English, environmental sciences, film studies, French, geology, geophysics, German, Germanic languages and literature, Hispanic studies, history, interdisciplinary studies, international studies, Japanese, Latin American studies, (pre)law sequence, literature, marine biology, mathematics, (pre)medicine sequence, modern languages, molecular biology, music, music education, music history, neurosciences, painting/drawing, philosophy, physical fitness/exercise science, physical sciences, physics, political science/government, psychobiology, psychology, public affairs and policy studies, religious studies, Romance languages, Russian, sculpture, sociology, Spanish, studio art, theater arts/drama, (pre)veterinary medicine sequence, women's studies.

Oglethorpe University

Accounting, American studies, art/fine arts, art history, biology/biological sciences, business administration/commerce/management, business economics, chemistry, communication, computer science, (pre)dentistry sequence, early childhood education, economics, education, elementary education, engineering (general), English, history, interdisciplinary studies, international studies, (pre)law sequence, mathematics, medical technology, (pre)medicine sequence, middle school education, philosophy, physics, political science/government, psychology, secondary education, social work, sociology, urban studies, (pre)veterinary medicine sequence.

Ohio Northern University

Accounting, art education, art/fine arts, biochemistry, biology/biological sciences, broadcasting, business administration/commerce/management, ceramic art and design, chemistry, civil engineering, communication, computer science, criminal justice, (pre)dentistry sequence, economics, electrical engineering, elementary education, English, environmental studies, finance/banking, French, graphic arts, health education, history, industrial arts, industrial engineering technology, international studies, (pre)law sequence, marketing/retailing/merchandising, mathematics, mechanical engineering, medical technology, (pre)medicine sequence, music, music education, painting/drawing, pharmacy/pharmaceutical sciences, philosophy, physical education, physics, political science/government, printmaking, psychology, public relations, religious studies, sculpture, sociology, Spanish, special education, speech/rhetoric/public address/debate, sports administration, sports medicine, theater arts/drama, (pre)veterinary medicine sequence.

The Ohio State University

Accounting, actuarial science, aerospace engineering, African studies, agricultural business, agricultural economics, agricultural education, agricultural engineering, agronomy/soil and crop sciences, animal sciences, anthropology, Arabic, architectural engineering, architecture, art education, art/fine arts, art history, Asian/Oriental studies, astronomy, audio engineering, aviation administration, aviation technology, behavioral sciences, biochemistry, biology/biological sciences, black/African-American studies, botany/plant sciences, business administration/commerce/management, business economics, business education, cell biology, ceramic engineering, chemical engineering, chemistry, child care/child and family studies, child psychology/child development, Chinese, civil engineering, classics, cognitive science, communication, computer engineering, computer information systems, computer programming, computer science, consumer services, criminal justice, criminology, dairy sciences, dance, dental services, (pre)dentistry sequence, dietetics, early childhood education, earth science, East Asian studies, East European and Soviet studies, ecology, economics, education, electrical engineering, elementary education, engineering (general), engineering physics, English, entomology, environmental biology, environmental education, environmental sciences, ethnic studies, European studies, experimental psychology, family and consumer studies, family services, fashion merchandising, film studies, finance/banking, fish and game management, flight training, food marketing, food sciences, food services management, forestry, French, genetics, geography, geology, German, gerontology, Greek, health education, Hebrew, history, home economics, home economics education, horticulture, hospitality services, hotel and restaurant management, human development, human ecology, humanities, human resources, illustration, industrial engineering, information science, insurance, interdisciplinary studies, interior design, international business, international economics, international studies, Islamic studies, Italian, Japanese, jazz, journalism, Judaic studies, labor and industrial relations, landscape architecture/design, land use management and reclamation, linguistics, marketing/retailing/merchandising, materials engineering, materials sciences, mathematics, mechanical engineering, medical illustration, medical records services, medical technology, (pre)medicine sequence, medieval studies, metallurgical engineering, microbiology, music, music education, music history, natural resource management, Near and Middle Eastern studies, nursing, nutrition, occupational therapy, parks management, pharmacy/pharmaceutical sciences, philosophy, physical education, physical therapy, physics, piano/organ, political science/government, Portuguese, poultry sciences, psychology, public relations, radiological technology, reading education, real estate, recreation and leisure services, religious studies, respiratory therapy, Russian, Russian and Slavic studies, science education, secondary education, Slavic languages, social work, sociology, South Asian studies, Southeast Asian studies, Spanish, special education, speech pathology and audiology, statistics, stringed instruments, surveying engineering, systems engineering, technical writing, textiles and clothing, theater arts/drama, transportation engineering, transportation technologies, (pre)veterinary medicine sequence, vocational education, voice, welding engineering, wildlife management, wind and percussion instruments, women's studies, zoology.

Ohio University

Accounting, advertising, African studies, anthropology, applied art, applied mathematics, art education, art/fine arts, art history, Asian/Oriental studies, athletic training, aviation administration, biochemistry, biology/biological sciences, biomedical sciences, black/African-American studies, botany/plant sciences, broadcasting, business administration/commerce/management, business economics, business education, cartography, cell biology, ceramic art and design, chemical engineering, chemistry, child care/child and family studies, civil engineering, classics, commercial art, communication, communication equipment technology, community services, computer engineering, computer information systems, computer science, creative writing, criminal justice, criminology, dance, (pre)dentistry sequence, dietetics, early childhood education, ecology, economics, education, electrical engineering, elementary education, English, environmental biology, environmental health sciences, environmental studies, European studies, family services, fashion merchandising, film studies, finance/banking, food services management, forensic sciences, French, geography, geology, German, graphic arts, health education, health services administration, history, home economics, home economics education, human resources, industrial arts, industrial engineering, interior design, international business, international studies, journalism, labor and industrial relations, Latin, Latin American studies, (pre)law sequence, liberal arts/general studies, linguistics, literature, management information systems, marine biology, marketing/retailing/merchandising, mathematics, mechanical engineering, medical laboratory technology, (pre)medicine sequence, microbiology, middle school education, mining and mineral engineering, music, music education, music history, music therapy, nursing, nutrition, occupational safety and health, painting/drawing, philosophy, photography, physical education, physical fitness/exercise science, physics, physiology, piano/organ, political science/government, printmaking, psychology, public administration, public health, public relations, radio and television studies, reading education, recreational facilities management, recreation and leisure services, recreation therapy, science education, sculpture, secondary education, social work, sociology, Southeast Asian studies, Spanish, special education, speech pathology and audiology, speech/rhetoric/public address/debate, speech therapy, sports administration, stringed instruments, studio art, systems engineering, teaching English as a second language, telecommunications, theater arts/drama, (pre)veterinary medicine sequence, voice, water resources, wildlife biology, wind and percussion instruments, zoology.

Ohio Wesleyan University

Accounting, anthropology, art education, art/fine arts, art history, art therapy, astronomy, bacteriology, biology/biological sciences, black/African-American studies, botany/plant sciences, broadcasting, business administration/commerce/management, chemistry, classics, computer science, creative writing, (pre)dentistry sequence, earth science, economics, education, elementary education, engineering sciences, English, environmental sciences, ethnic studies, French, genetics, geography, geology, German, health education, history, humanities, international business, international studies, journalism, (pre)law sequence, literature, mathematics, (pre)medicine sequence, medieval studies, music, music education, philosophy, physical education, physics, political science/government, psychology, public administration, religious studies, secondary education, sociology, Spanish, statistics, studio art, theater arts/drama, urban studies, (pre)veterinary medicine sequence, women's studies, zoology.

Oklahoma State University

Accounting, advertising, aerospace engineering, aerospace sciences, agricultural business, agricultural economics, agricultural education, agricultural engineering, agricultural sciences, agronomy/soil and crop sciences, animal sciences, architectural engineering, architecture, art education, art/fine arts, aviation administration, aviation technology, biochemistry, biology/biological sciences, biotechnology, botany/plant sciences, broadcasting, business administration/commerce/

management, business economics, cell biology, chemical engineering, chemistry, child care/child and family studies, child psychology/child development, civil engineering, communication, community services, computer engineering, computer information systems, computer management, computer programming, computer science, computer technologies, construction management, construction technologies, consumer services, dietetics, drafting and design, early childhood education, ecology, economics, education, electrical and electronics technologies, electrical engineering, electronics engineering technology, elementary education, engineering (general), engineering technology, English, entomology, family and consumer studies, family services, farm and ranch management, fashion design and technology, fashion merchandising, finance/banking, fire protection engineering, fish and game management, flight training, forestry, French, geography, geology, German, gerontology, graphic arts, health education, health science, history, home economics, home economics education, horticulture, hotel and restaurant management, human resources, industrial arts, industrial engineering, industrial engineering technology, information science, interior design, international business, journalism, laboratory technologies, landscape architecture/design, (pre)law sequence, management information systems, manufacturing technology, marketing/retailing/merchandising, marriage and family counseling, mathematics, mechanical design technology, mechanical engineering, mechanical engineering technology, medical technology, (pre)medicine sequence, microbiology, middle school education, military science, molecular biology, music, music education, nutrition, philosophy, physical education, physical sciences, physics, physiology, political science/government, psychology, public relations, radio and television studies, range management, recreation and leisure services, Russian, safety and security technologies, science education, secondary education, social science, social work, sociology, Spanish, special education, speech pathology and audiology, speech/rhetoric/public address/debate, statistics, studio art, technical writing, textiles and clothing, theater arts/drama, (pre)veterinary medicine sequence, vocational education, wildlife management, zoology.

Pacific Lutheran University

Accounting, anthropology, art education, art/fine arts, art history, biblical studies, biochemistry, biology/biological sciences, broadcasting, business administration/commerce/management, chemistry, classics, communication, computer engineering, computer science, (pre)dentistry sequence, early childhood education, earth science, ecology, economics, education, electrical engineering, elementary education, engineering physics, engineering sciences, English, finance/banking, French, geology, German, history, international business, international studies, jazz, journalism, (pre)law sequence, legal studies, literature, management information systems, marketing/retailing/merchandising, mathematics, medical technology, (pre)medicine sequence, modern languages, music, music education, nursing, philosophy, physical education, physical fitness/exercise science, physics, piano/organ, political science/government, psychology, public relations, publishing, radio and television studies, reading education, recreational facilities management, recreation and leisure services, recreation therapy, religious studies, sacred music, Scandinavian languages/studies, science education, secondary education, social work, sociology, Spanish, special education, speech/rhetoric/public address/debate, sports medicine, stringed instruments, studio art, theater arts/drama, (pre)veterinary medicine sequence, voice.

Parsons School of Design, New School for Social Research

Architecture, art education, art/fine arts, ceramic art and design, commercial art, environmental design, fashion design and technology,

graphic arts, illustration, industrial design, interior design, jewelry and metalsmithing, painting/drawing, photography, sculpture, textile arts.

Pennsylvania State University University Park Campus

Accounting, actuarial science, adult and continuing education, advertising, aerospace engineering, African studies, agricultural business, agricultural education, agricultural engineering, agricultural sciences, agronomy/soil and crop sciences, American studies, animal sciences, anthropology, architectural engineering, architecture, art education, art/fine arts, art history, astronomy, astrophysics, biochemistry, biology/biological sciences, biotechnology, black/African-American studies, botany/plant sciences, broadcasting, business administration/commerce/management, cell biology, ceramic engineering, chemical engineering, chemistry, child care/child and family studies, civil engineering, classics, communication, comparative literature, computer engineering, computer science, criminal justice, dairy sciences, early childhood education, earth science, East Asian studies, ecology, economics, education, educational media, electrical engineering, elementary education, engineering (general), engineering sciences, English, entomology, family and consumer studies, film and video production, finance/banking, fish and game management, food sciences, forestry, forest technology, French, geography, German, health education, health services administration, history, horticulture, hotel and restaurant management, human development, industrial engineering, insurance, interdisciplinary studies, international business, international studies, Italian, journalism, labor and industrial relations, landscape architecture/design, landscaping/grounds maintenance, Latin American studies, law enforcement/police sciences, (pre)law sequence, liberal arts/general studies, linguistics, marketing/retailing/merchandising, materials engineering, materials sciences, mathematics, mechanical engineering, (pre)medicine sequence, medieval studies, meteorology, microbiology, mining and mineral engineering, molecular biology, music, music education, nuclear engineering, nursing, nutrition, operations research, parks management, petroleum/natural gas engineering, philosophy, physical fitness/exercise science, physics, political science/government, poultry sciences, psychology, real estate, recreation and leisure services, rehabilitation therapy, religious studies, Russian, science, secondary education, social work, sociology, Spanish, special education, speech/rhetoric/public address/debate, theater arts/drama, wildlife management, women's studies, wood sciences.

Pepperdine University (Malibu)

Accounting, advertising, American studies, art/fine arts, Asian/Oriental studies, biology/biological sciences, broadcasting, business administration/commerce/management, chemistry, communication, computer science, creative writing, (pre)dentistry sequence, economics, education, elementary education, English, French, German, history, humanities, interdisciplinary studies, international studies, journalism, (pre)law sequence, liberal arts/general studies, literature, mathematics, (pre)medicine sequence, music, music education, natural sciences, nutrition, philosophy, physical education, political science/government, psychology, public relations, recreation and leisure services, religious education, religious studies, secondary education, social science, sociology, Spanish, speech/rhetoric/public address/debate, sports medicine, telecommunications, theater arts/drama.

Pitzer College

American studies, anthropology, art/fine arts, Asian/Oriental studies, biochemistry, biology/biological sciences, black/African-American studies, ceramic art and design, chemistry, child psychology/child development, Chinese, classics, East Asian studies, economics, English, environmental sciences, environmental studies, European studies, film studies, folklore, French, German, Hispanic studies, history, human development, international studies, Japanese, Latin American studies, linguistics, literature, management engineering, mathematics, (pre)medicine sequence, Mexican-American/Chicano studies, natural sciences, philosophy, physics, political science/government, psychobiology, psychology, religious studies, Romance languages, Russian, science, sociology, Spanish, studio art, theater arts/drama, women's studies.

Polytechnic University, Brooklyn Campus

Actuarial science, aerospace engineering, chemical engineering, chemistry, civil engineering, computer engineering, computer information systems, computer science, electrical engineering, environmental engineering, environmental sciences, humanities, journalism, mathematics, mechanical engineering, physics, social science, technical writing.

Polytechnic University, Farmingdale Campus

Aerospace engineering, chemical engineering, civil engineering, computer engineering, computer science, electrical engineering, environmental engineering, environmental sciences, management information systems, mechanical engineering.

Pomona College

American studies, anthropology, art/fine arts, art history, Asian/Oriental studies, astronomy, biochemistry, biology/biological sciences, black/African-American studies, cell biology, chemistry, Chinese, classics, computer science, dance, East Asian studies, ecology, economics, English, environmental studies, film studies, French, geochemistry, geology, German, Germanic languages and literature, Hispanic studies, history, humanities, interdisciplinary studies, international relations, international studies, Japanese, liberal arts/general studies, linguistics, mathematics, (pre)medicine sequence, Mexican-American/Chicano studies, microbiology, modern languages, molecular biology, music, neurosciences, philosophy, physics, political science/government, psychology, public affairs and policy studies, religious studies, Romance languages, Russian, sociology, Spanish, studio art, theater arts/drama, women's studies.

Presbyterian College

Accounting, art/fine arts, biology/biological sciences, business administration/commerce/management, chemistry, (pre)dentistry sequence, early childhood education, economics, education, elementary education, English, French, German, history, (pre)law sequence, mathematics, (pre)medicine sequence, modern languages, music, music education, philosophy, physics, political science/government, psychology, religious studies, social science, sociology, Spanish, special education, theater arts/drama, (pre)veterinary medicine sequence.

Princeton University

Aerospace engineering, African studies, American studies, anthropology, applied mathematics, archaeology, architectural engineering, architecture, art/fine arts, art history, astrophysics, bioengineering, biology/biological sciences, black/African-American studies, chemical engineering, chemistry, Chinese, civil engineering, classics, cognitive science, comparative literature, computer engineering, computer science, creative writing, East Asian studies, ecology, economics, electrical engineering, energy management technologies, engineering and applied sciences, engineering management, engineering physics, English, environmental engineering, environmental sciences, European studies, evolutionary biology, geological engineering, geology, geophysics, Germanic languages and literature, history, humanities, international studies, Latin American studies, linguistics, management engineering, mathematics, mechanical engineering, molecular biology, music, Near and Middle Eastern studies, philosophy, physics, political science/government, psychology, public affairs and policy studies, religious studies, robotics, Romance

languages, Russian and Slavic studies, Slavic languages, sociology, statistics, theater arts/drama, transportation engineering, women's studies.

Providence College

Accounting, American studies, art/fine arts, art history, biology/biological sciences, business administration/commerce/management, business economics, chemistry, community services, computer science, economics, education, elementary education, English, finance/banking, French, health services administration, history, humanities, instrumentation technology, Italian, Latin American studies, liberal arts/general studies, marketing/retailing/merchandising, mathematics, modern languages, music, painting/drawing, philosophy, photography, political science/government, psychology, secondary education, social science, social work, sociology, Spanish, special education, studio art, systems science, theater arts/drama, theology.

Purdue University (West Lafayette)

Accounting, actuarial science, advertising, aerospace engineering, agricultural business, agricultural economics, agricultural education, agricultural engineering, agricultural sciences, agricultural technologies, agronomy/soil and crop sciences, aircraft and missile maintenance, air traffic control, American studies, animal sciences, anthropology, applied mathematics, art education, art/fine arts, art history, athletic training, atmospheric sciences, aviation administration, aviation technology, biochemistry, bioengineering, biology/biological sciences, biomedical engineering, biomedical sciences, black/African-American studies, botany/plant sciences, business administration/commerce/management, business economics, cell biology, ceramic art and design, chemical engineering, chemistry, child care/child and family studies, child psychology/child development, civil engineering, clinical psychology, commercial art, communication, community services, comparative literature, computer engineering, computer programming, computer science, computer technologies, conservation, construction engineering, construction management, construction technologies, consumer services, creative writing, criminal justice, criminology, (pre)dentistry sequence, dietetics, drafting and design, early childhood education, earth science, ecology, economics, education, educational media, electrical engineering, electrical engineering technology, elementary education, engineering (general), engineering management, engineering sciences, engineering technology, English, entomology, environmental biology, environmental engineering, environmental health sciences, environmental sciences, evolutionary biology, family and consumer studies, farm and ranch management, fashion design and technology, fashion merchandising, film studies, finance/banking, fish and game management, flight training, food marketing, food sciences, food services management, forestry, forest technology, French, genetics, geochemistry, geological engineering, geology, geophysics, German, Germanic languages and literature, graphic arts, guidance and counseling, health education, health science, history, home economics, home economics education, horticulture, hospitality services, hotel and restaurant management, human resources, illustration, industrial administration, industrial arts, industrial design, industrial engineering, industrial engineering technology, interdisciplinary studies, interior design, journalism, landscape architecture/design, landscaping/grounds maintenance, (pre)law sequence, linguistics, management engineering, management information systems, manufacturing engineering, manufacturing technology, marketing/retailing/merchandising, materials engineering, materials sciences, mathematics, mechanical engineering, mechanical engineering technology, medical technology, (pre)medicine sequence, medieval studies, metallurgical engineering, meteorology, microbiology, middle school education, molecular biology, natural resource management, neurosciences, nuclear engineering, nuclear physics, nursing, nutrition, occupational safety and health, ocean engineering, operations research, painting/drawing, paleontology, parks management, pharmacology, pharmacy/pharmaceutical sciences, philosophy, photography, physical education, physical fitness/exercise science, physical sciences, physics, physiology, political science/government, poultry sciences, psychology, public relations, radio and television studies, radiological sciences, range management, reading education, recreational facilities management, recreation and leisure services, religious studies, retail management, robotics, Russian, science, science education, secondary education, social science, sociology, soil conservation, Spanish, special education, speech pathology and audiology, speech therapy, sports medicine, statistics, surveying engineering, systems engineering, technical writing, telecommunications, theater arts/drama, tourism and travel, transportation engineering, (pre)veterinary medicine sequence, veterinary sciences, vocational education, water resources, wildlife biology, wildlife management, wood sciences.

Quincy University

Accounting, art education, art/fine arts, art history, arts administration, athletic training, biology/biological sciences, business administration/commerce/management, chemistry, communication, computer information systems, computer science, criminal justice, (pre)dentistry sequence, elementary education, English, environmental studies, finance/banking, history, humanities, human resources, interdisciplinary studies, international studies, (pre)law sequence, liberal arts/general studies, marketing/retailing/merchandising, mathematics, medical technology, (pre)medicine sequence, music, music business, music education, peace studies, philosophy, physical education, political science/government, psychology, radio and television studies, religious education, secondary education, social work, sociology, special education, sports administration, studio art, theology, (pre)veterinary medicine sequence.

Randolph-Macon Woman's College

Anthropology, art/fine arts, art history, biology/biological sciences, business economics, chemistry, classics, communication, creative writing, dance, economics, English, French, German, Germanic languages and literature, Greek, history, international relations, Latin, literature, mathematics, museum studies, music, music history, philosophy, physics, political science/government, psychology, religious studies, Russian and Slavic studies, sociology, Spanish, studio art, theater arts/drama, voice.

Reed College

American studies, anthropology, art/fine arts, art history, biochemistry, biology/biological sciences, biophysics, chemistry, Chinese, classics, dance, economics, English, French, German, Germanic languages and literature, history, international studies, linguistics, literature, mathematics, medieval studies, music, philosophy, physics, political science/government, psychology, religious studies, Russian, sociology, Spanish, studio art, theater arts/drama.

Rensselaer Polytechnic Institute

Accounting, aerospace engineering, applied mathematics, architectural engineering, architecture, astrophysics, biochemistry, biology/biological sciences, biomedical engineering, biomedical sciences, biophysics, business administration/commerce/management, cell biology, ceramic engineering, chemical engineering, chemistry, civil engineering, communication, computer engineering, computer graphics, computer management, computer programming, computer science, (pre)dentistry sequence, ecology, economics, electrical engineering, electronics engineering, engineering (general), engineering and applied sciences, engineering management, engineering physics, engineering sciences, environmental biology, environmental engineering, environmental sciences, environmental

studies, finance/banking, French, genetics, geochemistry, geological engineering, geology, geophysics, industrial engineering, interdisciplinary studies, international business, (pre)law sequence, management engineering, management information systems, manufacturing engineering, materials engineering, mathematics, mechanical engineering, (pre)medicine sequence, metallurgy, microbiology, military science, molecular biology, music, natural sciences, naval sciences, nuclear engineering, nuclear physics, optics, philosophy, physical sciences, physics, physiology, planetary and space sciences, polymer science, psychology, science, science education, systems engineering, technical writing, technology and public affairs.

Rhode Island School of Design

Architecture, art/fine arts, ceramic art and design, fashion design and technology, film studies, graphic arts, illustration, industrial design, interior design, jewelry and metalsmithing, landscape architecture/design, painting/drawing, photography, printmaking, sculpture, textile arts, textiles and clothing.

Rhodes College

Anthropology, art/fine arts, art history, biochemistry, biology/biological sciences, business administration/commerce/management, chemistry, classics, computer science, economics, English, French, German, Greek, history, interdisciplinary studies, international business, international economics, international studies, Latin, Latin American studies, mathematics, museum studies, music, philosophy, physics, political science/government, psychology, religious studies, Russian and Slavic studies, sociology, Spanish, studio art, theater arts/drama, urban studies.

Rice University

Anthropology, architecture, art/fine arts, art history, Asian/Oriental studies, behavioral sciences, biochemistry, biology/biological sciences, business administration/commerce/management, chemical engineering, chemistry, civil engineering, classics, computer engineering, computer science, ecology, economics, electrical engineering, English, environmental engineering, evolutionary biology, French, geology, geophysics, German, history, linguistics, materials sciences, mathematics, mechanical engineering, music, neurosciences, philosophy, physical education, physics, political science/government, psychology, public affairs and policy studies, religious studies, Russian and Slavic studies, sociology, Spanish, statistics.

Ripon College

Anthropology, art/fine arts, behavioral sciences, biochemistry, biology/biological sciences, business administration/commerce/management, chemistry, computer science, (pre)dentistry sequence, economics, education, elementary education, English, French, German, history, interdisciplinary studies, (pre)law sequence, literature, mathematics, (pre)medicine sequence, modern languages, music, music education, natural sciences, philosophy, physical education, physical sciences, physics, political science/government, psychobiology, psychology, Romance languages, science, secondary education, sociology, Spanish, speech/rhetoric/public address/debate, theater arts/drama, (pre)veterinary medicine sequence.

Rochester Institute of Technology

Accounting, advertising, aerospace engineering, applied art, applied mathematics, art/fine arts, biochemistry, biology/biological sciences, biomedical sciences, biomedical technologies, biotechnology, business administration/commerce/management, ceramic art and design, chemistry, civil engineering technology, commercial art, communication, computer engineering, computer graphics, computer information systems, computer programming, computer science, computer technologies, criminal justice, (pre)dentistry sequence, dietetics, ecology, economics, electrical and electronics technologies, electrical engineering, electrical engineering technology, engineering (general), engineering technology, environmental engineering, environmental sciences, film and video production, finance/banking, food marketing, food services management, genetics, graphic arts, hotel and restaurant management, illustration, industrial design, industrial engineering, information science, interdisciplinary studies, interior design, international business, jewelry and metalsmithing, law enforcement/police sciences, (pre)law sequence, management information systems, manufacturing engineering, manufacturing technology, marketing/retailing/merchandising, mathematics, mechanical engineering, mechanical engineering technology, medical illustration, medical technology, (pre)medicine sequence, nuclear medical technology, nutrition, painting/drawing, photography, physician's assistant studies, physics, polymer science, printing technologies, printmaking, publishing, science, social work, statistics, studio art, telecommunications, textile arts, tourism and travel, (pre)veterinary medicine sequence.

Rockhurst College

Accounting, biology/biological sciences, business administration/ commerce/management, chemistry, communication, computer information systems, computer science, cytotechnology, economics, education, elementary education, English, finance/banking, French, health science, history, human resources, international studies, labor and industrial relations, marketing/retailing/merchandising, mathematics, medical technology, nursing, philosophy, physics, political science/government, psychology, secondary education, sociology, Spanish, theater arts/drama, theology.

Rollins College

Anthropology, art/fine arts, art history, biology/biological sciences, chemistry, classics, computer science, (pre)dentistry sequence, economics, education, elementary education, English, environmental sciences, French, German, history, interdisciplinary studies, international studies, Latin American studies, (pre)law sequence, mathematics, (pre)medicine sequence, music, music history, philosophy, physics, political science/government, psychology, religious studies, sociology, Spanish, studio art, theater arts/drama, (pre)veterinary medicine sequence.

Rose-Hulman Institute of Technology

Chemical engineering, chemistry, civil engineering, computer engineering, computer science, economics, electrical engineering, mathematics, mechanical engineering, optics, physics.

Rutgers, The State University of New Jersey, College of Engineering

Aerospace engineering, agricultural engineering, biomedical engineering, ceramic engineering, chemical engineering, civil engineering, computer engineering, electrical engineering, engineering and applied sciences, industrial engineering, mechanical engineering.

Rutgers, The State University of New Jersey, College of Pharmacy

Pharmacy/pharmaceutical sciences.

Rutgers, The State University of New Jersey, Cook College

Agricultural economics, agricultural education, agricultural engineering, agricultural sciences, agronomy/soil and crop sciences, animal sciences, atmospheric sciences, biochemistry, biology/biological sciences, biomedical sciences, biotechnology, botany/plant sciences, business economics, cell biology, chemistry, chemistry, foods, and nutrition, communication, computer science, conservation, (pre)dentistry sequence, dietetics, earth science, ecology, education, entomology, environmental and business economics, environmental design,

environmental education, environmental health sciences, environmental sciences, evolutionary biology, fish and game management, food sciences, forestry, genetics, geography, geology, health, physical education, and sports studies, horticulture, human ecology, interdisciplinary studies, international studies, journalism, landscape architecture/design, (pre)law sequence, (pre)medicine sequence, meteorology, microbiology, molecular biology, natural resource management, nutrition, oceanography, physical fitness/exercise science, physiology, public health, radiological sciences, recreation and leisure services, sports administration, (pre)veterinary medicine sequence, vocational education, water resources, wildlife management.

Rutgers, The State University of New Jersey, Douglass College

Accounting, African studies, American studies, anthropology, art/fine arts, art history, Asian/Oriental studies, atmospheric sciences, biochemistry, biology/biological sciences, biomedical sciences, biometrics, biotechnology, botany/plant sciences, business administration/commerce/management, cell biology, chemistry, chemistry, foods, and nutrition, Chinese, classics, communication, comparative literature, computer science, dance, East European and Soviet studies, ecology, economics, education, English, evolutionary biology, finance/banking, food sciences, French, genetics, geography, geology, German, Greek, health, physical education, and sports studies, Hispanic studies, history, human ecology, interdisciplinary studies, Italian, journalism, Judaic studies, labor studies, Latin, Latin American studies, (pre)law sequence, linguistics, management information systems, marketing/retailing/merchandising, mathematics, medical technology, (pre)medicine sequence, medieval studies, microbiology, molecular biology, music, Near and Middle Eastern studies, nutrition, philosophy, physical fitness/exercise science, physics, physiology, political science/government, Portuguese, psychology, public health, recreation and leisure services, religious studies, Russian, Russian and Slavic studies, sociology, Spanish, sports administration, statistics, theater arts/drama, urban studies, women's studies.

Rutgers, The State University of New Jersey, Mason Gross School of the Arts

Art/fine arts, ceramic art and design, dance, film studies, graphic arts, jazz, music, music education, painting/drawing, photography, printmaking, sculpture, theater arts/drama.

Rutgers, The State University of New Jersey, Rutgers College

Accounting, African studies, American studies, anthropology, art/fine arts, art history, Asian/Oriental studies, biochemistry, biology/ biological sciences, biomedical sciences, biometrics, black/ African-American studies, botany/plant sciences, business administration/commerce/management, cell biology, chemistry, chemistry, foods, and nutrition, Chinese, classics, communication, comparative literature, computer science, criminal justice, dance, (pre)dentistry sequence, East European and Soviet studies, ecology, economics, education, English, evolutionary biology, finance/banking, French, genetics, geography, geology, German, Greek, health, physical education, and sports studies, Hispanic studies, history, interdisciplinary studies, Italian, journalism, Judaic studies, labor studies, Latin, Latin American studies, (pre)law sequence, linguistics, management information systems, marketing/retailing/merchandising, mathematics, (pre)medicine sequence, medieval studies, microbiology, molecular biology, music, Near and Middle Eastern studies, philosophy, physical fitness/exercise science, physics, physiology, political science/government, Portuguese, psychology, public health, recreation and leisure services, religious studies, Russian, Russian and Slavic studies, sociology, Spanish, sports administration, statistics, theater arts/drama, urban studies, women's studies.

St. John's College (MD)
Interdisciplinary studies, liberal arts/general studies, Western civilization and culture.

St. John's College (NM)
Classics, liberal arts/general studies, Western civilization and culture.

Saint John's University (MN)
Accounting, art education, art/fine arts, art history, biology/biological sciences, business administration/commerce/management, chemistry, classics, communication, computer science, (pre)dentistry sequence, dietetics, economics, education, elementary education, English, forestry, French, German, Greek, history, humanities, Latin, (pre)law sequence, mathematics, medical technology, (pre)medicine sequence, medieval studies, ministries, music, music education, natural sciences, nursing, nutrition, occupational therapy, peace studies, philosophy, physical therapy, physics, political science/government, psychology, religious education, religious studies, sacred music, secondary education, social science, social work, sociology, Spanish, studio art, theater arts/drama, theology, (pre)veterinary medicine sequence.

Saint Joseph's University
Accounting, art/fine arts, biology/biological sciences, business administration/commerce/management, chemistry, classics, computer science, criminal justice, (pre)dentistry sequence, economics, education, elementary education, English, finance/banking, food marketing, French, German, health services administration, history, humanities, human services, international business, international relations, labor studies, (pre)law sequence, management information systems, marketing/retailing/merchandising, mathematics, (pre)medicine sequence, modern languages, philosophy, physics, political science/government, psychology, public administration, secondary education, social science, sociology, Spanish, theology.

St. Lawrence University
Anthropology, art/fine arts, Asian/Oriental studies, biology/biological sciences, biophysics, Canadian studies, chemistry, computer science, creative writing, ecology, economics, English, environmental sciences, French, geology, geophysics, German, history, literature, mathematics, modern languages, music, philosophy, physical education, physics, political science/government, psychology, recreation and leisure services, religious studies, Romance languages, sociology, Spanish, theater arts/drama.

St. Louis College of Pharmacy
Pharmacy/pharmaceutical sciences.

Saint Louis University
Accounting, aerospace engineering, aircraft and missile maintenance, American studies, art/fine arts, atmospheric sciences, aviation administration, aviation technology, biology/biological sciences, business administration/commerce/management, business economics, chemistry, classics, communication, community services, computer science, criminal justice, (pre)dentistry sequence, early childhood education, earth science, economics, education, electrical engineering, elementary education, engineering physics, English, finance/banking, flight training, French, geology, geophysics, German, Greek, history, humanities, information science, international business, labor and industrial relations, Latin, (pre)law sequence, management information systems, marketing/retailing/merchandising, mathematics, mechanical design technology, medical laboratory technology, medical records services, medical technology, (pre)medicine sequence, meteorology, middle school education, modern languages, nuclear medical technology, nursing, occupational therapy, philosophy, physical therapy, physician's assistant studies, physics, political science/government, Portuguese, psychology, religious studies, Russian,

secondary education, social work, sociology, Spanish, special education, speech pathology and audiology, speech therapy, theology, tourism and travel, transportation technologies, urban studies, (pre)veterinary medicine sequence.

Saint Mary's College (IN)
Accounting, anthropology, art education, art/fine arts, biology/biological sciences, business administration/commerce/management, chemistry, communication, creative writing, economics, elementary education, English, finance/banking, French, history, humanities, international business, literature, marketing/retailing/merchandising, mathematics, music, music education, nursing, philosophy, piano/organ, political science/government, psychology, religious studies, social work, sociology, Spanish, theater arts/drama, voice.

Saint Mary's College of California
Accounting, anthropology, art education, art/fine arts, art history, biology/biological sciences, business administration/commerce/management, chemistry, communication, dance, (pre)dentistry sequence, economics, education, engineering (general), English, French, German, Greek, health education, history, Latin, (pre)law sequence, liberal arts/general studies, mathematics, (pre)medicine sequence, modern languages, music, philosophy, physical education, physics, political science/government, psychology, religious studies, secondary education, sociology, Spanish, theater arts/drama, theology, (pre)veterinary medicine sequence, women's studies.

St. Mary's College of Maryland
Anthropology, art/fine arts, biology/biological sciences, chemistry, economics, English, history, human development, mathematics, modern languages, music, natural sciences, philosophy, physics, political science/government, psychology, public affairs and policy studies, sociology, theater arts/drama.

St. Norbert College
Accounting, anthropology, applied art, art education, art/fine arts, biology/biological sciences, business administration/commerce/management, chemistry, communication, computer information systems, computer science, creative writing, (pre)dentistry sequence, early childhood education, economics, education, elementary education, English, environmental sciences, French, geology, German, graphic arts, history, humanities, human services, international business, international economics, international studies, (pre)law sequence, literature, management information systems, mathematics, medical technology, (pre)medicine sequence, middle school education, music, music education, natural sciences, philosophy, physics, political science/government, psychology, religious education, religious studies, secondary education, social science, sociology, Spanish, theater arts/drama, (pre)veterinary medicine sequence.

St. Olaf College
American studies, art education, art/fine arts, art history, Asian/Oriental studies, biology/biological sciences, black/African-American studies, chemistry, classics, computer science, dance, (pre)dentistry sequence, East Asian studies, East European and Soviet studies, economics, education, elementary education, English, ethnic studies, French, German, Greek, health science, Hispanic studies, history, home economics education, Latin, (pre)law sequence, literature, mathematics, (pre)medicine sequence, medieval studies, music, music education, nursing, philosophy, physical education, physics, piano/organ, political science/government, psychology, religious studies, Russian, Russian and Slavic studies, sacred music, Scandinavian languages/studies, secondary education, social work, sociology, Spanish, speech/rhetoric/public address/debate, stringed instruments, theater arts/

drama, urban studies, (pre)veterinary medicine sequence, voice, Western civilization and culture, wind and percussion instruments, women's studies.

Samford University

Accounting, adult and continuing education, art education, art/fine arts, athletic training, biology/biological sciences, business administration/commerce/management, chemistry, commercial art, communication, community services, computer information systems, computer science, (pre)dentistry sequence, early childhood education, education, educational administration, elementary education, engineering physics, English, environmental sciences, family and consumer studies, fashion merchandising, food services management, French, geography, German, graphic arts, health education, history, home economics, home economics education, human resources, interior design, journalism, (pre)law sequence, liberal arts/general studies, literature, mathematics, (pre)medicine sequence, ministries, music, music education, nursing, nutrition, painting/drawing, paralegal studies, pastoral studies, physical education, physics, piano/organ, political science/government, psychology, public administration, public affairs and policy studies, recreation and leisure services, religious education, religious studies, sacred music, science education, secondary education, sociology, Spanish, speech/rhetoric/public address/debate, sports medicine, stringed instruments, theater arts/drama, (pre)veterinary medicine sequence, voice.

San Francisco Conservatory of Music

Music, opera, piano/organ, stringed instruments, voice, wind and percussion instruments.

Santa Clara University

Accounting, anthropology, art/fine arts, biology/biological sciences, business administration/commerce/management, business economics, chemistry, civil engineering, classics, communication, computer engineering, computer information systems, computer science, (pre)dentistry sequence, economics, education, electrical engineering, engineering (general), engineering physics, English, finance/banking, French, German, history, humanities, information science, interdisciplinary studies, international business, Italian, (pre)law sequence, liberal arts/general studies, marketing/retailing/merchandising, mathematics, mechanical engineering, (pre)medicine sequence, modern languages, music, philosophy, physics, political science/government, psychology, religious studies, retail management, science, sociology, Spanish, theater arts/drama, (pre)veterinary medicine sequence.

Sarah Lawrence College

American studies, anthropology, art/fine arts, art history, Asian/Oriental studies, biology/biological sciences, black/African-American studies, ceramic art and design, chemistry, child psychology/child development, classics, comparative literature, computer science, creative writing, dance, (pre)dentistry sequence, early childhood education, East European and Soviet studies, ecology, economics, English, environmental sciences, environmental studies, European studies, film studies, French, genetics, geology, German, Greek, history, human development, humanities, interdisciplinary studies, international studies, Italian, Latin, (pre)law sequence, liberal arts/general studies, literature, marine biology, mathematics, (pre)medicine sequence, modern languages, music, music history, natural sciences, painting/drawing, philosophy, photography, physics, piano/organ, political science/government, psychology, public affairs and policy studies, religious studies, Romance languages, Russian, science, sculpture, social science, sociology, Spanish, stringed instruments, studio art, theater arts/drama, voice, wind and percussion instruments, women's studies.

Scripps College

Accounting, American studies, anthropology, art/fine arts, art history, Asian/Oriental studies, astronomy, biochemistry, biology/biological sciences, black/African-American studies, chemistry, Chinese, classics, comparative literature, computer science, dance, East Asian studies, ecology, economics, engineering (general), English, environmental studies, ethnic studies, European studies, film studies, folklore, French, geography, geology, German, Germanic languages and literature, Hispanic studies, history, humanities, interdisciplinary studies, international relations, international studies, Italian, Japanese, Latin, Latin American studies, legal studies, linguistics, literature, mathematics, Mexican-American/Chicano studies, modern languages, music, philosophy, photography, physics, political science/government, psychobiology, psychology, religious studies, Russian, sociology, South Asian studies, Southeast Asian studies, Spanish, studio art, theater arts/drama, women's studies.

Shepherd College

Accounting, applied art, applied mathematics, art education, art/fine arts, athletic training, biochemistry, biology/biological sciences, botany/plant sciences, broadcasting, business administration/commerce/management, business economics, business education, chemistry, child care/child and family studies, commercial art, communication, computer information systems, computer management, computer programming, computer science, data processing, (pre)dentistry sequence, early childhood education, earth science, economics, education, elementary education, English, European studies, family and consumer studies, fashion merchandising, finance/banking, food services management, graphic arts, health education, history, home economics, home economics education, hotel and restaurant management, international studies, journalism, (pre)law sequence, library science, literature, management information systems, marketing/retailing/merchandising, mathematics, (pre)medicine sequence, middle school education, molecular biology, music, music education, music history, nursing, painting/drawing, photography, physical education, physical fitness/exercise science, physical sciences, piano/organ, political science/government, printmaking, psychology, public administration, recreational facilities management, recreation and leisure services, recreation therapy, science, science education, sculpture, secondary education, secretarial studies/office management, social work, sociology, sports administration, sports medicine, studio art, textiles and clothing, theater arts/drama, (pre)veterinary medicine sequence, voice, Western civilization and culture, wind and percussion instruments, women's studies, zoology.

Siena College

Accounting, American studies, biology/biological sciences, business economics, chemistry, classics, computer science, (pre)dentistry sequence, economics, English, finance/banking, French, history, marketing/retailing/merchandising, mathematics, (pre)medicine sequence, philosophy, physics, political science/government, psychology, religious studies, secondary education, social work, sociology, Spanish.

Simon's Rock College of Bard

American studies, applied mathematics, art/fine arts, art history, biology/biological sciences, cell biology, chemistry, comparative literature, dance, ecology, English, environmental sciences, environmental studies, French, German, graphic arts, history, interdisciplinary studies, international relations, international studies, literature, mathematics, (pre)medicine sequence, molecular biology, music, natural sciences, painting/drawing, philosophy, physics, psychology, Romance languages, Russian, science, social science, sociology, Spanish, theater arts/drama, women's studies.

Simpson College (IA)

Accounting, advertising, art education, art/fine arts, athletic training, biology/biological sciences, business administration/commerce/ management, chemistry, commercial art, communication, computer information systems, computer management, computer science, criminal justice, (pre)dentistry sequence, early childhood education, economics, education, elementary education, English, environmental biology, French, German, history, international business, international relations, (pre)law sequence, mathematics, medical technology, (pre)medicine sequence, music, music education, philosophy, physical education, physical therapy, political science/government, psychology, religious studies, science, secondary education, social science, sociology, Spanish, sports administration, theater arts/drama, (pre)veterinary medicine sequence.

Skidmore College

American studies, anthropology, art/fine arts, art history, biochemistry, biology/biological sciences, business administration/commerce/ management, business economics, chemistry, classics, computer science, creative writing, dance, (pre)dentistry sequence, economics, elementary education, English, French, geology, German, history, literature, mathematics, (pre)medicine sequence, music, philosophy, physical education, physics, political science/government, psychology, social work, sociology, Spanish, studio art, theater arts/drama, (pre)veterinary medicine sequence.

Smith College

American studies, anthropology, architecture, art/fine arts, art history, astronomy, biochemistry, biology/biological sciences, black/ African-American studies, chemistry, classics, comparative literature, computer science, dance, economics, education, English, French, geology, German, Germanic languages and literature, Greek, history, interdisciplinary studies, Italian, Latin, Latin American studies, mathematics, medieval studies, music, Near and Middle Eastern studies, philosophy, physics, political science/government, Portuguese, psychology, religious studies, Russian, Russian and Slavic studies, sociology, Spanish, studio art, theater arts/drama, women's studies.

South Dakota School of Mines and Technology

Chemical engineering, chemistry, civil engineering, computer engineering, computer science, electrical engineering, geological engineering, geology, industrial engineering, interdisciplinary studies, mathematics, mechanical engineering, metallurgical engineering, mining and mineral engineering, physics.

Southern Methodist University

Accounting, advertising, African studies, anthropology, art/fine arts, art history, behavioral sciences, biochemistry, bioengineering, biology/ biological sciences, biomedical engineering, black/African-American studies, broadcasting, business administration/commerce/ management, business economics, chemistry, communication, computer engineering, computer science, creative writing, dance, (pre)dentistry sequence, earth science, economics, electrical engineering, English, environmental sciences, ethnic studies, European studies, film studies, finance/banking, French, geology, geophysics, German, Germanic languages and literature, history, humanities, international business, international studies, journalism, Latin American studies, (pre)law sequence, literature, management information systems, marketing/ retailing/merchandising, mathematics, mechanical engineering, (pre)medicine sequence, Mexican-American/Chicano studies, modern languages, music, music education, music therapy, philosophy, physics, piano/organ, political science/government, psychology, public relations, radio and television studies, real estate, religious studies,

Russian, Russian and Slavic studies, social science, sociology, Spanish, statistics, stringed instruments, studio art, theater arts/drama, voice, wind and percussion instruments.

Southwestern University

Accounting, American studies, animal sciences, art education, art/fine arts, art history, biology/biological sciences, business administration/ commerce/management, chemistry, communication, computer science, economics, English, experimental psychology, French, German, history, international studies, literature, mathematics, modern languages, music, music education, music history, philosophy, physical education, physics, piano/organ, political science/government, psychology, religious studies, sacred music, social science, sociology, Spanish, studio art, theater arts/drama, (pre)veterinary medicine sequence, women's studies.

Spelman College

Art/fine arts, biochemistry, biology/biological sciences, chemistry, child psychology/child development, computer science, economics, engineering (general), English, French, history, mathematics, music, natural sciences, philosophy, physics, political science/government, psychology, religious studies, sociology, Spanish, theater arts/drama.

Stanford University

Aerospace sciences, African studies, American studies, anthropology, art/fine arts, art history, Asian/Oriental studies, biology/biological sciences, black/African-American studies, chemical engineering, chemistry, Chinese, civil engineering, classics, communication, comparative literature, computer engineering, computer science, earth science, East Asian studies, economics, electrical engineering, engineering (general), English, environmental sciences, European studies, French, geology, geophysics, German, history, humanities, industrial design, industrial engineering, interdisciplinary studies, international relations, Italian, Japanese, journalism, Latin American studies, linguistics, materials engineering, materials sciences, mathematics, mechanical engineering, medieval studies, microbiology, music, petroleum/natural gas engineering, philosophy, physics, political science/government, Portuguese, psychology, public affairs and policy studies, religious studies, Russian, Slavic languages, sociology, Spanish, statistics, theater arts/drama, urban studies, women's studies.

State University of New York at Binghamton

Accounting, African studies, American studies, anthropology, Arabic, art/fine arts, art history, biochemistry, biology/biological sciences, black/African-American studies, business administration/commerce/ management, chemistry, classics, comparative literature, computer information systems, computer science, (pre)dentistry sequence, economics, electrical engineering, English, environmental studies, film studies, French, geography, geology, geophysics, German, Germanic languages and literature, Hebrew, history, interdisciplinary studies, Italian, Judaic studies, Latin American studies, (pre)law sequence, liberal arts/general studies, linguistics, literature, mathematics, mechanical engineering, (pre)medicine sequence, medieval studies, music, nursing, painting/drawing, philosophy, physics, political science/government, psychobiology, psychology, Romance languages, social science, sociology, Spanish, studio art, theater arts/drama, (pre)veterinary medicine sequence.

State University of New York at Buffalo

Accounting, aerospace engineering, American studies, anthropology, architecture, art education, art/fine arts, art history, biochemistry, biology/biological sciences, biophysics, black/African-American studies, business administration/commerce/management, cell biology, chemical engineering, chemistry, civil engineering, classics, communication, computer science, dance, (pre)dentistry sequence, early childhood education, ecology, economics, electrical engineering, engineering (general), engineering physics, engineering sciences, English, environmental biology, environmental design, film studies, French, geography, geology, German, gerontology, health science, history, human services, industrial engineering, interdisciplinary studies, international studies, Italian, Judaic studies, (pre)law sequence, legal studies, linguistics, mathematics, mechanical engineering, medical technology, (pre)medicine sequence, modern languages, molecular biology, music, music education, Native American studies, nuclear medical technology, nursing, occupational therapy, painting/drawing, pharmacology, pharmacy/pharmaceutical sciences, philosophy, photography, physical fitness/exercise science, physical therapy, physics, political science/government, psychology, public affairs and policy studies, radio and television studies, religious studies, Russian, science education, secondary education, social science, sociology, Spanish, speech pathology and audiology, statistics, studio art, theater arts/drama, urban studies, (pre)veterinary medicine sequence, women's studies.

State University of New York College at Geneseo
Accounting, American studies, anthropology, applied art, art/fine arts, art history, biochemistry, biology/biological sciences, biophysics, black/African-American studies, broadcasting, business administration/commerce/management, chemistry, communication, comparative literature, computer science, (pre)dentistry sequence, early childhood education, economics, education, elementary education, English, French, geochemistry, geography, geology, geophysics, history, (pre)law sequence, mathematics, medical technology, (pre)medicine sequence, music, natural sciences, philosophy, physics, political science/government, psychology, radio and television studies, sociology, Spanish, special education, speech pathology and audiology, speech/rhetoric/public address/debate, speech therapy, studio art, theater arts/drama, (pre)veterinary medicine sequence.

State University of New York College of Environmental Science and Forestry
Biochemistry, biology/biological sciences, botany/plant sciences, chemistry, (pre)dentistry sequence, ecology, entomology, environmental biology, environmental design, environmental education, environmental engineering, environmental sciences, fish and game management, forest engineering, forestry, landscape architecture/design, land use management and reclamation, (pre)law sequence, (pre)medicine sequence, molecular biology, natural resource management, paper and pulp sciences, polymer science, science education, (pre)veterinary medicine sequence, wildlife biology, wildlife management, wood sciences, zoology.

State University of New York Maritime College
Business administration/commerce/management, electrical engineering, environmental sciences, humanities, marine engineering, marine sciences, maritime sciences, mechanical engineering, meteorology, naval architecture, naval sciences, oceanography.

Stetson University
Accounting, American studies, art/fine arts, biology/biological sciences, business administration/commerce/management, business economics, chemistry, communication, computer science, (pre)dentistry sequence, economics, education, elementary education, English, environmental studies, finance/banking, French, geography, German, history, humanities, journalism, Latin American studies, (pre)law sequence, marketing/retailing/merchandising, mathematics, medical technology, (pre)medicine sequence, music, music education, philosophy, physical education, physics, piano/organ, political

science/government, psychology, religious studies, Russian and Slavic studies, sacred music, social science, sociology, Spanish, speech/rhetoric/public address/debate, theater arts/drama, urban studies, (pre)veterinary medicine sequence, voice.

Stevens Institute of Technology
Applied mathematics, biochemistry, biology/biological sciences, chemical engineering, chemistry, civil engineering, computer engineering, computer information systems, computer science, construction engineering, construction management, (pre)dentistry sequence, electrical engineering, engineering (general), engineering and applied sciences, engineering management, engineering physics, engineering sciences, English, environmental engineering, geological engineering, history, history of science, humanities, (pre)law sequence, liberal arts/general studies, management engineering, management information systems, manufacturing engineering, marine engineering, materials engineering, materials sciences, mathematics, mechanical engineering, (pre)medicine sequence, metallurgical engineering, metallurgy, nuclear engineering, ocean engineering, optics, philosophy, physics, plastics engineering, polymer science, robotics, science, statistics, systems science, technology and public affairs, telecommunications, transportation engineering, water resources.

Swarthmore College
Anthropology, art/fine arts, art history, Asian/Oriental studies, astronomy, astrophysics, biochemistry, biology/biological sciences, black/African-American studies, chemistry, civil engineering, classics, computer science, economics, education, electrical engineering, engineering (general), English, environmental sciences, environmental studies, French, German, Greek, history, international relations, international studies, Latin, linguistics, literature, mathematics, mechanical engineering, medieval studies, music, peace studies, philosophy, physics, political science/government, psychobiology, psychology, public affairs and policy studies, religious studies, Russian, sociology, Spanish, theater arts/drama, women's studies.

Sweet Briar College
American studies, anthropology, art history, biochemistry, biology/biological sciences, chemistry, classics, computer science, creative writing, dance, economics, English, European studies, French, German, Greek, Hispanic studies, history, interdisciplinary studies, international studies, Italian, Latin, mathematics, modern languages, music, philosophy, physics, political science/government, psychology, religious studies, sociology, Spanish, studio art, theater arts/drama.

Syracuse University
Accounting, advertising, aerospace engineering, American studies, anthropology, applied art, architecture, art education, art/fine arts, art history, behavioral sciences, bilingual/bicultural education, biochemistry, bioengineering, biology/biological sciences, black/African-American studies, broadcasting, business administration/commerce/management, ceramic art and design, chemical engineering, chemistry, child care/child and family studies, civil engineering, classics, communication, comparative literature, computer engineering, computer graphics, computer information systems, computer science, consumer services, (pre)dentistry sequence, dietetics, early childhood education, economics, education, electrical engineering, elementary education, engineering physics, English, environmental design, environmental engineering, environmental studies, European studies, family services, fashion design and technology, film studies, finance/banking, food services management, forestry, French, geography, geology, German, gerontology, health education, health science, history, human development, human resources, illustration, industrial design, information science, interdisciplinary studies, interior design, international relations, Italian,

jewelry and metalsmithing, journalism, Latin American studies, (pre)law sequence, linguistics, management information systems, manufacturing engineering, marketing/retailing/merchandising, mathematics, mechanical engineering, (pre)medicine sequence, medieval studies, middle school education, modern languages, music, music business, music education, natural sciences, nursing, nutrition, painting/drawing, peace studies, philosophy, photography, physical education, physical fitness/exercise science, physics, piano/organ, political science/government, printmaking, psychology, public affairs and policy studies, public relations, radio and television studies, rehabilitation therapy, religious studies, retail management, Russian, Russian and Slavic studies, science education, sculpture, secondary education, social science, social work, sociology, Spanish, special education, speech pathology and audiology, speech/rhetoric/public address/debate, statistics, stringed instruments, studio art, telecommunications, textile arts, textiles and clothing, theater arts/drama, (pre)veterinary medicine sequence, voice, wind and percussion instruments, women's studies.

Taylor University
Accounting, art education, art/fine arts, athletic training, biblical languages, biblical studies, biology/biological sciences, broadcasting, business administration/commerce/management, chemistry, communication, computer information systems, computer programming, computer science, creative writing, (pre)dentistry sequence, economics, education, elementary education, English, environmental biology, environmental sciences, French, graphic arts, history, international business, international economics, international studies, journalism, (pre)law sequence, liberal arts/general studies, literature, mathematics, medical laboratory technology, medical technology, (pre)medicine sequence, middle school education, ministries, music, music education, natural sciences, philosophy, physical education, physics, political science/government, psychology, recreation and leisure services, religious education, religious studies, sacred music, science education, secondary education, social science, social work, sociology, Spanish, speech/rhetoric/public address/debate, theater arts/drama, theology, (pre)veterinary medicine sequence, voice.

Texas A&M University (College Station)
Accounting, aerospace engineering, agricultural business, agricultural economics, agricultural education, agricultural engineering, agricultural sciences, agronomy/soil and crop sciences, animal sciences, anthropology, applied mathematics, architecture, bilingual/bicultural education, biochemistry, bioengineering, biology/biological sciences, biomedical sciences, biophysics, botany/plant sciences, business administration/commerce/management, chemical engineering, chemistry, civil engineering, communication, computer engineering, computer science, construction management, dairy sciences, economics, educational administration, electrical engineering, elementary education, engineering technology, English, entomology, environmental design, environmental sciences, finance/banking, fish and game management, food sciences, forestry, French, genetics, geography, geology, geophysics, German, health education, history, horticulture, industrial administration, industrial engineering, interdisciplinary studies, international studies, Italian, journalism, landscape architecture/design, management information systems, marine biology, marine engineering, marine sciences, maritime sciences, marketing/retailing/merchandising, mathematics, mechanical engineering, meteorology, microbiology, nuclear engineering, nutrition, ocean engineering, ornamental horticulture, parks management, petroleum/natural gas engineering, philosophy, physical education, physics, political science/government, poultry sciences, psychology, range management, recreation and leisure services, Russian, safety and security technologies, sociology, soil conservation, Spanish,

speech/rhetoric/public address/debate, theater arts/drama, tourism and travel, veterinary sciences, wildlife management, zoology.

Thomas Aquinas College
Interdisciplinary studies, liberal arts/general studies, Western civilization and culture.

Transylvania University
Anthropology, art education, art/fine arts, biology/biological sciences, business administration/commerce/management, chemistry, computer science, economics, education, elementary education, English, French, history, mathematics, music, music education, philosophy, physical education, physical fitness/exercise science, physics, political science/government, psychology, religious studies, secondary education, sociology, Spanish, studio art, theater arts/drama.

Trenton State College
Accounting, art education, art/fine arts, art therapy, biology/biological sciences, business administration/commerce/management, business economics, chemistry, commercial art, communication, computer graphics, computer science, criminal justice, early childhood education, economics, education, elementary education, engineering sciences, English, finance/banking, graphic arts, health education, history, interior design, international business, journalism, (pre)law sequence, marketing/retailing/merchandising, mathematics, (pre)medicine sequence, music, music education, nursing, philosophy, physical education, physical fitness/exercise science, physics, political science/government, psychology, public administration, radio and television studies, secondary education, sociology, Spanish, special education, statistics, studio art.

Trinity College (CT)
American studies, art/fine arts, art history, Asian/Oriental studies, biochemistry, biology/biological sciences, biomedical engineering, black/African-American studies, chemistry, classics, comparative literature, computer science, dance, East European and Soviet studies, ecology, economics, education, electrical engineering, engineering (general), English, French, German, Greek, history, international relations, Italian, Judaic studies, Latin, Latin American studies, literature, mathematics, mechanical engineering, modern languages, music, neurosciences, philosophy, physical sciences, physics, political science/government, psychology, public affairs and policy studies, religious studies, Romance languages, Russian, Russian and Slavic studies, sociology, Spanish, studio art, theater arts/drama, women's studies.

Trinity University
Accounting, American studies, anthropology, art/fine arts, art history, Asian/Oriental studies, biochemistry, biology/biological sciences, business administration/commerce/management, business economics, chemistry, classics, communication, computer science, (pre)dentistry sequence, earth science, economics, education, engineering (general), engineering sciences, English, European studies, French, geology, German, history, interdisciplinary studies, international studies, journalism, (pre)law sequence, mathematics, (pre)medicine sequence, music, philosophy, physics, political science/government, psychology, religious studies, Russian, sociology, Spanish, speech/rhetoric/public address/debate, studio art, theater arts/drama, urban studies, (pre)veterinary medicine sequence.

Truman State University
Accounting, agricultural economics, agricultural sciences, agronomy/soil and crop sciences, animal sciences, applied art, art/fine arts, art history, biology/biological sciences, business administration/commerce/management, chemistry, classics, commercial art, communication, computer science, criminal justice, (pre)dentistry

sequence, economics, English, equestrian studies, finance/banking, French, German, graphic arts, health science, history, journalism, law enforcement/police sciences, (pre)law sequence, mathematics, (pre)medicine sequence, music, nursing, philosophy, physical fitness/exercise science, physics, piano/organ, political science/government, psychology, public health, religious studies, Russian, sociology, Spanish, speech pathology and audiology, speech/rhetoric/public address/debate, studio art, theater arts/drama, (pre)veterinary medicine sequence, voice.

Tufts University

American studies, anthropology, archaeology, architectural engineering, art/fine arts, art history, Asian/Oriental studies, astronomy, behavioral sciences, biology/biological sciences, black/African-American studies, chemical engineering, chemistry, child care/child and family studies, child psychology/child development, Chinese, civil engineering, classics, computer engineering, computer science, early childhood education, ecology, economics, electrical engineering, elementary education, engineering and applied sciences, engineering design, engineering physics, engineering sciences, English, environmental engineering, environmental sciences, experimental psychology, French, geology, geophysical engineering, German, Greek, history, international relations, international studies, Latin, manufacturing engineering, mathematics, mechanical engineering, mental health/rehabilitation counseling, music, philosophy, physics, political science/government, psychology, public health, Romance languages, Russian, Russian and Slavic studies, secondary education, sociobiology, sociology, Southeast Asian studies, Spanish, special education, theater arts/drama, urban studies, women's studies.

Tulane University

Accounting, American studies, anthropology, architecture, art/fine arts, art history, Asian/Oriental studies, biochemistry, biology/biological sciences, biomedical engineering, business administration/commerce/management, cell biology, chemical engineering, chemistry, civil engineering, classics, cognitive science, communication, computer engineering, computer information systems, computer science, (pre)dentistry sequence, early childhood education, earth science, ecology, economics, electrical engineering, engineering sciences, English, environmental biology, environmental engineering, environmental studies, evolutionary biology, finance/banking, French, geology, German, Germanic languages and literature, Greek, Hispanic studies, history, international relations, Italian, Judaic studies, Latin, Latin American studies, (pre)law sequence, liberal arts/general studies, linguistics, marketing/retailing/merchandising, mathematics, mechanical engineering, medical illustration, (pre)medicine sequence, medieval studies, molecular biology, music, paralegal studies, philosophy, physical fitness/exercise science, physics, political science/government, Portuguese, psychology, public affairs and policy studies, Russian, Russian and Slavic studies, sociology, Spanish, special education, sports administration, studio art, theater arts/drama, (pre)veterinary medicine sequence, women's studies.

Union College (NY)

African studies, American studies, anthropology, art/fine arts, biology/biological sciences, business economics, chemistry, civil engineering, classics, computer engineering, computer science, East Asian studies, East European and Soviet studies, economics, electrical engineering, English, environmental studies, geology, history, humanities, interdisciplinary studies, Latin American studies, mathematics, mechanical engineering, (pre)medicine sequence, modern languages, philosophy, physics, political science/government, psychology, science, social science, sociology, women's studies.

Union University

Accounting, art education, art/fine arts, biology/biological sciences, business administration/commerce/management, business economics, business education, chemistry, communication, computer information systems, computer science, dental services, (pre)dentistry sequence, early childhood education, economics, education, elementary education, English, finance/banking, French, Greek, history, interdisciplinary studies, journalism, (pre)law sequence, marine biology, marketing/retailing/merchandising, mathematics, medical technology, (pre)medicine sequence, music, music education, nursing, philosophy, physical education, piano/organ, psychology, radio and television studies, religious studies, sacred music, science, science education, secondary education, social work, sociology, Spanish, special education, telecommunications, theater arts/drama, theology, (pre)veterinary medicine sequence, voice.

United States Air Force Academy

Aerospace engineering, aerospace sciences, behavioral sciences, biochemistry, biology/biological sciences, business administration/commerce/management, chemistry, civil engineering, computer science, economics, electrical engineering, engineering (general), engineering mechanics, engineering sciences, English, environmental engineering, geography, history, humanities, legal studies, materials sciences, mathematics, mechanical engineering, meteorology, modern languages, operations research, philosophy, physics, planetary and space sciences, political science/government, science, social science.

United States Coast Guard Academy

Business administration/commerce/management, civil engineering, electrical engineering, marine engineering, marine sciences, mechanical engineering, naval architecture, operations research, political science/government.

United States Merchant Marine Academy

Marine engineering, maritime sciences.

United States Military Academy

Aerospace engineering, American studies, applied mathematics, Arabic, automotive engineering, behavioral sciences, biology/biological sciences, business administration/commerce/management, chemical engineering, chemistry, Chinese, civil engineering, computer engineering, computer information systems, computer science, East Asian studies, East European and Soviet studies, economics, electrical engineering, engineering and applied sciences, engineering management, engineering physics, English, environmental engineering, environmental sciences, environmental studies, European studies, French, geography, German, history, humanities, interdisciplinary studies, international studies, Latin American studies, (pre)law sequence, literature, management engineering, mathematics, mechanical engineering, (pre)medicine sequence, military science, modern languages, Near and Middle Eastern studies, nuclear engineering, operations research, philosophy, physical sciences, physics, political science/government, Portuguese, psychology, public affairs and policy studies, Russian, science, social science, sociology, Spanish, systems engineering.

United States Naval Academy

Aerospace engineering, chemistry, computer science, economics, electrical engineering, engineering (general), engineering and applied sciences, English, history, marine engineering, mathematics, mechanical engineering, naval architecture, ocean engineering, oceanography, physics, political science/government, systems engineering.

University at Albany, State University of New York

Accounting, African studies, anthropology, applied mathematics, art/fine arts, art history, Asian/Oriental studies, atmospheric sciences, biochemistry, biology/biological sciences, black/African-American studies, business administration/commerce/management, chemistry, Chinese, classics, communication, computer science, criminal justice, earth science, East Asian studies, East European and Soviet studies, economics, education, English, French, geography, geology, German, Hispanic studies, history, information science, interdisciplinary studies, Italian, Japanese, Judaic studies, Latin, Latin American studies, linguistics, management information systems, mathematics, medical technology, medieval studies, meteorology, molecular biology, music, philosophy, physical education, physics, political science/government, psychology, public affairs and policy studies, religious studies, Romance languages, Russian, Russian and Slavic studies, secondary education, Slavic languages, social work, sociology, Spanish, speech/rhetoric/public address/debate, studio art, theater arts/drama, urban studies, women's studies.

The University of Alabama in Huntsville

Accounting, art/fine arts, biology/biological sciences, business administration/commerce/management, business economics, chemical engineering, chemistry, civil engineering, communication, computer engineering, computer science, education, electrical engineering, English, finance/banking, French, German, history, industrial engineering, international business, management information systems, marketing/retailing/merchandising, mathematics, mechanical engineering, music, music education, nursing, optics, philosophy, physics, political science/government, psychology, purchasing/inventory management, Russian and Slavic studies, sociology, Spanish, systems engineering.

University of Arizona

Accounting, aerospace engineering, agricultural economics, agricultural education, agricultural engineering, agricultural technologies, agronomy/soil and crop sciences, animal sciences, anthropology, architecture, art education, art/fine arts, art history, Asian/Oriental studies, astronomy, atmospheric sciences, biochemistry, biology/biological sciences, black/African-American studies, botany/plant sciences, broadcasting, business administration/commerce/management, business economics, cell biology, chemical engineering, chemistry, child care/child and family studies, child psychology/child development, city/community/regional planning, civil engineering, classics, communication, computer engineering, computer information systems, computer science, consumer services, creative writing, criminal justice, dance, early childhood education, earth science, East Asian studies, East European and Soviet studies, ecology, economics, education, electrical engineering, elementary education, energy management technologies, engineering physics, English, environmental sciences, evolutionary biology, family and consumer studies, farm and ranch management, fashion merchandising, finance/banking, fish and game management, food sciences, food services management, French, geography, geological engineering, geology, German, Greek, health education, health services administration, history, home economics, home economics education, human ecology, humanities, human resources, human services, industrial engineering, information science, interdisciplinary studies, interior design, Italian, jazz, Judaic studies, Latin, Latin American studies, liberal arts/general studies, linguistics, management information systems, marine biology, marketing/retailing/merchandising, materials engineering, materials sciences, mathematics, mechanical engineering, medical technology, metallurgical engineering, Mexican-American/Chicano studies, microbiology, mining and mineral engineering, molecular biology, music, music education, music history, Native American studies, natural

resource management, Near and Middle Eastern studies, nursing, nutrition, occupational safety and health, optics, parks management, pharmacy/pharmaceutical sciences, philosophy, photography, physical fitness/exercise science, physics, piano/organ, planetary and space sciences, political science/government, Portuguese, psychology, public administration, radio and television studies, range management, recreation and leisure services, rehabilitation therapy, religious studies, Romance languages, Russian, Russian and Slavic studies, secondary education, social science, sociology, Spanish, speech pathology and audiology, speech/rhetoric/public address/debate, stringed instruments, studio art, systems engineering, textiles and clothing, theater arts/drama, urban studies, (pre)veterinary medicine sequence, veterinary sciences, voice, water resources, wildlife management, wind and percussion instruments, women's studies.

University of California, Berkeley

American studies, anthropology, applied mathematics, architecture, art/fine arts, art history, Asian/Oriental studies, astrophysics, bioengineering, biology/biological sciences, black/African-American studies, botany/plant sciences, business administration/commerce/management, cell biology, chemical engineering, chemistry, Chinese, civil engineering, cognitive science, communication, comparative literature, computer engineering, computer science, conservation, dance, dietetics, earth science, East Asian studies, ecology, economics, electrical engineering, engineering physics, engineering sciences, English, entomology, environmental sciences, ethnic studies, film studies, food sciences, forestry, forest technology, French, geography, geology, geophysical engineering, geophysics, German, Greek, history, humanities, industrial engineering, interdisciplinary studies, Italian, Japanese, landscape architecture/design, Latin, Latin American studies, legal studies, linguistics, literature, manufacturing engineering, materials sciences, mathematics, mechanical engineering, Mexican-American/Chicano studies, mining and mineral engineering, molecular biology, music, Native American studies, naval architecture, Near and Middle Eastern studies, nuclear engineering, nutrition, optometry, paleontology, peace studies, petroleum/natural gas engineering, philosophy, physical education, physical sciences, physics, political science/government, psychology, religious studies, Russian and Slavic studies, Scandinavian languages/studies, Slavic languages, social science, social work, sociology, soil conservation, South Asian studies, Southeast Asian studies, Spanish, speech/rhetoric/public address/debate, statistics, theater arts/drama, women's studies.

University of California, Davis

Aerospace engineering, agricultural business, agricultural economics, agricultural education, agricultural engineering, agricultural sciences, agronomy/soil and crop sciences, American studies, animal sciences, anthropology, applied art, art/fine arts, art history, Asian/Oriental studies, atmospheric sciences, bacteriology, behavioral sciences, biochemistry, bioengineering, biology/biological sciences, black/African-American studies, botany/plant sciences, chemical engineering, chemistry, child psychology/child development, Chinese, civil engineering, classics, comparative literature, computer engineering, computer science, dietetics, early childhood education, East Asian studies, ecology, economics, electrical engineering, engineering and applied sciences, English, entomology, environmental biology, environmental design, environmental sciences, environmental studies, ethnic studies, family and consumer studies, farm and ranch management, fish and game management, food sciences, food services management, French, genetics, geology, German, graphic arts, Greek, history, horticulture, human development, interdisciplinary studies, interior design, international relations, Italian, Japanese, landscape architecture/design, Latin, linguistics, materials engineering, materials sciences, mathematics, mechanical engineering, medieval studies, meteorology, Mexican-American/Chicano studies, microbiology, military science, music, music history, Native American studies, natural resource management, nutrition, ornamental horticulture, philosophy, physical education, physics, physiology, political science/government, polymer science, poultry sciences, psychology, public affairs and policy studies, range management, religious studies, Russian, sociology, soil conservation, Spanish, speech/rhetoric/public address/debate, statistics, studio art, textile arts, textiles and clothing, theater arts/drama, toxicology, water resources, wildlife biology, women's studies, zoology.

University of California, Los Angeles

Aerospace engineering, African languages, African studies, anthropology, applied art, applied mathematics, Arabic, art/fine arts, art history, Asian/Oriental studies, astronomy, astrophysics, atmospheric sciences, biochemistry, biology/biological sciences, black/African-American studies, business economics, cell biology, chemical engineering, chemistry, Chinese, civil engineering, classics, cognitive science, communication, computer engineering, computer science, dance, earth science, East Asian studies, economics, electrical engineering, engineering (general), engineering and applied sciences, English, environmental studies, film studies, French, geochemistry, geography, geological engineering, geology, geophysical engineering, geophysics, German, Greek, Hebrew, history, international economics, international studies, Italian, Japanese, Judaic studies, Latin, Latin American studies, linguistics, materials engineering, materials sciences, mathematics, mechanical engineering, Mexican-American/Chicano studies, microbiology, music, music education, music history, natural resource management, Near and Middle Eastern studies, neurosciences, nursing, philosophy, physical fitness/exercise science, physics, physiology, planetary and space sciences, political science/government, Portuguese, psychobiology, psychology, radio and television studies, religious studies, Russian, Russian and Slavic studies, Scandinavian languages/studies, Slavic languages, sociology, Spanish, systems science, theater arts/drama, Western civilization and culture, women's studies.

University of California, Riverside

Agronomy/soil and crop sciences, anthropology, art/fine arts, art history, Asian/Oriental studies, biochemistry, biology/biological sciences, biomedical sciences, botany/plant sciences, business administration/commerce/management, business economics, chemical engineering, chemistry, Chinese, classics, comparative literature, computer science, creative writing, dance, economics, electrical engineering, English, entomology, environmental engineering, environmental sciences, ethnic studies, French, geography, geology, geophysics, German, history, human development, humanities, Latin American studies, (pre)law sequence, liberal arts/general studies, linguistics, mathematics, mechanical engineering, modern languages, music, philosophy, physical sciences, physics, political science/government, psychobiology, psychology, public administration, religious studies, Russian and Slavic studies, social science, sociology, Spanish, statistics, studio art, theater arts/drama, women's studies.

University of California, San Diego

Aerospace engineering, anthropology, applied mathematics, art/fine arts, art history, Asian/Oriental studies, biochemistry, bioengineering, biology/biological sciences, biophysics, cell biology, chemical engineering, chemistry, Chinese, classics, cognitive science, communication, computer engineering, computer science, creative writing, earth science, ecology, economics, electrical engineering, engineering (general), engineering and applied sciences, engineering physics, engineering sciences, English, environmental sciences, ethnic studies, evolutionary biology, experimental psychology, film studies, French, German, Germanic languages and literature, history, information science, interdisciplinary studies, international studies,

Italian, Judaic studies, linguistics, literature, mathematics, mechanical engineering, microbiology, molecular biology, music, music history, philosophy, physics, physiology, political science/government, psychology, religious studies, Russian, sociology, Spanish, studio art, systems engineering, theater arts/drama, urban studies, women's studies.

University of California, Santa Barbara

Accounting, anthropology, archaeology, art/fine arts, art history, Asian/Oriental studies, biochemistry, biology/biological sciences, biomedical sciences, black/African-American studies, botany/plant sciences, business economics, cell biology, chemical engineering, chemistry, Chinese, classics, communication, comparative literature, computer science, creative writing, criminal justice, dance, ecology, economics, electrical engineering, English, environmental studies, evolutionary biology, film studies, French, geography, geology, geophysics, Germanic languages and literature, history, interdisciplinary studies, international relations, Italian, Japanese, Latin American studies, legal studies, linguistics, marine biology, mathematics, mechanical engineering, medieval studies, Mexican-American/Chicano studies, microbiology, molecular biology, music, operations research, painting/drawing, pharmacology, philosophy, physics, physiology, piano/organ, political science/government, Portuguese, psychobiology, psychology, public affairs and policy studies, religious studies, sculpture, Slavic languages, sociology, Spanish, statistics, studio art, theater arts/drama, voice, water resources, women's studies, zoology.

University of California, Santa Cruz

American studies, anthropology, applied mathematics, art/fine arts, art history, biochemistry, biology/biological sciences, botany/plant sciences, business economics, cell biology, chemistry, classics, clinical psychology, comparative literature, computer engineering, computer science, creative writing, dance, earth science, East Asian studies, ecology, economics, English, environmental sciences, ethnic studies, evolutionary biology, experimental psychology, film and video production, film studies, French, geology, geophysics, German, Greek, history, information science, Italian, Japanese, Latin American studies, legal studies, linguistics, literature, marine biology, mathematics, medieval studies, molecular biology, music, natural resource management, painting/drawing, peace studies, philosophy, photography, physics, political science/government, printmaking, psychobiology, psychology, religious studies, Russian, Russian and Slavic studies, sculpture, sociology, South Asian studies, Southeast Asian studies, Spanish, studio art, theater arts/drama, Western civilization and culture, women's studies.

University of Chicago

African studies, American studies, anthropology, applied mathematics, Arabic, art/fine arts, art history, Asian/Oriental studies, behavioral sciences, biblical languages, biochemistry, biology/biological sciences, black/African-American studies, chemistry, Chinese, classics, computer science, creative writing, East Asian studies, East European and Soviet studies, economics, English, environmental studies, French, geography, geophysics, German, Germanic languages and literature, Greek, history, history of science, humanities, interdisciplinary studies, Italian, Japanese, Judaic studies, Latin, Latin American studies, liberal arts/general studies, linguistics, mathematics, medieval studies, modern languages, music, music history, Near and Middle Eastern studies, philosophy, physics, political science/government, psychology, public affairs and policy studies, religious studies, Romance languages, Russian, Russian and Slavic studies, Slavic languages, social science, sociology, South Asian studies, Southeast Asian studies, Spanish, statistics, studio art.

University of Colorado at Boulder

Accounting, advertising, aerospace engineering, American studies, anthropology, applied mathematics, architectural engineering, architecture, art education, art/fine arts, art history, Asian/Oriental studies, biochemistry, biology/biological sciences, broadcasting, business administration/commerce/management, cell biology, chemical engineering, chemistry, Chinese, civil engineering, classics, communication, computer engineering, computer information systems, computer science, dance, (pre)dentistry sequence, East Asian studies, East European and Soviet studies, economics, education, electrical engineering, engineering physics, English, environmental biology, environmental design, environmental engineering, environmental sciences, environmental studies, ethnic studies, film studies, finance/banking, French, geography, geology, Germanic languages and literature, history, humanities, interdisciplinary studies, international studies, Italian, Japanese, journalism, Latin, Latin American studies, linguistics, management information systems, marketing/retailing/merchandising, mathematics, mechanical engineering, (pre)medicine sequence, microbiology, molecular biology, music, music education, music history, philosophy, physical fitness/exercise science, physics, political science/government, psychology, religious studies, Russian and Slavic studies, sociology, Spanish, speech pathology and audiology, studio art, theater arts/drama, women's studies.

University of Connecticut (Storrs)

Accounting, actuarial science, aerospace sciences, agricultural economics, agricultural education, agricultural sciences, agronomy/soil and crop sciences, animal sciences, anthropology, applied mathematics, art/fine arts, art history, biology/biological sciences, biophysics, business administration/commerce/management, cell biology, ceramic art and design, chemical engineering, chemistry, civil engineering, classics, communication, computer engineering, computer science, cytotechnology, dietetics, East European and Soviet studies, ecology, economics, education, electrical engineering, elementary education, English, environmental sciences, evolutionary biology, family and consumer studies, finance/banking, French, geography, geology, geophysics, German, graphic arts, health services administration, history, horticulture, human development, illustration, insurance, interdisciplinary studies, Islamic studies, Italian, journalism, landscape architecture/design, Latin American studies, liberal arts/general studies, linguistics, management engineering, management information systems, marketing/retailing/merchandising, materials engineering, mathematics, mechanical engineering, medical technology, military science, molecular biology, music, music education, natural resource management, natural sciences, nursing, nutrition, painting/drawing, pharmacy/pharmaceutical sciences, philosophy, photography, physical education, physical fitness/exercise science, physical therapy, physics, physiology, political science/government, Portuguese, printmaking, psychology, real estate, recreational facilities management, recreation and leisure services, Russian, sculpture, secondary education, social science, sociology, Spanish, special education, sports medicine, statistics, theater arts/drama, urban studies, women's studies.

University of Dallas

Art education, art/fine arts, art history, biochemistry, biology/biological sciences, chemistry, classics, (pre)dentistry sequence, economics, education, elementary education, English, French, German, history, (pre)law sequence, mathematics, (pre)medicine sequence, philosophy, physics, political science/government, psychology, secondary education, Spanish, theater arts/drama, theology.

University of Delaware

Accounting, agricultural business, agricultural economics, agricultural education, agricultural engineering, agricultural sciences, agronomy/soil and crop sciences, animal sciences, anthropology, applied art,

art/fine arts, art history, astronomy, athletic training, bilingual/bicultural education, biochemistry, biology/biological sciences, biotechnology, black/African-American studies, botany/plant sciences, business administration/commerce/management, business economics, chemical engineering, chemistry, child care/child and family studies, child psychology/child development, civil engineering, cognitive science, communication, community services, comparative literature, computer engineering, computer science, criminal justice, (pre)dentistry sequence, dietetics, early childhood education, East Asian studies, ecology, economics, education, electrical engineering, elementary education, English, entomology, environmental engineering, environmental engineering technology, environmental sciences, European studies, family and consumer studies, family services, fashion design and technology, fashion merchandising, film studies, finance/banking, food marketing, food sciences, French, geography, geology, geophysical engineering, geophysics, German, Germanic languages and literature, graphic arts, health education, historic preservation, history, home economics, horticulture, hotel and restaurant management, human development, information science, international business, international studies, Italian, jazz, journalism, Judaic studies, Latin, Latin American studies, (pre)law sequence, legal studies, liberal arts/general studies, linguistics, management information systems, marketing/retailing/merchandising, mathematics, mechanical engineering, medical technology, (pre)medicine sequence, medieval studies, music, music education, nursing, nutrition, ocean engineering, ornamental horticulture, paleontology, parks management, philosophy, physical education, physical fitness/exercise science, physics, piano/organ, political science/government, psychology, public administration, recreational facilities management, religious studies, Russian, science education, secondary education, sociology, soil conservation, Spanish, special education, statistics, technical writing, textiles and clothing, theater arts/drama, transportation engineering, (pre)veterinary medicine sequence, voice, wildlife management, women's studies.

University of Denver

Accounting, animal sciences, anthropology, art/fine arts, art history, biochemistry, biology/biological sciences, business administration/commerce/management, chemistry, classics, communication, comparative literature, computer science, construction management, creative writing, (pre)dentistry sequence, economics, electrical engineering, engineering (general), English, environmental sciences, finance/banking, French, geography, German, graphic arts, Greek, history, hotel and restaurant management, interdisciplinary studies, international business, international studies, Italian, Japanese, jazz, journalism, Latin, Latin American studies, (pre)law sequence, marketing/retailing/merchandising, mathematics, mechanical engineering, (pre)medicine sequence, music, music business, music education, natural sciences, philosophy, physics, political science/government, psychology, public affairs and policy studies, real estate, religious studies, Russian, science, social science, sociology, Spanish, statistics, studio art, theater arts/drama, (pre)veterinary medicine sequence, women's studies.

University of Detroit Mercy

Accounting, architecture, behavioral sciences, biochemistry, biology/biological sciences, broadcasting, business administration/commerce/management, chemical engineering, chemistry, child psychology/child development, civil engineering, classics, communication, computer engineering, computer information systems, computer programming, computer science, computer technologies, criminal justice, dental services, (pre)dentistry sequence, drug and alcohol/substance abuse counseling, early childhood education, economics, education, electrical engineering, elementary education, engineering (general), English, finance/banking, health education, health services administration, history, hotel and restaurant management, humanities, human resources, human services, industrial administration, information science, international business, journalism, labor and industrial relations, (pre)law sequence, legal studies, management information systems, marketing/retailing/merchandising, mathematics, mechanical engineering, (pre)medicine sequence, nursing, philosophy, physical education, plastics engineering, plastics technology, political science/government, polymer science, psychology, public administration, public relations, radio and television studies, religious studies, science education, secondary education, social work, sociology, Spanish, special education, sports medicine, systems engineering, theater arts/drama.

University of Evansville
Accounting, advertising, anthropology, archaeology, art education, art/fine arts, art history, arts administration, biology/biological sciences, business administration/commerce/management, business economics, ceramic art and design, chemistry, civil engineering, communication, computer engineering, computer science, creative writing, criminal justice, (pre)dentistry sequence, economics, electrical engineering, elementary education, engineering management, English, environmental studies, finance/banking, French, German, graphic arts, health services administration, history, international business, international studies, journalism, (pre)law sequence, legal studies, liberal arts/general studies, literature, marketing/retailing/merchandising, mathematics, mechanical engineering, medical technology, (pre)medicine sequence, music, music business, music education, music therapy, nursing, painting/drawing, philosophy, physical education, physical fitness/exercise science, physical therapy, physics, political science/government, psychobiology, psychology, public relations, religious studies, science education, sculpture, secondary education, sociology, Spanish, special education, telecommunications, theater arts/drama, (pre)veterinary medicine sequence.

University of Florida
Accounting, advertising, aerospace engineering, agricultural business, agricultural economics, agricultural education, agricultural engineering, agronomy/soil and crop sciences, American studies, animal sciences, anthropology, architecture, art education, art/fine arts, art history, Asian/Oriental studies, astronomy, botany/plant sciences, business administration/commerce/management, chemical engineering, chemistry, civil engineering, classics, computer engineering, computer science, conservation, construction management, criminal justice, dairy sciences, dance, East Asian studies, ecology, economics, electrical engineering, elementary education, engineering sciences, English, entomology, environmental engineering, environmental sciences, finance/banking, food sciences, forestry, French, geography, geology, German, graphic arts, health education, health science, history, horticulture, industrial engineering, insurance, interdisciplinary studies, interior design, journalism, Judaic studies, landscape architecture/design, linguistics, management information systems, marketing/retailing/merchandising, materials engineering, mathematics, mechanical engineering, microbiology, music, music education, natural resource management, nuclear engineering, nursing, nutrition, occupational therapy, pharmacy/pharmaceutical sciences, philosophy, photography, physical education, physical therapy, physician's assistant studies, physics, political science/government, Portuguese, poultry sciences, psychology, public relations, real estate, recreation and leisure services, religious studies, Russian, sociology, soil conservation, Spanish, special education, speech pathology and audiology, statistics, studio art, surveying engineering, telecommunications, theater arts/drama, zoology.

University of Georgia
Accounting, advertising, agricultural business, agricultural economics, agricultural education, agricultural engineering, agricultural sciences,

agricultural technologies, agronomy/soil and crop sciences, animal sciences, anthropology, applied art, art education, art/fine arts, art history, astronomy, biochemistry, biology/biological sciences, black/African-American studies, botany/plant sciences, broadcasting, business administration/commerce/management, business education, cell biology, chemistry, child care/child and family studies, child psychology/child development, Chinese, classics, communication, comparative literature, computer science, criminal justice, dairy sciences, dance, (pre)dentistry sequence, dietetics, early childhood education, economics, education, elementary education, English, entomology, environmental health sciences, family and consumer studies, fashion merchandising, film studies, finance/banking, fish and game management, food sciences, food services management, forestry, forest technology, French, genetics, geography, geology, German, Germanic languages and literature, graphic arts, Greek, health education, history, home economics, home economics education, horticulture, hotel and restaurant management, human resources, industrial arts, insurance, interdisciplinary studies, interior design, international business, international studies, Italian, Japanese, journalism, labor and industrial relations, landscape architecture/design, landscaping/grounds maintenance, Latin, Latin American studies, (pre)law sequence, linguistics, literature, management information systems, marketing/retailing/merchandising, mathematics, medical technology, (pre)medicine sequence, medieval studies, microbiology, middle school education, music, music education, music history, music therapy, nursing, nutrition, operations research, optometry, painting/drawing, pest control technology, pharmacy, pharmaceutical sciences, philosophy, photography, physical education, physical fitness/exercise science, physics, piano/organ, political science/government, poultry sciences, psychology, public relations, publishing, radio and television studies, reading education, real estate, recreation and leisure services, religious studies, Romance languages, Russian, science education, sculpture, secondary education, Slavic languages, social science, social work, sociology, Spanish, special education, speech pathology and audiology, speech/rhetoric/public address/debate, statistics, stringed instruments, studio art, telecommunications, textiles and clothing, theater arts/drama, theology, (pre)veterinary medicine sequence, vocational education, voice, water resources, wildlife biology, wildlife management, wind and percussion instruments, zoology.

The University of Iowa
Accounting, actuarial science, advertising, African studies, American studies, anthropology, art education, art/fine arts, art history, Asian/Oriental studies, astronomy, athletic training, biochemistry, biology/biological sciences, biomedical engineering, black/African-American studies, botany/plant sciences, broadcasting, business administration/commerce/management, business economics, ceramic art and design, chemical engineering, chemistry, child psychology/child development, Chinese, civil engineering, classics, clinical psychology, communication, comparative literature, computer engineering, computer science, creative writing, dance, (pre)dentistry sequence, earth science, East European and Soviet studies, economics, education, electrical engineering, elementary education, engineering (general), English, environmental engineering, environmental studies, experimental psychology, film and video production, film studies, finance/banking, French, geography, geology, German, Greek, health education, history, humanities, human resources, industrial engineering, interdisciplinary studies, international business, international studies, Italian, Japanese, jazz, jewelry and metalsmithing, journalism, labor and industrial relations, Latin, Latin American studies, (pre)law sequence, liberal arts/general studies, linguistics, literature, management engineering, marketing/retailing/merchandising, materials engineering, mathematics, mechanical engineering, medical

technology, (pre)medicine sequence, microbiology, museum studies, music, music education, music history, music therapy, Native American studies, Near and Middle Eastern studies, nuclear medical technology, nursing, opera, painting/drawing, pharmacy/pharmaceutical sciences, philosophy, photography, physical education, physical fitness/exercise science, physics, piano/organ, political science/government, Portuguese, printmaking, psychology, public relations, radio and television studies, recreational facilities management, recreation and leisure services, recreation therapy, religious studies, Russian, science education, sculpture, secondary education, social science, social work, sociology, Spanish, speech pathology and audiology, speech/rhetoric/public address/debate, speech therapy, sports administration, sports medicine, statistics, stringed instruments, studio art, theater arts/drama, urban studies, (pre)veterinary medicine sequence, voice, wind and percussion instruments, women's studies, zoology.

University of Kansas

Accounting, advertising, aerospace engineering, African studies, American studies, anthropology, applied art, archaeology, architectural engineering, architecture, art education, art/fine arts, art history, Asian/Oriental studies, astronomy, atmospheric sciences, biochemistry, biology/biological sciences, black/African-American studies, broadcasting, business administration/commerce/management, cell biology, ceramic art and design, chemical engineering, chemistry, child care/child and family studies, child psychology/child development, Chinese, civil engineering, classics, computer engineering, computer science, creative writing, cytotechnology, dance, (pre)dentistry sequence, East Asian studies, East European and Soviet studies, ecology, economics, electrical engineering, elementary education, engineering physics, English, environmental studies, film studies, French, genetics, geography, geology, German, Germanic languages and literature, graphic arts, health education, history, human development, humanities, industrial design, interior design, Japanese, jewelry and metalsmithing, journalism, Latin American studies, (pre)law sequence, liberal arts/general studies, linguistics, mathematics, mechanical engineering, medical records services, medical technology, (pre)medicine sequence, microbiology, music, music education, music history, music therapy, nursing, occupational therapy, painting/drawing, petroleum/natural gas engineering, pharmacy/pharmaceutical sciences, philosophy, physical education, physical fitness/exercise science, physics, piano/organ, political science/government, psychology, radio and television studies, religious studies, respiratory therapy, Russian, Russian and Slavic studies, science education, sculpture, secondary education, Slavic languages, social work, sociology, Spanish, speech pathology and audiology, speech/rhetoric/public address/debate, stringed instruments, studio art, textile arts, theater arts/drama, voice, wind and percussion instruments, women's studies.

University of Maryland College Park

Accounting, advertising, aerospace engineering, agricultural business, agricultural economics, agricultural education, agricultural engineering, agricultural sciences, agronomy/soil and crop sciences, American studies, animal sciences, anthropology, architecture, art education, art/fine arts, art history, astronomy, biochemistry, biology/biological sciences, black/African-American studies, botany/plant sciences, broadcasting, business administration/commerce/management, business education, cartography, chemical engineering, chemistry, child care/child and family studies, Chinese, city/community/regional planning, civil engineering, classics, community services, computer science, conservation, consumer services, criminal justice, criminology, dairy sciences, dance, (pre)dentistry sequence, dietetics, early childhood education, East Asian studies, economics, education, educational administration, electrical engineering, elementary education, engineering (general), English, entomology, family and

consumer studies, fashion design and technology, fashion merchandising, finance/banking, fire protection engineering, fire science, food sciences, French, geography, geology, German, Germanic languages and literature, health education, history, home economics, home economics education, horticulture, human ecology, industrial arts, interior design, Italian, Japanese, journalism, Judaic studies, labor and industrial relations, landscape architecture/design, Latin, law enforcement/police sciences, (pre)law sequence, liberal arts/general studies, linguistics, marketing/retailing/merchandising, mathematics, mechanical engineering, (pre)medicine sequence, microbiology, music, music education, music history, natural resource management, nuclear engineering, nutrition, philosophy, physical education, physical fitness/exercise science, physical sciences, physics, political science/government, Portuguese, poultry sciences, psychology, public relations, Romance languages, Russian, Russian and Slavic studies, science education, secondary education, secretarial studies/office management, Slavic languages, sociology, soil conservation, Spanish, special education, speech pathology and audiology, speech/rhetoric/public address/debate, statistics, studio art, textiles and clothing, theater arts/drama, transportation technologies, urban studies, vocational education, wildlife management, women's studies, zoology.

University of Massachusetts Amherst

Accounting, agricultural economics, agronomy/soil and crop sciences, animal sciences, anthropology, art education, art/fine arts, art history, astronomy, biochemistry, biology/biological sciences, black/African-American studies, botany/plant sciences, business administration/commerce/management, chemical engineering, chemistry, Chinese, civil engineering, classics, communication, comparative literature, computer engineering, computer science, dance, (pre)dentistry sequence, drafting and design, East European and Soviet studies, economics, education, electrical engineering, English, entomology, environmental design, environmental sciences, fashion merchandising, finance/banking, food sciences, forestry, French, geography, geology, German, history, home economics, hotel and restaurant management, industrial engineering, interdisciplinary studies, Italian, Japanese, journalism, Judaic studies, landscape architecture/design, (pre)law sequence, legal studies, liberal arts/general studies, linguistics, marketing/retailing/merchandising, mathematics, mechanical engineering, medical technology, (pre)medicine sequence, microbiology, music, natural resource management, Near and Middle Eastern studies, nursing, nutrition, philosophy, physical fitness/exercise science, physics, political science/government, Portuguese, psychology, Russian, science, sociology, Spanish, speech pathology and audiology, sports administration, studio art, theater arts/drama, (pre)veterinary medicine sequence, wildlife biology, women's studies, wood sciences.

University of Miami

Accounting, actuarial science, advertising, aerospace engineering, African studies, American studies, anthropology, applied mathematics, architectural engineering, architecture, art education, art/fine arts, art history, astronomy, audio engineering, biochemistry, biology/biological sciences, biomedical engineering, black/African-American studies, broadcasting, business administration/commerce/management, ceramic art and design, chemistry, civil engineering, communication, computer engineering, computer information systems, computer science, criminology, cytotechnology, (pre)dentistry sequence, economics, electrical engineering, electronics engineering, elementary education, engineering sciences, English, environmental engineering, environmental health sciences, environmental sciences, film and video production, film studies, finance/banking, French, geography, geology, German, graphic arts, health science, health services administration, history, human services, illustration, industrial administration, industrial engineering, insurance, international business, international studies, jazz, journalism, Judaic studies, landscape architecture/design, Latin American studies, (pre)law sequence, legal studies, liberal arts/general studies, manufacturing engineering, marine biology, marine sciences, marketing/retailing/merchandising, mathematics, mechanical engineering, medical technology, (pre)medicine sequence, meteorology, microbiology, music, music business, music education, music therapy, nuclear engineering, nuclear medical technology, nursing, ocean engineering, oceanography, painting/drawing, philosophy, photography, physical therapy, physics, piano/organ, political science/government, printmaking, psychobiology, psychology, public affairs and policy studies, public relations, radio and television studies, radiological technology, real estate, religious studies, science education, secondary education, sociology, Spanish, special education, speech/rhetoric/public address/debate, statistics, stringed instruments, studio art, systems science, telecommunications, theater arts/drama, transportation engineering, voice, wildlife management, wind and percussion instruments, women's studies.

University of Michigan (Ann Arbor)
Accounting, aerospace engineering, African studies, American studies, anthropology, applied art, applied mathematics, Arabic, archaeology, architecture, art education, art history, Asian/Oriental studies, astronomy, atmospheric sciences, biblical studies, biochemistry, biology/biological sciences, biomedical sciences, biometrics, biophysics, black/African-American studies, botany/plant sciences, business administration/commerce/management, cell biology, ceramic art and design, chemical engineering, chemistry, Chinese, civil engineering, classics, communication, comparative literature, computer engineering, computer information systems, computer science, creative writing, dance, dental services, (pre)dentistry sequence, ecology, economics, education, electrical engineering, electronics engineering, elementary education, engineering (general), engineering physics, engineering sciences, English, environmental design, environmental education, environmental engineering, environmental sciences, environmental studies, European studies, film studies, fish and game management, French, geography, geology, German, graphic arts, Greek, Hebrew, Hispanic studies, history, humanities, industrial design, industrial engineering, interdisciplinary studies, interior design, international studies, Islamic studies, Italian, Japanese, jazz, jewelry and metalsmithing, journalism, Judaic studies, landscape architecture/design, Latin, Latin American studies, liberal arts/general studies, linguistics, literature, marine engineering, materials engineering, materials sciences, mathematics, mechanical engineering, (pre)medicine sequence, medieval studies, metallurgical engineering, meteorology, Mexican-American/Chicano studies, microbiology, molecular biology, music, music education, music history, natural resource management, naval architecture, Near and Middle Eastern studies, nuclear engineering, nursing, nutrition, oceanography, painting/drawing, pharmacy/pharmaceutical sciences, philosophy, photography, physical education, physical fitness/exercise science, physics, piano/organ, political science/government, printmaking, psychology, recreation and leisure services, religious studies, Romance languages, Russian, Russian and Slavic studies, Scandinavian languages/studies, sculpture, secondary education, social science, sociology, Spanish, special education, speech pathology and audiology, speech/rhetoric/public address/debate, sports administration, statistics, stringed instruments, textile arts, theater arts/drama, voice, wildlife biology, wind and percussion instruments, women's studies, zoology.

University of Michigan–Dearborn
American studies, anthropology, art education, art history, arts administration, behavioral sciences, bilingual/bicultural education, biochemistry, biology/biological sciences, business administration/ commerce/management, chemistry, child care/child and family studies, child psychology/child development, communication equipment technology, comparative literature, computer information systems, computer science, early childhood education, economics, education, electrical engineering, elementary education, engineering (general), English, environmental sciences, environmental studies, finance/banking, French, German, health services administration, Hispanic studies, history, humanities, industrial engineering, information science, interdisciplinary studies, international studies, liberal arts/general studies, manufacturing engineering, marketing/ retailing/merchandising, mathematics, mechanical engineering, medieval studies, microbiology, middle school education, music, music history, natural sciences, philosophy, physical sciences, physics, political science/government, psychology, public administration, science, science education, secondary education, social science, sociology, Spanish, speech/rhetoric/public address/debate, women's studies.

University of Minnesota, Morris
Art history, biology/biological sciences, business administration/ commerce/management, business economics, chemistry, communication, computer science, (pre)dentistry sequence, economics, education, elementary education, English, European studies, French, geology, German, history, human services, Latin American studies, (pre)law sequence, mathematics, (pre)medicine sequence, music, philosophy, physics, political science/government, psychology, secondary education, social science, sociology, Spanish, speech/ rhetoric/public address/debate, studio art, theater arts/drama, (pre)veterinary medicine sequence.

University of Minnesota, Twin Cities Campus
Accounting, actuarial science, aerospace engineering, African studies, agricultural business, agricultural education, agricultural engineering, agricultural sciences, agronomy/soil and crop sciences, American studies, animal sciences, anthropology, applied art, architecture, art/fine arts, art history, astronomy, astrophysics, biochemistry, biology/biological sciences, black/African-American studies, botany/ plant sciences, business administration/commerce/management, business education, cell biology, chemical engineering, chemistry, child psychology/child development, Chinese, civil engineering, classics, communication, comparative literature, computer science, criminology, dance, dental services, (pre)dentistry sequence, early childhood education, East Asian studies, ecology, economics, education, electrical engineering, elementary education, engineering (general), engineering and applied sciences, English, environmental design, environmental studies, film studies, fish and game management, food sciences, forestry, forest technology, French, funeral service, genetics, geography, geological engineering, geology, geophysics, German, Greek, Hebrew, Hispanic studies, history, home economics, home economics education, human development, humanities, interdisciplinary studies, interior design, international relations, Italian, Japanese, journalism, Judaic studies, landscape architecture/design, Latin, Latin American studies, (pre)law sequence, linguistics, marketing/retailing/merchandising, materials engineering, materials sciences, mathematics, mechanical engineering, medical technology, (pre)medicine sequence, Mexican-American/Chicano studies, microbiology, modern languages, music, music education, music therapy, Native American studies, natural resource management, Near and Middle Eastern studies, nursing, nutrition, occupational therapy, parks management, pharmacy/pharmaceutical sciences, philosophy, physical education, physical fitness/exercise science, physical therapy, physics, physiology, political science/government, Portuguese, psychology, recreational facilities management, recreation and leisure services, religious studies, Russian, Russian and Slavic studies, Scandinavian languages/studies, secondary education, social science, sociology, South Asian studies,

Spanish, speech pathology and audiology, speech therapy, statistics, technical writing, textiles and clothing, theater arts/drama, urban studies, (pre)veterinary medicine sequence, vocational education, wildlife management, women's studies.

University of Missouri–Columbia
Accounting, advertising, agricultural economics, agricultural education, agricultural engineering, agricultural sciences, agricultural technologies, agronomy/soil and crop sciences, animal sciences, anthropology, archaeology, art education, art/fine arts, art history, atmospheric sciences, behavioral sciences, biochemistry, biology/biological sciences, broadcasting, business administration/commerce/management, business economics, business education, chemical engineering, chemistry, child care/child and family studies, child psychology/child development, civil engineering, classics, communication, computer engineering, computer science, cytotechnology, dietetics, early childhood education, economics, education, electrical engineering, elementary education, English, environmental design, family and consumer studies, fashion merchandising, finance/banking, fish and game management, food sciences, forestry, French, geography, geology, German, guidance and counseling, history, home economics education, horticulture, hotel and restaurant management, human development, industrial arts, industrial engineering, insurance, interdisciplinary studies, interior design, international business, international studies, journalism, liberal arts/general studies, marketing/retailing/merchandising, mathematics, mechanical engineering, medical laboratory technology, microbiology, music, music education, nuclear medical technology, nursing, nutrition, occupational therapy, parks management, philosophy, photography, physical therapy, physics, political science/government, psychology, publishing, radio and television studies, radiological sciences, reading education, real estate, recreation and leisure services, religious studies, respiratory therapy, Russian, Russian and Slavic studies, science education, secondary education, social work, sociology, South Asian studies, Spanish, special education, speech/rhetoric/public address/debate, statistics, textiles and clothing, theater arts/drama, tourism and travel, vocational education.

University of Missouri–Kansas City
Accounting, American studies, art/fine arts, art history, biology/biological sciences, business administration/commerce/management, chemistry, civil engineering, communication, computer science, criminal justice, dance, dental services, earth science, economics, education, electrical engineering, elementary education, English, French, geography, geology, German, history, interdisciplinary studies, Judaic studies, liberal arts/general studies, mathematics, mechanical engineering, medical technology, music, music education, music therapy, nursing, pharmacy/pharmaceutical sciences, philosophy, physical education, physics, piano/organ, political science/government, psychology, secondary education, sociology, Spanish, stringed instruments, studio art, theater arts/drama, urban studies, voice, wind and percussion instruments.

University of Missouri–Rolla
Aerospace engineering, applied mathematics, biochemistry, biology/biological sciences, ceramic engineering, chemical engineering, chemistry, civil engineering, computer science, (pre)dentistry sequence, economics, electrical engineering, engineering management, English, geological engineering, geology, geophysics, history, (pre)law sequence, management information systems, mechanical engineering, (pre)medicine sequence, metallurgical engineering, mining and mineral engineering, nuclear engineering, nursing, petroleum/natural gas engineering, philosophy, physics, polymer science, psychology.

University of New Hampshire (Durham)
Accounting, adult and continuing education, agricultural business, agricultural sciences, agronomy/soil and crop sciences, American studies, animal sciences, anthropology, art education, art/fine arts, art history, athletic training, biochemistry, biology/biological sciences, biomedical technologies, botany/plant sciences, business administration/commerce/management, cell biology, chemical engineering, chemistry, child care/child and family studies, city/community/regional planning, civil engineering, classics, communication, computer engineering, computer science, conservation, dairy sciences, dance, dietetics, early childhood education, earth science, ecology, economics, electrical engineering, electrical engineering technology, engineering technology, English, environmental engineering, environmental sciences, environmental studies, equestrian studies, evolutionary biology, family and consumer studies, forestry, French, geography, geology, German, Greek, health services administration, history, home economics, horticulture, hotel and restaurant management, humanities, interdisciplinary studies, international studies, journalism, Latin, linguistics, literature, marine biology, marine sciences, mathematics, mechanical engineering, mechanical engineering technology, medical laboratory technology, (pre)medicine sequence, microbiology, modern languages, molecular biology, music, music education, music history, natural resource management, natural sciences, nursing, nutrition, occupational therapy, ocean engineering, oceanography, parks management, philosophy, physical education, physics, piano/organ, political science/government, psychology, recreation and leisure services, recreation therapy, Romance languages, Russian, science, science education, social work, sociology, soil conservation, Spanish, special education, speech pathology and audiology, speech therapy, sports administration, sports medicine, statistics, stringed instruments, studio art, theater arts/drama, tourism and travel, (pre)veterinary medicine sequence, vocational education, voice, water resources, wildlife biology, wildlife management, wind and percussion instruments, women's studies, zoology.

University of North Carolina at Asheville
Accounting, actuarial science, applied mathematics, art/fine arts, atmospheric sciences, biology/biological sciences, business administration/commerce/management, chemistry, classics, communication, computer information systems, computer science, economics, education, English, environmental sciences, finance/banking, French, German, Greek, health services administration, history, Latin, literature, marketing/retailing/merchandising, mathematics, music, philosophy, physics, political science/government, psychology, sociology, Spanish, statistics, theater arts/drama.

University of North Carolina at Chapel Hill
Accounting, advertising, African studies, American studies, anthropology, applied mathematics, art education, art/fine arts, art history, Asian/Oriental studies, astronomy, biology/biological sciences, black/African-American studies, business administration/commerce/management, chemistry, city/community/regional planning, classics, communication, comparative literature, criminal justice, dental services, early childhood education, East Asian studies, economics, education, elementary education, engineering and applied sciences, English, environmental engineering, environmental sciences, folklore, French, geography, geology, German, health education, health services administration, history, industrial administration, interdisciplinary studies, international studies, Italian, journalism, Latin American studies, linguistics, mathematics, medical technology, middle school education, music, music education, nursing, nutrition, operations research, peace studies, pharmacy/pharmaceutical sciences, philosophy, physical education, physics, political science/government, Portuguese, psychology, public administration, public affairs and policy

studies, public health, radiological sciences, reading education, recreation and leisure services, religious studies, Russian, Russian and Slavic studies, science, secondary education, social science, sociology, Spanish, speech/rhetoric/public address/debate, statistics, studio art, theater arts/drama, women's studies.

University of Notre Dame

Accounting, aerospace engineering, American studies, anthropology, architecture, art/fine arts, art history, biochemistry, biology/biological sciences, black/African-American studies, business administration/ commerce/management, business economics, chemical engineering, chemistry, civil engineering, classics, communication, computer engineering, computer science, (pre)dentistry sequence, earth science, economics, electrical engineering, engineering (general), engineering sciences, English, environmental engineering, environmental sciences, film and video production, finance/banking, French, geology, German, Germanic languages and literature, Greek, history, humanities, interdisciplinary studies, international relations, international studies, Italian, Japanese, Latin, Latin American studies, liberal arts/general studies, literature, management information systems, marketing/ retailing/merchandising, mathematics, mechanical engineering, (pre)medicine sequence, medieval studies, microbiology, modern languages, music, painting/drawing, peace studies, philosophy, photography, physics, political science/government, psychology, Romance languages, Russian, science education, sculpture, secondary education, sociology, Spanish, studio art, theater arts/drama, theology, Western civilization and culture.

University of Oklahoma

Accounting, advertising, aerospace engineering, African studies, anthropology, architectural engineering, architecture, art/fine arts, art history, Asian/Oriental studies, astronomy, astrophysics, biochemistry, botany/plant sciences, broadcasting, business administration/ commerce/management, business economics, ceramic art and design, chemical engineering, chemistry, civil engineering, classics, communication, computer engineering, computer science, construction technologies, creative writing, dance, (pre)dentistry sequence, early childhood education, earth science, economics, education, electrical engineering, elementary education, engineering (general), engineering physics, English, environmental design, environmental engineering, environmental sciences, European studies, film and video production, film studies, finance/banking, French, geography, geological engineering, geology, geophysics, German, history, industrial engineering, interior design, international business, jewelry and metalsmithing, journalism, laboratory technologies, land use management and reclamation, Latin American studies, liberal arts/ general studies, linguistics, management information systems, marketing/retailing/merchandising, mathematics, mechanical engineering, (pre)medicine sequence, meteorology, microbiology, music, music education, music history, Native American studies, painting/drawing, petroleum/natural gas engineering, petroleum technology, philosophy, photography, physical education, physics, piano/organ, political science/government, printmaking, psychology, public administration, public affairs and policy studies, public relations, radio and television studies, real estate, religious studies, Russian, Russian and Slavic studies, science education, sculpture, secondary education, social work, sociology, Spanish, special education, stringed instruments, studio art, theater arts/drama, (pre)veterinary medicine sequence, voice, wind and percussion instruments, women's studies, zoology.

University of Pennsylvania

Accounting, actuarial science, adult and continuing education, African languages, African studies, American studies, anthropology, applied art, Arabic, archaeology, art/fine arts, art history, Asian/Oriental

studies, astronomy, astrophysics, behavioral sciences, biochemistry, bioengineering, biology/biological sciences, biomedical engineering, biophysics, black/African-American studies, botany/plant sciences, business administration/commerce/management, chemical engineering, chemistry, child psychology/child development, Chinese, city/community/regional planning, civil engineering, communication, comparative literature, computer engineering, computer programming, computer science, creative writing, (pre)dentistry sequence, early childhood education, East Asian studies, East European and Soviet studies, ecology, economics, education, electrical engineering, electrical engineering technology, elementary education, engineering (general), engineering and applied sciences, English, environmental design, environmental sciences, ethnic studies, European studies, finance/ banking, folklore, French, geology, German, Germanic languages and literature, Greek, Hebrew, Hispanic studies, history, history of science, insurance, interdisciplinary studies, international business, international economics, international relations, international studies, Italian, Japanese, Judaic studies, labor and industrial relations, Latin, Latin American studies, (pre)law sequence, legal studies, liberal arts/general studies, linguistics, literature, marketing/retailing/merchandising, materials engineering, materials sciences, mathematics, mechanical engineering, mechanical engineering technology, (pre)medicine sequence, microbiology, military science, modern languages, molecular biology, music, music history, natural sciences, naval sciences, Near and Middle Eastern studies, nursing, painting/drawing, peace studies, philosophy, physics, political science/government, Portuguese, psychobiology, psychology, real estate, religious studies, robotics, Romance languages, Russian, Russian and Slavic studies, Scandinavian languages/studies, secondary education, Slavic languages, social work, sociology, South Asian studies, Southeast Asian studies, Spanish, statistics, systems engineering, systems science, theater arts/drama, transportation engineering, urban studies, (pre)veterinary medicine sequence, women's studies.

University of Pittsburgh

Accounting, anthropology, applied mathematics, architectural technologies, art/fine arts, art history, astronomy, biology/biological sciences, black/African-American studies, business administration/ commerce/management, business education, chemical engineering, chemistry, child care/child and family studies, child psychology/child development, Chinese, civil engineering, classics, communication, computer science, criminal justice, dietetics, ecology, economics, electrical engineering, engineering physics, English, film studies, finance/banking, French, geology, German, health education, history, history of science, humanities, industrial engineering, information science, interdisciplinary studies, Italian, Japanese, laboratory technologies, legal studies, liberal arts/general studies, linguistics, literature, marketing/retailing/merchandising, materials engineering, materials sciences, mathematics, mechanical engineering, medical records services, medical technology, metallurgical engineering, microbiology, molecular biology, music, natural sciences, neurosciences, nursing, nutrition, occupational therapy, pharmacy/ pharmaceutical sciences, philosophy, physical education, physics, political science/government, psychology, public administration, religious studies, Russian, Slavic languages, social science, social work, sociology, Spanish, speech/rhetoric/public address/debate, statistics, studio art, theater arts/drama, urban studies, vocational education.

University of Pittsburgh at Johnstown

Accounting, American studies, biology/biological sciences, business administration/commerce/management, business economics, chemistry, civil engineering technology, communication, computer science, creative writing, (pre)dentistry sequence, ecology, economics, education, electrical engineering technology, elementary education, engineering technology, English, finance/banking, geography, geology, history, humanities, journalism, (pre)law sequence, literature, mathematics, mechanical engineering technology, medical technology, (pre)medicine sequence, natural sciences, political science/government, psychology, science education, secondary education, social science, sociology, theater arts/drama, (pre)veterinary medicine sequence.

University of Puget Sound

Art/fine arts, art history, Asian/Oriental studies, biology/biological sciences, business administration/commerce/management, chemistry, communication, computer science, (pre)dentistry sequence, economics, English, French, geology, German, history, international economics, (pre)law sequence, mathematics, (pre)medicine sequence, music, music business, music education, natural sciences, occupational therapy, philosophy, physical education, physical fitness/exercise science, physics, political science/government, psychology, religious studies, sociology, Spanish, theater arts/drama, (pre)veterinary medicine sequence.

University of Redlands

Accounting, anthropology, applied mathematics, art/fine arts, art history, Asian/Oriental studies, behavioral sciences, biology/biological sciences, business administration/commerce/management, ceramic art and design, chemistry, computer science, creative writing, economics, education, elementary education, English, environmental sciences, environmental studies, ethnic studies, French, German, history, humanities, international relations, (pre)law sequence, liberal arts/general studies, literature, mathematics, (pre)medicine sequence, modern languages, music, music education, music history, philosophy, physics, piano/organ, political science/government, psychology, religious studies, secondary education, social science, sociology, Spanish, speech pathology and audiology, speech therapy, stringed instruments, studio art, technical writing, voice, wind and percussion instruments, women's studies.

University of Richmond

Accounting, American studies, art education, art/fine arts, art history, biology/biological sciences, business administration/commerce/management, business economics, chemistry, classics, computer science, criminal justice, early childhood education, East European and Soviet studies, economics, education, elementary education, English, European studies, finance/banking, French, German, Greek, health education, health science, history, interdisciplinary studies, international business, international economics, international studies, journalism, Latin, Latin American studies, management information systems, marketing/retailing/merchandising, mathematics, middle school education, music, music education, music history, philosophy, physical education, physics, political science/government, psychology, religious studies, secondary education, sociology, Spanish, speech/rhetoric/public address/debate, studio art, theater arts/drama, urban studies, women's studies.

University of Rochester

Anthropology, applied mathematics, art history, astronomy, biochemistry, biology/biological sciences, cell biology, chemical engineering, chemistry, classics, cognitive science, computer science, earth science, economics, electrical engineering, engineering and applied sciences, engineering sciences, English, environmental sciences, environmental studies, evolutionary biology, film studies, French, genetics, geology, German, health science, history, interdisciplinary studies, Japanese, linguistics, mathematics, mechanical engineering, microbiology, music, music education, music history, natural sciences, neurosciences, nursing, optics, philosophy, physics, political science/government, psychology, religious studies, Russian, science, Spanish, statistics, studio art, women's studies.

University of Scranton

Accounting, advertising, biochemistry, biology/biological sciences, biophysics, broadcasting, business administration/commerce/management, business economics, chemistry, classics, communication, computer engineering, computer information systems, computer science, criminal justice, (pre)dentistry sequence, early childhood education, economics, education, electronics engineering, elementary education, English, environmental sciences, film and video production, finance/banking, French, German, gerontology, Greek, health services administration, history, human services, international business, international studies, journalism, Latin, (pre)law sequence, marketing/retailing/merchandising, mathematics, medical technology, (pre)medicine sequence, modern languages, neurosciences, nursing, occupational therapy, operations research, philosophy, physical therapy, physics, political science/government, psychology, public administration, radio and television studies, religious studies, Romance languages, science education, secondary education, sociology, Spanish, theology, (pre)veterinary medicine sequence.

University of Southern California

Accounting, aerospace engineering, American studies, anthropology, architecture, art/fine arts, art history, astronomy, audio engineering, biology/biological sciences, biomedical engineering, black/African-American studies, broadcasting, business administration/commerce/management, chemical engineering, chemistry, city/community/regional planning, civil engineering, classics, communication, comparative literature, computer engineering, computer science, creative writing, dental services, East Asian studies, economics, education, electrical engineering, English, environmental engineering, environmental studies, ethnic studies, film and video production, film studies, French, geography, geology, German, gerontology, Greek, history, history of philosophy, industrial engineering, interdisciplinary studies, international relations, Italian, jazz, journalism, Judaic studies, Latin, linguistics, mathematics, mechanical engineering, Mexican-American/Chicano studies, molecular biology, music, music education, nursing, occupational therapy, petroleum/natural gas engineering, philosophy, photography, physical fitness/exercise science, physical sciences, physician's assistant studies, physics, piano/organ, political science/government, polymer science, psychobiology, psychology, public administration, public affairs and policy studies, public relations, radio and television studies, religious studies, Russian, safety and security technologies, sociology, Spanish, stringed instruments, studio art, systems engineering, theater arts/drama, voice, water resources, wind and percussion instruments, women's studies.

University of Tennessee, Knoxville

Accounting, adult and continuing education, advertising, aerospace engineering, agricultural business, agricultural economics, agricultural education, agricultural engineering, agricultural sciences, agronomy/soil and crop sciences, American studies, animal sciences, anthropology, applied art, applied mathematics, archaeology, architecture, art education, art/fine arts, art history, Asian/Oriental studies, astronomy, behavioral sciences, biochemistry, biology/biological sciences, biomedical engineering, black/African-American studies, botany/plant sciences, broadcasting, business administration/commerce/management, business economics, business education, cell biology, ceramic art and design, chemical engineering, chemistry, child care/child and family studies, child psychology/child development, city/community/regional planning, civil engineering, classics, communication, comparative literature, computer engineering, computer science, creative writing, criminal justice, cytotechnology, dance, (pre)dentistry sequence, dietetics, early childhood education, East Asian studies, East European and Soviet studies, ecology, economics, education, electrical engineering, elementary education, engineering and applied sciences, engineering mechanics, engineering physics, engineering sciences, English, environmental sciences, family and consumer studies, fashion merchandising, film studies, finance/banking, fish and game management, food sciences, forestry, French, geography, geology, German, graphic arts, Greek, health education, history, home economics education, horticulture, hotel and restaurant management, human ecology, humanities, human services, illustration, industrial engineering, interdisciplinary studies, interior design, international business, Italian, jazz, journalism, landscape architecture/design, Latin, Latin American studies, liberal arts/general studies, linguistics, literature, marketing/retailing/merchandising, materials engineering, mathematics, mechanical engineering, medical laboratory technology, medical records services, medical technology, (pre)medicine sequence, medieval studies, metallurgical engineering, metallurgy, microbiology, music, music education, music history, natural sciences, nuclear engineering, nursing, nutrition, ornamental horticulture, painting/drawing, philosophy, physical education, physical fitness/exercise science, physics, piano/organ, political science/government, psychology, public administration, public health, public relations, recreation and leisure services, religious studies, retail management, Romance languages, Russian, Russian and Slavic studies, sacred music, science, science education, sculpture, secondary education, Slavic languages, social science, social work, sociology, Spanish, special education, speech pathology and audiology, speech/rhetoric/public address/debate, sports administration, statistics, stringed instruments, studio art, textiles and clothing, theater arts/drama, urban studies, (pre)veterinary medicine sequence, vocational education, voice, wildlife management, wind and percussion instruments, women's studies, zoology.

University of Texas at Austin

Accounting, advertising, aerospace engineering, African languages, African studies, American studies, anthropology, applied art, archaeology, architectural engineering, architecture, art education, art/fine arts, art history, Asian/Oriental studies, astronomy, bilingual/bicultural education, biochemistry, biology/biological sciences, black/African-American studies, botany/plant sciences, broadcasting, business administration/commerce/management, chemical engineering, chemistry, child psychology/child development, civil engineering, classics, communication, computer science, dance, (pre)dentistry sequence, dietetics, East European and Soviet studies, ecology, economics, education, electrical engineering, elementary education, English, ethnic studies, European studies, evolutionary biology, fashion design and technology, fashion merchandising, film studies, finance/banking, French, geography, geology, geophysics, German, Greek, Hebrew, history, home economics, humanities, interdisciplinary studies, interior design, international business, international studies, Italian, Japanese, journalism, Latin, Latin American studies, (pre)law sequence, liberal arts/general studies, linguistics, management information systems, marketing/retailing/merchandising, mathematics, mechanical engineering, medical technology, (pre)medicine sequence, Mexican-American/Chicano studies, microbiology, molecular biology, music, music education, Near and Middle Eastern studies, nursing, nutrition, painting/drawing, petroleum/natural gas engineering, pharmacy/pharmaceutical sciences, philosophy, photography, physical education, physics, political science/government, Portuguese, psychology, public relations, radio and television studies, reading education, Russian, Russian and Slavic studies, Scandinavian languages/studies, Slavic languages, social work, sociology, Spanish, special education, speech pathology and audiology, studio art, textiles and clothing, theater arts/drama, (pre)veterinary medicine sequence, zoology.

University of the South

American studies, anthropology, applied art, art/fine arts, art history, Asian/Oriental studies, biology/biological sciences, chemistry, classics, comparative literature, computer science, economics, English, environmental sciences, European studies, forestry, French, geology, German, Greek, history, international studies, Latin, literature, mathematics, medieval studies, music, music history, natural resource management, painting/drawing, philosophy, physics, political science/government, psychology, religious studies, Russian, Russian and Slavic studies, social science, Spanish, studio art, theater arts/drama.

University of Tulsa

Accounting, advertising, anthropology, applied mathematics, art education, art/fine arts, art history, athletic training, biochemistry, biology/biological sciences, broadcasting, business administration/commerce/management, cell biology, ceramic art and design, chemical engineering, chemistry, commercial art, communication, comparative literature, computer information systems, computer science, (pre)dentistry sequence, earth science, ecology, economics, education, electrical engineering, elementary education, engineering and applied sciences, engineering physics, English, environmental biology, environmental studies, finance/banking, French, geological engineering, geology, geophysics, German, health education, health science, history, interdisciplinary studies, international business, international studies, journalism, (pre)law sequence, literature, management information systems, marketing/retailing/merchandising, mathematics, mechanical engineering, (pre)medicine sequence, music, music education, nursing, painting/drawing, petroleum/natural gas engineering, philosophy, photography, physical sciences, physics, piano/organ, political science/government, printmaking, psychology, public relations, radio and television studies, real estate, religious studies, Russian and Slavic studies, science, science education, sculpture, secondary education, social science, sociology, Spanish, special education, speech pathology and audiology, sports administration, sports medicine, stringed instruments, studio art, theater arts/drama, (pre)veterinary medicine sequence, voice, wind and percussion instruments.

University of Utah

Accounting, anthropology, Arabic, architecture, art/fine arts, art history, Asian/Oriental studies, behavioral sciences, biology/biological sciences, biomedical sciences, broadcasting, business administration/commerce/management, chemical engineering, chemistry, child care/child and family studies, child psychology/child development, Chinese, civil engineering, classics, communication, computer engineering, computer science, dance, early childhood education, economics, electrical engineering, elementary education, English, environmental sciences, family and consumer studies, film studies, finance/banking, food sciences, French, geography, geological engineering, geology, geophysics, German, Greek, health education, history, home economics education, human development, Japanese, journalism, liberal arts/general studies, linguistics, marketing/retailing/merchandising, materials engineering, materials sciences, mathematics, mechanical engineering, medical laboratory technology, metallurgical engineering, meteorology, mining and mineral engineering, music, music education, Near and Middle Eastern studies, nursing, pharmacy/pharmaceutical sciences, philosophy, physical education, physical fitness/exercise science, physical therapy, physics, political science/government, psychology, public relations, radio and television studies, recreation and leisure services, Russian, science education, secondary education, social science, sociology, Spanish, speech pathology and audiology, speech/rhetoric/public address/debate, theater arts/drama, urban studies, women's studies.

University of Vermont

Accounting, agricultural economics, agricultural sciences, agricultural technologies, agronomy/soil and crop sciences, animal sciences, anthropology, applied mathematics, art education, art/fine arts, art history, Asian/Oriental studies, biochemistry, biology/biological sciences, botany/plant sciences, business administration/commerce/management, Canadian studies, chemistry, child care/child and family studies, child psychology/child development, civil engineering, classics, computer science, consumer services, dairy sciences, (pre)dentistry sequence, dietetics, early childhood education, East European and Soviet studies, ecology, economics, education, electrical engineering, elementary education, engineering (general), engineering management, English, environmental biology, environmental education, environmental sciences, environmental studies, European studies, family and consumer studies, fashion design and technology, fashion merchandising, finance/banking, fish and game management, food sciences, forestry, French, geography, geology, German, Greek, health education, history, home economics, home economics education, horticulture, human development, industrial arts, Latin, Latin American studies, (pre)law sequence, marine biology, marketing/retailing/merchandising, mathematics, mechanical engineering, medical technology, (pre)medicine sequence, microbiology, modern languages, molecular biology, music, music education, music history, natural resource management, nursing, nutrition, parks management, philosophy, physical education, physical therapy, physics, political science/government, psychology, reading education, recreational facilities management, recreation and leisure services, religious studies, Romance languages, Russian, Russian and Slavic studies, science education, secondary education, social work, sociology, soil conservation, Spanish, special education, speech pathology and audiology, speech therapy, statistics, studio art, textiles and clothing, theater arts/drama, (pre)veterinary medicine sequence, vocational education, water resources, wildlife biology, wildlife management, zoology.

University of Virginia

Aerospace engineering, anthropology, applied mathematics, architecture, astronomy, biology/biological sciences, black/African-American studies, business administration/commerce/management, chemical engineering, chemistry, city/community/regional planning, civil engineering, classics, comparative literature, computer science, economics, electrical engineering, engineering sciences, English, environmental sciences, ethnic studies, French, German, history, interdisciplinary studies, international studies, Italian, mathematics, mechanical engineering, music, nursing, philosophy, physical education, physics, political science/government, psychology, religious studies, Slavic languages, sociology, Spanish, speech pathology and audiology, studio art, systems engineering, theater arts/drama.

University of Washington

Accounting, aerospace engineering, anthropology, Arabic, architecture, art/fine arts, art history, Asian/Oriental studies, astronomy, atmospheric sciences, biochemistry, biology/biological sciences, black/African-American studies, botany/plant sciences, business administration/commerce/management, business economics, Canadian studies, cell biology, ceramic art and design, ceramic engineering, chemical engineering, chemistry, Chinese, city/community/regional planning, civil engineering, classics, communication, comparative literature, computer engineering, computer information systems, computer science, construction management, construction technologies, creative writing, criminal justice, dance, data processing, dental services, (pre)dentistry sequence, East Asian studies, East European and Soviet studies, ecology, economics, education, electrical engineering, elementary

education, engineering (general), English, environmental engineering, environmental health sciences, environmental studies, ethnic studies, European studies, finance/banking, forest engineering, forestry, French, genetics, geography, geology, German, Germanic languages and literature, graphic arts, Greek, Hebrew, Hispanic studies, history, history of science, human resources, industrial design, industrial engineering, interdisciplinary studies, international business, international studies, Italian, Japanese, journalism, Judaic studies, labor and industrial relations, landscape architecture/design, Latin, Latin American studies, liberal arts/general studies, linguistics, management information systems, marketing/retailing/merchandising, materials engineering, materials sciences, mathematics, mechanical engineering, medical technology, (pre)medicine sequence, metallurgical engineering, metallurgy, meteorology, Mexican-American/Chicano studies, microbiology, molecular biology, music, music education, music history, Native American studies, Near and Middle Eastern studies, nursing, occupational therapy, ocean engineering, oceanography, painting/drawing, paper and pulp sciences, peace studies, pharmacy/pharmaceutical sciences, philosophy, photography, physical therapy, physics, piano/organ, political science/government, Portuguese, psychology, rehabilitation therapy, religious studies, Romance languages, Russian, Russian and Slavic studies, Scandinavian languages/studies, sculpture, secondary education, Slavic languages, social work, sociology, South Asian studies, Spanish, speech pathology and audiology, statistics, stringed instruments, studio art, technical writing, theater arts/drama, (pre)veterinary medicine sequence, voice, wildlife management, women's studies, wood sciences, zoology.

University of Wisconsin–Madison

Accounting, actuarial science, advertising, African languages, African studies, agricultural business, agricultural economics, agricultural education, agricultural engineering, agricultural sciences, agronomy/soil and crop sciences, American studies, animal sciences, anthropology, applied art, applied mathematics, art education, art/fine arts, art history, Asian/Oriental studies, astronomy, bacteriology, biochemistry, biology/biological sciences, black/African-American studies, botany/plant sciences, broadcasting, business administration/commerce/management, cartography, cell biology, chemical engineering, chemistry, child care/child and family studies, child psychology/child development, Chinese, civil engineering, classics, communication, comparative literature, computer engineering, computer science, construction management, consumer services, dairy sciences, dietetics, early childhood education, earth science, economics, electrical engineering, elementary education, engineering and applied sciences, engineering mechanics, engineering physics, English, entomology, environmental engineering, experimental psychology, family and consumer studies, farm and ranch management, fashion merchandising, finance/banking, food sciences, forestry, French, genetics, geography, geology, geophysics, German, Greek, Hebrew, Hispanic studies, history, history of science, home economics, home economics education, horticulture, industrial engineering, insurance, interior design, international studies, Italian, Japanese, journalism, labor and industrial relations, landscape architecture/design, Latin, Latin American studies, linguistics, mathematics, mechanical engineering, medical technology, metallurgical engineering, mining and mineral engineering, molecular biology, music, music education, music history, natural resource management, nuclear engineering, nursing, nutrition, occupational therapy, pharmacology, pharmacy/pharmaceutical sciences, philosophy, physical education, physician's assistant studies, physics, political science/government, Portuguese, poultry sciences, psychology, public relations, radio and television studies, real estate, recreation and leisure services, Russian, Scandinavian languages/studies, science education, secondary education, Slavic languages, social science, social work, sociology, Southeast Asian studies, Spanish, special education, speech therapy, statistics, surveying engineering, textiles and clothing, theater arts/drama, toxicology, urban studies, water resources, wildlife management, women's studies, zoology.

Ursinus College
Accounting, anthropology, applied mathematics, art/fine arts, athletic training, biology/biological sciences, business administration/commerce/management, chemistry, classics, communication, computer science, creative writing, (pre)dentistry sequence, East Asian studies, ecology, economics, education, English, French, German, Greek, health education, health science, history, international relations, international studies, Japanese, Latin, (pre)law sequence, liberal arts/general studies, mathematics, (pre)medicine sequence, modern languages, music, philosophy, physical education, physical therapy, physics, political science/government, psychology, religious studies, Romance languages, secondary education, sociology, South Asian studies, Spanish, sports medicine, (pre)veterinary medicine sequence.

Utica College of Syracuse University
Accounting, actuarial science, anthropology, art/fine arts, biology/biological sciences, business administration/commerce/management, business economics, chemistry, child psychology/child development, communication, computer science, construction management, corrections, criminal justice, (pre)dentistry sequence, economics, English, gerontology, history, human development, international business, international studies, journalism, law enforcement/police sciences, (pre)law sequence, liberal arts/general studies, mathematics, (pre)medicine sequence, nursing, occupational therapy, philosophy, physical therapy, physics, political science/government, psychology, public relations, recreation therapy, secondary education, social science, sociology, speech/rhetoric/public address/debate, theater arts/drama, (pre)veterinary medicine sequence.

Valparaiso University
Accounting, American studies, art education, art/fine arts, art history, Asian/Oriental studies, astronomy, athletic training, behavioral sciences, biblical languages, biblical studies, biochemistry, biology/biological sciences, biomedical sciences, broadcasting, business administration/commerce/management, chemistry, city/community/regional planning, civil engineering, classics, communication, computer information systems, computer science, criminal justice, (pre)dentistry sequence, East Asian studies, economics, education, electrical engineering, elementary education, engineering (general), engineering sciences, English, finance/banking, French, geography, geology, German, Greek, health science, history, humanities, human resources, interdisciplinary studies, international economics, journalism, land use management and reclamation, Latin, (pre)law sequence, liberal arts/general studies, literature, marketing/retailing/merchandising, mathematics, mechanical engineering, medical technology, (pre)medicine sequence, meteorology, modern languages, music, music business, music education, music history, natural sciences, nursing, philosophy, physical education, physics, piano/organ, political science/government, psychology, public relations, radio and television studies, reading education, religious studies, Romance languages, sacred music, science education, secondary education, social science, social work, sociology, Spanish, special education, stringed instruments, studio art, theater arts/drama, theology, (pre)veterinary medicine sequence, voice, wind and percussion instruments.

Vanderbilt University
African studies, American studies, anthropology, art/fine arts, astronomy, biology/biological sciences, biomedical engineering, black/African-American studies, chemical engineering, chemistry, civil engineering, classics, cognitive science, communication, computer engineering, computer science, early childhood education, East Asian studies, East European and Soviet studies, ecology, economics, education, electrical engineering, elementary education, engineering (general), engineering sciences, English, European studies, French, geology, German, history, human development, interdisciplinary studies, Latin American studies, mathematics, mechanical engineering, molecular biology, music, philosophy, physics, piano/organ, political science/government, Portuguese, psychology, religious studies, Russian, secondary education, sociology, Spanish, special education, stringed instruments, theater arts/drama, urban studies, voice, wind and percussion instruments.

Vassar College
African studies, American studies, anthropology, art/fine arts, art history, Asian/Oriental studies, astronomy, biochemistry, biology/biological sciences, chemistry, classics, cognitive science, computer science, economics, elementary education, English, environmental sciences, film studies, French, geography, geology, German, Greek, Hispanic studies, history, interdisciplinary studies, international studies, Italian, Latin, Latin American studies, mathematics, medieval studies, music, philosophy, physics, political science/government, psychobiology, psychology, religious studies, Russian, sociology, studio art, technology and public affairs, theater arts/drama, urban studies, women's studies.

Villanova University
Accounting, art history, astronomy, astrophysics, biochemistry, biology/biological sciences, business administration/commerce/management, business economics, chemical engineering, chemistry, civil engineering, classics, communication, computer engineering, computer science, criminal justice, (pre)dentistry sequence, economics, education, electrical engineering, elementary education, English, environmental education, finance/banking, French, geography, German, history, humanities, human services, interdisciplinary studies, international business, (pre)law sequence, liberal arts/general studies, marketing/retailing/merchandising, mathematics, mechanical engineering, (pre)medicine sequence, meteorology, military science, natural sciences, naval sciences, nursing, philosophy, physics, political science/government, psychology, religious studies, secondary education, sociology, Spanish, special education, (pre)veterinary medicine sequence.

Virginia Polytechnic Institute and State University
Accounting, aerospace engineering, agricultural economics, agricultural education, agricultural engineering, agronomy/soil and crop sciences, animal sciences, architecture, art/fine arts, art history, biochemistry, biology/biological sciences, black/African-American studies, broadcasting, business administration/commerce/management, business economics, business education, chemical engineering, chemistry, child care/child and family studies, civil engineering, classics, communication, computer engineering, computer science, construction management, dairy sciences, (pre)dentistry sequence, dietetics, early childhood education, economics, education, electrical engineering, elementary education, engineering sciences, English, environmental sciences, family and consumer studies, farm and ranch management, fashion design and technology, fashion merchandising, finance/banking, fish and game management, food sciences, forestry, French, geography, geology, geophysics, German, health education, history, home economics, home economics education, horticulture, hotel and restaurant management, human development, human resources, human services, industrial design, industrial engineering, interior design, international studies, journalism, landscape architecture/design, (pre)law sequence, liberal arts/general studies, management information systems, marketing/retailing/

merchandising, materials engineering, mathematics, mechanical engineering, medical technology, (pre)medicine sequence, medieval studies, mining and mineral engineering, music, music education, music history, nutrition, ocean engineering, operations research, parks management, philosophy, physical education, physical fitness/exercise science, physics, political science/government, poultry sciences, psychology, public administration, public relations, religious studies, Russian and Slavic studies, science education, secondary education, sociology, Spanish, speech/rhetoric/public address/debate, sports administration, statistics, studio art, textiles and clothing, theater arts/drama, tourism and travel, urban studies, (pre)veterinary medicine sequence, vocational education, wildlife management, women's studies, wood sciences.

Wabash College

Art/fine arts, biology/biological sciences, chemistry, classics, economics, English, French, German, Greek, history, Latin, (pre)law sequence, mathematics, (pre)medicine sequence, music, philosophy, physics, political science/government, psychology, religious studies, Spanish, speech/rhetoric/public address/debate, theater arts/drama, (pre)veterinary medicine sequence.

Wake Forest University

Accounting, anthropology, art history, biology/biological sciences, business administration/commerce/management, chemistry, classics, communication, computer science, economics, education, elementary education, English, French, German, Greek, health science, history, Latin, (pre)law sequence, mathematics, (pre)medicine sequence, middle school education, music, philosophy, physical education, physician's assistant studies, physics, political science/government, psychology, religious studies, Russian, sociology, Spanish, speech/rhetoric/public address/debate, studio art, theater arts/drama.

Wartburg College

Accounting, art education, art/fine arts, arts administration, biology/biological sciences, broadcasting, business administration/commerce/management, chemistry, communication, computer information systems, computer science, early childhood education, economics, education, elementary education, English, finance/banking, French, German, health science, history, international business, journalism, law enforcement/police sciences, liberal arts/general studies, marketing/retailing/merchandising, mathematics, medical technology, music, music education, music therapy, occupational therapy, philosophy, physical education, physical fitness/exercise science, physics, political science/government, psychology, public health, public relations, religious education, religious studies, secondary education, social work, sociology, Spanish.

Washington and Jefferson College

Accounting, art education, art history, biology/biological sciences, business administration/commerce/management, chemistry, (pre)dentistry sequence, economics, education, English, French, German, history, (pre)law sequence, mathematics, medical technology, (pre)medicine sequence, philosophy, physics, political science/government, psychology, secondary education, sociology, Spanish, (pre)veterinary medicine sequence.

Washington and Lee University

Accounting, anthropology, art/fine arts, art history, biology/biological sciences, business administration/commerce/management, chemical engineering, chemistry, classics, cognitive science, communication, computer science, (pre)dentistry sequence, East Asian studies, economics, engineering physics, English, environmental sciences, equestrian studies, forestry, French, geology, geophysics, Germanic languages and literature, history, interdisciplinary studies, journalism, (pre)law sequence, marine biology, mathematics, (pre)medicine

sequence, medieval studies, music, natural sciences, neurosciences, philosophy, physics, political science/government, psychology, public affairs and policy studies, religious studies, Romance languages, Russian and Slavic studies, sociology, Spanish, studio art, theater arts/drama, (pre)veterinary medicine sequence.

Washington College

American studies, art/fine arts, biology/biological sciences, business administration/commerce/management, chemistry, (pre)dentistry sequence, economics, English, French, German, history, humanities, international studies, Latin American studies, (pre)law sequence, mathematics, (pre)medicine sequence, music, philosophy, physics, political science/government, psychology, sociology, Spanish, theater arts/drama, (pre)veterinary medicine sequence.

Washington University

Accounting, African studies, anthropology, applied art, applied mathematics, Arabic, archaeology, architectural technologies, architecture, art/fine arts, art history, Asian/Oriental studies, biochemistry, biology/biological sciences, biomedical engineering, black/African-American studies, business administration/commerce/management, business economics, ceramic art and design, chemical engineering, chemistry, Chinese, civil engineering, classics, cognitive science, commercial art, comparative literature, computer engineering, computer information systems, computer science, creative writing, (pre)dentistry sequence, earth science, East Asian studies, economics, education, electrical engineering, elementary education, engineering (general), engineering and applied sciences, engineering physics, engineering sciences, English, environmental sciences, environmental studies, ethnic studies, European studies, fashion design and technology, finance/banking, French, German, Germanic languages and literature, graphic arts, Greek, Hebrew, history, illustration, interdisciplinary studies, international business, international economics, international studies, Islamic studies, Italian, Japanese, Judaic studies, Latin, Latin American studies, (pre)law sequence, liberal arts/general studies, linguistics, literature, marketing/retailing/merchandising, mathematics, mechanical engineering, (pre)medicine sequence, medieval studies, modern languages, music, natural sciences, Near and Middle Eastern studies, painting/drawing, philosophy, photography, physical sciences, physics, planetary and space sciences, political science/government, printmaking, psychology, religious studies, Romance languages, Russian, science education, sculpture, secondary education, social science, Spanish, studio art, systems engineering, systems science, technology and public affairs, theater arts/drama, urban studies, (pre)veterinary medicine sequence, women's studies.

Webb Institute

Marine engineering, naval architecture.

Wellesley College

African studies, American studies, anthropology, archaeology, architecture, art/fine arts, art history, astronomy, biochemistry, biology/biological sciences, black/African-American studies, chemistry, Chinese, classics, cognitive science, computer science, East Asian studies, economics, English, European studies, French, geology, German, Greek, history, international relations, Italian, Japanese, Judaic studies, Latin, Latin American studies, linguistics, mathematics, (pre)medicine sequence, medieval studies, music, peace studies, philosophy, physics, political science/government, psychobiology, psychology, religious studies, Russian, Russian and Slavic studies, sociology, Spanish, studio art, theater arts/drama, women's studies.

Wells College

American studies, art/fine arts, art history, biology/biological sciences, chemistry, computer science, dance, (pre)dentistry sequence, economics, elementary education, engineering (general), English, environmental studies, French, German, history, international studies, Italian, (pre)law sequence, mathematics, (pre)medicine sequence, music, political science/government, psychology, public affairs and policy studies, religious studies, Russian, secondary education, sociology, Spanish, studio art, theater arts/drama, (pre)veterinary medicine sequence, women's studies.

Wesleyan College
Art history, biology/biological sciences, business administration/commerce/management, chemistry, communication, early childhood education, education, elementary education, English, history, interdisciplinary studies, international business, international relations, international studies, journalism, mathematics, middle school education, music, music history, philosophy, piano/organ, political science/government, psychology, religious studies, science education, secondary education, sociology, Spanish, studio art, voice.

Wesleyan University
African studies, American studies, anthropology, art/fine arts, art history, Asian/Oriental studies, astronomy, behavioral sciences, biochemistry, biology/biological sciences, black/African-American studies, chemistry, Chinese, classics, computer science, dance, earth science, East Asian studies, East European and Soviet studies, ecology, economics, English, environmental sciences, film studies, French, German, Germanic languages and literature, Greek, history, humanities, interdisciplinary studies, Italian, Japanese, Latin American studies, liberal arts/general studies, mathematics, medieval studies, molecular biology, music, neurosciences, philosophy, physics, political science/government, psychobiology, psychology, religious studies, Romance languages, Russian, Russian and Slavic studies, social science, sociology, Spanish, studio art, technology and public affairs, theater arts/drama, women's studies.

Westminster Choir College of Rider University
Liberal arts/general studies, music, music education, piano/organ, sacred music, voice.

Wheaton College (IL)
Anthropology, archaeology, art education, art/fine arts, art history, biblical languages, biblical studies, biology/biological sciences, business economics, chemistry, communication, computer science, economics, elementary education, engineering (general), environmental sciences, French, geology, German, history, interdisciplinary studies, linguistics, literature, mathematics, music, music business, music education, music history, nursing, philosophy, physical education, physics, piano/organ, political science/government, psychology, religious education, religious studies, sociology, Spanish, speech/rhetoric/public address/debate, stringed instruments, studio art, theater arts/drama, voice, wind and percussion instruments.

Whitman College
Anthropology, art/fine arts, art history, Asian/Oriental studies, biology/biological sciences, chemistry, computer science, economics, English, environmental biology, environmental studies, French, geology, German, history, literature, mathematics, music, philosophy, physics, political science/government, psychology, sociology, Spanish, theater arts/drama.

Whittier College
Anthropology, applied art, art/fine arts, athletic training, biochemistry, biology/biological sciences, business administration/commerce/management, chemistry, child psychology/child development, (pre)dentistry sequence, early childhood education, economics, education, elementary education, English, French, geology, history, international studies, Latin American studies, (pre)law sequence, liberal

arts/general studies, literature, mathematics, (pre)medicine sequence, modern languages, music, philosophy, physical education, physical sciences, physics, political science/government, psychology, religious studies, Romance languages, secondary education, social science, social work, sociology, Spanish, speech pathology and audiology, theater arts/drama, urban studies, (pre)veterinary medicine sequence.

Willamette University
American studies, art/fine arts, art history, Asian/Oriental studies, biology/biological sciences, business economics, chemistry, computer science, (pre)dentistry sequence, East European and Soviet studies, economics, English, environmental sciences, European studies, French, German, Hispanic studies, history, humanities, international studies, (pre)law sequence, literature, mathematics, (pre)medicine sequence, music, music education, music therapy, philosophy, physical education, physics, political science/government, psychology, religious studies, Russian and Slavic studies, sociology, Spanish, speech/rhetoric/public address/debate, studio art, theater arts/drama, (pre)veterinary medicine sequence.

William Jewell College
Accounting, art/fine arts, biology/biological sciences, business administration/commerce/management, chemistry, communication, computer science, data processing, (pre)dentistry sequence, economics, education, elementary education, English, French, German, history, international business, international relations, (pre)law sequence, mathematics, medical technology, (pre)medicine sequence, music, music education, nursing, philosophy, physics, political science/government, psychology, religious studies, secondary education, Spanish, (pre)veterinary medicine sequence.

Williams College
American studies, anthropology, art history, Asian/Oriental studies, astronomy, astrophysics, biology/biological sciences, chemistry, classics, computer science, economics, English, French, geology, German, history, literature, mathematics, music, philosophy, physics, political science/government, psychology, religious studies, Russian, sociology, Spanish, studio art, theater arts/drama.

William Smith College
American studies, anthropology, architecture, art/fine arts, art history, Asian/Oriental studies, biochemistry, biology/biological sciences, black/African-American studies, chemistry, Chinese, classics, comparative literature, computer science, dance, (pre)dentistry sequence, economics, English, environmental sciences, environmental studies, French, geology, German, Greek, history, interdisciplinary studies, Japanese, Judaic studies, Latin, (pre)law sequence, mathematics, (pre)medicine sequence, medieval studies, modern languages, music, philosophy, physics, political science/government, psychology, religious studies, Russian, Russian and Slavic studies, sociology, Spanish, studio art, theater arts/drama, urban studies, (pre)veterinary medicine sequence, women's studies.

Wofford College
Accounting, art history, biology/biological sciences, business economics, chemistry, computer science, (pre)dentistry sequence, economics, English, finance/banking, French, German, history, humanities, international studies, (pre)law sequence, mathematics, (pre)medicine sequence, philosophy, physics, political science/government, psychology, religious studies, sociology, Spanish, (pre)veterinary medicine sequence.

Worcester Polytechnic Institute
Actuarial science, aerospace engineering, applied mathematics, biochemistry, bioengineering, biology/biological sciences, biomedical engineering, biomedical sciences, biotechnology, business

administration/commerce/management, cell biology, chemical engineering, chemistry, city/community/regional planning, civil engineering, computer engineering, computer information systems, computer management, computer science, construction engineering, construction management, (pre)dentistry sequence, economics, electrical engineering, electronics engineering, engineering (general), engineering and applied sciences, engineering design, engineering management, engineering mechanics, engineering physics, engineering sciences, environmental engineering, environmental sciences, environmental studies, fire protection engineering, fluid and thermal sciences, genetics, geophysical engineering, history, history of science, humanities, industrial engineering, information science, interdisciplinary studies, (pre)law sequence, management engineering, management information systems, manufacturing engineering, materials engineering, materials sciences, mathematics, mechanical engineering, (pre)medicine sequence, metallurgical engineering, metallurgy, microbiology, molecular biology, music, natural sciences, nuclear engineering, nuclear physics, operations research, optics, philosophy, physics, political science/government, science, social science, statistics, systems engineering, technical writing, technology and public affairs, transportation engineering, (pre)veterinary medicine sequence.

Xavier University

Accounting, adult and continuing education, advertising, art education, art/fine arts, art history, athletic training, biology/biological sciences, broadcasting, business administration/commerce/management, business economics, chemistry, classics, communication, computer information systems, computer science, criminal justice, (pre)dentistry sequence, economics, education, elementary education, English, finance/banking, French, German, graphic arts, health education, history, humanities, human resources, international business, international studies, (pre)law sequence, liberal arts/general studies, management information systems, marketing/retailing/merchandising, mathematics, medical technology, (pre)medicine sequence, military science, modern languages, music, music education, natural sciences,

nursing, occupational therapy, painting/drawing, philosophy, physical education, physics, political science/government, psychology, public relations, radio and television studies, science education, secondary education, social work, sociology, Spanish, special education, sports administration, sports medicine, textile arts, theology, (pre)veterinary medicine sequence, voice.

Yale University

African studies, American studies, anthropology, applied mathematics, archaeology, architecture, art/fine arts, art history, Asian/Oriental studies, astronomy, biochemistry, biology/biological sciences, biophysics, black/African-American studies, chemical engineering, chemistry, Chinese, classics, comparative literature, computer science, East Asian studies, East European and Soviet studies, ecology, economics, electrical engineering, engineering mechanics, engineering sciences, English, environmental studies, European studies, film studies, forestry, French, geology, geophysics, German, Greek, history, history of science, humanities, interdisciplinary studies, international studies, Italian, Japanese, Judaic studies, Latin, Latin American studies, linguistics, literature, mathematics, mechanical engineering, music, Near and Middle Eastern studies, philosophy, physics, political science/government, psychology, religious studies, Russian, Russian and Slavic studies, sociology, Spanish, theater arts/drama, women's studies.

Yeshiva University

Accounting, biology/biological sciences, business administration/commerce/management, chemistry, classics, communication, computer science, (pre)dentistry sequence, early childhood education, economics, education, elementary education, English, finance/banking, French, Hebrew, history, interdisciplinary studies, (pre)law sequence, management information systems, marketing/retailing/merchandising, mathematics, (pre)medicine sequence, music, philosophy, physics, political science/government, psychology, sociology, speech pathology and audiology, speech/rhetoric/public address/debate, theater arts/drama.

COMPETITIVE COLLEGES INDEXES

The indexes that follow show which of the competitive colleges share certain characteristics in which students are very often interested. To get in-depth information on any of the colleges in these indexes, turn back to the individual college listings in the Comparative Descriptions section.

Colleges Costing $7000 or Less   431

Colleges Reporting 50% or More Need-Based Financial Aid Recipients   431

Colleges Reporting 20% or More Non-Need-Based Financial Aid Recipients   432

Ten Largest Colleges   434

Ten Smallest Colleges   434

Colleges Accepting Fewer than Half of Their Applicants   434

Single-Sex Colleges   434

Predominantly African-American Colleges   434

Colleges with Religious Affiliation   434

Public Colleges   436

Colleges Costing $7000 or Less

Deep Springs College	$0
United States Air Force Academy	$0
United States Coast Guard Academy	$0
United States Merchant Marine Academy	$0
United States Military Academy	$0‡
United States Naval Academy	$0‡
University of North Carolina at Asheville	$4386†
Texas A&M University (College Station)	$4488†‡
New Mexico Institute of Mining and Technology	$5354†
Oklahoma State University	$5514†
North Carolina State University	$5542†‡
University of Tennessee, Knoxville	$5582†
University of Kansas	$5726†
University of Oklahoma	$5770†
New College of the University of South Florida	$5913†
Iowa State University of Science and Technology	$5956†
The University of Alabama in Huntsville	$5990†
University of Florida	$6015†
Shepherd College	$6034†
University of North Carolina at Chapel Hill	$6035†
The University of Iowa	$6108†
Clemson University	$6112†
University of Arizona	$6140†
Brigham Young University	$6190
Louisiana State University and Agricultural and Mechanical College	$6273†
Florida State University	$6298†
University of Georgia	$6328†
South Dakota School of Mines and Technology	$6481†
Truman State University	$6514†
University of Texas at Austin	$6758†
University of Colorado at Boulder	$6892†
Colorado State University	$6931†

*Full room and board not available; estimated cost figured in.
†Cost for in-state students.
‡Figures are for 1996–97.

Colleges Reporting 50% or More Need-Based Financial Aid Recipients

Hiram College	95%
Fordham University	90%
Thomas Aquinas College	90%
University of Texas at Austin	90%
Millikin University	88%
Simpson College (IA)	87%
Capital University	85%
Central College (IA)	85%
College of St. Scholastica	85%
Simon's Rock College of Bard	85%
Albertson College of Idaho	84%
Clarkson University	83%
Concordia College (Moorhead, MN)	83%
Marietta College	83%
Houghton College	82%
Northwestern College (IA)	82%
State University of New York College of Environmental Science and Forestry	82%
University of Pittsburgh at Johnstown	82%
Belmont University	80%
Juniata College	80%
Knox College	80%
Quincy University	80%
Stevens Institute of Technology	80%

University of Scranton	80%
Ursinus College	80%
Wells College	80%
La Salle University	79%
Allegheny College	78%
Bennington College	78%
Mills College	78%
Ohio Northern University	78%
Kentucky Wesleyan College	77%
LeTourneau University	77%
Wartburg College	77%
Alma College	76%
GMI Engineering & Management Institute	76%
Hamline University	76%
Albright College	75%
Coe College	75%
Harvey Mudd College	75%
Loyola University Chicago	75%
Marlboro College	75%
Ripon College	75%
The University of Iowa	75%
University of Tulsa	75%
Westminster Choir College of Rider University	75%
Worcester Polytechnic Institute	75%
Yeshiva University	75%
Baldwin-Wallace College	74%
Elizabethtown College	74%
Pacific Lutheran University	74%
Utica College of Syracuse University	74%
College of Saint Benedict	73%
Gustavus Adolphus College	73%
Siena College	73%
Wesleyan College	73%
Illinois College	72%
Luther College	72%
Lake Forest College	71%
Bellarmine College	70%
Colorado School of Mines	70%
Dickinson College	70%
Harding University	70%
Le Moyne College	70%
Macalester College	70%
Maryland Institute, College of Art	70%
Rochester Institute of Technology	70%
Saint John's University (MN)	70%
St. Lawrence University	70%
University of Dallas	70%
Valparaiso University	70%
Beloit College	69%
Goshen College	69%
Rutgers, The State University of New Jersey, College of Pharmacy	69%
Whittier College	69%
Agnes Scott College	68%
Augustana College (IL)	68%
Bard College	68%
Eugene Lang College, New School for Social Research	68%
John Carroll University	68%
Linfield College	68%
California Institute of Technology	67%
Drake University	67%
Fairfield University	67%
Lyon College	67%
Saint Mary's College (IN)	67%

University of Rochester	67%	Claremont McKenna College	57%
Wabash College	67%	Hope College	57%
Willamette University	67%	Millsaps College	57%
Calvin College	66%	New College of the University of South Florida	57%
Grinnell College	66%	Union College (NY)	57%
New York University	66%	University of California, Riverside	57%
Oglethorpe University	66%	Case Western Reserve University	56%
William Jewell College	66%	Hobart College	56%
Colgate University	65%	Northwestern University	56%
Furman University	65%	Rutgers, The State University of New Jersey, Rutgers College	56%
Hillsdale College	65%	Taylor University	56%
Illinois Wesleyan University	65%	Bradley University	55%
Monmouth College	65%	Christian Brothers University	55%
St. John's College (NM)	65%	Drew University	55%
University of Puget Sound	65%	Hamilton College	55%
College of the Holy Cross	64%	Oberlin College	55%
Earlham College	64%	Providence College	55%
St. Norbert College	64%	St. John's College (MD)	55%
St. Olaf College	64%	Saint Mary's College of California	55%
Santa Clara University	64%	Smith College	55%
Clark University	63%	University of Denver	55%
Georgetown College	63%	Wellesley College	55%
Syracuse University	63%	Bates College	54%
Austin College	62%	Centenary College of Louisiana	54%
The College of Wooster	62%	Pomona College	54%
Nebraska Wesleyan University	62%	Rutgers, The State University of New Jersey, College of Engineering	54%
Occidental College	62%	University of Massachusetts Amherst	54%
University of Delaware	62%	Wheaton College (IL)	54%
William Smith College	62%	Bryn Mawr College	53%
Guilford College	61%	Columbia University, Columbia College (NY)	53%
Hampshire College	61%	Creighton University	53%
Hofstra University	61%	Muhlenberg College	53%
Iowa State University of Science and Technology	61%	Pepperdine University (Malibu)	53%
Rhode Island School of Design	61%	Purdue University (West Lafayette)	53%
Sarah Lawrence College	61%	Rutgers, The State University of New Jersey, Cook College	53%
Southwestern University	61%	Boston University	52%
University of Oklahoma	61%	Cedarville College	52%
University of Southern California	61%	Christendom College	52%
Barnard College	60%	Colorado State University	52%
Birmingham-Southern College	60%	Lehigh University	52%
Bucknell University	60%	Lewis & Clark College	52%
Butler University	60%	Rutgers, The State University of New Jersey, Douglass College	52%
New Jersey Institute of Technology	60%	DePauw University	51%
State University of New York at Buffalo	60%	Franklin and Marshall College	51%
Sweet Briar College	60%	Gettysburg College	51%
University of Notre Dame	60%	Kalamazoo College	51%
University of Redlands	60%	Lafayette College	51%
Vassar College	60%	University of California, Berkeley	51%
Washington College	60%	The Colorado College	50%
Whitman College	60%	The George Washington University	50%
Albion College	59%	Hampden-Sydney College	50%
Brandeis University	59%	Johns Hopkins University	50%
Carleton College	59%	New Mexico Institute of Mining and Technology	50%
Carnegie Mellon University	59%	University of Arizona	50%
Carroll College (MT)	59%		
Massachusetts Institute of Technology	59%		
Ohio Wesleyan University	59%		
Saint Louis University	59%		
Stetson University	59%		
University of New Hampshire (Durham)	59%		
The Catholic University of America	58%		
Eckerd College	58%		
Illinois Institute of Technology	58%		
Centre College	57%		

Colleges Reporting 20% or More Non-Need-Based Financial Aid Recipients

Capital University	95%
Oglethorpe University	89%
Carroll College (MT)	84%

University of Dallas	80%
Presbyterian College	78%
Goshen College	76%
John Carroll University	76%
Case Western Reserve University	74%
Nebraska Wesleyan University	68%
Quincy University	68%
Colorado Technical University	66%
Georgetown College	66%
Alma College	65%
Westminster Choir College of Rider University	65%
Illinois College	60%
Kentucky Wesleyan College	60%
Truman State University	59%
New College of the University of South Florida	57%
Rockhurst College	56%
Allegheny College	55%
Samford University	53%
Augustana College (IL)	51%
University of Missouri–Rolla	51%
St. Mary's College of Maryland	50%
The Catholic University of America	48%
Drew University	48%
New Mexico Institute of Mining and Technology	47%
Agnes Scott College	46%
Pepperdine University (Malibu)	46%
Kalamazoo College	45%
University of Tulsa	45%
Butler University	44%
Rutgers, The State University of New Jersey, College of Pharmacy	44%
Carnegie Mellon University	43%
Rice University	43%
Transylvania University	42%
Elizabethtown College	40%
Goucher College	40%
University of Puget Sound	40%
Shepherd College	39%
University of Oklahoma	39%
Miami University	38%
Monmouth College	38%
Rutgers, The State University of New Jersey, College of Engineering	38%
Valparaiso University	38%
Centenary College of Louisiana	37%
Louisiana State University and Agricultural and Mechanical College	37%
University of Florida	37%
Hiram College	36%
Hofstra University	36%
Illinois Institute of Technology	36%
Rutgers, The State University of New Jersey, Douglass College	36%
Trenton State College	36%
Christian Brothers University	35%
Harding University	35%
New Jersey Institute of Technology	35%
University of Colorado at Boulder	35%
Florida Institute of Technology	34%
Rutgers, The State University of New Jersey, Rutgers College	34%
Wake Forest University	34%
Creighton University	33%
University of Richmond	33%

Bradley University	32%
Grove City College	32%
Rhodes College	32%
Southern Methodist University	32%
Michigan Technological University	31%
Rutgers, The State University of New Jersey, Cook College	31%
University of New Hampshire (Durham)	31%
University of Pittsburgh at Johnstown	31%
William Jewell College	31%
Bellarmine College	30%
Birmingham-Southern College	30%
Davidson College	30%
DePauw University	30%
Le Moyne College	30%
Maryville University of Saint Louis	30%
Ohio University	30%
Stetson University	30%
University of Wisconsin–Madison	30%
Denison University	29%
Centre College	28%
College of William and Mary	28%
Hope College	28%
Wabash College	28%
Austin College	27%
Whitman College	27%
Wofford College	27%
Auburn University	26%
Calvin College	26%
Hampden-Sydney College	25%
Mary Washington College	25%
St. Norbert College	25%
Trinity University	25%
Yeshiva University	25%
Christendom College	24%
Eckerd College	24%
Guilford College	24%
James Madison University	24%
University of North Carolina at Asheville	24%
Wartburg College	24%
Bennington College	23%
Drake University	23%
Taylor University	23%
Albion College	22%
Cedarville College	22%
College of St. Scholastica	22%
Colorado State University	22%
Millsaps College	22%
Ohio Northern University	22%
Wesleyan College	22%
The George Washington University	21%
Ohio Wesleyan University	21%
Tulane University	21%
University of Denver	21%
Vanderbilt University	21%
Illinois Wesleyan University	20%
Marietta College	20%
Northwestern College (IA)	20%
Rochester Institute of Technology	20%
Rollins College	20%
University of Scranton	20%
Washington College	20%

Ten Largest Colleges

The Ohio State University	48,676
University of Texas at Austin	47,905
Texas A&M University (College Station)	41,790
Michigan State University	40,647
Pennsylvania State University University Park Campus	39,646
University of Florida	39,439
University of Wisconsin–Madison	37,890
University of Minnesota, Twin Cities Campus	36,995
University of Michigan (Ann Arbor)	36,687
New York University	35,825

Ten Smallest Colleges

Deep Springs College	25
Webb Institute	79
Christendom College	178
Thomas Aquinas College	232
Marlboro College	270
Simon's Rock College of Bard	304
Eugene Lang College, New School for Social Research	345
Bennington College	387
Westminster Choir College of Rider University	407
Wells College	425

Colleges Accepting Fewer than Half of Their Applicants

Amherst College
Babson College
Barnard College
Bates College
Boston College
Bowdoin College
Brown University
California Institute of Technology
Claremont McKenna College
Colby College
Colgate University
College of William and Mary
Columbia University, Columbia College (NY)
Cooper Union for the Advancement of Science and Art
Cornell University
Dartmouth College
Davidson College
Deep Springs College
Duke University
Georgetown University
Grove City College
Hamilton College
Harvard University
Harvey Mudd College
Haverford College
Johns Hopkins University
Lyon College
Massachusetts Institute of Technology
Middlebury College
New York University
Northwestern University
Ohio Northern University
Pomona College
Princeton University
Rice University
Rutgers, The State University of New Jersey, College of Pharmacy
Smith College
Spelman College

Stanford University
State University of New York at Binghamton
State University of New York College of Environmental Science and Forestry
Swarthmore College
Trenton State College
Tufts University
United States Air Force Academy
United States Coast Guard Academy
United States Merchant Marine Academy
United States Military Academy
United States Naval Academy
University of California, Berkeley
University of California, Los Angeles
University of California, San Diego
University of North Carolina at Chapel Hill
University of Notre Dame
University of Pennsylvania
University of Virginia
Vassar College
Wake Forest University
Washington and Lee University
Webb Institute
Wellesley College
Wesleyan University
Westminster Choir College of Rider University
Whitman College
Williams College
Yale University

Single-Sex Colleges

Agnes Scott College	W
Barnard College	W
Bryn Mawr College	W
College of Saint Benedict	W
Deep Springs College	M
Hampden-Sydney College	M
Hobart College	M
Mills College	W
Morehouse College	M
Mount Holyoke College	W
Randolph-Macon Woman's College	W
Rutgers, The State University of New Jersey, Douglass College	W
Saint John's University (MN)	M
Saint Mary's College (IN)	W
Scripps College	W
Smith College	W
Spelman College	W
Sweet Briar College	W
Wabash College	M
Wellesley College	W
Wells College	W
Wesleyan College	W
William Smith College	W

Predominantly African-American Colleges

Fisk University
Morehouse College
Spelman College

Colleges with Religious Affiliation

Baptist

Baylor University
Belmont University

Bethel College (MN)
Cedarville College
Georgetown College
Linfield College
Samford University
Union University
University of Richmond
William Jewell College

Brethren
Elizabethtown College
Messiah College

Christian Church (Disciples of Christ)
Hiram College
Transylvania University

Churches of Christ
David Lipscomb University
Harding University
Pepperdine University (Malibu)

Episcopal
Hobart College
University of the South

Friends
Earlham College
Guilford College

Interdenominational
Illinois College

Jewish
Albert A. List College, Jewish Theological Seminary of America

Latter-day Saints (Mormon)
Brigham Young University

Lutheran
Augustana College (IL)
Augustana College (SD)
Capital University
Concordia College (Moorhead, MN)
Gustavus Adolphus College
Luther College
Muhlenberg College
Pacific Lutheran University
St. Olaf College
Valparaiso University
Wartburg College

Mennonite
Goshen College

Methodist
Albion College
Albright College
Allegheny College
American University
Baldwin-Wallace College
Birmingham-Southern College
Centenary College of Louisiana
Cornell College
DePauw University
Drew University
Duke University
Emory University
Hamline University
Hendrix College

Kentucky Wesleyan College
Millsaps College
Mount Union College
Nebraska Wesleyan University
North Central College
Ohio Northern University
Ohio Wesleyan University
Randolph-Macon Woman's College
Simpson College (IA)
Southern Methodist University
Southwestern University
University of Evansville
Wesleyan College
Willamette University
Wofford College

Nondenominational
LeTourneau University
Wheaton College (IL)

Presbyterian
Agnes Scott College
Alma College
Austin College
Buena Vista University
Coe College
The College of Wooster
Davidson College
Eckerd College
Grove City College
Hampden-Sydney College
Lafayette College
Lyon College
Macalester College
Millikin University
Monmouth College
Presbyterian College
Rhodes College
Trinity University
University of Tulsa

Reformed Churches
Calvin College
Central College (IA)
Hope College
Northwestern College (IA)

Roman Catholic
Bellarmine College
Boston College
Carroll College (MT)
The Catholic University of America
Christendom College
Christian Brothers University
College of Saint Benedict
College of St. Scholastica
College of the Holy Cross
Creighton University
DePaul University
Fairfield University
Fordham University
Georgetown University
John Carroll University
La Salle University
Le Moyne College
Loyola College
Loyola University Chicago

Marquette University
Providence College
Quincy University
Rockhurst College
Saint John's University (MN)
Saint Joseph's University
Saint Louis University
Saint Mary's College (IN)
Saint Mary's College of California
St. Norbert College
Santa Clara University
Siena College
Thomas Aquinas College
University of Dallas
University of Detroit Mercy
University of Notre Dame
University of Scranton
Villanova University
Xavier University

United Church of Christ
Fisk University
Ursinus College

Wesleyan
Houghton College

Public Colleges
Auburn University
Clemson University
College of William and Mary
Colorado School of Mines
Colorado State University
Florida State University
Georgia Institute of Technology
Iowa State University of Science and Technology
James Madison University
Louisiana State University and Agricultural and
    Mechanical College
Mary Washington College
Miami University
Michigan State University
Michigan Technological University
New College of the University of South Florida
New Jersey Institute of Technology
New Mexico Institute of Mining and Technology
North Carolina State University
The Ohio State University
Ohio University
Oklahoma State University
Pennsylvania State University University Park Campus
Purdue University (West Lafayette)
Rutgers, The State University of New Jersey, College of
    Engineering
Rutgers, The State University of New Jersey, College of
    Pharmacy
Rutgers, The State University of New Jersey, Cook
    College
Rutgers, The State University of New Jersey, Douglass
    College
Rutgers, The State University of New Jersey, Rutgers
    College

St. Mary's College of Maryland
Shepherd College
South Dakota School of Mines and Technology
State University of New York at Binghamton
State University of New York at Buffalo
State University of New York College at Geneseo
State University of New York College of Environmental
    Science and Forestry
State University of New York Maritime College
Texas A&M University (College Station)
Trenton State College
Truman State University
United States Air Force Academy
United States Coast Guard Academy
United States Merchant Marine Academy
United States Military Academy
United States Naval Academy
University at Albany, State University of New York
The University of Alabama in Huntsville
University of Arizona
University of California, Berkeley
University of California, Davis
University of California, Los Angeles
University of California, Riverside
University of California, San Diego
University of California, Santa Barbara
University of California, Santa Cruz
University of Colorado at Boulder
University of Connecticut (Storrs)
University of Delaware
University of Florida
University of Georgia
The University of Iowa
University of Kansas
University of Maryland College Park
University of Massachusetts Amherst
University of Michigan (Ann Arbor)
University of Michigan–Dearborn
University of Minnesota, Morris
University of Minnesota, Twin Cities Campus
University of Missouri–Columbia
University of Missouri–Kansas City
University of Missouri–Rolla
University of New Hampshire (Durham)
University of North Carolina at Asheville
University of North Carolina at Chapel Hill
University of Oklahoma
University of Pittsburgh
University of Pittsburgh at Johnstown
University of Tennessee, Knoxville
University of Texas at Austin
University of Utah
University of Vermont
University of Virginia
University of Washington
University of Wisconsin–Madison
Virginia Polytechnic Institute and State University

GEOGRAPHICAL INDEX OF COLLEGES

Alabama
Auburn University   23
Birmingham-Southern College   39
Samford University   245
The University of Alabama in
   Huntsville   288

Arizona
University of Arizona   289

Arkansas
Harding University   129
Hendrix College   133
Lyon College   165

California
California Institute of Technology   51
Claremont McKenna College   65
Deep Springs College   92
Harvey Mudd College   131
Mills College   181
Occidental College   198
Pepperdine University   207
Pitzer College   208
Pomona College   211
Saint Mary's College of California   241
Santa Clara University   246
Scripps College   248
Stanford University   259
Thomas Aquinas College   272
University of California, Berkeley   290
University of California, Davis   291
University of California, Los Angeles   292
University of California, Riverside   293
University of California, San Diego   294
University of California, Santa
   Barbara   295
University of California, Santa Cruz   296
University of Redlands   328
University of Southern California   332
Whittier College   364

Colorado
The Colorado College   78
Colorado School of Mines   79
Colorado State University   80
Colorado Technical University   81
United States Air Force Academy   282
University of Colorado at Boulder   298
University of Denver   302

Connecticut
Fairfield University   106
Trinity College   275
United States Coast Guard Academy   283
University of Connecticut   299
Wesleyan University   360
Yale University   372

Delaware
University of Delaware   301

District of Columbia
American University   21
The Catholic University of America   58
Georgetown University   114
The George Washington University   115

Florida
Eckerd College   102
Florida Institute of Technology   108
Florida State University   109
New College of the University of
   South Florida   189
Rollins College   226
Stetson University   265
University of Florida   305
University of Miami   311

Georgia
Agnes Scott College   13
Berry College   37
Emory University   104
Georgia Institute of Technology   116
Morehouse College   184
Oglethorpe University   199
Spelman College   258
University of Georgia   306
Wesleyan College   359

Idaho
Albertson College of Idaho   15

Illinois
Augustana College   24
Bradley University   43
DePaul University   94
Illinois College   140
Illinois Institute of Technology   141
Illinois Wesleyan University   142
Knox College   151
Lake Forest College   153
Loyola University Chicago   163
Millikin University   179
Monmouth College   183
North Central College   194
Northwestern University   196
Quincy University   216
University of Chicago   297
Wheaton College   362

Indiana
Butler University   50
DePauw University   95
Earlham College   101
Goshen College   119
Purdue University   215
Rose-Hulman Institute of Technology   227
Saint Mary's College   240
Taylor University   270
University of Evansville   304
University of Notre Dame   322
Valparaiso University   344
Wabash College   349

Iowa
Buena Vista University   49
Central College   61
Coe College   69
Cornell College   86
Drake University   97
Grinnell College   121
Iowa State University of Science and
   Technology   143

Luther College   164
Northwestern College   195
Simpson College   252
The University of Iowa   307
Wartburg College   351

Kansas
University of Kansas   308

Kentucky
Bellarmine College   33
Centre College   62
Georgetown College   113
Kentucky Wesleyan College   149
Transylvania University   273

Louisiana
Centenary College of Louisiana   60
Louisiana State University and
   Agricultural and Mechanical
   College   161
Tulane University   279

Maine
Bates College   31
Bowdoin College   42
Colby College   70

Maryland
Goucher College   120
Johns Hopkins University   146
Loyola College   162
Maryland Institute, College of Art   170
St. John's College   233
St. Mary's College of Maryland   242
United States Naval Academy   286
University of Maryland College Park   309
Washington College   354

Massachusetts
Amherst College   22
Babson College   27
Boston College   40
Boston University   41
Brandeis University   44
Clark University   67
College of the Holy Cross   75
Hampshire College   128
Harvard University   130
Massachusetts Institute of Technology   173
Mount Holyoke College   185
Simon's Rock College of Bard   251
Smith College   254
Tufts University   278
University of Massachusetts Amherst   310
Wellesley College   357
Williams College   367
Worcester Polytechnic Institute   370

Michigan
Albion College   16
Alma College   20
Calvin College   52
GMI Engineering & Management
   Institute   118
Hillsdale College   134
Hope College   138

Kalamazoo College — 148
Michigan State University — 176
Michigan Technological University — 177
University of Detroit Mercy — 303
University of Michigan — 312
University of Michigan–Dearborn — 313

Minnesota

Bethel College — 38
Carleton College — 54
College of Saint Benedict — 73
College of St. Scholastica — 74
Concordia College — 84
Gustavus Adolphus College — 124
Hamline University — 126
Macalester College — 166
Saint John's University — 235
St. Olaf College — 244
University of Minnesota, Morris — 314
University of Minnesota, Twin Cities Campus — 315

Mississippi

Millsaps College — 180

Missouri

Drury College — 99
Maryville University of Saint Louis — 171
Rockhurst College — 225
St. Louis College of Pharmacy — 238
Saint Louis University — 239
Truman State University — 277
University of Missouri–Columbia — 316
University of Missouri–Kansas City — 317
University of Missouri–Rolla — 318
Washington University — 355
William Jewell College — 366

Montana

Carroll College — 56

Nebraska

Creighton University — 88
Nebraska Wesleyan University — 188

New Hampshire

Dartmouth College — 89
University of New Hampshire — 319

New Jersey

Drew University — 98
New Jersey Institute of Technology — 190
Princeton University — 213
Rutgers, The State University of New Jersey, College of Engineering — 228
Rutgers, The State University of New Jersey, College of Pharmacy — 229
Rutgers, The State University of New Jersey, Cook College — 230
Rutgers, The State University of New Jersey, Douglass College — 231
Rutgers, The State University of New Jersey, Rutgers College — 232
Stevens Institute of Technology — 266
Trenton State College — 274
Westminster Choir College of Rider University — 361

New Mexico

New Mexico Institute of Mining and Technology — 191
St. John's College — 234

New York

Albert A. List College, Jewish Theological Seminary of America — 14
Alfred University — 18
Bard College — 29
Barnard College — 30
Clarkson University — 66
Colgate University — 71
College of Insurance — 72
Columbia University, Columbia College — 82
Columbia University, School of Engineering and Applied Science — 83
Cooper Union for the Advancement of Science and Art — 85
Cornell University — 87
Eugene Lang College, New School for Social Research — 105
Fordham University — 110
Hamilton College — 125
Hobart College — 136
Hofstra University — 137
Houghton College — 139
Le Moyne College — 157
New York University — 192
Polytechnic University, Brooklyn Campus — 209
Polytechnic University, Farmingdale Campus — 210
Rensselaer Polytechnic Institute — 219
Rochester Institute of Technology — 224
St. Lawrence University — 237
Sarah Lawrence College — 247
Siena College — 250
Skidmore College — 253
State University of New York at Binghamton — 260
State University of New York at Buffalo — 261
State University of New York College at Geneseo — 262
State University of New York College of Environmental Science and Forestry — 263
State University of New York Maritime College — 264
Syracuse University — 269
Union College — 280
United States Merchant Marine Academy — 284
United States Military Academy — 285
University at Albany, State University of New York — 287
University of Rochester — 330
Utica College of Syracuse University — 343
Vassar College — 346
Webb Institute — 356
Wells College — 358
William Smith College — 368
Yeshiva University — 373

North Carolina

Davidson College — 91
Duke University — 100
Guilford College — 123
North Carolina State University — 193
University of North Carolina at Asheville — 320
University of North Carolina at Chapel Hill — 321
Wake Forest University — 350

Ohio

Baldwin-Wallace College — 28
Capital University — 53
Case Western Reserve University — 57
Cedarville College — 59
The College of Wooster — 77
Denison University — 93
Hiram College — 135
John Carroll University — 145
Kenyon College — 150
Marietta College — 167
Miami University — 175
Mount Union College — 186
Oberlin College — 197
Ohio Northern University — 200
The Ohio State University — 201
Ohio University — 202
Ohio Wesleyan University — 203
Xavier University — 371

Oklahoma

Oklahoma State University — 204
University of Oklahoma — 323
University of Tulsa — 336

Oregon

Lewis & Clark College — 159
Linfield College — 160
Reed College — 218
Willamette University — 365

Pennsylvania

Albright College — 17
Allegheny College — 19
Bryn Mawr College — 47
Bucknell University — 48
Carnegie Mellon University — 55
Dickinson College — 96
Elizabethtown College — 103
Franklin and Marshall College — 111
Gettysburg College — 117
Grove City College — 122
Haverford College — 132
Juniata College — 147
Lafayette College — 152
La Salle University — 154
Lehigh University — 156
Messiah College — 174
Muhlenberg College — 187
Pennsylvania State University University Park Campus — 206
Saint Joseph's University — 236
Swarthmore College — 267
University of Pennsylvania — 324
University of Pittsburgh — 325
University of Pittsburgh at Johnstown — 326
University of Scranton — 331
Ursinus College — 342
Villanova University — 347
Washington and Jefferson College — 352

Rhode Island

Brown University — 46
Providence College — 214
Rhode Island School of Design — 220

South Carolina

Clemson University — 68
Furman University — 112
Presbyterian College — 212
Wofford College — 369

South Dakota

Augustana College	25
South Dakota School of Mines and Technology	255

Tennessee

Belmont University	34
Christian Brothers University	64
David Lipscomb University	90
Fisk University	107
Rhodes College	221
Union University	281
University of Tennessee, Knoxville	333
University of the South	335
Vanderbilt University	345

Texas

Austin College	26
Baylor University	32
LeTourneau University	158
Rice University	222
Southern Methodist University	256
Southwestern University	257
Texas A&M University	271
Trinity University	276
University of Dallas	300
University of Texas at Austin	334

Utah

Brigham Young University	45
University of Utah	337

Vermont

Bennington College	36
Marlboro College	168
Middlebury College	178
University of Vermont	338

Virginia

Christendom College	63
College of William and Mary	76
Hampden-Sydney College	127
James Madison University	144
Mary Washington College	172
Randolph-Macon Woman's College	217
Sweet Briar College	268
University of Richmond	329
University of Virginia	339
Virginia Polytechnic Institute and State University	348
Washington and Lee University	353

Washington

Pacific Lutheran University	205
University of Puget Sound	327
University of Washington	340
Whitman College	363

West Virginia

Shepherd College	249

Wisconsin

Beloit College	35
Lawrence University	155
Marquette University	169
Milwaukee School of Engineering	182
Ripon College	223
St. Norbert College	243
University of Wisconsin–Madison	341